Lecture Notes in Computer Science 700

Edited by G. Goos and J. Hartmanis

Advisory Board: W. Brauer D. Gries J. Stoer

A. Lingas R. Karlsson S. Carlsson (Eds.)

Automata, Languages
and Programming

20th International Colloquium, ICALP 93
Lund, Sweden, July 5-9, 1993
Proceedings

Springer-Verlag
Berlin Heidelberg NewYork
London Paris Tokyo
Hong Kong Barcelona
Budapest

A. Lingas R. Karlsson S. Carlsson (Eds.)

Automata, Languages and Programming

20th International Colloquium, ICALP 93
Lund, Sweden, July 5-9, 1993
Proceedings

Springer-Verlag

Berlin Heidelberg New York
London Paris Tokyo
Hong Kong Barcelona
Budapest

Series Editors

Gerhard Goos
Universität Karlsruhe
Postfach 69 80
Vincenz-Priessnitz-Straße 1
D-76131 Karlsruhe, FRG

Juris Hartmanis
Cornell University
Department of Computer Science
4130 Upson Hall
Ithaca, NY 14853, USA

Volume Editors

Andrzej Lingas
Rolf Karlsson
Department of Computer Science, Lund University
Box 118, S-22100 Lund, Sweden

Svante Carlsson
Department of Computer Science, University of Luleå
S-95187 Luleå, Sweden

CR Subject Classification (1991): F, D.1, E.1, E.3, G.2, I.3.5

ISBN 3-540-56939-1 Springer-Verlag Berlin Heidelberg New York
ISBN 0-387-56939-1 Springer-Verlag New York Berlin Heidelberg

© Springer-Verlag Berlin Heidelberg 1993
Printed in Germany

Typesetting: Camera ready by author
Printing and binding: Druckhaus Beltz, Hemsbach/Bergstr.
45/3140-543210 - Printed on acid-free paper

FOREWORD

The International Colloquium on Automata, Languages and Programming (ICALP) is an annual conference series sponsored by the European Association for Theoretical Computer Science (EATCS). It is intended to cover all important areas of theoretical computer science, such as: computability, automata, formal languages, term rewriting, analysis of algorithms, computational geometry, computational complexity, symbolic and algebraic computation, cryptography, data types and data structures, theory of data bases and knowledge bases, semantics of programming languages, program specification, transformation and verification, foundations of logic programming, theory of logical design and layout, parallel and distributed computation, theory of concurrency, and theory of robotics.

ICALP 93 was held at Lund University, Sweden, from July 5 to July 9, 1993.

Previous colloquia were held in Wien (1992), Madrid (1991), Warwick (1990), Stresa (1989), Tampere (1988), Karlsruhe (1987), Rennes (1986), Nafplion (1985), Antwerp (1984), Barcelona (1983), Aarhus (1982), Haifa (1981), Amsterdam (1980), Graz (1979), Udine (1978), Turku (1977), Edinburgh (1976), Saarbrücken (1974) and Paris (1972). ICALP 94 will be held in Jerusalem from July 11 to July 15, 1994.

The number of papers submitted was 151. Each submitted paper was sent to at least four Programme Committee members, who were often assisted by their referees. The Programme Committee meeting took place at Lund University on the 5th and 6th of February 1993 (the names of those participating in the meeting are underlined below). This volume contains the 51 papers selected at the meeting plus the five invited papers.

We would like to thank all the Programme Committee members and the referees who assisted them in their work. The list of referees is as complete as we can achieve and we apologize for any omissions or errors.

The members of the Organizing Committee, the members of the algorithm group at our department sometimes assisted by their families, our departmental secretaries, and many other members of the department deserve our gratitude for their contributions throughout the preparations.

We also gratefully acknowledge support from Swedish Natural Science Research Council, Apple Computer AB, the Department of Computer Science at Lund University, Lund Institute of Technology, Lund University, and the city of Lund.

Svante Carlsson, Rolf Karlsson, and Andrzej Lingas
April 1993, Lund University

Invited Lecturers

S. Abiteboul, INRIA Rocquencourt;
M. Blum, Berkeley;
D. Dolev, IBM San José and Jerusalem;
L. Hemachandra, Rochester;
I. Simon, Sao Paulo.

Programme Committee

S. Abiteboul, Paris
J. Diaz, Barcelona
R. Freivalds, Riga
F. Gécseg, Szeged
G. Gonnet, Zurich
Y. Gurevich, Ann Arbor
D. Harel, Rehovot
T. Harju, Turku
I. M. Havel, Prague
J. Håstad, Stockholm
J.-P. Jouannaud, Paris
D. Kirkpatrick, Vancouver
H.-J. Kreowski, Bremen
W. Kuich, Vienna
G. Levi, Pisa
A. Lingas, Lund (chairman)
T. Maibaum, London
A. Mazurkiewicz, Warsaw
M. Nielsen, Aarhus
M. H. Overmars, Utrecht
W. Thomas, Kiel
U. Vishkin, Tel-Aviv and Maryland
P. Wolper, Liege

Organizing Committee

Arne Andersson, Lund;
Svante Carlsson, Luleå (co-chairman);
Rolf Karlsson, Lund (co-chairman);
Andrzej Lingas, Lund;
Ola Petersson, Växjö.

List of Referees

Abrahamson K.
Alur R.
Anderson R.
Andersson A.
Anstee R.P.
Arnborg S.
Arnold A.
Baaz M.
Balcázar J.L.
Bang-Jensen J.
Bartha M.
Beauquier D.
Berman P.
Bernot G.
Berry G.
Best E.
Bhattacharia B.
Boasson L.
Bodlaender H.L.
Bonatti P.
Breazu-Tannen V.
Carlsson S.
Casas R.
Cassaigne J.
Choffrut C.
Comon
Compton K.
Courcelle B.
Craig T.S.
Crochemore N.
Csakany B.
Csirik J.
Culberson J.
Damgaard I.B.
Delorme
Dessmark A.
Diaconescu
Diekert V.
Dovier A.
Drewes F.
Droste M.
Emerson E.A.
Engberg U.H.
Enjalbert P.
Farvardin N.
Frandsen G.
Fuchs N.E.

Fülöp Z.
Gabarró J.
Gallo G.
Garrido O.
Gavaldá R.
Giacobazzi R.
Godefroid P.
Goldmann M.
Goldreich O.
Goltz U.
Graedel E.
Grandjean E.
Grosse-Rhode M.
Habel A.
Hajnal P.
Hankin C.L.
Hansen M.R.
Higham L.
Hodkinson I.M.
Honkala J.
Hortmann M.
Horváth G.
Inverardi P.
JaJa J.
Jancar P.
Jantzen M.
Jebelean T.
Jenner B.
Jennings E.
Juras M.
Kameda T.
Karhumäki J.
Kari J.
Kari L.
Karlsson R.
Kasif S.
Khuller S.
Klarlund N.
Klop J.W.
Kluge W.
Knoop J.
Koubek V.
Krivánek M.
Kudlek M.
La Poutré J.A.
Lagergren J.
Landau G.M.

Lazard D.
Leduc G.
Leroy X.
Levcopoulos C.
Liestman A.
Luccio F.
Maggs B.M.
Magnusson B.
Manorioci D.
Manovssakis Y.
Martini S.
Masini A.
Matias Y.
Mattsson C.
Milo T.
Miltersen P.B.
Moggi E.
Montanari U.
Moreau L.
Moscowitz Y.
Mossakowski T.
Nagarajan R.
Nickl F.
Niemi V.
Nilsson B.
Nilsson S.
Olderog E.-R.
Pacholski L.
Padawitz P.
Paz A.
Petersson O.
Pin J.E.
Pippenger N.
Plump D.
Poigné A.
Potthoff A.
Prodinger H.
Qian Z.
Rajasekaran S.
Raman R.
Raz D.
Regnier M.
Renvall A.
Reynolds M.A.
Richter M.M.
Ruthing O.
Sahinalp S.

Sales T.
Salomaa A.
Sannella D.
Sassone V.
Schieber B.
Schmid U.
Schmidt E.M.
Séébold P.
Seibert S.
Seidl H.
Serna M.
Skyum S.
Staiger L.
Steffen B.
Steinby M.
Stevenne J.-M.
Steyaert J.-M.
Stirling C.
Storlind R.
Stout Q.
Taylor Paul
Tel G.
Thurimella R.
Tison
Torán J.
Treinen R.
Tsantilas T.
Turán G.
Upfal E.
Valkema E.
Varricchio S.
Vianu V.
Vickers S.J.
Wagner A.
Weber A.
Wiehagen R.
Wilke T.
Willem J.
Winskel G.
Wojciechowski S.
Woo Ryu K.
Yesha Y.
Young N.
Zielonka W.

TABLE OF CONTENTS

Program Result Checking:
A New Approach to Making Programs More Reliable

Manuel Blum[1]

Computer Science Division
University of California at Berkeley
94720

Abstract. Program result checking is concerned with designing programs to check their work. For example, after solving an equation for x, a result-checking program would substitute x back into the equation to make sure that the answer obtained is correct. There are many ways to check results, but there has been no theory to say what constitutes a good check. It is not a good check, for example, to redo a computation without change a second time. Such recomputation may uncover an intermittent hardware fault, but it will not uncover a software fault, and the discovery and elimination of software faults is the principal goal of this work. This talk discusses the concept of result checking, gives several examples, and outlines the basic theory.

1. Introduction

This talk restricts attention to program result checkers for a certain clean class of computational problems. These problems are completely described by specifying what constitutes correct input/output and acceptable running time, ie. by describing

1. what is an allowable *input* (to any program for the problem),

2. for each such input, what is an acceptable (ie. correct) *output*, and

3. what is an (easily computable) upper bound on the running time of a (reasonably fast) program for the problem.

For each (such) computational problem π, discussion will center on two classes of programs. The first will be a (possibly faulty) program for solving problem π. The second will be a (possibly faulty) checker for π. The latter *result checker* for computational problem π is an efficient program for checking the correctness of *any given program* (supposedly) for problem π on *any particular input* to the program. Notice that a checker does *not* check that the given program for π is correct on *all* inputs, but only that it is correct on the *given* input. This is one reason why it is generally easier to *check* a program (on a given input) than it is to *verify* a program (*prove* the program correct on all inputs).

---

[1] This work was supported in part by NSF grant CCR92-01092, in part by IBM Research Division, T.J. Watson Research Center, and in part by ICSI, the International Computer Science Institute, Berkeley, CA.

A preliminary version of this paper appeared in Blum and Raghavan [BR].

Author's e-mail address: blum@cs.berkeley.edu

More precisely, a *result checker* for problem π is an algorithm that is supplied with:

1. a (possibly faulty) program for solving computational problem π, given as a black box, which the checker may run on inputs of its choice; and
2. a particular input for this program.

The checker must determine either that the output is correct or the program is faulty. (It may be that *both* are true!) To this end, the checker is designed to do efficient computations that are permitted to include calling the given program on various allowable inputs of the checkers own choosing. If the checker outputs CORRECT, then this implies that the checker has verified that the output of the given program on the given input is correct; if it outputs FAULTY, then this implies that the checker has verified the existence of a fault in the given program. The latter fault may manifest itself when the program is run on an input different from the given input.

Notice above that when a faulty program gives a correct output despite its fault, the checker is permitted to output either CORRECT or FAULTY. In particular, the checker is permitted to output FAULTY even when the given program outputs a correct answer on the given input, provided the program is indeed faulty. While this may at first appear strange, it is exactly what is wanted: for example, a trivial program that gives the same answer on all inputs may be perfectly correct on the given input for *no good reason*! The checker that discovers the program is junk has good reason to declare it faulty.

2. Program Result Checkers

Let π denote a (computational) decision and/or search problem. For x an input to π, let $\pi(x)$ denote the output of π. Let P be a program (supposedly for π) that halts on all instances of π. We say that such a program P, viewed as a program for π, has a *fault* (or *bug*) if for some instance x of π, $P(x) \neq \pi(x)$.

Define an *(efficient) program result checker* C_π for problem π as follows: $C_\pi^P(I;k)$ is any probabilistic (expected-poly-time) oracle Turing machine that satisfies the following conditions, for any program P (supposedly for π) that halts on all instances of π, for any instance I of π, and for any positive integer k (the so-called "security parameter") presented in unary:

1. If P has no bugs, i.e., $P(x) = \pi(x)$ for all instances x of π, then with probability[2] $\geq 1 - 2^{-k}$, $C_\pi^P(I;k) = CORRECT$ (i.e., $P(I)$ is correct).
2. If $P(I) \neq \pi(I)$, then with probability[2] $\geq 1 - 2^{-k}$, $C_\pi^P(I;k) = BUGGY$ (i.e., P has a fault).

In the above, it is assumed that any program P for problem π halts on all instances of π. This is done in order to help focus on the problem at hand. In general, however, programs do not always halt, and the definition of a "bug" must be

---

[2] This probability is computed over the sample space of all finite sequences of coin flips that C could have tossed. In most examples, including all those in this paper, program P definitely (rather than probably) has a bug when $C_\pi^P(I;k) = BUGGY$.

3

extended to cover programming errors that slow a program down or cause it to diverge altogether. In this case, the definition of a program checker must also be extended to require the additional condition:

3. If $P(x)$ exceeds a precomputed bound $\Phi(x)$ on the running time for $x = I$, the given instance, or for any other value of x submitted by the checker to the oracle, then the program checker is to output a warning, namely $C_\pi^P (I;k) = TIME\_EXCEEDED$.

In the remainder of this paper, it is assumed that any program P for a problem π halts on all instances of π, so condition 3 is everywhere suppressed.

Some definitions and remarks are in order:

i. The *actual running time* of C will be the number of steps taken by C *including* the number of steps taken by the program it calls. The *funny (running) time* of C counts whatever time it takes C to do its computations and to submit inputs to and receive outputs from P, but *excludes* the time it takes for P to do its computations. More about this below.

ii. In the above definition, if P has bugs but $P(I) = \pi(I)$, ie. buggy program P gives the correct output on input I, then $C_\pi^P (I;k)$ may output *CORRECT* or *BUGGY*. Intuitively, if $C_\pi^P (I;k) = CORRECT$, then we may rely with a specific high (but not absolute!) degree of confidence on the output of P on this particular I; if $C_\pi^P (I;k) = BUGGY$, then with high probability P has a bug. Note that in this latter case, $P(I)$ may nevertheless be correct.

Regarding this model for ensuring program correctness the question naturally arises: if one cannot be sure that a program is correct, how then can one be sure that its checker is correct? This is a major serious problem![3] One solution is to *prove* the checker *correct*. Sometimes, this is easier than proving the original program correct, as in the case of the *Euclidean GCD* checker of section 5. Another possibility is to try and make the checker to some extent independent of the program it checks. To this end, we make the following definition: Say that (probabilistic) program checker C has the *little oh* property with respect to program P if and only if the (expected) funny time of C is little oh of the running time of P. We shall generally require that a checker have this little oh property with respect to any program it checks. The principal reason for this is to ensure that the checker is programmed *differently* from the program it checks.[4] The little oh property forces the programmer *away* from simply

---

[3] The author was privileged to hear Dr. Warren S. McCulloch at the First Bionics Symposium, where he described how farmers at a county fair weigh pigs: "First they lay a plank across a rock and set a pig at one end. Then they heap rocks at the other end until the rocks balance the pig. Finally, they *guess* the weight of the rocks and *compute* the weight of the pig!" Our approach to program checking is similar: Instead of proving a program checker correct, we *test* it. Then we *prove* that a (debugged) program checker will discover all output errors.

[4] A second reason (to ask that the checker have the "little oh" property) arises whenever the program checker is the type that runs the program P just once (to determine $O = P(I)$). In that case, P and C can be run consecutively without increasing the asymptotic running time over that of running just P.

running his program a second time. Whatever else he does, he must think more about his problem:

4.   The funny time of the checker must be little oh of the running time of the program being checked.

Checkers satisfying condition 4 will be specifically referred to as having the little oh property. The specific examples of program checkers sprinkled throughout this paper all have the little oh property with respect to all known programs for the given problem.

3. Example: Graph Isomorphism

The graph isomorphism decision problem is defined as follows:

Graph Isomorphism (GI):
Input: Two graphs G and H.
Output: YES if G is isomorphic to H; NO otherwise.

Our checker is an adaptation of Goldreich, Micali and Wigderson's [GMW] demonstration that Graph Isomorphism has interactive proofs. The [GMW] model relies on the existence of an all-powerful prover. The latter is replaced here by the program being checked. As such, ours is a concrete application of their abstract idea. Indeed, the following program checker is a sensible practical way to check computer programs including heuristic programs for graph isomorphism:

$C_{GI}^P (G, H; k) =$
Input: $P = $ a program (supposedly for Graph Isomorphism) that always halts, to be used as an oracle by C_{GI};
              $G, H = $ two graphs, each having n nodes;
              $k = $ a positive integer.
Output: The output must be *CORRECT* or *BUGGY* (sometimes either one is correct). It is only required that the implications hold:
              CORRECT $\Rightarrow$ $P(G, H)$ is probably correct. This means that the probability that output $= CORRECT$ in case $P(G, H) \neq GI(G, H)$ is at most 2^{-k} (see previous footnote).
              BUGGY $\Rightarrow$ P definitely has a bug.

Begin
Compute $P(G, H)$.
If $P(G, H) = YES$, **then**
       Use P (as if it were fault-free) to search for an isomorphism from G to H. (This is done by attaching an appropriately selected "gadget," say a clique on $n+1$ nodes, to node 1 of G. Denote the resulting graph by G_1. Then search for a node of H such that when the same gadget is attached to that node, the resulting H_1 is, according to P, isomorphic to G_1, that is, $P(G_1, H_1) = YES$. If no such H_1 is found **then return**

5

> *BUGGY*. Continue as above to build a correspondence between the
> nodes of G_1 and the nodes of H_1, until the resulting "isomorphism"
> is completed and checked. Isomorphism is in quotes here because P
> is unreliable.)

Check if the resulting correspondence is an isomorphism.
If not, **return** *BUGGY*; **if** yes, **return** *CORRECT*.
If $P(G, H) = NO$, **then**
    Do k times:
        Toss a fair coin.
        If coin = heads **then**
            generate a random[5] permutation G_i of G.
            Compute $P(G, G_i)$.
            If $P(G, G_i) = NO$, **then return** *BUGGY*.
        If coin = tails **then**
            generate a random permutation H_j of H.
            Compute $P(G, H_j)$.
            If $P(G, H_j) = YES$, **then return** *BUGGY*.
    End-do
Return *CORRECT*.
End

The above program checker correctly tests *any* computer program *whatsoever* that is purported to solve the graph isomorphism problem. Even the most bizarre program designed specifically to fool the checker will be caught, when it is run on any input that causes it to output an incorrect answer. The following Theorem formally proves this:

Theorem: The program checker for Graph Isomorphism runs efficiently and works correctly (as specified). Formally:
    C_{GI}^P is efficient.

Let P be any decision program (a program that halts on all inputs and always outputs YES or NO). Let G and H be any two graphs. Let k be a positive integer.

If P is a correct program for *GI*, ie. one without bugs, then $C_{GI}^P(G,H;k)$ will definitely output *CORRECT*.

If $P(G,H)$ is incorrect on this input, i.e., $P(G,H) \neq GI(G,H)$, then *prob* $\{C_{GI}^P(G,H;k) = CORRECT\}$ is at most 2^{-k}.

Proof: Clearly, C_{GI}^P runs in expected polynomial time.

If P has no bugs and G is isomorphic to H, then $C_{GI}^P(G,H;k)$ constructs an isomorphism from G to H and (correctly) outputs *CORRECT*.

If P has no bugs and G is not isomorphic to H, then $C_{GI}^P(G,H;k)$ tosses coins. It discovers that $P(G, G_i) = YES$ for all G_i, and $P(G, H_j) = NO$ for all H_j, and so

---

[5] By a "random" permutation we mean that every permutation of G, i.e., every relabeling of the n nodes of G with the integers $1, \cdots, n$, is equally likely.

(correctly) outputs *CORRECT*.

If $P(G,H)$ outputs an incorrect answer, there are two cases:

1.   If $P(G,H) = YES$ but G is not isomorphic to H then C fails to construct an isomorphism from G to H, and so C (correctly) outputs *BUGGY*.

Finally, the most interesting case:

2.   If $P(G,H) = NO$ but G is isomorphic to H, then what? The only way that C will return *CORRECT* is if $P(G, G_i \text{ or } H_j) = YES$ whenever the coin comes up heads, *NO* when it comes up tails. But G is isomorphic to H. Since the permutations of G and H are random, G_i has the same probability distribution as H_j. Therefore, P correctly distinguishes G_i from H_j only by chance, i.e., for just 1 of the 2^k possible sequences of C's coin tosses.

Qed

Remark: If $C_{GI}^P(I;k) = BUGGY$, then the above program checker must actually have obtained a proof that P has a bug, e.g., for $P(G,H) = NO$ it might have found H_j such that $P(G, H_j) = YES$. This proof points to instances of π, in this case (G,H) and (G, H_j), that exercise the part of P that has a bug. In general, one can always modify C, using the results of the next section, so that $C_\pi^P(I;k)$ outputs such a pointer whenever it discovers that P has a bug.

4. Beigel's Trick

Richard Beigel [Be] has pointed out to the author the following fundamental fact:

Theorem (Beigel's trick): Let π_1, π_2 be two polynomial-time equivalent computational (decision or search) problems. Then from any efficient program checker C_{π_1} for π_1 it is possible to construct an efficient program checker C_{π_2} for π_2.

Remark: Observe that this theorem requires $\pi_1 \equiv \pi_2$. It does not suffice to have just one of these problems reduce to the other.

Proof: Our proof of this theorem will be for the special case in which decision problems π_1, π_2 are polynomial-time equivalent by Karp-reductions, but it goes through as well for search/optimization problems π_1, π_2, that are polynomial-time equivalent by Cook-reductions.

Let f_{ij} be two polynomial-time functions that map YES-instances of π_i to YES-instances of π_j and NO-instances of π_i to NO-instances of π_j, for $\{i,j\} = \{1,2\}$. In what follows, P_i will denote a program for π_i and I_i will denote an instance of π_i, for $i \in \{1,2\}$.

$C_{\pi_2}^{P_2}(I_2;k)$ works as follows: it checks if $P_2(I_2) = \pi_2(I_2)$ by verifying two conditions:

1. $P_2(I_2) = P_2(f_{12}(f_{21}(I_2)))$, and

2.   setting $I_1 =_{def} f_{21}(I_2)$,   and   defining P_1 by $P_1(x_1) =_{def} P_2(f_{12}(x_1))$ for all instances x_1 of π_1, check the correctness of $P_1(I_1) = \pi_1(I_1)$ (and therefore of $P_2(I_2) = \pi_2(I_2)$) by using $C_{\pi_1}^{P_1}(I_1, k)$.

If conditions one or two fail, then $C_{\pi_2}^{P_2}(I_2; k) := BUGGY$. Otherwise, $C_{\pi_2}^{P_2}(I_2; k) := CORRECT$.

Observe that if P_2 is correct (i.e., $P_2 = \pi_2$), then conditions one and two hold. In particular, P_1 is correct, whence $C_{\pi_1}^{P_1}(I_1; k) = CORRECT$. So $C_{\pi_2}^{P_2}(I_2; k) = CORRECT$.

On the other hand, if $P_2(I_2) \neq \pi_2(I_2)$, then either condition one fails, i.e., $P_2(I_2) \neq P_2(f_{12}(f_{21}(I_2)))$, in which case $C_{\pi_2}^{P_2}(I_2; k) = BUGGY$, or else condition 1 holds, whence

$$P_1(I_1) = P_1(f_{21}(I_2))$$
$$= P_2(f_{12}(f_{21}(I_2))) \quad \text{since } P_1 =_{def} P_2 f_{12},$$
$$= P_2(I_2) \quad \text{because condition one holds}$$
$$\neq \pi_2(I_2) \quad \text{by assumption}$$
$$= \pi_1(f_{21}(I_2)) = \pi_1(I_1),$$

in which case $C_{\pi_1}^{P_1}(I_1; k)$, and therefore also $C_{\pi_2}^{P_2}(I_2; k)$ will correctly return $BUGGY$ with high probability, i.e., with probability of error $\leq 1/2^k$.
Qed

Problems that are polynomial-time equivalent to *Graph Isomorphism* include that of finding generators for the automorphism group of a graph, determining the order of the automorphism group of a graph, and counting the number of isomorphisms between two graphs. It follows from Beigel's trick that all these problems have efficient program checkers.

5. Problems in P

In this section, program checkers use their oracle just once (to determine $O = P(I)$) rather than several times. In such cases, instead of the program checker being denoted by $C_\pi^P(I; k)$, it will be denoted by $C_\pi(I, O; k)$. The latter notation has the advantage of clarifying what must be tested for. In cases where the checker is nonprobabilistic, it will be denoted by $C_\pi(I, O)$ instead of $C_\pi(I, O; k)$.

Many problems in P have efficient program checkers, and it is a challenge to find them. In what follows, we give a fairly complete description of program checkers for just two problems in P: *Euclidean-GCD* (because it is one of the oldest nontrivial algorithms on the books), and *Sorting* (because it is one of the most frequently run algorithms).

5.1. A Program Checker for Euclidean GCD

> **Euclidean-GCD**
> **Input:** Two positive integers a,b.
> **Output:** $d = gcd\,(a,b)$, and integers u,v such that $a \cdot u + b \cdot v = d$.

Observe that *Euclidean-GCD* is a specific computational problem, not an algorithm. In particular, it does not have to be solved by Euclid's algorithm. Problems *GCD* and *Euclidean-GCD* both output $d = gcd\,(a,b)$, but *Euclidean-GCD* also outputs two integers u,v such that $a \cdot u + b \cdot v = d$. We know how to check programs for *Euclidean-GCD* but not *GCD*.

For our model of computation, we choose a standard RAM and count only arithmetic operations $+, -, \cdot, /$ as steps.

> $C_{Euclidean\text{-}GCD}$
> **Input:** positive integers a,b; positive integer d and integers u,v.
> **Output:** BUGGY   if $d \nmid a$ or $d \nmid b$ or $a \cdot u + b \cdot v \neq d$,
>   CORRECT   if the given program P computes *Euclidean-GCD* correctly.
>
> **Begin**
>   1. If $d \nmid a$ or $d \nmid b$, return BUGGY, else
>   2. If $a \cdot u + b \cdot v \neq d$, return BUGGY, else
>   3. Return CORRECT.
> **End**

Here, line 1 checks that d is a *divisor* of a and b; line 2 checks that d is the *greatest* divisor of a and b. This checker takes just 5 steps: 2 division steps + 2 multiplication steps + 1 addition step. By comparison, the running time of all known *GCD* programs requires at least log n division steps on certain inputs.

5.2. A Program Checker for Sorting

> **Sorting**
> **Input:** An array of integers $X = [x_1, \cdots, x_n]$, representing a multiset.
> **Output:** An array Y consisting of the elements of X listed in non-decreasing order.

A checker for *Sorting* must do *more* than just check that Y is in order. It must also check that $X = Y$ (as multisets)!

> $C_{Sorting}$
> **Input:** Two arrays of integers $X = [x_1, \cdots, x_n]$ and $Y = [y_1, \cdots, y_{n'}]$
> **Output:** BUGGY   if Y is *not* in order or if $X \neq Y$ as multisets.
>   CORRECT   if the given program P correctly sorts.

Model of computation: The computer has a fixed number of tapes, including one that contains X and another that contains Y. X and Y each have at most n elements, and each such element is an integer in the range $[0,a]$. The random access memory has $O(lg\,n + lg\,a)$ words of memory, and each of its words is capable of holding any integer in the range $[0,a]$, in particular each can hold any element of $X \cup Y$.

Single precision operations: $+, -, \times, /, <, =$ each take one step. Here, $/$ denotes "integer divide."

Multi-precision operations: $+, -, <, =$ on integers that are m words long take m steps;

$\times, /$ on integers that are m words long take m^2 steps.

Each shift of a tape, and each copy of a word on tape to a word in RAM or vice versa counts 1 step.

In this model of computation, it is easy to check that Y is in order in just $O(n)$ steps. To check that $X = Y$ as multisets can be done in probabilistic $O(n)$ steps, but the right method depends in general on the the comparative sizes of a and n. Here is a precise statement of multiset equality and a way to check for it:

Multiset Equality Test
Input: Two arrays of integers X, Y; and a positive integer k.
Output: YES if X and Y represent the same multiset, NO otherwise, with probability of error $\leq 2^{-k}$. The latter means that for any two sets X and Y selected by adversary, the probability of an incorrect output (measured over the distribution of coin-toss-sequences generated by the algorithm) should be at most 2^{-k}.

Method: This idea was first suggested by Lipton [L3] and more recently by Ravi Kannan [K2]. Let $f(z) = (z - x_1) \cdots (z - x_n)$ and $g(z) = (z - y_1) \cdots (z - y_n)$. Then $x = y$ if and only if $f = g$. Since f and g are polynomials of degree n, either $f(z) = g(z)$ for all z (if $f = g$) or $f(z) = g(z)$ for at most n values of z (if $f \neq g$). A probabilistic algorithm can decide if $f = g$ by selecting k values for z at random from a set of $2n$ (or more) possibilities, say from $[1, 2n]$, then comparing $f(z)$ to $g(z)$ for these k values. The computations can be kept to reasonable size by doing the subtractions and multiplications modulo randomly chosen (small) primes.

6. Overview and Conclusions

6.1. An Alternative to Proving Correctness

The thrust of this paper is to show that in many cases, it is possible to check a program's output for a given input, thereby giving *quantitative mathematical evidence* that the program works correctly on that input. By allowing the possibility of an incorrect answer (just as one would if computations were done by hand), the program designer confronts the possibility of a bug and considers *what to do* if the answer is wrong. This gives an *alternative* to proving a program correct that may be achievable and sufficient for many situations.

A proper way to develop this theory would be to require that the program checker itself be proved correct. This paper, however, is about *pure* checking, meaning no proofs of correctness whatsoever. Instead, we require the checker C to be different from the program P that it checks in two ways: First, the input-output specifications for C are different from those for P (C gets P's output and it responds *CORRECT* or *BUGGY*). Second, we demand that the running time of the checker be $o(S(x))$, where $S(x)$ is the running time of any program for the problem on input x. This prevents a programmer from undercutting this approach, which he could otherwise do by simply running his program a second time and calling that a check. Whatever else the programmer does, he *must* think more about his problem.

6.2. Suggestions for the Program Check Designer

This raises the issue that checkers can be difficult to construct. We offer three suggestions for the program check designer:

1. Test the program on random inputs. Use the fact that it has been tested and found to work correctly on random inputs to check/correct it on the given input. An example due to Lipton [L] appears in the next section.

2. A library of programs may be easier to check than a single program. See Blum, Luby, and Rubinfeld [BLR] for an example of this.

3. Sometimes, when it is not evident how to construct a checker, there is another possibility:

   • Demand that the program compute certain *additional variables*, then
   • Construct a *partial checker* that uses those additional variables to check the correctness of the (originally desired) output.

The checker is *partial* because it does not necessarily have to check the correctness of the computed additional variables, only the correctness of the originally desired output.

For example, to check that a *GCD* program

Input: positive integers a,b
Output: $d = gcd(a,b)$

outputs the correct value, it suffices to require it to compute additional integers u,v such that $a \cdot u + b \cdot v = d$ and then to check that $d \mid a$ and $d \mid b$ and $a \cdot u + b \cdot v = d$. This example is worked in detail in section 5.

For another example, to check that a *MOD* program

Input: integers a,b with $b > 0$.
Output: $c = a \bmod b =_{def}$ remainder (a/b).

outputs the correct value, it suffices to require it to compute the additional variable $q = \lfloor a/b \rfloor$ and then to check that $a = bq + c$ and that $0 \le c < b$.

For a final example, to check that a *Max Flow* program

Input: A network with one source, one sink, and positive integer capacities assigned to edges.

Output: A nonnegative integer F = the maximum flow that can be pushed from source to sink.

outputs the correct value, it suffices to require the program to output the edge flow f, f = an assignment of integers to all edges, then to

2.1. check that f is a flow, that is to say:

    2.1.1. the sum of flows into a node = the sum of flows out of that node, for all nodes $\notin$ {source, sink}, and

    2.1.2. the flow in each edge is nonnegative and $\leq$ the capacity of that edge, and

2.2. check that a depth-first search that is started at the source and is turned back at every forward edge that is filled to capacity and at every backward edge that is empty will terminate at the source without ever reaching the sink, and

2.3. check that F = the sum of flows into the sink.

7. A Selection of Related and Relevant Works

The theory of result checking introduced above and in Blum [B1], provides an attractive supplement to traditional approaches for verifying that a program is correct. See also Blum Kannan [BK], Blum Ragahavan [BR], and Kannan [K1]. Others have considered approaches along these lines, some independently, some based on the work above.

Vainstein [V1, V2] based on work of Karpovsky has independently introduced a notion of checking for numerical computation of any algebraic functions that satisfy a polynomial relation. His checks make sure that the polynomial relation is satisfied on (several distinct) inputs that include the given one. Typical functions include such as

$$f(x) = \frac{(\sin(\frac{x}{11} + \frac{\pi}{7}) + e^x)^{3/5} + x^2\cos^4 x}{x^5 + (x^4 + x^2(\sin 2x + xe^x)^3)^{\frac{1}{3}}}.$$

Vainstein's theory builds on information and communication theory; it uses the theory of mathematical fields as its principal tool. His checkers are weaker than ours: large classes of distinct functions may satisfy the same check on ALL inputs, and therefore be indistinguishable to the checker. Nevertheless, the results have the potential to be turned into result checkers along the stronger lines advocated here. Troy Shahoumian, one of my graduate students, is currently hard at work extending the theory in that direction.

Sullivan & Mason [SM1 SM2] independently introduce a very useful idea for checking, that of the certification trail. The idea is that a program should be required to leave a trail of information that can then be used by the checker to guarantee that the output is correct. This idea is similar to the idea, introduced independently by

Blum, that a program that is hard to check may be made easier to check by requiring it to give additional information, as in the GCD and the Max Flow problems above. The first Sullivan & Masson paper gives a particularly nice application of their idea to the minimum spanning tree problem.

Although a result checker can be used to verify whether $P(x) = f(x)$, it does not give a method for computing the correct answer in the case that P is found to be faulty. To remedy this problem, Rubinfeld [R] and Blum, Luby, and Rubinfeld [BLR] introduce a theory of self-testing/correcting, which extends the theory of result checkers. Intuitively, a probabilistic program T_f is a *self-tester* for f if, for any program P that supposedly computes f, T_f can make calls to P to estimate the probability that $P(x) \neq f(x)$ for a random input x. This is the error probability of P. A probabilistic program C_f is a *self-corrector* for f if, for any program P such that the error probability of P is sufficiently low, for any input x, C_f can make calls to P to compute $f(x)$ correctly.

A self-testing/correcting pair for a function f implies a result checker for f. A result checker for f imples a self-tester for f, but it is not known whether a result checker also implies a self-corrector.

Lipton [L] independently of this work discusses the concept of self-correcting programs and for several functions uses it to construct a testing program with respect to any distribution assuming that the programs are not too faulty with respect to a particular distribution. His most important example, based on work of Beaver and Feigenbaum [BF], gives a checker/corrector for the permanent problem: consider a program for computing the permanent of an nxn matrix over a finite field GF[q] with q > n+1. The permanent of $[a_{ij}]$ can be computed by a checker/corrector as follows. Observe that PERM$[a_{ij} + x \cdot r_{ij}]$ is a polynomial $f(x)$ of degree n over the field. Here x is a variable. Each of the n^2 elements r_{ij} is chosen uniformly at random from the field. The checker/corrector calls the permanent program to compute f(x) for x = 1, 2, ..., n+1. Because the r_{ij} are randomly chosen, the PERM$[a_{ij} + x \cdot r_{ij}]$ is random (albeit dependent) for each of x = 1, 2, ..., n+1, and because the given program computes PERM correctly with high probability on random nxn matrices, linear algebra determines all the coefficients of f(x) correctly with high probability. The desired value for PERM $[a_{ij}]$ is then equal to f(0) with high probability.

The above can be extended to give a result checker for any #P-complete problem. It is interesting that this enables to check any program for a #P-complete problem, but not necessarily any program for an NP-complete problem. The output of a program for an NP-complete problem is easy to check, using self-reduction, when the answer is YES, but it is not clear how to check when the answer is NO. Indeed, Fortnow and Feigenbaum [FF] have given an argument that such a checker may not exist, but they do not completely show this.

The above two results taken together point out something not contradicted by Beigel's theorem: there can (indeed do) exist checkers for #P complete problems even though there may not exist checkers for NP-complete problems, whose programs just output YES or NO, Programs for the former can be checked even when they output 0 (same as NO). The specific numbers output when the answer is YES are just what's needed to check an answer of 0. Thus we do not have a checker for the problem of deciding if a graph has a Hamilton Cycle, but we do have a checker for the problem of deciding HOW MANY Hamilton Cycles a graph has.

Rubinfeld [R] originated and developed the idea of bootstrap self-testing.

Nisan [N] uses the bootstrap self-testing/correcting and the observation about the permanent problem in Lipton to construct a two-prover interactive proof system for the permanent problem. This led to the eventual discovery that IP = PSPACE [FKLN], Shamir [S], Babai [Ba]. Shamir's proof that IP=PSPACE supplies a result checker for any problem in PSPACE (as well as a result checker for any problem in #P). One must look at the proof carefully to see that the Prover in the interactive proof need only have the power of PSPACE (resp. #P), which suffices to make the interactive proof a check. The reason it does not prove that NP-complete problems have checkers is that the prover for NP-complete problems must have the power of #P in the proof. The program for the NP-complete problem may not have the necessary power.

Babai, Fortnow and Lund [BFL] have proved that NEXP = 2IP. Their proof shows that NonDeterministic exponential time complete problems have polynomial time result checkers. This also takes some care to see, that the interactive provers require no more power than nondeterministic exponential time. One needs 2 provers, neither of which knows what answers is given by the other. A program that is reinitialized each time it is run is just such a multi-prover.

The above theory is all for exact computations. Ar, Blum, Codenotti, and Gemmell [ABCG] and Gemmell [G] have initiated the development of a theory to check approximate computations (such as floating point).

References

[ABCG]   S. Ar, M. Blum, B. Codenotti, and P. Gemmell, "Checking Approximate Computations Over the Reals." to appear in STOC 93, 10 pp.

[Ba]   L. Babai, "E-mail and the power of interaction," Proc 5th Structures in Complexity Theory Conference, (1990).

[Be]   R. Beigel, personal communication.

[Bl]   M. Blum, "Designing Program to Check their Work," ICSI Tech. Report TR-88-009.

[BK]   M. Blum and S. Kannan, "Designing Programs that Check Their Work," Proc. 21st ACM STOC (1989).

[BF]   D. Beaver and J. Feigenbaum, "Hiding Instances in Multioracle Queries," Proc. 7th STACS90, Springer-Verlag vol. 415, 37-48 (1990).

[BFL]   L. Babai, L. Fortnow, and C. Lund, "Nondeterministic Exponential Time has Two-Prover Interactive Protocols," Computational Complexity, vol. 1, 3-40 (1991).

[BLR]   M. Blum, M. Luby and R. Rubinfeld, "Self-Testing/Correcting with Applications to Numerical Problems," to appear in special issue of JCSS (1993).

[BR]   M. Blum and P. Raghavan, "Program Correctness: Can One Test for It?," IBM T.J. Watson Research Center Technical Report RC 14038 (#62902) (Sept. 1988), 12 pp.

[FF]   J. Feigenbaum and L. Fortnow, "On the Random Self-Reducibility of Complete Sets," Proc. IEEE Structure in Complexity Theory, 124-132 (1991); to appear in SIAM J. Comp., vol. 22, No. 5 (1993).

[FKLN]   L. Fortnow, H. Karloff, K. Lund, and N. Nisan, "The Polynomial Hierarchy has Interactive Proofs," Proc 31st IEEE FOCS, (1990).

[G]   P. Gemmell, "Checking for Approximate Programs and Unconditionally Secure Authentication," Ph.D. Dissertation, Department of Computer Science, U. C. Berkeley (1993).

[GMW]   O. Goldreich, S. Micali and A. Wigderson, "Proofs that Yield Nothing but their Validity and a Methodologyof Cryptographic Design," Proc. 27th IEEE Symposium on Foundations of Computer Science, 174-187 (1986).

[K1]   S. Kannan, "Program Checkers for Algebraic Problems." Ph.D. thesis to be submitted to the Computer Science Division of the University of California at Berkeley.

[K2]   R. Kannan, personal communication through S. Rudich.

[L]   R. Lipton, "New Directions in Testing," DIMACS Series on Discrete Mathematics and Theoretical Computer Science, vol. 2, pp. 191-202, (1991).

[N]   N. Nisan, "Co-SAT Has Multi-Prover Interactive Proofs," e-mail announcement, (Nov 1989).

[R]   R. Rubinfeld, "A Mathematical Theory of Self-Checking, Self-Testing, and Self-Correcting Programs, Ph.D. thesis, Computer Science Departement, U.C. Berkeley, 1990.

[S]   A. Shamir, "IP = PSPACE," Proc 31st IEEE FOCS (1990).

[SM1]   G.F. Sullivan and G.M. Masson, "Using Certification Trails to Achieve Software Fault Tolerance," Digest of the 1990 Fault Tolerant Computing Symposium, pp. 423-431, IEEE Computer Society Press, 1990.

[SM2]   G.F. Sullivan and G.M. Masson, "Certification Trails for Data Structures," Digest of the 1991 Fault Tolerant Computing Symposium, pp. 240-247, IEEE Computer Society Press, 1991.

[V1]   F. Vainstein "Error Detection and Correction in Numerical Computations by Algebraic Methods," Lecture Notes in Computer Science 539, Springer-Verlag, 1991, pp 456-464.

[V2]   F. Vainstein "Algebraic Methods In Hardware/Software Testing," Ph.D. Dissertation, Boston University, 1993.

Dynamic Interpolation Search in $o(\log \log n)$ Time

Arne Andersson* and Christer Mattsson**

Department of Computer Science, Lund University, Box 118, S-221 00 Lund, Sweden

Abstract. A new efficient data structure, based on the augmentation technique used in the interpolation search tree by Mehlhorn and Tsakalidis, is presented. We achieve:

- a trade-off between input distribution and search cost for dynamic interpolation search.
- $\Theta(\log \log n)$ expected time for search and update operations for a larger class of densities than Mehlhorn and Tsakalidis.
- $o(\log \log n)$ expected time for search and update operations for a large class of densities. As an example, we give an unbounded density for which we achieve $\Theta(\log^* n)$ expected time. We also show $\Theta(1)$ expected time for all bounded densities, in particular, the uniform distribution.
- improved worst-case cost from $\Theta(\log^2 n)$ to $\Theta(\log n)$ for searches and from $\Theta(n)$ to $\Theta(\log n)$ for updates.

We also include a discussion of terminology: which methods should be termed "interpolation search"?

1 Introduction

1.1 History

One finds many applications in practice for search methods that use a favorable distribution of input to achieve low costs. A classical method of this kind is interpolation search, presented by Peterson in 1957 [10]. For independent random data taken from the uniform distribution, the expected search cost of interpolation search is $\Theta(\log \log n)$ [3, 12]. Willard [11] introduced a modified version which works efficiently for an extended class of distributions: *regular* distributions.

A natural extension of interpolation search is to adapt it to a dynamic data structure. Frederickson [2] presented an implicit data structure, supporting updates in time $O(n^\epsilon)$, $\epsilon > 0$. In this structure, a variant of interpolation search may be used to achieve $O(\log \log n)$ expected search time on uniformly distributed elements.

If an additional space of $\Theta(n)$ is allowed, the complexity can be further improved. Itai, Konheim, and Rodeh [4] achieved $O(\log n)$ average cost and

---

* Arne.Andersson@dna.lth.se
** Christer.Mattsson@dna.lth.se

$O(\log^2 n)$ worst-case cost for insertions. They claimed without proof that interpolation search could be applied efficiently.

An improved result was given by Mehlhorn and Tsakalidis [5]. Their data structure, the *interpolation search tree*, represents the state of the art in the area of dynamic interpolation search. It requires an average cost of $\Theta(\log \log n)$ for search operations and a worst case cost of $\Theta(\log^2 n)$. Insertions and deletions can be executed in $\Theta(\log \log n)$ average time and $\Theta(\log n)$ amortized time. The worst case update time is $\Theta(n)$.

The interpolation search tree may be viewed as a dynamization of the search algorithm by Perl and Reingold [9]: a tree containing n elements has a degree of $\Theta(\sqrt{n})$ in the root, the children of the root have a degree of $\Theta(\sqrt[4]{n})$, etc. Each node is associated with an array of sample elements, one element for each subtree. By interpolating in this array, we can determine in which subtree the search is to be continued. It can be shown that constant expected time is spent at each node when the stored set is independent random data taken from the uniform distribution. This, together with the fact that the height of the tree is $\Theta(\log \log n)$, yields the search cost. The dynamization of the interpolation search tree is based on the fact that the Perl-Reingold algorithm works also when the tree is not ideally balanced, i.e. we may allow the sizes of the subtrees to vary within certain limits. By periodical reconstruction of subtrees (and the entire tree), enough balance will be maintained to allow element location at low cost.

The data structure described above, the simple interpolation search tree, is only efficient when input is taken from uniform distributions. In order to make their data structure more robust for variations in the distribution of input, Mehlhorn and Tsakalidis introduced the technique of *augmented* interpolation search. The idea is to achieve a close approximation of the inverse distribution function by adding extra information. At the root of a subtree p, containing n_p elements, and having a degree of $\Theta(\sqrt{n_p})$, a table, denoted the ID array, is used to divide the interval covered by p in n_p^α subintervals, where $\frac{1}{2} \leq \alpha < 1$. Each interval is associated with a pointer to a subtree of p. During a search, the ID is used to estimate the position of the proper subtree.

The augmented interpolation search tree handles *smooth* distributions efficiently, see Definition 1 below. Given a density $\mu(x)$ we denote the truncated and standardized density on the interval $[a, b]$ as $\mu[a, b]$. More precisely

$$\mu[a, b](x) = \begin{cases} \mu(x)/\int_a^b \mu(t)dt, & a \leq x \leq b \\ 0, & x < a \text{ or } x > b. \end{cases} \tag{1}$$

Definition 1. A density $\mu = \mu[a, b]$ is *smooth* for a parameter α, $1/2 \leq \alpha < 1$, if there exists a constant d, such that for all $c_1, c_2, c_3, a \leq c_1 < c_2 < c_3 \leq b$, and all integers n,

$$\int_{c_2 - \frac{c_3 - c_1}{\lceil n^\alpha \rceil}}^{c_2} \mu[c_1, c_3](x)dx \leq \frac{d}{\sqrt{n}}. \tag{2}$$

It should be noted that the class of smooth densities contains the regular densities.

1.2   Our results

In this abstract, we improve the method of dynamic interpolation search both regarding simplicity and efficiency. The improvements are based on the following observations:

- It is well known that if the stored items are randomly and independently drawn from a known distribution, the expected error of an estimated position among n elements is $\Theta(\sqrt{n})$. This is the reason why the interpolation search tree has a degree of $\Theta(\sqrt{n_p})$ at each node p. No matter how well the distribution is known, to use a higher branching factor does not seem to be a good idea. However, a fact which was overlooked by Mehlhorn and Tsakalidis is that this rule does not apply when the technique of augmentation is used. Instead of an approximation of the inverse distribution function, we get an estimation of the *sample density*. The paradox is that this gives us *more* information! Using this observation, we may achieve a search cost of $o(\log \log n)$ for a large class of distributions, in "contradiction" to known lower bounds.
- In order to achieve a low search cost for a large class of densities, the ID array should be as large as possible at each node. We show how the length of this array can be better tuned, still using only linear space. In this way an access cost of $\Theta(\log \log n)$ may be achieved for a larger class than the smooth densities.
- The update algorithms may be simplified by the use of a static, implicit interpolation search tree associated with binary search trees at the bottom. The implicit tree is reconstructed after $\Theta(n)$ updates. Not only will the implementation be simpler, but the analysis will also be simpler, and the worst case performance will be better.

As the result of these observations, we present a new data structure, the *augmented sampled forest*, or ASF. This structure may be tuned for a large class of distributions.

We start by introducing a more general definition of densities. Informally, the definition of smooth densities, Definition 1, states that among a number of consecutive subintervals, no subinterval should be too dense compared to the others. We feel that the two functions $\lceil n^\alpha \rceil$ and $\sqrt{n}$, determining the number of subintervals and the local density respectively, are not particularly natural; they are tailored for the augmented interpolation search tree. By replacing them with arbitrary functions, we get the following definition:

Definition 2. Given two functions f_1 and f_2, A density $\mu = \mu[a, b]$ is (f_1, f_2)-smooth if there exists a constant d, such that for all $c_1, c_2, c_3, a \leq c_1 < c_2 < c_3 \leq b$, and all integers n,

$$\int_{c_2 - \frac{c_3 - c_1}{f_1(n)}}^{c_2} \mu[c_1, c_3](x)dx \leq \frac{d \cdot f_2(n)}{n}. \tag{3}$$

Using this definition, the smooth densities studied by Mehlhorn and Tsakalidis, are $(\lceil n^\alpha \rceil, \sqrt{n})$-smooth.

Let $H(n)$ be an increasing function, representing the height of our tree structure, we show that an expected search cost of $\Theta(H(n))$ can be achieved when the input is $\left(n \cdot g(H(n)), H^{-1}(H(n) - 1)\right)$-smooth, where g is a function satisfying $\sum_{i=1}^{\infty} g(i) = \Theta(1)$.

Our findings lead to a deeper understanding of augmented interpolation search, which in turn leads us to a discussion of terminology. We argue that it is doubtful whether the augmentation technique really should be termed interpolation search. Instead, we suggest the term *guided* search.

No matter which term is used, we feel that our data structure has a high potential to be a practical alternative in many applications where data is stored and retrieved. It can also be generalized to handle multidimensional data.

Due to space limitations all proofs except the proof of Theorem 6 are omitted.

2 Model of computation

The model of computation considered is the *uniform cost* RAM.

Without loss of generality, we assume that all functions determining height, branching factors, and sizes of augmentation arrays are non-decreasing and invertible with a second derivative less than or equal to zero.

We assume that the operations are made by an adversary that knows both the distribution μ and the number of stored elements, but not the exact stored set. The adversary is allowed to chose any sequence of the following operations:

μ-Random insertion: Insert an element chosen randomly from the density μ.
Random deletion: Delete an element randomly chosen from the stored set.
Search y: Search for the element y, or its nearest neighbor. The value of y is chosen by the adversary.
Range search between x and y: Both values are chosen by the adversary.

In general, when we analyze a distribution-dependent algorithm, we can not use an adversary which exactly knows the stored set. In that case, he could simply perform repeated (random) updates until a bad instance of input occurs (which eventually happens if he is patient enough), and make a large number of queries at the weak point.

3 Warm-up: An observation on dynamization

The interpolation search tree by Mehlhorn and Tsakalidis keeps a sample of elements in each node, a new sample is taken each time the subtree is reconstructed. In this section we discuss an alternative method, the *sampled forest*, or SF. Instead of using a tree with degree $\Theta(\sqrt{n})$, we use an array of length $\Theta(n)$. As we will show, this method is both simpler and more efficient than the sampling technique used by Mehlhorn and Tsakalidis.

In detail: let n_0 be the number of stored elements at the latest reconstruction. The sampled forest consists of two arrays of length n_0:

1. REP, containing, in sorted order, the n_0 key values of the elements present at the moment when the structure was reconstructed.
2. TREE, containing n_0 binary search trees. An element x is stored in TREE[i] if REP[$i-1$]$< x \leq$ REP[i], for $i \in [2..n_0]$. If $x \leq$ REP[1] then x is stored in TREE[1], and if $x >$ REP[n_0] then x is stored in TREE[n_0].

Each time the fraction (number of updates)/n_0 exceeds some predefined value, we reconstruct the structure. After reconstruction, TREE contains single-node trees.

Search and update operations are performed in two steps. First, by searching in REP, we locate the proper binary search tree. Second, the search or update is performed in the tree. The first step may be performed in several ways, by binary search, interpolation search, or with the assistance of some auxiliary information. We start our study by showing some basic properties of the sampled forest.

Lemma 3. *The following is true for an* SF:
  space $\Theta(n)$;
  search cost *average:* $\Theta(1)$, *worst case:* $\Theta(\log n)$;
  update cost *average:* $\Theta(1)$, *amortized:* $\Theta(\log n)$, *worst case* $\Theta(n)$
  range and neighbor search *average:* $\Theta(1 + r)$, *where* r *is the number of reported elements, worst case:* $\Theta(n)$.
The time bounds do not include the time required to locate the proper search tree.

The worst case costs of $\Theta(n)$ are due to the reconstruction and the fact that during a neighbor search, we may have to scan a linear number of empty trees. These costs can be improved by the following two modifications.

First, by maintaining two sampled forests, using the technique of global rebuilding [7], the linear work spent during a global reconstruction may be spread out on the updates in such a way that a rebuilding cost of $O(1)$ is spent at each update.

Second, for range and neighbor searches we can guarantee a worst case cost of $O(\log n + r)$, where r is the number of reported elements, and still keep low average costs for all operations by keeping all elements in a binary search tree, as described by Levcopoulos and Overmars [8]. In this tree, an element can be inserted at a worst case cost of $O(1)$ when the insertion position (i. e. the position of its neighbors) is known.

Altogether, we have the following lemma.

Lemma 4. *In combination with global rebuilding and a binary search tree, the* SF *supports insert, delete, search, range search, and neighbor search operations at a worst case cost of* $O(\log n + r)$, *where* r *is the number of reported elements.*

Before we discuss auxiliary structures, we recognize the fact that the plain sampled forest can be used for dynamic interpolation search simply by using

interpolation search in REP. Compared to the simple (non-augmented) interpolation search tree, it has some important advantages. First, it is simple, almost trivial, both to understand and to implement. Second, it is not tailored
for uniform distributions; we may use any interpolation search method, such as
Willard's algorithm to handle other distributions than the uniform. Third, it has
a better worst-case behavior.

Theorem 5. *When the interpolation search method by Willard is used, the following is true for an* SF *if the elements are drawn from a regular distribution:*
   space $\Theta(n)$;
   search cost *average:* $\Theta(\log \log n)$, *worst case:* $\Theta(\log n)$;
   update cost *average:* $\Theta(\log \log n)$, *worst case:* $\Theta(\log n)$;
   range and neighbor search *average:* $\Theta(\log \log n + r)$, *worst:* $\Theta(\log n + r)$,
   where r *is the number of reported elements.*

4 Main result: the augmented sampled forest

As we mentioned in the introduction, the technique of augmentation gives us
an approximation of the *sample density*. We also claimed that when the sample
density is used as a base for interpolation search, the lower bound of $\Theta(\log \log n)$
does not apply. In this section, we give a constructive proof of this claim by
presenting the *augmented sampled forest*, or ASF. This data structure consists
of a static implicit tree with binary search trees at the bottom, maintained
as described in the previous section. That is, updates are made in the binary
search trees and the implicit tree contains the sample. In this way we avoid
all the cumbersome trouble with bookkeeping, reconstruction, and allocation of
varying-length arrays.

We characterize our implicit tree by three nondecreasing functions $H(n)$,
$R(n)$, and $I(n)$. A (sub-)tree containing n elements has a height of $H(n)$, the
root of the tree has degree of $R(n)$, and at the root we use an ID array of
length $I(n)$. There is an obvious relation between $H(n)$ and $R(n)$: choosing
$R(n) = H^{-1}(H(n) - 1)$ we obtain the desired height $H(n)$. In order to handle
a large class of densities, the approximation of the sample density should be as
detailed as possible, that is, the function $I(n)$ should be large. Basically, we can
allow $I(n)$ to grow without any restriction, the only limitation being the amount
of memory available. For $I(n) = n \cdot g(H(n))$, where $\sum_{i=1}^{\infty} g(i) = \Theta(1)$, the total
space occupied by the tree will be linear.

In detail, let n be the size of the stored set at the last global reconstruction.
As parameters to our data structure, the *augmented sampled forest*, or ASF, we
use two functions $R(n)$ and $I(n)$. We use an implicit tree containing n elements,
$x_1, \ldots, x_n$. The root of the tree is represented in the following way:

- An array, REP, of length $R(n)$. $\text{REP}[i] = x_{in/R(n)}$, $1 \le i \le R(n)$. Each entry
  in REP is associated with a subtree, defined recursively. The tree associated
  with $\text{REP}[i]$ contains elements x such that $\text{REP}[i-1] < x \le \text{REP}[i]$, $2 \le i \le$

$R(n) + 1$. If $x \leq \text{REP}[1]$ then x is stored in the tree associated with $\text{REP}[1]$, if $x \geq \text{REP}[R(n)]$ then x is stored in the tree associated with $\text{REP}[R(n)]$.

- An array, ID, of length $I(n)$. $\text{ID}[i] = j$ iff $\text{REP}[j] < x_1 + i(x_n - x_1)/I(n) \leq \text{REP}[j+1]$. In other words, we split the interval between the smallest and largest element in $I(n)$ subintervals of equal size. $\text{ID}[i]$ contain the index of the smallest element falling in the ith subinterval. If the subinterval is empty, $\text{ID}[i]$ equal $\text{ID}[i+1]$. $\text{ID}[1] = 1$.

Since the tree is implicit, all ID and REP arrays are concatenated.

During a search for an element x we use ID to estimate the position of x in REP. From this position an exponential and binary search is made. Below, in Figure 1, we present the algorithm for searching an element in an ASF. Algorithms for the update operations can be obtained from the search algorithm with minor changes.

```
procedure FindTree(x, T)
(* min and max denotes the endpoints of *)
(* the interval covered by the (sub-)tree T. *)
(* I denotes the length of the ID array. *)
      j := trunc((x − min) · ─────I─────)
                              max − min
      if j < 1 then
            return   The first subtree
      elseif j > I then
            return   The last subtree
      else
            Perform an exponential and binary search
            in REP starting at position ID[j]
            return   Correct subtree of REP
      endif
endproc FindTree
```

```
procedure Search(x, T)
      repeat
            T := FindTree(x, T)
      until T is a binary tree
      SearchBinaryTree(x, T)
endproc Search
```

Figure 1. Algorithms for searching an element in an ASF.

Theorem 6. *If the density is* $(n \cdot g(H(n)), H^{-1}(H(n) - 1))$-*smooth, where* $\sum_{i=1}^{\infty} g(i) = \Theta(1)$, *there is an* ASF *which supports searches and updates at an expected cost of* $\Theta(H(n))$ *and uses* $\Theta(n)$ *space.*

Proof. Without loss of generality, we assume that the number of stored elements = size of the sample = n. We claim that the conditions of the theorem are fulfilled by an ASF with the following parameters:

$$R(n) = \frac{n}{H^{-1}(H(n) - 1)} \quad \text{and} \quad I(n) = n \cdot g(H(n)). \tag{4}$$

The height $H(n)$ of the implicit tree is given by

$$H(n) = 1 + H\left(\frac{n}{R(n)}\right). \tag{5}$$

It is easily verified that our choice of $R(n)$ satisfies (5).

The space is given by the recurrence relation

$$S(n) = C_1 I(n) + C_2 R(n) + R(n) S\left(\frac{n}{R(n)}\right), \tag{6}$$

where C_1 and C_2 are constants depending on the implementation. We substitute $S(n) = nP(n)$, giving

$$P(n) = \frac{C_1 I(n)}{n} + \frac{C_2 R(n)}{n} + P\left(\frac{n}{R(n)}\right). \tag{7}$$

If $n \cdot g(H(n))$ is substituted for $I(n)$ and (4) is used in (7) we get:

$$P(n) \leq C_1 g(H(n)) + \frac{C_2}{H^{-1}(H(n) - 1)} + P(H^{-1}(H(n) - 1))$$

$$= C_1 g(H(n)) + \frac{C_2}{H^{-1}(H(n) - 1)} +$$

$$C_1 g(H(n) - 1) + \frac{C_2}{H^{-1}(H(n) - 2)} + \cdots + P(\Theta(1)). \tag{8}$$

Since the height is $H(n)$ and $P(\Theta(1)) = \Theta(1)$, we have:

$$P(n) \leq \sum_{i=1}^{H(n)-1} \left(C_1 g(H(n) - i + 1) + \frac{C_2}{H^{-1}(H(n) - i)}\right) + \Theta(1)$$

$$= C_1 \sum_{i=2}^{H(n)} g(i) + C_2 \sum_{i=1}^{H(n)-1} \frac{1}{H^{-1}(i)} + \Theta(1). \tag{9}$$

From the properties of the function g it follows that the first sum is $\Theta(1)$. The second sum increases as $H(n)$ grows. For reasons to be discussed below, see Example 4 in the next section, $H(n)$ will always be $O(\log n)$. This implies that the second sum is bounded by a constant. Thus, the total space is $\Theta(n)$.

The expected costs of $\Theta(H(n))$ follows from Lemma 3 together with the fact that the expected time spent at each node is constant. This can be shown from the definition of (f_1, f_2)-smooth densities. Let p be a node on the search path and let n_p be the number of elements in the subtree rooted at p. Further, let c_1 and c_3 be the endpoints of the interval covered by p. The length of the ID-array at p is $n_p g(H(n_p))$. When we arrive at p, we make an interpolation step in order to find the proper entry of ID. The element searched for is contained in an interval $[c_2 - (c_3 - c_1)/n_p g(H(n_p)), c_2]$ for some constant c_2. This interval is covered by one entry in ID. Let X be the number of the n_p elements that belong to this interval, then X is binomially distributed with

$$E[X] = n_p \int_{c_2 - \frac{c_3 - c_1}{n_p g(H(n_p))}}^{c_2} \mu[c_1, c_3](x)dx \leq n_p \frac{dH^{-1}(H(n_p) - 1)}{n_p} = \frac{dn_p}{R(n_p)}. \quad (10)$$

Since every subtree of p is of size $n_p/R(n_p)$, the cost to find the proper subtree is $O(XR(n_p)/n_p)$. From this fact it is simple to prove, in a similar manner as seen in [6], that the expected number of elements to probe in REP is $\Theta(1)$. $\quad\square$

Theorem 7. *The worst case cost of a search or update in the ASF is $\Theta(\log n)$.*

5 On the relation between expected cost and density

Theorem 6 gives a trade-off between expected cost and distribution. It is natural to believe that when the height of the implicit tree increases, the class of densities gets larger. However, this is not always the case!

In this section, we study the relation between search cost and distribution. In Lemma 8, we show that a higher search cost corresponds to a larger class of distributions, as long as $H(n)$ is increasing. In Lemma 9 we show the fact that $(n \cdot g(H(n)), H^{-1}(H(n) - 1))$-smooth densities may not be zero on an interval, as long as $H(n)$ is increasing and $H(n) = o(\log n)$. There are two exceptions, occurring at the extremas of $H(n)$; when $H(n) = \Theta(1)$ and when $H(n) = \Theta(\log n)$.

Lemma 8. *The class of $(n \cdot g(H(n)), H^{-1}(H(n) - 1))$-smooth densities contains the class of $(n \cdot g(P(n)), P^{-1}(P(n) - 1))$-smooth densities if $H(n)$, $P(n)$, and $\frac{H(n)}{P(n)}$ are increasing functions.*

Lemma 9. *Let μ be a $(n \cdot g(H(n)), H^{-1}(H(n) - 1))$-smooth density such that $H(n)$ is not $O(1)$ and $H(n) = o(\log n)$, then μ is not zero on an interval.*

5.1 Example 1: the augmented interpolation search tree revisited

If we choose $R(n) = \sqrt{n}$ and $I(n) = \lceil n^\alpha \rceil$, $1/2 \leq \alpha < 1$, we achieve a data structure with the same expected cost as the augmented interpolation search tree [5]. It supports search efficiently with an expected cost of $\Theta(\log \log n)$ when the input is $(n^\alpha, \sqrt{n})$-smooth.

However, the ASF allows us to do better. If we replace $H(n)$ by $\Theta(\log \log n)$ in Theorem 6 and use $g(x) = 1/x^{1+\epsilon}$ where $\epsilon > 0$, we get the following corollary:

Corollary 10. *A average cost of $\Theta(\log \log n)$ for searches and updates can be achieved for any $(n/(\log \log n)^{1+\epsilon}, n^{1-\delta})$-smooth density μ, where $\epsilon > 0$ and $0 < \delta < 1$.*

This fact allows us to achieve the same time bounds as Mehlhorn and Tsakalidis for a larger class of distributions.

Lemma 11. $(\lceil n^{\alpha} \rceil, \sqrt{n}) - smooth \subset (n/(\log \log n)^{1+\epsilon}, \sqrt{n}) - smooth$, for $1/2 \leq \alpha < 1, \epsilon > 0$.

Hence, the augmented interpolation search tree is reduced to a non-optimized special case, cumbersome to implement.

5.2 Example 2: $\Theta(1)$ expected cost for bounded densities

Another interesting special case occurs when the height of the implicit tree is set to $\Theta(1)$. In this case, our data structure behaves in the same manner as the well known method of bucketing [1]. In detail, we set

$$H(n) = \begin{cases} 0, n = 1 \\ 1, n > 1 \end{cases} \tag{11}$$

This function is only invertible at zero, but $H^{-1}(H(n) - 1)$ is computable and equals one. The densities are $(n, 1)$-smooth, which is equivalent to the class of bounded densities.

Corollary 12. *An expected cost of $\Theta(1)$ for searches and updates can be achieved for any distribution which is bounded.*

Note that a bounded density may be zero on an interval. From this fact and Lemma 9 we conclude that an increased search cost does not always give a larger class of densities.

5.3 Example 3: $o(\log \log n)$ expected cost for an unbounded density

In [6], it is mentioned that an expected search cost of $\Theta(\log \log n)$ can be achieved for an unbounded density. For some unbounded densities, the ASF allows even faster searches. As an example, when the outdegree $R(n)$ is chosen as $\frac{n}{\log^2 n}$, we achieve an expected cost of $\Theta(\log^* n)$ for $\mu(x) = \mu[0, 1] = -\ln(x)$.

Lemma 13. $\mu[0, 1](x) = -\ln x$ is $(n/(\log^* n)^{1+\epsilon}, \log^2 n)$-smooth.

Lemma 14. *If $R(n) = n/\log^2 n$ then the height of the implicit tree is $\Theta(\log^* n)$.*

The following corollary follows immediately from Lemma 13, Lemma 14, and Theorem 6.

Corollary 15. *There is an ASF which support searches and updates at an expected cost of $\Theta(\log^* n)$ for $\mu(x) = \mu[0, 1](x) = -\ln(x)$.*

5.4 Example 4: $\Theta(\log n)$ expected cost for any distribution

If we chose $H(n) = \Theta(\log n)$, the density may be $(n \cdot g(\Theta(\log n)), \Theta(n))$-smooth. This class contains all densities, and we get $R(n) = \Theta(1), R(n) \geq 2$. Since the degree of the nodes in the implicit tree is constant, the time spent at each node will be constant, even without the ID array. However, in many cases, the constant factor will be improved by the ID. Using $I(n) = n/\Theta(\log^{1+\epsilon} n)$, we still use only linear space. Note that this class of densities may be zero on an interval.

5.5 Relation between densities

In Figure 2 we show the relation between the densities discussed above. The hierarchy discussed in Lemma 8 is represented by the $(n \cdot g(H(n)), H^{-1}(H(n) - 1))$-smooth densities and the $(n, 1)$-smooth densities represent the special case when $H(n) = O(1)$. We also illustrate the fact that the class of regular densities [11] is quite small. Of course, the densities discussed in Example 4 contains all classes in the figure.

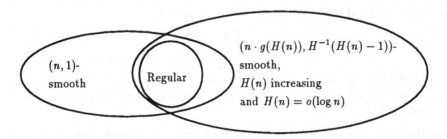

Figure 2. Density relation.

6 Concluding discussion

Compared to previous methods for dynamic interpolation search, our data structure shows a number of interesting features.

Simple implementation The data structure consists of two arrays, one of which is associated with binary search trees. Both the global reconstruction and the updates in the trees are easy to implement. In particular, we feel that the simplicity becomes evident when we compare our data structure with the interpolation search tree.

Improved tradeoff between distribution and search cost The ASF can be adapted to a large variety of distributions. In particular, we extend the class of distribution for which a search cost of $O(\log \log n)$ can be achieved. Furthermore, for a large class of distributions, we obtain a search cost of $o(\log \log n)$. A comparison between the interpolation search tree and the sampled forest is shown in Table 1.

What does the tradeoff between distribution and search time tell us about the ASF? In practice, it is rarely the case that the input is independent, randomly chosen from a distribution which can be classified. In this sense our (f_1, f_2)-smooth densities are neither more nor less natural than regular densities or the densities studied by Mehlhorn and Tsakalidis. However, the fact that a method can theoretically handle a wide class of distributions gives an *indication* that it is well suited for practical use.

Table 1. Results obtained: the sampled forest compared with the interpolation search tree. By simple sampled forest, we mean the data structure described in Theorem 1. $H(n)$ is an increasing function and $H(n) = o(\log n)$.

	interpolation search tree		sampled forest	
	simple	augmented	simple	augmented
distribution	uniform	smooth	regular	$(n \cdot g(H(n)), H^{-1}(H(n) - 1))$-smooth
search cost				
average	$\Theta(\log \log n)$	$\Theta(\log \log n)$	$\Theta(\log \log n)$	$\Theta(H(n))$
worst case	$\Theta(\log^2 n)$	$\Theta(\log^2 n)$	$\Theta(\log n)$	$\Theta(\log n)$
update cost				
average	$\Theta(\log \log n)$	$\Theta(\log \log n)$	$\Theta(\log \log n)$	$\Theta(H(n))$
amortized	$\Theta(\log n)$	$\Theta(\log n)$	$\Theta(\log n)$	$\Theta(\log n)$
worst case	$\Theta(n)$	$\Theta(n)$	$\Theta(\log n)$	$\Theta(\log n)$

Facing a practical application, it is possible to change the function $H(n)$ at each global reconstruction until a suitable choice is found. Since the worst case costs are logarithmic, we can afford to make a bad choice every now and then.

A discussion of terminology. We believe that the results presented here shed some new light on the topic of dynamic interpolation search. For this reason, we end this abstract with a short discussion of terminology.

We would like to emphasize the fact that our augmented sampled forest uses interpolation search in the same sense as the augmented interpolation search tree by Mehlhorn and Tsakalidis. In both cases, we use a table as an approximation of the distribution. By interpolating in this table, we get a good estimation of in which subtree the search should be continued.

The purpose of the augmentation technique was to achieve an approximation of the distribution μ. However, there is a major difference between knowing μ and the augmentation technique, a difference which was overlooked by Mehlhorn and Tsakalidis: by taking a sample of the current set we get an estimation of the *sample density*. This is the reason why we achieve a search cost of $o(\log \log n)$ for a large class of distributions, in "contradiction" to known lower bounds.

We feel that the method of augmentation should be distinguished from classical interpolation search. It should reside somewhere between interpolation search and distributive partitioning (bucketing and trie structures). Note the difference between our structure and the partitioning method used in tries and bucketing. In our case, the elements are recursively split into groups of equal size and the augmentation is used to search efficiently among these groups. In a trie or bucketing scheme, the domain is split into subintervals of equal size, and the number of elements in each subinterval (subtree) may vary considerably. The two methods are similar only at one extreme, as described in Example 2.

To distinguish between the methods, we suggest the term "guided search" for the augmented interpolation search tree and the augmented sampled forest. In our opinion, only the two *simple* structures should be termed dynamic interpolation search. Among these two, the simple sampled forest has obvious advantages.

A final comment. We end this presentation reminding the reader that dynamic dictionaries are used in many, many applications. Regardless of whether the ASF should be called dynamic interpolation search or not, we believe that it has a high potential as a practical data structure.

Acknowledgments. We would like to thank Dr. Christos Levcopoulos for valuable comments.

This work was partially supported by projects F-FU 8992-317, TFR 91-357, and TFR 92-82.

References

1. L. Devroye. *Lecture Notes on Bucket Algorithms.* Birkhäuser, 1985. ISBN 0-8176-3328-6.
2. G. Frederickson. Implicit Data Structures for the Dictionary Problem. *Journal of the ACM*, 30(1):80–94, 1983.
3. G. H. Gonnet. *Interpolation and Interplation Hash Searching.* PhD thesis, University of Waterloo, February 1977.
4. A. Itai, A.G. Konheim, and M. Rodeh. A sparse table implementation of priority queues. In *Proc. 8th ICALP*, pages 417–431, 1981.
5. K. Mehlhorn and A. Tsakalidis. Dynamic interpolation search. In *Proc. 12th ICALP*, 1985.
6. K. Mehlhorn and A. Tsakalidis. Dynamic interpolation search. To appear in Journal of the ACM, 1993.
7. M. H. Overmars. *The Design of Dynamic Data Structures*, volume 156 of *Lecture Notes in Computer Science.* Springer Verlag, 1983. ISBN 3-540-12330-X.
8. M. H. Overmars and C. Levcopoulos. A balanced search tree with O(1) worst-case update time. *Acta Informatica*, 26:269–277, 1988.
9. Y. Perl and E. M. Reingold. Understanding the Complexity of Interpolation Search. *Information Processing Letters*, 6(6):219–222, December 1977.
10. W. W. Peterson. Addressing for Random-Access Storage. *IBM J. Res. Development*, 1(4):130–146, April 1957.
11. D. E. Willard. Searching Unindexed and Nonuniformly Generated Files in $\log \log N$ Time. *SIAM Journal on Computing*, 14(4), 1985.
12. A. C. Yao and F. F. Yao. The Complexity of Searching an Ordered Random Table. In *Proceeding Seventeenth Annual Symposium on Foundations of Computer Science*, pages 173–177, HOUSTON TX, October 1976. IEEE.

Searching among Intervals and Compact Routing Tables

Greg N. Frederickson[1]

Department of Computer Science, Purdue University
West Lafayette, Indiana 47907, USA

Abstract. Shortest paths in weighted directed graphs are considered within the context of compact routing tables. Strategies are given for organizing compact routing tables so that extracting a requested shortest path will take $o(k \log n)$ time, where k is the number of edges in the path and n the number of vertices in the graph. The first strategy takes $O(k + \log n)$ time to extract a requested shortest path. A second strategy takes $O(K/n^2)$ average time, if all requested paths are equally likely, where K is the total number of edges (counting repetitions) in all $n(n-1)$ shortest paths. Both strategies introduce techniques for storing collections of disjoint intervals over the integers from 1 to n, so that identifying the interval within which a given integer falls can be performed quickly.

1 Introduction

This paper addresses a connection between two fundamental problems: data structures for handling subsets of the integers from 1 to m [vBKZ], [FKS], [TY], [Wi] [Y], and shortest paths in graphs [AHU], [CLR], [DP], [D], [Fl], [Fs3], [Fm], [FT], [Wa]. We consider representing shortest paths in special classes of graphs by compact routing tables [Fs4], [Fs5], [FJ]. Each such table can be characterized as containing a set of disjoint intervals over the integers from 1 to n, the number of vertices. A search in a table consists of determining in which of the intervals a requested value is contained. The compact routing tables in [Fs4], [Fs5] and [FJ] can be searched by a modified binary search. Thus extracting a shortest path whose length is k edges takes $O(\log n)$ time per edge, or $O(k \log n)$ overall. We propose new strategies for organizing these tables that allow for faster extraction of a requested shortest path.

Identifying the interval that contains a given value reduces to the problem of finding a predecessor of that value in the set of first values of the intervals. The problem of handling predecessor queries with respect to a static subset of q integer values drawn from the range 1 to m was first addressed in [vBKZ], in which a data structure of size $\Theta(m \log \log m)$ is used to answer a query in $\Theta(\log \log m)$ time. In [Wi] a data structure of size $O(q)$ is designed that can be constructed so that each query can be handled in $O(\log \log m)$ time. The data structure in [Wi] includes a number of tables for answering membership queries for the subset of q integer values drawn from the range 1 to m. These tables [FKS] allow membership queries to be answered in constant time, but their construction time is large, $O(q^3 \log m)$.

An alternative to the tables in [Fs4], [Fs5] and [FJ] is given in [DPZ], such that extracting a shortest path takes $O(k + \log n)$ time. Unfortunately, those tables are less compact, using $\Omega(n \log n)$ space and preprocessing time, even in the case that the graph is outerplanar. Another alternative is suggested by the data structure in [Wi], which would use $O(n)$ space and allow for a shortest path to be extracted in $O(k \log \log n)$ time. Unfortunately, $O(n^3 \log n)$ preprocessing time would be used.

We present two approaches. For simplicity, we state our results in this introduction relative to outerplanar graphs, but in the paper itself extend the results to graphs that are not outerplanar. The extension uses the partial hammock decomposition techniques of [Fs4] and [Fs5], as does the approach in [DPZ]. Our first approach allows us to reorganize compact routing tables in $O(n)$ time and space so that extracting a shortest path takes $O(k + \log n)$ time. This matches the extraction time of [DPZ] but has better space and preprocessing time. It matches the space of [Wi], has a much better preprocessing time, and a better extraction time when k is $\omega(\log n / \log \log n)$. Our second approach removes the additive term of $\log n$, but only for a certain type of average. A shortest path can be extracted in expected time proportional to the average number of edges in a shortest path, assuming that any source-destination pair is equally likely. The preprocessing time and space remain $O(n)$.

Our contribution lies in designing two techniques for organizing tables for intervals. The first technique assigns a weight to each interval and organizes the table to have access times sensitive to the weights. The choice of the particular weighting function and its effect on the search time analysis makes this technique interesting. The second technique uses a compressed representation of the set of intervals such that at least half of the searches terminate successfully on an initial probe, with any unresolved search continuing recursively within the compressed representation of the remaining intervals. A charging system that takes into account where shortest paths might have gone but didn't(!) makes the second technique interesting.

Our paper is organized as follows. In section 2 we review the notion of compact routing tables based on the work in [Fs4] and [Fs5]. In section 3 we present weight-adjusted compact routing tables. In section 4 we present our compressed representation, called a multi-level indexing table.

A full version of this paper is available from the author (email contact: gnf@cs.purdue.edu).

2   Review of compact routing tables

Compact routing tables appear in [FJ], [Fs4] and [Fs5] and are based on ideas in [SK], [vLT]. They encode all pairs shortest paths information for a directed graph with real-valued edge weights, but no negative cycles. They are of use only if graph G is sparse, i.e., that the number of edges is $O(n)$. The approach relies on an appropriate renaming of the vertices. The compact routing tables can be found in time that ranges from $O(n)$ up to $O(n^2 \log n)$ as a certain topological measure of G ranges from 0 up to $O(n)$. This encoding helps to avoid a lower bound of $\Omega(n^2)$ time that would be needed if the output were required to be in the form of n shortest path trees or a distance matrix. The topological measure is $\tilde{\gamma}(G)$, the minimum number of a special type of outerplanar graph called a *hammock* into which G can be partitioned. The algorithm in [Fs4] and [Fs5] partitions G into *partial hammocks*, which are similar to hammocks in structure, i.e., they are a special type of outerplanar graph. The algorithm then constructs compact routing tables of total size $O(\tilde{\gamma}(G)n)$ using $O(\tilde{\gamma}(G)n + (\tilde{\gamma}(G))^2 \log \tilde{\gamma}(G))$ time. Compact routing tables are suitable for a distributed network, in which each table is local to a node in the network. If global tables are allowed, then the approach in [Fs4] and [Fs5] can be modified to generate tables of total size $O(n + (\tilde{\gamma}(G))^2))$ in $O(n + (\tilde{\gamma}(G))^2 \log \tilde{\gamma}(G))$ time.

Let the vertices be assigned names from 1 to n in a manner to be discussed. Assume preprocessing so that edges satisfy the generalized triangle inequality, i.e., each edge $\langle v, w \rangle$ is a shortest path from v to w. For every edge $\langle v, w \rangle$ incident from any given vertex v, let $S(v, w)$ be the set of vertices such that there is a shortest path from v to each vertex in $S(v, w)$ with the first edge on this path being $\langle v, w \rangle$. When there are two or more shortest paths between a pair of vertices, an appropriate tie-breaking rule is employed so that for each pair of vertices v and $u \neq v$, u is in just one set $S(v, w)$ for some w. We assume that a shortest path from v to w will have the fewest number of edges among all paths from v to w of shortest distance.

Let each set $S(v, w)$ be described as a union of a minimum number of subintervals of $[1, n]$. We allow a subinterval to wrap around from n back to 1, i.e., a set $\{i, i+1, \ldots, n, 1, 2, \ldots, j\}$, where $i > j+1$ will be described by $[i, j]$. We also use open interval notation, and half-open interval notation, so that $\{i+1, \ldots, j-1\}$ is described by (i, j), and $\{i, \ldots, j-1\}$ is described by $[i, j)$. All intervals are assumed to be nonempty, so that for example $[v, v]$ contains all vertices.

Consider an outerplanar graph. (A graph is outerplanar if it can be embedded in the plane such that all vertices are on one face [H].) It was observed in [Fs5] that if the vertices of a directed outerplanar graph are named in clockwise order around this one face, then each set $S(v, w)$ is a single interval $[l, h]$. A compact routing table for v consists of a list of initial values l of each interval, along with pointers to the corresponding edges. The list is a rotated list [MS], [Fs1], and can be searched using a modified binary search. For a graph that is not outerplanar, an edge label $S(v, w)$ can consist of more than one subinterval. A compact routing table then has an entry for each of the subintervals contained in an edge label at v.

3 Weight-adjusted compact routing tables

We consider first a directed graph whose undirected counterpart is outerplanar. Assume that the vertices are named in clockwise order around the exterior face of an outerplane embedding of this graph. Consider this outerplane embedding. Let v be a vertex with at least 2 edges incident from it. Consider these edges ordered clockwise around v in the embedding. Let $\langle v, w \rangle$ be one of these edges, $\langle v, w' \rangle$ the edge counterclockwise from $\langle v, w \rangle$, and $\langle v, w'' \rangle$ the edge clockwise from $\langle v, w \rangle$. Define the *weight* $W(v, w)$ of edge $\langle v, w \rangle$ to be the number of integers in the interval $[w', w'']$. The total weight of all edges incident from v is $2n$.

For each vertex v, form a dictionary in which each element is an interval $S(v, w)$. Associated with interval $S(v, w)$ will be w. The basic approach in section 2 of [Fs2] is used to implement the dictionary, where $W(v, w)$ is the weight of element $S(v, w)$. The elements will be grouped together on the basis of weights and arranged within groups as lists ordered by the first value of each interval. Let A_i be the i-th group, $i = 0, 1, ..., s$, with the weight of any element in A_i being no larger than the weight of any element in A_{i-1}, for $i = 1, 2, ..., s$. Set the size of A_i to be $2^{2^i} - 1$ for $i = 0, 1, ..., s - 1$, and the size of A_s to be at most $2^{2^s} - 1$. Call the above structure a *weight-adjusted compact routing table*.

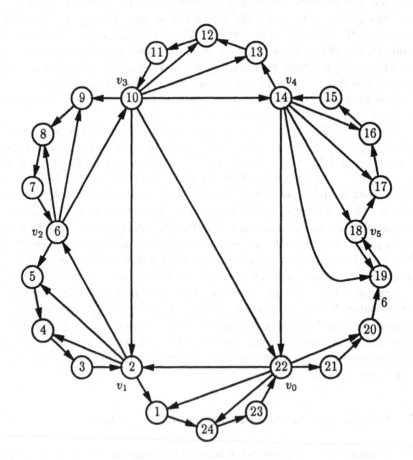

Fig. 1. A directed strongly connected outerplanar graph

Consider the outerplanar graph in Fig. 1. Each edge shown has cost 1 except for the edge $\langle 20, 19 \rangle$, which has cost 6. For vertex 22 we have $S(22, 24) = [23, 24]$, $S(22, 1) = [1, 1]$, $S(22, 2) = [2, 19]$, $S(22, 20) = [20, 20]$ and $S(22, 21) = [21, 21]$. The corresponding weights are $W(22, 24) = 4$, $W(22, 1) = 2$, $W(22, 2) = 19$, $W(22, 20) = 19$ and $W(22, 21) = 4$. The weight-adjusted compact routing table for vertex 22 is shown in Fig. 2. It has as its list of intervals $[2, 19]$, $[20, 20]$, $[21, 21]$, $[23, 24]$, $[1, 1]$. The associated list of neighbors of 22 will be $2, 20, 21, 24, 1$. Group 0 consists of the first element in the table, group 1 consists of the next 3, and group 2 consists of the remaining element.

[2, 19]	[20, 20]	[21, 21]	[23, 24]	[1, 1]
2	20	21	24	1

Fig. 2. The weight-adjusted compact routing table for vertex 22

A weight-adjusted compact routing table is searched for u as follows. Examine each group in turn, starting with group A_0, until an interval containing u is found. Within a group, search the list of intervals using binary search. It follows from the proof of Thm. 1 in [Fs2] that finding the interval $S(v, w)$ that contains u will take $O(\log r)$ time, where r is the rank of $W(v, w)$. As discussed in [Fs2], the above structure can be constructed in time proportional to the number of elements it contains if the elements are presented in sorted order. The elements for all of the weight-adjusted compact routing tables of an outerplanar graph can together be sorted in a total of $O(n)$ time by performing a two-pass bucket-sort of the pairs consisting of v and the first value in an interval labeling an edge incident from v.

Theorem 1. *Let G be a directed graph of n vertices, whose undirected counterpart is outerplanar. The time to extract a shortest path $v_0, v_1, \cdots, v_k$ using weight-adjusted compact routing tables is $O(k + \log n)$.*

Proof. (Sketch) The rank of $W(v_0, v_1)$ with respect to the weights of edges incident from v_0 is at most $2n/W(v_0, v_1)$. Let $[w_i, u_i]$ be the interval that need not be searched when determining v_{i+1}. Clearly, $w_0 = v_0$ and $u_0 = v_0$. For $i = 1, 2, \ldots, d-1$, we define w_i and u_i as follows. If there is an edge $\langle v_{i-1}, x \rangle$ such that x is in the interval (v_i, w_{i-1}), then let $\langle v_{i-1}, w_i \rangle$ be the next such edge clockwise from $\langle v_{i-1}, v_i \rangle$. Otherwise, set w_i to w_{i-1}. If there is an edge $\langle v_{i-1}, x' \rangle$ such that x' is in the interval (u_{i-1}, v_i), then let $\langle v_{i-1}, u_i \rangle$ be the previous edge clockwise from $\langle v_{i-1}, v_i \rangle$. Otherwise, set u_i to u_{i-1}. Let $size(u_i, w_i)$ be the number of integers in the open interval (u_i, w_i).

Consider determining vertex v_{i+1} given v_i. Edges incident from v_i whose S sets contain vertices from the interval $[w_i, u_i]$ are *backpath edges* $\langle v_j, v_i \rangle$, where $i + 1 < j < k$, and at most two other edges. Let b_i be the number of backpath edges incident from vertex v_i. The total number of backpath edges is at most $k - 2$. The remaining edges incident from v_i will have a total weight of at most $2size(u_i, w_i)$. Thus the rank of $W(v_i, v_{i+1})$ will be at most $b_i + 2 + 2size(u_i, w_i)/W(v_i, v_{i+1}) \leq b_i + 2 + 2size(u_i, w_i)/size(u_{i+1}, w_{i+1})$.

The total search time will then be no worse than proportional to

$$\sum_{i=0}^{k-1} \log(b_i + 2 + 2size(u_i, w_i)/size(u_{i+1}, w_{i+1}))$$

$$\leq (k - 2) + k + k + \log \prod_{i=0}^{k-1} size(u_i, w_i)/size(u_{i+1}, w_{i+1})$$

$$\leq 3k - 2 + \log size(u_0, w_0) \leq 3k + \log n.$$

We next discuss graphs that are not outerplanar. The challenge here is to avoid using time that has an additive $\log n$ term per partial hammock. We modify the naming of vertices slightly from that used in [Fs4] so that all attachment vertices are named consecutively. Each vertex v will then have a table *to_AV*, giving for each attachment vertex a the neighbor w from v such that a is in $S(v, w)$.

Each vertex will have a second table *to_all*, accessing vertices in the whole graph. This table will be similar to a weight-adjusted compact routing table, but each interval in the table will have associated with it not only the next edge in a shortest path to each vertex in the interval, but also the furthest attachment vertex through which such a shortest path would go, if the shortest path leaves the partial hammock. These tables are most likely longer, since an interval in the unmodified compact routing table may need to be split to reflect the sixteen different pairs of attachment vertices per pair of partial hammocks. However, these new compact routing tables will still have total size $O(\tilde{\gamma}(G)n)$, since the size of the the tables cannot exceed the time to generate them, which is $O(\tilde{\gamma}(G)n)$.

If a vertex v is not an attachment vertex, then it has a table *within_hamm*, a weight-adjusted compact routing table for the partial hammock, with weights W for edges computed as though the partial hammock were in isolation. Finally, every attachment vertex a has a table *from_AV* that is a complete routing table from a to every other vertex. The above set of tables together constitute *distrib_tables1*.

Algorithm *distrib_route1* for extracting the shortest path from v to u is the following. First use *to_all* and *to_AV* to find the portion of the shortest path that is not contained in the partial hammock containing u. Then use *from_AV* and *within_hamm* to find the remaining portion of the shortest path.

Theorem 2. *Let G be a directed graph of n vertices. The total time for algorithm distrib_route1 to extract a shortest path $v_0, v_1, \cdots, v_k$ from distrib_tables1 is $O(k + \log n)$. The time and space to set up distrib_tables1 are $O(\widetilde{\gamma}(G)n + (\widetilde{\gamma}(G))^2 \log \widetilde{\gamma}(G))$ and $O(\widetilde{\gamma}(G)n)$, resp., where $\widetilde{\gamma}(G)$ is the hammock number of G.*

Proof. The time for the search algorithm is established as follows. The initial search for u in the table *to_all* associated with v will take $O(\log n)$ time. Each index into a table *to_AV* or a table *from_AV* will take constant time, and advance the shortest path by one edge. The search of the final partial hammock will take $O(k' + \log n')$ time, where k' is the number of edges in that portion of the shortest path within the final partial hammock, and n' is the size of the final partial hammock.

We finally discuss the second version of the method for handling general graphs. In this version not all information is stored in tables associated with particular vertices. The preprocessing time and the space can then be reduced. A key idea taken from section 9 of [Fs5] is to keep distances between all pairs of attachment vertices. If v is in partial hammock H and u be in partial hammock $H' \neq H$, and let a_1, a_2, a_3 and a_4 be the attachment vertices of H, and let b_1, b_2, b_3 and b_4 be the attachment vertices of H'. Then choose i and j to minimize $d(v, a_i) + d(a_i, b_j) + d(b_j, u)$.

Theorem 3. *The total time for algorithm nondistrib_route1 to extract a shortest path $v_0, v_1, \cdots, v_k$ from nondistrib_tables1 is $O(k + \log n)$. The time and space to set up nondistrib_tables1 are $O(n + (\widetilde{\gamma}(G))^2 \log \widetilde{\gamma}(G))$ and $O(n + (\widetilde{\gamma}(G))^2)$, resp.*

4   Multi-level indexing tables

In this section we discuss our second variation of compact routing tables that allows for faster retrieval of paths. This variation allows a shortest path to be retrieved in expected time proportional to the average length of a shortest path if all source and destination pairs are equally likely. This solution is presented in two parts. First, multi-level indexing tables are presented for vertices in a directed outerplanar graph, and they are shown to work well in finding the first edge on a shortest path. Then the tables are modified, so that good performance is achieved in retrieving the whole path. This method is extended to handle directed graphs.

We consider as a motivating example the undirected outerplanar graph in Fig. 3, with each edge of cost 1. A shortest path between any pair of vertices v and u is of length no greater than 2, since there is a path from v to 5 to u. Considering shortest paths starting from any given vertex, all but at most 5 of them must contain but not terminate at vertex 5. Using a comparison-based approach, the average time to extract a shortest path will be $\Omega(\log n)$. An obvious alternative organization is to keep the compact routing tables at every vertex other than 5, but use a standard routing table at vertex 5, and index into it in constant time. The total space would be $O(n)$, and the time to extract any shortest path would be constant.

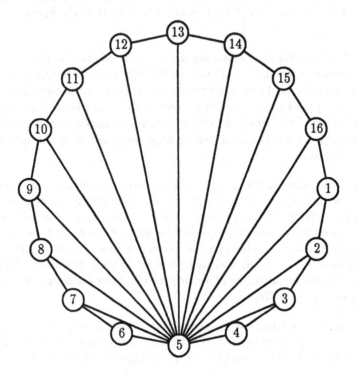

Fig. 3. A second outerplanar graph

Can direct indexing be used even when the graph is not as regular as in Fig. 3? Our solution is to introduce a compressed representation of the intervals, into which we shall index. This compressed representation will allow for a large number of searches to be resolved in constant time, but yet not use an excessive amount of storage. For those searches that are not immediately resolved, we shall have a compressed representation for what remains, which can then be searched recursively.

A *multi-level indexing table* for vertex v and interval $[x, y]$ representing the union of one or more S sets for v is the following. Let r be the number of integers in $[x, y]$. For a given positive integer i, consider a partition of $[x, y]$ into subintervals, each of size $2^{\lfloor \log_2 r \rfloor - i}$ except possibly the last, which is at most that size. Choose the smallest $i \geq 0$ such that at least half of the resulting subintervals are homogeneous. An interval that intersects precisely one S set for v is said to be *homogeneous*. Form a list of these subintervals in order. For each subinterval $[x', y']$ in the list, store the neighbor w such that x' is in $S(v, w)$, and the neighbor t such that y' is in $S(v, t)$. For each subinterval $[x', y']$ that is not homogeneous, let $[x'', y''] = [x', y'] - (S(v, w) \cup S(v, t))$. If $[x'', y'']$ is not empty, we associate with interval $[x', y']$ in the list a pointer to a multi-level indexing table for $[x'', y'']$.

The next edge in a shortest path from v to u is identified as follows. Let s be the size of all but perhaps the last subinterval in the list. Index into the list to examine the $\lceil (u - x + 1)/s \rceil$-th subinterval $[x', y']$. Extract the neighbors w and t of v that are stored with x' and y', resp. If u is contained in $S(v, w)$, then return w, else if u is contained in $S(v, t)$, then return t. Otherwise, search the multi-level indexing table pointed to by the pointer associated with $[x', y']$.

Lemma 4. *The size of a multi-level indexing table for vertex v and interval $[x, y]$ is proportional to the number of S sets contained in $[x, y]$. The expected time to search the table is constant if all vertices in $[x, y]$ are equally likely to be searched for.*

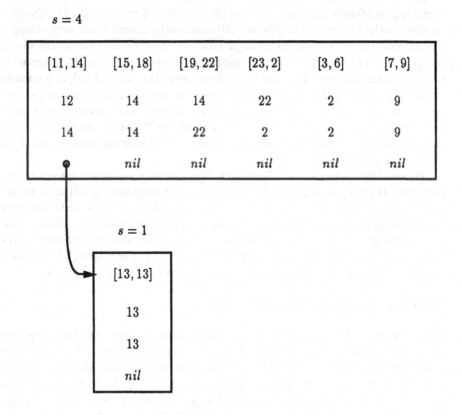

Fig. 4. The multi-level indexing table for vertex 10 and interval $[11, 9]$

We consider the graph in Fig. 1, and construct a multi-level indexing table for vertex 10 and interval $[11, 9]$. This table is shown in Fig. 4. The S sets for vertex 10 are $S(10,2) = [1,6]$, $S(10,9) = [7,9]$, $S(10,12) = [11,12]$, $S(10,13) = [13,13]$, $S(10,14) = [14,19]$, and $S(10,22) = [20,24]$. For $i = 2$, there are six subintervals: $[11,14]$, $[15,18]$, $[19,22]$, $[23,2]$, $[3,6]$, and $[7,9]$. Exactly half of these are homogeneous, namely $[15,18]$, $[3,6]$ and $[7,9]$. The w values for the six intervals in order are 12, 14, 14, 22, 2, and 9, and the t values for the six intervals in order are 14, 14, 22, 2, 2, and 9. Only one of the nonhomogeneous intervals, $[11,14]$, has anything left in it after $S(v,w)$ and $S(v,t)$ are removed from it, namely $[13,13]$. Thus subinterval $[11,14]$ has a pointer to a multi-level indexing table for $[13,13]$. That table is very simple.

Consider constructing tables to minimize the average time to extract a shortest path, given that any pair of source and destination are equally likely. This is trickier, since a shortest path to a vertex u may not go through v, thus rendering Lemma 4 unusable. To overcome this problem, we modify our data structures slightly, and use a charging method in our analysis.

Let $\langle v, w \rangle$ be an edge incident from v, and let $\langle v, w' \rangle$ and $\langle v, w'' \rangle$ be the preceding and following edges, resp., in the clockwise direction out of v. Consider shortest paths to vertices in $S(v,w)$. All such paths except those originating in the interval (w', w'') must go through either v or w' or w''. We would like to charge either the edge $\langle v, w \rangle$ or the appropriate vertex in the path, either w' or w'', a constant amount. To make this scheme work the interval (w', w'') must be sufficiently small so that costs related to source vertices inside interval (w', w'') can be charged to source vertices outside the interval. Also, a vertex such as w' or w'' should not get charged more than twice for the same shortest path. To accomplish this, we remove certain S sets from consideration when we build the multi-level indexing tables.

We identify these sets as follows. Let $R(v)$ be the vertices w adjacent from v such that $W(v,w) \geq n/2$. Let $R'(v)$ be the set of neighbors w adjacent from v such that w is in $R(v)$ or $\langle v, w \rangle$ is the next edge clockwise or counterclockwise from an edge $\langle v, w' \rangle$ and w' is in $R(v)$. Let $R''(v)$ be the vertices w adjacent from v such that w is in $R'(v)$ or $\langle v, w \rangle$ is the next edge clockwise or counterclockwise from an edge $\langle v, w' \rangle$ and w' is in $R'(v)$. The set $R''(v)$ contains the vertices w whose sets $S(v,w)$ we exclude from the multi-level indexing table for v.

Lemma 5. *For any vertex v, $|R''(v)| \leq 6$.*

Proof. (Sketch) The proof considers various cases. If there are two neighbors w and w' adjacent from v, with $W(v,w) = n/2$ and $W(v,w') = n/2$, then it follows that $|R''(v)| = |R'(v)| = 4$. Suppose instead that there are no two such neighbors w and w'. Then it follows that $|R(v)| \leq 3$. If $|R(v)| = 3$, then there are exactly three edges in total that are incident from v. It follows that $|R''(v)| = |R'(v)| = 3$. Otherwise $|R(v)| \leq 2$. If $|R(v)| = 2$, then it follows that $|R'(v)| \leq 4$, and $|R''(v)| \leq 6$. If $|R(v)| = 1$, then it follows that $|R'(v)| \leq 3$, and $|R''(v)| \leq 5$.

We set up a *modified multi-level indexing table* for v as follows. Construct a *front list* of the $S(v,w)$ sets for all w in $R''(v)$. For each remaining subinterval from (v, v) after these $S(v, w)$ sets are removed, construct a multi-level indexing table. To search this table for a destination u, first search the front list to locate an interval containing u. If such an interval is not found, search the appropriate multi-level indexing table.

Theorem 6. *Using modified multi-level indexing tables for an n-vertex outer-planar graph, the expected time to extract a shortest path is proportional to the average number of edges in a path, when all source-destination pairs are equally likely.*

Proof. (Sketch) Consider the shortest path P from q to u, where u is in $S(v, w)$. If $S(v, w)$ is not in the front list for v, and q is not in the interval $[w', w'']$, where $\langle v, w' \rangle$ and $\langle v, w'' \rangle$ are the preceding and following edges clockwise from $\langle v, w \rangle$, charge double the expected access cost of the multi-level indexing table to P as follows. If P actually goes through v, then charge the edge $\langle v, w \rangle$ of P that is used. If shortest path P does not go through v, then charge the vertex w' or w'' through which P actually goes. Using the characterization of S sets on the front list, we argue by contradiction that no vertex on P gets charged more than once.

For directed graphs that are not outerplanar, we do the following. We set up *distrib_tables2* that are similar to *distrib_tables1*, except that modified multi-level indexing tables are used and the effect of attachment vertices is counteracted as follows. Table *within_hamm* is modified, as follows. At any vertex v with at least two edges incident from it, let $\langle v, w \rangle$ be incident from v, and let $\langle v, w' \rangle$ and $\langle v, w'' \rangle$ be the preceding and following edges, resp., in the clockwise direction out of v. If an attachment vertex is in the interval (within the partial hammock) (w', w''), then insert $S(v, w)$ into the front list of v, if it isn't there already. Algorithm *distrib_route2* is similar to *distrib_route1*.

Theorem 7. *When all source-destination pairs are equally likely, the expected time for distrib_route2 to extract a shortest path from distrib_tables2 is proportional to the average number of edges in a path. The time and space to set up the tables are $O(\tilde{\gamma}(G)n + (\tilde{\gamma}(G))^2 \log \tilde{\gamma}(G))$ and $O(\tilde{\gamma}(G)n)$, resp.*

A nondistributed version uses similar ideas to those already discussed.

Theorem 8. *When all source-destination pairs are equally likely, the expected time for nondistrib_route2 to extract a shortest path from nondistrib_tables2 is proportional to the average number of edges in a path. The time and space to set up the set of tables are $O(n + (\tilde{\gamma}(G))^2 \log \tilde{\gamma}(G))$ and $O(n + (\tilde{\gamma}(G))^2)$, resp.*

References

[AHU] A. V. Aho, J. E. Hopcroft, and J. D. Ullman. *The Design and Analysis of Computer Algorithms.* Addison-Wesley, Reading, Massachusetts, 1974.

[vBKZ] P. Van Emde Boas, R. Kaas, and E. Zijlstra. Design and implementation of an efficient priority queue. *Math. Systems Theory*, 10:99–127, 1977.

[CLR] T. H. Cormen, C. E. Leiserson, and R. L. Rivest. *Introduction to Algorithms*. McGraw-Hill, New York, 1990.

[DP] N. Deo and C. Pang. Shortest-path algorithms: taxonomy and annotation. *Networks*, 14:275–323, 1984.

[D] E. W. Dijkstra. A note on two problems in connexion with graphs. *Numerische Mathematik*, 1:269–271, 1959.

[DPZ] H. N. Djidjev, G. E. Pantziou, and C. D. Zaraliagis. Computing shortest paths and distances in planar graphs. In *Proceedings of the International Colloquium on Automata, Languages and Programming, Lecture Notes in Computer Science vol. 510*, pages 327–338. Springer-Verlag, 1991.

[Fl] R. W. Floyd. Algorithm 97: shortest path. *Comm. ACM*, 5:345, 1962.

[Fs1] G. N. Frederickson. Implicit data structures for the dictionary problem. *J. ACM*, 30:80–94, 1983.

[Fs2] G. N. Frederickson. Implicit data structures for weighted elements. *Information and Control*, 66:61–82, 1985.

[Fs3] G. N. Frederickson. Fast algorithms for shortest paths in planar graphs, with applications. *SIAM J. on Computing*, 16:1004–1022, 1987.

[Fs4] G. N. Frederickson. Using cellular embeddings in solving all pairs shortest paths problems. In *Proceedings of the 30th IEEE Symposium on Foundations of Computer Science*, pages 448–453, 1989. revised version in Purdue University technical report CSD-TR-897, 1992.

[Fs5] G. N. Frederickson. Planar graph decomposition and all pairs shortest paths. *J. ACM*, 38:162–204, 1991.

[FJ] G. N. Frederickson and R. Janardan. Designing networks with compact routing tables. *Algorithmica*, 3:171–190, 1988.

[Fm] M. L. Fredman. New bounds on the complexity of the shortest path problem. *SIAM J. on Computing*, 5:83–89, 1976.

[FKS] M. L. Fredman, J. Komlos, and E. Szemeredi. Storing a sparse table with $O(1)$ worst case access. *J. ACM*, 31:538–544, 1984.

[FT] M. L. Fredman and R. E. Tarjan. Fibonacci heaps and their uses in improved network optimization algorithms. *J. ACM*, 34:596–615, 1987.

[H] F. Harary. *Graph Theory*. Addison-Wesley, Reading, Massachusetts, 1969.

[MS] J. I. Munro and H. Suwanda. Implicit data structures for fast search and update. *J. Computer and System Sciences*, 21:236–250, 1980.

[SK] N. Santoro and R. Khatib. Labelling and implicit routing in networks. *Computer Journal*, 28:5–8, 1985.

[TY] R. E. Tarjan and A. C.-C. Yao. Storing a sparse table. *Comm. ACM*, 21:606–611, 1979.

[vLT] J. van Leeuwen and R. B. Tan. Computer networks with compact routing tables. In G. Rozenberg and A. Salomaa, editors, *The Book of L*, pages 259–273. Springer-Verlag, New York, 1986.

[Wa] S. Warshall. A theorem on boolean matrices. *J. ACM*, 9:11–12, 1962.

[Wi] D. E. Willard. Log-logarithmic worst-case range queries are possible in space $\Theta(n)$. *Info. Proc. Lett.*, 17:81–84, 1983.

[Y] A. C.-C. Yao. Should tables be sorted? *J. ACM*, 28:615–628, 1981.

The Approximation of Maximum Subgraph Problems

(Extended Abstract)

Carsten Lund and Mihalis Yannakakis

AT&T Bell Laboratories Murray Hill, NJ 07974, USA

Abstract. We consider the following class of problems: given a graph, find the maximum number of nodes inducing a subgraph that satisfies a desired property π, such as planar, acyclic, bipartite, etc. We show that this problem is hard to approximate for any property π on directed or undirected graphs that is nontrivial and hereditary on induced subgraphs.

1 Introduction

The *maximum (induced) subgraph problem* for a fixed property π is the following problem: Given a graph, find the maximum number of nodes that induces a subgraph satisfying the property π. There is a distinct problem for each property π. For example, if the property π is "complete graph", then we have the maximum clique problem. If π is "planar graph", then we wish to find the largest (induced) planar subgraph of a given graph. Many other graph optimization problems of interest can be formulated as maximum subgraph problems by specifying appropriately the property π.

The maximum subgraph problem for many interesting properties is NP-hard. This was shown for some particular properties in [10] and [15], and a general result was obtained in [19]. Specifically, they proved that the maximum subgraph problem is NP-hard for a large class of natural properties on (directed or undirected) graphs, namely for the properties that are *nontrivial* and *hereditary* on induced subgraphs. A property is nontrivial if it is true for infinitely many graphs and false for infinitely many graphs. It is easy to see that if this is not the case, then the maximum subgraph problem can be solved trivially in polynomial time by an exhaustive search algorithm. A property π is hereditary if it cannot be destroyed by removing nodes from the graph; i.e., whenever a graph G satisfies the property π then also every induced subgraph of G satisfies π. Most of the well-studied graph properties are hereditary. Examples include: complete graph, independent set, planar, outerplanar, bipartite, complete bipartite, acyclic, degree-constrained, interval, circular-arc, circle graph, chordal, comparability, permutation, perfect, line graph or digraph, transitive digraph. (See [6], [12] or [13] for definitions.)

Some examples of properties that are not hereditary are: connected, biconnected, etc. Note that in these particular cases, the maximum subgraph problem amounts to finding the largest connected (or biconnected) component, and thus can be solved in polynomial time.

In this paper we study the approximability of the maximum subgraph problem for the class of hereditary properties. Until very recently, no positive or negative (NP-hardness) approximation result was known for any specific property. In 1991 Feige et al [8] used the theory of interactive proof systems to prove a strong negative result on the approximation of the maximum clique and maximum independent set problem, which was then tightened in [3] and [2] to show that there is some $\epsilon > 0$ such that these problems cannot be approximated in polynomial time with ratio n^ϵ unless P = NP. Simon showed that finding the maximum complete bipartite subgraph is related to the maximum independent set problem via approximation-preserving reductions [23], and thus the same result applies also to the property "complete bipartite".

Our goal in this paper is to prove a general negative result on the approximation of the maximum subgraph problem for the whole class of hereditary properties. It is well known that typically polynomial transformations do not preserve approximations. This is true in particular for the general transformations of [19] with respect to the maximum subgraph problem. So we have to develop new general transformations. Our proofs utilize the new results and techniques based on interactive proof systems from [2, 9].

First, we shall give in the next section some basic definitions and notation. In Section 3 we study graph properties that are not satisfied either by some clique or by some independent set. This subclass includes for example all properties that are monotone with respect to the deletion of edges (or with respect to addition of edges), such as planar, acyclic, bipartite, etc. We show that for any property in this subclass there is an $\epsilon > 0$ such that the corresponding maximum subgraph problem cannot be approximated in polynomial time with ratio n^ϵ unless P = NP. The proof builds on the construction of [2] for the maximum independent set problem.

In Section 4 we examine the general case of hereditary graph properties. We prove that the maximum subgraph problem cannot be approximated with ratio $2^{\log^c n}$, for any $c < 1/2$, unless $\tilde{P} = \widetilde{NP}$, where $\tilde{P}$ (respectively $\widetilde{NP}$) is the class of languages that can be recognized in quasipolynomial time, i.e., time $2^{\log^d n}$ for some constant d, by a deterministic (resp. nondeterministic) algorithm. Our proof for this result uses a different construction that is based on two-prover one-round interactive proof systems [9]. In Section 5 we discuss properties on directed graphs and note that completely analogous results hold for them.

In Section 6 we consider the variant of the problem where the induced subgraph is required to be connected in addition to satisfying a hereditary property π. Note that the conjunction with the connectivity requirement typically destroys hereditariness; for example, the property "tree" (= connected acyclic) is not hereditary. In [24] it was shown that the maximum connected subgraph problem for any hereditary property is NP-hard. Regarding the approximation, Berman and Schnitger showed in [7] a negative result for two properties, namely for the problems of finding the longest induced path in a graph and finding the maximum induced connected chordal subgraph (they make essential use of the connectivity requirement in these proofs). In Section 6 we show that for any hereditary property, the addition of a connectivity requirement does not make the approximation of the maximum subgraph problem any easier, and in fact in many cases it makes it even harder.

In Section 7 we discuss briefly the class of node-deletion problems, and in Section 8 we conclude and state related open problems.

2 Definitions and Notation

For a graph G, we use $n(G)$ to denote its number of nodes and $\alpha(G)$ to denote the size of the largest independent set. If π is a property, we let $\alpha_\pi(G)$ denote the maximum number of nodes which induce a subgraph that satisfies the property π.

If π is a hereditary property and a graph H does not satisfy it, then any supergraph of H also fails to satisfy it. H is called a *forbidden subgraph* for π; and it is *minimal* if every proper (induced) subgraph of it satisfies π. Any hereditary property is characterized by its set of minimal forbidden subgraphs. In fact much work in graph theory aims at finding such characterizations for graph properties of interest. We say that a graph is *H-free* if it does not contain H as an induced subgraph. Abusing slightly the notation, we will use $\alpha_H(G)$ to denote the size of the largest H-free subgraph of a graph G, i.e., the parameter $\alpha_\pi(G)$ for π the property with H as its only minimal forbidden subgraph.

We use K_n to denote the complete graph (clique) on n nodes and I_n to denote an independent set with n nodes. A *complete k-partite graph* is a graph whose nodes can be partitioned into k parts so that each part induces an independent set and there are edges joining all pairs of nodes from different parts. An independent set is a complete 1-partite graph and a clique K_n is a complete n-partite graph with one node in each part.

The quality of a solution to an optimization problem is measured by the ratio of its value to that of the optimal solution. The performance of an approximation algorithm A is measured then by the worst-case ratio of the solution that it finds over all instances of a given size. An algorithm for a maximization (resp. minimization) problem achieves ratio $r(n)$ if for every instance of size n it computes a solution with value at least $1/r(n)$ (resp. at most $r(n)$) times the optimal value. For graph problems we will measure the size of an instance (graph) by its number n of nodes.

We say that an algorithm *distinguishes* between two disjoint languages L_1 and L_2 if on input x, it outputs "Yes" if $x \in L_1$ and "No" if $x \in L_2$; the output is irrelevant if x is in neither L_1 nor in L_2.

3 Properties with a forbidden clique

In this section we study properties that have either a forbidden clique K_c (for some c) or a forbidden independent set I_c. Note in particular that any nontrivial property π that is *edge-monotone* falls into this subclass. For, if π is monotone with respect to the deletion of edges and is satisfied by all cliques, then it is satisfied by all graphs because every graph can be obtained from a clique of the same size by deleting edges. Similarly, if π is monotone with respect to the addition of edges then it must be violated by some independent set of nodes.

For every property π we can define a complementary property π^c as follows: a graph G satisfies π^c if and only if its complement G^c satisfies π. It follows immediately from the definitions that π^c is nontrivial and hereditary if and only if π is. Furthermore, the maximum subgraph problems for the two properties are obviously equivalent: by complementing the input graph, we can use an approximation algorithm for one property to approximate the problem for the other property with the same ratio. If π does not hold for an independent set, then π^c does not hold for a clique. Thus, by considering if necessary the complementary property, we can assume from now on without loss of generality that our property π is not satisfied by some clique K_c.

It follows from Ramsey's theorem that every nontrivial hereditary property is satisfied either by all cliques or by all independent sets [19]. Thus, we may assume that π is satisfied by all independent sets. We shall prove the following theorem.

Theorem 1. *There exists an $\epsilon > 0$ such that the following holds for every integer constant $c \geq 2$. If there is a polynomial time algorithm which, when given an input graph G with n nodes and a number z, can distinguish between the case that G contains an independent set with z nodes and the case that the maximum K_c-free subgraph of G has less than z/n^ϵ nodes, then $P = NP$.*

From this we can derive then the following:

Theorem 2. *There exists an $\epsilon > 0$ such that the maximum subgraph problem cannot be approximated with ratio n^ϵ in polynomial time for any nontrivial hereditary property that is false for some clique or independent set, or more generally is false for some complete multipartite graph, unless $P = NP$.*

We list below some specific properties that satisfy the conditions of the theorem.

Corollary 3. *The conclusion of Theorem 2 applies among others to the following graph properties: planar, outerplanar, bipartite, complete bipartite, acyclic, degree-constrained, chordal, interval.*

Proof of Theorem 1. Arora et al [2] reduced the Satisfiability problem (SAT) to the approximation of the maximum independent set problem. They showed that from a given Boolean formula x one can construct in polynomial time a graph G such that, when $x \in SAT$ then $\alpha(G)$ is equal to some number r, and if $x \notin SAT$ then $\alpha(G) < r/N^\delta$ for some $\delta > 0$, where $N = n(G)$.

For a positive integer k, let G^k be the graph which has one node for every k-tuple of independent nodes of G and has an edge joining any two nodes whose corresponding k-tuples contain two adjacent nodes of G. An independent set I of G gives rise to an independent set I^k in G^k consisting of all k-tuples of nodes from I. Conversely, if T is an independent set in G^k, then the set I of G consisting of all the nodes that appear in the tuples in T forms an independent set; thus, $|T| \leq |I|^k$. Therefore, $\alpha(G^k) = (\alpha(G))^k$. If $x \in SAT$ then $\alpha(G^k) = r^k$.

Suppose that $x \notin SAT$. Let $\alpha_{K_{c+1}}(G^k)$ be the size of the largest K_{c+1}-free subgraph of G^k, and let $\gamma(c, k) = \alpha_{K_{c+1}}(G^k)/N^k$. Thus, for $c = k = 1$, $\gamma(1, 1) = \alpha(G)/N$. We show in Lemma 4 below that when $k \geq c$:

$$\gamma(c, k) < 2^k[\gamma(1, 1)]^{k-c}.$$

Let $\epsilon > 0$ be any constant smaller than δ. Assume without loss of generality that $N \geq 4^{1/(\delta - \epsilon)}$, and choose $k \geq 2c/(\delta - \epsilon)$. It follows that the ratio between $\alpha(G^k)$ in the satisfiable case and $\alpha_{K_{c+1}}(G^k)$ in the unsatisfiable case is

$$\frac{r^k}{\gamma(c, k)N^k} > \frac{r^k}{2^k[\gamma(1,1)]^{k-c}N^k} = \frac{r^k}{2^k[\alpha(G)]^{k-c}N^c}$$

$$= (\frac{r}{\alpha(G)})^{k-c}(\frac{r}{N})^c\frac{1}{2^k}$$

$$> \frac{N^{\delta k}}{N^c 2^k} \geq N^{\epsilon k} \geq [n(G^k)]^\epsilon. \square$$

Lemma 4. *For any* $1 \leq c \leq k$ *we have that* $\gamma(c, k) < 2^k[\gamma(1, 1)]^{k-c}$.

Proof. We shall use induction on k and c. By definition, $\gamma(1, k) = \alpha(G^k)/N^k = [\gamma(1, 1)]^k$. If $c \geq k$ then we use the fact that $\gamma(c, k) \leq 1$.

Assume that $k > c$ and that the lemma is true for all k', c' where $k' < k$ and $c' \leq c$.

Let S be a K_{c+1}-free subgraph of G^k. Recall that every node of G^k is a k-tuple of nodes of G. Let S_1 be the projection of S onto the first component. We partition the nodes of S_1 (and accordingly of S) into two groups as follows. If a node u of S_1 is not adjacent in G to any component of any tuple of S, then we say that u is *pure*; otherwise it is *mixed*. We partition the nodes of S into pure and mixed according to their first component.

The pure nodes of S_1 form an independent set in G. Such a node can be the projection of at most $\gamma(c, k - 1)N^{k-1}$ nodes of S. Thus the contribution to $\gamma(c, k)$ of the pure nodes is at most $\gamma(1, 1)\gamma(c, k - 1)$.

Let u be a mixed node of S_1. Then there is a node w in S whose tuple contains a node of G that is adjacent to u. Therefore, w is adjacent to every node of S with first component u. Thus, S contains at most $\gamma(c - 1, k - 1)N^{k-1}$ nodes with first component u. Consequently, the contribution to $\gamma(c, k)$ of the mixed nodes is at most $\gamma(c - 1, k - 1)$.

Hence if $k > c$ then

$$\gamma(c, k) \leq \gamma(1, 1)\gamma(c, k - 1) + \gamma(c - 1, k - 1)$$
$$< 2^{k-1}\gamma(1, 1)[\gamma(1, 1)]^{k-c-1} + 2^{k-1}[\gamma(1, 1)]^{k-c}$$
$$= 2^k[\gamma(1, 1)]^{k-c}. \square$$

4 The general undirected case

Let π be an arbitrary nontrivial hereditary property. We can assume again without loss of generality that π is satisfied by all independent sets of nodes. Let H be any forbidden subgraph. Thus, H must be nonempty (i.e. has at least one edge). We shall prove the following theorem.

Theorem 5. *The following holds for every $\epsilon > 0$ and every nonempty graph H. If there is a quasipolynomial time algorithm which, when given an input graph G with n nodes and a number z, can distinguish between the case that G contains an independent set with z nodes and the case that the maximum H-free subgraph of G has less than $z/2^{\log^{1/2-\epsilon} n}$ nodes, then $\tilde{P} = \widetilde{NP}$.*

From this it follows easily then that:

Theorem 6. *For any nontrivial hereditary property and every $\epsilon > 0$, the maximum subgraph problem cannot be approximated with ratio $2^{\log^{1/2-\epsilon} n}$ in (quasi)-polynomial time unless $\tilde{P} = \widetilde{NP}$.*

Corollary 7. *The conclusion of Theorem 6 applies to the following graph properties: comparability, permutation, perfect, circular-arc, circle, line graph.*

Proof of Theorem 5. The proof of Theorem 5 has two parts. First we construct in Lemma 8 below a graph G with N nodes for which it is hard to distinguish between the case that it contains an independent set with some number h of nodes and the case that the maximum K_l-free subgraph, with $l = O(\log N)$ has less than $h/2^{\log^{1/2-\epsilon} N}$ nodes.

Using this graph G we next construct a collection $\mathcal{G}$ of graphs, such that for every graph F in the collection we have $\alpha(F) \geq \alpha(G)$, and for at least one half of them we have $\alpha_H(F) \leq \alpha_{K_l}(G)$. We construct the collection $\mathcal{G}$ as a pseudo-random subset of all partial subgraphs of G.

From [1] we obtain for any $m, \delta > 0$ a set S of m-bit vectors such that for any m-bit vector v and any $I \subset \{1, 2, \ldots, m\}$:

$$\left| Prob_{w \in S}[\forall i \in I : w_i = v_i] - \frac{1}{2^{|I|}} \right| \leq \delta.$$

Furthermore $|S| = O((m \log m)^2 \delta^{-2})$ and S is constructible in time polynomial in $|S|$.

Let m equal the number of edges in G and for any m-bit vector v, let G_v be the subgraph of G where the ith edge has been removed if and only if $v_i = 1$. Define $\mathcal{G} = \{G_v\}_{v \in S}$.

Lemma 9 shows that this collection of graphs has the above stated property.
$\square$

Lemma 8. *For any constant c and for any $\epsilon > 0$ we can construct from a formula x in quasipolynomial time a graph G on N nodes with the following properties: If $x \in SAT$ then $\alpha(G)$ is equal to some number h, and if $x \notin SAT$ then the maximum K_l free subgraph of G, where $l = c \log N$ has size at most $h/2^{\log^{1/2-\epsilon} N}$.*

Proof Sketch. Using a construction of one-round two-prover interactive proof systems [17, 9] and using a more careful analysis [5] we obtain a 1-round 2-prover interactive proof system for SAT that uses $R(n) = O(\log n \log^2 e^{-1}(n))$ random bits, the number of bits communicated is $Q(n) = O(\log n \log^2 e^{-1}(n))$ and errs with probability at most $e(n)$, where $n = |x|$ and $e(n) \leq 1/n$.

From this proof system build a graph G using the construction in [8]. Every node of G corresponds to a pair (r, a) consisting of a random seed r and a pair a of answers from the two provers. If $x \in SAT$ then $\alpha(G) = 2^{R(n)}$.

Suppose that $x \notin SAT$. Any subset S of the nodes of G that is K_l-free corresponds to at most $l-1$ strategies for the first prover and $l-1$ strategies for the second prover. (Note that for any query there will be at most $l-1$ different answers.) For any pair $(r, a) \in S$ there exist a pair of strategies for the provers among these $l-1$ strategies that makes the verifier accept. Hence there exists one strategy for the first prover and one strategy for the second prover that makes the verifier accept with probability at least $|S|/((l-1)^2 2^{R(n)})$.

Hence we know that if $x \notin SAT$ then $\alpha_{K_l}(G) \leq e(n)(l-1)^2 2^{R(n)}$. Furthermore $N = |n(G)| = 2^{R(n)+Q(n)}$. Hence if $e(n) = O(2^{-\log^{1/4\epsilon} n})$ then we get that $\alpha_{K_l}(G) \leq 2^{R(n)}/2^{\log^{1/2-\epsilon} N}$ for large enough N. $\square$

Lemma 9. *Let H be a graph on k nodes. For sufficiently large N, for any graph G on N nodes and for all $l = \Omega(\log N)$, a pseudo-random subgraph G' of G does not, with probability $1/2$, contain a subset S of l nodes that is a clique in G but H is not an induced subgraph of $G'|_S$.*

Proof. First note that there are $\binom{N}{l}$ subsets of l nodes. Furthermore observe that the complete graph on l nodes contains at least $l^2/4k^2$ edge disjoint k-cliques (see Lemma 10 below). Fix a clique C of G with l nodes. Let C' be a random partial subgraph of C where each edge has probability $1/2$. Each of the $l^2/4k^2$ edge disjoint k-cliques of C has probability $p = 1/2^{\binom{k}{2}}$ of becoming equal to H and these events are independent because the cliques are edge-disjoint. Thus C' is H-free with probability at most $(1-p)^{l^2/4k^2}$.

Now let C'' be a pseudo-random subgraph of C. It follows that C'' is H-free with probability at most $(1-p)^{l^2/4k^2} + 2^{\binom{l}{2}}\delta$, where δ is from the pseudo-random construction. This is because any fixed subgraph C'' happens with probability at least $1/2^{\binom{l}{2}} - \delta$, thus the probability that $G'|_C$ is not H-free is

$$\sum_{C'': \text{ not } H-\text{free}} Prob(G'|_C = C'') \geq \sum_{C'': \text{ not } H-\text{free}} 1/2^{\binom{l}{2}} - \delta$$

$$\geq (1 - (1-p)^{l^2/4k^2})(1 - 2^{\binom{l}{2}}\delta)$$

$$\geq 1 - \left((1-p)^{l^2/4k^2} + 2^{\binom{l}{2}}\delta\right)$$

Thus the probability that G contains a l-clique C such that $G'|_C$ does not contain H is at most

$$\binom{N}{l}\left((1-p)^{l^2/4k^2} + 2^{\binom{l}{2}}\delta\right) \leq 1/2$$

if $l = \Omega(\log N)$ and $\delta^{-1} = 2^{\Omega(l^2)}$. □

Lemma 10. *The complete graph on l nodes contains at least $l^2/4k^2$ edge disjoint k-cliques.*

Proof. Omitted from this extended abstract. □

5 Directed graph properties

The results of the previous sections can be extended to properties on directed graphs. We say that a digraph on n nodes is a *bidirectional clique*, denoted B_n, if it contains for every pair of nodes u, v, both directed edges between them $u \to v$ and $v \to u$. A digraph is a *unidirectional clique*, denoted U_n, if there is an ordering of its nodes $u_1, \cdots, u_n$ so that the graph contains all edges $u_i \to u_j$ with $i < j$ (i.e., U_n is an acyclic tournament). In [19] it is shown that a nontrivial hereditary property on digraphs is satisfied either by all independent sets, or by all bidirectional cliques or by all unidirectional cliques.

Theorem 11. *Let π be any nontrivial hereditary property on digraphs that is false for some bidirectional or unidirectional clique or for some independent set. Then there exists an $\epsilon > 0$ such that the maximum subgraph problem for π cannot be approximated with ratio n^ϵ in polynomial time unless $P = NP$.*

Proof. Suppose first that property π is satisfied by all independent sets. Then π is false either for some bidirectional clique B_c or some unidirectional clique U_c. We reduce from the problem of Theorem 1. Let G be an undirected graph for that problem for the same constant c. If B_c violates π, then we replace every edge of G by two opposite directed edges. If U_c violates π then we order arbitrarily the nodes of G as $u_1, \cdots, u_n$ and replace every edge $[u_i, u_j]$ of G by a single directed edge $u_i \to u_j$ for $i < j$.

Suppose that π is satisfied by all unidirectional cliques but it is false for some independent set of nodes I_c. Let G be an undirected graph for the problem of Theorem 1 for the same constant c. Order its nodes arbitrarily and construct a directed graph D with the same nodes as follows. If two nodes u_i, u_j are adjacent in G then we do not include an edge between them in D; if they are not adjacent in G then we include a single directed edge $u_i \to u_j$ for $i < j$.

Finally, if π is satisfied by all bidirectional cliques, then we can consider the equivalent problem for its complementary property π^c, which falls in the first case. □

Similarly, we can prove the analogue of Theorem 6 for the general case.

Theorem 12. *For any nontrivial hereditary property on directed graphs and every $\epsilon > 0$, the maximum subgraph problem cannot be approximated with ratio $2^{\log^{1/2-\epsilon} n}$ in (quasi)polynomial time unless $\tilde{P} = \widetilde{NP}$.*

Corollary 13. *The conclusions of the above theorems apply to the following digraph properties: acyclic, transitive, symmetric, antisymmetric, tournament, degree-constrained, line digraph.*

In [19] it is shown that the maximum subgraph problem remains NP-hard even when the problem is restricted to acyclic digraphs or to planar graphs or digraphs, provided that the property is still nontrivial under the restriction. It is easy to see that Theorems 11 and 12 hold also for the acyclic case; i.e., the approximation problem restricted to acyclic digraphs is equally hard. This is not the case for the restriction to planar graphs. Lipton and Tarjan [18] showed that the maximum independent set on planar graphs has a polynomial time approximation scheme by a divide and conquer algorithm that uses the small separator theorem for planar graphs (see also [4] for a different technique and a more efficient algorithm). The method can be applied to approximate a large class of hereditary properties on planar graphs [21].

6 Connected Subgraphs

In certain situations we may wish to find a subgraph which does not only satisfy a property π but is also connected. Finding the maximum subgraph problem remains NP-hard under this requirement [24]. We show in this section that the same fact holds also for the approximation.

Consider the undirected case first. Every property π that is nontrivial and hereditary on connected graphs, is satisfied either by all cliques or by all stars or by all paths [24]. If the property is satisfied by all cliques but not by some star, or vice-versa, if it is satisfied by all stars but not by some clique, then we can use the construction of Theorem 2 to show a similar result for the maximum connected subgraph problem, i.e., it cannot be approximated with ratio n^{ϵ} for some $\epsilon > 0$. If all cliques and stars satisfy π then we can use the construction of Theorem 5 for the complementary property to show that the problem cannot be approximated with ratio $2^{\log^{1/2-\epsilon} n}$ unless $\tilde{P} = \widetilde{NP}$.

If some clique and some star violates the property, then it is satisfied by all paths. In this case things are worse. We can show the following.

Theorem 14. *Suppose that π is a property that is nontrivial and hereditary on connected graphs, is satisfied by all paths and does not hold for some complete bipartite graph. Then, for every $\epsilon > 0$, the maximum connected subgraph problem for π cannot be approximated with ratio $n^{1-\epsilon}$ in polynomial time unless $P = NP$.*

Examples of properties that satisfy the conditions of this theorem include: path, tree, planar, outerplanar, bipartite, chordal, interval and others. Obviously, "clique" does not satisfy the conditions. Although no approximation algorithm for the clique problem is known that achieves ratio $n^{1-\epsilon}$ for any ϵ, it is open whether this is in fact intractable (and it may well be possible). Examples of some other properties that do not satisfy the conditions of the above theorem are "star", "complete bipartite"; both of these are essentially equivalent (up to a constant factor) to clique in approximation.

A similar analysis can be carried out for properties on directed graphs, there are only some more cases that have to be considered. Summarizing, we have in general:

Theorem 15. *For every property that is nontrivial and hereditary on connected graphs or digraphs, and for every $\epsilon > 0$, the maximum connected subgraph problem cannot be approximated with ratio $2^{\log^{1/2-\epsilon} n}$ in (quasi)polynomial time unless $\tilde{P} = \widetilde{NP}$.*

7 Node-deletion problems

In the case of node-deletion problems, we wish to delete the minimum number of nodes from the graph so that the remaining subgraph satisfies a property π. In terms of finding the exact optimal solution, the node-deletion and the maximum subgraph problem for a property are obviously equivalent. However, the two can be very different in terms of their approximation ratios because in the one case we measure the quality of the solution by the number of nodes deleted, whereas in the other case we measure it in terms of the number of nodes that are left. For example, the maximum independent set problem cannot be approximated within any constant ratio (in fact ratio n^ϵ), whereas the corresponding node-deletion problem, which is simply the node cover problem can be approximated within a factor of 2 [11]. This approximability within a constant factor holds for more problems.

Theorem 16. *The node-deletion problem for any hereditary property with a finite number of minimal forbidden subgraphs can be approximated with a constant ratio.*

Examples of such properties include: transitive digraph (partial order), symmetric, antisymmetric, tournament, line graph, interval and others. We conjecture that for every nontrivial, hereditary property with an infinite number of minimal forbidden subgraphs the node-deletion problem cannot be approximated with constant ratio. For some such properties there are algorithms that approximate the node-deletion problem with a better (though not constant) ratio than it is possible for the corresponding maximum subgraph problem according to our results. For example, the feedback node set in directed graphs (corresponding to $\pi =$ "acyclic") can be approximated with ratio $O(\log^2 n)$ [16]. In undirected graphs it can be approximated with ratio $O(\log n)$ and the same is true for the property $\pi =$ "bipartite". On the negative side, the results of [19], [22] and [2] imply the following theorem.

Theorem 17. *The node-deletion problem for every nontrivial hereditary property is MAX SNP-hard; thus, it does not have a polynomial time approximation scheme unless $P = NP$.*

8 Discussion and Open Problems

We have shown strong negative results on the approximation of the whole class of maximum induced subgraph problems for hereditary properties. There is a number of related open problems that one could explore. First, one technical question is to improve the conclusion of Theorem 6 to say that the problems cannot be approximated with ratio n^ϵ for some $\epsilon > 0$ unless $P = NP$, as in the case of Theorem 2. Second, we would like to characterize the approximability of the class of node-deletion problems. In particular, is the conjecture of the previous section true? The techniques of [20] for the set cover problem may be relevant here.

Finally, a related well-studied, important class of problems is that of maximum *partial* subgraph, or *edge-deletion problems*, where we wish to obtain a property by removing edges from the graph [25]. As has been often observed, edge problems tend to be computationally easier. For example, the maximum partial subgraph problem for the property "forest" is trivial; the problem for the property "degree ≤ 1" can be solved in polynomial time (this is the maximum matching problem). The maximum partial subgraph problem for the properties "acyclic digraph" and "bipartite graph" (this is the Max Cut problem) can be approximated with ratio 2, although they are both NP-hard and in fact also MAX SNP-hard. It would be interesting to prove some general results for the approximation of maximum partial subgraph problems, along the same lines as in the present paper.

References

1. N. Alon, O. Goldreich, J. Håstad, and R. Peralta. Simple constructions of almost k-wise independent random variables. In *Proc. of the 31st IEEE Symp. on Foundations of Computer Science*, pp. 544–553, 1990.
2. S. Arora, C. Lund, R. Motwani, M. Sudan, and M. Szegedy. Proof verification and the hardness of approximation problems. In *Proc. of the 33rd IEEE Symp. on Foundations of Computer Science*, pages 14–23, 1992.
3. S. Arora, and S. Safra. Probabilistic checking of proofs. In *Proc. of the 33rd IEEE Symp. on Foundations of Computer Science*, pp. 2–13, 1992.
4. B. S. Baker. Approximation algorithms for NP-complete problems on planar graphs. In *Proc. of the 24th IEEE Symp. on Foundations of Computer Science*, pp. 265–273, 1983.

5. M. Bellare, S. Goldwasser, C. Lund and A. Russell. Efficient Probabilistically Checkable Proofs: Applications to Approximation. In *Proc. of the 25th ACM Symp. on the Theory of Computing*, 1993.

6. C. Berge. *Graphs and Hypergraphs*. North-Holland, Amsterdam, 1973.

7. P. Berman and G. Schnitger. On the complexity of approximating the independent set problem. In *Information and Computation*, 96, pp. 77-94, 1992.

8. U. Feige, S. Goldwasser, L. Lovász, S. Safra, and M. Szegedy. Approximating clique is almost NP-complete. In *Proc. of the 32nd IEEE Symp. on Foundations of Computer Science*, pp. 2-12, 1991.

9. U. Feige and L. Lóvasz. Two-prover one-round proof systems: Their power and their problems. In *Proc. of the 24th ACM Symp. on the Theory of Computing*, pp. 733-744, 1992.

10. M. R. Garey, D. S. Johnson, and L. Stockmeyer. Some simplified NP-complete graph problems. *Theoretical Computer Science*, pp. 237-267, 1976.

11. M. R. Garey and D. S. Johnson. *Computers and Intractability: A guide to the theory of NP-completeness*. W. H. Freeman and co., San Fransisco, 1979.

12. M. C. Golumbic. *Algorithmic Graph Theory and Perfect Graphs*. Academic Press, New York, 1980.

13. F. Harary. *Graph Theory*. Addison-Wesley, Reading, Mass., 1970.

14. V. Kann. *On the approximability of NP-complete optimization problems*. Ph.D. Thesis, Royal Institute of Technology, Stockholm, 1992.

15. M. S. Krishnamoorthy and N. Deo. Node-deletion NP-complete problems. In *SIAM J. on Computing*, pp. 619-625, 1979.

16. F. T. Leighton, and S. Rao. An approximate max-flow min-cut theorem for uniform multicommodity flow problems with applications to approximation algorithms. In *Proc. of the 28th IEEE Symp. on Foundations of Computer Science*, pp. 256-269, 1988.

17. D. Lapidot and A. Shamir. Fully parallelized multi prover protocols for NEXPtime. In *Proc. of the 32nd IEEE Symp. on Foundations of Computer Science*, pp. 13-18, 1991.

18. R. J. Lipton, and R. E. Tarjan. Applications of a planar separator theorem. In *SIAM J. on Computing*, pp. 615-627, 1980.

19. J. M. Lewis, and M. Yannakakis. The node-deletion problem for hereditary properties is NP-complete. In *J. of Computer and System Sciences*, pp. 219-230, 1980.

20. C. Lund and M. Yannakakis. On the hardness of approximating minimization problems. In *Proc. of the 25th ACM Symp. on the Theory of Computing*, 1993.

21. T. Nishizeki, and N. Chiba. *Planar Graphs: Theory and Algorithms*. Vol. 32 of Annals of Discrete Mathematics, Elsevier Pub. co., Amsterdam, 1988.

22. C. H. Papadimitriou, and M. Yannakakis. Optimization, approximation and complexity classes. In *J. of Computer and System Sciences*, pp. 425-440, 1991.

23. H. U. Simon. On approximate solutions for combinatorial optimization problems. *SIAM J. Disc. Meth.*, 3, pp. 294-310, 1990.

24. M. Yannakakis. The effect of a connectivity requirement on the complexity of maximum subgraph problems. In *J. of the ACM*, pp. 618-630, 1979.

25. M. Yannakakis. Edge-deletion problems. In *SIAM J. on Computing*, pp. 297-309, 1982.

Polynomially Bounded Minimization Problems which are Hard to Approximate

Viggo Kann*

Department of Numerical Analysis and Computing Science,
Royal Institute of Technology, S-100 44 Stockholm, Sweden

Abstract. MIN PB is the class of minimization problems whose objective functions are bounded by a polynomial in the size of the input. We show that there exist several problems which are MIN PB-complete with respect to an approximation preserving reduction. These problems are very hard to approximate; in polynomial time they cannot be approximated within n^ε for some $\varepsilon > 0$, where n is the size of the input, provided that P $\neq$ NP. In particular, the problem of finding the minimum independent dominating set in a graph, the problem of satisfying a 3-SAT formula setting the least number of variables to one, and the minimum bounded $0-1$ programming problem are shown to be MIN PB-complete. We also present a new type of approximation preserving reduction that is designed for problems whose approximability is expressed as a function in some size parameter. Using this reduction we obtain good lower bounds on the approximability of the treated problems.

1 Introduction

Approximation of NP-complete optimization problems is a very interesting and active area of research. Since all NP-complete problems are reducible to each other one could suspect that they should have similar approximation properties, but this is not at all the case.

For example the TSP (Travelling Salesperson Problem) with triangular inequality can be solved approximately within a factor $3/2$, i.e. one can in polynomial time find a trip of length at most $3/2$ times the shortest trip possible, while the general TSP cannot be approximated within any constant factor if P $\neq$ NP [4].

The range of approximability of NP-complete problems stretches from problems which can be approximated within every constant in polynomial time, e.g. the knapsack problem [7], to problems which cannot be approximated within n^ε for some $\varepsilon > 0$, where n is the size of the input instance, unless P = NP. A problem which is this hard to approximate is the minimum independent dominating set problem (minimum maximal independence number) [5, 8].

In the middle of this range we find the important class MAX SNP, which is syntactically defined [14]. All problems in MAX SNP can be approximated

---

* E-mail: `viggo@nada.kth.se`, supported by grants from TFR.

within a constant in polynomial time and several maximization problems have been shown to be complete in MAX SNP under L-reduction (a type of reduction that preserves approximability within constants) [14]. A recent result says that it is impossible to find an algorithm that approximates a MAX SNP-complete problem within every constant, unless P = NP [1]. Thus showing a problem to be MAX SNP-complete describes the approximability of the problem very well: it can be approximated within a constant, but it cannot be approximated within every constant.

Even optimization problems whose objective function is bounded by a polynomial in the size of the input may be hard to approximate. Krentel has defined a class of optimization problems called OPTP[$\log n$], which consists of all NP optimization problems that are polynomially bounded [12]. OPTP[$\log n$] can be divided into two classes, MAX PB and MIN PB, containing maximization and minimization problems respectively [11]. Berman and Schnitger proved that there are MAX PB-complete problems, i.e. MAX PB problems to which every MAX PB problem can be reduced using an approximation preserving reduction [2]. Several problems are now known to be MAX PB-complete [9, 10].

In this paper we investigate if there, in the same manner, exist problems which are MIN PB-complete. We show that SHORTEST COMPUTATION is a generic MIN PB-complete problem and find reductions to several other MIN PB problems, for example MIN INDEPENDENT DOMINATING SET and MIN PB $0-1$ PROGRAMMING, thereby proving them to be MIN PB-complete. If a problem is MIN PB-complete (or MAX PB-complete) it cannot be approximated within n^ε for some $\varepsilon > 0$, where n is the size of the input, provided that P $\neq$ NP.

The nonapproximability of the minimum independent dominating set problem was proved by Irving [8] and the limit was recently improved by Halldórsson to $n^{1-\varepsilon}$ for any $\varepsilon > 0$, where n is the number of nodes in the input graph [5]. Thus our results give another way of showing the nonapproximability of this problem, but the most important conclusion is the structural result that every polynomially bounded minimization problem can be reduced to the minimum independent dominating set problem.

2 Definitions

Definition 1. [3] An NPO problem (over an alphabet Σ) is a four-tuple $F = (\mathcal{I}_F, S_F, m_F, opt_F)$ where

- $\mathcal{I}_F \subseteq \Sigma^*$ is the space of *input instances*. It is recognizable in polynomial time.
- $S_F(x) \subseteq \Sigma^*$ is the space of *feasible solutions* on input $x \in \mathcal{I}_F$. The only requirement on S_F is that there exist a polynomial q and a polynomial time computable predicate π such that for all x in $\mathcal{I}_F$, S_F can be expressed as $S_F(x) = \{y : |y| \leq q(|x|) \wedge \pi(x,y)\}$ where q and π only depend on F.
- $m_F : \mathcal{I}_F \times \Sigma^* \to \mathbb{N}$, the *objective function*, is a polynomial time computable function. $m_F(x,y)$ is defined only when $y \in S_F(x)$.
- $opt_F \in \{\max, \min\}$ tells if F is a *maximization* or a *minimization* problem.

Solving an optimization problem F given the input $x \in \mathcal{I}_F$ means finding a $y \in S_F(x)$ such that $m_F(x, y)$ is optimum, that is as big as possible if $opt_F = \max$ and as small as possible if $opt_F = \min$. Let $opt_F(x)$ denote this optimal value.

Approximating an optimization problem F given the input $x \in \mathcal{I}_F$ means finding any $y' \in S_F(x)$. How good the approximation is depends on the relation between $m_F(x, y')$ and $opt_F(x)$.

We often demand that there exist a trivial solution $triv_F(x)$ for each input x so that we can ensure that an approximation algorithm always finds a feasible solution. The trivial solution should be given in the definition of the problem and does not need to be an ordinary feasible solution. The set of formal feasible solutions is really the union of $\{triv_F(x)\}$ and the ordinary feasible solutions $S_F(x)$. A typical trivial solution to a maximization problem is the empty set. For a minimization problem $triv_F(x)$ is usually a special solution with $m_F(x, triv_F(x)) \geq \max_{y \in S_F(x)} m_F(x, y)$. The trivial solution is only defined for technical reasons. It is not important in practice.

Definition 2. The *relative error* of a feasible solution with respect to the optimum of an NPO problem F is defined as

$$\mathcal{E}_F^r(x, y) = |opt_F(x) - m_F(x, y)| / opt_F(x)$$

where $y \in S_F(x)$. In order to avoid division by zero we may either define the problems so that the optimal value is always positive or change the denominator in the definition of the relative error to $opt_F(x) + 1$.

Definition 3. The *performance ratio* of a feasible solution with respect to the optimum of an NPO problem F is defined as

$$R_F(x, y) = \begin{cases} opt_F(x)/m_F(x, y) & \text{if } opt_F = \max, \\ m_F(x, y)/opt_F(x) & \text{if } opt_F = \min, \end{cases}$$

where $x \in \mathcal{I}_F$ and $y \in S_F(x)$.

Definition 4. We say that an optimization problem F *can be approximated within* $p(n)$ for a function $p : \mathbb{Z}^+ \rightarrow \mathbb{R}^+$ if there exists a polynomial time algorithm A such that for every $n \in \mathbb{Z}^+$ and for all instances $x \in \mathcal{I}_F$ with $|x| = n$ we have that $A(x) \in S_F(x)$ and $R_F(x, A(x)) \leq p(n)$.

In order to relate optimization problems we need an approximation preserving reduction. The following reduction is generalized variant of the L-reduction.

Definition 5. Given two NPO problems F and G, a *linear reduction* from F to G is a triple $f = (t_1, t_2, c)$ such that

1. t_1, t_2 are polynomial time computable functions and $c \in \mathbb{Q}^+$.
2. $t_1 : \mathcal{I}_F \rightarrow \mathcal{I}_G$ and $\forall x \in \mathcal{I}_F$ and $\forall y \in S_G(t_1(x))$, $t_2(x, y) \in S_F(x)$.
3. $\forall x \in \mathcal{I}_F$ and $\forall y \in S_G(t_1(x))$, $\mathcal{E}_G^r(t_1(x), y) \leq c \cdot \varepsilon \Rightarrow \mathcal{E}_F^r(x, t_2(x, y)) \leq \varepsilon$.

If there is a linear reduction from F to G we write $F \leq G$.

Definition 6. Definitions of the problems treated in the text.

Shortest computation (SHORTEST COMPUTATION)
$\mathcal{I} = \{\langle M, x \rangle : M$ nondeterministic Turing machine, x binary string$\}$
$S(\langle M, x \rangle) = \{c : |c| < |x|\}$ where c is a computation of M on input x and $|c|$
denotes the length of c.
$triv(\langle M, x \rangle) = 1^{|x|}$, $m(\langle M, x \rangle, c) = |c|$, $opt = \min$.

Shortest path with forbidden pairs (SP WITH FORBIDDEN PAIRS)
$\mathcal{I} = \{G = \langle V, E \rangle : G$ is a graph, $s \in V, f \in V, P \subset V \times V\}$
$S(\langle V, E, s, f, P \rangle) = \{(v_1, \ldots, v_k)$ a sequence of k different nodes in V s.t. $v_1 = s$,
$v_k = f$ and $\forall i \in [1..k-1] ((v_i, v_{i+1}) \in E \wedge \forall j \in [i+1..k](v_i, v_j) \notin P)\}$
$triv(\langle V, E, s, f, P \rangle) = V$, $m(\langle V, E, s, f, P \rangle, (v_1, \ldots, v_k)) = k$, $opt = \min$.

Minimum independent dominating set (MIN IND DOM SET)
$\mathcal{I} = \{G = \langle V, E \rangle : G$ is a graph$\}$
$S(\langle V, E \rangle) = \{V' \subseteq V : (\forall v_1 \in V - V' \exists v_2 \in V' : (v_1, v_2) \in E) \wedge$
$$\wedge (\forall v_1 \in V' \not\exists v_2 \in V' : (v_1, v_2) \in E)\}$$
$triv(\langle V, E \rangle) = V$, $m(\langle V, E \rangle, V') = |V'|$, $opt = \min$.

Minimum number of distinguished ones (MIN DONES)
$\mathcal{I} = \{\langle X, Z, C \rangle : X$ and Z finite set of variables, C set of disjunctive clauses,
each involving at most 3 literals$\}$
$S(\langle X, Z, C \rangle) = \{\langle X', Z' \rangle : X' \subseteq X \wedge Z' \subseteq Z \wedge$ every clause in C is satisfied when
the variables in X' and Z' are set to 1 and the variables in $X - X'$ and $Z - Z'$
are set to 0$\}$
$triv(\langle X, Z, C \rangle) = \langle \emptyset, Z \rangle$, $m(\langle X, Z, C \rangle, \langle X', Z' \rangle) = |Z'|$, $opt = \min$.

Minimum number of ones (MIN ONES)
$\mathcal{I} = \{\langle U, F \rangle : U$ finite set of variables, F boolean formula in 3CNF$\}$
$S(\langle U, F \rangle) = \{U' \subseteq U : F$ is satisfied when the variables in U' are set to 1 and
the variables in $U - U'$ are set to 0$\}$
$triv(\langle U, F \rangle) = U$, $m(\langle U, F \rangle, U') = |U'|$, $opt = \min$.

Minimum number of satisfiable formulas (MIN # SAT)
$\mathcal{I} = \{\langle U, Z \rangle : U$ finite set of variables, Z set of 3CNF formulas$\}$
$S(\langle U, Z \rangle) = \{U' \subseteq U\}$
$m(\langle U, Z \rangle, U') = |\{F \in Z : F$ is satisfied when the variables in U' are set to 1
and the variables in $U - U'$ are set to 0$\}|$
$m(\langle U, Z \rangle, triv(\langle U, Z \rangle)) = |Z|$, $opt = \min$.

Minimum bounded 0 − 1 programming (MIN PB 0 − 1 PROGRAMMING)
$\mathcal{I} = \{A \in \{-1, 0, 1\}^{m \cdot n}$ integer $m \times n$-matrix, $b \in \{-1, 0, 1\}^m$ integer m-vector$\}$
$S(\langle A, b \rangle) = \{x \in \{0, 1\}^n : Ax \geq b\}$
$triv(\langle A, b \rangle) = 1^n$, $m(\langle A, b \rangle, x) = \sum_{i=1}^{n} x_i$, $opt = \min$.

Definition 7. An NPO problem F is *polynomially bounded* if there is a polynomial p such that $\forall x \in \mathcal{I}_F \forall y \in S_F(x), m_F(x, y) \leq p(|x|)$. The class of all polynomially bounded NPO problems is called NPO PB. This class was called $\mathrm{OPTP}[\log n]$ by Krentel [12].

All problems defined in Definition 6 are included in NPO PB. Integer programming and TSP are examples of problems not in NPO PB.

Definition 8. [11] Let MAX PB be the maximization problems which have polynomially bounded objective function, and let MIN PB be the minimization problems which have polynomially bounded objective function. Thus NPO PB = MAX PB ∪ MIN PB.

Definition 9. Given an NPO problem F and a class C. We say that F *is C-complete* if $F \in C$ and $G \leq F$ for all $G \in C$. We say that F *is C-hard* if $G \leq F$ for all $G \in C$.

3 MIN PB-Complete Problems

In this section we will prove that some problems are MIN PB-complete with respect to the linear reduction. These problems are very hard to approximate. It is in fact easy to show that a MIN PB-complete problem cannot be approximated within n^ε for some $\varepsilon > 0$, where n is the size of the input, provided that P $\neq$ NP.

We consider an NP-complete language $\{x : \exists y\, R(x, y)\}$ and we assume, without loss of generality, that $R(x, y) \Rightarrow |x| = |y|$. Define a MIN PB problem F with the same input instances, with $S_F(x) = \{y : R(x, y)\}$, $m_F(x, y) = 1$ if $R(x, y)$ and $m_F(x, y) = |x| + 1$ otherwise.

If this problem could be approximated within $n = |x|$, then we would have a polynomial algorithm which could solve the original NP-complete problem, and thus P = NP. If F cannot be approximated within n, then any MIN PB-complete problem G cannot be approximated within n^ε for some $\varepsilon > 0$, since there is a linear reduction from F to G.

The proofs of the MIN PB-completeness of SHORTEST COMPUTATION and SP WITH FORBIDDEN PAIRS below are inspired by [2].

Theorem 10. SHORTEST COMPUTATION *is* MIN PB-*complete.*

Proof. First we note that SHORTEST COMPUTATION is included in MIN PB (it is a minimization problem where the objective function is bounded by the length of the input and where each feasible solution is a computation of bounded length and therefore can be recognized in polynomial time).

In order to prove that SHORTEST COMPUTATION is MIN PB-complete we will describe a linear reduction from any MIN PB problem to SHORTEST COMPUTATION.

Let $F = (\mathcal{I}_F, S_F, m_F, \min)$ be a MIN PB problem and $p(|x|)$ be a polynomial which bounds both the size of the feasible solutions and the size of the objective function, i.e. for all $x \in \mathcal{I}_F$, $y \in S_F(x) \Rightarrow |y| \leq p(|x|) \wedge m_F(x, y) \leq p(|x|)$.

Construct a Turing machine M which first nondeterministically chooses a solution y (which is at most of size $p(|x|)$) and then deterministically checks if $y \in S_F(x)$. In that case M computes $m_F(x, y)$. We can assume that M so far has computed at most $(|x| + 1)^k$ steps where k is a sufficiently large integer. If y was

57

feasible then M proceeds to compute until a total of $m_F(x,y)(|x|+1)^k$ steps is reached. If y was not feasible then M proceeds to compute until it has computed at least as many steps as the length of the input to M. We see that the input to M must contain $p(|x|)$ and x, and must be longer than $p(|x|)(|x|+1)^k$.

Let x' denote the word resulting from x by replacing each 0 by 01 and each 1 by 10. Let the input to the Turing machine be $1^{p(|x|)}0x'0^{p(|x|)(|x|+1)^k}$.

Let $t_1 = (M, 1^{p(|x|)}0x'0^{p(|x|)(|x|+1)^k})$ and let $t_2 = y$ if y was feasible and $t_2 = triv_F(x)$ otherwise. The reduction from any MIN PB problem to a SHORTEST COMPUTATION problem described by t_1 and t_2 is a linear reduction since for every $y \in S_G(t_1(x))$, $\mathcal{E}_F^r(x, t_2(x,y)) \leq \mathcal{E}_G^r(t_1(x), y)$. $\qquad\square$

Theorem 11. SHORTEST PATH WITH FORBIDDEN PAIRS *is* MIN PB-*complete.*

Proof. We consider a Turing machine M and an input $x = (x_1, \ldots, x_n)$. Without loss of generality we can assume that M is a 1-tape, 1-head Turing machine with oblivious head movement and that M does not write and move in the same step, that is starts in state q_0 and halts in state q_h [2, 15].

From M and x we will construct a graph $G = \langle V, E \rangle$, a start node s, a final node f and a set of forbidden pairs P such that legal paths from s to f correspond to computations of M.

We label the nodes V by (a, q, t) where a is a tape symbol of M, q is a state in M and t is a step number ($0 \leq t \leq n$). Let the start node s be $(x_1, q_0, 0)$.

There is an edge between (a, q, t) and $(b, r, t+1)$ if M can change its state from q to r after reading a. If it is a writing step we demand that b is the written tape symbol. If the tape head is not moved by the step we demand that $b = a$. If the tape head is moved and it is the first time M visits the new tape square we demand that b is the initial content of this square.

Moreover, there is a special final node f and edges between every node of the form (a, q_h, t) and f.

Every pair of nodes labelled by the same step number t is included in P, together with every pair of the form $\{(a, q, t_1), (b, r, t_2)\}$ such that $a \neq b$, and that during step t_1 the tape head leaves a tape square and t_2 is the next step when the head revisits the same square.

We can see that every path of length $k+1$ from s to f without forbidden pairs corresponds to a computation of M on input x running in time k and, in the opposite direction, that every computation corresponds to a path from s to f without forbidden pairs.

Therefore this reduction is a linear reduction. Since SP WITH FORBIDDEN PAIRS is a polynomially bounded minimization problem we conclude that it is MIN PB-complete. $\qquad\square$

We are now ready to state our main theorem.

Theorem 12. MIN IND DOM SET *is complete for* MIN PB.

Proof. We will show that MIN IND DOM SET is MIN PB-hard by reducing from SP WITH FORBIDDEN PAIRS. Suppose we have an instance $\langle V, E, s, f, P \rangle$ of SP WITH FORBIDDEN PAIRS and that $V = \{v_1, \ldots, v_n\}$ where $v_1 = s$ and $v_n = f$.

We construct a graph $G' = \langle V', E' \rangle$ as follows. Let m be a large positive integer whose value will be specified later. V' consists of $n + 2$ parts which we call $A, K_1, K_2, \ldots, K_n$, and B. Let $A = \{a_1, \ldots, a_m\}$, $B = \{b_1, \ldots, b_m\}$ and for each $j \in [1..n]$, $K_j = \{v_1^j, \ldots, v_n^j, w_1^j, \ldots, w_m^j\}$. We will call these four types of nodes a-, b-, v- and w-nodes. Thus V' contains a total of $2m + n(n + m)$ nodes.

The idea is to include at most one node in each K_i in the solution and the fact that v_j^i is included should correspond to node v_j being the i-th node in a valid path in G.

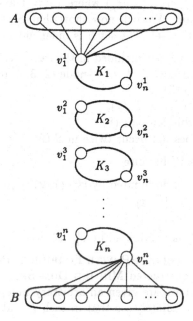

Fig. 1. The constructed instance of MIN IND DOM SET in the reduction from SP WITH FORBIDDEN PAIRS. Only some of the edges are shown in the figure. In each K_i only two nodes, v_1^i and v_n^i, are shown, but K_i contains a total of n v-nodes and m w-nodes.

We include edges in E' in the following way.

$$\forall i, j, k \in [1..n], i \neq k \Rightarrow (v_i^j, v_k^j) \in E' \tag{1}$$

$$\forall i, j \in [1..n], \forall k \in [1..m], (v_i^j, w_k^j) \in E' \tag{2}$$

$$\forall k \in [1..m], (a_k, v_1^1) \in E' \tag{3}$$

$$\forall j \in [1..n], \forall k \in [1..m], (v_n^j, b_k) \in E' \tag{4}$$

$$\forall j, k, l \in [1..n], l > j \Rightarrow (v_n^j, v_k^l) \in E' \tag{5}$$

$$\forall j, l \in [1..n], \forall k \in [1..m], l > j \Rightarrow (v_n^j, w_k^l) \in E' \tag{6}$$

$$\forall i, k \in [1..n], \forall j \in [1..n-1], (v_i, v_k) \notin E \Rightarrow (v_i^j, v_k^{j+1}) \in E' \tag{7}$$

$$\forall i, j, k, l \in [1..n], (v_i, v_k) \in P \Rightarrow (v_i^j, v_k^l) \in E' \tag{8}$$

$$\forall i, j, l \in [1..n], j \neq l \Rightarrow (v_i^j, v_i^l) \in E' \tag{9}$$

In words this means that each K_j is an n-clique of v-nodes (1) extended by m w-nodes which are connected to each v-node (2). Each node in A is connected to v_1^1, i.e. the first v-node in K_1 (3). The last v-node in each K_j is connected to all nodes below it in Fig. 1 (4, 5, 6). Node v_i in K_j and node v_k in K_{j+1} are connected whenever there is no edge between v_i and v_k in the original graph G (7). Node v_i in K_j and node v_k in K_l are connected whenever (v_i, v_k) is a forbidden pair (8). Finally all v-nodes with the same number in different K_j:s are connected (9).

Suppose that $(v_{L_1}, v_{L_2}, \ldots, v_{L_p})$ where $L_1 = 1$ and $L_p = n$ is a path in G without forbidden pairs. We will now show that $S = \{v_{L_1}^1, v_{L_2}^2, \ldots, v_{L_p}^p\}$ is an independent dominating set. The set S is independent because

- no two nodes from S are included in the same K_j (1),
- S does not contain any a-, b- or w-node (2, 3, 4, 6),
- $v_{L_i} \neq v_n$ for $i < p$ (5),
- $(v_{L_i}, v_{L_{i+1}})$ is an edge in E (7),
- S contains no forbidden pair (8),
- the same node does not occur twice in S (9).

The set S dominates V' because

- for $1 \leq j \leq p$, K_j is dominated by $v_{L_j}^j$ (1, 2),
- A is dominated by $v_{L_1}^1$ (3),
- B is dominated by $v_{L_p}^p$ (4),
- for $p < j \leq n$, K_j is dominated by $v_{L_p}^p$ (5, 6).

Thus every solution of the SP WITH FORBIDDEN PAIRS instance corresponds to a solution of the constructed MIN IND DOM SET instance of the same size.

Now suppose that we are given an arbitrary independent dominating set S with $|S| \leq n$. We immediately see that in each K_j, at most one v-node may be included in S.

We would like to prevent any w-node from occurring in S. If a w-node does occur in S, then all w-nodes in the same K_j must be included in order to dominate K_j (because otherwise some v-node in K_j must be included, which is forbidden since S must be independent), which means that we need m nodes to dominate just one K_j. Since $|S| \leq n$ this will be impossible if we choose $m \geq n$. The same argument can be used to show that there cannot be any a-node or b-node in S.

Thus S consists solely of v-nodes, at most one from each K_j.

The fact that $A \cap S = \emptyset$ must be due to that $v_1^1 \in S$, because v_1^1 is the only v-node which has edges to any a-node. Since $B \cap S = \emptyset$ we must have that $v_n^p \in S$ for some p. Suppose that $v_n^p \in S$ for a fixed p, then $K_j \cap S = \emptyset$ for all $j > p$ by (5). We cannot have that $K_j \cap S = \emptyset$ for some $j < p$, because then K_j must be dominated by some v_n^k with $k < j < p$, which is impossible since $(v_n^k, v_n^p) \in E'$.

Apparently there must be exactly one v-node from each K_j with $1 \leq j \leq p$ included in S and these are the only nodes in S. Hence we can skip the superscripts of the nodes in S, read from top to bottom and write $(v_{L_1}, v_{L_2}, \ldots, v_{L_p})$ where $L_1 = 1$ and $L_p = n$. Now we use that S is independent to show that

- for all $1 \leq i < p$, $(v_{L_i}, v_{L_{i+1}}) \in E$ (7),
- for all $1 \leq i < j \leq p$, (v_{L_i}, v_{L_j}) is not a forbidden pair (8),
- for all $1 \leq i < j \leq p$, $L_i \neq L_j$ (9).

Thus S describes a path from s to f in G without forbidden pairs, i.e. a feasible solution to the problem. Moreover this solution is of the same size as S.

If we are given an independent dominating set S of size greater than n we can directly choose the trivial solution of SP WITH FORBIDDEN PAIRS.

We have shown that the described reduction from SP WITH FORBIDDEN PAIRS to MIN IND DOM SET is a linear reduction. Since MIN IND DOM SET is included in MIN PB we can conclude that MIN IND DOM SET is MIN PB-complete. □

The following theorem was independently of us obtained by Höffgen, Simon and van Horn [6]. It is easy to prove it using Theorem 12.

Theorem 13. MIN DONES *is complete for* MIN PB.

Proof. We will describe a linear reduction from MIN IND DOM SET to MIN DONES. Given an instance $\langle V, E \rangle$ of MIN IND DOM SET, let $Z = \{z_1, \ldots, z_{|V|}\}$ be a set of $|V|$ boolean variables, one for each node in V. We would like a node to be included in a dominating independent set if and only if the corresponding variable is true. In order to obtain this we describe the independence and domination properties using a CNF formula F.

For every edge $\langle v_i, v_j \rangle \in E$ we add the clause $\overline{z}_i \vee \overline{z}_j$ in order to assure the independence. For every node v_i with its neighbours $v_{i_1}, v_{i_2}, \ldots, v_{i_k}$ we add the clause $z_i \vee z_{i_1} \vee z_{i_2} \vee \cdots \vee z_{i_k}$, thus assuring that v_i is dominated.

This gives us $|E| + |V|$ clauses some of which may consist of more than three literals. We use the standard transformation to obtain only clauses with at most three literals: each clause $z_0 \vee z_1 \vee \cdots \vee z_k$ transforms into $k - 1$ clauses $(z_0 \vee z_1 \vee x_1) \wedge (\overline{x}_1 \vee z_2 \vee x_2) \wedge \cdots \wedge (\overline{x}_{k-2} \vee z_{k-1} \vee z_k)$ where $x_1, \ldots, x_{k-2}$ are new variables (different for each original clause). Let X be the set of new variables. We can see that X consists of less than $2E$ variables and that we have increased the number of clauses with $|X|$ to $|E| + |V| + |X| < 3|E| + |V|$.

Now we have a MIN DONES problem $\langle X, Z, C \rangle$ which exactly corresponds to the original MIN IND DOM SET problem. Even the objective values agree. □

Theorem 14. MIN ONES *is complete for* MIN PB.

Proof. This is a sketch of the proof. We reduce MIN DONES to MIN ONES. The reduction is based on the reduction between the corresponding maximization problems MAX DONES and MAX ONES by Panconesi and Ranjan [13].

The idea is to make a lot of copies of the distinguished variables to make each such variable more valuable than all the nondistinguished variables together. If there are k distinguished variables and l nondistinguished variables we introduce, for each distinguished variable z, $2l$ new variables $z_1, \ldots, z_{2l}$ and $2l$ pairs of clauses $(z_i \vee \overline{z}_{i+1}) \wedge (\overline{z}_i \vee z_{i+1})$ to assure that $z = z_1 = \cdots = z_{2l}$. A solution

of this MIN ONES problem with objective value m can be transformed to a
solution of the original MIN DONES problem with objective value $\lfloor m/(2l+1) \rfloor$.
The reduction is a linear reduction. $\qquad\square$

Theorem 15. MIN # SAT *is complete for* MIN PB.

Proof. We reduce from MIN DONES. Let $\langle X, Z, C \rangle$ be an input instance of this
problem. Construct $|Z|$ 3CNF formulas such that the i-th formula is $z_i \wedge C$.
This means that the number of true distinguished variables in an assignment
satisfying C is equal to the number of satisfied formulas $z_i \wedge C$ using the same
assignment. Thus the reduction is a linear reduction. $\qquad\square$

Theorem 16. MIN PB $0-1$ PROGRAMMING *is complete for* MIN PB.

Proof. We reduce from MIN IND DOM SET. Given an input instance $\langle V, E \rangle$ of
MIN IND DOM SET, first construct the set of $|E| + |V|$ clauses in the same way
as in the proof of Theorem 13. We represent each clause as a linear inequality in
the binary variables $x_1, \ldots, x_{|V|}$. Each clause of the type $\overline{z}_i \vee \overline{z}_j$ corresponds to
an inequality $-x_i - x_j \geq -1$ and each clause of the type $z_i \vee z_{i_1} \vee z_{i_2} \vee \cdots \vee z_{i_k}$
corresponds to an inequality $x_i + x_{i_1} + \cdots + x_{i_k} \geq 1$. This is a MIN PB $0-1$
PROGRAMMING problem with $m = |E| + |V|$ and $n = |V|$ and the reduction is a
linear reduction. $\qquad\square$

The five original MAX PB-complete problems were LONGEST COMPUTA-
TION, LP WITH FORBIDDEN PAIRS, MAX PB $0-1$ PROGRAMMING, LARGEST
INDUCED CONNECTED CORDAL SUBGRAPH and LONGEST INDUCED PATH [2].

We have shown that the minimization problems corresponding to the first
three problems (SHORTEST COMPUTATION, SP WITH FORBIDDEN PAIRS and
MIN PB $0-1$ PROGRAMMING) are MIN PB-complete. The "smallest induced
connected cordal subgraph problem" is obviously uninteresting.

A natural question would be to ask whether the shortest induced path between two given nodes, the minimization problem corresponding to the last problem above, is also MIN PB-complete. The answer is no, because this problem
is solvable in polynomial time using for example Dijkstra's algorithm (since the
shortest path is always an induced path).

4 A Parameter Dependent Reduction

The relative error preserving reductions, like the L-reduction and the linear
reduction, work very well when reducing to problems with bounded approximation. When analyzing approximation algorithms for problems which cannot
be approximated within a constant, like the MIN PB-complete problems, one
usually specifies the approximability using a one variable function where the
parameter concerns the size of the input instance. Which quantity of the input
instance to choose as the parameter depends on the problem and the algorithm.

When reducing between two such problems, say from F to G, the relative
error preserving reductions are not perfect. The trouble is that these reductions

may transform an input instance of F to a much larger input instance of G. One purpose of a reduction is to be able to use an approximation algorithm for G to construct an equally good approximation algorithm for F. Because of the size amplification the constructed algorithm will not be as good as the original.

In order to tell how the approximability, when given as a function, will be changed by a reduction, we have to specify how the size of the input instance will be amplified. For every reduction we may add a statement *with size amplification* $f(n)$ in order to specify this. If the size amplification is $O(n)$, i.e. if the size of the constructed structure is a constant times the size of the original structure, we say that the reduction is *without amplification*. Moreover we introduce a completely new size dependent reduction which we think is well suited for reductions between problems which cannot be approximated within a constant.

Definition 17. Given two NPO problems F and G, an *S-reduction with size amplification* $a(n)$ from F to G is a tuple $f = (t_1, t_2, a, c)$ such that

1. t_1, t_2 are polynomial time computable functions, a is a monotonously increasing positive function and c is a positive constant.
2. $t_1 : \mathcal{I}_F \to \mathcal{I}_G$ and $\forall x \in \mathcal{I}_F$ and $\forall y \in S_G(t_1(x))$, $t_2(x, y) \in S_F(x)$.
3. $\forall x \in \mathcal{I}_F$ and $\forall y \in S_G(t_1(x))$, $R_F(x, t_2(x, y)) \le c \cdot R_G(t_1(x), y)$.
4. $\forall x \in \mathcal{I}_F$, $|t_1(x)| \le a(|x|)$.

Proposition 18. *Given two* NPO *problems F and G, if $F \le G$ with size amplification $a(n)$ and G can be approximated within some monotonously increasing positive function $u(n)$ of the size of the input instance, then F can be approximated within $c \cdot u(a(n))$, which is a monotonously increasing positive function.*

Proof. For each $x \in \mathcal{I}_F$ of size n we use the approximation function for G to find a solution $y \in S_G(t_1(x))$ so that $R_F(x, t_2(x, y)) \le c \cdot R_G(t_1(x), y) \le c \cdot u(|t_1(x)|) \le c \cdot u(a(|t_1(x)|)) = c \cdot u(a(n))$ since u is monotonously increasing and positive. $\square$

For constant and polylogarithmic approximable problems the S-reduction preserves approximability within a constant for any polynomial size amplification, since $c \log^k(n^p) = p^k c \log^k n = O(\log^k n)$. For n^c approximable problems it only does this for size amplification $O(n)$, since $c \cdot (O(n))^c = O(n^c)$.

We apply Proposition 18 to the reductions in Theorem 13–16, use the fact that MIN IND DOM SET cannot be approximated within $n^{1-\varepsilon}$, and get:

Corollary 19. *If* P$\neq$NP *the following statements are true.*

a) MIN DONES *cannot be approximated within $n^{1-\varepsilon}$ for any $\varepsilon > 0$, where n is the number of distinguished variables.*

b) MIN ONES *cannot be approximated within $n^{1/3-\varepsilon}$ for any $\varepsilon > 0$, where n is the number of variables.*

c) MIN # SAT *cannot be approximated within $n^{1-\varepsilon}$ for any $\varepsilon > 0$, where n is the number of formulas.*

d) MIN PB $0-1$ PROGRAMMING *cannot be approximated within $n^{1-\varepsilon}$ for any $\varepsilon > 0$, where n is the number of unknown variables.*

Note that all four problems can trivially be approximated within n. Thus the lower bounds in a), c) and d) are optimal.

Acknowledgements

I would like to thank Magnús Halldórsson for asking me if MIN IND DOM SET is MIN PB-complete. Thanks also to Johan Håstad and Klaus-Uwe Höffgen for discovering some unclear points in the proofs.

References

1. S. Arora, C. Lund, R. Motwani, M. Sudan, and M. Szegedy. Proof verification and hardness of approximation problems. In *Proc. of 33rd Annual IEEE Sympos. on Foundations of Computer Science*, pages 14–23, 1992.
2. P. Berman and G. Schnitger. On the complexity of approximating the independent set problem. *Information and Computation*, 96:77–94, 1992.
3. P. Crescenzi and A. Panconesi. Completeness in approximation classes. *Information and Computation*, 93(2):241–262, 1991.
4. M. R. Garey and D. S. Johnson. *Computers and Intractability: a guide to the theory of NP-completeness*. W. H. Freeman and Company, San Fransisco, 1979.
5. M. M. Halldórsson. Approximating the minimum maximal independence number. Technical Report IS-RR-93-0001F, ISSN 0918-7553, Japan Advanced Institute of Science and Technology, JAIST, 1993.
6. K-U. Höffgen, H-U. Simon, and K. van Horn. Robust trainability of single neurons. Manuscript, 1992.
7. O. H. Ibarra and C. E. Kim. Fast approximation for the knapsack and sum of subset problems. *Journal of the ACM*, 22(4):463–468, 1975.
8. R. W. Irving. On approximating the minimum independent dominating set. *Information Processing Letters*, 37:197–200, 1991.
9. V. Kann. *On the Approximability of NP-complete Optimization Problems*. PhD thesis, Department of Numerical Analysis and Computing Science, Royal Institute of Technology, Stockholm, 1992.
10. V. Kann. On the approximability of the maximum common subgraph problem. In *Proc. 9th Annual Symposium on Theoretical Aspects of Computer Science*, pages 377–388. Springer-Verlag, 1992. Lecture Notes in Computer Science 577.
11. P. G. Kolaitis and M. N. Thakur. Logical definability of NP optimization problems. Technical Report UCSC-CRL-90-48, Board of Studies in Computer and Information Sciences, University of California at Santa Cruz, 1990. To be published in Information and Computation.
12. M. W. Krentel. The complexity of optimization problems. *Journal of Computer and System Sciences*, 36:490–509, 1988.
13. A. Panconesi and D. Ranjan. Quantifiers and approximation. In *Proc. Twenty second Annual ACM symp. on Theory of Comp.*, pages 446–456. ACM, 1990.
14. C. H. Papadimitriou and M. Yannakakis. Optimization, approximation, and complexity classes. *Journal of Computer and System Sciences*, 43:425–440, 1991.
15. N. Pippenger and M. J. Fischer. Relations among complexity measures. *Journal of the ACM*, 26(2):361–381, 1979.

Primal-Dual Approximation Algorithms for Integral Flow and Multicut in Trees, with Applications to Matching and Set Cover

(Extended Abstract)

Naveen Garg[1], Vijay V. Vazirani[1], Mihalis Yannakakis[2]

[1] Department of Computer Science and Engg.
Indian Institute of Technology, Delhi
[2] AT & T Bell Laboratories, Murray Hill, NJ 07974

1 Introduction

The classical max flow problem plays a central role in combinatorial optimization. More recently, the importance of various formulations of the multicommodity flow problem has been realized in the context of developing good approximation algorithms for NP-hard optimization problems. Approximate max-flow min-cut theorems for these formulations were first derived for general graphs [15, 12, 9, 20] and later the bounds were improved for special classes of graphs (see for example [13, 23] for planar graphs).

In this paper, we consider multicommodity flow in trees; the formulation we deal with requires maximizing the sum of the flows routed subject to capacity and flow conservation constraints. This setting captures a surprisingly rich collection of problems, as described below. Our main result is an efficient algorithm for finding an integral flow, F, and a multicut, M, such that $F \geq \frac{1}{2}M$. This gives a factor 2 approximate max-flow min-multicut theorem, as well as approximation algorithms for integral flow and multicut in trees. Both problems are shown to be NP-hard and MAX SNP-hard [19], which implies that no polynomial time approximation scheme exists unless P=NP [1].

A specially interesting feature of our work lies in the methodology used for designing the algorithm - it is based on a primal-dual approach. The primal-dual method has been used extensively in the past for solving problems in P. In fact, the solutions of some of the corner-stone problems in combinatorial optimization, including matching, flow and shortest paths are based on this method [18]. More recently, the usefulness of this method to approximation algorithms has been demonstrated, particularly in the work of [10], followed by [24]. [24] also formally identifies the elements of the primal-dual approach to approximation algorithms, and indicates why the method holds considerable promise in this setting.

The problem of finding a maximum integral flow is the same as that of finding a maximum cardinality set of edge-disjoint paths between the specified source-sink pairs, and has been extensively studied [7, 21]. We do not know of approximation algorithms for any other NP-hard cases besides ours. We give some explanation by showing that even for planar graphs, the integrality gap for flow is unbounded, thus indicating that LP duality based methods would not be useful for obtaining approximation algorithms. Our algorithm for integral flow has potential applications to problems of routing paths in networks that are configured as trees.

As stated above, the formulation studied in this paper captures a rich collection of problems. When restricted to trees of height one and unit edge capacities, integral max flow is essentially the maximum matching problem on general graphs, and multicut is the vertex cover problem on general graphs. The best approximation factor known for vertex cover is 2 (see eg. [2]), indicating that improving our result would be quite difficult. If the trees are of height one and edge capacities are arbitrary, integral max flow corresponds to the maximum b-matching problem in general graphs. On the other hand, if the edge capacities are unity and the trees are of arbitrary height, integral max flow corresponds to a generalization of matching, which we call the *cross-free-cut matching* problem. This problem inherits many nice combinatorial properties of matching. For instance, we can characterize the facets of the polytope defined by the convex hull of all cross-free-cut matchings, thereby generalizing Edmonds' celebrated theorem [6]. We also give a polynomial time algorithm for finding a maximum cross-free-cut matching, and hence also for integral max flow in trees having unit edge capacities.

Finally, we also show that the multicut problem in trees is equivalent to the set cover problem for a special class of set systems, which we call *tree-representable set systems*. Interestingly enough, the problem of recognizing this class in polynomial time has been extensively studied in a different context [22] (it is the same as testing if a given binary matroid is graphic), and efficient algorithms have been discovered [3]. Hence, we also get a factor 2 approximation algorithm for the tree-representable set cover problem. The best approximation factor known for the set cover problem is $O(\log n)$, where n is the number of elements being covered, and the recent result of [16] shows that modulo constant factors, it is not possible to do better unless $NP \subseteq TIME(n^{\log n})$.

2 Relationship with other problems

Given a tree $T = (V, E)$, a capacity function $c : E \to \mathcal{Z}^+$, and k pairs of vertices (not necessarily distinct) $\{s_i, t_i\}$ $1 \le i \le k$, we associate a commodity i with the pair $\{s_i, t_i\}$ and designate s_i as the source and t_i the sink for this commodity. A *multicommodity flow* is a way of simultaneously routing commodities from their sources to sinks, subject to capacity and conservation constraints.

A multicommodity flow in which the sum of the flows over all the commodities is maximized will be called a *generalized max flow*. A flow is integral if each commodity has an integral flow through each edge. The *integral max flow* problem is to find an integral multicommodity flow that is maximum. A *multicut* is defined as a set of edges whose removal disconnects each $\{s_i, t_i\}$ pair. The weight of the multicut is the sum of the capacities of the edges in it. The *minimum multicut* problem is to find a multicut of minimum weight.

Closely related to the multicut is the notion of a *multiway cut* [5]. Given a set of vertices $s_1, s_2, \ldots s_k$ a multiway cut is a set of edges whose removal disconnects each pair s_i, s_j, $1 \leq i, j \leq k$. The *minimum multiway cut* problem is to find a multiway cut of minimum weight.

The generalized maxflow problem for trees can be formulated as

$$\text{maximize} \quad \sum_{i=1}^{k} f_i$$
$$\text{subject to } \sum_{i=1}^{k} f_i q_i(e) \leq c_e \ \forall e \in E$$
$$f_i \geq 0 \ \forall i : 1 \leq i \leq k$$

where q_i denotes the unique path from s_i to t_i in T and $q_i(e)$ is the characteristic function of this path, i.e. $q_i(e) = 1$ if $e \in q_i$, 0 otherwise. The variable f_i denotes the flow of commodity i. The additional constraint, $f_i \in \mathcal{Z}^+$, yields a program for the integral max flow problem.

The dual of this LP is

$$\text{minimize} \quad \sum_{e \in E} d_e c_e$$
$$\text{subject to } \sum_{e \in E} d_e q_i(e) \geq 1 \ \forall i : 1 \leq i \leq k$$
$$d_e \geq 0 \ \forall e \in E$$

and can be viewed as an assignment of non-negative distance labels, d_e, to edges $e \in E$, so as to minimize $\sum_{e \in E} d_e c_e$, subject to the constraint that each $\{s_i, t_i\}$ pair be at least a unit distance apart. An integral solution to the dual problem corresponds to a multicut; the edges with $d_e = 1$ form a multicut.

Following standard terminology, two cuts $(S, \overline{S})$ and $(T, \overline{T})$ are said to be *crossing* iff $S \cap T$, $S \cap \overline{T}$, $\overline{S} \cap T$ and $\overline{S} \cap \overline{T}$ are all non-empty. A family of cuts is *non-crossing* if no pair is crossing.

Given a graph $G = (U, F)$ and a family, $\mathcal{F}$, of non-crossing cuts; a *cross-free-cut matching* is a set of edges, $F' \subseteq F$, such that F' contains at most one edge from each cut, $(S, \overline{S}) \in \mathcal{F}$. If $\mathcal{F}$ is the set of all singleton cuts, $(u, U - u)$ $u \in U$, then a cross-free-cut matching is simply a matching in G (note that this family of cuts is non-crossing). Thus a cross-free-cut matching generalizes the notion of a matching. The *maximum cross-free-cut matching* problem is to find a cross-free-cut matching of maximum cardinality.

A well studied generalization of matching is the b-matching. Given a graph $G = (U, F)$ and a function $b : U \to \mathcal{Z}^+$, a b-matching is a set (with multiplicities) of edges, $F' \subseteq F$, such that each vertex, $u \in U$, has at most $b(u)$ edges incident at it. Viewed differently, F' contains at most $b(u)$ edges from the singleton cut $(u, U - u)$ $u \in U$. We generalize the notion of b-matchings by allowing constraints for any family of non-crossing cuts (not just singleton cuts) and call this a *cross-free-cut b-matching*. Thus, given a graph $G = (U, F)$, a family, $\mathcal{F}$, of non-crossing cuts and a function $b : \mathcal{F} \to \mathcal{Z}^+$; a cross-free-cut b-matching is a set of edges that contains at most $b((S, \overline{S}))$ edges from the cut $(S, \overline{S}) \in \mathcal{F}$. The *maximum cross-free-cut b-matching* problem is to find a cross-free-cut b-matching of maximum cardinality.

We now establish a relationship between the maximum cross-free-cut matching problem and the integral max flow problem on trees. As a first step we relate the integral max flow and minimum multicut problems on trees of height one to the maximum matching and minimum vertex cover problems respectively.

Proposition 1. *For trees of height one and unit edge capacities, the integral max flow problem is equivalent to the maximum matching problem on general graphs, while the minimum multicut problem is the same as the minimum vertex cover problem on general graphs. When the edge capacities are arbitrary, integral max flow is equivalent to maximum b-matching and minimum multicut is the same as the minimum weight vertex cover on general graphs.*

Proof. From a tree T of height one, we can construct a graph G as follows. Let r be the root and $v_1, v_2, \ldots v_d$ be the leaves of the tree, T. Construct graph $G = (U, F)$ where $U = \{v_1, v_2, \ldots v_d\}$. If v_i, v_j form the source-sink pair for some commodity, add edge (v_i, v_j) to G. Conversely, to every graph G we can associate a tree T of height one that has one leaf v_i for every vertex of G and one commodity for every edge.

Routing a unit flow from v_i to v_j corresponds to picking edge (v_i, v_j) in G. Since all edges of T have unit capacity, an integral flow in T is a matching in G of the same size. The converse is also true; a matching in G of size f corresponds to an integral flow of f units in T. Thus computing the integral max flow in T is equivalent to finding a maximum matching in G.

If edge $e_i = (r, v_i)$ has capacity c_i then corresponding to an integral flow in T we would be picking at most c_i edges incident to v_i in G. Thus, computing an integral max flow in T now corresponds to finding a maximum b-matching in G, where $b(v_i) = c_i$.

If the edges $e_{i_1}, e_{i_2}, \ldots e_{i_p}$ form a multicut in T, they separate all source sink pairs. The corresponding vertices $v_{i_1}, v_{i_2}, \ldots v_{i_p} \in U$ hence form a vertex cover in G. Thus, finding the minimum multicut in T is equivalent to finding a minimum weight vertex cover in G; the vertex v_i has weight c_i. $\quad\Box$

We now extend Proposition 1 to trees of arbitrary height.

Proposition 2. *The integral max flow problem on trees with unit capacity edges is equivalent to the maximum cross-free-cut matching problem on general graphs. When edge capacities are arbitrary it is the same as the maximum cross-free-cut b-matching problem.*

3   Trees with Unit Capacity Edges

The minimum multicut problem for trees can be solved in polynomial time for fixed k. This is so because the multicut contains at most k edges; we can in time $O(n^k)$ enumerate all subsets of edges of cardinality at most k and pick one that is a multicut and has the minimum weight. However, for arbitrary k the problem is NP-hard.

Theorem 3. *The minimum multicut problem is NP-hard and MAX SNP-hard for trees, even if all edge capacities are unity.*

The proof follows from the equivalence between the minimum multicut problem and the minimum vertex cover problem, established in Proposition 1. Contrast this with the minimum multiway cut problem for trees which is polynomial time solvable even for arbitrary k; this follows from a straight-forward dynamic programming approach [4].

The integral max flow problem on trees with unit edge capacities is equivalent to the maximum cross-free-cut matching problem (Proposition 2).

3.1 The Cross-free-cut Matching Polytope

The cross-free-cut matching polytope is the convex hull of the incidence vectors of all cross-free-cut matchings. In a celebrated result, Edmonds [6] provided the first description of the matching polytope as a linear set of inequalities. Subsequently, Pulleyblank [17] proved that every inequality of this set indeed defines a facet. Lovasz [14] provided a simpler proof of the theorem characterizing the facets of this polytope. We use ideas from this proof to obtain a complete characterization of the facets of the cross-free-cut matching polytope.

Given $G = (U, F)$ and a family $\mathcal{F}$ of non-crossing cuts (an instance of the maximum cross-free-cut matching problem); let $T = (V, E)$ be the tree and $\{s_i, t_i\}$ $1 \le i \le k$, be pairs of vertices for the instance of the integral max flow problem corresponding to the given instance of the maximum cross-free-cut matching problem. Let $t \in V$ be an internal vertex of T and $T_1, T_2, \ldots T_d$ be the subtrees incident at t. Each vertex of G corresponds to a vertex of T. The subtrees $T_1, T_2, \ldots T_d$ thus partition the vertex set U. Let $S_1, S_2, \ldots S_d \subseteq U$ be the sets in the partition. Coalesce each set S_i, to a single vertex u_i and remove any self loops so formed. Define G_t as the multi-graph induced over the vertices $u_1, u_2, \ldots u_d$.

A graph is *matching-critical* if the removal of any vertex leaves a graph that has a perfect matching.

Theorem 4. *The following inequalities define the facets of the cross-free-cut matching polytope.*

(a) $x_f \ge 0 \quad \forall f \in F$

(b) $\sum_{f \in C} x_f \le 1$

   where $C \equiv (S, \overline{S}) \in \mathcal{F}$ is such that if $S(\overline{S})$ has only one neighbor, u, then $S \cup \{u\}$ is a connected component of G and if $S(\overline{S})$ has exactly two neighbors then they are not adjacent.

(c) $\sum_{f \in E(W)} x_f \le \frac{|W| - 1}{2}$
   where W spans a 2-connected matching-critical subgraph of G_t, t is an internal vertex of T.

3.2 An Efficient Algorithm for Integral Maxflow

Using a slight extension of Theorem 4 and the ellipsoid method, we can obtain a polynomial time algorithm for the maximum cross-free-cut matching problem.

In this subsection we present a more efficient algorithm, based on a dynamic programming approach.

Since all edge capacities are unity, and we want an integral flow, at most one commodity can flow through an edge. As shown in Proposition 1, for a tree of height one, this is simply a maximum matching problem.

Our algorithm starts by rooting the tree at an arbitrary vertex. It then does two passes over the tree, level by level, - an upward pass followed by a downward pass. Consider a tree of height 2. At a vertex v at level 1, we could solve a maximum matching problem to route flow in the subtree rooted at v. However, it may also be advantageous to send a commodity along the edge from v to the root, r. This will be strictly advantageous only if we can still route the previous amount of flow in the subtree rooted at v. We determine the commodities for which we get a strict advantage, by solving a maximum matching problem for each commodity (on the downward pass, we will pick one of these commodities for the (v, r) edge; once this is done, the rest of the routing in the subtree rooted at v can be accomplished). Vertex v can now be considered the source/sink of these commodities. This is done for all vertices at level 1. Then a height one problem is solved at the root. In solving this, we pick the commodity that is routed on the (v, r) edge. As remarked earlier, the rest of the routing in the subtree rooted at v can now be fixed.

This is the essential idea of the algorithm for arbitrary height trees as well. In the upward pass, we consider vertices level by level. At a vertex v we solve, for each choice of commodity being routed on the $(v, parent(v))$ edge, a height one problem. The commodities giving strict advantage are thought of as originating at v itself.

In the downward pass, we start at the root, fixing commodities. The vertex $parent(v)$ decides which commodity gets routed on $(v, parent(v))$. Once this is done vertex v fixes the commodities coming up from its children.

Theorem 5. *There is a polynomial time algorithm for finding a maximum integral flow on trees with unit capacity edges, and for the maximum cross-free-cut matching problem.*

4 Integral Flow and Multicut in Trees

We now consider the case when the edge capacities are integral and not just one. Computing the maximum integral flow is now NP-hard and so good approximation algorithms are required.

4.1 NP-hardness of integral maxflow

In this subsection we show that the integral max flow problem for trees with arbitrary edge capacities is NP-hard, and so is the maximum cross-free-cut b-matching problem. It is intriguing that generalizing the maximum matching problem to a family of non-crossing cuts results in a polynomial time solvable problem (the maximum cross-free-cut matching problem), whereas the same generalization of the maximum b-matching problem results in an NP-hard problem.

Theorem 6. *The integral max flow problem is* NP-*hard and* MAX SNP-*hard for trees with edge capacities 1 and 2.*

We reduce the 3D-matching problem to the integral max flow problem. Given three disjoint sets X, Y, Z, $|X| = |Y| = |Z| = n$ and a set of triples $S = \{(x_i, y_j, z_k) | x_i \in X, y_j \in Y, z_k \in Z\}$, the 3D-matching problem is to find the maximum number of disjoint triples.

Given an instance of the 3D-matching problem, we construct a tree, T, of height 3. The root has one child corresponding to each element of $X \cup Y \cup Z$. A vertex corresponding to the element $x_i \in X$ has p_i children; p_i is the number of occurences of x_i in S. We label these vertices $\underline{x_i, l}$, $1 \le l \le p_i$. Each of these vertices $\underline{x_i, l}$ has 2 children labelled $\underline{x_i, l, \alpha}$ and $\underline{x_i, l, \beta}$. Edges $(x_i, \underline{x_i, l}), 1 \le l \le p_i, 1 \le i \le n$, and $(r, x_i), 1 \le i \le n$, have a capacity 2. All other edges have unit capacity.

The occurences of x_i in S are numbered arbitrarily from 1 to p_i, and the lth occurence corresponds to $\underline{x_i, l}$. If $(x_i, y_j, z_k) \in S$ corresponds to the lth occurence of x_i, we add three source-sink pairs, $\{\underline{x_i, l, \alpha}, \underline{x_i, l, \beta}\}$, $\{\underline{x_i, l, \alpha}, y_j\}$ and $\{\underline{x_i, l, \beta}, z_k\}$. Thus the instance of the integral max flow problem constructed has $3|S|$ commodities. Theorem 6 now follows from:

Lemma 7. *The instance of the 3D-matching problem has t disjoint triples iff T has an integral flow of $t + |S|$ units.*

MAX SNP-hardness follows from the fact that the 3D-matching problem is MAX SNP-hard even if every element occurs a bounded number of times [11], and in this case the above transformation is an L-reduction [19].

4.2 Approximation Algorithm for Integral Flow and Multicut

Theorem 8 Approximate max-integral-flow min-multicut theorem. *For trees, the maximum integral flow, F_{opt}, and the minimum multicut, M_{opt}, are related as*

$$\frac{1}{2}M_{opt} \le F_{opt} \le M_{opt}$$

We prove Theorem 8 by showing an algorithm that finds an integral flow, F, and a multicut, M, such that $\frac{1}{2}M \le F$. Since the maximum integral flow, F_{opt}, is less than the minimum multicut, M_{opt}, we obtain

$$\frac{1}{2}M \le F \le F_{opt} \le M_{opt} \le M$$

which implies $\frac{1}{2}F_{opt} \le F \le F_{opt}$ and $M_{opt} \le M \le 2M_{opt}$. Thus the integral flow, F, and multicut, M, found by our algorithm are good approximations to the optimal.

Theorem 9 Approximating integral max flow and minimum multicut.
One can, in polynomial time, approximate integral max flow within a factor $\frac{1}{2}$ and minimum multicut within a factor 2.

Our algorithm follows a primal-dual approach. In [24], the elements of the primal-dual approach have been enunciated. We will use their framework to describe our algorithm. The approach consists of starting with arbitrary solutions to the primal and dual LP's, and making alternate improvements to each, until 'good' integral solutions to both are found. The improvements are guided by the complementary slackness conditions. The two complementary slackness conditions are:

1. *Primal complementary slackness condition:* $f_i > 0 \Rightarrow \sum_{e \in E} d_e q_i(e) = 1$,
   i.e. if the commodity i has a non-zero flow then the sum of the distance labels along path q_i is exactly 1.
2. *Dual complementary slackness condition:* $d_e > 0 \Rightarrow \sum_{i=1}^{k} f_i q_i(e) = c_e$,
   i.e. an edge with a non-zero distance label is saturated.

Since we are seeking 'good' integral solutions to the primal and dual LP's, we should not be enforcing all the complementary slackness conditions (because then we will end up with optimal solutions to both LP's, and these may not be integral). As proposed in [24], we shall enforce the dual complemetary slackness condition and relax the primal condition to:

$$f_i > 0 \Rightarrow 1 \le \sum_{e \in E} d_e q_i(e) \le 2$$

If F is the integral flow, and M the multicut found under these conditions, then $F \ge \frac{1}{2} M$.

For this, notice that ensuring the following is sufficient.

1. only saturated edges are picked in the multicut.
2. for each commodity i, the multicut contains at least one edge of the path q_i.
3. for each commodity i that is routed, the multicut contains at most two edges from the path q_i.

We root the tree at an arbitrary vertex say r. The level of a vertex is its distance from the root. An edge e_1 is an *ancestor* of an edge e_2 if e_1 lies on the path from e_2 to the root. The algorithm proceeds in two phases

Phase 1. In this phase we move up, from the leaves to the root, one level at a time, routing flow as we go along and picking edges tentatively (a subset of these edges will be retained as the multicut in Phase 2). If v is a vertex in the current level, check if there exists a path completely contained in the subtree rooted at v, along which flow can be routed. If yes, send as much flow as can be sent along this path. Repeat this procedure till all paths in this subtree are saturated.

Let Q be the set of edges saturated in this step. Define *frontier*(v) to be the largest subset of Q such that no edge of Q is an ancestor of an edge in *frontier*(v).

We augment the flow in this manner, level by level. A path along which some flow is sent will be called a *flow path*. Since all capacities are integral the flow along each flow path is also integral.

Phase 2. In this phase we work top down picking an appropriate subset of the frontier edges so as to form a small multicut. Let S denote the set of edges picked. Initially $S \leftarrow \phi$. We move down one level at a time. For each vertex in the current level do

$\forall e \in frontier(v)$
if $\not\exists e' \in S$ such that e' lies on the path from e to v then $S \leftarrow S \cup \{e\}$

Lemma 10. *The set, S, of edges picked forms a multicut.*

We also need to show that condition 3. holds, i.e. the multicut picked, S, contains at most two edges from each flow path. We begin by making the following two claims.

Claim *Let s_i-t_i be a flow path, and v the least common ancestor of s_i, t_i. If $e \in$ frontier(u) is an edge on this path then u is an ancestor of v.*

Proof. For contradiction, assume that v is an ancestor of u. Hence, u is considered before v in Phase 1. Since $e \in frontier(u)$, e is saturated while considering vertex u and flow is sent along the path s_i-t_i later (while processing vertex v). However, this is not possible as edge e lies on the path s_i-t_i. $\square$

Claim *If u is an ancestor of v then no edge of frontier(v) is an ancestor of an edge of frontier(u).*

Proof. Suppose, $e_1 \in frontier(v)$ is an ancestor of $e_2 \in frontier(u)$. Since u is an ancestor of v, vertex v is considered before u in Phase 1. As $e_1 \in frontier(v)$, e_1 is saturated while considering vertex v and $e_2 \in frontier(u)$ is saturated later (while processing vertex u). However, this is not possible as edge e_1 is an ancestor of e_2 and lies on the path from e_2 to u. $\square$

Lemma 11. *Let s_i-t_i be a flow path and v the least common ancestor of s_i, t_i. Then S contains at most one edge from the path s_i-$v(t_i$-$v)$.*

Proof. Let S contain two edges e_1, e_2 from the path s_i-v. Further, let $e_1 \in frontier(v_1)$ be an ancestor of $e_2 \in frontier(v_2)$. By the above two claims it follows that v_1 is an ancestor of v_2 which is an ancestor of v. Thus, e_1 occurs on the path from e_2 to v_2 and so while picking edges from $frontier(v_2)$ (Phase 2) we would not have included e_2 in S. $\square$

5 The Tree-representable Set Cover Problem

The minimum multicut problem for trees can be viewed as a weighted set cover problem. The elements, P, of the set system, (P, E), are the s_i-t_i paths in the tree, $1 \leq i \leq k$. The sets, E, correspond to edges of the tree. A set includes all s_i-t_i paths (elements) that use this edge; the set has weight equal to the capacity of the edge. Finding the minimum weight multicut for the tree is the same as finding the minimum weight set cover of this set system.

Note however, that not all set cover problems can be viewed as a minimum multicut problem on trees. A set system (P, E) is called a *tree-representable set system* if there exists a tree T, whose set of edges is E such that every path $p \in P$ is a path in T. The problem of deciding whether a given set system is a tree-representable set system is well-studied and efficient algorithms known [3]. Thus, given a set cover problem, one can, in almost linear time, check if it corresponds to the minimum multicut problem on some tree, T, and if so, find T and the $\{s_i, t_i\}$ pairs.

Theorem 12. *There exists a polynomial time algorithm that achieves a factor 2 approximation for the minimum weight set cover problem for set systems that are tree-representable.*

6 Integrality Gap for Planar Graphs

The approximation algorithm for integral max flow on trees uses, implicitly, the fact that the ratio between the fractional and integral max flow for trees is at most 2. This, however, is not true for general graphs. In fact, even for planar graphs this gap is quite large.

Proposition 13. *The gap between integral max flow and the maximum fractional flow for planar graphs can be as high as $\frac{k}{2}$, where k is the number of commodities.*

Proof. The graph G is a union of k paths, $p_1, p_2, \ldots p_k$; the end points of the path p_i form the source-sink pair for commodity i. Every pair of paths p_i, p_j, $i \neq j$, intersect in a unique edge.

The graph G can be embedded on an $k \times k$ grid. If the origin $(0,0)$ is the left bottom corner of the grid then $s_i = (0, k - i + 1)$ and $t_i = (i, 0)$. The path p_i is then the path from $(0, k - i + 1)$ to $(i, k - i + 1)$ to $(i, 0)$. Any two paths intersect at a unique vertex. To ensure that they intersect in a unique edge we replace each intersection $v \equiv (i, j)$ by two vertices v_a, v_b. The edges incident at vertices v_a, v_b are $(v_a, (i - 1, j))$, $(v_a, (i, j - 1))$, $(v_b, (i + 1, j))$, $(v_b, (i, j + 1))$ and (v_a, v_b).

The integral max flow for this instance is one unit as by routing any one commodity we block the paths of all other commodities. However, the maximum fractional flow is $k/2$ units; half unit of each commodity can be routed simultaneously. This yields a gap of $k/2$ between the maximum fractional flow and the integral max flow. $\qquad\square$

Note that the preceeding discussion also applies to the gap between the integral max flow and the minimum multicut.

7 Discussion and open problems

The notion of a cross-free family of cuts is quite basic and comes up in several contexts (e.g. in approximating TSP by solving the LP relaxation, and doing subtour elimination). It will be interesting to interpret and apply our results to these contexts.

In particular, understanding better the link between our problem and the setting of [10, 24] seems especially promising. The problem considered in [10] is to find a small subgraph that satisfies specified cut requirements. Let $G = (V, E)$ be a graph, $c : E \rightarrow \mathcal{Z}^+$ capacities on the edges and $f : 2^V \rightarrow \{0, 1\}$ a function specifying cut requirements. The LP relaxation (primal) and dual of their problem is

$$
\begin{array}{ll}
\text{minimize} & \sum_{e \in E} x_e c_e \\
\text{subject to } \forall S \subset V, & \sum_{e : e \in \nabla(S)} x_e \geq f(S) \\
\forall e \in E, & x_e \geq 0
\end{array}
$$

$$
\begin{array}{ll}
\text{maximize} & \sum_{S \subset V} f(S) y_S \\
\text{subject to } \forall e \in E, & \sum_{S : e \in \nabla(S)} y_S \leq c_e \\
\forall S \subset V, & y_S \geq 0
\end{array}
$$

This primal and our primal form a complementary pair - this is a covering problem and ours is the corresponding packing problem. The above-stated dual is a cut packing problem. The approximation algorithm of [10] finds a dual solution in which the non-zero y_S's correspond to a non-crossing family of cuts. Furthermore, our algorithm, as well as those of [10, 24] are primal-dual algorithms. These relationships seem to suggest a deeper connection.

Is there a generalization of the maximum cross-free-cut matching problem, allowing certain crossing cuts, that is in P? We can show that allowing arbitrary crossing cuts leads to NP-hardness. Our reduction from the maximum independent set problem is approximation preserving and hence no polynomial time algorithm can achieve an approximation factor of n^ε.

Can our primal-dual approximation algorithm be generalized beyond trees? Proposition 13 shows that any such algorithm attempting to approximate the integral max flow, will have to compare it to the non-integral flow.

Acknowledgement We wish to thank Clyde Momna and Alex Schaffer for providing references for the tree-representable set systems.

References

1. S. Arora, C. Lund, R. Motwani, M. Sudan, and M. Szegedy: Proof verification and the hardness of approximation problems. Proc. 33rd IEEE Symp. on Foundations of Computer Science, 14-23 (1992).

2. R. Bar-Yehuda, S. Even: A linear time approximation algorithm for the weighted vertex cover problem. J. Algorithms 2, 198-203 (1981).

3. R.E. Bixby, D.K. Wagner: An almost linear time algorithm for graph realization. Mathematics of Operations Research 13, 99-123 (1988)

4. S. Chopra, M.R. Rao: On the multiway cut polyhedron. Networks 21, 51-89 (1991).

5. E. Dalhaus, D.S. Johnson, C.H. Papadimitriou, P.D. Seymour, M. Yannakakis: The complexity of multiway cuts. Proc. 24th ACM Symposium on Theory of Computing (1992).

6. J. Edmonds: Maximum matching and a polyhedron with (0,1) vertices. J. Res. Nat. Bur. Standards Sect. B 69B, 125-130 (1965).

7. A. Frank: Packing paths, circuits and cuts - a survey. In: B. Korte, L. Lovasz, H.J. Promel A. Schrijver (eds.): Paths, Flows and VLSI-Layout. Algorithms and Combinatorics 9. Springer, pp. 47-100.

8. M. Grotschel, L. Lovasz, A. Schrijver: The ellipsoid method and its consequences in combinatorial optimization. Combinatorica 1, 169-197 (1981).

9. N. Garg, V.V. Vazirani, M. Yannakakis: Approximate max-flow min-(multi)cut theorems and their applications. 25th ACM Symposium on Theory of Computing (1993).

10. M.X. Goemans, D.P. Williamson: A general approximation technique for constrained forest problems. 3rd Annual ACM-SIAM Symposium on Discrete Algorithms (1992).

11. V. Kann. On the approximability of NP-complete optimization problems. Ph.D. Thesis, Royal Institute of Technology, Stockholm, 1992.

12. P. Klein, A. Agrawal, R. Ravi, S. Rao: Approximation through multicommodity flow. 31st Symposium on Foundations of Computer Science, 726-737 (1990).

13. P. Klein, S. Plotkin, S. Rao: Excluded minors, network decomposition, and multicommodity flow. 25th ACM Symposium on Theory of Computing (1993).

14. L. Lovasz: Graph theory and integer programming, Discrete Optimization I. In: P.L. Hammer, E.L. Johnson, B. Korte (eds.): Ann. Discrete Math. 4. Amsterdam: North-Holland 1979, pp. 141-158.

15. F.T. Leighton, S. Rao: An approximate max-flow min-cut theorem for uniform multicommodity flow problems with application to approximation algorithms. 29th Symposium on Foundations of Computer Science, 422-431 (1988).

16. C. Lund, M. Yannakakis: On the hardness of approximating minimization problems. 25th ACM Symposium on Theory of Computing (1993).

17. W.R. Pulleyblank: Faces of matching polyhedra. Ph.D. Thesis: Univ. of Waterloo: Dept. Combinatorics and Optimization, 1973.

18. C.H. Papadimitriou, K. Steiglitz: Combinatorial Optimization: Algorithms and Complexity. New Jersey: Prentice Hall Inc., 1982.

19. C. H. Papadimitriou, and M. Yannakakis. Optimization, approximation and complexity classes. J. of Computer and System Sciences, 425-440 (1991).

20. S. Plotkin, E. Tardos: Improved bounds on the max-flow min-cut ratio for multicommodity flows. 25th ACM Symposium on Theory of Computing (1993).

21. A. Schrijver: Homotopic routing methods. In: B. Korte, L. Lovasz, H.J. Promel, A. Schrijver (eds.): Paths, Flows and VLSI-Layout. Algorithms and Combinatorics 9, Springer, pp. 329-371, 1990.

22. W. T. Tutte: An algorithm for determining whether a given binary matroid is graphic. Proc. Amer. Math. Soc. 11, 905-917 (1960).

23. E. Tardos, V.V. Vazirani: Improved bounds for the max-flow min-multicut ratio for planar and $K_{r,r}$-free graphs. submitted for publication (1992).

24. D.P. Williamson, M.X. Goemans, M. Mihail, V.V. Vazirani: A primal-dual approximation algorithm for generalized steiner network problems. 25th ACM Symposium on Theory of Computing (1993).

The Complexity of Approximating PSPACE-Complete Problems for Hierarchical Specifications [1] (Extended Abstract)

M. V. Marathe   H. B. Hunt III   S.S.Ravi

Department of Computer Science
University at Albany, SUNY,
Albany, NY 12222

Abstract

We extend the concept of polynomial time approximation algorithms to apply to problems for hierarchically specified graphs, many of which are PSPACE-complete. Assuming P $\neq$ PSPACE, the existence or nonexistence of such efficient approximation algorithms is characterized, for several standard graph theoretic and combinatorial problems. We present polynomial time approximation algorithms for several standard problems considered in the literature. In contrast, we show that unless P = PSPACE, there is no polynomial time ϵ-approximation for any $\epsilon > 0$, for several other problems, when the instances are specified hierarchically.

1 Introduction

Hierarchical system design is becoming increasingly important with the development of VLSI technology. At present, many VLSI circuits already have over a million transistors. (For example the *Intel i860* chip has about 2.5 million transistors.) Although VLSI circuits can have millions of transistors, they usually have highly regular structures. These regular structures often make them amenable to hierarchical design, specification and analysis.

Over the last decade several theoretical models have been put forward to succinctly represent objects hierarchically [2, 4, 14, 18]. Here, we use the model defined in Lengauer [6, 11, 14, 15] to describe hierarchically specified graphs. Using this model, Lengauer et al. [12, 13, 14] have given efficient algorithms to solve several graph theoretic problems including minimum spanning forests, planarity testing etc.

Here we extend the concept of polynomial time approximation algorithms so as to apply to problems for hierarchically specified graphs including PSPACE-complete such problems. We characterize the existence or nonexistence (assuming P $\neq$ PSPACE) of polynomial time approximation algorithms, for several standard graph problems. Both positive and negative results are obtained (see

---

[1] Research supported in part by NSF Grants CCR 89-03319 and CCR 89-05296. Email addresses of authors: {madhav, hunt, ravi}@cs.albany.edu.

Tables 1 and 2). Our study of approximation algorithms for hierarchically specified problems is motivated by the following two facts:

1. $\Theta(n)$ size hierarchical specifications can specify $2^{\Omega(n)}$ size graphs.

2. Many basic graph theoretic properties are PSPACE-complete [7, 11], rather than NP-complete.

For these reasons the known approximation algorithms in the literature are not applicable to graph problems, when graphs are specified hierarchically.

What we mean by a *polynomial time approximation algorithm* for a graph problem, when the graph is specified hierarchically, can be best understood by means of an example.

Example: Consider the minimum vertex cover problem, where the input is a hierarchical specification of a graph G. We wish to compute the size of a minimum vertex cover of G. Our polynomial time approximation algorithm for the vertex cover problem computes the size of an approximate vertex cover and runs in time *polynomial* in the *size* of the hierarchical description, rather than the *size* of G. Moreover, it also solves in polynomial time (in the size of the hierarchical specification) the following **query problem**: Given any vertex v of G and the path from the root to the node in the *hierarchy tree* in which v occurs, determine whether v belongs to the approximate vertex cover so computed. ∎

This is a natural extension of the definition of approximation algorithms in the flat (i.e. non-hierarchical) case. This can be seen as follows: In the flat case, the number of vertices is polynomial in the size of the description. Given this, any polynomial time algorithm to determine if a vertex v of G is in the approximate minimum vertex cover can be modified easily into a polynomial time algorithm that lists all the vertices of G in the approximate minimum vertex cover. For an optimization problem or a query problem, our algorithms use space and time which is a low level polynomial in the size of the hierarchical specification and thus $O(poly \log N)$ in the size of the specified graph, when the size N of the graph is exponential in the size of the specification. Moreover, when we need to output the subset of vertices, subset of edges, etc. corresponding to a vertex cover, maximal matching, etc., in the expanded graph, our algorithms take essentially the same time but substantially less (often exponentially less) space than algorithms that work directly on the expanded graph.

We believe that this is the first time efficient approximation algorithms with good performance guarantees have been provided both for hierarchically specified graph problems and for PSPACE-complete problems.[2] Thus by providing algorithms which exploit the underlying structure, we extend the range of applicability of standard algorithms. Our results are summarized as follows.

---

[2] Independently, Condon et al. [3] have investigated the approximability of other PSPACE-complete problems.

Table 1. Performance Guarantees

Problem	Performance guarantee in hierarchical case	Best known guarantee in flat case
MAX 3SAT	2	4/3
MIN Vertex Cover	2	2
MIN Maximal Matching	2	2
Bounded Degree (B) MAX Independent Set	B	B
Bounded Degree (B) MIN Dominating Set	B	B
MAX CUT	2	2

The results mentioned in the last column of the above table can be found in [5, 20].

Table 2. Hardness Results

Problem	Hierarchical Case	Flat Case
Maximum Number of True Gates in a circuit	PSPACE-hard to approximate any ϵ	Log-hard for P to approximate to within any ϵ of the optimal
Optimal Value of Objective Function of a Linear Program	PSPACE-hard for any ϵ	Log-hard for P to approximate for any ϵ
High Degree Subgraph	PSPACE-hard for $\epsilon < 2$	Log-hard for P to approximate for $\epsilon < 2$
$k-$ Vertex Connectivity	PSPACE-hard for $\epsilon < 2$	Log-hard for P to approximate for $\epsilon < 2$
$k-$ Edge Connectivity	PSPACE-hard for $\epsilon < 2$	Log-hard for P to approximate for $\epsilon < 2$

The results mentioned in the last column of the above table can be found in [1, 9, 16].

2 Definitions and Description of the Model

The following two definitions are from Lengauer [12].

Definition 2.1 *A hierarchical specification* $T = (G_1, ..., G_n)$ *of a graph is a sequence of undirected simple graphs* G_i *called cells. The graph* G_i *has* m_i *edges and* n_i *vertices.* p_i *of the vertices are distinguished and are called pins. The other* $(n_i - p_i)$ *vertices are called inner vertices.* r_i *of the inner vertices are distinguished and are called nonterminals. The* $(n_i - r_i)$ *vertices are called terminals.*

Note that there are $n_i - p_i - r_i$ vertices defined explicitly in G_i. We call these *explicit vertices*. Each pin of G_i has a unique label, its *name*. The pins are assumed to be numbered between 1 and p_i. Each nonterminal in G_i has two labels, a *name* and a *type*. The type is a symbol from $G_1, ..., G_{i-1}$. If a nonterminal vertex v is of the type G_j, then the terminal vertices which are the neighbors of G_j are in one-to-one correspondence with the pins of G_j. (Note that all the neighbors of a nonterminal vertex must be terminals. Also, a terminal vertex may be a neighbor of several nonterminal vertices.) Without loss of generality we assume that for each G_i there is a nonterminal node associated with it. The size of T is $n = \sum_{1 \le i \le k} n_i$, and the edge number is $m = \sum_{1 \le i \le k} m_i$.

Definition 2.2 *The expansion* $E(T)$ *(i.e. the graph associated with* T*) of the hierarchical specification* T *is done as follows:*
$k = 1 : E(T) = G_1$.
$k > 1$: *Repeat the following step for each nonterminal* v *of* G_k*, say of the type* G_j*: delete* v *and the incident edges. Insert a copy of* $E(T_j)$ *by identifying the* l^{th} *pin of* $E(T_j)$ *with the node in* G_k *that is labeled* (v, l)*. The inserted copy of* $E(T_j)$ *is called the subcell of* G_k*. (Observe that the expanded graph can have multiple edges although none of the* G_i *have multiple edges.)*

The expansion $E(T)$ is the graph associated with the hierarchical definition T. With T one can associate a natural tree structure depicting the sequence of calls made by the successive levels. We call it the *hierarchy tree. We note again that our approximation algorithms answer query problems without explicitly expanding the hierarchical specification.*

A hierarchical specification is 1-*level restricted* if every edge passes through at most one pin (i.e. if (x, y) is an edge with x defined in G_i and y defined in G_j, then, $|i - j| \le 1$).

Let the length of the encoding of T be n, and let the numbers be represented in binary. Then the total number of nodes in $E(T)$ can be $2^{\Omega(n)}$.

We assume that the reader is familiar with the definition of the *Circuit Value problem* (CVP). We use $MVCP_{HG}$ to denote the monotone circuit value problem when the circuit is defined hierarchically. It is shown in [11] that the $MCVP_{HG}$ is PSPACE-complete. Furthermore, we can show that this problem remains PSPACE-complete, even when the hierarchical specifiction of the circuit is 1-level restricted and $O(\log(N))$ bandwidth bounded.

Definition 2.3 *An instance of Hierarchical Linear Program (HLP) is of the form*

$$F_i(X^i) = (\bigcup_{1 \le i_j \le i} F_{i_j}(X_i^j, Z_i^j)) \bigcup f_i(X^i, Z^i)$$

for $1 \le i \le n$ where f_i are set of linear inequalities, X_j, X_j^i, Z^i, Z_j^i are vectors of variables such that $X_j^i \subseteq X^i$, $Z_j^i \subseteq Z^i$, $1 \le i_j \le i$. Thus F_1 is just a set of linear inequalities. An instance of HLP defines a hierarchically specified linear program $F_n(X^n)$ obtained after expanding F_j $(1 \le j \le n)$ as macros where the Z's in different expansions are considered distinct.

We assume that each inequality is of the form $\sum a_i x_i + b \le 0$. The *HLP* feasibility problem is to determine whether there exists an assignment to the variables used in the *HLP* (over the reals) such that all the inequalities are satisfied. In the case of the *HLP* optimization problem, one is given a linear objective function and linear inequalities both defined hierarchically. The aim is to find an assignment to the variables so as to maximize the value of the objective function subject to the inequality constraints. Using Lengauer's definition of hierarchical graphs, one can represent graphically a *HLP* by associating a node with each variable and with each inequality. Further, a variable node has an edge to an inequality node iff the corresponding variable occurs in the inequality.

The definitions of High Degree Subgraph problem and the k-vertex connectivity problems are omitted in this abstract. Readers can refer to [1, 9] for these definitions.

3 Approximation Algorithm for Vertex Cover

Here we discuss our heuristic for computing the size of a near-optimal vertex cover for a hierarchically defined graph. This problem was shown to be PSPACE-complete in Lengauer [11]. Our heuristic extends the well known vertex cover heuristic for the flat case, where one computes a maximal matching as an approximate vertex cover. The algorithm in the non-hierarchical case has a performance guarantee of 2 [5].

We note that the straightforward greedy approach for obtaining a maximal matching in a flat graph cannot be directly extended to the hierarchical case. Two reasons for this are as follows. First, the degree of a vertex in a hierarchical graph can be exponential in the size of the description, and so it is not possible to keep track of the neighbors of a node explicitly. Secondly, an edge between a pair of nodes can pass through several *pins*, and thus need not be explicitly present at any level. Therefore edges cannot be handled as simply as in the flat case. This complicates our heuristic since we can keep track of only a polynomial amount of information at each level.

We use a *bottom up* method for processing hierarchical graphs. This method has been used in Lengauer et al. [11, 14], and Williams et al. [19] for designing efficient algorithms for hierarchical graphs. The bottom up method aims at finding a small graph G_i^{bt} called the *burnt graph* which can replace each occurrence of G_i in such a way that G_i and G_i^{bt} behave identically with respect to the problem under consideration. The bottom up method should produce such burnt graphs efficiently.

Before we present the heuristic we give some notation which we use throughout this section. Given a graph G, $MM(G)$ denotes a maximal matching in the subgraph induced by the explicit vertices in G (i.e. no pins and no nonterminals). $V(MM(G))$ denotes the vertices in the subgraph induced by $MM(G)$. $MxM(G)$ denotes a maximum matching of G. $V(MxM(G))$ denotes the vertices in the subgraph induced by $MxM(G)$. The following lemma recalls known properties of a maximum matching in a bipartite graph.

Lemma 3.1: Let $G = (S, T, E)$ be a bipartite graph. Let V_1^S and V_1^T denote the set of vertices in S and T included in $V(MxM(G))$. Let V_2^S and V_2^T denote the set of vertices in S and T not included in $V(MxM(G))$. Then the following statements hold:

1. For all $\alpha \in V_2^S$ and $\beta \in V_2^T$, $(\alpha, \beta) \notin E$.

2. For all $v_x \in V_1^S$, $v_y \in V_1^T$, $v_z \in V_2^S$ and $v_w \in V_2^T$, if $(v_x, v_y) \in E$ and $(v_y, v_z) \in E$ then $(v_z, v_w) \notin E$.

3. For all $v_x' \in V_1^S$, $v_y' \in V_1^T$, $v_z' \in V_2^S$, and $v_w' \in V_2^T$, if $(v_x', v_y') \in E$ and $(v_x', v_w') \in E$ then $(v_z', v_w') \notin E$.

4. $|V(MxM(G))|$ is equal to the size of a minimum vertex cover for G. ∎

For simplicity, we assume that in the given hierarchical specification there is no edge between two pins which are defined in the same cell. It is possible to modify the heuristic to handle this case also. In the following description, we use $\psi(G_i)$ to denote the size of an approximate vertex cover for the expanded version of G_i. We also use $EM(G_i)$ to denote the set of edges implicitly chosen by the heuristic from the expanded version of G_i.

Heuristic HVC
Input: *A hierarchical specification* $T = (G_1, ..., G_n)$ *of a graph* G.

1. (a) Construct a maximal matching $MM(G_1)$ for G_1.
   $\psi(G_1) = |V(MM(G_1))|$.
   Remark: At this point, $EM(G_1)$ is equal to $MM(G_1)$.

   (b) Let V_1' denote the explicit vertices in V_1 which are not included in $MM(G_1)$. Let G_1^b denote the vertex induced subgraph on V_1' and the set of pins in G_1.

   (c) Construct a maximum matching $MxM(G_1^b)$ on this graph G_1^b. (Observe that G_1^b is a bipartite graph.) Let G_1^{bt} denote the subgraph induced on $V(MxM(G_1^b))$.

2. Repeat the following steps for $2 \leq i \leq n$.

(a) Compute $MM(G_i)$.

(b) Let V_i^l denote the vertices not in $V(MM(G_i))$. Also let $G_{i_1}, ..., G_{i_k}$ be the nonterminals in the definition of G_i. (Recall that $i_j \leq i$.)

(c) Vertices in V_i^l which are connected to pins in one of $G_{i_1}, ..., G_{i_k}$ are the endpoints of those edges that have their other endpoints in one of G_{i_j} where $1 \leq i_j < i$. For each such vertex, arbitrarily choose (if available) one of the matching partners of the pins in the corresponding burnt graph $G_{i_1}^{bt}, ..., G_{i_k}^{bt}$. Following this, construct a maximal matching on the set of vertices remaining in V_1^l and the burnt graphs of nonterminals called in G_i.

(d) For the bipartite graph G_i^b induced by the vertices left over in G_i including those in $G_{i_1}^{bt}, ..., G_{i_k}^{bt}$, and the pins in G_i, construct $MxM(G_i^b)$. This corresponds to the burnt graph G_i^{bt}.

(e) $\psi(G_i) = |V(MM(G_i))| +$ Number of explicit vertices matched

in Step 2(c) $+ \sum_{j=1}^{k} \psi(G_{i_j})$.

Remark: $EM(G_i)$ consists of $MM(G_i)$, the edges chosen in Step 2(c) and $(\cup_{j=1}^{k} EM(G_{i_j}))$. Note that $EM(G_i)$ is only needed in the proof; it is not explicitly computed. Further, $\psi(G_i)$ is at most $2 \times |EM(G_i)|$.

3. Output $\psi(G_n)$.

Theorem 3.1 *Given a hierarchical graph G, the above approximation algorithm runs in time polynomial in the size of the specification, and the size of the vertex cover computed by the algorithm is within 2 of the optimal value. Furthermore, given any vertex v, we can determine in polynomial time if the vertex is in the approximate vertex cover so computed.*

Proof Sketch: We show that the set $EM(G_n)$ is a maximal matching for $E(T)$.

$EM(G_n)$ is a matching since at each individual level we construct a valid matching, and the only vertices in V_i^l which are considered for computing the maximum matching to obtain G_i^{bt} are the ones which have no edges between them. Further, each time a pair of vertices is matched up in Step 2(c), they are never considered again. Hence no two edges in the set so constructed have a common endpoint.

The proof that $EM(G_n)$ is maximal is nontrivial. We need to prove that each edge in the expanded graph $E(T)$ has at least one of its endpoints in $E(G_n)$. The details are omitted in this abstract. ∎

Corollary 3.1 *Given a hierarchical specification of a graph G, we can compute in time polynomial in the size of the specification, the size of an approximate minimum maximal matching which is within a factor of 2 of the optimal.*

3.1 Approximating Simple Max Cut

Given an undirected graph $G(V, E)$, the goal of the simple max cut problem is to partition the set V into two sets V_1 and V_2 such that the number of edges in E having one end point in V_1 and the other in V_2 is maximized.

Again for simplicity, we assume that in the given hierarchical specification there is no edge between two pins which are defined in the same cell. It is possible to modify the heuristic to handle the case when this restriction does not hold.

We first give a brief overview of the algorithm. As in the case of the vertex cover algorithm, we process the input specification in a bottom up fashion. At each level, we construct a burnt graph G_i^b starting from the original description of the level G_i. At this point, it is useful to recall the idea behind the known heuristic for the flat case. That heuristic (referred to as FMax-Cut in the following discussion) processes the nodes in arbitrary order, and assigns each node v either to V_1 or to V_2 depending upon which of these sets has the fewer number of edges to v. We use the heuristic FMax-Cut to partition the explicit vertices at each stage. The burnt graph for G_i then just consists of two super nodes denoting an implicit partition of all the vertices defined in levels below. The edges go from a super node to the pins in G_i. Each edge has a weight associated with it. The edge weight basically keeps count of the number of edges the ancestor of the pin has to the vertices in that partition.

Heuristic HMax-Cut
Input: *A hierarchical specification* $T = (G_1, ..., G_n)$ *of a graph* G.

1. (a) Process G_1 as follows: Let A_1 be the set of explicit vertices in G_1. Execute FMax-Cut on the vertex induced subgraph $G(A_1)$. Let V_1 and V_2 be the sets produced by FMax-Cut. (Observe that we did not need to process any edge from a pin p_i to an explicit vertex until now.)

   (b) The burnt graph G_1^b for G_1 is constructed as follows: The pins in G_1^b are the same as the pins in the original graph. There are two super vertices V_1^1 and V_2^1 in G_1^b; these correspond to sets V_1 and V_2 computed in Step 1. Construct a complete bipartite graph with the set of pins on one side and the two super vertices on the other. The weights on the edges are computed as follows: For a pin p_i, the weight of edge (p_i, V_j^1) $(j = 1, 2)$ is equal to the number of edges (p_i, v_j) such that $v_j \in V_j^1$. (The weight basically gives the number of edges the ancestor of the pin will have to the set V_j^1.)

2. Repeat the following steps for $2 \le i \le n$.

   (a) Let A_i be the set consisting of all the explicit vertices in G_i which are not adjacent to any nonterminals in the definition of G_i. Further, let $G(A_i)$ denote the subgraph induced on the nodes in A_i. Use Algorithm FMax-Cut to obtain a partition of A_i into two sets X_1

and X_2. (Again realize that we need not consider any edges which are from these explicit vertices to the pins.)

(b) Let $V_1 = X_1 \cup \bigcup_j V_1^j$ and $V_2 = X_2 \cup \bigcup_j V_2^j$ where G_j, $j < i$ appears in the definition of G_i.

(c) Let B_i denote the set of all the explicit vertices remaining after Step 2(b). Note that each of these explicit vertices is adjacent to at least one nonterminal in the definition of G_i. We consider the vertices in B_i one at a time. For each vertex $v \in B_i$, we place it in one of the sets V_1^i or V_2^i according to the following criterion. Let

$Count(V_1^i)$ = number of vertices in the set V_1^i that are adjacent to v.
$Count(V_2^i)$ = number of vertices in the set V_2^i that are adjacent to v.

If $(Count(V_1^i) \geq Count(V_2^i))$ then $V_2^i = V_2^i \cup \{v\}$ else $V_1^i = V_1^i \cup \{v\}$.

(d) Now construct the burnt graph G_i^b as follows: The pins in G_i^b are the same as the pins in G_i, and we have two super vertices V_1 and V_2 which implicitly represent the partition constructed so far. Again, as in Step 1, we construct a complete bipartite graph with the set of pins on one side and the super vertices on the other. The weight of an edge is computed similar to Step 1 by just adding the weights of all the edges which are incident on the pin.

We note that in Step 2(c) of the above algorithm, the sets V_1^i and V_2^i are updated after the addition of each vertex. Also, we do not maintain these sets explicitly. We just need the number of vertices in V_1^i and V_2^i to which each $v \in B_i$ is adjacent. This information can be maintained by keeping track of the partition of explicit vertices in G_i processed so far and the weights on the edges from the pins to the super vertices of the burnt graphs of all the nonterminals defined in G_i. It is easy to modify the above algorithm (along the lines of the approximate vertex cover algorithm) to output the number of edges in the approximate max cut.

Theorem 3.2 *Let $H(G)$ be a hierarchical specification of a graph G. Then the above algorithm computes in time polynomial the size of $H(G)$, an approximate max cut which comes to within two times the size of an optimal max cut. Moreover, given any vertex v in the graph G, we can determine in time polynomial in the size of $H(G)$, the set to which v belongs.*

Proof Sketch: We need to show that the two sets V_1 and V_2 indeed partition the original set of nodes and also that the number of edges going across the partition is at least $1/2$ of the total number of edges in the graph. This can be proven by induction on the number of distinct cells in the hierarchical description. We omit the details of this proof due to lack of space. ∎

The algorithms for weighted MAX 3SAT, bounded degree dominating set, and bounded degree independent set will appear in a complete version of this paper. The algorithms for each of the problems also process the hierarchical specification in a bottom up fashion and compute burnt graphs efficiently.

4 Hardness Results

4.1 Approximating Number of True Gates in MVCP

Here we give a number of hardness results for hierarchically specified instances. All our hardness results hold for $O(\log N)$ bandwidth bounded hierarchical specifications, where N denotes the number of vertices the expanded graph.

Theorem 4.1 *Unless P=PSPACE, no polynomial time algorithm can approximate the maximum number of true gates in a $MCVP_{HG}$, to within any constant factor, even when the hierarchical description is 1-level restricted.*

Proof Sketch: Given an instance $C = \{C_1, C_2, ..., C_k\}$ of $MCVP_{HG}$ with m gates and an ϵ where $0 < \epsilon \leq 1$, we construct an instance $D = \{D_1, D_2, ..., D_k\}$ of $MVCP_{HG}$ with $m + \lceil m/\epsilon \rceil$ gates such that D has at least $\lceil m/\epsilon \rceil$ true gates iff C outputs the value 1. The basic idea is to construct for each C_i a corresponding D_i such that if C_i calls k copies of C_{i-1} then D_i calls k copies of D_{i-1}. D is similar to C except for an additional series of AND gates. The output of C forms the input to the first of these AND gates and the output of the last AND gate is the output of D. If the output of C is 1 all the additional AND gates will output a 1; otherwise, less than $\lceil m/\epsilon \rceil$ of those gates will output a 1. ∎

The above construction can be done carefully so as to ensure that the circuit D can be specified using a $O(\log N)$ bandwidth bounded hierarchical specification. We note that if the circuit is allowed to be non-monotone, the above result can be extended to $O(\log N)$ bandwidth bounded hierarchically specified planar circuits.

Given Theorem 4.1, the proof that approximating the objective function of a hierarchical linear program is hard unless P=PSPACE is an extension of the proof in [16] showing that approximating linear programming is log-complete for P. In contrast, the problem of determining the solvability of a system of hierarchically specified linear equations is polynomial [10]. We omit the proofs for showing that the high degree subgraph problem and the k-vertex(edge) connectivity problems are not only PSPACE-complete, but it is hard to approximate them to within a factor of $\epsilon < 2$ of the optimal. Again, these proofs are extensions of the proofs in [1, 9] that these problems are log-complete for P.

5 Conclusions

We have shown that many PSPACE-complete problems for hierarchical specification have efficient polynomial time approximation algorithms. Intriguingly enough, most of the problems listed in Table 1 are known to have NC approximation algorithms when the problem instances are specified non-hierarchically [8, 17]. Moreover, each of the problems shown to have a polynomial time optimal solution in [14, 12, 13, 19] (eg. minimum spanning tree, planarity testing) when the problem is specified hierarchically, has an NC algorithm, when the problem instance is presented non-hierarchically. The above results suggest that there is a strong relationship between a problem having an NC algorithm in the non-hierarchical case and a polynomial time algorithm in the hierarchical case. Understanding this relationship may well lead to a paradigm for for translating known NC algorithms in the literature, for problems when specified non-hierarchically, to yield polynomial time algorithms for the same problems when the instances are specified hierarchically.

Acknowledgements: We would like to thank Venkatesh Radhakrishnan and Professor Richard Stearns for numerous constructive suggestions.

References

[1] R.J. Anderson and E.W. Mayr "Approximating P-complete problems," *Tech Report, Stanford University*, 1986.

[2] J.L. Bentley, T. Ottmann, P. Widmayer, "The Complexity of Manipulating Hierarchically Defined set of Intervals," *Advances in Computing Research, ed. F.P. Preparata* Vol. 1, (1983), pp. 127-158.

[3] A. Condon, J. Feigenbaum, C. Lund and P. Shor, "Probabilistically Checkable Debate Systems and Approximation Algorithms for PSPACE-Hard Functions", to appear in *Proc. 25th ACM Symposium on Theory of Computing* , 1993.

[4] H. Galperin and A. Wigderson, "Succinct Representation of Graphs," *Information and Control* , Vol.56, 1983, pp. 183-198.

[5] M.R. Garey, D.S. Johnson, *Computers and Intractability. A Guide to the Theory of NP-Completeness*, Freeman, San Francisco CA, 1979.

[6] F. Höfting, T. Lengauer and E. Wanke, "Processing of Hierarchically Defined Graphs and Graph Families", in *Data Structures and Efficient Algorithms* (Final Report on the DFG Special Joint Initiative), LNCS 594, Springer-Verlag, 1992, pp. 44-69.

[7] H.B. Hunt III, V. Radhakrishnan, R.E. Stearns, "On The Complexity of Generalized Satisfiability and Hierarchically Specified Generalized Satisfiability Problems," in preparation.

[8] R.M. Karp, A. Wigderson, "A Fast Parallel Algorithm for the Maximal Independent Set Problem", *J.ACM* , Vol.32, No.4, July 1985, pp. 762-773.

[9] L. Kirousis, M. Serna and P. Spirakis, "The Parallel Complexity of the Subgraph Connectivity problem," *Proc. 30th IEEE-FOCS*, 1989, pp. 294-299.

[10] T. Lengauer and C. Weiner, "Efficient Solutions hierarchical systems of linear equations," *Computing*, Vol 39, 1987, pp. 111-132.

[11] T. Lengauer, K.W. Wagner, "The correlation between the complexities of non-hierarchical and hierarchical versions of graph problems", *JCSS*, Vol. 44, 1992, pp. 63-93.

[12] T. Lengauer, "Hierarchical Planarity Testing," *J.ACM* , Vol.36, No.3, July 1989, pp. 474-509.

[13] T. Lengauer, "Efficient Solutions for Connectivity Problems for Hierarchically Defined Graphs ," *SIAM J. Computing*, Vol. 17, No. 6, 1988, pp. 1063-1080.

[14] T. Lengauer, "Efficient Algorithms for Finding Minimum Spanning Forests of Hierarchically Defined graphs ," *Journal of Algorithms*, Vol. 8, 1987, pp. 260-284.

[15] T. Lengauer, "Exploiting Hierarchy in VLSI Design," *Proc. AWOC '86*, LNCS 227, Springer-Verlag, 1986, pp. 180-193.

[16] M. Serna, "Approximating Linear Programming is log-space complete for P," *Inf. Proc. Letters*, Vol. 37, No. 4, 1991, pp. 233-236.

[17] G. Pantziou, P. Spirakis, C. Zaroliagis, "Fast Parallel Approximations of the Maximum Weighted Cut Problem Through Derandomization," *Proc. 9th Foundations of Software Technology and Theoretical Computer Science, FCT-TCS*, 1989, pp. 20-29.

[18] K.W. Wagner, "The complexity of Combinatorial Problems with Succinct Input Representation," *Acta Informatica* , Vol.23, No.3, 1986, pp. 325-356.

[19] M. Williams, "Efficient Processing of Hierarchical Graphs ," *TR 90-06*, Dept of Computer Science, Iowa Sate University. (Parts of the report appeared in WADS'89 and SWAT'90 coauthored with F. Baca.)

[20] M. Yannakakis, "On the Approximation of Maximum Satisfiability," *Proc. Third Annual ACM-SIAM Symp. on Discrete Algorithms*, Jan. 1992, pp 1-9.

Problems on Pairs of Trees and the Four Colour Problem of Planar Graphs

(Extended Abstract)

Artur Czumaj[1] and Alan Gibbons[2]

[1] Department of Mathematics, Warsaw University, Institute of Informatics,
ul. Banacha 2, 02-097 Warszawa, Poland
[2] Department of Computer Science, University of Warwick, Coventry, CV4 7AL, UK

1 Introduction

One of the most famous and fascinating problems in mathematics and graph theory is the *Four-Colour Problem* [8, 9] which is to show that every planar graph is vertex-colourable using at most four colours. Appel and Haken [1, 2] provided a computer based solution in 1977. Their proof is immensely long and follows from successive reductions of the input graph, each corresponding to the removal of one of roughly 1500 reducible subgraphs. Appel and Haken also described an algorithm which runs in $O(n^4)$ time. The hidden constant is very large so that their construction seems to be rather impractical.

The first contribution of this paper is a proof that the Four-Colour Problem is equivalent by a fast reduction to the problem of *Colouring Pairs of Trees* defined as follows. Let T_1 and T_2 be any two binary trees of the same size. The problem is then to find a 3-edge colouring of T_1 and of T_2 such that for every i, the edge adjacent to the i-th leaf (from the left) will have the same colour in both trees (see figure 1).

The second contribution is to show that three different problems, which generally require exponential time, can be solved in polynomial time if they are restricted to non-trivial subclasses of the problems defined on trees. The problems involve: finding a common word of two regular languages, finding an integer solution of a set of linear equations and finding a common evaluation of two expressions over a certain algebra.

In restricted form these problems reduce to the problem of finding a common element which satisfies some function of two trees. The set of all elements which hold this property can be computed for each tree independently, generally taking exponential time. We show how a common element satisfying the appropriate function can be found in polynomial time and we also prove that such an element always exists.

---

[1] E-mail aczumaj@mimuw.edu.pl. This work was partially supported by grant KBN 2-1190-91-01 and done while the author was visiting the University of Warwick.
[2] E-mail amg@dcs.warwick.ac.uk. This work was partially supported by the ESPRIT BRA Programme under contract No. 7141 and by SERC grant GR/H/76487.

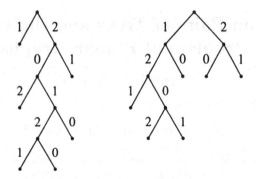

Fig. 1. 3-edge colouring of two trees of the same size.

2 Preliminaries

Throughout we generally use standard graph-theoretic definitions (see, for example [4]). By a planar graph we will always mean its planar embedding. In a *cubic* graph, every vertex is of degree three. We use two non-standard definitions. By a *k-cut* we mean a set of k edges which disconnects a graph into at least two connected components *each with more than one* vertex. A graph G is *bridgeless* if it contains no bridge, that is, an edge whose removal disconnects G. We will call a planar graph G *3-normalized* if it is cubic, bridgeless and does not contain either a 2- or a 3-cut.

Let vertices v, w disconnect a cubic bridgeless planar graph G such that $(v, w) \notin E$ and let one component be $G_1 = (V_1, E_1)$. Suppose also that the degrees of both v and w are two in G. Then we define the *cubic 2-complementary* graph of G_1 to be the graph $G_1' = (V_1, E_1 \cup \{(v, w)\})$. Clearly G_1' is a cubic bridgeless planar graph.

Let (v_1, w_1), (v_2, w_2), (v_3, w_3) be a 3-cut in a 3-connected cubic planar graph G which disconnects G into $G_1 = (V_1, E_1)$ and $G_2 = (V_2, E_2)$ such that $v_1, v_2, v_3 \in V_1$ and $w_1, w_2, w_3 \in V_2$. Define the *cubic 3-complementary* of G_1 to be $G_1' = (V_1 \cup \{v\}, E_1 \cup \{(v_1, v), (v_2, v), (v_3, v)\})$ where v is a new vertex. That is, G_1' is obtained from G_1 after adding the new vertex v and three edges (v_1, v), (v_2, v) and (v_3, v). Similarly $G_2' = (V_2 \cup \{w\}, E_2 \cup \{(w_1, w), (w_2, w), (w_3, w)\})$ is the cubic 3-complementary of G_2. Define a *ladder* $\mathcal{L}$ with respect to vertices v_1, w_1, v_k, w_k to be a subgraph of a cubic graph G with the vertex set $V_{\mathcal{L}} = \{v_1, w_1, \ldots, v_k, w_k\}$ (for $k > 1$) which contains $3k - 4$ edges of the following forms (v_i, v_{i+1}), for $i = 1, 2, \ldots, k - 1$, (w_i, w_{i+1}), for $i = 1, 2, \ldots, k - 1$ and (v_i, w_i), for $i = 2, 3, \ldots, k$. We will call a graph $\mathcal{L}' = (V_{\mathcal{L}'}, E_{\mathcal{L}'})$ the *complementary of a ladder* $\mathcal{L} = (V_{\mathcal{L}}, E_{\mathcal{L}})$ with respect to vertices v_1, w_1, v_k, w_k if $V_{\mathcal{L}'} = V_{\mathcal{L}}$ and $E_{\mathcal{L}'} = E_{\mathcal{L}} \cup \{(v_1, w_1), (v_k, w_k)\}$. By a *binary tree* we mean a rooted tree in which every non-leaf node has exactly two sons. We define a *free binary tree* to be a tree in which every non-leaf node is of degree three.

We will use the following two well-known Lemmas.

Lemma 1. *Every planar graph is 4-vertex colourable if and only if every cubic bridgeless planar graph is 3-edge colourable. (see, for example, [9, p. 102]).*

Lemma 2. *Every 4-connected planar graph is Hamiltonian. [10].*

Reduction between the problems of Lemma 1 can be done in linear time. Chiba and Nishizeki have shown that a Hamiltonian cycle of a 4-connected planar graph can be found in $O(n)$ time [3].

3 Colouring 3-normalized graphs

From Lemma 1, to establish equivalence between a particular problem and the Four-Colour Problem it is enough to establish equivalence beween the particular problem and the problem of 3-edge colouring of cubic bridgeless planar graphs.

Lemma 3. *To show that every cubic bridgeless planar graph is 3-edge colourable, it is enough to show that every 3-normalized planar graph is 3-edge colourable.*

Proof. By induction. The lemma holds trivially for graphs with no more than four vertices. Consider any cubic bridgeless planar graph G with $n > 4$ vertices and with a 2- or a 3-cut. We show how to colour G using colourings of smaller graphs. Since G is bridgeless and cubic it is connected and has no 1-cut.

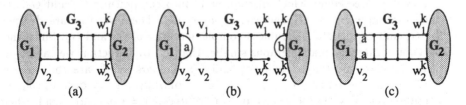

Fig. 2. Colouring of a planar graph G with a 2-cut. (a) situation before colouring, (b) situation after colouring G_1 and G_2, (c) final colouring

If G has a 2-cut (see figure 2) then let $(v_1, w_1), (v_2, w_2)$ be two edges whose removal produces two components G_1 and $\overline{G_1}$. We choose these edges so that in G_1 there is no 2-cut. Assume that $v_1, v_2 \in G_1$ and $w_1, w_2 \in \overline{G_1}$. Note that since G is bridgeless we have $v_1 \neq v_2$ and $w_1 \neq w_2$.

Now consider the case when there is an edge between w_1 and w_2 in $\overline{G_1}$. Since $\deg(w_1) = \deg(w_2) = 3$, there is exactly one neighbour w_1^2 of w_1 and w_2^2 of w_2 in $\overline{G_1}$. Thus edges (w_1, w_1^2) and (w_2, w_2^2) disconnect G. If $(w_1^2, w_2^2) \in E$ then define similarly vertices w_1^3 and w_2^3 such that (w_1^2, w_1^3) and $(w_2^2, w_2^3) \in E$ and $w_1^3 \neq w_1^1$, $w_2^3 \neq w_2^1$. These edges also disconnect G. Repeat this process until $(w_1^k, w_2^k) \notin E$. Edges (w_1^{k-1}, w_1^k) and (w_2^{k-1}, w_2^k) disconnect G into two subgraphs G_2 and $\overline{G_2}$. Let $w_1^k, w_2^k \in G_2$ and $w_1^{k-1}, w_2^{k-1} \in \overline{G_2}$. Denote $w_1^1, w_2^1, w_1^0, w_2^0$

respectively by w_1, w_2, v_1, v_2. Note that there is no edge (v_1, v_2) in G because G_1 does not contain a 2-cut.

Divide G into three edge-disjoint subgraphs G_1, G_2 and $G_3 = G - G_1 - G_2$, G_3 is the ladder with respect to $w_1^0, w_2^0, w_1^k, w_2^k$. Let G_1' and G_2' denote the cubic 2-complementaries of G_1 and G_2. Since G_1' and G_2' are cubic bridgeless planar graphs smaller than G we assume, by the induction hypothesis, colourings of G_1' and G_2'. Then we colour G_3 such that $\mathrm{COLOUR}(w_1^0, w_1^1) = \mathrm{COLOUR}(v_1, v_2)$, and for all $1 \leq i \leq k$, $\mathrm{COLOUR}(w_1^{i-1}, w_1^i) = \mathrm{COLOUR}(w_2^{i-1}, w_2^i)$. Such a colouring can be easily found. Now we rename colours in G_2' such that $\mathrm{COLOUR}(w_1^k, w_2^k) = \mathrm{COLOUR}(w_1^{k-1}, w_2^{k-1})$. This gives a proper colouring of G.

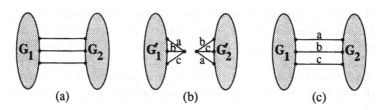

Fig. 3. Colouring of a planar graph G with a 3-cut. (a) situation before colouring, (b) situation after colouring G_1' and G_2', (c) final colouring

If G has a 3-cut but not a 2-cut (see figure 3) then let $(v_1, w_1), (v_2, w_2)$, (v_3, w_3) be three edges which disconnect G into components G_1 and G_2. Assume that $v_1, v_2, v_3 \in G_1$ and $w_1, w_2, w_3 \in G_2$. These vertices are distinct. Let G_1' and G_2' denote the cubic 3-complementaries of G_1 and G_2. Since they are cubic bridgeless planar graphs smaller than G, by induction we can colour them. Now we must join again G_1' and G_2'. Colours in G_1 are the same as in G_1'. In G_2 we rename colours such that $\mathrm{COLOUR}(v_1, v) = \mathrm{COLOUR}(w_1, w)$, $\mathrm{COLOUR}(v_2, v) = \mathrm{COLOUR}(w_2, w)$ and $\mathrm{COLOUR}(v_3, v) = \mathrm{COLOUR}(w_3, w)$, where v and w are vertices of $G_1' - G_1$ and $G_2' - G_2$. This gives proper colours for G.

4 Colouring pairs of trees

We show here that the Four-Colour Problem is equivalent to the problem of Colouring Pairs of Trees defined earlier. Consider the dual graph H of a 3-normalized planar graph G. Since G is cubic bridgeless, H is a triangulation (each face of H is bounded by three edges). Lemma 4 shows that such a triangulation is 4-connected. This, together with lemma 2 ensures that H is Hamiltonian.

Lemma 4. *If planar G is 3-normalized then its dual graph H is 4-connected.*

Proof. By contradiction. Suppose that H is not 4-connected. There then exists a set of vertices $V_0^* = \{v_1^*, v_2^*, v_3^*\}$ in H, whose removal disconnects H into two non-empty subgraphs H_1 and H_2. We start with the case that any subset of such a set does not disconnect H (i.e., H is 3-connected). Since H is a triangulation there are edges between each pair of vertices from set V_0^*. Let $e_1^* = (v_1^*, v_2^*)$, $e_2^* = (v_2^*, v_3^*)$ and $e_3^* = (v_3^*, v_1^*)$. Clearly we may assume without loss of generality that cycle e_1^*, e_2^*, e_3^* contains graph H_1 in the inside and graph H_2 in the outside of this cycle. So let e_1, e_2 and e_3 be edges in G corresponding to crosses of respectively e_1^*, e_2^* and e_3^* in H. These edges therefore disconnect G into subgraph G_1 which is dual of H_1 and G_2 which dual of H_2.

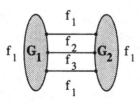

Fig. 4. Partitioning of a planar graph G when its dual H is 3- and not 4-connected.

Since graph G is 3-cut free, the only case when such edges may exist is when either G_1 or G_2 contains exactly one vertex. Assume this is G_2. But when G_2 has only one vertex it contains no face. Thus the corresponding graph H_2 is empty and we obtain a contradiction.

When H is not 3-connected then there exist one or two vertices which disconnect H. Existence of such vertices implies the existence of 1- or 2-cut in G. Using similar arguments we obtain contradictions.

Corollary 5. *If planar G is 3-normalized then its dual graph H is Hamiltonian.*

For the proof of Theorem 7 we need the following observation concerning the colouring of free binary trees. Here $\#_T(\alpha)$ is the number of edges adjacent to leaves having the colour α.

Observation 6. *In any proper 3-edge colouring in colours $\{0, 1, 2\}$ of T either all $\#_T(0), \#_T(1)$, and $\#_T(2)$ are odd or all of them are even.*

Theorem 7 (Main Theorem). *The Four-Colour Problem is equivalent to the problem of Colouring Pairs of Trees.*

Proof of Theorem. If we can 3-edge colour cubic bridgeless planar graphs we can clearly solve the Colouring Pairs of Trees problem. We only show that Colouring Pairs of Trees allows 3-edge colouring of 3-normalized planar graphs.

Consider a 3-normalized planar graph G and its dual H. Define a *cycle of faces* to be a sequence of faces $(f_1, f_2, \ldots, f_k)$ such that $f_1 = f_k$, and for all other $i \neq j$, $f_i \neq f_j$, and for every i, f_i and f_{i+1} have a common edge, e_i. Since H has a Hamiltonian cycle, there is a simple cycle C_H of all faces of G.

Define a new graph G^* built from G by dividing all edges $e_1, e_2, \ldots, e_k$ of C_H into two parts. That is, if $e_i = (v, w)$ then we obtain two edges $e_{i_1} = (v, x_i)$ and $e_{i_2} = (x_i, w)$. In G all edges e_i lie on a hamiltonian cycle of faces (see figure 5).

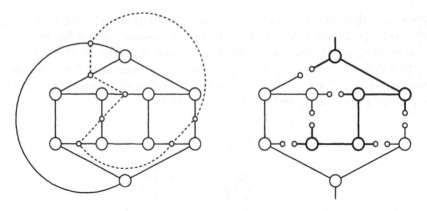

Fig. 5. (a) Hamiltonian cycle of faces in a graph G is shown by dotted line,
(b) Subgraphs G_1 and G_2

Thus if we join all vertices x_i in G^* into a cycle C_G then we divide graph G^* into two subgraphs G_1 and G_2. The first, G_1, contains all edges and vertices from the inside of C_G while the second, G_2, contains all vertices and edges from the outside of C_G. These subgraphs have vertices $x_1, \ldots, x_n$ in common. Both G_1 and G_2 have only one outer face. Therefore both G_1 and G_2 are connected and acyclic and thus are free trees. Because every vertex which does not lie on C_G has degree 3 and every vertex from C_G has degree 1 both these free trees are binary.

3-edge colouring of G corresponds to 3-edge colourings of G_1 and G_2 with a restriction that for each x_i edges (v, x_i) and (x_i, w) have the same colours. Thus to prove the theorem we must only show that after selecting roots of both trees we can remove the restriction of the same colouring of the edge connecting roots of G_1 and G_2. This follows from Observation 6, since for any rooted binary tree with n leaves only colours of leaves (not the shape of the tree) fix colour of the edge above the root of tree.

5 Some problems on pairs of trees

Here we describe applications of Theorem 7 which are concerned with problems on pairs of trees. These are non-trivial subclasses of well-known problems which generally need exponential time to solve. Rather surprisingly, we are able to show that all these problems can be solved in polynomial time. This follows from reductions of these problems to the problem of Colouring Pairs of Trees.

5.1 Intersection of regular languages defined by trees

Let $\Sigma = \{0, 1, 2\}$ be an alphabet. For given binary tree T and $\alpha \in \Sigma$ define language $L(T, \alpha)$ recursively as follows (in fact this language is also generated by a regular grammar without Kleene closure, although in this form the equivalent problem has input size $O(2^n)$, where n is the input size for our problem defined by trees):

- If the root of T has no son (i.e., T is a tree with exactly one node) then $L(T, \alpha) = \{\alpha\}$.
- If tree T has the left nonempty subtree T_l and the right nonempty subtree T_r then $L(T, \alpha) = L(T_l, \beta) \bullet L(T_r, \gamma) \cup L(T_l, \gamma) \bullet L(T_r, \beta)$, where $\beta, \gamma \in \Sigma$, such that all α, β, γ are different, and $\bullet$ denotes concatenation of languages. That is $L_1 \bullet L_2 = \{xy \mid x \in L_1 \text{ and } y \in L_2\}$.

Problem of Intersection of Regular Languages on Trees: *Given two binary trees T_1 and T_2 of the same size find $w \in L(T_1, 0) \cap L(T_2, 0)$.*

Example 1. Consider the two distinct trees of figure 6. Word $102110 \in L(T_1, 0)$, while $001121 \in L(T_2, 0)$ and 110201 is a common word of $L(T_1, 0)$ and $L(T_2, 0)$.

For a fixed T with n leaves, $L(T, \alpha)$ defines a set of words of length n over the alphabet Σ. This set is easily computed in $\Omega(2^n)$ time. The finite automaton for recognizing this language has also exponential size. The problem of finding a common word of two regular languages is known to need in general exponential time (the square of the size of automaton). A similar time is needed to test whether the intersection of the languages is non-empty. Thus a polynomial time solution of our problem seems unlikely.

5.2 Integer linear equations

Consider a set of $n + 1$ linear equations in arithmetic modulo 3. We have an $(n + 1) \times n$ matrix A_n of values $\{-1, 0, 1\}$ defined recursively as follows.

$$A_n = \begin{pmatrix} A_k & \theta & \mathcal{I} \\ \theta & A_{n-k-1} & -\mathcal{I} \end{pmatrix} \tag{1}$$

where k may be any integer from the range $[0 \dots n - 1]$, θ is a matrix containing all 0 and $\mathcal{I}$ is a column matrix containing all 1. A_k and A_{n-k-1} are smaller matrices of sizes $(k + 1) \times k$ and respectively $(n - k) \times (n - k - 1)$.

When either $k = 0$ or $n - k - 1 = 0$ then there is no column corresponding to this A_0. Thus, e.g., $A_1 = \begin{pmatrix} 1 \\ -1 \end{pmatrix}$ and A_2 may be either $\begin{pmatrix} 1 & 1 \\ -1 & 1 \\ 0 & -1 \end{pmatrix}$ or $\begin{pmatrix} 0 & 1 \\ 1 & -1 \\ -1 & -1 \end{pmatrix}$.

This matrix corresponds to a labeling of a binary tree T with $n + 1$ leaves. The left subtree of T has $k + 1$ leaves and corresponds to matrix A_k while the right subtree has $n - k$ leaves and corresponds to matrix A_{n-k-1}. We label each edge by 1 or 2 such that if vertex v has two sons then edges to its sons are differently labelled. For every edge (w, v) we assign a final label to be the sum of all labels on the path from v to the root of T in arithmetic modulo 3. Note that in this arithmetic we have $1 \equiv -2$ and $2 \equiv -1$. Let $x = (x_1, \dots, x_n)^T$ be a vector of values from the set $\{1, 2\}$. Matrix A_n is defined such that for a given

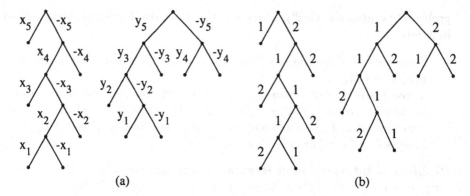

Fig. 6. Labeling of two trees. (a) trees with corresponding variables; (b) certain solution; the corresponding matrices A_n and B_n are as follows:

$$A_5 = \begin{pmatrix} 0 & 0 & 0 & 0 & 1 \\ 0 & 0 & 1 & 1 & -1 \\ 1 & 1 & -1 & 1 & -1 \\ -1 & 1 & -1 & 1 & -1 \\ 0 & -1 & -1 & 1 & -1 \\ 0 & 0 & 0 & -1 & -1 \end{pmatrix} \quad \text{and} \quad B_5 = \begin{pmatrix} 0 & 1 & 1 & 0 & 1 \\ 1 & -1 & 1 & 0 & 1 \\ -1 & -1 & 1 & 0 & 1 \\ 0 & 0 & -1 & 0 & 1 \\ 0 & 0 & 0 & 1 & -1 \\ 0 & 0 & 0 & -1 & -1 \end{pmatrix}$$

vector x, vector $v \equiv A_n x \pmod 3$ contains the final labels (defined by x) of all leaves in the tree. That is, if $v = (v_1, \ldots, v_{n+1})^T$ then the i-th leaf has final label v_i. See also figure 6.

Problem of Integer Linear Equations on Trees: *Let A_n and B_n be two $(n+1) \times n$ arrays defined by equation (1) and let $x = (x_1, \ldots, x_n)^T$, $y = (y_1, \ldots, y_n)^T$ be $2n$ unknowns from the set $\{1, 2\}$. Find some x and y which satisfy the equation*

$$A_n x \equiv B_n y \pmod 3 \tag{2}$$

This problem can be solved using integer linear programming or the integer linear equation problem. These require (unless $P = NP$) exponential time algorithms. Hence a polynomial time algorithm for our problem does not seem likely.

5.3 Algebraic problem

Consider the algebra with carrier $A = \{a, b, c, f\}$ and a binary operator $\diamond$ defined as follows:

$\diamond$	a	b	c	f
a	f	c	b	f
b	c	f	a	f
c	b	a	f	f
f	f	f	f	f

Define an expression over a sequence of variables $(v_1, \ldots, v_n)$ to be an expression defined by any binary parenthesisation of $v_1 \diamond v_2 \diamond \ldots v_{n-1} \diamond v_n$.

The Algebraic Problem: *For two given expressions over the same sequence $(v_1, \ldots, v_n)$ find an instantiation such that the result of both is a.*

Example 2. Consider two expressions corresponding to trees from figure 6.

$$a = (v_1 \diamond ((v_2 \diamond ((v_3 \diamond v_4) \diamond v_5)) \diamond v_6)) \qquad a = (((v_1 \diamond (v_2 \diamond v_3)) \diamond v_4) \diamond (v_5 \diamond v_6))$$

The following instantiation solves this algebraic problem

$$(v_1, v_2, v_3, v_4, v_5, v_6) = (b, c, b, a, a, b)$$

since $(b \diamond ((c \diamond ((b \diamond a) \diamond a)) \diamond b)) = a$ and $(((b \diamond (c \diamond b)) \diamond a) \diamond (a \diamond b)) = a$.

There is an exponential number of different possible instantiations and so a polynomial solution to the problem seems unlikely.

Fact 8. *The Problem of Intersection of Regular Languages on Trees, the Problem of Integer Linear Equations on Trees and the Algebraic Problem are equivalent to the Four-Colour Problem. We can solve all of them in polynomial time. Also, for each of these problems there always exists a solution.*

6 Complexity of reduction

In this section we show how reductions between the Four-Colour Problem and the problem of Colouring Pairs of Trees can be performed rapidly.

Theorem 9. *We can reduce the problem of Colouring Pairs of Trees to the Four-Colour Problem in $O(n\alpha(n,n))$ time. Reductions from the Four-Colour Problem to the problem of colouring pairs of trees can be performed in $O(n)$ time.*

It is well known that reductions between the Four-Colour Problem and the problem of 3-edge colouring cubic bridgeless planar graphs can be done in linear time. Also 3-edge colouring of cubic bridgeless planar graphs gives a solution for Colouring Pairs of Trees. This is because any pair of trees after joining edges adjacent to leaves is (essentially) a subgraph of a cubic bridgeless planar graph. Note also that Colouring of Pairs of Trees implies 3-edge colouring of 3-normalized planar graphs. First, from Observation 6 follows 3-edge colouring of pairs of free trees. Then, from the proof of Lemma 4 and from an $O(n)$-time algorithm for Hamiltonian cycle in four-connected planar graphs [3] we obtain a linear time algorithm for 3-edge colouring of 3-normalized planar graphs. Thus to describe an algorithm for conversion between the Four-Colour Problem and the problem of Colouring Pairs of Trees we need only give an algorithm for 3-edge colouring cubic bridgeless planar graphs using 3-edge colouring of 3-normalized ones. We describe such an algorithm which runs in only $O(n\alpha(n,n))$ time.

Our algorithm is based on Lemma 3. This gives a recursive algorithm for colouring cubic bridgeless planar graphs. First we check whether there is any

2-cut in G. If there is, we decompose G into three components G_1, G_2 and G_3 as for Lemma 3. After modification of G_1 and G_2 to cubic 2-complementaries G_1' and G_2' we colour these components recursively. When there is no 2-cut in G we find any 3-cut. Each 3-cut decomposes G into two vertex-disjoint subgraphs G_1 and G_2. We create the cubic 3-complementaries G_1' and G_2' and colour them recursively. We show that to find any 2-cut of a cubic planar graph it is enough to find any separating pair, thus reducing this problem to the problem of finding triconnected components. Moreover such a decomposition allows us to find all 2-cuts which may occur in the recursive algorithm. Then we consider a cubic bridgeless planar graph G with no 2-cut. We describe an equivalent condition for edges to be in a 3-cut which enables us to consider only dual graph of G and any separating triplets in it. To avoid the cost of recursion we can use a decomposition of the dual graph into four-connected components.

6.1   2-cuts in cubic bridgeless planar graphs

In cubic bridgeless planar graphs there is a one-to-one correspondence between 2-cuts and separating pairs of vertices, thus the problem of finding 2-cuts reduces to finding triconnected components. Hence using standard algorithms we can split in $O(n)$ time every cubic bridgeless planar graph into components such that their cubic 2-complementaries are either a ladder or do not contain a 2-cut.

Lemma 10. *A cubic bridgeless planar graph G has no 2-cut iff G is a cubic triconnected planar graph. Also, a pair of vertices v_1, v_2 disconnects G into G_1 and G_2 iff a pair of edges (v_1, w_1), (v_2, w_2) is a 2-cut in G, where w_1, w_2 are neighbours of respectively v_1, v_2 such that if $w_1 \in G_1 - G_2$ ($w_2 \in G_1 - G_2$) then all others neighbours of v_1 (respectively v_2) are in G_2, and otherwise $w_1 \in G_2 - G_1$ ($w_2 \in G_2 - G_1$) and all others neighbours of v_1 (respectively v_2) are in G_1.*

Corollary 11. *Finding a 2-cut in a cubic bridgeless planar graph G is equivalent to finding a separating pair in G and can be solved in $O(n)$ time.*

Decomposition of a biconnected graph into triconnected components.
Hopcroft and Tarjan [5] gave a linear time algorithm for the decomposition of a biconnected graph into triconnected components of three types: (i) a triconnected graph, (ii) a simple cycle (a *polygon*) or (iii) a pair of vertices with at least three edges between them (a *bond*). The decomposition is unique [11], takes $O(n + m)$ time and is defined as follows. The decomposition of a biconnected graph G into triconnected components may be defined as follows. If G is triconnected, then G itself is the unique triconnected component of G. Otherwise, let v, w be a separating pair of vertices in G. We partition the edges of G into two disjoint subsets E_1 and E_2, such that $|E_1| \geq 2, |E_2| \geq 2$, and subgraphs G_1 and G_2 (induced by E_1 and E_2) have in common only v and w. Graphs $G_1' = G_1 \cup (v, w)$ and $G_2' = G_2 \cup (v, w)$ are called the *split graphs* of G. We allow multiple edges in G_1' and G_2'. The split components are created after recursively splitting G_1' and G_2' until no more splits are possible. The split components of a multigraph are

of three types: triple *bonds* of the form $(\{v, w\}, \{(v, w), (v, w), (v, w)\})$, *triangles* of the form $(\{v, w, u\}, \{(v, w), (w, u), (u, v)\})$, and triconnected graphs. To get unique triconnected components, we partially reassemble the split components. Suppose $G_1 = (V_1, E_1)$ and $G_2 = (V_2, E_2)$ are two split components, both containing a virtual edge $(v, w)_i$. Let $G = (V_1 \cup V_2, (E_1 - \{(v, w)_i\}) \cup (E_2 - \{(v, w)_i\}))$. Then G is a *merge graph* of G_1 and G_2. The triconnected components of G are obtained from the split components by merging the triple bonds into maximal sets of multiple edges (bonds) and the triangles into maximal simple cycles (polygons). The Hopcroft-Tarjan algorithm outputs the decomposition tree of a biconnected graph, enabling the splitting as well as the merging operation.

Finding 2-cut's decomposition in linear time. We focus on decomposing cubic bridgeless planar graphs into ladders and 2-cut free graphs as in Lemma 3. We outline a $O(n)$-time algorithm. We match all 2-cut free components and ladders using the Hopcroft-Tarjan decomposition. Every triconnected subgraph is a 2-cut free component while the complementary of a ladder is found by merging bonds and polygons. We recursively decompose with respect to 2-cut free components and colour in $O(n)$ time using the Hopcroft-Tarjan decomposition.

We test for 2-cuts in $G = (V, E)$. If one exists, we decompose G into three edge disjoint components as in Lemma 3. That is, $G_1 = (V_1, E_1)$ is a graph which is disconnected from graph $G - G_1$ by edges $(w_1^0, w_1^1), (w_2^0, w_2^1)$ and $w_1^0, w_2^0 \in V_1$, $w_1^1, w_2^1 \notin V_1$, and $(w_1^0, w_2^0) \notin E$. $G_3 = (V_3, E_3)$ is a ladder with respect to $w_1^0, w_2^0, w_1^k, w_2^k$ of graph G such that $(w_1^k, w_2^k) \notin E$. Graph $G_2 = (V_2, E_2)$ is defined to be $G - G_1 - G_3$, Vertices w_1^0, w_2^0 and w_1^k, w_2^k are separating pairs.

Perform the splitting of G with respect to vertices w_1^0, w_2^0. Let S_1 and S_2 be the split graphs of G. Without loss of generality, S_1 is the cubic complementary of G_1. Consider split graph S_2. Clearly $S_2 = G_2 \cup G_3 \cup \{(w_1^0, w_2^0)\}$, hence w_1^k, w_2^k is a separating pair in S_2. Perform the splitting of S_2 with respect to w_1^k, w_2^k and let S_3, S_4 be the splitting graphs of S_2. We may assume that S_3 is the complementary of the ladder G_3 while S_4 is the cubic complementary of G_2.

Thus in the splitting of G we obtain three split graphs S_1 (the cubic complementary of G_1), S_4 (the cubic complementary of G_2) and S_3 (the complementary of ladder G_3). Dividing G with respect to 2-cuts (as in Lemma 3) reduces to the splitting algorithm of [5]. Since triconnected components are unique we can use them in the algorithm for dividing G into ladders and 2-cut free components.

Lemma 12. *We can perform a decomposition of a cubic bridgeless planar graph into ladders and 2-cut free components in $O(n)$ time.*

6.2   3-cuts in triconnected cubic planar graphs

Consider a cubic bridgeless planar graph G which contains no 2-cut. This is equivalent (Lemma 10) to dealing only with triconnected cubic planar graphs. We show how to find a 3-cut in G in $O(n\alpha(m, n) + m)$ time. The main lemma claims a one-to-one correspondence between 3-cuts in a triconnected cubic planar graph G and separating triplets of vertices in its dual H. We avoid the cost of recursion for finding other 3-cuts in splitting parts of G. Using a decomposition of H into four-connected components we perform all decompositions into 3-cut free components of G.

Lemma 13 (Main Lemma). *Let G be a triconnected cubic planar graph and H be its dual. There is one-to-one correspondence between 3-cuts in G and separating triplets in H as follows. Edges e_1, e_2, e_3 are a 3-cut in G iff vertices v_1, v_2, v_3 are a separating triplet in H such that they form a cycle of dual edges of e_1, e_2, e_3. We call edges e_1, e_2, e_3 in G and vertices v_1, v_2, v_3 in H siblings.*

This lemma gives an algorithm for finding a 3-cut in cubic bridgeless planar graph G with no 2-cut. To find any separating triplet in H we can use the $O(n\alpha(m, n) + m)$ time algorithm for four-connectivity of [7]. We now show how to find a decomposition of a cubic planar graph G with no 2-cut into edge disjoint components not containing a 3-cut.

Lemma 14. *Let G be a triconnected cubic planar graph and let e_1, e_2, e_3 be a 3-cut disconnecting G into graphs T_1 and T_2. Then the cubic 3-complementaries of graphs T_1 and T_2 are triconnected cubic planar graphs.*

So we can divide the algorithm for reduction from 3-normalized planar graphs to cubic bridgeless ones into the following two phases: remove all 2-cuts and ladders and then remove all 3-cuts.

Let a separating triplet $\tau = \{v_1, v_2, v_3\}$ of vertices in $H = (V, E)$ disconnect the graph into $H_1 = (V_1, E_1)$ and $H_2 = (V_2, E_2)$. That is, H_1 and H_2 are maximal subgraphs of H such that no edge of H_1 and H_2 connects two vertices of τ, and any two vertices of H_1 or H_2 can be joined by a path with no edges or intermediate vertices in τ. H_1 and H_2 are edge-disjoint and they contain all edges of H except $\{(v_1, v_2), (v_2, v_3), (v_1, v_3)\}$. Define $H'_1 = (V_1, E_1 \cup \{(v_1, v_2), (v_2, v_3), (v_1, v_3)\})$ and $H'_2 = (V_2, E_2 \cup \{(v_1, v_2), (v_2, v_3), (v_1, v_3)\})$ to be *complementaries* of triconnected triangulations H_1 and H_2.

Lemma 15. *Let edges e_1, e_2, e_3 be a 3-cut disconnecting G into graphs T_1 and T_2 and let v_1, v_2, v_3 be its siblings disconnecting H into graphs H_1 and H_2. Then the complementary graph of H_1 (similarly H_2) is the dual graph of the cubic 3-complementary of T_1 (respectively T_2). Also the complementary graph of H_1 (and H_2) is a triconnected triangulation.*

Decomposition of triconnected graphs into 4-connected components. We recall ideas of an $O(n\alpha(m, n) + m)$ time algorithm [6, 7]. Kanevsky *et al.* [7] define a *decomposition tree* of a triconnected graph G with respect to wheels and flowers. Hsu [6] modified this structure and derived the *four-block tree* 4-blk(G) in which there are three types of nodes corresponding to wheels, flowers and four-connected graphs (4-blocks). The following lemma simplifies our presentation.

Lemma 16. *There are no wheels in triconnected triangle planar graphs.*

Consider removing a separating triplet of vertices $\tau = \{v_1, v_2, v_3\}$ from a triconnected graph $G = (V, E)$. Let $G_1 = (V_1, E_1)$ be any connected component of the remaining graph. Every vertex from τ is adjacent to a vertex in V_1. Let $\tau_0 \subseteq \tau$ be the set of vertices adjacent to at least two vertices in G_1. Denote by $\widetilde{G_1}$ the graph (called the bridge in [7] and [6]) with the vertex set $V_1 \cup \tau_0$ and the edge set $E_1 \cup \{(x, y) \in E : x \in V_1 \text{and } y \in \tau_0\}$. The definition of 4-blk(G) in [6] corresponds to the following splitting of triconnected graph G:

- If G is four-connected or contains at most four vertices, then G itself is the unique component of 4-blk(G).
- Otherwise G contains a separating triplet $\tau = \{v_1, v_2, v_3\}$ which may or not be in a wheel. Since in our case it is not in a wheel, it is a flower. 4-blk(G) has the root corresponding to this flower. Let τ disconnect G into connected components $G_1, \ldots, G_k$. Split recursively all graphs $\widetilde{G_1}, \ldots, \widetilde{G_k}$. All trees 4-blk$(\widetilde{G_i})$ are subtrees of the node corresponding to flower τ.

Lemma 17. *For every triconnected G we can create 4-blk(G) in $O(n\alpha(m, n) + m)$ time. Hence we can perform the splitting algorithm in the same time [6, 7].*

4-blk trees of triconnected triangle planar graphs. Let H be a triconnected triangle planar graph. From Lemma 17 and that in planar graphs $m = O(n)$, we can build 4-blk(H) in $O(n\alpha(m, n))$ time. We outline the decomposition of triconnected cubic planar graph G with respect to a flower $\tau = \{v_1, v_2, v_3\}$ in its dual graph H. Let removing τ in H create two components H_1 and H_2. This corresponds to a 3-cut disconnecting G into G_1 and G_2. Let G_1' and G_2' be the cubic 3-complementaries of G_1 and G_2. Their duals are induced by vertices in H_1 and τ and in H_2 and τ. Let H_1^* and H_2^* denote these graphs.

In the 4-blk decomposition of H with respect to flower τ we obtain two graphs $\widetilde{H_1}$ and $\widetilde{H_2}$ and 4-blk$(\widetilde{H_1})$ and 4-blk$(\widetilde{H_2})$. We show how to decompose H_1^* and G_1' using 4-blk$(\widetilde{H_1})$. Let τ_0 be the set of vertices in τ adjacent in H to at least two vertices of $\widetilde{H_1}$. One can show that $|\tau - \tau_0| \le 1$. We consider two cases.

$\tau_0 = \tau$, we may add three edges $(v_1, v_2), (v_1, v_3), (v_2, v_3)$ to obtain H_1^* from graph $\widetilde{H_1}$. Using the algorithm for dynamic updates of graph $\widetilde{H_1}$ from [7] we can create 4-blk(H_1^*) in amortized $O(\alpha(n, n))$ time. Thus we can recursively decompose H_1^* and G_1' using 4-blk(H_1^*).

$|\tau_0| < |\tau|$, let v be the only vertex in H_1 adjacent to v_3 in H. Vertices v_1, v_2, v form a separating triplet in H_1^* corresponding to decomposition of G_1' into $G_{1,1}'$ which corresponds to vertices v_1, v_2, v_3, v and $G_{1,2}'$. The dual graph of the cubic 3-complementary of $G_{1,2}'$ is exactly $\widetilde{H_1}$ plus edge (v_1, v_2). As before, we can add this edge in amortized $O(\alpha(n, n))$ time to get 4-blk(H_1^*). Hence we can recursively perform decomposition using 4-blk(H_1^*).

Lemma 18. *Let G be a triconnected cubic planar graph. There exists a decomposition algorithm which divides G into 3-cut free components and runs in $O(n\alpha(n, n))$ time.*

Lemma 19 (Implying theorem 9). *If we can colour every 3-normalized planar graph in $O(f(n))$ time, then we can colour every cubic bridgeless planar graph in $O(f(n) + n\alpha(n, n))$ time.*

7 Conclusions

We described a new characterization of the Four-Colour Problem in terms of its equivalence to a problem of 3-edge colouring pairs of binary trees each with m leaves with the restriction that for every i, $1 \leq i \leq m$, edges adjacent to the i-th leaf have the same colour in both trees. This problem is equivalent to non-trivial subclasses of many problems in mathematics and computer science of which we described three. These provide new and enticing opportunities in the search for shorter proofs of the Four-Colour Theorem and efficient algorithms for Four-Colouring. Conversely, taking the polynomial time solution for Four-Colouring, our equivalences provide unexpected polynomial time solutions for non-trivial sub-classes of problems for which in general only exponential time algorithms are known. The reductions between the various problems were shown to be rapid (in at worst $O(n\alpha(n, n))$ time) and are of interest in themselves. It is likely, because of the nature of the problem of Colouring Pairs of Trees, that many other non-trivial subclasses of important problems defined on trees will find unexpected polynomial time solutions.

References

1. K. Appel, W. Haken, "Every planar map is four colorable, Part I: discharging", *Illinois Journal of Mathematics*, Vol. 21, 1977, pp. 429–490.
2. K. Appel, W. Haken, J. Koch, "Every planar map is four colorable, Part II: reducibility", *Illinois Journal of Mathematics*, Vol. 21, 1977, pp. 491–567.
3. N. Chiba, T. Nishizeki, "The hamiltonian cycle problem is linear-time solvable for 4-connected planar graphs", *Journal of Algorithms*, Vol. 10, 1989, pp. 187–211.
4. A. M. Gibbons, *"Algorithmic Graph Theory"*, Cambridge University Press, 1985.
5. J.E. Hopcroft, R.E. Tarjan, "Dividing a graph into triconnected components", *SIAM Journal of Computing*, 1973, pp. 135–158.
6. T-s. Hsu, "On four-connecting a triconnected graph", *Proceedings of the 33rd Annual Symposium on Foundations of Computer Science*, 1992, pp. 70–79.
7. A. Kanevsky, R. Tamassia, G. Di Battista, J. Chen, "On-line maintenance of the four-connected components of a graph", *Proceedings of the 32nd Annual Symposium on Foundations of Computer Science*, 1991, pp. 793–801.
8. O. Ore, *"The Four Color Problem"*, New York, Academic Press, 1967.
9. T.L. Saaty, P.C. Kainen, *"The Four-Color Problem. Assaults and Conquest"*, McGraw-Hill, 1977.
10. W.T. Tutte, "A theorem on planar graphs", *Trans. Amer. Math. Soc.*, Vol. 82, 1956, pp. 99–116.
11. H. Whitney, "2-isomorphic graphs", *Amer. J. Math.*, Vol. 55, 1933, pp. 245–254.

Constructing Competitive Tours
From Local Information

Bala Kalyanasundaram[1]   Kirk R. Pruhs[2]

Computer Science Department, University of Pittsburgh
Pittsburgh, PA 15260, USA

Abstract

We consider the problem of a searcher exploring an initially unknown weighted planar graph G. When the searcher visits a vertex v, it learns of each edge incident to v. The searcher's goal is to visit each vertex of G, incurring as little cost as possible. We present a constant competitive algorithm for this problem.

1 Introduction

In this paper we consider an online version of *traveling salesperson problem*, online TSP for short. We model it graph theoretically in the following manner. We assume that the roads form an edge-weighted planar connected graph $G = (V, E)$. Then G is learned by a searcher under what we call the *fixed graph scenario*. That is, when the searcher visits a vertex v, it learns of each vertex w adjacent to v in G, as well as the length $|vw|$ of the edge vw. Note that $|vw|$ need not be the Euclidean distance between v and w in the planar embedding. We only require that the distances are nonnegative. So, for example, the distances need not satisfy the triangle inequality. In addition, n, the number of vertices of G, is not known in advance to the searcher. As in the standard traveling salesperson problem [15], the salesperson's goal is to visit all of the vertices, traveling only on the edges, with his/her path being as short as possible.

Since the searcher/salesperson lacks complete information, it is generally not possible to construct the optimal tour. Instead, the searcher's goal is to construct a tour that is as close to optimal as possible. We take as our measure of closeness the ratio of the length of the searcher's tour to the length of the optimal tour. This ratio is called the *competitiveness* of the tour. An online algorithm is α-*competitive*, or alternatively, has a *competitive factor* of α, if the supremum, over all possible instances, of this ratio is α. For us a "good" algorithm is one that has a competitive factor that is bounded by a constant. We simply say that such an algorithm is *competitive*.

---

[1] Supported in part by NSF under grants CCR-9009318 and CCR-9202158
[2] Supported in part by NSF under grant CCR-9209283

The main result of this paper is a competitive algorithm, ShortCut, for online TSP in a planar graph. ShortCut is described in section 2. In section 3, we show that the competitive factor for ShortCut is at most 16. We use the fact that the graph is planar only in the analysis. We also show how this algorithm can be extended to planar graphs that additionally have vertex weights. The total computation time for ShortCut is asymptotically equivalent to the time required by the standard algorithms for solving the all-pairs shortest path problem on a sparse graph.

At this point we should note that the standard heuristics for approximating offline TSP do not seem to be applicable in the online setting. The competitive factor of the nearest neighbor algorithm [19] on an arbitrary graph is $\Theta(\log n)$. The proof that an online algorithm such as ShortCut is competitive seems to require a more general technique than finding a one-to-one correspondence with edges in the minimum spanning tree.

We should also note that we have essentially determined how much local information is necessary to construct online a competitive tour of a planar graph. If all edges incident to a vertex v do not need to be revealed when v is visited, then no competitive algorithm exists. To see this consider the following situation. The edge weights in G are the Euclidean distances between the points. Initially the searcher only knows of one vertex v_1 far from the starting vertex s. After visiting v_1 the searcher learns of another vertex v_2 near s, and after visiting v_2 learns of another vertex v_3 near v_1, etc. Since the searcher is forced to repeatedly travel back and forth between two points, the resulting competitive factor is $n-1$, where n is the number of vertices in G.

Our original motivation for considering online TSP arose from an online mapping problem, apparently first proposed in the literature by Deng and Papadimitriou [8]. In this problem a robot searcher inhabits a plane littered with opaque polygonal objects. The searcher learns about the environment only through visual information. More precisely, the searcher only learns about a part of an object when it comes into the searcher's line of sight. The goal of the searcher is to create a complete map of the scene. In this mapping problem it is the case that the searcher is allowed to map arbitrarily minute details from arbitrarily large distances. At least in some situations, it seems more realistic to assume that one must be close to an object to completely map it. This assumption leads us to define the following problem, which we call the *visual traveling salesperson problem*, or visual TSP for short. In visual TSP the searcher's goal is to visit and traverse the perimeter of each polygonal object.

In section 4, we modify our algorithm for online TSP to obtain a competitive algorithm for visual TSP. The main difficultly in developing the algorithm for visual TSP is that the visibility graph of the objects is not necessarily planar. This result shows that the ability of the adversary to map from a distance is the reason that competitive algorithms can not be achieved for the Deng and Papadimitriou's mapping problem.

As far as we know this paper is the first one to examine constructing short tours online under the fixed graph scenario. However, we will now briefly survey some related work to place our results in perspective. Baeza-Yates, Culberson, and Rawlins [2] seem to have initiated the recent line of research into problems involving searching with incomplete information. They studied several problems that deal with finding a short path to an unknown destination in some simple types of metrics.

Papadimitriou and Yannakakis [17] introduced the problem of finding a short path to some vertex under the fixed graph scenario. Related results can be found in [4]. One application cited by Bar-noy and Schieber [4] is the problem of establishing a point to point connection in a communication network with unreliable links. Computing a tour online under the fixed graph scenario has some relation to broadcasting in a network with unknown topology. Note that the combinatorics of finding shortest paths under the fixed graph scenario differs significantly from the combinatorics of finding tours under the fixed graph scenario. For more information regarding online searching and mapping using visual information, we refer the readers to [5, 8, 9, 13, 14, 17].

Several researchers have considered constructing spanning trees and Steiner trees online under what we call the *point by point* scenario. In this scenario the points are revealed one at a time. When the ith point is revealed, all edges to previously revealed points are also revealed, and the online algorithm must extend (without the deletion of any edges) the previous tree to include the new point. Chandra and Vishwanathan [6], and Imase and Waxman [10] showed that it is possible to maintain a $O(\log n)$ competitive spanning tree under the point by point scenario. Alon and Azar [1] give an $\Omega(\log n / \log \log n)$ lower bound on the competitiveness achievable for constructing a Steiner tree point by point in the plane. Further results can be found in [3, 10]. The main difference between this scenario and the fixed graph scenario is in what information in known to the online algorithm about "explored" vertices. In the point by point scenario the online algorithm may not be aware of all edges incident to revealed points.

We denote an edge between vertices x and y by xy, with $|xy|$ being the length of xy. We think of graphs as being multisets of edges and perform set operations accordingly. If S is a multiset of edges then $|S|$ is the aggregate length of the edges in S. We say a vertex v is a member of a graph S if an edge in S is incident to v. We use OPT for the optimal offline path, and MST for the minimum spanning tree of G.

2   The Algorithm ShortCut

Intuitively, the algorithm ShortCut performs depth first search on different localities in G, with occasional jumps from one locality to another. Before being more specific we need some definitions.

Definition 1 *Throughout the algorithm each vertex will be classified in one of three mutually exclusive ways:*

1. Visited: A visited vertex is one that has been visited by the searcher.

2. Boundary: A boundary vertex is an unvisited vertex adjacent to a visited vertex.

3. Unknown: An unknown vertex is one that the searcher has not yet seen.

Definition 2 *Throughout the algorithm each edge in G will be classified in one of three mutually exclusive ways:*

1. Explored: An edge is explored if both endpoints are visited.

2. Boundary: A boundary edge is one for which exactly one endpoint has been visited.

3. Unknown: An unknown edge is one for which neither endpoint has been visited.

As mentioned previously we will need to occasionally shift our search from one portion of G to another via a known path in G. Conceptually, this shift can be viewed as traversing a new edge, which we will call a *jump edge*, that is added to G. Throughout the rest of this paper whenever we refer to a boundary edge, say vw, we will always list the visited vertex first. So, in this case v would be a visited vertex, and w would be a boundary vertex.

Definition 3 *At any particular time, let $d(v,w)$ denote the length of the shortest path known between vertices v and w using only explored and boundary edges.*

The following definition is the crucial one for understanding the algorithm ShortCut. We will define the constant $\delta > 0$ later so as to minimize the competitive factor.

Definition 4 *A boundary edge xy blocks a boundary edge vw if $|xy| < |vw|$ and $d(v,x) + |xy| < (1+\delta)|vw|$. A boundary edge vw is a shortcut if no other boundary edge blocks vw.*

We are now ready to continue the explanation of ShortCut. The searcher begins as if it were performing a standard depth first search on G. Assume that the searcher is at a vertex v and is considering whether to traverse a boundary edge vw. If vw is a shortcut then vw is traversed at this time. In our later analysis, we will say that vw is a *charged edge*. Otherwise, the traversal of vw is delayed, perhaps indefinitely.

Assume that the searcher just traversed a boundary edge xy, causing y to become visited and xy to become explored. It may then be the case that some other boundary edge vw, whose traversal was delayed at some previous point in time, now becomes a shortcut. In this case a jump edge is added from y to w. Conceptually, the searcher can traverse this jump edge like any other edge. If at some time ShortCut directs the searcher to traverse this jump edge, then the searcher will actually traverse the shortest path that it is aware of from y to w. We will prove later that $d(y,w) \leq (2+\delta)|vw|$. In this case we will say that vw is a *charged edge*, and it will pay for the cost of moving from y to w.

We now give pseudo-code for ShortCut. For each vertex v, ShortCut maintains a list, $Incident(v)$, of edges incident to v. For each boundary edge e, ShortCut maintains a list, $Block(e)$, of boundary edges that block e.

```
Procedure ShortCut(x, y: Vertices; G:Graph);
Comment: Traveling from x, the searcher visits y for the first time
begin
For each boundary edge vw do
        If visiting y caused Block(vw) to became empty then
                add a jump edge yw at the end of Incident(y) and Incident(w)
EndFor
For each edge yz ∈ Incident(y) do
    If z is a boundary vertex and yz is a jump edge then
        Traverse the shortest known path from y to z
        ShortCut(y, z, G)
    EndIf
    If z is a boundary vertex and yz is a shortcut then
        Traverse the edge yz
        ShortCut(y, z, G)
    EndIf
EndFor
Return to x along the shortest known path
end;
```

3 Algorithm Analysis

In this section we prove that ShortCut constructs a competitive tour, and analyze the total computation time required. It is important to mention the possibility that there is no one-to-one correspondence between the edges used by the algorithm to the edges in minimum spanning trees. Proofs found in [7, 16] also face similar problem. The proof that the tour is competitive (as well as proofs found in [7, 16]) overcome this problem by performing an amortized cost-accounting.

Theorem 1 *The searcher, using ShortCut, visits all the vertices.*

Proof Sketch: Assume to reach a contradiction that upon termination the algorithm does not visit all the vertices. At the time of termination let xy be the boundary edge minimizing $|xy|$. Hence, during the visit of some vertex z (which need not be x), xy will be a shortcut. Therefore, y will be visited either through the jump edge from z or directly from x.   ◇

Observation 1 *If at some point in time a boundary edge xy blocks a boundary edge vw, then xy will continue to block vw until either y or w is visited.*

This observation follows since both xy and vw remain boundary edges until either y or w are visited.

Lemma 1 *Assume that after traversing a boundary edge xy another boundary edge vw became a shortcut and a jump edge was added from y to w. Then $d(y, w) \leq (2 + \delta)|vw|$.*

Proof Sketch: After visiting y no edge blocks vw. By observation 1, before y was visited it must be the case that there was a boundary edge incident on y that blocked vw. Hence by definition 4, $d(y, v) < (1 + \delta)|vw|$. Therefore, $d(y, w) < (2 + \delta)|vw|$.   ◇

Theorem 2 *The algorithm ShortCut is 16-competitive.*

Proof Sketch: Let P be the set of *charged edges*. Recall that an edge xy is said to be charged if it is the shortcut edge that allowed y to be visited for the first time (though xy need not have been traversed on this visit). We know that the total length of the tour is at most $2(2 + \delta)|P|$, with the factor of $(2 + \delta)$ coming from lemma 1, and the factor of 2 coming from the fact that depth first search traverses each edge once in each direction. Let MST be the minimum spanning tree that minimizes the number of edges in $P - MST$ (this assumption is unnecessary if edge lengths are distinct). Note $|MST| \leq |OPT|$. We show that $|P| \leq (1 + \frac{2}{\delta})|MST|$. The theorem then follows by selecting $\delta = 2$, which minimizes $2(2 + \delta)(1 + \frac{2}{\delta})$.

Consider a fixed planar embedding of $MST \cup P$ (note that each edge in $P \cap MST$ is only included once in this embedding). We call an edge in $P - MST$ a *chord*. Let R be the closed walk obtained by walking around the planar embedding of MST. Note that each edge in MST is included exactly twice in R. We then give each vertex in R a new identifier. It will likely aid the reader's intuition to imagine blowing R up like a balloon so that R becomes the perimeter of a polygon, with the chords embedded on the outside of R. Let z be any vertex on the exterior face of the embedding. Now imagine making a cut that passes through z from the interior of R to the exterior face. We henceforth consider this planar embedding. Note that R is now an open curve. For example, the graph in the upper left portion of figure 1 shows a planar graph, where MST is shown with solid edges, and edges in $P - MST$ are shown as dashed lines. The closed walk of MST is shown in solid lines in the upper right portion of figure 1. On the bottom is the blown-up version of R and the chords. By cutting at d, we can get the open curve $R = dc'ec''b'fb''abcd'$.

Since $|R| = 2|MST|$, to prove $|P| \leq (1 + \frac{2}{\delta})|MST|$, it suffices to show that the cumulative weight of edges in $P - MST$ is at most $|R|/\delta$. We say that a chord xy is *inside* a chord vw if in traversing R we encounter these points in the order $vxyw$, $vyxw$, $wyxv$, or $wxyv$. We now recursively consider the chords from inside out, changing R in the process.

Let xy be the chord under consideration. Denote by $R(x, y)$ the portion of R between x and y. We first prove that $|R(x, y)| \geq (1 + \delta)|xy|$. Suppose to reach a contradiction that $|R(x, y)| < (1 + \delta)|xy|$. We say an edge vw is *big* if

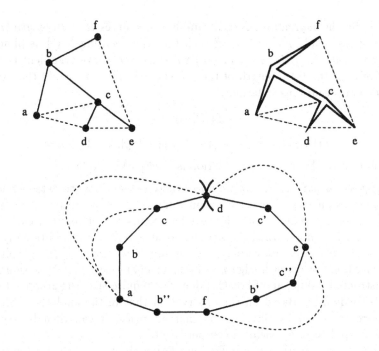

Figure 1: Construction of R

$vw \in R(x,y)$ and $|xy| \leq |vw|$. We first show that there is at least one big edge. Consider the time that xy was charged, or equivalently, the time that y was first visited. At that time there must be one other boundary edge in $R(x,y)$ since $R(x,y)$ is a path from a visited vertex to a boundary vertex. Let vw be the first such boundary edge encountered when traveling from x to y on $R(x,y)$. Since at that time $d(x,v) + |vw| < (1+\delta)|xy|$, it must be the case that $|xy| \leq |vw|$, or xy would not have been charged when y was visited.

Among big edges in $R(x,y)$, consider the big edge vw that is charged last. Assume, without loss of generality that v is visited before w, and consider the time that the boundary edge vw was charged. Let ab be the first boundary edge encountered when traversing the path $R(x,y) + \{xy\} - \{vw\}$ from v to w. Note that $d(v,a) + |ab| \leq |R(x,y)| + |xy| - |vw|$. Then using the fact that $|vw| \geq |xy|$, and the assumption that $|R(x,y)| < (1+\delta)|xy|$, we can conclude that $d(v,a) + |ab| < (1+\delta)|vw|$. It must then be the case that $|vw| \leq |ab|$, or vw would not have been charged at this time. Therefore, ab is a big edge that is not charged by ShortCut.

If an edge $ab \in R(x,y)$ is not charged, then $ab \in MST$. We can then derive a contradiction since either $MST - \{ab\} + \{xy\}$ has smaller cost than MST, or has fewer chords (induced by P) than MST.

We can now assume that $|R(x,y)| \geq (1+\delta)|xy|$. We let R be the curve formed by replacing $R(x,y)$ by xy, and repeat the argument recursively. Let

$T(|R|, k)$ be the supremum, over all simple open curves R, with length $|R|$, and over all ways to add k chords to R such that the resulting graph is planar and each chord satisfies $|R(x, y)| \geq (1 + \delta)|xy|$ when the above argument is applied recursively, of the total length of these k chords. Then $T(|R|, k)$ then satisfies the following recurrence relation:

$$T(|R|, 0) = 0$$

$$T(|R|, k) \leq T(|R| - (1 + \delta)|xy| + |xy|, k - 1) + |xy|$$

The solution to this recurrence relation is $T(|R|, k) \leq |R|/\delta$. ◇

Using a standard trick [15] we now briefly explain how to extend ShortCut to handle graphs with vertex costs in addition to edge costs. That is each vertex x has a cost $w(x)$ and the searcher incurs a cost of $w(x)$ each time it visits x. Furthermore, when the searcher is at a vertex x it additionally knows the cost of each adjacent vertex. We modify G to create a new graph G' by increasing the cost on each edge xy to $|xy| + (w(x) + w(y))/2$. Note that G' can be constructed online, and ShortCut does not require that the graph satisfy the triangle inequality. Based on the observation that in the analysis of ShortCut each edge traversed by ShortCut is charged twice, it can then be seen that ShortCut applied to G' yields a competitive tour.

We finish this section by briefly considering the total computation time required by ShortCut. By maintaining two lists *Blocked* and *BlockedBy* for each vertex we can show that the total computation time is $O(n^2 \log n)$, which is the same as the time required for the standard all-pairs shortest path algorithms for sparse graphs.

4 Visual TSP

We now show how to use the algorithm ShortCut, presented in section 2, to develop a competitive algorithm for visual TSP. Notice that our analysis of ShortCut holds only when the underlying graph is planar. In addition we require that the planar graph used by the searcher must contain a minimum spanning tree as a subgraph. In this section, we show how to construct online such a planar subgraph.

Let V be the set of all the vertices of the objects. In the *visibility graph*, VG for short, two vertices $v, w \in V$ are adjacent if they are mutually visible. We consider adjacent corners of an object as mutually visible since we are dealing with polygonal objects. The shortest object avoiding path between two object vertices is the shortest path between these vertices in VG. We use the notation $d(x, y)$ to denote the distance between vertices x and y in VG, and $|xy|$ for the Euclidean distance between x and y.

Definition 5 *For two points $v, w \in V$, the lune(v, w) consists of those points contained strictly inside both the circle with radius $|vw|$ centered at v, and the circle with radius $|vw|$ centered at w. Hence, $x \in$ lune(v, w) is equivalent to $|vx| < |vw|$ and $|wx| < |vw|$.*

Definition 6 *An edge $vw \in VG$ is an edge in the object neighborhood graph, denoted ONG, if v and w are consecutive vertices on the perimeter of some object, or if there is no vertex $x \in lune(v, w)$ that is mutually visible from both v and w. In the first case, vw is called a perimeter edge.*

An object neighborhood graph is a generalization of a relative neighborhood graph [21]. The constrained relative neighborhood graph, $CRNG$, defined in [11, 20], is almost identical to ONG.

Definition 7 *For a nonperimeter edge vw in ONG, the $Olune(v, w)$ is the intersection of $lune(v, w)$ with the region of the plane mutually visible from v and w.*

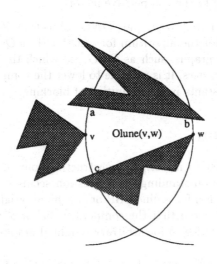

Figure 2: Olune

Lemma 2 *Let vw be a nonperimeter edge in ONG and assume that ONG is drawn so that vw is horizontal. Then $Olune(v, w)$ consists of $lune(v, w)$ minus possibly two straight line cuts, one above vw and one below.*

Proof: Omitted. See figure 2 for an example of an *Olune*. ◇

Lemma 3 *When the searcher is at a vertex v it can determine all of the edges from ONG incident to v from visual information.*

The proof of the following lemma is very similar to the proof of $CMST(G) \subseteq CRNG(G)$ in [11].

Lemma 4 *ONG is a planar graph that contains the minimum spanning tree of VG as a subgraph.*

111

Proof: Omitted. ◇

If the searcher wishes to visit each object vertex it now need only apply ShortCut to ONG. In visual TSP, however, we are also asked to traverse each perimeter edge. This can be accomplished by modifying ShortCut so that when the searcher visits an object for the first time it circumnavigates the perimeter of that object. This circumnavigation does not change the status of any of the edges or vertices, and ShortCut then continues as if it had not performed this circumnavigation.

Theorem 3 *There is a 17-competitive algorithm for visual TSP.*

Proof: The proof is the same as theorem 2, except that the cost of the circum-navigations adds one to the competitive factor. ◇

The total time required to compute ONG online from VG is $O(n^2)$. Thus the total time required for the algorithm for visual TSP is $O(n^2 \log n)$. We should note that for planar graphs, such as ONG, for which the edge lengths are the actual Euclidean distances, it is possible to lower the competitive factor slightly by changing the constants in the definition of blocking.

5 Conclusion

This paper is the first to investigate constructing tours online under the fixed graph scenario. The outstanding open question seems to be whether there is a competitive algorithm for online TSP on a general weighted graph under the fixed graph scenario. Note that the competitive factor of the greedy algorithm Nearest Neighbor is $O(\log n)$ for arbitrary weighted graphs [19].

Acknowledgments: We would like to thank Sundar Vishwanathan, Gautam Das, Giri Narasimhan, and Harry Plantinga for helpful discussions.

References

[1] N. Alon, and Y. Azar, On-line Steiner trees in the Euclidean plane, in: *Proceedings of the 8th ACM Symposium on Computational Geometry* (1992).

[2] R. Baeza-Yates, J. Culberson, and G. Rawlins, Searching with uncertainty, to appear in: *Information and Computation*.

[3] V. Bafna, B. Kalyanasundaram, and K. Pruhs, Not all insertion methods yield constant approximate tours in the plane, Technical Report, Computer Science Department, University of Pittsburgh, 1992.

[4] A. Bar-Noy, and B. Schieber, The Canadian travelers problem, in: *Proceedings of the Second Annual ACM/SIAM Symposium on Discrete Algorithms* (1991) 261–270.

[5] A. Blum, P. Raghavan, and B. Schieber, Navigating in unfamiliar geometric terrain, in: *Proceedings of the Twenty Third Annual ACM Symposium of Theory of Computing* (1991) 494–504.

[6] B. Chandra, and S. Vishwanathan, Constructing reliable communication networks of small weight online, Manuscript.

[7] G. Das and D. Joseph, Which triangulations approximate the complete graph, in: *Proceedings of International Symposium on Optimal Algorithms* (1989) 168–192.

[8] X. Deng, and C. Papadimitriou, Exploring an unknown graph, in: *Proceedings of the Thirty First Annual Symposium on Foundations of Computer Science* (1990) 355–361.

[9] X. Deng, Kameda, and C. Papadimitriou, How to learn an unknown environment, in: *Proceedings of the Thirty Second Annual Symposium on Foundations of Computer Science* (1991), 298–303.

[10] M. Imase, and B. Waxman, Dynamic Steiner tree problem, *SIAM Journal of Discrete Mathematics* 4 (1991) 369–384.

[11] E. Jennings, and A. Lingas, On the Relationships among Constrained Geometric Structures, *Proceedings of the 3rd International Symposium on Algorithms and Computation (ISAAC)* (1992) 289–298.

[12] B. Kalyanasundaram, and K. Pruhs, Constructing competitive tours from local information, Technical Report, Computer Science Department, University of Pittsburgh, 1992.

[13] B. Kalyanasundaram, and K. Pruhs, A competitive analysis of nearest neighbor algorithms for searching unknown scenes, in: *Proceedings of the 9th Annual Symposium on Theoretical Aspects of Computer Science* (1992) 147–157.

[14] R. Klein, Walking an unknown street with bounded detour, in: *Proceedings of the Thirty Second Annual Symposium on Foundations of Computer Science* (1991) 304–313.

[15] E. Lawler, J. Lenstra, A. Rinnooy Kan, and D. Schmoys, *The Traveling Salesman Problem* (Wiley, New York, 1985).

[16] C. Levcopoulos, and A. Lingas, There are planar graphs almost as good as the complete graphs and as short as minimum spanning trees, in: *Proceedings of International Symposium on Optimal Algorithms* (1989) 9–13.

[17] C. Papadimitriou, and M. Yannakakis, Shortest paths without a map, in: *Proceedings of the Sixteenth Annual Internation Colloquium on Automata, Languages, and Programming* (1989) 610–620.

[18] F. Preparata, and M. Shamos, *Computational Geometry: An Introduction* (Springer-Verlag, New York, 1985).

[19] D. Rosenkrantz, R. Stearns, and P. Lewis, An analysis of several heuristics for the traveling salesman problem, *SIAM Journal of Computing* 6 (1977) 563–581.

[20] T. H. Su, and R.C. Chang, Computing the constrained relative neighborhood graphs and constrained Gabriel graphs in Euclidean Plane, in: *Pattern Recognition* **24**, **3**, (1991) 221–230.

[21] G. Toussaint, The relative neighborhood graph of a finite planar set, *Pattern Recognition* **12** (1980) 261–268.

Treewidth and Pathwidth of Permutation Graphs

Hans Bodlaender[1] and Ton Kloks[1]* and Dieter Kratsch[2]

[1] Department of Computer Science, Utrecht University, P.O. Box 80.089, 3508 TB
Utrecht, the Netherlands
[2] Fakultät Mathematik, Friedrich-Schiller-Universität, Universitätshochhaus, O-6900
Jena, Germany

Abstract. In this paper we show that the treewidth and pathwidth of a
permutation graph can be computed in polynomial time. In fact we show
that, for permutation graphs, the treewidth and pathwidth are equal. These
results make permutation graphs one of the few non-trivial graph classes for
which at the moment, treewidth is known to be computable in polynomial
time. Our algorithm to decide whether the treewidth (pathwidth) is at most
some given integer k, can be implemented to run in $O(nk^2)$ time, when the
matching diagram is given. We show that this algorithm can easily be adapted
to compute the pathwidth of a permutation graph in $O(nk^2)$ time, where k
is the pathwidth.

1 Introduction

In many recent investigations in computer science, the notions of treewidth and
pathwidth play an increasingly important role. One reason for this is that many
problems, including many well studied NP-complete graph problems, become solvable in polynomial and usually even linear time, when restricted to the class of
graphs with bounded tree- or pathwidth [1, 3, 5, 15]. Of crucial importance for these
algorithms is, that a tree-decomposition or path-decomposition of the graph is given
in advance. Much research has been done in finding a tree-decomposition with a reasonable small treewidth. Recent results [17, 7, 14] show that an $O(n \log n)$ algorithm
exists to find a suitable tree-decomposition for a graph with bounded treewidth.
However, the constant hidden in the 'big oh', is exponential in the treewidth, limiting the practicality of this algorithm.

For some *special classes* of graphs, it has been shown that the treewidth can
be computed efficiently. In this paper we discuss the problem of finding tree- and
path-decompositions for permutation graphs. We also show that for these graphs,
the treewidth and the pathwidth are the same. We give a $O(nk^2)$ time algorithm
which determines whether the pathwidth is at most k, when the matching diagram
is given. The algorithm can easily be adapted such that it computes the pathwidth
of a permutation graph within the same time bound.

---

* This author is supported by the foundation for Computer Science (S.I.O.N) of the Netherlands Organization for Scientific Research (N.W.O.).

2 Preliminaries

In this section we start with some definitions and easy lemmas. For more information on perfect graphs the reader is referred to [10, 8, 4].

Definition 1. A graph is *chordal* if it has no induced chordless cycle of length at least four.

Chordal graphs are also called triangulated. There are basically two ways two define the treewidth of a graph. One way is to use the concept of a *tree-decomposition*. For more information on tree-decompositions the reader is referred to the survey paper [5]. In this paper we introduce the treewidth of a graph by means of k-trees.

Definition 2. Let k be an integer. A k-tree is a graph which is defined recursively as follows. A clique with $k+1$ vertices is a k-tree. Given a k-tree T_n with n vertices, a k-tree with $n+1$ vertices can be constructed by making a new vertex adjacent to the vertices of a k-clique in T_n. A graph is a *partial k-tree* if either it has at most k vertices or it is a subgraph of a k-tree T with the same vertex set as T.

k-Trees are chordal and have $\omega(G) = k+1$ (where $\omega(G)$ is the maximum clique size). Notice that any graph is a partial k-tree for some k; take k equal to the number of vertices minus one.

Definition 3. The *treewidth* of a graph G is the minimum value k for which G is a partial k-tree.

Definition 4. A *triangulation* of a graph G is a graph H with the same vertex set as G, such that G is a subgraph of H and H is chordal.

For a proof of the following lemma see for example [15].

Lemma 5. *A graph G has treewidth $\leq k$ if and only if there is a triangulation H of G with $\omega(H) = \leq k+1$.*

It follows that the treewidth of a chordal graph is the maximum clique size minus one. The treewidth can be defined in terms of the minimum over all triangulations of the maximum clique size. We define the *pathwidth* of a graph using triangulations of a special kind.

Definition 6. An *interval graph* is a graph of which the vertices can be put into one to one correspondence with intervals on the real line, such that two vertices are adjacent if and only if the corresponding intervals have a nonempty intersection.

There are many ways to characterize interval graphs. We state only one of the first characterizations [16].

Lemma 7. *An undirected graph is an interval graph if and only if the following two conditions are satisfied:*

1. *G is chordal and*
2. *any three vertices of G can be ordered in such a way that every path from the first to the third vertex passes through a neighbor of the second vertex.*

Three vertices which do not satisfy the second condition are called an *astroidal triple*. These are pairwise non adjacent and for any pair of them there is a path that avoids the neighborhood of the remaining vertex.

Definition 8. Let k be an integer. A graph G has *pathwidth* $\leq k$ if and only if there is a triangulation H of G such that H is an interval graph with $\omega(H) =\leq k + 1$.

Determining the treewidth or the pathwidth of a graph is NP-complete [2]. However, for *constant* k, graphs with treewidth $\leq k$ are recognizable in $O(n \log n)$ time [17, 7, 14]. The large constants involved in these algorithms make them usually not very practical. It is therefore of importance to find fully polynomial algorithms for treewidth and pathwidth for special classes of graphs which are as large as possible.

One of the main reasons why there exist fast algorithms for many problems when restricted to graphs with bounded treewidth, is the existence of vertex separators of bounded size.

Definition 9. A subset $S \subseteq V$ is a a, b-separator for nonadjacent vertices a and b, if the removal of S separates a and b in distinct connected components. If no proper subset of S is an a, b-separator then S is a minimal a, b-separator. A minimal separator S is a subset such that S is a minimal a, b-separator for some nonadjacent vertices a and b.

The following lemma, which must have been rediscovered many times, appears for example as an exercise in [10].

Lemma 10. *Let S be a minimal a, b-separator, and let C_a and C_b be the connected components of $G[V - S]$, containing a and b respectively. Then every vertex of S has a neighbor in C_a and a neighbor in C_b.*

Theorem 11. *Let G be a partial k-tree. There exists a triangulation of G into a chordal graph H such that the following three statements hold:*

1. $\omega(H) \leq k + 1$.
2. *If a and b are nonadjacent vertices in H then every minimal a, b-separator of H is also a minimal a, b-separator in G.*
3. *If S is a minimal separator in H and C is the vertex set of a connected component of $H[V - S]$, then C induces also a connected component in $G[V - S]$.*

Proof. Take a triangulation H, with treewidth at most k and with a minimum number of edges (this exists by lemma 5). Suppose H has a minimal vertex separator C for nonadjacent vertices a and b, such that either C induces no minimal a, b-separator in G, or the vertex sets of the connected components of $H[V - C]$ are different from those of $G[V - C]$. Let $S \subseteq C$ be a minimal a, b-separator in G. Let $C_1, \ldots, C_t$ be the connected components of $G[V - S]$. Make a chordal graph H' as follows. For each $C_i \cup S$ take the chordal subgraph of H induced by these vertices. Since S is a clique in H, this gives a chordal subgraph H' of H. Notice that the vertex sets of the connected components of $H'[V - S]$ are the same as those of $G[V - S]$. We claim that the number of edges of H' is less than the number of edges of H, which is a contradiction. Clearly, the number of edges of H' does not exceed the number of edges of H. First assume that $S \neq C$, and let $x \in C \setminus S$. By lemma 10, in H, x has a neighbor in the component containing a and a neighbor in the component containing b. Not both these edges can be present in H'. Thus we may assume $S = C$. Then the vertex sets of the connected components of $H[V - C]$ are different from those of $H'[V - C]$. Since H' is a subgraph of H, every connected component $H'[V - C]$ is contained in some connected component of $H[V-C]$. It follows that there must be a connected component in $H[V-C]$ containing two different connected components of $H'[V-C]$. This can only be the case if there is some edge between these components in $H[V - C]$ (which is not there in $H'[V - C]$). This proves the theorem.

Definition 12. We call a triangulation of which the existence is guaranteed by theorem 11, a *minimal triangulation*.

Let $G = (V, E)$ be a graph and let C be a minimal vertex separator. Let $C_1, \ldots, C_t$ be the connected components of $G[V - C]$. We denote by $\overline{C}_i$ $(i = 1, \ldots, t)$ the graph obtained as follows. Take the induced subgraph $G[C \cup C_i]$, and add edges such that the subgraph induced by C is complete. The following lemma easily follows from theorem 11 (a similar result appears in [2]).

Lemma 13. *A graph G with at least $k + 2$ vertices is a partial k-tree if and only if there exists a minimal vertex separator C such that the graphs $\overline{C}_i$ are partial k-trees $(i = 1, \ldots, t)$.*

In this paper we show that the treewidth and pathwidth of a permutation graph can be computed in polynomial time. We think of a permutation π of the numbers $1, \ldots, n$ as the sequence $\pi = [\pi_1, \ldots, \pi_n]$.

Definition 14. If π is a permutation of the numbers $1, \ldots, n$, we can construct a graph $G[\pi] = (V, E)$ with vertex set $V = \{1, \ldots, n\}$ and edge set E:

$$(i, j) \in E \Leftrightarrow (i - j)(\pi_i^{-1} - \pi_j^{-1}) < 0$$

An undirected graph is a *permutation graph* if there is a permutation π such that $G \cong G[\pi]$.

The graph $G[\pi]$ is sometimes called the inversion graph of π. If the permutation is not given, it can be computed in $O(n^2)$ time ([18, 10]). In this paper we assume that the permutation is given and we identify the permutation graph with the inversion graph. A permutation graph is an intersection graph, which is illustrated by the matching diagram.

Definition 15. Let π be a permutation of $1, \ldots, n$. The matching diagram can be obtained as follows. Write the numbers $1, \ldots, n$ horizontally from left to right. Underneath, write the numbers $\pi_1, \ldots, \pi_n$, also horizontally from left to right. Draw straight line segments joining the two 1's, the two 2's, etc.

Notice that two vertices i and j of $G[\pi]$ are adjacent if and only if the corresponding line segments intersect. In figure 1 we give an example.

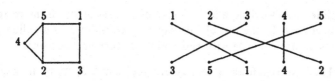

Fig. 1. permutation graph and matching diagram

3 Scanlines

In this section we show that every minimal separator in a permutation graph can be obtained by using a *scanline*. Recall the definition of the matching diagram. It consists of two horizontal lines, one above the other, and a number of straight line segments, one for each vertex, such that each line segment has one end vertex on each horizontal line. Two vertices are adjacent, if the corresponding line segments intersect. We say that two line segments *cross* if they have a nonempty intersection.

Definition 16. A *scanline* in the diagram is any line segment with one end vertex on each horizontal line. A scanline s is *between* two non-crossing line segments x and y if the top point of s is in the open interval bordered by the top points of x and y and the bottom point of s is in the open interval bordered by the bottom points of x and y.

If a scanline s is between line segments x and y then the intersection of each pair of the three line segments is empty. Consider two nonadjacent vertices x and y. The line segments in the diagram corresponding to x and y do not cross in the diagram. Hence we can find a scanline s between the lines x and y. Take out all the lines that cross the scanline s. Clearly this corresponds with an x,y-separator in the graph. The next lemma shows that we can find all minimal x,y-separators in this way.

Lemma 17. *Let G be a permutation graph, and let x and y be nonadjacent vertices in G. Every minimal x,y-separator consists of all line segments crossing a scanline which lies between the line segments of x and y.*

Proof. Let S be a minimal x,y-separator. Consider the connected components of $G[V-S]$. Let C_x be the component containing x and C_y be the component containing y. Clearly these must also be 'connected' parts in the diagram, and we may assume without loss of generality that the component containing x is completely to the left of the component containing y. Every vertex of S is adjacent to some vertex in C_x and to some vertex in C_y (lemma 10). Notice that we can choose a scanline s crossing no line segment of $G[V-S]$, and which is between x and y. Then all lines crossing the scanline must be elements of S. But for all elements of S the corresponding line segment must cross s, since it is intersecting with a line segment of C_x, which is to the left of s, and with a line segment of C_y, which is to the right of s.

Corollary 18. *There are $O(n^2)$ minimal separators in a permutation graph with n vertices.*

If s is a scanline, then we denote by S the set of vertices of which the corresponding line segments cross s. In the rest of this paper we consider only scanlines, of which the end points do not coincide with end points of other line segments.

Definition 19. Two scanlines s_1 and s_2 are *equivalent*, $s_1 \equiv s_2$, if they have the same position in the diagram relative to every line segment.

Hence, if $s_1 \equiv s_2$, then the set of line segments with the top (or bottom) end point to the left of the top (or bottom) end point of the scanline is the same for s_1 and s_2.

We are only interested in scanlines which do not cross too many line segments, since these correspond with suitable separators.

Definition 20. A scanline s is *k-small* if it crosses with at most $k+1$ line segments.

Lemma 21. *There are $O(nk)$ pairwise non-equivalent k-small scanlines.*

Proof. Consider the matching diagram, with numbers $1, \ldots, n$ written from left to right and underneath written $\pi_1, \ldots, \pi_n$. Consider a scanline t and assume the top end point is between i and $i+1$ and the bottom end point is between π_j and π_{j+1}. Assume that s line segments are such that the top end point is to the left of the top of t and the bottom end point to the left of the bottom of t. Then the number of line segments crossing t is $i + j - 2s$. Since $s \leq i$ and $s \leq j$, it follows that $i - k - 1 \leq j \leq i + k + 1$ must hold. This proves the lemma.

4 Treewidth = pathwidth

In this section we show that a permutation graph can be triangulated optimally such that the result is an interval graph.

Theorem 22. *Let G be a permutation graph, and let H be a minimal triangulation of G. Then H is an interval graph.*

Proof. Assume H has an astroidal triple x, y, z. Since x, y and z are pairwise non-adjacent, the corresponding line segments in the matching diagram pairwise do not cross. We may assume without loss of generality that the line segment of y is between those of x and z. Take a path p between x and z which avoids the neighborhood of y. Then each line of the path lies totally to the left or totally to the right of y. It follows that there are x' to the left of y and z' to the right of y such that x' and z' are adjacent in H, but neither x' or z' is a neighbor of y in H. Let S be a minimal x', y-separator in H. Since H is a minimal triangulation, S is also a minimal x', y-separator in G. By lemma 17 S consists of all lines crossing some scanline s between x' and y. Clearly, the connected component of $G[V - S]$ containing x' lies totally to the left of s and the connected component containing z' in $G[V - S]$ lies totally to the right of s (notice $z' \notin S$ since z' lies totally to the right of y). It follows that x' and z' must be in different components of $G[V - S]$. Since H is minimal, by theorem 11 they must also be in different components of $H[V - S]$. But then x' and z' can not be adjacent in H. It follows that there can not be an astroidal triple, and by the characterization of Lekkerkerker and Boland ([16], stated in lemma 7), H is an interval graph.

Corollary 23. *For a permutation graph G, the pathwidth of G is equal to the treewidth of G.*

5 Candidate components

Consider the matching diagram of G.

Definition 24. Let s_1 and s_2 be two scanlines of which the intersection is either empty or one of the end points of s_1 and s_2. A *candidate component* $C = C(s_1, s_2)$ is a subgraph of G induced by the following sets of lines:

- All lines that are *between* the scanlines (in case the scanlines have a common end point, this set is empty).
- All line crossing at least one of the scanlines.

We identify the candidate component $C = C(s_1, s_2)$ with the diagram containing s_1, s_2 and the set of lines corresponding with vertices of C.

Definition 25. Let k be an integer. A candidate component $C = C(s_1, s_2)$ is k-*feasible* if there is a triangulation H of C such that $\omega(H) \leq k + 1$ and such that for each scanline s_i $(i = 1, 2)$ the set of lines crossing this scanline forms a clique in H.

Notice that, if a candidate component has at most $k + 1$ vertices then it is k-feasible.

Definition 26. Let $C = C(s_1, s_2)$ be a candidate component. We define the *realizer* $R(C)$ as the graph obtained from C, by adding all edges between vertices of S_1 and between vertices of S_2 (i.e. the two subgraphs of $R(C)$ induced by S_1 and by S_2 are cliques).

A candidate component $C = C(s_1, s_2)$ is k-feasible if and only if the realizer $R(C)$ has treewidth at most k.

Lemma 27. *If $C = C(s_1, s_2)$ is a candidate component, then the realizer $R(C)$ is a permutation graph.*

Proof. Consider the matching diagram. Assume s_1 is to the left of s_2. First consider lines that cross only s_1 and with top end point to the right of the top end point of s_1. Let $(a_1, b_1), \ldots, (a_r, b_r)$ be these line segments with top end points $a_1, \ldots, a_r$. Assume $a_1 < a_2 < \ldots < a_r$. Change the order of $b_1, \ldots, b_r$ such that $b_1 > b_2 > \ldots > b_r$. This is illustrated in figure 2. Now consider the line segments crossing s_1 of which the top end point is to the left of the top end point of s_1. Reorder in the same way the *top end points* of these line segments. The lines crossing s_2 are handled similarly. The resulting diagram is a matching diagram for $R(C)$.

Let $C = C(s_1, s_2)$ be a candidate component such that C has at least $k + 2$ vertices. The realizer $R(C)$ has treewidth at most k if and only if there is a minimal vertex separator S with at most k vertices such that all components, with S added as a clique, have treewidth at most k (see lemma 13). Consider the diagram of $R(C)$, obtained from the diagram of C by the method described in the proof of lemma 27. By lemma 17 a minimal separator can be found by a scanline. Let H be a minimal

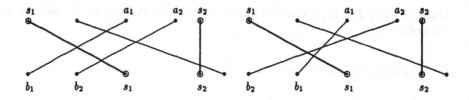

Fig. 2. diagrams of candidate component and realizer

triangulation of $R(C)$ and let the scanline s represent a minimal vertex separator in H for non-adjacent vertices a and b. The separator consists exactly of the lines crossing this scanline s.

Definition 28. Let $C = C(s_1, s_2)$ be a candidate component with realizer $R(C)$. A scanline t is *nice* if the top point of t is in the closed interval between the top points of s_1 and s_2, and the bottom point of t is in the closed interval between the bottom points of s_1 and s_2.

Lemma 29. *There is a scanline $s^* \equiv s$ such that s^* is nice.*

Proof. Consider the diagram of $R(C)$ with the scanlines s_1, s_2 and s. Without loss of generality, we assume s_1 is to the left of s_2. s Separates non adjacent vertices a and b. Let the line segment of a be to the left of the line segment of b. The scanline s lies between the line segments of a and b. Assume s is not nice. Without loss of generality assume it crosses s_1. Then $a \in S_1$ and $b \notin S_1$ (since a and b are not adjacent). (see the left diagram in figure 3). Let s^* be the line segment with top point the top of s_1 and bottom point the bottom of s. We want to proof that $s \equiv s^*$. This clearly is the case if there is no line segment of which the top point is between the top points of s and s_1. Assume there is such a vertex p (see the right diagram in figure 3). Notice that, since p and a both cross s_1 they are adjacent. We claim

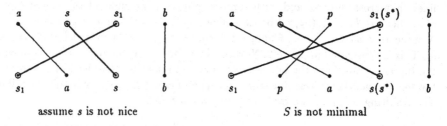

assume s is not nice S is not minimal

Fig. 3. there is an equivalent nice scanline

that $S^* \subset S$. Let x be a line segment crossing s^*. If the bottom end of x is to the left of the bottom end of s^*, then the segment x clearly also crosses s. Assume the bottom vertex of x is to the right of the bottom vertex of s^*. Then the line segment also crosses s_1. But then x and a are adjacent, hence the top vertex of x must be to the left of the top vertex of a. This implies that x also crosses s. Clearly, S^* is an a, b-separator in $R(C)$. Since $p \in S \setminus S^*$, S can not be a minimal a, b-separator in $R(C)$, and since H is a minimal triangulation of $R(C)$, it can not be a minimal a, b-separator in H (theorem 11). This is a contradiction.

This proves that all lines crossing the scanline s are in C, and the next lemma follows.

Lemma 30. *Let $C = C(s_1, s_2)$ be a candidate component with at least $k+2$ vertices. Then C is k-feasible if and only if there is a nice scanline s such that the two candidate components $C_1 = C(s_1, s)$ and $C_2 = C(s, s_2)$ are both smaller than C and are both k-feasible.*

We are now ready to proof our main theorem.

Theorem 31. *Let $C = C(s_1, s_2)$ be a candidate components with s_2 to the right of s_1. Then C is k-feasible if and only if there exists a sequence of scanlines $s_1 = t_1, t_2, \ldots, t_r = s_2$ such that the following conditions are satisfied:*

- *t_i and t_{i+1} have an endpoint in common for $i = 1, \ldots, r-1$, and the other end point of t_{i+1} lies to the right of the other end point of t_i.*
- *Each $C(t_i, t_{i+1})$ has at most $k+1$ vertices $(i = 1, \ldots, r-1)$.*

Proof. First assume such a sequence exists. Let $t_1, \ldots t_r$ be the sequence of scanlines. If C has at most $k+1$ vertices, then C is k-feasible. Hence we may assume that C has at least $k+2$ vertices. Then $r \geq 3$. By induction we show that $C(t_1, t_i)$ is k-feasible for $i = 2, \ldots r$. If $i = 2$ then $C(t_1, t_2)$ has at most $k+1$ vertices and hence it is k-feasible. Assume $C(t_1, t_{i-1})$ is k-feasible and $C(t_1, t_i) \neq C(t_1, t_{i-1})$. Then t_{i-1} is a nice scanline in $C(t_1, t_i)$. $C(t_1, t_{i-1})$ and $C(t_{i-1}, t_i)$ are both k-feasible, hence, by lemma 30, also $C(t_1, t_i)$ is k-feasible.

Now assume that C is k-feasible. Consider the case that C has at most $k+1$ vertices. If s_1 and s_2 have an end point in common we can take $r = 2$. If s_1 and s_2 do not have an end point in common, take a scanline t which has one end point in common with s_1 and the other end point in common with s_2. The sequence of scanlines s_1, t, s_2 satisfies the requirements. Assume C has at least $k+2$ vertices. Then by lemma 30 the is a nice scanline s^* such that $C(s_1, s^*)$ and $C(s^*, s_2)$ are both k-feasible. The theorem follows by induction on the number of vertices of C.

6 Algorithm

In this section we show how to compute the treewidth (and pathwidth) of a permutation graph G. Let k be an integer. The algorithm we present checks whether the treewidth of the permutation graph does not exceed k.

Make a directed acyclic graph $W_k(G)$ as follows. The vertices of the graph are the pairwise non-equivalent k-small scanlines. Direct an arc from scanline s to t if:

- The intersection of s and t is one end point of s and t, and the other end point of t is to the right of the other end point of s.
- The candidate component $C(s,t)$ has at most $k+1$ vertices.

We call this graph the *scanline graph*.

Lemma 32. *Let s_L be the scanline which lies totally to the left of all line segments and let s_R be the scanline which lies totally to the right of all line segments. G has treewidth at most k if and only if there is a directed path in the scanline graph from s_L to s_R.*

Proof. Clearly s_L and s_R are k-small. The result follows immediately from theorem 31.

Lemma 33. *The scanline graph has $O(nk)$ vertices and each vertex is incident with $O(k)$ arcs.*

Proof. The bound on the number of vertices is proved in lemma 21. The bound on the number of arcs incident with a vertex can be seen as follows. Let s be a k-small scanline. First we count the number of scanlines t which which have an incoming arc from s in $W_k(G)$ and such that s and t have the same top end point. Consider the matching diagram and assume the top point of s and t is between i and $i+1$, the bottom vertex of s is between π_j and π_{j+1}, and the bottom point of t is between π_m and π_{m+1} (hence $m > j$). Clearly, the number of vertices in $C(s,t)$ is at least $m - j$. Since there is an arc from s to t, $m - j \leq k+1$. The other cases are similar and this proves that s is incident with $O(k)$ arcs.

We now describe the algorithm which determines if the treewidth of G is at most k.

Step 1 Make a maximal list $\mathcal{L}$ of pairwise non-equivalent k-small scanlines.

Step 2 Construct the acyclic digraph $W_k(G)$.

Step 3 If there exists a path in $W_k(G)$ from s_L to s_R, then the pathwidth of G is at most k. If such a path does not exist, then the pathwidth of G is larger than k.

We now discuss the running time of the algorithm in more detail.

Lemma 34. *The algorithm can be implemented to run in $O(nk^2)$ time.*

Proof. By lemma 21 each k-small scanline can be characterized by two indices i and θ with $0 \leq i \leq n$ and $-(k+1) \leq \theta \leq k+1$. The scanline with these indices has top end point between i and $i+1$ and bottom end point between $\pi_{i+\theta}$ and $\pi_{i+\theta+1}$ (with obvious boundary restrictions). Let $A(i,\theta)$ be the number of line segments of which the top end point is to the left of the top endpoint of this scanline and which cross the scanline. Notice that $A(0,\theta) = 0$ for $\theta = 0,\ldots,k+1$. The rest of the table follows from:

$$A(i,\theta) = \begin{cases} A(i,\theta-1) & \text{if } \pi_{i+\theta} > i \\ A(i,\theta-1) - 1 & \text{if } \pi_{i+\theta} \leq i \end{cases} \quad \text{if } \theta > -\min(k+1,i)$$

$$A(i,\theta) = \begin{cases} A(i-1,\theta+1)+1 & \text{if } \pi_i^{-1} > i+\theta \\ A(i-1,\theta+1) & \text{if } \pi_i^{-1} \leq i+\theta \end{cases} \quad \text{if } i \geq 1 \text{ and } \theta = -\min(k+1,i)$$

The number of line segments crossing the scanline with indices i and θ is $2A(i,\theta)+\theta$. It follows that the list $\mathcal{L}$ of k-small scanlines can be made in $O(nk)$ time.

We now show that the scanline graph $W_k(G)$ can be constructed in $O(nk^2)$ time. Consider two k-small scanlines s and t, which have a top end point in common, say between i and $i+1$. Assume the bottom end point of s is between π_j and π_{j+1} and the bottom end point of t is between π_m and π_{m+1}. According to lemma 33 we must have $|m-j| \leq k+1$, otherwise there can not be an arc between s and t. Assume without loss of generality that $j < m$. Notice that the number of vertices of $C(s,t)$ is $m-i+A(i,m-i)+A(i,j-i)$. This shows that the adjacency list for each k-small scanline can be computed in $O(k)$ time. Computing a path in W from s_L to s_R, if it exists, clearly also takes $O(nk^2)$ time. Hence the total algorithm can be implemented to run in $O(nk^2)$ time.

Theorem 35. *Let G be a permutation graph. Then the pathwidth and treewidth of G are the same, and there is an $O(nk^2)$ algorithm that correctly determines whether the treewidth of G is at most k.*

We end this section by remarking that the algorithm can be adapted such that it computes, within the same time bound, the pathwidth of a permutation graph (when the matching diagram is given). This can be seen as follows. Let the treewidth of G be k. First compute a number L such that $L \leq k \leq 2L$. This can be done, using the algorithm described above $O(\log k)$ times, in time $O(nk^2)$. Now construct the scanline graph $W_{2L}(G)$, and put weights on the arcs, saying how many vertices are in the corresponding candidate component. Then search for a path from s_L to s_R, such that the maximum over weights of arcs in the path is minimized. This maximum weight minus one gives the exact treewidth k of G.

7 Conclusions

In this paper we described a very simple and efficient algorithm to compute the treewidth and pathwidth of a permutation graph. There are some other classes of graphs for which the exact pathwidth and treewidth can be computed efficiently. For example cographs [6], splitgraphs and interval graphs. The treewidth can also be computed efficiently for chordal graphs, circular arc graphs [19] and chordal bipartite graphs [13]. In this respect we like to mention the result of [11] which shows that the pathwidth of chordal graphs is NP-complete. Permutation graphs are exactly the graphs that are comparability and cocomparability. It is easy to see that treewidth is NP-complete for bipartite graphs. Hence our result can not be generalized to the class of comparability graphs. However, an open problem is whether the results of this paper can be generalized to the class of cocomparability graphs. One of the other open problems we like to mention is whether the running time of our algorithm can be improved. Notice that there is a *linear* time (i.e. $O(nk)$) approximation algorithm for treewidth and pathwidth of permutation graph with performance ratio 2 ([12]).

Acknowledgements

We like to thank A. Brandstädt, H. Müller, A. Jacobs, D. Seese and B. Reed for valuable discussions.

References

1. S. Arnborg, Efficient algorithms for combinatorial problems on graphs with bounded decomposability — A survey. *BIT* **25**, 2 − 23, 1985.
2. S. Arnborg, D.G. Corneil and A. Proskurowski, Complexity of finding embeddings in a *k*-tree, *SIAM J. Alg. Disc. Meth.* **8**, 277 − 284, 1987.
3. S. Arnborg and A. Proskurowski, Linear time algorithms for NP-hard problems restricted to partial *k*-trees. *Disc. Appl. Math.* **23**, 11 − 24, 1989.
4. C. Berge and C. Chvatal, *Topics on Perfect Graphs*, Annals of Discrete Math. **21**, 1984.
5. H.L. Bodlaender, A tourist guide through treewidth, Technical report RUU-CS-92-12, Department of Computer Science, Utrecht University, Utrecht, The Netherlands, 1992. To appear in: *Proceedings 7th Int. Meeting of Young Computer Scientists*.
6. H. Bodlaender and R.H. Möhring, The pathwidth and treewidth of cographs, In *Proceedings 2nd Scandinavian Workshop on Algorithm Theory*, 301 − 309, Springer Verlag, Lect. Notes in Comp. Sc., vol. 447, 1990. To appear in: *SIAM J. Discr. Math.*
7. H. Bodlaender and T. Kloks, Better algorithms for the pathwidth and treewidth of graphs, *Proceedings of the 18th Int. Coll. on Automata, Languages and Programming*, 544 − 555, Springer Verlag, Lect. Notes in Comp. Sc., vol. 510, 1991.
8. A. Brandstädt, Special graph classes — a survey, Schriftenreihe des Fachbereichs Mathematik, SM-DU-199 (1991) Universität Duisburg Gesamthochschule.
9. S. Even, A. Pnueli and A. Lempel, Permutation graphs and transitive graphs, *J. Assoc. Comput. Mach.* **19**, 400 − 410, 1972.
10. M.C. Golumbic, *Algorithmic Graph Theory and Perfect Graphs*, Academic Press, New York, 1980.
11. J. Gustedt, Pathwidth for chordal graphs is NP-complete. To appear in: *Discr. Appl. Math.*
12. T. Kloks and H. Bodlaender, Approximating treewidth and pathwidth of some classes of perfect graphs. *3th Ann. Int. Symp. on Algorithms and Computation (ISAAC'92)*, 116 − 125, Springer Verlag, Lect. Notes in Comp. Sc., vol. 650, 1993.
13. T. Kloks and D. Kratsch, Treewidth of chordal bipartite graphs. In: *Proc. 10th Ann. Symp. on Theoretical Aspects of Computer Science*, 80 − 89, Springer Verlag, Lect. Notes in Comp. Sc., vol. 665, 1993.
14. J. Lagergren and S. Arnborg, Finding minimal forbidden minors using a finite congruence, *Proceedings of the 18th Int. Coll. on Automata, Languages and Programming*, 532 − 543, Springer Verlag, Lect. Notes in Comp. Sc., vol. 510, 1991.
15. J. van Leeuwen, Graph algorithms. In *Handbook of Theoretical Computer Science, A: Algorithms an Complexity Theory*, 527 − 631, Amsterdam, 1990. North Holland Publ. Comp.
16. C.G. Lekkerkerker and J.Ch. Boland, Representation of a finite graph by a set of intervals on the real line, *Fund. Math.* **51**, 45 − 64, 1962.
17. B. Reed, Finding approximate separators and computing treewidth quickly, *Proc. 24th Ann. ACM Symp. on Theory of Computing*, 221 − 228, 1992.
18. J. Spinrad, On comparability and permutation graphs, *SIAM J. Comp.* **14**, 658 − 670, 1985.
19. R. Sundaram, K. Sher Singh and C. Pandu Rangan, Treewidth of circular arc graphs, Manuscript, 1991, to appear in SIAM J. Disc. Math..

A Theory of Even Functionals
and Their Algorithmic Applications

by

Jerzy W. Jaromczyk[*] and Grzegorz Świątek[†]

Abstract

We present a theory of even functionals of degree k. Even functionals are homogeneous polynomials which are invariant with respect to permutations and reflections. These are evaluated on real symmetric matrices. Important examples of even functionals include functions for enumerating embeddings of graphs with k edges into a weighted graph with arbitrary (positive or negative) weights and computing kth moments (expected values of kth powers) of a binary form. This theory provides a uniform approach for evaluating even functionals and links their evaluation with expressions with matrices as operands. In particular, we show that any even functional of degree less than 7 can be computed in time $O(n^\omega)$, the time required to multiply two $n \times n$ matrices.

1 Introduction

We shall develop a new theory leading to fast computation of polynomials in a class of so-called even functionals of degree k. These are directly related to a variety of discrete algorithmic problems. The theory of even functionals presented in this paper has been originally motivated by our study on efficient algorithms for fast evaluation of expected values of binary quadratic forms. Such forms arise in a natural way in combinatorial optimization, see [3, 5, 7, 8]. The theory, however, has much wider applications due to its strong, and non-trivial links with fundamental problems in graph theory. Even functionals arise in enumerating graph embeddings, in computing the order of a graph automorphism group, in detecting and counting cycles of a given size in an input graph , see [1, 4, 6], just to list a few applications. It is necessary to emphasize that most of the results offered by even functionals hold for arbitrary weighted graphs both with positive and negative weights. It addresses a well known limitation of many graph algorithms which are sensitive to the presence of negative cycles, see [6].

Specific examples of even functionals investigated in this paper include:

kth moments of binary quadratic forms Consider a polynomial $p(A) = \sum_{1 \leq i < j \leq n} a_{ij} x_i x_j$. This quadratic form is fully described by a symmetric matrix $A = (a_{ij})$; the matrix entry is 0 if the corresponding term in the polynomial is absent. Expectation of the kth power of $p(A)$, i.e. the kth moment, where x_i are identically distributed, independent random variables, with the distribution concentrated with probability $\frac{1}{2}$ on 1 and -1 is an even functional of degree k. Binary quadratic forms arise in many optimization problems.

Even multigraphs Let g be a multigraph with k edges and all vertex degrees even, i.e., g is an even multigraph of size k. The number of (weighted) embeddings of g into a weighted graph G with arbitrary weights and n vertices is an even functional of degree k. (In other words, the number of different occurrences of a pattern graph g in G can be expressed as an even functional on the incidence matrix of G.)

[*]Department of Computer Science, University of Kentucky, Lexington, KY 40506-0027
[†]Department of Mathematics, SUNY at Stony Brook, Stony Brook, NY 11794

Simple cycles Let g be a simple cycle with k edges. There is an even functional of degree k such that the number of embeddings of g into a graph G with n vertices is equal to the value of this functional on an incidence matrix of G. If $k \leq 7$ then this functional can be evaluated in time proportional to matrix multiplication.

All of the even functionals mentioned above can be explicitly constructed. In further sections we will show that they form a linear space whose dimension is equal to the number of even multigraphs with k edges. This, in turn, will lead to a special class of even functionals, called matrix expressions, which provide a linear basis for small values of k. Each even functional is a linear combination of the elements of basis. This implies, for an example, that the kth moment for $k \leq 7$ can be found in amount of time proportional to matrix multiplication; note that the size of the probabilistic space is 2^n.

Here is the organization of the paper. In the next section we will define even functionals of degree k. Then, we will prove that the dimension of the linear space of even functionals of degree k is equal to the number of even multigraphs with k edges. In Section 4 we will introduce a class of matrix expressions, i.e., even functionals which can be quickly computed. These will be used for efficient evaluation of even functionals of small degree ($k \leq 8$). Next, important examples of even functionals will be discussed and some final remarks will conclude the paper.

2   Even functionals of degree k

Let $M(n)$ be the set of $n \times n$ symmetric matrices with all elements on the main diagonal equal to 0. Let $\mathcal{M} = \bigcup_{n \in N} M(n)$. We define $\mathcal{F}_k$ to be a family of functions from $\mathcal{M}$ to R which have the following properties:

For each n and $M \in M(n)$

- $f \in \mathcal{F}_k$ is a polynomial of degree k that is homogeneous with respect to the matrix entries as indeterminates.
- $f \in \mathcal{F}_k$ is invariant with respect to the conjugation with a matrix from the group $O(n, Z)$. That is, if U is a matrix in $O(n, Z)$ then $f(UMU^{-1}) = f(M)$.

$O(n, Z)$ is the group of $n \times n$ orthogonal matrices with integer entries. It is generated by linear transformations corresponding to permutations (and therefore, transpositions) of the basis vectors and by transformations corresponding to reflections with respect to a basis vector.

Elements of $\mathcal{F}_k$ are called *even functionals of degree k*. Let us recall that a permutation matrix has a single entry 1 in each row and in each column and all other entries are 0. A reflection matrix is a diagonal matrix with all entries 1 or -1.

Clearly, for any k the even functionals $\mathcal{F}_k$ form a linear space over the field of real numbers. Examples of even functionals will be given in the next sections.

3   Even multigraphs with k edges - $\mathcal{G}(k)$

Let $\mathcal{G}(k)$ be a set of all multigraphs (not necessarily connected) with k edges such that the degree of each vertex is an even positive number, see [4]. The number of edges between two vertices v_i and v_j will be denoted by λ_{ij}. In particular, $\lambda_{ij} = 0$ if there is no edge between v_i and v_j. Clearly, each connected component of a multigraph in the $\mathcal{G}(k)$ has an Euler cycle - a closed tour which traces each edge exactly once.

The objective of this section is to establish a connection between $\mathcal{G}(k)$ and the class of even functionals. Every graph in $\mathcal{G}(k)$ defines in a natural way an element in $\mathcal{F}_k$. Specifically, for every k we can define a mapping $\rho : \mathcal{G}(k) \to \mathcal{F}_k$.

Let $g \in \mathcal{G}(k)$ and $A = (a_{ij}) \in \mathcal{M}$. Assume that $V = \{v_1, \ldots, v_p\}$ are vertices of g. A one-to-one map from V to V that preserves adjacency and multiplicities of edges is called an automorphism of g. The order of the automorphism group $\Gamma(g)$ of g is denoted by $s(g)$; it is the number of symmetries of g.

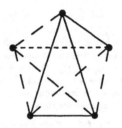

Figure 1: A multigraph and its embedding into a 5-clique

Let θ be a one-to-one function from $\{1,\ldots,p\}$ to $\{1,\ldots,n\}$. Θ denotes a set of all such functions. Now, $\rho(g)(A)$ is defined as

$$\rho(g)(A) = \frac{1}{s(g)}\sum_{\theta \in \Theta}\prod_{1 \le i < j \le p} a_{\theta(i)\theta(j)}^{\lambda_{ij}}.$$

Clearly, $\rho(g)(A) = 0$ if $k > n$. (As a convention we assume that $0^0 = 1$.) That is, $\rho(g)(A)$ is the sum of the products of the weights of edges (with their multiplicities) over all one-to-one embeddings of the vertices of the graph g into a weighted graph g' with the incidence matrix A. Specifically, if v_1, v_2 are mapped into w_1 and w_2 in g' then the contribution of the edge $v_1 v_2$ to the $\rho(g)$ is equal to $a_{12}^{\lambda_{12}}$.

Example: Consider a multigraph g with 5 edges and an incidence matrix A of a complete graph with 5 vertices and all weights equal to 1; see Figure 1. Clearly, the weight of each embedding of g is equal to 1. Hence, $\rho(g)$ is equal to the number of the embeddings of (unlabeled) g into a complete graph with 5 vertices. □

We have an important theorem which bridges even multigraphs with k edges and even functionals of degree k.

Theorem 1 *The image of $\mathcal{G}(k)$ under ρ spans the linear space $\mathcal{F}_k$. If $k \le n$ then this image is a basis of $\mathcal{F}_k$.*

Proof: We will show that every $f \in \mathcal{F}_k$ is a linear combination of the elements from the image of $\mathcal{G}(k)$ under ρ. Let f represent a sum of monomials of the order k. Each monomial

$$x_{i_1 j_1}^{\lambda_{i_1 j_1}} \ldots x_{i_l j_l}^{\lambda_{i_l j_l}}$$

determines its equivalence class, namely the set constituted by the monomials

$$x_{\sigma(i_1)\sigma(j_1)}^{\lambda_{i_1 j_1}} \ldots x_{\sigma(i_l)\sigma(j_l)}^{\lambda_{i_l j_l}}$$

where σ is a permutation of $\{1,\ldots,n\}$.

Two monomials are equivalent if (up to multiplicative constants) they belong to the same equivalence class. Let α denote an equivalence class. Clearly, α is determined by a vector $(\lambda_{i_1 j_1},\ldots,\lambda_{i_l j_l})$. Let f_α denote the sum of all monomials in f (with their scalar multiplicative constants) that belong to the equivalence class α. Then, $f = \sum_\alpha f_\alpha$ and since f is symmetric with respect to permutations σ of $\{1,\ldots,n\}$, we have

$$f = \sum_\alpha f_\alpha = \frac{1}{n!}\sum_\sigma \sum_\alpha f_\alpha = \frac{1}{n!}\sum_\alpha \sum_\sigma f_\alpha. \tag{1}$$

Let c_α denote the sum of all scalars in f_α and $\sum w_\alpha$ denote the sum of all different representatives in the equivalence class α. We have $\sum_\sigma f_\alpha = c_\alpha s_\alpha \sum w_\alpha$ where s_α denotes the number of permutations σ that do not change w_α.

Letting $C_\alpha = c_\alpha s_\alpha / n!$ we finally obtain that

$$f = \sum_\alpha C_\alpha (\sum w_\alpha). \tag{2}$$

We will show that $\sum w_\alpha$ is equal to $\rho(g)$ for some even graph g with $k = \sum_t \lambda_{i_t j_t}$ edges. Let $w_\alpha = x_{i_1 j_1}^{\lambda_{i_1 j_1}} \ldots x_{i_l j_l}^{\lambda_{i_l j_l}}$ be a representative in the equivalence class α. The graph g is defined explicitly based on w_α. It has a vertex v_i for each index i in the indeterminates (each indeterminate has two indices). The edges correspond to indeterminates: each $x_{i_p j_p}$ induces an edge of strength $\lambda_{i_p j_p}$ between the pair of vertices v_{i_p} and v_{j_p}. The above correspondence defines a function from the equivalence classes of monomials of degree k to even graphs with k edges. We will denote this function by τ. The function τ^{-1} is defined since τ is one-to-one and onto. We can think about $\tau^{-1}(g)$ as an arbitrary monomial in the corresponding equivalence class.

Example 1 *The mapping τ maps both monomials $x_{12}^2 x_{23} x_{24} x_{34}$ and $x_{43}^2 x_{12} x_{13} x_{23}$, which are equivalent by the permutation $(1\ 4)(2\ 3)$, onto the even graph from Figure 1. Also, either of these monomials can be viewed as the value of τ^{-1} on the graph.*

Now, each embedding of g into an $n \times n$ matrix M corresponds to some representative in the equivalence class of w_α. All embeddings give $\sum w_\alpha$ and the sum of their weights is exactly $\rho(g)$.

To finish the proof we need to demonstrate that g is an even graph with k edges. Clearly, the number of edges in g is equal to k. The degree of each vertex is even. To prove this, assume that the degree of a vertex v_{i_0} is odd. Then in at least one monomial μ with an indeterminate $x_{i_0 j_0}$ (for some j_0) the corresponding $\lambda_{i_0 j_0}$ is odd. Consider the incidence matrix M of of the graph g and a reflection R of this matrix with respect to the i_0-th vector in the basis. The value of $\rho(g)$ on M is nonnegative. On the other hand, at least one monomial (specifically, μ) is negative on the matrix $R \cdot M \cdot R^{-1}$. Hence, $\rho(g)(M) > \rho(g)(R \cdot M \cdot R^{-1})$ which is a contradiction because f is invariant with respect to reflections.

Finally, we will show that all $\rho(g)$, where $g \in \mathcal{G}(k)$, are linearly independent. Consider an even functional f and its representation as a sum of monomials. This representation is unique (if monomials with coefficients equal to 0 are ignored) and therefore the representation of f given in Eq. (2) is unique as well. We will show that $\rho(g_1) \neq \rho(g_2)$ for two non-isomorphic even graphs g_1, g_2. Let us assume that the contrary holds true. Consider $w_1 = \tau^{-1}(g_1)$ and $w_2 = \tau^{-1}(g_2)$. The assumption $\rho(g_1) = \rho(g_2)$ and the definition of ρ imply that there is a permutation of indices σ such that $w_1 = \sigma w_2$. Hence, $\tau^{-1}(g_1) = \sigma(\tau^{-1}(g_2))$. Now, based on the definition of τ and σ we show that $\tau \sigma \tau^{-1}$ is an isomorphism of g_1, g_2 which implies that $g_1 = g_2$. This contradiction ends the proof.

□

The above proof immediately implies the following

Corollary 3.1 *If $k \leq n$ then the number of even graphs of size k is equal to the dimension of the linear space of even functionals of degree k.*

Note that the above corollary holds for any n. On the other hand the number of even multigraphs of size k depends only on k. Additionally, $\rho(g)(A)$ for an even multigraph g of degree k and an $n \times n$ matrix A can be found in $O(n^k)$ time. As an immediate implication we obtain the following lemma.

Corollary 3.2 *Every even functional of degree k, if k is viewed as a constant, can be computed in polynomial time $O(n^k)$.* □

In the next sections we will show a faster method to compute even functionals for small values of k in time proportional to matrix multiplication, see [2, 9].

We will finish this section with a theorem pertaining to even functionals with integer coefficients.

Theorem 2 *If f is an even functional of degree k with integer coefficients then f is a linear combination of $\rho(g_i)$, $g_i \in \mathcal{G}(k)$, with integer coefficients.*

Proof: Assume that an even functional with integer coefficient $f = \sum_{i=1}^l a_i \rho(g_i)$ where not all a_i are integers. Consider $S = \{i : a_i \notin \mathbf{Z}\}$ ($\mathbf{Z}$ is the set of integers.) Take $s \in S$ such that g_s does not contain any proper subgraph g_i with $i \in S$. Here we consider subgraphs in the sense of graphs and not multigraphs; that is, edge multiplicities are ignored. Let A be the incidence matrix of g_s; $a_{ij} = 1$ if and only if there is at least one edge in g_s between v_i and v_j. Clearly $f(A)$ is an integer. On the other hand, $\rho(g_i)(A)$ is always an integer. Moreover, it is 0 if g_i is not a subgraph of g_s, and $\rho(g_s) = 1$. Hence, $\sum_{i=1}^l a_i \rho(g_i) = a_s + \sum_j a_j \rho(g_j)(A)$ where g_j are proper subgraphs of g_s. By the choice of s all a_j are integers and $a_s + \sum_j a_j \rho(g_j)(A) \notin \mathbf{Z}$. A contradiction. This ends the proof.

□

4 Matrix expressions

In this section we will define an important class of even functionals of degree k. Functionals in this class will be called matrix expressions.

Let $A = (a_{ij})$ be a matrix. We consider the following operations on matrices and numbers:

- two-argument standard matrix multiplication denoted by $\cdot$,

- two-argument entrywise matrix multiplication denoted by $\circ$, in which we multiply corresponding entries, i.e., $(a_{ij}) \circ (b_{ij}) = (c_{ij})$ where $c_{ij} = a_{ij}b_{ij}$,

- one-argument operation diag which is equivalent to the entrywise multiplication by an identity matrix.

Definition 1 *Let A be a matrix. An expression which uses the above operations with A as the only operands and whose result is a matrix is called an elementary matrix expression.*

Definition 2 *A matrix expression is defined as $c\,Tr(W)$ where W is an elementary matrix expression for a matrix A, c is a scalar, and Tr is the trace operation, i.e., $Tr((a_{ij})) = \sum_i a_{ii}$. The product of matrix expressions is also a matrix expression.*

Each matrix expression determines a function from $\mathcal{M}$ to the set of real numbers. Moreover, a matrix expression is a homogeneous polynomial of the matrix entries as indeterminates. The degree of homogeneity is simply referred to as the degree of a matrix expression.

Example 2 *Consider a symmetric 3 by 3 matrix A and a matrix expression $Tr(A \cdot A)$. This expression defines a function given by the following polynomial:*

$$a_{1,1}^2 + 2\,a_{1,2}^2 + 2\,a_{1,3}^2 + a_{2,2}^2 + 2\,a_{2,3}^2 + a_{3,3}^2.$$

The value of this expression for the matrix

$$\begin{bmatrix} 0 & 1 & -1 \\ 1 & 0 & 2 \\ -1 & 2 & 0 \end{bmatrix}$$

is equal 12.

Example 3 *Consider a symmetric 3 by 3 matrix A and a matrix expression of degree 5 given by $Tr((A \cdot (A \circ A)) \cdot diag(A \cdot A))$. This expression defines a function given by the following polynomial:*

$$a_{1,1}^3 a_{1,2}^2 + a_{1,1}^3 a_{1,3}^2 + a_{1,2}^3 a_{1,1}^2 + a_{1,2}^3 a_{1,3}^2 + a_{1,3}^3 a_{1,1}^2 + a_{1,3}^3 a_{1,2}^2 +$$
$$a_{1,2}^3 a_{2,2}^2 + a_{1,2}^3 a_{2,3}^2 + a_{2,2}^3 a_{1,2}^2 + a_{2,2}^3 a_{2,3}^2 + a_{2,3}^3 a_{1,2}^2 + a_{2,3}^3 a_{2,2}^2 +$$
$$a_{1,3}^3 a_{2,3}^2 + a_{1,3}^3 a_{3,3}^2 + a_{2,3}^3 a_{1,3}^2 + a_{2,3}^3 a_{3,3}^2 + a_{3,3}^3 a_{1,3}^2 + a_{3,3}^3 a_{2,3}^2 +$$
$$2\,a_{1,2}^5 + a_{1,1}^5 + a_{3,3}^5 + 2\,a_{2,3}^5 + a_{2,2}^5 + 2\,a_{1,3}^5$$

which is equal to 80 for

$$A = \begin{bmatrix} 0 & 1 & -1 \\ 1 & 0 & 2 \\ -1 & 2 & 0 \end{bmatrix}.$$

For elementary matrix expressions we define parity as follows. Let A be a $n \times n$ matrix and R be a matrix of a reflection with respect to a basis vector.

Definition 3 *We say that the parity of an elementary matrix expression W is defined and is odd if $W(RAR^{-1}) = RW(A)R^{-1}$ and is even if $W(RAR^{-1}) = W(A)$, for every reflection in $O(n, Z)$.* □

The parity of an elementary matrix expression describes its behavior with respect to conjugations with reflections. Note also that a parity of an elementary expression can be undefined.

Example 4

1. $A \cdot A$ has an odd parity.

2. $A \circ A$ has an even parity.

3. $A \cdot (A \circ A)$ has an undefined parity and similarly the functional in Example 3 has an undefined parity. □

We have the following lemma which helps to determine the parity of an elementary expression.

Lemma 4.1

(i) The parity of any matrix A is odd;

(ii) if the matrix expressions W_1 and W_2 have equal parity then $W_1 \cdot W_2$ has the same parity;

(iii) if the matrix expressions W_1 and W_2 have equal parity then $W_1 \circ W_2$ has even parity; if they have opposite parity then $W_1 \circ W_2$ has odd parity;

(iv) if the parity of a matrix expression W is defined then diag(W) has both even and odd parity.

Proof:
Let R be a matrix of a reflection with respect to one basis vector. RAR^{-1} is a matrix obtained from A by multiplying elements in the ith row and then elements in jth column by -1. In particular, this operation doesn't change the main diagonal.

Let W_1 and W_2 be elementary matrix expressions. If both are odd then $(W_1(RAR^{-1})) \cdot (W_2(RAR^{-1})) = R(W_1(A) \cdot W_2(A))R^{-1}$. If both are even then $(W_1(RAR^{-1})) \cdot (W_2(RAR^{-1})) = (W_1(A) \cdot W_2(A))$.

Reflections do not affect the main diagonal and for any matrix B diag(RBR^{-1}) = diag(B). Hence, diag($W_1(RAR^{-1})$) = diag($W_1(A)$) = diag($RW_1(A)R^{-1}$) if the parity of W_1 is defined.

By the above mentioned property of reflections and by the definition of the entrywise multiplication we have $(W_1(RAR^{-1})) \circ (W_2(RAR^{-1})) = RW_1(A)R^{-1} \circ RW_2(A)R^{-1} = W_1(A) \circ W_2(A)$ if both W_1 and W_2 have odd parity. Clearly, $(W_1(RAR^{-1})) \circ (W_2(RAR^{-1})) = W_1(A) \circ W_2(A)$ for even parity elementary expressions. If W_1 has an odd parity and W_2 has an even parity then $(W_1(RAR^{-1})) \circ (W_2(RAR^{-1})) = RW_1(A)R^{-1} \circ W_2(A) = RW_1(A) \circ W_2(A)R^{-1}$. Now, the lemma is implied by the above identities.

□

This lemma provides a useful tool to find the parity of a given elementary matrix expression. For a given elementary expression $W(A)$ we can consider its expression tree labeling the leaves with A and the internal nodes with the operations. A bottom-up traversal of this tree determines, with the help of Lemma 4.1, the parity of W.

We have an important theorem about matrix expressions and even functionals:

Theorem 3 *The trace of an elementary expression of degree k whose parity is defined is an even functional of degree k.*

Proof: Consider a matrix expression $c\text{Tr}(W(A))$, $W(A)$ being an elementary matrix expression of degree k with defined parity, for a matrix A. This expression is a homogeneous polynomial of degree k for the matrix entries as indeterminants.

By definition, the elementary matrix expression $W(A)$ satisfies either $W(RAR^{-1}) = W(A)$ or $W(RAR^{-1}) = RW(A)R^{-1}$. In both cases $\text{Tr}\,W(RAR^{-1}) = \text{Tr}\,W(A)$.

Let P be a matrix of an elementary permutation. Then PAP^{-1} is a matrix with i and j columns and rows of A transposed. In particular, the i and j elements on the main diagonal are also transposed.

Clearly, $(PAP^{-1})(PBP^{-1}) = P(AB)P^{-1}$ and diag(PAP^{-1}) = Pdiag(A)P^{-1}.

For the entrywise multiplication we have $(PAP^{-1}) \circ (PBP^{-1}) = P(A \circ B)P^{-1}$ since permuting the ith and jth columns and rows before or after multiplying the corresponding entries doesn't affect the result.

Consequently, $W(PAP^{-1}) = PW(A)P^{-1}$ independently of the parity of W. Since P only permutes the main diagonal elements we have $\operatorname{Tr} W(PAP^{-1}) = \operatorname{Tr} W(A)$ and thus ends the proof.

□

The significance of the matrix expressions with a defined parity is based on their simplicity and on the fact that they can be used to build the linear basis for $\mathcal{F}_k$. Specifically,

1. each matrix expression of fixed degree k for an $n \times n$ matrix can be computed in $O(n^\omega)$, where $O(n^\omega)$ is the time required to multiply two $n \times n$ matrices

2. matrix expressions of degree k for $k \leq 7$ form a basis of $\mathcal{F}_k$.

We will elaborate on this in the following sections.

5 Even functionals of a small degree

As we know from the above sections the even functionals form a linear space. This becomes advantageous if we can find a "computationally efficient" basis of the linear space $\mathcal{F}_k$. Obviously, matrix expressions are attractive candidates for such a basis because they can be computed in $O(n^\omega)$ time. In fact, we have the following theorem.

Theorem 4 *Matrix expressions of degree 7 span $\mathcal{F}_7$.*

Proof: By virtue of Theorem 1 we know that the dimension of $\mathcal{F}$, is equal to the number r_7 of even graphs with 7 edges. This can be effectively found by enumerating these graphs. Let r_7 stand for the number of even functionals of degree 7 ($r_7 = 21$.) We consider a set of r_7 matrix expressions of degree 7. To check their linear independence we evaluate each matrix expression on a set of r_7 matrices. By elementary linear algebra, the system of matrix expressions is linearly independent provided that the obtained system of evaluated expressions is linearly independent. Therefore, the problem reduces to finding a rank of an $r_7 \times r_7$ matrix which can be done in a straightforward way using, for example, the symbolic manipulation facilities provided by system Maple. Now, the independent set of r_7 elements (r_7 - the dimension of the space) must be a basis of the space. This ends the proof.

□

Theorem 1 suggests a heuristic which helps to find matrix expressions which are elements of the basis. The mapping ρ defined in Section 3 provides another tool. We will not, however, elaborate on these heuristic here. The linear basis for $\mathcal{F}_7$ has 21 elements and, in fact, they can be listed. We will show, as an illustration, a basis for $\mathcal{F}_5$.

Example 5 *The following set of 4 matrix expressions form a basis of the linear space $\mathcal{F}_5$ of even functionals of degree 5.*
$\operatorname{Tr}(A \cdot A \cdot A \cdot A \cdot A)$;
$\operatorname{Tr}(diag(A \cdot A \cdot A) \circ diag(A \cdot A))$;
$\operatorname{Tr}((A \cdot A) \cdot (A \circ A \circ A))$;
$\operatorname{Tr}(A \cdot A \cdot A) \times \operatorname{Tr}(A \cdot A)$;

□

The structure of the even functionals for higher degrees becomes richer what causes the linear dimension to grow. Interestingly, even multigraph counterparts of cliques (complete graphs) come to game here. Denote the even connected graph with 4 vertices and 8 edges showed in Figure 2 by $g(4,8)$.

For degree 8 we have:

Theorem 5 *Matrix expressions of degree 8 and $\rho(g(4,8))$, span $\mathcal{F}_8$.* □

Figure 2: graph $g(4,8)$

This theorem can be demonstrated similarly to Theorem 4.

A computationally important consequence of the above theorems is phrased in the following corollary.

Corollary 5.1 *Any even functional of degree 7 can be evaluated in time $O(n^\omega)$ where $O(n^\omega)$ is time required for fast matrix multiplication. Any even functional of degree 8 can be evaluated in time $O(n^4)$.*

□

This is a strong result in view of interesting functions which happen to be even functionals. We will provide examples in the next section.

The complexity of computing even functionals of degree k grows with k.

6   Expectation of powers of binary quadratic forms

Binary quadratic forms are polynomials defined as

$$\sum_{1 \le i < j \le n} a_{ij} x_i x_j$$

where x_i are identically distributed, independent random variables, with the distribution concentrated with probability $\frac{1}{2}$ on 1 and -1.

Clearly, a binary quadratic polynomial (form) is fully described by a real matrix A of the coefficients a_{ij}. The matrix A is completely defined by the requirement that if the corresponding term in the form is absent, the matrix entry is 0, and that the matrix is symmetric.

Binary quadratic forms arise in many optimization problems, e.g., unconstrained quadratic 0-1 programming, weighted 2-satisfiability, and maximum cut problem.

We have the following theorem.

Theorem 6 *The expectation of the kth power of a binary quadratic form $Q(x)$ with the matrix of coefficients A is an even functional of degree k. That is, there is an even functional of degree k whose value on A is equal to the expectation of kth power $Q(x)$.*

Proof: The claim follows directly from the definition of the expected value. The kth power of $Q(x)$ is a homogeneous polynomial. Clearly, this is invariant with respect to permutations. Also, since the summation in computing the expected value is done over all possible vectors of $\{-1, 1\}$ this polynomial is also invariant with respect to reflections.

□

By virtue of Theorem 4 we have

Corollary 6.1 *If $k \le 7$ then the expectation of the k-th power of a quadratic form with the matrix A is equal to*

$$\sum c_j(k) w_j^k(A)$$

where w_j^k are the matrix expressions of degree k, numbered with j. In particular, the coefficients $c_j(k)$ are independent of A.

This implies immediately, that

Corollary 6.2 *The expectation of the k-th power of any quadratic form can be computed in $O(n^\omega)$ time, for $k \leq 7$.*

For $k = 8$ the basis contains $\rho(g(4,8))$, in addition to matrix expressions. Hence, the expectation of 8th power of a binary quadratic form can be computed in $O(n^4)$ time.

7 Simple cycles

Based on the previous sections we know that the weighted embedding of a simple cycle of size k into a weighted graph G is an even functional of degree k evaluated on the matrix of G. For short cycles, $k \leq 7$, this functional is a linear combination of matrix expressions. For $k = 8$ it is a linear combination of matrix expressions of degree 8 and $\rho(g(4,8))$. It leads to an efficient algorithm for enumeration of simple cycles of the length $k \leq 8$ in a given graph.

Specifically, we have the following theorem:

Theorem 7 *If $k \leq 7$ then the number of simple cycles with k edges in a given graph of the order n can be found in time $O(n^\omega)$. If $k = 8$ then this number can be found in $O(n^4)$ time.* $\Box$

Using the same linear representation we can compute the total weight of all cycles of the length k in a given weighted graph with n vertices. Clearly, the same results apply to enumerating the number of occurrences of an arbitrary even graph with at most 8 edges.

To illustrate the theorem we will show how the even functional counting the embeddings of a simple cycle with 7 vertices is represented as a linear combination of matrix expressions of degree 7

Example 6 *The following linear combination of 15 matrix expressions is an even functional that counts the embeddings of a simple cycle C_7 with 7 vertices into a weighted graph with incidence matrix A. Recall that there are 21 even graphs of size 7; six of them are disconnected.*

$$
\begin{aligned}
\rho(C_7)(A) \;=\; & 2\,Tr(A \cdot (A \circ A \circ A) \cdot (A \circ A \circ A)) \\
+\; & \tfrac{1}{2}\,Tr(A \cdot ((A \cdot A) \circ (A \cdot A) \circ (A \cdot A))) \\
+\; & 2\,Tr((A \cdot A) \cdot (A \circ A \circ A \circ A \circ A)) \\
-\; & \tfrac{1}{2}\,Tr(diag(A \cdot A \cdot A) \circ diag(A \cdot A \cdot A \cdot A)) \\
-\; & Tr(diag(A \cdot A \cdot A) \circ diag((A \circ A) \cdot (A \circ A))) \\
-\; & 4\,Tr((A \cdot A) \cdot diag(A \cdot A) \cdot (A \circ A \circ A)) \\
-\; & \tfrac{1}{2}\,Tr(A \cdot diag(A \cdot A) \cdot A \cdot (A \circ A \circ A)) \\
+\; & Tr(diag(A \cdot A \cdot A) \circ diag(A \cdot A) \circ diag(A \cdot A)) \\
-\; & 2\,Tr(((A \cdot A) \circ (A \circ A) \cdot (A \circ A)) \cdot A) \\
+\; & \tfrac{1}{2}\,Tr((A \cdot A) \cdot diag(A \cdot A) \cdot A \cdot diag(A \cdot A)) \\
+\; & \tfrac{3}{2}\,Tr(((A \cdot A \cdot A) \circ (A \cdot A)) \cdot (A \circ A)) \\
+\; & \tfrac{1}{2}\,Tr(A \cdot diag(A \cdot A \cdot A) \cdot A \cdot diag(A \cdot A)) \\
+\; & \tfrac{1}{2}\,Tr((A \cdot A \cdot A \cdot A) \cdot (A \circ A \circ A)) \\
-\; & \tfrac{1}{2}\,Tr(diag(A \cdot A \cdot A \cdot A \cdot A) \cdot (A \cdot A)) \\
+\; & \tfrac{1}{14}\,Tr(A \cdot A \cdot A \cdot A \cdot A \cdot A \cdot A)
\end{aligned}
$$

Example 7 *For completeness we include representations of $\rho(C_k)$, simple cycles, for $k = 3, 4, 5,$ and 6 in terms of matrix expressions.*

$$\rho(C_6)(A) = \frac{1}{3} Tr(diag(A \cdot A) \circ diag(A \cdot A) \circ diag(A \cdot A))$$

$$+ \frac{1}{2} Tr((A \circ A \circ A) \cdot (A \cdot A \cdot A))$$

$$- Tr(diag(A \cdot A) \circ diag((A \circ A) \cdot (A \circ A)))$$

$$+ \frac{1}{3} Tr((A \circ A \circ A) \cdot (A \circ A \circ A))$$

$$+ \frac{1}{4} Tr(diag(A \cdot A) \circ diag(A \cdot diag(A \cdot A) \cdot A))$$

$$- \frac{1}{3} Tr((A \circ A) \cdot (A \circ A) \cdot (A \circ A))$$

$$+ \frac{3}{4} Tr(((A \cdot A) \circ (A \cdot A)) \cdot (A \circ A))$$

$$- \frac{1}{4} Tr(diag(A \cdot A \cdot A) \circ diag(A \cdot A \cdot A))$$

$$- \frac{1}{2} Tr(diag(A \cdot A) \circ diag(A \cdot A \cdot A \cdot A))$$

$$+ \frac{1}{12} Tr(A \cdot A \cdot A \cdot A \cdot A \cdot A)$$

$$\rho(C_5)(A) = \frac{1}{10} Tr(A \cdot A \cdot A \cdot A \cdot A)$$

$$- \frac{1}{2} Tr(diag(A \cdot A) \circ diag(A \cdot A \cdot A))$$

$$+ \frac{1}{2} Tr((A \cdot A) \circ (A \cdot A \cdot A))$$

$$\rho(C_4)(A) = \frac{1}{8} Tr(A \cdot A \cdot A \cdot A)$$

$$- \frac{1}{4} Tr(diag(A \cdot A) \circ diag(A \cdot A))$$

$$+ \frac{1}{8} Tr((A \circ A) \cdot (A \circ A))$$

$$\rho(C_3)(A) = \frac{1}{6} Tr(A \cdot A \cdot A)$$

8 Discussion and remarks

We have presented a theory of even functionals. The major motivation to study these objects stems from the fact that many complex algorithmic problems may be reduced to evaluating such functionals.

We have shown that the even functionals of degree k form a linear space whose dimension is equal to the number of even multigraphs with k edges. This result provides an effective tool for constructing a linear basis for this space. Now, such algebraic and symbolic manipulation systems, as Maple or Mathematica, are helpful to carry out this task.

We have also demonstrated that matrix expressions span the linear space of even functionals of degree $k \leq 7$. Interestingly, for $k = 8$, the basis includes an even functional for a multigraph that corresponds to a 4-clique with doubled diagonals. An immediate implication is that for, $k \leq 7$, any even functional can be evaluated in $O(n^\omega)$, time required for matrix multiplication. For $k = 8$ this time is $O(n^4)$.

The theory of even functionals combines results in linear algebra, matrix theory, and graph theory. Examples of applications for even functionals include efficient counting graph embeddings and computing the expected value of the kth powers of a binary quadratic form. Moreover, the theory offers a uniform approach for analyzing graphs with arbitrary real weights (positive or negative). Because of the strong connections of even functionals to central algorithmic problems we expect that this theory will prove useful in further applications.

Acknowledgements We are grateful to a referee for valuable remarks and suggestions. We also thank G. Cusick for his careful proofreading of the manuscript.

References

[1] A. V. Aho and J. E. Hopcroft and J. D. Ullman, The Design and Analysis of Computer Algorithms, Addison-Wesley, 1974.

[2] D. Coppersmith and S. Winograd, Matrix multiplications via arithmetic progressions, in Proc. 19th Annual Acm Symp. on Theory of Computing, pp. 1-6, 1987.

[3] P. Hansen, Methods of nonlinear 0-1 programming, Ann. Discrete Math., 5 (1979), pp.53-70.

[4] F. Harary and E. M. Palmer, Graphical Enumeration, Academic Press (1973)

[5] S. Kirkpatrick, C. D. Gelatt Jr., and M.P. Vecchi, Optimization by Simulated Annealing, *Science*, 220, 671-680, 1983.

[6] J. van Leeuwen, Graph Algorithm, pp.526-631, in "Handbook of Theoretical Computer science", Elsevier Science Publishers, 1990.

[7] A. Schrijver, Theory of Linear and Integer Programming, John Wiley, New York, 1986.

[8] J. Spencer *Ten lectures on the probabilistic methods*, SIAM, 1987.

[9] B. L. van der Waerden, Modern algebra, Frederick Ungar Publishing Co., New York, 1950.

Exact Asymptotics of Divide-and-Conquer Recurrences

Philippe FLAJOLET[1] and Mordecai GOLIN[2]

[1] Algorithms Project, INRIA Rocquencourt, F-78153 Le Chesnay, France
[2] Department of Computer Science, HKUST, Clear Water Bay, Kowloon, Hong Kong

Abstract. The divide–and–conquer principle is a majoı paradigm of algorithms design. Corresponding cost functions satisfy recurrences that directly reflect the decomposition mechanism used in the algorithm.
This work shows that periodicity phenomena, often of a fractal nature, are ubiquitous in the performances of these algorithms. Mellin transforms and Dirichlet series are used to attain precise asymptotic estimates. The method is illustrated by a detailed average case, variance and distribution analysis of the classic top–down recursive mergesort algorithm.
The approach is applicable to a large number of divide–and–conquer recurrences, and a general theorem is obtained when the partitioning–merging toll of a divide–and–conquer algorithm is a sublinear function. As another illustration the method is also used to provide an exact analysis of an efficient maxima-finding algorithm.

Many algorithms are based on a recursive *divide–and–conquer* strategy. Accordingly, their complexity is expressed by recurrences of the usual divide–and–conquer form [10]. Typical examples are heapsort, mergesort, Karatsuba's multiprecision multiplication, discrete Fourier transforms, binomial queues, sorting networks, etc. It is relatively easy to determine general orders of growth for solutions to these recurrences as explained in standard texts, see the "master theorem" of [10, p. 62]: if for example

$$f_n = f_{\lfloor n/2 \rfloor} + f_{\lceil n/2 \rceil} + e_n \qquad (1)$$

and $e_n = O(n)$ then $f_n = O(n \log n)$ while if $e_n = O(n^{1-\epsilon})$ for some $\epsilon > 0$ then $e_n = O(n)$. However, a precise asymptotic analysis is often appreciably more delicate.

At a more detailed level, divide–and–conquer recurrences tend to have solutions that involve *periodicities*, many of which are of a *fractal* nature. It is our purpose here to discuss the analysis of such periodicity phenomena while focussing on the analysis of the standard top–down recursive mergesort algorithm. We will show for example that the average number of comparisons performed by mergesort satisfies

$$U(n) = n \lg n + n B(\lg n) + O(n^{1/2}),$$

while the variance is of the form $n C(\lg n) + O(n^{1/2})$: $B(u)$ and $C(u)$ are both periodic functions that are *fractal*–like and which are everywhere continuous but not differentiable at a dense set of points on the line.

Our approach consists in introducing for this range of problems techniques – Mellin transforms, Dirichlet series, and Perron's formula – that are borrowed from classical analytic number theory [4]. These techniques lead to *exact* analyses. For example, we find exact formulas for the functions $B(u)$ and $C(u)$ above. They are of a very wide applicability in this range of problems, a fact that we demonstrate by applying the techniques to the analysis of a maxima finding algorithm in multidimensional space.

The general character of the results attained is attested by Theorem 9. This theorem gives the precise asymptotic form of solutions to divide and conquer recurrences of the form (1), when the partitioning (or dually merging) cost is sublinear.

This paper is only an extended abstract of a full article [15].

1 Mergesort

First, we recall the schema of the Mergesort algorithm.

Algorithm MergeSort($a[1..n]$);
- MergeSort($a[1..\lfloor n/2\rfloor]$);
- MergeSort($a[\lfloor n/2\rfloor + 1..n]$);
- Merge($a[1..\lfloor n/2\rfloor]$, $a[\lfloor n/2\rfloor + 1..n]$);

Let $T(n)$ denote the worst time cost measured in the number of comparisons that are required for sorting n elements by the MergeSort procedure, and let $U(n)$ be the corresponding average cost. We have

$$T(n) = T(\lfloor \frac{n}{2}\rfloor) + T(\lceil \frac{n}{2}\rceil) + n - 1, \qquad U(n) = U(\lfloor \frac{n}{2}\rfloor) + U(\lceil \frac{n}{2}\rceil) + n - \gamma_n \quad (2)$$

for $n \geq 2$, with $T(1) = U(1) = 0$, and $\gamma_n = \frac{\lfloor\frac{n}{2}\rfloor}{\lceil\frac{n}{2}\rceil+1} + \frac{\lceil\frac{n}{2}\rceil}{\lfloor\frac{n}{2}\rfloor+1}$. This results from the cost of merging two files of size a and b which is

$$a + b - 1 \quad \text{and} \quad a + b - \frac{a}{b+1} - \frac{b}{a+1},$$

in the worst case and average cases respectively (see [19, p. 165] for a fuller description of recursive mergesort and [18, ex. 5.2.4-2] for a derivation of the average case cost of merging).

The precise behavior of $T(n)$ is essentially known. The main term is $n \lg n$ and $T(n)$ also contains a simple periodic function in $\lg n \equiv \log_2 n$. (Recall the usual notation for fractional parts, $\{u\} = u - \lfloor u\rfloor$.) The periodicities are apparent from Fig. 1 with "cusps" whenever $\lg n$ is an integer.

Theorem 1. *The worst case cost $T(n)$ satisfies*

$$T(n) = n \lg n + nA(\lg n) + 1,$$

where $A(u)$ is the periodic function

$$A(u) = 1 - \{u\} - 2^{1 - \{u\}}.$$

Proof. It is easy to check that

$$T(n) = \sum_{k=1}^{n} \lceil \lg n\rceil = n\lceil \lg n\rceil - 2^{\lceil \lg n\rceil} + 1.$$

(See [17, p. 400], where a closely related function is discussed.) The statement then follows from writing $\lceil \lg n\rceil = \lg n + 1 - \{\lg n\}$, for any n not a power of 2. □

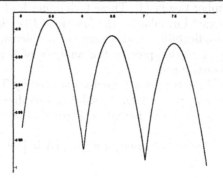

Fig. 1. The fluctuation in the worst case behavior of Mergesort, in the form of the coefficient of the linear term, $\frac{1}{n}[T(n) - n\lg n]$, as a function of $\lg n \equiv \log_2 n$ for $n = 32..256$. From Theorems 1 and 2, the periodic function involved, $A(u)$, fluctuates in $[-1, -0.91392,]$ with mean value $a_0 = -0.94269$.

Knuth analyzes a bottom up version of Mergesort in the average case (Algorithm L, see [18, 5.2.4 and 5.2.4-13]), when n is power of 2. Knuth's analysis is also valid for top down recursive Mergesort in this special case. When $n = 2^k$, the recurrence for $U(n)$ can be unfolded to derive $U(2^k) = n\lg n + \beta n + o(n)$ where $\beta = -\sum_{j \geq 0} \frac{1}{2^j+1} = -1.26449\,97803$.

For general n, no such formula is known. (See however Equation (13) at the end of Section 4 for some related analyses.) In what follows we will outline an approach that permits the analysis of mergesort type recurrences and demonstrate it by analyzing $U(n)$.

2 The Mergesort Recurrences

We approach the analysis of $T(n)$ and $U(n)$ via the computation of some associated Dirichlet series.

Let $\{w_n\}$ be a sequence of numbers. The Dirichlet generating function of w_n is defined to be

$$W(s) = \sum_{n=1}^{\infty} \frac{w_n}{n^s}.$$

The coefficients of Dirichlet series can be recovered by an inversion formula known as the Mellin–Perron formula which belongs to the galaxy of methods relating to Mellin transform analysis.

Lemma 2 (Mellin–Perron). *Assume the Dirichlet series $W(s)$ converges absolutely for $\Re(s) > 2$. Then,*

$$\frac{n}{2i\pi} \int_{3-i\infty}^{3+i\infty} W(s)n^s \frac{ds}{s(s+1)} = \sum_{k=1}^{n-1}(n-k)w_k. \tag{3}$$

The proof is based on contour integration and the residue theorem; see [4, p. 243] for a closely related result in the context of classic analytic number theory. An iterated sum

$$\sum_{k=1}^{n-1}(n-k)w_k = \sum_{k=1}^{n-1}\sum_{l=1}^{k} w_l$$

of coefficients of a Dirichlet series is thus expressible by an integral applied to the series itself.

In order to recover the mergesort quantities $T(n)$ and $U(n)$, we will determine the Dirichlet series of their second differences. Then we will use the Mellin-Perron formula to derive an integral representation of the given quantity. We conclude by evaluating the integral via the residue theorem. As in other Mellin type analyses, this provides an asymptotic expansion for the quantities of interest.

This technique, which is familiar from analytic number theory, is analogous to a common technique in combinatorial counting. In the latter case, generating functions are ordinary, their singularities play a crucial rôle, and the asymptotic behavior of the coefficients of the power series is found by utilizing the Cauchy integral formula.

Consider the general divide-and-conquer recurrence scheme

$$f_n = f_{\lfloor n/2 \rfloor} + f_{\lceil n/2 \rceil} + e_n, \tag{4}$$

for $n \geq 2$, where e_n is a known sequence and f_n is the sequence to be analyzed. An initial condition fixing the value f_1 is also assumed. In order to make the notation unambiguous we formally set $e_0 = f_0 = e_1 = 0$. The functions $T(n)$ and $U(n)$ both satisfy this scheme: for $T(n)$, $e_n = n - 1$ and for $U(n)$, $e_n = n - \gamma_n$. Take the backward differences $\nabla f_n = f_n - f_{n-1}$ and $\nabla e_n = e_n - e_{n-1}$ and then the double differences (forward of backward) $\Delta\nabla f_n = \nabla f_{n+1} - \nabla f_n$ and $\Delta\nabla e_n = \nabla e_{n+1} - \nabla e_n$. Working through the details we find

$$\begin{cases} \Delta\nabla f_{2m} = \Delta\nabla f_m + \Delta\nabla e_{2m} \\ \Delta\nabla f_{2m+1} = \Delta\nabla e_{2m+1}, \end{cases} \tag{5}$$

for $m \geq 1$, with $\Delta\nabla f_1 = f_2 - 2f_1 = e_2 = \Delta\nabla e_1$.

Define the Dirichlet generating function corresponding to $w_n = \Delta\nabla f_n$,

$$W(s) = \sum_{n=1}^{\infty} \frac{\Delta\nabla f_n}{n^s}. \tag{6}$$

Then, from (5), multiplying w_n by n^{-s}, summing over n, and solving for $W(s)$, we attain the explicit form

$$W(s) = \frac{1}{1 - 2^s}\left(\Delta\nabla f_1 + \sum_{n=2}^{\infty} \frac{\Delta\nabla e_n}{n^s}\right). \tag{7}$$

Since $\sum_{k=1}^{n-1}(n-k)\Delta\nabla f_k = f_n - nf_1$ the Mellin-Perron formula yields a direct integral representation of f_n:

Lemma 3. *Consider the recurrence*

$$f_n = f_{\lfloor n/2 \rfloor} + f_{\lceil n/2 \rceil} + e_n,$$

for $n \geq 2$, with f_1 given and $e_n = O(n)$. The solution satisfies

$$f_n = nf_1 + \frac{n}{2i\pi}\int_{3-i\infty}^{3+i\infty} \frac{\Xi(s)n^s}{1-2^{-s}}\frac{ds}{s(s+1)},$$

where $\Xi(s) = \sum_{n=1}^{\infty}\frac{\Delta\nabla e_n}{n^s}$.

(The growth condition on e_n ensures existence of associated Dirichlet series when $\Re(s) > 2$, in accordance with the conditions of Lemma 1.)

3 Worst Case of Mergesort

As an application of Lemma 3 we quickly sketch how it can be used to derive an alternate expression involving a Fourier series for the value $T(n)$, the *worst case* number of comparisons performed by mergesort.

Theorem 4. *The worst case cost $T(n)$ satisfies*

$$T(n) = n \lg n + n A(\lg n) + 1$$

where $A(u)$ is a periodic function with mean value $a_0 = \frac{1}{2} - \frac{1}{\log 2} = -0.94269\,50408$, and $A(u)$ has the explicit Fourier expansion, $A(u) = \sum_{k \in \mathbb{Z}} a_k e^{2ik\pi u}$, where, for $k \in \mathbb{Z} \setminus \{0\}$,

$$a_k = \frac{1}{\log 2} \frac{1}{\chi_k(\chi_k + 1)} \quad \text{with} \quad \chi_k = \frac{2ik\pi}{\log 2}.$$

The extreme values of $A(u)$ are

$$-\frac{1 + \log \log 2}{\log 2} = -0.91392, \text{and} \; -1.$$

Proof. We apply Lemma 3 with $f_n = T(n)$. For this case we have $e_n = n - 1$ and $f_1 = 0$ so $\Delta \nabla e_1 = e_2 = 1$ and $\Delta \nabla e_n = 0$ for all $n \geq 2$. Thus $\Xi(s) = 1$ and

$$\frac{f_n}{n} = \frac{1}{2i\pi} \int_{3-i\infty}^{3+i\infty} \frac{n^s}{1 - 2^{-s}} \frac{ds}{s(s+1)}. \tag{8}$$

We can evaluate this integral using residue computations. Fix $\alpha < -1$. Let $R > 0$ and Γ be the counterclockwise contour around $\Gamma_1 \cup \Gamma_2 \cup \Gamma_3 \cup \Gamma_4$ where

$$\Gamma_1 = \{3 + iy : |y| \leq R\}, \qquad \Gamma_2 = \{x + iR : \alpha \leq x \leq 3\}, \tag{9}$$
$$\Gamma_3 = \{\alpha + iy : |y| \leq R\}, \qquad \Gamma_4 = \{x - iR : \alpha \leq x \leq 3\}.$$

(We further assume that R is of the form $(2j+1)\pi/\log 2$ for integer j, so that the contour passes halfway between poles of the integrand.) Set $I(s) = \frac{n^s}{1-2^{-s}} \frac{1}{s(s+1)}$ to be the kernel of the integral in (8). Letting $R \uparrow \infty$ we find that $\frac{1}{2i\pi} \int_{\Gamma_1} I(s) \, ds$ becomes the integral in (8), $|\int_{\Gamma_2} I(s) ds|$ and $|\int_{\Gamma_4} I(s) ds|$ are both $O\left(1/R^2\right)$ and

$$\left| \int_{\Gamma_3} I(s) ds \right| \to \left| \int_{\alpha+i\infty}^{\alpha-i\infty} I(s) ds \right| \leq 4n^\alpha.$$

The residue theorem therefore yields that f_n/n equals $O(n^\alpha)$ plus the sum of the residues of $I(s)$ inside Γ.

We can actually do better. Since $I(s)$ is analytic for *all* s with $\Re(s) < -1$ we may let α go to $-\infty$ getting progressively smaller and smaller error terms. This shows that f_n/n is *exactly* equal to the sum of the residues of $I(s)$ inside Γ. The singularities of $I(s)$ are

1. A double pole at $s = 0$ with residue $\lg n + \frac{1}{2} - \frac{1}{\log 2}$.
2. A simple pole at $s = -1$ with residue $\frac{1}{n}$.
3. Simple poles at $s = 2ki\pi/\log 2$, $k \in \mathbb{Z} \setminus \{0\}$ with residues $a_k e^{2ik\pi \lg n}$.

Thus, as promised, we have shown that $T(n) = n \lg n + n A(\lg n) + 1$. $\square$

142

We note that a computation of the Fourier series of $A(u)$ directly from Theorem 1 is also feasible and in fact yields the Fourier series derived in the last theorem (providing a convenient check on the validity of the theorem). However, the calculations performed above are needed in the analysis of the average case behavior in the next section.

4 Average Case of Mergesort

We now proceed with the main purpose of this paper, the analysis of the *average* number of comparisons performed by mergesort, $U(n)$.

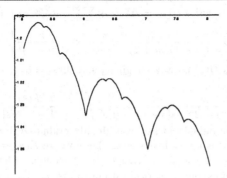

Fig. 2. The fluctuation in the average case behavior of Mergesort, graphing the coefficient of the linear term, $\frac{1}{n}[U(n) - n \lg n]$, using a logarithmic scale for $n = 32..256$. From Theorem 3, the periodic function involved, $B(u)$, fluctuates in $[-1.26449, -1.24075]$ with mean value $b_0 = -1.24815$.

Theorem 5. *(i). Let $\epsilon > 0$. The average case cost $U(n)$ of Mergesort satisfies*
$$U(n) = n \lg n + n B(\lg n) + O(n^\epsilon),$$
where $B(u)$ is periodic with period 1 and everywhere continuous but non-differentiable at every point $u = \{\lg n\}$. Furthermore, B has an explicit Fourier expansion.

(ii). The mean value $b_0 = -1.24815\,20420\,99653\,88489\ldots$ of $B(u)$ is
$$\frac{1}{2} - \frac{1}{\log 2} - \frac{1}{\log 2} \sum_{m=1}^{\infty} \frac{2}{(m+1)(m+2)} \log\left(\frac{2m+1}{2m}\right).$$

(iii). $B(u) = \sum_{k \in \mathbb{Z}} b_k e^{2ik\pi u}$ where b_0 is as above and the other Fourier coefficients of $B(u)$ are, for $k \in \mathbb{Z} \setminus \{0\}$,
$$b_k = \frac{1}{\log 2} \frac{1 + \Psi(\chi_k)}{\chi_k(\chi_k + 1)} \qquad \text{where } \chi_k = \frac{2ik\pi}{\log 2},$$
and
$$\Psi(s) = \sum_{m=1}^{\infty} \frac{2}{(m+1)(m+2)} \left[\frac{-1}{(2m)^s} + \frac{1}{(2m+1)^s}\right].$$

This Fourier series is uniformly convergent to $B(u)$.

(iv). The extreme values of $B(u)$ are

$$\beta = -1.26449\,97803\ldots \quad and \quad -1.24075\,0572 \pm 10^{-9}.$$

Proof. The proof follows the paradigm laid down by Theorem 5. We first use Lemma 3 to derive an integral form for $f_n = U(n)$ and then use residue analysis to evaluate the integral.

For $f_n = U(n)$ we are given $f_1 = 0$ and $\Delta\nabla e_1 = e_2 = 1$. We are also given that for all $m > 0$

$$\begin{cases} e_{2m} &= 2m - 2 + \frac{2}{m+1} \\ e_{2m+1} &= 2m - 1 + \frac{2}{m+2}, \end{cases} \tag{10}$$

and thus

$$-\Delta\nabla e_{2m} = \frac{2}{(m+1)(m+2)} = \Delta\nabla e_{2m+1}.$$

Summing over all m we may write $\Xi(s) = \Delta\nabla e_1 + \sum_{n=2}^{\infty} \frac{\Delta\nabla e_n}{n^s} = 1 + \Psi(s)$ where

$$\Psi(s) = \sum_{m=1}^{\infty} \frac{2}{(m+1)(m+2)} \left[\frac{-1}{(2m)^s} + \frac{1}{(2m+1)^s} \right]$$

converges absolutely and is $O(1)$ on any imaginary line $\Re(s) = \alpha \geq -1 + \epsilon$. Lemma 3 therefore tells us that

$$\frac{f_n}{n} = \frac{1}{2i\pi} \int_{3-i\infty}^{3+i\infty} \frac{n^s}{1 - 2^{-s}} \frac{ds}{s(s+1)} + \frac{1}{2i\pi} \int_{3-i\infty}^{3+i\infty} \frac{n^s \Psi(s)}{1 - 2^{-s}} \frac{ds}{s(s+1)}. \tag{11}$$

The first integral on the right-hand side was already evaluated during the proof of Theorem 4 and shown to be equal to $\lg n + A(\lg n) + 1$ where $A(u) = \sum_k a_k 2^{ik\pi u}$.

The second integral can be evaluated using similar techniques (details omitted).

Differentiability properties and numerical estimates are discussed below. □

Non Differentiability. There is an interesting decomposition of the periodic part of the average case behavior $B(u)$ in terms of the periodic part of the worst case $A(u)$. Define first

$$A^*(u) = A(u) - a_0, \quad B^*(u) = B(u) - b_0,$$

both functions having mean value 0. By exchanging summations, we find

$$B^*(u) - A^*(u) = \sum_{m=1}^{\infty} \psi_m A^*(u - \lg m), \tag{12}$$

where the ψ_m are the coefficients of the Dirichlet series $\Psi(s) = \sum_{m\geq 2} \frac{\psi_m}{m^s}$:

$$-\psi_{2m} = \frac{2}{(m+1)(m+2)} = \psi_{2m+1}.$$

This unusual decomposition (12) explains the behavior of $U(n)$ in Fig. 2. First, $A(u)$ and $A^*(u)$ have a cusp at $u = 0$, where the derivative has a finite jump. The function $B^*(u)$ is $A^*(u)$ to which is added a sum of pseudo–harmonics $A^*(u - \lg m)$ with decreasing amplitudes ψ_m. The harmonics corresponding to $m = 2, 4, 8$ are the same as those of $A^*(m)$ up to scaling, and their presence explains the cusp of $B^*(u)$ at $u = 0$ which is visible on the graph of Fig. 2. We also have two less pronounced cusps at $\{\lg 3\} = 0.58$ and at $\{\lg 5\} = 0.32$ induced by the harmonics corresponding to $m = 3$ and $m = 5$. More generally, this decomposition allows us to prove the following property: *The function $B(u)$ is non differentiable (cusp–like) at any point of the form $u = \lg(p/2^r)$.* Stated differently, $B(\lg v)$ has a cusp at any dyadic rational $v = p/2^r$.

Numerical Computations. These have been carried out with the help of the Maple system. The computation of the *mean value* b_0 to great accuracy can be achieved simply by appealing to a general purpose series acceleration method discussed by Vardi in his entertaining book [21]. We have $\Psi'(0) = \sum_{m=1}^{\infty} \theta(1/m)$, for some function $\theta(y)$ analytic at the origin. Such sums can be transformed into fast converging sums involving the Riemann zeta function, $\zeta(s) = \sum_{n \geq 1} n^{-s}$. In this way, we evaluate $\Psi'(0)$ to 50 digits in a matter of one minute of computation time.

Extreme values. Regarding the computation of *extreme values* of $B(u)$ accurately, the approach via the Fourier series does not seem to be practicable, since the Fourier coefficients only decrease as $O(k^{-2})$. Consider instead the sequence $U(a2^k)$ for some fixed integer a. By unwinding the recurrence, we find

$$U(a2^k) = ak2^k + 2^k U(a) - a2^k \sum_{j=0}^{k-1} \frac{1}{a2^j + 1}.$$

Rewriting $U(a2^k)$ in terms of $n = a2^k$, and taking care of the error terms yields for these particular values of n,

$$U(n) = n \lg n + \beta(a)n + o(n) \quad \text{where} \quad \beta(a) = \frac{U(a)}{a} - \lg a - \sum_{j=0}^{\infty} \frac{1}{a2^j + 1}. \quad (13)$$

This formula is a *real* formula that generalizes the one given by Knuth for the average case, when $n = 2^k$. Comparing with Theorem 3, we find that

$$\beta(a) = B(\lg a).$$

The computation of $\beta(a)$ for all values a in an integer interval like $[2^{15} .. 2^{16}]$ (again in a matter of minutes) then furnishes the values of B with the required accuracy.

From these estimates, Mergesort has been found to have an average case complexity about
$$n \lg n - (1.25 \pm 0.01)n + o(n).$$
This is not far from the information theoretic lower bound,
$$\lg n! = n \lg n - n \lg e + o(n) = n \lg n - 1.44n + o(n).$$

5   Variance of Mergesort

The cost of Mergesort is the sum of the costs of the individual merges, which are independent random variables with a known distribution. Merging two files of size m and n costs $m + n - S$, where the random variable S has distribution [18, p. 620]

$$\Pr\{S \geq s\} = \frac{\binom{m+n-s}{m} + \binom{m+n-s}{n}}{\binom{m+n}{n}}. \quad (14)$$

Then, the variance $V(n)$ of Mergesort applied to random data of size n is a solution to the another divide–and–conquer recurrence. Applying Lemma 3 we find:

Theorem 6. *The variance of the MergeSort algorithm applied to data of size n satisfies*
$$V(n) = n \cdot C(\log_2 n) + o(n),$$

where $C(u)$ is a continuous periodic function with period 1 and mean value

$$c_0 = \frac{1}{\log 2} \sum_{m=1}^{\infty} \frac{2m(5m^2 + 10m + 1)}{(m+1)(m+2)^2(m+3)^2} \log \frac{2m+1}{2m}$$

which evaluates to $c_0 \approx 0.34549\,95688$.

Like the function $B(u)$ that describes the fluctuation of the average cost the function $C(u)$ is continuous but non-differentiable with cusps at the logarithms of dyadic rationals, a dense set of points. Numerically, its range of fluctuation is found to lie in the interval $[0.30, 0.36]$.

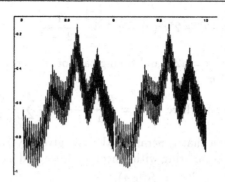

Fig. 3. The clearly fractal fluctuation in the best case behavior of Mergesort, graphing the coefficient of the linear term $\frac{1}{n}[Y(n) - \frac{1}{2}n \lg n]$ using a logarithmic scale for $n = 256 .. 1024$.

6 Best Case of Mergesort

The best case of a merge occurs each time all elements in the larger file dominate the largest element of the smaller file. Thus, the quantity $Y(n)$ representing the smallest number of comparisons—the *best case*—of mergesort satisfies the divide and conquer recurrence:

$$Y(n) = Y(\lfloor \tfrac{n}{2} \rfloor) + Y(\lceil \tfrac{n}{2} \rceil) + \lfloor \tfrac{n}{2} \rfloor. \tag{15}$$

Let $\nu(n)$ denote the sum of the digits of n represented in binary, for instance $\nu(13) = \nu([1101]_2) = 3$. Then by comparing recurrences, we find that

$$Y(n) = \sum_{m \leq n} \nu(m). \tag{16}$$

Equation (16) has been already noticed by several authors (see, e.g., [3]). The function $Y(n)$ has been studied by Delange [11] using elementary real analysis. It can also be subjected to the methods of this paper (see [16] for a discussion of exact summatory formulæ), and one gets:

Theorem 7. *The best case cost* $Y(n)$ *satisfies*

$$Y(n) = \frac{1}{2} n \lg n + n D(\lg n),$$

where $D(u)$ *has Fourier coefficients* $d_0 = \lg \sqrt{\pi} - \frac{1}{2 \log 2} - \frac{1}{4}$,

$$d_k = -\frac{1}{\log 2} \frac{\zeta(\chi_k)}{\chi_k(\chi_k + 1)}, \quad k \neq 0, \ \chi_k = \frac{2ik\pi}{\log 2}.$$

Delange already proved that the periodic function $D(n)$ is continuous but nowhere differentiable.

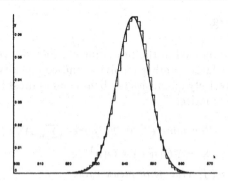

Fig. 4. The histogram of the exact probability distribution of the comparison cost of Mergesort for $n = 100$ and its fitting Gausian curve.

7 Distribution of Mergesort

The distribution of the cost of mergesort is computable exactly, as well as numerically using the resources of computer algebra systems. The probability generating function of the single merge intervening in the sorting of n elements is found from (14). The probability generating function of the cost of merge sort then satisfies the divide–and–conquer product recurrence,

$$\Xi_n(z) = \xi_n(z) \cdot \Xi_{\lfloor n/2 \rfloor} \cdot \Xi_{\lceil n/2 \rceil}.$$

Unwinding the recurrence yields

$$\Xi_n(z) = \prod_{m \leq n} \xi_m(z),$$

the summation being taken over the multiset of all m that appear as subfile sizes in mergesorting n elements. For instance:

$$\Xi_{23} = \xi_{23} \cdot \xi_{12} \cdot \xi_{11} \cdot \xi_6^3 \cdot \xi_5 \cdot \xi_3^7 \cdot \xi_2^8.$$

For $n = 100$, the mergesort comparison costs lie in the interval $[316..573]$ with mean value 541.84. The standard deviation is 5.78, and Figure 4 shows the histogram of the distribution computed from these formulæ. The numerical data strongly suggest convergence to a Gaussian law with matching mean and variance that is also plotted on the same diagram.

Actually, using Lyapounov's extensions of the central limit theorem [8, p. 371] to sums of independent—but not necessarily identically distributed—random variables, we find:

Theorem 8. *The cost X_n of Mergesort applied to random data of size n converges in distribution to a normal variable,*

$$\Pr\left\{\frac{X_n - U(n)}{\sqrt{V(n)}} \leq \mu\right\} \to \frac{1}{\sqrt{2\pi}} \int_{-\infty}^{\mu} e^{-t^2/2}\, dt.$$

8 Maxima-Finding

The tools that we have developed in the preceding sections are very general and can be used to analyze a large number of divide-and-conquer type algorithms. The following theorem precisely quantifies the behaviour of most linearly growing recurrences occurring in practice.

Theorem 9. *Assume that for some $\epsilon > 0$ the series $(\sum_n \Delta \nabla e_n \cdot n^\epsilon)$ converges absolutely. Then*

$$f_n = nQ(\lg n) + O(n^{1-\epsilon}),$$

where $Q(u)$ is periodic and fractal, with mean value

$$q_0 = \frac{1}{\log 2} \sum_{n=2}^{\infty} e_n \log\left(\frac{n^2}{n^2 - 1}\right).$$

As an application of this theorem, we briefly sketch how to analyze the expected running time of a maxima-finding algorithm. The interesting feature of this analysis is that the running time will grow as $nQ(\lg n)$ where $Q(u)$ is a continuous, fractal like function which is non differentiable. Thus here, unlike in the running time of mergesort, the periodic term appears in the highest order asymptotics.

A d-dimensional point $P = (p_{(1)}, \ldots p_{(d)})$ *dominates* a point $Q = (q_{(1)}, \ldots q_{(d)})$ if $P \neq Q$ and $p_{(j)} \geq q_{(j)}$. A maximal element of a finite set $\{P_1, \ldots, P_n\}$ is a point in the set which is not dominated by any other point in the set. Maximal elements are of interest for a variety of reasons and much work has therefore been done on devising algorithms to identify them, e.g. [6] [7]. One of these algorithms is the divide–and–conquer one discussed by [12]: given a set of n points, split the set into two subsets of size $\lfloor n/2 \rfloor$, $\lceil n/2 \rceil$, recursively find the maxima in each of the subsets and then determine the maxima of the entire set by pairwise comparisons of all the maxima in the first subset to all of the maxima in the second.

It is known [9] that if n points are drawn independently identically distributed (IID) from the uniform distribution over a hypercube or, in fact, from any component-independent distribution then the expected number of the points that will be maximal is

$$\mu_n^{(d)} = \sum_{k_{d-1}=1}^{n} \frac{1}{k_{d-1}} \sum_{k_{d-2}=1}^{k_{d-1}} \frac{1}{k_{d-1}} \cdots \sum_{k_2=1}^{k_3} \frac{1}{k_2} \sum_{k_1=1}^{k_2} \frac{1}{k_1}.$$

For example $\mu_n^{(2)} = H_n = \sum_{k \leq n} 1/k$ is the harmonic number. The average running time of the divide-and-conquer maxima finding algorithm when run on inputs chosen IID from a d-dimensional hypercube (or component independent distribution) therefore satisfies $f_1 = 1$ with

$$f_n = f_{\lfloor n/2 \rfloor} + f_{\lceil n/2 \rceil} + 2u_{\lfloor n/2 \rfloor}^{(d)} \cdot \mu_{\lceil n/2 \rceil}^{(d)} \tag{17}$$

for $n \geq 2$.

It is not difficult to see that $\mu_n^{(d)} = O(\log^{d-1} n)$ so we find automatically (as is done in [12]) that $f_n = O(n)$. Observe that this seemingly naïve algorithm has linear expected case, and thus beats a simple sweepline algorithm already in dimension $d = 2$, the latter requiring sorting. Using the techniques introduced earlier in this paper, we can go much further and derive the *exact* asymptotics of f_n.

Theorem 10. *Let $\epsilon > 0$. The expected running time of the maxima finding algorithm when run on inputs chosen IID from a d-dimensional hypercube satisfies*

$$f_n = nQ^{(d)}(\lg n) + O(n^\epsilon)$$

where $Q^{(d)}(u)$ is a continuous, periodic, non-differentiable function with mean value

$$q_0^{(d)} = 2 \sum_{m=1}^{\infty} (\mu_m^{(d)})^2 \log(1 - (2m)^{-2})^{-1} + 2 \sum_{m=1}^{\infty} \mu_m^{(d)} \mu_{m+1}^{(d)} \log(1 - (2m+1)^{-2})^{-1},$$

and $\mu_n^{(d)} = [u^{d-1}] \exp(\frac{u}{1} H_n^{(1)} + \frac{u^2}{2} H_n^{(2)} + \cdots)$.

With computer algebra, the mean values can be calculated to high accuracy using relations between the Dirichlet series of generalized harmonic numbers and derivatives of the Riemann Zeta function [5], as well as the techniques discussed previously. For example, we have

$$q_0^{(2)} = 6.32527\ldots, \quad q_0^{(3)} = 21.64397\ldots, \quad q_0^{(4)} = 76.77212\ldots.$$

9 Conclusion

Divide–and–conquer recurrences are naturally associated with Dirichlet series that satisfy various sorts of functional relations (see also the case of 'automatic' sequences in [1, 2, 13]) so that they can be proven to have continuations in the whole of the complex plane. As we have seen here and as in [16], the Mellin–Perron formula then allows us to recover asymptotic properties of the original sequence with great accuracy, revealing periodicities and fractal behaviour for these recurrences.

ACKNOWLEDGEMENTS: The work of both authors was supported in part by the Basic Research Action of the E.C. under contract No. 7141 (Project ALCOM II). the second author was also supported by NSF CCR-8918152.

Authors' electronic mail addresses: Philippe.Flajolet@inria.fr and golin@cs.ust.hk.

References

1. ALLOUCHE, J.-P. Automates finis en théorie des nombres. *Expositiones Mathematicae 5* (1987), 239–266.
2. ALLOUCHE, J.-P., AND COHEN, H. Dirichlet series and curious infinite products. *Bulletin of the London Mathematical Society 17* (1985), 531–538.
3. ALLOUCHE, J.-P., AND SHALLIT, J. The ring of k-regular sequences. *Theoretical Computer Science 98* (1992), 163–197.
4. APOSTOL, T. M. *Introduction to Analytic Number Theory.* Springer-Verlag, 1976.
5. APOSTOL, T. M., AND VU, T. H. Dirichlet series related to the Riemann zeta function. *Journal of Number Theory 19* (1984), 85–102.
6. BENTLEY, J. L., CLARKSON, K. L., AND LEVINE, D. B. Fast linear expected-time algorithms for computing maxima and convex hulls. In *First Symposium on Discrete Algorithms (SODA)* (1990).
7. BENTLEY, J. L., KUNG, H., SCHKOLNICK, M., AND THOMPSON, C. On the average number of maxima in a set of vectors and applications. *Journal of the Association for Computing Machinery 25*, 4 (October 1978), 536–543.
8. BILLINGSLEY, P. *Probability and Measure*, 2nd ed. John Wiley & Sons, 1986.
9. BUCHTA, C. On the average number of maxima in a set of vectors. *Information Processing Letters 33* (Nov. 1989), 63–65.
10. CORMEN, T. H., LEISERSON, C. E., AND RIVEST, R. L. *Introduction to Algorithms.* MIT Press, New York, 1990.
11. DELANGE, H. Sur la fonction sommatoire de la fonction somme des chiffres. *L'enseignement Mathématique XXI*, 1 (1975), 31–47.
12. DEVROYE, L. Moment inequalities for random variables in computational geometry. *Computing 30* (1983), 111–119.
13. DUMAS, P. *Récurrences Mahlériennes, suites automatiques, et études asymptotiques.* Doctorat de mathématiques, Université de Bordeaux I, 1992. In preparation.
14. DUMONT, J.-M., AND THOMAS, A. Systèmes de numération et fonctions fractales relatifs aux substitutions. *Theoretical Computer Science 65* (1989), 153–169.
15. FLAJOLET, P., AND GOLIN, M. Mellin transforms and asymptotics: The mergesort recurrence. Preprint submitted to *Acta Informatica.*, Jan. 1993.
16. FLAJOLET, P., GRABNER, P., KIRSCHENHOFER, P., PRODINGER, H., AND TICHY, R. Mellin transforms and asymptotics: Digital sums. Research Report 1498, Institut National de Recherche en Informatique et en Automatique, Sept. 1991. 23 pages. To appear in *Theoretical Computer Science*, December 1993.
17. KNUTH, D. E. *The Art of Computer Programming*, vol. 1: Fundamental Algorithms. Addison-Wesley, 1968. Second edition, 1973.
18. KNUTH, D. E. *The Art of Computer Programming*, vol. 3: Sorting and Searching. Addison-Wesley, 1973.
19. SEDGEWICK, R. *Algorithms*, second ed. Addison–Wesley, Reading, Mass., 1988.
20. STOLARSKY, K. B. Power and exponential sums of digital sums related to binomial coefficients. *SIAM Journal on Applied Mathematics 32*, 4 (1977), 717–730.
21. VARDI, I. *Computational Recreations in Mathematica.* Addison Wesley, 1991.

Optimal Bounds for the Change-Making Problem

Dexter Kozen[1] and Shmuel Zaks[2]

[1] Computer Science Department, Cornell University
Ithaca, New York 14853, USA
kozen@cs.cornell.edu

[2] Computer Science Department, Technion
Haifa, Israel
zaks@cs.technion.ac.il

Abstract. The *change-making problem* is the problem of representing a given value with the fewest coins possible. We investigate the problem of determining whether the greedy algorithm produces an optimal representation of all amounts for a given set of coin denominations $1 = c_1 < c_2 < \cdots < c_m$. Chang and Gill [1] show that if the greedy algorithm is not always optimal, then there exists a counterexample x in the range

$$c_3 \leq x < \frac{c_m(c_m c_{m-1} + c_m - 3c_{m-1})}{c_m - c_{m-1}}.$$

To test for the existence of such a counterexample, Chang and Gill propose computing and comparing the greedy and optimal representations of all x in this range. In this paper we show that if a counterexample exists, then the smallest one lies in the range

$$c_3 + 1 < x < c_m + c_{m-1},$$

and these bounds are tight. Moreover, we give a simple test for the existence of a counterexample that does not require the calculation of optimal representations. In addition, we give a complete characterization of three-coin systems and an efficient algorithm for all systems with a fixed number of coins. Finally, we show that a related problem is *coNP-complete*.

1 Introduction

The *change-making problem* is the problem of representing a given value with the fewest coins possible from a given set of coin denominations. Unboundedly many coins of each denomination are available.

Formally, given a finite system $c_1 < c_2 < \cdots < c_m = n$ of positive integers (the *coins*) and a positive integer x, we wish to determine nonnegative integer coefficients x_i, $1 \leq i \leq m$, so as to minimize

$$\sum_{i=1}^{m} x_i \tag{1}$$

subject to

$$x = \sum_{i=1}^{m} x_i c_i . \tag{2}$$

The sequence of coefficients $x_1, \ldots, x_m$ is called a *representation* of x. The quantity (1) that we wish to minimize is called the *size* of the representation. A representation is *optimal* if it is of minimum size. If $x_i > 0$, then we say that the coin c_i is *used* in the representation. We restrict our attention here to systems containing a penny (*i.e.*, $c_1 = 1$), so that every x has a representation.

The change-making problem is a form of knapsack problem. Martello and Toth devote an entire chapter to it in their text on knapsack problems [4], and a good summary of the state of knowledge can be found there. In general, the problem is *NP*-complete when the coin values are large and represented in binary [3]; however, it can be solved in time polynomial in the number of coins and the value of the largest coin. In this regard, a number of algorithms have been investigated, the simplest of which is the *greedy algorithm*, which repeatedly takes the largest coin less than or equal to the amount remaining. Equivalently and more efficiently: for each of $i = m, m - 1, \ldots, 2, 1$ in that order, let x_i be the integer quotient $\lfloor x/c_i \rfloor$, and set $x := x \bmod c_i$. This produces the greedy representation in time $O(m \log n)$. Note that this is the unique representation $x_1, \ldots, x_m$ such that for all i, $1 < i \le m$,

$$\sum_{j=1}^{i-1} x_j c_j < c_i . \tag{3}$$

The greedy representation is not necessarily optimal. For example, given the system 1,3,4, the greedy algorithm produces the representation 2,0,1 for the number 6; this representation is of size 3, whereas the optimal representation is 0,2,0 of size 2. For some systems, however, the greedy algorithm always produces an optimal representation for any given value; as a matter of practical interest, we note that this is the case for the system 1,5,10,25,50,100 of American coins and the system 1,5,10,50,100,500 of Israeli coins. The question thus arises: how does one determine whether the greedy algorithm is always optimal for a given system?

Definition 1. Given a system of coins, let $M(x)$ denote the minimum size over all representations of the number x in that system, and let $G(x)$ denote the size of the greedy representation of x. Following [4], we call the system *canonical* if $G(x) = M(x)$ for all x. If a system is not canonical, then a value x for which $M(x) < G(x)$ is called a *counterexample* for the system.

Example 1. For any nonnegative integer k, the system $1, 2, 4, \ldots, 2^k$ is canonical. The *Fibonacci system* $1, 2, 3, 5, 8, \ldots, F_k$ is canonical, where F_k is the kth Fibonacci number. The system $1, k, k + 1$ for $k > 2$ is not canonical: the counterexample $2k$ has optimal representation $0, 2, 0$ of size 2, whereas the greedy representation is $k - 1, 0, 1$ of size k.

Chang and Gill [1] show that it suffices to search for a counterexample among the members of a certain finite set; if no counterexample is found in this set, then no counterexample exists and the system is canonical. The size of the set to be checked is polynomial in the largest coin value. Specifically,

Theorem 2 Chang and Gill [1]. *Let* $1 = c_1 < \cdots < c_m$ *be any system of coins. If* $M(x) = G(x)$ *for all* x *in the range*

$$c_3 \leq x < \frac{c_m(c_m c_{m-1} + c_m - 3c_{m-1})}{c_m - c_{m-1}} , \tag{4}$$

then the system is canonical.

In order to check for a counterexample in this set, Chang and Gill propose computing the greedy and optimal representations of each element of the set and comparing their sizes. Martello and Toth comment [4, p. 142]:

> The proof [of Theorem 2] is quite involved and will not be reported here. Furthermore, application of the theorem is very onerous, calling for optimality testing of a usually high number of greedy solutions.

Example 2. Consider the system $1, 2, 4, 8, 10, 16$ (this example is taken from [4, Example 5.2, p. 143]). In order to test whether this system is canonical according to the algorithm of Chang and Gill, we must compute and compare the sizes of the greedy and optimal representations of all 385 values x in the range (4).

In Section 2 below we give two results that simplify the process of testing for the existence of a couterexample:

- We give tight bounds for Theorem 2. Specifically, we show that if a counterexample exists at all, then the smallest one lies in the range

$$c_3 + 1 < x < c_m + c_{m-1} ,$$

and these bounds are tight for an infinity of systems. Note that the upper bound is linear in the largest coin value, whereas (4) is cubic. Thus in order to check the system of Example 2, we need only check a set of size 20.
- We show that it is not necessary to compute optimal representations for the numbers in the given range as suggested by Chang and Gill. There is a much simpler test involving only the sizes of the greedy representations, which are trivial to compute in time $O(n)$ using the recurrence

$$G(x) = 1 + G(x - c) \tag{5}$$

where c is the largest coin value less than or equal to x.

These results give rise to an $O(mn)$ algorithm for testing whether a given system of coins is canonical.

In Section 3 we give a characterization of systems of three coins and a simple $O(\log n)$ test for determining when such a system in canonical.

In Section 4 we extend these results to systems with any fixed number of coins.

In Section 5 we consider the related problem of determining whether the greedy representation of a given number x in a given system is optimal. We show that this problem is *coNP*-complete. It remains open whether there is an algorithm that is polynomial in m and $\log n$ for testing whether a given system is canonical.

2   Optimal Bounds

In this section we derive optimal bounds for the change-making problem. Many of our arguments hinge on the following lemma, which describes the behavior of the function M.

Lemma 3. *Let* $1 = c_1 < \cdots < c_m$ *be any system of coins. For all* x *and coins* $c_i \leq x$,

$$M(x) \leq M(x - c_i) + 1 , \qquad (6)$$

with equality holding if and only if there exists an optimal representation of x *that uses the coin* c_i.

Proof. Certainly (6) holds, since any optimal representation of $x - c_i$ gives a representation of x of size $M(x - c_i) + 1$ by adding one to the coefficient of c_i. If in addition $M(x) = M(x - c_i) + 1$, then the representation of x so obtained is optimal and uses the coin c_i. Conversely, given an optimal representation of x that uses c_i, we can obtain a representation of $x - c_i$ of size $M(x) - 1$ by subtracting one from the coefficient of c_i, and (6) implies that this representation is optimal.

Theorem 4. *Let* $1 = c_1 < \cdots < c_m$ *be any system of coins. If there exists an* x *such that* $M(x) < G(x)$, *then the smallest such* x *lies in the range*

$$c_3 + 1 < x < c_m + c_{m-1} . \qquad (7)$$

Moreover, these bounds are tight.

Proof. Certainly $M(x) = G(x)$ for all $x < c_3$, since c_1, c_2 is a canonical system. In addition, neither c_3 nor $c_3 + 1$ provides a counterexample, since in both cases the greedy representation is optimal. This establishes the lower bound.

To prove the upper bound, let $x \geq c_m + c_{m-1}$ and assume inductively that $G(y) = M(y)$ for all $y < x$. Let c_i be any coin used in some optimal representation of x. If $i = m$, then

$$
\begin{aligned}
G(x) &= G(x - c_m) + 1 && \text{by definition of } G \\
&= M(x - c_m) + 1 && \text{by induction hypothesis} \\
&= M(x) && \text{by Lemma 3.}
\end{aligned}
$$

If $i < m$, then

$$
\begin{aligned}
G(x) &= G(x - c_m) + 1 && \text{by definition of } G \\
&= M(x - c_m) + 1 && \text{by induction hypothesis} \\
&\leq M(x - c_m - c_i) + 2 && \text{by Lemma 3} \\
&\leq G(x - c_m - c_i) + 2 && \text{by definition of } M \\
&= G(x - c_i) + 1 && \text{by definition of } G \\
&= M(x - c_i) + 1 && \text{by induction hypothesis} \\
&= M(x) && \text{by Lemma 3} \\
&\leq G(x) && \text{by definition of } M.
\end{aligned}
$$

Thus in either case $G(x) = M(x)$.

For $k > 2$, the systems $1, k, 2k - 2$ give an infinity of systems for which the smallest counterexample is $c_3 + 2$, and the systems $1, k, k + 1$ give an infinity of systems for which the smallest counterexample is $c_m + c_{m-1} - 1$. Thus the bounds (7) are tight.

Our simplified algorithm is based on the observation that we can avoid computing optimal representations by checking for the existence of *witnesses* instead of counterexamples:

Definition 5. A *witness* is an x for which

$$
G(x) > G(x - c) + 1
$$

for some coin $c < x$.

Lemma 6. *(i) Every witness is a counterexample.*
(ii) If a counterexample exists, then the smallest one is a witness.

Proof. (i) Suppose x is a witness; thus

$$
G(x - c) + 1 < G(x)
$$

for some coin c. Then

$$
\begin{aligned}
M(x) &\leq M(x - c) + 1 && \text{by Lemma 3} \\
&\leq G(x - c) + 1 && \text{by definition of } M \\
&< G(x).
\end{aligned}
$$

(ii) If x is a counterexample but not a witness, and if c is any coin used in an optimal representation of x, then $x - c$ is also a counterexample:

$$
\begin{aligned}
M(x - c) \;=\;& M(x) - 1 && \text{by Lemma 3} \\
<\;& G(x) - 1 \\
\leq\;& G(x - c)\;.
\end{aligned}
$$

Therefore the smallest counterexample must be a witness.

The converse of Lemma 6(i) is false: in the system $1, 4, 5$, the value 12 is a counterexample but not a witness. In this example, the coin 4 is used in the optimal representation $0, 3, 0$ of 12, therefore $8 = 12 - 4$ is also a counterexample. It is in fact the smallest counterexample, thus is also a witness.

Theorem 7. *For a given system to be canonical, it is necessary and sufficient that there exist no witness in the range (7).*

Proof. Immediate from Theorem 4 and Lemma 6.

Theorem 7 implies that to test whether a given system is canonical, it suffices to check whether

$$
G(x) \;\leq\; G(x - c) + 1
$$

for all x in the range (7) and coins $c < x$; we need not calculate any optimal representations. All necessary values of $G(x)$ can be computed in time $O(n)$ using the recurrence (5); thus the entire algorithm takes time $O(mn)$.

3 A Characterization of Three-Coin Systems

In this section we characterize completely all systems of three coins. This characterization gives a trivial $O(\log n)$ test for determining whether the system is canonical.

Let $1 < c < d$ and let q and r be the quotient and remainder, respectively, obtained from the integer division of d by c. Thus q and r are the unique integers such that

$$
d \;=\; qc + r\;, \tag{8}
$$
$$
0 \;\leq\; r \;<\; c\;. \tag{9}
$$

Theorem 8. *The system $1, c, d$ is not canonical if and only if $0 < r < c - q$.*

Proof. If $0 < r < c - q$, then the value $d + c - 1$ is a counterexample: the greedy representation $c - 1, 0, 1$ is of size $c > r + q$, whereas the representation $r - 1, q + 1, 0$ is of size $r + q$.

Conversely, suppose $1 < c < d$ is not canonical, and let x be the smallest counterexample. The greedy representation of x must be of the form $e, 0, 1$ with

$0 < e < c$, since $d+1 < x < c+d$ by Theorem 4. Moreover, there is a unique optimal representation of x of the form $0, k, 0$ with $k > 0$, since if either the coefficient of 1 or d were nonzero, then by Lemma 3 we could subtract one and get a smaller counterexample. Since $x = d + e = kc$, we have

$$\begin{aligned}
d &= kc - e = (k-1)c + (c-e) \\
0 &< (d+c) - x = (d+c) - (d+e) = c - e < c,
\end{aligned}$$

and since q and r are unique numbers satisfying (8) and (9), we must have $q = k - 1$ and $r = c - e$. Since x is a counterexample, we have that $k < 1 + e$, thus $q = k - 1 < e$ and $0 < c - e = r$, from which the desired inequalities $0 < r < c - q$ follow.

4 Large Coins

The characterization of the previous section yields a simple $O(\log n)$ algorithm for determining whether a given system of three coins is canonical. In this section we give an algorithm whose time complexity is $O(\log n)$ for any fixed number of coins m. The complexity of the algorithm is $O(m^2 2^{m-1} \log n)$.

Recall that $\lfloor x/c \rfloor$ and $x \bmod c$ denote the integer quotient and remainder, respectively, obtained when dividing x by c. Thus

$$\begin{aligned}
x &= \lfloor x/c \rfloor c + x \bmod c \\
0 &\le x \bmod c < c
\end{aligned}$$

and $\lfloor x/c \rfloor$ and $x \bmod c$ are the unique numbers for which these two statements hold.

Let $\gamma_i(x)$ denote the greedy representation of x in the system $1 = c_1 < \cdots < c_i$. Thus

$$\begin{aligned}
\gamma_1(x) &= x \\
\gamma_i(x) &= \langle \gamma_{i-1}(x \bmod c_i), \lfloor x/c_i \rfloor \rangle, \quad i > 1
\end{aligned}$$

where $\langle \alpha, z \rangle$ denotes the sequence obtained by appending the integer z to the end of the sequence α.

Define the equivalence relation $\equiv_k^i$ on integers $x \ge k$ by:

$$x \equiv_k^i y \quad \leftrightarrow \quad \gamma_i(x) - \gamma_i(x-k) = \gamma_i(y) - \gamma_i(y-k),$$

where $-$ applied to the sequences $\gamma_i(\ )$ denotes componentwise difference. Note that $x \equiv_{c_m}^m y$ for every $x, y \ge c_m$. It follows from the observation

$$G(x) - G(x-c) = \sum_{i=1}^m (\gamma_m(x) - \gamma_m(x-c))_i$$

that if $x \equiv_c^m y$ for a coin c, then x satisfies the property

$$G(x) \le G(x-c) + 1 \tag{10}$$

if and only if y does. Thus in order to find a witness, it suffices to check (10) for one representative x from each $\equiv_c^m$-class for each coin c. We will show below (Theorem 10) that for each coin c there are at most 2^{m-1} $\equiv_c^m$-classes, and representatives can be constructed efficiently.

The formal statement and proof of Theorem 10 do not adequately reflect the intuition behind them, so we preface the formalities with the following intuitive argument.

Fix k and consider the difference $\gamma_m(x) - \gamma_m(x - k)$ of the greedy representations of x and $x - k$ as x increases. The last coefficient of this difference, namely $\lfloor x/c_m \rfloor - \lfloor (x-k)/c_m \rfloor$, alternates periodically between two values r and $r + 1$ (unless k is a multiple of c_m, in which case there is only one value). We can thus think of x as being in one of two states, depending on the value of this coefficient. The state changes whenever either x or $x - k$ skips over a multiple of c_m. In between the times when this state changes, the next-to-last coefficient of $\gamma_m(x) - \gamma_m(x - k)$ alternates periodically between two states in a similar fashion, but with period c_{m-1}; and so on. Thus each coin value c_i, $i \geq 2$, accounts for two states (there is only one state for $c_1 = 1$), giving 2^{m-1} global states.

Formally, let x, y, and c be integers, c positive. Define

$$t_c(x, y) \;=\; \lfloor (x \bmod c + y \bmod c)/c \rfloor \;\in\; \{0, 1\} \, .$$

The function t_c formalizes the "state" for coin c as described above. The following lemma establishes some basic observations regarding this function.

Lemma 9. *The function t_c satisfies the following properties:*

$$
\begin{aligned}
(x + y) \bmod c &= x \bmod c + y \bmod c - c\, t_c(x, y) \\
\lfloor (x + y)/c \rfloor &= \lfloor x/c \rfloor + \lfloor y/c \rfloor + t_c(x, y) \\
t_c(x, y) = 0 &\leftrightarrow x \bmod c \leq (x + y) \bmod c \\
t_c(x, y) = 1 &\rightarrow t_c(y + x, -x) = 0 \, .
\end{aligned}
$$

These properties follow immediately from the definitions.
Now define the sets

$$
\begin{aligned}
A_k^1 &= \{k\} \\
A_k^i &= \{\lfloor k/c_i \rfloor c_i + u \mid u \in A_{k \bmod c_i}^{i-1}\} \cup \{k + v \mid v \in A_{(-k) \bmod c_i}^{i-1}\} , \quad i > 1 \, .
\end{aligned}
$$

Theorem 10. *The set A_k^i contains the minimum element of each $\equiv_k^i$-class. In other words, for all $x \geq k$ there exists a $y \in A_k^i$ such that*

$$k \;\leq\; y \;\leq\; x \tag{11}$$

$$y \;\equiv_k^i\; x \, . \tag{12}$$

Proof. The proof is by induction on i. The basis is immediate from the definition of A_k^1 and γ_1.

For $i > 1$, let $t_i = t_{c_i}$. We break the proof into two cases, depending on the value of $t_i(k, x - k)$. First suppose $t_i(k, x - k) = 0$. Then $k \bmod c_i \leq x \bmod c_i$. By the induction hypothesis, there exists a $u \in A_{k \bmod c_i}^{i-1}$ such that

$$k \bmod c_i \ \leq \ u \ \leq \ x \bmod c_i \tag{13}$$

$$u \ \equiv_{k \bmod c_i}^{i-1} \ x \bmod c_i \ . \tag{14}$$

Let

$$y \ = \ \lfloor k/c_i \rfloor c_i + u \ \in \ A_k^i \ .$$

By (13) and the fact that $k \leq x$, we have

$$
\begin{aligned}
k \ &= \ \lfloor k/c_i \rfloor c_i + k \bmod c_i \\
&\leq \ \lfloor k/c_i \rfloor c_i + u \ \ (= y) \\
&\leq \ \lfloor x/c_i \rfloor c_i + x \bmod c_i \\
&= \ x \ .
\end{aligned}
$$

This establishes (11). By Lemma 9, we also have that $t_i(k, y - k) = 0$, since

$$k \bmod c_i \ \leq \ u \ = \ y \bmod c_i \ .$$

By (14) and the fact that $t_i(k, x - k) = t_i(k, y - k) = 0$, we have

$$
\begin{aligned}
&\gamma_{i-1}(x \bmod c_i) - \gamma_{i-1}((x - k) \bmod c_i) \\
= \ &\gamma_{i-1}(x \bmod c_i) - \gamma_{i-1}(x \bmod c_i - k \bmod c_i) \\
= \ &\gamma_{i-1}(u) - \gamma_{i-1}(u - k \bmod c_i) \\
= \ &\gamma_{i-1}(y \bmod c_i) - \gamma_{i-1}(y \bmod c_i - k \bmod c_i) \\
= \ &\gamma_{i-1}(y \bmod c_i) - \gamma_{i-1}((y - k) \bmod c_i) \ .
\end{aligned}
\tag{15}
$$

Now suppose $t_i(k, x - k) = 1$. By Lemma 9, $t_i(x, -k) = 0$, thus $(-k) \bmod c_i \leq (x - k) \bmod c_i$. By the induction hypothesis, there exists a $v \in A_{(-k) \bmod c_i}^{i-1}$ such that

$$(-k) \bmod c_i \ \leq \ v \ \leq \ (x - k) \bmod c_i \tag{16}$$

$$v \ \equiv_{(-k) \bmod c_i}^{i-1} \ (x - k) \bmod c_i \ . \tag{17}$$

Let

$$y \ = \ k + v \ \in \ A_k^i \ .$$

By (16) and the fact that $k \leq x$, we have

$$
\begin{aligned}
k &\leq k + v \quad (= y) \\
&\leq k + (x - k) \bmod c_i \\
&\leq x \, .
\end{aligned}
$$

This establishes (11). We also have that $t_i(k, y - k) = 1$:

$$
\begin{aligned}
k \bmod c_i + (y - k) \bmod c_i &= k \bmod c_i + v \bmod c_i \\
&\geq k \bmod c_i + (-k) \bmod c_i \\
&= c_i \, ,
\end{aligned}
$$

since $k \bmod c_i \neq 0$ by Lemma 9. By (17) and the fact that $t_i(k, x - k) = t_i(k, y - k) = 1$, we have

$$
\begin{aligned}
&\gamma_{i-1}(x \bmod c_i) - \gamma_{i-1}((x - k) \bmod c_i) \\
&= -(\gamma_{i-1}((x - k) \bmod c_i) - \gamma_{i-1}(x \bmod c_i)) \\
&= -(\gamma_{i-1}(v) - \gamma_{i-1}(v - (-k) \bmod c_i)) \\
&= \gamma_{i-1}(y \bmod c_i) - \gamma_{i-1}((y - k) \bmod c_i) \, .
\end{aligned}
\tag{18}
$$

Now for either value of $t_i(k, x - k)$, we have $t_i(k, x - k) = t_i(k, y - k)$. Then by Lemma 9,

$$
\begin{aligned}
\lfloor x/c_i \rfloor - \lfloor (x - k)/c_i \rfloor &= \lfloor k/c_i \rfloor + t_i(k, x - k) \\
&= \lfloor k/c_i \rfloor + t_i(k, y - k) \\
&= \lfloor y/c_i \rfloor - \lfloor (y - k)/c_i \rfloor \, .
\end{aligned}
\tag{19}
$$

Thus in either case, using (15), (18), and (19), we have

$$
\begin{aligned}
&\gamma_i(x) - \gamma_i(x - k) \\
&= \langle \gamma_{i-1}(x \bmod c_i), \lfloor x/c_i \rfloor \rangle - \langle \gamma_{i-1}((x - k) \bmod c_i), \lfloor (x - k)/c_i \rfloor \rangle \\
&= \langle \gamma_{i-1}(x \bmod c_i) - \gamma_{i-1}((x - k) \bmod c_i), \lfloor x/c_i \rfloor - \lfloor (x - k)/c_i \rfloor \rangle \\
&= \langle \gamma_{i-1}(y \bmod c_i) - \gamma_{i-1}((y - k) \bmod c_i), \lfloor y/c_i \rfloor - \lfloor (y - k)/c_i \rfloor \rangle \\
&= \langle \gamma_{i-1}(y \bmod c_i), \lfloor y/c_i \rfloor \rangle - \langle \gamma_{i-1}((y - k) \bmod c_i), \lfloor (y - k)/c_i \rfloor \rangle \\
&= \gamma_i(y) - \gamma_i(y - k) \, ,
\end{aligned}
$$

which establishes (12).

It is easily shown by induction that the set A_k^m contains at most 2^{m-1} elements, and each element of A_k^m is less than

$$
\sum_{i=1}^{m} c_i \leq k + mn \, .
$$

Moreover, the straightforward method of constructing A_k^m according to its inductive definition takes time $O(m 2^{m-1} \log n)$. Thus to check whether the system is canonical, we need only determine (10) for all coins c and $x \in A_c^m$. There are $m 2^{m-1}$ such x to check, and each check takes time $O(m \log n)$.

5 An *NP*-Completeness Result

Lueker [3] shows that when the coin values are large and represented in binary, the problem of finding an optimal representation of a given x is *NP*-hard. Here we show:

Theorem 11. *It is coNP-complete to determine, given a system of coins and a number x represented in binary, whether the greedy representation of x is optimal.*

Proof. The problem is clearly in *coNP*: we can compute the greedy representation of x in linear time, then find a better one if it exists by guessing.

To show *coNP*-hardness, we will encode the problem of *exact cover by three-sets*: given a set X and a family $\mathcal{E}$ of three-element subsets of X, can X be represented as a disjoint union of elements of $\mathcal{E}$? This problem is known to be *NP*-complete (see [2]).

Assume without loss of generality that $X = \{1, 2, \ldots, 3n\}$. Let $p = n + 1$. Consider the system of coins

$$c_A = 1 + \sum_{i \in A} p^i , \quad A \in \mathcal{E}$$

$$c_X = \sum_{i=1}^{3n} p^i$$

and a penny. Let

$$x = n + c_X .$$

The greedy algorithm gives a representation of x of size $n + 1$ consisting of c_X and n pennies. This is optimal unless there is an exact cover, in which case a better representation is obtained by taking c_A for A in the cover.

The problem of Theorem 11 differs from the problem of determining whether a given system of coins is canonical in that in the former, we are asking whether greedy is optimal for a given x, whereas in the latter, we are asking whether greedy is optimal for all x. We know by Theorems 7 and 11 that both problems are in *coNP*, and the former is complete. An interesting question that we have not succeeded in answering is whether the latter is complete, or whether there is an algorithm whose time complexity is polynomial in m and $\log n$.

Acknowledgements

We thank Gudmund Frandsen, Kim Skak Larsen, Peter Bro Miltersen, Mike Paterson, Erik Meineche Schmidt, and Sven Skyum for valuable suggestions.

Dexter Kozen was supported by the Danish Research Academy, the National Science Foundation, the John Simon Guggenheim Foundation, and the

U.S. Army Research Office through the ACSyAM branch of the Mathematical Sciences Institute of Cornell University under contract DAAL03-91-C-0027. Shmuel Zaks was supported by the ESPRIT II Basic Research Actions Program of the EC under contract No. 3075 (Project ALCOM).

References

1. S. K. Chang and A. Gill. Algorithmic solution of the change-making problem. *J. Assoc. Comput. Mach.*, 17(1):113–122, January 1970.
2. M. R. Garey and D. S. Johnson. *Computers and Intractability: a Guide to the Theory of NP-Completeness*. W. H. Freeman, 1979.
3. G. S. Lueker. Two *NP*-complete problems in nonnegative integer programming. Technical Report 178, Computer Science Laboratory, Princeton University, 1975.
4. S. Martello and P. Toth. *Knapsack Problems*. John Wiley and Sons, 1990.

The Complexity of N-body Simulation*

John H. Reif and Stephen R. Tate

Computer Science Department, Duke University, Durham, NC 27706

Abstract. The *n-body simulation problem* is stated as follows: Given initial positions and velocities of n particles that have pair-wise force interactions, simulate the movement of these particles so as to determine the positions of the particles at a future time.

In this paper, we give the first known n-body simulation algorithms with rigorous proofs of bounded error. The *reachability problem* is to determine if a specific particle will reach a certain region at some specified target time. In the case we require $poly(n)$ bits of accuracy and where the target time is $poly(n)$, our complexity bounds are surprisingly PSPACE.

We also have matching lower bounds for n-body simulation problem (in comparison all previous lower bound proofs required either artificial external forces or obstacles). We show that the reachability problem for a set of interacting particles in three dimensions is PSPACE-hard.

1 Introduction

The *n-body problem*, is the problem of simulating a set of n charged particles in three dimensions, where the particles interact under the induced electrostatic or gravitational potential field. Generally the simulations are done by time stepping. See [1, 6, 7, 8, 10] for details. These simulations are one of the heaviest users of super computer cycles (for example at the CRAY-YMP, at RTP, a study by MCNC recent showed that over 30 percent of all compute time was used for n-body simulation by molecular chemists), and are widely used by astronomers, chemists, and biochemists, and to a lesser degree physicists (note: certain physicists prefer other methods based on energy minimization).

The equations of motion for each body are in fact given by Newton's second law of motion applied to each body; this results in a system of n ordinary differential equations. These equations can be approximately solved from initial positions and velocities by stepping in time, using the equations of motion and numerical integration to determine approximations to incremental movements and velocity changes of the bodies due to the forces exerted by the other particles. The force vector associated with these potentials is calculated by taking the partial derivatives of the potential in each direction. This is the basis for most computer simulations of n-body systems. The main computational task

* This research was supported by DARPA/ISTO Contracts N00014-88-K-0458, DARPA N00014-91-J-1985, N00014-91-C-0114, NASA subcontract 550-63 of prime contract NAS5-30428, US-Israel Binational NSF Grant 88-00282/2, and NSF Grant NSF-IRI-91-00681.

is the calculation of the potential field due to all other bodies, at the current location of each body. The naive algorithm for this potential computation requires quadratic work; however, the potential can be approximated to p bits of accuracy in $O(np^2 \log p)$ time using the multipole method of Greengard and Rokhlin [4, 5], or by the recent modified multipole method of Reif and Tate [11] that has time complexity $O(np^2)$.

1.1 The n-body Reachability Problem

In this paper, we consider the complexity of simulating a set of n charged particles in three dimensions, where the particles interact under the induced electrostatic potential field.

Throughout this paper, n denotes the number of bodies. We require that the number of bits of the input description is polynomial in n. A k-bit rational is a ratio of two k-bit integers. Consider a set of n points satisfying a fixed electrostatic potential law. We assume that we are given an initial $poly(n)$-bit rational position and velocity as well as a destination position, given by a ball, where the ball's position and radius is n-bit rational. The *n-body reachability problem* concerns the trajectories of these bodies; in particular we wish to determine if a given particle reaches a position within the given destination ball within a given time bound, where the ball's position and radius are $poly(n)$-bit rationals.

We give the first known n-body simulation algorithms with rigorous proofs of bounded error. In the case we require $poly(n)$ bits of accuracy and where the target time is $poly(n)$, our complexity bounds are surprisingly PSPACE. Our algorithm requires the additional assumption that there is at least an exponentially small separation between all pairs of particles at all times during the simulation.

Molecular Computers, Molecular Castles, and Our Lower Bounds for the n-body Simulation Problem. We also give the first lower bounds for these simulations, and show that the *reachability problem* for n-body simulations is PSPACE-hard. We prove this lower bound for the most practical version of this problem: inverse-square law forces in three dimensions.

The hardness proof is via a reduction to machine simulation, and is novel due to the nature of the problem under study. In particular, non-trivial problems to overcome include the fact that machines work in discrete time steps and particle simulations are continuous, and the fact that realistic machines perform transitions based on local state whereas the particle simulations have the property that all particles induce a force on all other particles (so all effects are global). To our knowledge, this is the first hardness proof to overcome these problems.

The techniques involved in our lower bound proof include constructions in which the time-averaged potential of a small set of particles is almost identical to the potential due to solid, uniformly-charged plates which persists for exponential time. A side effect of this construction is a proof that given any set of polygons fixed at rational positions in 3D with f faces and sides (say a castle), we can construct in 3D a stable configuration (for exponential time) of a set of $O(f)$ charged particles (which move according to Newton's and Coulomb's laws) which generate a time averaged very close approximation (with exponentially small error) to this set of polygons. The physical implications of such a construction is interesting in its own right.

Our PSPACE results for n-body reachability indicate that there is no polynomial time computable closed form representation of the equations for the motion or trajectory of n-body systems with above a certain constant number of particles n, unless P = PSPACE.

Theoretically, if the particles are placed with initial position and velocity of sufficient precision (polynomial bit precision will suffice), these PSPACE-hard n-body systems can be viewed as general computing machines executing in the real time at molecular sizes. However, we strongly caution that these n-body systems may not be practical, since the above assumptions of the classical laws of potential theory may not always hold in the physical world for small displacements. Our constructions can be scaled to as small a dimension as possible, and quantum mechanical effects minimized by using large mass, large charge particles at a small spatial scale — in this case, as the masses and charges of the particles increase, the motion of the particles approaches the motion of an ideal Newtonian system. While this is fine in theory, actual subatomic particles with fixed charge and mass do indeed exhibit quantum mechanical effects that deviate from the simple Newtonian force laws that we use in this paper.

Related Work in Hardness Results. Here we note that all previous hardness results for n-body simulation depend on sharp discontinuities in space (i.e., obstacles) or force in order for the proof to work. In contrast, our lower bound applies when the forces are realistic inverse-square law forces, and there are no obstacles present to produce discontinuities.

A related result has been obtained by Moore [9] who investigated unpredictability in dynamical systems. He showed that motion of a body with as few as three degrees of freedom in the presence of a fixed, immobile potential field can simulate universal computation. His construction requires an artificially defined potential field that does not satisfy the usual potential laws for far distances (in fact, potentials from even moderately distant interactions are assumed by Moore to be 0, contradicting the classical potential laws). In contrast, in our work on the complexity of the n-body reachability problem, we assume the classical potential laws are in effect and no other external potential fields are assumed; therefore our lower bound requires a sophisticated construction to overcome the errors which accrue from each pair of bodies potential force. This causes a difficult to overcome accumulation of error due to the fact that all n bodies exert non-zero potential on each other, depending only on their distance.

In addition, it follows from the "Billiard Ball Computer" construction of Fredkin and Toffoli [3] that the reachability problem for particles under elastic collisions (but no potential fields) is PSPACE-hard. However, this construction relies on the presence of fixed non-movable obstacles and thus is not applicable to n-body simulations. A related lower bound result was obtained by Reif and Yoshida for the optical ray tracing problem [12]. Again, the use of fixed polygonal obstacles is vital to their proof.

2 Simulation Algorithm and Error Bounds

In this section, we present an algorithm for simulating a system of n charged particles under the induced electrostatic forces for some time T. The algorithm is the basic Euler method for evaluating a system of differential equations, and we prove error bounds that are specific to the problem of n-body simulation. In order for the error bounds to be reasonable, we require that no pair of particles is ever closer than unit distance apart (we explain below how we can handle situations where the particles can get exponentially close).

The input to the simulation consists of the following information:

Notation	Description
$m_1, m_2, \cdots, m_n$	Particle masses
$q_1, q_2, \cdots, q_n$	Particle charges
$\mathbf{x}_1, \mathbf{x}_2, \cdots, \mathbf{x}_n$	Initial positions
$\mathbf{v}_1, \mathbf{v}_2, \cdots, \mathbf{v}_n$	Initial velocities
C	Constant for Coulombic forces
T	The amount of time to simulate
ϵ	The maximum allowable (position) error

The simulation time T must be bounded by n^c for some constant c, all masses must be at least n^{-c}, and the *lengths of the binary representations* of all the remaining variables must be bounded by n^c. The constant C is such that the force magnitude between two particles i and j is

$$C \frac{q_i q_j}{\|\mathbf{x}_i - \mathbf{x}_j\|^2} \ .$$

From this equation, it is clear that if the distance between all pairs of particles is lower bounded by $\Delta = 2^{-n^c}$ for some constant c, we can rescale space and particle charges by a factor of $1/\Delta$ so that there is at least unit distance between all pairs of particles and the motion of all the particles is exactly the same as in the original system (but on the larger spatial scale). Specifically, we can create a new system with $\mathbf{x}_{\text{new},i} = (1/\Delta)\mathbf{x}_i$, $\mathbf{v}_{\text{new},i} = (1/\Delta)\mathbf{v}_i$, $q_{\text{new},i} = (1/\Delta)q_i$, and $C_{\text{new}} = (1/\Delta)C$. The induced force is thus a factor of $(1/\Delta)$ of the force in the original system, which is exactly what we need for the increased spatial scale. This system induces the exactly same particle motion as the original system, and yet it meets all of the assumptions in our problem statement — the length of each scaled variable grows at most by an additive polynomial factor, and the minimum distance between pairs of particles is always at least 1.

The simulation takes place by taking discrete time steps of length τ, which defines approximate trajectories for each particle. The continuation of the discrete approximation position and velocity functions are $\tilde{\mathbf{x}}_k(t)$ and $\tilde{\mathbf{v}}_k(t)$, and we denote the discrete "samples" as $\tilde{\mathbf{x}}_{k,j} = \tilde{\mathbf{x}}(j\tau)$ and $\tilde{\mathbf{v}}_{k,j} = \tilde{\mathbf{v}}(j\tau)$. The simulation can then be described by

$$\tilde{\mathbf{v}}_{k,j} = \begin{cases} \tilde{\mathbf{v}}_{k,j-1} + \frac{\tilde{\mathbf{f}}_{k,j-1}}{m_k}\tau & \text{if } j > 0 \\ \mathbf{v}_k & \text{if } j = 0 \end{cases}$$

and

$$\tilde{\mathbf{x}}_{k,j} = \begin{cases} \tilde{\mathbf{x}}_{k,j-1} + \tilde{\mathbf{v}}_{k,j-1}\tau + \frac{\tilde{\mathbf{f}}_{k,j-1}}{2m_k}\tau^2 & \text{if } j > 0 \\ \mathbf{x}_k & \text{if } j = 0 \end{cases}.$$

In order to bound the error of these approximations, it is useful to note that the velocity and position are easily upper bounded. It is a simple calculation to calculate the total energy of the system to be simulated. Since all pairs of particles are required to stay unit distance apart at all times, we can lower bound the potential energy at any time, and thus upper bound the kinetic energy of the system, since the total energy is conserved. In particular, let B_x denote the bound on the position norm, and B_v denote the bound on the velocity norm. It can easily be seen that B_x and B_v are both bounded by e^{n^c}, for some constant c. This ensures us that the velocity and position of all particles can always be represented by a polynomial number of bits, and since the only changing state in the simulation is the velocity and position of each particle, the described simulation is clearly in PSPACE.

We use $\epsilon_{x,k,j}$, $\epsilon_{v,k,j}$, and $\epsilon_{f,k,j}$ to denote the error in the approximation $\tilde{\mathbf{x}}_{k,j}$, $\tilde{\mathbf{v}}_{k,j}$, and $\tilde{\mathbf{f}}_{k,j}$, respectively. For example, $\epsilon_{x,k,j} = \mathbf{x}_k(j\tau) - \tilde{\mathbf{x}}_{k,j}$. The error values are vectors, and we will denote the norm of the vectors by replacing the ϵ with a δ. For example, $\delta_{x,k,j} = \|\epsilon_{x,k,j}\|$.

Our main result for this problem is the following:

Theorem 1. *If $T \leq n^b$ for some constant b, there exists a constant c such that if the above simulation is run with timestep $\tau = e^{-n^c}$, then the final approximate position of each particle after simulating T/τ time steps is within ϵ of it's correct position. Furthermore, all of the values required in the simulation can be represented by n^c bits, so the simulation is in PSPACE.*

Proof. (Sketch) Now we sketch the proof of this theorem. More careful analysis of the constants involved will be included in the full paper. We first notice that at step j the exact velocity of particle k can be written as

$$\mathbf{v}_k(j\tau) = \mathbf{v}_k((j-1)\tau) + \frac{\mathbf{f}_k((j-1)\tau)}{m_k}\tau + \frac{1}{2}\mathbf{x}_k^{(3)}(\xi_1)\tau^2 \;,$$

where $\mathbf{x}_k^{(3)}(t)$ is the third derivative of the position function, and $(j-1)\tau \leq \xi_1 \leq j\tau$. The updated approximation velocity is therefore

$$\begin{aligned}
\tilde{\mathbf{v}}_{k,j} &= \mathbf{v}_k((j-1)\tau) + \epsilon_{v,k,j-1} + \frac{\mathbf{f}_k((j-1)\tau) + \epsilon_{f,k,j-1}}{m_k}\tau \\
&= \mathbf{v}_k((j-1)\tau) + \frac{\mathbf{f}_k((j-1)\tau)}{m_k}\tau + \epsilon_{v,k,j-1} + \frac{\epsilon_{f,k,j-1}}{m_k}\tau \\
&= \mathbf{v}_k(j\tau) - \frac{1}{2}\mathbf{x}_k^{(3)}(\xi_1)\tau^2 + \epsilon_{v,k,j-1} + \frac{\epsilon_{f,k,j-1}}{m_k}\tau \;.
\end{aligned}$$

The error is therefore updated as

$$\epsilon_{v,k,j} = \epsilon_{v,k,j-1} + \frac{\epsilon_{f,k,j-1}}{m_k}\tau - \frac{1}{2}\mathbf{x}_k^{(3)}(\xi_1)\tau^2 \ .$$

Similarly, the position error is updated as

$$\epsilon_{x,k,j} = \epsilon_{x,k,j-1} + \epsilon_{v,k,j-1}\tau + \frac{1}{2}\frac{\epsilon_{f,k,j-1}}{m_k}\tau^2 - \frac{1}{6}\mathbf{x}_k^{(3)}(\xi_2)\tau^3 \ .$$

By writing

$$\mathbf{f}_k(t) = \sum_{\substack{i=1 \\ i \neq j}}^{n} \frac{\mathbf{x}_k - \mathbf{x}_i}{\|\mathbf{x}_k - \mathbf{x}_i\|^3}Cq_iq_k \ , \tag{1}$$

some algebraic manipulation yields

$$\delta_{f,k,j} \leq 4n\delta_{x,k,j} + \delta_c \ ,$$

where δ_c is the error introduced in the computation of (1), say by multipole approximation. We can, of course, choose δ_c to be such that $\delta_{f,k,j} \leq 8n\delta_{x,k,j}$. Furthermore, by noticing that $\mathbf{x}_k''(t) = \mathbf{f}_k(t)/m_k$, we can bound

$$\|\mathbf{x}_k^{(3)}(t)\| \leq \sum_{\substack{i=1 \\ i \neq j}}^{n} \|\mathbf{x}_k'(t)\| + \frac{3}{2}\|\mathbf{x}_k(t)\|\|\mathbf{x}_k'(t) - \mathbf{x}_i'(t)\|$$

$$< nB_v + \frac{3}{2}nB_xB_v = nB_v(1 + \frac{3}{2}B_x) \ .$$

Set $B_3 = nB_v(1 + \frac{3}{2}B_x)$, so B_3 is a bound on the third derivative of the position. Putting all of this together we can bound the error propagation by the following formula.

$$\begin{pmatrix} \delta_{x,k,j} \\ \delta_{v,k,j} \end{pmatrix} \leq \begin{pmatrix} 1 + \frac{4n}{m_k}\tau^2 & \tau \\ \frac{8n}{m_k}\tau & 1 \end{pmatrix}\begin{pmatrix} \delta_{x,k,j-1} \\ \delta_{v,k,j-1} \end{pmatrix} + \begin{pmatrix} \frac{1}{6}B_3\tau^3 \\ \frac{1}{2}B_3\tau^2 \end{pmatrix} \ . \tag{2}$$

For any linear recurrence $\mathbf{y}_j \leq A\mathbf{y}_{j-1} + \mathbf{b}$ with $\mathbf{y}_0 = 0$, we can bound the norm of vector $\mathbf{y}_j$ by

$$\|\mathbf{y}_j\| \leq \frac{\lambda_{\max}^j - 1}{\lambda_{\max} - 1}\|\mathbf{b}\| \ , \tag{3}$$

where $\lambda_{\max}$ is the largest eigenvalue of A. By the Gerschgorin Circle Theorem (see, for example, [2, p. 489]), it is easy to bound

$$\lambda_{\max} \leq 1 + \left(\frac{4n}{m_k}\tau + \frac{8n}{m_k} + 1\right)\tau$$

for matrix equation (2). Using (3), we can bound

$$\delta_{x,k,T/\tau} \le \frac{m_k}{(4n\tau+8n+m_k)\tau} \left(1 + \frac{4n\tau+8n+m_k}{m_k}\tau\right)^{T/\tau} \frac{1}{2}B_3\tau^2$$

$$= \left(1 + \frac{4n\tau+8n+m_k}{m_k}\tau\right)^{\frac{m_k}{(4n\tau+8n+m_k)\tau}T\frac{4n\tau+8n+m_k}{m_k}} \frac{m_k B_3}{2(4n\tau+8n+m_k)}\tau$$

$$< e^{T\frac{4n\tau+8n+m_k}{m_k}} \frac{m_k B_3}{2(4n\tau+8n+m_k)}\tau$$

$$< e^{n^c}\tau ,$$

for some constant c. Therefore, setting $\tau = \epsilon e^{-n^c}$ insures that $\delta_{x,k,T/\tau} \le \epsilon$ for all k. $\qquad\qquad\square$

3 The N-body Reachability Problem is PSPACE-hard

In this section we examine the *n-body reachability problem*: given an n-body system (namely, a set of n bodies that interact according to a harmonic potential function, and with no external forces present), an initial position and velocity of each body, and some fixed ball B, does a given body eventually reach B? We always assume that the initial position and velocity of each of the bodies are vectors of rationals, and that the destination ball B has rational coordinates. We prove a lower bound for the most practical version of this problem: inverse-square law (repulsive) forces in three dimensions.

Our PSPACE-hardness proof uses a number of log-space reductions [13] between various problems, of interest themselves. In the following, let a *rectangular obstacle environment* be a finite set of immobile rectangular surfaces in three dimensional space whose face-planes are described by linear equations with $poly(n)$-bit rational coefficients. The problems we consider are the following:

1. *n-body reachability problem*, as defined above,
2. The *fixed potential field 1-body reachability problem* is the 1-body reachability problem augmented with a fixed potential field generated by a rectangular obstacle environment, where each obstacle is a surface with uniform electrostatic charge.
3. The *bouncing particle reachability problem* is a 1-body reachability problem with no potential fields, but with a rectangular obstacle environment where we assume that the body bounces on the obstacle surfaces with perfect elastic collisions. We actually consider a restricted version of this problem, called the $\sigma(n)$-*centered obstacle bouncing particle reachability problem*, where we guarantee that if the particle hits an obstacle, it hits it "near" the center of the obstacle. Specifically, if d_c is the distance from the point of impact to the center of the obstacle and d_e is the distance to the closest edge, then $\frac{d_e}{d_c} \ge \sigma(n)$.

The following class of functions will be useful in the following discussion.

169

Definition 2. We use the notation $\exp(f(n))$ to denote the function $2^{f(n)}$. By writing simply exp-poly, we mean the class of all functions bounded by an $\exp(n^c)$ function. In other words,

$$\text{exp-poly} = \bigcup_{c>0} O(2^{n^c}) \ .$$

The functions $\exp(n^c)$ have a very important property, and that is that for any two constants $1 < c_1 < c_2$ and sufficiently large n, it is true that $2^n \exp(n^{c_1}) << \exp(n^{c_2})$. In other words, $\exp(n^{c_2})$ is more than an *exponential* factor greater than $\exp(n^{c_1})$, so any $O(2^n)$ factor of $\exp(n^{c_1})$ is negligible when compared to $\exp(n^{c_2})$.

In the remaining part of this section, we give the reductions between the three previously mentioned problems. To keep the goal in mind, we quote our final result here.

Theorem 8. *The n-body reachability problem, as defined above, is PSPACE-hard.*

First, modifying the PSPACE-hardness result for the ray tracing problem of Reif, Tygar, and Yoshida [12] to the $\sigma(n)$-centered bouncing particle reachability problem is straightforward.

Theorem 3. *For any $\sigma(n) \in$ exp-poly, the $\sigma(n)$-centered bouncing particle reachability problem is PSPACE-hard.*

Proof. The proof of Reif, Tygar, and Yoshida that the raytracing problem with only reflective surfaces is PSPACE-hard [12] can be directly extended to show that the bouncing particle reachability problem is PSPACE hard. To show that the $\sigma(n)$-centered bouncing particle reachability problem uses a similar construction, but a base $\sigma(n)$ encoding is used to encode the tape contents. In particular, if the tape of the simulated reversible Turing machine has contents $(a_{n-1}, ..., a_1, a_0)$, this is represented by the distance

$$\sum_{i=0}^{n-1} a_i (\sigma(n))^{n-i} \ .$$

In this way, all configurations with $a_0 = 0$ are within distance $\sigma(n)^{n-1}$ of each other, but are distance at least $\frac{\sigma(n)^n}{2}$ away from all configurations with $a_0 = 1$. In this way, the splitter obstacles (the only mirrors that violate the $\sigma(n)$-centered constraint in [12]) can be centered in such a way that the collisions are all $\sigma(n)$ centered. □

We next give a reduction from the $\sigma(n)$-centered bouncing particle reachability problem to the fixed potential field 1-body reachability problem. Every obstacle of the bouncing particle particle problem will be replaced by a box containing a single charged plate. Ideally, a particle entering the box should be repelled by the plate in such a way that, to an observer standing outside the box, the particle seems to have bounced off the obstacle in the same way as in the bouncing particle problem. For our traveling particle, we choose a particle with unit charge and unit mass — all other parts of the construction will be scaled to these units.

To see how a particle can be repelled in such a way, consider the following special case: the point of the particle's closest approach to the plate is directly over the center of the plate (see Fig. 3). When the traveling particle is far away from the plate, the force on the particle is very small and the particle travels in approximately a straight line. In fact, as the distance is taken to infinity, the trajectory of the particle is a straight line. This line is marked on Fig. 3 as the dashed asymptote. By a simple symmetry argument, it can be shown that fixed potential field problems like this one have the following property: if a particle has trajectory $x(t)$ from time 0 to time T, then if the particle is *started* at position $x(T)$ with velocity $-x'(T)$, then the trajectory will be exactly $x(T-t)$ — it exactly reverses the original trajectory.

Let p be the position of the particle's closest approach to the charge plate, and let v_p be the velocity vector at this point. By the above property, if we start a particle at point p with velocity $-v_p$, it should exactly reverse the original trajectory. Since the potential field is symmetric about the center line, this is exactly the reflected outgoing trajectory of the original trajectory, so the entire trajectory is symmetric about this line. The immediate consequence of this argument is that the angle at which the particle is repelled from the plate is exactly the same as the angle at which the angle approaches the plate. As simple as this seems, there are two non-trivial problems that arise in this construction.

First, it is impossible to make a charged plate act exactly as an obstacle in the bouncing particle problem. In particular, if the particle's closest approach to the plate is not exactly above the center of the plate, then the reflected angle will be different from the incoming angle. We avoid this by guaranteeing that the closest approach of the particle is above a point on the plate that is *near* the center of the plate while never reaching the plate itself (recall the definition of the $\sigma(n)$-centered bouncing particle reachability problem from above). Thus we can bound the error induced in the potential field model.

Secondly, in the bouncing particle problem, when the particle is traveling between boxes it always follows a straight line, since there are no forces acting upon it. However, in the potential field problem, there is an electrostatic force at *all* points in space, including at points between the boxes.

Both of the above problems involve error induced by approximating the bouncing particle with repelling potential fields. If the path that the bouncing particle takes is defined by the function $x_b(t)$, and the path the potential field particle takes is defined by the function $x_p(t)$, then we define an error function err(t) by

$$\text{err}(t) = x_b(t) - x_p(t) \ .$$

Let $f(t)$ denote the electrostatic force acting on the particle traveling in the potential field problem. We will decompose this force into two components, intuitively the "good" force $f_g(t)$ and the "bad" force $f_b(t)$. The good force will be the force necessary to simulate the bouncing particle, and the bad force will be the part that induces errors. Clearly, whenever the particle is outside of a box there should be no force acting on it, so all of the force is bad force. Inside a box, the good force is exactly the force needed to turn the path of the particle so that it leaves the box exactly the same way as it would have in the bouncing particle problem. Any additional force is defined to be bad force. Defined in this way, *all* of the error is induced by bad force, so if we can bound $f_b(t)$, then we can bound the error of our bouncing particle simulation.

By the careful construction given below, we can ensure that at all times $\|f_b(t)\| \le \exp(-n^{c+1})$ for any constant c, so for a time $T = \exp(n^c)$ simulation the accumulated error is at most

$$\|\mathrm{err}(T)\| \le \frac{1}{2}\exp(-n^{c+1})\left(\exp(n^c)\right)^2 \le \exp(-n^c) \ ,$$

for n sufficiently large.

To bound the bad force, we use the following lemma.

Lemma 4. *Consider a point p with unit electrostatic charge, and a plate with uniform electrostatic charge Q. If d is the distance from p to the closest point on the plate, then the magnitude of the force induced on p is at most $\frac{Q}{d^2}$.*

To build a box that simulates a particle bouncing off an obstacle, we will place a uniformly charged, square plate centered at the location of the original obstacle. For a box with sides of length s, we want to set the distance of the particle's closest approach to the plate to be d. Noticing that the kinetic energy of the particle at infinity is $\frac{1}{2}$ plus the error (which is $\exp(-n^c)$), we would like for the potential energy at the point distance d above the center of the plate to be exactly $\frac{1}{2}$. We can achieve this by setting the total charge of the plate appropriately. We should note here that the charge required on the plate grows linearly in d.[2] By using obstacles that are only $\frac{s}{2}$ wide (so the distance from the plate to the edge of the box is at least $\frac{s}{4}$) and setting $d = s\exp(-n^c)$ for a c that we specify in the following proof, we can insure a small error.

Theorem 5. *The fixed potential field 1-body reachability problem is PSPACE-hard.*

Proof. The proof of this theorem is essentially an analysis of the error introduced in our simulation, which will be shown to be very small. In this construction,

---

[2] The exact equation for potential over the plate is quite messy, but the growth rate can be proved to be linear in d by considering the growth rate of Q for a uniformly charged disk. The potential due to a charged disk is a fairly simple formula that grows as $Q(\sqrt{d^2 + r^2} - d)$, where r is the radius of the disk. It is easy to see that Q grows linearly in x when solving for a fixed potential, and this must be the same as the growth rate of the charge required by a square plate (consider inscribed and circumscribed disks).

assume we want to achieve a simulation in which the bad force is always bounded by $\exp(-n^{c_1})$. We perform the above construction with $c_2 = c_1 + 1$.

To analyze the amount of "bad" force due to this construction, first consider the bad force at positions outside of any box. The bad force due to any particular box of side-length s can be bounded by $\frac{16Q}{s^2} = O(\frac{s \exp(-n^{c_2})}{s^2}) = O(\exp(-n^{c_2}))$. Therefore, the total bad force at points outside a box is $O(n \exp(-n^{c_2}))$, which is much smaller than $\exp(-n^{c_1})$ since $c_2 > c_1$.

We now bound the bad force within a box can be bounded by defining regions of the plate that induce the bad force. In particular, for a particle entering the box, we hit "near" the center of the box. Clearly, there is some subset of the plate that can be used to generate the good force: we take a subset such that the closest approach of the traveling particle is above the center of this plate. Now the trajectory due to the force induced by the subplate looks exactly like a reflection, by the previous argument. Since we hit near the center of the plate, the parts of the plate not included in our "good" region are small and at the boarder of the plate. We can easily bound the distance to the closest point on the "bad" region by $\frac{s}{8}$, and the total charge of the bad region is significantly less than Q; a very loose bound on the bad force induced is therefore $\frac{8Q}{s^2} = O(\frac{s \exp(-n^{c_2})}{s^2})$. Once again, this is much smaller than $\exp(-n^{c_1})$. □

3.1 Molecular Castles

Finally, we reduce the fixed potential field 1-body reachability problem to the n-body reachability problem by simulating surfaces by rapidly moving points. For example, consider the simple problem of simulating the effect of a potential field generated by a line segment with uniform charge distribution. To simulate this, consider a point moving very quickly back and forth between two massive particles of similar charge (see Fig. 1).

In the following discussion, we make the simplifying assumption that the outside masses are stationary; we will show how to remove the assumption later. In this idealized case, the lighter particle would bounce back and forth between the outside particles forever, repeating the same exact trajectory over and over. Let Δt denote the amount of time it takes the bouncing particle to trace out its trajectory once. In other words, if $x(t)$ and $x'(t)$ denote the position and velocity of the particle at time t, then $x(t) = x(t + i\Delta t)$ and $x'(t) = x'(t + i\Delta t)$ for all $i = 1, 2, \dots$. Now it can be seen that if the potential at a point x is averaged over one time span (0 to Δt, for example) we can see that the average potential is a good approximation of the potential of the line segment. In fact, if we restrict our attention to the potential at points that are in an area of width $\exp(-n^c)$ times the distance between the endpoints, then we see that the velocity of the bouncing particle is constant with an error term of $\exp(-n^c)$. Furthermore, the charge of the bouncing particle is chosen so that the contribution to the average potential from times when the particle is outside this range is another exponentially small, $\exp(-n^c)$. This means that at all points in our range of interest, the average potential of the bouncing particle approximates the potential of the bar with an error term of $\exp(-n^c)$.

Of course, there is additional error involved because the above discussion made the simplifying assumption that the outside masses were stationary. Of course, in the general n-body problem, no particles have fixed position, so the outside masses will move slightly. However, by making the outside masses exponentially more massive than the inside masses, they will move too little to cause any problems in our limited-time simulation. In particular, if the mass of the bouncing particle is $\exp(n^{c_1})$, then by making the outside masses have mass $\exp(n^{c_2})$ for some $c_2 > c_1$, the outside masses will move only an exponentially small amount over the polynomially bounded time of the simulation. By increasing c_2 above, we can make the amount of movement in the outside masses arbitrarily small. The only additional error introduced into the system is related to the ratio of the time-step and the inverse of the velocity of the approaching particle. This error is analyzed in the proof of the following lemma.

Lemma 6. *Let c_1 and c_2 be constants such that $1 < c_1 < c_2$. In the above construction, if the bouncing particle bounces between its endpoints with frequency $\exp(n^{c_2})$, then the trajectory of a unit velocity particle approaching the line of the bouncing particle will differ from the trajectory of the same particle approaching a uniformly charged bar by at most $\exp(-n^{c_1})$.*

Proof. In the text preceding the lemma, we showed that the average potential field of the bouncing point can be made arbitrarily close to the potential field of a uniformly charged bar, where the average is taken over a time interval of length Δt. To bound the error on the trajectory of the moving particle, we can consider the following equivalent formulation: the particle is moving toward a uniformly charged bar, but the force on the particle over time in the range $(i\Delta t, (i+1)\Delta t]$ is taken to constant with the value of the force at the beginning of the interval. Since we have assumed that the traveling particle has unit mass, the acceleration is identical to the force at all times. Next we bound the error introduced by using this approximation for a single time step.

Let $a_{err} = \max_{0 \le t \le \Delta t}(a(t) - a(0))$. Then the position error (denoted x_{err}) induced between time 0 and time Δt can be bounded using elementary equations of motion:

$$ x_{err} = \int_0^{\Delta t} \int_0^\tau (a(t) - a(0))dtd\tau \le \int_0^{\Delta t} \int_0^\tau a_{err}dtd\tau \frac{1}{2}a_{err}(\Delta t)^2. $$

If we do this repeatedly over time T, then the number of steps required is $\frac{T}{\Delta t}$, so the accumulated error is $a_{max}\Delta t T$, where a_{max} is the maximum acceleration induced on the particle by the bar over the simulation time T. This is obviously bounded since there is a finite minimum distance between the particle and the bar. By taking $\Delta t = \exp(-n^{c_2})$ we make this error negligible.

Therefore, the total error introduced by our simulation is bounded by the error of the average potential field plus the error from the discrete time stepping. Both quantities can be made $\exp(-n^{c_2})$ for arbitrarily large c_2, so by making $c_2 > c_1$ the simulation meets the desired error bound of $\exp(-n^{c_1})$. $\square$

To construct the more complex structure of a square sheet with uniform potential, we can use the above construction to make the four repelling line segments that bound the desired square, and then set another particle sweeping out the area enclosed by the line segments (see Fig. 2). If viewed from a distance, the average potential (taken over the time of an entire sweep of the square) induced by the bouncing particle is very close to that of a uniformly charged plate. If the horizontal distance between successive vertical sweeps is $\exp(-n^{c_2})$, then any particle at distance $\exp(-n^{c_1})$ will experience an average potential field that differs from the potential field of a square plate by only an exponentially small amount, say $\exp(-n^{c_3})$ for $c_3 > c_2$. This is formalized in the following lemma.

Lemma 7. *Let c_1, c_2, and c_3 be constants such that $1 < c_1 < c_2 < c_3$. Assume that the particle sweeping out the area of the square makes $\exp(n^{c_3})$ sweeps of the entire square (each one involving $\exp(n^{c_2})$ vertical sweeps) per time unit. Then the difference between the trajectory of a unit-velocity particle approaching this construction differs from the trajectory of the same particle approaching a uniformly charged plate by at most $\exp(-n^{c_1})$.*

Proof. First, we need to prove that the average potential of the sweeping particle is a good approximation of a charged plate. If we could sweep a solid bar over the area, then the proof of this fact would be identical to the proof in the preceding lemma. The vertical sweeps of the sweeping particle look (on the average) like a set of vertical bars, with small error as described in the previous lemma. Intuitively, one would expect that if the vertical bars are packed densely enough, then the average potential field of all these bars would be only slightly different from the potential field of the plane, and in fact, this is true. The potential due to a charged plate can be calculated by integrating the potential due to a bar over the width of the square. By using discretely placed bars, we are essentially using numerical integration to estimate the potential of the charged plate, and by making the integration step small enough ($\exp(-n^{c_2})$ of the square width), we make the numerical integration error very small ($\exp(-n^c)$).

We have shown that the average potential over a small timestep ($\exp(-n^{c_3})$) has an exponentially small error from that of a charged plate, so we can do a timestepping error analysis exactly like the previous lemma to complete the proof here. $\square$

By replacing each uniformly charged plate in the 1-body fixed potential field problem with the above construction, we have reduced the 1-body problem to the n-body reachability problem. We can make the error of the new simulation $\exp(-n^c)$ for arbitrarily large c, completing the proof of our main lower bound result.

Theorem 8. *The n-body reachability problem, as defined above, is PSPACE-hard.*

References

1. D. Beveridge and W.L. Jorgensen, Eds. *Computer Simulation of Chemical and Biochemical Systems.* Ann NY Acad. Sci. Vol. 482, 1986. Proceedings of a 1986 conference.

2. R. L. Burden, and J. D. Faires. *Numerical Analysis, Fourth Edition*, PWS-KENT Publishing Company, Boston, MA, 1989.

3. E. Fredkin and T. Toffoli. Conservative Logic. In *Int. J. of Theo. Phys.*, Vol. 21, pp. 219–253, 1982.

4. L. Greengard and V. Rokhlin. Rapid Evaluation of Potential Fields in Three Dimensions. Yale University Research Report YALEU/DCS/RR-515, 1987.

5. L. Greengard and V. Rokhlin. On the Efficient Implementation of the Fast Multipole Algorithm. Technical Report RR-602, Yale University Department of Computer Science, 1988.

6. W.F. van Gunsteren and P.K. Weiner, Eds. Computer Simulations of Biomolecular Systems. ESCOM, Leiden, 1989.

7. R.W. Hockney and J.W. Eastwood. *Computer Simulation Using Particles.* McGraw-Hill, New York, 1981.

8. M. Karpus and G.A. Petsko. Molecular Dynamics Simulations in Biology. In *Nature* 347, pp. 631-639, 1990.

9. C. Moore. Unpredictability and Undecidability in Dynamical Systems. In *Phy. Rev. Lett.* **64**, pp. 2354-2357, 1990.

10. K. Nabors and J. White. Fastcap: A Multipole Accelerated 3-D Capacitance Extraction Program. Technical Report, MIT Department of Electrical Engineering and Computer Science, 1991.

11. J. Reif and S. Tate. Fast Approximation Algorihtms for Trummer's Problem and n-body Potential Field Evaluation. Technical Report, Duke University, July 1992.

12. J. Reif, D. Tygar, and A. Yoshida. The Computability and Complexity of Optical Beam Tracing. In *Proc. 31st Annual Symposium on Foundations of Computer Science* **I**, pp. 106-114, 1990.

13. W.J. Savitch. Relations Between Nondeterministic and Deterministic Tape Complexities. In *J. Comput. Systems Sci.*4, pp. 177-192, 1970.

$$\text{Mass}(M_1) = \text{Mass}(M_2) >> \text{Mass}(M_s)$$

Fig. 1. Simulating the potential field of a line segment using three points.

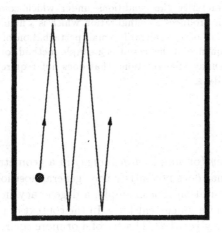

Fig. 2. Simulating the potential field of a planar region.

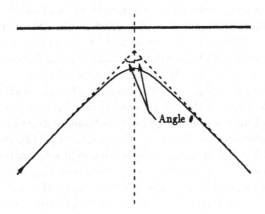

Fig. 3. A particle being repelled by a uniformly charged plate with the closest point of approach being over the center of the plate.

A Simple Method for Resolving Degeneracies in Delaunay Triangulations

Michael B. Dillencourt* and Warren D. Smith†

Abstract. We characterize the conditions under which completing a Delaunay tessellation produces a configuration which is a nondegenerate Delaunay triangulation of an arbitrarily small perturbation of the original sites. One consequence of this result is a simple method for resolving degeneracies in Delaunay triangulations that does not require symbolic perturbation of the data.

1 Introduction

A *data-induced degeneracy* (or simply *degeneracy*) in a geometric computation is a subset of the input that does not satisfy the "general position" assumptions appropriate for the computation. For example, a degeneracy in a line arrangement is a set of three or more concurrent lines. In the context of planar Delaunay triangulations, a degeneracy is either (1) a set of 4 or more cocircular generating sites such that the circle through the sites contains no other generating site in its interior, or (2) a set of three or more collinear generating sites on the boundary of the convex hull.

Handling degeneracies correctly is an important, and subtle, practical issue that arises in the implementation of geometric algorithms. It is generally desirable to resolve a data-induced degeneracy by computing a nondegenerate output that can be realized by an arbitrarily small perturbation of the input. General techniques, based on symbolic perturbation schemes, are developed in [10, 11, 24]. All of these techniques involve considerable computational overhead.

In this paper, we consider the special case of two-dimensional Delaunay triangulations. It is well-known that not all possible triangulations have combinatorially equivalent realizations as Delaunay triangulations [7, 13]. Indeed, only an exponentially small fraction of triangulations have such a realization [23]. Hence one would expect that some care is necessary when removing degeneracies from Delaunay triangulations and indeed, this turns out to be the case. However, the amount of care required turns out to be modest. In particular, we show that general symbolic-perturbation schemes are unnecessary, and that a much simpler method of resolving degeneracies suffices.

Our main result (Theorem 3.1) is a characterization of the conditions under which completing a degenerate Delaunay tessellation yields a configuration which

---

* Information and Computer Science Department, University of California, Irvine, CA 92717. The support of a UCI Faculty Research Grant is gratefully acknowledged.

† NEC Research Institute, 4 Independence Way, Princeton NJ 08540

is the nondegenerate triangulation of an arbitrarily small perturbation of the input. The proof of Theorem 3.1 is given in Section 5. The proof is based on a characterization of the conditions under which adding an edge to an inscribable polyhedron preserves inscribability (Theorem 5.1), which may be of independent interest. A specific example showing that the (minor) restrictions imposed by Theorem 3.1 are indeed necessary is given in Section 6. Practical consequences for Delaunay triangulation algorithms are discussed in Section 7. In Section 8, we apply Theorem 3.1 to show that any triangulation of a simple polygon may be realized as a Delaunay triangulation of an "almost cocircular" set of points.

Edelsbrunner has defined a *globally equiangular triangulation* to be a triangulation that maximizes lexicographically the angle sequence (sorted in increasing order) [9]. Mount and Saalfeld have given an efficient algorithm to compute the globally equiangular triangulation of a set of cocircular points [16]. When points are in general position, the Delaunay triangulation is the globally equiangular triangulation. In Section 9, we show that if a set of points has a degenerate Delaunay tessellation, the globally equiangular triangulation need not be realizable as the nondegenerate Delaunay triangulation of a small perturbation of the sites, even if the globally equiangular triangulation is unique.

Somewhat related to Theorem 3.1 is a recent algorithm by Fortune for computing "approximate" Delaunay triangulations using fixed-precision arithmetic [12]. Fortune's algorithm uses $O(n^2)$ fixed-precision operations and produces a triangulation that satisfies an approximate Delaunay condition. However, there is no guarantee that the output of his algorithm will be the Delaunay triangulation of any input. Our theorem, like the general schemes of [10, 11, 24], is only applicable if exact arithmetic is being used (since otherwise it is impossible to correctly detect degeneracies.) If exact arithmetic is used, our theorem provides a means of ensuring that the output is a Delaunay triangulation of an arbitrarily small perturbation of the input.

2 Preliminaries

Except as noted, we use the graph-theoretical notation and definitions of [2]. In particular, $V(G)$ and $E(G)$ denote the set of vertices and edges of a graph G, respectively. A *triangulation* is a 2-connected plane graph in which all faces except possibly the outer face are bounded by triangles. A *maximal planar graph* is a planar graph in which all faces (including the outer face) are bounded by triangles. A graph G is *1-tough* [4] if for all nonempty $S \subseteq V(G)$, $c(G - S) \leq |S|$. (Here $|\cdot|$ denotes cardinality, and $c(\cdot)$ denotes the number of connected components.) G is *1-supertough* if, for all $S \subseteq V(G)$ with $|S| \geq 2$, $c(G - S) < |S|$.

The *Delaunay tessellation*, DT(S), of a planar set of points S is the unique graph with $V(G) = S$ such that the outer face is bounded by the convex hull of S, all vertices on the boundary of a common interior face are cocircular, the vertices of an interior face are exactly the points of S lying on the circumcircle of the face, and no points of S lie in the interior of a circumcircle of any interior face. DT(S) is said to be *nondegenerate* if it is a triangulation and all convex hull vertices of S are extreme points of S, *degenerate* otherwise. If DT(S) is nondegenerate, it is called the Delaunay triangulation. Elementary properties of the Delaunay tessellation/triangulation, and the more conventional definition as the dual of the Voronoi diagram, are developed in [1, 9, 17].

Let S be a set of generating sites, DT(S) its Delaunay tessellation. Define a *completion* of DT(S) to be a triangulation obtained by

(C1) Declaring each non-extreme site on the convex hull of S to be either "extreme" or "non-extreme."

(C2) Adding new edges so that the sites incident on the outer face are exactly the sites that either are extreme sites or were declared "extreme" in step (C1).

(C3) Adding diagonals to non-triangular interior faces of DT(S).

If DT(S) is nondegenerate, it has only one completion, namely itself. If DT(S) is degenerate, there is more than one way to complete it. In this case, we call *any* completion of DT(S) a *degenerate Delaunay triangulation*.

3 The Main Result

We say a Delaunay triangulation is *valid* if it can be realized as a nondegenerate Delaunay triangulation of an arbitrarily small perturbation of its input. Obviously, any nondegenerate Delaunay triangulation is valid. Theorem 3.1, below, characterizes the completions of Delaunay tessellations that produce valid Delaunay triangulations.

The *augmented Delaunay tessellation* of S, ADT(S), is the graph obtained from DT(S) by adding a new vertex ∞, representing the point at infinity, and connecting all extreme points of S to ∞. Obtaining a completion of the Delaunay tessellation, as defined in Section 2, is equivalent to adding diagonals to faces of ADT(S) to make it maximal planar. Indeed, declaring a non-extreme site on the convex hull of S to be "extreme" in step (C1) corresponds to connecting the site with ∞ in ADT(S), while edges added in steps (C2) and (C3) correspond directly to edges added to ADT(S).

If ADT(S) is a bipartite graph, assume that its vertices are two-colored red and blue. In this case, a *weakly symmetric* completion of DT(S) is a completion obtained by first adding edges to ADT(S) to obtain a maximal planar graph, in such a way that at least one red-red edge and at least one blue-blue edge are added, and then removing the vertex ∞ (and all attached edges).

Theorem 3.1. *Let S be a set of planar points.*

(a) *If the augmented Delaunay tessellation ADT(S) is not bipartite, then any completion of DT(S) is valid.*

(b) *If ADT(S) is bipartite, then a completion of DT(S) is valid if and only if it is weakly symmetric. If the completion is not weakly symmetric, then it is not the Delaunay triangulation of any input.*

The proof of this theorem is given in Section 5.

Theorem 3.1(a) says that except in highly degenerate cases, *any* completion of a Delaunay tessellation yields a valid Delaunay triangulation. In particular, if $ADT(S)$ is bipartite, every face of $DT(S)$ has even valence (so $DT(S)$ has no triangular faces!) and no two extreme points of S appear consecutively on the convex hull of S. Such behavior, while pathological, can occur: we give an example in Section 6. Since testing $ADT(S)$ for bipartiteness (and ensuring weak symmetry of the completion, if necessary) is straightforward, Theorem 3.1 provides a simple method for postprocessing a degenerate Delaunay triangulation to obtain a triangulation that is a nondegenerate Delaunay triangulation of an arbitrarily small perturbation of the input. We discuss this in more detail in Section 7.

4 Some Facts about Inscribable Graphs

The proof of Theorem 3.1 uses some theoretical results about inscribable graphs, which we summarize here. A graph G is *polyhedral* if it can be realized as the edges and vertices of the convex hull of a noncoplanar set of points in 3-space. A famous theorem of Steinitz (see [13]) asserts that a graph is polyhedral if and only if it is 3-connected and planar. A graph G is *inscribable* if it can be realized as the edges and vertices of the convex hull of a noncoplanar set of points on the surface of a sphere in 3-space. An *inscription* of G is an assignment of coordinates to the vertices of G achieving this realization. A *cutset* in a graph is a minimal set of edges whose removal increases the number of components. A cutset is *noncoterminous* if its edges do not all have a common endpoint.

The following result is due to Rivin [19] (also see [14, 18, 22]).

Characterization 4.1. *A graph is inscribable if and only if it is polyhedral and weights w can be assigned to its edges such that:*

(W1) *For each edge e, $0 < w(e) < 1/2$.*
(W2) *For each vertex v, the total weight of all edges incident on v is equal to 1.*
(W3) *For each noncoterminous cutset $C \subseteq E(G)$, the total weight of all edges in C is strictly greater than 1.*

The weights in Characterization 4.1 correspond to certain normalized hyperbolic angles in a realization of the polyhedron as a convex polyhedron in hyperbolic 3-space with vertices on the ideal sphere. It can be shown [21] that these angles uniquely determine an inscription, up to homothetic transformations. Furthermore, there is a continuity relation between the weights and the inscription, which is precisely formulated in the following lemma.

Lemma 4.2 [21]. *Let G be an inscribable graph, w a weighting, I an inscription of G that realizes w, $\epsilon > 0$.*

(a) *There exists a real number $\delta = \delta(G, w, \epsilon)$ such that if w' is any other weighting of G satisfying conditions (W1)–(W3) and for which $|w(e) - w'(e)| < \delta$ for all $e \in E(G)$, then there is an inscription I' of G realizing w' with $d(I(v), I'(v)) < \epsilon$ for all $v \in V(G)$.*

(b) *Let H be a planar graph obtained from G by adding edges $e_1, \ldots, e_k$. There exists a real number $\delta = \delta(G, w, \epsilon)$ such that if w' is any weighting of H satisfying conditions (W1)–(W3) and the additional conditions that $|w(e) - w'(e)| < \delta$ for all $e \in E(G)$ and $0 < w'(e_i) < \delta$ for $1 \leq i \leq k$, then there is an inscription I' of H realizing w' with $d(I(v), I'(v)) < \epsilon$ for all $v \in V(G)$.*

The following lemma describes the connection between Delaunay tessellations and inscribable graphs. It is a different formulation from that in [3]. The operation of *stellating* a face f in a plane graph G consists of adding a vertex inside the face f and then connecting all vertices incident on f to the new vertex.

Lemma 4.3. *A plane graph G is realizable as $\mathrm{DT}(S)$ for some set S, with f as the unbounded face, if and only if the graph G' obtained from G by stellating f is inscribable. In this case, G' is realizable as $\mathrm{ADT}(S)$.*

Proof. The lemma follows immediately from the fact that stereographic projection of a plane (together with the point at ∞) onto a sphere maps lines onto circles passing through the pole, and circles onto circles not passing through the pole. See [5] for a discussion of stereographic projection. □

5 Proof of Theorem 3.1

In this section, we prove Theorem 3.1. We first establish the circumstances under which adding an edge to an inscribable graph preserves inscribability.

Theorem 5.1. *Let G be an inscribable graph. Suppose that H is obtained from G by performing any of the following transformations in such a way that H remains planar.*

(T1) *If G is nonbipartite, adding an edge to G.*
(T2) *If G is bipartite, adding a red-blue edge to G.*
(T3) *If G is bipartite, adding a red-red edge and a blue-blue edge to G.*

Then H is inscribable, and can be realized through an arbitrarily small perturbation of the vertices of G.

Proof. Since G is polyhedral, so is H. Let $\epsilon > 0$ be given. Let w be a weighting of the edges of G satisfying (W1)–(W3) of Characterization 4.1, and extend this weighting to H by (temporarily) assigning the new edge(s) a weight of 0. Let α be less than the minimum slack in all the strict inequalities in (W1) and (W3) in the weighting of G, and let n be the number of vertices in G. Finally, let $\delta = \min(\alpha/n, \epsilon)/2$. We show that the temporary weights assigned to H can be modified so that (1) the modified weights provide a weighting of H satisfying (W1)–(W3), and (2) no edge weight is modified by more than 2δ. The theorem then follows from Characterization 4.1 and Lemma 4.2.

Suppose first that a single edge $e = vx$ is added (Transformation (T1) or (T2)). Since H is planar and G is 3-connected, v and x are nonconsecutive vertices incident on a common face f of G. Adding e splits f into two new faces, f_1 and f_2. If either of these two faces has even valence, alternately modify the weights of edges about this face by $\pm\delta$, with e being modified by $+\delta$, as shown in Figure 1(a). Notice that when (T2) is applied, this case must occur.

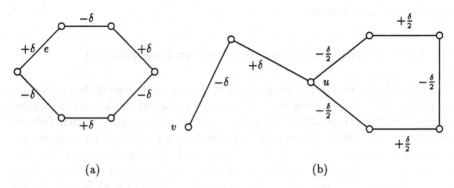

(a)   (b)

Fig. 1. (a) Adding an edge e when at least one face of H incident on e has even valence. (b) Adding an edge e when some face of G has odd valence.

When (T1) is applied, if both f_1 and f_2 have odd valence, then f must have even valence. Since G is nonbipartite, there must be a face of G (and hence of H) with odd valence. Let Z be the cycle bounding this face. Choose a path Φ in G from v to a vertex u of Z. Modify the weights of the edges along Φ by $\pm\delta$, alternating signs, so that the edge incident on v is modified by $-\delta$. Modify the weights along Z by $\pm\delta/2$, alternating signs, so that the two edges of Z incident on u have the opposite sign from the edge of Φ incident on u. (See Figure 1(b)). Process vertex x in a similar fashion. Assign edge e a weight of δ. It is easy to see that this modification satisfies the necessary properties.

Finally, consider Transformation (T3), and let e_1 and e_2 be the two new edges. Choose any cycle Z in H passing through e_1 and e_2. Increment the weights along Z by $\pm\delta$, alternating signs, so that $w(e_1)$ is incremented by $+\delta$. Since G is bipartite, e_1 is red-red, and e_2 is blue-blue, it follows that Z has even length and $w(e_2)$ is also incremented by $+\delta$. Hence all (W1) constraints are preserved. $\square$

Proof of Theorem 3.1. Suppose first that the hypotheses of Theorem 3.1(a) or (b) hold. By Lemma 4.3, ADT(S) is inscribable. It then follows from repeated applications of Theorem 5.1 that the completion of ADT(S) is inscribable, and the inscription may be achieved through an arbitrarily small perturbation of the inscription of ADT(S). Hence (a), and the "if" part of (b), follow from Lemma 4.3 and the fact that stereographic projection is a bicontinuous mapping between the sphere and the extended plane.

Now suppose that ADT(S) is bipartite, but that the completion is not weakly symmetric. Let K' be the maximal planar graph obtained by adding edges to ADT(S) and assume, without loss of generality, that all the edges are blue-blue. Let K be the graph obtained by deleting ∞ from K'. Let b and r denote, respectively, the number of blue and red vertices of ADT(S). Since all inscribable graphs are 1-tough ([7, Theorem 3.2]), $r = b$. Hence removing the b blue vertices from K' decomposes it into b components, each consisting of a single red vertex. Since K' is maximal planar and not 1-supertough, K' cannot be inscribable ([8, Theorem 2.2]). It follows from Lemma 4.3 that K is not realizable as a Delaunay triangulation of any input. □

6 An Example of a Non-Realizable Completion

Theorem 3.1 provides a characterization of those completions of degenerate Delaunay tessellations that can be realized as Delaunay triangulations of arbitrarily small perturbations of the input. An example of a completion that fails the weak symmetry test of Theorem 3.1(b) is shown in Figure 2. This example was originally described by Kantabutra in a somewhat different context [15]. The set S of generating sites consists of the three vertices of an equilateral triangle, the midpoints of the edges, and the centroid. DT(S) is shown on the left of the figure. The two triangulations obtained by completing DT(S) in a non-weakly-symmetric fashion are shown on the right of the figure. Neither of these triangulations is realizable as a Delaunay triangulation, as they fail to satisfy the necessary conditions of Theorems 3.1 and 3.2 of [7], respectively. By Theorem 3.1 of this paper, any completion of the tessellation in Figure 2, other than the two shown, can be realized by an arbitrarily small perturbation of the vertices of S.

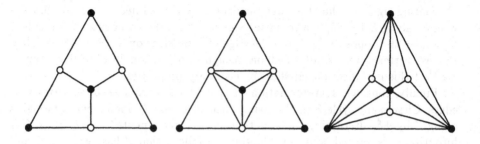

Fig. 2. A degenerate Delaunay tessellation, DT(S) such that ADT(S) is bipartite (shown on the left), and the two triangulations resulting from non-weakly-symmetric completions of $ADT(S)$.

7 Consequences for Delaunay Triangulation Algorithms

Suppose that a Delaunay triangulation algorithm is correct in the sense that it produces the Delaunay triangulation if its input is nondegenerate and produces *some* degenerate Delaunay triangulation if its input is degenerate. We can ensure that the algorithm always produces a valid Delaunay triangulation by postprocessing its output as follows. Let S be an input to such an algorithm, G its output.

1. Add a new vertex to G, and label it ∞. Connect every vertex on the outer face of G to ∞. Call the augmented graph, which is maximal planar, G'.
2. Label each edge $e = uv$ of G' as either "real" or "artificial" as follows:
   (a) If either u or v is ∞, (assume $u = \infty$), label e as "real" if v is an extreme point of S, "artificial" otherwise. Notice that this can be done in constant time by determining whether angle $xvw = 180°$, where x and w are the two neighbors of v adjacent to u about v.
   (b) If e is an edge of the outer face of G, let x be the (unique) vertex such that $x \neq \infty$ and uxv bounds a face of G'. Label e as "real" if angle $uxv < 180°$, "artificial" if angle $uxv = 180°$.
   (c) If neither of the preceding two cases apply, e is an interior edge of G. Let w and x be the two vertices of G such that uwv and uxv bound faces of G. Label e "artificial" if u, v, w, and x are cocircular, "real" otherwise.
3. Determine whether the subgraph of G' induced by the "real" edges is bipartite. If so, 2-color the vertices of this graph red and blue, and proceed to Step 4. Otherwise, exit.
4. If there is at least one red-red "artificial" edge and at least one blue-blue "artificial" edge, exit.
5. Choose any "artificial" edge of G', say uv and delete it, creating a 4-valent face $uxvw$. Add the "opposite diagonal" xw to G'. Make the corresponding changes in G (i.e., delete uv if $u \neq \infty$ and $v \neq \infty$, add xw if $x \neq \infty$ and $w \neq \infty$).

It follows from Theorem 3.1 that the preceding postprocessing sequence produces a graph G that is a valid Delaunay triangulation of S. In the worst case, $O(|S|)$ operations are required. It is never necessary to perform more than one edge deletion and one edge addition.

8 A Delaunay Realizability Theorem

It was shown in [6] that any triangulation of a simple polygon (that is, any triangulation obtained by adding diagonals to the interior of a simple polygon) is combinatorially realizable as a Delaunay triangulation. Theorem 3.1 provides a simple proof of a stronger version of this result:

Theorem 8.1. *Let T be any triangulation of a simple polygon with n vertices, $v_1, \ldots, v_n$ (listed in order along the boundary of the polygon). Then T can be realized as a (combinatorially equivalent) Delaunay triangulation. Furthermore, if $p_1, \ldots, p_n$ are any set of distinct cocircular points in the plane (listed in counterclockwise order about their common circle), and ϵ is any prescribed positive real number, then the vertices in the Delaunay realization of T can be chosen so that for each i, the vertex in the realization corresponding to v_i is at a distance of at most ϵ from p_i.*

Proof. Let $S = \{p_1, p_2, \ldots, p_n\}$. Since the set S is cocircular, the Delaunay tessellation $DT(S)$ is the polygon $p_1 p_2 \ldots p_n p_1$. Since each point in S is an extreme point, the augmented Delaunay Tessellation $ADT(S)$ is nonbipartite. Hence, by Theorem 3.1, any completion of $DT(S)$ is realizable as the nondegenerate Delaunay triangulation of an arbitrarily small perturbation of the vertices $\{p_i\}$. In particular, this is true of the completion obtained by adding a diagonal $p_i p_j$ if and only if $v_i v_j$ is an edge of T. □

Notice that Theorem 8.1 implies, in particular, that the realization of T may be chosen so that the vertices come arbitrarily close to forming the vertices of a regular polygon.

9 Globally Equiangular Triangulations

A globally equiangular triangulation is a triangulation that achieves the lexicographic maximum of the angle sequence, sorted in nondecreasing order. Theorem 8.1 implies that any triangulation of a cocircular planar point set is a valid Delaunay triangulation, and hence any globally equiangular triangulation of a cocircular point set is a valid Delaunay triangulation.

It is shown on [9, page 302] that any globally equiangular triangulation is necessarily a completion of the Delaunay tessellation. Here we show that a globally equiangular triangulation need not be a *valid* completion of the Delaunay tessellation.

Consider the (degenerate) Delaunay tessellation shown in Figure 3(a). The sites consist of the vertices of a 2×2 square grid, with the four corner vertices perturbed. For each corner vertex, the perturbation consists of rotating it clockwise on the circumcircle of the small square containing it, through an angle of θ degrees. The resulting point set still has a convex hull that is a square, a central point in the center of the square, and four rotational symmetries. However, the four vertices along the square's sides are no longer the midpoints of the sides.

Quadrilateral $ABCD$ may be triangulated in one of two ways. The left (respectively, right) half of the following table gives the angles that would be obtained if edge BD (respectively, AC) were added to the triangulation.

Angle	Value	Angle	Value
BDA	$45-\theta/2$	BCA	$45-\theta/2$
DBC	45	DAC	45
CDB	45	CAB	45
ABD	$45+\theta/2$	ACD	$45+\theta/2$
DAB	90	CDA	$90-\theta/2$
BCD	90	ABC	$90+\theta/2$

These values and the symmetry of the figure imply that the (unique) globally equiangular triangulation is the triangulation shown in Figure 3(b). This triangulation represents a completion of the Delaunay tessellation that is not weakly symmetric. Hence, by Theorem 3.1, it is not combinatorially equivalent to the Delaunay triangulation of any input, so in particular, it is not a valid completion of the Delaunay tessellation of Figure 3(a).

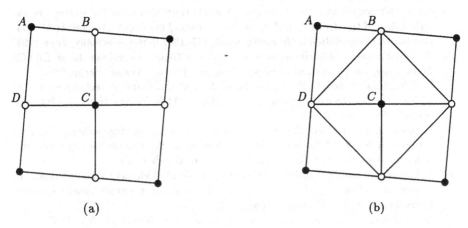

(a)   (b)

Fig. 3. The globally equiangular triangulation of a point set with a degenerate Delaunay tessellation need not be combinatorially equivalent to the nondegenerate Delaunay triangulation of any point set.

10 Final Remark

The proofs given in this paper are constructive, in the sense that they describe how to manipulate the edge weightings described in Characterization 4.1. Once appropriate weightings are computed, a corresponding inscription (or the coordinates of a Delaunay realization) can be found using algorithms sketched in [20, 21].

Acknowledgment

It is a pleasure to acknowledge stimulating conversations with Igor Rivin.

References

1. F. Aurenhammer. Voronoi diagrams—a survey of a fundamental geometric data structure. *ACM Computing Surveys*, 23(3):345–405, September 1991.

2. J. A. Bondy and U. S. R. Murty. *Graph Theory with Applications*. North-Holland, New York, NY, 1976.

3. K. Q. Brown. Voronoi diagrams from convex hulls. *Information Processing Letters*, 9(5):223–228, December 1979.

4. V. Chvátal. Tough graphs and Hamiltonian circuits. *Discrete Mathematics*, 5(3):215–228, July 1973.

5. H. S. M. Coxeter. *Introduction to Geometry*. John Wiley and Sons, New York, NY, second edition, 1969.

6. M. B. Dillencourt. Realizability of Delaunay triangulations. *Information Processing Letters*, 33(6):283–287, February 1990.

7. M. B. Dillencourt. Toughness and Delaunay triangulations. *Discrete & Computational Geometry*, 5(6):575–601, 1990.

8. M. B. Dillencourt and W. D. Smith. A linear-time algorithm for testing the inscribability of trivalent polyhedra. In *Proceedings of the Eighth Annual ACM Symposium on Computational Geometry*, pages 177–185, Berlin, Germany, June 1992.

9. H. Edelsbrunner. *Algorithms in Combinatorial Geometry*, volume 10 of *EATCS Monographs on Theoretical Computer Science*. Springer-Verlag, Berlin, 1987.

10. H. Edelsbrunner and E. P. Mücke. Simulation of simplicity: A technique to cope with degenerate cases in geometric algorithms. *ACM Transactions on Graphics*, 9(1):66–104, January 1990.

11. I. Emiris and J. Canny. A general approach to removing degeneracies. In *Proceedings of the 32nd Annual IEEE Symposium on the Foundations of Computer Science*, pages 405–413, San Juan, Puerto Rico, October 1991.

12. S. Fortune. Numerical stability of algorithms for 2D Delaunay triangulations. In *Proceedings of the Eighth Annual ACM Symposium on Computational Geometry*, pages 83–92, Berlin, Germany, June 1992.

13. B. Grünbaum. *Convex Polytopes*. Wiley Interscience, New York, NY, 1967.

14. C. D. Hodgson, I. Rivin, and W. D. Smith. A characterization of convex hyperbolic polyhedra and of convex polyhedra inscribed in the sphere. *Bulletin of the AMS*, 27(2):246–251, October 1992. See also Erratum, *Bulletin of the AMS*, 28(1):213, January 1993.

15. V. Kantabutra. Traveling salesman cycles are not always subgraphs of Voronoi duals. *Information Processing Letters*, 16(1):11–12, January 1983.

16. D. M. Mount and A. Saalfeld. Globally-equiangular triangulations of co-circular points in $O(n \log n)$ time. In *Proceedings of the Fourth ACM Symposium on Computational Geometry*, pages 143–152, Urbana-Champaign, IL, June 1988.

17. F. P. Preparata and M. I. Shamos. *Computational Geometry: An Introduction*. Springer-Verlag, New York, NY, 1985.

18. I. Rivin. On the geometry of ideal polyhedra in hyperbolic 3-Space. To appear, *Topology*.

19. I. Rivin. A characterization of ideal polyhedra in hyperbolic 3-space. Preprint, 1992.

20. I. Rivin. Some applications of the hyperbolic volume formula of Lobachevskii and Milnor. Preprint, 1992.

21. I. Rivin and W. D. Smith. Ideal polyhedra in H^3 are determined by their dihedral angles. Manuscript, NEC Research Institute, Princeton, NJ, 1991.

22. I. Rivin and W. D. Smith. Inscribable graphs. Manuscript, NEC Research Institute, Princeton, NJ, 1991.

23. W. D. Smith. On the enumeration of inscribable graphs. Manuscript, NEC Research Institute, Princeton, NJ, 1991.

24. C-K. Yap. A geometric consistency theorem for a symbolic perturbation scheme. In *Proceedings of the Fourth Annual ACM Symposium on Computational Geometry*, pages 134–142, Urbana-Champaign, IL, June 1988.

Fault-Tolerance and Complexity
(Extended Abstract)

*Lane A. Hemachandra**
Department of Computer Science
University of Rochester
Rochester, NY 14627

Abstract

Robust computation—a radical approach to fault-tolerant database access—was explicitly defined one decade ago, and in the following year this notion was presented at ICALP in Antwerp. A decade's study of robust computation by many researchers has determined which problems can be fault-tolerantly solved via access to databases of many strengths. This paper surveys these results and mentions some interesting unresolved issues.

1 Introduction

Suppose we wish to compute with some help from a database. So as we compute we may every once in a while send a question to the database, which will send back an answer. In the best of all worlds, the communication would be complete reliable, and we could depend on a correct answer coming back. However, for reasons varying from noise on phone lines to outright malicious tampering with an answer, this is not such a world. Faced with often unreliable access to external databases, it is natural to seek to tolerate faults.

How should one approach this? One natural avenue would be to make statistical assumptions about the errors. The problem with such assumptions is that they fail to model actual error patterns—as error patterns may change dramatically from day to day and hour to hour.

Perhaps the most radical approach we could take would be to require our computer to solve correctly whatever problem it is working on *regardless of the fault pattern*. This is exactly the radical approach proposed by Schöning [46]. Now, at this point the reader may well say: Whoa... what if a demon is sitting on the communication line and replaces each answer with a "0"? Note that the demon ensures that essentially no information is obtained from the database. Schöning dealt with this possibility by the following concession: Though our computer must correctly solve its problem regardless of whether faults occur in the communication with the database, we require the computer to solve a problem *quickly* only if there happen to be no faults during its database communications.

Can we now say: So the computer just asks the database to solve the problem and then immediately uses the answer unless there was a fault, in which case the computer solves the problem by brute force? Not quite. The standard deadly point, of

* Supported in part by the National Science Foundation under grants NSF-CCR-8957604 and NSF-INT-9116781/JSPS-ENG-207.

course, is that when the computer gets an answer from our database, it doesn't know offhand whether it is a good answer or a faulty answer. After all, if the computer were powerful enough to solve quickly any problem it sent to the database, it wouldn't need the database in the first place.

However, the previous paragraph is a bit deceptive. As we'll see, the true question is less whether the computer can compute what the database computes than whether the computer can *check* what the database claims. And, even better, the computer need not be able to check every answer instantly, but merely needs, after some pattern of interaction—many questions and many answers—to feel secure that our database has been non-faulty. This issue is at the heart of most of the results discussed in this paper.

That, in a nutshell, is Schöning's [46] notion of robust computation. It requires a machine (with access to a database) to compute correctly regardless of faults, and to compute quickly if there happen (on a given run) to be no faults. Schöning's motivation was not fault-tolerance, but rather was artificial intelligence; he likened robust computation to both man-machine interaction [47] and to heuristic strategies for improving branch and bound search [46].

Section 2 states the formal definition of robust computation. It also surveys the power of fault-tolerant access to databases of various complexities, and in particular to databases chosen from certain central nondeterministic classes such as NP.

Section 3 turns to the issue of fault-tolerance's interactions with probabilistic computation. Indeed, fault-tolerance completely characterizes many key probabilistic classes.

Section 4 discusses why robustness is of interest of itself as a complexity-theoretic notion. Robustness in fact refers not only to machines whose *languages* are unchanged by faults, but also to machines having some computational property that is unchanged by faults. We'll see that robustly maintaining nontrivial properties exacts a telling toll on a machine's ability to accept complex sets.

Section 5 gives pointers to some other issues important in the theory of robustness, and highlights some interesting open questions.

At points, both for space and flow, we eschew detailed definitions, and instead give intuitive descriptions of the aspect of computation a given notion models (along with references to full definitions).

2 Robust Machines and Access to Nondeterministic Information

Definitions and the NP Case

The notion of robustness described in the introduction is formalized in the definition of "helping" below, and its basic properties are discussed.

Throughout this paper, we restrict our attention to the case in which the queries to the database are simply membership tests in some set. (Note that databases returning functions can be placed into this model by making a new database that allows one to query whether the answer to question y has an ith bit and to query what that bit is.) Thus, we view the database as a set, D, and queries are of the form "$y \in D$?" Similarly, we assume, as is standard in complexity theory, that the "problems" our machines are solving are also set membership problems. Again, function computing can coerced into this form if need be.

We'll take $\Sigma = \{0, 1\}$ to be our alphabet throughout. Furthermore, we assume that a query to a database is effectively a unit-time operation: After writing down its question, the machine gets an answer right away. Using the standard notation from the literature, we describe a machine M given (non-faulty, unit-time) access to (set-membership format) database D as M^D, and we use $L(M^D)$ to describe the language accepted. Furthermore, we'll use $L(M)$ to denote $L(M^\emptyset)$, where $\emptyset$ is the empty set.

Recall that robust machines are expected to compute correctly even if given faulty replies. Note that getting some set of faulty replies is essentially the same as having the wrong set as one's database.[2] Thus, we henceforward speak of machines whose language is unchanged by their database, rather than about access to a single database with faults in the replies. Keeping this in mind, we state the basic definitions.

Definition 1. [46] A machine M is *robust* if for every database E (that is, for every set $E \in 2^{\Sigma^*}$) we have $L(M) = L(M^E)$.

A set A is *helped* by database E if it is fault-tolerantly accepted (in the sense described in the Introduction) via access to E.

Definition 2. [46]

1. Set A is *helped* by database D if there is a deterministic robust Turing machine M such that (a) $L(M) = A$, and (b) M^D runs in polynomial time.

2. For any database D, we define

$$P_{help}(D) = \{A \mid A \text{ is helped by } D\}.$$

3. For any collection $\mathcal{D}$ of databases, we define

$$P_{help}(\mathcal{D}) = \{A \mid (\exists D \in \mathcal{D})[A \in P_{help}(D)]\}.$$

---

[2] We say "essentially" due to the following point. A "wrong database" will nonetheless answer the same query *consistently* if the query is asked more than once on the same input. On the other hand, if running in the presence of faults, a question might be answered inconsistently. However, from the standpoint of robustness this difference isn't interesting (at least for the vanilla—deterministic Turing—version of robustness), as the moment we see the same query answered inconsistently, we know that faults have occurred and we can take as long as we like to solve the problem by brute force. Thus we safely make the shift above from speaking of faults to speaking of machines that may have a "wrong" database substituted for the right one. Even for nondeterministic or probabilistic access (for which there is a valid worry regarding the same query being asked in different parts of a computation tree and the computation being unable to notice this), consistent and inconsistent access are know to be essentially equivalent for all database classes that have certain natural "padding" properties ([15], but compare this with the comment in [48, p. 104] regarding databases lacking that property).

The result of Schöning's first robustness paper is:

Theorem 3. [46] $P_{help}(2^{\Sigma^*}) = P_{help}(NP) = NP \cap coNP$.

That is, any set that is fault-tolerantly accepted via access to *any* database is fault-tolerantly accepted via access to a database in NP, and both these classes are exactly equal to NP $\cap$ coNP. (Exercise for reader: Fill in the proof! Hint: it follows quickly from the definitions, as the acceptance of a helping machine itself proves membership or nonmembership, and, going the other way, sets in NP $\cap$ coNP are exactly the sets having short proofs of membership and nonmembership so we may take as a helping database a database made up of inputs paired with prefixes of the inputs' certificates.)

Ko [36] defines another key notion: one-sided helping. One-sided helping is identical to helping except the "no faults $\Rightarrow$ fast" condition is relaxed to "no faults $\Rightarrow$ fast for elements in the set."

Definition 4. [36]

1. Set A is *1-helped* by database D if there is a deterministic robust Turing machine M such that (a) $L(M) = A$, and (b) there is a polynomial $q(\cdot)$ such that for every $x \in A$ it holds that $M^D(x)$ runs in time $q(|x|)$.

2. For any database D, we define
$$P_{1\text{-help}}(D) = \{A \mid A \text{ is 1-helped by } D\}.$$

3. For any collection $\mathcal{D}$ of databases, we define
$$P_{1\text{-help}}(\mathcal{D}) = \{A \mid (\exists D \in \mathcal{D})[A \in P_{1\text{-help}}(D)]\}.$$

Ko proved the following.

Theorem 5. [36] $P_{1\text{-help}}(2^{\Sigma^*}) = P_{1\text{-help}}(NP) = NP$.

The proof essentially is that NP sets (by definition) have succinct membership certificates, and that the quick acceptance of a robust machine is itself a clear certificate of membership. Balcázar has made formal the intuition that 1-helping is identical to providing certifications [9]. Immediate relationships between helping and 1-helping include:

Proposition 6. [36]

1. For every set or class F, it holds that $P_{help}(F) \subseteq P_{1\text{-help}}(F) \subseteq P^F$.

2. For any sets A and B: $A \in P_{1\text{-help}}(B)$ and $\overline{A} \in P_{1\text{-help}}(B) \iff A \in P_{help}(B)$.

Ko proved that sets hard for NP and NP $\cap$ coNP naturally enough suffice to fault-tolerantly accept the entire classes.

Theorem 7. [36] For each database A:

1. $NP \subseteq P_{1\text{-help}}(A) \iff A$ is $\leq_T^p$-hard for NP.

2. $NP \cap coNP \subseteq P_{1\text{-help}}(A) \iff A$ is $\leq_T^p$-hard for NP $\cap$ coNP.

Fault-Tolerance and Unambiguous Computation

Much of the research in the area of robustness has gone into finding, for other natural classes of databases, results that are as clean and complete as Theorems 3 and 5. In particular, Schöning's and Ko's original papers raised the issues of probabilistic database sets (discussed in the following section) and of unambiguous database sets.

Valiant [56] defined UP, unambiguous polynomial time, as the class of languages accepted by nondeterministic polynomial-time Turing machines that (as usual reject by having zero accepting paths and) when they accept do so along exactly one accepting path; clearly $P \subseteq UP \subseteq NP$. These sets may be thought of, loosely, as an NP analog of the unambiguous context-free languages. Unambiguous computation is believed to be deeply incomparable with probabilistic computation [44,18], and suggests a line of attack for improving Savitch's Theorem [13,43].

Ko proved the following result.

Theorem 8. [36]

1. $UP \subseteq P_{1\text{-help}}(UP)$.

2. $UP \cap coUP = P_{help}(UP \cap coUP)$.

Motivated by the analogous equality for NP (Theorem 5), Ko posed as an open question whether the first part of the above theorem can be improved to $UP = P_{1\text{-help}}(UP)$. Recent work by Cai, Hemachandra, and Vyskoč shows that equality is unlikely. Though $P_{1\text{-help}}(NP)$ is equal to NP, $P_{1\text{-help}}(UP)$ contains not only UP, but also all sets that reduce to UP via a type of positive reduction—namely the ℓpos reduction introduced by Hemachandra and Jain ([29], see Section 4). Intuitively, $A \leq^p_{\ell pos} B$ if A polynomial-time Turing reduces to B via a machine such that for every C, it holds that $L(M^{B-C}) - L(M^B)$ is empty—that is, removing elements from the database makes the set accepted shrink (perhaps non-strictly). Let $R^p_{\ell pos}(UP) = \{A \mid (\exists B \in UP)[A \leq^p_{\ell pos} B]\}$.

Theorem 9. [15] $P_{1\text{-help}}(UP) = R^p_{\ell pos}(UP)$.

As an additional piece of evidence against the potential equality of UP and $P_{1\text{-help}}(UP)$, Cai, Hemachandra, and Vyskoč [15] construct a "relativized world" [7] in which UP does not equal $P_{1\text{-help}}(UP)$.

We make three final remarks about the first part of Theorem 8. Ko uses this result to obtain the following theorem, which intuitively says that $P = UP$ if every UP language is accepted by a P machine given an "advice" string [33] that depends on only the input's length and whose length is logarithmic in the input's length. Ko's proof [36] avoids any reliance on a complete set having specific "self-reducibility" properties (see also [59]).

Theorem 10. [36] $UP \subseteq P/\log \Rightarrow P = UP$.

Yamakami [61] has noted that the first part of Theorem 8 can be strengthened if one introduces the (intuitive) notion of truth-table [38] access (intuitively, all questions must be asked simultaneously—thus answers to one question cannot determine other questions). He proves that $\mathrm{UP} \subseteq \mathrm{P}_{1\text{-tt-help}}(\mathrm{UP})$.[3]

Finally, Ko [36] discusses a method—redefining helping by requiring the helping to itself be unambiguous in a certain sense—different from that of Theorem 9 for making the first part of Theorem 8 more satisfying.

Limited Nondeterminism

Kintala and Fisher [34] suggested an approach to "thinning down" that is different from Valiant's unambiguous computation notion. They suggest limiting not the number of accepting paths (as Valiant does), but rather limiting the amount of nondeterminism. They define, for each $k \in \{0, 1, 2, ...\}$, the class β_k ([34], see also [17], which introduced the β notation) as the class of sets accepted by NP machines that on inputs of length n make at most $\mathcal{O}(\log^k n)$ nondeterministic guesses on each computation path; of course, $\beta_0 = \beta_1 = \mathrm{P}$, and $\mathrm{P} \subseteq \beta_2 \subseteq \beta_3 \subseteq \cdots \subseteq \mathrm{NP}$. These classes have recently been shown to be merely a reflection of the structure of greedy algorithms [54], and have been shown to have truly bizarre translation properties on tally sets [30]. Díaz and Torán characterized the β classes in terms of 1-helping (below, "[...]" indicates a bound on the number of queries that may be made to the database on inputs of length n).

Theorem 11. [17] For every $k \geq 0$:

$$\beta_k = \mathrm{P}_{1\text{-help}}(\beta_k[\mathcal{O}(\log^k n)]) = \mathrm{P}_{1\text{-help}}(\mathrm{NP}[\mathcal{O}(\log^k n)]) = \mathrm{P}_{1\text{-help}}(2^{\Sigma^*}[\mathcal{O}(\log^k n)]).$$

Clearly, we also have: For every $k \geq 0$, $\beta_k \cap \mathrm{co}\beta_k = \mathrm{P}_{\text{help}}(\beta_k[\mathcal{O}(\log^k n)]) = \mathrm{P}_{\text{help}}(\mathrm{NP}[\mathcal{O}(\log^k n)]) = \mathrm{P}_{\text{help}}(2^{\Sigma^*}[\mathcal{O}(\log^k n)])$. Díaz and Torán provide evidence for the necessity of the $\mathcal{O}(\log^k n)$ query bounds in Theorem 11 by showing that for any $k \geq 2$ there is a relativized world in which β_k is strictly contained in $\mathrm{P}_{1\text{-help}}(\beta_k)$ (note: for the cases $k = 0$ and $k = 1$, equality trivially holds with or without the bounds, and the equality safely relativizes).

3 Robustness and Probabilistic Computation

Section 2 discussed fault-tolerant access to databases capturing the power of nondeterministic computation. This section discusses the connections between the robustness fault-tolerance paradigm and probabilistic computation; robust computation exactly characterizes many basic probabilistic complexity classes.

---

[3] And, as a technical aside, his generalization of this claim to FewP [2], the "polynomial ambiguity" version of UP, is an early example of the so-called parallel census technique ([51], see also [60,3]). Yamakami [61] also obtains results for the "constant ambiguity" generalizations of UP [58,32].

195

Probabilistic Databases

In their seminal papers, Schöning and Ko proved inclusions for the class of sets helped by BPP, bounded probabilistic polynomial time.

(ZPP is the class of sets accepted in expected polynomial time by probabilistic Turing machines that never err; R is the class of sets accepted by probabilistic polynomial-time Turing machines that for strings out of the language always detect that and for strings in the language detect that with probability at least 99 percent[4]; BPP is the class of sets accepted by probabilistic Turing machines that on each input are correct with probability above 75 percent[5] [24]. Known relations include $P \subseteq ZPP = R \cap coR \subseteq R \subseteq BPP$, $R \subseteq NP$, and $BPP \subseteq NP^{NP}$ [24,52,39].)

Theorem 12.

1. [36] $P_{1\text{-help}}(BPP) \subseteq R$.

2. [46] $P_{\text{help}}(BPP) \subseteq ZPP$.

Both Schöning and Ko asked whether equality holds in Theorem 12. Recently, Cai, Hemachandra, and Vyskoč [14] have proven that equality holds in the arbitrary failure model, a model, indicated by $\widehat{BPP}$, in which if the "promise" that THE PROBABILITY OF ACCEPTANCE IS NOT BETWEEN 25 PERCENT AND 75 PERCENT is broken by some query, then the answer returned on that query is unreliable and yet *not* considered a fault. This offers a complete characterization of ZPP and R in terms of fault-tolerant access.

Theorem 13. [14]

1. $R = P_{1\text{-help}}(\widehat{BPP})$.

2. $ZPP = P_{\text{help}}(\widehat{BPP})$.

The "obvious" proof (amplifying sharply and then walking the tree towards the subtree with the greater density of accepting computations) does not succeed, and instead a somewhat more involved combination of gap-computing [19,25] and imprecise computation is needed—loosely speaking, the machine doesn't always correctly find the subtree with the greater density of accepting computations, but it does in the cases when the subtrees differ greatly, and if they don't differ greatly, erring doesn't matter much anyway.

Theorem 13 shows how a probabilistic database can fault-tolerantly accept R and ZPP sets. This should be contrasted with the following result showing how low density sets in the polynomial hierarchy [42,53] can fault-tolerantly accept R and ZPP. Recall that SPARSE is the class of sets whose number of length n elements is bounded by some polynomial in n (see, e.g., the survey [31]).

Theorem 14. ([61], see also Open Question 24 in Section 5)

1. $R \subseteq P_{1\text{-help}}(\Sigma_3^p \cap SPARSE)$.

---

[4] Any constant probability c, $0 < c < 1$, is equivalent.
[5] Any constant probability c, $1/2 < c < 1$, is equivalent.

2. $\text{ZPP} \subseteq P_{\text{help}}(\Sigma_3^p \cap \text{SPARSE})$.

Returning to the first part of Theorem 12, $P_{1\text{-help}}(\text{BPP}) \subseteq \text{R}$, Vyskoč [57] noted a nice application: if $A \in P_{1\text{-help}}(\mathcal{C})$ and $\mathcal{C} \subseteq \text{BPP}$, then $A \in \text{R}$, and so for any class with $\mathcal{C} \subseteq P_{1\text{-help}}(\mathcal{C})$, it follows that $\mathcal{C} \subseteq \text{BPP} \Rightarrow \mathcal{C} \subseteq \text{R}$. Note that by Theorems 5, 11, and 8 this condition is satisfied by NP, $\{\beta_k \mid k \geq 0\}$, UP, and UP $\cap$ coUP.

Theorem 15. [57]

1. If $\text{UP} \subseteq \text{BPP}$, then $\text{UP} \subseteq \text{R}$.

2. If $\text{UP} \cap \text{coUP} \subseteq \text{BPP}$, then $\text{UP} \cap \text{coUP} \subseteq \text{R}$.

3. For each $k \geq 0$: If $\beta_k \subseteq \text{BPP}$, then $\beta_k \subseteq \text{R}$.

4. [35][6] If $\text{NP} \subseteq \text{BPP}$, then $\text{NP} \subseteq \text{R}$.

We note that one can state the analogous result for helping: If $A \in P_{\text{help}}(\mathcal{C})$ and $\mathcal{C} \subseteq \text{BPP}$, then $A \in \text{ZPP}$.

A Probabilistic Version of Robustness

We now briefly mention some results on probabilistic helping. Schöning alluded to this notion in [46] and it was explicitly defined by Fortnow, Rompel, and Sipser [21], under the name MIP, and Schöning [48] (see also [4]), to whose papers we refer the reader for an exact definition (we mention here only that the definition is but one of various possible definitions, and is not a tight analog of the case of standard helping: the definition allows the BPP machine to have its "bounded probability" condition broken and indeed the machine may not be a robust machine at all!). The recent result that MIP=NEXP (one direction each in [20] and [5]) comprises the first part below, and the second part is due to Torán. For a definition of MA see [6]; as a technical aside, a textbook's claim to the contrary notwithstanding, to the best of the author's knowledge it remains open whether MA=$\exists \cdot$ BPP, though certainly $\exists \cdot \text{BPP} = \text{NP}^{\text{BPP}}$. The *bounded-query* subscript below indicates that the set of strings queried in the tree is polynomial in size; the issue of whether the bound applies to only the correct database or to all databases is moot, as it is possible to see from the proof in [4] that for the case below the two notions are equivalent.

Theorem 16.

1. [20,5] $\text{BPP}_{1\text{-help}}(2^{\Sigma^*}) = \text{NEXP}$, where $\text{NEXP} = \bigcup_{k>0} \text{NTIME}[2^{n^k}]$.

2. (Torán, as cited in [48]) $\text{BPP}_{1\text{-help, bounded-query}}(2^{\Sigma^*}) = \text{MA}$.

Arvind, Schöning, and Schuler [4] discuss the above two theorems, and, via the probabilistic analog of Ko's Proposition 6, Part 2, derive from the above that $\text{BPP}_{\text{help}}(2^{\Sigma^*}) = \text{NEXP} \cap \text{coNEXP}$ and establish a characterization of MA $\cap$ coMA closely related to Torán's result.

---

[6] The proof found therein relies indirectly on an incorrectly proven theorem—which was latter proven by Zachos [62], thus reestablishing the result.

4 Robustness: Beyond Fixed Languages

Section 2 discussed machines robust in the sense that they accept the same language regardless of faults—and as we said, in the model of that section, being oblivious to faults is equivalent to accepting the same language with respect to any database. Hartmanis and Hemachandra [27] studied machines that maintain, with respect to any database, other computational properties. Generally put, it is so taxing for machines to maintain such properties that such machines cannot accept hard sets with respect to *any* database.

We state here just two examples. The first says that if two nondeterministic languages accept complementary languages for every database, then with respect to every database they accept only easy sets. Let N_0, N_1, ... be a standard enumeration of nondeterministic polynomial-time Turing machines.

Theorem 17. [27] $(\forall A)[L(N_i^A) = \overline{L(N_j^A)}]$ $\Rightarrow$ $(\forall A)[L(N_i^A) \in \mathrm{P}^{\mathrm{NP} \oplus A}]$.

Corollary 18. ([27,11], see also [55])   If P = NP and N_i and N_j are robustly complementary (i.e., $(\forall A)[L(N_i^A) = \overline{L(N_j^A)}]$), then for every database A it holds that $L(N_i^A) \in \mathrm{P}^A$.

The following theorem says machines that accept all strings with respect to every database of low density do so for relatively transparent reasons. This should be compared with the results of Borodin and Demers [12] and Hartmanis and Hemachandra [26] showing that complexity-theoretic assumptions generally believed true imply the existence of nondeterministic machines that accept all input strings but not for polynomial-time computable reasons.

Theorem 19. [27] $(\forall \text{ sparse } S)[L(N_i^S) = \Sigma^*]$ $\Rightarrow$ $(\forall \text{ sparse } S)(\exists f \text{ computable in } \mathrm{P}^{\mathrm{NP} \oplus S})(\forall x)[f(x) \text{ prints an accepting path of } N_i^S(x)]$.

Corollary 20. [27]   If P = NP and N_i robustly accepts Σ^* on sparse databases (i.e., $(\forall \text{ sparse } T)[L(N_i^T) = \Sigma^*]$), then for every sparse database S, there is a function f computable in P^S so that on any input x, $f(x)$ prints an accepting path of $N_i^S(x)$.

Crescenzi and Silvestri [16] have recently shown that the sparseness condition of the above theorem is essential; without the condition there are relativized worlds in which the result fails.

In addition to the above results, Hartmanis and Hemachandra [27] prove similar results for robustly unambiguous machines, robustly Σ^*-spanning machine collections, and so on, and Crescenzi and Silvestri [16] prove a similar result for machines that are simultaneously complementary and unambiguous.

We mention briefly two other computational properties for which robustness has been studied.

Positive reductions have played an important role in complexity theory—for example in the study of P-selective [49] and NP-selective [28] sets—ever since they were introduced into complexity theory by Ladner, Lynch, and Selman [38] and Selman [50]. Hemachandra and Jain [29] recently compared robustly positive reductions with nonrobustly positive reductions. (Curiously enough, the standard definition of positive reductions had been the less natural one—robust positivity.) They showed that if P = NP then robustly and nonrobustly positive truth-table reductions coincide. For the case of Turing reductions they show that, though nonrobust Turing reductions are potentially more flexible than robust positive Turing reductions, most of the key results that hold for robust positive Turing reductions also (with some exceptions, for which they display explicit relativized counterexamples) hold even for nonrobust positive Turing reductions.

Gavaldà and Balcázar [23] compared robust and nonrobust "strong"[7] nondeterministic Turing machines with access to sparse databases. Gavaldà and Balcázar characterize the power of both robust and nonrobust strong nondeterministic machines in terms of "advice" classes, and prove that if the two classes coincide, then an unlikely structural condition follows: If $NP \subseteq coNP^{SPARSE}$ then the polynomial hierarchy collapses to NP^{NP}.

5   Further Issues and Open Questions

In this section, we briefly bring to the reader's attention to some further issues related to robustness.

Lowness theory—originally defined by Schöning by analogy with the recursion-theoretic notion and since repeatedly refined [45,10,1,41]—studies the level at which databases stop increasing the power of the polynomial hierarchy, e.g., $L_0 = \{A \mid P^A = P\} = P$, $L_1 = \{A \mid NP^A = NP\} = NP \cap coNP$, $L_2 = \{A \mid NP^{NP^A} = NP^{NP}\}$, etc. A stream of results shows that sets that can be fault-tolerantly accepted inhabit only small levels of the low hierarchy [48,36,61,4].

No-helpers, introduced by Ko [36], are sets that fail to help in any nontrivial way, e.g., sets D such that $P_{help}(D) = P_{help}(\emptyset)$. No-helpers of various forms have been studied [36,8,4,61], yielding various classes of sets that are no-helpers (e.g., very sparse sets are always no-helpers [36]). Similarly, Ko introduced the notion of self-helpers, sets that (1-)help themselves ([36], see also [9]).

Open issues related to robust computation abound. We mention in particular the following questions.

Open Question 21. The current definition of robustness is "all or nothing"—a single detected fault allows one all the time in the world. Can one develop a theory of robustness in which the time bound depends more naturally on the faults, i.e., so that the machine is allowed time "polynomial + f(number of faults)" for various reasonable functions f?

Open Question 22. Prove that $R = P_{1\text{-help}}(BPP)$ or show some unlikely result that equality would imply. Similarly for $ZPP = P_{help}(BPP)$ and $UP = P_{1\text{-help}}(UP)$.

Open Question 23. What can be said about helping by parity-based and mod-based classes (see [61])?

---

[7] Strong machines, introduced by Long [40] and Selman [50], are machines that, loosely put, have certificates for rejection as well as for acceptance; thus, if they have access to no database, they accept exactly the $NP \cap coNP$ languages.

Open Question 24. Can Theorem 14 be improved (see Gavaldà [22] and Köbler [37])?

Open Question 25. For each known lowness result (see earlier this section for pointers), show some likely structural consequence that would follow were it improved (compare with the different lower bounding approach of [1]).

Acknowledgments

I thank J. Balcázar, J. Cai, L. Fortnow, R. Gavaldà, K. Ko, M. Ogiwara, U. Schöning, R. Schuler, R. Silvestri, S. Toda, J. Vyskoč, O. Watanabe, and T. Yamakami for their kind help in providing pointers to the literature and access to manuscripts.

References

1. E. Allender and L. Hemachandra. Lower bounds for the low hierarchy. *Journal of the ACM*, 39(1):234–250, 1992.

2. E. Allender and R. Rubinstein. P-printable sets. *SIAM Journal on Computing*, 17(6):1193–1202, 1988.

3. V. Arvind, Y. Han, L. Hemachandra, J. Köbler, A. Lozano, M. Mundhenk, M. Ogiwara, U. Schöning, R. Silvestri, and T. Thierauf. Reductions to sets of low information content. In K. Ambos-Spies, S. Homer, and U. Schöning, editors, *Complexity Theory*. Cambridge University Press. To appear.

4. V. Arvind, U. Schöning, and R. Schuler. On helping probabilistic oracle machines. Draft, Mar. 1993.

5. L. Babai, L. Fortnow, and C. Lund. Non-deterministic exponential time has two-prover interactive protocols. *Computational Complexity*, 1(1):3–40, 1991.

6. L. Babai and S. Moran. Arthur-Merlin games: A randomized proof system, and a hierarchy of complexity classes. *Journal of Computer and System Sciences*, 36(2):254–276, 1988.

7. T. Baker, J. Gill, and R. Solovay. Relativizations of the P=?NP question. *SIAM Journal on Computing*, 4(4):431–442, 1975.

8. J. Balcázar. Only smart oracles help. Technical Report LSI-88-9, Universitat Politècnica de Catalunya, Facultat d'Informatica, Barcelona, Spain, 1988.

9. J. Balcázar. Self-reducibility structures and solutions of NP problems. Technical Report LSI-88-19, Universitat Politècnica de Catalunya, Facultat d'Informatica, 1988. Also appears as pages 175–184 of *Revista Matematica de la UCM 2 (1989)*.

10. J. Balcázar, R. Book, and U. Schöning. Sparse sets, lowness and highness. *SIAM Journal on Computing*, 15(3):739–746, 1986.

11. M. Blum and R. Impagliazzo. Generic oracles and oracle classes. In *Proceedings of the 28th IEEE Symposium on Foundations of Computer Science*, pages 118–126, October 1987.

12. A. Borodin and A. Demers. Some comments on functional self-reducibility and the NP hierarchy. Technical Report TR 76-284, Cornell Department of Computer Science, Ithaca, NY, July 1976.

13. G. Buntrock, L. Hemachandra, and D. Siefkes. Using inductive counting to simulate nondeterministic computation. *Information and Computation*, 102(1):102–117, 1993.

14. J. Cai, L. Hemachandra, and J. Vyskoč. Promise problems and access to unambiguous computation. In *Proceedings of the 17th Symposium on Mathematical Foundations of Computer Science*, pages 162–171. Springer-Verlag *Lecture Notes in Computer Science #629*, Aug. 1992.

15. J. Cai, L. Hemachandra, and J. Vyskoč. Promises and fault-tolerant database access. Technical Report TR-447, University of Rochester, Department of Computer Science, Rochester, NY, 1993. Preliminary version appears in *Proceedings of the 17th Symposium on Mathematical Foundations of Computer Science (1992)*.

16. P. Crescenzi and R. Silvestri. Sperner's lemma and robust machines. In *Proceedings of the 8th Structure in Complexity Theory Conference*. IEEE Computer Society Press, 1993. To appear.

17. J. Díaz and J. Torán. Classes of bounded nondeterminism. *Mathematical Systems Theory*, 23(1):21–32, 1990.

18. D. Eppstein, L. Hemachandra, J. Tisdall, and B. Yener. Simultaneous strong separations of probabilistic and unambiguous complexity classes. *Mathematical Systems Theory*, 25(1):23–36, 1992.

19. S. Fenner, L. Fortnow, and S. Kurtz. Gap-definable counting classes. In *Proceedings of the 6th Structure in Complexity Theory Conference*, pages 30–42. IEEE Computer Society Press, June/July 1991.

20. L. Fortnow, J. Rompel, and M. Sipser. On the power of multiple-prover interactive protocols. Manuscript. Preliminary version appears as [21].

21. L. Fortnow, J. Rompel, and M. Sipser. On the power of multiple-prover interactive protocols. In *Proceedings of the 3rd Structure in Complexity Theory Conference*, pages 156–161. IEEE Computer Society Press, June 1988. Erratum appears in the same conference's 1990 proceedings, pp. 318–319.

22. R. Gavaldà. Bounding the complexity of advice functions. In *Proceedings of the 7th Structure in Complexity Theory Conference*, pages 249–254. IEEE Computer Society Press, June 1992.

23. R. Gavaldà and J. Balcázar. Strong and robustly strong polynomial time reducibilities to sparse sets. *Theoretical Computer Science*, 88(1):1–14, 1991.

24. J. Gill. Computational complexity of probabilistic Turing machines. *SIAM Journal on Computing*, 6(4):675–695, 1977.

25. S. Gupta. The power of witness reduction. In *Proceedings of the 6th Structure in Complexity Theory Conference*, pages 43–59. IEEE Computer Society Press, June/July 1991.

26. J. Hartmanis and L. Hemachandra. Complexity classes without machines: On complete languages for UP. *Theoretical Computer Science*, 58:129–142, 1988.

27. J. Hartmanis and L. Hemachandra. Robust machines accept easy sets. *Theoretical Computer Science*, 74(2):217–226, 1990.

28. L. Hemachandra, A. Hoene, M. Ogiwara, A. Selman, T. Thierauf, and J. Wang. Selectivity. In *Proceedings of the 5th International Conference on Computing and Information*. IEEE Computer Society Press, 1993. To appear.

29. L. Hemachandra and S. Jain. On the limitations of locally robust positive reductions. *International Journal of Foundations of Computer Science*, 2(3):237–255, 1991.

30. L. Hemachandra and S. Jha. Defying upward and downward separation. In *Proceedings of the 10th Annual Symposium on Theoretical Aspects of Computer Science*, pages 185–195. Springer-Verlag *Lecture Notes in Computer Science #665*, Feb. 1993.

31. L. Hemachandra, M. Ogiwara, and O. Watanabe. How hard are sparse sets? In *Proceedings of the 7th Structure in Complexity Theory Conference*, pages 222–238. IEEE Computer Society Press, June 1992.

32. L. Hemachandra and E. Spaan. Quasi-injective reductions. *Theoretical Computer Science*. To appear.

33. R. Karp and R. Lipton. Some connections between nonuniform and uniform complexity classes. In *Proceedings of the 12th ACM Symposium on Theory of Computing*, pages 302–309, Apr. 1980.

34. C. Kintala and P. Fisher. Refining nondeterminism in relativized polynomial-time bounded computations. *SIAM Journal on Computing*, 9(1):46–53, 1980.

35. K. Ko. Some observations on the probabilistic algorithms and NP-hard problems. *Information Processing Letters*, 14(1):39–43, 1982.

36. K. Ko. On helping by robust oracle machines. *Theoretical Computer Science*, 52:15–36, 1987.

37. J. Köbler. Locating P/poly optimally in the extended low hierarchy. In *Proceedings of the 10th Annual Symposium on Theoretical Aspects of Computer Science*, pages 28–37. Springer-Verlag *Lecture Notes in Computer Science #665*, Feb. 1993.

38. R. Ladner, N. Lynch, and A. Selman. A comparison of polynomial time reducibilities. *Theoretical Computer Science*, 1(2):103–124, 1975.

39. C. Lautemann. BPP and the polynomial hierarchy. *Information Processing Letters*, 14:215–217, 1983.

40. T. Long. Strong nondeterministic polynomial-time reducibilities. *Theoretical Computer Science*, 21:1–25, 1982.

41. T. Long and M. Sheu. A refinement of the low and high hierarchies. Technical Report OSU-CISRC-2/91-TR6, Ohio State University, Department of Computer Science, Columbus, Ohio, Feb. 1991.

42. A. Meyer and L. Stockmeyer. The equivalence problem for regular expressions with squaring requires exponential space. In *Proceedings of the 13th IEEE Symposium on Switching and Automata Theory*, pages 125–129, 1972.

43. R. Niedermeier and P. Rossmanith. Unambiguous simulations of auxiliary pushdown automata and circuits. In *Proceedings, 1st Latin American Symposium on Theoretical Informatics*, pages 387–400. Springer-Verlag *Lecture Notes in Computer Science #583*, Apr. 1992.

44. C. Rackoff. Relativized questions involving probabilistic algorithms. *Journal of the ACM*, 29(1):261–268, 1982.

45. U. Schöning. A low and a high hierarchy in NP. *Journal of Computer and System Sciences*, 27:14–28, 1983.

46. U. Schöning. Robust algorithms: A different approach to oracles. *Theoretical Computer Science*, 40:57–66, 1985.

47. U. Schöning. Complexity theory and interaction. In R. Herken, editor, *The Universal Turing Machine: A Half-Century Survey*, pages 561–580. Oxford University Press, 1988.

48. U. Schöning. Robust oracle machines. In *Proceedings of the 13th Symposium on Mathematical Foundations of Computer Science*, pages 93–106. Springer-Verlag *Lecture Notes in Computer Science #324*, August/September 1988.

49. A. Selman. P-selective sets, tally languages, and the behavior of polynomial time reducibilities on NP. *Mathematical Systems Theory*, 13:55–65, 1979.

50. A. Selman. Reductions on NP and P-selective sets. *Theoretical Computer Science*, 19:287–304, 1982.

51. A. Selman. A note on adaptive vs. nonadaptive reductions to NP. Technical Report 90-20, State University of New York at Buffalo Department of Computer Science, Buffalo, NY, Sept. 1990.

52. M. Sipser. Borel sets and circuit complexity. In *Proceedings of the 15th ACM Symposium on Theory of Computing*, pages 61–69, 1983.

53. L. Stockmeyer. The polynomial-time hierarchy. *Theoretical Computer Science*, 3:1–22, 1977.

54. R. Szelepcsényi. β_k-complete problems and greediness. Manuscript, Mar. 1993.

55. G. Tardos. Query complexity, or why is it difficult to separate $NP^A \cap coNP^A$ from P^A by random oracles A. *Combinatorica*, 9:385–392, 1989.

56. L. Valiant. The relative complexity of checking and evaluating. *Information Processing Letters*, 5:20–23, 1976.

57. J. Vyskoč, Mar. 1993. Personal Communication.

58. O. Watanabe. On hardness of one-way functions. *Information Processing Letters*, 27:151–157, 1988.

59. O. Watanabe. On intractability of the class UP. *Mathematical Systems Theory*, 24:1–10, 1991.

60. O. Watanabe and S. Toda. Structural analysis on the complexity of inverting functions. In *Proceedings of the 1990 SIGAL International Symposium on Algorithms*, pages 31–38. Springer-Verlag *Lecture Notes in Computer Science #450*, Aug. 1990.

61. T. Yamakami. Polynomial helpers of robust machines. Manuscript, Dec. 1990.

62. S. Zachos. Probabilistic quantifiers and games. *Journal of Computer and System Sciences*, 36:433–451, 1988.

Reversal-Space Trade-offs For Simultaneous Resource-Bounded Nondeterministic Turing Machines

Hiroaki YAMAMOTO

Department of Information Engineering, Faculty of Engineering, Shinshu University,
Nagano-shi, 380 Japan

Abstract. Studying trade-offs among computational complexities is one of the important topics in the computer science. In this paper, we are concerned with two important complexities, reversal and space, and show reversal-space trade-off results for nondeterministic Turing machines (NTMs for short). For example, the following results are shown: Let $Nreve, space_k(R(n), S(n))$ and off-$Nreve, space_k(R(n), S(n))$ be classes of languages accepted by k-tape NTMs and off-line k-tape NTMs running simultaneously within $O(R(n))$ reversals and $O(S(n))$ space, respectively. Then we have the following: (1) $Nreve, space_1(R(n), S(n))$ $= Nreve, space_1 (S(n), R(n))$, where $R(n) \geq n$ and $S(n) \geq n$, and (2) off-$Nreve, space_1 (R(n)n^{O(1)}, S(n)(\log n)^{O(1)}) =$ off-$Nreve, space_1 (S(n)(\log n)^{O(1)}, R(n)n^{O(1)})$. Moreover we consider multitape NTMs and obtain the following: For any $k \geq 1$, (1) $Nreve, space_k(R(n)^{O(1)}, S(n)^{O(1)}) = Nreve, space_1 (S(n)^{O(1)}, R(n)^{O(1)})$, where $R(n) \geq S(n) \geq n$, and (2) off-$Nreve, space_k (R(n)^{O(1)}, S(n)^{O(1)}) =$ off-$Nreve, space_1 (S(n)^{O(1)}, R(n)^{O(1)})$, where $R(n) \geq S(n) \geq \log n$ and $R(n)S(n) \geq n \log n$. Such reversal-space trade-off results for deterministic Turing machines is still not known.

1 Introduction

Studying trade-offs among computational complexities is one of the important topics in the computer science. In this paper, we are concerned with two important complexities, reversal and space, and show reversal-space trade-off results for nondeterministic Turing machines (NTM for short) bounded simultaneously by these complexities. Up to now, reversal and space complexities have been widely studied [1, 3, 4, 6, 7, 9]. As a reversal-space trade-off result, Greibach [4] is very famous. She studied the relationships between the reversal complexity classes and the space complexity classes, and showed that the classes of languages accepted by $R(n) \log n$ space-bounded NTMs are equal to the classes of languages accepted by $R(n)$ reversal-bounded NTMs. However, she never considered simultaneous resource bounded classes. Moriya [6] studied simultaneous resource bounded classes for off-line 1-tape NTMs. He considers time, reversal and space complexities and obtained some interesting relations, such as relations between the time-space bounded complexity classes and the reversal-space bounded complexity classes. He there introduced restricted off-line NTMs, called sweep NTMs, which are NTMs without any stationary move. By a stationary move, we mean a move such that an NTM changes only the state, the input head position and the tape symbol, and does not move the storage-tape head at all. Although he obtained a reversal-space trade-off for such models, there are no fine reversal-space trade-offs for general models. By focusing on reversal-space bounded complexity classes, we will show fine reversal-space trade-offs for general models.

Our results are as follows: Let $Nreve, space_k(R(n), S(n))$ and off-$Nreve, space_k(R(n), S(n))$ be classes of languages accepted by k-tape NTMs and off-line k-tape NTMs running simultaneously within $O(R(n))$ reversals and $O(S(n))$ space, respectively. A k-tape Turing machine is a Turing machine having k storage-tapes. An off-line k-tape Turing machine is a Turing machine having k storage-tapes and a read-only two-way input tape. Then we have the following fine trade-offs: For 1-tape NTMs, $Nreve, space_1(R(n), S(n)) = Nreve, space_1(S(n), R(n))$, where $R(n) \geq n$ and $S(n) \geq n$. For off-line 1-tape NTMs, off-$Nreve, space_1(R(n), S(n)) \subseteq$ off-$Nreve, space_1(S(n), R(n)n)$ and off-$Nreve, space_1(R(n), S(n)) \subseteq$ off-$Nreve, space_1(S(n)n^2/f(n), R(n)f(n))$, where $f(n)$ is any function satisfying $n \geq f(n) \geq \log n$. As an immediate corollary of results for sweep NTMs in [6], Moriya also can get off-$Nreve, space_1(R(n), S(n)) \subseteq$ off-$Nreve, space_1(S(n)n^2, R(n) \log n)$. However, our second result clearly leads to a finer trade-off if $f(n) = \log n$, that is, off-$Nreve, space_1(R(n), S(n)) \subseteq$ off-$Nreve, space_1(S(n)n^2/\log n, R(n) \log n)$. Moreover it is clear that our results are more general. Some interesting results follow from the main results. For example, we immediately have the following for any functions $R(n)$ and $S(n)$: off-$Nreve, space_1(R(n)n^{O(1)}, S(n)(\log n)^{O(1)}) =$ off-$Nreve, space_1(S(n)(\log n)^{O(1)}, R(n)n^{O(1)})$.

Finally we consider multitape NTMs. For such models, we will get the following: (1) If $R(n) \geq S(n) \geq n$, then we have $Nreve, space(R(n)^{O(1)}, S(n)^{O(1)}) = Nreve, space_1(S(n)^{O(1)}, R(n)^{O(1)})$, where $Nreve, space(R(n), S(n)) = \cup_{k \geq 1} Nreve, space_k(R(n), S(n))$. (2) If $R(n) \geq S(n) \geq \log n$ and $R(n)S(n) \geq n \log n$, then we have off-$Nreve, space(R(n)^{O(1)}, S(n)^{O(1)}) =$ off-$Nreve, space_1(S(n)^{O(1)}, R(n)^{O(1)})$, where off-$Nreve, space(R(n), S(n))$ is also defined similarly. For example, this result leads to off-$Nreve, space(n^{O(1)}, (\log n)^{O(1)}) =$ off-$Nreve, space_1((\log n)^{O(1)}, n^{O(1)})$.

For reversal- and space-bounded deterministic Turing machines (DTM for short), there are two well-known classes, that is, NC and SC. The class NC (SC, respectively) is the class of languages accepted by $(\log n)^{O(1)}$ reversal- and $n^{O(1)}$ space-bounded DTMs ($n^{O(1)}$ reversal- and $(\log n)^{O(1)}$ space-bounded DTMs, respectively). The class NC is known as one which includes problems with an efficient parallel algorithm. From the view point of the parallel complexity, the reversal complexity corresponds to the parallel time and the space complexity corresponds to the number of processors. Thus the question whether NC=SC or not is related to the time-processor trade-off in parallel algorithms and important. However, it remains open. In [2], Cook conjectured that NC and SC are incomparable by showing some candidates for NC≠SC. Moriya [6] showed the affirmative answer for one tape nondeterministic version of this problem. This result can be put forward as a corollary of our results. Moreover, by our results, if Cook's conjecture is true, then NC and SC are proper subsets of off-$Nreve, space((\log n)^{O(1)}, n^{O(1)})$, and thus we can get a difference between nondeterminism and determinism for subsets of the classes P and NP.

2 Preliminaries

In this section, we give some definitions. Throughout the paper, by a function, we mean a non-decreasing function from natural numbers to real numbers.

In this paper, we are concerned with two type of Turing machines, k-tape Turing machines and off-line k-tape Turing machines. A k-tape Turing machine is a Turing machine having k storage-tapes. An off-line k-tape Turing machine is a Turing machine having k storage-tapes and a read-only two-way input tape.

Definition 1. Let $R(n)$ and $S(n)$ be functions. It is said that an NTM runs in reversal $R(n)$ (respectively, space $S(n)$) if, for every accepted input of length n, there is an accepting computation such that the number of times storage-tape heads change directions on its computation is at most $O(R(n))$ (respectively, the number of squares used by the machine is at most $O(S(n))$). Also such NTMs are called $R(n)$ reversal-bounded NTMs ($S(n)$ space-bounded NTMs, respectively). If an accepting computation satisfies two complexity conditions, we say that an NTM runs simultaneously in these complexities. For example, it is said that an NTM runs simultaneously in reversal $R(n)$ and space $S(n)$ if, for every accepted input of length n, there is an accepting computation such that the number of times storage-tape heads change directions on its computation is at most $O(R(n))$ and the amount of space used by the machine is at most $O(S(n))$. Such an NTM is also called an $R(n)$ reversal- and $S(n)$ space-bounded NTM. Note that for off-line NTMs, the space complexity and the reversal complexity are defined only for storage-tapes.

Definition 2. Let $R(n)$ and $S(n)$ be functions. $Nreve, space_k(R(n), S(n))$ denotes a class of languages accepted by k-tape NTMs running simultaneously in reversal $R(n)$ and space $S(n)$. Similarly, off-$Nreve, space_k(R(n), S(n))$ is defined for off-line k-tape NTMs. If there are no suffixes for the number of tapes, it means the union over the number of tapes. For example,
$Nreve, space(R(n), S(n)) = \cup_{k \geq 1} Nreve, space_k(R(n), S(n))$

Two well-known classes for DTMs, NC and SC, are defined as follows:
NC=off-$Dreve, space((\log n)^{O(1)}, n^{O(1)})$,
SC=off-$Dreve, space(n^{O(1)}, (\log n)^{O(1)})$.

3 1-tape Nondeterministic Turing Machines

Without loss of generality, we may assume that every 1-tape NTM M moves as follows: The input of length n stands originally on the tape squares $1, \ldots, n$, and the head of M stands originally on square 0. M starts by going in initial state to square 1 and visits square 0 again only if it is in the accepting state, where tape squares are numbered from 0 from the left-end. Moreover, in one move, M changes the state and the tape-symbol, and then moves the tape head. The following is what we first got in [9]. Since the proof includes the basic idea used in the subsequent section, we give it. Note that the proof in [9] is made for more general models.

Proposition 3. *Let $R(n) \geq n$ and $S(n) \geq n$ be functions. Then,*
$Nreve, space_1(R(n), S(n)) \subseteq Nreve, space_1(S(n), R(n))$.

(Proof) Let $\in Nreve, space_1(R(n), S(n))$ and N be an $R(n)$ reversal- and $S(n)$ space-bounded 1-tape NTM accepting L. A 1-tape NTM M accepting L is constructed as follows.

The tape of M has three tracks. The input is given to the first track and the second, and the third, tracks are used to store crossing sequences. They are stored from square $n + 1$. The squares from 1 to n are used to indicate the position of each crossing sequence if it is in the squares from 1 to n.

The action of M is as follows: First M guesses the crossing sequences s_1 and s_2 at both boundaries of a square. Next M checks the consistency of the guessed crossing sequences. For that reason, we describe how to store the crossing sequences.

The time interval from a reversal to the next reversal is called a phase. The first phase is defined as the time interval from the start to the first reversal. M provides two squares, $n + 2t - 1$ and $n + 2t$, in each track for the tth phase of a computation of N. Now, let a crossing sequence of N be $q_1 \cdots q_s$ and assume that $q_j (1 \leq j \leq s)$ is generated by the t_jth phase. Then, each q_j is stored according to the following rules.

(a) In the case where this crossing sequence corresponds to s_1, if t_j is odd, then q_j is stored in square $n + 2t_j - 1$, otherwise in square $n + 2t_j$.
(b) In the case where this crossing sequence corresponds to s_2, if t_j is even, then q_j is stored in square $n + 2t_j - 1$, otherwise in square $n + 2t_j$.

Procedure CONSIST($s_1, s_2, squarenum$)
This procedure does for checking the consistency of s_1 and s_2, where $s_1 = q_1 \cdots q_m$, $s_2 = p_1 \cdots p_{m'}$. Then this is done in the following way:

(1) M sets the state to q_1. If $squarenum \leq n$, then M reads the $squarenum$th symbol of the input into the finite control and marks the input-symbol; otherwise reads a blank symbol. Thus since the input-symbols which have been already processed are marked, it is easy for M to find out the $squarenum$th symbol.
(2) In order to check whether or not there exists a computation of M such that s_1 and s_2 are consistent with the crossing sequences of both sides of the $squarenum$th square, M simulates N using the finite control. If there exists such a computation, then M returns, otherwise M enters the rejecting state.

MAIN

Step 1 Set *squarenum* to 1.

Step 2 If *squarenum* $= 1$, then $s_1 \leftarrow q_0 q_a$, where q_0 and q_a are the initial state and an accepting state of N, respectively. If *squarenum* $\neq 1$, then $s_1 \leftarrow s_2$.

Step 3 Guess s_2.

Step 4 CONSIST($s_1, s_2, squarenum$).

Step 5 If $s_2 = \epsilon$, then M enters the accepting state and halts, otherwise *squarenum* $\leftarrow$ *squarenum* $+ 1$ and go to Step 2.

End of **MAIN**

Analysis of complexities: The space complexity is $O(R(n))$ because it depends on the space to store the crossing sequences. The procedure CONSIST requires only $O(1)$ reversals if the crossing sequences are stored under the rules (a) and (b). Since CONSIST is called at most $O(S(n))$ times, the reversal complexity is $O(S(n))$. $\qquad$ Q.E.D.

Corollary 4. *Let $R(n) \geq n$ and $S(n) \geq n$ be functions. Then,*
$Nreve, space_1(R(n), S(n)) = Nreve, space_1(S(n), R(n))$.

(Proof) This corollary follows from Proposition 1 directly. $\qquad$ Q.E.D.

4 Off-line 1-Tape Nondeterministic Turing Machines

In this section, we will be concerned with off-line 1-tape NTMs. As with 1-tape NTMs, without loss of generality, we may assume that every 1-tape NTM M moves as follows: The storage-tape head of M stands originally on square 0. M starts by going in initial state to square 1 and visits square 0 again only if it is in the accepting state, where storage-tape squares are numbered from 0 from the left-end. Moreover, in one move, M changes the state and the tape-symbol, moves the input head, and then moves the storage-tape head. Basically the proofs of the following theorems use the technique checking the consistency of crossing sequences (for example, see [5] or [9]).

Theorem 5. *Let $R(n)$ and $S(n)$ be functions. Then,*
$off\text{-}Nreve, space_1(R(n), S(n)) \subseteq off\text{-}Nreve, space_1(S(n), R(n)n)$.

(Proof) Let $L \in$ off-$Nreve, space_1(R(n), S(n))$ and N be an $R(n)$ reversal- and $S(n)$ space-bounded off-line 1-tape NTM accepting L. Then we construct an off-line 1-tape NTM M accepting L within $O(S(n))$ reversals and $O(R(n)n)$ space as follows: The storage-tape of M has two tracks, which are used to store crossing sequences. For off-line 1-tape NTMs, crossing sequences are defined as sequences of tuples $(state, ihp)$, where ihp is for an input head position, and is represented as a unary number. As with the proof of Proposition 1, M guesses crossing sequences, s_1 and s_2, at the left and the right boundaries of a square, respectively, and checks the consistency of s_1 and s_2. This time, s_1 and s_2 are stored in the first track and the second track, respectively.

We first describe how to store the crossing sequences. The storage-tape of M is divided into blocks in which a tuple $(state, ihp)$ is stored. The time interval from a reversal to the next reversal is called a phase. The first phase is defined as the time interval from the start to the first reversal. M provides two blocks, $2t - 1$ and $2t$, in each track for the tth phase of a computation of N. Now, let a crossing sequence of N be $\alpha_1 \cdots \alpha_s$ and assume that $\alpha_j (1 \leq j \leq s)$ is generated by the t_jth phase. Then, each α_j is stored according to the following rules.

(a) In the case where this crossing sequence corresponds to s_1, if t_j is odd, then α_j is stored in block $2t_j - 1$, otherwise in block $2t_j$.

(b) In the case where this crossing sequence corresponds to s_2, if t_j is even, then α_j is stored in block $2t_j - 1$, otherwise in block $2t_j$.

Procedure CONSIST(s_1, s_2)

This procedure checks the consistency of s_1 and s_2, where $s_1 = \alpha_1 \cdots \alpha_m$, $s_2 = \beta_1 \cdots \beta_{m'}$. Let $\alpha_1 = (q_1, i_1)$. Then this is done in the following way:

(1) M reads a blank symbol into the finite control, sets the state to q_1 and puts the input head on the position i_1. Note that these actions require only $O(1)$ reversals.

(2) In order to check whether or not there exists a computation of M such that s_1 and s_2 are consistent with the crossing sequences of both sides of a square, M simulates N using the finite control and the input tape. During the simulation, each time the storage-tape head of N goes out from the square, M must check the state and the input head position in the guessed crossing sequences. The check of the state is done by comparing the state in the finite control with the state specified in s_1 and s_2. The check of the input head position is done as follows: Let (q, i) be the currently checked tuple of the crossing sequence. Then M compares the current position of the input head with i by moving the input head to the left. Thus M requires only $O(1)$ reversals. If there exists a consistent computation, then M returns, otherwise M enters the rejecting state.

End of CONSIST

MAIN

Step 1 Set *squarenum* to 1.

Step 2 If *squarenum* $= 1$, then $s_1 \leftarrow (q_0, 1)(q_a, i)$, where q_0 and q_a are the initial state and an accepting state of N, respectively. If *squarenum* $\neq 1$, then $s_1 \leftarrow s_2$, that is, M copies s_2 into the first track according to rule (a) as follows: By one sweep from the left to the right over the storage-tape, for the t_j phase (t_j is even), M copies block $2t_j - 1$ in the second track to block $2t_j$ in the first track, and by one sweep from the right to the left, for the t_j phase (t_j is odd), M copies block $2t_j - 1$ in the second track to block $2t_j$ in the first track. Thus, if M uses the input tape, this is done in $O(1)$ reversals.

Step 3 Guess s_2.

Step 4 CONSIST(s_1, s_2).

Step 5 If $s_2 = \epsilon$, then M enters the accepting state and halts; otherwise $squarenum \leftarrow squarenum + 1$ and go to Step 2.

End of MAIN

Analysis of complexities: The space complexity is $O(R(n)n)$ because it depends on the space to store the crossing sequences. The reversal complexity depends on CONSIST. This procedure requires only $O(1)$ reversals. Hence, since this is called $O(S(n))$ times in MAIN, the reversal complexity is $O(S(n))$.Q.E.D.

In what follows, we show another fine trade-off. The similar result can be seen in Moriya [6]. However, Moriya showed it for restricted NTMs, called sweep NTMs, which are NTMs without any stationary move. By using crossing sequences, we obtain the result for more general models. As stated in Introduction, the next result shows a finer trade-off than Moriya's.

Theorem 6. *Let $R(n)$ and $S(n)$ be functions. Then, for any function $f(n)$ satisfying $n \geq f(n) \geq \log n$,*
$off\text{-}Nreve, space_1(R(n), S(n)) \subseteq off\text{-}Nreve, space_1(S(n)n^2/f(n), R(n)f(n))$.

(Proof) Let $L \in off\text{-}Nreve, space_1(R(n), S(n))$ and N be an $R(n)$ reversal- and $S(n)$ space-bounded off-line 1-tape NTM accepting L. Let $m = \lceil f(n) \rceil$. Then we construct an off-line 1-tape NTM M accepting L within $O(S(n)n^2/f(n))$ reversals and $O(R(n)f(n))$ space as follows.

The storage-tape of M has five tracks, where the first and the second tracks are used to store the guessed crossing sequences, the third and the fourth tracks is used to check the consistency, and the fifth track is used as binary counters. For off-line NTMs, crossing sequences are defined as sequences of tuples,
$(state_1, tsym_1, ttmp, ihp_1, in_0, d_1, in_1, \ldots, in_{m-1}, d_m, rnum, ihp_2, tsym_2, state_2)$,
where ihp_1 and ihp_2 represent input head positions, each in_i is used to store the input symbol, $d_i \in \{-1, 0, 1\}$ represents the direction of the input head movement and $rnum$ is $-\sum_{i=1}^{m} d_i$. These are used for stationary moves. The elements ihp_1 and ihp_2 are given as binary representations and $rnum$ is given as a unary representation. The elements $tsym_1$, $ttmp$ and $tsym_2$ are used for tape symbols in the square which the storage-head enters with the tuple, and $tsym_1 = ttmp$ when crossing sequences are guessed. As with the proof of Proposition 1, M guesses crossing sequences, s_1 and s_2, at the left and the right boundaries of a square, respectively, and checks the consistency of s_1 and s_2. This time, s_1 and s_2 are stored in the first track and the second track, respectively.

We first describe how to store the crossing sequences. The storage-tape of M is divided into blocks in which a tuple $(state_1, tsym_1, ttmp, ihp_1, in_0, d_1, in_1, \ldots, in_{m-1}, d_m, in_m, rnum, ihp_2, tsym_2, state_2)$ is stored. The time interval from a reversal to the next reversal is called a phase. The first phase is defined as the time interval from the start to the first reversal. M provides two blocks, $2t - 1$ and $2t$, in each track for the tth phase of a computation of N. Now, let a crossing sequence of N be $\alpha_1 \cdots \alpha_s$ and assume that $\alpha_j (1 \leq j \leq s)$ is generated by the t_jth phase. Then, each α_j is stored according to the following rules.

(a) In the case where this crossing sequence corresponds to s_1, if t_j is odd, then α_j is stored in block $2t_j - 1$, otherwise in block $2t_j$.

(b) In the case where this crossing sequence corresponds to s_2, if t_j is even, then α_j is stored in block $2t_j - 1$, otherwise in block $2t_j$.

Following the above rule, the sequence of tuples of s_1 and s_2 is viewed as a sequence $\gamma_1 \cdots \gamma_m$ such that, for every odd number $j \geq 1$, N enters a square with γ_j and goes out from it with γ_{j+1}. We call such a sequence a *legal sequence* of s_1 and s_2.

We first describe some procedures used by the main program.

Procedure POS_CHECK1(s)

The argument s is a crossing sequence. The elements ihp_1 and ihp_2 of each tuple in s need to be equal to simulate N correctly. This procedure checks whether ihp_1 and ihp_2 are equal or not.

(1) $i \leftarrow 1$.

(2) M puts the storage-tape head on the left-end of the tape. And then, by moving the head from the left-end to the right-end, M checks whether the ith bits of ihp_1 and ihp_2 is equal or not. If equal, then go to (3), otherwise M enters the rejecting state.

(3) If M has checked all bits, then M returns; otherwise $i \leftarrow i + 1$ and go to (2).

End of POS_CHECK1

Procedure POS_CHECK2(s_1,s_2)

The argument s_1 and s_2 are crossing sequences. Let $\gamma_1 \cdots \gamma_m$ be a legal sequence of s_1 and s_2. This procedure is used in the procedure CONSIST. In CONSIST, to check the consistency of the crossing sequences, M must check whether or not the current input head position is equal to ihp_1 in γ_{j+1} for every odd number $j \geq 1$ when the storage-tape head goes out from a square. For that reason, M adds $rnum$ to the element ihp_2 for every γ_j, and then it is compared with ihp_1 in γ_{j+1}.

(1) For every γ_j with odd number $j \geq 1$, M adds $-rnum$ to ihp_2 in γ_j. Since $|rnum| \leq m$, M requires only $O(m)$ reversals, that is, $O(f(n))$ reversals.

(2) $i \leftarrow 1$.

(3) M puts the storage-tape head on the left-end of the tape. And then, by moving the head from the left-end to the right-end, M checks whether the ith bit of ihp_2 in γ_j is equal to the ith bit of ihp_1 in γ_{j+1} or not for every γ_j with odd number $j \geq 1$. If equal, then go to (4), otherwise M enters the rejecting state.

(4) If M has checked all bits, then M returns; otherwise $i \leftarrow i + 1$ and go to (3).

End of POS_CHECK2

Procedure INPUT(s)

The argument s is a crossing sequence. When a crossing sequence is guessed, every element in_i is empty. This procedure reads the input symbol into each in_i.

(1) For every tuple in s, M checks whether $rnum = -\sum_i d_i$ or not. This can be done in $O(1)$ reversals if M uses the input tape.

(2) M makes a binary counter for each tuple of s. Namely, the binary counter is made in the fifth track beneath ihp_1. M puts the input head on the left-end.

(3) M does the following each time it moves the input head to the right one square:

First M adds one to all counters. Next, by moving the storage-tape head the left-end to the right-end, M checks whether counter is equal to ihp_1 or not. If equal, then M reads the input symbol currently scanned by the input head into in_0. M then moves the input head according to $d_1, \ldots, d_{m-1}$ and reads the input symbols into $in_1, \ldots, in_{m-1}$. After that, M moves the input head to the left or the right $|rnum|$ squares (if $rnum$ is positive, the right, otherwise the left). Thus $rnum$ is used to return the input head to the position indicated by the counters.

End of INPUT

Procedure CONSIST(s_1, s_2)

This procedure checks the consistency of s_1 and s_2. Let $\gamma_1 \cdots \gamma_m$ be a legal sequence of s_1 and s_2. First M copies s_1 and s_2 into the third and the fourth tracks, respectively. After that, checking the consistency of s_1 and s_2 is done in the following way, using the third and the fourth tracks:

(1) For every odd number $j \geq 1$, M does the following (1-1) to (1-3) for γ_j being not marked.
Let $\gamma_j = (q_1^j, t_1^j, tmp^j, x_1^j, a_0^j, d_1^j, a_1^j, \ldots, a_{m-1}^j, d_m^j, rnum^j, x_2^j, t_2^j, q_2^j)$. Note that, in the beginning, every γ_j is not marked and $t_1^j = tmp^j$. Moreover, since every γ_j can be processed in one sweep from the left-end to the right-end over the storage-tape, the steps (1-1) and (1-2) require only $O(1)$ reversals.

(1-1) M sets the state to q_1^j and reads tmp^j into the finite control.

(1-2) While reading the input symbols $a_0^j, \ldots, a_{m-1}^j$, M simulates N until N moves the storage-tape head. This time, M checks also the correctness of $d_1^j, \ldots, d_m^j$. After having processed a_{m-1}^j, M sets the current tape symbol and the current state in the finite control to t_2^j and q_2^j, respectively. If N continues stationary moves, then M goes to (1-3). If N has moved the storage-tape head, then M marks γ_j and goes to (1-3).

(1-3) If every γ_j is marked, then go to (2). Otherwise, for γ_j being not marked, M updates it. That is, M guesses a new tuple γ_j',
$(q_1, t_1, tmp, x_1, a_0, d_1, \ldots, a_{m-1}, d_m, rnum, x_2, t_2, q_2)$,
where $q_1 = q_2^j$, $t_1 = t_1^j$, $tmp = t_2^j$, and $x_1 = x_1^j + rnum^j$. This can be done in $O(|rnum|)$ reversals, that is, $O(f(n))$ reversals. After that, M calls INPUT(s_1') and INPUT(s_2') to read input symbols, where s_1' and s_2' are s_1 and s_2 updated by the above process, respectively, and then M goes to (1-1), regarding γ_j' as γ_j.

(2) For every odd number $j \geq 1$, M does the following: Let γ_j' be an updated tuple of γ_j. M checks whether t_1^j in γ_j' is equal to t_2^{j+2} in γ_{j+2}' or not. If all is equal, then go to (3), otherwise M enters the rejecting state. This step also requires only $O(1)$ reversals.

(3) For every odd number $j \geq 1$, M checks whether q_2^j in γ_j' is equal to q_1^{j+1} in γ_{j+1} or not. This also requires only $O(1)$ reversals. If all is equal, then M runs POS_CHEC2(s_1', s_2'); otherwise M enters the rejecting state.

End of CONSIST

MAIN

Step 1 Set *squarenum* to 1.

Step 2 If *squarenum* $= 1$, then $s_1 \leftarrow (q_0, B, B, 1, a_0, d_1, \ldots, a_{m-1}, d_m, rnum_1,$ $1, t_2, q_2)(q_a, t_2, t_2, i, \epsilon, i, t_2, q_a)$ and INPUT(s_1), where q_0 and q_a are the initial state and an accepting state of N, respectively, and B is a blank symbol. If *squarenum* $\neq 1$, then $s_1 \leftarrow s_2$.

Step 3 Guess s_2 and then POS_CHECK1(s_2).

Step 4 INPUT(s_2).

Step 5 CONSIST(s_1, s_2).

Step 6 If $s_2 = \epsilon$, then M enters the accepting state and halts, otherwise *squarenum* $\leftarrow$ *squarenum* $+ 1$ and go to Step 2.

End of MAIN

Analysis of complexities: The space complexity depends on the space to store the crossing sequences and the binary counter. Both of them require $O(R(n)f(n))$ squares. Thus the space complexity is $O(R(n)f(n))$.

We first see the number of reversals that each procedure requires. The procedure POS_CHECK1 requires $O(\log n)$ reversals. The procedure INPUT requires $O(n)$ reversals. The procedure POS_CHECK2 requires $O(\log n)$ reversals. Hence, since CONSIST calls INPUT at most $O(n/f(n))$ times, CONSIST requires $O(n^2/f(n))$ reversals. Since these procedures are called $O(S(n))$ times in MAIN, the reversal complexity is $O(S(n)n^2/f(n))$. Q.E.D.

We have the following if $f(n) = \log n$.

Corollary 7. *Let $R(n)$ and $S(n)$ be functions. Then, for $\forall i \geq 0$, the following holds:*

(1) $off\text{-}Nreve, space_1(R(n)n^i, S(n)(\log n)^i)$
   $\subseteq off\text{-}Nreve, space_1(S(n)(\log n)^i, R(n)n^{i+1})$,
(2) $off\text{-}Nreve, space_1(R(n)(\log n)^i, S(n)n^i)$
   $\subseteq off\text{-}Nreve, space_1(S(n)n^{i+2}/\log n, R(n)(\log n)^{i+1})$.

Corollary 8. *Let $R(n)$ and $S(n)$ be functions. Then,*
$off\text{-}Nreve, space_1(R(n)(\log n)^{O(1)}, S(n)n^{O(1)})$
$= off\text{-}Nreve, space_1(S(n)n^{O(1)}, R(n)(\log n)^{O(1)})$.

(Proof) This follows from the above corollary directly. Q.E.D.

The following is the same as Moriya's [6].

213

Corollary 9.
$off\text{-}Nreve, space_1((\log n)^{O(1)}, n^{O(1)}) = off\text{-}Nreve, space_1(n^{O(1)}, (\log n)^{O(1)}).$

5 Multitape Nondeterministic Turing Machines

We consider k-tape Turing machines below. First we show the interesting proposition. This proposition means that it is sufficient to consider only 2-tape NTMs for multitape NTMs. For the time complexity, the similar result is already known (see [8]). The proof uses the same technique as that of the time complexity, and appears in the final version.

Proposition 10. *The following holds:*

1. *Let $R(n)$ and $S(n) \geq n$ be functions. Then,*
   $Nreve, space_k(R(n), S(n)) = Nreve, space_2(R(n), S(n)).$
2. *Let $R(n)$ and $S(n)$ be functions. Then,*
   $off\text{-}Nreve, space_k(R(n), S(n)) = off\text{-}Nreve, space_2(R(n), S(n)).$

By using the technique used in the above proposition, we obtain the following for 1-tape NTMs.

Proposition 11. *The following holds:*

1. *Let $R(n)$ and $S(n) \geq n$ be functions. Then,*
   $Nreve, space_k(R(n), S(n)) \subseteq Nreve, space_1(R(n)S(n), S(n)).$
2. *Let $R(n)$ and $S(n)$ be functions. Then,*
   $off\text{-}Nreve, space_k(R(n), S(n)) \subseteq off\text{-}Nreve, space_1(R(n)S(n), S(n)).$

Hence, from Corollary 4, Corollary 8 and Proposition 11, we have the following:

Theorem 12. *The following holds:*

1. *Let $R(n) \geq n$ and $S(n) \geq n$ be functions. Then,*
   $Nreve, space_1(R(n), S(n))$
   $\subseteq Nreve, space(S(n), R(n))$
   $\subseteq Nreve, space_1(R(n), S(n)R(n)).$
2. *Let $R(n)$ and $S(n)$ be functions. Then,*
   $off\text{-}Nreve, space_1(R(n)(\log n)^{O(1)}, S(n)n^{O(1)})$
   $\subseteq off\text{-}Nreve, space(S(n)n^{O(1)}, R(n)(\log n)^{O(1)})$
   $\subseteq off\text{-}Nreve, space_1(R(n)(\log n)^{O(1)}, S(n)R(n)n^{O(1)}).$

The next corollaries follows from Theorem 12 immediately.

Corollary 13. *The following holds:*

1. *Let $R(n) \geq S(n) \geq n$ be functions. Then,*
   $Nreve, space(R(n)^{O(1)}, S(n)^{O(1)}) = Nreve, space_1(S(n)^{O(1)}, R(n)^{O(1)}).$

2. *Let $R(n) \geq S(n) \geq \log n$ be functions satisfying $R(n)S(n) \geq n\log n$. Then,*
   $off\text{-}Nreve, space(R(n)^{O(1)}, S(n)^{O(1)}) = off\text{-}Nreve, space_1(S(n)^{O(1)}, R(n)^{O(1)}).$

Corollary 14. *The following holds:*
$off\text{-}Nreve, space_1((\log n)^{O(1)}, n^{O(1)}) = off\text{-}Nreve, space(n^{O(1)}, (\log n)^{O(1)}).$

Cook [2] showed some candidates for $NC \subsetneq SC$ and $SC \subsetneq NC$. Hence if his conjecture is true, the above corollary leads to the next interesting results:
(1) $NC \subsetneq off\text{-}Nreve, space((\log n)^{O(1)}, n^{O(1)})$,
(2) $SC \subsetneq off\text{-}Nreve, space((\log n)^{O(1)}, n^{O(1)})$.
This gives a difference of power between nondeterminism and determinism.

6 Conclusions

We have shown the reversal-space trade-offs for NTMs. Especially, for one-tape NTMs, the fine trade-offs hold. We think that the results obtained in this paper do not hold for DTMs. The interesting question for multitape NTMs remains open. Namely, we do not know whether $off\text{-}Nreve, space_2(R(n)^{O(1)}, S(n)^{O(1)}) \subseteq off\text{-}Nreve, space_1(R(n)^{O(1)}, S(n)^{O(1)})$ holds or not for any functions $R(n)$ and $S(n)$. If this holds, then we could have $off\text{-}Nreve, space(R(n)^{O(1)}, S(n)^{O(1)}) = off\text{-}Nreve, space(S(n)^{O(1)}, R(n)^{O(1)})$. However, we conjecture that this does not hold.

References

1. B.S. Baker and R.V. Book : "Reversal bounded multipushdown machines", J. Comput. System. Sci.,8, 315-322(1974).
2. S.A.Cook : "Towards a complexity theory of synchronous parallel computation",L Enseignement mathematique,T.XXVII,fasc.1-2,99-124(1981).
3. P.C. Fischer : "The reduction of tape reversals for off-line one tape Turing machines", J. Comput. Syst. Sci.,2,136-147(1968).
4. S.A. Greibach : "Visits, crosses and reversals for off-line one-tape Turing machines ",Inform. and Control,36,174-216(1978).
5. J.E. Hopcroft and J.D. Ullman : "Introduction to automata theory language and computation", Addison Wesley,Reading Mass,1979.
6. E. Moriya, S. Iwata and T. Kasai: "A Note on Some Simultaneous Relations among Time, Space, and Reversal for Single Work Tape Nondeterministic Turing Machine", Information and Control,70,2/3, 179-185(1986).
7. N. Pipenger : "On simultaneous resource bounds", Proc. 20th Annu. Found. of Comput. Sci., 307-311(1979).
8. J.I. Seiferas, M.J. Fischer and A.R. Meyer : "Separating nondeterministic time complexity classes", J. Assoc. Comput. Mach.,25,1, 146-167(1978).
9. H. Yamamoto and S. Noguchi : "Comparison of the power between reversal bounded ATMs and reversal bounded NTMs", Information and Computation, 75,2, 144-161(1987).

On the Computational Power of Discrete Hopfield Nets

Pekka Orponen

Department of Computer Science, University of Helsinki
Teollisuuskatu 23, SF–00510 Helsinki, Finland
E-mail: orponen@cs.helsinki.fi

Abstract. We prove that polynomial size discrete synchronous Hopfield networks with hidden units compute exactly the class of Boolean functions PSPACE/poly, i.e., the same functions as are computed by polynomial space-bounded nonuniform Turing machines. As a corollary to the construction, we observe also that networks with polynomially bounded interconnection weights compute exactly the class of functions P/poly.

1 Background

Recurrent, or cyclic, neural networks are an intriguing model of massively parallel computation. In the recent surge of research in neural computation, such networks have been considered mostly from the point of view of two types of applications: pattern classification and associative memory (e.g. [16, 18, 21, 24]), and combinatorial optimization (e.g. [1, 7, 20]). Nevertheless, recurrent networks are capable also of more general types of computation, and issues of what exactly such networks can compute, and how they should be programmed, are becoming increasingly topical as work on hardware implementations progresses. (See, for instance, the several designs for analog, digital, hybrid, and optoelectronic implementations of recurrent networks contained in the compendium [32].) In this paper we address the task of comparing the computational power of the most basic recurrent network model, the *discrete Hopfield net* [18], to more traditional models of computation.

More precisely, our main interest is in the problem of Boolean function computation by undirected, or *symmetric* networks of weighted threshold logic units; but for the constructions, we also have to consider directed, or *asymmetric* nets.

In our model of network computation, the input to a net is initially loaded onto a set of designated input units; then the states of the units in the network are updated repeatedly, according to their local update rules until the network (possibly) converges to some stable global state, at which point the output is read from a set of designated output units. We only consider finite networks of units with binary states.

Since our networks in general contain cycles, their behavior may depend significantly on the update order of the units. (Note that we only deal with *discrete-time* networks here.) The updates may be *synchronous*, in which case all the units are updated simultaneously in parallel, or *asynchronous*, in which case the units are selected for updating one at a time in some order. We concentrate here on synchronous networks; not only because they are easier to deal with, but also because we do not want the notion of a function computed by a network to depend on an arbitrary choice of an update order.

Following the early work of McCulloch and Pitts [26] and Kleene [23] (see also [27]), it has been customary to think of finite networks of threshold units as equivalent to finite automata. However, in Kleene's construction for this equivalence, the input to a net is given as a sequence of pulses, whereas from most of the current applications' point of view, it is more natural to think of all of the input as being loaded onto the network in the beginning of a computation. (Also, this input convention relates network computations more closely to standard circuit complexity theory [34].) Of course, this makes the network model nonuniform, as any single net operates on only fixed-length inputs, and to compute a function on an infinite domain one needs a *sequence* of networks.

Since a cyclic net of s units converging in time t may be "unwound" into an acyclic net of size $s \cdot t$, the class of Boolean functions computed by polynomial size, polynomial time asymmetric nets coincides with the class P/poly of functions computed by polynomial size circuits or, equivalently, polynomial time Turing machines with polynomially bounded, nonuniform "advice" [4, 22][1]. On the other hand, if the computation time of a cyclic network is not bounded, then it is fairly easy to see that the class of functions computed by polynomial size asymmetric nets equals the class PSPACE/poly of functions computed by polynomial space bounded Turing machines with polynomially bounded advice. (Parberry in [29] attributes this result to an early unpublished report [25], but for completeness we outline a proof in Section 3.) Unbounded computation time might not be a totally unreasonable modeling assumption when one considers systems with a potential for extremely fast analog or optical implementations. Other characterizations of the class PSPACE/poly have been presented in [3].

Thus, the computational power of asymmetric nets is fairly easy to characterize. However, in the theory of neural computation, symmetric nets have attracted much more attention than general asymmetric ones, because of their very regular convergence behavior. The fundamental result here is Hopfield's [18] observation that a symmetric simple net (i.e, a net with no self-loops) using an asynchronous update rule always converges to a stable state. This was improved in [8] to show that in a symmetric simple net of p units with integer weights w_{ij}, the convergence requires at most a total of

$$3 \sum_{i,j} |w_{ij}| = O(p^2 \cdot \max_{i,j} |w_{ij}|)$$

unit state changes, under an asynchronous update rule. Under synchronous up-

---

[1] In a recent paper [33], Siegelmann and Sontag prove that also *bounded* size asymmetric cyclic nets with *real-valued* unit states and connection weights, and a saturated-linear transfer function compute in polynomial time exactly the functions in P/poly. Further complexity aspects of this model are studied in [5].

dates, a similar bound holds also for non-simple nets [6, 9, 30], but under such updates the network may also converge to oscillate between two alternating states instead of a unique stable state.

Thus, in particular, symmetric networks with polynomially bounded weights converge in polynomial time. On the other hand, networks with exponentially large weights may indeed require an exponential time to converge, as was first shown in [12] for synchronous updates (a simplified construction appears in [10]), and in [14] for a particular asynchronous update rule. A network requiring exponential time to converge under any asynchronous update rule was demonstrated in [13]. Related work appears in [6, 11].

In this paper, we prove that despite their apparently very constrained behavior also symmetric polynomial size networks are capable of computing all functions in PSPACE/poly. The idea, presented in section 4, is to start with the simulation of space-bounded Turing machines by asymmetric nets, and then replace each of the asymmetric edges by a sequence of symmetric edges whose behavior is sequenced by clock pulses. The appropriate clock can be obtained from, e.g., the construction in [10] of a symmetric network that takes an exponential number of steps to converge. Obviously, such a clock network cannot run forever (in this case it is not sufficient to have a network that simply oscillates between two states), but the exponentially long sequence of pulses it generates is sufficient to simulate a polynomially space-bounded computation. Applying the same technique to polynomial size nets with polynomially bounded weights shows that also in this case symmetric nets are computationally equivalent to asymmetric ones, i.e., capable of computing all of P/poly.

For a general introduction to neural computation, see the excellent textbook [17]; for aspects of recurrent networks, see [21]; and for computational complexity issues, see the survey papers [28, 29, 35].

2 Preliminaries

As in [29], we define a *(discrete) neural network* as a 6-tuple $N = (V, I, O, A, w, h)$, where V is a finite set of *units*, which we assume are indexed as $V = \{1, \ldots, p\}$; $I \subseteq V$ and $O \subseteq V$ are the sets of *input* and *output units*, respectively; $A \subseteq V$ is a set of *initially active units*, of which we require that $A \cap I = \emptyset$; $w : V \times V \to Z$ is the *edge weight matrix*, and $h : V \to Z$ is the *threshold vector*. The *size* of a network is its number of units, $|V| = p$, and the *weight* of a network is defined as its sum total of edge weights, $\sum_{i,j \in V} |w_{ij}|$. A *Hopfield net (with hidden units)* is a neural network N whose weight matrix is symmetric, i.e. $w_{ij} = w_{ji}$ for all $i, j \in V$.

Given a neural network N, let us denote $|I| = n$, $|O| = m$; moreover, assume that the units are indexed so that the input units appear at indices 1 to n. The network then computes a partial mapping

$$f_N : \{0,1\}^n \to \{0,1\}^m$$

as follows. Given an input x, $|x| = n$, the "states" s_i of the input units are initialized as $s_i = x_i$. The states of the units in set A are initialized to 1, and the states of the remaining units are initialized to 0. Then new states s_i', $i = 1, \ldots, p$, are computed simultaneously for all the units according to the rule

$$s_i' = \text{sgn}(\sum_{j=1}^{p} w_{ij} s_j - h_i),$$

where $\text{sgn}(t) = 1$ for $t \geq 0$, and $\text{sgn}(t) = 0$ for $t < 0$. (Thus, we only consider synchronous updating.) This updating process is repeated until no more changes occur, at which point we say that the network has *converged*, and the output value $f_N(x)$ can be read off the output units (in order). If the network does not converge on input x, the value $f_N(x)$ is undefined.

For simplicity, we consider from now on only networks with a single output unit; the extensions to networks with multiple outputs are straightforward. The *language recognized* by a single-output network N, with n input units, is defined as

$$L(N) = \{x \in \{0,1\}^n \mid f_N(x) = 1\}.$$

Given a language $A \subseteq \{0,1\}^*$, denote $A^{(n)} = A \cap \{0,1\}^n$. We consider the following complexity classes of languages:

PNETS $= \{A \subseteq \{0,1\}^* \mid$ for some polynomial q, there is for each n a network of size at most $q(n)$ that recognizes $A^{(n)}$ $\}$,

PNETS(symm) $= \{A \subseteq \{0,1\}^* \mid$ for some polynomial q, there is for each n a Hopfield net of size at most $q(n)$ that recognizes $A^{(n)}$ $\}$,

PNETS(symm, small) $= \{A \subseteq \{0,1\}^* \mid$ for some polynomial q, there is for each n a Hopfield net of weight at most $q(n)$ that recognizes $A^{(n)}$ $\}$.

Let $\langle x, y \rangle$ be some standard pairing function mapping pairs of binary strings to binary strings (see, e.g. [4, p. 7]). A language $A \subseteq \{0,1\}^*$ belongs to the nonuniform complexity class PSPACE/poly ([3], [4, p. 100], [22]), if there are a polynomial space bounded Turing machine M, and an "advice" function $f : N \rightarrow \{0,1\}^*$, where for some polynomial q and all $n \in N$, $|f(n)| \leq q(n)$, and for all $x \in \{0,1\}^*$,

$$x \in A \quad \Leftrightarrow \quad M \text{ accepts } \langle x, f(|x|) \rangle.$$

The class P/poly is defined analogously, using polynomial time instead of space bounded Turing machines.

3 Simulating Turing Machines with Asymmetric Nets

Simulating space-bounded Turing machines with asymmetric neural nets is fairly straightforward.

Theorem 1. PNETS = PSPACE/poly.

Proof. To prove the inclusion PNETS ⊆ PSPACE/poly, observe that given (a description of) a neural net, it is possible to simulate its behavior *in situ*. Hence, there exists a universal neural net interpreter machine M that given a pair $\langle x, N \rangle$ simulates the behavior of net N on input x in linear space. Let then language A be recognized by a polynomial size bounded sequence of nets (N_n). Then $A \in$ PSPACE/poly via the machine M and advice function $f(n) = N_n$.

To prove the converse inclusion, let $A \in$ PSPACE/poly via a machine M and advice function f. Let the space complexity of M on input $\langle x, f(|x|) \rangle$ be bounded by a polynomial $q(|x|)$. Without loss of generality (see, e.g. [4]) we may assume that M has only one tape, halts on any input $\langle x, f(|x|) \rangle$ in time $c^{q(|x|)}$, for some constant c, and indicates its acceptance or rejection of the input by printing a 1 or a 0 on the first square of its tape.

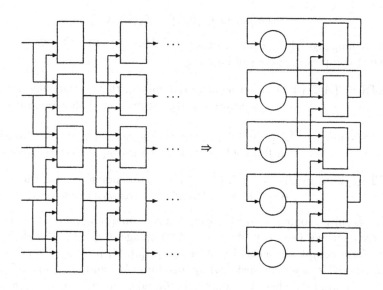

Fig. 1. Simulation of a space bounded Turing machine by an asymmetric cyclic net.

Following the standard simulation of Turing machines by combinational circuits [4, pp. 106–112], it is straightforward to construct for each n an *acyclic* network that simulates the behavior of M on inputs of length n. (More precisely, the network simulates computations $M(\langle x, f(n) \rangle)$, where $|x| = n$.) This network consists of $c^{q(n)}$ "layers" of $O(q(n))$ parallel wires, where the tth layer represents the configuration of the machine M at time t (Fig. 1, left). Each two consecutive layers of wires are interconnected by an intermediate layer of $q(n)$ constant-size subcircuits, each implementing the local transition rule of machine M at a single position of the simulated configuration. The input x is entered to the network along input wires; the advice string $f(n)$ appears as a constant input on another set of wires; and the output is read from the particular wire at the end of the circuit that corresponds to the first square of the machine tape.

One may now observe that the interconnection patterns between layers are very uniform: all the local transition subcircuits are similar, with a structure that depends only on the structure of M, and their number depends only on the length of x. Hence we may replace the exponentially many consecutive layers in the acyclic circuit by a single transformation layer that feeds back on itself (Fig. 1, right). The size of the cyclic network thus obtained is then only $O(q(n))$. When initialized with input x loaded onto the appropriate input units, and advice string $f(n)$ mapped to the appropriate initially active units, the network will converge in $O(c^{q(n)})$ update steps, at which point the output can be read off the unit corresponding to the first square of the machine tape.

$\square$

4 Simulating Asymmetric Nets with Symmetric Nets

Having now shown how to simulate polynomial space-bounded Turing machines by polynomial size asymmetric nets, the remaining problem is how to simulate the asymmetric edges in a network by symmetric ones. This is not possible in general, as is shown by the different convergence behaviors of asymmetric and symmetric nets. However, in the special case of *convergent* computations of asymmetric nets the simulation can be achieved.

Theorem 2. PNETS(symm) = PSPACE/poly.

Proof. Because PNETS(symm) $\subseteq$ PNETS, and by the previous theorem PNETS $\subseteq$ PSPACE/poly, it suffices to show the inclusion PSPACE/poly $\subseteq$ PNETS(symm).

Given any $A \in$ PSPACE/poly, there is by Theorem 1 a sequence of polynomial size asymmetric networks recognizing A. Rather than show how this specific sequence of networks can be simulated by symmetric networks, we shall show how to simulate the convergent computations of an *arbitrary* asymmetric network of n units and e edges of nonzero weight on a symmetric network of $O(n + e)$ units and $O(n^2)$ edges.

The construction combines two network "gadgets": a simplified version of a mechanism due to Hartley and Szu [15] for simulating an asymmetric edge by a sequence of symmetric edges and their interconnecting units, whose behavior is coordinated by a system clock (Figs. 2, 3); and a binary counter network due to Goles and Martínez ([10], [11, pp. 88–95]) that can count up to 2^n using about $3n$ units and $O(n^2)$ symmetric edges (Fig. 4). An important observation here is that any convergent computation by an asymmetric network of n units has to terminate in 2^n synchronous update steps, because otherwise the network repeats a configuration and goes into a loop; hence, the exponential counter network can be used to provide a sufficient number of clock pulses for the simulation to be performed.

Let us first consider the gadget for a symmetric simulation of an asymmetric edge of weight w from a unit i to a unit j (Fig. 2) [15]. Here the idea is that

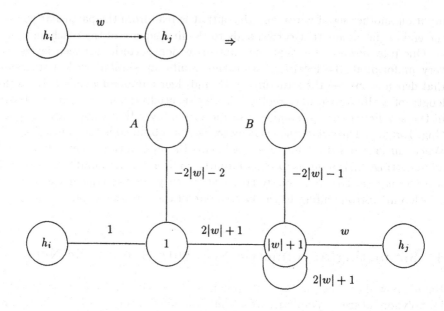

Fig. 2. A sequence of symmetric edges simulating an asymmetric edge of weight w.

the two units inserted between the units i and j in the synchronous network function as locks in a canal, permitting information to move only from left to right. The locks are sequenced by clock pulses emanating from the units labeled A and B, in cycles of length three as presented in Fig. 3.

At time 0 clock A is on, setting the first intermediate unit to zero, and clock B is off, permitting the state of the second intermediate unit to influence the state computation at unit j. At time 1 clock B turns on, clearing the second intermediate unit at time 2 (note that the connection from unit j is not strong enough to turn this unit back on). This will make the state of unit j indeterminate at time 3. At time 2, clock A turns off, permitting a new state to be copied from unit i to the first intermediate unit at time 3 (i.e., just before the state of unit i becomes indeterminate). At time 3, clock A turns on again, clearing the first intermediate unit at time 4; but simultaneously at time 4 the new state is copied from the first to the second intermediate unit, from where it can then influence the computation of the new state of unit j at time 5.

The next question is how to generate the clock pulses A and B. It is not possible to construct a symmetric clock network that runs forever: at best such a network can end up oscillating between two states, but this is not sufficient to generate the period 3 pulse sequences required for the previous construction. However, Fig. 4 presents the first two stages in the construction of a $(3n - 4)$-unit symmetric network with a convergence time of more than 2^n (actually, $2^n + 2^{n-1} - 3$) synchronous update steps [10]. The idea here is that the n units

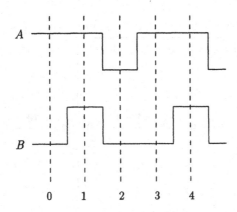

Fig. 3. The clock pulse sequence used in the edge simulation of Fig. 2.

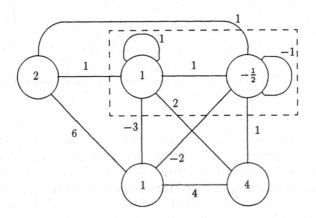

Fig. 4. The first two stages in the construction of a binary counter network [10].

in the upper row implement a binary counter, counting from all 0's to all 1's (in the figure, the least significant unit is to the right). For each "counter" unit added to the upper row, after the two initial ones, two "control" units are added to the lower row. The purpose of the latter is to first turn off all the "old" units, when the new counter unit is activated, and from then on balance the input coming to the old units from the new units, so that the old units may resume counting from zero[2].

---

[2] Following the construction in [10], we have made use of one negative self-loop in the counter network. If desired, this can be removed by making two copies of the least significant unit, both with threshold $-\frac{1}{2}$, interconnected by an edge of weight -1, and with the same connections to the rest of the network as the current single unit. All the other weights and thresholds in the network must then be doubled.

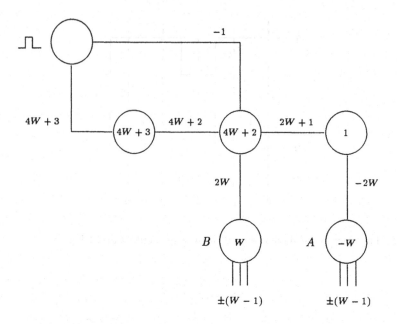

Fig. 5. A delay line for generating clock pulses from the binary counter network in Fig. 4.

It is possible to derive from such a counter network a sufficient number of the A and B pulse sequences by means of the delay line network presented in Fig. 5. Here the unit at the upper left corner is some sufficiently slow oscillator; since we require pulse sequences of period three, this could be the second counter unit in the preceding construction, which is "on" for four update steps at a time. (Thus, a 2^{n+1}-counter suffices to sequence computations of length up to $2^n - 1$.) The delay line operates as follows: when the oscillator unit turns on, it "primes" the first unit in the line; but nothing else happens until the oscillator turns off. At that point the "on" state begins to travel down the line, one unit per update step, and the pulses A and B are derived from the appropriate points in the line.

The value W used in the construction has to be chosen so large that the states of the units in the underlying network have no effect back on the delay line. It is sufficient to choose W larger than the total weight of the underlying network. Similarly, the weights and thresholds in the counter network have to modified so that the connections to the delay line do not interfere with the counting. Assuming that $W \geq 3$, it is here sufficient to multiply all the weights and thresholds by $6W$, and then subtract one from each threshold.

□

Concerning the edge weights in the above constructions, one can see that in the network implementing the machine simulation (Figs. 1, 2), the weights actually are bounded by some constant that depends only on the simulated machine M; in the delay line, the weights are proportional to the total weight of the underlying network; and the weights in the counter network (Fig. 4) are proportional to the length of the required simulation and, less significantly, to the weight of the delay line. Thus, we obtain as a corollary to the construction that if the simulated Turing machine (or, more generally, asymmetric network) is known to converge in polynomial time, then it is sufficient to have polynomially bounded weights in the simulating symmetric network. Formulating this in terms of nonuniform complexity classes, we obtain:

Corollary 3. PNETS(symm, small) = P/poly.

□

A somewhat interesting further observation is that this implies that large (i.e., superpolynomial) weights are necessary in polynomial size symmetric nets if and only if P/poly $\neq$ PSPACE/poly. In asymmetric nets, large weights are never required (in fact, bounded weights suffice).

5 Conclusion and Open Problems

We have characterized the classes of Boolean functions computed by asymmetric and, more interestingly, symmetric polynomial size cyclic networks of threshold logic units under a synchronous network state update rule. When no restrictions are placed on either computation time or the sizes of interconnection weights, both of these classes of networks compute exactly the class of functions PSPACE/poly. If interconnection weights are limited to be polynomial in the size of the network, the class of functions computed by symmetric networks reduces to P/poly. This limitation has no effect on the computational power of asymmetric nets.

Some of the open problems remaining from this work are the following. In Hopfield's original paper [18], and much of subsequent work, asynchronous update rules are used. Are also asynchronous Hopfield nets capable of computing all of PSPACE/poly? Or, with the small weights restriction, all of P/poly? (To address such questions, one would first need to formulate a proper notion of the function computed by an asynchronous network. One reasonable approach might be to require that for the function value to be defined at a given input point, all update orders must lead to the same result.) The synchronous Goles/Martínez counting network could possibly be replaced by an asynchronous counter due to A. Haken [13], but it is not clear how to effect the rest of the construction.

Also in Hopfield's original model, all the units are used for both input and output, and no hidden units are allowed. Although this is a somewhat artificial restriction from the function computation point of view, it would nevertheless be of interest to neural network theory to characterize the class of mappings computable by such networks.

In the neural networks literature, much attention has been paid to the *continuous-time* version of Hopfield's network model [19, 20]. It would be an interesting broad research task to define the appropriate notions of computability and complexity in this model, and attempt to characterize its computational power.

225

Acknowledgment

I wish to thank Mr. Juha Kärkkäinen for improving on my initial attempts at simplifying the Hartley/Szu network, and suggesting the elegant construction presented in Fig. 2.

References

1. Aarts, E., Korst, J. *Simulated Annealing and Boltzmann Machines.* John Wiley & Sons, Chichester, 1989.
2. Anderson, J. A., Rosenfeld, E. (eds.) *Neurocomputing: Foundations of Research.* The MIT Press, Cambridge, MA, 1988.
3. Balcázar, J. L., Díaz, J., Gabarró, J. On characterizations of the class PSPACE/poly. *Theoret. Comput. Sci. 52* (1987), 251–267.
4. Balcázar, J. L., Díaz, J., Gabarró, J. *Structural Complexity I.* Springer-Verlag, Berlin Heidelberg, 1988.
5. Balcázar, J. L., Gavaldà, R., Siegelmann, H. T., Sontag, E. D. Some structural complexity aspects of neural computation. Presented at the *8th Ann. Conf. on Structure in Complexity Theory (San Diego, CA, May 1993).*
6. Bruck, J. On the convergence properties of the Hopfield model. *Proc. of the IEEE 78* (1990), 1579–1585.
7. Durbin, R., Willshaw, D. An analogue approach to the Travelling Salesman Problem using an elastic net method. *Nature 326* (1987), 689–691.
8. Fogelman, F., Goles, E., Weisbuch, G. Transient length in sequential iterations of threshold functions. *Discr. Appl. Math. 6* (1983), 95–98.
9. Goles, E., Fogelman, F., Pellegrin, D. Decreasing energy functions as a tool for studying threshold networks. *Discr. Appl. Math. 12* (1985), 261–277.
10. Goles, E., Martínez, S. Exponential transient classes of symmetric neural networks for synchronous and sequential updating. *Complex Systems 3* (1989), 589–597.
11. Goles, E., Martínez, S. *Neural and Automata Networks.* Kluwer Academic, Dordrecht, 1990.
12. Goles, E., Olivos, J. The convergence of symmetric threshold automata. *Info. and Control 51* (1981), 98–104.
13. Haken, A. Connectionist networks that need exponential time to converge. Manuscript, 10 pp., January 1989.
14. Haken, A., Luby, M. Steepest descent can take exponential time for symmetric connection networks. *Complex Systems 2* (1988), 191–196.
15. Hartley, R., Szu, H. A comparison of the computational power of neural networks. In: *Proc. of the 1987 Internat. Conf. on Neural Networks, Vol. 3.* IEEE, New York, 1987. Pp. 15–22.
16. Hinton, G. E., Sejnowski, T. E. Learning and relearning in Boltzmann machines. In [31], pp. 282–317.
17. Hertz, J., Krogh, A., Palmer, R. G. *Introduction to the Theory of Neural Computation.* Addison-Wesley, Redwood City, CA, 1991.
18. Hopfield, J. J. Neural networks and physical systems with emergent collective computational abilities. *Proc. Nat. Acad. Sci. USA 79* (1982), 2554–2558. Reprinted in [2], pp. 460–464.

19. Hopfield, J. J. Neurons with graded response have collective computational properties like those of two-state neurons. *Proc. Nat. Acad. Sci. USA 81* (1984), 3088–3092. Reprinted in [2], pp. 579–583.

20. Hopfield, J. J., Tank, D. W. "Neural" computation of decisions in optimization problems. *Biol. Cybern. 52* (1985), 141–152.

21. Kamp, Y., Hasler, M. *Recursive Neural Networks for Associative Memory.* John Wiley & Sons, Chichester, 1990.

22. Karp, R. M., Lipton, R. J. Turing machines that take advice. *L'Enseignement Mathématique 28* (1982), 191–209.

23. Kleene, S. C. Representation of events in nerve nets and finite automata. In: *Automata Studies* (ed. C. E. Shannon, J. McCarthy). Annals of Mathematics Studies n:o 34. Princeton Univ. Press, Princeton, NJ, 1956. Pp. 3–41.

24. Kohonen, T. *Self-Organization and Associative Memory.* Springer-Verlag, Berlin Heidelberg, 1989 (3rd Edition).

25. Lepley, M., Miller, G. Computational power for networks of threshold devices in an asynchronous environment. Unpublished manuscript, Dept. of Mathematics, Massachusetts Inst. of Technology, 1983.

26. McCulloch, W. S., Pitts, W. A logical calculus of the ideas immanent in nervous activity. *Bull. Math. Biophys. 5* (1943), 115–133. Reprinted in [2], pp. 18–27.

27. Minsky, M. L. *Computation: Finite and Infinite Machines.* Prentice-Hall, Englewood Cliffs, NJ, 1972.

28. Orponen, P. Neural networks and complexity theory. In: *Proc. of the 17th Internat. Symp. on Mathematical Foundations of Computer Science* (ed. I. M. Havel, V. Koubek). Lecture Notes in Computer Science 629, Springer-Verlag, Berlin Heidelberg, 1992. Pp. 50–61.

29. Parberry, I. A primer on the complexity theory of neural networks. In: *Formal Techniques in Artificial Intelligence: A Sourcebook* (ed. R. B. Banerji). Elsevier – North-Holland, Amsterdam, 1990. Pp. 217–268.

30. Poljak, S., Sura, M. On periodical behaviour in societies with symmetric influences. *Combinatorica 3* (1983), 119–121.

31. Rumelhart, D. E., McClelland, J. L., et al. (eds.) *Parallel Distributed Processing: Explorations in the Microstructure of Cognition, Vol. 1.* The MIT Press, Cambridge, MA, 1986.

32. Sánchez-Sinencio, E., Lau, C. *Artificial Neural Networks: Paradigms, Applications, and Hardware Implementations.* IEEE Press, New York, 1992.

33. Siegelmann, H. T., Sontag, E. D. Analog computation via neural networks. Presented at the *2nd Israel Symp. on Theory of Computing and Systems (Natanya, Israel, June 1993).*

34. Wegener, I. *The Complexity of Boolean Functions.* John Wiley & Sons, Chichester, and B. G. Teubner, Stuttgart, 1987.

35. Wiedermann, J. Complexity issues in discrete neurocomputing. In: *Aspects and Prospects of Theoretical Computer Science. Proc. of the 6th Meeting of Young Computer Scientists* (ed. J. Dassow, J. Kelemen). Lecture Notes in Computer Science 464, Springer-Verlag, Berlin Heidelberg, 1990. Pp. 93–108.

On Randomized Versus Deterministic Computation

Marek Karpinski*   Rutger Verbeek†

Abstract. In contrast to deterministic or nondeterministic computation, it is a fundamental open problem in randomized computation how to separate different randomized time classes (at this point we do not even know how to separate linear randomized time from $O(n^{\log n})$ randomized time) or how to compare them relative to corresponding deterministic time classes. In another words we are far from understanding the power of *random coin tosses* in the computation, and the possible ways of simulating them deterministically.

In this paper we study the relative power of linear and polynomial randomized time compared with exponential deterministic time. Surprisingly, we are able to construct an oracle A such that exponential time (with or without the oracle A) is simulated by linear time Las Vegas algorithms using the oracle A. For Las Vegas polynomial time (ZPP) this will mean the following equalities of the time classes:

$$ZPP^A = EXPTIME^A = EXPTIME(= DTIME(2^{poly})).$$

Furthermore, for all the sets

$$M \subseteq \Sigma^* : M \leq_{UR} \bar{A} \Longleftrightarrow M \in EXPTIME$$

($\leq_{UR}$ being unfaithful polynomial random reduction, c.f. [Jo 90]).
Thus $\bar{A}$ is $\leq_{UR}$ complete for EXPTIME, but interestingly not NP-hard under (deterministic) polynomial reduction unless EXPTIME=NEXPTIME. We are also able to prove, for the first time, that randomized reductions are exponentially more powerful than deterministic or nondeterministic ones (cf. [AM 77]). Moreover, a set B is constructed such that Monte Carlo polynomial time (BPP) under the oracle B is exponentially more powerful than deterministic time with nondeterministic oracles, more precisely:

$$BPP^B = \Delta_2 EXPTIME^B = \Delta_2 EXPTIME(= DTIME(2^{poly})^{NTIME(n)}).$$

This strengthens considerably a result of Stockmeyer [St 85] about the polynomial time hierarchy that for some decidable oracle B, $BPP^B \not\subseteq \Delta_2 P^B$. Under

* Dept. of Computer Science, University of Bonn, 5300 Bonn 1, and International Computer Science Institute, Berkeley, California. Supported in part by the Leibniz Center for Research in Computer Science, by the DFG Grant KA 673/4-1 and by the ESPRIT BR Grant 7097. Email: marek@cs.uni-bonn.de
† Dept. of Computer Science, FernUniversität Hagen, 5800 Hagen 1. Part of the research was done while visiting the International Computer Science Institute, Berkeley, California. Email: verbeek@fernuni-hagen.de

our oracle BPP^B is exponentially more powerful than $\Delta_2 P^B$, and B does not add any power to $\Delta_2 EXPTIME$.

1 Randomized Computation

A probabilistic Turing machine (PTM) is a standard Turing machine with the ability to *toss* a *random coin*, and can be viewed as a nondeterministic machine with a different accepting condition: an input $x \in \Sigma^*$ is accepted (in time $T(n)$) if more than a half of the computations (of length $T(|x|)$) are accepting.

The probability of accepting (rejecting) can be defined as the fraction of accepting (rejecting) paths in the normalized computation tree (i.e. all the paths have the same number of binary branching points). We will restrict ourselves to machines with a clock: all computations have the length at most $T(|x|)$.

We shall study the following classes of probabilistic (bounded error) Turing machines:

- **Monte Carlo machines** (Bounded error PTMs, **MTMs**)
  any input is accepted either with probability $> \frac{3}{4}$ or with probability $< \frac{1}{4}$.
- **Randomized machines** (one sided error PTMs, **RTMs**):
  any input is accepted with probability $> \frac{3}{4}$ or 0.
- **Las Vegas machines** (zero error PTMs, **ZPTMs**):
  either x is accepted with probability $> \frac{3}{4}$ and rejected with probability 0 or x is rejected with probability $> \frac{3}{4}$ and accepted with probability 0.

We denote the corresponding complexity classes by

$$PrTIME(T) = \{L(\mathcal{M}) \mid \mathcal{M} \text{ is an } O(T)\text{-bounded PTM}\}$$
$$BPTIME(T) \quad \text{(same for MTMs)}$$
$$RTIME(T) \quad \text{(same for RTMs)}$$
$$ZPTIME(T) \quad \text{(same for ZPTMs)}$$

Other than in the deterministic case it is not clear that the "linear speed up" is valid for Monte Carlo, Randomized, and Las Vegas machines.

The polynomial time classes are denoted as usual by

$$PP \left(= \bigcup_k PrTIME(n^k)\right), \; BPP, \; RP, \; and \; ZPP.$$

All these machines can be relativized in a canonical way. The relativized machines, sets, complexity classes (with oracle A) are (as usual) denoted by $\mathcal{M}^A$,

$L(\mathcal{M}^A)$, e.g. BPP^A; if C is a set of oracle sets, the union of relativized classes with oracle $A \in C$ is denoted by superscript C (e.g. $BPP^{NP} = \bigcup_{A \in NP} BPP^A$).

Other than deterministic or nondeterministic machines, PTMs with bounded error (MTMs, RTMs, or ZPTMs) cannot be described by the syntactical properties only. The MTMs (RTMs, ZPTMs) form nonenumerable subsets of the PTMs. Thus ZPP, RP and BPP have probably no complete sets. Therefore, we do not have any method for proving that $BPTIME(n) \neq BPTIME(n^{\log n})$ [KV 88] and we cannot exclude the situation that (at least under some oracle) $ZPTIME(n) = BPP$. In [FS 89] the existence of such an oracle is claimed but unfortunately the construction used in the proof seems to have an irreparable flow [F 92]. The paper [FS 89] was also a starting point of our investigation.

A related notion of a probabilistic Turing machine with an oracle was introduced recently by A. Yao in a context of program checkers [Y 90].

Under the random oracle BPP (and RP, ZPP) equals P and reasonable hierarchy theorems are valid ([BG 81]). Most researchers believe that the power of ZPP does not (or not by much) exceed P. BPP is included in Σ_2^P and thus in the polynomial hierarchy. On the other hand, under some oracle, $BPP \not\subseteq \Delta_2^P$ [St 85]. We will show that under appropriate oracles ZPP=EXPTIME and $BPP = \Delta_2 EXPTIME$. This means: under some oracle the zero-error PTMs are exponentially more powerful that their deterministic counterparts, and bounded error PTMs are exponentially more powerful than nondeterministic machines.

The results have also consequences for the unrelativized world: we can show that the Las Vegas reductions are exponentially more powerful than deterministic reductions, and the Monte Carlo reductions are exponentially more powerful than γ-reductions.

We will need a generalization of the well known polynomial hierarchy (in a relativized version):

$$\Sigma_0 TIME(T)^A = \Pi_0 TIME(T)^A = \Delta_0 TIME(T)^A = DTIME(T)^A$$
$$\Delta_{k+1} TIME(T)^A = DTIME(T)^{\Sigma_k TIME(n)^A}$$
$$\Sigma_{k+1} TIME(T)^A = NTIME(T)^{\Sigma_k TIME(n)^A}$$
$$\Pi_{k+1} TIME(T)^A = \text{co-}NTIME(T)^{\Sigma_k TIME(n)^A} = \{\Sigma^* \setminus A \mid A \in \Sigma_k TIME(T)^A\}.$$

To avoid confusion with oracle classes we prefer $\Sigma_k P$ etc. for the classes of the polynomial hierarchy $\Sigma_k^P = \bigcup_i \Sigma_k TIME(n^i)$; e.g. $NP = \Sigma_1 P$. It is easy to see that for all at least linearly increasing T

$$\Sigma_{k+1} TIME(T)^A \supseteq NTIME(n)^{\Sigma_k TIME(T)^A}$$

and this inclusion is strict for some oracle A.

Let EXTIME denote $\bigcup_k DTIME(2^{kn})$, and let NEXTIME, BPEXTIME, $\Sigma_k EXTIME$, etc. denote the other exponential time classes. In the same way let EXPTIME (NEXPTIME etc.) denote $\bigcup_k DTIME(2^{n^k})$ ($\bigcup_k NTIME(2^{n^k})$ etc.).

2 Oracle A with $ZPP^A = EXPTIME^A = EXPTIME$

We will construct an oracle A such that for all deterministic oracle machines $\mathcal{M}_i$ running in time 2^n and all $x \in \Sigma^*$ with $|x| = n > i$

$$x \notin L(\mathcal{M}_i^A) \Longrightarrow \forall \rho \in \Sigma^{4n}, < i, x, \rho > \notin A$$

$$x \in L(\mathcal{M}_i^A) \Longrightarrow \#\{\rho \in \Sigma^{4n} \mid < i, x, \rho >\in A\} > \frac{3}{4} \cdot 2^{4n}$$

This set A has the property

$$DTIME(2^n)^A \subseteq DTIME(2^{6n}).$$

By standard padding arguments we can conclude

Theorem 1. *There exists an oracle A, such that*

$$ZPTIME(n)^A = EXTIME^A = EXTIME,$$
$$ZPP^A = EXPTIME^A = EXPTIME.$$

The (surprisingly simple) construction uses the fact, that deterministic exponential time machines cannot query all oracle strings of linear length.

First of all some notations:

- $< i, x, \rho >$ will denote the string $\$^i x \$ \rho$. The oracles will be subsets of $\{0, 1, \$\}^* = (\Sigma \cup \{\$\})^*$.
- The following ordering of pairs $(i, x) \in \mathbb{N} \times \Sigma^*$ is used:
  $(i, x) < (j, y)$ if one of the following holds
  (1) $|x| < |y|$
  (2) $|x| = |y|$ and $x < y$ (lexicographically)
  (3) $x = y$ and $i < j$.
- (Restricted to pairs (i, x) with $i < |x|$ this is a linear ordering of (ordinal) type ω.)

Without loss of generality we restrict ourselves to the input alphabet $\Sigma = \{0, 1\}$.

Construction of the Oracle A

A is constructed in stages following the above defined ordering. The (initially empty) set A is augmented during the construction at stage (i, x) by strings $< i, x, \rho >$, when $x \in L(M_i^A)$. Queries "$< i, x, \rho >\in A$?" on previous stages are recorded in a set D; these are not changed when "$x \in L(M_i^A)$" is encoded.

Stage $(0, \epsilon)$: $A := \emptyset; D := \emptyset$.
Stage (i, x), $i < |x|$:
    Simulate at most $2^{|x|}$ steps of $M_i^A(x)$.
    If M_i^A asks "$< j, y, \rho >\in A$?", $(j, y) > (i, x)$, and $|\rho| = 4 \cdot |y|$,
        then $D := D \cup \{< j, y, \rho >\}$ (i.e. $< j, y, \rho >\notin A$ is fixed).
    If M_i^A accepts x, then $A := A \cup (\{< i, x, \rho >| \, |\rho| = 4 \cdot |x|\} \setminus D)$.   □

Lemma 1. *For all i, x ($i < |x|$) the following holds:*

(1) If M_i^A accepts $x \in \Sigma^n$ within 2^n steps, then $< i, x, \rho >\notin A$ for at most $2n \cdot 2^{2n}$ strings $< i, x, \rho >$ with $|\rho| = 4n$.
(2) If M_i^A does not accept $x \in \Sigma^n$ within 2^n steps, then $< i, x, \rho >\notin A$ for all ρ.

Proof. Though the oracle is changed during the construction, all oracle queries are answered consistently. A new string is added to A only if it was not queried during previous steps.

(1) If M_i^A accepts $x \in \Sigma^n$ within the time bound, all strings $< i, x, \rho >$ not in D with $|\rho| = 4n$ are added to A. D contains all strings $< i, x, \rho >$ queried in earlier stages. Since there are less than $n \cdot 2^{n+1}$ earlier stages and on each stage at most 2^n strings are queried, $\#D < 2n \cdot 2^{2n}$.
(2) is obvious, since $< i, x, \rho >$ is added to A only if M_i^A accepts x within 2^n steps.   □

Our next lemma shows that A is not only decidable in exponential time, but A does not add much power to deterministic time bounded machines. A universal set for all sets decidable in time 2^n with oracle A is itself decidable in exponential time. (From "$A \in DTIME(2^n)$" we could only conclude "$DTIME(2^n)^A \subseteq DTIME(2^n)^{DTIME(2^n)} = DTIME(2^{2^n})$".)

Lemma 2. $L_A := \{\$^i x \mid M_i^A \text{ accepts } x \text{ in time } 2^{|x|}, |x| > i\} \in DTIME(2^{6n})$.

Proof. We construct a machine $\mathcal{M}$ which accepts L_A (without oracle) in time 2^{6n}.

On input $\$^i x$ ($i < |x|$) $\mathcal{M}$ simulates all $M_j^A(y)((j, y) \leq (i, x), j < |y|)$ for $2^{|y|}$ steps in the order of the oracle construction, recording the set D (as list of oracle strings) and the outcome of these machines. Oracle queries "$a \in A$?" are replaced by the following procedure:

(1) If a has not the form $< k, z, \rho >$ with $|z| > k$ and $|\rho| = 4|z|$, then $a \notin A$.
(2) Otherwise, if $a =< k, z, \rho >$ and $(k, z) \geq (j, y)$, then $a \notin A$. If $a \notin D$, $D := D \cup \{a\}$.
(3) Otherwise, if $a \in D$, then $a \notin A$.
(4) Otherwise $(a =< k, z, \rho >, (k, z) < (j, y), a \notin D)$, then $a \in A \iff \mathcal{M}_k^A$ accepts z (which was recorded on stage (k, z)).

If $\mathcal{M}_j^A(y)$ enters an accepting configuration, this fact is recorded and the next machine is simulated. After $2^{|y|}$ steps of simulation we know that $\mathcal{M}_j^A(y)$ does not accept within the time bound and record this fact. After stage (i, x) we know whether or not $\mathcal{M}_i^A$ accepts x within the time bound and thus have decided "is $\$^i x \in L_A$?".

Thus $\mathcal{M}$ accepts L_A.

On stage (i, x) D contains at most $2|x| \cdot 2^{2|x|}$ strings of length at most $2^{|x|}$. Thus the simulation of a single oracle query costs $O(|x| \cdot 2^{3|x|})$ steps. The other simulation steps are cheaper. Thus the simulation of $\mathcal{M}_j^A(y)$ $((j, y) \leq (i, x))$ can be done in $O(|x| \cdot 2^{4|x|})$ steps, which yields the total costs for all stages up to (i, x) of $O(|x|^2 \cdot 2^{5|x|}) \subseteq O(2^{6|x|})$. $\qquad \Box$

Proof of Theorem 1.

- "$EXTIME^A = EXTIME$"

  Suppose $L \in EXTIME^A$. Then there is an oracle machine $\mathcal{M}_i^A$ and some k such that $\mathcal{M}_i^A$ decides L within $2^{k \cdot n}$ steps. Let $L' = \{x10^m \mid x \in L, m \geq k \cdot |x|\}$ be the appropriately padded set. Then $y = x10^m \in L'$ can be decided by some $\mathcal{M}_j^A$ in time $|y| + 2^m \leq 2^{|y|}$.
  Hence by Lemma 2,

  $$L = \{x \mid \$^j x10^{k \cdot |x|+j} \in L_A\} = \{x \mid x10^{k \cdot |x|+j} \in L'\}$$
  $$\in DTIME(2^{6(2j+(k+1) \cdot |x|)}) = DTIME(2^{6(k+1) \cdot |x|})$$
  $$\subseteq EXTIME.$$

- "$ZPTIME(n)^A \supseteq EXTIME^{A}$"

  Since[D $EXTIME^A$ is closed under complement and $ZPTIME(n)^A = RTIME(n)^A \supseteq EXTIME^A \cap \text{co-}RTIME(n)^A$, it is sufficient to show "$RTIME(n)^A \supseteq EXTIME^{A}$".
  Suppose $L \in DTIME(2^{k \cdot n})^A$.
  Let $L' = L(\mathcal{M}_j^A)$ as above, $\mathcal{M}_i^A$ runs in time 2^n. An R-machine $\mathcal{M}$ accepts $L = \{x \mid x10^{k \cdot |x|+j} \in L'\}$ as follows:

On input x, $\mathcal{M}$ computes $y = x10^{k \cdot |x|+j}$. Then $\mathcal{M}$ chooses a random string ρ of length $4 \cdot |y|$. $\mathcal{M}$ accepts iff $< j, y, \rho > \in A$.

Obviously, $\mathcal{M}$ runs in time $O(n)$. From Lemma 1 we conclude for all x:

$$x \notin L \Longrightarrow y \notin L' \Longrightarrow \forall \rho \; < j, y, \rho > \notin A \Longrightarrow \text{Prob}[< j, y, \rho > \in A] = 0 \,,$$

$$x \in L \Longrightarrow \text{Prob}[< j, y, \rho > \in A] > \frac{3}{4} \,.$$

- "$ZPTIME(n)^A \subseteq EXTIME^A$" is obvious:

$$ZPTIME(n)^A \subseteq PrTIME(n)^A \subseteq DTIME(2^{O(n)})^A$$

for any oracle A.

The corresponding statements for ZPP^A, $EXPTIME^A$, and EXPTIME are proved in similar way using polynomial instead of linear padding. $\qquad \Box$

3 Oracle B with $BPP^B = \Delta_2 EXPTIME^B = \Delta_2 EXPTIME$

The construction of the oracle B follows a similar idea as for the oracle A. The main difference is that we must introduce strings $< i, x, \rho >$ into the oracle before $\mathcal{M}_i^B(x)$ is encoded. This yields a small two-sided error for the probabilistic machine.

B will have the property that for all Δ_2-oracle machines $\mathcal{M}_i$ running in time 2^n and all x with $|x| = n > i$ the following holds:

$$x \in L(\mathcal{M}_i^B) \Longrightarrow \#\{\rho \in \Sigma^{4n} \; |< i, x, \rho > \in B\} > \frac{3}{4} \cdot 2^{4n}$$

$$x \notin L(\mathcal{M}_i^B) \Longrightarrow \#\{\rho \in \Sigma^{4n} \; |< i, x, \rho > \in B\} < \frac{1}{4} \cdot 2^{4n} \,.$$

Furthermore

$$\Delta_2 TIME(2^n)^B \subseteq \Delta_2 TIME(2^{21n}) \,.$$

Again we can conclude

Theorem 2. *There exists an oracle B, such that*

$$BPTIME(n)^B = \Delta_2 EXTIME^B = \Delta_2 EXTIME \,,$$

$$BPP^B = \Delta_2 EXPTIME^B = \Delta_2 EXPTIME \,.$$

Construction of the Oracle B

During the construction we record all oracle queries in (initially empty) sets B (strings with positive answer) and C (strings with negative answer), $B \cap C = \emptyset$. $E = \{0, 1, \$\}^* \setminus (B \cup C)$ contains all strings with yet undetermined outcome.

Recall that a Δ_2-machine with an oracle X is a deterministic machine which can query arbitrary nondeterministic linear time machines with the oracle X.

Let us denote the j-th nondeterministic linear time machine with oracle X by $\mathcal{N}_j^X$.

Stage $(0, \epsilon)$:
$\quad B := \emptyset$;
$\quad E := \{< i, x, \rho >| \ |\rho| = 4 \cdot |x|, i < |x|\}$;
$\quad C := \{0, 1, \$\}^* \setminus E$;
Stage (i, x) $(i < |x|)$:
$\quad$ Simulate up to $2^{|x|}$ steps of $\mathcal{M}_i(x)$.
$\quad$ If $\mathcal{M}_i(x)$ queries "$y \in L(\mathcal{N}_j^B)$?", do the following:

$\qquad$ If there is a set $D \subseteq E$ such that $y \in L(\mathcal{N}_j^{B \cup D})$, then $\mathcal{N}_j^{B \cup D}$ has at least one accepting path of length $|y|$. Suppose F is the set of all oracle queries on this path. Set $B := B \cup (F \cap D)$; $C := C \cup (F \cap (E \setminus D))$; $E := E \setminus F$. Otherwise for all $D \subseteq E$ $y \notin L(\mathcal{N}_j^{B \cup D})$.
$\quad$ If $\mathcal{M}_i$ accepts x, encode this:
$\qquad B := B \cup \{< i, x, \rho > \in E\}$; $E := E \setminus B$.
$\quad$ If $\mathcal{M}_i$ rejects x or does not accept x within $2^{|x|}$ steps
$\qquad C := C \cup \{< i, x, \rho > \in E\}$; $E := E \setminus C$. $\qquad\qquad \square$

Lemma 3. *Suppose B is constructed as described above. Then for all i, x $(i < |x|)$ the following holds:*

(1) If $\mathcal{M}_i^B$ accepts $x \in \Sigma^n$ within 2^n steps, then $< i, x, \rho > \notin B$ for at most $2n \cdot 2^{3n}$ strings $< i, x, \rho >$ with $|\rho| = 4n$.
(2) If $\mathcal{M}_i^B$ does not accept $x \in \Sigma^n$ within 2^n steps, then $< i, x, \rho > \in B$ for at most $2n \cdot 2^{3n}$ strings $< i, x, \rho >$ with $|\rho| = 4n$.

Proof. At the end of stage (i, x) all $< i, x, \rho > \in E$ are added to B (case (1)) or to C (case (2)). Since there are less than $2n \cdot 2^n$ stages $(j, y) \leq (i, x)$, it is sufficient to show that at most 2^{2n} strings $< i, x, \rho >$ are removed from E during stage $(j, y) < (i, x)$ and during but before the end of stage (i, x).

$\mathcal{M}_j(y)$ $(j, |y| \leq n)$ performs at most 2^n queries of the form "$z \in L(\mathcal{N}_k^B)$?" with $|z| \leq 2^n$. For each of these queries the size of F (in the oracle construction) is bounded by $|z| \leq 2^n$. Thus for each query "$z \in L(\mathcal{N}_k^B)$?" at most $\#F \leq 2^n$ strings (possibly of the form $< i, x, \rho >$) are removed from E. At the end of stage (j, y) only strings $< j, y, \rho >$ are added to B or C and thus removed from E. □

Our next lemma asserts that B does not add much power to Δ_2-machines. The proof of this fact is much more difficult than the proof of the corresponding Lemma 2.

Recall that the construction of B does not completely determine the oracle B: when "$y \in L(\mathcal{N}_k^B)$" is fixed, we can choose different sets $D \subseteq E$ such that $y \in L(\mathcal{N}_j^{B \cup D})$ and for every such D select several accepting computation paths of $\mathcal{N}_j^{B \cup D}(y)$. Thus by appropriate choice arbitrary complex (even undecidable) oracle sets B may turn out. The proof of Lemma 4 yields the construction of one oracle set B consistent with the above described construction and thus with the properties of Lemma 3. In the rest of the paper B denotes this set.

Lemma 4. *There is an oracle B (which is one of the possible sets that turn out from the "construction of oracle B") such that*

$$L_B = \{\$^i x \mid \mathcal{M}_i^B \text{ is a } \Delta_2\text{-machine accepting } x \text{ in time } 2^{|x|}, i < |x|\}$$
$$\in \Delta_2 TIME(2^{21n}) \,.$$

Proof. Similarly as in the proof of Lemma 2 the Δ_2-machine $\mathcal{M}$ with input $\$^i x$ will simulate all stages of the oracle construction up to stage (i, x).

Again we record the outcome of $\mathcal{M}_j^B(y)$ on stage (j, y) in a list Z. The positive or negative answers to the oracle queries are recorderd in the additional lists X and Y. X and Y are (initially empty) lists of oracle strings of the form $< k, z, \rho >$ ($|\rho| = 4 \cdot |z|$, $k < |z|$) which are known to be in B (or not in B, respectively). Let E be defined as in the "construction of oracle B", i.e. on stage (j, y)

$$E = \{< k, z, \rho >\mid (k, z) \geq (j, y), \, k < |z|, |\rho| = 4 \cdot |z|\} \setminus (X \cup Y) \,.$$

In order to simulate queries "$z \in L(\mathcal{N}_k^B)$?" we will use the following universal set L, which determines on stage (j, y) whether or not there is an augmentation of the current B consistent with the previous oracle queries (recorded in X, Y, Z) such that the nondeterministic machine $\mathcal{N}_k^{B \cup D}$ starting in same configuration C can reach an accepting configuration within t steps:

$\$^k c \$ X \$ Y \$ Z \$^j \$ y \$^i \in L \iff \mathcal{N}_k$ starting in configuration accepts within t
 steps, where the oracle queries "$a \in B$?" are
 replaced as follows:

(1) "$a \notin B$" if a has not the form $< l, u, \rho >$ with $l < |u|$, $|\rho| = 4 \cdot |u|$.
 For the other cases assume $a = < l, u, \rho >$.

(2) "$a \in B$" if a is contained in the list X or if $(l, u) < (j, y)$, $a \notin Y$ and $(l, u) \in Z$.

(3) "$a \notin B$" if $a \in Y$ or if $(l, u) < (j, y)$, $a \notin X$ and $(l, u) \notin Z$.

(4) Otherwise ($a \in E$) replace the query by a nondeterministic choice.

It is easy to see that $L \in NTIME(k \cdot t \cdot (|X| + |Y| + |Z|)) \subseteq NTIME(n^3)$.

Suppose we are simulating stage $(j, y) \leq (i, x)$.

Using L a query of $\mathcal{M}_j(y)$ of the form "$z \in L(\mathcal{N}_k^B)$?" can be replaced by a sequence of queries "$p \in L$?", which yields a stepwise simulation of an accepting path of N_k^B, and appropriate augmentation of X or Y:

$c :=$ initial configuration of $\mathcal{N}_k(z)$;
$t := |z|$;
IF $\$^k c \$ X \$ Y \$ Z \S^j \$ y \$^t \in L$ THEN
WHILE $t > 0$ AND c is not accepting DO
BEGIN
  IF the next step of $\mathcal{N}_k$ is an oracle query "$a \in B$?"
  and a is not yet recorded in X or Y THEN
  BEGIN
    add a to X;
    $c' :=$ next configuration if $a \in B$;
    IF $\$^k c' \$ X \$ Y \$ Z \$\$^j Y \$^{t-1} \notin L$ THEN
    BEGIN
      remove a from X;
      add a to Y;
      $c' :=$ next configuration if $a \notin B$
    END
  END
  ELSE { the next step is a nondeterministic choice }
    determine a next configuration c' with $\$^k c' \$ X \$ Y \$ Z \$\$^j y \$^{t-1} \in L$
    { at least one c' has this property };
  $t := t - 1$;
  $c := c'$
END;
IF c is an accepting configuration of $\mathcal{N}_k$
THEN "$z \in L(\mathcal{N}_k^B)$" ELSE "$z \notin L(\mathcal{N}_k^B)$".

At the end of the stage (j, y) (i.e. when $\mathcal{M}_j$ reaches an accepting configuration or else after $2^{|y|}$ simulation steps) record the outcome of $\mathcal{M}_j(y)$: if $\mathcal{M}_j$ accepts y within $2^{|y|}$ steps, add (j, y) to Z.

The oracle B constructed by this procedure is determined by

$a \in B \iff a =< i, x, \rho >$, $i < |x|$, $|\rho| = 4 \cdot |x|$ and after stage (i, x) of the simulation either $a \in X$ or $a \notin Y$ and $(i, x) \in Z$.

On stage $(j, y) \leq (i, x)$ $\mathcal{M}$ simulates at most 2^n $(n = |x|)$ steps. The simulation of a query "$z \in L(\mathcal{N}_k^B)$" costs $|z| \leq 2^n$ steps and 2^n queries to the oracle B times the cost for looking at and updating the lists X, Y and Z. These can contain up to $2n \cdot 2^{3n}$ elements of length 2^{2n}. Thus the total costs for all $2n \cdot 2^n$ stages up to (i, x) are bounded by $4n^2 \cdot 2^{6n}$ and

$$L_B \in DTIME(2^{7n})^{NTIME(n^3)} \subseteq DTIME(2^{21n})^{NTIME(n)} = \Delta_2 TIME(2^{21n}).$$

□

Proof of Theorem 2. Follows from Lemma 3 and Lemma 4 in the same way as Theorem 1 from Lemma 1 and Lemma 2. □

4 Consequences

The sets A and B have many interesting properties. Perhaps the most interesting is that randomized reduction can be exponentially more powerful than deterministic or nondeterministic reduction (cf. [AM 77]).

Definition (Reducibilities)

$X \leq_\gamma Y :\iff$ there is a polynomial time bounded NTM $\mathcal{M}$ with:

    (1) For every input x there is at least one computation which produces an output.
    (2) $\forall(x, y)$ $\mathcal{M}(x) = y \Rightarrow [x \in X \iff y \in Y]$

$X \leq_{UR} Y :\iff$ there is a polynomial time bounded PTM $\mathcal{M}$ with:

    (1) every computation produces an output
    (2a) $x \in X \Rightarrow \mathcal{M}(x) \in Y$
    (2b) $x \notin X \Rightarrow \text{Prob}[\mathcal{M}(x) \notin Y] > \frac{3}{4}$ (unfaithful R-reduction)

$X \leq_{BPP} Y :\iff$ as $\leq_{UR}$ with (1'), (2b), and (2a')

    (2a') $x \in X \Rightarrow \text{Prob}[x \in X \Rightarrow \mathcal{M}(x) \in Y] > \frac{3}{4}$.

Obviously $X \leq_\gamma Y \Rightarrow X \in NP^Y$, $X \leq_{DTIME(T)} Y \Rightarrow X \in DTIME(T)^Y$.

Theorem 3. *UR-Reductions are exponentially more powerful than DTIME-reductions.*

(1) $\forall X \in EXPTIME$, $X \leq_{UR} \bar{A}$ and $\bar{X} \leq_{UR} \bar{A}$
(2) $\forall k \, \forall T \in O(2^{n^k}) \, \exists X \in EXPTIME$, $X \not\leq_{DTIME(T)} \bar{A}$.

Proof.

(1) follows (by polynomial padding) from Lemma 1.

(2) Suppose $T \in O(2^{n^k})$.

$X \leq_{DTIME(T)} \bar{A} \Rightarrow X \in DTIME(T)^{\bar{A}} \Rightarrow X \in DTIME(2^{6 \cdot n^k})$ (by Lemma 2), which is not true for all $X \in EXPTIME$. $\qquad\Box$

Theorem 4. *BPP-reductions are exponentially more powerful than nondeterministic (and than γ-) reductions (cf. [AM 77]):*

(1) $\forall X \in \Delta_2 EXPTIME, X \leq_{BPP} B$

(2) $\forall k, \forall T \in O(2^{n^k}), \Delta_2 TIME(T)^B \not\supseteq \Delta_2 EXPTIME$.

Proof.

(1) follows from Lemma 3.

(2) as Proof of Theorem 3 using Lemma 4. $\qquad\Box$

Since the oracle queries used for the $\leq_{UR}$ and $\leq_{BPP}$ are extremely simple, they can be computed by NC^1-circuits. Thus $\leq_{UR}$ and $\leq_{BPP}$ in Theorems 3 and 4 can be replaced even by Las Vegas NC^1-reducibility and Monte Carlo NC^1-reducibility (defined in an obvious way).

Since Monte Carlo machines have small nonuniform circuits it is an easy consequence from Lemma 3 that relative to oracle B, $\Delta_2 EXTIME$ has linear size circuits (for a weaker version of it see [W 83], cf. also [K 82]).

We list some other consequences for our oracles with hints how to prove them (to shorten the formulas we denote EXPTIME by E):

(1) $P^A \subsetneqq ZPP^A = NP^A = PH^A = E = E^A \subsetneqq ZPE^A = E^E = DTIME(2^{2^n})$.

(2) $P^B \subsetneqq NP^B \subsetneqq \Delta_2 P^B \subsetneqq BPP^B = \Sigma_2 P^B = PH^B = \Delta_2 E =$
$\Delta_2 E^B \subsetneqq BPE^B = \Sigma_2 E^B = EH^B = E^{\Delta_2 E}$
$= \Delta_2 TIME(2^{2^n})$.

(The inclusions 1 to 4 are strict because otherwise the polynomial hierarchy collapses and $\Delta_2 P^B = \Sigma_2 P^B = \Delta_2 E^B$, which is impossible.)

(3) If $E \neq ZPE$, then $P^A \not\supseteq ZPP$.

$(P^A \supseteq ZPP \Rightarrow E = E^A = E^{P^A} \supseteq E^{ZPP} = ZPE)$

(4) If $\Delta_2 E \neq \Delta_3 E$, then $P^B \not\supseteq NP$ (i.e. B is not NP-hard, but complete for $\Delta_2 E$ under $\leq_{BPP}$). $(P^B \supseteq NP \Rightarrow \Delta_2 E = \Delta_2 E^{P^B} \supseteq \Delta_2 E^{NP} = \Delta_3 E.)$

(5) If $\Delta_2 E \neq \Delta_3 E$, then $NP^B \not\supseteq coNP$.

$\quad (NP^B \supseteq coNP \Rightarrow NP^{NP} \subseteq NP^B \Rightarrow \Delta_3 E \subseteq \Delta_2 E^B = \Delta_2 E)$

(6) If $\Delta_2 E \neq \Sigma_2 E$, then $\Delta_2 P^B \not\supseteq \Sigma_2 P$.

$\quad (\Delta_2 P^B \supseteq \Sigma_2 P \Rightarrow \Delta_2 E = \Delta_2 E^B = E^{\Delta_2 P^B} \supseteq E^{\Sigma_2 P} = \Sigma_2 E)$

5 Conclusion

Our results show that the randomized computation can be extremely powerful when compared with deterministic computation in a relativized context, even though randomization has almost no additional power in the presence of random oracles.

We have constructed oracles A and B with maximal collapse between polynomial and exponential classes without known strict inclusion:

$$ZPP^A = \Sigma_1 P^A \cap \Pi_1 P^A = \Delta_1 E^A = \Delta_1 E \ (= EXPTIME),$$
$$BPP^B = \Sigma_2 P^B \cap \Pi_2 P^B = \Delta_2 E^B = \Delta_2 E.$$
$$(BPP^B \subseteq \Sigma_2 P^B \cap \Pi_2 P^B, \text{ see [S 83]})$$

It is an open question, if such oracles with maximal collapse exist also on other levels of the polynomial and exponential hierarchies, i.e. whether there exists C such that for some $k > 2$,

$$\Sigma_k P^C \cap \Pi_k P^C = \Delta_k E^C = \Delta_k E.$$

It seems that the methods presented in this paper cannot be applied directly to higher levels, since no probabilistic class is known below $\Sigma_k P$ and not below $\Delta_k P$ ($k > 2$).

Acknowledgments. We thank Eric Allender, Klaus Ambos-Spies, Richard Beigel, Yuri Gurevich, and Johan Håstad for the number of interesting discussions connected to the topic of this paper.

References

[A 78]   Adleman, L., *Two Theorems on Random Polynomial Time*, Proc. 19th IEEE FOCS, 1978, pp. 75-83.

[AM 77]   Adleman, L., Manders, K., *Reducibility, Randomness, and Intractibility*, Proc. 9th ACM STOC, 1977, pp. 151-163.

[ABHH 92]   Allender, E., Beigel, R., Hertrampf, U., Homer, S., *Almost-Everywhere Complexity Hierarchies for Nondeterministic Time*, Manuscript, 1992; A preliminary version has appeared in Proc. STACS '90, LNCS 415, Springer-Verlag, 1990, pp. 1-11.

[BG 81]   Bennett, Ch. H., Gill, J., *Relative to a Random Oracle A, $P^A \neq NP^A \neq co-NP^A$ with Probability* 1, SIAM J. on Computing **10**, 1981, pp. 96-113.

[F 92]   Fortnow, L., *Personal Communication*, 1992.

[FS 89]   Fortnow, L., Sipser, M., *Probabilistic Computation and Linear Time*, Proc. 21st ACM STOC, 1989, pp. 148-166.

[F 79]   Freivalds, R., *Fast Probabilistic Algorithms*, Proc. MFCS'79, LNCS **75**, 1979, Springer-Verlag, pp. 57-69.

[Jo 90]   Johnson, P.S., *A Catalog of Complexity Classes*, in Handbook of Theoretical Computer Science, Vol. A., Algorithms and Complexity, Elsevier-MIT Press, 1990, pp. 69-161.

[K 82]   Kannan, R., *Circuit-Size Lower Bounds and Non-reducibility to Sparse Sets*, Information and Control **55**, 1982, pp. 40-46.

[KV 87]   Karpinski, M., Verbeek, R., *On the Monte Carlo Space Constructible Functions and Separation Results for Probabilistic Complexity Classes*, Information and Computation **75**, 1987, pp. 178-189.

[KV 88]   Karpinski, M., Verbeek, R., *Randomness, Provability, and the Separation of Monte Carlo Time and Space*, LNCS 270, Springer-Verlag, 1988, pp. 189-207.

[R 82]   Rackoff, C., *Relational Questions Involving Probabilistic Algorithms*, J. ACM **29**, 1982, pp. 261-268.

[S 83]   Sipser, M., *A Complexity Theoretic Approach to Randomness*, Proc. 15th ACM STOC, 1983, pp. 330-335.

[St 85]   Stockmeyer, L., *On Approximation Algorithms for #P*, SIAM J. Comput. **14**, 1985, pp. 849-861.

[W 83]   Wilson, C., *Relativized Circuit Complexity*, 24th IEEE FOCS, 1983, pp. 329-334.

[Y 90]   Yao, A. C., *Coherent Functions and Program Checkers*, Proc. 22nd ACM STOC, 1990, pp. 84-94.

Lower Bounds for One-way Probabilistic Communication Complexity

*Farid Ablayev**

Department of Theoretical Cybernetics
Kazan University
Kazan 420008, Russia

Abstract

We prove three different types of complexity lower bounds for the one-way unbounded-error and bounded-error error probabilistic communication protocols for boolean functions. The lower bounds are proved for arbitrary boolean functions in the common way in terms of the deterministic communication complexity of functions and in terms of the notion "probabilistic communication characteristic" that we define.

Our lower bounds are good enough for proving proper hierarchies for various one-way probabilistic communication complexity classes (namely for unbounded error probabilistic communication, for bounded error probabilistic communication, and for errors of probabilistic communication).

1 Introduction

The model of a communication protocol we are using is based on that of Yao [16], who introduced the notion of deterministic and probabilistic communication complexity.

Two processors P_0 and P_1 wish to compute a boolean function of two arguments. The first argument, x, of the Boolean function $f : \{0,1\}^n \times \{0,1\}^n \to \{0,1\}$ is known to P_0, and the second argument, y, is known to P_1. With the function f, we associate a $2^n \times 2^n$ communication matrix $F(n)$ whose (x,y)th entry, $F(n)[x,y]$ is $f(x,y)$. We will also use the notation F instead of $F(n)$.

Given the inputs x, y to P_0, P_1 respectively, the computation, according to some protocol ϕ, will be as follows: P_0 is always the first one to send a message (sequences of bits). The processors communicate in turns. The output produced by P_1 or by P_0 is a single bit b.

---

*Work done in part while visiting the University of Rochester. Supported in part by a Fulbright grant and by the National Science Foundation under grant CCR-8957604.

Papadimitrio and Sipser [13] defined the notion of k-round protocols in which up to k messages between P_0 and P_1 are exchanged and proved some relations between the complexity of k-round protocols and $(k-1)$-round protocols. Duris, Galil and Schnitger [6] generalized [13] results. They proved an exponential gap in complexity between deterministic k-round protocols and $(k-1)$-round protocols.

If $k = 1$ then following [13] we call such a protocol a *one-way* protocol. So a one-way communication protocol is a restricted model in which only one processor, P_0, is allowed to send messages. If $k > 1$ then we call such a protocol a *two-way* protocol.

Paturi and Simon [14] exhibited a one-way probabilistic protocol for each two-way probabilistic protocol (with non bounded error) such that both compute the same function with the same probability and their communication complexities differ by at most 1.

Yao [17] presented a boolean function for which he proved an exponential gap between one-way (one-round) and two-round probabilistic protocols with bounded error. Halstenberg and Reischuk [8] generalized the results of [17] and [6]. They proved an exponential gap in complexity between deterministic k-round protocols and probabilistic $(k-1)$-round protocols with fixed error of probability.

This paper is the conference version of the [1]. In this paper we consider the worst case complexity for probabilistic communication.

We define the notion of *probabilistic communication characteristic* of boolean functions. We prove three main different types of complexity lower bounds for the one-way unbounded-error (theorem 1) and bounded-error error (theorem 2 and theorem 3) probabilistic communication protocols for boolean functions. Theorems 4 and 5 are corollary of main theorem 3.

The lower bounds are proved for arbitrary boolean functions in the common way in terms of the deterministic communication complexity of functions and in terms of the notion of probabilistic communication characteristics. The lower bounds technique has probabilistic finite automata methods background. Namely the Phan Dinh Dieu method [5] for the theorem 1, "metric" interpretation of Rabin's [15] reduction theorem proof for the theorem 2, and the "entropy" method [2] for the theorem 3.

We present boolean functions with the different probabilistic communication characteristics which demonstrates that each of these lower bounds can be more precise than the others depending on the probabilistic communication characteristics of a function. The communication complexity of this function shows that the lower bounds of the paper can not be strongly generalized.

Our lower bounds for communication complexity for probabilistic one-way protocols with bounded errors are powerful enough to prove proper hierarchy for different one-way probabilistic communication complexity classes (for unbounded error probabilistic communications, for bounded error probabilistic communications, and for probabilistic communications depends on a measure of bounded error).

As one corollary of the influences of the communication structure of boolean functions on communication complexity we demonstrate the following "magic" for the boolean functions $f_1^{g'}$, f_2^g. The deterministic communication complexity of f_2^g is less than the deterministic communication complexity of $f_1^{g'}$, but in the probabilistic case, on the contrary, the probabilistic communication complexity of f_2^g is greater than the probabilistic communication complexity of $f_1^{g'}$.

As the additional application of the theorem 3 (theorem 5) we obtain the lower bound for almost all functions for small error case. Note that lower bounds for almost all boolean functions have been investigated by several authors [4, 3, 12, 16]. It is proved in this papers that most boolean functions have linear communication complexity in different probabilistic sense.

2 Preliminaries

The one-way probabilistic protocol Φ can be completely specified by two functions $\mu, \nu : \{0,1\}^n \times M_\Phi \to [0,1]$, where $M_\Phi = \{\beta_1, \beta_2, ..., \beta_d\}$ is the set of all messages that are sent by P_0 for some input and $[0,1]$ is the closed interval on the real line with end points 0 and 1. μ and ν can be represented as d-dimensional vectors $\mu(x) = (p_1(x), p_2(x), \ldots, p_d(x))$, $\nu(y) = (q_1(y), q_2(y), \ldots, q_d(y))$, where $d = |M_\Phi|$, $p_i(x)$ is the probability that P_0 sends the messages β_i when reading x and $q_i(y)$ is the probability that P_1, on the receipt of β_i and reading the input y, outputs 1. In the computation $T_\Phi(x, y)$, the probability of outputting the bit $b = 1$ is $\sum_{i=1}^d p_i(x)q_i(y)$ and the bit $b = 0$ is $1 - \sum_{i=1}^d p_i(x)q_i(y)$.

Definition 1 *The probabilistic protocol Φ p-computes, $p \geq 1/2$, a function f if $f(x,y) = b$ iff the probability of outputting the bit b in the computation $T_\Phi(x,y)$ is no less than p when $p = 1/2 + \epsilon$, $\epsilon > 0$ and is greater than p when $p = 1/2$.(The last is important because the probabilistic protocol which computes the function with the probability exactly $1/2$ can compute any function without any communication between processors).*

As usually, we call ϵ the advantage of the protocol Φ and $er = 1 - p$ — the error probability of the protocol Φ.

Definition 2 (Worst case complexity) *The probabilistic communication complexity $C_\Phi(x, y)$ of the probabilistic protocol Φ on the inputs x, y is $\lceil \log d \rceil$, d is the total number of messages used by Φ.*
$C_\Phi(n) = \max_{|x|=n, |y|=n}\{C_\Phi(x, y)\}$.
The number d of distinct messages used is also called the dimension of probabilistic protocol Φ and denoted $dim(\Phi)$.
The probabilistic communication complexity $PC_p(f, n)$ of a boolean function f is $\min\{C_\Phi(n) \mid$ the probabilistic protocol Φ p-computes f for the inputs of the length $n\}$.
We will use the notation $PC_p(f)$ instead of $PC_p(f, n)$.

The one-way deterministic protocol ϕ is a particular case of the one-way probabilistic protocol. In the deterministic one-way model, P_0 deterministically sends one message $\beta \in M_\phi$ determined by the input at P_0 alone, and is not influenced by the input at P_1. P_1 on the receipt of β, deterministically outputs bit b depending only on its input and the message β received.

The one-way deterministic protocol ϕ can be completely specified by two functions $\mu, \nu : \{0,1\}^n \times M_\phi \to \{0,1\}$.

The one-way deterministic protocol ϕ computes a function f if $f(x,y) = b$ iff the computation $T_\phi(x,y)$ outputs the bit b.

Definition 3 *The deterministic communication complexity $C_\phi(x,y)$ of the deterministic protocol ϕ on the inputs x, y is $\lceil \log d \rceil$.*

$C_\phi(n) = \max_{|x|=n,|y|=n} \{C_\phi(x,y)\}$.

The number d of distinct messages used is also called the dimension of the deterministic protocol ϕ and is denoted $dim(\phi)$.

The deterministic communication complexity $DC(f,n)$ of a boolean function f is $\min\{C_\phi(n) \mid$ the deterministic protocol ϕ computes f for the inputs of the length $n\}$. We will, also, use the notation $DC(f)$ instead of $DC(f,n)$.

$DC(f)$ and $PC_p(f)$ will denote the complexity of one-way, left-right communication complexity of a boolean function f in the paper. Of course if the complexity of one-way, right-left communication complexity of a boolean function f is less than the complexity of one-way, left-right communication complexity then the reverse right-left protocol is better. We will consider that the left-right communication complexity of a boolean function is less throughout the paper.

The case of a two-way communication will be formulated separately.

3 Lower bounds

As it is mentioned in [16] the one-way deterministic communication complexity $DC(f)$ of a boolean function f is easily seen to be $\lceil \log(nrow(f)) \rceil$, where $nrow(f)$ is the number of distinct rows of communication matrix F.

Let us fix an $X \subseteq \{0,1\}^n$, $X = \{x_1, x_2, ..., x_{nrow(f)}\}$, such that for $x, x' \in X$ it holds that $F[x] \neq F[x']$, where $F[x]$ denotes the x-th rows of the communication matrix F.

Let us choose a $Y \subseteq \{0,1\}^n$, $Y = \{y_1, y_2, ..., y_t\}$, such that for an arbitrary two words $x, x' \in X$ there exists a word $y \in Y$ such that $f(x,y) \neq f(x',y)$.

Definition 4 *Let us call such a set Y of words the test for the boolean function f. Let us denote $ts(f,n) = \min\{|Y| \, / \, Y \text{ is a test for } f\}$.*

We will use the notation $ts(f)$ instead of $ts(f,n)$.

The notion of test is well known and widely used in circuits theory. It is evident that $\lceil \log(nrow(f)) \rceil \leq ts(f) \leq nrow(f)$ or $DC(f) \leq ts(f) \leq 2^{DC(f)}$.

The notion of the set of representatives and the notion of test defined above, more precisely can be called the set of left representatives and right test respectively. In a similar way we can define the notions of the set of right representatives and the notion of left test. In the case that the reverse point of view gives more less complexity then the reverse one-way protocol is better.

Theorem 1 For an arbitrary boolean function $f : \{0,1\}^n \times \{0,1\}^n \to \{0,1\}$, for $p = 1/2$

$$PC_p(f) \geq \log DC(f) - \log \log ts(f) - 1.$$

Theorem 2 For an arbitrary boolean function $f : \{0,1\}^n \times \{0,1\}^n \to \{0,1\}$, for arbitrary $\epsilon \in (0, 1/2]$, $p = 1/2 + \epsilon$

$$PC_p(f) \geq \log DC(f) - \log \log(1 + 1/\epsilon) - 1.$$

Definition 5 For a boolean function $f : \{0,1\}^n \times \{0,1\}^n \to \{0,1\}$, for a number $p \in [1/2, 1]$, let us define $dcc(f, n) = ts(f, n)/DC(f, n)$. We call $dcc(f, n)$ the deterministic communication characteristic of the boolean function f.

We will, also, use the notation $dcc(f)$ instead of $dcc(f, n)$.

Definition 6 For a boolean function $f : \{0,1\}^n \times \{0,1\}^n \to \{0,1\}$, for a number $p \in [1/2, 1]$, let us define $pcc_p(f, n) = dcc(f, n)h(p)$, where $h(p) = -p \log p - (1 - p) \log(1 - p)$ is a Shannon entropy. We call $pcc_p(f, n)$ the p-probabilistic communication characteristic of the boolean function f.

We will use the notation $pcc_p(f)$ instead of $pcc_p(f, n)$.

From the definitions it follows that for an arbitrary boolean function f $1 \leq dcc(f) \leq 2^n/n$ holds and for $p \in [1/2, 1]$ $h(p) \leq dcc(f) \leq 2^n h(p)/n$ holds.

Theorem 3 For an arbitrary boolean function $f : \{0,1\}^n \times \{0,1\}^n \to \{0,1\}$, for arbitrary $\epsilon \in (0, 1/2]$, $p = 1/2 + \epsilon$

$$PC_p(f) \geq DC(f)(1 - pcc_p(f)) - 1.$$

Using the Tailor expansion for the entropy function $h(1/2 + \epsilon)$, when $\epsilon \to 0$ one can verify the following fact

$$h(1/2 + \epsilon) = 1 - \epsilon^2(2/\ln 2) + \epsilon^5(7/960 \ln 2) + \ldots$$

As a corollary from theorem 3 and the expansion for the entropy function $h(1/2 + \epsilon)$ we have the following statement.

Theorem 4 If for a boolean function $f : \{0,1\}^n \times \{0,1\}^n \to \{0,1\}$ $dcc(f, n) = const$, then for arbitrary $\epsilon(n) \in (0, 1/2]$, $\epsilon(n) \to 0$ when $n \to \infty$, $p(n) = 1/2 + \epsilon(n)$

$$PC_{p(n)}(f, n) \geq O(DC(f, n)\epsilon^2(n)).$$

As a corollary from theorem 3 and the fact that $h(p) \sim (1 - p) \log(1 - p)^{-1}$ when $p \to 1$ we have the following statement.

Theorem 5 If for a boolean function $f : \{0,1\}^n \times \{0,1\}^n \to \{0,1\}$ $dcc(f, n) = const$, then for arbitrary $er(n) \in [0, 1/2)$, $er(n) \to 0$ when $n \to \infty$, $p(n) = 1 - er(n)$

$$PC_{p(n)}(f, n) \geq DC(f, n) - O(DC(f, n)er(n) \log er(n)^{-1}).$$

4 Functions with different communication characteristic

4.1 Two functions with different communication characteristics

We present two main boolean functions and their modifications with absolutely different communication structures, which demonstrate the different aspects of the lower bounds from the section 3.

Let us consider to simplify, (in order not to use ceiling and floor brackets) that n is of the form $n = 2^k$ where k is the integer throughout this section (it is easy to generalize all the results of the section to the common case).

Function $f_1(x, y) = 1$ iff $x = y$ is well known. One can easily see that the communication matrix F_1 for the boolean function f_1 is an $2^n \times 2^n$ identity matrix and it holds that

- $ts(f_1) = 2^n$,

- $DC(f_1) = n$,

- $dcc(f_1) = 2^n/n$ and for $p \in [1/2, 1]$ $pcc_p(f_1) = 2^n h(p)/n$

Theorem 4.1 For an arbitrary $\epsilon \in (0, 1/2)$, $p = 1/2 + \epsilon$ it holds that

$$\log n - \log \log(1 + 1/\epsilon) - 1 \leq PC_p(f_1) \leq 4 \log n.$$

Proof: The randomized protocol, based on the "prime numbers algorithm" of [7] is well known. It incurs restricted error while transmitting only $O(\log n)$ bits. So, for an arbitrary $\epsilon \in (0, 1/2)$, $p = 1/2 + \epsilon$ it holds that (see for example [11])

$$PC_p(f_1) \leq 4 \log n.$$

Theorem 2 gives the lower bound. ∎

- The lower bounds from theorems 1 and 2 can not be improved in the general case and for the boolean function f_1 we have an optimal bounded error probabilistic communication protocol.

- Theorem 1 and Theorem 3 give a trivial lower bound $PC_p(f_1) \geq 0$.

- There is no better unbounded error probabilistic protocol than the one-way bounded error probabilistic protocol for f_1.

Now we define function $f_2(x, y)$. Let Z_1 denote the following subset of $\{0, 1\}^n$. $Z_1 = \{x(i)/i \in \{1, 2, ..., n\}\}$, where $x(i)$, $i \in \{1, 2, ..., n\}$, is a word which i-th bit is 1 and the rest bits are 0. Let S denote the following subset of $\{0,1\}^n \times \{0,1\}^n$. $S = \{0,1\}^n \times Z_1 \bigcup Z_1 \times \{0,1\}^n$

$$f_2(x,y) = \begin{cases} \bigvee_{i=1}^n x_i \wedge y_i & \text{if } x,y \in S \\ 0 & \text{otherwise} \end{cases}$$

¿From the definition of function f_2 it follows that f_2 is equal to *inner product* function and *set intersection* function on the subset S of inputs. One can easily see that the communication matrix F_2 for the boolean function f_2 is a $2^n \times 2^n$ matrix with 2^n different rows, and columns and it holds that the set Z_1 is a test for f_2. So we have

- $ts(f_2) = n$,

- $DC(f_2) = n$,

- $dcc(f_2) = 1$ and for $p \in [\frac{1}{2}, 1]$ $pcc_p(f_2) = h(p)$

Theorem 4.2 There exists a 2-round deterministic protocol ϕ which computes the boolean function f_2 and

$$C_\phi(n) \leq 2 \log n + 1.$$

Proof: Evident. ∎

Let us describe the probabilistic one-way protocol Φ for the boolean function f_2.

If $x \in Z_1$, $x = x(i)$, $i \in \{1, 2, \ldots, n\}$ then protocol Φ works as follows. P_0 send a message $x \in Z_1$ and the message i to P_1. P_1 outputs the correct answer with probability 1.

If $x \notin Z_1$, then protocol Φ works as follows. Let us consider, to simplify, that $z = 2^m$ where m is an integer (it is easy to generalize this protocol to the common case). The processor P_0 divides its input x on the z equal parts of the length n/z each. Then P_0 uniformly randomly chooses one of the parts $x(j)$, $j \in \{1, 2, \ldots, z\}$, of the input x and sends a message $x \notin Z_1$, j and $x(j)$ to P_1.

P_1 works as follows. P_1 checks its input y. If $y \notin Z_1$, then P_1 outputs the correct answer with probability 1. If $y \in Z_1$, $y = y(i)$, $i \in \{1, 2, \ldots, n\}$, $x(j)$ contains i-th bit (in the common numeration of x) and this bit is 1, then P_1 outputs $b = 1$, else with the probability $q = 1/2 - 1/(4z - 2)$ P_1 outputs $b = 1$, and with the probability $1 - q$ outputs $b = 0$.

So for the probabilistic protocol Φ we have

$$Pr(\Phi \text{ outputs } b = 1 \text{ when } f_2(x,y) = 1) \geq 1/z + (1 - 1/z)q = 1/2 + 1/(4z - 2),$$

$$Pr(\Phi \text{ outputs } b = 0 \text{ when } f_2(x,y) = 0) \geq 1 - q = 1/2 + 1/(4z - 2).$$

¿From the description of the probabilistic one-way protocol Φ for $p = 1/2 + 1/(4z - 2)$, for the boolean function f_2 it follows

$$PC_p(f_2, n) \leq n/z + \log z + 2.$$

Theorem 4.3 For the boolean function f_2, for $p = 1/2$

$$\log n - \log \log n - 1 \ \le \ PC_p(f_2) \ \le \ \log n \ + \ 3.$$

Proof: Let $z = n$. Then the upper bound follows from the description of the probabilistic one-way protocol Φ for the boolean function f_2. So in our case parts x_i are trivial and are exactly the i-th bit of the input x.

Theorem 1 gives the lower bound. ∎

- From the description of the probabilistic one-way protocol Φ for the boolean function f_2 we have that $\epsilon(n) = 1/(4n - 2)$ for the probabilistic communication protocol described.

- Comparing the lower bounds of theorems 1,2,3, and 4 shows that in this case the lower bound of theorem 1 is the best.

Theorem 4.4 For the boolean function f_2, for a constant $z \ge 1$, $p = 1/2 + 1/(4z - 2)$

$$n(1 - h(p)) - 1 \ \le \ PC_p(f_2) \ \le \ n/z \ + \log z \ + \ 2.$$

Proof: The upper bound follows from the description of the probabilistic one-way protocol Φ for the boolean function f_2.

The lower bound follows from the fact that $pcc_p(f_2) = h(p)$ and from the theorem 3 lower bound. ∎

- Theorem 3 gives the best lower bound in this case.

We say that for a boolean function f and the numbers $p, p' \in [0, 1]$, $PC_p(f) < PC_{p'}(f)$ if there exists an n_0 such that for all $n \ge n_0$ $PC_p(f, n) < PC_{p'}(f, n)$.

Corollary 1 There exists an infinite sequence of numbers $1/2 < p_1 < p_2 < \cdots < p_i < \cdots < 1$ such, that for each $i \ge 1$

$$PC_{p_i}(f_2) \ < \ PC_{p_{i+1}}(f_2).$$

Theorem 4.5 For the boolean function f_2, for a $\epsilon(n) \to 0$, $p(n) = 1/2 + \epsilon(n)$

$$O(n\epsilon^2(n)) \ \le \ PC_{p(n)}(f_2) \ \le \ O(n\epsilon(n)).$$

Proof: The upper bound follows from the description of the probabilistic one-way protocol Φ for the boolean function f_2.

Theorem 4 gives the lower bound. ∎

Corollary 2 For the boolean function f_2, for a constant $t \ge 2$, $z(t, n) = \lceil n^{1/t} \rceil$, $p(t, n) = 1/2 + 1/(4z(t, n) - 2)$

$$O(n^{(1-2/t)}) \ \le \ PC_{p(t,n)}(f_2) \ \le \ O(n^{(1-1/t)}).$$

We say that for a boolean function f and for $p(n), p'(n) \in \{0,1\}$, $PC_{p(n)}(f) \prec PC_{p'(n)}(f)$ if $PC_{p(n)}(f,n)/PC_{p'(n)}(f,n) \to 0$ when $n \to \infty$.

Corollary 3 There exists an infinite sequence of integers $2 < t_1 < t_2 < \cdots < t_i < \cdots$ such, that for each $i \geq 1$

$$PC_{p(t_i,n)}(f_2) \prec PC_{p(t_{i+1},n)}(f_2).$$

Let $g : \{1,2,\ldots\} \to \{1,2,\ldots\}$ be a function such that $g(n) \leq n$ for all $n \geq 1$. Let $k(n) = n - g(n)$.

Let us define the function $f_1^g(x,y)$ as follows. $f_1^g(x,y) = 1$ iff $x = y$ and first $g(n)$ bits in x are 0. This function is similar to function f_1 and it is easy to verify that f_1^g has the following characteristics.

- $ts(f_1^g) = 2^{k(n)}$,

- $DC(f_1^g = k(n)$,

- $dcc(f_1^g) = 2^{k(n)}/n$.

- For a $\epsilon \in (0,1/2)$, for $p = 1/2 + \epsilon$ it holds

$$\log(k(n)) - \log\log(1 + 1/\epsilon) - 1 \leq PC_p(f_1^g) \leq 4\log(k(n)).$$

Let us define the function $f_2^g(x,y)$ similar to $f_2(x,y)$ as follows. Let $Z_1^g = \{x(i) \in Z_1/i \in \{1,2,\ldots,k(n)\}\}$, $S^g = \{0,1\}^n \times Z_1^g \bigcup Z_1^g \times \{0,1\}^n$

$$f_2^g(x,y) = \begin{cases} \bigvee_{i=1}^{n} x_i \wedge y_i & \text{if } x,y \in S^g \\ 0 & \text{otherwise} \end{cases}$$

One can easily see that for $k(n) = n - g(n)$ the boolean function f_2^g has the following properties.

- $ts(f_2^g) = k(n)$,

- $DC(f_2^g) = k(n)$,

- $dcc(f_2^g) = 1$, for $p \in (1/2,1)$ $pcc_p(f_2^g) = h(p)$.

- for $p = 1/2$ it holds that

$$\log k(n) - \log\log k(n) - 1 \leq PC_p(f_2^g) \leq 2\log k(n) + 1.$$

- For a proper $z \geq 2$, for $p = 1/2 + 1/(4z - 2)$ it holds that

$$k(n)(1 - h(p)) - 1 \leq PC_p(f_2^g) \leq k(n)/z + \log z + 2.$$

The following theorem for this function is similar to theorem 4.2 for the function f_2.

Theorem 4.6 For function $g(n)$ $(O(1) \prec g(n) \leq n)$ there exists a 2-round deterministic protocol ϕ which computes the boolean function f_2^g and

$$C_\phi(n) \leq 2 \log k(n) + 1.$$

¿From the properties of the functions f_1^g and f_2^g the following hold.

Theorem 4.7 For functions $g(n)$ and $g'(n)$ such that $\log g'(n) \prec g(n) \prec g'(n) \leq n$

$$DC(f_2^g) \prec DC(f_1^{g'}),$$

but for an arbitrary $p \in (1/2, 1)$

$$PC_p(f_2^g) \succ PC_p(f_1^{g'}).$$

4.2 Complexity for almost all functions

Denote by $\mathbf{F}(n, n)$ the set of all boolean functions $f(x, y)$. Let E be some property of functions from $\mathbf{F}(n, n)$. Denote by $\mathbf{F}^E(n, n)$ the subset of functions from $\mathbf{F}(n, n)$ without property E. We say that almost all functions have the property E if

$$| \mathbf{F}^E(n, n) | / | \mathbf{F}(n, n) | \to 0$$

as $n \to \infty$.

Lemma 4.1 Almost all functions have the following property

1. $DC(f) = n$,

2. For an arbitrary $\theta \in (0, 1)$ it holds that $n \leq ts(f) < (2 + \theta)n$.

   Proof: Omitted. ∎

   As a corollary from theorem 5 and the lemma above we can formulate the following statements.

Theorem 4.8 For almost all functions, for an $er(n) \to 0$, $p(n) = 1 - er(n)$

$$PC_{p(n)}(f, n) \geq n - O(n \, er(n) \log er(n)^{-1}) - 1$$

Note that in the case $en(n) \prec 1/n$ the lower bound of the theorem above is more preciese than Yao [16] lower bound $n - \log n - 2$ for an arbitrary fixed error probability.

Concluding Remarks

It is an interesting open problem to prove results similar to the results of this paper for probabilistic k-round protocols and more general optimal partition model (see [16, 9, 10] for the most recent results and complete references) allows the partition to be chosen arbitrarily, each processor still receiving n bits. As it is mentioned in [10], communication complexity in the optimal partition model is closely related to the area/time complexity of VLSI circuits.

Acknowledgment

I wish to thank L. Hemachandra for his invitation to me to spend the spring
semester at the University of Rochester and for his permanent attention to my
research and helpfulness in all my problems and J. Seiferas for extensive comments on an earlier draft of this paper. I wish also to thank P.Dietz for his
comments, which helped to simplify the proof of lemma 4.1.

References

[1] F.Ablayev: Lower Bounds for One-way Probabilistic Communication Complexity. University of Rochester, Computer Science Department, July 1992 TR422.

[2] F.Ablayev: On Comparing Probabilistic and Deterministic Automata Complexity of Languages. In: Proceedings of MFCS'89,
Lecture Notes in Computer Science, 379, (1989), 599-605.

[3] N.Alon, P.frankl, V.Rodl: Geometrical realization of set systems
and probabilistic communication complexity. In: Proc. 26th Annual
IEEE Symposium on Foundations of Computer Science, (1985),
277-280.

[4] B.Chor, O.Goldreich: Unibased bits from sourcesof weak randomness and probabilistic communication complexity. SIAM J. Comput. 17, 2, (1988), 230-261.

[5] Phan Dinh Dieu: On a Necessary Condition for Stochastic Languages. Elektronische Informationsverarbeitung und Kybernetik, 8
(1972), 575-588.

[6] P.Duris, Z.Galil, G.Schnitger: Lower bounds on Communication
Complexity. In: Proc. of the 16th Annual ACM Symposium on the
Theory of Computing, (1984), 81-89.

[7] R.Freivalds: Fast Probabilistic Algorithms. In: Proc. of the Conference Mathematical Foundation of Computer Science 1979, Lect.
Notes in Comput. Science, 74 (1979), 57-69.

[8] B.Halstenberg, R.Reischuk: On Different Modes of Communication. In: Proc. of the 20th Annual ACM Symposium on the Theory
of Computing, (1988), 162-172.

[9] J.Ja'Ja', V.K.Prasana Kumar, J.Simon: Information transfer under
different sets of protocols. SIAM J. Comput. 13 (1984), 840-849.

[10] T. Wah Lam and W. Ruzzo: Results on Communication Complexity Classes. Journal of Computer and System Sciences, 44 (1992),
324-342.

[11] L. Lovasz: Communication Complexity: A Survey. In: Korte, Lovasz, Promel, Schrijver (eds.): "Paths, Flows and VLSI Layout", , Springer 1990, pp.235-266.

[12] A.Orlitsky, A. El Gamal: Communication complexity. In Yaser S. Abu-Mostafa(ed.): Complexity in information theory. Springer 1988, pp. 17-61.

[13] C.H.Papadimitrio, M.Sipser. Communication Complexity. In: Proc. 14th ACM Annual ACM Symposium on the Theory of Computing, (1983), 196-200.

[14] H. Paturi and J.Simon: Probabilistic Communication Complexity. Journal of Computer and System Sciences, 33 (1986), 106-123.

[15] M.O Rabin: Probabilistic automata. Information and Control, 6 (1963), 230-244.

[16] A.C.Yao: Some Complexity Questions Related to Distributive Computing. In: Proc. of the 11th Annual ACM Symposium on the Theory of Computing, (1979), 209-213.

[17] A.C.Yao: Lower Bounds by Probabilistic Arguments. In: Proc. of the 24th Annual IEEE Symposium on Foundations of Computer Science, (1983), 420-428.

Maintaining Discrete Probability Distributions Optimally[*]

Torben Hagerup,[1] Kurt Mehlhorn,[1] and J. Ian Munro[2]

[1] Max-Planck-Institut für Informatik, Im Stadtwald, W–6600 Saarbrücken, Germany.
[2] Dept. of Computer Science, University of Waterloo, Waterloo, Ontario, Canada N2L 3G1.

Abstract. Consider a *distribution* as an abstract data type that represents a probability distribution f on a finite set and supports a *generate* operation, which returns a random value distributed according to f and independent of the values returned by previous calls. We study the implementation of *dynamic* distributions, which additionally support changes to the probability distribution through *update* operations, and show how to realize distributions on $\{1, \ldots, n\}$ with constant expected generate time, constant update time, $O(n)$ space, and $O(n)$ initialization time. We also consider *generalized distributions*, whose values need not sum to 1, and obtain similar results.

1 Introduction

The problem of generating sequences of independent random values with a specified discrete probability distribution is fundamental in the area of discrete-event simulation [BFS87]. If the probability distribution is invariant over time, the well-known *alias method* [BFS87, Section 5.2.8] can generate each successive value in constant time (following $O(n)$ preprocessing time). We generalize this to a dynamic setting, where the probability distribution is allowed to change over time, extending work of Fox [Fox90] and Rajasekaran and Ross [RR91] and complementing work of Matias, Vitter, and Ni [MVN93]. Our results lead to more efficient simulations of an important class of queueing networks, the so-called open Jackson networks (see [Kle75, Section 4.8] and [Fox90]).

A *distribution* f on a finite set D assigns a probability to each element of D, i.e., f is a nonnegative function defined on D with $\sum_{x \in D} f(x) = 1$. We study the problem of maintaining a distribution f on a finite domain D under the operations *generate*, which returns a random value distributed according to f and independent of the values generated by previous calls, and *update*, which shifts a specified amount of probability from one element of D to another. Our first result is

Theorem 1. *Distributions on $\{1, \ldots, n\}$ can be maintained with constant expected generate time, constant update time, $O(n)$ space, and $O(n)$ initialization time.*

In some applications, notably the simulation of open Jackson networks mentioned above, it is more natural to view a distribution on a set D as induced by an arbitrary nonnegative function f on D, whereby the probability of each $x \in D$ is proportional to $f(x)$. We model this situation by defining a *generalized distribution* on a finite domain D as any nonnegative function f on D. The values of f are called *weights*, and $W = \sum_{x \in D} f(x)$ is the *total weight* of f. A *generate* operation produces each element $x \in D$ with probability proportional to $f(x)$, i.e., with probability $f(x)/W$, and an *update*

[*] Supported by the ESPRIT Basic Research Actions Program of the EC under contract No. 7141 (project ALCOM II). The research was carried out in part while the first author was with the Departament de LSI of the Universitat Politècnica de Catalunya in Barcelona, Spain, and in part while the third author was visiting the MPI für Informatik.

operation changes a single weight arbitrarily. A generalized distribution on a set of size n is called *polynomially-bounded* if its weights remain integral and bounded by a fixed polynomial in n. We show

Theorem 2. *Polynomially-bounded generalized distributions on $\{1, \ldots, n\}$ can be maintained with constant expected generate time, constant update time, $O(n)$ space, and $O(n)$ initialization time.*

Our results are valid in the standard randomized real RAM model. More specifically, we assume that the following operations take constant time: arithmetic (addition, subtraction, multiplication, and integer division) on integers of absolute value polynomial in n, real arithmetic and the floor function, and drawing a random number from the uniform distribution on the interval $[0, 1]$.

Theorem 1 completely settles the problem of maintaining a distribution. For generalized distributions we achieve optimality only under the assumption that the weights are integral and polynomially bounded; this is definitely the setting of greatest practical relevance. Matias, Vitter, and Ni [MVN93] recently showed in independent work that arbitrary generalized distributions can be maintained with $O(\log^* n)$ expected update and generate times in a more powerful model that assumes constant-time operations on integers of arbitrary size. A combination of their original methods and those described here yields a solution in the more powerful model with constant expected update and generate times [MVN93]. Previous to [MVN93] and the present paper, the only method that could deal with general update operations and put no restrictions on the (generalized) distribution had generate and update times of $\Theta(\log n)$ (store the weights at the leaves of a complete binary tree, with each internal node storing the total weight at its leaf descendants). Sublogarithmic methods were only known under the assumption that there are known and fixed generalized distributions $\underline{f}$ and $\overline{f}$ such that always $\underline{f}(x) \leq f(x) \leq \overline{f}(x)$, for all $x \in D$. Under this assumption, Rajasekaran and Ross [RR91] achieve update and generate times of $O(\overline{\alpha}/\underline{\alpha})$, where $\underline{\alpha} = (1/n) \sum_{x \in D} \underline{f}(x)$ and $\overline{\alpha} = (1/n) \sum_{x \in D} \overline{f}(x)$.

2 Maintaining Distributions

2.1 Two Simple Methods

The problem of generating a random value distributed according to a generalized distribution f on $\{1, \ldots, n\}$ has a trivial $O(n)$-time solution whose correctness is obvious: Compute the prefix sums of f, i.e., let $s_i = \sum_{j=1}^{i} f(j)$, for $i = 0, \ldots, n$, and then pick a random value z from the uniform distribution on $(0, s_n]$ and return the unique $i \in \{1, \ldots, n\}$ with $s_{i-1} < z \leq s_i$.

Lemma 1. *Given a generalized distribution f on $\{1, \ldots, n\}$, a random value distributed according to f can be generated in $O(n)$ time using $O(n)$ space.*

The algorithm described above will be called the *prefix-sums algorithm* or the naive algorithm. We next develop another algorithm, based on the *rejection method* [BFS87, Section 5.2.5], that performs efficiently in a very special case, namely for so-called *flat generalized distributions*. A generalized distribution is *flat* if its nonzero weights all lie in $[r, 2r]$, for some known $r > 0$.

First consider the following problem: Given a real number p with $0 \leq p \leq 1$, accept with probability p and reject with probability $1 - p$; here accepting and rejecting are symbolic actions without any concrete meaning. The problem is trivial to solve in constant time: Simply draw a random value z from the uniform distribution on $[0, 1]$ and accept if and only if $z \leq p$. When p has been fixed, an algorithm with this behavior will be called a *p-acceptor*.

Lemma 2. *A generalized distribution f on $\{1,\ldots,n\}$ whose nonzero weights lie in the interval $[r, 2r]$, for some known (but possibly time-dependent) $r > 0$, can be maintained with constant expected generate time, constant update time, $O(n)$ space, and $O(n)$ initialization time.*

Proof. Store the elements of $D' = \{j : 1 \le j \le n \text{ and } f(j) > 0\}$ in the first $|D'|$ cells of an array $A[1..n]$, and also record $n' = |D'|$. For $j = 1,\ldots,n$, store in the jth cell of another array $B[1..n]$ the weight $f(j)$ and, if $j \in D'$, the position of j in A. In order to generate a random value distributed according to f, first pick a random value l from the uniform distribution on $\{1,\ldots,n'\}$. Then convert l to a random element j of D' by indexing into A, i.e., let $j = A[l]$, and run an $f(j)/(2r)$-acceptor. If the acceptor accepts, output the value j; otherwise restart the algorithm, i.e., pick a new random value l, etc.

It is easy to see that the value j is output with probability proportional to $f(j)$, for $j = 1,\ldots,n$, i.e., the algorithm is correct. The algorithm carries out successive trials until some trial succeeds. Each trial can be executed in constant time and succeeds with probability $(1/n') \sum_{j \in D'} f(j)/(2r) \ge 1/2$. The required number of trials is therefore geometrically distributed with expected value at most 2.

An update is straightforward, except when n' changes. When D' gains an element, store it in the first unused cell in A and increment n'; when D' loses an element, exchange it with the element stored in the last used cell in A and decrement n'. $\qquad\square$

2.2 Reducing the Domain Size

In this subsection we discuss a simple way of combining data structures designed to maintain different "parts" of a single generalized distribution. It can be viewed as a dynamic version of the *composition method* [BFS87, Section 5.2.7].

It is convenient to divide the universe of weights into discrete *ranges*: For every integer i, let $R_i = (2^i, 2^{i+1}]$. Given a generalized distribution f on a domain D and an integer i, we call $D_i = \{j \in D : f(j) \in R_i\}$ the ith *layer domain* of f and the restriction of f to D_i the ith *layer* of f. Since each layer of a generalized distribution is flat, we know from Lemma 2 that any given layer can be maintained with constant expected generate time and constant update time. Our goal now is to put together solutions for different layers in order to obtain an overall solution. The idea is quite simple: To generate a random value, first somehow decide on a layer, and then generate the value using the data structure for that layer. "Somehow deciding on a layer" in fact again is generating a value according to a given generalized distribution, which now assigns weight $\sum_{j \in D_i} f(j)$ to i, for all integers i — we call it the *layer distribution*.

To *locate* an element $x \in D$ with respect to a partition $D_1,\ldots,D_m$ of a set D is to determine the unique $i \in \{1,\ldots,m\}$ with $x \in D_i$. If the partition $D_1,\ldots,D_m$ is successively changed by a sequence of updates, it will be called *slowly dynamic* if each update causes only a constant number of elements of D to move between sets in the partition, and if the set of moving elements can be determined in constant time.

Suppose now that f is a distribution on $D = \{1,\ldots,n\}$, and that $D_1,\ldots,D_m$ is a slowly dynamic partition of D such that any $x \in D$ can be located with respect to $D_1,\ldots,D_m$ in constant time. The *dynamic composition method* applied to f and $D_1,\ldots,D_m$ maintains the restriction f_i of f to D_i, for $i = 1,\ldots,m$, as well as the *group distribution* g on $\{1,\ldots,m\}$ with $g(i) = W_i = \sum_{x \in D_i} f(x)$, for $i = 1,\ldots,m$. To generate a random value z according to f, first select a group D_i by choosing i according to the group distribution g, and then generate z according to f_i. Since we choose between groups with the correct probabilities and between the elements of the chosen group with the correct relative probabilities, z is indeed distributed according to f, i.e., the algorithm is correct.

Lemma 3. *In the situation described above, suppose that f_i can be maintained with expected generate time T_i, constant update time, space S_i, and initialization time I_i, for $i = 1, \ldots, m$, and that g can be maintained with expected generate time T, update time U, space S, and initialization time I. Then the dynamic composition method maintains f with expected generate time $\sum_{i=1}^{m} W_i T_i + T + O(1)$, update time $O(U)$, space $\sum_{i=1}^{m} S_i + S + O(n)$, and initialization time $\sum_{i=1}^{m} I_i + I + O(n)$.*

Proof. The expected time needed is T for the generation according to g, $\sum_{i=1}^{m} W_i T_i$ for the generation according to a restriction of f, and $O(1)$ for miscellaneous overhead. An update to f entails at most two updates to restrictions of f and one update to g, plus whatever updates are caused by changes in the partition $D_1, \ldots, D_m$. By assumption, these updates can be executed in $O(U)$ time. □

In attempting to combine Lemmas 2 and 3 directly as sketched above, we are faced with the difficulty that we cannot put a bound on the number of layers, since weights may be arbitrarily small. The weighted average $\sum_{i=1}^{m} W_i T_i$ appearing in Lemma 3, however, shows that we can allow a very bad method (a large T_i) for very small weights (a small W_i). In concrete terms, we can use the naive method of Lemma 1 to handle all weights no larger than $1/n^2$. Since these weights sum to at most $1/n$ and Lemma 1 guarantees a generate time of $O(n)$, the contribution of the small weights to the overall expected generate time will be constant. This means that we need only maintain $m = \lceil 2 \log_2 n \rceil$ layers according to Lemma 2; the remaining layers are lumped together and handled by the naive algorithm.

Lemma 4. *A distribution on $D = \{1, \ldots, n\}$ can be maintained with constant expected generate time, constant update time, $O(n \log n)$ space, and $O(n \log n)$ initialization time, plus the time and space needed to maintain a distribution on a fixed domain of size $O(\log n)$.*

Proof. We combine Lemmas 1, 2 and 3 as described above. For $i = 1, \ldots, m = \lceil 2 \log_2 n \rceil$, maintain the restriction f_i of f to $D_{-i} = \{j \in D : f(j) \in R_{-i}\}$ according to Lemma 2, and maintain the restriction f_{m+1} of f to $D_{-m-1} = D \setminus \bigcup_{i=1}^{m} D_{-i}$ according to Lemma 1. Then put the $m + 1$ data structures together using Lemma 3; we already argued above that the resulting expected generate time is constant. The space and initialization time needed by each of the $O(\log n)$ data structures is $O(n)$.

The dynamic composition method requires that given $j \in D$, constant time must suffice to determine the unique $i \in \{1, \ldots, m+1\}$ with $j \in D_{-i}$. While at first glance this might appear to require the extraction of binary logarithms ($i = \min\{\lceil \log_2(2/f(j)) \rceil, m+1\}$), an appendix argues that in fact we are not going beyond our stated instruction repertoire. □

Lemma 4 still does not provide us with a complete data structure, since we are left with the problem of maintaining a layer distribution on a domain of size $O(\log n)$. Applying Lemma 4 a second time, we can reduce this problem to one of maintaining a distribution on a domain of size $O(\log \log n)$. Continuing in this fashion until the remaining problem is of constant size and hence trivial to solve, we could derive a solution with $O(\log^* n)$ expected generate time and $2^{O(\log^* n)}$ update time. We can do better, however, by exploiting the fact that after a constant number of reduction steps, the problem has become so small that it can be solved by means of table lookup. This is pursued in the next subsection.

2.3 Table Lookup

Our approach will be to approximate the given distribution by a suitable generalized distribution, to store the generalized distribution in a single memory word, and to use this word to index into tables that indicate the outcomes of all possible operations. For this to have any hope of succeeding, the generalized distribution must be defined on a very small domain, which is certainly the case, and its weights must be small integers. As described in the proof of Lemma 6, we achieve this by scaling and rounding the weights of the original distribution. Assume first that this has already taken place.

Lemma 5. *A generalized distribution f on $\{1,\ldots,m\}$ and with integer weights in the range $\{0,\ldots,m-1\}$ can be maintained with constant generate time, constant update time, $m^{O(m)}$ space and initialization time, and a word length of $O(m\log m)$ bits.*

Proof. It suffices to encode f as a single integer F and to realize the following functions in constant time:

Generate: Given F and an integer l from the set $\{1,\ldots,\sum_{j=1}^{m} f(j)\}$ (l will be chosen randomly from this set), return the integer that would be output by the prefix-sums algorithm applied to the generalized distribution f and the random number l, i.e., return the unique $i \in \{1,\ldots,m\}$ with $\sum_{j=1}^{i-1} f(j) < l \leq \sum_{j=1}^{i} f(j)$.

Update: Given F and integers i and j with $1 \leq j \leq m$ and $0 \leq i \leq m-1$ (representing a request to set $f(j)$ to i), return an integer F' representing the generalized distribution f' on $\{1,\ldots,m\}$ with $f'(j) = i$, and $f'(l) = f(l)$ for all $l \in \{1,\ldots,m\}\setminus\{j\}$.

Any reasonable encoding of f will do, e.g., take F as the integer $\sum_{j=1}^{m} f(j)m^{j-1}$ with m-ary representation $f(m)\cdots f(1)$. The functions Generate and Update can be realized via table lookup, whereby the arguments of a function are used as indices into an (up to three-dimensional) array whose entries are the desired answers. The tables have $m^{O(m)}$ entries, and it is easy to compute any given entry in $O(m)$ time. Hence the space and initialization time are $m^{O(m)}$, the necessary word length is $O(m\log m)$ bits, and the generate and update times are constant. $\quad\square$

Before we can apply the above result in the context of the previous subsection, we have to deal with the rounding problem mentioned above.

Lemma 6. *A distribution f on $\{1,\ldots,m\}$ can be maintained with constant expected generate time, constant update time, $m^{O(m^2)}$ space and initialization time, and a word length of $O(m^2\log m)$ bits.*

Proof. Consider the following derived distribution f' on $\{1,\ldots 2m\}$: For $j = 1,\ldots,m$, $f'(j) = (1/m^2)\lfloor m^2 f(j)\rfloor$, and $f'(m+j) = f(j) - f'(j)$. To generate a random value according to f, we can generate a random value according to f' and subtract m if the value generated is larger than m. On the other hand, an update to f translates into a constant number of updates to f'. It hence suffices to maintain f' within the stated bounds.

The values $f'(1),\ldots,f'(m)$ are obviously multiples of $1/m^2$, so that the first half of f' (i.e., the restriction of f' to $\{1,\ldots,m\}$) can be maintained with constant generate and update time and $m^{O(m^2)}$ space and initialization time according to Lemma 5 — maintaining a generalized distribution of integers scaled by a common and fixed factor obviously is as easy as maintaining the generalized distribution of the integers themselves. On the other hand, the values $f'(m+1),\ldots,f'(2m)$ are bounded by $1/m^2$ and therefore sum to at most $1/m$. We can hence maintain the second half of f according to the naive algorithm and use Lemma 3 to combine the data structures for the first and second halves of f, incurring only a constant expected generate time for the second half. $\quad\square$

As outlined at the end of the previous subsection, Lemmas 4 (applied twice) and 6 combine to show that distributions on $\{1,\ldots,n\}$ can be maintained with constant expected generate time, constant update time, and $O(n\log n)$ space and initialization time.

258

2.4 The Complete Data Structure

In this section we improve the result formulated above by showing how to reduce the space and initialization time to $O(n)$. For this it is necessary to take a second look at the data structures implied by the proof of Lemma 4.

The superlinear resource requirements can be traced to the fact that $m = \Theta(\log n)$ layers of a distribution f are maintained simultaneously using the construction of Lemma 2; for each layer, $\Theta(n)$ space and initialization time are set aside for the arrays A and B. Since layer domains are disjoint, however, all layers can in fact share the same array B — two layers never access the same cell in B. Furthermore, the sizes of those parts of the arrays A actually in use never sum to more than n. We are hence left with the problem of maintaining a collection of dynamic arrays that grow and shrink, but whose total size remains bounded by n. We solve this problem in a way suggested by the known methods for dynamizing static data structures [OvL81].

Our general strategy is as follows: We represent each array by an *array segment*, trying to keep these near the beginning of a large *base segment*, the part of which following the last array segment forms a *free segment*. When an array needs to expand but has no room to do so within its segment, it abandons its segment, which becomes *garbage*, and a new, larger, segment is allocated for it from the beginning of the free segment. Of course, if this were the entire scheme, array segments would tend to migrate towards still higher memory addresses, eating up ever more of the free segment, and no linear bound would apply. To counteract this drift we run a *garbage collector* in parallel with the algorithm. The garbage collector continuously sweeps the base segment and moves the array segments closer to the beginning of the base segment, squeezing out garbage cells as it does so. What is to be shown, basically, is that the garbage collector can keep up with the garbage-producing capability of the algorithm.

Lemma 7. *Suppose that an algorithm maintains a collection $\mathcal{A}$ of dynamic one-dimensional arrays indexed from 1, and that in each step of the algorithm a single array in $\mathcal{A}$ may expand or contract by a single memory cell. Then $\mathcal{A}$ can be represented in a fixed contiguous block of $O(n)$ memory cells, where n is a fixed known upper bound on the total size of the arrays in $\mathcal{A}$.*

Proof. Imagine a *base segment* to be laid out from left to right. An array $A \in \mathcal{A}$ of size m is usually stored in an *array segment* of m consecutive cells in the base segment; cells in array segments are said to be *used*. When a segment of initial size m is created for an array A, the m cells to its right are *reserved* for future expansions of A. When A expands, the leftmost cell reserved for it becomes used. When A contracts, the block of cells reserved for it, if nonempty, expands by one cell on the left, but contracts by two cells on the right (i.e., A altogether loses one reserved cell); if no cells were reserved for A before the contraction, this remains so. The cells to the right of the rightmost used or reserved cell are said to be *free* and to form a *free segment*; a *free pointer* to the leftmost free cell is maintained. Cells that are neither used nor reserved nor free are called *garbage cells*.

When an array A of size m needs to expand but has used up all its reserved cells, it abandons its current array segment and moves to a new array segment of initial size $m+1$ allocated for it from the left end of the free segment. In each of the m subsequent accesses to A, a single cell of its old segment is *vacated*, i.e., its contents are copied to the new segment, and it becomes garbage (or free). Since the $m+1$ (additional) cells reserved for A disappear at the rate of at most one per access to A, the old segment of A can be completely vacated before A must move again; hence at any given time A spreads over at most two segments, and it is not difficult to carry out the accesses to A correctly.

The original *user algorithm*, modified as described above, and a *garbage collector* algorithm are run as coroutines: The execution is divided into *rounds*; in each round, the user algorithm is run for one step (in particular, it executes at most one access to an array in $\mathcal{A}$), after which the garbage collector processes 9 cells. The garbage collector needs access to information about the current size and the number of cells reserved for each array segment; we can assume that this information is kept in a cell associated with the first cell of the segment. To understand the workings of the garbage collector, note that we actually employ two base segments, a *foreground segment* and a *background segment*, and that each cell of the foreground segment has an associated *cross pointer*. The garbage collector maintains a *foreground pointer* into the foreground segment and a *background pointer* into the background segment. It always next processes the cell γ pointed to by the foreground pointer. If γ is a garbage cell, processing γ simply increments the foreground pointer. Otherwise the contents of γ are copied to the cell pointed to by the background pointer, the current value of the background pointer is copied to the cross pointer of γ, and the foreground and background pointers are both advanced. The user algorithm normally operates on the foreground segment, but uses the cross pointers to execute any modifications behind the foreground pointer in the background segment as well. Hence when the foreground pointer reaches the free pointer, the information recorded in the two base segments will be identical, except that the background segment may contain less garbage. At this point the roles of the two base segments are switched, the foreground and background pointers are reset to point to the left end of their respective arrays, and the free pointer is set appropriately.

We claim that no sweep of the garbage collector takes more than n rounds, which implies that the total space used is $O(n)$. To see the truth of the claim, assume that it holds for a particular sweep S. Since in each round the user algorithm can produce at most 3 cells of garbage (two by contracting an array, and one by vacating a cell), during S and the n rounds following S it produces at most $6n$ cells of garbage. No garbage from before S can persist after S. Hence at any point during the n rounds following S there are at most $6n$ cells of garbage. Furthermore, the total number of used and reserved cells at any given time is at most $3n$, for an array of size m occupies at most m used cells in one (new) segment, m used cells in another (old) segment, and m reserved cells. Hence during the n rounds following S the number of cells that are not free never exceeds $9n$, which implies that the sweep following S takes at most n rounds. □

Theorem 1. *Distributions on $\{1, \ldots, n\}$ can be maintained with constant expected generate time, constant update time, $O(n)$ space, and $O(n)$ initialization time.*

3 Maintaining Polynomially-Bounded Generalized Distributions

3.1 Table Lookup Revisited

In this subsection we extend the table lookup method of Lemma 6 from distributions to polynomially-bounded generalized distributions. Recall that the basic idea used in the original scheme was to split each weight in a "significant" part and a small remainder, to maintain the significant parts using table lookup proper, and to maintain the remainders naively. We will use the same approach here, the main obstacle being that the meaning of "significant" changes over time. Because of this, we are actually unable to maintain the remainder weights explicitly.

Lemma 8. *For every fixed $c \geq 0$, a generalized distribution f on $\{1, \ldots, m\}$ and with integer weights bounded by n^c can be maintained with constant expected generate time, constant update time, $O(n + m \log n) + m^{O(m)}$ space and initialization time, and a word length of $O(\log n + m \log m)$ bits.*

Proof. It will be convenient to view each weight as expressed as a sequence of digits in the positional system with base m. Let $t = \lfloor c \log_2 n \rfloor + 1$, a certain upper bound on the maximum number of digits needed. A central data structure will be an $m \times t$ table A that records the most significant part of each weight. Informally, A has a row for each weight and a column for each digit position and stores the three most significant digits of each weight in the three corresponding cells (see Fig. 1).

$$
\begin{aligned}
f(1) &= 35824 \\
f(2) &= 401075 \\
&\quad\;\; 67 \\
&\vdots \\
&\quad 9243380 \\
f(m) &= 6921
\end{aligned}
$$

		3	5	8		
	4	0	1			
					6	7
9	2	4				
			6	9	2	

Fig. 1. The table A in a decimal example ($m = 10$). Empty squares denote zero entries. The columns of A are numbered from right to left.

More precisely, let us number the rows and columns of A starting from 1 and 0, respectively, and denote the entry in row i and column j of A by $A_{i,j}$, for $i = 1, \ldots, m$ and $j = 0, \ldots, t-1$. For $i = 1, \ldots, m$, if $f(i) = \sum_{j=0}^{l_i} w_{i,j} m^j$ with $w_{i,l_i} \neq 0$ and $w_{i,j} \in \{0, \ldots, m-1\}$, for $j = 0, \ldots, l_i$, then take $A_{i,j} = w_{i,j}$ for all integers j with $\max\{l_i - 2, 0\} \leq j \leq l_i$, and take $A_{i,j} = 0$ for all other j, i.e., for $j \in \{0, \ldots, t-1\} \setminus \{l_i, l_i - 1, l_i - 2\}$.

For $j = 0, \ldots, t-1$, we furthermore record the jth column sum $S_j = \sum_{i=1}^{m} A_{i,j}$ and maintain the generalized distribution f_j on $\{1, \ldots, m\}$ defined by the jth column of A, i.e., $f_j(i) = A_{i,j}$, for $i = 1, \ldots, m$. Since a column holds m integers in the range $\{0, \ldots, m-1\}$, the latter can be done using the simple table-lookup scheme of Lemma 5. Because only three digits of each weight are recorded in A, it is possible to update all this information in constant time whenever a weight changes. We also record the total weight $W = \sum_{i=1}^{m} f(i)$.

Imagine now that we *scale* S_j as well as the entries in the jth column of A by multiplying them by the factor m^j of the corresponding digit position, for $j = 0, \ldots, t-1$. Scaled in this way, the table A corresponds in a natural way to a generalized distribution on a domain of size mt. If we had recorded all digits of each weight in A instead of just three digits, we could have generated a random value z distributed according to f in the following way: First choose a column of A according to the generalized distribution defined by the scaled column weights, then generate z according to the generalized distribution maintained for the chosen column. As it is, however, only the generalized distributions maintained for the leftmost nonzero column of A and the two columns immediately to its right can be trusted.

We actually proceed as follows: Suppose that the index of the leftmost nonzero column of A is $l \geq 2$. Then we use the scaled column weights of columns l, $l-1$ and $l-2$ together with the total weight W to make a 4-way branch in the style of the composition method: To column l, column $l-1$, column $l-2$, or neither of these. In the first three cases we simply proceed to generate a random value according to the generalized distribution maintained for the column in question. In the forth case we spend $\Theta(m)$ time calculating the remainder weights not "covered" by columns l, $l-1$ and $l-2$ and then generate the random value according to these remainder weights using the prefix-sums algorithm of Lemma 1.

The algorithm is easily seen to be correct. It takes constant time, except in the forth case above, which uses $\Theta(m)$ time. Most of the scaled weight is found in the leftmost nonzero column of A or near it, however, and it is not difficult to see that the forth case occurs with probability at most $1/m$. Hence, by Lemma 3, the overall expected generate time is constant.

The above description skirted the question of how to determine the index l of the leftmost nonzero column of A. In order to do this efficiently, we additionally maintain the integer $V = \sum_{j=0}^{t-1} b_j \cdot 2^j$, where $b_j = 1$ if $S_j > 0$ and $b_j = 0$ if $S_j = 0$, for $j = 0, \ldots, t-1$, i.e., V is a bit vector representation of the set of indices of nonzero columns in A. Now l can be obtained as $\lfloor \log_2 V \rfloor$; we again appeal to the description in the appendix of how to compute logarithms. Individual bits in V can be updated using shifts, i.e., multiplications and integer divisions by powers of 2; the need to change a bit is signalled by the transition of the corresponding column sum from zero to nonzero, or vice versa. □

3.2 A Refined Reduction

Recall that the scheme of Lemma 4 maintains a distribution f on $D = \{1, \ldots, n\}$ essentially by taking $m = \lceil 2 \log_2 n \rceil$, maintaining a layer distribution g on the fixed set $I = \{-1, \ldots, -m\}$, maintaining the restriction of f to $D_i = \{j \in D : f(j) \in R_i\}$ for all $i \in I$ using the method of Lemma 2, and maintaining the restriction of f to $D \backslash \bigcup_{i \in I} D_i$ using the naive algorithm. The same approach works when f is a generalized distribution, except that the index set I must be allowed to change over time. Define an integer i to be *nonempty* if $f(j) \in R_i$ for at least one $j \in D$. Then the requirement essentially is that I should contain (at least) the largest nonempty integer and the $m-1$ integers directly below it. In other words, we move a sliding window over the ranges, always focusing on the currently largest weights.

As is clear from the above description, we must make sure that I is slowly dynamic in the sense that an update causes only a constant number of elements to enter or leave I. If this is the case, it is easy to keep the elements of I consecutively numbered (i.e., g can continue to be defined on a fixed set after all) and to carry out the required updates on g. If we furthermore maintain the ith layer of f for all integers i, not just for those currently in I, a generate operation can proceed precisely as before.

Let I_0 be the set of all nonempty integers. The set $I' = \{l, l-1, \ldots, l-m+1\}$, where $l = \max I_0$, is probably the most natural choice for I, but I' is not slowly dynamic. We therefore define I not as I', but instead as the set of the $\min\{m, |I_0|\}$ largest elements of I_0. As can easily be verified, this set is indeed slowly dynamic. The only remaining problem is to actually maintain I.

Recall from the end of the previous subsection that a bit vector can be used to maintain an arbitrary set of layer numbers such that the operations *insert*, *delete*, and *findmax* (which returns the maximum) can be executed in constant time. Storing the reversed bit vector as well, we can also execute *findmin* in constant time. We use this to maintain the two sets I and $J = I_0 \backslash I$.

When a new element enters I_0, a comparison with $\min I$ determines whether it is to be inserted in J or in I; if in the latter case subsequently $|I| = m+1$, we also move $\min I$ from I to J. When an element leaves I and $J \neq \emptyset$, we also move $\max J$ from J to I. This maintains I correctly and takes only constant time per update operation.

3.3 The Complete Data Structure

The previous subsection extended Lemma 4 from distributions to polynomially-bounded generalized distributions; furthermore, Lemma 7 still allows us to get by with linear space and initialization time. Applying the reduction twice to a polynomially-bounded generalized distribution on $\{1, \ldots, n\}$, we are left with the problem of maintaining a generalized distribution on a domain of size $O(\log\log n)$ and with weights polynomial in n, at which point we can appeal to Lemma 8.

Theorem 2. *Polynomially-bounded generalized distributions on* $\{1,\dots,n\}$ *can be maintained with constant expected generate time, constant update time, $O(n)$ space, and $O(n)$ initialization time.*

4 Maintaining Unrestricted Generalized Distributions

What prevents us from extending the result of the previous section beyond polynomially-bounded generalized distributions is the convention that all integers must be of $O(\log n)$ bits, which restricts the length of the bit vectors used in Subsections 3.1 and 3.2, as well as our inability to compute logarithms of superpolynomial integers in constant time. If these obstacles were removed, i.e., given unit-cost implementations of the arithmetic operations on arbitrary integers and of the function $\text{LOG}_2 : I\!N \to I\!N \cup \{0\}$ with $\text{LOG}_2(m) = \lfloor \log_2 m \rfloor$, our scheme could handle arbitrary integer weights. The space used by a straightforward implementation would no longer be bounded, since both the table-lookup method of Lemma 8 and the reduction of Section 3.2 would need an infinite array. Since each weight is recorded in only a constant number of places, however, the distribution data structure could be run in such a way that at any given point in time, only $O(n)$ (known) memory cells would contain essential values. Dynamic perfect hashing could then be employed to pack the $O(n)$ used cells into a fixed storage area of size $O(n)$, i.e., linear space requirements could be achieved. Given the ability to handle arbitrary integer weights, it is easy to handle arbitrary real weights, provided that LOG_2 can be applied to arbitrary positive real numbers: Our data structure allows all current weights to be scaled by a power of 2 in constant time, since all this requires is fixing a new "origin" for the infinite arrays mentioned above. Use this to make sure that all nonzero weights are at least n^2, maintain their integer parts in the data structure for integer weights, and maintain the remainders in the naive way.

A more complicated scheme operating essentially according to these principles was described by Matias, Vitter, and Ni [MVN93]. Their result is that in the stronger model considered above, augmented with the operation $\text{EXP}_2 : I\!N \to I\!N$ with $\text{EXP}_2(m) = 2^m$, arbitrary generalized distributions on $\{1,\dots,n\}$ can be maintained in $O(n)$ space with constant expected generate and update times. In the remainder of this section we sketch a different solution to the same problem in a closely related model. An important parameter in a comparison between the scheme described below and that of Matias, Vitter, and Ni or the one outlined above is the size of the integers manipulated. In all three cases this size is data-dependent and grows to infinity as the maximum ratio between two nonzero weights presented to the data structures grows to infinity. For any fixed sequence of updates, however, the algorithm described below uses integers of roughly n times more bits than its competitors. It also needs the additional operation of bitwise AND on arbitrary nonnegative integers (represented in binary). On the other hand, the algorithm is simple, and it has extremely small constant factors.

Assume first that all weights are integers. The basic idea is to store all prefix sums of the current weights together in a single memory word. Applying the prefix-sums algorithm, we need to locate a random value with respect to the sequence of prefix sums; we do this in constant time using a variant of an essentially parallel algorithm described by Paul and Simon [PS80].

The algorithm manipulates words that conceptually consist of n *fields* of $k+1$ bits each, where k is a positive integer chosen so large that the current total weight fits in k bits. The most significant bit of each field is called its *test bit*, while the remaining k bits form its *main part*. The n fields of each word are packed tightly in its least significant $n(k+1)$ bit positions. For $j = 1,\ldots,n$, define the jth field of a word as its jth least significant field (i.e., the jth field "from the right").

We store a generalized distribution f as the word F whose jth field contains 0 in its test bit and $s_{j-1} = \sum_{i=1}^{j-1} f(i)$ in its main part, for $j = 1,\ldots,n$.

In order to generate a random value z distributed according to f, we begin by drawing a random value l from the uniform distribution on $\{0,\ldots,W-1\}$, where $W = \sum_{j=1}^{n} f(j)$ is the total weight of f. We then create the word L, each of whose n fields contains 1 in its test bit and l in its main part. Observe that if we now subtract F from L, then the test bit in the jth field "survives" if and only if $l \geq s_{j-1}$, for $j = 1,\ldots,n$ (see Fig. 2).

| 1 | 12 | 1 | 12 | 1 | 12 | 1 | 12 | 1 | 12 | 1 | 12 | 1 | 12 | 1 | 12 | L |

$-$

| 0 | 27 | 0 | 23 | 0 | 15 | 0 | 12 | 0 | 8 | 0 | 8 | 0 | 3 | 0 | 0 | F |

$=$

| 0 | | 0 | | 0 | | 1 | | 1 | | 1 | | 1 | | 1 | |

Fig. 2. One subtraction carries out n comparisons.

Hence the number of surviving test bits is precisely the value that we want to output. We can compute this value by masking away all but the test bits, taking the logarithm of the result, adding 1, and dividing by $k+1$.

In order to facilitate the computation of L, we store also the word C, each of whose fields contains 0 in its test bit and 1 in its main part. Then L can be obtained simply as $(l + 2^k) \cdot C$. Assuming that *Random* returns a random value drawn from the uniform distribution on $[0, 1)$, the whole algorithm for generating z hence takes the form

$$z := \frac{\text{LOG}_2\Big(\big((\lfloor W \cdot Random\rfloor + 2^k) \cdot C - F\big) \text{ AND } (2^k \cdot C)\Big) + 1}{k+1}.$$

An update, replacing $f(j)$ by $f'(j)$, say, takes two forms depending on whether the new total weight $W' = W + f'(j) - f(j)$ still fits in k bits. If this is the case, all that is required is to add $i = f'(j) - f(j)$ to all except the j first fields of F; this is realized by the instruction

$$F := F + \left\lfloor \frac{i \cdot C}{2^{j(k+1)}} \right\rfloor \cdot 2^{j(k+1)},$$

which shifts $i \cdot C$ first right and then left in order to clear the j rightmost fields.

If W' does not fit in k bits, it is necessary to increase k, i.e., to "pull apart" the fields in F, after which the update can proceed as above.

We choose the new field size as $k' + 1$ bits, where $k' = \max\{\text{LOG}_2(W') + 1, (n+1)(k+1)\}$, i.e., the new total weight fits in a new field, but in addition each new field can contain at least $n + 1$ old fields. Let us call a field of $k+1$ bits a *small field*, and a field of $k' + 1$ bits a *large field*.

For all integers $l \geq 2$, let $G(l) = \sum_{j=0}^{n-1} 2^{jl}$; in particular, the new value C' of C is $G(k' + 1)$. By the identity $\frac{1}{1-x} = \sum_{j=0}^{\infty} x^j$, for $0 < x < 1$, $2^{nl}/(2^l - 1) = \sum_{j=1}^{\infty} 2^{(n-j)l}$, so that $G(l)$ can be obtained in constant time as $\lfloor 2^{nl}/(2^l - 1)\rfloor$. In order to increase the field size from $k+1$ to $k' + 1$, begin by multiplying F by $G(k' - k)$. This creates n copies of the old value of F, but the jth copy "lags behind" the jth large field by $j - 1$ small fields, which has the effect of placing the jth old field of F in the leftmost small field of the jth large field, for $j = 1, \ldots, n$; note that the condition $k' \geq (n+1)(k+1)$ ensures that the n copies of F do not overlap. Now simply eliminate all bits outside the leftmost small fields of the large fields using the mask $(2^k - 1) \cdot C'$. Altogether, the expansion of the fields takes the form

$$C := G(k' + 1)$$
$$F := \left(F \cdot G(k' - k)\right) \text{ AND } \left((2^k - 1) \cdot C\right).$$

The code fragments given above clearly execute in constant time. We hence have

Theorem 3. *In a model that includes constant-time operations on integers of arbitrary size, LOG$_2$, EXP$_2$, and bitwise AND, integer-valued generalized distributions on $\{1, \ldots, n\}$ can be maintained with constant generate and update times and $O(n)$ space and initialization time.*

The above result is weaker than that of Matias, Vitter, and Ni [MVN93] in that it applies only to integer weights (and in needing the AND operation), but stronger in that the bounds on the generate and update times are worst-case, rather than expected. As argued above, a scheme for arbitrary integer weights can handle arbitrary real weights, provided that it allows all weights to be multiplied by 2^q in constant time, where q is an integer that can be chosen by the algorithm, except that it should be larger than some given q_0. Since this operation essentially reduces to the expansion of fields described above, Theorem 3 holds for arbitrary weights as well, except that "constant generate time" becomes "constant expected generate time".

References

[BFS87] P. Bratley, B. L. Fox, and L. E. Schrage, *A Guide to Simulation (2nd ed.)*, Springer-Verlag, 1987.

[Fox90] B. L. Fox, Generating Markov-chain transitions quickly: I, *Operations Research Society of America Journal on Computing* **2** (1990), pp. 126–135.

[Kle75] L. Kleinrock, *Queueing Systems. Vol. 1: Theory*, John Wiley & Sons, 1975.

[MVN93] Y. Matias, J. S. Vitter, and W. C. Ni, Dynamic generation of discrete random variates, In Proc. 4th Annual ACM-SIAM Symposium on Discrete Algorithms (1993), pp. 361–370.

[OvL81] M. H. Overmars and J. van Leeuwen, Worst-case optimal insertion and deletion methods for decomposable searching problems, *Information Processing Letters* **12** (1981), pp. 168–173.

[PS80] W. J. Paul and J. Simon, Decision trees and random access machines, In Proc. International Symposium on Logic and Algorithmic, Zürich (1980), pp. 331–340.

[RR91] S. Rajasekaran and K. W. Ross, Fast algorithms for generating discrete random variates with changing distributions, Technical Report No. MS-CIS-91-52, Dept. of CIS, Univ. of Pennsylvania, 1991.

Appendix: Computing Logarithms

We argue that given any fixed $c \in I\!N$ and $O(n)$ space and initialization time, LOG$_2(x) = \lfloor \log_2 x \rfloor$ can be computed in constant time for any real $x \in [n^{-c}, n^c]$.

It is easy to set up a table that gives LOG$_2(x)$ for all $x \in \{1, \ldots, n\}$. For $x \in [1, n^c]$, let $i_0 = \max\{i \geq 0 : \bar{n}^i \leq x\}$, where $\bar{n}$ is the largest power of 2 no larger than n, and then use LOG$_2(x) = i_0 \cdot$ LOG$_2(\bar{n}) +$ LOG$_2(\lfloor x/\bar{n}^{i_0} \rfloor)$. For $x \in [n^{-c}, 1)$, use LOG$_2(x) \in \{-$LOG$_2(1/x), -$LOG$_2(1/x) - 1\}$ and choose the correct element of the right-hand set using a precomputed table of powers of 2.

Secure and Efficient Off-Line Digital Money
(extended abstract)

Matthew Franklin*
Columbia University
Computer Science Department,
New York, NY 10027

Moti Yung
IBM Research Division,
T.J. Watson Center,
Yorktown Heights, NY 10598

Abstract

No off-line electronic coin scheme has yet been proposed which is both provably secure with respect to natural cryptographic assumptions and efficient with respect to reasonable measures. We show that off-line coin schemes can be implemented securely and efficiently, where security is proven based on the hardness of the discrete log function and a pre-processing stage, and where efficiency is in a new sense that we put forth in this work: "a protocol is efficient if its communication complexity is independent of the computational complexity of its participants" (and thus the communication length and number of encryption operations is only a low-degree polynomial of the input).

1 Introduction

1.1 What is an Off-Line Electronic Coin Scheme?

An electronic coin scheme [4] is a set of cryptographic protocols for withdrawal (by a customer from the bank), purchase (by a customer to a vendor while possibly involving the bank), and deposit (by a vendor to the bank), such that the security needs of all participants are satisfied: anonymity of purchase for the customer, assurance of authenticity for the vendor, impossibility of undetected reuse or forgery for the bank.

A coin scheme has the interesting "off-line" property [5] if the purchase protocol does not involve the bank; everyday non-digital money is of course off-line. To balance the customer's need for anonymity (so that her/his spendings, and thus her/his lifestyle, cannot be traced by the bank/government) with the bank's need for protection against reuse (to prevent counterfeit money), each coin in an off-line scheme must somehow "embed" the customer's identity in a way that is accessible only if the same coin is used for more than one purchase. Moreover, to balance the customer's need for anonymity with the bank's need for protection against forgery, each coin must somehow get an authentication from the bank (e.g., a digital signature) without being seen by the bank!

Meeting all of these security needs simultaneously is a difficult task. In fact, no scheme has yet been proposed which is both provably secure with respect to natural cryptographic assumptions

*Partially supported by an AT&T Bell Laboratories Scholarship. Work supported in part by NSF Grant CCR-9014605 and NSF CISE Institutional Infrastructure Grant CDA-90-24735

and efficient with respect to reasonable measures. We review previous approaches to the problem and present our new approach and contributions.

1.2 Previous Approaches to Off-Line Coin Schemes

There have been two main approaches to off-line coin schemes in the literature. One direction is based on blind signatures, and the other is based on zero knowledge proofs of knowledge.

1.2.1 Schemes Based on Blind Signatures

A blind signature scheme of Chaum [4] is a protocol that enables one party (i.e., a customer) to receive a signature of a message of its choice under the second party's (i.e., the bank's) private signature key. The second party learns nothing about the message it helped to sign. For use in an off-line coin scheme, the bank must be sure that the message it never sees has a certain form (i.e., that it embeds the customer's identity in the proper way). This can be done by combining the blind signature scheme with a zero knowledge proof [15, 13] or "cut-and-choose" check [26] that the message has the right form. The first off-line coin scheme, due to Chaum, Fiat, and Naor [5] takes this approach, using the blind signature scheme based on RSA [28]. This approach is efficient but heuristic; no proof of security has been given that relies on assumptions about RSA that are simple or natural. In fact, refinements to their protocol [1] were later found to introduce security flaws [17], which underscores the risk of relying on heuristics.

It is also possible to implement blind signatures using general secure 2-party computation protocols [30], as shown by Pfitzmann and Waidner [25], building on work of Damgård [6]. A circuit to compute signatures is jointly computed by the bank and the customer, with the bank contributing one input (secret signature key), the customer contributing the other input (message to be signed), and the customer alone receiving the output (signed message). The security of a scheme of this type can be reduced to general cryptographic assumptions. However, the message complexity (number of bits sent between parties) and encryption complexity (number of applications of encryption operations) of all known secure computation protocols is proportional to the size of the circuit being computed. It is unreasonable for a coin scheme to have a communication cost that depends on the computational complexity of the underlying signature function algorithm (which should be only a "local" computation for the bank)— the same way it is unreasonable to have a one cent coin weigh fifty kilograms. Thus, a scheme of this type is secure, but definitely not efficient.

1.2.2 Schemes Based on Zero Knowledge Proofs of Knowledge

A zero knowledge proof of knowledge [15] is a protocol between a prover and a verifier, in which the verifier is convinced that the prover possesses a witness (e.g., for membership in a language) without learning anything about that witness. In a non-interactive zero knowledge proof of knowledge [2], a single message is sent (from prover to verifier); in this case, the two parties are assumed to share a random string. DeSantis and Persiano [8] show that, when non-interactive zero knowledge proofs of knowledge are possible, blind signatures are not necessary for an off-line coin scheme (see also [23]). The basic idea is that the bank gives an ordinary signature to the customer, but no one ever sees that signature again. Instead of presenting the signature to validate a coin at purchase time, the customer presents the vendor with a proof that it possesses a valid signature from the bank. To deposit the coin, the vendor presents the bank with a proof that it possesses a valid proof of possession from the customer. The security of this type of scheme can be proven with respect to general cryptographic assumptions. However, the message complexity and encryption complexity is prohibitively large, e.g, the length of a proof of possession of a valid signature depends on the complexity of the signing function itself. Thus a scheme of this type is secure, but again it is not efficient.

In the next four subsections, we discuss our new notion of efficiency (1.3), the overview of our off-line coin scheme (1.4), and then a closer look at two building blocks for our scheme (1.5, 1.6).

1.3 Security and Efficiency: A Closer Look

We want an off-line coin scheme that is both secure and efficient. Let us clarify more formally what we mean by security and by efficiency.

Security of protocols means that the claimed properties can be proven based on some intractability assumption. This is the typical notion of complexity-theoretic security.

Efficiency of protocols, which is a notion we try to capture in this work, can be formalized by requiring that "the communication complexity of the protocol is independent of the computational complexity of the participants". In schemes which lead to practical implementations, like identification schemes [11] and basic practical operations like signature and encryption, this is the case (the communication is a low-degree polynomial function of the security parameter and the input size). On the other hand, general protocols which encrypt computations of results (like general zero-knowledge schemes for NP and IP, and secure computation schemes) are considered impractical by users of cryptography, since the local computation is typically a much higher-degree polynomial function of the input and the security parameters. This makes them prohibitively expensive – as they require much communication and, more crucially, similarly many applications of cryptographic operations. We feel that it is important to make this distinction to further develop a sound theory of cryptography with robust notions of efficiency; our effort here is to be considered as a first step in this direction. (We note that there are other measures of efficiency of interest; in particular we also measure and try to minimize the number of rounds).

In this paper, we show that a secure and efficient off-line coin scheme is possible, based on what we call "oblivious authentication" and the hardness of the discrete log function. We implement oblivious authentication (to be described later) based on any one-way function together with a pre-processing stage independent from the withdrawal, purchase, and deposit protocols. The communication complexity of our scheme is $O(k^2 s)$ bits where k is a security parameter and s is the size of a signed bit; $O(k^2)$ encryption operations are performed. Purchase and deposit are non-interactive, while withdrawal requires two rounds of interaction.

1.4 Off-Line Coin = Passport + Witness + Hints

Next we informally (and metaphorically) describe the building blocks and mechanisms which underlie the efficient off-line digital coin scheme. In real life, a "passport" is an authorized document from a trusted source (the government) that identifies its owner. We can also imagine an anonymous passport without any name or picture, but still stamped by the proper authority, allowing

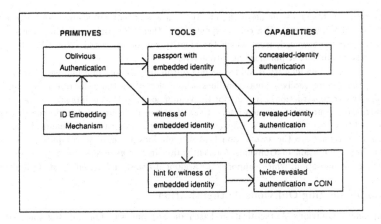

Figure 1: Building an off-line coin scheme from basic primitives

a sort of anonymous authentication. Off-line coin schemes make use of yet another type of passport, in which the identity of its owner is only *somewhat* present, embedded in the document in a complexity theoretic sense (through the use of what we call an Identity Embedding Mechanism).

A primitive that we call Oblivious Authentication lets an authorizing agency issue a digital passport with an embedded identity, together with a "witness" of the embedded identity. The issuing process is oblivious in the sense that the authorizing agency cannot later connect any passport to the time it was issued. Use of the passport without the witness would allow repeated authentication while concealing forever the identity of the user (against a resource bounded attack). Use of the passport with the witness would authenticate the user and reveal the user's embedded identity. We will use the passport with a "hint" of the witness, where any two hints, but no single hint, is enough to recover the witness[1]. This is the crux of an off-line coin scheme (see Figure One).

Withdrawal is an instance of Oblivious Authentication (using an Identity Embedding Mechanism), in which the bank issues a passport (with embedded identity) and a witness to the customer. To make a purchase, the customer gives the passport and a unique hint (extracted from the witness) to the vendor. To deposit, the vendor forwards the passport and the hint to the bank.

1.5 Identity Embedding Mechanism

The goal of an Identity Embedding Mechanism is to hide the customer's identity so that it is concealed unless a witness is known, and to allow for the extraction of verifiable hints (any two of which reveal a witness). The only prior Identity Embedding Mechanism for an efficient off-line coin scheme, due to Chaum, Fiat, and Naor [5], hides the identity in a collection of nested one-way functions that each hide a pair of xor shares of the customer's identity. During purchase, the vendor

---

[1] We can generalize to hints that reveal the witness at thresholds greater than two, which is useful (e.g., for multiple access authorization tokens) but not considered in this paper.

challenges the customer to "de-nest" the functions in a way that reveals one xor share from each pair ("hint" of the witness). If a coin is spent twice, then with high probability both xor shares from some pair are revealed, from which the identity can be recovered. Note that the challenge and response requires that purchase be interactive.

In our method, the identity is hidden as bits of the discrete logs of a number of values. During purchase, the vendor receives points on lines whose slopes are these discrete logs ("hint" of the witness). By our construction, it is easy for the vendor to verify that points are on lines as claimed; thus purchase in our scheme is non-interactive. If a coin is spent twice, then the points can be interpolated to recover the identity. Efficiency is the same as the scheme of Chaum, Fiat, and Naor, while security reduces to the assumption that discrete logs are hard to compute (and plugging a heuristic implementation of Oblivious Authentication in our general scheme gives an improved-efficiency implementation, which supports our argument about and definition of efficient schemes).

1.6   Implementing Oblivious Authentication

We implement Oblivious Authentication based on any one-way function together with a pre-processing stage. The purpose of the pre-processing stage is to produce generic strings that are sent to any customer that asks for them. Each string enables a customer to withdraw a single coin from the bank. These strings are generic in the sense that any string could go to anyone, so long as no string goes to more than one party (like "blank withdrawal slips").

The pre-processing stage of our Oblivious Authentication protocol can be based on the presence of some trusted agent that is separate from the bank, vendors, and customers and is present at initiation. This agent, which we call a "trusted manufacturer," might fill each user's smart card memory once with a large number of strings and then destroy its records. Unlike some physically based schemes [10], the smart card memory does not need to be shielded in any way from the owner of the smart card (i.e., no read or write restrictions are needed). The only issue is that the manufacturer is trusted to produce strings of the proper form, and to never give the same string to more than one party. This mild assumption, as argued above, still leaves the major problems of off-line money scheme security with no trivial answer.

How reasonable is this assumption? Many cryptographic systems need a trusted center. Any complete public key system needs a trusted center of our kind to certify the connection between keys and users without risking impersonation attacks. The zero-knowledge identification scheme of Feige, Fiat, and Shamir [11] uses a trusted center to publish a modulus with unknown factorization and to maintain a public key directory; in the "keyless" version of their system, the trusted center issues tamper-resistant (unreadable, unwritable) smart cards to all participants.

Alternatively, pre-processing can be done inefficiently (high degree polynomial communication), under general cryptographic assumptions, as a general secure protocol between bank and customer. The efficiency of the withdrawal, purchase and deposit protocols would be unaffected. Our stated principle of efficiency would be violated only at initiation, which can be a background computation independent of money-exchanging transactions. When Oblivious Authentication is realized in this way with an inefficient preparatory stage and an efficient main stage, it has a form similar to the "on-line/off-line" signature scheme of Even, Goldreich, and Micali [9].

2 Oblivious Authentication

2.1 Definition of Oblivious Authentication Schemes

Informally, an oblivious authentication scheme is a protocol between a requestor and an authenticator. The requestor ends up being able to compute a request string z, an authentication string a, and a witness wit. The authentication a reflects not only that the requestor actually went through the protocol (i.e., could not compute a otherwise), but also that z somehow refers to the identity id of the requestor (i.e., wit is a witness that some predicate $\psi(z, id)$ is true). At the same time, the protocol is "oblivious" from the point of view of the authenticator, i.e., after several executions of the protocol, the authenticator must not be able to connect any $[z, a]$ pair to the instance of the protocol that produced it. Using terminology from the Introduction, the authenticator issues a "passport" $[z, a]$ with the requestor's identity embedded in it.

Definition 1 *An oblivious authentication scheme is $[R, A, k, ID, REQ, AUT, WIT, g, wf, \psi]$ where R (requestor) and A (authenticator) are communicating p.p.t Turing Machines, k is a security parameter, ID is the space of requestor identifiers, REQ is the space of request strings, AUT is the space of authentication strings, WIT is the space of witness strings, g is a p.p.t. computable function from views of R (after a joint execution of R and A) to $REQ \times AUT \times WIT$, wf is a p.p.t. computable boolean predicate on $REQ \times AUT$, and ψ is a (not necessarily p.p.t.) computable boolean predicate on $REQ \times ID$ (for which consistent req, wit pairs can be efficiently sampled for any $id \in ID$). Let V_R^i be the view of R after R and A begin with $id^i \in ID$ and k on the shared input tape; let $V_{\bar{R}}^i$ b the view if R is cheating. The following requirements must be satisfied:*

1. *(Correct) For all $id_i \in ID$, $g(V_R^i) = [z, a, wit]$ where $wf(z, a)$ is true, and wit is a witness that $\psi(z, id_i)$ is true, except with negligible probability (in k).*

2. *(Oblivious) Let M be any p.p.t. TM that on input $V_A^0, V_A^1, z, a, f(z)$, can output $b_M \in \{0, 1\}$, where $[z, a, wit] = g(V_R^b)$ for $b \in_R \{0, 1\}$, and where f is any (not necessarily efficiently) computable function. Then there exists a p.p.t. TM M' that on input $z, f(z)$ can output $b_{M'} \in \{0, 1\}$ such that $|Prob(b_M = b) - Prob(b_{M'} = b)|$ is negligible (in k).*

3. *(Unexpandable) No p.p.t. TM on input $V_{\bar{R}}^1, \cdots V_{\bar{R}}^n$ can output $[z_1, a_1], \cdots, [z_{n+1}, a_{n+1}]$ such that $wf(z_j, a_j)$ is true for $1 \leq j \leq n + 1$, except with negligible probability (in k).*

4. *(Unforgeable) No p.p.t. TM on input $V_{\bar{R}}^1, \cdots V_{\bar{R}}^n$ can output $[z, a]$ such that $wf(z, a)$ is true while $\psi(z, id_i)$ is false for all $1 \leq i \leq n$, except with negligible probability (in k).*

The function g enables the requestor to extract a valid $[z, a]$ and witness wit at the end of the protocol. The predicate wf enables anyone to check that $[z, a]$ is genuine. The predicate ψ reflects the requestor's identity embedded in z, but is typically not easy to compute or verify without a witness. If ψ were easy to compute, and if ψ is never true for the same z with different id, then the second requirement (obliviousness) would be trivially satisfied whenever $id_0 \neq id_1$. For the off-line coin scheme of Chaum, Fiat, and Naor [5], ψ is easy to compute but hard to witness, and in fact is true almost everywhere on $REQ \times ID$. For our off-line coin scheme, ψ is hard to compute without a witness under the Discrete Log Assumption (DLA), and never true for the same z with different id.

For all of the instances of oblivious authentication schemes that will be discussed in this paper, we can make the following assumptions (since all rely on a cut-and-choose procedure). Instead of one large space REQ from which request strings come, there is a smaller space REQ' such that $REQ = (REQ')^k$. Moreover, there is a boolean predicate ψ' defined on $REQ' \times ID$ such that $\psi(rec, id)$ is true if and only if $\psi'(rec.i, id)$ is true for a majority of $i \in [1..k]$.

2.2 Heuristic Oblivious Authentication via RSA

Most off-line electronic money schemes in the literature have used what can be abstracted as a heuristic Oblivious Authentication protocol based on RSA public-key encryption [28] (i.e., multiple blinding plus cut-and-choose). When actually used in electronic money schemes, the predicate ψ' looks for redundancy in z, or incorporates one-way functions, as a way to hope to satisfy the requirements of unexpandability and unforgeability despite the "nice" algebraic properties of RSA (e.g., multiplicative homomorphism). For example, in the off-line coin scheme of Chaum, Fiat, and Naor [5], $\psi'(z', id)$ is true if $z' = f(g(r_1, r_2), g(r_1 \oplus id, r_3))$ for some r_1, r_2, r_3, where f, g are two-argument collision-free functions, and where f is "similar to a random oracle." Here the predicate ψ' is in fact easy to compute (i.e., it is true almost always), but hard to witness (i.e., with a particular r_1, r_2, r_3).

Note that the security of this type of scheme is heuristic, and has never been reduced simply to the difficulty of inverting RSA. In particular, proving that the scheme is unexpandable and unforgeable seems to require additional assumptions about RSA which are neither natural nor simple.

3 Secure Off-Line Money Scheme

Informally, an off-line electronic coin scheme [4] is the simplest useful electronic payment system. Any customer can withdraw a coin from the bank, as the bank debits the customer's account. That coin can then be used to purchase from any vendor. The vendor will be able to trust that the coin is valid without assistance from the bank. A vendor can later deposit a coin, and the bank will credit the vendor's account. The rights and privileges of customers, vendors, and the bank are all protected within the scheme. The customer is guaranteed anonymity of purchase, i.e., that the bank cannot link a deposited coin to its corresponding withdrawal. The vendor is guaranteed that any acceptable purchase will lead to an acceptable deposit. The bank is guaranteed that no number of withdrawals can lead to a greater number of deposits.

3.1 Definition of Secure Off-Line Coins

There is a bank B, a collection of vendors $\{V_i\}$, and a collection of customers $\{C_i\}$, all of whom are assumed to be communicating Turing Machines. There is a security parameter k.

An off-line coin scheme consists of three protocols: a withdrawal protocol between B and any C_i; a purchase protocol between any C_i and any V_j; and a deposit protocol between any V_j and B. The withdrawal protocol begins with C_i and B having id_i on their shared input tape, and ends with C_i having a "coin" τ on its private output tape. The purchase protocol begins with C_i having a coin τ on its input tape, and ends with V_j having a "spent coin" τ' on its private output tape.

The deposit protocol begins with V_j having a spent coin τ' on its input tape and ends with B having a "deposited coin" τ'' on its private output tape.

Definition 2 *An off-line coin scheme is secure if the following requirements are satisfied:*

1. *(Unreusable) If any C_i begins two successful purchase protocols with the same coin τ on its input tape, then the fact of reuse and the identity id_i can be computed in p.p.t. from the two corresponding deposited coins τ_1'', τ_2'', except with negligible probability (in k).*

2. *(Unexpandable) From the views of the customers of n withdrawal protocols, no p.p.t. Turing Machine can compute $n + 1$ distinct coins that will lead to successful purchase protocols (or $n + 1$ distinct spent coins that will lead to successful deposit protocols), except with negligible probability (in k).*

3. *(Unforgeable) If, from the views of the customers of n withdrawal protocols, some p.p.t. Turing Machine can compute a single coin that will lead to two successful purchase protocols, then the fact of reuse and the identity of at least one of these customers can be efficiently computed from the two corresponding deposited coins, except with negligible probability (in k).*

4. *(Untraceable) Let V_B^i (V_V^i) be the view of B (V) for a withdrawal (purchase) protocol with C_i. Then, for all i, j, no p.p.t Turing Machine on input V_B^i, V_B^j, and $V_V^l \in_R \{V_V^i, v_V^j\}$, can output a guess for $l \in \{i, j\}$ non-negligibly better than random guessing (in k).*

3.2 Discrete Log Based Secure Off-Line Coins

For this scheme, we use oblivious authentication for which the space of authentication strings is $REQ = (REQ')^k$, where $(REQ') = (\{0,1\}^{\log p})^{2m}$. A request string z is interpreted as a k-tuple of m pairs of elements from Z_p^* (and each pair is interpreted as elements whose discrete logs are the slope and intercept of a line over Z_{p-1}^*). We assume that p is prime, such that $p - 1$ has one large factor q.

The predicate ψ' on $REQ' \times ID$ is true if the m pairs encode the requestor's identity id in the following way: for every i, the ith bit of id is equal to the hard bit h of the discrete log of the first element of the ith pair. Notice that ψ' (and hence ψ, the "majority vote" of ψ') is hard to compute under the DLA. A witness for $\psi'(z, id)$ is the set of discrete logs for all m pairs of z.

The secure coin scheme is given in Figure Two. The intuition behind the scheme is that a coin is a pair $[z, a]$ ("passport") produced by an Oblivious Authentication protocol with REQ' and ψ' as described above. To spend a coin, $[z, a]$ is given, together with a point on every "line" under the interpretation of z described above ("hint" of the witness). The x coordinate of each of these points is the same deterministic combination of the vendor's id and the current time, to guarantee that different purchases with the same coin involve different points on each line. The algebra underlying the coin ensures that a correct purchase can be verified easily and non-interactively (i.e., verify that each point is indeed on the line it is supposed to be on), while multiple spending will reveal the identity of the customer (i.e., interpolate to recover the coefficients of the lines and hence the majority identity encoded in z) with high probability. The following holds (proof omitted).

Theorem 1 *If oblivious authentication is possible, and if discrete log has a hard bit, then this off-line coin scheme is secure.*

Withdrawal

1. C and B engage in an O.A. protocol with id_C on the shared input tape, where $REQ' = (\{0,1\}^{\log p})^{2m}$ and where

   (a) $\psi'(req', id)$ is true if and only if, for all $1 \leq i \leq m$, $DL_{g,p}(req'_{i1}) < q$ and $h(req'_{i1}) = id.i$, where $req' = (req'_{11}||req'_{12}||\cdots||req'_{m1}||req'_{m2})$, and where h is a hard bit for the discrete log.

2. C finds the coin $g(V_C) = [z, a, wit]$, where $z = z_1||\cdots||z_k$, and each $z_i = z_{i11}||z_{i12}||\cdots||z_{im1}||z_{im2}$. C stores $wit = [DL_{g,p}(z_{ijl}) : 1 \leq i \leq k, 1 \leq j \leq m, l \in \{0,1\}]$.

Purchase

1. $C \to V$: $[z, a, x, [y_{ij} : 1 \leq i \leq k, 1 \leq j \leq m]]$ where

   (a) $x = id_V||time$, where $time$ is the current clock reading.

   (b) $y_{ij} = x DL_{g,p}(z_{ij1}) + DL_{g,p}(z_{ij2}) \bmod p - 1$, for all $1 \leq i \leq k$, $1 \leq j \leq m$.

2. V accepts if $wf(z,a)$, and $(z_{ij1})^x(z_{ij2}) = g^{y_{ij}} \bmod p$ for all $1 \leq i \leq k$, $1 \leq j \leq m$.

Deposit

1. $V \to B$: exactly what C gave to V during Purchase.

2. B accepts under exactly the same circumstances as for V to accept during Purchase.

Figure 2: Secure Coin Scheme

3.3 Practical Off-Line Coins

How practical is this off-line coin scheme? Assume that Oblivious Authentication based on RSA is used. Further assume that, instead of a single hard bit, there are as many hard bits in the discrete log as the size of the id of a customer. In this case, each element of REQ' is only $2 \log p$ bits long (hiding the coefficients of a single line, whose slope encodes all of id), and the authenticating string is only $\log N$ bits long (where N is the bank's RSA modulus). Thus the total length of a coin at purchase or deposit time is only $O(\log N + k \log p)$ bits (and encryption complexity is $O(k)$ modular exponentiations), which is quite reasonable. Withdrawal requires only two rounds of interaction, while purchase and deposit are non-interactive.

This is an example of taking a secure scheme (for off-line coins) that is "efficient" in the sense discussed in the Introduction, and plugging in a heuristic implementation (for Oblivious Authentication). The low complexity of the resulting practical scheme helps to demonstrate how our notion of efficiency of protocols coincides with practical efficiency.

4 Oblivious Authentication via Pre-processing

In this section, we describe an implementation of oblivious authentication that depends on a pre-processing stage. This pre-processing stage can be done directly by a "trusted manufacturer." A "trusted manufacturer" is an entity that can perform computations, and can send information to a requestor without it being seen by the authenticator, and without the requestor having to identify itself. For example, data may be put by the manufacturer into the memory of a smart card that is then sold to a requestor. It is not necessary to shield the smart card memory from the requestor, only that the authenticator learns nothing about the data (e.g., by eavesdropping on the transfer of data to the requestor, or by corrupting the manufacturer).

Alternatively, pre-processing can be implemented inefficiently using a general secure 2-party computation protocol between the requestor and the authenticator. As shown by Kilian [20], the assumption that Oblivious Transfer [27] (a basic cryptographic primitive) is possible suffices.

Intuitively, the pre-processing stage supplies encrypted windows, where each window presigns both a zero and a one for a given bit position in the message. Each signature is concealed in a half-window as a pair of elements, where the first element is a (secret-key) encryption of a random mask, and the second element is the xor of the mask with the signature. In this way, the authenticator is needed to reveal either of the signatures in a window (by decrypting the mask), but the authenticator cannot later recognize a signature he helped reveal.

A collection of m windows (called a "row") can be used to sign a string of m bits. However, to prevent signed bits from one message being substituted in a second message, the windows must be "linked" together. In fact, all pairs of adjacent half-windows are connected, so that the same collection of windows is capable of signing any possible message. Links are also pairs of elements, where the first element is a (secret-key) encryption of a random mask, and the second element is the xor of the mask with a signature of the two half-windows that are being linked. When half-windows are "opened" (i.e., when their masks are decrypted), the corresponding links are opened as well.

A cut-and-choose procedure is used to guarantee that the predicate $\psi(z, id)$ is true at the end. There will be $2k$ strings that are presented to the authenticator, each of which satisfies some predicate $\psi'(z', id)$, and for each of which the requestor knows a witness wit'. The authenticator challenges half of the strings, and receives witnesses that the predicate is true for them. The authenticator then sends decrypted masks for all half-windows and links for all unchallenged strings. The predicate ψ is defined to hold if and only if a majority of the k unchallenged strings satisfy ψ'.

A second type of link is needed to prevent cheating with the cut-and-choose procedure. Rows of windows need to be linked together, to prevent a new collection of k rows from being pieced together from two or more runs of the protocol. This is achieved by providing links between half-windows at the end of one row to half-windows at the beginning of the next row.

The entire data structure, windows and links, is called a "struct" (see Figure Three). We assume that the pre-processing stage (via trusted manufacturer or secure 2-party computation) has sent a supply of structs to the requestor. The following holds (proof omitted).

Theorem 2 *Oblivious authentication with a pre-processing stage (assuming trusted manufacturer or Oblivious Transfer) is possible if one-way functions exist.*

This protocol requires two rounds of communication between the requestor and the authenticator. The size of $[z, a]$ is $O(mk)$ signed elements; this is also the communication complexity of the protocol. By hashing elements in REQ', m can be reduced to $O(k)$.

If a trusted manufacturer is present, then the pre-processing stage for each customer consists of a single transfer of structs, upon request, from the trusted manufacturer to the customer (or more frequent transfers, upon request, as needed); the manufacturer does not need to know the identity of the customer for this pre-processing stage. If a general secure 2-party computation protocol were to be used, then the pre-processing stage would have round and message complexities that are polynomial in the size of the circuit to compute a struct from jointly produced random values.

275

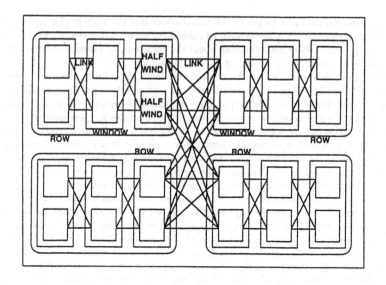

Figure 3: Struct Data Structure (informal picture: 4 out of $2k$ rows, $m = 3$

Acknowledgments

We thank David Chaum, Tony Eng, Zvi Galil, Stuart Haber, Rafael Hirschfeld, Rafi Ostrovsky, Venkie Ramarathnam, and Yacov Yacobi for helpful discussions.

References

[1] C. van Antwerpen, "Electronic cash," Master's thesis, Eindhoven University of Technology, 1990.

[2] M. Blum, A. De Santis, S. Micali, and G. Persiano, "Non-interactive zero knowledge," SIAM J. Comput. 6 (1991), 1084-1118.

[3] M. Blum and S. Micali, "How to generate cryptographically strong sequences of pseudo random bits", SIAM J. Comput. 13, 850-864, 1984.

[4] D. Chaum, "Security without identification: transaction systems to make big brother obsolete," CACM 28, 10 (October 1985).

[5] D. Chaum, A. Fiat, and M. Naor, "Untraceable electronic cash," Crypto 88, pp. 319-327.

[6] I. Damgård, "Payment systems and credential mechanisms with provable security against abuse by individuals," Crypto 88, pp. 328-335.

[7] W. Diffie and M. Hellman, "New directions in cryptography," IEEE Transaction on Information Theory, vol. IT-22, 1976, pp. 644-654.

[8] A. De Santis and G. Persiano, "Communication efficient zero-knowledge proofs of knowledge (with applications to electronic cash)," STACS 1992, pp. 449-460.

[9] S. Even, O. Goldreich, and S. Micali, "On-line/off-line digital signatures," Crypto 1989, pp. 263-275.

[10] S. Even, O. Goldreich, and Y. Yacobi, "Electronic Wallet," Crypto 83, pp. 383-386.

[11] U. Feige, A. Fiat, and A. Shamir, "Zero-Knowledge Proofs of Identity," J. Cryptology, Vol.1, No. 2, 1988, pp. 77-94.

[12] O. Goldreich and L. Levin, "A hard-core predicate for all one-way functions," STOC 1989, pp. 25-32.

[13] O. Goldreich, S. Micali, and A. Wigderson, "Proofs that yield nothing but the validity of the assertion, and a methodology of cryptographic protocol design," FOCS 1986, 174-187.

[14] S. Goldwasser and S. Micali, "Probabilistic encryption," JCSS 28, pp. 644-654, 1984.

[15] S. Goldwasser, S. Micali, and C. Rackoff, "The knowledge complexity of interactive proof systems," SIAM J. Comput., Vol. 18, 1989, pp. 186-208.

[16] J.T. Hastad, "Pseudo-random generators under uniform assumptions," STOC 1990, 395-404.

[17] R. Hirschfeld, "Making electronic refunds safer," Crypto 1992 abstracts, 3.7-3.10.

[18] R. Impagliazzo and M. Luby, "One-way functions are essential for complexity based cryptography," FOCS 1989, 236-243.

[19] R. Impagliazzo, L. Levin, and M. Luby, "Pseudorandom generation from one-way functions," STOC 1989, pp. 12-24.

[20] J. Kilian, "Uses of Randomness in Algorithms and Protocols," ACM Distinguished Dissertation, MIT Press, 1990.

[21] T. Long and A. Wigderson, "The discrete logarithm hides $O(\log n)$ bits," SIAM J. Comput. 17, 1988, 363-372.

[22] M. Naor and M. Yung, "Universal one-way hash functions and their cryptographic applications," STOC 1989, pp. 33-43.

[23] T. Okamoto and K. Ohta, "Disposable zero-knowledge authentications and their applications to untraceable electronic cash," Crypto 1989, pp. 481-496.

[24] T. Okamoto and K. Ohta, "Universal electronic cash," Crypto 1991, pp. 324-337.

[25] B. Pfitzmann and M. Waidner, "How to break and repair a 'provably secure' untraceable payment system," Crypto 91, pp. 338-350.

[26] M. Rabin, "Digital signatures," in Foundations of Secure Computation, R. DeMillo, D. Dobkin, A. Jones, and R. Lipton (editors), Academic Press, NY, 1978, 155-168.

[27] M. Rabin, "How to exchange secrets by oblivious transfer," Tech. Memo TR-81, Aiken Computation Laboratory, Harvard University, 1981.

[28] R. Rivest, A. Shamir, and L. Adleman, "A method for obtaining digital signatures and public-key cryptosystems," CACM, vol. 21, 1978, pp. 120-126.

[29] J. Rompel, "One-way functions are necessary and sufficient for secure signatures," STOC 1990, pp. 387-394.

[30] A. Yao, "How to generate and exchange secrets," FOCS 1986, pp. 162-167.

Computational Depth and Reducibility [*]
(Extended Abstract)

David W. Juedes, James I. Lathrop, and Jack H. Lutz
Department of Computer Science
Iowa State University
Ames, IA 50011

Abstract. This paper investigates Bennett's notions of strong and weak computational depth (also called logical depth) for infinite binary sequences. Roughly, an infinite binary sequence x is defined to be *weakly useful* if every element of a non-negligible set of decidable sequences is reducible to x in recursively bounded time. It is shown that every weakly useful sequence is strongly deep. This result (which generalizes Bennett's observation that the halting problem is strongly deep) implies that every high Turing degree contains strongly deep sequences. It is also shown that, in the sense of Baire category, almost every infinite binary sequence is weakly deep, but not strongly deep.

1 Introduction

Algorithmic information theory, as developed by Solomonoff [35], Kolmogorov [13, 14, 15], Chaitin [7, 8, 9, 10], Martin-Löf [27, 28], Levin [39, 17, 18, 20, 21, 19, 22], Schnorr [31], Gács [11], Shen' [32, 33], and others, gives a satisfactory, quantitative account of the information content of individual binary strings (finite) and binary sequences (infinite). However, a given quantity of information may be organized in various ways, rendering it more or less useful for various computational purposes. In order to quantify the degree to which the information in a computational, physical, or biological object has been organized, Bennett [3, 4] has extended algorithmic information theory by defining and investigating the *computational depth* of binary strings and binary sequences.

Roughly speaking, the computational depth (called "logical depth" by Bennett [3, 4]) of an object is the amount of time required for an algorithm to derive the object from its shortest description. Since this shortest description contains all the information in the object, the depth thus represents the amount of "computational work" that has been "added" to this information and "stored in the organization" of the object. (Depth is closely related to Adleman's notion of "potential" [1] and Koppel's notion of "sophistication" [16].)

One way to investigate the computational usefulness of an object is to investigate the class of computational problems that can be solved efficiently, given access to the object. When the object is an infinite binary sequence, i.e., a sequence $x \in \{0,1\}^{\infty}$, this typically amounts to investigating the class of binary

[*] This research was supported in part by National Science Foundation Grant CCR-9157382, with matching funds from Rockwell International.

strings $y \in \{0,1\}^\infty$ that are Turing reducible to x in some recursive time bound $s : \mathbf{N} \to \mathbf{N}$. For example, consider the *diagonal halting problem* $\chi_K \in \{0,1\}^\infty$, whose n^{th} bit $\chi_K[n]$ is 1 if and only if M_n, the nth Turing machine, halts on input n. It is well-known that χ_K is useful, in the sense that every recursive sequence (in fact, every recursively enumerable sequence) $y \in \{0,1\}^\infty$ is Turing reducible to χ_K in polynomial time.

An interesting feature of this example is that χ_K has relatively low information content. In fact, an n-bit prefix of χ_K, denoted $\chi_K[0..n-1]$, contains only $O(\log n)$ bits of algorithmic information [2]. This is because $\chi_K[0..n-1]$ is completely specified by the *number* of indices $i \in \{0, \ldots, n-1\}$ such that the ith Turing machine M_i halts on input i. Once this $O(\log n)$-bit number is known, direct simulation of $M_0, M_1, \cdots, M_{n-1}$ on inputs $0, 1, \ldots, n-1$, respectively, will eventually determine all n bits of $\chi_K[0..n-1]$.

In contrast, consider a sequence $z \in \{0,1\}^\infty$ that is *algorithmically random* in the equivalent senses of Martin-Löf [27], Levin [17], Schnorr [31], Chaitin [9], Solovay [36], and Shen' [32, 33]. An n-bit prefix $z[0..n-1]$ of an algorithmically random sequence z contains approximately n bits of algorithmic information [27], so the information content of z is exponentially greater than that of χ_K. On the other hand, z is much less useful than χ_K, in the following sense. While *every* recursive sequence is Turing reducible to χ_K in polynomial time, a recursive sequence $y \in \{0,1\}^\infty$ is Turing reducible to z in polynomial time if and only if y is in the complexity class BPP [4, 6]. Since BPP contains only the simplest recursive sequences, this means that, for the purpose of efficiently deciding recursive sequences, χ_K is much more useful than an algorithmically random sequence z.

Bennett has argued that the computational usefulness of χ_K derives not from its algorithmic information content (which is relatively low), but rather from its computational depth. In support of this thesis, Bennett [4] has proven that χ_K is *strongly deep*, while no algorithmically random sequence can even be *weakly deep*.

This paper furthers Bennett's investigation of the computational depth of infinite binary sequences. We pay particular, quantitative attention to interactions between computational depth and time-bounded Turing reductions.

In order to further investigate the above-discussed notion of the computational usefulness of a sequence $x \in \{0,1\}^\infty$, we quantify the *size* of the set of recursive sequences that are Turing reducible to x within some recursive time bound. For this purpose, let REC be the set of all recursive (i.e., decidable) sequences, and, for a recursive time bound $s : \mathbf{N} \to \mathbf{N}$, let $\mathrm{DTIME}^x(s)$ be the set of all sequences $y \in \{0,1\}^\infty$ such that $y \leq_{\mathrm{T}}^{\mathrm{DTIME}(s)} x$. We are interested in the size of $\mathrm{DTIME}^x(s) \cap \mathrm{REC}$ *as a subset of* REC. To quantify this, we use a special case of the *resource-bounded measure theory* of Lutz [24, 25]. Intuitively, this theory, a generalization of classical Lebesgue measure theory, defines a set X of infinite binary sequences to have *measure* 0 *in* REC if $X \cap \mathrm{REC}$ is a *negligibly small* subset of REC.

In this paper, we define a sequence $x \in \{0,1\}^\infty$ to be *weakly useful* if there exists a recursive time bound $s : \mathbf{N} \to \mathbf{N}$ such that $\mathrm{DTIME}^x(s)$ does *not* have measure 0 in REC. Returning to the two examples discussed earlier, χ_K is weakly useful because *every* element of REC is in $\mathrm{DTIME}^{\chi_K}(s)$, provided that s is superpolynomial, e.g. if $s(n) = n^{\log n}$. On the other hand, if z is algorithmically random, then z is *not* weakly useful, by the following two facts.

(i) For every recursive time bound $s : \mathbf{N} \to \mathbf{N}$ there exists a recursive time bound $\widehat{s} : \mathbf{N} \to \mathbf{N}$ such that, for all algorithmically random sequences z, $\mathrm{DTIME}^z(s) \cap \mathrm{REC} \subseteq \mathrm{DTIME}(\widehat{s})$ [4, 6, 5].

(ii) For every recursive time bound $\widehat{s} : \mathbf{N} \to \mathbf{N}$, $\mathrm{DTIME}(\widehat{s})$ has measure 0 in REC [24].

Our main result, Theorem 3.4 below, establishes that *every* weakly useful sequence is strongly deep. This implies that every high Turing degree contains strongly deep sequences (Corollary 3.8). Since the Turing degree of χ_K is one of many high Turing degrees, our main result thus generalizes Bennett's result [4] that χ_K is strongly deep.

More importantly, our main result rigorously confirms Bennett's intuitive arguments relating the computational usefulness of χ_K to its depth. The fact that the useful sequence χ_K is strongly deep is no coincidence. *Every* sequence that is even weakly useful *must* be strongly deep.

Bennett [4] also defines the class of *weakly deep* binary sequences. (As noted by Bennett, this class has been investigated in other guises by Levin and V'jugin [39, 19, 37, 23, 38, 22].) A sequence $x \in \{0,1\}^\infty$ is weakly deep if there do *not* exist a recursive time bound $s : \mathbf{N} \to \mathbf{N}$ and an algorithmically random sequence z such that $x \leq_{\mathrm{T}}^{\mathrm{DTIME}(s)} z$. Bennett [4] notes that every strongly deep sequence is weakly deep, but that there exist weakly deep sequences that are not strongly deep. In section 4 below we strengthen the separation between these two notions by proving that, in the sense of Baire category, *almost every* sequence $x \in \{0,1\}^\infty$ is weakly deep, but not strongly deep. In particular, this implies that weakly deep sequences are "topologically abundant." In contrast, weakly deep sequences are "probabilistically scarce," in the sense that, with respect to Lebesgue measure, almost every sequence $x \in \{0,1\}^\infty$ is algorithmically random [27], hence not weakly deep.

In order to provide a basis for further investigation of Bennett's fundamental ideas, this paper also includes a self-contained mathematical treatment of the weak and strong computational depth of infinite sequences. In section 2 we introduce our basic terminology and notation. Section 3 is the main section of the paper. In this section, we present the strong computational depth of infinite binary sequences in a unified, self-contained framework using a convenient family of parametrized depth classes, D_g^t. This framework is used to prove our main result (Theorem 3.4), that every weakly useful sequence is strongly deep. In the course of our development, we prove several results, some of which were already proven by Bennett [4], giving precise, quantitative relationships among depth, randomness, and recursiveness. We also prove (Theorem 3.9) that strongly deep sequences are extremely rare, in that they form a meager, measure 0 subset of

$\{0,1\}^{\infty}$. In section 4 we give a brief discussion of weak computational depth, including a proof that, in the sense of Baire category, almost every sequence is weakly deep, but not strongly deep. In section 5 we mention possible directions for further research.

All proofs and lemmas are omitted from this extended abstract.

2 Preliminaries

We work primarily in the set $\{0,1\}^{\infty}$ of all (infinite, binary) *sequences*. We also use the set $\{0,1\}^*$ of all (finite, binary) *strings*. We write $|x|$ for the length of a string x, and λ for the empty string. The *standard enumeration* of $\{0,1\}^*$ is the sequence $s_0, s_1, \ldots,$ in which shorter strings precede longer ones and strings of the same length are ordered lexicographically.

Given a sequence $x \in \{0,1\}^{\infty}$ and $m, n \in \mathbf{N}$ with $m \leq n$, we write $x[m..n]$ for the string consisting of the mth through n^{th} bits of x. In particular, $x[0..n-1]$ is the string consisting of the first n bits of x. We write $x[n]$ for $x[n..n]$, the nth bit of x.

We write $\llbracket \varphi \rrbracket$ for the Boolean value of a condition φ, i.e., $\llbracket \varphi \rrbracket = 1$ if φ is true and $\llbracket \varphi \rrbracket = 0$ if φ is false. The *characteristic sequence* of a set $A \subseteq \mathbf{N}$ is then the sequence $\chi_A \in \{0,1\}^{\infty}$ defined by $\chi_A[n] = \llbracket n \in A \rrbracket$ for all $n \in \mathbf{N}$.

We say that a condition $\varphi(n)$ holds *infinitely often* (*i.o.*) if it holds for infinitely many $n \in \mathbf{N}$. We say that a condition $\varphi(n)$ holds *almost everywhere* (*a.e.*) if it holds for all but finitely many $n \in \mathbf{N}$.

Given a recursive time bound $s : \mathbf{N} \to \mathbf{N}$, we say that an oracle Turing machine M is *s-time-bounded* if, given any input $n \in \mathbf{N}$ and oracle $y \in \{0,1\}^{\infty}$, M decides a bit $M^y(n) \in \{0,1\}$ in at most $s(l)$ steps, where l is the number of bits in the binary representation of n. In this case, if $x \in \{0,1\}^{\infty}$ satisfies $x[n] = M^y(n)$ for all $n \in \mathbf{N}$, then we say that x is *Turing reducible to y in time s via M*, and we write $x \leq_{\mathrm{T}}^{\mathrm{DTIME}(s)} y$ via M. We say that x is *Turing reducible to y in time s*, and we write $x \leq_{\mathrm{T}}^{\mathrm{DTIME}(s)} y$, if there is some oracle Turing machine M such that $x \leq_{\mathrm{T}}^{\mathrm{DTIME}(s)} y$ via M. For $y \in \{0,1\}^{\infty}$ and $s : \mathbf{N} \to \mathbf{N}$, we write

$$\mathrm{DTIME}^y(s) = \left\{ x \in \{0,1\}^{\infty} \mid x \leq_{\mathrm{T}}^{\mathrm{DTIME}(s)} y \right\}.$$

(Note that the time bound here is "sharp"; there is no "big-O.") The unrelativized complexity class $\mathrm{DTIME}(s)$ is then defined to be $\mathrm{DTIME}^{0^{\infty}}(s)$, where 0^{∞} is the sequence consisting entirely of 0's.

A sequence $x \in \{0,1\}^{\infty}$ is *truth-table reducible* to a sequence $y \in \{0,1\}^{\infty}$, and we write $x \leq_{\mathrm{tt}} y$, if there exists a recursive time bound $s : \mathbf{N} \to \mathbf{N}$ such that $x \leq_{\mathrm{T}}^{\mathrm{DTIME}(s)} y$. (This definition is easily seen to be equivalent to standard textbook definitions of truth-table reducibility [29, 34].) We write REC for the set of all recursive (i.e., decidable) sequences $x \in \{0,1\}^{\infty}$. A sequence $x \in \{0,1\}^{\infty}$ is *Turing reducible* to a sequence $y \in \{0,1\}^{\infty}$, and we write $x \leq_{\mathrm{T}} y$, if there is an oracle Turing machine M such that $M^y(n) = x[n]$ for every $n \in \mathbf{N}$.

Two sequences $x, y \in \{0,1\}^\infty$ are *Turing equivalent*, and we write $x \equiv_T y$, if $x \leq_T y$ and $y \leq_T x$. A *Turing degree* is an equivalence class of $\{0,1\}^\infty$ under the equivalence relation $\equiv_T$.

The *complement* of a set $X \subseteq \{0,1\}^\infty$ is $X^c = \{0,1\}^\infty - X$.

3 Strong Computational Depth

Here we investigate Bennett's notion of strong computational depth for infinite binary sequences. We first present the necessary notation. We write $K(x)$ for the self-delimiting Kolmogorov complexity of a string $x \in \{0,1\}^*$ and we write U for the efficient universal Turing machine used to define $K(x)$. For $t : \mathbf{N} \to \mathbf{N}$, $K^t(x)$ denotes the $t(|x|)$-time-bounded self-delimiting Kolmogorov complexity of x and

$$\text{PROG}^t(x) = \{\pi \in \{0,1\}^* \mid U(\pi) \text{ in } \leq t(|x|) \text{ steps}\}.$$

A sequence $x \in \{0,1\}^\infty$ is *(algorithmically) random*, and we write $x \in \text{RAND}$, if there is a constant $c \in \mathbf{N}$ such that

$$K(x[0..n-1]) \geq n - c \text{ a.e.}$$

Although Bennett's notion of strong computational depth for infinite binary sequences can be defined in several equivalent ways, we use the definition most convenient for our purposes.

__Definition.__ For $t, g : \mathbf{N} \to \mathbf{N}$ and $n \in \mathbf{N}$, we define the sets

$$\mathbf{D}_g^t(n) = \{x \in \{0,1\}^\infty \mid (\forall \pi \in \text{PROG}^t(x[0..n-1]))K(\pi) \leq |\pi| - g(n)\}$$

and

$$\mathbf{D}_g^t = \bigcup_{m=0}^{\infty} \bigcap_{n=m}^{\infty} \mathbf{D}_g^t(n) = \{x \in \{0,1\}^\infty \mid x \in \mathbf{D}_g^t(n) \text{ a.e.}\}.$$

A sequence $x \in \{0,1\}^\infty$ is *strongly deep*, and we write $x \in \text{strDEEP}$, if for every recursive time bound $t : \mathbf{N} \to \mathbf{N}$ and every constant $c \in \mathbf{N}$, $x \in \mathbf{D}_c^t$.

Intuitively, then, a sequence $x \in \{0,1\}^\infty$ is in $\mathbf{D}_g^t(n)$ if every t-fast program π for $x[0..n-1]$ can be compressed by at least $g(n)$ bits. Note that, if $t(n) \leq \hat{t}(n)$ and $g(n) \leq \hat{g}(n)$, then $\mathbf{D}_{\hat{g}}^{\hat{t}}(n) \subseteq \mathbf{D}_g^t(n)$. Thus, if $t(n) \leq \hat{t}(n)$ a.e. and $g(n) \leq \hat{g}(n)$ a.e., then $\mathbf{D}_{\hat{g}}^{\hat{t}} \subseteq \mathbf{D}_g^t$. In particular, if $g(n) = c$ and $\hat{g}(n) = \hat{c}$ are constant, then we have the situation depicted in Figure 1.

We start by examining the relationship between randomness and strong depth. Bennett [4] has noted that no algorithmically random sequence is strongly deep. We prove this fact. Moreover, we show that it holds in a very strong way. Intuitively, we show that every algorithmically random sequence lies "very near the top" of the diagram in Figure 1.

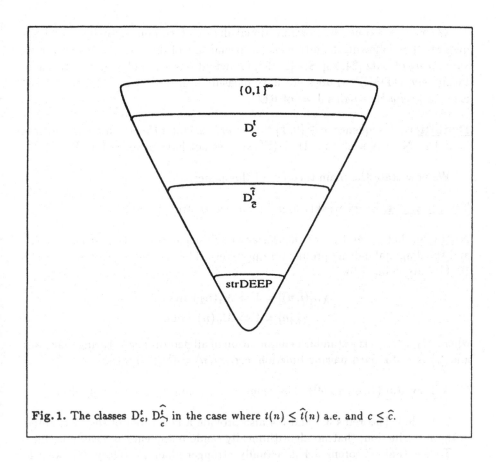

Fig. 1. The classes D_c^t, $D_{\hat{c}}^{\hat{t}}$, in the case where $t(n) \leq \hat{t}(n)$ a.e. and $c \leq \hat{c}$.

Theorem 3.1 (Bennett [4]). RAND∩strDEEP $= \emptyset$. In fact, there exist a recursive function $t(n) = O(n\log n)$ and a constant $c \in \mathbf{N}$ such that RAND∩$D_c^t = \emptyset$.

We note that a strongly deep sequence cannot be truth-table reducible (equivalently, reducible in recursively bounded time) to a sequence that is not also strongly deep. This implies the fact, noted by Bennett [4], that strong depth is invariant under truth-table equivalence.

Theorem 3.2. Let $x, y \in \{0, 1\}^\infty$. If $y \leq_{tt} x$ and y is strongly deep, then x is strongly deep.

We now note that no recursive sequence is strongly deep.

Corollary 3.3 (Bennett [4]). REC∩strDEEP $= \emptyset$.

Up to this point, this section has largely followed the line of Bennett's work. We now build on this work to prove some new results.

We now examine the computational depth of computationally useful sequences. The following definition uses a special case of the *resource-bounded measure theory* of Lutz [24, 25]. See [24, 25] for definitions, examples, and motivation. Intuitively, $\mathrm{DTIME}^x(s)$ does not have measure 0 in REC if $\mathrm{DTIME}^x(s) \cap \mathrm{REC}$ is not a *negligibly small* subset of REC.

Definition. A sequence $x \in \{0,1\}^\infty$ is *weakly useful* if there is a recursive time bound $s : \mathbf{N} \to \mathbf{N}$ such that $\mathrm{DTIME}^x(s)$ does not have measure 0 in REC.

We now state the main theorem of this paper.

Theorem 3.4. Every weakly useful sequence is strongly deep.

Notation. Let χ_H and χ_K be the characteristic sequences of the halting problem and the diagonal halting problem, respectively. That is, the sequences $\chi_H, \chi_K \in \{0,1\}^\infty$ are defined by

$$\chi_H[\langle i, n \rangle] = 1 \Leftrightarrow M_i(n) \text{ halts,}$$
$$\chi_K[n] = 1 \Leftrightarrow M_n(n) \text{ halts,}$$

where $M_0, M_1, \ldots$ is a standard enumeration of all deterministic Turing machines and $\langle, \rangle$ is a standard pairing function, e.g., $\langle i, n \rangle = \binom{i+n+1}{2} + n$.

Corollary 3.5 (Bennett [4]). The sequences χ_H and χ_K are strongly deep.

Note that Theorems 3.1 and 3.4 also provide a new proof of the fact, noted in the introduction, that no algorithmically random sequence is weakly useful.

To see that Theorem 3.4 is actually stronger than Corollary 3.5, we use two known facts concerning high Turing degrees. We first review the relevant definitions. (More detailed discussion can be found in a standard recursion theory text, e.g. [34].)

Recall from section 2 that the characteristic sequence of a set $A \subseteq \mathbf{N}$ is the sequence $\chi_A \in \{0,1\}^\infty$ such that $A = \{n \in \mathbf{N} \mid \chi_A[n] = 1\}$. A sequence $x \in \{0,1\}^\infty$ is *recursively enumerable (r.e.)* if $x = \chi_A$ for some r.e. set $A \subseteq \mathbf{N}$. The *diagonal halting problem relative to* a sequence $x \in \{0,1\}^\infty$ is the set

$$K^x = \{n \in \mathbf{N} \mid M_n^x(n) \text{ halts}\},$$

where M_n is the nth oracle Turing machine in a standard enumeration. The *jump* of a sequence $x \in \{0,1\}^\infty$ is the sequence

$$jump(x) = \chi_{K^x}.$$

A sequence $x \in \{0,1\}^\infty$ is *high* if $x \leq_T \chi_K$ and $jump(x) \equiv_T jump(\chi_K)$. A Turing degree is *high* if it contains a high sequence. It is clear that χ_K and its Turing degree are high.

A set $X \subseteq \{0,1\}^\infty$ is *uniformly recursive in* a sequence $x \in \{0,1\}^\infty$ if there is a sequence $y \in \{0,1\}^\infty$ with the following two properties.

(i) $y \leq_T x$.

(ii) $X \subseteq \{y_k \mid k \in \mathbf{N}\}$, where each $y_k \in \{0,1\}^\infty$ is defined by $y_k[n] = y[\langle k,n \rangle]$ for all $n \in \mathbf{N}$. (Here we are using the standard pairing function $\langle k, n \rangle = \binom{k+n+1}{2} + n$.)

We use the following two known facts.

Theorem 3.6 (Sacks [30]). There exist r.e. sequences that are high and not Turing equivalent to χ_K.

Theorem 3.7 (Martin [26]). A Turing degree **a** is high if and only if there exists $x \in \mathbf{a}$ such that REC is uniformly recursive in x.

Corollary 3.8. Every high Turing degree contains a strongly deep sequence.

Taken together, Theorem 3.6 and Corollary 3.8 show that Theorem 3.4 does indeed strengthen Bennett's result, Corollary 3.5.

We conclude this section by proving that strongly deep sequences are extremely rare, both in the sense of Lebesgue measure and in the sense of Baire category.

Theorem 3.9. The set strDEEP is meager and has measure 0. In fact, if t and c are as in Theorem 3.1, then D_c^t is meager and has measure 0.

4 Weak Computational Depth

In Theorem 3.9, we saw that strongly deep sequences are very rare, both in the sense of Lebesgue measure and in the sense of Baire category. In this brief section, we show that the situation is different for weakly deep sequences. We first recall the definition.

Definition (Bennett [4].) A sequence $x \in \{0,1\}^\infty$ is *weakly deep*, and we write $x \in \mathrm{wkDEEP}$, if there is no sequence $z \in \mathrm{RAND}$ such that $x \leq_{tt} z$.

We use the notation

$$\mathrm{REC}_{tt}(\mathrm{RAND}) = \{x \in \{0,1\}^\infty \mid (\exists z \in \mathrm{RAND})x \leq_{tt} z\}.$$

We thus have

$$\mathrm{wkDEEP} = \mathrm{REC}_{tt}(\mathrm{RAND})^c.$$

Since $\mathrm{REC} \cup \mathrm{RAND} \subseteq \mathrm{REC}_{tt}(\mathrm{RAND})$, it follows immediately that

$$\mathrm{wkDEEP} \cap \mathrm{REC} = \mathrm{wkDEEP} \cap \mathrm{RAND} = \emptyset,$$

i.e., that no weakly deep sequence can be recursive or algorithmically random. As the terminology suggests, every strongly deep sequence is weakly deep.

Theorem 4.1 (Bennett [4]). strDEEP $\subseteq$ wkDEEP.

In particular, Theorems 3.4 and 4.1 imply that weakly deep sequences exist. It should be noted that Gács [12] has proven that, for *every* sequence $x \in \{0,1\}^\infty$, there exists a sequence $z \in \text{RAND}$ such that $x \leq_T z$. Thus $\leq_T$-reducibility cannot be used in place of $\leq_{tt}$-reducibility in the definition of wkDEEP.

We have already noted that wkDEEP∩RAND = $\emptyset$. Since RAND has Lebesgue measure 1, it follows that wkDEEP, like strDEEP, has Lebesgue measure 0. The situation for Baire category is quite different. While strDEEP is meager by Theorem 3.9, wkDEEP is comeager by the following result.

Theorem 4.2. The set wkDEEP is comeager.

Bennett [4] noted that there exist sequences that are weakly deep, but not strongly deep. The following corollary shows that such sequences are, in the sense of Baire category, commonplace.

Corollary 4.3. The set wkDEEP − strDEEP is comeager.

Thus, in the sense of Baire category, almost every sequence $x \in \{0,1\}^\infty$ is weakly deep, but not strongly deep.

Corollary 4.4 (Bennett [4]). strDEEP $\subsetneq$ wkDEEP.

Figure 2 summarizes the relationships among REC, RAND, wkDEEP, and strDEEP. In the sense of Lebesgue measure, almost every binary sequence is in RAND. On the other hand, in the sense of Baire category, almost every binary sequence is in wkDEEP − strDEEP.

5 Conclusion

We have shown that every weakly useful sequence is strongly deep. This result generalizes Bennett's observation that χ_K is strongly deep, and gives support to Bennett's thesis that the computational usefulness of χ_K is related to its computational depth. We mention two open questions that are suggested by this result.

Recall that a sequence $x \in \{0,1\}^\infty$ is weakly useful if there is a recursive time bound $s : N \to N$ such that $\text{DTIME}^x(s)$ does not have measure 0 in REC. Define a sequence $x \in \{0,1\}^\infty$ to be *strongly useful* if there is a recursive time bound $s : N \to N$ such that REC $\subseteq \text{DTIME}^x(s)$. Clearly, every strongly useful sequence is weakly useful.

Question 5.1. Do there exist sequences that are weakly useful, but not strongly useful? (We conjecture in the affirmative.)

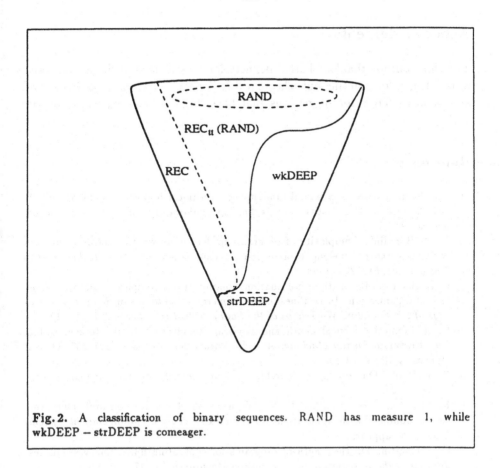

Fig. 2. A classification of binary sequences. RAND has measure 1, while wkDEEP − strDEEP is comeager.

Our main result implies that every high Turing degree contains a strongly deep sequence. A well-known generalization of high sequences and degrees defines a sequence $x \in \{0,1\}^\infty$ to be $high_n$ ($n \in \mathbb{N}$) if $x \leq_T \chi_K$ and $jump^{(n)}(x) \equiv_T jump^{(n)}(\chi_K)$, where $jump^{(n)}$ is the n-fold iteration of the jump operation. A Turing degree $\mathbf{a}$ is then $high_n$ if it contains a $high_n$ sequence. (See [34], for example.) If a sequence or degree is $high_n$, then it is clearly $high_{n+1}$. The Turing degree of χ_K is clearly the only $high_0$ degree. It is also clear that a sequence or degree is $high_1$ if and only if it is high. Thus, by Corollary 3.8, every $high_1$ Turing degree contains a strongly deep sequence.

Question 5.2. For $n > 1$, is it necessarily the case that every $high_n$ Turing degree contains a strongly deep sequence?

Answers to Question 5.1 and 5.2 may well improve our understanding of computational depth *vis-á-vis* computational usefulness. More generally, further investigation of Bennett's fundamental notions may yield profound insights into the role of depth in the organization of computational, physical, and biological information.

287

Acknowledgments

The third author thanks Charles Bennett for several helpful discussions, and Stuart Kurtz for pointing out Theorem 3.7. We also thank Ron Book and two anonymous referees for suggestions that have improved the exposition of this paper.

References

1. L. Adleman. Time, space, and randomness. Technical Report MIT/LCS/79/TM-131, Massachusettes Institute of Technology, Laboratory for Computer Science, March 1979.
2. Y. M. Barzdin'. Complexity of programs to determine whether natural numbers not greater than n belong to a recursively enumerable set. *Soviet Mathematics Doklady*, 9:1251–1254, 1968.
3. C. H. Bennett. Dissipation, information, computational complexity and the definition of organization. In D. Pines, editor, *Emerging Syntheses in Science, Proceedings of the Founding Workshops of the Santa Fe Institute*, pages 297–313, 1985.
4. C. H. Bennett. Logical depth and physical complexity. In R. Herken, editor, *The Universal Turing Machine: A Half-Century Survey*, pages 227–257. Oxford University Press, 1988.
5. R. V. Book. On languages reducible to algorithmically random languages. submitted, 1993.
6. R. V. Book, J. H. Lutz, and K. W. Wagner. An observation on probability versus randomness with applications to complexity classes. *Mathematical Systems Theory*. to appear.
7. G. J. Chaitin. On the length of programs for computing finite binary sequences. *Journal of the Association for Computing Machinery*, 13:547–569, 1966.
8. G. J. Chaitin. On the length of programs for computing finite binary sequences: statistical considerations. *Journal of the ACM*, 16:145–159, 1969.
9. G. J. Chaitin. A theory of program size formally identical to information theory. *Journal of the Association for Computing Machinery*, 22:329–340, 1975.
10. G. J. Chaitin. Incompleteness theorems for random reals. *Advances in Applied Mathematics*, 8:119–146, 1987.
11. P. Gács. On the symmetry of algorithmic information. *Soviet Mathematics Doklady*, 15:1477, 1974.
12. P. Gács. Every sequence is reducible to a random one. *Information and Control*, 70:186–192, 1986.
13. A. N. Kolmogorov. Three approaches to the quantitative definition of 'information'. *Problems of Information Transmission*, 1:1–7, 1965.
14. A. N. Kolmogorov. Logical basis for information theory and probability theory. *IEEE Transactions on Information Theory*, IT-14:662–664, 1968.
15. A. N. Kolmogorov and V. A. Uspenskii. Algorithms and randomness. translated in *Theory of Probability and its Applications*, 32:389–412, 1987.
16. M. Koppel. Structure. In R. Herken, editor, *The Universal Turing Machine: A Half-Century Survey*, pages 435–452. Oxford University Press, 1988.
17. L. A. Levin. On the notion of a random sequence. *Soviet Mathematics Doklady*, 14:1413–1416, 1973.

18. L. A. Levin. Laws of information conservation (nongrowth) and aspects of the foundation of probability theory. *Problems of Information Transmission*, 10:206–210, 1974.

19. L. A. Levin. On the principle of conservation of information in intuitionistic mathematics. *Soviet Mathematics Doklady*, 17:601–605, 1976.

20. L. A. Levin. Uniform tests of randomness. *Soviet Mathematics Doklady*, pages 337–340, 1976.

21. L. A. Levin. Various measures of complexity for finite objects (axiomatic description). *Soviet Mathematics Doklady*, 17:522–526, 1976.

22. L. A. Levin. Randomness conservation inequalities; information and independence in mathematical theories. *Information and Control*, 61:15–37, 1984.

23. L. A. Levin and V. V. V'jugin. Invariant properties of informational bulks. *Proceedings of the Sixth Symposium on Mathematical Foundations of Computer Science*, pages 359–364, 1977.

24. J. H. Lutz. Almost everywhere high nonuniform complexity. *Journal of Computer and System Sciences*, 44:220–258, 1992.

25. J. H. Lutz. Resource-bounded measure, 1992. in preparation.

26. D. A. Martin. Classes of recursively enumerable sets and degrees of unsolvability. *Z. Math. Logik Grundlag. Math.*, 12:295–310, 1966.

27. P. Martin-Löf. On the definition of random sequences. *Information and Control*, 9:602–619, 1966.

28. P. Martin-Löf. Complexity oscillations in infinite binary sequences. *Zeitschrift für Wahrscheinlichkeitstheorie und Verwandte Gebiete*, 19:225–230, 1971.

29. H. Rogers, Jr. *Theory of Recursive Functions and Effective Computability*. McGraw - Hill, 1967.

30. G. E. Sacks. *Degrees of Unsolvability*. Princeton University Press, 1966.

31. C. P. Schnorr. Process complexity and effective random tests. *Journal of Computer and System Sciences*, 7:376–388, 1973.

32. A. Kh. Shen'. The frequency approach to defining a random sequence. *Semiotika i Informatika*, 19:14–42, 1982. (In Russian.).

33. A. Kh. Shen'. On relations between different algorithmic definitions of randomness. *Soviet Mathematics Doklady*, 38:316–319, 1989.

34. R. I. Soare. *Recursively Enumerable Sets and Degrees*. Springer-Verlag, 1987.

35. R. J. Solomonoff. A formal theory of inductive inference. *Information and Control*, 7:1–22, 224–254, 1964.

36. R. M. Solovay, 1975. reported in [10].

37. V. V. V'jugin. On Turing invariant sets. *Soviet Mathematics Doklady*, 17:1090–1094, 1976.

38. V. V. V'jugin. The algebra of invariant properties of finite sequences. *Problems of Information Transmission*, 18:147–161, 1982.

39. A. K. Zvonkin and L. A. Levin. The complexity of finite objects and the development of the concepts of information and randomness by means of the theory of algorithms. *Russian Mathematical Surveys*, 25:83–124, 1970.

Learnability:
Admissible, Co-finite, and Hypersimple Languages*

Ganesh Baliga and John Case

Department of Computer and Information Sciences
University of Delaware
Newark, DE 19716
USA

Abstract. Presented is a surprising characterization of hypersimple sets in algorithmic learning theory. It is used herein to obtain an elegant, tight separation result for learnability criteria. It is argued that such separation results may yield insight for eventual characterizations.

1   Introduction

In Gold's paradigm [Gol67] for language learning (or in variants of it [OSW86, Cas88]), an algorithmic device is fed *positive* membership information about a (formal) language, and it attempts eventually to conjecture reasonably accurate grammars for that language. This eventual algorithmic learning of reasonably accurate grammars for languages from positive information is difficult, yet Gold [Gol67] cites [McN66] for psycholinguistic evidence that positive information seems to be enough for people. Beginning just below, we will present some examples of what can and cannot be learned from positive information. These examples will help us introduce the results of the present paper.

We suppose for convenience and without loss of generality that every language consists of nothing but non-negative integers. Let $\mathcal{FIN}$ be the class of all finite languages. From [Gol67], for $\mathcal{L} = \mathcal{FIN}$, there is an algorithmic device d such that

> given any language in $\mathcal{L}$, d eventually converges to a single final, perfectly correct grammar generating that language. $\hfill (1)$

Suppose $L \notin \mathcal{FIN}$. By contrast, for $\mathcal{L} = \mathcal{FIN} \cup \{L\}$, there is no algorithmic device d such that (1) [Gol67, OSW86]. We call $\mathcal{FIN}$ *supersaturated* because of this contrast: learnability breaks down if *any* single language not in $\mathcal{FIN}$ is added to it; no language is *admissible* to $\mathcal{FIN}$ without loss of learning power.

Some classes of languages $\mathcal{L}$ are merely *saturated*: adding *some* r.e. $L \notin \mathcal{L}$ to such $\mathcal{L}$ results in a loss of learning power. For saturated classes some r.e. languages are not admissible, but others may be. An example will be presented shortly below and again in Corollary 1.

---

* The respective email addresses of the authors are baliga@cis.udel.edu and case@cis.udel.edu.

A language L is *co-finite* $\overset{\text{def}}{\Leftrightarrow}$ it is missing at most finitely many non-negative integers, i.e., $\overset{\text{def}}{\Leftrightarrow}$ it is a finite variant of N, the entire set of non-negative integers. Let $\mathcal{COF}$ = the class of all co-finite languages. For $\mathcal{L} = \mathcal{COF}$, there is no algorithmic device d such that (1) [OW82a, OSW86]. Hence, even a class of languages as simple as $\mathcal{COF}$ is difficult to learn from positive information. However, $\mathcal{COF}$ can be learned if we relax a bit our criterion for successful learning: trivially, for $\mathcal{L} = \mathcal{COF}$, there is an algorithmic device d such that

$$\text{given any language in } \mathcal{L}, d \text{ eventually converges to a single final grammar} \quad (2)$$
$$\text{which generates a finite variant of that language.}$$

Hence, $\mathcal{COF}$ witnesses that more can be learned with respect to the criterion of success specified by (2) than from that specified by (1) [OW82a, OSW86]. We say, then, that $\mathcal{COF}$ witnesses a *separation* result for learning criteria.

More generally, and in some cases surprisingly, simple subclasses of $\mathcal{COF}$ witness separation results for learning criteria. An example from [CL82, Cas92] appears in (4) at the beginning of Section 3 below. In some cases, separation results, originally obtained by self-referential examples, can be witnessed more simply by natural subclasses of $\mathcal{COF}$. An example such separation, which improves on self referential separation witnesses in [Cas88, Cas92], is presented as Theorem 3 in Section 3 below.

We show (Corollary 1 in Section 3 below) that, with respect to the learning criterion specified by (2), $\mathcal{COF}$ is saturated, but not supersaturated.

We say that a language L is *co-infinite* $\overset{\text{def}}{\Leftrightarrow}$ it is not co-finite. A language L is called *hypersimple* $\overset{\text{def}}{\Leftrightarrow}$ [L is recursively enumerable and co-infinite $\land$ the function enumerating the complement of L in increasing order is not bounded above by any computable function] [Rog67]. Post [Pos44] originally defined hypersimple sets by a different characterization which is presented below in Definition 1 (Section 2.1) and exploited in the proof of our main theorem (Theorem 4 in Section 3 below). This theorem provides a very surprising characterization of hypersimple sets within learnability theory. It says that, with respect to the learning criterion specified by (2), for r.e. L, L is inadmissible to $\mathcal{COF}$ (i.e., L witnesses that $\mathcal{COF}$ is saturated) $\Leftrightarrow$ L is hypersimple. In Corollary 4 below in Section 3 we use $\mathcal{COF} \cup \{L\}$, where L is hypersimple, as a particularly elegant witness to a learning criteria separation result from [OW82a, CL82].

Why are hypersimple sets involved in a separation result in learnability? Actually, hypersimple sets seem, more generally, to capture an essence of many separation and independence results in a wide diversity of contexts besides learning theory. Originally hypersimple sets were used to separate T-complete sets from tt-complete sets [Pos44, Rog67]. Hypersimple sets are crucial in a surprising characterization of recursively axiomatizable theories that have no independent axiomatization which is recursive [Kre57, PE68]. Furthermore, hypersimple sets have played a role in independence results for both complexity theory [JY81] and control structures [Roy87]. We expect that an important understanding of the role of hypersimple sets in separation and independence in general can be obtained by a careful comparative study of the examples referenced in this paragraph.

Lastly (Theorem 5) we present a self-referential witness to a saturation result for a case where $\mathcal{COF}$ would not work. N is the inadmissible set we use to witness this saturation result. Saturated (or supersaturated) classes are just barely inside the boundary of the power of the underlying learning criteria, and the inadmissible sets used to witness the saturation are just on the other side of that boundary. We believe, then, that further study of saturated classes and corresponding inadmissible sets will give us a greater understanding of the underlying learning criteria, and, may, in some cases, lead to insightful characterizations.

2 Preliminaries

2.1 Notation

Any unexplained recursion theoretic notation is from [Rog67]. N denotes the set of natural numbers, $\{0, 1, 2, 3, \ldots\}$. Unless otherwise specified, $e, i, j, k, m, n, p, s, w, x, y, z$, with or without decorations[2], range over N. $*$ denotes a nonmember of N and is assumed to satisfy $(\forall n)[n < * < \infty]$. a and b, with or without decorations, range over $N \cup \{*\}$. $\emptyset$ denotes the empty set. $\subseteq$ denotes subset. $\subset$ denotes proper subset. $\supseteq$ denotes superset. $\supset$ denotes proper superset. P and S, with or without decorations, range over sets of N. $\text{card}(S)$ denotes the cardinality of S. $S_1 \triangle S_2$ denotes the symmetric difference between S_1 and S_2. For $n \in N$ and sets S_1 and S_2, $S_1 =^n S_2$ means that $\text{card}(\{x \mid x \in S_1 \triangle S_2\}) \leq n$; $S_1 =^* S_2$ means that $\text{card}(\{x \mid x \in S_1 \triangle S_2\})$ is finite. D_x denotes the finite set with canonical index x [Rog67].

$\uparrow$ denotes undefined. $\max(\cdot), \min(\cdot)$ denote the maximum and minimum of a set, respectively, where $\max(\emptyset) = 0$ and $\min(\emptyset) = \uparrow$.

η ranges over *partial* functions with arguments and values from N. $\eta(x)\downarrow$ denotes that $\eta(x)$ is defined; $\eta(x)\uparrow$ denotes that $\eta(x)$ is undefined.

f and g, with or without decorations, range over *total* functions with arguments and values from N. $\text{domain}(\eta)$ and $\text{range}(\eta)$ denote the domain and range of the function η, respectively.

φ denotes a fixed *acceptable* programming system for the partial computable functions: $N \to N$ [Rog58, Rog67, MY78]. φ_i denotes the partial computable function computed by program i in the φ-system. Φ denotes an arbitrary fixed Blum complexity measure [Blu67, HU79] for the φ-system.

W_i denotes $\text{domain}(\varphi_i)$. W_i is, then, the r.e. set/language ($\subseteq N$) accepted (or equivalently, generated) by the φ-program i. $\mathcal{E}$ will denote the class of all r.e. sets. L, with or without decorations, ranges over $\mathcal{E}$. $\overline{L}$ denotes the complement of L.

Definition 1 A *hypersimple set* [Pos44] L is an r.e., co-infinite set for which there does not exist a recursive f such that, for all x, $D_{f(x)} \cap \overline{L} \neq \emptyset$ and for all x, y such that $x \neq y$, $D_{f(x)} \cap D_{f(y)} = \emptyset$.

---

[2] Decorations are subscripts, superscripts and the like.

It is well known that hypersimple sets exist [Rog67]. $\mathcal{L}$, with or without decorations, ranges over subsets of $\mathcal{E}$. $W_i^s \overset{\text{def}}{=} \{x \leq s \mid \Phi_i(x) \leq s\}$. The class of finite languages $\mathcal{FIN} \overset{\text{def}}{=} \{L \mid \text{card}(L) < \infty\}$. The class of co-finite sets $\mathcal{COF} \overset{\text{def}}{=} \{L \mid \text{card}(N - L) < \infty\}$.

The quantifiers '$\overset{\infty}{\forall}$', and '$\overset{\infty}{\exists}$' essentially from [Blu67], mean 'for all but finitely many' and 'there exist infinitely many', respectively.

2.2 Learning Machines

We now consider language learning machines. Definition 2 below introduces a notion that facilitates discussion about elements of a language being fed to a learning machine.

Definition 2 A *sequence* σ is a mapping from an initial segment of N into $(N \cup \{\#\})$. The *content* of a sequence σ, denoted content(σ), is the set of natural numbers in the range of σ. The *length* of σ, denoted by $|\sigma|$, is the number of elements in σ.

Intuitively, #'s represent pauses in the presentation of data. We let σ and τ, with or without decorations, range over finite sequences. We say that $\sigma \subseteq \tau$ $(\sigma \subset \tau)$ iff σ is an (proper) initial subsequence of τ. We say that $\sigma \supseteq \tau$ $(\sigma \supset \tau)$ iff τ is an (proper) initial subsequence of σ. $\sigma.\tau$ denotes the initial sequence obtained by concatenating τ at the end of σ. SEQ denotes the set of all finite sequences. The set of all finite sequences of natural numbers and #'s, SEQ, can be coded onto N.

Definition 3 A *language learning machine* is an algorithmic device which computes a mapping from SEQ into N.

We let M, with or without decorations, range over learning machines.

2.3 Fundamental Language Identification Paradigms

Definition 4 A *text* T for a language L is a mapping from N into $(N \cup \{\#\})$ such that L is the set of natural numbers in the range of T. The *content* of a text T, denoted content(T), is the set of natural numbers in the range of T.

Intuitively, a text for a language is an enumeration or sequential presentation of all the objects in the language with the #'s representing pauses in the listing or presentation of such objects. For example, the only text for the empty language is just an infinite sequence of #'s.

We let T, with or without decorations, range over texts. $T[n]$ denotes the finite initial sequence of T with length n. Hence, domain$(T[n]) = \{x \mid x < n\}$. For $n \leq |\sigma|$, $\sigma[n]$ denotes the finite initial sequence of σ with length n.

Finite Vacillatory Language Identification Definitions 5 through 8 were defined, sometimes for special cases, in [Gol67, OW82a, Cas86, Cas88].

Definition 5 Suppose $\mathbf{M}$ is a learning machine and T is a text. We say $\mathbf{M}(T)\Downarrow$) $\Leftrightarrow$ $\{\mathbf{M}(\tau) \mid \tau \subset T\}$ is finite. If $\mathbf{M}(T)\Downarrow$, then $\mathbf{M}(T)$ is defined $= \{p \mid (\overset{\infty}{\exists} \tau \subset T)[\mathbf{M}(\tau) = p]\}$; otherwise, $\mathbf{M}(T)$ is undefined.

We now introduce criteria for a learning machine to be considered successful on languages.

Definition 6 For $n > 0$, a language learning machine, $\mathbf{M}$, $\mathbf{TxtFex}_n^a$-*identifies* an r.e. language L (written: $L \in \mathbf{TxtFex}_n^a(\mathbf{M})$) $\Leftrightarrow$ ($\forall$ texts T for L)[$\mathbf{M}(T)\Downarrow$ = a set of cardinality $\leq n$ and ($\forall p \in \mathbf{M}(T))[W_p =^a L]$].

Definition 7 A language learning machine, $\mathbf{M}$, $\mathbf{TxtFex}_*^a$-*identifies* an r.e. language L (written: $L \in \mathbf{TxtFex}_*^a(\mathbf{M})$) $\Leftrightarrow$ ($\forall$ texts T for L)[$\mathbf{M}(T)\Downarrow \wedge$ ($\forall p \in \mathbf{M}(T))[W_p =^a L]$].

In $\mathbf{TxtFex}_b^a$-identification the b is a "bound" on the number of final grammars and the a a "bound" on the number of anomalies allowed in these final grammars. In general a "bound" of $*$ just means *unbounded*, but *finite*.

Definition 8 $\mathbf{TxtFex}_b^a = \{\mathcal{L} \mid (\exists \mathbf{M})[\mathcal{L} \subseteq \mathbf{TxtFex}_b^a(\mathbf{M})]\}$.

Intuitively, $\mathcal{L} \in \mathbf{TxtFex}_b^a \Leftrightarrow$ there is an effective procedure $\mathbf{p}$ such that, if $\mathbf{p}$ is given any listing of any language $L \in \mathcal{L}$, it outputs a sequence of grammars *converging* in a non-empty *set* of no more than b grammars, and each of these grammars makes no more than a mistakes in generating L.

$\mathbf{TxtFex}_1^0$-identification is equivalent to Gold's [Gol67] seminal notion of *identification*, also referred to as $\mathbf{TxtEx}$-identification in [CL82] and (indirectly) as **INT** in [OW82b, OW82a, OSW86]. $\mathbf{TxtFex}_1^a$-identification is just $\mathbf{TxtEx}^a$-identification from [CL82]. For $n > 0$, $\mathbf{TxtFex}_n^0$-identification is just the notion of $\mathbf{TXTFEX}_n$-identification from [Cas86]. Osherson and Weinstein [OW82a] were the first to define $\mathbf{TxtFex}_*^0$ and $\mathbf{TxtFex}_*^*$. The influence of Gold's paradigm [Gol67] on human language learning is discussed by Pinker [Pin79], Wexler and Culicover [WC80], Wexler [Wex82], and Osherson, Stob, and Weinstein [OSW82, OSW84, OSW86].

Behaviorally Correct Language Identification Next are introduced the cases of success criteria for which the number of final grammars is possibly infinite, not necessarily finite as it is for $\mathbf{TxtFex}_b^a$-identification. Definitions 9 and 10 are from [CL82]. The $a \in \{0, *\}$ cases were independently introduced in [OW82a, OW82b].

Definition 9 $\mathbf{M}$ $\mathbf{TxtBc}^a$-*identifies* L (written: $L \in \mathbf{TxtBc}^a(\mathbf{M})$) $\Longleftrightarrow$ ($\forall$ texts T for L)($\overset{\infty}{\forall} n$)[$W_{\mathbf{M}(T[n])} =^a L$].

Definition 10 $\mathbf{TxtBc}^a = \{\mathcal{L} \mid (\exists \mathbf{M})[\mathcal{L} \subseteq \mathbf{TxtBc}^a(\mathbf{M})]\}$.

We sometimes write $\mathbf{TxtBc}$ for $\mathbf{TxtBc}^0$.

Some Basic Results We now enumerate the connections between various learning criteria defined above.

Theorem 1. *For all n, the following hold.*

(a) $\mathbf{TxtFex}_1^{n+1} - \mathbf{TxtFex}_*^n \neq \emptyset$.
(b) $\mathbf{TxtFex}_{n+2}^0 - \mathbf{TxtFex}_{n+1}^* \neq \emptyset$.
(c) $\mathbf{TxtBc}^{n+1} - \mathbf{TxtBc}^n \neq \emptyset$.
(d) $\mathbf{TxtFex}_1^{2n+1} - \mathbf{TxtBc}^n \neq \emptyset$.
(e) $\mathbf{TxtFex}_1^* - \bigcup_n \mathbf{TxtBc}^n \neq \emptyset$.
(f) $\mathbf{TxtBc} - \mathbf{TxtFex}_*^* \neq \emptyset$.
(g) $\mathbf{TxtBc}^* - (\bigcup_n \mathbf{TxtBc}^n \cup \mathbf{TxtFex}_*^*) \neq \emptyset$.
(h) $\mathbf{TxtFex}_*^{2n} \subset \mathbf{TxtBc}^n$.
(i) $\mathcal{E} \notin \mathbf{TxtBc}^*$.

Most of the above results were announced in [CL82, Cas88] and are all proved in [Cas92]. Recall that $\mathbf{TxtEx}^a \stackrel{\text{def}}{=} \mathbf{TxtFex}_1^a$. Osherson and Weinstein [OW82a] independently proved that $\mathbf{TxtFex}_0^* \subset \mathbf{TxtFex}_*^*$ and that $\mathbf{TxtFex}_1^0 \subset \mathbf{TxtFex}_*^0$. They also showed that $\mathbf{TxtBc} - \mathbf{TxtEx}^* \neq \emptyset$ and noted that $\mathcal{COF} \in \mathbf{TxtEx}^* - \mathbf{TxtBc}$. We note that the former along with part (c) of the above theorem imply that $\mathbf{TxtEx}^* \subset \mathbf{TxtBc}^*$. [CL82] proved this result by first proving part (c) and then showing that $\mathbf{TxtBc} - \mathbf{TxtEx}^* \neq \emptyset$. They used the self–referential class of languages

$$\mathcal{L}_0 = \{L \mid L \text{ is recursive, infinite and } (\stackrel{\infty}{\forall} x \in L)[W_x = L]\} \tag{3}$$

to prove the latter result (we further consider this class in Theorem 6). Herein, we achieve the same separation via our characterization of the hypersimple sets in Theorem 4 below.

We now introduce some important definitions and technical concepts which will be used in our proofs.

Let $Progs(\mathbf{M}, \sigma) \stackrel{\text{def}}{=} \{p \mid (\exists n \leq |\sigma|)[\mathbf{M}(\sigma[n]) = p]\}$.

Definition 11 We say that σ is a *hypostabilizing sequence for* $\mathbf{M}$ *on* L $\stackrel{\text{def}}{\Leftrightarrow}$ $[[\text{content}(\sigma) \subseteq L] \wedge (\forall \sigma' \supseteq \sigma \mid \text{content}(\sigma') \subseteq L)[\mathbf{M}(\sigma') \in Progs(\mathbf{M}, \sigma)]]$.

Fulk defined the notion of stabilizing sequences [Ful85, Ful90] which differs slightly from the above notion. Next are presented the crucial notions of $\mathbf{TxtEx}^a$, $\mathbf{TxtFex}_*^a$ and $\mathbf{TxtBc}^a$ *locking sequences* which are extensively used in the proofs presented in this paper.

Definition 12 [BB75, OW82a] σ is a $\mathbf{TxtEx}^a$-*locking sequence for* $\mathbf{M}$ *on* L $\stackrel{\text{def}}{\Leftrightarrow}$ $[[\text{content}(\sigma) \subseteq L] \wedge (\forall \sigma' \mid \text{content}(\sigma') \subseteq L \wedge \sigma \subseteq \sigma')[\mathbf{M}(\sigma') = \mathbf{M}(\sigma)] \wedge [W_{\mathbf{M}(\sigma)} =^a L]]$.

Definition 13 We say that σ is a **TxtFex$_*^a$**-*locking sequence for* **M** *on* L $\overset{\text{def}}{\Longleftrightarrow}$ $[[\sigma$ is a hypostabilizing sequence for **M** on $L] \wedge (\forall \sigma' \supseteq \sigma \mid \text{content}(\sigma') \subseteq L)[W_{M(\sigma')} =^a L]]$.

Definition 14 We say that σ is a **TxtBc^a**-*locking sequence for* **M** *on* L $\overset{\text{def}}{\Longleftrightarrow}$ $[[\text{content}(\sigma) \subseteq L] \wedge (\forall \sigma' \supseteq \sigma \mid \text{content}(\sigma') \subseteq L)[W_{\mathbf{M}(\sigma')} =^a L]]$.

The following important lemma in learning theory which is essentially due to L. Blum and M. Blum [BB75] will be an important tool used in our proofs in this paper.

Lemma 2. [BB75, OW82a] *If* **M** **TxtEx^a**-*identifies* L, *then there is a* **TxtEx^a** - *locking sequence for* **M** *on* L.

A similar lemma asserts the existence of **TxtFex$_*^a$** and **TxtBc^a**-locking sequences. We omit formal statements of these lemmata; nonetheless, we will use these facts in the proofs of Theorem 3 and Theorem 6.

3 Results

Classes of co-finite sets witness many separation results in language learning. For instance, from [CL82, Cas92],

$$\{L \mid L =^{2n+1} N\} \in \mathbf{TxtEx}^{2n+1} - \mathbf{TxtBc}^n. \tag{4}$$

At the same time, other separation results such as $\mathbf{TxtFex}_1^{n+1} - \mathbf{TxtFex}_*^n \neq \emptyset$ [Cas92] have been proved using self referential classes of languages. We prove the same separation using a natural class of co-finite sets.

Theorem 3. *Let* $\mathcal{L}_{n+1} = \{L \mid L =^{n+1} N\}$. *Then* $\mathcal{L}_{n+1} \in \mathbf{TxtFex}_1^{n+1} - \mathbf{TxtFex}_*^n$.

Proof. Clearly $\mathcal{L}_{n+1} \in \mathbf{TxtFex}_1^{n+1}$.

Suppose by way of contradiction that $\mathcal{L}_{n+1} \in \mathbf{TxtFex}_*^n(\mathbf{M})$. Then, let σ_N be a $\mathbf{TxtFex}_*^n$-locking sequence for **M** on N. By a variant of Lemma 2, such a σ_N exists. From the definition of locking sequence, it follows that, for all $\sigma \supseteq \sigma_N$, $\mathbf{M}(\sigma) \in Progs(\mathbf{M}, \sigma_N)$. Let $GoodProgs = \{p \in Progs(\mathbf{M}, \sigma_N) \mid W_p =^* N\}$.

We consider 2 cases.

Case 1: $GoodProgs = \emptyset$.

Then clearly $N \notin \mathbf{TxtFex}_*^n(\mathbf{M})$.

Case 2: $GoodProgs \neq \emptyset$.

For $p \in GoodProgs$, let

$$Last(p) = \begin{cases} x_p, & \text{if } [W_p \neq N] \wedge [x_p = \max(N - W_p)]; \\ 0, & \text{otherwise;} \end{cases}$$

Since each $p \in GoodProgs$ satisfies $W_p =^* N$, it is clear that $Last$ is well defined. Let $m = \max(\{Last(p) \mid p \in GoodProgs\})$. Let S be a set of cardinality $n+1$ such that $\min(S) > m$ and $S \cap \text{content}(\sigma_N) = \emptyset$. Let $L = N - S$. Clearly, $L \in \mathcal{L}_{n+1}$. Also, for all $p \in GoodProgs$, it is clear that $L \neq^n W_p$. Thus, for all $p \in Progs(\mathbf{M}, \sigma_N)$, $L \neq^n W_p$. Let $T \supset \sigma_N$ be any text for L. It is clear that $\mathbf{M}$ does not $\mathbf{TxtFex}_*^n$-identify L on T.

Thus, $\mathcal{L}_{n+1} \notin \mathbf{TxtFex}_*^n$. ∎

$\mathcal{COF}$ does not witness that $\mathbf{TxtBc}^*$ separates from $\mathbf{TxtEx}^*$, i.e., $\mathcal{COF} \notin \mathbf{TxtBc}^* - \mathbf{TxtEx}^*$. Perhaps if $\mathcal{COF}$ were augmented by another language the result would witness the separation. This partly motivates the following. Intuitively we think of $\mathcal{I}$ in Definition 15 as an identification criterion.

Definition 15 Let $\mathcal{I}$ be a set of classes of languages.

(a) We say L is $\mathcal{I}$–admissible to $\mathcal{L} \overset{\text{def}}{\Leftrightarrow} \mathcal{L} \cup \{L\} \in \mathcal{I}$. We say L is $\mathcal{I}$–inadmissible to $\mathcal{L} \overset{\text{def}}{\Leftrightarrow} L$ is not $\mathcal{I}$–admissible to $\mathcal{L}$.

(b) We say that $\mathcal{L}$ is $\mathcal{I}$–saturated $\overset{\text{def}}{\Leftrightarrow} [[\mathcal{L} \in \mathcal{I}] \wedge (\exists L)[L$ is $\mathcal{I}$–inadmissible to $\mathcal{L}]]$.

(c) We say that $\mathcal{L}$ is $\mathcal{I}$–supersaturated $\overset{\text{def}}{\Leftrightarrow} [[\mathcal{L} \in \mathcal{I}] \wedge (\forall L \in \mathcal{E} - \mathcal{L})[L$ is $\mathcal{I}$–inadmissible to $\mathcal{L}]]$.

[OSW86] define variants of the saturatedness and supersaturatedness notions above (they call their variants 'maximal' and 'saturated' respectively). Their definitions pertain to not necessarily algorithmic language learning.

As an example of supersaturated language classes, consider $\mathcal{FIN}$, the class of all finite languages. Clearly, $\mathcal{FIN} \in \mathbf{TxtEx}^*$. Also, for *any* infinite language L, it can be proved that $\mathcal{FIN} \cup \{L\} \notin \mathbf{TxtEx}^*$ [OW82a, CL82]. Thus, $\mathcal{FIN}$ is $\mathbf{TxtEx}^*$–supersaturated (it can also be proved that it is $\mathbf{TxtBc}^*$–supersaturated). In fact, it is easily proved that $\mathcal{FIN}$ is the only $\mathbf{TxtEx}^*$–supersaturated class of languages [OSW86]. On the other hand, from our next and surprising main theorem, one can see that (all and) only the hypersimple sets are $\mathbf{TxtEx}^*$–inadmissible to $\mathcal{COF}$.

Theorem 4. L *hypersimple* $\Leftrightarrow L$ *is* $\mathbf{TxtEx}^*$–*inadmissible to* $\mathcal{COF}$.

Proof. ($\Rightarrow$)

Suppose L is hypersimple. Suppose by way of contradiction that $\mathcal{COF} \cup \{L\} \in \mathbf{TxtEx}^*(\mathbf{M})$. Then, let σ_L be a locking sequence for $\mathbf{M}$ on L. By Lemma 2, such a σ_L exists. Let g be a recursive function such that, for all σ, $D_{g(\sigma)} = \text{content}(\sigma)$. Now consider program p which on all inputs x computes as specified below.
$\varphi_p(0) = g(\min(\overline{L}))$.
For $x \geq 1$, $\varphi_p(x)$ is computed as follows.

1. First compute $\varphi_p(x-1)$.
2. Search for σ such that $\text{content}(\sigma) \subset \{x \mid x \geq 1 + \max(D_{\varphi_p(x-1)})\}$ and $\mathbf{M}(\sigma_L.\sigma) \neq \mathbf{M}(\sigma_L)$. If (at all) such a σ is found, let $\varphi_p(x) = g(\sigma)$.

This completes the specification of program p. We now consider 2 cases.

Case 1: φ_p is not total.

Let x be the least value such that $\varphi_p(x)\uparrow$. Clearly $x \geq 1$. Since x is the least value such that $\varphi_p(x)\uparrow$, step 1 in the computation of $\varphi_p(x)$ terminates. Let $m = 1+\max(D_{\varphi_p(x-1)})$. Let T' be a text for the language $\{x \mid x \geq m\}$. Let $T = \sigma_L.T'$. T is clearly a text for the co-finite set $L' = \text{content}(\sigma_L) \cup \{x \mid x \geq m\}$. Now $\mathbf{M}(T) = \mathbf{M}(\sigma_L)$ (otherwise, step 2 in the computation of program p on input x would have terminated as well; hence, $\varphi_p(x)$ would have been defined). Thus, from our supposition that $\mathcal{COF} \cup \{L\} \in \mathbf{TxtEx}^*(\mathbf{M})$, it follows that $L =^* W_{\mathbf{M}(\sigma_L)} = W_{\mathbf{M}(T)} =^* L'$. Thus we conclude that $L' =^* L$, which is a contradiction since L' is co-finite and L, a hypersimple set, is co-infinite.

Case 2: φ_p is total.

Since σ_L is a locking sequence for $\mathbf{M}$ on L, it follows from the specification of program p that for all x, $D_{\varphi_p(x)} \cap \overline{L} \neq \emptyset$ and that for all x, y such that $x \neq y$, $D_{\varphi_p(x)} \cap D_{\varphi_p(y)} = \emptyset$. Thus, $f = \varphi_p$ witnesses that L is not hypersimple which is a contradiction.

($\Leftarrow$)

Suppose that L is not hypersimple. If L is co-finite, then clearly $\mathcal{COF} \cup \{L\} = \mathcal{COF} \in \mathbf{TxtEx}^*$. So, suppose L is not co-finite. Then there exists a recursive f such that, for all x, $D_{f(x)} \cap \overline{L} \neq \emptyset$ and for x, y such that $x \neq y$, $D_{f(x)} \cap D_{f(y)} = \emptyset$. Let p_L and p_N be such that $W_{p_L} = L$ and $W_{p_N} = N$. Consider $\mathbf{M}$ defined as follows.

$$\mathbf{M}(\sigma) = \begin{cases} p_N, & \text{if } (\exists x \leq |\sigma|)[D_{f(x)} \subseteq \text{content}(\sigma)]; \\ p_L, & \text{otherwise.} \end{cases}$$

Let T be a text for a language in $\mathcal{COF} \cup \{L\}$. We consider 2 cases.

Case 1: T is a text for L.

Since it is the case that for all x, $D_{f(x)} \cap \overline{L} \neq \emptyset$, it follows that $(\forall \sigma \subset T)(\forall x)[D_{f(x)} \nsubseteq \text{content}(\sigma)]$. Thus, for all n, $\mathbf{M}(T[n]) = p_L$. Thus, $\mathbf{M}$ $\mathbf{TxtEx}^*$-identifies L.

Case 2: T is a text for $L' \in \mathcal{COF}$.

Since L' is co-finite, it follows that $(\overset{\infty}{\forall} x \in \overline{L})[x \in L']$ and $(\overset{\infty}{\forall} x \in L)[x \in L']$. Note also that $\text{card}(x \mid (x \in \overline{L} \text{ and } (\exists y)[x \in D_{f(y)}])$ is infinite. Thus, it is clear that there exists n such that $(\exists x \leq n)[D_{f(x)} \subseteq \text{content}(T[n])]$. From the definition of $\mathbf{M}$, it follows that for all $n' \geq n$, $\mathbf{M}(T[n']) = p_N$. Since L' was an arbitrary co-finite language, it is clear that $\mathbf{M}$ $\mathbf{TxtEx}^*$-identifies $\mathcal{COF}$.

Thus $\mathbf{M}$ $\mathbf{TxtEx}^*$-identifies $\mathcal{COF} \cup \{L\}$. ∎

Corollary 1 $\mathcal{COF}$ *is* **TxtEx****-saturated, but not* **TxtEx****-supersaturated.*

Proof. By Theorem 4, any hypersimple set is **TxtEx***–inadmissible to $\mathcal{COF}$, yet r.e. non-hypersimple, co-infinite sets are **TxtEx***–admissible. ∎

Corollary 2 $\mathcal{COF}$ *is* **TxtFex**$^*_*$*-saturated, but not* **TxtFex**$^*_*$*-supersaturated.*

Proof. This follows from a modification of Theorem 4. We omit details. ∎

Theorem 5. $\mathcal{COF}$ *is not* **TxtBc****-saturated.*

Proof. Let L be any arbitrary language. We will prove that $\mathcal{COF} \cup \{L\} \in$ **TxtBc***.

Let p_L be such that $W_{p_L} = L$. Then, let f be a recursive function such that, for all σ, $W_{f(\sigma)}$ is defined as follows.

1. Initially $W_{f(\sigma)}$ is empty.
2. $i = 0$.
   repeat
       Enumerate i into $W_{f(\sigma)}$.
       $i = i + 1$.
   until content$(\sigma) \subseteq W^i_{p_L}$
3. Enumerate all the elements of W_{p_L} into $W_{f(\sigma)}$.

Suppose σ is such that content$(\sigma) \subseteq L$. Then, there exists an i such that content$(\sigma) \subseteq W^i_{p_L}$. Thus, in the enumeration of $W_{f(\sigma)}$, the **repeat**–loop in step 2 terminates giving $W_{f(\sigma)} =^* L$.

Now suppose σ is such that content$(\sigma) \not\subseteq L$. Then, in the enumeration of $W_{f(\sigma)}$, the **repeat**–loop in step 2 does not terminate. Thus, $W_{f(\sigma)} = N$.

Consider **M** such that, for all σ, $\mathbf{M}(\sigma) = f(\sigma)$. From the preceding assertions, it is clear that **M** **TxtBc***-identifies $\mathcal{COF} \cup \{L\}$. ∎

In fact, the proof of Theorem 5 can be generalized to prove the following. We omit details here.

Corollary 3 ($\forall$ *finite* $\mathcal{L}$)$[\mathcal{COF} \cup \mathcal{L} \in$ **TxtBc***]. ∎

The following separation result from [CL82, OW82a] now follows as a corollary of Theorems 4 and 5.

Corollary 4 **TxtBc*** $-$ **TxtEx*** $\neq \emptyset$.

Proof. Let L be a hypersimple set. Let $\mathcal{L} = \mathcal{COF} \cup \{L\}$. From Theorem 5, $\mathcal{L} \in$ **TxtBc*** and from Theorem 4, $\mathcal{L} \notin$ **TxtEx***. ∎

$\mathcal{L}_0$ is defined in (3) in Section 2.3 above. $\mathcal{L}_0$ is the self referential class used in [CL82] to witness Corollary 4 just above.

Theorem 6. $\mathcal{L}_0$ *is* **TxtBc***-*saturated.*

Proof. We observe first that $\mathcal{COF} \cap \mathcal{L}_0 = \emptyset$ (since any co-finite set contains infinitely many indices for $L_1 = \emptyset$ and $L_2 = N \neq^* L_1$). Now we prove the following claim.

Claim 1 $(\forall$ *finite* $S)(\exists L \in \mathcal{L}_0)[S \subset L]$.

Proof. Fix S. Then, by the operator recursion theorem [Cas74], there exists a monotone increasing recursive function f such that, for all x, $W_{f(x)} = S \cup \{f(w) \mid w \in N\}$.

Let $L = S \cup \{f(x) \mid x \in N\}$. Since $L =^*$ range(f), for monotone increasing recursive function f, it is clear that L is infinite and recursive. Also, $(\overset{\infty}{\forall} x \in L)[W_x = L]$. Hence $L \in \mathcal{L}_0$. This completes the proof of Claim 1. ∎

We now prove that N is **TxtBc***-inadmissible to $\mathcal{L}_0$. Suppose by way of contradiction that $\mathcal{L}_0 \cup \{N\} \in$ **TxtBc***(M). Then, let σ_N be a **TxtBc***-locking sequence for **M** on N.

Let $L \in \mathcal{L}_0$ be such that content$(\sigma_N) \subset L$. From Claim 1, such an L exists. Let $T \supset \sigma_N$ be a text for L. Since $L \notin \mathcal{COF}$, it follows that $(\overset{\infty}{\forall} n)[W_{\mathbf{M}(T[n])} =^* N \neq^* L]$. ∎

Corollary 5 *For all* n, $\mathcal{L}_0$ *is* **TxtBc^n**-*saturated.*

Proof. This corollary follows from Theorem 6 and the fact that, for all n, $\mathcal{L}_0 \in$ **TxtBc^n** $\subset$ **TxtBc***. ∎

References

[BB75]   L. Blum and M. Blum. Toward a mathematical theory of inductive inference. *Information and Control*, 28:125–155, 1975.

[Blu67] M. Blum. A machine independent theory of the complexity of recursive functions. *Journal of the ACM*, 14:322–336, 1967.

[Cas74] J. Case. Periodicity in generations of automata. *Mathematical Systems Theory*, 8:15–32, 1974.

[Cas86] J. Case. Learning machines. In W. Demopoulos and A. Marras, editors, *Language Learning and Concept Acquisition*. Ablex Publishing Company, 1986.

[Cas88] J. Case. The power of vacillation. In D. Haussler and L. Pitt, editors, *Proceedings of the Workshop on Computational Learning Theory*, pages 133–142. Morgan Kaufmann Publishers, Inc., 1988. Expanded in [Cas92].

[Cas92] J. Case. The power of vacillation in language learning. Technical Report 93-08, University of Delaware, 1992. Expands on [Cas88]; journal article under review.

[CL82]   J. Case and C. Lynes. Machine inductive inference and language identification. In M. Nielsen and E. M. Schmidt, editors, *Proceedings of the 9th International Colloquium on Automata, Languages and Programming*, volume 140, pages 107–115. Springer-Verlag, Berlin, 1982.

[Ful85]   M. Fulk. *A Study of Inductive Inference machines.* PhD thesis, SUNY at Buffalo, 1985.

[Ful90]   M. Fulk. Prudence and other conditions on formal language learning. *Information and Computation*, 85:1–11, 1990.

[Gol67]   E. M. Gold. Language identification in the limit. *Information and Control*, 10:447–474, 1967.

[HU79]   J. Hopcroft and J. Ullman. *Introduction to Automata Theory Languages and Computation.* Addison-Wesley Publishing Company, 1979.

[JY81]   D. Joseph and P. Young. Independence results in computer science? *Journal of Computer and System Sciences*, pages 205–222, 1981.

[Kre57]   G. Kreisel. Independent recursive axiomizability. *Journal of Symbolic Logic*, 22:109, 1957.

[McN66]   D. McNeill. Developmental psycholinguistics. In F. Smith and G. A. Miller, editors, *The Genesis of Language*, pages 15–84. MIT Press, 1966.

[MY78]   M. Machtey and P. Young. *An Introduction to the General Theory of Algorithms.* North Holland, New York, 1978.

[OSW82]   D. Osherson, M. Stob, and S. Weinstein. Ideal learning machines. *Cognitive Science*, 6:277–290, 1982.

[OSW84]   D. Osherson, M. Stob, and S. Weinstein. Learning theory and natural language. *Cognition*, 17:1–28, 1984.

[OSW86]   D. Osherson, M. Stob, and S. Weinstein. *Systems that Learn, An Introduction to Learning Theory for Cognitive and Computer Scientists.* MIT Press, Cambridge, Mass., 1986.

[OW82a]   D. Osherson and S. Weinstein. Criteria of language learning. *Information and Control*, 52:123–138, 1982.

[OW82b]   D. Osherson and S. Weinstein. A note on formal learning theory. *Cognition*, 11:77–88, 1982.

[PE68]   M. Pour-El. Independent axiomatization and its relation to the hypersimple set. *Zeitschr. j. math. Logik und Grundlagen d. Math. Bd.*, 14:449–456, 1968.

[Pin79]   S. Pinker. Formal models of language learning. *Cognition*, 7:217–283, 1979.

[Pos44]   E. Post. Recursively enumerable sets of positive integers and their decision problems. *Bulletin of the American Mathematical Society*, 50:284–316, 1944.

[Rog58]   H. Rogers. Gödel numberings of partial recursive functions. *Journal of Symbolic Logic*, 23:331–341, 1958.

[Rog67]   H. Rogers. *Theory of Recursive Functions and Effective Computability.* McGraw Hill, New York, 1967. Reprinted, MIT Press 1987.

[Roy87]   J. Royer. *A Connotational Theory of Program Structure.* Lecture Notes in Computer Science 273. Springer Verlag, 1987.

[WC80]   K. Wexler and P. Culicover. *Formal Principles of Language Acquisition.* MIT Press, Cambridge, Mass, 1980.

[Wex82]   K. Wexler. On extensional learnability. *Cognition*, 11:89–95, 1982.

Inclusion is Undecidable for Pattern Languages *

(Extended Abstract)

Tao Jiang[†] Arto Salomaa[‡] Kai Salomaa[§] Sheng Yu[§]

Abstract

The inclusion problem for (nonerasing) pattern languages was raised by Angluin [1] in 1980. It has been open ever since. In this paper, we settle this open problem and show that inclusion is undecidable for (both erasing and nonerasing) pattern languages. In addition, we show that a special case of the inclusion problem, i.e., the inclusion problem for terminal-free erasing pattern languages, is decidable.

Keywords: patterns, pattern languages, inclusion problems, equivalence problems, decidability

1   Introduction

Instead of an exhaustive definition for a language, [6], it is sometime better to give more leeway in the definition, and try to find *patterns* common to all words in a sample set. Such an approach is especially appropriate if the sample set is growing, for instance, through some learning process. It does not matter if several "equally good" patterns are found. The study of *pattern languages* in the sense understood in this paper was initiated by Angluin, [1], [2].

Trying to infer a pattern common to all words in a given sample is a very typical instance of the process of *inductive inference*, that is, the process of inferring general rules from specific examples. The interrelation with the *theory of learning* is also obvious, especially if the sample is not fixed but is supplemented by new words, or, even better, if one may enquire whether or not some specified words belong to the set.

We refer to [2], [8], and [11] for such interrelations and to [9] for some background information and interconnections with random numbers and Kolmogorov complexity.

---

*The work reported here has been supported by the Natural Sciences and Engineering Research Council of Canada grants OGP0041630 and OGP0046613, an NSERC International Fellowship, and the Project 11281 of the Academy of Finland.

[†]Dept. of Computer Science, McMaster University, Hamilton, Ontario, Canada L8S 4K1

[‡]Academy of Finland and Mathematics Dept., University of Turku, 20500 Turku, Finland

[§]Dept. of Computer Science, University of Western Ontario, London, Ontario, Canada N6A 5B7

Our main result can be stated very simply, without assuming any previous knowledge on the part of the reader. Our alphabet, if not being explicitly specified, is the union $V \cup \Sigma$, where the letters of V are referred to as *variables* and those of Σ as *terminals*. A *pattern* is a word α over $V \cup \Sigma$. The language $L(\alpha)$ defined by the pattern α consists of all words obtained from α by leaving the terminals unchanged and substituting a terminal word for each variable x. The substitution has to be *uniform*: different occurrences of x have to be replaced by the same terminal word. In Angluin's original approach [1] the variables have to be replaced always by *nonempty* words. Such patterns will be referred to as *nonerasing*, or *NE-patterns*, in the sequel. The situation is essentially different if the empty word is allowed in the substitutions (that still have to be uniform). The study of such *erasing*, or *E-patterns*, was initiated in [9]. Thus, both the NE-pattern and the E-pattern α look exactly the same; only their languages $L(\alpha)$ are defined differently. In order to distinguish the two languages, we use $L_E(\alpha)$ and $L_{NE}(\alpha)$ to denote the E-pattern language of α and the NE-pattern language of α, respectively, in the sequel. Whenever the terminal alphabet Σ of a pattern language must also be explicitly specified, we use the notation $L_{E,\Sigma}(\alpha)$ or $L_{NE,\Sigma}(\alpha)$.

A little reflection will show that two NE-patterns define the same language if and only if they are identical, up to an eventual renaming of the variables (cf. [1]). Hence, the decidability of the *equivalence problem* for nonerasing pattern languages is trivial.

In view of the simplicity of the equivalence problem, our main result is very surprising: the *inclusion problem* is undecidable for nonerasing pattern languages. It seems also that people who have worked with this problem (for instance, see [1]) would have expected the opposite result.

As regards E-patterns α and β, we show that the inclusion $L_E(\alpha) \subseteq L_E(\beta)$ is undecidable. The decidability status of the equivalence problem for E-pattern languages is still open.

In the next section, we discuss relationship between the inclusion problem and some classical problems concerning strings, and argue why the inclusion problem is hard. In Section 3, we introduce some basic definitions and notations. In Sections 4 and 5, we prove the undecidability of the inclusion problems for E-pattern languages and NE-pattern languages, respectively. Due to the limit on the number of pages, we only give an abbreviated version of each proof. In the final section, we prove that a special case of the inclusion problem, i.e., the inclusion problem for terminal-free E-pattern languages, is decidable.

2 Why is the inclusion problem hard

The inclusion $L_{NE}(\alpha) \subseteq L_{NE}(\beta)$ can hold for two patterns α and β without α and β having seemingly any connection. The inclusion holds if $\alpha = h(\beta)$, for some nonerasing morphism h that keeps the terminals fixed, but the existence of such a morphism is by no means necessary for the inclusion to hold. For instance, if $\Sigma = \{0, 1\}$ and α is an arbitrary pattern with length at least 6, then

$L_{NE}(\alpha)$ is included in $L_{NE}(xyyz)$. The pattern α is not necessarily a morphic image of $xyyz$; the position of the square yy varies in different words of $L_{NE}(\alpha)$.

Thue's classical results, [12, 6], can be expressed in terms of non-inclusion among NE-pattern languages as follows.

If Σ consists of two letters then, for all n, $L_{NE}(x_1x_2\ldots x_n)$ contains words not belonging to $L_{NE}(xyyyz)$. If Σ contains at least three letters then, for all n, $L_{NE}(x_1x_2\ldots x_n)$ contains words not belonging to $L_{NE}(xyyz)$.

The above results concerning squares and cubes have been extended to arbitrary terminal-free patterns in [4]. We present the definitions in our terminology.

A terminal-free pattern α is termed *unavoidable* (on an alphabet Σ) iff, for some n,

$$L_{NE}(x_1x_2\ldots x_n) \subseteq L_{NE}(x\alpha z),$$

where the x_i's are distinct variables, and x and z are variables not occurring in α. Otherwise, α is *avoidable*.

Thus, yy is unavoidable on two letters but avoidable on three letters. The pattern yyy is avoidable also on two letters. The paper [4] gives a recursive characterization of unavoidable terminal-free patterns. A rather tricky example is the pattern

$$\alpha = xyxzx'yxy'xyx'zx'yx',$$

unavoidable for a suitable Σ. Given a pattern α unavoidable on Σ, it is of interest to find the *smallest n* such that every word of length at least n possesses a subword of pattern α. The following result, obvious from the definitions, shows the interconnection with the inclusion problem.

Any algorithm for solving the inclusion problem for NE-pattern languages can be converted into an algorithm for computing the smallest n such that a given unavoidable pattern cannot be avoided on words of length at least n.

It has been a challenging task in language theory to find natural examples of language families with a decidable equivalence problem and an undecidable inclusion problem. Of course, reverse examples are not possible. This is also one way to approach the borderline between decidable and undecidable.

We mention here the following four such examples: (i) deterministic context-free languages, (ii) simple languages (s-languages) [6], (iii) languages accepted by deterministic multi-tape finite automata [5], and (iv) nonerasing pattern languages. Note that for each of these four language families, (a) the inclusion problem is undecidable, whereas (b) the equivalence problem is decidable except that for (i) the decidability of the equivalence problem is still open [6]. Since we are crossing here the borderline of decidability, it is intuitively clear that if one of the proofs for *(a)* and *(b)* is easy, the other one is difficult. In (iii) the inclusion part is easy and, hence, the equivalence part is difficult. The same holds true as regards (i). (In fact, the equivalence part will be difficult also if undecidability holds, because this part will then be much closer to the borderline.) In (ii) the situation is rather balanced: neither part is very difficult. Among these examples, (iv) is the only one where the equivalence part is easy.

3 Basic notations

Consider two disjoint alphabets Σ (the alphabet of *terminals*) and V (the alphabet of *variables*). Words over $\Sigma \cup V$ are referred to as *patterns*. The length of a word α is denoted $|\alpha|$. Naturally, the length of the empty word λ, $|\lambda|$, is zero. The number of occurrences of $a \in \Sigma \cup V$ in α is denoted $|\alpha|_a$. The set of variables of V appearing in α is denoted $\mathrm{var}(\alpha)$. For an arbitrary set S, the cardinality of S is denoted $card(S)$.

Let Σ and V be given, and let $H_{\Sigma,V}$ be the set of morphisms $h : (\Sigma \cup V)^* \to (\Sigma \cup V)^*$. The language generated by an E-pattern $\alpha \in (\Sigma \cup V)^*$ is defined as

$$L_{E,\Sigma}(\alpha) = \{w \in \Sigma^* | w = h(\alpha) \text{ for some } h \in H_{\Sigma,V} \text{ such that }$$

$$h(a) = a \text{ for each } a \in \Sigma\}.$$

The language generated by an NE-pattern $\alpha \in (\Sigma \cup V)^*$ is

$$L_{NE,\Sigma}(\alpha) = \{w \in \Sigma^* | w = h(\alpha) \text{ for some } \lambda\text{-free } h \in H_{\Sigma,V} \text{ such that }$$

$$h(a) = a \text{ for each } a \in \Sigma\}.$$

If Σ is understood, we use also the notations $L_E(\alpha)$ and $L_{NE}(\alpha)$. A morphism $h \in H_{\Sigma,V}$ such that $h(a) = a$ for each $a \in \Sigma$ is usually defined just as a mapping $V \to (\Sigma \cup V)^*$ in the following.

4 The inclusion problem for E-pattern languages

In this section, we show that the inclusion problem for E-pattern languages is undecidable by reducing to this problem the question whether a nondeterministic two-counter automaton without input has an accepting computation. A nondeterministic 2-counter automaton without input is denoted as a quintuple

$$(1) \qquad\qquad M = (Q, q_0, Q_F, 0, \delta),$$

where Q is the finite set of states, $q_0 \in Q$ is the initial state, $Q_F \subseteq Q$ is the set of final states, $0 \notin Q$ is the single symbol of the stack alphabet, and $\delta \subseteq Q \times \{0,1\}^2 \times Q \times \{-1,0,1\}^2$ is the transition relation of the automaton. In a transition $(q_1, x_1, x_2, q_2, y_1, y_2) \in \delta$, q_1 denotes the present state, q_2 the new state, x_i is 0 or 1 depending on whether the ith, $1 \leq i \leq 2$, counter is empty or not, and the value of y_i determines the change of contents of the ith counter in the corresponding transition. We assume that if $x_i = 0$ then $y_i \geq 0$, $i = 1, 2$. For a formal definition see e.g. [7]. The set of configurations of M is $\mathrm{conf}(M) = 0^* Q 0^*$. The computation relation $\Rightarrow_M$ on the set of configurations is determined by the transition relation δ in the natural way.

Let $\#$ be a new symbol not appearing in $Q \cup \{0\}$. An accepting computation of M is a word $W_c \in (Q \cup \{0, \#\})^*$ that can be written as follows:

$$(2) \qquad\qquad W_c = \#C_1 \# C_2 \# \cdots \# C_m \#,$$

where $m \geq 1$, $C_1 = q_0$, $C_m = u_1 q u_2$, $q \in Q_F$, $u_1, u_2 \in 0^*$, $C_i \in \mathrm{conf}(M)$, $i = 2, \ldots, m-1$, and $C_i \Rightarrow_M C_{i+1}$, $i = 1, \ldots, m-1$. It is well known that the emptiness problem for deterministic 2-counter automata is undecidable, cf. e.g. [3, 7, 10]. Thus it is also clearly undecidable whether a nondeterministic 2-counter automaton without input has an accepting computation. Now we can state the main result of this section.

Theorem 4.1 *Given a terminal alphabet Σ, a set of variables V, and two arbitrary patterns $\beta_1, \beta_2 \in (\Sigma \cup V)^*$, it is in general undecidable whether*

$$L_{E,\Sigma}(\beta_1) \subseteq L_{E,\Sigma}(\beta_2).$$

Proof. Let $M = (Q, q_0, Q_F, 0, \delta)$ be an arbitrary 2-counter automaton as in (1). We construct patterns $\beta_1, \beta_2 \in (\Sigma \cup V)^*$ such that $L_{E,\Sigma}(\beta_1) \not\subseteq L_{E,\Sigma}(\beta_2)$ iff M has an accepting computation. Choose $\Sigma = Q \cup \{0, \$, \star, @, \#, \&\}$, where $\$$, $\star$, @, $\#$, $\&$ are new symbols not belonging to $Q \cup \{0\}$. The set of variables V will consist of all variables appearing in the patterns β_1 and β_2 constructed below.

Define

$$\beta_1 = \star\$ \star x \star y \star \$ \star \star p_0 \star \star \$@,$$

where x and y are variables and p_0 is a constant pattern (over Σ) of the form

$$p_0 = @@w_1 @@w_2 @@ \cdots @@w_k @@, \quad w_i \in \Sigma^*, i = 1, \ldots, k.$$

The choice of the integer k and of the words $w_1, \ldots, w_k \in \Sigma^*$ will be explained later.

The pattern β_2 is defined as $\beta_{21}\$\beta_{22}$ where

$$\beta_{21} = x_1 \cdots x_k \$ x_1 r_1 x_1 s_1 x_1 \cdots x_k r_k x_k s_k x_k,$$

$$\beta_{22} = x_1 x_1 z_1^{left} t_1 z_1^{right} x_1 x_1 \cdots x_k x_k z_k^{left} t_k z_k^{right} x_k x_k \$ z_1 \cdots z_k.$$

Here $x_1, \ldots, x_k$, $z_1, \ldots, z_k$ are distinct variables and for $i \in \{1, \ldots, k\}$:

$$z_i^{left} = z_i z_i y_{i,1} z_i z_i y_{i,2} z_i z_i \cdots z_i z_i y_{i,i-1} z_i z_i, \text{ and, } z_i^{right} = z_i z_i y_{i,i+1} z_i z_i \cdots z_i z_i y_{i,k} z_i z_i.$$

Above $y_{i,j}$ is a distinct variable for each pair (i, j). The symbols r_i, s_i, t_i denote terminal-free patterns (in V^*) and their construction will be explained later. We always assume that for every $i \in \{1, \ldots, k\}$, the variables of $\mathrm{var}(r_i) \cup \mathrm{var}(s_i) \cup \mathrm{var}(t_i)$ do not appear anywhere else in β_2 except in the subpatterns r_i, s_i, and t_i.

The set of all mappings $\{x, y\} \to \Sigma^*$ is denoted by H. For each $i = 1, \ldots, k$ we define a unary predicate P_i on the set H as follows. For $h \in H$: $h \in P_i$ iff there exists a mapping

$$g : \mathrm{var}(r_i) \cup \mathrm{var}(s_i) \cup \mathrm{var}(t_i) \to \Sigma^* \text{ such that } g(r_i) = h(x), \ g(s_i) = h(y), \ g(t_i) = w_i.$$

We denote $\mathrm{var}(P_i) = \mathrm{var}(r_i) \cup \mathrm{var}(s_i) \cup \mathrm{var}(t_i)$, $i = 1, \ldots, k$. Our aim is to choose k and the tuples (w_i, r_i, s_i, t_i), $i = 1, \ldots, k$, so that for all $h \in H$:

(i) $h(\beta_1) \in L_{E,\Sigma}(\beta_2)$ iff $h \in \bigcup_{i=1}^{k} P_i$;

(ii) $h \notin \bigcup_{i=1}^{k} P_i$ iff $h(x)$ is an accepting computation of M (as in (2)) and $h(y) \in 0^*$ is longer than the catenation of any two 0-subwords of $h(x)$. (The latter condition on $h(y)$ enables us to define the condition "$h(x)$ is an accepting computation" using the predicates P_i.)

We say that a mapping $h \in H$ is of *good form* if

(3) $$h(x) \in (\Sigma - \{\$, \star, @, \&\})^* \text{ and } h(y) \in 0^*.$$

First for a suitable $k_1 < k$ we define the predicates $P_1, \ldots, P_{k_1}$ so that for $h \in H$: h is not of good form iff $h \in \bigcup_{i=1}^{k_1} P_i$. Let $k_1 = \text{card}(\Sigma) + 3$. The predicates P_i, $i = 1, 2, 3$, are given by the condition:

(4) $$r_i = a_1 b a_2, \ s_i = c, \ t_i = b, \ w_i = A,$$

where a_1, a_2, b, c are variables and A assumes the values $\$, \star, \&$. Then clearly $h \in H$ satisfies P_i defined by (4) iff the word $h(x)$ contains the symbol A.

Because of technical reasons for the symbol @ we need a slightly different predicate P_4:

$$r_4 = a_1 b a_2, \ s_4 = c, \ t_4 = dbd, \ w_4 = \&@\&,$$

where a_1, a_2, b, c, and d are variables. Again it is clear that $h \in P_4$ iff $|h(x)|_@ \neq 0$.

Similarly, the predicates P_i, $i = 5, \ldots, k_1 - 1$, are defined by the condition

$$r_i = c, \ s_i = a_1 b a_2, \ t_i = b, \ w_i = A,$$

where a_1, a_2, b, c are variables and the constant A assumes all values from $\Sigma - \{0, @\}$. We define the predicate P_{k_1} corresponding to the symbol @:

$$r_{k_1} = c, \ s_{k_1} = a_1 b a_2, \ t_{k_1} = dbd, \ w_{k_1} = \&@\&.$$

Thus $h \notin \bigcup_{i=5}^{k_1} P_i$ iff $h(y) \in 0^*$. The following claim follows immediately from the above observations.

Claim 1. $h \in H$ is of good form iff $h \notin \bigcup_{i=1}^{k_1} P_i$.

In the following, the predicates $P_1, \ldots, P_{k_1}$ are called BAD_FORM predicates and the as yet undefined predicates P_i, $k_1 < i \leq k$, are called INV_COMP (invalid computation) predicates. Exactly two of the constant words w_i, $1 \leq i \leq k_1$, are equal to $\$$ (resp. $\star$) and in all other cases w_i does not contain the symbol $\$$ (resp. $\star$). Similarly, exactly two of the words w_i, $1 \leq i \leq k_1$, are equal to $\&@\&$ and in all other cases w_i does not contain the symbol @. We still postpone the definition of the INV_COMP predicates but we here make the restriction that none of the constant words w_i, $k_1 < i \leq k$, contains any of the symbols $\$$, $\star$ or @. Thus the following conditions hold:

(5) $$| p_0 |_\$ = 2;$$

(6) $$| p_0 |_\star = 2, \ p_0 \notin \{\star\}\Sigma^* \cup \Sigma^*\{\star\} \cup \Sigma^*\{\star\star\}\Sigma^*;$$

(7) p_0 contains $k+1$ occurrences of the subword @@ that are all pairwise non-overlapping.

The following claim holds independently of how we define the INV_COMP predicates, assuming only the above mentioned restrictions on the words w_i guaranteeing (5), (6) and (7).

Claim 2. Let $h \in H$. Then $h(\beta_1) \in L_{E,\Sigma}(\beta_2)$ iff $h \in \bigcup_{i=1}^k P_i$.

Proof of Claim 2. Assume first that $h \in P_i$ for some i, $1 \le i \le k$, i.e., there exists a mapping $g : \mathrm{var}(P_i) \to \Sigma^*$ such that $g(r_i) = h(x)$, $g(s_i) = h(y)$, and $g(t_i) = w_i$. It is straightforward to construct an extension of g, $g' : \mathrm{var}(\beta_2) \to \Sigma^*$ such that $g'(\beta_2) = h(\beta_1)$ which implies then that $h(\beta_1) \in L_{E,\Sigma}(\beta_2)$.

Conversely, assume that $h(\beta_1) \in L_{E,\Sigma}(\beta_2)$. By Claim 1, if h is not of good form then h satisfies one of the BAD_FORM predicates. Thus without loss of generality we may assume that $h(x)$ and $h(y)$ are as in (3). Let $g : \mathrm{var}(\beta_2) \to \Sigma^*$ be a mapping such that $g(\beta_2) = h(\beta_1)$. Since h is of good form it follows from (5) that $h(\beta_1)$ contains exactly 5 occurrences of the symbol $\$$. Thus clearly none of the words $g(x_i)$, $i = 1, \ldots, k$, contains the symbol $\$$ and this implies that necessarily $g(x_1 \cdots x_k) = \star$, i.e., there exists $m \in \{1, \ldots, k\}$ such that

$$g(x_j) = \begin{cases} \star, & \text{if } j = m; \\ \lambda, & \text{if } j \ne m, 1 \le j \le k. \end{cases}$$

Again by (5), none of the words $g(z_i)$, $i = 1, \ldots, k$, contains the symbol $\$$ and thus there exists $n \in \{1, \ldots, k\}$ such that

$$g(z_j) = \begin{cases} @, & \text{if } j = n; \\ \lambda, & \text{if } j \ne n, 1 \le j \le k. \end{cases}$$

Since h is of good form it follows from (6) that $h(\beta_1)$ contains exactly two occurrences of the subword $\star\star$. These must coincide with the two subwords $g(x_m x_m) = \star\star$ of the word $g(\beta_2)$ and it follows that necessarily $m = n$. This implies that

$$g(r_m) = h(x), \ g(s_m) = h(y),$$

(8)
$$g(z_m^{left} t_m z_m^{right}) = p_0,$$

and for all $j \ne m$,

$$g(r_j) = g(s_j) = g(t_j) = g(z_j^{left}) = g(z_j^{right}) = \lambda.$$

By (7), p_0 contains exactly $k+1$ non-overlapping occurrences of the subword @@ and by (8) these must coincide with the $k+1$ subword occurrences $g(z_m z_m) = @@$ in the word $g(z_m^{left} t_m z_m^{right})$. Hence necessarily $g(t_m) = w_m$ and $g(y_{m,j}) = w_j$, $j = 1, \ldots, m-1, m+1, \ldots, k$. Thus $h \in P_m$ and this concludes the proof of the claim. $\square$

It remains to define the INV_COMP predicates $P_{k_1+1}, \ldots, P_k$ so that if h does not satisfy any of the BAD_FORM or INV_COMP predicates then $h(x)$ is necessarily a coding of an accepting computation of the automaton M. First we define a predicate P_i such that the negation of P_i forces $h(y)$ to be longer than the catenation of any two 0-subwords of the word $h(x)$. This property of $h(y)$ will be useful in defining the other INV_COMP predicates that are used to check that $h(x)$ is not a coding of an accepting computation. Below the symbols a, b, c, d, e with possible subscripts denote always new variables that do not appear in any other predicate.

- "$h(y)$ is a catenation of two subwords of $h(x)$": The predicate P_i is defined by

$$r_i = a_1 b_1 a_2 b_2 a_3, \ s_i = b_1 b_2, \ t_i = w_i = \lambda.$$

- "$h(x)$ begins with some symbol other than #": For each $A \in Q \cup \{0\}$ we define a predicate P_i by

$$r_i = ba, \ s_i = c, \ t_i = b, \ w_i = A.$$

Analogously one defines: "$h(x)$ ends with some symbol other than #."

If $h \in H$ does not satisfy any of the BAD_FORM predicates or the predicates defined above then we can write

(9) $$h(x) = \#f_1\#f_2\# \cdots \#f_m\#,$$

$m \geq 0$, $f_i \in (Q \cup \{0\})^*$, $i = 1, \ldots, m$, and $h(y) = 0^n$, $n \geq 1$, where 0^n is longer than the catenation of any two 0-subwords of $h(x)$.

It is easy to define predicates whose negations guarantee that each f_j, $1 \leq j \leq m$, belongs to conf(M), $f_1 = q_0$, $q_m \in 0^* Q_F 0^*$, and the transition from f_j to f_{j+1}, $1 \leq j \leq m-1$, increments or decrements the counters by at most one symbol. The details are omitted in this extended abstract. Finally, assuming that any transition from f_j to f_{j+1} makes a change of at most one symbol in both counters we can describe the invalid computation steps using a finite number of the predicates P_i. We give one such predicate as an example below. By going through all possibilities whether the counters are initially empty or not, and whether the transition increments, decrements or does not change the contents of each counter, for given states q_1 and q_2 one defines analogously the remaining 24 different conditions describing an invalid computation step with state transition from q_1 to q_2.

- "Assuming that in f_j both counters are nonempty, the transition from f_j to f_{j+1} changes the state from q_1 to q_2, increments the first counter (by one) and decrements the second counter (by one) but this is not a valid computation step": For every pair of states $(q_1, q_2) \in Q^2$ such that $(q_1, 1, 1, q_2, 1, -1) \notin \delta$ define the condition P_i by

$$r_i = ac_1 db_1 c_2 dac_1 ddb_2 c_2 a, \ s_i = c_1 c_2 c_3, \ t_i = aeb_1 eb_2 ed, \ w_i = \#\&q_1\&q_2\&0.$$

Note that here we need the assumption that $h(y)$ is longer than the catenation of any two 0-subwords of $h(x)$.

309

If $h \in H$ does not satisfy any of the BAD_FORM or INV_COMP predicates, then $h(x)$ given by (9) describes an accepting computation of the automaton M. Conversely, assume that M has an accepting computation W_c as in (2). Denote $n = \max\{ j \mid 0^j$ is a subword of $W_c \}$ and define $h \in H$ by setting $h(x) = W_c$, $h(y) = 0^{2n+1}$. Then clearly $h \notin \bigcup_{i=1}^{k} P_i$. By Claim 2 it follows thus that $L_{E,\Sigma}(\beta_1) \subseteq L_{E,\Sigma}(\beta_2)$ iff M does not have an accepting computation. This concludes the proof. $\square$

In the proof of Theorem 4.1 the pattern β_2 does not contain any other terminal symbols than \$. Thus the following result is an immediate consequence of the proof of Theorem 4.1.

Corollary 4.1 *Given two arbitrary patterns $\beta_1 \in (\Sigma \cup V)^*$ and $\beta_2 \in (\{c\} \cup V)^*$ where Σ is a terminal alphabet, $c \in \Sigma$, and V is a set of variables, it is in general undecidable whether or not $L_{E,\Sigma}(\beta_1) \subseteq L_{E,\Sigma}(\beta_2)$.*

5 The inclusion problem for NE-pattern languages

The decidability of the inclusion problem for NE-patterns was left open in [1]. Here we show that the inclusion problem is undecidable for NE-pattern languages. This is done by reducing the question of deciding inclusion of E-pattern languages to the inclusion problem for NE-pattern languages. The former question was shown to be undecidable in the previous section. In the reduction we use the slightly strengthened form of the undecidability result in Corollary 4.1. First we need a simple technical lemma.

Lemma 5.1 *Let V be a set of variables, Σ be a terminal alphabet and $\Omega \subseteq \Sigma$. Consider a pattern $p \in (\Omega \cup V)^*$. Then there exist effectively $m \geq 1$ and patterns $p_1, \ldots, p_m \in (\Omega \cup V)^*$ such that*

$$L_{E,\Sigma}(p) = \bigcup_{i=1}^{m} L_{NE,\Sigma}(p_i).$$

Theorem 5.1 *Given a terminal alphabet Σ, a set of variables V and two patterns $\alpha_1, \alpha_2 \in (\Sigma \cup V)^*$ it is undecidable in general whether*

(10) $$L_{NE,\Sigma}(\alpha_1) \subseteq L_{NE,\Sigma}(\alpha_2).$$

Proof. We proceed by contradiction. Assuming that for given patterns α_1 and α_2 one can decide whether (10) holds we show that the problem of Corollary 4.1 would also be decidable. For this purpose let Σ be a terminal alphabet, $0 \in \Sigma$ a fixed symbol, V a set of variables, and $\beta_1 \in (\Sigma \cup V)^*$, $\beta_2 \in (\{0\} \cup V)^*$ arbitrary given patterns. By Lemma 5.1 there exist patterns $p_1, \ldots, p_m \in (\Sigma \cup V)^*$ and $q_1, \ldots, q_n \in (\{0\} \cup V)^*$, $m, n \geq 1$, such that

$$L_{E,\Sigma}(\beta_1) = \bigcup_{i=1}^{m} L_{NE,\Sigma}(p_i), \text{ and, } L_{E,\Sigma}(\beta_2) = \bigcup_{j=1}^{n} L_{NE,\Sigma}(q_j).$$

Thus to decide whether $L_{E,\Sigma}(\beta_1) \subseteq L_{E,\Sigma}(\beta_2)$, it is sufficient to decide for each $i = 1, \ldots, m$, whether

$$(11) \qquad L_{NE,\Sigma}(p_i) \subseteq \bigcup_{j=1}^{n} L_{NE,\Sigma}(q_j).$$

Let i be an arbitrary number in $\{1, \ldots, m\}$. We construct a terminal alphabet Ω, a set of variables Y and patterns $p'_i, q \in (\Omega \cup Y)^*$ such that (11) holds iff

$$(12) \qquad L_{NE,\Omega}(p'_i) \subseteq L_{NE,\Omega}(q).$$

We introduce two new terminal symbols \$ and $\star$ and let $\Omega = \Sigma \cup \{\$, \star\}$. The set Y will consist of all variables appearing in the patterns p'_i and q constructed below.

By renaming the variables in q_j, $1 \le j \le n$, we can assume that $\mathrm{var}(q_j) \cap \mathrm{var}(q_l) = \emptyset$ for all $1 \le j, l \le n$, $j \ne l$. Denote $k = \sum_{j=1}^{n} |q_j|$. The pattern p'_i is defined by

$$p'_i = 0^{2n+8} \star \star 0^{2n+8} \$\$ 0^{2n+k+18} \star p_i \star 0^{2n+k+18} \$\$ p_0 \$\$ p_0 \$\$ p_0 \$\$ p_0,$$

where $p_0 = 0^4 \star \$ \star \star \star \star 0^4$. Let $x_1, \ldots, x_{n+4}$, y_j, y'_j, $j = 1, \ldots, 6$, u_l, z_l, $l = 1, \ldots, 4$, be distinct variables not belonging to $\bigcup_{j=1}^{n} \mathrm{var}(q_j)$. We denote

$$r_1 = u_1 z_1, \quad r_2 = z_2 u_2, \quad r_3 = z_3 u_3 z_4, \quad r_4 = u_4.$$

Now the pattern q is defined as

$$q = Q_1 \$\$ Q_2 \$\$ Q_3 \$\$ Q_4 \$\$ Q_5 \$\$ Q_6,$$

where

- $Q_1 = y_1 x_1 x_1 x_2 x_2 \cdots x_{n+4} x_{n+4} y'_1$,

- $Q_2 = y_2 x_1 q_1 x_1 \cdots x_n q_n x_n x_{n+1} r_1 x_{n+1} \cdots x_{n+4} r_4 x_{n+4} y'_2$,

- $Q_j = y_j x_{n+j-2} u_{j-2} x_{n+j-2} y'_j$, $j = 3, \ldots, 6$.

Due to the limit on the number of pages, we omit the formal proof of the equivalence of (11) and (12). The idea is similar to that of the proof of Theorem 4.1 and below we only outline it briefly.

Assume that (11) holds and let h be an arbitrary mapping $\mathrm{var}(p'_i) \to \Omega^+$. If $h(p_i) \in \Sigma^+$, then by (11) there exist $j \in \{1, \ldots, n\}$ and $f : \mathrm{var}(q_j) \to \Sigma^+$ such that $f(q_j) = h(p_i)$. Then we can define $g : \mathrm{var}(q) \to \Omega^+$ such that $h(p'_i) = g(q)$ by "matching" the subpattern p_i of p'_i to the subpattern q_j of q. If $h(p_i)$ contains a symbol \$ or $\star$ then p_i is "matched" to a suitable subpattern r_l, $1 \le l \le 4$, of q.

Conversely, assume that (12) holds and let h be an arbitrary mapping $\mathrm{var}(p_i) \to \Sigma^+$. Then $h(p'_i) \in L_{NE,\Omega}(q)$ and from the construction of the patterns p'_i and q it can be verified that the subpattern p_i of p'_i necessarily has to be matched with some subpattern q_j, $1 \le j \le n$, of q. From this it follows that $h(p_i) \in \bigcup_{j=1}^{n} L_{NE,\Sigma}(q_j)$. $\square$

6   Other results

The main result of this section is that the inclusion problem for terminal-free E-pattern languages is decidable. The equivalence problem for E-pattern languages in general is still open.

Let $V = \{x_1, \ldots, x_n\}$ be a set of variables and Σ be an alphabet such that $card(\Sigma) \geq 2$. For each pair of letters a, b in Σ, $a \neq b$, and an integer $k > 0$, we define a morphism $\tau_{k,a,b} : V^* \to V^*$ by

$$\tau_{k,a,b}(x_i) = ab^{ki+1}aab^{ki+2}a \ldots ab^{k(i+1)}a, \ 1 \leq i \leq n.$$

Lemma 6.1 *Let $\alpha, \beta \in V^+$ be two arbitrary terminal-free patterns, and a, b be two distinct letters in Σ. Then $\tau_{|\beta|,a,b}(\alpha) \in L_{E,\Sigma}(\beta)$ if and only if there exists a morphism $h : V^* \to V^*$ such that $h(\beta) = \alpha$.*

Proof. The *if* part of the lemma is trivially true. We prove the *only if* part as follows.

Let $k = |\beta|$. Since $\tau_{k,a,b}(\alpha)$ is in $L_{E,\Sigma}(\beta)$, there exists a morphism $\nu : V^* \to \Sigma^*$ such that $\nu(\beta) = \tau_{k,a,b}(\alpha)$. For each $x \in V$, according to the definition of $\tau_{k,a,b}$, $\tau_{k,a,b}(x)$ consists of k segments of the form $ab^j a$. Therefore, for each $x_i \in var(\alpha)$, there must exist at least one segment $ab^{j_i}a$, $ki + 1 \leq j_i \leq k(i+1)$, such that none of the appearance(s) of this segment in $\nu(\beta)$ is split by any partition of $\nu(\beta)$ into $\nu(\beta_1)$ and $\nu(\beta_2)$ such that $\beta = \beta_1\beta_2$. For each $x \in var(\alpha)$, we choose one such segment to be named as the anchor segment of x in $\tau_{k,a,b}(\alpha)$ with respect to β. We also say that this segment anchors x.

We define a morphism $h : V^* \to V^*$ by the following: For each $y \in var(\beta)$, let

$$ab^{j_{i_1}}aab^{j_{i_2}}a \ldots ab^{j_{i_r}}a, \ r \geq 0$$

be the word obtained from $\nu(y)$ by deleting all the incomplete segments and segments that are not anchor segments. Note that the indices $i_1, i_2, \ldots, i_r$ are not necessarily distinct. Here, a segment $ab^{j_{i_s}}a$ anchors a variable $x_{i_s} \in var(\alpha)$, $1 \leq i_s \leq n$. Then we define

$$h(y) = x_{i_1}x_{i_2} \ldots x_{i_r}.$$

For each $y \notin var(\beta)$, $h(y) = \lambda$. It easy to see that $h(\beta) = \alpha$ since each appearance of x in α has exactly one anchor segment with respect to β. □

Theorem 6.1 *Let $\alpha, \beta \in X^+$ be two arbitrarily given terminal-free patterns. Then $L_{E,\Sigma}(\alpha) \subseteq L_{E,\Sigma}(\beta)$ if and only if there exists a morphism $h : V^* \to V^*$ such that $h(\beta) = \alpha$.*

Proof. The *only if* part is proved by Lemma 6.1. The *if* part is trivial. □

From the above results, we can easily obtain the following corollaries.

Corollary 6.1 *Let $\alpha, \beta \in V^+$ be two arbitrary terminal-free patterns and Σ be an alphabet, $card(\Sigma) \geq 2$. Then $L_{E,\Sigma}(\alpha) \subseteq L_{E,\Sigma}(\beta)$ if and only if $\tau_{|\beta|,a,b}(\alpha) \in L_{E,\Sigma}(\beta)$ for $a, b \in \Sigma$ and $a \neq b$.*

Corollary 6.2 *Given two terminal-free patterns $\alpha, \beta \in V^+$ and an alphabet Σ, the inclusion problem, i.e., the question of whether or not $L_{E,\Sigma}(\alpha) \subseteq L_{E,\Sigma}(\beta)$, is decidable.*

Note that the inclusion problem for terminal-free NE-pattern languages is still open, as well as the equivalence problem for general E-pattern languages. We conjecture that the latter problem is decidable. We have proved strong necessary conditions for the equivalence of two E-pattern languages. The result will be presented in the full version of this paper.

References

[1] D. Angluin, "Finding patterns common to a set of strings", *Journal of Computer and System Sciences* 21 (1980) 46-62.

[2] D. Angluin, "Inductive inference of formal languages from positive data", *Information and Control* 45 (1980) 117-135.

[3] B.S. Baker and R.V. Book, "Reversal-bounded multipushdown machines", *Journal of Computer and System Sciences* 8 (1974) 315–332.

[4] D. R. Bean, A. Ehrenfeucht, and G. F. McNulty, "Avoidable patterns in strings of symbols", *Pacific Journal of Mathematics* 85 (1979) 261-294.

[5] T. Harju and J. Karhumäki, "The equivalence problem of multitape finite automata", *Theoretical Computer Science* 78 (1991) 347-355.

[6] M. A. Harrison, *Introduction to Formal Language Theory*, Addison-Wesley, Reading, 1978.

[7] O.H. Ibarra, "Reversal-bounded multicounter machines and their decision problems", *Journal of the Association for Computing Machinery* 25 (1978) 116–133.

[8] O. Ibarra and T. Jiang "Learning regular languages from counterexamples", *Journal of Computer and System Sciences*, 43 (1991) 299-316.

[9] T. Jiang, E. Kinber, A. Salomaa, K. Salomaa, S. Yu, "Pattern languages with and without erasing", to appear in the *International Journal of Computer Mathematics*.

[10] M.L. Minsky, "Recursive unsolvability of Post's problem of 'Tag' and other topics in theory of Turing machines", *Annals of Mathematics* 74 (1961) 437–455.

[11] N. Tanida and T. Yokomori, "Polynomial-time identification of strictly regular languages in the limit", *IEICE Trans. Inf. and Syst.* E75-D (1992) 125-132.

[12] A. Thue, "Über unendliche Zeichenreihen", *Norske Vid. Selsk. Skr., I Mat. Nat. Kl., Christiania* 7 (1906) 1-22.

New Decidability Results Concerning Two-way Counter Machines and Applications

Oscar H. Ibarra*, Tao Jiang**, Nicholas Tran*, Hui Wang***

Abstract. We look at some decision questions concerning two-way counter machines and obtain the strongest decidable results to date concerning these machines. In particular, we show that the emptiness, containment, and equivalence problems are decidable for two-way counter machines whose counter is reversal-bounded (i.e., the counter alternates between increasing and decreasing modes at most a fixed number of times). We use this result to give a simpler proof of a recent result that the emptiness, containment, and equivalence problems for two-way reversal-bounded pushdown automata accepting bounded languages (i.e., subsets of $w_1^* \ldots w_k^*$ for some nonnull words $w_1, \ldots, w_k$) are decidable. Other applications concern decision questions about simple programs. Finally, we show that nondeterministic two-way reversal-bounded multicounter machines are effectively equivalent to finite automata on unary languages, and hence their emptiness, containment, and equivalence problems are decidable also.

1 Introduction

A fundamental decision question concerning any class C of language recognizers is whether there exists an algorithm to decide the following question: given an arbitrary machine M in C, is the language accepted by M empty? This is known as the emptiness problem (for C). Decidability (existence of an algorithm) of emptiness leads to the decidability of other questions such as containment and equivalence (given arbitrary machines M_1 and M_2 in C, is the language accepted by M_1 contained (respectively, equal to) the language accepted by M_2) if the class of languages defined by C is effectively closed under union and complementation.

The simplest recognizers are the finite automata. It is well known that all the different varieties of finite automata (one-way, two-way, etc.) are effectively equivalent, and the class has decidable emptiness, containment, and equivalence (ECE, for short) problems.

When the two-way finite automaton is augmented with a storage device, such as a counter, a pushdown stack or a Turing machine tape, the ECE problems become undecidable (no algorithms exist). In fact, it follows from a result in [Min61] that the emptiness problem is undecidable for two-way counter machines even over a unary

* Department of Computer Science, University of California, Santa Barbara, CA 93106. Research supported in part by NSF Grant CCR89-18409.

** Department of Computer Science and Systems, McMaster University, Hamilton, Ontario L8S 4K1, Canada. Research supported in part by NSERC Operating Grant OGP 0046613.

*** Department of Computer Science, University of Alabama in Huntsville, AL 35899.

input alphabet. If one restricts the machines to make only a finite number of turns on the input tape, the ECE problems are still undecidable, even for the case when the input head makes only one turn [Iba78]. However, for one-way counter machines, it is known that the equivalence (hence also the emptiness) problem is decidable, but the containment problem is undecidable [VP75]. The situation is different when we restrict both the input and counter. It has been shown that the ECE problems are decidable for counter machines with a finite-turn input and a reversal-bounded counter (the number of alternation between increasing and decreasing modes is finite, independent of the input) [Iba78]. It is also known that the ECE problems are decidable for two-way counter machines with a reversal-bounded counter accepting bounded languages (subsets of $w_1^* \ldots w_k^*$ for some nonnull words $w_1, \ldots, w_k$) [GI82]. Note that these machines can accept fairly complex languages. For example, it can recognize the language consisting of strings of the form $0^i 1^j$ where i divides j. The decidability for the general case when the input is not over a bounded language was left open in [GI82]. We resolve this question here: we show that the ECE problems are decidable for two-way reversal-bounded counter machines. We believe this is the largest known class of machines, which are a natural generalization of the two-way finite automaton, for which the ECE problems are decidable. This result has some nice applications. We use it to give a simpler proof of a recent result that the emptiness, containment, and equivalence problems for two-way reversal-bounded pushdown automata accepting bounded languages (i.e., subsets of $w_1^* \ldots w_k^*$ for some nonnull words $w_1, \ldots, w_k$) are decidable. Other applications of this result concern decision questions about some special classes of simple programs.

Finally, we consider the nondeterministic version of reversal-bounded multicounter machines. We show that when the input alphabet is unary, these machines accept only regular languages. Since the proof is constructive, we obtain as corollaries that the emptiness, containment, and equivalence problems for these machines are also decidable. This resolves an open question raised in [GI79], where a similar result was shown for deterministic such machines. This is the strongest result one can obtain since it is known that deterministic reversal-bounded 2-counter machines over $a_1^* \ldots a_k^*$ (for distinct symbols $a_1, \ldots, a_k$ for some k) can accept nonsemilinear sets and have an undecidable emptiness problem [Iba78].

The rest of this paper is organized as follows. In Section 2, we show the decidability of the ECE problems for two-way reversal-bounded counter machines. We give the applications in Section 3. Finally, we show the effective equivalence of two-way reversal-bounded nondeterministic multicounter machines and finite automata over unary languages, along with the decidability of their ECE problems in Section 4.

In the remainder of this section, we define the models of computation of interest and related concepts. A *language* L is a subset of $\{0, 1\}^*$. A language is *strictly bounded* over k letters $a_1, a_2, \ldots, a_k$ if it is a subset of $a_1^* a_2^* \ldots a_k^*$. A language is *bounded* over k nonnull words $w_1, w_2, \ldots, w_k$ if it is a subset of $w_1^* w_2^* \ldots w_k^*$. A *counter machine* is a finite automaton augmented with a counter, whose value can be incremented, decremented, or tested for zero. An r-input reversal 2DCM is a two-way counter machine whose input head makes at most r reversals (but the counter is unrestricted). A two-way machine is *sweeping* if the input head reverses only on the endmarkers. *2DCM(c, r)* denotes the class of deterministic machines having a two-way input head and c counters, each of which makes at most r reversals in any computation. *2NCM(c, r)* denotes the corresponding nondeterministic class. *2DPDA(r)* denotes the class of two-way deterministic pushdown automata whose pushdown stack makes at most r reversals. *2NPDA(r)* denotes the nondeterministic class.

In the following sections, we will study the emptiness problems for the above machines on bounded languages. A straightforward argument shows that a machine of any type studied in this paper accepts a nonempty bounded language if and only if there is another machine of the same type that accepts a nonempty *strictly* bounded language. So when we are dealing with the emptiness question for machines over bounded languages, we need only handle the case when the machines accept strictly bounded languages.

Note: Due to the space constraint, we omit or abbreviate some proofs in this paper. They will appear in the full version.

2 Reversal-Bounded Counter Machines

It was shown in [Iba78] that many decision problems such as emptiness, containment, and equivalence for the class $2DCM(c,r)$ for $c \geq 2$ and $r \geq 1$ are undecidable. The same paper raised the question of the decidability of these problems for $2DCM(1,r)$ for $r \geq 1$. A partial answer was given in [GI82], where it was shown that the emptiness problem for $2DCM(1,r)$ for $r \geq 1$ over bounded languages is decidable.

In this section we give a complete answer to this question; we show that the emptiness, equivalence, and containment problems for the class $2DCM(1,r)$, where $r \geq 1$, are decidable. First, we consider the emptiness problem and improve the result of Gurari and Ibarra by removing the requirement that the language be bounded.

Theorem 1. *The emptiness problem for 2DCM(1,r) is decidable for every $r \geq 1$.*

Proof. Fix an $r \geq 1$, and let M be a *2DCM(1,r)* with q states. We show that if $L(M) \neq \emptyset$, then M must accept an input in some bounded language over k words $w_1, w_2, \ldots, w_k$, where k and $w_1, w_2, \ldots, w_k$ are effectively computable from M. Suppose M accepts some input x. Without loss of generality, we assume there are exactly $r + 1$ phases in the computation of M on x, such that in each phase the counter is either increasing or decreasing.

Define the *phase crossing sequence* C_i at the boundary of two inputs squares to be the sequence (s, d) of M's states and input head directions at the times the input head crosses this boundary during phase i. During an increasing phase, the input head crosses any boundary at most $2q$ times, or else M, being deterministic, would get into an infinite loop. Hence, there are at most $(q + 1)^{2q}$ different crossing sequences for an increasing phase. During a decreasing phase, the input head may get into a loop which terminates only when the counter becomes empty, and in this case the input head may cross some boundary $O(|x|)$ times. Suppose the loop is repeated j times for some $j \geq 0$. Then the input head either crosses a boundary a constant number of times, or $O(j)$ times, depending on whether the boundary is involved in the loop. Thus any crossing sequence during this phase can be written in the form $C_i = uv^j w$ where $|u|/2, |v|, |w| \leq 2q$. Hence there are at most $(q + 1)^{8q}$ different crossing sequences during a decreasing phase.

Define the *crossing sequence* at the boundary of two input squares to be the string $C_1 \# C_2 \# \ldots \# C_{2r}$ of the phase crossing sequences at that boundary. From the above paragraph, we can see that the number of different crossing sequences is bounded by $c = (q+1)^{8q(r+1)}$, which is independent of x. Hence we can rewrite x as $u_0 v_1 u_1 \ldots v_k u_k$, such that $0 \leq |u_j|, |v_j| \leq c$ for $j = 1, \ldots, k$ and the crossing sequences at the left and right boundaries of each v_j are identical. Call each v_j a *movable segment* and each u_j a *separator segment*. We say two movable segments v_m and v_n are of the same type if they are identical and have the same crossing sequences at the left and right boundaries. There are at most c^3 different types. From the definition, we can see that M does not make a counter reversal while the input head is on a movable segment.

We now transform x to another string x' by performing the following operation repeatedly on x. If $x = z_1 v_1 z_2 v_2 z_3$, where v_1 and v_2 are movable segments of the same type, then we rewrite x as $z_1 v_1 v_2 z_2 z_3$, i.e. we group movable segments of the same type together. It is easy to see that at the end of each phase, the state and counter value of M in the computation on x are the same as those in the computation on x', and therefore, M accepts x iff M accepts x'. Apply the same process of partitioning and transforming recursively on z_1 and $z_2 z_3$ (at most $|x|$ times), so that at the end, x can be written as a bounded word $x' \in w_1^* w_2^* \ldots w_k^*$ where $|w_i| \leq c$, $k \leq c^3$, c is independent of x, and M accepts x iff M accepts x'. But since the emptiness problem for *2DCM(1,r)* on bounded languages is decidable [GI82], the theorem follows.

In contrast to Theorem 1 we state the following result from [Iba78].

Theorem 2. *[Iba78] The emptiness problem for 1-input reversal 2DCM is undecidable.*

Next, we show the decidability of the equivalence and containment problems. To do that, we need to ensure that each machine *2DCM(1, r)* halts on every input. Below we prove that this is in fact true for every *2DCM(c, r)*. We first prove a lemma which shows how to modify a 2DFA to make it halt on every input. This lemma is slightly stronger than a similar result by Sipser [Sip80], since our simulating 2DFA behaves exactly as the original machine until it detects that looping has occurred.

Lemma 3. *For every 2DFA N we can construct an equivalent halting 2DFA N' such that on each input N' moves exactly like N until N enters a loop.*

Proof. Let $x = a_1 a_2 \ldots a_n$ be an input. For simplicity, assume N moves every step. For each $i, 1 \leq i \leq n$, define a relation $R(i)$ as follows: for any two states p and q of N, the pair (p, q) is in $R(i)$ iff in state p, N will leave cell i to the right and return to cell i in state q the next time. Clearly N doesn't halt iff it moves to some cell i in state q and (q, q) is in the transitive closure of $R(i)$. We construct a 2DFA N' which simulates N and at the same time tries to construct the relation $R(i)$ for each cell being visited. To simplify the presentation, here we will allow N' to construct the relation $R(i)$ nondeterministically. The nondeterminism can be eliminated by the standard subset construction technique. Let δ_N be the transition function of N, and suppose N starts at cell 1.

N' initializes $R(1)$ to $\emptyset$. In general, suppose that N is at cell j. If N moves to the left, N' constructs deterministically $R(j-1)$ from the current $R(j)$ as follows. For each pair (p,q), N' puts (p,q) in $R(j-1)$ iff

1. $\exists s[\delta_N(p, a_{j-1}) = (s, right) \ \& \ \delta(s, a_j) = (q, left)]$, or
2. $\exists s_1, \ldots, s_k[\delta_N(p, a_{j-1}) = (s_1, right), \delta_N(s_k, a_j) = (q, left) \ \& \ (s_1, s_2), \ldots, (s_{k-1}, s_k) \in R(j)]$.

If N moves to the right, N' constructs (nondeterministically) $R(j+1)$ from the current $R(j)$ as follows: For each pair (p, q) in $R(j)$, M' guesses a sequence of distinct states $s_1, \ldots, s_k$, such that $\delta_N(p, a_j) = (s_1, right)$ and $\delta_N(k, a_{j+1}) = (q, left)$, and puts all $(s_1, s_2), \ldots, (s_{k-1}, s_k)$ in $R(j+1)$. In doing this, N' also makes sure that no two pairs in the resulting $R(j+1)$ share the same first state. Moreover, N' also checks the validity of the current $R(j)$ and abandons the computation if some pair (p,q) in $R(j)$ is non-realizable, i.e., $\delta_N(p, a_j) = (p', left)$ for some state p' or there exists no state q' such that $\delta_N(q', a_{j+1}) = (q, left)$.

N' halts if it detects that at some cell j, N is in state q and (q, q) is in current $R(j)$. Clearly, during the simulation, a relation $R(j)$ may contain some non-realizable pairs. But it is not hard to see that these non-realizable pairs will not cause a false loop detection. Thus we can establish the following claims. Suppose that N is at cell j.

1. If N is in state q and (q, q) is in the current $R(j)$, then N is in a loop.
2. Suppose that the rightmost cell that N has visited so far is cell k. Then for any pair (p, q) such that in state p, M will leave cell j to the right, stay in the cells $j+1$ through k, and return to cell j for the first time in state q, (p, q) is contained in $R(j)$.

Hence, N' can detect if N will enter a loop correctly.

Theorem 4. *For any c and $r \geq 1$, we can effective convert a $2DCM(c, r)$ to a $2DCM(c, r)$ that halts on every input.*

Proof. For simplicity, we prove the theorem for the case $c = 1$. The idea is the same for $c > 1$. Let M be a $2DCM(1, r)$ machine. We construct an equivalent halting $2DCM(1, r)$ machine M'. M' basically simulates M faithfully. We know that M can enter a loop only when (i) M is in an increasing phase or (ii) M is in an decreasing phase but the moves do not affect (i.e., really decrease) the counter (for otherwise M would not be reversal-bounded). Call the latter a zero-decrease period. So besides simulating M, M' also checks if M will enter a loop in each increasing phase and each zero-decrease period. The fact that M' is able to realize this follows from the observation that M behaves like a 2DFA in an increasing phase and a zero-decrease period, and the above lemma.

Corollary 5. *For each c, $\bigcup_r 2DCM(c, r)$ is effectively closed under complementation, intersection, and union. In particular, the class of languages recognized by two-way deterministic reversal-bounded multicounter machines is effectively closed under boolean operations.*

318

Corollary 6. *The containment and equivalence problems for $\bigcup_r 2DCM(1,r)$ are decidable.*

Open Question: Is 2DCM(c,r) closed under union or intersection ?

We state below a related interesting halting result, where $2DCM(1,\infty)$ denotes a two-way deterministic 1-counter machine whose counter can make unrestricted (unbounded) number of reversals. (Its proof appears in the full version of this paper.)

Theorem 7. *Each $2DCM(1,\infty)$ machine accepting a bounded language can be made halting.*

We obtain from the above theorem the next corollary.

Corollary 8. *The class of $2DCM(1,\infty)$ on bounded languages is effectively closed under complementation, intersection and union.*

Open Question: Is $2DCM(1,\infty)$ closed under complementation or union ?

3 Some Applications

We give three applications of Theorem 1 in this section. First we give a simpler proof of the decidability of the ECE problems concerning reversal-bounded deterministic pushdown automata on bounded languages. This result first appeared in [IJTW] as a corollary of a rather difficult theorem.

Theorem 9. *The emptiness problem for 2DPDA(r) for $r \geq 1$ on bounded languages is decidable.*

The proof follows from Theorem 1 and the following lemma.

Lemma 10. *Let M be a 2DPDA(r) accepting a strictly bounded language over $a_1^* \ldots a_k^*$. We can effectively construct a $2DCM(1,r)$ machine M' (not necessarily accepting the same language) such that $L(M)$ is empty iff $L(M')$ is empty.*

Proof. We may assume, without loss of generality, that on every step, M pushes exactly 1 symbol on top of the stack, does not change the top of the stack, or pops exactly 1 symbol, i.e., M is not allowed to rewrite the top of the stack. In the discussion that follows, we assume M is processing an input that is accepted, i.e., the computation is halting.

A writing phase is a sequence of steps which starts with a push and the stack is never popped (i.e., the stack height does not decrease) during the sequence. A writing phase is periodic if there are strings u,v,w with v nonnull such that for the entire writing phase, the string written on the stack is of the form uv^iw for some i (the multiplicity) , and the configuration of M (state, symbol, top of the stack) just before the first symbol of the first v is written is the same as the configuration just before the first symbol of the second v is written. Note that w is a prefix of v. Clearly, a writing phase can only end when the input head reaches an endmarker or a boundary between the a_i's. A writing phase can only be followed by a popping of the stack (i.e. reversal) or another writing phase with possibly different triple (u, v, w).

By enlarging the state set, we can easily modify M so that all writing phases are periodic. One can easily verify that because M is reversal-bounded, there are at most a fixed number t of writing phases (in the computation), and t is effectively computable from the specification of M.

We now describe the construction of M. Let $x = a_1^{i_1} \ldots a_k^{i_k}$ be the input to M. The input to M' is of the form: $y \# c_1 \# c_2 \# \ldots \# c_t$, where the c_i's are unary strings; y is x but certain positions are marked with markers $m_1, m_2, \ldots, m_t$. Note that a position of y can have $0, 1, \ldots$ at most t markers.

M simulates M' on the segment y ignoring the markers. The c_i's are used to remember the counter values. Informally, every time the counter enters a new writing phase, the machine "records" the current value of the counter by checking the c_i's.

M' begins by simulating M on y (ignoring the marks). When a writing phase is entered, M' records the triple (u_1, v_1, w_1) in its finite control and the multiplicity in the counter. Suppose M enters another writing phase. Then M' checks that the input head is on a symbol marked by marker m_1; hence M' can "remember" the input head position. (If it's not marked m_1, M' rejects.) Then it "records" the current value of the counter on the input by checking that the current value is equal to c_1. (If it's not, M' rejects.) M' restores the input head to the position marked m_1 and resets the counter to 0. It can then proceed with the simulation. Next time M' has to record the value of the counter, M' use the input marker m_2 and checks c_2, while storing the triple (u_2, v_2, w_2) in its finite control, etc. Popping of the counter is easily simulated using the appropriate triple (u, v, w) and the counter value. Note that if in the simulation of a sequence of pops, the counter becomes 0, M' must first retrieve the appropriate c_i (corresponding to the pushdown segment directly below the one that was just consumed) and restore it in the counter before it can continue with the simulation; retrieving and restoring the count in the counter requires the input head to leave the input position, but M' can remember the "new" position with a new "marker". If after a sequence of pops M enters a new writing phase before the counter becomes 0, the "residual" counter value is recorded as a new c_i like before. We leave the details to the reader. It is clear that M' in in 2DCM(1,r) for some r.

Since the proof of Theorem 4 can be trivially modified to show that reversal-bounded 2DPDA's can be made halting (even for those accepting unbounded languages), the class of languages they define is effectively closed under complementation. In particular, we have

Corollary 11. *The containment and equivalence problems for* 2DPDA(r) *for* $r \geq 1$ *on bounded languages are decidable.*

As a second application, we use Theorem 1 to show the decidability of the emptiness problem for some classes of simple programs. The motivation for the following definition comes from the study of real-time verification [AHV].

Definition 12. A *simple program* P is a triple (V, X, I), where $V = \{A_1, A_2, \ldots, A_n\}$ is a finite set of *input variables*, $X \notin V$ is the *accumulator*, and $I = (i_1; i_2; \ldots; i_l)$ is a finite list of *instructions* of the form

- label s: $X \leftarrow X + A_i$
- label s: $X \leftarrow X - A_i$
- label s: if $X = 0$ goto label t
- label s: if $X > 0$ goto label t
- label s: if $X < 0$ goto label t
- label s: goto label t
- label s: halt

Note that the program is not allowed to change the value of an input variable.

Definition 13. For a program P, EMPTY(P) = yes if there are integers (positive, negative, or zero) $a_1, a_2, \ldots, a_n$ such that P on this input halts; otherwise EMPTY(P) = no. The emptiness problem for simple programs is deciding given P if EMPTY(P) is yes.

At present, we do not know if the emptiness problem for simple programs is decidable. However, for some special cases, we are able to show that the problem is decidable.

One such special case is a program whose accumulator crosses the 0 axis (alternates between positive values and negative values) at most k times for some positive integer k independent of the input. Call such a program k-*crossing*, and in general, a program *finite-crossing* if it is k-crossing for some $k \geq 1$.

For example, a program with three inputs A, B, C that checks the relation $A = (B - C)i$ for some i can operate as follows: add A to the accumulator, and iterate adding B and subtracting C and checking if the accumulator X is zero after every iteration (the program halts if X is zero and goes into an infinite loop if X is negative). Although the accumulator alternates between increasing and decreasing modes arbitrarily many times (which depends on the input), the accumulator crosses the 0 axis at most once. So such a program is 1-crossing.

Again, we apply Theorem 1 to show the emptiness problem for finite-crossing simple programs is decidable.

Theorem 14. *The emptiness problem for finite-crossing simple programs is decidable, even when instructions of the form $X \leftarrow X + 1$ and $X \leftarrow X - 1$, are allowed.*

Proof. We give an algorithm to decide whether a finite-crossing simple program P halts on any input. Suppose P has l instructions and n input variables $A_1, A_2, \ldots, A_n$. Define the instantaneous description (abbreviated as ID) $(c_t, sign(X_t))$ of P at time t to be the label of the instruction being executed and the sign of the accumulator, which is either negative or nonnegative.

Consider a halting computation of P on some set of input values $a_1, a_2, \ldots, a_n$ as given by a sequence of ID's of P from start to finish. Since the accumulator of P alternates between positive and negative values at most k times for some $k \geq 1$, this computation can be divided into at most $k + 1$ phases such that every ID in a phase has the same second component. Because P is deterministic, some ID must be repeated after the first l steps in each phase, and hence the sequence of ID's in each phase can be written in the form of $uv^i w$, where each $u, v,$ and w is a concatenation of at most l ID's.

Using this observation about finite-crossing simple programs, we construct a reversal-bounded counter machine M such that M accepts some input if and only if P halts on some input. Since M can make only a finite number of reversals on its counter, it cannot simulate P faithfully. Rather, M uses the "padding" technique described in Lemma 10. For each phase in the computation of P, M precomputes the effect made on the counter by each possible loop v of instructions and "stores" it in the input, i.e. M verifies that its input is padded with this extra information. From then on, to simulate a loop M needs only add its corresponding net effect to the counter, and hence to simulate a phase, M needs at most a constant number of counter reversals. Also, to simulate the increment and decrement instructions, M introduces two new variables a_+ and a_- which holds $+1$ and -1 respectively. It is easy to see that M accepts some input iff P halts on some input. By Theorem 1, it is decidable whether $L(M) = \emptyset$.

Remark Allowing the use of "constant" instructions of the form $X \leftarrow X + 1$ and $X \leftarrow X - 1$ makes simple programs computationally more powerful. For example, the relation $R = \{A : 2|A\}$ can easily be verified by a finite-crossing program with constant instructions, but not by any program without constant instructions, even if it is not finite-crossing.

Although finite-crossing programs can accept fairly complicated relations, they cannot verify multiplication and squaring.

Define MULT $= \{(A, B, C)|C = A * B\}$ and SQUARE $= \{(A, B)|B = A^2\}$.

Claim 15. *MULT and SQUARE cannot be verified by finite-crossing programs.*

Although finite-crossing simple programs may seem equivalent at first glance to counter machines whose counters can become zero only a finite number of times regardless of its input (we call those *finite-reset* counter machines), the latter are in fact much more powerful computational devices. For example, there is a finite-reset counter machine M that accepts a set S similar to MULT, namely, $S = \{0^x \#(0^y \#)^x : x, y \geq 1\}$. Hence the emptiness problem for finite-reset counter machines is undecidable, because they can multiply and hence compute the value of any polynomial $p(y, x_1, x_2, \ldots, x_n)$ (see [Cha87] for the proof of an analogous result). This contrasts with Theorem 14. We can use the same technique in Theorem 14 to show that the emptiness problem is decidable for finite-reset counter machines on *strictly bounded languages* (and hence bounded languages also; see the remark at the bottom of Section 1). From this and Corollary 8, we have

Theorem 16. *The emptiness, containment, and equivalence problems for finite-reset counter machines over strictly bounded languages are decidable.*

It is interesting to note that there are strictly bounded languages that can be recognized by a finite-reset counter machine but not by any finite-reversal counter machine. Using an easy cut-and-paste argument, one can show that the language $L = \{0^a 1^b 2^c : a = n(b - c) \text{ for some } n \geq 0\}$ is such an example.

There is a restricted class of simple programs allowing "nondeterminism" that arises in the theory of real-time verification [AHV]:

Definition 17. A *restricted nondeterministic simple program* is a simple program that allows more than one choice of instruction for each label and has the property that the accumulator X is nonnegative (nonpositive) after each instruction of the form $X \leftarrow X + A_i$ $(X \leftarrow X - A_i)$.

It is an open question whether the emptiness problem for this class of simple programs is decidable. However, we can show that the emptiness problem is decidable for restricted *deterministic* simple programs.

Theorem 18. *The emptiness problem for restricted deterministic simple programs is decidable.*

We can allow comparisons between input variables and the emptiness problem still remains decidable.

Corollary 19. *The emptiness problem is decidable for finite-crossing simple programs and restricted deterministic simple programs which use additional instructions of the form:*

$$\text{if } p(A_i, A_j) \text{ goto } label$$

where A_i and A_j are input variables, and the predicate p is $|$ (for divides) , $>, <$, or $=$.

4 Nondeterministic Reversal-bounded Multicounter Machines

We do not know if the emptiness problem for $\bigcup_r 2NCM(1, r)$ is decidable. In fact, the question is open even for $\bigcup_r 2NCM(1, r)$ machines accepting only bounded languages. However, we can show that the emptiness, equivalence, and containment problems are decidable for $\bigcup_c \bigcup_r 2NCM(c, r)$ on unary alphabet. More precisely, we prove that unary languages accepted by $\bigcup_c \bigcup_r 2NCM(c, r)$ machines are effectively regular. This settles a conjecture of Gurari and Ibarra [GI79]. In [GI79] it was only shown that unary languages accepted by $\bigcup_c \bigcup_r 2DCM(c, r)$ machines are effectively regular. Our technique is totally different. We first state a lemma that characterizes regular unary languages.

Lemma 20. *A unary language L is regular iff there is a constant c such that for every $x \in L$, $|x| > c$, there is some j, $1 \leq j \leq c$, such that $x' = 0^{jn}0^{|x|-j} \in L$ for all $n \geq 1$.*

Theorem 21. *Every unary language accepted by a 2NCM(c, r) is regular for $c, r \geq 1$.*

Proof. It suffices to show the theorem for 2NCM(c, 1), since we can reduce the number of counter reversals by any 2NCM(c, r) to 1 by adding more counters. We first show the theorem for $c = 1$, using the characterization given in Lemma 20, and then extend the proof to the general case.

Suppose L is accepted by some 2NCM(1, 1) M with q states. To avoid stating unnecessary constants, we will use the word "bounded" in the following to mean "bounded by some constant depending only on q".

Let 0^x be in L, and let C be an accepting computation of M on 0^x. C has a *simple loop* if there are some $t_1 < t_2$ such that at times t_1 and t_2 M is in the same state and on the same input square, and furthermore M does not visit an endmarker during $[t_1, t_2]$. A simple loop is called *positive* or *negative* depending on the net change it makes to the counter value. C has a *sweep* if there are some $t_1 < t_2$ such that at times t_1 and t_2 M is on an endmarker, and M does not visit an endmarker during (t_1, t_2).

So given a computation C, we decompose C into sweeps of length $O(|x|)$ after first removing all simple loops. Since each input square is visited at most q times in any sweep, the number of different crossing sequences is bounded by $t = (q + 1)^{2q} + 1$, and so we can divide each sweep into a bounded number of clusters of identical movable segments (segments which have the same crossing sequences at both ends) separated by separator segments as explained in the proof of Theorem 1. Let b be the least common multiple of the lengths of all types of movable segments. After consolidating, we may assume that every movable segment has length b, and each sweep has exactly m movable segments for some $m = \Omega(|x|)$. (We consider sweeps that start and end on the same marker to have "empty" movable segments whose net change to the counter is zero.) We use $v(F)$ to denote the net change to the counter value by a computation fragment F (such as a loop or a sweep) of C. For example, $v(C) = 0$.

Suppose we add a segment of length b to the input 0^x. We can obtain from C an "almost" valid computation C' by duplicating one arbitrary movable segment in each sweep. (The simple loops are not affected since the input head never visits the endmarkers during a simple loop.) We call a set of movable segments obtained by taking one movable segment from each sweep a *cross-section* E of C. A cross-section E is called *positive* or *negative* depending on the sign of $v(E)$. Our strategy is to manipulate the sweeps, loops, and cross-sections to obtain from C an accepting computation of M on 0^{x+kbn} for some bounded k and all $n \geq 1$.

We have four cases:

1. C has a negative cross-section and a positive cross-section
2. C has only positive cross-sections, but also negative simple loops
3. C has only positive cross-sections, but also positive simple loops
4. C has only positive cross-sections, and no simple loops

In all cases, it can be shown (proof omitted) that some bounded k exists such that 0^{x+kbn} is in L for all $n \geq 1$. Hence by Lemma 20, L is regular. This concludes the proof of the theorem for $c = 1$.

Now we show how to extend the above proof to the general case. Suppose L is accepted by some 2NCM(c, 1) M. Let 0^x be in L, and let C be an accepting computation of M on 0^x. We partition C into simple loops, movable segments, and sweeps as for the case of 2NCM(1, 1), except that now these units are defined relative to a single counter. So there are c different partitions of C, each concerning with net changes to only one counter and ignoring the other counters. Proceed as in the construction above to find the size of the segment to be added for each case, say $k_1 b$, $k_2 b$, ..., $k_c b$. Then the final input segment to be added is $k_1 k_2 \dots k_c b^c$.

The proof of Theorem 21 also works even if we shorten instead of lengthen the input. Thus, to decide whether a 2NCM(c, r) accept some input, we only need to check all inputs of length at most a bounded constant. Since the membership problem for 2NCM(c, r) is decidable [Cha81], we have

Corollary 22. *The emptiness, containment, and equivalence problems for* $\bigcup_c \bigcup_r 2NCM(c, r)$ *on unary alphabet are decidable.*

This is the strongest result one can obtain since it is known that deterministic reversal-bounded 2-counter machines over strictly bounded languages can accept nonsemilinear sets and have an undecidable emptiness problem [Iba78].

References

[AHV] R. ALUR, T. HENZINGER, AND M. VARDI, *Parametric delays in real-time reasoning.* In preparation.

[Cha81] T.-H. CHAN, *Reversal complexity of counter machines*, in Proc. 13th Symp. on Theory of Computing, ACM, 1981, pp. 146–157.

[Cha87] T.-H. CHAN, *On two-way weak counter machines*, Math. System Theory, 20 (1987), pp. 31–41.

[GI79] E. M. GURARI AND O. H. IBARRA, *Simple counter machines and number-theoretic problems*, J. Comput. System Sci., 19 (1979), pp. 145–162.

[GI82] ———, *Two-way counter machines and diophantine equations*, J. Assoc. Comput. Mach., 29 (1982), pp. 863–873.

[Iba78] O. H. IBARRA, *Reversal-bounded multicounter machines and their decision problems*, J. Assoc. Comput. Mach., 25 (1978), pp. 116–133.

[IJTW] O. IBARRA, T. JIANG, N. TRAN, AND H. WANG, *On the equivalence of two-way pushdown automata and counter machines over bounded languages.* Accepted for STACS 93.

[Min61] M. MINSKY, *Recursive unsolvability of Post's problem of tag and other topics in the theory of Turing machines*, Ann. of Math., 74 (1961), pp. 437–455.

[Sip80] M. SIPSER, *Halting space-bounded computations*, Theoretical Computer Science, 10 (1980), pp. 335–338.

[VP75] L. G. VALIANT AND M. S. PATERSON, *Deterministic one-counter automata*, J. Comput. System Sci., 10 (1975), pp. 340–350.

Cobham's Theorem seen through Büchi's Theorem

Christian Michaux
Faculté des Sciences
Université de Mons-Hainaut
Mons, Belgium
sboffa@bmsuem11.bitnet

Roger Villemaire
Département de mathématiques et d'informatique
Université du Québec à Montréal
Montréal (Québec), Canada H3C 3P8
villem@math.uqam.ca

Abstract

Cobham's Theorem says that for k and l multiplicatively independent (i.e. for any nonzero integers r and s we have $k^r \neq l^s$), a subset of $\mathbb{N}$ which is k- and l-recognizable is recognizable.

Here we give a new proof of this result using a combinatorial property of subsets of $\mathbb{N}$ which are not first-order definable in Presburger Arithmetic (i.e. which are not ultimately periodic). The crucial lemma shows that an $L \subseteq \mathbb{N}$ is first-order definable in Presburger Arithmetic iff any subset of $\mathbb{N}$ first-order definable in $< \mathbb{N}, +, L >$ is non-expanding (i.e. the distance between two consecutive elements is bounded).

1. Introduction. Let Σ be an *alphabet*, i.e. a finite set. Σ^* will denote the set of *words* of finite length on Σ containing the *empty* word λ formed of no symbol. Any subset L of Σ is called a *language* on the alphabet Σ.

Definition Let Σ be an alphabet. A Σ-*automaton* $\mathcal{A}$ is a finite labelled directed graph G whose vertices are called *states* and which satisfies the following properties.

a) There is a distinguished state called the *initial state*.

b) Some of the states are said to be *final states*.

c) From any state q and any element σ of the alphabet Σ there is one and only one arrow labelled by σ leaving q.

Furthermore we have the following definitions.

Definition A word $\alpha \in \Sigma^*$ is said to be *accepted* by the Σ-automaton G if starting at the initial state of G and reading α from left to right taking arrows labelled by the letters of α, one reaches a final state.

Definition A language L on Σ is said to be Σ-*recognizable* if there exists a Σ-automaton such that the set of words accepted by this automaton is exactly L.

Let Σ_k be the alphabet $\{0, 1, \ldots, k-1\}$. For $n \in \mathbb{N}$ let $[n]_k$ be the word on Σ_k which is the inverse representation of n in base k, i.e. if $n = \Sigma_{i=0}^s \lambda_i k^i$ with $\lambda_i \in \{0, \ldots, k-1\}$, then $[n]_k = \lambda_0 \cdots \lambda_s$.

Definition For $k \in \mathbb{N}$. We say that a subset L of $\mathbb{N}$ is k-*recognizable* if $\{[n]_k; n \in L\}$ is Σ_k-recognizable.

It is quite useful to have a notion of k-recognizability for subsets of $\mathbb{N}^n$ for any positive natural number n. For this we follow the approach of [7] which is different of the definition normally used in language theory. Nevertheless it is a natural point of view since it will allow Büchi's Theorem to work in full generality (see below).

It is possible to represent tuples of natural numbers by words on $(\Sigma_k^n)^*$ in the following way. Let $(m_1, \ldots, m_n) \in \mathbb{N}^n$. Add on the right of each $[m_i]_k$ the minimal number of 0 in order to make them all of the same length and call these words ω_i. Let $\omega_i = \lambda_{i1} \cdots \lambda_{is}$ where $\lambda_{ij} \in \Sigma_k$. We represent $(m_1, \ldots, m_n)$ by the word

$$[(m_1, \ldots, m_n)]_k = (\lambda_{11}, \lambda_{21}, \ldots, \lambda_{n1})(\lambda_{12}, \lambda_{22}, \ldots, \lambda_{n2}) \cdots (\lambda_{1s}, \lambda_{2s}, \ldots, \lambda_{ns}) \in (\Sigma_k^n)^*.$$

Definition For $k \in \mathbb{N}$. We say that a subset L of $\mathbb{N}^n$ is k-*recognizable* if $\{[x]_k; x \in L\}$ is Σ_k^n-recognizable.

Definition Let $V_k : \mathbb{N} \setminus \{0\} \to \mathbb{N}$ be the function which sends x to $V_k(x)$, the greatest power of k which divides x.

Definition We say that a subset R of $\mathbb{N}^n$ is *definable* in $< \mathbb{N}, +, V_k >$ if it can be defined by a formula built up from $=$, $+$ and V_k using only $\wedge$ ("and"), $\vee$ ("or"), $\neg$ ("not"), $\to$ ("if ... then ..."), $\exists x$ ("there exists $x \in \mathbb{N}$ ...", where x is a symbol for a variable) and $\forall x$ (" for all $x \in \mathbb{N}$ ...", where x is a symbol for a variable). In the same way we say that R is *definable* in $< \mathbb{N}, + >$ if it can be define by a formula of the above type, without using V_k. Finally for L a subset of $\mathbb{N}$, a subset R of $\mathbb{N}^n$ is say to be definable in $< \mathbb{N}, +, L >$ or $< \mathbb{N}, +, V_k, L >$ if we can define it in the above way using now also the relation $L(x)$, meaning $x \in L$ (x being either a natural number or tuples of natural numbers according to the case).

In [2,Theorem 9] Büchi almost states the following theorem. Actually Büchi claimed that an X is k-recognizable if and only if it is first-order definable in the structure $< \mathbb{N}, +, P_k >$, where P_k is the set of powers of k. Unfortunately, as remarked by McNaughton in [9], his proof is incorrect. Furthermore Büchi's statement has been disproved by Semenov in [14, Corollary 4]. Thanks to the work of Bruyère [1], we know that the ideas of Büchi can be used to show the following theorem. (See [1] for a proof among the lines of Büchi's, [10] for a different proof or also [15]).

Theorem 1.1 **Büchi's Theorem** A set $X \subseteq \mathbb{N}^n$ is k-recognizable if and only if it is first-order definable in the structure $< \mathbb{N}, +, V_k >$.

There is another version of Büchi's Theorem in terms of weak monadic logic. See [16] for the relationship of that version with the one stated here.

Using Büchi's Theorem as a motivation, we introduce the following definition.

Definition We say that a subset L of $\mathbb{N}^n$ is *recognizable* if it is definable in $< \mathbb{N}, + >$.

Remark One normally defines a subset of $\mathbb{N}$ to be 1-recognizable if $\{a^n; n \in L\}$ is $\{a\}$-recognizable ($\{a\}$ is the alphabet formed of one single letter a). It is well known that a set is 1-recognizable if and only if it is recognizable according to our definition. Note that if we extend the definition of 1-recognizability to subsets of $\mathbb{N}^n$ in the way we did it for k-recognizability ($k > 1$) then it would not be equivalent to the notion of recognizability.

Definition We say that two natural numbers k and l are multiplicatively independent if $k^n \neq l^m$, for any n and m nonzero natural numbers.

We now give some well known facts about recognizability of natural numbers.

• If k and l are multiplicatively dependent then any set $X \subseteq \mathbb{N}$ which is k-recognizable is also l-recognizable (see [4, Corollary 3.7]).

• A set $L \subseteq \mathbb{N}$ is recognizable if and only if it is a finite union of arithmetic progressions if and only if there exists a nonzero natural number d and a natural number c such that for all $x > c$, we have that $x \in L$ is equivalent to $x + d \in L$, i.e. L is ultimately periodic (see [5]).

• A set $L \subseteq \mathbb{N}$ which is recognizable is k-recognizable for any $k \in \mathbb{N}$ (see [4,

Proposition 3.4])

and finally

Theorem 1.2 **Cobham's Theorem** For k, l multiplicatively independent, a subset of $\mathbb{N}$ which is k- and l-recognizable is recognizable, hence it is m-recognizable for any m (see [3] or also [6] and [13]).

This paper is about a new proof of this last result.

2. About the proofs of Cobham's Theorem.

Definition Let $L = \{l_n; n \in \mathbb{N}\}$ be a subset of $\mathbb{N}$ in increasing order. Let (as in [4]) D_L be the smallest natural number s such that there exists a $c \in \mathbb{N}$ satisfying $l_{n+1} - l_n \leq s$ for all $n > c$ if it exists and ∞ otherwise.

Definition We say that L a subset of $\mathbb{N}$ is *expanding* if $D_L = \infty$.

G. Hansel in [6] (see also [13], which is a more accessible source or [11]), broke up the proof of Cobham's Therorem in two parts. First he shows that

(1) if $L \subseteq \mathbb{N}$ is k- and l-recognizable, then it is non-expanding (he says *syndetic*).

Secondly he uses this fact to show that L must be recognizable.

In this paper we first show in section 3 that

(1′) if L is non-expanding, k- and l-recognizable and not recognizable (i.e. not first-order definable in $< \mathbb{N}, + >$), then we can find an $L' \subseteq \mathbb{N}$ which is expanding and first-order definable in $< \mathbb{N}, +, L >$.

We therefore have a definition of L' in terms of $+$ and L. Replacing L in this definition by its definition in terms of $+$ and V_k (we use Büchi's Theorem here) we get a definition of L' in terms of $+$ and V_k. Hence, again by Büchi's Theorem, L' is k-recognizable. In the same way we can show that L' is also l-recognizable. Therefore we have that L' is expanding and k- and l-recognizable. This is in contradiction with Hansel's result (1) and forms a simple proof of Cobham's Theorem.

A. Muchnik gave in [12] a proof of Cobham's Theorem which is different of the original one, of Hansel's and of ours. He first proves that for all natural numbers $n > 0$ there exists a formula $\varphi_n(X_n)$ in the language $\{+, X_n\}$ of Presburger arithmetic extended by a n-ary predicate X_n, such that the following property holds.

(∗) for all $A \subseteq \mathbb{N}^n$, A is definable in Presburger arithmetic (i.e. is definable in $< \mathbb{N}, + >$) if and only if $\varphi_n(A)$ holds.

In the second part of his paper (using the result (∗)), he proves :

(a) that it is decidable whether a k-recognizable subset of $\mathbb{N}$ is recognizable.

(b) Cobham's Theorem and also a generalization due to Semenov.

In the proof of (b), Muchnik introduces an interesting notion of (k, l)-automata for k and l multiplicatively independent natural numbers.

Let us mention a formula $\varphi_1(X_1)$, which is not the one used by Muchnik (for technical reason), but which satisfies (∗) for $n = 1$. Take $\varphi_1(X_1)$ to be

$$\exists d\, \exists c\, (\forall x \geq c\ X_1(x) \leftrightarrow X_1(x + d)).$$

(As we said before $X_1(x)$ means $x \in X_1$.)

It is clear by the second fact stated at the end of section 1., that $\varphi_1(A)$ is satisfied for $A \subseteq \mathbb{N}$ if and only if A is definable in $< \mathbb{N}, + >$.

Remark The result (a) has also been proved by J. Honkala in [8].

We can now begin with our proof of Cobham's Theorem.

3. L non-expanding.

We show in this section that if $L \subseteq \mathbb{N}$ is not definable in $< \mathbb{N}, + >$ and if $D_L < \infty$ then there exists an $L' \subseteq \mathbb{N}$, such that L' is definable in $< \mathbb{N}, +, L >$ and $D_{L'} = \infty$. As we showed in section 2. using this fact and a result of Hansel, we have a proof of Cobham's Theorem.

We will need the following notation.

Notation For $L \subseteq \mathbb{N}$ and n, $m \in \mathbb{N}$ let

$L[n, m] = \{x \in \mathbb{N}; n + x \in L \text{ and } n + x \leq m\}.$

We will say that $L[n, m]$ is a *factor* of L of length $m - n$.

Remark Often in language theory one identifies $L \subseteq \mathbb{N}$ with the infinite word w_L on $\{0, 1\}$, having a 1 in position i if and only if $i \in L$. With this point of view $L[n, m]$ is the analog of the factor $w_L[n, m]$ of the infinite word w_L. Hence we have that $L[n, m] = L[n', m']$ if and only if $w_L[n, m] = w_L[n', m']$.

For n, m, $k \in \mathbb{N}$ such that $n < m$ and $m - n = k$, we have that $L[n, m] \subseteq \{0, 1, \ldots, k\}$. Hence for a fixed k there are only finitely many possibilities for $L[n, m]$. Therefore for any k there is some factor of length k which is repeated. We will make use of this fact.

We will first define two functions $\tilde{d}_L$ and $\tilde{\alpha}_L$ and then modify them slightly in order to obtain two increasing functions d_L and α_L.

Definition Let $L \subseteq \mathbb{N}$. Define $\tilde{d}_L : \mathbb{N} \to \mathbb{N}$ to be the function which sends $n \in \mathbb{N}$ to the smallest natural number $d \neq 0$ such that there exists an $a \in \mathbb{N}$ with

$$L[a, a + n] = L[a + d, a + d + n].$$

As said before there are only finitely many factors of length n, hence there is at least one of them which is repeated. Therefore $\tilde{d}_L$ is really a function of $\mathbb{N}$ into $\mathbb{N}$. Actually $\tilde{d}_L(n)$ is the smallest distance by which you can move a factor of length n in order to recover another copy of it.

The following fact will be useful.

Lemma 3.1 Let $L \subseteq \mathbb{N}$ and a, b, $d \in \mathbb{N}$. If $L[a, b] = L[a + d, b + d]$, then for any α, $\beta \in \mathbb{N}$ such that $a \leq \alpha \leq \beta \leq b$, we have that $L[\alpha, \beta] = L[\alpha + d, \beta + d]$.

Proof Trivial, if one thinks in terms of factors (see the remark after the definition of $L[n, m]$).

Proposition 3.2 $\tilde{d}_L$ is an increasing function.

Proof Trivial, if one thinks in terms of factors (see the remark after the definition of $L[n, m]$).

Definition Let $L \subseteq \mathbb{N}$. Define $\tilde{\alpha}_L : \mathbb{N} \to \mathbb{N}$ to be the function which sends $n \in \mathbb{N}$ to the smallest natural number a such that

$$L[a, a + n] = L[a + \tilde{d}_L(n), a + \tilde{d}_L(n) + n].$$

It would be convenient to have that $\tilde{\alpha}_L$ is increasing. Since this is not always the case, we will need the following definitions.

Definition Let $U \subseteq \mathbb{N}$ be defined as follows. There are two cases.

Case 1. If $\{\tilde{\alpha}_L(n); n \in \mathbb{N}\}$ is finite then take $U = \tilde{\alpha}_L^{-1}(s)$, for some $s \in \{\tilde{\alpha}_L(n); n \in \mathbb{N}\}$ such that $\tilde{\alpha}_L^{-1}(s)$ is infinite.

Case 2. If $\{\tilde{\alpha}_L(n); n \in \mathbb{N}\}$ is infinite, then let U be the set of $x \in \mathbb{N}$ such that $\tilde{\alpha}_L(y) \leq \tilde{\alpha}_L(x)$, for all $y \leq x$.

In both cases U is infinite.

Definition Define $d_L : \mathbb{N} \to \mathbb{N}$ to be the function which sends $n \in \mathbb{N}$ to $\tilde{d}_L(m)$, where m is the smallest element of U which is greater than n.

Definition Define $\alpha_L : \mathbb{N} \to \mathbb{N}$ to be the function which sends $n \in \mathbb{N}$ to $\tilde{\alpha}_L(m)$, where m is the smallest element of U which is greater than n.

Hence it is obvious that

Proposition 3.3 The functions d_L and α_L are increasing and also

$$L[\alpha_L(n), \alpha_L(n) + n] = L[\alpha_L(n) + d_L(n), \alpha_L(n) + d_L(n) + n].$$

Proposition 3.4 d_L and α_L are functions first-order definable in the structure $< \mathbb{N}, +, L >$.

Proof We first notice that $x \leq y$ is easily defined in $< \mathbb{N}, +, L >$ by the formula $\exists z \; x + z = y$ and $x < y$ is defined by $x \leq y \land \neg(x = y)$.

Furthermore $z \in L[x, y]$ is defined in $< \mathbb{N}, +, L >$ by the formula $\chi(x, y, z)$:

$$L(x + z) \land x + z \leq y.$$

Now $L[x, y] = L[v, w]$ is easily defined as $\forall z \; \chi(x, y, z) \leftrightarrow \chi(v, w, z)$.

If $\varphi(x, \bar{y})$, where $\bar{y}$ is some tuple of variables, is some formula in the language of $< \mathbb{N}, +, L >$, then $\varphi(x, \bar{y}) \land \forall x'(\varphi(x', \bar{y}) \to x \leq x')$ expresses the fact that x is the smallest value satisfing $\varphi(x, \bar{y})$. Hence it follows that $\tilde{d}_L(x) = y$ is defined by

$$\neg(y = 0) \land \exists u(L[u, u + x] = L[u + y, u + y + x]) \land$$
$$\forall y'(\neg(y' = 0) \land \exists u L[u, u + x] = L[u + y', u + y' + x] \to y \leq y').$$

It is now easy to show that d_L is first-order definable because U is first-order definable.

In a similar way one can now easily find a formula defining $\alpha_L(x) = y$ in $< \mathbb{N}, +, L >$. This completes the proof.

The main lemma is now of combinatorial nature.

Lemma 3.5 If $\{d_L(n); n \in \mathbb{N}\}$ and $\{\alpha_L(n); n \in \mathbb{N}\}$ are non-expanding, then d_L is eventually constant.

Proof Suppose that $\{d_L(n); n \in \mathbb{N}\}$ and $\{\alpha_L(N); n \in \mathbb{N}\}$ are non-expanding and that d_L is not eventually constant.

332

Let u, v be natural numbers such that $d_L(n+1) - d_L(n) \leq u$ and $\alpha_L(n+1) - \alpha_L(n) \leq v$, for all $n \in \mathbb{N}$.

Let $k \in \mathbb{N}$. We will find natural numbers r, s such that $r - s \geq k$ and $L[r, s] = L[r+d, s+d]$ for some $d \leq u$. Therefore it will follow that $\tilde{d}_L$ is bounded and since it is increasing it will be constant. Hence d_L is also constant.

Take $n \geq k + v$ such that $d_L(n+1) > d_L(n)$. We have that

(1) $L[\alpha_L(n), \alpha_L(n) + n] = L[\alpha_L(n) + d_L(n), \alpha_L(n) + d_L(n) + n]$

and

(2) $L[\alpha_L(n+1), \alpha_L(n+1) + n + 1] =$

$L[\alpha_L(n+1) + d_L(n+1), \alpha_L(n+1) + d_L(n+1) + n + 1]$.

Consider $L[\alpha_L(n+1), \alpha_L(n) + n]$. Note that $\alpha_L(n) + n - \alpha_L(n+1) = n - (\alpha_L(n+1) - \alpha_L(n)) \geq k + v - v = k$.

Applying Lemma 3.1 to (1) one sees that

$L[\alpha_L(n+1), \alpha_L(n) + n] = L[\alpha_L(n+1) + d_L(n), \alpha_L(n) + d_L(n) + n]$.

The same Lemma applied to (2) yields

$L[\alpha_L(n+1), \alpha_L(n) + n] = L[\alpha_L(n+1) + d_L(n+1), \alpha_L(n) + d_L(n+1) + n]$.

Hence
$$L[\alpha_L(n+1) + d_L(n), \alpha_L(n) + d_L(n) + n] =$$
$$L[\alpha_L(n+1) + d_L(n+1), \alpha_L(n) + d_L(n+1) + n].$$

Take $r = \alpha_L(n+1) + d_L(n)$, $s = \alpha_L(n) + d_L(n) + n$ and $d = d_L(n+1) - d_L(n)$. We have that $d \leq u$ and also that $L[r, s] = L[r+d, s+d]$. Furthermore $s - r = \alpha_L(n) + d_L(n) + n - (\alpha_L(n+1) + d_L(n)) = n - (\alpha_L(n+1) - \alpha_L(n)) \geq k$. This completes the proof.

The final Lemma is the following.

Lemma 3.6 If $\{\alpha_L(n); n \in \mathbb{N}\}$ is non-expanding and d_L is eventually constant, then L is a finite union of arithmetic progressions.

Proof To show the conclusion it is sufficient to prove that for all y greater than some constant we have that

(**) $y \in L$ if and only if $y + d \in L$

for some natural number d and all but finitely many $y \in L$.

We will show that this is the case with d equal to the constant value that d_L eventually takes.

Since $L[\alpha_L(n), \alpha_L(n) + n] = L[\alpha_L(n) + d, \alpha_L(n) + d + n]$ we have (∗∗) for $y \in [\alpha_L(n), \alpha_L(n) + n]$. Hence we now just need to show that the intervals $[\alpha_L(n), \alpha_L(n) + n]$ ($n \in \mathbb{N}$) cover all of $\mathbb{N}$ but finitely many points. Since α_L is non-expanding this is clearly the case.

We therefore have the following theorem.

Theorem 3.7 Let $L \subseteq \mathbb{N}$. If L is not first-order definable in $< \mathbb{N}, + >$ then either $\{d_L(n); n \in \mathbb{N}\}$ or $\{\alpha_L(n); n \in \mathbb{N}\}$ is expanding.

Proof This follows from Lemma 3.5 and 3.6.

Corollary 3.8 Let $L \subseteq \mathbb{N}$. If L is not definable in $< \mathbb{N}, + >$ then there exists a $L' \subseteq \mathbb{N}$ definable in $< \mathbb{N}, +, L >$ such that $D_{L'} = \infty$.

Proof This follows from Theorem 3.7 and Proposition 3.4.

Acknowledgements This work has been done with the financial support of La Fondation de l'UQAM, the second author holding the J.A. de Sève post-doctoral scholarship. The second author would also like to thank the Laboratoire de combinatoire et d'informatique-mathématique de l'Université du Québec à Montréal, especially Professor André Joyal for financial support.

We also thank Véronique Bruyère for reading the original proof and helping us to simplify it.

References

[1] V. Bruyère, Entiers et automates finis, U.E. Mons (mémoire de licence en mathématiques) 1984-85

[2] J.R. Büchi, Weak second-order arithmetic and finite automata, Z. Math. Logik Grundlagen Math. 6 (1960), pp 66-92

[3] A. Cobham, On the Base-Dependence of Sets of Numbers Recognizable by Finite-Automata, Math. Systems Theory 3, 1969, pp 186-192.

[4] S. Eilenberg, Automata, Languages and Machines, Academic Press 1974.

[5] H.B. Enderton, A Mathematical Introduction to Logic. Academic Press, 1972.

[6] G. Hansel, A propos d'un théorème de Cobham, in: D. Perrin, ed., Actes de

334

la Fête des Mots, Greco de Programmation, CNRS, Rouen (1982).

[7] B. Hodgson, Décidabilité par automate fini, Ann. Sc. math. du Québec, 1985, Vol 7, No 1, p 39-57.

[8] J. Honkala, A decision method for the recognizability of sets defined by number systems. Informatique théorique et Applications. vol. 20, no 4, 1986, pp 395-403.

[9] R. McNaughton, Review of [2], J. Symbolic Logic 28 (1963), pp 100-102.

[10] C. Michaux, F. Point, Les ensembles k-reconnaissables sont définissables dans $< \mathbb{N}, +, V_k >$, C.R. Acad. Sc. Paris t. 303, Série I, no 19, 1986, p.939-942.

[11] C. Michaux, R. Villemaire, A new proof of Cobham's Theorem on recognizability of natural numbers by finite automata (in preparation).

[12] A. Muchnik, Definable criterion for definability in Presburger Arithmetic and its applications. (Russian) (Preprint, Institut of new technologies, 1991).

[13] D. Perrin, Finite Automata, in: J. van Leeuwen, Handbook of Theoretical Computer Science, Elsevier 1990.

[14] A.L. Semenov, On certain extensions of the arithmetic of addition of natural numbers, Math. USSR. Izvestiya, vol 15 (1980), 2, p.401-418

[15] R. Villemaire, $< \mathbb{N}, +, V_k, V_l >$ is undecidable, Theoretical Computer Science 106 (1992) pp. 337-349.

[16] R. Villemaire, Joining $k-$ and $l-$ recognizable sets of natural numbers Proceeding of the 9th Symposium on Theoretical Aspects of Computer Science, (STACS'92) Paris, France, (1992) Springer lectures notes in Computer Science, vol. 577.

Logical Definability on Infinite Traces *

Werner Ebinger and Anca Muscholl

Universität Stuttgart, Institut für Informatik,
Breitwiesenstr. 20-22, D 70565 Stuttgart

Abstract. The main results of the present paper are the equivalence of
monadic second order logic and recognizability for real trace languages,
and that first order definable, star-free, and aperiodic real trace languages
form the same class of languages. This generalizes results on infinite
words [Tho90a, for an overview] and on finite traces [Tho90b, GRS91]
to infinite traces. It closes the last gap in the different characterizations
of recognizable infinitary trace languages.

1 Introduction

Due to model checking applications and to Büchi's work in the field of infinitary
word languages, it is of great interest to investigate the power of logic in describing sets of infinite traces. In the present paper we provide an answer on some
of the remaining open problems in the theory of infinite traces [DE92, for some
recent open problems]. We show for example that monadic second order logic
again corresponds to recognizability. Our proof is independent of any special
kind of trace automata.

For the weaker first order logic, we generalize results from the theory of words
and finite traces and show that the family of star-free (aperiodic, respectively)
sets of real traces is equivalent to the family of first order definable languages.

Thus we have completed the different characterizations for recognizable infinitary trace languages.

The paper is organized as follows: In Section 2 we recall some basic notions
of trace theory. Further we exhibit known characterizations of recognizability in
the context of infinitary word and real trace languages. In Section 3 we show
the equivalence of monadic second order logic and recognizability for real trace
languages. This is a generalization of the corresponding results for infinite words
[Tho90a, for an overview] and finite traces [Tho90b]. Together with a result
of Section 4 this provides a new proof for Métivier's [Mét86, Theorem 2.3] and
Ochmanski's [Och85, Lemma 8.2] result on the recognizability of the *-iteration
of connected recognizable trace languages. In Section 4, we consider first order logic on real traces. First we describe how to transform in the finitary case
formulae for words to formulae for traces, and vice versa. Then we show that
first order definable languages are exactly the star-free languages. Finally, we

---

* This research has been supported by the EBRA working group No. 6317 ASMICS2.

show the equivalence of star-freeness and aperiodicity by using results for finite traces [GRS91]. Some of our ideas have been proposed independently by H. J. Hoogeboom, W. Thomas, and W. Zielonka (personal communication).

2 Preliminaries

2.1 Basic Notions

We denote by (Σ, D) a finite *dependence alphabet*, with Σ being a finite alphabet and $D \subseteq \Sigma \times \Sigma$ a reflexive and symmetric relation called *dependence relation*. The complementary relation $I = (\Sigma \times \Sigma) \setminus D$ is called *independence relation*. The notations $D(a) = \{ b \in \Sigma \mid (a, b) \in D \}$ and $D(\Sigma') = \bigcup_{a \in \Sigma'} D(a)$, with $\Sigma' \subseteq \Sigma$, (analogously for I) will be used throughout the paper.

The monoid of *finite traces*, $\mathbf{M}(\Sigma, D)$, is defined as a quotient monoid with respect to the congruence relation induced by I, i.e. $\mathbf{M}(\Sigma, D) = \Sigma^* / \{ ab \equiv ba \mid (a, b) \in I \}$. The empty trace (and the empty word as well) is denoted by 1. Traces can be identified with their *dependence graph*, i.e. with (isomorphism classes of) labelled, acyclic, directed graphs $[V, E, \ell]$, where V is a set of vertices labelled by $\ell : V \to \Sigma$ and E is a set of edges between vertices with dependent labels. More precisely, we have for every $x, y \in V$, $(\ell(x), \ell(y)) \in D$ if and only if $x = y$ or $(x, y) \in E$ or $(y, x) \in E$. This notion provides a natural definition of infinite traces by means of infinite dependence graphs. We denote by $\mathbb{G}(\Sigma, D)$ the set of infinite dependence graphs having a countable set of vertices V such that $\ell^{-1}(a)$ is well-ordered for all $a \in \Sigma$. The set $\mathbb{G}(\Sigma, D)$ is a monoid by the operation $[V_1, E_1, \ell_1][V_2, E_2, \ell_2] = [V, E, \ell]$, where $[V, E, \ell]$ is the disjoint union of $[V_1, E_1, \ell_1]$ and $[V_2, E_2, \ell_2]$ together with new edges $(v_1, v_2) \in V_1 \times V_2$, whenever $(\ell_1(v_1), \ell_2(v_2)) \in D$ holds. The identity is the empty graph $[\emptyset, \emptyset, \emptyset]$. The concatenation is immediately extendable to infinite products. Let $(g_n)_{n \geq 0} \subseteq \mathbb{G}(\Sigma, D)$. The infinite product $g = g_0 g_1 \ldots \in \mathbb{G}(\Sigma, D)$ is defined as the disjoint union of the g_n, together with new edges from g_n to g_m for $n < m$ between vertices with dependent labels. Thus, we can now define the ω-*iteration* of $A \subseteq \mathbb{G}(\Sigma, D)$ as $A^\omega = \{ g_0 g_1 \ldots \mid g_n \in A, \forall n \geq 0 \}$.

We denote by Σ^ω the set of infinite words over the alphabet Σ (i.e. mappings from $\mathbb{N}$ to Σ), and by Σ^∞ the set of all words $\Sigma^* \cup \Sigma^\omega$. The *canonical mapping* $\varphi : \Sigma^* \to \mathbf{M}(\Sigma, D)$ can be extended to Σ^∞, i.e. $\varphi : \Sigma^\infty \to \mathbb{G}(\Sigma, D)$. The image $\varphi(\Sigma^\infty) \subseteq \mathbb{G}(\Sigma, D)$ is called the set of *real traces* and is denoted by $\mathbb{R}(\Sigma, D)$. Real traces correspond to those (in)finite graphs, where every vertex has finitely many predecessors. Throughout this paper we denote $\mathbb{R}(\Sigma, D)$ ($\mathbf{M}(\Sigma, D)$, respectively) by $\mathbb{R}$ ($\mathbf{M}$, respectively).

Observe that $\mathbb{R}(\Sigma, D)$ is not a submonoid of $\mathbb{G}(\Sigma, D)$, since, in general, φ commutes neither with concatenation nor with ω-iteration. The solution to this concatenation problem is given by considering complex traces [Die91]. Since we consider real traces only, we choosed the approach of viewing the concatenation as a partially defined operation on $\mathbb{R}$, i.e., $t = t_1 t_2$ for $t_1, t_2 \in \mathbb{R}$ is defined only if $t \in \mathbb{R}$. Note that this condition is always fulfilled for $t_1 \in \mathbf{M}$.

A word language $L \subseteq \Sigma^\infty$ is said to be *closed* (with respect to (Σ, D)) if $L = \varphi^{-1}\varphi(L)$ for the canonical mapping $\varphi : \Sigma^\infty \to \mathbf{R}$.

We denote by alph(t) the set of letters occuring in a trace t. We mean then by $I(t)$ the set $I(\text{alph}(t))$ (analogously for D). We also use the abbreviation $(t, u) \in I$ for alph(t) × alph(u) $\subseteq I$.

A trace is called *connected* if its dependence graph is connected. A language is called *connected* if all its elements are connected. Every trace $t \in \mathbf{R}$ can be decomposed in connected components $t = t_1 \dot\cup \ldots \dot\cup t_n$, i.e. every t_i is a connected factor of $t = t_1 t_2 \ldots$ and $(t_i, t_j) \in I$, for $1 \leq i \neq j \leq n$. Let $A \subseteq \mathbf{M}$, then the language of its connected components is defined as $\mathrm{CC}(A) = \{ u \in \mathbf{M} \mid u$ is a connected component of some $t \in A \}$.

The set of letters occuring infinitely often in a real trace t is denoted alphinf(t).

2.2 Recognizable Infinitary Word and Trace Languages

In this section we recall some properties of *recognizable* subsets of Σ^∞ and $\mathbf{R}$, which we denote by Rec(Σ^∞) and Rec($\mathbf{R}$), respectively. Recognizable infinitary word languages can be characterized in several ways. The most familiar one involves finite state *automata*, which are equipped with suitable acceptance conditions. These conditions specify (eventually partially) the set of states, which have to occur infinitely often in an accepting path. A further characterization is given by *ω-rational expressions*, which are built over finite languages of finite words by using the operations union, concatenation, Kleene-* and ω-iteration. Following the definition of the infinite product for dependence graphs, we have for $A \subseteq \Sigma^*$, $A^\omega = \{ w \in \Sigma^\infty \mid w = w_0 w_1 \ldots,$ with $w_n \in A$ for $n \geq 0 \}$. In particular, if $1 \in A$, then $A^\omega = A^* \cup (A \setminus \{1\})^\omega$.

Finally, from the logical viewpoint, recognizability of (infinitary) word languages corresponds to definability in a *monadic second order logic* framework [Büc60].

One possible way to define *recognizable infinitary trace languages* is by recognizing morphisms [Gas91]. Let $\eta : \mathbf{M} \to S$ be a morphism to a finite monoid S. A trace language $A \subseteq \mathbf{R}$ is recognized by η if for any sequence $(t_n)_{n \geq 0} \subseteq \mathbf{M}$:

$$t_0 t_1 t_2 \ldots \in A \quad \Longrightarrow \quad \eta^{-1}\eta(t_0)\, \eta^{-1}\eta(t_1)\, \eta^{-1}\eta(t_2) \ldots \subseteq A .$$

Moreover, in this case we may express A by $A = \bigcup_{(s,e) \in P_A} \eta^{-1}(s)\, \eta^{-1}(e)^\omega$ with $P_A = \{ (s, e) \in S^2 \mid se = s, e^2 = e$ and $\eta^{-1}(s)\, \eta^{-1}(e)^\omega \cap A \neq \emptyset \}$. An equivalent definition uses the *syntactic congruence* of Arnold [Arn85]. For $A \subseteq \mathbf{R}$, two finite traces $u, v \in \mathbf{M}$ are syntactically congruent if and only if for every $x, y, z \in \mathbf{M}$, $x(uy)^\omega \in A \Leftrightarrow x(vy)^\omega \in A$ and $xuyz^\omega \in A \Leftrightarrow xvyz^\omega \in A$ hold. We denote the syntactic congruence by $\equiv_A$ and consider the canonical morphism $\eta : \mathbf{M} \to \mathrm{Synt}(A)$, where $\mathrm{Synt}(A) = \mathbf{M}/\equiv_A$ is the *syntactic monoid* of A. Then $A \in \mathrm{Rec}(\mathbf{R})$ if and only if the syntactic congruence $\equiv_A$ has finite index and $\eta : \mathbf{M} \to \mathrm{Synt}(A)$ recognizes A. Furthermore, for $A \subseteq \mathbf{R}$ we have $\mathrm{Synt}(A) = \mathrm{Synt}(\varphi^{-1}(A))$ [Gas91].

Finally there exist characterizations of Rec($\mathbb{R}$) by asynchronous automata with suitable acceptance conditions. Very recently, Rec($\mathbb{R}$) has also been characterized in terms of *deterministic Muller asynchronous automata* [DM93].

Due to the partial commutativity there can be no equivalence between recognizability and rational expressions. Therefore, Ochmanski [Och85] introduced the concept of concurrent iteration. With this notion the family of recognizable finitary trace languages has been characterized as the family of *c-rational* (also called co-rational) languages. This characterization has been extended to the infinitary case [GPZ91]. Hereto we refer to Section 3.1.

3 Monadic Second Order Logic over Real Traces

For logical characterizations, a real trace $t \in \mathbb{R}$ can be represented as a labelled partial order $(V, <, \ell)$, which corresponds to the dependence graph of t. Logical *formulae* are defined over a *structure* with *signature* $(V, <, (P_a)_{a \in \Sigma})$. If we do not want to restrict ourselves to $\mathbb{R} \setminus \{1\}$, we have to allow the empty structure $V = \emptyset$. We use first order variables x, y, z, ... ranging over V and monadic second order variables X, Y, Z, ... ranging over $\mathcal{P}(V)$. Formulae are defined inductively as follows.

- *Atomic formulae:* First order predicates of the form $x < y$, $P_a(x)$ and monadic second order predicates of the form $X(x)$ are formulae, where x, y, X denote variables and $a \in \Sigma$.
- *Logical connectives:* If ψ_1 and ψ_2 are formulae, then $(\psi_1 \wedge \psi_2)$, $(\psi_1 \vee \psi_2)$, $(\psi_1 \rightarrow \psi_2)$, and $(\neg \psi_1)$ are formulae, too.
- *Quantifiers:* If ψ is a formula, then $\exists x \psi$, $\forall x \psi$, $\exists X \psi$, and $\forall X \psi$ are formulae, too.

We denote this monadic second order logic system by MSO. We will also write $x \in X$ instead of $X(x)$ and freely use abbreviations like $X \subseteq Y$ for $\forall x\, (x \in X \rightarrow x \in Y)$ and $x = y$ for $\forall Z\, (x \in Z \leftrightarrow y \in Z)$. A real trace t is a model for a sentence (i.e. a formula without free variables) ψ, if ψ is satisfied by t under the canonical interpretation (in symbols $t \models \psi$). This means that variables are mapped to (sets of) vertices of the dependence graph $G(t)$ of t, the relation $<$ is interpreted as the partial order in $G(t)$, and the predicate $P_a(x)$ means that x is labelled with $a \in \Sigma$.

In this monadic second order system, the power of logic does not depend on the difference between the $<$-relation and the edge relation of the Hasse diagram of $(V, <, \ell)$, which constitutes some kind of successor relation. The edge relation E of the Hasse diagram of $(V, <, \ell)$ is expressible by $<$ (even in first order logic): $x\ E\ y$ iff $x < y \wedge \neg \exists z\, (x < z \wedge z < y)$ and vice versa (in MSO): $x < y$ iff $\neg x = y \wedge \forall X (x \in X \wedge \forall z \forall z' (z \in X \wedge z\ E\ z' \rightarrow z' \in X) \rightarrow y \in X)$. Therefore we are free to use both, the $<$-relation and the edge relation E in monadic second order formulae.

3.1 Equivalence of Recognizability and Monadic Second Order Logic

Before introducing *c-rational languages* let us define for $A \subseteq \mathbf{M}$ the *concurrent $*$-iteration* $A^{c*} = (\text{CC}(A))^*$ and the *concurrent ω-iteration* $A^{c\omega} = (\text{CC}(A))^\omega$.

- All *finite subsets of* $\mathbf{M}$ are c-rational trace languages.
- If $A \subseteq \mathbf{M}$ and $B, C \subseteq \mathbf{R}$ are c-rational, then the *concatenation* $A\,B$ and the *union* $B \cup C$ are c-rational, too.
- If $A \subseteq \mathbf{M}$ is c-rational, then the *concurrent $*$-iteration* A^{c*} and the *concurrent ω-iteration* $A^{c\omega}$ are c-rational, too.

In the proof of the following theorem we use an equivalent definition af c-rational languages, where the last item above is replaced by the following one [Och85, GPZ91]:

- If $A \subseteq \mathbf{M}$ is c-rational and *connected*, then the $*$-*iteration* A^* and the ω-*iteration* A^ω are c-rational, too.

The proof of the next theorem is based on the corresponding equivalence for infinitary word languages [Büc60]. Furthermore, it makes use of the equivalence between $\text{Rec}(\mathbf{R})$ and the family of c-rational subsets of $\mathbf{R}$ [GPZ91].

Theorem 1. *A trace language $A \subseteq \mathbf{R}$ is recognizable if and only if A is definable in monadic second order logic.*

Proof. The figure below sketches what we intend to show.

$$
\begin{array}{ccccc}
 & & \varphi^{-1}(A) \text{ is} & (\text{Büchi}) & \varphi^{-1}(A) \text{ is} \\
 & \overset{(1)}{\Longrightarrow} & \text{definable} & \Longleftrightarrow & \text{recog-} & \overset{[\text{Gas91}]}{\Longleftrightarrow} \\
A \text{ is} & & \text{in MSO} & & \text{nizable} & & A \text{ is} \\
\text{definable} & & & & & & \text{recog-} \\
\text{in MSO} & \overset{(2)}{\Longleftarrow} & & & \overset{[\text{GPZ91}]}{\Longleftrightarrow} & & \text{nizable} \\
 & & A \text{ is} & & & & \\
 & & \text{c-rational} & & & &
\end{array}
$$

(1): It suffices (cf. Section 3) to express the edge relation E by the linear order on words, which we denote below by $<_{lin}$ in order to avoid confusion: $x\,E\,y$ if and only if

$$
\bigvee_{(a,b) \in D} \left(P_a(x) \wedge P_b(y) \wedge x <_{lin} y \wedge \forall z \left(x <_{lin} z \wedge z <_{lin} y \rightarrow \bigwedge_{c \in D(\{a,b\})} \neg P_c(z) \right) \right) .
$$

(2): For this implication of the diagram we perform an induction over c-rational expressions. Since we characterize both finite and infinite traces, every formula we give states implicitly whether the satisfying traces are finite or not.

- A is a finite subset of $\mathbf{M}$: We give a formula ψ_t for every single trace in A and combine them in a disjunction $\psi_A = \bigvee_{t \in A} \psi_t$.

- $A \cup B$ for c-rational sets A and B: Combine the formulae ψ_A and ψ_B for A and B to $\psi_{A \cup B} = \psi_A \vee \psi_B$.
- $A \cdot B$ for c-rational sets $A \subseteq \mathbf{M}$ and $B \subseteq \mathbf{R}$: For the formulae ψ_A and ψ_B we define formulae with restricted quantification. $\psi_A|_X$ for some set variable X is the formula ψ_A where we replace every subformula $\exists x \psi$ by $\exists x \, (x \in X \wedge \psi)$, $\forall x \psi$ by $\forall x \, (x \in X \rightarrow \psi)$, $\exists Y \psi$ by $\exists Y \, (Y \subseteq X \wedge \psi)$, and $\forall Y \psi$ by $\forall Y \, (Y \subseteq X \rightarrow \psi)$. The formula $\psi_{A \cdot B}$ is defined as

$$\bigvee_{0 \le k \le |\Sigma|} \exists x_1 \ldots \exists x_k \left(\psi_A|_{\{x| \bigvee_{1 \le i \le k} x \le x_i\}} \wedge \psi_B|_{\{x| \bigwedge_{1 \le j \le k} \neg x \le x_i\}} \right) ,$$

where the variables $x_1, \ldots, x_k$ stand for the possible maximal elements of the left part in A.
- A^*, A^ω for a connected c-rational set $A \subseteq \mathbf{M}$: Let ψ_A denote the sentence defining $A \subseteq \mathbf{M}$ and assume $1 \notin A$.
  The formula below is based on a colouring of the vertices of the dependence graph of a factorization $t_1 t_2 \ldots$, such that every factor t_i is one-coloured and if two different factors have the same colour, then there is no edge in the Hasse diagram between them. Two factors t_i, t_j will have the same colour only if $\mathrm{alph}(t_i) = \mathrm{alph}(t_j)$. For every $\Sigma' \subseteq \Sigma$ we take 2 colours and colour alternatingly the factors t_i with one of the colours of $\mathrm{alph}(t_i)$.
  We define ψ_{A^*} and ψ_{A^ω} as

$$\exists X_1 \ldots \exists X_k \, (\psi_1 \wedge \psi_2 \wedge \psi_3 \wedge \psi_4) ,$$

where $X_1, \ldots, X_k$ stand for the colouring mentioned above with $k = 2^{|\Sigma|+1}$. ψ_1 is a formula with the meaning that V is the disjoint union of all X_i. For the next two subformulae we define some abbreviations. By $mocs(X)$ we mean that X is a 'maximal one-coloured connected subgraph' of the Hasse diagram, or more formally, we define $mocs(X)$ as

$$\bigvee_{1 \le i \le k} \left(X \subseteq X_i \wedge \text{``}X \text{ is connected''} \right.$$
$$\left. \wedge \, \forall y \forall z \, \big((y \in X \wedge z \in X_i \wedge (z \, E \, y \vee y \, E \, z)) \rightarrow z \in X \big) \right) ,$$

where E stands for the edge relation of the Hasse diagram. The formula ψ_2 ensures that every $mocs$-component is an element of A and is defined as:

$$\forall X \, (mocs(X) \rightarrow \psi_A|_X) .$$

Note that since A is a finitary language, the $mocs$-components satisfying ψ_2 will automatically be finite.

The underlying interpretation of the $mocs$-components is that they are factors of the given trace. In order to ensure that the $mocs$-components can be ordered, we define $X \prec Y$ as $\exists x \exists y \, (x \in X \wedge y \in Y \wedge x < y)$. The formula ψ_3 ensures that there are no cycles in the relation $\prec$. Note that every cycle, which is longer than $|\Sigma|$ can be shortened. Therefore it is possible to define ψ_3 as follows:

$$\neg \bigvee_{2 \leq l \leq |\Sigma|} \exists Y_1 \ldots \exists Y_l \left(\bigwedge_{1 \leq i \leq l} mocs(Y_i) \wedge Y_1 \prec Y_2 \wedge \ldots \wedge Y_{l-1} \prec Y_l \wedge Y_l \prec Y_1 \right).$$

Finally ψ_4 determines whether the trace is finite or not, depending on the type of iteration. $\square$

Remark 2. In Section 4 we transform formulae on finite words to formulae on finite traces directly. Note that this provides, together with Theorem 1, a new proof for Métivier's [Mét86, Theorem 2.3] and Ochmanski's [Och85, Lemma 8.2] result on the recognizability of the *-iteration of connected recognizable finitary trace languages.

Remark 3. Theorem 1 can also be shown using Büchi asynchronous cellular automata defined by P. Gastin and A. Petit [GP92]. Considering runs of such an automaton as labellings of the dependence graph with local states, one can show [Ebi92] that a trace language $A \subseteq \mathbb{R}$ is accepted by some Büchi asynchronous cellular automaton if and only if A is definable in MSO.

4   First Order Logic on Real Traces

First order logical formulae are defined like second order formulae, but without second order variables. Note that for traces $x = y$ is equivalent to $\bigvee_{a \in \Sigma} (P_a(x) \wedge P_a(y) \wedge \neg(x < y) \wedge \neg(y < x))$. We denote this first order logic by FO.

In the (infinitary) word case [Tho90a, for an overview] star-free languages, aperiodic languages, and first order definable languages form the same class of languages. For finite traces it has been shown that star-free languages coincide with aperiodic languages [GRS91]. Independently from our work it has been shown for finite traces, that star-freeness and FO-definability are equivalent properties [TZ91].

4.1   Connection to the Word Case

Our first result connects the logical definability of finitary word languages to the logical definability of finitary trace languages (this theorem also holds for higher order logic). By our results in Sections 4.2, 4.3 the next theorem will immediately follow also in the general case of real trace languages.

Theorem 4. *A trace language $A \subseteq \mathbb{M}$ is definable in first order logic if and only if $\varphi^{-1}(A)$ is definable in first order logic.*

Proof. It suffices to express the partial order on traces by the linear order on words and vice versa.

"$\Rightarrow$": We express the partial order on traces by a first order formula using the linear order on words, which we denote again by $<_{lin}$: $x < y$ in the partial order on traces if and only if

$$
\bigvee_{\substack{1 \leq l \leq |\Sigma| \\ \text{with } (a_i, a_{i+1}) \in D \\ \text{for } 1 \leq i \leq l-1}} \bigvee_{\{a_1,\dots,a_l\} \subseteq \Sigma} \exists x_2 \dots \exists x_{l-1} \Big(P_{a_1}(x) \wedge P_{a_2}(x_2) \wedge \dots \wedge P_{a_{l-1}}(x_{l-1}) \wedge P_{a_l}(y) \wedge \\ x <_{lin} x_2 <_{lin} \dots <_{lin} x_{l-1} <_{lin} y \Big) .
$$

"$\Leftarrow$": In order to interpret a formula for words on traces, we view the trace t as one of its representing words, since the word formula is satisfied either by all representing words of t or by none. As representing word we choose the lexicographic normal form. For a linear ordering $<_\Sigma$ of Σ, there is a representing word $w \in \varphi^{-1}(t)$, which is lexicographically the first one. This word is called the *lexicographic normal form* of t. A word $w \in \Sigma^*$ is the lexicographic normal form of its trace if and only if for each factor aub of w with $a, b \in \Sigma$, $u \in \Sigma^*$, and $(au, b) \in I$, it holds $a <_\Sigma b$ [Per84a]. The use of the lexicographic normal form here was observed independently by W. Zielonka (personal communication). We have $x <_{lin} y$ in the linear order on the lexicographic normal form if and only if

$$
x < y \vee \Big(\neg x < y \wedge \neg y < x \wedge \bigvee_{\substack{(a,b) \in I \\ a <_\Sigma b}} (P_a(x) \wedge P_b(y)) \Big) .
$$

$\Box$

Remark 5. Clearly, the step from traces to words in the above proof holds for any language of real traces.

Since the lexicographic normal form is in general undefined for real traces, the above proof can be extended directly to real traces only for the special case where the considered language contains only traces t where alphinf(t) is connected.

4.2 Equivalence of Star-Free Expressions and First Order Logic

The family of *star-free* finitary trace languages SF(**M**) is the closure of singleton sets $\{t\}$ ($t \in$ **M**) by boolean operations and concatenation [GRS91].

Definition 6. The family SF(**R**) of *star-free* real trace languages is the smallest family $\mathcal{F}$ of subsets of **R** with
1. SF(**M**) $\subseteq \mathcal{F}$,
2. $AB \in \mathcal{F}$ for any $A, B \in \mathcal{F}$, $A \subseteq$ **M**, $B \subseteq$ **R**, and
3. $\mathcal{F}$ is closed under boolean operations (complement is meant w.r.t. **R**).

Note that since **M** $\in$ SF(**R**) holds, the complementation with respect to **M** can be obtained by complementing with respect to **R** and intersecting with **M**.

We will consider formulae and languages with *free variables*. For a set W of free variables we add to the structure $(V, <, \ell)$ a mapping $\sigma : W \to V$, which maps every free variable to a vertex in the dependence graph of the trace. Thus we obtain a new structure $(V, <, \ell, \sigma)$ for a trace. If a trace has no free variables, then σ is the empty mapping and the new structure $(V, <, \ell, \emptyset)$ may be identified with $(V, <, \ell)$. A set $\mathbf{M}$, $\mathbb{R}$, A, B, ... with free variables W is denoted by $\mathbf{M}_W$, $\mathbb{R}_W$, A_W, B_W, ..., a trace t with free variables W is denoted by t_W. Often we will omit the subscript of a set A_W and write W_A for the set of free variables of A. Concatenation of traces with free variables is defined only on traces with disjoint sets of free variables. If $u = (V_u, <_u, \ell_u, \sigma_u)$ and $v = (V_v, <_v, \ell_v, \sigma_v)$ are traces with sets W_u, W_v of free variables and $W_u \cap W_v = \emptyset$, then the dependence graph of the concatenation $t = uv = (V_t, <_t, \ell_t, \sigma_t)$ is defined as the usual concatenation of the two traces together with the mapping $\sigma_t = \sigma_u \cup \sigma_v$. The complement of a language $A \subseteq \mathbb{R}_W$ is taken w.r.t. $\mathbb{R}_W$.

The following lemma states some useful properties of star-free trace languages over the extended structure defined above. We define the left and right quotients $t^{-1}A$ and At^{-1} for $t \in \mathbb{R}_U$, $A \subseteq \mathbb{R}_W$ as $t^{-1}A = \{v \mid tv \in A\}$ and $At^{-1} = \{v \mid vt \in A\}$. Note that the partial monoid of real traces is not cancellative. If uv, uv', vu, and $v'u$ are defined, we have $uv = uv' \Rightarrow v = v'$, but $vu = v'u \not\Rightarrow v = v'$. Especially it does not hold that $\{t\}t^{-1} = \{1\}$, for example $\{a^\omega\}(a^\omega)^{-1} = a^* \neq \{1\}$. The proof of the next lemma is omitted for lack of space.

Lemma 7. *1. For any $\Sigma' \subseteq \Sigma$, the languages $(\Sigma'^*)_W$ and $(\Sigma'^\omega)_W$ are star-free.*
2. Let $t \in \mathbb{R}_U$ and $A \subseteq \mathbb{R}_W$ ($U \subseteq W$). Then the left and right quotients $t^{-1}A$ and At^{-1} commute with $\cup$ and $\cap$. Moreover, $\overline{t^{-1}A} = t^{-1}\overline{A} \cup \{u \in \mathbb{R}_{W \setminus U} \mid tu \notin \mathbb{R}_W\}$ holds (analogously, $\overline{At^{-1}} = \overline{A}t^{-1} \cup \{u \in \mathbb{R}_{W \setminus U} \mid ut \notin \mathbb{R}_W\}$).
3. Let $A \in SF(\mathbb{R}_W)$ and $U \subseteq W$. Then the set of left (right) quotients $\{t^{-1}A \mid t \in \mathbb{R}_U\}$ ($\{At^{-1} \mid t \in \mathbb{R}_U\}$) is a finite subset of $SF(\mathbb{R}_{W \setminus U})$.

Theorem 8. *A trace language $A \subseteq \mathbb{R}$ is definable in first order logic if and only if it is star-free.*

Proof. "$\Leftarrow$": In order to construct logical formulae from star-free expressions, we replace the set operations by the corresponding logical operations. For concatenation we can use the first order formula we gave in Section 3.

"$\Rightarrow$": We give a proof by induction on the construction of formulae.

Predicates: The set of infinite traces with a set of free variables W satisfying $x < y$ for some variables x, y, is the star-free trace language (we omit the subscripts for $\mathbf{M}, \mathbb{R}$)

$$\bigcup_{\text{finite}} \quad \bigcup_{\substack{a_1 \in \Sigma_X, a_l \in \Sigma_Y, \ x \in X, \ y \in Y \\ \text{with } (a_i, a_{i+1}) \in D \text{ for } 1 \leq i \leq l-1}} \quad \mathbf{M}a_1 \mathbf{M} \ldots \mathbf{M}a_l \mathbb{R} \ .$$

Note that the variable sets omitted above form a partition of W and $l \leq |\Sigma|$.

The language for $P_a(x)$ with a set of free variables W is $\bigcup_{\text{finite}} \mathbf{M}a\mathbb{R}$ with $x \in W_a$. For $x = y$ we have $\bigcup_{\text{finite}} \bigcup_{\substack{a \in \Sigma \\ x, y \in W_a}} \mathbf{M}a\mathbb{R}$.

Induction step: For $\wedge$, $\vee$, $\neg$ we use the corresponding set operations. Finally, for quantified formulae, if $A \in SF(\mathbb{R})$ is a language defined by ψ and $x \in W_A$, then we can write [PP86] $A = \bigcup_{ua \in \mathbb{R}, \ x \in W_a, \ a \in \Sigma} B(u)\,a\,C(u)$ with $C(u) =$

$(ua)^{-1}A$, $B(u) = \bigcap_{v \in C(u)} A(av)^{-1}$. By Lemma 7 the union above is finite. Finally, the language defined by the formula $\exists x \psi$ is $A' = \bigcup_{ua \in R} B(u) \, a \, C(u)$ with $W_{A'} = W_A \setminus \{x\}$. □

4.3 Aperiodic and Star-Free Real Trace Languages

A monoid is called *aperiodic* if it satisfies the equation $x^n = x^{n+1}$ for some $n > 0$. Let $A \subseteq \mathbb{R}$ be a real trace language. A is called *aperiodic* if there exists a morphism $\eta : \mathbf{M} \to S$ to an aperiodic, finite monoid S recognizing A.

We denote the family of aperiodic real (finitary, respectively) trace languages by $\mathrm{AP}(\mathbb{R})$ ($\mathrm{AP}(\mathbf{M})$, respectively). We use analogous notations for word languages. We recall that the equivalence between aperiodicity and star-freeness holds for finitary word languages by Schützenberger's theorem [Sch65], for infinitary word languages by a result of D. Perrin [Per84b] and for finitary trace languages by Guaiana et. al. [GRS91].

If $A \in \mathrm{Rec}(\Sigma^\infty)$ ($A \in \mathrm{Rec}(\mathbb{R})$, resp.) is recognized by a morphism $\eta : \Sigma^* \to S$ ($\eta : \mathbf{M} \to S$, resp.) to a finite monoid S, then we use the following notations for $s \in S$:

$$X_s = \eta^{-1}(s) \quad (\mathbf{M}_s = \eta^{-1}(s), \text{ resp.}) ,$$
$$P_s = X_s \setminus X_s \Sigma^+ \quad (P_s = \mathbf{M}_s \setminus \mathbf{M}_s \mathbf{M}_+, \text{ resp., with } \mathbf{M}_+ = \mathbf{M} \setminus \{1\}) .$$

Thus, P_s is the prefix-free subset of X_s ($\mathbf{M}_s$, resp.).

Moreover, we may assume that $\mathrm{alph}(t) = \mathrm{alph}(t')$ for all $t, t' \in \mathbf{M}$ with $\eta(t) = \eta(t')$ holds, since we may replace S by $S \times \mathcal{P}(\Sigma)$, with the multiplication defined by $(s, \Gamma)(s', \Gamma') = (ss', \Gamma \cup \Gamma')$ and $(1, \emptyset)$ as identity. Moreover we replace $\eta(a)$ with $(\eta(a), \{a\})$ for $a \in \Sigma$. Hence, $\mathrm{alph}(s)$ for $s \in S$ is well-defined and will be an abbreviation for $\mathrm{alph}(\mathbf{M}_s)$. Note that any aperiodic monoid S remains aperiodic if we replace it by $S \times \mathcal{P}(\Sigma)$.

For $\Sigma' \subseteq \Sigma$, let $\mathbb{R}_{\Sigma'} = \{ t \in \mathbb{R} \mid D(\mathrm{alphinf}(t)) = D(\Sigma') \}$. Note that in the word case (i.e. $D = \Sigma \times \Sigma$) we have $\mathbb{R}_{\Sigma'} = \Sigma^\omega$, for every $\emptyset \neq \Sigma' \subseteq \Sigma$ and $\mathbb{R}_\emptyset = \Sigma^*$. In particular, we denote by $\mathbb{R}_s$ for $s \in S$ the set $\mathbb{R}_{\Sigma'}$ with $\Sigma' = \mathrm{alph}(s)$. In the definition below the notion of upper bound (resp. least upper bound $\sqcup$) is meant with respect to the prefix order on traces.

Definition 9. [DM93] Let $A \subseteq \mathbf{M}$. We define

$$\overrightarrow{A} = \{ t \in \mathbb{R} \mid t = \sqcup B \text{ with } B \text{ directed and } B \subseteq A \} .$$

A set $B \subseteq \mathbf{M}$ is called directed if for every $t, t' \in B$, there exists an upper bound of t, t' which also belongs to B.

Lemma 10. [DM93] *Let S be a finite monoid, $\eta : \mathbf{M} \to S$ a morphism and $e \in S$ such that $e^2 = e$. Then we have $\mathbf{M}_e^\omega = \overrightarrow{\mathbf{M}_e P_e} \cap \mathbb{R}_e$.*

Theorem 11. *The family of star-free subsets of $\mathbb{R}$ coincides with the family of aperiodic real trace languages.*

Proof. "⇐": Let us first show that every aperiodic language $A \subseteq \mathbb{R}$ is star-free. To this purpose, consider $\eta : \mathbf{M} \to S$ a morphism to a finite, aperiodic monoid S recognizing A. Then, $A = \bigcup_{(s,e) \in P} \mathbf{M}_s \mathbf{M}_e^\omega$, with $P = \{ (s,e) \in S^2 \mid se = s, e^2 = e, \mathbf{M}_s \mathbf{M}_e^\omega \cap A \neq \emptyset \}$. Since $\mathbf{M}_s \in \mathrm{SF}(\mathbf{M})$ [GRS91], it suffices to show that $\mathbf{M}_e^\omega \in \mathrm{SF}(\mathbb{R})$. Due to Lemma 10 and since $\mathbb{R}_e$ is easily shown to be star-free, it suffices to show $\overrightarrow{\mathbf{M}_e P_e} \in \mathrm{SF}(\mathbb{R})$. More generally, if $B \in \mathrm{AP}(\mathbf{M})$ is recognized by a morphism $\eta : \mathbf{M} \to M$ to a finite, aperiodic monoid M, then we may write the complement of $\overrightarrow{B}$ as a star-free expression (in analogy to the word case [Per84b]):

$$\overline{\overrightarrow{B}} = \bigcup_{p \in M} \left(\mathbf{M}_p \left(\mathbb{R} \setminus \bigcup_{q \text{ with } pq \in \eta(B)} \mathbf{M}_q \mathbb{R} \right) \right) .$$

"⇒": For this inclusion, it suffices to show that $A \in \mathrm{SF}(\mathbb{R})$ implies $\varphi^{-1}(A) \in \mathrm{SF}(\Sigma^\infty)$, since $\mathrm{SF}(\Sigma^\infty) = \mathrm{AP}(\Sigma^\infty)$ and $\mathrm{Synt}(A) = \mathrm{Synt}(\varphi^{-1}(A))$. We proceed by induction on the star-free expression denoting $A \in \mathrm{SF}(\mathbb{R})$. For $A \in \mathrm{SF}(\mathbf{M})$ we have $A \in \mathrm{AP}(\mathbf{M})$ by [GRS91], hence $\varphi^{-1}(A) \in \mathrm{AP}(\Sigma^*) = \mathrm{SF}(\Sigma^*)$. Furthermore, let $A = A_1 \cup A_2$ ($A = A_1 \cap A_2$, $A = \overline{A_1}$ respectively) with $\varphi^{-1}(A_1), \varphi^{-1}(A_2) \in \mathrm{SF}(\Sigma^\infty)$. Then $\varphi^{-1}(A) \in \mathrm{SF}(\Sigma^\infty)$ holds, since φ^{-1} commutes with the Boolean operations.

Finally, let $A = A_1 A_2$ with $A_1' = \varphi^{-1}(A_1) \in \mathrm{SF}(\Sigma^*)$, $A_2' = \varphi^{-1}(A_2) \in \mathrm{SF}(\Sigma^\infty)$. Then, $\varphi^{-1}(A) = A_1' \sqcup\!\sqcup_D A_2'$, with $\sqcup\!\sqcup_D$ denoting the dependent shuffle operation (with respect to D), defined by $K_1 \sqcup\!\sqcup_D K_2 = \{ u_0 v_0 u_1 v_1 \ldots \mid u_n, v_n \in \Sigma^*, u_0 u_1 \ldots \in K_1, v_0 v_1 \ldots \in K_2 \text{ and } (v_n, u_m) \in I, \text{ for } n < m \}$, where $K_1, K_2 \subseteq \Sigma^\infty$. In particular, we have

$$A_1' \sqcup\!\sqcup_D A_2' = \{ u_0 v_0 \ldots u_n v_n w \mid u_k, v_k \in \Sigma^*, w \in \Sigma^\infty, u_0 u_1 \ldots u_n \in A_1', $$
$$v_0 v_1 \ldots v_n w \in A_2' \text{ and } (v_i, u_k) \in I, \text{ for } i < k \leq n \} .$$

Since $A_1' \in \mathrm{SF}(\Sigma^*) = \mathrm{AP}(\Sigma^*)$ [Sch65] and $A_2' \in \mathrm{SF}(\Sigma^\infty) = \mathrm{AP}(\Sigma^\infty)$ [Per84b], let $\eta_i : \Sigma^* \to S_i$ ($i = 1, 2$) denote the syntactic morphism recognizing A_i', and S_i the aperiodic syntactic monoid. Furthermore, we assume $A_2' \subseteq \Sigma^\omega$ and consider the set $P = \{ (s_2, e_2) \in S_2^2 \mid s_2 e_2 = s_2, e_2^2 = e_2, X_{s_2} X_{e_2}^\omega \cap A_2' \neq \emptyset \}$. Thus, we have $A_2' = \bigcup_{(s_2, e_2) \in P} X_{s_2} X_{e_2}^\omega$ and $A_1' = \eta_1^{-1} \eta_1(A_1')$. It is not hard to see that we may express $A_1' \sqcup\!\sqcup_D A_2'$ by

$$A_1' \sqcup\!\sqcup_D A_2' = \bigcup_{s_1 \in \eta_1(A_1')} \bigcup_{(s_2, e_2) \in P} (X_{s_1} \sqcup\!\sqcup_D X_{s_2}) X_{e_2}^\omega .$$

Therefore, since both X_{s_1} and X_{s_2} are aperiodic, closed finitary word languages (due to A_i' being closed languages), we have $X_{s_1} \sqcup\!\sqcup_D X_{s_2} \in \mathrm{SF}(\Sigma^*)$ [GRS91]. Moreover, since e_2 is an idempotent element of S_2, with S_2 aperiodic, we also have $X_{e_2}^\omega \in \mathrm{SF}(\Sigma^\infty)$ [Per84b]. Hence, $A_1' \sqcup\!\sqcup_D A_2' = \varphi^{-1}(A) \in \mathrm{SF}(\Sigma^\infty)$. □

Summary. Since for every $A \subseteq \mathrm{Rec}(\mathbb{R})$, $\mathrm{Synt}(A) = \mathrm{Synt}(\varphi^{-1}(A))$ holds, we obtained by the results of Section 4 the following equivalent characterizations: 1. A is first order definable. 2. $\varphi^{-1}(A)$ is first order definable. 3. A is star-free. 4. $\mathrm{Synt}(A)$ is aperiodic.

Acknowledgements

We want to thank V. Diekert, P. Gastin, H. J. Hoogeboom, and W. Thomas for many fruitful discussions and the anonymous referee from ICALP for many valuable comments which helped improving this paper.

References

[Arn85]   A. Arnold. A syntactic congruence for rational ω-languages. *Theoretical Computer Science*, 39:333–335, 1985.

[Büc60]   J.R. Büchi. On a decision method in restricted second order arithmetic. In E. Nagel et al., editor, *Proc. Internat. Congr. on Logic, Methodology and Philosophy of Science*, pages 1–11. Stanford Univ. Press, Stanford, CA, 1960.

[DE92]   V. Diekert and W. Ebinger, editors. *Infinite Traces. Proceedings of a workshop of the ESPRIT Basic Research Action No 3166: Algebraic and Syntactic Methods in Computer Science (ASMICS), Tübingen, Germany, 1992*, number 4/92. Universität Stuttgart, Fakultät Informatik, 1992.

[Die91]   V. Diekert. On the concatenation of infinite traces. In Choffrut C. et al., editors, *Proc. 8th STACS, Hamburg 1991*, LNCS 480, pages 105–117. Springer, 1991.

[DM93]   V. Diekert and A. Muscholl. Deterministic asynchronous automata for infinite traces. In P. Enjalbert, A. Finkel, and K. W. Wagner, editors, *Proc. 10th STACS, Würzburg 1993*, LNCS 665, pages 617–628. Springer, 1993.

[Ebi92]   W. Ebinger. On logical definability of ω-trace languages. In Volker Diekert and Werner Ebinger, editors, *Proceedings ASMICS Workshop Infinite Traces, Tübingen*, Bericht 4/92, pages 106–122. Universität Stuttgart, Fakultät Informatik, 1992.

[Gas91]   P. Gastin. Recognizable and rational trace languages of finite and infinite traces. In Choffrut C. et al., editors, *Proc. 8th STACS, Hamburg 1991*, LNCS 480, pages 89–104. Springer, 1991.

[GP92]   P. Gastin and A. Petit. Asynchronous automata for infinite traces. In W. Kuich, editor, *Proc. 19th ICALP, Vienna (Austria) 1992*, LNCS 623, pages 583–594. Springer, 1992.

[GPZ91]   P. Gastin, A. Petit, and W. Zielonka. A Kleene theorem for infinite trace languages. In J. Leach Albert et al., editors, *Proc. 18th ICALP, Madrid (Spain) 1991*, LNCS 510, pages 254–266. Springer, 1991.

[GRS91]   G. Guaiana, A. Restivo, and S. Salemi. On aperiodic trace languages. In Choffrut C. et al., editors, *Proc. 8th STACS, Hamburg 1991*, LNCS 480, pages 76–88. Springer, 1991.

[Mét86]   Y. Métivier. Une condition suffisante de reconnaissabilité dans un monoïde partiellement commutatif. *R.A.I.R.O. — Informatique Théorique et Applications*, 20:121–127, 1986.

[Och85]   E. Ochmanski. Regular behaviour of concurrent systems. *Bulletin of the European Association for Theoretical Computer Science (EATCS)*, 27:56–67, Oct 1985.

[Per84a] D. Perrin. Words over a partially commutative alphabet. Report no. 84-59, LITP Université de Paris VII, 1984. Also appeared in A. Apostolico, editor, *Combinatorial Algorithms on Words*, Springer NATO-ASI Series, Vol. F12, p.329-340, 1986.

[Per84b] D. Perrin. Recent results on automata and infinite words. In M. P. Chytil and V. Koubek, editors, *Proc. 11th MFCS, Praha (CSFR) 1984*, LNCS 176, pages 134–148. Springer, 1984.

[PP86]   D. Perrin and J.-E. Pin. First-order logic and star-free sets. *Journal of Computer and System Sciences*, 32:393–406, 1986.

[Sch65]   M. P. Schützenberger. On finite monoids having only trivial subgroups. *Information and Control*, 8:190–194, 1965.

[Tho90a] W. Thomas. Automata on infinite objects. In Jan van Leeuwen, editor, *Handbook of Theoretical Computer Science*, chapter 4, pages 133–191. Elsevier Science Publishers B. V., 1990.

[Tho90b] W. Thomas. On logical definability of trace languages. In V. Diekert, editor, *Proceedings of a workshop of the ESPRIT Basic Research Action No 3166: Algebraic and Syntactic Methods in Computer Science (ASMICS), Kochel am See, Bavaria, FRG (1989)*, Report TUM-I9002, Technical University of Munich, pages 172–182, 1990.

[TZ91]   W. Thomas and W. Zielonka. Logical definability of trace languages. unpublished manuscript, 1991.

Algebras for Classifying Regular Tree Languages and an Application to Frontier Testability

(Extended Abstract)

Thomas Wilke*

Christian-Albrechts-Universität zu Kiel, Institut für Informatik und Praktische
Mathematik, Hermann-Rodewald-Str. 3, 24118 Kiel, Germany

Abstract. Point-tree algebras, a class of equational three-sorted algebras, are introduced for the purpose of characterizing and classifying
regular tree languages. Any tree over an alphabet A can be identified
with some element of the free point-tree algebra $\mathbf{T}(A)$ generated by A.
A set L of finite binary trees over A is proved to be regular if and only if
L is recognized by a finite point-tree algebra $\mathbf{B}$, i.e. if L (as a subset of
$\mathbf{T}(A)$) is an inverse image under a homomorphism from $\mathbf{T}(A)$ into $\mathbf{B}$.
For each regular tree language a smallest recognizing point-tree algebra,
its syntactic point-tree algebra, is shown to exist and to be effectively
computable.
For the class of frontier testable tree languages a finite set of equations characterizing the corresponding syntactic point-tree algebras is
presented. This is in contrast with other algebraic approaches to the classification of tree languages (the semigroup and the universal-algebraic
approach) where such equations are not possible resp. not known. As
a byproduct one obtains an alternative proof of the decidability of the
class of frontier testable tree languages.

Introduction

Since the sixties a great number of classes of regular languages of finite words,
such as the classes of star-free, locally testable, or piecewise testable languages,
have been characterized algebraically in a very succinct way by giving descriptions of the corresponding syntactic semigroups. These results are in contrast
with the situation for regular sets (languages) of finite trees: only for the class of
root testable tree languages, which corresponds to definiteness in the word case,
an algebraic description is known [5].

There are to mention two basically different approaches to an algebraic treatment of regular tree languages. On the one hand, there is the so-called semigroup
approach [11, 3, 5, 6] which tries to extended the results and methods from the
word case directly to trees. It provides the important instrument of decomposing

* Supported by ESPRIT Basic Research Action No. 6317 Algebraic and Syntactic
Methods in Computer Science 2 (ASMICS 2).

trees along a path (corresponding to decompositions of words), but it ignores the two-dimensional structure which each tree has. So it is not surprising that a class such as the class of frontier testable tree languages cannot be classified in the semigroup framework (Example 2). On the other hand, the universal-algebraic approach proposed in [10] provides an abstract classification theory as represented by Samuel Eilenberg's variety theorem [2] for word languages, but characterizations of concrete classes (in non-trivial cases) are not known.

In this paper we introduce a new kind of algebra for the characterization and classification of regular languages of finite binary trees. We call these point-tree algebras. Within the new framework we give an equational characterization of the class of frontier testable tree languages (which corresponds to the class of reverse definite word languages).[2]

The concept of point-tree algebras can be viewed as an extension of the semigroup approach: apart from associative operations for the (de-) composition of trees along a path point-tree algebras have a ternary operation that connects a letter and two trees to a new tree, taking into account the two-dimensional aspect of every tree.

We show the following general results about point-tree algebras and regular tree languages: the set of trees over a given alphabet forms the free point-tree algebra generated by the elements of the given alphabet (Theorem 1), tree (semi-) automata and finite point-tree algebras correspond to each other in a natural way,[3] a tree language is regular if and only if it is the inverse image of a homomorphism from a free point-tree algebra into a finite point-tree algebra (Proposition 2), for every regular tree language a smallest recognizing point-tree algebra (syntactic point-tree algebra) exists and can effectively be computed (Lemma 3).

In the second part frontier testable tree languages are characterized. Recall that, as for reverse definite word languages, a language of finite trees is called frontier testable if membership to it depends only on the set of subtrees of bounded depth (the bound fixed for the language) occurring at the frontier of a given tree, cf. [3], where it was shown that the class of frontier testable languages is decidable. This was achieved by bounding the degree of frontier testability of a given language by the number of states of a recognizing automaton. We complement this by presenting for each degree k of frontier testability (given by the depth k of the considered frontier trees) a finite set of equations such that a tree language is k-frontier testable iff its syntactic point-tree algebra satisfies these equations.[3] Over the signature of point-tree algebras extended by the (implicit) ω-operation as known from finite semigroup theory, we characterize frontier testability in general by a finite base of identities (Theorem 5).

By means of the close connection between syntactic point-tree algebras and

---

[2] We restrict ourselves to finite binary trees throughout. The nodes of our trees are all labelled with letters of the same alphabet, i.e. we do not have different alphabets for the inner nodes and the leaves.

[3] Because of the page limit this is cut down to a few sentences here. We refer the reader to the full version for more details.

minimal automata the presented equations help to understand the structure of the (minimal) automata of frontier testable languages.

The combinatorial properties of frontier testable languages used in the second part were, in a weaker form, established jointly with T. Scholz (cf. [9]).

Point-Tree algebras

Let A be an arbitrary alphabet. We consider the set $T(A)$ of *(binary) trees* over A, that is, the set of all terms over the ranked alphabet $\Sigma = \Sigma_{(0)} \cup \Sigma_{(2)}$ where $\Sigma_{(0)} = \Sigma_{(2)} = A$.[4] Furthermore we are interested in the set $S(A)$ of all *special trees* [11] over A which can be obtained from the elements of $T(A)$ by substituting $\cdot$ *(point)* for exactly one leaf, i.e. $S(A)$ is the set of all terms over the ranked alphabet $\Sigma' = \Sigma'_{(0)} \cup \Sigma'_{(2)}$ with $\Sigma'_{(0)} = A \cup \{\cdot\}$ and $\Sigma'_{(2)} = A$, where point occurs exactly once. We do not allow the trivial term $\cdot$ in $S(A)$. Special trees are also called *pointed trees* [5].[5] When we want to stress that we are dealing with elements of $T(A)$ and not of $S(A)$ we speak of *ordinary trees* (in contrast to special trees).

In the following we shall describe the relationships between the three sets A, $S(A)$, and $T(A)$ in terms of six functions: $\iota, \rho, \lambda, \sigma, \tau, \kappa$, which we now introduce. (For a graphical illustration see Fig. 1.)

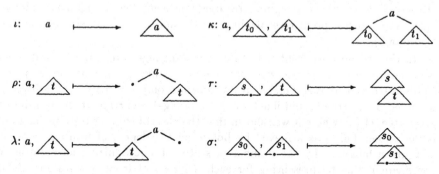

Fig. 1. The six operations on A, $T(A)$, and $S(A)$

$[\iota: A \rightarrow T(A)]$ The function ι identifies each letter a with the one-node tree a.
$[\rho: A \times T(A) \rightarrow S(A)]$ The function ρ takes a letter a and a tree t as arguments and maps them on the special tree with root a and right subtree t, i.e. $\rho(a, t) = a(\cdot, t)$.

---

[4] Here and below we use parantheses in subscripts to indicate the arity of a function symbol, the type of an operation, or the sort of a set.

[5] Our notion of special tree is in fact a slightly modified version of what is called a 'pointed tree' in [5].

$[\lambda: A \times T(A) \to S(A)]$ This is the same function as ρ but placing the given tree to the left of the given letter, i.e. $\lambda(a,t) = a(t, \cdot)$.

$[\kappa: A \times T(A) \times T(A) \to T(A)]$ The function κ associates with a letter a and two trees t_0 and t_1 the tree with root a, left subtree t_0 and right subtree t_1, i.e. $\kappa(a, t_0, t_1) = a(t_0, t_1)$.

$[\tau: S(A) \times T(A) \to T(A)]$ Given a special tree s and a tree t, the function τ substitutes t for point in s, i.e. $\tau(s,t) = s[\cdot/t]$.

$[\sigma: S(A) \times S(A) \to S(A)]$ Given special trees s_0, s_1, the function σ substitutes s_1 for point in s_0, i.e. $\sigma(s_0, s_1) = s_0[\cdot/s_1]$.

Example 1. Let $A = \{0,1\}$. The tree $0(1(0,1(0,1)),0(0,0))$ can be obtained in several ways starting from the letters $0, 1 \in A$. In Fig. 2 a graphical representation of t is given and some of the possible representations in terms of the $\rho, \lambda, \ldots$ are listed.

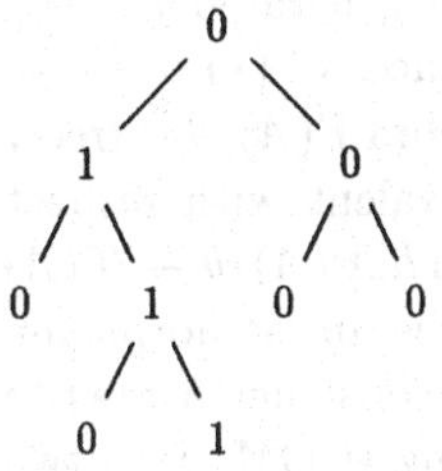

$$
\begin{cases}
\kappa(0, \kappa(1, \iota(0), \kappa(1, \iota(0), \iota(1))), \kappa(0, \iota(0), \iota(0))) \\
\kappa(0, \kappa(1, \iota(0), \kappa(1, \iota(0), \iota(1))), \tau(\rho(0, \iota(0)), \iota(0))) \\
\tau(\sigma(\sigma(\rho(0, \kappa(0, \iota(0), \iota(0))), \lambda(1, \iota(0))), \rho(1, \iota(1))), \iota(0)) \\
\tau(\sigma(\rho(0, \kappa(0, \iota(0), \iota(0))), \sigma(\lambda(1, \iota(0)), \rho(1, \iota(1)))), \iota(0)) \\
\tau(\tau(\rho(0, \kappa(0, \iota(0), \iota(0))), \tau(\sigma(\lambda(1, \iota(0)), \rho(1, \iota(1))), \iota(0)))) \\
\tau(\lambda(0, \tau(\sigma(\lambda(1, \iota(0)), \rho(1, \iota(1))), \iota(0))), \kappa(0, \iota(0), \iota(0)))
\end{cases}
$$

Fig. 2. Different representations of the same tree

Obviously the following identities hold for an arbitrary letter $a \in A$, special trees $s_0, s_1, s_2 \in S(A)$, and ordinary trees $t, t_0, t_1 \in T(A)$.

$$
\left.
\begin{aligned}
&\text{(ASS1)} && \sigma(s_0, \sigma(s_1, s_2)) = \sigma(\sigma(s_0, s_1), s_2) \\
&\text{(ASS2)} && \tau(s_0, \tau(s_1, t)) = \tau(\sigma(s_0, s_1), t) \\
&\text{(COM)} && \tau(\lambda(a, t_0), t_1) = \tau(\rho(a, t_1), t_0) = \kappa(a, t_0, t_1)
\end{aligned}
\right\} (*)
$$

Each of the identities is reflected by at least one of the different presentations given for the tree of Example 1. Equations (ASS1) and (ASS2) express the associativity of the substitution operation used in the definition of σ and τ. Equation (COM) takes into account that it is the same whether we put first a tree to the left of a node and then another tree to the right of that node or do it in the reversed order. In some sense ρ and λ 'commute'.

The equations in $(*)$ are the starting point for the definition of our notion of point-tree algebra. Consider the sort set $S = \{l, s, t\}$, where we think of l as being the sort of letters, of s as being the sort of special trees, and of t as being the sort of ordinary trees. Besides consider the typed signature $\Sigma = \{\iota_{(l,t)}, \lambda_{(lt,s)}, \rho_{(lt,s)}, \kappa_{(ltt,t)}, \sigma_{(ss,s)}, \tau_{(st,t)}\}$. Now $T(A) = A_{(l)} \cup S(A)_{(s)} \cup T(A)_{(t)}$ is the universe (as an S-sorted set) of a Σ-algebra $\mathbf{T}(A)$,[6] which, in addition, sat-

---

[6] We adopt the convention that bold face symbols stand for entire structures.

isfies (∗). In general a Σ-algebra satisfying (∗) will be called a *point-tree algebra*.

Notice that if **B** is a point-tree algebra, then the set $B_{(s)}$ together with the binary operation $\sigma^{\mathbf{B}}$ is a semigroup.

We introduce some conventions concerning the notation of terms over Σ. Let a stand for l-terms, ϕ, ϕ_0, and ϕ_1 for s-terms, and ψ, ψ_0, ψ_1 for t-terms. We simply write $\phi_0\phi_1$ instead of $\sigma(\phi_0,\phi_1)$ and $\phi\psi$ instead of $\tau(\phi,\psi)$ since we have associativity of σ and τ. We also replace $\kappa(a,\psi_0,\psi_1)$ by $a(\phi_0,\phi_1)$ and sometimes write $a(\cdot,\psi)$ for $\rho(a,\psi)$ and $a(\psi,\cdot)$ for $\lambda(a,\psi)$. The single letter a stands for $\iota(a)$.

Our first theorem tells us that the point-tree algebra $\mathbf{T}(A)$ is uniquely determined (up to isomorphism) by (∗).

Theorem 1 (Free point-tree algebras). *Let A be an arbitrary set (possibly infinite). Then $\mathbf{T}(A)$ is a Σ-algebra freely generated by $A_{(l)}$ in the class of point-tree algebras, i.e. in the class of all Σ-algebras satisfying (∗).*

Proof sketch. Let $\mathbf{F}(A)$ denote the (free) Σ-term algebra generated by $A_{(l)}$, and let θ be the congruence relation generated by the instances of (∗) in $\mathbf{F}(A)$. Then, by Birkhoff's theorem, we know that the quotient algebra $\mathbf{F}(A)/\theta$ is freely generated by A/θ. Since distinct letters of A are non-equivalent with respect to θ and $\mathbf{T}(A)$ satisfies (∗), there is a unique homomorphism $h:\mathbf{F}(A)/\theta \to \mathbf{T}(A)$ with $h(a/\theta) = a$ for every $a \in A$. We have to show that h is an isomorphism. It is not hard to see that h is onto. For the injectivity we construct a rewrite system over $\mathbf{F}(A)$ (by reading (∗) from left to right, splitting (COM) into two rules $\tau(\lambda(a,t_0),t_1) \to \kappa(a,t_0,t_1)$ and $\tau(\rho(a,t_1),t_0) \to \kappa(a,t_0,t_1)$) such that the reflexive-symmetric-transitive closure of the corresponding reduction relation coincides with θ, the system terminates, and the classes of two irreducible elements go to distinct elements of $\mathbf{T}(A)$ under h. Then h is one-to-one.□

As indicated in the introduction we leave out most of the part on the relation between tree (semi-) automata and finite point-tree algebras. We mention only the definition of recognizing homomorphism and the fundamental result characterizing regular tree languages in terms of finite point-tree algebras.

A homomorphism h from a point-tree algebra $\mathbf{T}(A)$ into a finite point-tree algebra **B** is called a *recognizing homomorphism*. A tree language L over A is *recognized* by a homomorphism $h:\mathbf{T}(A) \to \mathbf{B}$ if h is recognizing, i.e. if B is finite, and if $L = h^{-1}(P)$ for some subset P of $B_{(t)}$.

Proposition 2. *A tree language over A is regular iff it is recognized by a homomorphism defined on $\mathbf{T}(A)$.*

The proof shows how tree semi-automata can be transformed into recognizing homomorphisms and vice versa. We outline the transformation of a tree semi-automaton into a recognizing homomorphism.

Let $\mathfrak{A} = (Q,\delta,i)$ be a tree semi-automaton over A, i.e. Q is a finite set of states, δ is a function $A \times Q \times Q \to Q$, and i is a function $A \to Q$. (Such an automaton associates with every tree $t \in T(A)$ a state $t_{\mathfrak{A}}$ by $a_{\mathfrak{A}} = i(a)$ and $a(t',t'') = \delta(a,t'_{\mathfrak{A}},t''_{\mathfrak{A}})$. It recognizes a tree language L over A if there is a subset P of Q such that $L = \{t:t_{\mathfrak{A}} \in P\}$.) We define a point-tree algebra **B**.

Let $B_{(1)}$ be the set A modulo the equivalence χ defined by $a\chi b$ iff $i(a) = i(b)$ and $\delta(a, q, q') = \delta(b, q, q')$ for all choices $q, q' \in Q$. Let $B_{(t)} = Q$ and $B_{(s)}$ the smallest set of functions $Q \to Q$ closed under composition and containing $(q' \mapsto \delta(a, q, q'))$ and $(q' \mapsto \delta(a, q', q))$ for every $q \in Q$; i.e. the elements of $B_{(s)}$ are just the functions on Q induced by the special trees. The operations of $\mathbf{B}$ are defined by the following rules.

$$
\begin{aligned}
\iota^{\mathbf{B}}(a/\chi) &= i(a) && \text{for } a \in A, \\
\kappa^{\mathbf{B}}(a/\chi, q, q') &= \delta(a, q, q') && \text{for } a \in A \text{ and } q, q' \in Q, \\
\rho^{\mathbf{B}}(a/\chi, q) &= (q' \mapsto \delta(a, q', q)) && \text{for } a \in A \text{ and } q \in Q, \\
\lambda^{\mathbf{B}}(a/\chi, q) &= (q' \mapsto \delta(a, q, q')) && \text{for } a \in A \text{ and } q \in Q, \\
\sigma^{\mathbf{B}}(f, f') &= f \circ f' && \text{for } f, f \in B_{(s)}, \\
\tau^{\mathbf{B}}(f, q) &= f(q) && \text{for } f \in B_{(s)} \text{ and } q \in Q.
\end{aligned}
$$

Then, as one can easily check, B together with these operations forms a finite point-tree algebra.

Since $\mathbf{T}(A)$ is free on $A_{(1)}$ (Theorem 1) there is a unique homomorphism h from $\mathbf{T}(A)$ into $\mathbf{B}$ with $h(a) = a/\chi$ for every $a \in A$. It turns out that for every set $P \subseteq Q$ we have $h^{-1}(P) = \{t : t_{\mathfrak{A}} \in P\}$, i.e. h recognizes a tree language L iff L is recognized by the given automaton $\mathfrak{A}$.$\Box$

Next we will transform the concept of syntactic congruence resp. syntactic algebra to our situation of regular tree languages and point-tree algebras. We shall see that for every regular tree language L there exists a smallest (up to isomorphism) finite point-tree algebra that recognizes the given language. This algebra is called the syntactic point-tree algebra of L and we will obtain it as the factor algebra of the free point-tree algebra modulo an appropriate congruence $\cong_L$, called the syntactic congruence of L. Furthermore, as a consequence of the correspondence between recognizing homomorphisms and tree semi-automata the syntactic congruence and the syntactic point-tree algebra turn out to be effectively computable.

Assume L is a tree language over A. Let $\cong_L$ be the relation on $T(A)$ defined as follows.

For $a, a' \in A$ let $a \cong_L a'$ iff

$$
\begin{aligned}
a \in L &\iff a' \in L, \\
sa \in L &\iff sa' \in L && \text{for all } s \in \mathcal{S}(A), \\
sa(t, t') \in L &\iff sa'(t, t') \in L && \text{for all } s \in \mathcal{S}(A),\ t, t' \in \mathcal{T}(A).
\end{aligned}
$$

For $s, s' \in \mathcal{S}(A)$ let $s \cong_L s'$ iff

$$
\begin{aligned}
st \in L &\iff s't \in L && \text{for all } t \in \mathcal{T}(A), \\
s_0 st \in L &\iff s_0 s't \in L && \text{for all } s_0 \in \mathcal{S}(A) \text{ and } t \in \mathcal{T}(A).
\end{aligned}
$$

For $t, t' \in \mathcal{T}(A)$ let $t \cong_L t'$ iff,

$$
\begin{aligned}
t \in L &\iff t' \in L, \\
st \in L &\iff st' \in L && \text{for all } s \in \mathcal{S}(A).
\end{aligned}
$$

In other words, two elements of the same sort are equivalent if and only if they relate to L the same in every possible context. In fact, the relation $\cong_L$ on $\mathbf{T}(A)$ is a congruence and called the *syntactic congruence* of L. The algebra $\mathbf{SA}(L) = \mathbf{T}(A)/\cong_L$ is called the *syntactic point-tree algebra* of L. As indicated above the properties of $\cong_L$ resp. $\mathbf{SA}(L)$ can be summed up as follows.

Lemma 3 (Syntactic congruence). *Let L be a tree language over A.*

(1) *The relation $\cong_L$ is the greatest congruence on $\mathbf{T}(A)$ such that L is a union of classes.*

(2) *L is regular iff $\cong_L$ is of finite index.*

(3) *If L is regular, then the syntactic point-tree algebra $\mathbf{SA}(L)$ is effectively computable.*

Hints to the proof. The proof of this lemma is similar to corresponding proofs for the syntactic congruence of regular sets of finite words, infinite words, or arbitrary algebras. For a version concerning regular sets of finite trees see, for instance, the recent contribution [4]. However, in this paper the recognizing structures are not point-tree algebras.□

To conclude this section we want to emphasize that (3) of the above lemma is relevant from the point of view of classification of regular tree languages. We have the following result.

Theorem 4 (Classification). *If C is a class of regular tree languages and B is a decidable class of finite point-tree algebras such that a language L belongs to C iff its syntactic point-tree algebra belongs to B, then C is also decidable.*□

Frontier testable tree languages

A language of finite words is reverse definite if membership is determined by the prefix of fixed maximal length of a given word. In the case of tree languages this corresponds to the set of frontier trees of fixed maximal depth.

The set of *frontier trees* of a given tree (either ordinary or special) is defined as follows: $\mathrm{front}(a) = \{a\}$ if $a \in A$ or $a = \cdot$, and

$$\mathrm{front}(a(t_0, t_1)) = \mathrm{front}(t_0) \cup \mathrm{front}(t_1) \cup \{a(t_0, t_1)\},$$

if $a \in A$ and t_0, t_1 are trees.

The *depth* of a tree is inductively defined by the following rules: $\mathrm{depth}(a) = 1$ if $a \in A$ or $a = \cdot$, and

$$\mathrm{depth}(a(t_0, t_1)) = \max\{\mathrm{depth}(t_0), \mathrm{depth}(t_1)\} + 1,$$

if $a \in A$ and t_0, t_1 are trees.

Now the set of frontier trees of depth less than or equal to k of a tree $t \in \mathcal{T}(A)$ is defined by $\mathrm{front}_{\leq k}(t) = \{t' \in \mathrm{front}(t) \mid \mathrm{depth}(t') \leq k\}$.

A tree language L over A is *k-frontier testable* if, for $t, t' \in T(A)$, the equivalence $t \in L \iff t' \in L$ holds, whenever $\text{front}_{\leq k}(t) = \text{front}_{\leq k}(t')$. The language L is *frontier testable* if it is k-frontier testable for some k.

The primary aim is to present a (finite) base of identities for frontier testable tree languages (where the parameter k is not fixed). As in the case of reverse definite languages of finite words, it is impossible to find such a set of equations over the given signature Σ. (In the proof of this we show that two arbitrary trees can be distinguished by some frontier testable tree language. This means that every possibly occurring equation could be violated.) However, one could appropriately adjust the notion of 'ultimately defined by an infinite sequence of equations' known from finite semigroup theory (e.g., see [7]) to the tree case. But introducing implicit operations (see [8]) is an even better remedy, for in our case the base of identities turns out to be finite. We do not want to transform the entire machinery of implicit operations and implicit equations (as elaborated in [1]) to tree algebras, but confine ourselves to equations involving only (apart from symbols of Σ) the ω-operation from finite semigroup theory.

As pointed out before, if $\mathbf{B}$ is a finite point-tree algebra, then $B_{(s)}$ together with the binary function $\cdot: B_{(s)} \times B_{(s)} \to B_{(s)}$ defined by $s \cdot s' = \sigma^{\mathbf{B}}(s, s')$ forms a finite semigroup. Thus for every $s \in B_{(s)}$ there is a unique element e in $\{s, s \cdot s, \ldots\}$ with $e \cdot e = e$ (i.e. e is idempotent). This element is denoted by s^{ω}. Existence and uniqueness of s^{ω} justify the following convention.

Convention. From now on every finite point-tree algebra $\mathbf{B}$ is viewed as a structure over the signature $\Sigma \cup \{^{\omega}{}_{(s,s)}\}$, where ω maps every element $s \in B_{(s)}$ onto the unique element s^{ω}. This operation may also be used in terms and equations for characterizing finite point-tree algebras.

Consider, for instance, the term $s_0 s_1^{\omega} t$ with variables s_0, s_1 of sort s and a variable t of sort t. This term covers all 'sufficiently deep' trees in the following sense: if $h: \mathbf{T}(A) \to \mathbf{B}$ is a recognizing epimorphism and m is the cardinality of $B_{(s)}$, then t' belongs to the range of $s_0 s_1^{\omega} t$ in $\mathbf{B}$ iff there exists a tree t'' of depth at least $m+1$ with $h(t'') = t'$. This is due to the fact that in a finite semigroup S of cardinality m an element s can be written as a product of at least m factors iff there are elements s_0, s_1, s_2 such that $s = s_0 s_1^{\omega} s_2$.

We have the following result.

Theorem 5 (Frontier testability). *Let L be a tree language over $S(A)$. The following are equivalent:*

(A) *L is frontier testable.*

(B) *The syntactic point-tree algebra of L satisfies the identities*

$$
\left.
\begin{array}{ll}
\text{(Sym)} & a(s_0 s_1^{\omega} t_0, t) = b(t, s_0 s_1^{\omega} t_0) \\[4pt]
\text{(Idp)} & a(s_0 s_1^{\omega} t_0, s_0 s_1^{\omega} t_0) = s_0 s_1^{\omega} t_0 \\[4pt]
\text{(Can)} & a(b(s_0 s_1^{\omega} t_0, st), t) = a(s_0 s_1^{\omega} t_0, st) \\[4pt]
\text{(Rot)} & a(b(t, s_0 s_1^{\omega} t_0), t') = c(t, d(s_0 s_1^{\omega} t_0, t'))
\end{array}
\right\} (+)
$$

for variables a, b, c, d of sort l, variables s, s_0, s_1 of sort s, and variables t_0, t, t' of sort t.

(C) *L is recognized by a point-tree algebra satisfying the identities under* (+).

An illustration of the four equations is given in Fig. 3; there δ stands for the term $s_0 s_1^\omega t$. The pictures in Fig. 3 also explain the names of the equations: (Sym) stands for 'symmetry', (Idp) for 'idempotence', (Can) for 'cancellation', and (Rot) for 'rotation'. Equation (Sym) says that deep trees can be turned around its root. Equation (Idp) allows a duplication of a deep tree, (Can) allows the elimination of the occurrence of a frontier tree which also occurs in the neighbourhood of a deep tree. Finally (Rot) expresses that trees can be rotated around a deep tree.

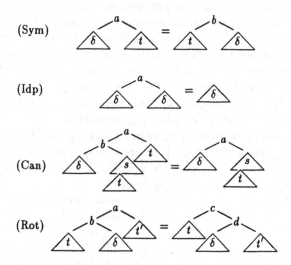

Fig. 3. Graphical illustration of (+)

Proof sketch. The proof of the theorem relies on an analogous result (henceforth called 'parametric version') characterizing the class of k-frontier testable tree languages for a fixed parameter k, the statement of which is like the one above except for that frontier-testability has to be replaced by k-frontier testability and the term $s_0 s_1^\omega t_0$ must be replaced by the term $s_{k-2} \ldots s_0 t_0$ (which covers exactly the trees of depth at least k.)

We want to give an outline of the proof of the parametric version. Since equations are preserved under the application of homomorphisms we obtain, by using Lemma 3(2), that (B) and (C) are equivalent. So it is only necessary to prove the implication from (A) to (C) (correctness) and the implication from (C) to (A) (completeness).

For the correctness it is sufficient to show that there exists a finite point-tree algebra **B** satisfying the parametric version of (+) such that a homomorphism

$h\colon \mathbf{T}(A) \to \mathbf{B}$ recognizes a given k-frontier testable tree language L over A. We obtain the algebra $\mathbf{B}$ as the quotient of $\mathbf{T}(A)$ modulo the congruence $\approx_k$ defined below.

For $a, a' \in A$ we define $a \approx_k a'$ iff $a = a'$. For $s, s' \in \mathcal{S}(A)$ we define $s \approx_k s'$ iff $\text{front}_{\leq k}(s) = \text{front}_{\leq k}(s')$, and for $t, t' \in \mathcal{T}(A)$ we define $t \approx_k t'$ iff $\text{front}_{\leq k}(t) = \text{front}_{\leq k}(t')$. Notice that we treat, according to the definition, special trees simply as trees (over an extended alphabet).

As indicated above the following holds.

Lemma 6 (k-testability). *Let $k > 0$.*

(1) *The binary relation $\approx_k$ is a congruence of finite index (on $\mathbf{T}(A)$).*
(2) *A tree language over A is k-frontier testable iff it is a union of $\approx_k$-classes (of ordinary trees).*
(3) *The quotient algebra $\mathbf{T}(A)/\approx_k$ satisfies $(+)$.*

For the completeness proof we fix a recognizing homomorphism $h\colon \mathbf{T}(A) \to \mathbf{B}$ where $\mathbf{B}$ satisfies the parametric version of $(+)$. We have to show $h(t) = h(t')$ whenever $t \approx_k t'$ for $t, t' \in \mathcal{T}(A)$. If $\text{depth}(t) < k$ then $t = t'$ and the claim is trivial. To prove the claim for $\approx_k$-equivalent trees of depth at least k we proceed in two steps: first we define a set of trees in so-called normal form that contains for every tree t of depth at least k an $\approx_k$-equivalent tree t' such that $t \approx_k t'$ and $h(t) = h(t')$; secondly we show that all $\approx_k$-equivalent trees in normal form have the same image under h.

We finish the proof sketch with a presentation of the normal forms. Let $a \in A$ be a fixed letter. We say that a tree t is a *comb* with *teeth* $u_0, \ldots, u_n$ and width $n+1$ if t has the form $a(u_0, a(u_1, \ldots, a(u_{n-1}, u_n)\ldots))$. The tree is denoted by $\eta(u_0, \ldots, u_n)$. We say that a comb $\eta(u_0, \ldots, u_n)$ is in *normal form* if its width is at least 2, $\text{depth}(u_n) = k$ and, for $0 \leq i \leq n$, $\text{depth}(u_i) \leq k$. Furthermore, we demand $\text{front}_{\leq k}(t) = \{u_0, \ldots, u_n\}$. $\square$

As a consequence of the Theorem 4 and 5, using also the fact that the ω-operation is effectively computable in finite semigroups, we obtain that the class of frontier testable tree languages is decidable.

Corollary 7 (Decidability) [3]. *The class of frontier testable tree languages is decidable.*

We conclude with an example showing that within the semigroup approach frontier testability cannot be characterized.

Example 2. Let $A = \{0, 1, 2\}$. The language L consists of all trees over A such that some leaf is labelled with 0. Besides these trees the language L' consists also of all trees having some node labelled with 2. Then L and L' have isomorphic syntactic semigroups (in the sense of [5], cf. [6, Example 3.1, p. 251]), and L is frontier testable, whereas L' is not.

Discussion

We have seen that point-tree algebras are an appropriate structure for the characterization of the class of frontier testable tree languages. There is some hope that the results can be viewed as the starting point of a more exhaustive algebraic classification of regular tree languages. For instance, it is not hard to extend the results to the more general case of generalized definite tree languages. One only needs to combine them with the results on root testable languages presented in [5]. This is worked out in [9]. Presumably a transformation of the known results from universal algebra [1] could provide an abstract framework for the classification of regular tree languages — we think of an EILENBERG correspondence as known for regular languages of finite [2] and infinite [12] words. (However, working with more than one sort, this might not be straightforward.) It would be desirable to try to characterize other, more complicated, classes of regular tree languages by using point-tree algebras. Perhaps a characterization of locally testable tree languages [3, 10], a natural class of regular tree languages, can be obtained along these lines. In the corresponding word case the use of the wreath product is essential. Therefore it would be interesting to know what the appropriate notion of wreath product for point-tree algebras should be.

References

1. J. Almeida. On pseudovarieties, varieties of languages, filters of congruences, pseudoidentities and related topics. *Algebra Universalis*, 27:333–350, 1990.
2. S. Eilenberg. *Automata, Languages and Machines*, vol. B. Academic Press, New York, 1976.
3. U. Heuter. Zur Klassifizierung regulärer Baumsprachen. doctoral thesis, RWTH Aachen, June 1989.
4. D. Kozen. On the Myhill-Nerode theorem for trees. *Bull. European Assoc. Theoret. Comput. Sci.*, 47:170–173, June 1992.
5. M. Nivat and A. Podelski. Definite tree languages. *Bull. European Assoc. Theoret. Comput. Sci.*, 38:186–190, June 1989.
6. P. Péladeau and A. Podelski. On reverse and general definite tree languages. In W. Kuich, editor, *Automata, Languages and Programming: 19th International Colloquium, Wien, July 1992*, volume 623 of *Lecture Notes in Computer Science*, pages 150–161, Springer.
7. J.-E. Pin. *Varieties of Formal Languages*. North Oxford Academic Press, London, 1986.
8. J. Reiterman. The Birkhoff Theorem for finite algebras. *Algebra Universalis*, 14:1–10, 1982.
9. T. Scholz. Charakterisierung definiter Baumsprachen durch Gleichungen in der Termalgebra. Diploma thesis, Inst. f. Inform. u. Prakt. Math., Univ. Kiel, Germany, Sept. 1992.
10. M. Steinby. A theory of tree language varieties. In M. Nivat and A. Podelski, editors, *Tree Automata and Languages*, pages 57–81. Elsevier Science Publishers, Amsterdam, 1992.

11. W. Thomas. Logical aspects in the study of tree languages. In B. Courcelle, editor, *Ninth Coll. on Trees in Algebra and Programming*, pages 31–51. Cambridge Univ. Press, 1984.

12. Th. Wilke. An Eilenberg theorem for ∞-languages. In J. Leach Albert, B. Monien, and M. Rodríguez Artalejo, editors, *Automata, Languages and Programming: 18th Intern. Coll., Madrid, 1991*, volume 510 of *Lecture Notes in Computer Science*, pages 588–599, Springer.

Finite automata as characterizations of minor closed tree families (Extended Abstract)

Arvind Gupta *

School of Computing Science
Simon Fraser University
Burnaby, British Columbia
Canada, V5A 1S6
email: arvind@cs.sfu.ca.

Abstract. The theory of graph minors has posed some interesting problems in graph representations. The work of Robertson and Seymour directly implies the existence of polynomial time algorithms for any family of graphs closed under the minor ordering. Such algorithms rely on knowledge of the entire obstruction set of the graph family. One common question concerns finding other polynomial-time algorithm for membership in the graph family being considered. As the graph family is normally infinite, the encoding of the family becomes an issue. In this paper we investigate this question by showing that any family of trees closed under minors can be recognized by a finite automaton. Towards this goal, we present a new representation of trees which may have other applications. We also show that many structural questions are easily answered using this representation. Finally we give algorithms for transforming between our regular expression characterization and the obstruction set characterization.

1 Introduction

The work of Robertson and Seymour [9] on the theory of graph minors has had significant ramifications in the theory of algorithms. An extremely large class of problems have been shown to have low-order polynomial-time algorithms (although admittedly with large constants). These algorithms proceed as follows: By the key theorem of Robertson and Seymour, every minor closed graph family has some fixed number of obstructions (minor-minimal graphs not in the family). Now, checking whether or not a graph is in the family involves a minor test involving these obstructions, an $O(n^3)$ time procedure.

A question often asked concerns the complexity of finding obstructions, and more generally, finding polynomial time algorithms for minor closed graph families. For graph families with certain properties, extensive work has been done (see, for example, [2], [3], [7], [1]). However, the general problem remains elusive partially because the question itself is not well-formed. A graph family must be given as part of the input to a procedure which finds obstructions of that family. Fellows and Langston have shown that if a Turing Machine for that is family is used, the problem of computing obstructions is undecidable. Clearly any oracle for the family does not help since nothing would be known about elements larger than the largest query. This leads to the following interesting question: What formal languages can be used to describe minor closed graph families

---

* Research supported by the Natural Sciences and Engineering Research Council of Canada, the Centre for System Sciences and a President's Research Grant, Simon Fraser University. A detailed exposition of these results appear in the author's dissertation [4].

such that natural questions about the graph family can be answered in a constructive manner? This question is, in some sense, circular. Certainly the language of obstruction sets seems like a good candidate. However, we would like a language which captures the structure of the family directly – after all if we knew the obstructions we could directly obtain the polynomial time algorithm. As well, it is natural to ask about the expressiveness of the language required to describe minor closed graph families.

In this paper we investigate this problem when restricted to trees. We give a new tree representation based on the depth-first-traversal of a tree and show that such representations for trees in a proper lower ideal are regular. We show that to solve a large number of problems on these families, it suffices to present, as input, a regular expression for the tree family. Recently, Robertson, Seymour and Thomas [10] have independently given descriptions of lower ideals of trees under the more general embedding relation. The relationship between their descriptions and ours are not clear, especially as they relate to computational questions.

The outline of the remainder of this paper is as follows. In §2 we give background material. In §3 we present our new tree representation. In §4 we define an ordering on this representation and show that this ordering captures the notion of topological embedding on trees. In §5 we give our regular expression characterization of proper tree lower ideal. Finally in §6 we use this characterization to obtain computational results.

2 Preliminaries

2.1 Definitions

For T a tree, $V(T)$ and $E(T)$ are its vertex and edge sets. We treat rooted trees as directed graphs with edges directed away from the root. A *planar-planted* tree is a rooted tree with an ordering on the children of every internal vertex. We will write the children of a vertex as a sequence, say $(c_1, \ldots, c_k)$ to indicate this ordering. A *planar-planting* of a rooted tree T is a planar-planted tree T' which, as a rooted tree, is isomorphic to T. Notice that for any two vertices v and w in a planar-planted tree, if one is not the ancestor of the other, we can speak of v as either *left* or *right* of w.

For G a graph and e an edge of G, the *contraction* of e in G is formed by identifying the endpoints of e. That is, if $e = \{x, y\}$ then we delete x and y and add a new vertex z adjacent to every vertex w which was adjacent to x or y.

Definition 1. Let G and H be graphs. H is a *minor* of G ($H \leq_m G$) if there is a subgraph S of G such that H is isomorphic to a graph formed by a sequence of edge contractions on S.

We extend the definition of minor to rooted and planar-planted trees.

Definition 2. Let T and T' be planar-planted trees. Then T is a *rooted minor* of T' ($T \leq_{m^r} T'$) if $T \leq_m T'$ and for $v \in V(T)$, $v \neq root(T)$, all vertices in $im(v)$ are descendants of some vertex of the parent of v. T is a *planar-planted minor* of T', ($T \leq_{m^p} T'$), if $T \leq_{m^r} T'$ and for every $u, v \in V(T)$, if u is to the left of v in T then $im(u)$ is to the left of $im(v)$ in T'.

Lemma 3. Let T_1 and T_2 be non-null trees. For $i \in \{1, 2\}$, choose $v_i \in V(T_i)$ and let $T'(i)$ be the rooted tree formed by rooting T_i at v_i. For $i \in \{1, 2\}$, let T_i'' be any planar-planting of T_i'. Then,

$$T_1'' \leq_{m^p} T_2'' \Rightarrow T_1' \leq_{m^r} T_2' \Rightarrow T_1 \leq_m T_2.$$

By placing a restriction on contractions we form the related notion of *topological embedding*.

Definition 4. Let G and H be graphs. Then, H is *(topologically) embedded* in G if there is a subgraph S of G such that H is isomorphic to a graph formed by a sequence of edge contractions on S where edges having an endpoint of degree 2 are the only ones which may be contracted.

Intuitively a graph H is embedded in a graph G as follows: Distinct vertices of H map to distinct vertices of G. Distinct edges of H map to distinct (internally) vertex disjoint paths of G.

Lemma 5. *Let H and G be graphs. H is embedded in G if and only if there is a pair of injective functions (im_1, im_2), the embedding functions, such that*

1. $im_1 : V(H) \to V(G)$ and $im_2 : E(H) \to \{simple\ paths\ in\ G\}$.
2. *if $e = \{x, y\} \in E(H)$ then $im_2(e)$ has endpoints $im_1(x)$ and $im_1(y)$.*
3. *for $e, e' \in E(H)$, if $e \neq e'$ then $im_2(e)$ and $im_2(e')$ are vertex disjoint except possibly at their endpoints.*

We extend the definition of topological embedding to rooted and planar-planted trees (ie $\leq_{e^r}$ and $\leq_{e^p}$) analogously to that for minors. Notice that if $H \leq_e G$ then $H \leq_m G$ but the converse does not hold (see Figure 1). However, Lemma 6 gives a partial converse.

$$T \qquad\qquad\qquad T'$$

Fig. 1. $T \leq_m T'$ but $T \not\leq_e T'$

Lemma 6. *For every graph G there is a sequence of graphs $G_1, \ldots, G_k$ with $G \leq_m G_i$ for $1 \leq i \leq k$ such that for any graph H, $G \leq_m H$ if any only if for some G_i, $G_i \leq_e H$.*

We will be dealing extensively with finite sequences of numbers. For p and q sequences, $p^\frown q$ is the *concatenation* of p and q, $|p|$ is the length of p and $\pi_i(p)$ is the ith element of p.

2.2 An Overview of Graph Minor Theory

A binary relation is a well-quasi-order if it is transitive, reflexive and for every infinite sequence there are two elements such that the first is smaller than the second. In 1960 K. Wagner conjectured, and in 1985 Robertson and Seymour proved [9], that finite graphs are well-quasi-ordered under the minor relation. It follows that for every minor closed graph family (a *lower ideal*) there are only a finite number of minimal elements not in the family (the *obstruction set*). This set characterizes the lower ideal in that a graph G is not in the lower ideal if and only if for some obstruction graph H, $H \leq_m G$.

Only results about a few specific lower ideals were known previous to the Robertson and Seymour work. The most renowned is Kuratowski's Theorem [6] which states that a graph is planar if and only if it does not contain either K_5 or $K_{3,3}$ as a minor. Since planar graphs are closed under the minor ordering, they form a lower ideal with obstruction set $\{K_5, K_{3,3}\}$. In fact, Robertson and Seymour's theorems immediately show that for the family of graphs embeddable on a fixed surface have a finite obstruction set, a problem previously open for even the torus.

Obstruction sets give one easy method of presenting lower ideals. However, in general, they characterize lower ideals in terms of structures not in the ideal. As such, it can be difficult to obtain useful information about the ideal from the obstruction set. For example, if we are given a set of graphs and are told they are the obstructions of a lower ideal is it possible to obtain useful structural information about the graphs in the ideal? Without Kuratowski's theorem, would it be obvious that the lower ideal with obstructions $\{K_5, K_{3,3}\}$ consists exactly of planar graphs?

One method of building lower ideals is to consider operations which preserve the closure property. For example, the union of two lower ideals is also a lower ideal. However, given the obstruction sets of two ideals, computing the obstructions of the union of two ideals (called the intertwines) seems to be a difficult problem. Recently, Gupta and Impagliazzo [5] and Seymour and Thomas [11] have shown that the number of obstructions in the union is bounded by towers of towers of 2. However, it is very natural to obtain tree obstructions using our representation.

Clearly different representations of lower ideals will yield different structural information about the ideal. With planar graphs, the topological definition seems to be much more useful than the obstruction set characterization. This leads to the issue of whether it is possible to design representations of lower ideals which yield structural results about the graphs in the ideal. This paper deals with such representations for tree lower ideals.

3   Trees as Sequences of Numbers

In this section we outline a two step transformation of planar-planted trees into sequences of triples of numbers. First, planar-planted trees are transformed into a sequence of pairs where each pair corresponds to a vertex in the depth-first-traversal of the tree. Second each pair is augmented into a triple so as to capture the notion of topological embedding. The third element of a triple will allow edges in the original tree to be mapped to paths. In the next section we will define an ordering on these sequences which preserves the topological embedding relationship.

3.1   Tree Linearizations

Definition 7. Let T be a planar-planted tree and $(v_1, v_2, \ldots, v_n)$ be a (preorder) depth-first-traversal of the vertices of T. For $i \in \mathbb{N}$, $1 \leq i \leq n$ define

$$\alpha_i = \{v_j : j \leq i \text{ and there is a } k \geq i \text{ such that } v_k \text{ is a child of } v_j\}$$

In the depth-first-traversal of the vertices, we list a vertex the first time it is visited. α_i consists of all vertices on the path from the root to v_i which either contain unvisited chilren as well as v_i and the parent of v_i. One intuitive method of thinking about α_i is to consider a stack implementation of depth-first-traversal. Then α_i is the contents of the stack just after v_i has been pushed on.

For the remainder of this section, let T be a planar-planted tree and $(v_1, \ldots, v_n)$ be the depth-first-traversal of T. We transform $(\alpha_1, \ldots \alpha_n)$ into the required sequence.

Definition 8. For $1 \leq i \leq n$, define p_i to be a sequence on $\mathbb{N} \times \{0,1,2,3\}$ as follows. $p_1 = ((1,0)), p_n = ((2,3))$. For $1 < i < n$,

$$
p_i = \begin{cases}
(((|\alpha_i|,0)) & \text{if } \alpha_i \subseteq \alpha_{i+1}; \\
(((|\alpha_i|,1),(|\alpha_i \cap \alpha_{i+1}|,0)) & \text{if } v_i \in \alpha_{i+1}, parent(v_i) \notin \alpha(v_i); \\
(((|\alpha_i|,2),(|\alpha_i \cap \alpha_{i+1}|,0)) & \text{if } v_i \notin \alpha_{i+1}, parent(v_i) \in \alpha(v_i); \\
(((|\alpha_i|,3),(|\alpha_i \cap \alpha_{i+1}|,0)) & \text{if } v_i, parent(v_i) \notin \alpha_{i+1}.
\end{cases}
$$

The *tree linearizaton of T*, $\tau(T)$ is the sequence $p_1 \frown p_2 \frown \cdots \frown p_n$. In Figure 2 we give an example of a tree linearization. Intuitively, for a pair $p = (a,b)$ in the tree linearization, a represents the height of the stack (and is denoted by $size(p)$) and b is an indication of why the stack changed height (and is denoted by $type(p)$). When $b = 0$, the child of the current vertex is visited next (vertex 1). When $b = 2$ or $b = 3$, the current vertex is a leaf and either one or two vertices must be popped off the stack depending on whether the leaf is the last child of its parent (vertex 3 and 4). When $b = 1$, the top node of the stack is internal but the last child of its parent to be visited (vertex 6). In this case, its parent can safely be removed from the stack.

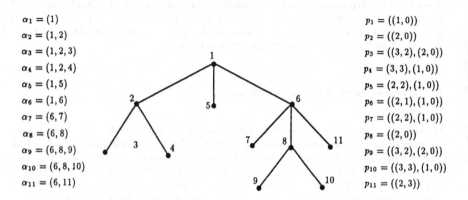

$\alpha_1 = (1)$ $p_1 = ((1,0))$
$\alpha_2 = (1,2)$ $p_2 = ((2,0))$
$\alpha_3 = (1,2,3)$ $p_3 = ((3,2),(2,0))$
$\alpha_4 = (1,2,4)$ $p_4 = ((3,3),(1,0))$
$\alpha_5 = (1,5)$ $p_5 = ((2,2),(1,0))$
$\alpha_6 = (1,6)$ $p_6 = ((2,1),(1,0))$
$\alpha_7 = (6,7)$ $p_7 = ((2,2),(1,0))$
$\alpha_8 = (6,8)$ $p_8 = ((2,0))$
$\alpha_9 = (6,8,9)$ $p_9 = ((3,2),(2,0))$
$\alpha_{10} = (6,8,10)$ $p_{10} = ((3,3),(1,0))$
$\alpha_{11} = (6,11)$ $p_{11} = ((2,3))$

Fig. 2. The tree linearization $\tau(T)$.

There is a one-to-one correspondence between tree linearizations and planar-planted trees (upto isomorphisms). However, we will only require the following Lemma.

Lemma 9. *For non-isomorphic planar-planted trees T and T', $\tau(T) \neq \tau(T')$.*

Define the *width* of the tree linearization, of a tree T, $width(T)$, as $\max\{size(p)|p \in \tau(T)\}$. By computing the size of the smallest binary tree with contains T as a minor, we can show:

Theorem 10. *Let T and T' be rooted trees such that $T \not\leq_{mr} T'$. Then there is a planar-planting T'' of T' such that $width(T'') \leq |V_T|$.*

3.2 Augmented Tree Linearizations

Although tree linearizations give nice linear representations of trees, it is not clear how to define an ordering on them which corresponds to the minor ordering. Instead, we augment the linearizations in such a manner that we can define the topological embedding ordering on them. Using these, Theorem 10 and Lemma 6 we will obtain the required ordering for minors.

Definition 11. Let $\tau(T) = (p_1,\ldots,p_r)$. For $1 \leq i \leq n$, the *vertex associated* with p_i is defined inductively as follows: When $i = 1$, $vertex(p_i)$ is $root(T)$. For, $i > 1$, suppose $vertex(p_{i-1}) = v_j$. Then, if $type(p_{i-1}) = 0$, $vertex(p_i) = v_{j+1}$. If $type(p_{i-1}) \neq 0$ then choose the maximal k such that $k \leq j$ and v_k is in $\alpha(v_j)$. Then, $vertex(p_i) = v_k$.

Intuitively, $vertex(p_i)$ is the top vertex of the stack whenever a change is made to the stack. For example, in Figure 2, the sequence $vertex(p_1),\ldots,vertex(p_{18})$ would be $(1,2,3,2,4,1,5,1,6,6,7,6,8,9,8,10,6,11)$. The two adjacent 6's occur because 6 is at the top of the stack when it is first visited and again when 1 is removed from the stack.

Definition 12. Let T be a planar-planted tree such that $\tau(T) = (p_1,\ldots,p_r)$. An *augmented tree-linearization* of T, $\overline{\tau}(T)$, is a finite sequence $(q_1,\ldots,q_r)$ such that for every i, q_i is a triple $(size(p_i), type(p_i), \theta_i)$ where $\theta_i \in \mathbf{N}$, the *offset* of q_i, satisfies the following conditions:

1. $\theta_1 \geq 0$;
2. For $2 \leq i,j \leq r$, if $p_i = p_j$ and $vertex(p_i) = vertex(p_j)$ then $\theta_i = \theta_j$;
3. For $2 \leq i,j \leq r$, $i \neq j$, if $type(p_i) = type(p_j) = 0$ and $vertex(p_i)$ is an ancestor of $vertex(p_j)$ then $\theta_i \leq \theta_j$; and
4. If 1-3 do not hold then $\theta_i = \theta_{i-1}$.

We will denote the offset of q_i by $offset(q_i)$.

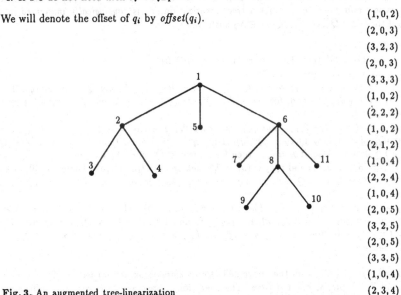

(1,0,2)
(2,0,3)
(3,2,3)
(2,0,3)
(3,3,3)
(1,0,2)
(2,2,2)
(1,0,2)
(2,1,2)
(1,0,4)
(2,2,4)
(1,0,4)
(2,0,5)
(3,2,5)
(2,0,5)
(3,3,5)
(1,0,4)
(2,3,4)

Fig. 3. An augmented tree-linearization

In Figure 3 we exhibit one possible augmented tree-linearization for the tree in Figure 2. Notice that leaves always have the same offset as there parent and that descendants of a vertex have an offset at least as large as the offset of the vertex. The offsets can be viewed as parenthesising the expression in that larger offsets are grouped inside smaller. Recall that in the definition of topological embedding, edges are mapped to paths. Consider such a mapping and suppose a vertex v in a tree T is mapped to a vertex v' in a tree T'. The key in defining this mapping in terms of tree linearizations is the number of ancestors with unvisited children of v versus the number of ancestors with unvisited children of v'. It is essentially straight-forward to show that, v' must have at least as many as v. The offset is the difference between these two numbers. This is the key to defining the ordering relation.

4 Topological Immersion

We now define an ordering, $\leq_T$, from augmented tree linearizations to tree linearizations. In this ordering, every $q \in \overline{\tau}(T)$ will essentially be associated with an interval of $\tau(T')$ which contains a pair q' such that $size(q') = size(q) + offset(q)$. We will then show that for trees T_1 and T_2, $T_1 \leq_{e'} T_2$ if and only if there is an augmented tree linearization $\overline{\tau}_1$ of T_1 and a tree linearization τ_2 of T_2 such that $\overline{\tau}_1 \leq_T \tau_2$.

We begin by giving a formal definition of the ordering. We warn the reader that this definition is fairly technical as there are many conditions to check for the mapping to be consistent. We have pictorially illustrated many of the conditions and have given a detailed discussion of the definition to help better motivate the mapping. It may be helpful to read both the definition and the detailed discussion simultaneously.

Definition 13. Let $\mathcal{N}_2$ be the set of finite sequences on $\mathbf{N}^2$. For $\overline{\tau}_1 = (p_1, \ldots, p_r)$ an augmented tree linearization and $\tau_2 = (q_1, \ldots, q_s)$ a tree linearization, $\overline{\tau}_1$ is *topologically immersed* in τ_2 ($\overline{\tau}_1 \leq_T \tau_2$) if there are $Q_0, Q_1, \ldots, Q_{r+1} \in \mathcal{N}_2$ such that

1. $\tau_2 = Q_0 {}^\frown Q_1 {}^\frown \cdots {}^\frown Q_{r+1}$.
2. $|Q_1| \geq 1$, say $Q_1 = Q'{}^\frown(q_1)$. Then, $q_1 = (1 + offset(p_1), 0)$.
3. For $i \geq 1$, suppose $p_i = (\sigma_i, 0, \theta_i)$. Then,
    (a) If $p_{i+1} = (\sigma_i + 1, 0, \theta_{i+1})$ where $\theta_{i+1} \geq \theta_i$, then $|Q_{i+1}| \geq 1$, say $Q_{i+1} = Q'{}^\frown(q)$. Then $q = (\sigma_i + 1 + \theta_{i+1}, 0)$ and, for every $q' \in Q'$, $size(q') \geq \sigma_i + \theta_i$ and $q' \neq (\sigma_i + 1 + \theta_i, 1)$. See Figure 4.
    (b) If $p_{i+1} = (\sigma_i + 1, 1, \theta_{i+1})$ and $p_{i+2} = (\sigma_i, 0, \theta_{i+2})$ where $\theta_{i+2} \geq \theta_i$ then $Q_{i+1} = \varnothing$ and $|Q_{i+2}| \geq 1$, say $Q_{i+2} = Q'{}^\frown(q)$. Then $q = (\sigma_i + \theta_{i+2}, 0)$ and, for every $q' \in Q'$, $\pi_1(q') \geq \sigma_i + \theta_i$. Also, if $\theta_i = \theta_{i+2}$ then for some $q' \in Q'$, $q' = (\sigma_i + 1 + \theta_i, 1)$. See Figure 5.
    (c) If $p_{i+1} = (\sigma_i + 1, 2, \theta_i)$ and $p_{i+2} = (\sigma_i, 0, \theta_i)$ then $Q_{i+1} = ((\sigma_i + 1, \bar{\delta}))$ where $\bar{\delta} \in \{0, 2\}$ and $|Q_{i+2}| \geq 1$ say $Q_{i+2} = Q'{}^\frown(q)$. Then $q = (\sigma_i + \theta_i, 0)$ and, for every $q' \in Q'$, $size(q') \geq \sigma_i + \theta_i$ and $q' \neq (\sigma_i + 1 + \theta_i, 1)$. See Figure 6.
    (d) Suppose $p_{i+1} = (\sigma_i + 1, 3, \theta_i)$. Then, $Q_{i+1} = ((\sigma_i + 1, \bar{\delta}))$ where $0 \leq \bar{\delta} \leq 3$. If $i + 1 < r$ then $p_{i+2} = (\sigma_i - 1, 0, \theta_{i+2})$ where $\theta_{i+2} \leq \theta_i$ and $|Q_{i+2}| \geq 1$ say $Q_{i+2} = Q'{}^\frown(q)$. Now $q = (\sigma_i + \theta_{i+2}, 0)$ and for every $q' \in Q'$, $size(q') \geq \sigma_i - 1 + \theta_{i+2}$ and $q' \neq (\sigma_i + \theta_{i+2}, 1)$. See Figure 7.

We will call $(Q_0, \ldots, Q_{r+1})$ in the above definition a *immersion decomposition* of τ_2 by $\overline{\tau}_1$.

Let T_1 and T_2 be planar-planted trees. The conditions above are necessary and sufficient to ensure that $T_1 \leq_{e'} T_2$ if and only if $\overline{\tau} \leq_T \tau(T_2)$ for some augmented tree linearization $\overline{\tau}$ of T_1. Let $\overline{\tau}(T_1) = (p_1, \ldots, p_r)$ and $v_i = vertex(p_i)$. Let $\tau(T_2) = (q_1, \ldots, q_s)$. The idea is to explicitly construct the embedding functions (im_1, im_2). Here we only describe the construction of im_1 since for trees there is only one possible choice for im_2 once im_1 is defined.

Suppose that $type(p_i) \neq 1$. Then $Q_i \neq \varnothing$ and we can write $Q_i = Q'_i{}^\frown(q_{j_i})$. The key idea is that our ordering is defined such that $im_1(v_i) = u_i$ where $u_i = vertex(q_{j_i})$. Notice that since

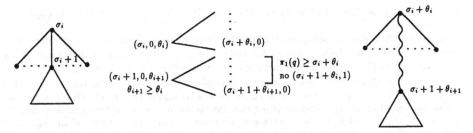

Fig. 4. Topological immersion when $type(p_i) = 0$

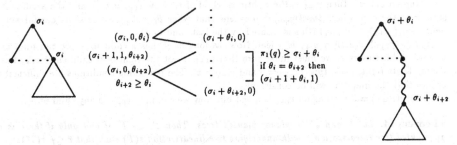

Fig. 5. Topological immersion when $type(p_i) = 1$

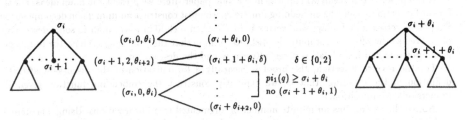

Fig. 6. Topological immersion when $type(p_i) = 2$

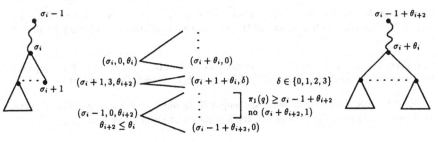

Fig. 7. Topological immersion when $type(p_i) = 3$

$v_i = vertex(p_k)$ for many different k, we must ensure that our mapping consistently maps v_i to the same vertex in T_2.

Condition 2 is used to define $im_1(root(T_1))$. Now suppose for some i, $1 \leq i \leq r$ for which $type(p_i) = 0$, we have defined $im_1(v_j)$ for every j, $1 \leq j \leq i$ in a consistent manner. Then $q_i = (size(p_i) + offset(p_i), 0)$. Now, either $i = r - 1$ or one of $type(p_{i+1}), type(p_{i+2}) = 0$.

Suppose $type(p_{i+1}) = 0$. Then, v_{i+1} is not the rightmost child of v_i. Also, $v_{i+1} \neq vertex(p_j)$ for $j < i+1$. Finally, u_{i+1} is a vertex of T_{u_i}, so for $k \leq j_i$, $u_{i+1} \neq vertex(q_k)$. Therefore, we can define $im_1(v_{i+1}) = u_{i+1}$ and our mapping remains consistent. We need the condition that for $q \in Q'_{i+1}$, $q \neq (\sigma_i + 1 + \theta_i, 1)$ since such a q would place u_{i+1} in the tree rooted at the rightmost child of u_i. However, this clearly should not occur since v_{i+1} has a sibling to the right which could no longer be mapped.

If $type(p_{i+1}) = 1$ then v_{i+1} is the rightmost child of v_i. Now $v_{i+2} = v_{i+1}$ and the argument is similar to the case where $type(p_{i+1}) = 0$ except that when $\theta_i = \theta_{i+2}$ we must be careful not to define $im_1(v_{i+2}) = im_1(v_i)$ (this is assured by the last condition).

If $type(p_{i+1}) = 2$ then v_{i+1} is a leaf. Now, as long as u_i has a child u_{i+1}, we can map v_{i+1} to that child. However, we must make sure that u_{i+1} is not the rightmost child since v_{i+1} has a sibling to its right. Now, $type(p_{i+2}) = 0$ and $v_{i+2} = v_i$. The remaining conditions are sufficient to ensure that the mapping will be consistent.

If $type(p_{i+1}) = 3$ then again v_{i+1} is a leaf but now we can map v_{i+1} to any child of u_i.

Theorem 14. *Let T and T' be planar-planted trees. Then $T \leq_{er} T'$ if and only if there is an augmented tree linearization $\bar{\tau}$ with underlying tree linearization $\tau(T)$ such that $\bar{\tau} \leq_T \tau(T')$.*

A full proof of this result will appear in the final paper. Here we present the main ideas. For the forward direction, given the embedding functions, we must construct an immersion decomposition. Suppose a vertex v in T maps to a vertex w in T'. Then a child of v will map to some descendant of w. We use the offset to compute the distance from w that the child maps. Then, the immersion decomposition can include all vertices between w and the descendant.

For the reverse direction, the proof is basically a formalization of the discussion after the definition of the ordering, that is, we explicitly construct the embedding function given the immersion decomposition.

Notice that a tree has an infinite number of augmented tree linearizations. Using Theorem 14 and Theorem 10 we can easily show that we need only consider a finite subset of them.

Definition 15. *For T a planar-planted tree, and $\bar{\tau} = (p_1, \ldots, p_r)$ be an augmented tree linearization of T. Then the width of $\bar{\tau}$, $width(\bar{\tau})$ is the maximum of $size(p) + offset(p)$ for all elements p of $\bar{\tau}$.*

Corollary 16. *Let T, T' be planar-planted trees such that $T \leq_{er} T'$. Let $\bar{\tau}$ be augmented tree linearization of T such that $\bar{\tau} \leq_T \tau(T')$. Then, $width(\bar{\tau}) \leq width(treeseq(T'))$.*

Since for any given tree T there are only a finite number of augmented tree sequences of a fixed width, it is possible to check if T topologically embeds in a tree T'.

5 Regular Expression Characterizations

We are now ready to define a regular expression which recognizes a given lower ideal of trees under minors. We first prove the following:

Theorem 17. *Let $n \in \mathbb{N}$, $n > 0$. Let T be the set of all planar-planted trees whose tree linearizations have width at most n. Let $\mathcal{D}$ be a lower ideal of T under planar-planted embeddings. Then there is a regular expression $\mathcal{E}$ such that $\mathcal{L}(\mathcal{E}) = \{\tau(T) : T \in \mathcal{D}\}$.*

For the remainder of this section we fix $\Sigma = \{1, \ldots, n\} \times \{0, 1, 2, 3\}$. We first show that there is a regular expression which recognizes all bounded width tree linearizations.

Lemma 18. *Let $n \in \mathbb{N}$, $n > 0$. Then there is a regular expression $\mathcal{E}$ over Σ such that $\mathcal{L}(\mathcal{E}) = \{\tau(T) : width(\tau(T)) \leq n\}$.*

Proof. We describe an automaton which accepts $\mathcal{L}(\mathcal{E})$. Let $\tau(T) = (p_1, \ldots, p_r)$. First note that $size(p_{i+1})$ is completely determined by $size(p_i)$. Also, if $type(p_i) \neq 0$ then $type(p_{i+1}) = 0$ and if $type(p_i) = 0$ then $type(p_{i+1})$ can be any value. Therefore, our automaton can have one state for every element of Σ and a transition to the next possible element labeled by that element. In the initial state, the automaton must read $(1, 0)$ and the last symbol it must read is $(2, 3)$ before entering an accepting state. □

Lemma 19. *For every planar-planted tree T with $width(\tau(T)) \leq n$ there is a regular expression $\mathcal{E}$ such that $\mathcal{L}(\mathcal{E}) = \{\tau(T') : width(\tau(T')) \leq n, \text{ and } T \leq_{e^p} T'\}$.*

Proof. Suppose $width(\tau(T)) \leq n$ and $T \leq_{e^p} T'$. Then there is an augmented tree linearization $\bar{\tau}$ of T such that $\bar{\tau} \leq_T \tau(T')$. By Lemma 16, there are only a finite number of possible augmented tree linearizations of T say, $\bar{\tau}_1, \ldots, \bar{\tau}_k$. We show that for every $\bar{\tau}_i$ there is a regular expression $\mathcal{E}_i$ such that $\mathcal{L}(\mathcal{E}_i) = \{\tau(T') : width(\tau(T')) \leq n, \text{ and } \bar{\tau}_i \leq_T \tau(T')\}$.

We describe an automaton which accepts $\mathcal{L}(\mathcal{E}_i)$. Let $\bar{\tau}_i = (p_1, \ldots, p_r)$. Our automaton is broken into subautomata $\mathcal{A}_i$, $1 \leq i \leq r$, where $\mathcal{A}_i$ will recognize a string Q_i from an immersion desomposition $(Q_0, \ldots, Q_{r+1})$. Suppose we have constructed $\mathcal{A}_i$. We only describe the construction of $\mathcal{A}_{i+1}$ when $type(p_i) = type(p_{i+1}) = 0$; the automata for the other cases can similarly be constructed. Suppose $p_i = (\sigma_i, 0, \theta_i)$ and $p_{i+1} = (\sigma_i + 1, 0, \theta_{i+1})$ where $\theta_{i+1} \geq \theta_i$ and assume that $\mathcal{A}_i$ recognizes strings Q_i of the appropriate form. Then, $\mathcal{A}_{i+1}$ will be a loop which checks for elements of Σ with first component at least $\sigma_i + \theta_i$. If an element $p \in \Sigma$ with $p = (\sigma_i + \theta_1 + 1, 1)$ or $size(p) < \sigma_i + \theta_i$ is read, $\mathcal{A}_{i+1}$ immediately enters a reject state. Otherwise, every time an element $p \in \Sigma$ with $size(p) = \sigma_i + 1 + \theta_{i+1}$ is read, $\mathcal{A}_{i+1}$ non-deterministically enter an accept state and loops back to the initial state. Finally, there is an edge from the final state of $\mathcal{A}_i$ to the initial state of $\mathcal{A}_{i+1}$. □

Proof. (Theorem 17) By Lemma 18 there is a regular expression $\mathcal{E}$ which recognizes T. Let $\mathcal{D}$ be a lower ideal of T under planar-planted embeddings and let $\mathcal{O}_{\mathcal{D}}$ be the obstruction set of $\mathcal{D}$, $\mathcal{O}_{\mathcal{D}} = \{T_1, \ldots, T_k\}$ (recall that $T \in \mathcal{D}$ if and only if for every T_i, $T_i \not\leq_{e^p} T$). By Lemma 19 there are regular expressions $\mathcal{E}_1, \ldots, \mathcal{E}_k$ such that for T a planar-planted tree, $\tau(T) \in \mathcal{E}_i$ if and only if $T_i \leq_{e^p} T$. Let $\mathcal{E}$ be the regular expression whose language is $\overline{\mathcal{L}(\mathcal{E}_1) \bigcap \ldots \bigcap \mathcal{L}(\mathcal{E}_k)}$ and clearly $\mathcal{E}$ is the required expression. □

We can now state the main theorem of the paper:

Theorem 20. *Let T be the set of all finite trees. Let $T' \subseteq T$ be a proper lower ideal of T under the minor relation. Then there is a regular expression $\mathcal{E}$ such that $T \in T'$ if and only if $\tau(T) \in \mathcal{L}(\mathcal{E})$ for some planar-planting of T.*

To prove this theorem, we first prove a number of Lemmas. First we use Lemma 6 and Theorem 17 to obtain:

Lemma 21. *Let* $n \in \mathbb{N}$, $n > 0$. *Let* $\mathcal{T}$ *be the set of all planar-planted trees whose tree linearizations have width at most* n. *Suppose* $\mathcal{D}$ *is a lower ideal of* $\mathcal{T}$ *under planar-planted minors. Then there is a regular expression* $\mathcal{E}$ *such that* $\mathcal{L}(\mathcal{E}) = \{\tau(T) : T \in \mathcal{D}\}$.

We next generalize Lemma 21 to rooted trees which have bounded width.

Lemma 22. *Let* $n \in \mathbb{N}$. *Let* T *be a rooted tree and* T' *be a planar-planted tree with* $T \leq_{m^r} T'$ *and* $width(\tau(T')) \leq n$. *Then there is a planar-planting of* T, T'', *such that* $T'' \leq_{m^r} T'$ *and* $width(\tau(T'')) \leq n$.

Corollary 23. *Let* $n \in \mathbb{N}$, $n > 0$. *Let* $\mathcal{T}$ *be the set of all rooted trees which have some planar-planting of width at most* n. *Suppose* $\mathcal{D}$ *is a lower ideal of* $\mathcal{T}$ *under rooted minors. Then there is a regular expression* $\mathcal{E}$ *such that* $\mathcal{L}(\mathcal{E}) = \{\tau(T') : T' \text{ is a planar-planting of } T, T \in \mathcal{D}\}$.

We want to remove the width constraint in Corollary 23. To do this, consider any proper lower ideal $\mathcal{D}$ of rooted trees under minors. Then, there is some rooted tree T not in $\mathcal{D}$. Now, for every T' in $\mathcal{D}$, $T \not\leq_{m^r} T'$ there is a planar-planting of T', T'' such that $width(\tau(T'')) \leq |V_T|$. Therefore, we conclude the following.

Lemma 24. *Let* $\mathcal{T}$ *be the set of all rooted trees. Suppose* $\mathcal{D}$ *is a proper lower ideal of* $\mathcal{T}$ *under rooted minors. Then there is a regular expression* $\mathcal{E}$ *such that for every tree* $T \in \mathcal{T}$, $T \in \mathcal{D}$ *if and only if there is some planar-planting* T' *of* T *such that* $\tau(T') \in \mathcal{L}(\mathcal{E})$.

To prove Theorem 20, we extend Lemma 24 to unrooted trees by trying all possible rootings of our target trees. More specifically, let T and T' be trees, $T \leq_m T'$. Then there is some vertex v of T and v' of T' such that if we root T at v and T' at v' then $T \leq_{m^r} T'$. Therefore, if we have a lower ideal of (unrooted) trees, say $\mathcal{D}$ and T is an obstruction then for every tree T' in $\mathcal{D}$ and every rooting of T and T', say T_1, T_1' respectively, $T_1 \not\leq_m T_1'$.

6 Computations on Lower Ideals

The characterizations of tree lower ideals discussed in the previous section have been in terms of regular expressions. In this section, we discuss the computational aspects of using regular expressions as characterizations. Throughout we will not distinguish between a planar-planted tree and its tree-linearization.

Let Σ_n be the set $\{(i, j) : 1 \leq i \leq n, 0 \leq j \leq 3\}$. Recall that for every proper family of trees closed under minors there is some number $n > 0$ such that the ideal is described by a regular expression over the alphabet Σ_n. The main computational result we discuss is the following.

Lemma 25. *Let* $n > 0$ *and let* $\mathcal{E}$ *be a regular expression over* Σ_n. *Then, there is a recursive procedure which determines whether or not* $\mathcal{E}$ *recognizes the tree-linearizations of a proper family* $\mathcal{D}$ *of trees under minors. Also, if* $\mathcal{E}$ *recognizes the family* $\mathcal{D}$ *then the procedure will generate the obstructions of* $\mathcal{D}$, $\mathcal{O}_{\mathcal{D}}$.

Proof. Recall that by Lemma 18 there is a regular expression $\mathcal{E}_0$ over Σ_n which recognizes all tree-linearizations of width at most n. We first check if $\mathcal{L}(\mathcal{E}) = \mathcal{L}(\mathcal{E}_0)$. If so, then $\mathcal{O}_{\mathcal{D}} = \{B_n\}$. If $\mathcal{L}(\mathcal{E}) \neq \mathcal{L}(\mathcal{E}_0)$ then $\mathcal{L}(\mathcal{E}) \subseteq \mathcal{L}(\mathcal{E}_0)$ (otherwise, $\mathcal{E}$ does not recognize a minor closed tree family). Therefore, there is some tree T_1 such that $\tau(T_1) \notin \mathcal{L}(\mathcal{E})$. Let $\mathcal{F}(T_1)$ be the regular expression recognizing all trees which do not contain T_1 as a minor and let $\mathcal{E}_1$ be the regular expression recognizing $\mathcal{L}(\mathcal{E}_0) \bigcap \mathcal{L}(\mathcal{F}(T_1))$.

If $\mathcal{L}(\mathcal{E}) = \mathcal{L}(\mathcal{E}_1)$ then either $\mathcal{O}_\mathcal{D} = \{T_1\}$ or $\mathcal{O}_\mathcal{D} = \{B_n, T_1\}$ depending on whether $T_1 \leq_m B_n$. If $\mathcal{L}(\mathcal{E}) = \mathcal{L}(\mathcal{E}_1)$ then we check if $\mathcal{L}(\mathcal{E}) \subseteq \mathcal{L}(\mathcal{E}_1)$. If not, then $\mathcal{E}$ does not recognize a minor closed tree family. Otherwise $\mathcal{L}(\mathcal{E}) \subseteq \mathcal{L}(\mathcal{E}_1)$ and we find a new tree T_2 such that $\tau(T_2) \notin \mathcal{L}(\mathcal{E})$. Recursively continuing this process yields the obstructions. The procedure is guaranteed to halt, since trees are well-quasi-ordered under minors. $\qquad\square$

Clearly by Lemma 25 any construction that can be made using obstructions can also be made using our regular expression characterization. One non-trivial place that this regular expression characterization helps is in computing unions of minor closed tree families.

Suppose $\mathcal{D}$ is a lower ideal of trees under minors. We now have recursive procedures which can generate the obstruction set of $\mathcal{D}$ from the regular expression characterization and the regular expression characterization from the obstruction set.

Finally notice that using the regular expression characterization of lower ideals we can easily compute the obstructions for the union of lower ideals of trees under minors (this problem is discussed in the introduction and in Appendix 1). Suppose $\mathcal{D}_1$ and $\mathcal{D}_2$ are lower ideals and $\mathcal{E}_1$ and $\mathcal{E}_2$ are the regular expression characterizations of $\mathcal{D}_1$ and $\mathcal{D}_2$ respectively. Since regular expressions are closed under unions we find a regular expression $\mathcal{D}$ such that $\mathcal{L}(\mathcal{D}) = \mathcal{L}(\mathcal{D}_1) \bigcup \mathcal{L}(\mathcal{D}_2)$. Now, using the procedure outlined in the proof of Lemma 25, we can compute the obstructions of the unions.

Similarly, we can compute the intertwine of two trees under minors and embeddings using our regular expression characterization. Recently alternate proofs of these problems have been found (see [5, 11]). It is not clear whether our techniques or their's give better bounds on the intertwines.

References

1. S. Arnborg, J. Lagergren, and D. Seese. Problems easy for tree-decomposable graphs. *Journal of Algorithms*, 12(2):308ff, 1991.

2. M. Fellows and M. Langston. Nonconstructive tools for proving polynomial-time decidability. *Journal of the Association for Computing Machinery*, 35(3):727–739, July 1988.

3. M. Fellows and M. Langston. On search, decision and the efficiency of polynomial-time algorithms. In *21st ACM Symposium on Theory of Computing*, pages 501–512, 1989.

4. A. Gupta. *Constructivity Issues in Tree Minors*. PhD thesis, Dept. of Computer Science, University of Toronto, Toronto, Canada, 1990. Also Appears as Technical Report 244/90, Dept. of Computer Science, University of Toronto.

5. A. Gupta and R. Impagliazzo. Computing planar intertwines. In *32nd Symposium on the Foundations of Computer Science*, pages 802–811, 1991.

6. C. Kuratowski. Sur le problème des courbes gauches en topologie. *Fund. Math.*, 15:271–283, 1930.

7. J. Lagergren. Efficient parallel algorithms for tree-decompositions and related problems. In *31th Symposium on Foundations of Computer Science*, pages 173–181, 1990.

8. N. Robertson. Personal communication, 1990.

9. N. Robertson and P. Seymour. Graph Minors XV. Wagner's conjecture. in preparation.

10. N. Robertson, P. Seymour, and R. Thomas. Lower ideals of tree-structures. in preperation, 1991.

11. P. Seymour and R. Thomas, 1991. Personal communication.

On Distributed Algorithms in a Broadcast Domain

Danny Dolev*, Dalia Malki**

The Hebrew University of Jerusalem, Israel

Abstract. This paper studies the usage of broadcast communication in distributed services. The approach taken is practical: all the algorithms are asynchronous, and tolerate realistic faults. We study four problems in a broadcast domain: clock synchronization, reliable and ordered broadcast, membership, and file replication. The clock synchronization algorithm shows for the first time how to utilize broadcast communication for synchronization. The master synchronizes any number of slaves while incurring a constant load. The approach taken in the file replication tool uses *snooping* in order to enhance the availability of file systems, at almost no cost.

1 Introduction

This paper presents algorithms that use broadcast communication. The broadcast primitive enables the dissemination of messages to multiple destinations via a single transmission. The motivation behind this work is practical: most computer networks nowadays essentially provide a datagram broadcast service. Most transport protocols do not utilize the broadcast capability, though, because the handling of faults and retransmissions is far more complicated than point to point communication. Future networks designs also appear to possess the broadcast capability (*e.g.* FDDI, MAN, wireless networks based on cellular communication).

Thus, it is important to define high level services over the datagram broadcast layer, and examine how applications can utilize broadcast communication. Our work incorporates the broadcast primitive into the system model. We show various algorithms in this model that are substantially different from their point-to-point counterparts. We focus on practical algorithms, and present their basic properties. Therefore, all the algorithms are asynchronous, and tolerate realistic faults.

The first algorithm we present is for a clock synchronization service. While it is rather obvious that broadcast messages are capable of carrying *data* to multiple destinations efficiently, we have not seen any use of it in synchronization. We show how multiple clients can synchronize with a single time-source ("master")

---

* also at IBM Almaden Research Center
** This work was supported in part by GIF I-207-199.6/91

using broadcast messages. The master incurs a constant overhead of emitting the broadcast messages, regardless of the number of clients being synchronized.

The second service presented is a reliable broadcast service, that delivers messages to a group of processes, while preserving their relative orders. This paper surveys some of the protocols suggested in the literature for these services. One of the interesting trade-offs manifested in these protocols is whether to employ a central coordinator for achieving an agreed order of delivery of the messages.

Another category of distributed algorithms that are examined in the broadcast domain are algorithms that need to achieve coordinated decisions. The impossibility result of [14] bounds all these problems within an asynchronous environment. The problem is the inability to distinguish between a slow machine and one that crashed. In practical asynchronous systems it is often preferable to give-up on a slow machine, rather than get stuck in waiting.

The membership protocol we present circumvents this problem by maintaining the set of machines that appear active *internally* at any point. Moreover, other protocols can use the membership service instead of explicitly handling the dynamicity in the system. The specific membership protocol presented here handles both failures and recoveries of machines, and network partitions and remerges. We provide an informal definition of the requirements of the membership service, while allowing partitions.

We conclude with a utility that exploits an unusual facet of broadcast communication, the ability to *snoop* and intercept broadcast messages. We show how to use the snooping ability in order to enhance availability of file system, at almost no cost.

None of the above protocols explicitly uses any known theoretical solution to coordination problems, even though these problems were extensively studied. Randomized protocols prove their usefulness in overcoming the impossibility of consensus ([14]). However, they proved to be too complicated for usage, and typically exchange too many messages. Specifically to this context, we note that there are no randomized protocols that utilize available broadcast as a primitive.

Another approach that was taken in many works, is to assume that the system is synchronized. Thus, all machines perform their operations in a synchronous lock step. There were a few variations to this approach, but shared by all of them is the need to guarantee a tight synchronization. In practice this is not a valid approach, since distance, temporary load, and the independence in operation of individual machines prevents us from guaranteeing such a synchronization. It is true that one can assume, for instance, that 90% of the messages arrive within a small window of time, but the rest of the messages may take a much longer time to arrive. Tight synchronization requires a single step of the protocol to be very large, so that all but few of the messages sent at that step will arrive correctly.

The algorithms presented in this paper operate within a realistic model, and were all implemented. We encourage other researchers to continue investigating the possibilities and tradeoffs within this framework, and explore the possibility of using randomized techniques in practice.

2 System Model

This section presents the assumed underlying model of the rest of the paper. We believe that the model below reflects the basic concepts shared by most distributed systems today. A distributed system comprises of a set of machines. that communicate using messages. The underlying network is completely connected and can transfer messages between any pair of machines. In addition, the network provides a broadcast service. A machine emits a broadcast message at once to all its destinations. A single copy of the message reaches all the machines, but might arrive at different times to them.

An essential property of the model is that broadcast messages incur the same processing overhead as unicast messages at the sending and at the receiving machines. Similarly, broadcast messages consume identical network capacity as unicast messages.

A broadcast message is sent "anonymously" and does not require specific addressees. In this paper we will not distinguish between broadcast, which sends a message to all the machines in the network, and a *multicast*, which sends a message to a selected subset via a group-designation. The broadcast capability also enables in some cases a non-targeted machine to *snoop* and intercept messages. This might be a security concern for some environments; in this paper we present an advantageous facet of this property.

A typical LAN architecture is composed of one or more broadcast segments, interconnected via bridging and gateway elements. The LAN might partition to two sets of machines, in case a bridging/gateway element fails. In case that some other machine fails or disconnects from the network, the remaining machines continue to be connected and to pass messages undisturbed. Machine failure is either fail stop or omission, thus a machine may fail to send messages, but will not produce messages that are not part of the basic protocol. Thus, no byzantine faults are assumed. Moreover, in the context of this paper it is assumed that if a message arrives to its destination, its data is assumed to be uncorrupted.

The broadcast service provided by the hardware media is an unreliable datagram service. A single transmission can potentially reach all the machines, but it may fail to go out, or a single machine might miss it. Although message loss rate is not specified explicitly, the protocols were designed under the assumption that it is low.

The Basic Impossibility Result

At the basis of any coordination problem in a distributed system lies some algorithm like atomic-broadcast and membership-maintenance which requires a consensus at one level or another. Fischer Lynch and Paterson ([14]) were the first to point out that there is no way to reach consensus in an asynchronous distributed system, when faults may occur. Moreover the asynchrony that produces the difficulty can be very limited, as can be seen in [11].

The basic idea behind all these impossibility results is that there is no way to distinguish between a very slow machine and a failed one. Since any nontrivial coordination problems should be determined on the fly according to the initial inputs to the individual machines, there should always be a case in which a single machine may determine the general outcome. Thus, as long as the input from this machine does not arrive, we cannot guarantee that all the correctly operating machines will perform the same operation (or reach the same decision).

The Practical Approach

In practice, coordination problems cannot be solved in "full", *i.e.* their solution may not comply with an outsider's view of the system and its view of "correct" processors. In order to be able to overcome the impossibility result, machines will use inaccurate fault detectors, based on timeout. The coordination decisions are reached only among the machines that are viewed *internally* as operational, and not necessarily "really" all the operational machines. Thus, in the cases that the fault detector errs, a correctly operating machine may be considered faulty, and will need to reconcile with the rest of the machines at some later time.

The basic differences can be summarized as follows: in our approach individual machines operate asynchronously, each one at its own pace. Prior to some decision points some machine may need to wait for others, but instead of a deadlock, a timeout will detect failures, and will enable the machines to resume operation.

3   Clock Synchronization

In this section we will describe a new approach to clock synchronization. The approach utilizes the broadcast domain environment and enables synchronizing many machines without explicitly exchanging messages with each one of them.

Common to all clock synchronization algorithms is the need to exchange messages between the synchronizer and the synchronized machine. This is true in master-slave protocols, as well as in all versions of distributed clock synchronization protocols. The need arises from the requirement to produce three events, two on one clock and a middle one on a different clock. Once such events are identified, one can obtain an estimate on the difference between the clock readings. This estimate is used to adjust one of the two clocks.

An access to an outside time source is a common way to obtain a precise time service. And several researchers have offered to use the machine having that input as the master clock that will occasionally synchronize the rest.

This approach seems to mean that in such a time service, if many machines are connected via a LAN, and one of them is the master, it will need to explicitly exchange messages with each one of them in order to synchronize all the clocks. When the LAN contains dozens of machines this becomes a real load on the master machine. The problem is to find a way to broadcast the time information to synchronize individual clocks without the need to explicitly exchange messages between the master and the slaves.

A Simplified Solution

First concentrate on a simplified model. Assume that the master machine has a direct access to the LAN in the sense that it does not use any buffer to store messages it sends out. Moreover, assume that there are no other messages produced at the master machine. Thus all it produces are clock synchronization messages.

Thus, when it decides to send a message it knows when this message is being sent out. Thus it can produce a sequence of messages, each one being produced after the previous one was actually sent out. The master will timestamp each message in such a sequence, and will broadcast it over the LAN.

Ignoring message loss, for a moment, we can study the flow of messages at each receiving machine. These machines naturally are busy with other functions, and when a machine reads its input, it may find several messages of the sequence at its input buffer at once. A machine needs to identify two events of the master that took place between one of its own events.

The receiving machine marks the time it first notices a partial sequence sent by the master at its buffer. Let this time be R_1 and let $x_1, ... x_k$ be the prefix of the sequence it noticed at its input buffer. At a later time, say R_2 it reads its input again and sees some more messages of the sequence sent by the master. Let this new subsequence be denoted $x_{k+1}, x_{k+2}, \cdots$. The simple model assures that each one of these messages was produced after the previous one was sent. On the other hand, we do not know that x_{k+1} was produced after time R_1, since it is possible that this message was in transit when the receiver was reading its input buffer. But in this case we know that x_{k+2} was not produced yet, thus its timestamp is an event that took place after time R_1 and before time R_2. This implies that the timestamp on this message, say T_{k+2}, can be used to synchronize the receiver clock. Figure 1 exemplifies these events.

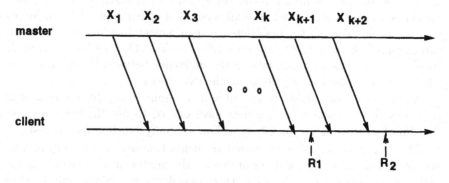

Fig. 1. Event X_{k+2} occurs between R_1 and R_2

Adapting ideas from previous clock synchronization protocols, the receiver can adjust its clock by,

$$R_2 - T_{k+2} + \frac{(R_2 - R_1)}{2}.$$

Notice that all receivers on the LAN can synchronize using the same method. Thus, the load on the master does not depend on the number of machines that are currently connected.

The general case

In the general case there may be specific architectures in which more than one message might be in transit at once. In such architectures, the number of such messages is still bounded by a small constant number. The basic idea above can easily be adopted to count for that.

There might be cases where the master doesn't necessarily know when its messages are being sent out. In this case we can borrow another idea from existing clock synchronization protocols. We can assign a specific machine to echo back to the master whenever it receives each message. The master waits for an echo on its previous message before time-stamping and sending the next one. In a sense, the master and this machine follow the basic idea of a master-slave protocol. The rest of the receivers synchronize their clocks just by listening in.

In the [13] the reader can find the complete study of this approach and various optimizations to the problem.

4 Reliable Broadcast

The topic of consistent dissemination of information in distributed systems has been the focus of many studies, both theoretical and practical. The pioneering work of the V system ([8]), deals with communication among groups of processes, via broadcast messages. In V, broadcast messages are not reliable, but provide "best effort" delivery semantics. In addition, if messages are sent concurrently from several sources, the order of their delivery at overlapping destinations is undefined. Later work in the ISIS system ([6]), deals with providing higher level services, and supports reliable delivery, as well as various orderings. Many distributed applications require such high degree of coordination among their processes. The main difficulty facing the designer of a distributed application is the consistency of information disseminated, and the control over the dissemination of that information. Thus, the designer of a distributed system would wish for a service that provides a guaranteed delivery-and-consistency of broadcast messages. Having such a service, most distributed applications become much easier to implement and to maintain.

In many systems, when a group of processes need to perform a coordinated work they interact via (reliable) point-to-point communication. This approach is costly when there are several participants. It would be preferable to use the available broadcast hardware where possible, for efficient dissemination of messages to multiple destinations via a single transmission. The problem is that current transport protocols provide only datagram broadcast services (*e.g.* UDP [22], IP-multicast [10]).

Today, there are several projects that develop protocols for reliable broadcast services while utilizing the broadcast hardware where possible, *e.g.* [18, 17, 3, 2] and the recent version of the ISIS system [7]. We discuss some of them in this section. In this section it is assumed that the system consists of a static set of machines (the Membership Section shows how to maintain the set of *active* machines up to date, and the protocols we present below can be extended to dynamic environments once the membership layer is present).

Causal Broadcast

This section presents the mechanism employed in the Transis communication sub-system ([2]) for guaranteeing delivery of messages to all their destinations. The principle idea of reliable message delivery in Transis is motivated by the Trans algorithm ([18]) and the Psync algorithm ([21]).

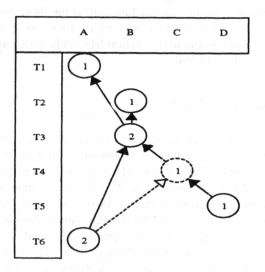

Fig. 2. A Transis Scenario

Messages are transmitted via a single transmission, using the available network broadcast. The "blobs" in Figure 2 represent broadcast messages. Each machine tags its messages with increasing serial numbers, serving as message-ids. For example, in the figure, machine A emits at the time-mark T1 the first message, machine B emits at T2 its first message, and so on. Acknowledgments to messages are piggybacked onto the next broadcast messages. The full arrows represent acknowledgments: from message B_2 to A_1 and to B_1, from C_1 to B_2, etc. An ACK consists of the sending machine-id and the serial number of the acknowledged message. A fundamental principle of the protocol is that each ACK need only be sent once. Further messages, that follow from other machines, form a "chain" of ACKs, which implicitly acknowledge former messages in the chain. For example, Figure 2 could depict the following scenario on the network:

$$A_1 , \quad B_1 , \quad \overset{A_1 B_1}{\hookrightarrow\hookrightarrow} B_2 , \quad \overset{B_2}{\hookrightarrow} C_1 , \quad \overset{C_1}{\hookrightarrow} D_1 , \quad ...$$

Machines on the LAN might experience message losses. They can recognize it by analyzing the received message chains. For example, machine A recognized that it lost C_1 after receiving the sequence: $A_1 , \quad B_1 , \quad \overset{A_1 B_1}{\hookrightarrow\hookrightarrow} B_2 , \quad \overset{C_1}{\hookrightarrow} D_1$. Therefore, A emits a *negative-ACK* on message C_1, requesting for its retransmission. In this case A acknowledges B_2 and not D_1, since messages that follow "causal holes" are not incorporated for delivery until the lost messages are recovered. In this way, the acknowledgments form the causal relation among messages directly.

The delivered messages are held for backup by all the receiving machines. In this way, retransmission requests can be honored by any one of the participants. Of course, messages cannot be kept for retransmission forever. When all the machines have acknowledged the reception of a message, it can be safely discarded.

If the LAN runs without losses then it determines a single total order of the messages. Since there are message losses, and machines receive retransmitted messages, the original total order is lost. The piggybacked acknowledgments are used for reconstructing the original partial order of the messages.

Agreed Broadcast

One of the characteristics of the Trans and the Transis protocols, is that they allow completely spontaneous transmission of messages by any machine. Consequently, two machines may send messages within a small interval apart, none receiving each other's message first. In this case, there will be no acknowledgment between these messages. This means that additional processing is required if there is a requirement to deliver the messages in the same total order at all their common destinations.

An *agreed broadcast* service guarantees that messages arrive reliably and in the same total-order to all their destinations. There are several completely distributed algorithms that build a total order from the local information and reach agreement ([18, 12, 21]). It is perhaps easiest to understand a naive *all-ack* algorithm that is also completely distributed. The above referred algorithms are essentially optimizations on this principle. The all-ack idea is:

– Wait until at least one message is received from each machine.

- Then go through the machines in ascending order, and deliver the first message from each machine unless it directly acknowledges another message.

The common characteristic of these algorithms, is that they do not incur any extra message exchange for achieving agreement on the total order. They have *post-transmission* delay, from the time a message is transmitted and received until it is ordered in the right place. Interestingly, this cost is most apparent when the system is relatively idle, and waiting for responses from all (or some) of the machines incurs the worst-case delay. On the other hand, these methods can sustain steady transmission loads that are close to the network limits, when all the machines are fairly uniformly active (*e.g.* the ToTo protocol was measured delivering around 500 1K messages per second over an Ethernet of 10 Indigo stations, see [12]).

A different family of protocols orders the messages in a total order by employing a centrally controlled ordering scheme ([7, 3, 17]). The Isis ABCAST protocol ([7]) employs a *token-holder* within each group of communicating processes. ABCAST messages are broadcast at will, and their delivery is delayed by all the receiving processes except for the token holder. Periodically, the token holder sends a message indicating its order of delivery for all received ABCAST messages, and all the other processes comply with it.

The Amoeba system contains a different variation of this scheme, implemented within the operating system kernel ([17]). A sequencer kernel is designated as the central controller. Every message is sent to it via point to point communication, and the sequencer broadcasts it to all the machines. The FIFO order of sequencer-transmissions determines a total order for all the messages.

The Totem protocol ([3]) uses a revolving token that holds a sequence-number for messages. The holder of the token can emit one or more broadcast messages, and update the token sequence accordingly. In order to transmit a broadcast message, a processor must obtain the token. The token itself regularly revolves among all the processors.

The cost in these protocols is in obtaining access to the central controller, be it a processor or a token. This cost is apparent both in the delay occurring until the control is obtained, and in extra messages exchanged. Once it is obtained, transmission and ordering is done immediately. Therefore, we say that they have a *pre-transmission* delay. The advantage of central control is that it regulates the flow of messages efficiently. It is not entirely clear what are the trade-offs between distributed and centralized control in these protocols. In particular, the behavior of these protocols when the communication pattern is "chaotic" need to be further investigated.

5 Membership in Broadcast Environments

A point to point communication protocol needs to maintain information about one machine, "the other party." A reliable broadcast communication system needs to maintain information about a set of machines of a variable size. The machines may fail and recover. The underlying communication network may partition and reconnect, thereby partitioning the set of participating machines. This dynamicity is one of the main reasons that reliable broadcast protocols are more complex than their point-to-point counterparts.

The *membership* problem is to maintain the set of participating machines in agreement among all the machines. This basic problem of distributed computing has received considerable attention in the past (see [9, 1, 19, 20, 23, 24, 16, 3, 4]). We are mainly interested in membership protocols for broadcast communication environments. In these environments, the membership changes are reported via special messages, that are delivered to the upper level application among the stream of regular messages.

In distributed applications, the machines typically act upon regular messages according to their installed membership. Thus, in addition to the agreement on membership changes, it is desired that the machines see the membership changes in the *same order*. Furthermore, in order for all the machines to respond in the same manner to broadcast messages, they should see the same messages between every pair of membership changes. This valuable principle is defined in [5], and is called *virtual synchrony*.

Informally, we require that membership changes maintain:

- Membership changes occur in the same order at all the machines that view them.
- Every failed or disconnected machine is removed from its membership within a finite time.
- Every two operational machines that are connected for sufficiently long time *join* in a common membership.
- Membership changes preserve virtual synchrony with respect to regular messages.

We briefly present a protocol that satisfies all these requirements here. The protocol relies on broadcast communication that preserves *causality*.[3] This protocol is completely symmetrical. Joining with other machine(s) is triggered when a message from a machine that does not belong to the current membership view is intercepted in the broadcast domain. Fault handling is triggered by timeout. (A closely related membership protocol that satisfies the above requisites is presented in [1]).

Whenever the membership protocol starts, each machine sends a message with the best *suggestion* it has for the current membership. Each membership suggestion contains two sets: all the known machines, called M, and all the suspected faulty/detached machines, called F. In order to *accept* the membership suggested in $< M, F >$, all the machines in $M \setminus F$ need to broadcast identical suggestions. If a membership suggestion $< M', F' >$ from $M \setminus F$ differs from $< M, F >$, then there are a few cases:

---

[3] We say that two messages m, m' are related in the causal order $\xrightarrow{cause}$, if they are in the transitive closure of: (1) $m \xrightarrow{cause} m'$ if $\text{deliver}_q(m, *) \rightarrow \text{broadcast}_q(m')$, (2) $m \xrightarrow{cause} m'$ if $\text{broadcast}_q(m) \rightarrow \text{broadcast}_q(m')$

- If $M' \subseteq M$ and $F \subseteq F'$, then this message is ignored.
- If M' or F' contains machines that are not contained in M, F, and the sender of this suggestion did not agree already to $< M, F >$, then M', F', are merged into M, F and a new membership suggestion is broadcast.
- If M' or F' contains machines that are not contained in M, F, and the sender of this message is already marked as agreeing to $< M, F >$, then the message is queued for future membership instances. This handling is crucial for the consistency of the membership decision.

  If there are machines in F' that are not included in F, they will not be required to agree to the $< M, F >$ suggestion (this could lead to a deadlock). In this case, all the machines in $M \setminus (F \cup F')$ must send their agreement both to the $< M, F >$ suggestion, and to the suspected machines in F'.

As shown in these cases, the suggestion of each participating machine may change during the execution of the membership protocol, one or more times. Therefore, this protocol cannot be classified as a k-phase protocol for any specific k, and the number of rounds of message exchanges depends on the specific scenario.

During an instance of the membership protocol, the suspected machines are **not** removed from M, but are only added to F. A machine that is suspected in F, cannot be removed from F either. This guarantees that the protocol will terminate within a finite time. For example, during a period of instability in the network, a certain machine might detach and re-connect frequently. The removal of this machine from M might lead to an endless process of removing and adding it to M. In our scheme, it can be added and removed at most once during the execution of the protocol. Consequently, our scheme might mistakenly remove from the membership an operational machine. This machine can later re-join the membership. Note that in an asynchronous environment, there is no way to prevent the removal of a slow machine from the membership. Thus, in our view, the means for reducing the potential of such mistakes are practical means: fine-tuning of the system timeouts, and a robust fault-detection mechanism, involving *consulting* with a few machines. These practical details are not relevant for the correctness of the membership protocol.

This protocol also preserves virtual synchrony with respect to other regular messages in the system. In order to understand the main difficulty in preserving virtual synchrony, envision a system of four machines, A, B, C, D. Machine D has crashed, and its last message m_d is received only by C. If C sends its membership suggestion $< \{A, B, C, D\}, \{D\} >$ (for excluding D) before it receives m_d, how will A and B know they must deliver this message before the membership-change? There may be more complicated scenarios, for example if first D crashes, and C is the only receiver of m_d, and then C crashes, but has sent a message m_c referring to m_d. The rule for message delivery in our protocol is the following: Between every two membership changes, all the messages that follow *any one of the identical membership suggestion-messages of the first membership-change* and do not follow *any one of the identical membership suggestion-messages of the second membership-change* are delivered. This set of messages can be proved to be identical among all the machines that install the same two membership-changes.

6   Warm Replication by Snooping

This section deals with a less obvious facet of broadcast communication, the ability to intercept messages by non-target machines (*snooping*). We propose a way to exploit this ability in order to enhance availability of system services. The snooping ability offers a novel way for cheaply replicating services in the network.

To exemplify our ideas, we use the Sun Network File System (NFS) environment, available at Unix environments. In an NFS environment, applications access files throughout the network in an automatic, transparent way. We can view the entire network as providing a global file system service that is distributed among different machines. While very convenient in all ways, this distribution leads to a reliability problem: The failure of any one of the machines that provide file-system services can block an application from running.

In these environments, local-area broadcast networks such as Ethernet and token-rings are becoming a standard de-facto. These broadcast media carry the point-to-point NFS messages and enable snooping by unlisted parties.

A *warm-backup service* (WB) provides a *per-application* replication service. The main mechanism of WB is quite simple: When an application asks for WB service, a second replica will be created for each file that the application opens. The *warm-backup service* will keep the two replicas up-to-date and consistent by snooping, and intercepting the file-modification messages. WB performs these changes on the replica. When that file is not needed any more, the new replica will be deleted. In order to enhance availability even more, the same scheme can work with any number of additional replicas for each file, instead of only one.

Another option of the WB service is to provide a *per-directory* warm replication service. When this option is specified for the WB server, then only files in the specified directory sub-hierarchy are automatically replicated. We anticipate this to be a most useful option for the WB tool.

The WB server differs from other known replication systems in that it provides a *per-application/per-directory* replication service in order to increase the accessibility of files throughout the application's lifetime. The main novelty is the use of *snooping* in broadcast environments for providing replication cheaply. It does not require any special hardware such as multiple-access disks, yet it provides warm replication that is consistent at every moment. In addition, unlike fully-replicated file systems, the WB architecture does not require modification to the basic file-system structure or semantics.

Concurrent-Write WB

In the general case, multiple processes from different machines may access the same file concurrently. In order to keep the primary file copy and its replica(s)

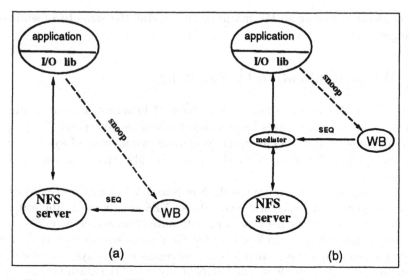

Fig. 3. Concurrent-Reader WB

consistent, the modifications to the file should be made at the same order in all
the replicas. For this case, we propose the architecture shown in Figure 3(a-b)
(for simplicity, we only discuss the single-replica case; similar results apply in
the multi-replica case). This paradigm works as follows:

1. The NFS and the WB server are notified by the application at startup
   whether it wishes to be warmly backed-up (and which directories to back
   up).
2. When the NFS server receives a modify-request from a WB application, it
   must wait for a sequence-message from its warm-backup.
3. The WB server *snoops* for all NFS messages. When it receives an NFS
   modify-request from a WB application, it issues the modify-operation on
   the replica, and sends a numbered sequence-message with an identification
   of the request to the NFS server in the site of the accessed file.
4. The NFS server executes the modify-requests it has received according to
   the order set by the sequence-messages it receives from the WB server. It
   returns the results to the application.
5. If either the NFS server or the WB server loses a message from the application, the application will time-out and re-issue the request (this is the
   standard fault handling protocol of the NFS).

The modification of the NFS server can be done internally (Figure 3(a)), or
by placing a special server on the NFS server's machine that mediates between
the application and the NFS server (Figure 3(b)).

Recovery

The modified NFS server and the WB server need to dynamically detect each other's failures and recoveries, and bring the system to a consistent state upon recoveries. In case of the primary NFS server failure, the WB server holds up-to-date copies of all the accessed file. The WB can also "take over" the primary NFS server role for those files, and allow currently running applications to continue. In order that a running application will turn to the WB server for backup file-service, it needs to be modified as well. It is sufficient to transparently replace the system-calls library and no change is required to the application itself. The details of the *takeover* algorithm, for moving the application from the primary server to the backup, are standard for such a system, and are beyond the scope of this compact presentation. Likewise, the matter of re-integrating an NFS server upon recovery are detailed elsewhere ([15]).

Exclusive-Write WB

One of the drawbacks of the above architecture is that it requires changes to the NFS server, thus affecting the entire system and not only the WB applications. In this section we offer a more restrictive solution, that does not require changes to the NFS server. This solution work under the assumption that there are no concurrent accesses by different applications to the same file.

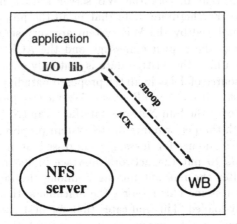

Fig. 4. Exclusive-Reader WB

It is a known belief that the majority of modify-accesses to files in Unix are done by processes exclusively and not concurrently. The Unix loose semantics on concurrent-modify on files encourages this style of usage. In order to replicate files for the exclusive writer case, we propose the architecture shown in Figure 4. Each application that wishes to obtain the WB services, links with a modified system-call library. The files accessed by this applications must be dedicated to the WB server, and should be not accessed by "regular" NFS clients. The modify accesses to files is done as follows:

1. The WB server is notified by the application at startup whether it wishes to be warmly backed-up (and which directories to back up).
2. When the application issues a modify request on a file, it sends the request as usual to the NFS server.
3. There is no change to the NFS server: it executes each received request and returns the results to the application.
4. The WB server "snoops" on the network for NFS requests. When it receives a modify-request from a WB application, it performs the modify-operation on the replica, and returns an acknowledgment (ACK) message to the application.
5. The application waits for the returned results from the NFS server and for the acknowledgment message from the WB server. If it times out on any one of them, it re-issues the request. If either the NFS server or the WB server loses a message, it will receive the retransmission.

Practical Considerations

The WB architecture is designed for incurring a minimal overhead on the message traffic in the system. All the dashed-arrows in Figures 3, 4 are almost cost-free, and are done by network snooping (the reason for saying that this *almost* cost free is that in case the WB server loses a message, it needs to be re-transmitted). Furthermore, note that in all the proposed paradigms, the extra-messages employed by the WB system are very short messages that do not carry data (*e.g.* the sequence-message and the ACK message). Thus, for write-operations on files, the written data is sent only once over the network.

The common source of delay in all the proposed paradigms is the need to wait for an extra message from the WB server. We have implemented a prototype of the WB server over the Sun Network Interface Tap (NIT), and are currently experimenting with the performance of the system proposed in Figure 4.

The WB server snoops for messages addressed at multiple NFS servers. Therefore, it needs to put the network-interface in its machine in promiscuous mode, and filter the relevant messages among the multitude of messages transferred in the system. This requires the machine(s) that run the WB server to be fairly lightly-loaded. This indicates that for best results, the WB server should probably run on a designated machine by itself, the *backup machine*.

7 Conclusions

The hardware media of computer networks provide the capability to broadcast messages. This offers an efficient way to disseminate messages to multiple destinations. Essentially, this is a practical consideration; however, if we incorporate the broadcast capability into the system model, we arrive at distributed algorithms that are quite different from their sequential counterparts. Moreover, in the case of the warm-replication application, the ability to snoop within a broadcast network has led us to devise a completely new scheme for replication. Thus, these practical considerations can be of significance to the designer of distributed services.

Future networks such as the high-speed FDDI ring, and wireless networks, also possess the broadcast capability. Therefore, understanding the potential in broadcast communication is important. Our experience with some of the protocols presented in this paper indicates that there are interesting tradeoffs that need to be exlored. The choice between having a distributed control and a centralized control is not fully understood yet. Similarly, we note that *quantitative* measures may effect their conduct. For example, the reliable broadcast protocols we presented behave quite differently under various communication-load conditions, and when different loss-rates of underlying network messages are exhibited.

Randomized techniques have proved their importance in the field of distributed algorithms by producing solutions to the consensus problem and others. Rarely, is any of the theoretical randomized protocols used in practical distributed environments. Typically, this is because they are too complicated, or involve too many message-exchanges. We propose to investigate the usage of randomization in more realistic models, and in particular, within a broadcast domain.

8 Acknowledgments

The work presented in this paper benefitted from many other works. The Transis reliable broadcast and the membership protocol are the results of joint work with the colleague Transis developers, Yair Amir and Shlomo Kramer. The Warm Backup service was enhanced and implemented by Yuval Harari. Yuval Yarom helped editing the section about the Warm Backup. Ray Strong and Rudigue Reischuk co-developed with one of the authors the clock synchronization scheme. Idit Keidar wrote the tool that automatically plotted Figure 2.

References

1. Y. Amir, D. Dolev, S. Kramer, and D. Malki. Membership Algorithms for Multicast Communication Groups. In *Intl. Workshop on Distributed Algorithms proceedings (WDAG-6), (LCNS, 647)*, number 6th, pages 292–312, November 1992.
2. Y. Amir, D. Dolev, S. Kramer, and D. Malki. Transis: A Communication Sub-System for High Availability. In *Annual International Symposium on Fault-Tolerant Computing*, number 22, pages 76–84, July 1992.
3. Y. Amir, L. E. Moser, P. M. Melliar-Smith, D. A. Agarwal, and P. Ciarfella. Fast Message Ordering and Membership Using a Logical Token-Passing Ring. In *Intl. conf. on Distributed Computing Systems*, 1993. to appear.
4. J. Auerbach, M. Gopal, M. Kaplan, and S. Kutten. Multicast group membership management in high speed wide area networks. In *proc. intl. conference on Distributed Computing Systems*, number 11, pages 231–238, May 1991.

5. K. Birman, R. Cooper, and B. Gleeson. Programming with Process Groups: Group and Multicast Semantics. TR 91-1185, dept. of Computer Science, Cornell University, Jan 1991.

6. K. Birman, R. Cooper, T. A. Joseph, K. Marzullo, M. Makpangou, K. Kane, F. Schmuck, and M. Wood. *The ISIS System Manual*. Dept of Computer Science, Cornell University, Sep 90.

7. K. Birman, A. Schiper, and P. Stephenson. Lightweight Causal and Atomic Group Multicast. *ACM Trans. Comput. Syst.*, 9(3):272–314, 1991.

8. D. R. Cheriton and W. Zwaenepoel. Distributed Process Groups in the V Kernel. *ACM Trans. Comput. Syst.*, 2(3):77–107, May 1985.

9. F. Cristian. Reaching Agreement on Processor Group Membership in Synchronous Distributed Systems. *Distributed Computing*, 4(4), April 1991.

10. S. E. Deering. Host extensions for IP multicasting. RFC 1112, SRI Network Information Center, August 1989.

11. D. Dolev, C. Dwork, and L. Stockmeyer. On the minimal synchrony needed for distributed consensus. *J. ACM*, 34(1):77–97, Jan. 1987.

12. D. Dolev, S. Kramer, and D. Malki. Early Delivery Totally Ordered Broadcast in Asynchronous Environments. In *Annual International Symposium on Fault-Tolerant Computing*, number 23, June 1993.

13. D. Dolev, R.Reischuk, and H.R.Strong. Clock Synchronization Algorithms on a LAN. in preparation, 1993.

14. M. Fischer, N. Lynch, and M. Paterson. Impossibility of Distributed Consensus with One Faulty Process. *J. ACM*, 32:374–382, April 1985.

15. Y. Harari. Warm Backup Tool for Unix Network File System. internal manuscript, 1992.

16. F. Jahanian and W. Moran. Strong, Weak and Hybrid Group Membership. unpublished, IBM internal draft, 1992.

17. M. F. Kaashoek, A. S. Tanenbaum, S. F. Hummel, and H. E. Bal. An Efficient Reliable Broadcast Protocol. *Operating Systems Review*, 23(4):5–19, October 1989.

18. P. M. Melliar-Smith, L. E. Moser, and V. Agrawala. Broadcast Protocols for Distributed Systems. *IEEE Trans. Parallel & Distributed Syst.*, (1), Jan 1990.

19. P. M. Melliar-Smith, L. E. Moser, and V. Agrawala. Membership Algorithms for Asynchronous Distributed Systems. In *Intl. Conf. Distributed Computing Systems*, May 91.

20. S. Mishra, L. L. Peterson, and R. D. Schlichting. A Membership Protocol based on Partial Order. In *proc. of the intl. working conf. on Dependable Computing for Critical Applications*, Feb 1991.

21. L. L. Peterson, N. C. Buchholz, and R. D. Schlichting. Preserving and Using Context Information in Interprocess Communication. *ACM Trans. Comput. Syst.*, 7(3):217–246, August 89.

22. J. B. Postel. User Datagram Protocol. RFC 768, SRI Network Information Center, August 1980.

23. A. M. Ricciardi and K. P. Birman. Using Process Groups to Implement Failure Detection in Asynchronous Environments. In *proc. annual ACM Symposium on Principles of Distributed Computing*, pages 341–352, August 1991.

24. A. M. Ricciardi, K. P. Birman, and P. Stephenson. The Cost of Order in Asynchronous Systems. In *Intl. Workshop on Distributed Algorithms proceedings (WDAG-6), (LCNS, 647)*, number 6th, pages 329–345, November 1992.

Sparse Networks Supporting Efficient Reliable Broadcasting

Bogdan S. Chlebus(1)   Krzysztof Diks(2)   Andrzej Pelc(3)

(1,2)Instytut Informatyki   (2,3)Département d'Informatique
Uniwersytet Warszawski   Université du Québec à Hull
ul. Banacha 2   C.P. 1250, succ. "B"
02-097 Warszawa, Poland   Hull, Québec J8X 3X7, Canada

Abstract. Broadcasting concerns transmitting information from a node of a communication network to all other nodes. We consider this problem assuming that links and nodes of the network fail independently with given probabilities $p<1$ and $q<1$, respectively. For a positive constant ε, broadcasting in an n-node network is said to be ε-safe, if source information is transmitted to all fault-free nodes with probability at least $1-n^{-\varepsilon}$. For any $p<1$, $q<1$ and $\varepsilon>0$ we show a class of n-node networks with maximum degree $O(\log n)$ and ε-safe broadcasting algorithms for such networks working in logarithmic time.

1 Introduction

Broadcasting concerns transmitting information from a node of a communication network to all other nodes. It is closely related to gossiping where each node of a network holds a piece of information and all nodes need to learn the total information. Messages may be directly transmitted to adjacent nodes only, and every node may communicate with at most one neighbor in a unit of time.

The following are two important parameters of a broadcasting or gossiping algorithm: the total time used and the total number of two-party transmissions ("phone calls"). Many papers have been devoted to the study of algorithms optimizing one or both of these parameters. An extensive bibliography can be found in [10].

Recently a lot of attention has been devoted to broadcasting and gossiping in the presence of faulty links [2-8,11]. Two alternative assumptions about faults are usually made: either an upper bound k on the total number of faults is supposed [2,7,8] or it is assumed that links fail independently with fixed probability p [3-6]. If an upper bound is imposed and the worst case is considered, the maximum number of faults that can be tolerated must be smaller than the connectivity of the network. Thus, for large networks, the stochastic approach seems to be more realistic.

(1,2)   partly supported by EC Cooperative Action IC-1000 (project ALTEC: Algorithms for Future Technologies).
(2)   partly supported by NSERC International Fellowship.
(3)   partly supported by NSERC grant OGP 0008136.

In the presence of faults two ways of constructing a broadcasting algorithm are possible. One way is non-adaptive, that is, all calls have to be predetermined by specifying in advance which pairs of nodes communicate in a given time unit, without the possibility of modifying the sequence of calls depending on which calls succeeded and which failed. Mostly this approach has been studied in literature [2,3,6,7,8]. (In [8] it was called static). Another way of broadcasting in the presence of faults is adaptive, that is, every node can decide which node it should call in a given time unit, depending on the outcome of previous calls. However, in making this decision, a node can only take advantage of the information currently available to it, that is, no existence of a central monitor supervising the execution f the scheme is assumed. Adaptive algorithms were studied in [4,5].

If random faults are assumed, we cannot expect to perform broadcasting with absolute certainty and thus we look for highly reliable algorithms. Let ε be a positive constant. A broadcasting algorithm working for an n-node network is called ε-safe if the probability of broadcasting information throughout the network is at least $1-n^{-\varepsilon}$.

Efficient ε-safe broadcasting algorithms working under assumption of random link failures and fault-free nodes were studied in [3-5,12]. Bienstock [3] constructed n-node networks with $O(n \log n)$ links for which a non-adaptive ε-safe broadcasting algorithm could be shown to work in logarithmic time. His construction, however, is quite involved in that it uses expander graphs. Moreover, although Bienstock's network has only $O(n \log n)$ links, it contains nodes of degrees $\Theta(n)$.

In this paper we study ε-safe broadcasting algorithms working under a more general assumption: both links and nodes fail independently with given probabilities $p < 1$ and $q < 1$, respectively. Under this scenario the aim of the algorithm is to transmit information to all fault-free nodes. For any $p, q < 1$ and $\varepsilon > 0$ we construct simple n-node networks with maximum degree $O(\log n)$; for those networks we show a non-adaptive ε-safe broadcasting algorithm working in logarithmic time. The algorithm uses $O(n \log n)$ calls. Thus, using a simpler construction we improve Bienstock's result [3] under a more general fault model. We also construct an adaptive ε-safe broadcasting algorithm working in worst case logarithmic time and using an expected linear number of calls. All these characteristics are of minimal possible order of magnitude.

The paper is organized as follows: in section 2 we give a precise description of the communication model used in this paper, in section 3 we construct the family of sparse networks supporting our broadcasting algorithms, in section 4 we describe the algorithms, and in section 5 their reliability and efficiency are analyzed.

We use the following notation. For any random event E, $\overline{E}$ denotes it complement. For a set X, |X| denotes its size. For any positive number x, we write $\log x$ instead of $\log_2 x$.

2 The Model

The communication network is represented as a simple undirected graph whose vertices are nodes of the network and edges are communication links. Information to be broadcasted is initially stored in a node called the source. It will be referred to as source information. Links fail with fixed probability $p < 1$ and nodes other than the source fail with fixed probability $q < 1$. All failures are stochastically independent and the fault status of all components is permanent, that is, it does not change during the execution of the algorithm. The source is assumed fault-free.

We consider only synchronous algorithms. A basic step of a broadcasting algorithm is an attempt made by a node v to communicate with its neighbor w. Such an attempt takes a unit of time and we say in this case that v calls w. We assume that a node v can call at most one neighbor or be called by at most one neighbor in a unit of time, these two possibilities being exclusive. We refer to this assumption by saying that every node is involved in at most one call in a unit of time. A call from v to w is successful if v, w and the joining link are fault-free. During such a call, the node which already has source information, transmits it to the other node and some control messages can also be exchanged between v and w. When a call from a fault-free node v to w does not succeed, v becomes aware of it but it does not know the reason of failure (faulty link, faulty destination node or both). In this case no information is transmitted. Faulty nodes do not make calls: if a call from a faulty node is scheduled by an algorithm, it is not executed.

We consider two types of broadcasting algorithms: non-adaptive, in which the sequence of calls made by every node is given in advance, and adaptive, in which each fault-free node can decide which node to call in a given time unit using information currently available to it.

We say that a broadcasting algorithm is successful if upon its completion all fault-free nodes get the source information. Let ε be a positive constant. A broadcasting algorithm working for an n-node network is called ε-safe, if it succeeds with probability at least $1-n^{-\varepsilon}$. Two complexity measures of a broadcasting algorithm are considered in this paper: the number of time units used by the algorithm and the total number of calls (both successful and not) made during its execution. For adaptive algorithms, both the time and the number of calls are random variables and in this case expected values of these parameters become appropriate measures of complexity. For non-adaptive algorithms both parameters are obviously fixed, regardless of the execution.

3 Construction of Networks

In this section we describe n-node networks with maximum degree $O(\log n)$ for which efficient ε-safe broadcasting algorithms will be presented later.

Let $c \geq 2$ be a positive integer defined later. For each $n \geq 2c$ we define an n-node network $G_n(c)$. The set of nodes of $G_n(c)$ is $\{1,...,n\}$. We assume 1 to be the source of broadcasting. Easy modifications of our algorithms allow to drop this assumption. Let $d=c\lfloor \log n \rfloor$ and $s = \lfloor n/d \rfloor$. For clarity of presentation we assume that d divides n and $s=2^{h+1}-1$, for some $h \geq 0$. Partition the set of all nodes into sets $S_1,...,S_s$ such that $S_1=\{1,...,d\}$, $S_2=\{d+1,...,2d\}$, ... ,$S_s=\{(s-1)d+1,...,n\}$. These sets will be often called groups. In every set S_i, $1 \leq i \leq s$, enumerate consecutive nodes from 0 to d-1. For any $i=1,...,s$ and $j=0,...,d-1$, denote by (i,j) the j-th node in the i-th group. Arrange all groups S_i into complete binary tree T with h+1 levels enumerated 0,1,...,h, starting from the level containing the root. The group S_1 is the root of T. For every $1 \leq i \leq \lfloor s/2 \rfloor$, S_{2i} is the left child of S_i and S_{2i+1} is the right child of S_i in the tree T. For every $1 < i \leq s$, the group $S_{\lfloor i/2 \rfloor}$ is the parent of the group S_i. If S_i is a parent or a child of S_j we say that these groups are adjacent in T.

The set of edges of $G_n(c)$ is defined as follows. If groups S_i and S_j are adjacent in T, there is an edge in $G_n(c)$ between every node from S_i and every node from S_j. There are no other edges in $G_n(c)$.

Notice that $G_n(c)$ has the following properties:

- for every $1 \le i \le s$, $|S_i| \in O(\log n)$;
- $G_n(c)$ has maximum degree $O(\log n)$;
- the height h of the tree T is less than $\log n$.

4 Broadcasting Algorithms

In this section we construct non-adaptive and adaptive ε-safe broadcasting algorithms working for graph $G_n(c)$ defined in section 3. We first describe three procedures used in these algorithms.

1. Procedure Multicall (S_i, S_j, k)

The aim of this procedure is communication between nodes of group S_i and nodes of group S_j. S_j is a child of S_i in the tree T. The procedure uses one time unit.

procedure Multicall (S_i, S_j, k);
begin
        for all $0 \le r < d$ **in parallel do**
            (i,r) calls $(j, (r+k) \pmod d)$
end;

2. Procedure One To All $((i,r), S_j)$

The aim of the procedure is communication between a node of group S_i and all nodes of group S_j. Groups S_i and S_j are adjacent in the tree T. The procedure uses d time units.

procedure One To All $((i,r), S_j)$;
begin
        for k:=0 **to** d-1 **do**
            (i,r) calls (j,k)
end;

3. Procedure Pipeline Calls (S_i, S_j)

This procedure is adaptive. For groups S_i and S_j adjacent in the tree T, nodes from S_i call consecutive nodes from S_j. A fault-free node u from S_i is called active if u does not have yet the source information; as soon as it gets it, it stops being active. Calls are made only by active nodes. The procedure uses 2d-1 time units.

procedure Pipeline Calls (S_i, S_j);
begin
        for k:=0 **to** 2d - 2 **do**
            for all $0 \le r < d$ **in parallel do**
                if (i,r) is active and $r \le k \le r+d$ **then**
                    (i,r) calls $(j, k-r)$
end;

We are now ready to describe the main broadcasting algorithms.

The Non-adaptive Broadcasting Algorithm (NBA)

The algorithm consists of 3 identical stages. The aim of the first stage is to disseminate source information originally stored in node 1 (the source) belonging to group S_1 (the root of T) down the tree T in such a way that at least one fault-free node in each group gets the information with high probability. Nodes which get information in the first stage are called leaders of their respective groups. Every group may have many leaders. In stages 2 and 3 leaders transmit information to other fault-free nodes in their group. In order to do that a leader of group S_i transmits source information to nodes of an adjacent group S_j in stage 2 and subsequently these nodes transmit source information to other nodes of group S_i in stage 3.

```
Algorithm NBA;
begin
for stage := 1 to 3 do
     for step := 0 to d-1 do
     begin
               for each Si on an even level in T, less then h do
               begin
                         MultiCall (Si, S2i, step);
                         MultiCall (Si, S2i+1, step);
               end;
               for each Si on an odd level in T, less than h do
               begin
                         MultiCall (Si, S2i, step);
                         MultiCall (Si, S2i+1, step);
               end
     end
end;
```

Since the algorithm NBA contains 3 stages, each consisting of d steps taking 4 time units each, it works in time $O(\log n)$. Clearly every node is involved in at most one call in a unit of time.

The Adaptive Broadcasting Algorithm (ABA)

The idea of the adaptive algorithm is fairly similar to the above. However, in the present case we need to avoid making too many calls on average, since NBA used $\Theta(n \log n)$ calls and our present goal is the expected number of $O(n)$ calls. As before, the algorithm consists of 3 stages. This time they are not identical but their role in the broadcasting process is similar as in the non-adaptive case.

A node u in group S_i is called a left sender (right sender) if $1 \leq i \leq \lfloor s/2 \rfloor$, and u has source information but it has not yet transmitted it to any node from S_{2i} (S_{2i+1}). Notice that at the beginning only node 1 is a left and right sender .

Stage 1
begin

    for step := 0 **to** d-1 **do**
    begin

        for each S_i on an even level in T **do**
        begin

            if (i,r) is a left sender in S_i **then**
                (i,r) calls (2i, (r+step) (mod d);
            if (i,r) is a right sender in S_i **then**
                (i,r) calls (2i+1, (r+step) (mod d))
        end;
        for each S_i on an odd level in T **do**
        begin

            if (i,r) is a left sender in S_i **then**
                (i,r) calls (2i, (r+step) (mod d));
            if (i,r) is a right sender in S_i **then**
                (i,r) calls (2i+1, (r+step) (mod d))

        end

    end
end;

Stage 1 of ABA takes 4d time units. Every group S_i can have at most one leader upon completion of this stage. When a node u becomes the leader of S_i (that is, it has obtained the source information from the leader of $S_{\lfloor i/2 \rfloor}$) and $2i \leq s$ $(2i+1 \leq s)$ then u becomes a left sender (right sender). If S_i is the left child (right child) of $S_{\lfloor i/2 \rfloor}$ then the leader of $S_{\lfloor i/2 \rfloor}$ stops being a left sender (right sender) at this point. A left sender (right sender) from S_i calls different nodes from S_{2i} (S_{2i+1}).

In the second stage the leader of every group S_i, $1 < i \leq s$, calls all nodes from $S_{\lfloor i/2 \rfloor}$. The leader of S_1 calls all nodes from S_2.

Stage 2
begin

    for each leader (i,r) such that
        S_i is on an even level in T and it is
        the left child of its parent **do**
            One To All ((i,r), $S_{\lfloor i/2 \rfloor}$);
    for each leader (i,r) such that
        S_i is on an even level in T and it is
        the right child of its parent **do**
            One To All ((i,r), $S_{\lfloor i/2 \rfloor}$);
    for each leader (i,r) such that
        S_i is on an odd level in T and it is
        the left child of its parent **do**
            One To All ((i,r), $S_{\lfloor i/2 \rfloor}$);
    for each leader (i,r) such that
        S_i is on an odd level in T and it is

the right child of its parent **do**
One To All $((i,r), S_{\lfloor i/2 \rfloor})$;
One to All $((1,0), S_2)$

end;

Stage 2 uses 5d time units.

In stage 3 those nodes from group S_i, $1 < i \leq s$, which do not have yet source information, call nodes from $S_{\lfloor i/2 \rfloor}$ in order to obtain this information transmitted there in stage 2 by the leader of S_i.

Stage 3
begin

Pipeline Calls (S_1, S_2);
for each S_i such that
$1 < i \leq s$, S_i is on an even level in T and it is the left child of its parent **do**
Pipeline Calls $(S_i, S_{\lfloor i/2 \rfloor})$;
for each S_i such that
$1 < i \leq s$, S_i is on an even level in T and it is the right child of its parent **do**
Pipeline Calls $(S_i, S_{\lfloor i/2 \rfloor})$;
for each S_i such that
$1 < i \leq s$, S_i is on an odd level in T and it is the left child of its parent **do**
Pipeline Calls $(S_i, S_{\lfloor i/2 \rfloor})$;
for each S_i such that
$1 < i \leq s$, S_i is on an odd level in T and it is the right child of its parent **do**
Pipeline Calls $(S_i, S_{\lfloor i/2 \rfloor})$

end;

Stage 3 uses less than 10d time units. Hence the entire algorithm ABA works in (worst case) logarithmic time. Clearly every node is involved in at most one call in a unit of time.

5 Reliability and Complexity of Broadcasting Algorithms

In this section we estimate the probability that the broadcasting algorithms described in section 4 are successful. We also discuss their complexity. The main result is:

Theorem 1.

Let $p < 1$ be the link failure probability and $q < 1$ be the node failure probability. For every $\varepsilon > 0$ there exist integers c, $n_0 > 0$ such that for every $n \geq n_0$, each of the algorithms NBA and ABA working for the network $G_n(c)$ is ε-safe.
Proof.
We give the proof only for algorithm NBA. The adaptive case is similar. Let

$$c = \max \left(\left\lceil \frac{-4(1+\varepsilon)}{\log(1-(1-p)^2(1-q))} \right\rceil, \left\lceil \frac{8(1+2\varepsilon)}{(1-p)(1-q)\log e} \right\rceil \right)$$

and $n_0 = \max (\min\{n: \frac{n}{c\lfloor \log n \rfloor} \geq 2\}, \min \{n: n^\varepsilon \geq 2\})$.

Let E denote the event that NBA is successful. Consider the following events:

E_1 -   upon completion of the first stage at least one node in every group S_i obtains source information (every group has a leader).

E_2 -   between every pair of nodes in the same group there exists a path of length 2 whose both links and the intermediate node are fault-free.

First notice that $E_1 \cap E_2 \subset E$. Indeed, in view of E_1, every group has a leader. In the second stage a leader u of group S_i transmits source information to all its fault-free neighbors, provided that the joining links are fault-free. In the third stage these neighbors transmit information to every fault-free node v in S_i, provided that respective joining links are fault-free. By E_2 there is a path of length 2 between u and v without faulty components and consequently v obtains source information upon completion of the third phase.

We will show that $Pr(\overline{E_1}) \leq n^{-2\varepsilon}$ and $Pr(\overline{E_2}) \leq n^{-2\varepsilon}$, thus $Pr(\overline{E}) \leq n^{-\varepsilon}$, for sufficiently large n. The event $\overline{E_1}$ implies that during the first stage of NBA source information has not been passed along some branch of the tree T (that is, some group of this branch does not have a leader). Fix such a branch $B = (S_{i_0}, S_{i_1}, ..., S_{i_h})$, where $S_{i_0} = S_1$, and estimate the probability of the event P that information has not been passed along this branch. Every fault-free node from group S_{i_j} calls different nodes from group $S_{i_{j+1}}$ in d consecutive steps. These attempts are independent and they have success probability $r_1 = (1-p)(1-q)$ (both the destination node and the joining link must be fault-free). Upon a successful call from a leader of S_{i_j}, some node of $S_{i_{j+1}}$ becomes a leader and information can be passed further along branch B. Hence $Pr(P)$ does not exceed the probability of at most h successes in d Bernoulli trials with success probability r_1.

Since $h < \lfloor \log n \rfloor$, $Pr(P)$ does not exceed the probability of at most $\lfloor \log n \rfloor$ successes in a series of d trials with success probability r_1. Consider such a series of trials and let X be the number of successes. By Chernoff bound (cf. [1,9]) we get $Pr(X \leq (1-\lambda)r_1 d) \leq e^{-\lambda^2 r_1 d/2}$, for any $0 < \lambda < 1$.

Since $c > 1/r_1$, we have

$$0 < \lambda = \frac{r_1 c - 1}{r_1 c} < 1$$

and $(1-\lambda)r_1 d = \frac{1}{r_1 c} \cdot r_1 c \lfloor \log n \rfloor = \lfloor \log n \rfloor$,

hence

$Pr(P) \leq Pr(X \leq \lfloor \log n \rfloor) \leq e^{-\lambda^2 r_1 c \lfloor \log n \rfloor/2}$.

Since there are less than n branches in the tree T, we get (for $n \geq 2$)

$$\Pr(\overline{E_1}) \le n \, \Pr(P) \le n \, e^{-\lambda^2 r_1 c \, \log n / 4} =$$

$$= n \cdot n^{-\lambda^2 r_1 c \, \log e / 4} = n^{1 - (r_1 c - 2 + \frac{1}{r_1 c}) \log e / 4}$$

$$\le n^{1 - r_1 \, c \, \log e / 8},$$

because $c \ge \lceil \frac{8(1+2\varepsilon)}{r_1 \log e} \rceil \ge \lceil 4/r_1 \rceil$ implies

$$r_1 c - 2 + \frac{1}{r_1 c} \ge \frac{r_1 c}{2} \quad .$$

Since $r_1 \, c \, \log e / 8 \ge 1 + 2\varepsilon$, we finally get

$$\Pr(\overline{E_1}) \le n^{-2\varepsilon} \quad .$$

Next, we estimate $\Pr(\overline{E_2})$. Every group contains at least d nodes. In view of $n/d \ge 2$ there are at least two groups. Between every pair of nodes in a group there exist at least d disjoint paths of length 2. The probability that in a single path u-w-v the intermediate node or one of the links are faulty is $r_2 = 1 - (1-p)^2 (1-q)$. Consider two fault-free nodes u, v in a group and fix d disjoint paths of length 2 between them. Since the events that these paths contain a faulty component are independent, the probability that each of them does, is r_2^d. Since there are less than n^2 pairs of nodes in the network, we get

$$\Pr(\overline{E_2}) \le n^2 r_2^d \le n^2 r_2^{c \, \log n / 2}, \text{ for } n \ge 2$$

and since $c \log r_2 \le -4(1+\varepsilon)$, we obtain

$$\Pr(\overline{E_2}) \le n^2 n^{c \, \log r_2 / 2} \le n^2 \cdot n^{-(2+2\varepsilon)} = n^{-2\varepsilon} \quad .$$

Since $n^\varepsilon \ge 2$ for $n \ge n_0$, this implies

$$\Pr(\overline{E}) \le \Pr(\overline{E_1}) + \Pr(\overline{E_2}) \le 2n^{-2\varepsilon} \le n^{-\varepsilon},$$

which concludes the proof.

∎

In section 4 we noticed that both algorithms NBA and ABA work in (worst case) logarithmic time. This order clearly cannot be decreased even without faults. It follows that the number of calls used by NBA is $O(n \log n)$ and the worst case number of calls used by ABA is also $O(n \log n)$. It is easy to see that in both cases order $n \log n$ is exact. Moreover it can be proved (cf. [5]) that every non-adaptive broadcasting algorithm using $o(n \log n)$ calls is successful with probability converging to 0, so NBA is asymptotically optimal among ε-safe algorithms, with respect to the number of calls. On the other hand, in case of ABA, the average number of calls is linear. Indeed, during the first two stages only leaders of groups make calls, and since there are $O(n/\log n)$ leaders, the number of calls in these phases is $O(n)$. In stage 3 every node u which does not yet have source information calls nodes from a group adjacent to its own group S_i until it finds a node previously informed by the leader of S_i. If this leader appeared in stage 1, the expected number of calls made by u in stage 3 is $\lceil 1/((1-p)^2(1-q)) \rceil$, otherwise u makes d calls. Hence the expected number of calls made by u in stage 3 is at most

$$\lceil 1/((1-p)^2(1-q)) \rceil + c \lfloor \log n \rfloor \cdot n^{-\varepsilon} \in O(1)$$

and consequently the total expected number of calls is linear.

Theorem 1 and the above remarks imply the following Corollary.

Corollary.
Let p < 1 be the link failure probability and q < 1 the node failure probability. There exists a family of n-node networks with maximum degree O(log n) which support a non-adaptive ε-safe broadcasting algorithm working in logarithmic time, as well as an adaptive ε-safe broadcasting algorithm working in (worst case) logarithmic time and using an average linear number of calls.

References.

1. D. Angluin, L.G. Valiant, Fast probabilistic algorithms for Hamiltonian circuits and matchings, J. Comput. System Sci. 18 (1979), 155-193.
2. K.A. Berman, M. Hawrylycz, Telephone problems with failures, SIAM J. Alg. Disc. Meth. 7 (1986), 13-17.
3. D. Bienstock, Broadcasting with random faults, Disc. Appl. Math. 20 (1988), 1-7.
4. B.S. Chlebus, K. Diks, A. Pelc, Optimal broadcasting in faulty hypercubes, Proc. 21st Int. Symp. on Fault-Tolerant Computing, Montreal, Canada (1991), 266-273.
5. K. Diks, A. Pelc, Reliable gossip schemes with random link failures, Proc. 28th Ann. Allerton Conf. on Comm. Control and Comp. (1990), 978-987.
6. K. Diks, A. Pelc, Almost safe gossiping in bounded degree networks, SIAM J. Disc. Math. 5 (1992), 338-344.
7. L. Gargano, Tighter time bounds on fault tolerant broadcasting and gossiping, Networks, to appear.
8. R.W. Haddad, S. Roy, A.A. Schaffer, On gossiping with faulty telephone lines, SIAM J. Alg. Disc. Meth. 8 (1987), 439-445.
9. T. Hagerup, C. Rub, A guided tour of Chernoff bounds, Inf. Proc. Letters 33 (1989/90), 305-308.
10. S.M. Hedetniemi, S.T. Hedetniemi, A.L. Liestman, A survey of gossiping and broadcasting in communication networks, Networks 18 (1988), 319-349.
11. D.W. Krumme, K.N. Venkataraman, G. Cybenko, Gossiping in minimal time, SIAM J. on Computing 21 (1992), 111-139.
12. E.R. Scheinerman, J.C. Wierman, Optimal and near-optimal broadcast in random graphs, Disc. Appl. Math. 25 (1989), 289-297.

Strongly Adaptive Token Distribution

Friedhelm Meyer auf der Heide*, Brigitte Oesterdiekhoff*, Rolf Wanka*

Fachbereich Mathematik-Informatik
and Heinz-Nixdorf-Institut
Universität-GH Paderborn
D-W-4790 Paderborn, Germany
email: {fmadh,brigitte,wanka}@uni-paderborn.de

Abstract. The token distribution (TD) problem, an abstract static variant of load balancing, is defined as follows: let M be a (parallel processor) network with processors $\mathcal{P}$. Initially each processor $P \in \mathcal{P}$ has a certain amount $\ell(P)$ of tokens. The goal of a TD algorithm, run on M, is to evenly distribute the tokens among the processors. In this paper, we introduce TD algorithms that are strongly adaptive, i. e. whose running times come close to the best possible runtime, the off-line complexity of the TD problem, for each individual initial token distribution ℓ. Until now, only weakly adaptive algorithms have been considered, where the running time is measured in terms of the maximum initial load $\max\{\ell(P) \mid P \in \mathcal{P}\}$.

We design an almost optimal, strongly adaptive algorithm on mesh-connected networks of arbitrary dimension. Furthermore, we exactly characterize the off-line complexity of arbitrary initial token distributions on arbitrary networks. As an intermediate result, we design almost optimal weakly adaptive algorithms for TD on mesh-connected networks of arbitrary dimension.

1 Introduction

We consider the token distribution (TD) problem, a static variant of the load balancing problem. The underlying parallel computation model is the (parallel processor) network. Such a network consists of a set of p processors $\mathcal{P} = \{P_1, \ldots, P_p\}$ pairs of which are connected via bidirectional links forming a communication graph $M = (\mathcal{P}, E)$ with E denoting the set of links. We identify the network with its communication graph. The network is assumed to be synchronized; in a computation step, each processor can do a constant amount of internal computation and can send a message to a neighbouring processor. We demand that each processor can receive at most one message per step.

Load balancing is one of the basic tasks to be performed in order to achieve efficient execution of parallel programs on a network: if a processor is overloaded with work during a computation, it tries to reduce its load by shifting part of it to less busy processors. The aim is to keep the load balanced among the processors.

Token distribution is an abstraction of a static variant of load balancing. Initially each processor P has a number $\ell(P)$ of tokens, i.e. the **initial load** is

---

* partially supported by DFG-Forschergruppe "Effiziente Nutzung massiv paralleler Systeme, Teilprojekt 4", by the ESPRIT Basic Research Action No. 7141 (ALCOM II), and by the Volkswagenstiftung.

given by a function $\ell : \mathcal{P} \to \mathbb{N}$. We refer to $N = \sum_{P \in \mathcal{P}} \ell(P)$ as the **total load**, to $k = \max\{\ell(P) \mid P \in \mathcal{P}\}$ as the **maximum load**, and to $\frac{N}{p}$ as the **average load**.

The goal of token distribution is to distribute the tokens given by the initial load so that the final load of each processor is close to the average load. More specifically, a TD algorithm is δ-**exact** if finally no processor holds more than $\left\lceil \frac{N}{p} \right\rceil + \delta$ tokens.

In order to be able to measure the performance of a TD algorithm, we first introduce a quantity which lower bounds the running time of any TD algorithm on M with initial load ℓ. For this purpose, we consider off-line algorithms for token distribution. In this case, with M, ℓ given, we allow an arbitrarily complex preprocessing that can be executed without being added to the complexity and that produces a protocol for each processor telling, for each time t, whether and, if yes, where to send a token. We assume that a processor can send and receive one token per time step. The **off-line complexity** of the TD problem (M, ℓ) is $T^{\text{off}}(M; \ell, \delta)$, the running time of a fastest δ-exact off-line TD algorithm.

On-line algorithms are designed for a fixed network M, but do not allow any free preprocessing given an initial load ℓ. Thus, a TD algorithm executes **distribution steps**, where each processor can send and receive one token, and **computation steps**, where computation and communication can take place (e. g. to gather information about the current load distribution). In such a step, no tokens are moved. The **on-line complexity** of (M, ℓ) is $T(M; \ell, \delta)$, the running time of a fastest δ-exact on-line TD algorithm on M started with initial load ℓ.

All papers mentioned below consider the following **adaptive complexity measure** for TD on M:

$$T_{\text{ad}}(M; N, k, \delta) = \max\{T(M; \ell, \delta) \mid \ell \text{ has maximum load} \leq k \text{ and total load} \leq N\}.$$

In this paper, we consider an even stronger version of adaptivity: we want to design on-line TD algorithms which come close to the performance of off-line algorithms of each individual initial load function, i.e. we design **strongly adaptive** TD algorithms, showing that their performance comes close to the lower bound, i.e. the off-line complexity.

Known results about token distribution. The token distribution problem was introduced by Peleg and Upfal [7]. For arbitrary networks M with p processors and total load $N = p$, the same authors show in [8] that for all $k \geq 2$,

$$T_{\text{ad}}(M; p, k, 0) = O(p) \quad \text{and} \quad T_{\text{ad}}(M; p, k, 0) = \Omega(k + \text{diam}(M)),$$

with $\text{diam}(M)$ denoting the diameter of M.

Matching upper bounds are shown in [8], by Herley [2], and by Broder et al. [1] for certain classes $\mathcal{K}$ of expander-related, bounded-degree, low-diameter networks, i.e.

$$T_{\text{ad}}(M; p, k, O(1)) = O(k + \log p)$$

for all $M \in \mathcal{K}$.

Plaxton [9] investigates the TD problem on the d-dimensional hypercube Q_d. He shows that for $k \geq 2 \cdot \frac{N}{p}$,

$$T_{\text{ad}}(Q_d; N, k, 0) = \Omega \left(k \cdot \sqrt{\frac{d}{d + \log(\frac{k}{N})}} \right) \quad \text{and} \quad T_{\text{ad}}(Q_d; \text{poly}(p), k, 0) = O(k\sqrt{d} + d^2).$$

Werchner [11] deals with TD on Q_d, where the total load is less than the number of processors. By carefully analyzing expansion properties of Q_d, he shows that

$$T_{ad}(Q_d; p^{1/2-\Omega(1)}, k, 0) = O(k + d^2 \cdot \log d) \ .$$

JáJá and Ryu [3] show for the cube-connected cycles network, shuffle-exchange network, and the butterfly network that for $k \geq 2 \cdot \frac{N}{p}$,

$$T_{ad}(M; N, k, 0) = \Omega\left(\frac{N \cdot \log p}{p} + k \cdot \sqrt{\frac{\log p}{\log(\frac{p \cdot k}{N})}}\right) \ ,$$

combining results from [9] and low bisection width considerations.

Makedon and Symvonis [5] address the many-to-one routing problem on the 2-dimensional $\sqrt{p}$-sided mesh $M(\sqrt{p}, 2)$. Their results can easily be modified to show that

$$T_{ad}(M(\sqrt{p}, 2); N, k, 0) = \Theta(\sqrt{k \cdot p}) \ .$$

New results about token distribution. In this paper, we characterize almost exactly the off-line complexity of TD. Furthermore, we consider TD on the d-dimensional n-sided mesh-connected network $M(n, d)$ and characterize its adaptive TD complexity up to a factor of $O(d^2)$ (resp. $O(d \cdot 2^d)$ if the maximum load is small). Finally, we present a strongly adaptive algorithm for TD on $M(n, d)$ which only differs by a factor of $O(d^3 \cdot \log k)$ (resp. $O(d \cdot 2^d + d^3 \cdot \log k)$) from the off-line bound. More specifically, we prove

Theorem 1 (Off-line Complexity of TD). *Let M be a network, ℓ be an initial load. For $X \subseteq \mathcal{P}$, let $I(X) := \sum_{P \in X} \ell(P)$ the load of X. $\mathcal{MM}(X)$ denotes the cardinality of a maximum matching between X and $\mathcal{P} \setminus X$.*

(a) $T^{\mathrm{off}}(M; \ell, 0) \geq \max\limits_{\emptyset \subsetneq X \subsetneq \mathcal{P}} \left\lceil \frac{I(X) - \lceil \frac{N}{p} \rceil \cdot |X|}{\mathcal{MM}(X)} \right\rceil$;

(b) $T^{\mathrm{off}}(M; \ell, 1) \leq \max\limits_{\emptyset \subsetneq X \subsetneq \mathcal{P}} \left\lceil \frac{I(X) - \lceil \frac{N}{p} \rceil \cdot |X|}{\mathcal{MM}(X)} \right\rceil$.

Thus, we obtain an exact characterization of the off-line complexity of TD with the restriction that the upper bound only holds if we allow that the final maximum load is by one token larger than desired. The following observation shows that this restriction is unavoidable.

Observation 1. There is an infinite family of TD problems (M, ℓ) with the following properties. $N = p$, $k = \max\limits_{\emptyset \subsetneq X \subsetneq \mathcal{P}} \left\lceil \frac{I(X) - \lceil \frac{N}{p} \rceil \cdot |X|}{\mathcal{MM}(X)} \right\rceil = \frac{1}{2} \cdot p + 1 =: T$, and

$$T^{\mathrm{off}}(M; \ell, 0) \geq T + 2 \cdot \sqrt{T - 1} - 4 \gg T \ .$$

Theorem 2 (Weakly Adaptive Complexity of TD on Meshes).

(a) For $k \geq 2 \cdot \frac{N}{n^d}$, $T_{ad}(M(n, d); N, k, 0) = \Omega(\frac{1}{d} \cdot \sqrt[d]{N \cdot k^{d-1}})$.

(b) $T_{ad}(M(n, d); N, k, 0) = \begin{cases} O(2^d \cdot \sqrt[d]{N \cdot k^{d-1}} + 2^d \cdot n) & \text{if } k < 2 \cdot \frac{N}{n^d} \\ O(d \cdot \sqrt[d]{N \cdot k^{d-1}} + d^2 \cdot n) & \text{if } k \geq 2 \cdot \frac{N}{n^d} \end{cases}$.

This theorem extends the result of [5] mentioned above. We use its basic ideas, but have to add further techniques to generalize for arbitrary total load and arbitrary dimension. Note that for constant d, the above bounds match. By using the weakly adaptive algorithms as subroutines, we show the following main result of this paper.

Theorem 3 (Strongly Adaptive Complexity of TD on Meshes).

$$T(M(n, d); \ell, 1) = \begin{cases} O((d \cdot 2^d + d^3 \cdot \log k) \cdot T^{\text{off}}(M(n, d), \ell, 0)) & \text{if } k < 2 \cdot \frac{N}{n^d} \\ O((d^3 \cdot \log k) \cdot T^{\text{off}}(M(n, d), \ell, 0)) & \text{if } k \geq 2 \cdot \frac{N}{n^d} \end{cases}$$

for each load ℓ with maximum load k.

This result shows that an on-line TD algorithm can come close to the optimal (off-line) bound for each individual initial load.

The results of this paper are part of the second author's Diploma Thesis [6].

2 The Off-line Complexity of Token Distribution

2.1 Off-line Lower Bound

The lower bound is based on expansion properties of M like Plaxton's lower bound [9]. It is similar to that mentioned by Peleg and Upfal [8].

Proof of Theorem 1 (a). Consider an arbitrary set X of processors, $\emptyset \subsetneqq X \subsetneqq \mathcal{P}$. Initially, X contains $I(X)$ tokens, finally at most $\lceil \frac{N}{P} \rceil \cdot |X|$. Thus, $I(X) - \lceil \frac{N}{P} \rceil \cdot |X|$ tokens have to leave X. At most $\mathcal{MM}(X)$ tokens can leave X per time step. Thus, any solution to the TD problem requires at least $\max_{\emptyset \subsetneqq X \subsetneqq \mathcal{P}} \left\lceil \frac{I(X) - \lceil \frac{N}{P} \rceil \cdot |X|}{\mathcal{MM}(X)} \right\rceil$ distribution steps. □

In what follows, we show that this bound is tight for arbitrary networks, if we allow preprocessing, and if some processors may eventually hold one token more than the average load. Note that in this case, the diameter of M does not influence the off-line running time.

2.2 An Almost Optimal Off-line Algorithm

Proof of Theorem 1 (b). We transform the TD problem (M, ℓ) with desired final maximum load m into a maximum flow problem on a directed flow graph $G_f(M, \ell, t, m)$ (or G_f for short) we describe in what follows. The parameter t stands for the running time we allow to solve the TD problem. For the terminology of network flow methods, see e. g. [10]. An example for the transformation of the linear array $M(3, 1)$ of length 3 with initial load ℓ, $\ell(P_1) = 4$, $\ell(P_2) = 3$, $\ell(P_3) = 5$, into the flow graph $G_f(M(3, 1), \ell, 2, 4)$ is given in Figure 1.

G_f consists of levels $V_0, \ldots, V_t$. Each level consists of copies of all processors of M. The flow from the source q to a vertex in V_i represents the load of the corresponding processor of M after i distribution steps of a possible TD algorithm. In particular, a path between two levels models a single distribution step.

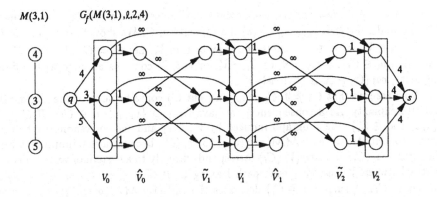

Fig. 1. Transformation of $(M(3,1), \ell)$ into the flow-graph $G_f(M(3,1), \ell, 2, 4)$

To establish the initial distribution of tokens, we have edges from the source q to the vertices in level V_0, where the capacities are chosen with respect to the initial load ℓ. As the vertices in V_t represent the token distribution at the end of a possible TD algorithm, these vertices are connected to the sink s via edges with capacity m.

To model the constraints of a single distribution step, we introduce two helping levels $\widehat{V_i}$ and $\widetilde{V_{i+1}}$ between each V_i and V_{i+1}, $i \in \{0, \ldots, t-1\}$. The reason is that we have to take care of the following mode of communication among processors as described in the introduction:

1. Each processor can send at most one token per time step (ensured by the edges with capacity 1 between V_i and $\widehat{V_i}$).
2. Each processor can receive at most one token per time step (ensured by the edges with capacity 1 between $\widetilde{V_{i+1}}$ and V_{i+1}).
3. Each processor holds the tokens not transmitted (ensured by the edges with infinite capacity between V_i and V_{i+1}).

For the details of realizing 1. through 3., see Figure 1. Finally, the helping levels are connected with respect to the links of M by edges with capacity ∞.

Following the description of G_f given above, it should be clear that, if there is a maximum flow with value N in G_f, the N tokens can be redistributed among M in t steps, so that eventually the maximum number of tokens in any processor is at most m. Of course, we want $m = \left\lceil \frac{N}{p} \right\rceil$ (average load) and t as small as possible. The following lemma implies Theorem 1 (b).

Lemma 4. *The value of a maximum flow in* $G_f = G_f\left(M, \ell, T, \left\lceil \frac{N}{p} \right\rceil + 1\right)$ *is* N, *if*

$$T = \max_{\emptyset \subsetneq X \subsetneq P} \left\lceil \frac{I(X) - \left\lceil \frac{N}{p} \right\rceil \cdot |X|}{\mathcal{MM}(X)} \right\rceil.$$

Proof of Lemma 4. We use the well-known Maxflow-Mincut Theorem. Let V_f be the vertices and c the capacities in G_f. Let $C \subset V_f$ be an arbitrary (q, s)-cut in G_f, i.e.

$q \in C$ and $s \notin C$. Let $out(C)$ denote the set of edges from nodes in C to nodes in $V_f \setminus C$, and $cap(C) = \sum_{e \in out(C)} c(e)$ the capacity of C. We show that $cap(C) \geq N$.

For $u \in V$, let $u_i \in V_i$ denote the copy of u in V_i. Let $C_i = C \cap V_i$, $orig(C_i) = \{u \in V \mid u_i \in C_i\}$. If $C_0 = \emptyset$, or $C_t = V_t$, or $out(C)$ contains an edge with infinite capacity, $cap(C) \geq N$ is obviously true.

Now assume that $C_0 \neq \emptyset$, $C_t \neq V_t$, and $out(C)$ contains none of the edges with infinite capacity. As a consequence, we have $C_{i+1} \supseteq \{u_{i+1} \mid u_i \in C_i\}$. If $C_{i+1} = \{u_{i+1} \mid u_i \in C_i\}$, the subgraph induced by V_i, V_{i+1} and the corresponding helping levels contributes at least $\mathcal{MM}(orig(C_i))$ to $cap(C)$, because a maximum matching between $orig(C_i)$ and $orig(V_i \setminus C_i)$ corresponds directly to a system of vertex-disjoint paths between V_i and V_{i+1} each path leaving C. If $C_{i+1} \supsetneq \{u_{i+1} \mid u_i \in C_i\}$, each vertex in $C_{i+1} \setminus \{u_{i+1} \mid u_i \in C_i\}$ decreases the capacity $\mathcal{MM}(orig(C_i))$ by at most 1 because the paths to them do not leave C. Thus, the contribution of the edges between V_i and V_{i+1} to $cap(C)$ is at least $\mathcal{MM}(orig(C_i)) - (|C_{i+1}| - |C_i|)$ for all $i < T$. Using this fact and that $T \geq \frac{I(orig(C_i)) - |C_i|}{\mathcal{MM}(orig(C_i))}$ for all i, we have the following estimation for $cap(C)$:

$$cap(C) \geq \sum_{u \in orig(V_0 \setminus C_0)} \ell(u) + \sum_{i=0}^{T-1} \left(\mathcal{MM}(orig(C_i)) - (|C_{i+1}| - |C_i|) \right) + \left(\left\lceil \frac{N}{p} \right\rceil + 1 \right) \cdot |C_T| \geq N$$

Thus, $C = \{q\}$ is a minimum cut with $cap(C) = N$. $\qquad\qquad\square$

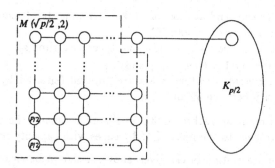

Fig. 2. 0-exact TD requires more than T steps

Proof of Observation 1. Consider the network M shown in Figure 2 and the given initial load. $K_{p/2}$ denotes the complete network consisting of $\frac{1}{2}p$ processors. For this TD problem, we have $T = \max_{\emptyset \subsetneq X \subsetneq P} \left\lceil \frac{I(X) - \lceil \frac{N}{p} \rceil \cdot |X|}{\mathcal{MM}(X)} \right\rceil = \frac{1}{2} \cdot p + 1$. But obviously, at least $\frac{1}{2} \cdot p + 1 + 2 \cdot \sqrt{\frac{1}{2}p} - 4$ distribution steps are necessary. $\qquad\square$

3 The Adaptive Complexity of Token Distribution on Meshes

3.1 Lower Bound

Proof of Theorem 2 (a). We construct a poor input for $M(n,d)$ as follows: Concentrate all tokens in a corner region of $M(n,d)$ that is isomorphic to $M((\frac{N}{k})^{1/d}, d)$. (The situations for $d=2$ and $d=3$ are shown in Figure 3). This corner region has

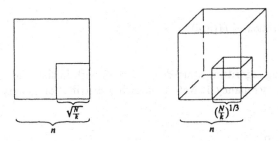

Fig. 3. All tokens are located at a corner of the mesh

$d \cdot \left(\frac{N}{k}\right)^{\frac{d-1}{d}}$ outgoing links. Arguing as in the proof of Theorem 1 (a), any solution to the problem described above requires at least

$$\frac{N - \frac{N}{n^d} \cdot \frac{N}{k}}{d \cdot \left(\frac{N}{k}\right)^{\frac{d-1}{d}}} = \left(1 - \frac{N}{n^d \cdot k}\right) \cdot \frac{1}{d} \cdot \sqrt[d]{N \cdot k^{d-1}} \geq \frac{1}{2} \cdot \frac{1}{d} \cdot \sqrt[d]{N \cdot k^{d-1}} = \Omega\left(\frac{1}{d} \cdot \sqrt[d]{N \cdot k^{d-1}}\right)$$

distribution steps. $\qquad\qquad\qquad\qquad\qquad\qquad\qquad\qquad\qquad\qquad\qquad\qquad\qquad\qquad\square$

Note that the condition $k \geq 2 \cdot \frac{N}{n^d}$ is true for each TD problem on $M(n,d)$ with total load $N = n^d$.

3.2 Adaptive Algorithm

In the rest of this paper, we investigate arbitrary TD problems on $M(n,d)$ with initial load ℓ, maximum load k, and total load N. Furthermore, we denote the maximum load difference of the processors by **discrepancy**.

Proof of Theorem 2 (b). We first present a TD algorithm requiring $O(2^d \cdot (\sqrt[d]{N \cdot k^{d-1}} + n))$ steps. Note that this is optimal when d is constant. For the case that $k \geq 2 \cdot \frac{N}{n^d}$, we present a faster algorithm.

Let $M_1, M_2, \ldots, M_n$ be a partition of $M(n,d)$ into n copies of $M(n, d-1)$, and $A_1, \ldots, A_{n^{d-1}}$ a partition into n^d linear arrays of length n where each vertex of an array belongs to a different M_r. The decomposition of $M(n,d)$ into $M_1, M_2, \ldots, M_n$ and one A_s is shown in Figure 4.

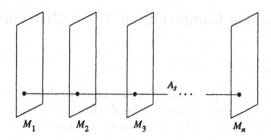

Fig. 4. Decomposition of $M(n, d)$

The following algorithm, started on $M(n, d)$ with initial load ℓ, generates a distribution with discrepancy 1. Note that such a distribution is 0-exact.

Algorithm TD

if $d = 1$ **then**
1. Distribute the tokens with discrepancy 1.

if $d > 1$ **then**
2. In each M_r, colour $\min\{a_r, \sqrt[d]{N^{d-1} \cdot k}\}$ of the a_r tokens in M_r black, and all remaining tokens white.
3. Recursively distribute the black tokens in each M_r with discrepancy 1.
4. Let k_r be such that each processor in M_r contains k_r or $k_r + 1$ black tokens. Select k_r of the black tokens in each processor of M_r.
5. Distribute the selected black tokens in each A_s with discrepancy 1.

Comment: Note that the current distribution of the black tokens has overall discrepancy 2.
6. Distribute the white tokens in each A_s with discrepancy 1.
7. Let h_s be such that each processor in A_s contains h_s or $h_s + 1$ white tokens. Select h_s of the white tokens in each processor of A_s.
8. Recursively distribute the selected white tokens in each M_r with discrepancy 1.

Comment: Note that the current distribution of the white tokens has overall discrepancy 2. Thus, the current distribution of all tokens has discrepancy 4.
9. Distribute the tokens in $M(n, d)$, so that the discrepancy decreases to 1.

Lemma 5. *The algorithm solves the TD problem on $M(n, d)$ in $O(2^d \cdot (\sqrt[d]{N \cdot k^{d-1}} + n))$ steps with discrepancy 1.*

Proof. $d = 1$: Obviously, Step 1 can be executed in time $O(N + n)$.

$d > 1$: The method of the algorithm is to split up the tokens into two sets and to balance one set at first in each M_r and then across each A_s and the other set at first across each A_s and then in each M_r.

To execute Step 2, the tokens in each M_r are counted at first. Then each processor knows, how many of its at most k tokens it has to colour black. In order to count the tokens, a prefix computation and a broadcast have to be done on a d-dimensional

n-sided mesh. Both of these computations can be realized in $O(d \cdot n)$ steps by running d phases in each phase communicating on linear arrays of n processors. Thus, Step 2 requires $O(d \cdot n + k) = O(d \cdot n + \sqrt[d]{N \cdot k^{d-1}})$ steps.

In Step 3, at most $\sqrt[d]{N^{d-1} \cdot k}$ black tokens in each M_r will be balanced with discrepancy 1. By inductive assumption, balancing of $\sqrt[d]{N^{d-1} \cdot k}$ black tokens in Step 3 needs $O(2^{d-1} \cdot (\sqrt[d]{N \cdot k^{d-1}} + n))$ steps.

In order to do Step 4, the value k_r has to be known by each processor of M_r. Obviously, this can be done in $O(d \cdot n)$ steps by a prefix computation and a broadcast.

Since the numbers of selected black tokens are the same in each A_s, there are at most $\frac{N}{n^d} \cdot n \leq \sqrt[d]{N \cdot k^{d-1}}$ selected black tokens in every A_s. Thus, balancing in Step 5 requires $O(\sqrt[d]{N \cdot k^{d-1}} + n)$ time steps.

Since in each M_r up to $\sqrt[d]{N^{d-1} \cdot k}$ tokens are coloured black, and since there are exactly N tokens in the mesh, there are less than $\frac{N}{\sqrt[d]{N^{d-1} \cdot k}} = \left(\frac{N}{k}\right)^{\frac{1}{d}}$ submeshes M_r containing white tokens. Thus, the total number of white tokens in each A_s is at most $\left(\frac{N}{k}\right)^{\frac{1}{d}} \cdot k = \sqrt[d]{N \cdot k^{d-1}}$. Thus, Step 6 requires $O(\sqrt[d]{N \cdot k^{d-1}} + n)$ steps.

Step 7 can be done in the same way as Step 4. After Step 7, there are at most $\frac{N}{n} \leq \sqrt[d]{N^{d-1} \cdot k}$ selected tokens in each M_r. Thus, Step 8 requires $O(2^{d-1} \cdot (\sqrt[d]{N \cdot k^{d-1}} + n))$ steps.

In Subsection 3.4.3 of [4], a monotone routing algorithm on d-dimensional hypercubes requiring $O(d)$ steps is described. It can easily be generalized for meshes, needing $O(d \cdot n)$ steps on $M(n, d)$. In Step 9, we redistribute the tokens in at most three phases, each phase reducing discrepancy by at least 1, performing monotone routing. Thus, Step 9 requires $O(d \cdot n)$ steps.

Altogether, the TD algorithm requires $O(2^d \cdot (\sqrt[d]{N \cdot k^{d-1}} + n))$ steps. $\square$

Now, we present an adaptive TD algorithm achieving a better performance for large maximum load, i.e. $k \geq 2 \cdot \frac{N}{n^d}$. It requires $O(d \cdot \sqrt[d]{N \cdot k^{d-1}} + d^2 \cdot n)$ steps. Note that the condition $k \geq 2 \cdot \frac{N}{n^d}$ is always true for TD problems with total load $N = n^d$.

Faster TD algorithm

   if $d = 1$ then
   1. Distribute the tokens with discrepancy 1.
   if $d > 1$ then
   2. In each M_r, colour $\min\{a_r, \frac{\sqrt[d]{2}-1}{\sqrt[d]{2}} \sqrt[d]{N^{d-1} \cdot k}\}$ of the tokens black, and the remaining tokens white.
   3. Distribute the white tokens in each A_s with discrepancy 1.
   4. Let k_s be such that each processor in A_s contains k_s or $k_s + 1$ white tokens. Select k_s of the white tokens in each processor of A_s.
   5. Recursively distribute the the black tokens together with the selected white tokens in each M_r with discrepancy 1.
   6. Let h_r be such that each processor in M_r contains exactly h_r, $h_r + 1$ or $h_r + 2$ tokens. Select h_r of the tokens in each processor of M_r.
   7. Distribute the tokens in each A_s with discrepancy 1.
   Comment: Note, the current distribution has discrepancy at most 3.
   8. Distribute the tokens in $M(n, d)$, so that the discrepancy is reduced to 1.

By methods similar to those used in the proof of Lemma 5, one can prove the correctness and the time complexity of the above algorithm.

4 The Strongly Adaptive Complexity of Token Distribution on Meshes

Proof of Theorem 3. Let $f(d)$ be a function, so that the (adaptive) complexity of the TD problem on $M(n,d)$ is $O(f(d) \cdot (\sqrt[d]{N \cdot k^{d-1}} + n))$. In Subsection 3.2, we presented algorithms with $f(d) = 2^d$ and $f(d) = d^2$, if $k \geq 2 \cdot \frac{N}{n^d}$, respectively. Let $T := T^{\text{off}}(M(n,d), \ell, 0)$ be the off-line complexity of the TD problem on $M(n,d)$. Now we present a strongly adaptive algorithm solving the problem 1-exactly in $O((d \cdot f(d) + d^3 \cdot \log k) \cdot T)$ steps. For that purpose, we partition $M(n,d)$ into submeshes $S(2dT, d)$ that are isomorphic to $M(2dT, d)$. For example, we have illustrated such partitionings for $d = 2$ and $d = 3$, resp., in Figure 5.

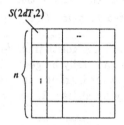
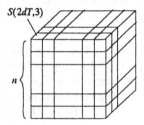

Fig. 5. Partitioning into submeshes

The following lemma shows that, if we solve the TD problem locally in each $S(2dT, d)$, the whole $M(n,d)$ is balanced 1-exactly.

Lemma 6. *Let S be an arbitrary submesh isomorphic to $M(m,d)$ in $M(n,d)$. Let L be the load of an arbitrary processor in S after balancing S. Then $\lfloor \lfloor \frac{N}{n^d} \rfloor - \frac{2dT}{m} \rfloor \leq L \leq \lceil \lceil \frac{N}{n^d} \rceil + \frac{2dT}{m} \rceil$.*

Proof. Let P be the total number of tokens initially located in an arbitrary submesh S of $M(n,d)$. Because of the definition of T, an optimal off-line algorithm balances each S in T off-line steps. At most $2d \cdot m^{d-1}$ tokens can leave S per time step, and at most $\lceil \frac{N}{n^d} \rceil \cdot m^d$ tokens may be in S after T time steps. Thus, $P - 2dT \cdot m^{d-1} \leq \lceil \frac{N}{n^d} \rceil \cdot m^d$. Analogously, at most $2dT \cdot m^{d-1}$ tokens can enter S per time step, and at least $\lfloor \frac{N}{n^d} \rfloor \cdot m^d$ tokens must be in S after T time steps. Thus, $P + 2dT \cdot m^{d-1} \geq \lfloor \frac{N}{n^d} \rfloor \cdot m^d$. After balancing each S, either $L = \lfloor \frac{P}{m^d} \rfloor$ or $L = \lceil \frac{P}{m^d} \rceil$. The estimation for L is concluded directly. $\square$

The following algorithm solves the TD on $M(n,d)$ 1-exactly by solving the problem locally in each $S(2dT, d)$.

Algorithm Local-TD (T)

1. For each $S(2dT, d)$: Determine the local maximum load k_s and broadcast this value to all processors.
2. Consider a decomposition of each $S(2dT, d)$ into submeshes $S(2 \cdot \frac{2dT}{k_s}, d)$. Balance the tokens in each $S(2 \cdot \frac{2dT}{k_s}, d)$ with discrepancy 1 by using one of the weakly adaptive algorithms described in Subsection 3.2.
3. for $\ell := 1$ to $\log k_s - 1$ do

    Combine $2d$ neighbouring balanced $S(2^\ell \cdot \frac{2dT}{k_s}, d)$ to one $S(2^{\ell+1} \cdot \frac{2dT}{k_s}, d)$ and reduce the discrepancy between all $S(2^\ell \cdot \frac{2dT}{k_s}, d)$ of each $S(2^{\ell+1} \cdot \frac{2dT}{k_s}, d)$ in the following way:

    (a) for $p := 0$ to $d - 1$ do

    Determine the discrepancy between the two $S(2^\ell \cdot \frac{2dT}{k_s}, d)$ neighboured in dimension p, and reduce the discrepancy between these two submeshes to at most 2.

    Comment: After (a) is executed, the discrepancy in each $S(2^{\ell+1} \cdot \frac{2dT}{k_s}, d)$ is at most $d + 1$.

    (b) for $p := d$ downto 1 do

    Distribute the tokens in each $S(2^{\ell+1} \cdot \frac{2dT}{k_s}, d)$, so that the discrepancy is decreased to at most p.

Lemma 7. Local-TD (T) *solves the TD problem on* $M(n, d)$ *1-exactly in* $O((d \cdot f(d) + d^3 \cdot \log k) \cdot T)$ *steps.*

Proof. To execute Phase 1, a prefix computation and a broadcast have to be performed on a d-dimensional $2dT$-sided mesh. Both of these computations can be realized in $O(d^2 \cdot T)$ steps by running d phases in each phase operating on linear arrays of length $2dT$. Since in each $S(2 \cdot \frac{2dT}{k_s}, d)$ the maximum load is at most k_s, and since the total number of tokens is at most $k_s \cdot (2 \cdot \frac{2dT}{k_s})^d$, the (adaptive) algorithm in Phase 2 requires $O(d \cdot f(d) \cdot T)$ steps. Because of Lemma 6, we know: when pass ℓ of the loop in Phase 3 is executed, the load of an arbitrary processor in each $S(2^{\ell+1} \cdot \frac{2dT}{k_s}, d)$ is at least $\lfloor \lfloor \frac{N}{n^d} \rfloor - \frac{k}{2^{\ell+1}} \rfloor$ and at most $\lceil \lceil \frac{N}{n^d} \rceil + \frac{k}{2^{\ell+1}} \rceil$. Hence, the discrepancy at the beginning of pass ℓ is $O(\frac{k}{2^\ell})$. Determining the discrepancy in Phase (a) can be done in $O(d^2 \cdot T)$ steps in the same way as in Phase 1. Balancing in Phase (a) can be done by moving one token of each processor in $S(2^\ell \cdot \frac{2dT}{k_s}, d)$ to the corresponding processor in the neighboured $S(2^\ell \cdot \frac{2dT}{k_s}, d)$. Since the discrepancy is at most $O(\frac{k}{2^\ell})$, balancing in Phase (a) needs $O(d^2 \cdot T)$ steps. Thus, Phase (a) requires $O(d^3 \cdot T)$ steps. The distribution of tokens in Phase (b) in order to decrease the discrepancy can be implemented in the same way as in the algorithms in Subsection 3.2. Hence, Phase (b) needs $O(d^3 \cdot T)$ steps. Thus, Phase 3 requires $O(d^3 \cdot \log k \cdot T)$ steps. □

In the above algorithm, we have assumed that the value of T is known by each processor in advance. In order to avoid this, we extend our network model by a global bus capable of storing one bit. Each processor is able to write on and to read from this bus in one time step. If the processors write different values, then the bus receives the logical "AND" of these values. Although the modified model does not rigorously fit into the fixed-connection network model, it is simple to realize in practice. The following algorithm solves the TD problem on $M(n,d)$ 1-exactly in $O((d \cdot f(d) + d^3 \cdot \log k) \cdot T)$ steps without knowing the value of T in advance by using the modified network model.

Algorithm TD

> $t := 1$.
> **Do**
> - $t := 2 \cdot t$.
> - Local-TD (t).
> - Each processor P writes the following bit on the bus
>
> $$\text{bus} := \begin{cases} 1 & \text{If the load } L_P \text{ of } P \text{ accomplishes: } \lfloor \frac{N}{n^d} \rfloor - 1 \leq L_P \leq \lceil \frac{N}{n^d} \rceil + 1 \\ 0 & \text{otherwise} \end{cases}$$
>
> **until** bus $= 1$.

Note that each processor has to know the total number N of tokens.

Lemma 8. *Algorithm* TD *solves the token distribution problem on* $M(n,d)$ *1-exactly in* $O((d \cdot f(d) + d^3 \cdot \log k) \cdot T)$ *steps.*

Proof. In TD, the algorithm Local-TD is started for $t = 2$, $t = 2^2$, ..., $t = 2^{\lceil \log T \rceil}$. Thus, TD requires $\sum_{i=1}^{\lceil \log T \rceil} O((d \cdot f(d) + d^3 \cdot \log k) \cdot 2^i) = O((d \cdot f(d) + d^3 \cdot \log k) \cdot T)$ time steps. $\qquad\square$

References

1. A. Z. Broder, A. M. Frieze, E. Shamir, and E. Upfal. Near-perfect token distribution. In *Proceedings of the 19th ICALP*, pages 308–317, 1992.
2. K. T. Herley. A note on the token distribution problem. *Inf. Process. Lett.*, 38:329–334, 1991.
3. J. JáJá and K. W. Ryu. Load balancing and routing on the hypercube and related networks. *Journal of Parallel and Distributed Computing*, 14:431–435, 1992.
4. F. T. Leighton. *Introduction to Parallel Algorithms and Architectures: Arrays, Trees, Hypercubes.* Morgan Kaufmann Publishers, 1992.
5. F. Makedon and A. Symvonis. Optimal algorithms for the many-to-one routing problem on 2-dimensional meshes. *Microprocessors and Microsystems*, 1993, to appear.
6. B. Oesterdiekhoff. Entwurf und Analyse adaptiver Lastbalancierungsverfahren. Diplomarbeit, Universität-GH Paderborn, Dez. 1992 (In German).
7. D. Peleg and E. Upfal. The generalized packet routing problem. *Theoretical Comput. Sci.*, 53:281–293, 1987.
8. D. Peleg and E. Upfal. The token distribution problem. *SIAM J. Comput.*, 18:229–243, 1989.
9. C. G. Plaxton. Load balancing, selection and sorting on the hypercube. In *Proceedings of the ACM-SPAA*, pages 64–73, 1989.
10. R. E. Tarjan. *Data Structures and Network Algorithms.* Society for Industrial and Applied Mathematics, Philadelphia, PA, 1983.
11. R. Werchner. Balancieren und Selection auf Expandern und auf dem Hyperwürfel. Diplomarbeit, J. W. Goethe-Universität, Frankfurt, Jan. 1991 (In German).

Fast Parallel Computation of Characteristic Polynomials by Leverrier's Power Sum Method Adapted to Fields of Finite Characteristic

Arnold Schönhage

Institut für Informatik II
der Universität Bonn
Römerstraße 164
D-5300 Bonn 1
Germany
Email: bach@informatik.uni-bonn.de

Abstract. Symmetric polynomials over F_p in n indeterminates $x_1, \ldots, x_n$ are expressible as rational functions of the first n power sums $s_j = x_1^j + \cdots + x_n^j$ with exponents j not divisible by p. There exist fairly simple *regular* specializations of these power sums by elements from F_p so that all denominators of such rational expressions remain nonzero. This leads to a new class of fast parallel algorithms for the determinant or the characteristic polynomial of $n \times n$ matrices over any field of characteristic p with arithmetic circuit depth $\mathcal{O}(\log n)^2$.

1 Introduction

For any $n \times n$ matrix A over some field F there is a suitable extension of F with eigenvalues $\alpha_1, \ldots, \alpha_n$ of A so that the coefficients of its characteristic polynomial

$$\det(tI - A) = \prod_{i=1}^{n}(t - \alpha_i) = t^n - \sigma_1 t^{n-1} + \sigma_2 t^{n-2} \ldots \pm \sigma_n$$

can be regarded as the elementary symmetric functions σ_k of these α_i. Leverrier's classical method [7] first to compute the n power sums

$$s_j = \sum_{i=1}^{n} \alpha_i^j = tr(A^j) \qquad \text{for } 1 \leq j \leq n$$

as the traces of the powers of A and then to obtain the σ's by means of the Newton identities has found renewed interest in Csanky's paper [4] and by others ([9], e.g.) for the construction of fast parallel algorithms for matrix inversion, for computing determinants etc., thus leading to bounds of order $\mathcal{O}(\log n)^2$ for arithmetic circuit depth. For fields of finite characteristic p, however, this method fails as soon as $n \geq p$, since resolving Newton's identities implies division by $n!$. Meanwhile this gap could be closed (with the same $\mathcal{O}(\log n)^2$ bound) by means of some other methods [2], [1], [3]. Nevertheless, the power sum approach appears to be so natural that, in order to deepen our insight and for methodological reasons, it remains desirable somehow to adapt it also to the finite characteristic case. – The aim of this paper is to show how that can be done.

The main idea is to compute a few additional power sums with exponents beyond n and then to obtain the σ's as *rational,,* expressions from the power sums. Switching to indeterminates x_i over $F_p = \mathbb{Z}/p\mathbb{Z}$, we can mention simple examples like $\sigma_2 = x_1 x_2 = (s_1^3 - s_3)/s_1$ for $p = 2, n = 2$, or $\sigma_2 = (s_1^2 s_3 - s_5)/(s_1^3 \pm s_3)$ for $p = 2, n = 3$, but the general case is more complicated, relying on an adequate substitute for the Newton identities. The corresponding foundations are developed in section 2.

Application to a given matrix A induces a homomorphism mapping the x_i upon the eigenvalues α_i. Hereby the denominators of those rational functions may become zero. This difficulty is circumvented by treating the *regularized* matrix $B = C + yA$ over the ring $F[[y]]$ of formal power series in an extra indeterminate y, where C is suitably chosen as a constant $n \times n$ matrix over F_p such that those denominators do not vanish for C (i.e., for $y = 0$), and then all computations may be carried out in the truncated form mod y^{n+1}. In section 3 we shall explicitly construct such matrices C; they are companion matrices of very simple 0-1 polynomials, for which the values of those denominators become ± 1.

Section 4 finally provides a parallel version of these new algorithmic ideas, again within the bound $\mathcal{O}(\log n)^2$ on arithmetic circuit depth. Regarding *size* (or number of processors) we get the bound $\mathcal{O} \cdot n^{\beta+2}$ for any β greater than the exponent of matrix multiplication over F_p. Certain improvements are possible, but in the search for much better size bounds this new method does not look very promising.

2 Fundamental systems of power sums over F_p

With regard to indeterminates $x_1, \ldots, x_n$ over a field F and the field $F(x_1, \ldots, x_n)/\mathrm{sym}$ of symmetric quolynomials, any set of power sums in these x's, $S(J) = \{s_j | j \in J\}$ for some $J \subset \mathbb{N}$, is called a *fundamental system* iff $F(x_1, \ldots, x_n)/\mathrm{sym} = F(S(J))$ and $\#J = n$. These conditions imply the algebraic independence of such systems $S(J)$, so the rational representations of the symmetric quolynomials by a fundamental system are essentially unique. In discussing suitable choices of J it is apparently sufficient to consider the prime fields F_p and $\mathbb{Q}$. For the characteristic zero case there is Kakeya's elegant criterion [5], [6] that $S(J)$ is a fundamental system iff $\mathbb{N} \setminus J$ is closed under addition. Things are different over F_p; then J cannot contain any multiple of p, since otherwise the uniqueness of representation would be violated by some identity $s_{ip} = s_i^p$. This shows, in particular, that $J = \{1, \ldots, n\}$ cannot be suitable for $n \geq p$. We need the following converse.

Proposition 1. *For any $J \subset \mathbb{N} \setminus p\mathbb{N}$ of size n, the system $S(J)$ of power sums in $x_1, \ldots, x_n$ is algebraically independent over F_p.*

Proof. We show that the determinant of the Jacobian matrix is nonzero. Its entries are $\partial_i s_j = j \cdot x_i^{j-1}$; division by the nonzero factors $j \in J$ leads to a Vandermonde type determinant $\det(x_i^{j-1} | i \leq n, j \in J) \neq 0$. $\square$

Here we are interested in the most natural choice $J = J(p, n)$ defined as the set of the *first* n elements of $\mathbb{N} \setminus p\mathbb{N}$ up to the maximal index

$$\ell = \max(J(p, n)) = m \cdot p + r \quad \text{with} \quad 1 \leq r \leq p - 1. \tag{1}$$

Counting the missing multiples $p, 2p, \ldots, mp,$ we find that $\ell = n + m,$

$$n = \ell - m = m(p - 1) + r, \qquad m = \lfloor (n - 1)/(p - 1) \rfloor, \qquad \ell < 2n. \tag{2}$$

For characteristic zero, these $J = J(p, n)$ are special cases satisfying Kakeya's criterion; the corresponding fundamental systems were studied by Vahlen [10] in 1900 already. But neither Vahlen's work nor studies by Nakamura [8] for Kakeya's general case are explicit enough to admit an immediate translation of the representations over $\mathbb{Q}$ to the F_p case. So we have to work by ourselves; the remainder of this section will be devoted to a direct constructive proof of the following basic result.

Theorem 2. *The $S(J)$ for $J = J(p, n)$ are fundamental systems over F_p; equivalently, the σ_k in $x_1, \ldots, x_n$ are expressible as rational functions of the corresponding power sums $s_j \in S(J)$.*

Instead of the σ's with their alternating signs we prefer to consider the coefficients $a_j = (-1)^j \sigma_j$ of the "master polynomial"

$$f(t) = \prod_{i=1}^{n}(1 - x_i t) = 1 + a_1 t + a_2 t^2 + \cdots + a_n t^n. \tag{3}$$

Logarithmic differentiation followed by multiplication with $t \cdot f(t)$ yields the decisive identity

$$t \cdot f'(t) = -(s_1 t + s_2 t + s_3 t^3 + \cdots) \cdot f(t) \tag{4}$$

from which all further conclusions are drawn. The power sums s_j in the first factor are given for all $j \leq \ell$, either directly as elements of the system $S(J)$, or by the identities $s_{ip} = s_i^p$ (possibly applied recursively). Comparing coefficients at this stage would lead to $\ell = n + m$ linear equations for the n unknown coefficients a_i, but then (for $m > 0$) it is hard to see how this redundant system should be solved or how to prove its solvability. Therefore we pursue a different course relying on the partition of the unknown a's according to the residue classes mod p. By means of the corresponding auxiliary polynomials

$$h_k(z) = a_k + a_{k+p} z + a_{k+2p} z^2 + \cdots \quad \text{for} \quad 0 \leq k \leq p - 1 \tag{5}$$

we have the handy representations

$$f(t) = \sum_{k=0}^{p-1} t^k \cdot h_k(t^p), \qquad t \cdot f'(t) = \sum_{k=1}^{p-1} k \cdot t^k \cdot h_k(t^p).$$

The crucial next step is now to divide (4) by $t \cdot h_0(t^p)$ and to rewrite everything in terms of the quolynomials

$$q_k(z) = \frac{h_k(z)}{h_0(z)} = \frac{a_k + a_{k+p}z + a_{k+2p}z^2 + \cdots}{1 + a_p z + a_{2p}z^2 + \cdots} = \sum_{i=0}^{\infty} q_{k,i} z^i \qquad (6)$$

for $1 \le k \le p - 1$, or with the coefficients $q_{k,i}$ of their formal power series expansions. In this way, (4) is translated into

$$q_1(t^p) + 2t \cdot q_2(t^p) + \cdots + (p-1)t^{p-2} \cdot q_{p-1}(t^p) =$$
$$-\left(\sum_{i=1}^{\infty} s_i t^{i-1} \right)\left(1 + t \cdot q_1(t^p) + t^2 \cdot q_2(t^p) + \cdots + t^{p-1} \cdot q_{p-1}(t^p) \right). \qquad (7)$$

The special structure of this new equation implies that, by comparing the coefficients of t^{j-1} for all $j \in J$, an initial portion of exactly n of the $q_{k,i}$ can be determined *recursively* from the given s_j; more precisely, these n coefficients $q_{k,i}$ are obtained as *polynomials* of the $s_j \in S(J)$ in antilexicographic order

$$q_{1,0}, \quad q_{2,0}, \ldots, q_{p-1,0}, \quad q_{1,1}, \ldots, q_{p-1,1}, \ldots \quad \text{up to} \quad q_{r,m}. \qquad (8)$$

The counting is compatible with (2), namely $m + 1$ coefficients (up to $q_{k,m}$) for each $k \le r$, but only m coefficients (up to $q_{k,m-1}$) for $k > r$.

Example 1. For $p = 5, n = 46$, we have $m = 11, r = 2$; so the number of coefficients known in (6) is 12 for q_1 and q_2 and 11 for q_3 and q_4.

No information is lost by this transition from the given power sums to the q's in (8). Division of (7) by the second factor of the second line shows that the s_j for $j \le \ell$ may conversely be expressed as polynomials of these q's. Combined with proposition 1, this proves that also the polynomials $q_{k,i}$ in (8) are algebraically independent.

There remains the task to solve the general *Padé approximation problem* described by (6): to find $p - 1$ numerator polynomials h_k and a proper denominator h_0 in agreement with the $p - 1$ right-hand power series, with a finite number of coefficients prescribed up to certain approximation orders for each k. For $p = 2$ this reduces to a standard problem of Padé approximation just with a single quotient, (sequentially) solvable by the extended Euclidean algorithm. But what can we say about degenerate cases, and what about the general problem for arbitrary p ?

It is convenient to rewrite (6) in the form

$$h_0(z)\left(\sum_{i \ge 0} q_{k,i} z^i \right) \equiv h_k(z) \bmod z^{m+1} \text{ for } 1 \le k \le r,$$
$$\bmod z^m \quad \text{for } r < k \le p - 1. \qquad (9)$$

In order to describe the possible formats of such problems, we have to use (2), the pattern in (8) plus some index arithmetic related to

$$n = \mu p + \rho \quad \text{with} \quad \mu = \lfloor n/p \rfloor, \quad 0 \leq \rho \leq p - 1. \tag{10}$$

The degrees of the polynomials h_k are μ for $k \leq \rho$, and $\mu - 1$ for $k > \rho$, corresponding to a total of $\mu p + \rho + 1 = n + 1$ coefficients, but $h_0(0) = 1$ is known already. Comparing the coefficients of z^j in the k-th equation of (9) for all admissible pairs (k, j) (they shall be taken in ascending lexicographic order) leads to a system of n linear equations for the n unknown coefficients $a_1, \ldots, a_n$. The μ coefficients $a_p, a_{2p}, \ldots, a_{\mu p}$ of h_0 appear only on the left-hand side of these equations, and the other a's form the right-hand sides of $n - \mu$ equations. So there are exactly μ linear equations only involving the coefficients of h_0 (and the known q's from (8)) with zeros on their right-hand sides. By treating the absolute term $h_0(0) = 1$ separately we can thus introduce a corresponding $\mu \times \mu$ matrix Q and a certain μ-vector q' by means of which this linear subsystem can be written in the form

$$q' + Qa' = 0 \quad \text{for} \quad a' = (a_p, a_{2p}, \ldots, a_{\mu p})^T. \tag{11}$$

It remains to show that $det(Q)$ does not vanish, because after having solved this subsystem, we can easily obtain the other h_k for $k > 0$ from (9) by polynomial multiplications. Furthermore, this shows that all denominators of the rational representations of the σ_k predicted by Theorem 2 will be divisors of this "resultant" $det(Q)$.

The μ equations of this subsystem correspond to the zero coefficients implicit in the right-hand sides of (9), where the degree of precision (m or $m - 1$) will usually exceed the degrees μ or $\mu - 1$ of the h_k. The precise number of equations resulting for each $k \geq 1$ is therefore

$$\mu_k = \begin{cases} m - \mu & \text{for } k \leq r \wedge k \leq \rho \quad \text{or} \quad k > r \wedge k > \rho, \\ m - \mu + 1 & \text{for } \rho < k \leq r, \\ m - \mu - 1 & \text{for } r < k \leq \rho. \end{cases} \tag{12}$$

All this is, of course, to be discussed for $n \geq p$ only (otherwise the Newton identities are sufficient), and then we have always $m \geq \mu \geq 1$. If $m = \mu$ (this happens for certain values $n \leq p^2 - p$), then necessarily $r = \rho + \mu$, and the third line of (12) does not apply, so always $\mu_k \geq 0$.

Continuing example 1, we find $\mu = 9$, $\rho = 1$, $\mu_1 = \mu_3 = \mu_4 = 2$, $\mu_2 = 3$. Another example, where the third case of (12) occurs, is obtained by choosing $p = 5$, $n = 37$ with $m = 9$, $\mu = 7$, $r = 1$, $\rho = 2$.

Now we are ready to take a closer look at the pattern by which the q's from (8) are placed in the matrix Q. The admissible pairs (k, j) were taken in lexicographic order, here restricted to the subsystem. Therefore the main diagonal of Q contains μ_1 copies of $q_{1,\tau(1)}$, μ_2 times $q_{2,\tau(2)}$, etc., where these "diagonal indices" $\tau(k)$ are given by

$$\tau(k) = \deg(h_1) - (\mu_1 + \cdots + \mu_{k-1}) = \sum_{i=k}^{p-1} \mu_i - \delta_{\rho,0}. \tag{13}$$

This definition will prove useful also for the void cases with $\mu_k = 0$. The correction by one comes from $\deg(h_1) = \mu - 1$ in case of $\rho = 0$.

The product of these diagonal elements differs from all the other monomials in the determinant of Q (expanded as a polynomial of the q's). Therefore, by the algebraic independence of the q's, also $det(Q)$ regarded as a polynomial of $x_1, \ldots, x_n$ (or of the power sums s_j for $j \in J$) does not vanish. This completes the proof of Theorem 2. □

3 Special matrices for the regular case

Replacing the x's by the eigenvalues of some concrete matrix A (equivalently, replacing the general power sums by the traces of the powers A^j, thereby staying in the ground field F) may lead to the singular case $det(Q) = 0$. This happens certainly, if there is another matrix having the same power sums but with a different characteristic polynomial. For $n \geq p$, the unit matrix $A = I$ is always such an example, since changing p of its diagonal elements (= eigenvalues) from one to zero does not alter the values of the power sums $tr(A^j)$. Nevertheless we have the following surprisingly simple recipe for the construction of special sparse matrices leading to the regular case.

Proposition 3. *Keep to the technical details of format $J = J(p, n)$ as described in section 2, in particular by (13), and choose C as an $n \times n$ companion matrix of the specialized polynomial*

$$\hat{f}(t) = det(I - tC) = t^{1+\tau(1)p} + t^{2+\tau(2)p} + \cdots + t^{p-1+\tau(p-1)p}. \qquad (14)$$

Then by specializing $s_j = tr(C^j)$, the matrix Q in (11) becomes the unit matrix I_μ. If $n \equiv 1 \bmod p$, then $det(C) = (-1)^n$.

Proof. Here the coefficients a_j have prescribed values, namely

$$a_j = 1 \text{ for } j \in \{k + \tau(k)p \mid 1 \leq k \leq p - 1\}, \quad a_j = 0 \text{ for all other } j \leq n.$$

In example 1, for instance, this is $\hat{f}(t) = t^{46} + t^{37} + t^{23} + t^{14}$. This leads to the specialized polynomials $\hat{h}_0 = 1$ and $\hat{h}_k(z) = z^{\tau(k)}$ for $k \geq 1$. So almost all the coefficients $q_{k,i}$ in (6) must be zero, except for $q_{k,\tau(k)} = 1$. Restricted to the indices k with $\mu_k > 0$, these are exactly the diagonal elements of Q, so we have $Q = I_\mu$. For the final assertion observe that $n = \mu p + \rho$ with $\rho = 1$ implies $\tau(1) = \mu$, whence $\deg(\hat{f}) = n$ with leading coefficient one. □

It is worthy to note that proposition 3 offers another direct way to justify the last step in the proof of Theorem 2; since we have found a specialization with $det(Q) = 1$, the general $det(Q) \in F_p[x_1, \ldots, x_n]$ cannot be zero.

4 Fast parallel algorithms

The inputs for our algorithms are arbitrary $n \times n$ matrices $A = (a_{i,j})$ over some field F of characteristic p (for $n \geq p$). Our constructions refer to the model of *arithmetic circuits* over F. Formally the gates of such a circuit may be considered as functions $g : F^{n \times n} \to F$. The *input gates* are the projections $A \mapsto a_{i,j}$ picking the entries of A or constant functions $c \in F$; each other gate g has two predecessors g' and g'' such that $g = g' \circ g''$ with some $\circ \in \{+, -, *\}$. (Zero test and division are not needed.) *Depth* and *size* are defined in the obvious way.

In order to avoid divisions the computations are carried out over the extended domain $F' = F[y]/(y^{n+1})$ thus dealing with vectors of length $n + 1$ over F. Multiplication in F' is possible by a subcircuit of depth $\mathcal{O} \cdot \log n$ and size $\mathcal{O} \cdot n \cdot \log n \cdot \log \log n$, multiplication of $n \times n$ matrices over F' in depth $\mathcal{O} \cdot \log n$ with size $\mathcal{O} \cdot n^{\beta+1}$ for any β greater than the exponent of matrix multiplication over F_p.

For computing the determinant of A we choose a matrix C as described in proposition 3 and apply the theory of section 2 to the F'-matrix $B = C + yA$ for the computation of the highest coefficient a_n in (3). Then $det(A)$ is obtained as the highest coefficient of the polynomial $(-1)^n a_n = det(B) = det(C) + \cdots + det(A) \cdot y^n$. Everything else is very similar to the more general case of computing the characteristic polynomial which shall now be discussed in greater detail.

Let us assume that $n \equiv 1 \bmod p$ is satisfied; otherwise we can extend A by an appropriate number of zero rows and columns without changing the reversed characteristic polynomial $det(I - yA)$. Thus $det(C) = (-1)^n$ by the last statement of proposition 3. Here we apply the theory of section 2 to the F'-matrix $B = C(I - yA)$, which leads to the simple identity $det(I - yA) = (-1)^n det(B) = a_n$.

Algorithm 1. Computes $det(I - yA)$ for $n \times n$ matrix A over field F of characteristic p, where $n = \mu p + 1$.

S0: Choose matrix C according to proposition 3, set $B := C - yCA$
    and perform the further steps in $F' = F[y]/(y^{n+1})$.

S1: $s_j := tr(B^j)$ for $1 \leq j \leq \ell = mp + r$, cf. (1), (2).

S2: Compute the q's in (8) by resolving (7).

S3: Compute the coefficients a_{ip} of h_0 by $a' := -Q^{-1}q'$ from (11).

S4: Compute $det(I - yA) = a_n := \sum_{i+j=\mu} a_{ip} \cdot q_{1,j}$.

Proposition 4. *All steps of algorithm 1 are possible by circuits over F (uniform in p, n) of depth $\mathcal{O}(\log n)^2$ and size $\mathcal{O} \cdot n^{\beta+2}$ for any β greater than the exponent of matrix multiplication over F_p.*

Proof. The most expensive step is S1. By means of $B^{2j} = B^j \cdot B^j$ and $B^{2j+1} = B^j \cdot B^{j+1}$ the powers B^j can be computed in about $\log n$ stages by $\ell - 1 < 2n$ matrix multiplications over F', which amounts to the bounds in 4. Compared to this, the work for S4 is negligible.

For S2 we have to parallelize the recursive computation of the q's in (8). Since the recurrence equations obtained from (7) by comparing coefficients have the form $k \cdot q_{k,i} = -s_{k+ip} - \Sigma s_\nu q_{\kappa,\iota}$ with index pairs (κ, ι) earlier than (k, i) the vector v of the q's (taken in this particular order) satisfies an equation $v - Dv = u$ with a given vector u and an easily computable nilpotent lower triangular matrix D. So one can use the identity $v = (I - D)^{-1}u = (I + D)(I + D^2)(I + D^4)\ldots u$ for computing v by means of $\mathcal{O} \cdot \log n$ matrix multiplications plus little extra work.

Due to the choice of C and B, step S3 can be done in a similar way. The matrix Q in (11) has the form $Q = I - yM$ with some $\mu \times \mu$ matrix M over F', whence $\mathcal{O} \cdot \log n$ matrix multiplications suffice to compute $Q^{-1} = (I + yM)(I + y^2M^2)(I + y^4M^2)\ldots$ $\qquad\square$

The size bound can be improved by exploiting the more economic formula $s_{j+id} = tr(B^j \cdot B^{id})$ for S1. Then only the d powers B^j for $j \le d$ (with entries of degree $\le d$ in y) and the powers of B^d for $i \le l/d$ are needed. By choosing $d \approx n^{2/3}$ one gets the better size bound $\mathcal{O} \cdot n^{\beta+4/3}$, but even this is worse than the exponent $\beta + 1$ in [1].

References

1. S.J. Berkowitz, On computing the determinant in small parallel time using a small number of processors, Inf. Proc. Letters 18 (1984), 147-150.
2. A. Borodin, J. von zur Gathen, and J.E. Hopcroft, Fast parallel matrix and GCD computations, Inf. Control 52 (1982), 241-256.
3. A.L. Chistov, Fast parallel calculation of the rank of matrices over a field of arbitrary characteristic, Proc. FCT '85, Lect. Notes Comp. Sci. 199 (1985), 63-69.
4. L. Csanky, Fast parallel matrix inversion algorithms, SIAM J. Comput. 5 (1976), 618-623.
5. S. Kakeya, On fundamental systems of symmetric functions, Jap. J. Math. 2 (1925), 69-80.
6. S. Kakeya, On fundamental systems of symmetric functions 2, Jap. J. Math. 4 (1927), 77-85.
7. U.J.J. Leverrier, Sur les variations séculaires des éléments elliptiques des sept planètes principales: Mercure, Vénus, la Terre, Mars, Jupiter, Saturne, et Uranus, J. Math. Pures Appl. 5 (1840), 220-254.
8. K. Nakamura, On the representation of symmetric functions by power-sums which form the fundamental system, Jap. J. Math. 4 (1927), 87-92.
9. F.P. Preparata, and D.V. Sarwate, An improved parallel processor bound in fast matrix inversion, Inf. Proc. Letters 7 (1978), 148-150.
10. K.T. Vahlen, über Fundamentalsysteme für symmetrische Funktionen, Acta Mathematica 23 (1900), 91-120.

Fast Parallel Constraint Satisfaction

Lefteris M. Kirousis[1,2]

Abstract

A Constraint Satisfaction Problem (CSP) involves searching for an assignment of values to a given set of variables so that the values assigned satisfy a given set of constraints. The general CSP is NP-complete. To confront the intractability of the general CSP, *relaxation procedures* have been devised: instead of searching for a globally consistent assignment of values to the variables, try to restrict the domain of values of each variable in a way that ensures local consistency only. The relaxation procedures are efficient, but have been proved to be inherently sequential. In this paper, we define a class of CSPs for which a global solution can be found by a fast parallel algorithm. No relaxation preprocessing is needed for the parallel algorithm to work. The result is motivated from the problem of labelling a 2-D line drawing of a 3-D object by the Clowes-Huffman-Malik labelling scheme—an important application of CSP in computer vision. For such a labelling CSP, the constraint graph can be general, but the constraint relations are usually of the type we call implicational. It is shown here that a CSP with this type of constraint relations (and no restrictions on its graph) can be solved by an efficient (i.e., with polynomial time complexity) sequential algorithm. Also, it is shown that it can be solved by a fast parallel algorithm that executes in time $O(\log^3 n)$ with $O((m + n^3)/\log n)$ processors on a Exlusive-Read-Exclusive-Write Parallel Random Access Machine (n is the number of variables and m is the number of constrain relations—the constraint relations may have arity more than two).

1 Introduction

A constraint satisfaction problem (CSP) involves assigning values from a given domain to a given set of variables so that a number of constraints between the values of these variables are satisfied (for a formal definition see next section). An often quoted example is the eight queens problem, where one is asked to place eight queens on a chessboard in a way that none of them "attacks" any other, i.e. no two of them lie on the same horizontal or vertical or diagonal line. This is equivalent to assigning to each column of the chessboard a number 1–8 indicating the row number on the column where a queen is to be placed. The columns are the variables of the CSP, the row numbers 1–8 are the legal values for the variables and finally the constraint that no two queens threaten each other may be viewed as a set of binary relations limiting the values (i.e., row numbers) that may ba assigned to pairs of columns.

The classical approach to solving a CSP is the backtracking method. Unfortunately, since the general CSP is NP-complete (the graph 3-colorability problem can be easily seen to be a CSP), exponential worst case complexity arises when applying backtracking

---

[1]This research was partially supported by the European Community ESPRIT Basic Research Program under contracts 7141 (project ALCOM II) and 6019 (project Insight II).

[2]Department of Computer Engineering and Informatics, University of Patras, Rio, 265 00 Patras, Greece and Computer Technology Institute, P.O. Box 1122, 261 10 Patras, Greece. E-address: kirousis@grpatvx1.bitnet.

(or any other known method) to the CSP. To confront this situation, the relaxation procedures were proposed. The general idea is to opt not for a complete solution of the CSP, but for an algorithm that restricts the domain of permissible values of each variable so that: (i) no constraint-consistent assignment of values to all variables (if any) is lost and (ii) any constraint-consistent assignment of values from the restricted domains to one or to a fixed number of variables can be extended, without any constraint violation, to include an arbitrary additional variable.

Obviously then, one can apply the backtracking method to the new CSP with the restricted domains in order to find a general solution within a shorter (but of course, in worst case, still exponential) time. A relaxation procedure was first described in [Waltz, 1975]. Several efficient sequential relaxation algorithms have been subsequently devised (see e.g., [Mackworth and Freuder, 1985], [Mohr and Henderson, 1986]). Also, conditions under which relaxation procedures can give a complete solution have been studied (e.g., [Montanari and Rossi, 1991], [Dechter, 1992]). Finally, Freuder ([1982] and [1985]) and van Beek [1992] give sufficient conditions under which a relaxation preprocessing leads to efficiently solvable CSPs. However, Kasif [1990] proved that even the weakest relaxation procedure is P-complete, therefore, most likely, algorithms depending on such a procedure are not amenable to parallelism. In other words, no parallel relaxation algorithm using $n^{O(1)}$ processors can achieve exponential speedup (for a presentation of issues related to parallel complexity see e.g., [Cook, 1985] or [Karp and Ramachandran, 1990]). Of course, there are parallel relaxation algorithms with constant speedup (e.g., [Samal and Henderson, 1986], [Cooper and Swain, 1992]) or sublinear parallel algorithms with superpolynomially many processors ([Swain, 1988]).

An important notion related to the CSP is that of the **constraint (hyper)graph**. The constraint graph of a CSP that has only binary constraints is the graph obtained by letting variables of the CSP be represented as vertices and binary relations constraining pairs of variables be represented as edges connecting the corresponding vertices. CSPs with constraints of higher order are represented as hypergraphs, where an edge of the hypergraph comprises all the variables constrained by the corresponding relation. It must be pointed out that the sufficient conditions of Freuder ([1982] and [1985]) under which a CSP with only binary relations is efficiently solvable by a sequential algorithm (under the assumption that a relaxation preprocessing has been previously applied) refer to the maximum degree of any induced subgraph of the constraint graph. However, it is known that computing the maximum subgraph degree of a given graph is again inherently sequential [Anderson and Mayr, 1984].

In this paper, I give a condition under which a CSP can be solved by a fast parallel algorithm (i.e., by an algorithm using $n^{O(1)}$ processors and $\log^{O(1)} n$ time). The condition refers not to the constraint hypergraph, which is assumed to be arbitrary, but to the type of allowed constraint relations. No relaxation preprocessing is necessary for the algorithm to work. Moreover, given a CSP, it can be trivially checked whether it satisfies this condition.

The motivation of the result comes from the problem of labelling a 2-D line drawing of a 3-D scene by the Clowes-Huffman-Malik scheme (see [Clowes, 1971], [Huffman, 1971] and [Malik, 1987]). The line drawing is assumed to be obtained by projecting the edges of a 3-D scene on a plane. The usual approach towards the problem of understanding the 3-D scene from its line drawing is to label the lines of the line drawing by a set of labels that reflect some geometric property of the corresponding edges (e.g., a certain label, usually '+', is given to lines that are projections of convex edges, the label '−' is for concave edges, etc). The fundamental tool in this area is that the requirement that the drawing is a projection of a real object severely restricts the permissible combinations of labellings of the lines incident onto a node belonging to each one of the types of a particular node-classification scheme (this classification scheme is based on the shape formed by the node together with its incident lines). Thus the line labelling problem can be seen as a CSP, where one has to assign values (labels) to the lines of a 2-D image so that the constraints imposed on the labels by the type of the incident nodes are satisfied. It turns out that the labellability problem is NP-complete even for scenes that contain only polyhedra [Kirousis and Papadimitriou, 1988]. However, polynomial time algorithms have been proposed for many interesting restricted types of permissible "worlds"of scenes. (see [Kirousis and Papadimitriou, 1988], [Alevizos, 1991], [Dendris et al., 1991], [Parodi and Torre, 1993]).

The key fact in these algorithms is the fact that a "good" case is attained when for any pair of lines incident onto the same node, any label on one of them either uniquely determines the label of the other (i.e. the label is uniquely propagated) or puts no extra restriction on it (i.e. the label propagation stops). This pheneomenon is quite often in drawings of "non-pathological" scenes and it possibly explains the reason that labelling algorithms work well in practice despite the intractability of the general problem.

The sufficient condition for fast parallel solution of a CSP that is formulated in this paper reflects this notion of unique label propagation. Constraints having this property are called *implicational* (several other types of constraint relations—all different from implicational—are defined in [Van Hentenryck et al., 1992] and [Perlin, 1992] and studied not in the context of finding efficiently solvable CSPs but rather in the context of improvising the relaxation technique). Here, I first show that a CSP with an arbitrary constraint hypergraph and with implicational constraints can be solved by an efficient sequential algorithm. It is interesting to note that this algorithm is not backtrack-free. However, it avoids the combinatorial explosion because the value of a variable can be changed only a bounded number of times. In Section 3, I show how to obtain a fast parallel version of the algorithm, which not only answers the decision CSP, but also produces a legal assignment of values, if there is one. This algorithm on an Exclusive-Read-Exclusive-Write (EREW) Parallel Random Access Machine (PRAM) requires $O(\log^3 n)$ time and $O((m + n^3)/\log n)$ processors, where n is the number of variables of the CSP, while m is the number of its relations (the arity of these relations may be more than two). The algorithm makes use of a fast parallel algorithm that produces a maximal independent set of vertices of a graph ([Luby, 1986], [Goldberg and Spencer, 1989]). Recall that although to find a maximum cardinality independent set is NP-complete, the maximal independent set problem is in NC.

2 Definitions and the Sequential Algorithm

Let $X_1, \ldots, X_n$ be a set of variables and let $D_1, \ldots, D_n$ be domains of values corresponding to the variables. The sets D_i are assumed to be finite and nonempty. Let a be the maximum cardinality of any of the sets $D_1, \ldots, D_n$. Suppose, moreover, that we have a class of m constraint relations. Each constraint relation R is a subset of a Cartesian product of the form $D_{j_1} \times \ldots \times D_{j_k}$, where $j_1, \ldots, j_k$ is a sequence of distinct integers from the set $\{1, \ldots, n\}$ and having length k, $(2 \leq k \leq n)$. The number k is called the **arity** of R. Also, we say that R **constrains** the variables $X_{j_1}, \ldots, X_{j_k}$. Let c be the maximum arity of any constraint relation. The parameters a and c are usually small constants. Because we assume that variables have names, the order of the variables constrained by a relation is not important, i.e., we follow the set-of-mappings formulation of relations (see [Ullman, 1982]). However, when no confusion may arise we use the set-of-lists formulation as well.

The general Constraint Satisfaction Problem is defined to be: given variables, domains and constraint relations as above, find all n-tuples $(d_1, \ldots, d_n) \in D_1 \times \ldots \times D_n$ such that for each relation R that constrains the variables $X_{j_1}, \ldots, X_{j_k}$ the k-tuple $(d_{j_1}, \ldots, d_{j_k}) \in R$. Such an n-tuple is called a **legal assignment** of values. Sometimes, one is interested not to find a legal assignment but only answer the question of whether there is at least one such. This existence question is the decision version of the CSP.

Given a CSP Π as above we define a hypergraph G_Π, where the nodes of G_Π represent the variables X_i, $i = 1, \ldots, n$, of Π and the edges represent sets of variables constrained by relations of Π. The hypergraph G_Π is called the **constraint hypergraph** of Π (if no confusion may arise, G_Π will be simply denoted by G). If all constraint relations of Π are binary, then the hypergraph G_Π is a graph.

Now, given a relation R of arity k, a variable X_i constrained by R and a value a_i form the domain D_i of X_i, we say that a_i is **arc consistent** with respect to R if there exist values for all the other variables that are constrained by R such that the k-tuple formed from a_i and these values satisfies R.

If a_i is arc consistent with respect to R and if X_j is another variable constrained by R we say that R and a_i **uniquely determine** the value of X_j, if there is a *unique* value a_j in the domain of X_j such that the pair (a_i, a_j) can be extended to a k-tuple of values satisfying R.

Finally, we say that R and a_i **bear no implication** on X_j, if for any arc consistent with respect to R value a_j of the domain of X_j, the pair (a_i, a_j) can be extended to a k-tuple of values satisfying R.

Definition 1 *A constraint relation R is called* implicational *if for any two variables X_i and X_j constrained by R and any arc consistent with respect to R value a_i from the domain of X_i, either a_i and R uniquely determine the value of X_j, or bear no implication on it.*

Notice that the property in the above definition that is required to be satisfied by the values a_i is vacuously true for a value a_i that is not arc consistent. This is intended to be so, since we do not want to assume that we have a preprocessing relaxation stage that guarantees arc consistency.

It is now trivial to check that:

Observation 1 *Given an instance of the CSP with at most a values per variable and m constraint relations each with arity at most c, then to check whether this instance is implicational requires $O(\log a)$ time on an EREW machine with $O(a^2 c^2 m)$ processors.*

Notice that given a constraint relation R and a value a_i of X_i arc consistent with R, as above, the partition of the other variables constrained by R into two sets, one with the variables whose values are uniquely determined by a_i and one with the variables onto which a_i bears no implication, may depend on the value a_i, i.e., for a different value a_i', a different partition may arise. That means that an implicational relation as defined above is not in general what in database theory is known as functional dependency relation, since in a functional dependency relations all values of a certain attribute must uniquely determine the values of certain other attributes (see, e.g., [Ullman, 1982] and [Hentenryck et al., 1992]). Notice also, that the "implications" of an implicational relation can be easily expressed in a suitable propositional language with Horn clauses having only two literals. However, the restriction that each variable must be assigned at least one value from its domain cannot be expressed by a clause of only two literals. So, the implicational CSP is not a case of 2SAT.

Now the following proposition is easy to prove but it is very useful in proving the correctness of the algorithms in this paper.

Proposition 1 *Suppose that X_i and X_j are constrained by an implicational relation R and that a value $a_i \in D_i$ together with R uniquely determine the value of X_j to be a_j. Then for any value $a_j' \in D_j$ such that $a_j' \neq a_j$ and such that a_j' is arc consistent with respect to R, there is a value $a_i' \in D_i$ such that $a_i' \neq a_i$ and such that a_j' together with R uniquely determine the value of X_i to be a_i'.*

Proof First notice that since $a_j \neq a_j'$, the pair (a_i, a_j') cannot be extended to a tuple satisfying R. Now, since R is implicational, a_j' together with R must either uniquely determine the value of X_i or bear no implication on it. If the first possibility is not the case, then a_i and a_j' must be compatible with respect to R, a contradiction. Therefore, a_j' together with R uniquely detrmine the value of X_i. It is trivial to check that this uniquely determined value cannot be a_i, QED.

Implicational relations of more than two arguments can have a very rich structure. This is testified by the fact that the problem of labelling a line drawing by the Clowes-Huffman-Malik scheme has only implicational relations for quite rich permissible worlds of 3-D scenes (see [Dendris et al., 1991]).

To the contrary, the bipartite graphs of *binary* implicational relations have less structure and are easily characterizable (here—and until the end of the Proof of Proposition 2—the term 'graph' stands for the graphical representation of a binary relation; it is not related to the notion of constraint graph). To formalize this, let us first define certain types of bipartite graphs. A bipartite graph is called a **bijection** if each vertex of any of its parts is connected with exactly one vertex from the other part. A bipartite graph is called a **one-to-all** bipartite graph if for each of its two parts there exists exactly one vertex that is connected to all vertices of the other part, while all other vertices have degree one. Now the following proposition can be easily proved.

Proposition 2 *If the graph of a binary implicational relation has no isolated vertices then it is either a bijection or a complete bipartite graph or a one-to-all bipartite graph (see Figure 1).*

Proof By the definition of an implicational relation and because it is assumed that no isolated vertices exist, any vertex of degree more than one must be connected to

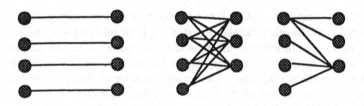

Figure 1: Types of binary implicational relations: the bijection, the complete and the one-to-all.

all vertices of the other part. Now notice that if in one part of the graph there are more than one vertices of degree more than one, then the graph is a complete bipartite graph. Moreover, if there is a vertex of degree more than one and the graph is not complete, then all other vertices on the same part as this vertex are connected with the same vertex of the other part, therefore the graph is one-to-all, QED.

I informally now describe the efficient sequential algorithm that solves a CSP with implicational relations: Choose arbitrarily a variable which has not been assigned a value and mark it "active". Assign to it a value from its domain. Propagate this value as far as it goes assuming, however, that all values assigned during the propagation are *provisional*. If an inconsistency is ever reached, undo all provisional assignments; backtrack to the active variable and try another value for it (if no such value is left, conclude that the CSP does not have a legal assignment). If no inconsistency is reached, then make permanent all provisional assignments and choose a new active variable.

Formally, the algorithm is given below.

- *activate:* if there is a variable to which no value has been assigned **then do** choose such a variable; mark it *active*; let the set of *values-to-be-tried* for this variable be its domain; go to *assign* **od**; **else** stop, a legal assignment has been produced.

- *assign:* if the set *values-to-be-tried* for the *active* variable is empty, stop and conclude that there is no legal assignment; **else do** assign a value to the *active* variable from its set of *values-to-be-tried*; mark this value as *provisional*; delete this value from the set of *values-to-be-tried* of the *active* variable; if this value is not arc consistent with respect to a relation that constrains the *active* variable then go to *assign* **else** go to *propagate* **od**.

- *propagate:* **repeat** choose a variable X_i not marked as *visited* and to which a value marked *provisional* has been assigned; mark the variable X_i as *visited*; for all R that constrain X_i and any X_j whose value is uniquely determined by a_i and R, assign to X_j the unique value determined by a_i (call it a_j); mark a_j as *provisional* **until**

    - Either an inconsistency appears, i.e., either X_j has already been assigned a different from a_j value (this value may be arbitrarily marked) or the value

a_j is not arc consistent with respect to some relation that constrains X_j. In this case, do undo all assignments of values marked *provisional*; undo all markings of variables as *visited*; go to *assign* od.

- Or there is no value marked *provisional* assigned to a variable not marked *visited* /*nothing is left to be propagated*/. In this case, do change all *provisional* markings into *permanent*; undo all markings of variables as *visited*; go to *activate*.

The proof of the correctness of this algorithm rests on the fact that once a value has been permanently assigned to a variable X it will not be contradicted by a different assigment on X made at a later stage. This is so because values are marked permanent if they bear no implication on any contiguous variable. But then, by Proposition 1, it is not possible that a contiguous variable of X will force a different value on X at a later stage. This argument is formalized in the proof of Theorem 2, where the correctness of the parallel version of the above algorithm is shown in detail.

To study the complexity of the algorithm, let n be the number of variables of the input CSP, m the number of its constraints, a the largest cardinal of any of its domains and c the largest arity of any of its constraint relations. Usually, and especially in applications of CSP in computer vision, the numbers a and c are considered to be constants, however, I will give the complexity regarding them as variables. I assume that $m = \Omega(n)$. This is not an essential restriction, it only makes the statement of complexity results more succinct. Moreover, in applications in computer vision where c is constant and small and the line drawing is assumed to be connected, this is always the case (if the line drawing is not connected, the labelling algorithms labels each component separately).

First observe that while the active variable remains the same, the step *assign* will be executed at most a times. This is so, because each call of *assign* deletes one value from the set of *values-to-be-tried* which is initialized to be the domain of the variable. Then observe that between two calls of *assign* the number of steps is at most ac^2m since this is the number of possible propagations (there are m constraint relations that may propagate a value and each can be used at most ac times to propagate values to at most $c - 1$ variables). Therefore, between two calls of *activate*, the number of steps is $O(a^2c^2m)$. Now the procedure *activate* can be called n times so the total complexity is $O(a^2c^2nm)$ and so we have proved:

Theorem 1 *The constraint propagation problem for implicational constraints can be solved by a sequential algorithm whose time complexity is $O(a^2c^2nm)$, where n is the number of variables, m is the number of constraints, a is the maximum cardinality of any of the domains and c is the maximum arity of any of the constraints.*

If a and c are constant then the complexity of the above algorithm is $O(nm)$. One could also design an efficient sequential algorithm by the transitive closure technique, where propagation of a value is represented as computation of the transitive closure of a graph (see next section). However the algorithm above has the following advantages: first not only does it solve the decision problem but also produces a legal assignment of values, if there is one, and second for graphs where $m = O(n)$—as is the case in applications in computer vision where m is the number of nodes of the line drawing and

n is the number of its edges—the complexity of the algorithm is $O(n^2)$, whereas finding the transitive closure entails matrix multiplication and so has complexity $O(M(n)) = n^{2.376}$ (see [Coppersmith and Winograd, 1987]).

3 The Parallel Algorithm

In this section, I will give a fast parallel algorithm for the CSP, which produces a legal assignment, if there is one. The algorithm is inspired from the way that Karp and Wigderson [1985] apply their fast parallel algorithm that finds a maximal independent set in order to solve the problem of 2SAT (however, as we argued in the previous section, implicational CSP is not a case of 2SAT). Also, it should be pointed out that Cook and Luby [1988] have given a simple fast parallel algorithm that finds a satisfying truth assignment for an instance of 2SAT and which does not make use of maximal independent sets. However, their method does not apply to the more general problem of finding a legal assignment for an implicational instance of the CSP.

The algorithm has four stages: The first one is to construct the *implication graph* G. This is a directed graph and has a vertex for each possible value a_i of each variable X_i. **Loops**, i.e., edges whose endpoints coincide, are allowed in the implication graph G. In the sequel, I will use the same symbol to denote values and their corresponding vertices. Also G has a special vertex, called the inconsistency vertex and denoted by □. Obviously, the number of vertices of the graph is $O(an)$. Two vertices a_i and a_j corresponding to values of the variables X_i and X_j are connected by an arc from a_i to a_j if there is a relation R that constrains X_i and X_j and such that a_i and R uniquely determine the value of X_j to be a_j. Moreover, a value that is not arc consistent with respect to a relation that constrains its corresponding variable is connected to the □. The connection is by an arc pointing to the □. Finally, all values are connected to themselves by a loop and □ is connected to all vertices by arcs pointing to them. Notice that the number of arcs of this directed graph is at most $O(ac^2m)$. Notice that G is not a hypergraph, even if there are constraint relations of arity greater than 2.

The second stage is to find the transitive closure G^* of G. Intuitively, G^* has an arc from a_i to a_j, if the value a_i of X_i is propagated as a_j on X_j.

The third step is the construction of the *conflict graph*. This is an (undirected) graph C which has the same set of vertices as G (loops, i.e. single-endpoint edges, are allowed in C). Two vertices a_i and b_j of C are connected by an edge if and only if there are two different vertices c_k and c'_k of C corresponding to values of the same variable X_k such that (a_i, c_k) and (b_j, c'_k) are both arcs of G^* (the vertex □ is considered to correspond to a value of any variable). Notice that thus two different values of the same variable are always connected by an edge in C. Also, if there is an arc in G^* from a vertex a_i to the inconsistency vertex □, then a_i belongs to a loop in C. The number of vertices of this graph is $O(an)$ and the number of its edges is $O(a^2n^2)$. Intuitively, two values are connected by an edge in the conflict graph if they imply different values onto the same variable.

Finally, the fourth step of the algorithm is to find a maximal independent set of vertices in the conflict graph C. It must be pointed out that by the definition of independence, no vertex which is incident on a loop in C can belong to an independent set (however, notice that by construction, all vertices in G^* are incident on loops).

Now, I claim the following:

Theorem 2 *An implicational instance of the CSP has a legal assignment of values if and only if the cardinality of any maximal independent set of its conflict graph is equal to n, the number of variables of the instance of the CSP. In this case, any maximal independent set defines a legal assignment of values.*

Before proving the theorem, I give a lemma:

Lemma *If a is an element of a maximal independent set M of vertices of C and if (a, b) is an edge in G^*, then $b \in M$.*

Proof of Lemma Suppose that b is not in M. Then, by the maximality of M, there must exist an edge $\{b, c\}$ in C with $c \in M$. Therefore, by the definition of C, there must be two different values d and d' of the same variable such that (b, d) and (c, d') are arcs in G^*. Therefore, since G^* is transitive, also (a, d) is an arc of G^*. So, both (a, d) and (c, d') are arcs in G^* and therefore a and c are connected by an edge in C, contradicting the fact that they both belong to M, QED.

I now give the proof of the Theorem.

Proof of Theorem 2 It is obvious that once the cardinality of a maximal independent set of vertices in C is n, this independent set must correspond to exactly one value for each variable (as was explained in the description of the conflict graph, different values of the same variable are always connected by an edge in C). It is also obvious that these values define a legal assignment. For the converse, let $M = \{a_{j_1}, \ldots, a_{j_r}\}$ be a maximal independent set of vertices of C corresponding to values of the variables $X_{j_1}, \ldots X_{j_r}$. Suppose, towards a contradiction, that $r < n$ and that there is a legal assignment to the variables of the CSP (notice, that at this point of the proof is not yet obvious that there necessarily exists a legal assignment that assigns the values $a_{j_1}, \ldots a_{j_r}$ to the variables $X_{j_1}, \ldots, X_{j_r}$). Let X_i be a variable not in $\{X_{j_1}, \ldots X_{j_r}\}$. Let a_i be a value of X_i which does not belong to a loop in C. Such a value exists, because, otherwise no value could be legally assigned to X_i. By definition of maximality, a_i is connected by an edge in C to at least one of the $a_{j_1}, \ldots, a_{j_r}$, say, without loss of generality, to the a_{j_1}. Then by the definition of C, there must exist two different values b and b' of the same variable, say Y, such that (a_i, b) and (a_{j_1}, b') are arcs of G^*. I now claim that there is a value a_i' of X_i such that (a_{j_1}, a_i') is an edge of G^*. This claim leads to a contradiction because then by the Lemma, M would also include a_i'.

To prove the last claim, first observe that since (a_i, b) is an arc in the transitive closure G^*, there must exist a sequence of values $a_i = b_0, b_1, \ldots, b_t = b$ such that (b_i, b_{i+1}), for $i = 0, \ldots, t-1$, is an arc in G. Then b_i uniquely determines, with respect to some constraint, say R_i, the value b_{i+1}. Let also the b_is, $i = 1, \ldots, t-1$, correspond to values of the variables Y_i (see Figure 2).

Now first observe that because (a_{j_1}, b') is an arc of G^*, we have by the Lemma that $b' \in M$. Therefore b' must be arc consistent with respect to all relations that constrain Y (otherwise, b' would be connected by an arc to the inconsistency vertex $\square$, and therefore, as explained in the description of the conflict graph, it could not belong to an independent set). Therefore, by Proposition 1 and because $b' \neq b$, b' and R_{t-1} must uniquely determine a value $b_{t-1}' \neq b_{t-1}$ for Y_{t-1}. Now observe that (a_{j_1}, b_{t-1}') must be

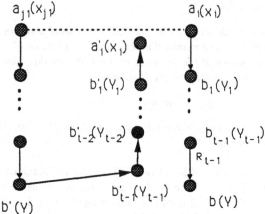

Figure 2: Arcs depict edges of G, dashed lines depict edges of C; next to the vertex names, inside parentheses, are the names of the corresponding variables.

an arc of G^* and therefore $(b'_{t-1} \in M$. Repeating the above argument recursively with b'_{t-1} in place of b' and so on all the way down to b'_1, we conclude that for the variable X_i there must be a value $a'_i \neq a_i$ such that (a_{j_i}, a'_i) is an arc in G^*, a contradiction, QED.

The above theorem shows that to answer the decision question for an instance of the CSP it suffices to find any maximal independent set of the corresponding conflict graph C. If the cardinality of such an independent set is equal to n, the number of variables of the CSP, then the vertices in it define a legal assignment for the given instance of the CSP. Notice that the vertex $\square$ of C is by construction incident on a loop, so it cannot belong to an independent set. Also, the cardinality of an independent set cannot exceed n, because two different values of the same variable are always connected by an edge in C.

Finally, notice that the above theorem also proves the correctness of the sequential algorithm described in the previous section. This is so because the values assigned to the variables by the sequential algorithm constitute a maximal independent set of the conflict graph.

Concerning the complexity of the above algorithm, first notice that constructing the implication graph requires $O(\log a)$ time with $O(a^2 c^2 m)$ processors. Then notice that constructing the transitive closure G^* requires time $O(\log^2(an))$ and $O(M(an))$ processors ($M(n) = n^{2.376}$, see [Coppersmith and Winograd, 1987]). The construction of the conflict graph requires constant time with $O(a^2 n^3)$ processors on a EREW machine. Now, by the fast parallel algorithm in [Goldberg and Spencer, 1989], the construction of a maximal independent set of the conflict graph requires $O(\log^3(an)$ time and $O(a^2 n^2 / \log n)$ processors. Summing these up, we get that our parallel algorithm requires $O(\log^3(an)$ time and $O((a^2 c^2 m + a^3 n^3) / \log(an))$ processors. Therefore, we have proved:

Theorem 3 *There is a fast parallel algorithm that on input an implicational instance of the CSP, it decides whether there is a legal assignment of values to the variables and moreover, if the answer is positive, it produces such an assignment. The algorithm re-*

quires $O(\log^3(an))$ time and $O((a^2c^2m+a^3n^3)/\log(an))$ processors on a EREW PRAM, where n is the number of variables of the CSP, a is the maximum cardinality of any of its domains, c is the maximum arity of any of its relations and m is the number of its relations.

Acknowledgment

I thank Paul Spirakis for many illuminating conversations. I also thank N. Dendris and I. Kalafatis because working with them on the problem of scene labelling provided the motivation for the results in this paper. Finally, I am thankful for all comments on previous drafts of this paper.

References

P. Alevizos, "A linear algorithm for labeling planar projections of polyhedra," Proc. IEEE/RSJ Int. Workshop on Intelligent Robots and Systems (Osaka, Japan, 1991), 595-601.

R. Anderson and E. Mayr, "Parallelism and greedy algorithms", *Advances in Computing Research* 4 (1987), 17-38.

M.B. Clowes, "On seeing things," *Artifical Intelligence*, 2 (1971), 79-116.

S.A. Cook and M. Luby, "A simple parallel algorithm for finding a satisfying truth assignment to a 2-CNF formula", *Information Processing Letters*, 27 (1988), 141-145.

S.A. Cook, "A taxonomy of problems with fast parallel algorithms," *Information and Control*, 64 (1985), 2-22.

D. Coppersmith and S. Winograd, "Matrix multiplication via arithmetic progressions," Proc. 28th Ann. ACM Symp. on Theory of Computing (1987), 1-6.

R. Dechter, "From local to global consistency," *Artificial Intelligence* 55 (1992), 87-107.

N. Dendris, I. Kalafatis and L.M. Kirousis, "Labelling images of the pottery world," Proc. 3rd Intl. Symp. on Algorithms and Computation, ISAAC '92 (Springer-Verlag).

P.R. Cooper and M.J. Swain, "Arc consistency: parallelism and domain dependence," *Artificial Intelligence* 58 (1992), 207-235.

E.C. Freuder, "A sufficient condition for backtrack-free search," *JACM*, 29 (1982), 24-32.

E.C. Freuder, "A sufficient condition for backtrack-bounded search," *JACM*, 32 (1985), 755-761.

M. Goldberg and T. Spencer, "Constructing a maximal independent set in parallel," *SIAM J. Discrete Mathematics*, 2 (1989), 322-328.

P.V. Hentenryck, Y. Deville, and C.-M. Teng, "A generic arc-consistency algorithm and its specializations," *Artificial Intelligence* 57 (1992), 291-321.

D.A. Huffman, "Impossible objects as nonsense sentences," *Machine Intelligence*, 6 (1971), 295-323.

R.M. Karp and V. Ramachandran, "Parallel algorithms for shared-memory machines," in: J. van Leeuwen (ed.), Handbook of Theoretical Computer Science, vol. A (Elsevier, 1990), 869–942.

R.M. Karp and A. Wigderson, "A fast parallel algorithm for the maximal independent set problem," J. Association of Computing Machinery, 32 (1985), 762–773.

S. Kasif, "On the parallel complexity of discrete relaxation in constraint satisfaction networks," Artificial Intelligence, 45 (1990), 275–286.

L.M. Kirousis and C.H. Papadimitriou, "The complexity of recognizing polyhedral scenes," Journal of Computer and System Sciences, 37 (1988), 14–38.

M. Luby, "A simple parallel algorithm for the maximal independent set problem," SIAM J. Computing 15 (1986), 1036–1053.

A.K. Mackworth and E.C. Freuder, "The complexity of some polynomial network consistency algorithms for constraint satisfaction problems," Artificial İntelligence 25 (1985), 65–74.

J. Malik, "Interpreting line drawings of curved objects," International J. of Computer Vision, 1 (1987), 73–103.

R. Mohr and T.C. Henderson, "Arc and path consistency revisited," Artificial Intelligence 28 (1986), 225–233.

U. Montanari and F. Rossi, "Constraint relaxation may be perfect," Artificial Intelligence, 48 (1991), 143–170.

P. Parodi and V. Torre, "On the complexity of labelling line drawings of polyhedral scenes", ICCV 1993, to appear.

M. Perlin, "Arc consistency for factorable relations," Artificial Intelligence 53 (1992), 329–342.

A. Samal and T. Henderson, "Parallel consistent labeling algorithms," Int. J. Parallel Programming, 16 (1987), 341–384.

M.J. Swain, "Comments on Samal and Henderson: 'Parallel consistent labeling algorithms'," Int. J. Parallel Programming, 17 (1988), 523–528.

J.D. Ullman, Principles of Database Systems, 2nd ed. Computer Science Press, 1982.

P. van Beek, "On the minimality and decomposability of constraint networks," Proc. AAAI, 1992

P. Van Hentenryck, Y. Deville, and C.-M. Teng, "A generic arc-consisstency algorithm and its specializations," Artificial Intelligence 57 (1992), 291–321.

D. Waltz, "Understanding line drawings of scenes with shadows," in: P.H. Winston (ed.), The Psychology of Computer Vision, (McGraw-Hill, New York, 1975), 19–91.

The Product of Rational Languages

Imre Simon*

Instituto de Matemática e Estatística
Universidade de São Paulo
05508-900 São Paulo, SP, Brasil
<is@ime.usp.br>

Abstract. The very basic operation of the product of rational languages is the source of some of the most fertilizing problems in the Theory of Finite Automata. Indeed, attempts to solve McNaughton's star-free problem, Eggan's star-height problem and Brzozowski's dot-depth problem, all three related to the product, already led to many deep and ever expanding connections between the Theory of Finite Automata and other parts of Mathematics, such as Combinatorics, Algebra, Topology, Logic and even Universal Algebra. We review some of the most significant results of the area, obtained during the last 35 years, and try to show their contribution to our understanding of the product.

1 Introduction and historical survey

Let us consider rational languages X and Y, subsets of the free monoid A^* and their product

$$XY = \{\, xy \in A^* \mid x \in X \text{ and } y \in Y \,\}.$$

In this lecture we wish to argue that this innocently looking operation is the source of much research and of some still unsolved problems, even though considerable progress has been achieved in the last decades, revealing many links between the Theory of Finite Automata and other fields of Mathematics.

The correct perspective to lead to our problem areas is from Kleene's theorem, so let us recall this cornerstone of the Theory of Finite Automata [17, 9].

Theorem 1 *For any finite alphabet A, $\operatorname{Rec} A^* = \operatorname{Rat} A^*$.*

Here, $\operatorname{Rec} A^*$ is the family of recognizable subsets of A^*, i.e. the ones recognized by (not necessarily deterministic) finite automata, while $\operatorname{Rat} A^*$ is the family of rational subsets of A^*, i.e. the least family of languages over A which contains the singleton sets $\{\, a \,\}$, for $a \in A$, and is closed under union, product and star.

The terms of Kleene's theorem are nondeterministic in nature. Indeed, $\operatorname{Rec} A^*$ was defined in terms of nondeterministic automata, even though we know that any set in $\operatorname{Rec} A^*$ is recognized by a deterministic automaton. The nondeterministic setting for $\operatorname{Rec} A^*$ is, however, the correct one since it is in this form

* This work was done with partial support from FAPESP, CNPq and BID/USP.

that Kleene's theorem generalizes to the case of multiplicities in any semiring in place of the Boolean semiring. The interested reader can find the details in Eilenberg's book [9]; we only note that we will make use of the multiplicity theory in section 4. On the other side of Kleene's equation we find $\operatorname{Rat} A^*$ which is also nondeterministic, in the sense that any given rational language is denoted by an infinity of rational expressions, i.e. there are different ways of obtaining a set using the rational operations. This will be our starting point, since all three problems we will address began with questions about the existence or the optimization of expressions, possibly of restricted forms, to denote a given rational language.

Historically, the first problem of our interest, related to the product, was posed by R. McNaughton in 1960 [25] and solved by M. P. Schützenberger in 1965 [36] in the first real breakthrough in the area. Very interesting historical remarks about the formulation of the star-height problem can be found throughout the monograph of McNaughton and Papert [27], especially on page 99.

Let us recall first that every recognizable set is recognized by some *deterministic* automaton; it immediately follows that the family $\operatorname{Rec} A^*$, hence also $\operatorname{Rat} A^*$, is closed under complementation.[2] McNaughton's question was to characterize the family of star-free languages, i.e. the ones which can be expressed using only the singletons and the operations of union, complement and product. For instance, consider the language[3] $L = (ab + ba)^*$. Even though the star is used in this particular expression for L it can also be expressed without the star, hence it is a star-free language. We leave it to the reader the interesting exercise of verifying that the following expressions define L over the alphabet $A = \{a, b\}$.[4]

$$I = A^* = \overline{\overline{\emptyset}},$$

$$J = (ab)^* = 1 + aI \cap Ib \cap \overline{IaaI} \cap \overline{IbbI},$$

$$L = (ab + ba)^* = \overline{\overline{IabJaI} + \overline{IbJabI}}$$

In section 2 we will return to the star-free question, state Schützenberger's theorem and comment its many consequences.

The next problem to appear was Eggan's star-height problem. The *star-height of a rational expression* is the maximum number of nested stars in it. For instance, the star-height of

$$a^*b + ((ab^*)c)^* + (((a^*b + c)^* + d)^*e$$

is three. We define the *star-height of a set* X as being the least star-height of rational expressions denoting X. The star-height problem consists in determining

---

[2] Note that this statement about $\operatorname{Rat} A^*$ is an algebraic property of an algebraically defined family. However, its proof goes through Kleene's theorem and uses the concept of a *finite* automaton, which, in principle, has nothing to do with the family $\operatorname{Rat} A^*$.

[3] We frequently denote a union by $X + Y$; the empty word is denoted by 1.

[4] Unfortunately, there are no methods to produce beautiful symmetric expressions for star-free languages as in our example. This problem probably merits further study.

the star-height of a given rational language X. This problem, formulated in 1963 has been shown to be algorithmically decidable by Hashiguchi in 1988 [15] but, unfortunately no practically executable algorithm is known to determine the star height of a given set. We shall say more about this problem and some of the tools used to attack it in section 4.

Connected to the star-height problem we mention another problem of Brzozowski, formulated in 1966, which had a great influence in the theory. A language X has the *finite power property* if its star is the union of finitely many of its powers, i.e. if there exists an $m \geq 0$, such that $X^* = (1+X)^m$. This is equivalent to saying that

$$X^* = 1 + X + X^2 + \cdots + X^m.$$

This problem, solved independently by Hashiguchi [12] and the author [40] was the starting point for further developments which ultimately led to Hashiguchi's solution of the star-height problem. Note that Brzozowski's condition is sufficient in order to replace a star by finitely many unions and products.

Interested in star-free languages and inspired by Eggan's star-height hierarchy, J. A. Brzozowski formulated the dot-depth problem in the late 60's [8] which is, in general, still unsolved, despite the combined efforts of many researchers. The *dot-depth of a star-free rational expression* is the maximum nested levels of concatenation used in the expression. The *dot-depth of a language* is the least dot-depth of star-free expressions denoting it. The dot-depth problem asks for the characterization of languages of any given dot-depth. For instance the previous star-free expressions show that the dot-depths of A^*, $(ab)^*$ and $(ab + ba)^*$ are at most 0, 1 and 2, respectively. However, it is a nontrivial journey to prove that 2 *is* the dot-depth of $(ab + ba)^*$ [38].

The dot-depth problem has an easy solution for dot-depth zero. The next step, i.e. the characterization of dot-depth one languages was achieved by R. Knast in 1983 [18]. For depth two or more the problem is open, but important partial results of Margolis, Pin, Straubing and Weil in that direction should be mentioned. We leave the details to section 3.

We close this introduction by mentioning that the first and third problems here described led to the discovery of many interesting families of rational languages, called varieties. The study of these varieties is mathematically sophisticated and it combines algebraic, combinatorial, logical and lately topological methods to attack linguistic problems. Reciprocally, linguistic properties are often used to establish algebraic results about pseudovarieties. Such mathematical diversity and richness is one of the main credentials of this theory. Extensive and modern accounts of these developments can be found in the books of Pin [31] and Almeida [3].

2 More on McNaughton's star-free problem

McNaughton's question on star-free languages was not motivated by its linguistic aspect but it appeared as a natural question related to the representation of rational languages by logical formulas. This area was pioneered by Trakhtenbrot

[56] and independently discovered by McNaughton [25]. See also the fundamental work of Büchi [7] and Elgot [11].

More precisely, following Büchi, rational languages can be defined by formulas in the monadic second order theory of successor. A restriction to first order formulas leads to the subfamily of star-free languages and this was the original motivation of McNaughton for his interest in star-free languages. The reader will find further details in [27, 51, 54, 28].

Now we recall that every language X has a syntactic monoid M and a syntactic morphism $f: A^* \to M$ which have the property that $f^{-1}fX$ equals X. Furthermore, M is the least monoid with this property in the sense that for every other morphism $f': A^* \to M'$, such that $f'^{-1}f'X = X$, M is a homomorphic image of M'. We will say that a monoid M is *aperiodic* if for every $x \in M$ there exists an $n > 0$, such that $x^n = x^{n+1}$. Here is Schützenberger's theorem.

Theorem 2 *A set X in $\mathrm{Rat}\, A^*$ is star-free iff the syntactic monoid of X is finite and aperiodic.*

We wish to comment now on three aspects of Schützenberger's paper [36] containing this theorem:

- the effective solution of a linguistic problem through the use of the syntactic monoid;
- the introduction of the Schützenberger product for finite monoids;
- the lead it contained for the introduction and investigation of pseudovarieties, one of the most significant aspects of the theory today.

Let us examine first the constructive aspect of Schützenberger's solution of the star-free problem. Note that the syntactic monoid can be constructed algorithmically for a recognizable set, given an automaton recognizing it or an expression denoting it. Since one can easily check whether the syntactic monoid of a language is aperiodic or not it follows that the theorem is an effective characterization of star-free sets. This is one of the theorem's major aspects, certainly the one which motivated McNaughton's question. Maybe it even stimulated and justified the study of the syntactic monoid. Indeed, this invariant has been known for a long time and both Schützenberger and Rhodes were directing some of the work of their respective schools to the investigation of these algebraic structures since the beginning of their activity. However, the structure only gained widespread acceptance after the appearance of Schützenberger's theorem, effectively characterizing star-free languages.

Next we comment on the Schützenberger product of monoids. Note that given languages X and Y, the syntactic monoid of $X + Y$ divides the direct product of the syntactic monoids of X and Y. One of the difficulties in handling the product of languages, our main concern here, is that we do not have a simple operation on monoids which would play the role of the direct product in the above statement. Such a product was introduced during the course of the original proof of theorem 2. This product is now called the Schützenberger product and it can be found in section 5.

The product was originally defined for two monoids. Straubing took this idea of the 2-fold Schützenberger product and generalized it for a k-fold product. His definition can be found in section 5. This was an essential step because the Schützenberger product is not associative and the iterated use of the 2-fold product introduces unnecessary and unwanted algebraic "complexities". Next, Straubing proved that the Schützenberger product is an operation on monoids which reflects the (k-fold) product of languages in the sense mentioned before. On the other hand, Reutenauer proved in 1979 [34] an inverse result for the 2-fold Schützenberger product, using the marked product of languages. More precisely, he proved that every language recognized by the 2-fold Schützenberger product of monoids M_1 and M_2 can be expressed as a Boolean combination of marked products $L_1 a L_2$, where L_i is recognized by M_i and a is a letter. Pin generalized this proof and showed [29] a similar property for the k-fold product. From all these developments we can conclude that the Schützenberger product is the monoid equivalent of the marked product of languages. This transforms the Schützenberger product in a major tool to attack product problems for rational languages. In section 5 we give a full proof of this basic property of the Schützenberger product, and this will be the only proof in our paper.

The last aspect we will comment is still another far reaching consequence of Schützenberger's work. It provides perhaps the earliest example of a pseudovariety of monoids, theme which dominates the modern research in the area.

A pseudovariety of monoids is a class of finite monoids which is closed under formation of submonoids, of homomorphic images and of finite direct products. These classes are the finite analogue of Birkhoff's varieties of algebras which are exactly the classes of algebras definable by equations. An example of a pseudovariety of monoids is given by the class $\mathbf{A}$ of finite aperiodic monoids. Schützenberger noted very early this connection [37] but the subject was to be developed only in the book of Eilenberg [10] in 1976. One problem is that on account of the finiteness the equational property of varieties, present in Birkhoff's theorem, is lost, i.e. it is not true that every pseudovariety is the class of finite monoids satisfying some set of equations. Nevertheless, Eilenberg and Schützenberger have shown [10] that the equational property can be partially recovered. Indeed, they proved that every pseudovariety of monoids is ultimately defined by equations. Another, very elegant proof of this fine theorem was found by Ash [4]. Let us illustrate this property by the example of $\mathbf{A}$. Consider the equation $x^n = x^{n+1}$, one for every $n \geq 1$. It is easy to see that only the idempotent monoids, in which $x = x^2$, satisfy all of these equations. It is equally easy to see that every aperiodic monoid satisfies all but finitely many of these equations: it is said therefore that those equations ultimately define the class $\mathbf{A}$.

Later on, Reiterman [33] improved the analogy with Birkhoff's theorem by introducing the topological algebra of the implicit operations on finite monoids (finite algebras in general). He proved that every pseudovariety is defined by pseudoidentities. For the case of $\mathbf{A}$, the pseudoidentity defining it is $x^\omega = x x^\omega$, where x^ω is a typical example of an implicit operation which is not a homomorphism. It associates to each element x of a monoid its unique power x^ω which is idempotent. The use and calculus of implicit operations for pseudovarieties of monoids was significantly developed by Jorge Almeida who recently wrote a comprehensive book about the subject [3]. This area still has many unanswered and interesting questions, the book of Almeida, for instance, lists 57 open problems.

3 More on Brzozowski's dot-depth problem

We begin with a precise linguistic statement of the dot-depth problem. For technical reasons we will initially restrict our attention to languages which do not contain the empty word, i.e. our universe for languages will be 2^{A^+}, for a fixed alphabet A. Let $\mathcal{E}$ be the family of singletons, one for each letter of A. For a family $\mathcal{F}$ of languages we denote by $B\mathcal{F}$ the smallest Boolean algebra containing $\mathcal{F}$, i.e. the closure of $\mathcal{F} \cup \{\emptyset\}$ under union and complementation. Let us denote by $S\mathcal{F}$ the smallest semigroup containing $\mathcal{F}$, i.e. the closure of $\mathcal{F}$ under multiplication. The dot-depth hierarchy is the sequence

$$\mathcal{B}_0 \subseteq \mathcal{B}_1 \subseteq \cdots \subseteq \mathcal{B}_n \subseteq \cdots$$

of Boolean algebras, where $\mathcal{B}_0 = B\mathcal{E}$ and $\mathcal{B}_{n+1} = BS\mathcal{B}_n$, for $n \geq 0$. Now, we say that a language $L \subseteq A^*$ is of *dot-depth* n if $L - \{1\}$ belongs to $\mathcal{B}_n$ but not to $\mathcal{B}_{n-1}$. The dot-depth problem consists in (effectively) characterizing the languages of each given dot-depth.

The idea here is to minimize the nested number of levels of concatenation in expressions denoting the star-free sets: $\mathcal{B}_n$ is the family of star-free languages which must use n nested levels of concatenation and for which that many levels are sufficient to denote them. Clearly, each $\mathcal{B}_n$ is a subfamily of the star-free sets, and each star-free set belongs to some $\mathcal{B}_n$, but not much more than this follows by intuitive arguments.

It can be shown without difficulty that each $\mathcal{B}_n$ is a +-variety of languages, in the terminology of Eilenberg [10], and this essentially means that the syntactic semigroups of languages in $\mathcal{B}_n$ form exactly the syntactic semigroups of some pseudovariety of semigroups. The corresponding pseudovariety of semigroups will be denoted by $\mathbf{B}_n$.

It is known that the hierarchy is proper but the proof of this result already requires sophisticated arguments. It was first proved by Brzozowski and Knast in 1978 [5]. A more informative and algebraic proof was later obtained by Straubing [46]. Another proof, logically oriented, was given by Thomas [52, 53].

Straubing proved initially that $\mathbf{B}_{n+1} = \Diamond\mathbf{B}_n$, where $\Diamond\mathbf{V}$ is the pseudovariety generated by the Schützenberger product of semigroups in $\mathbf{V}$. Straubing's proof of the properness of the dot-depth hierarchy was done then by a careful analysis of the algebraic properties of the Schützenberger product of semigroups.

As for the dot-depth problem the strongest known result is the characterization of dot-depth one languages, achieved by Knast [18]. Knast's condition is a bit complicated to be stated here; we only mention that it is an effective property on the syntactic semigroup of a language which gives a necessary and sufficient condition for a language to be of dot-depth one. The same problem for dot-depth two is still open, despite the many efforts of solving it. The closest results so far were obtained by Straubing and Weil in a series of papers [48, 58, 50]. Another line of attack tried to characterize the power operator **P**, since an effective characterization of **PJ** would solve the problem [45, 22, 32, 23, 24, 30, 1].

At this point we mention some early results on the dot-depth problem which had an influence on the forthcoming research in this area. These are contained in the Doctoral dissertation of the author [38], written in 1972. Three problems were tackled there: the characterization of locally testable languages, the characterization of piecewise testable languages and the localization of two infinite hierarchies of languages of dot-depth one.

A language X is said to be *locally testable* if pertinence of a word to X can be decided by looking only at segments of bounded length of the given word. The problem of effectively characterizing locally testable languages has been formulated by McNaughton and Papert in their monograph [27] and it was solved independently by McNaughton and by Brzozowski and Simon [26, 6]. It is easy to see that a language is locally testable iff it belongs to the Boolean algebra generated by the sets $A^* w A^*$, $A^* w$ and $w A^*$, for words w. This clearly implies that every locally testable language is of dot-depth one.

Theorem 3 *A subset of A^* is locally testable iff its syntactic semigroup S is finite and locally idempotent and commutative, i.e. for every idempotent $e = e^2$ in S the monoid eSe in S is idempotent and commutative.*

One of the major steps in our solution corresponded to a wreath-product decomposition of semigroups which are locally idempotent and commutative and which became known as "A theorem on graphs", after its reformulation by Eilenberg [10]. This result inspired Knast to obtain a technically more complex theorem on graphs [19] and which allowed him to characterize the whole family of languages of dot-depth one[18]. Later on, starting from these theorems on graphs, Tilson developed the Theory of Finite Categories as Algebras [55], as a generalization of the Theory of Finite Monoids and which is bound to play a crucial role in a possible solution of the dot-depth problem. Another very important result in this area is contained in the **V ∗ D** paper [47] of Straubing; theorem 3 is also the first discovered particular case of Straubings results on **V ∗ D**.

A language X is *piecewise testable* if pertinence of a word to X can be decided by looking at subwords of bounded length of the given word. Note that $u = a_1 a_2 \cdots a_n$, with $a_i \in A$, is a *subword* of v iff $v \in A^* a_1 A^* \cdots a_n A^*$. This last set is the shuffle product of u and A^*, denoted $u \sqcup A^*$. It is easy to see that a language is piecewise testable iff it belongs to the Boolean algebra generated by the sets $u \sqcup A^* = A^* a_1 A^* \cdots a_n A^*$. Piecewise testable languages were first considered by the author [38, 39] who also obtained several characterizations. The most important one is the following.

Theorem 4 *A subset of A^* is piecewise testable iff its syntactic monoid is finite and $\mathcal{J}$-trivial.*

We recall that a monoid M is $\mathcal{J}$-trivial iff every principal ideal of M has a unique generator. In other words, for any $m_1, m_2 \in M$, $Mm_1M = Mm_2M$ implies that $m_1 = m_2$. This is an important structural property of monoids and the corresponding pseudovariety **J** appears frequently especially in connection with the Schützenberger product and the dot-depth problem. Note, as a starter, that the shuffle product $u \sqcup A^*$ is a particular case (perhaps the simplest one) of the marked product of section 5.

The family of piecewise testable sets possesses today many characterizations, some of them having more than one proof. We do not have space to review these here but indicate some of the literature [10, 35, 44, 49, 2]. Perhaps the most outstanding proof so far is that of Almeida which contains a completely topological proof of theorem 4 staged in Universal Algebraic terms. Even though his proof is not constructive it yields an effective decision procedure for the problem of deciding whether or not a given recognizable set is piecewise testable.

The third aspect we mentioned was the identification of two infinite hierarchies inside $\mathcal{B}_1$, particular families of which were the locally testable languages and the piecewise testable ones. Again, we will not survey this aspect here and only mention that this subject was much expanded by Pin who in [29] introduced a formalism to construct many hierarchies inside the family of star-free sets and which are very closely related to the role of the Schützenberger product in the theory of pseudovarieties (see section 5). We even believe that a proper study of the algebraic properties of the hierarchies introduced by Pin might lead to a solution of the dot-depth problem.

4 More on Eggan's star-height problem

Instead of addressing the star-height problem in detail we shall try to describe here only the main tool developed to deal with this problem area, pointing out its connection with the product of rational languages. Even this we will do very briefly, a more detailed account can be found in our survey [41].

Consider initially the following problem. Let be given a finite family $\mathcal{F}$ of rational languages. Can we decide whether a given language, L belongs to the closure of $\mathcal{F}$ under certain operations? Hashiguchi solved this problem in 1983 for any subset of the rational operations: union, product and star [14]. Two cases are particularly interesting and difficult: the closure of $\mathcal{F}$ under product and its closure under union and product. Representing the elements of $\mathcal{F}$ by $X_1, X_2, \ldots, X_n$, in the first case we wish to know whether some monomial in the (noncommuting) X's (i.e. a product $X_{i_1} X_{i_2} \cdots X_{i_k}$) denotes L. In the second case one is interested in a polynomial in the X's, denoting L. But what is the relation to the star-height problem? Consider the following situation: we have already found expressions of star-height at most h for the sets X_i. We are given the language L. Can we express L^* as unions of products of the X_i's? If so, then we can guarantee that the height of L^* is at most h. This technique alone is not strong enough to solve Eggan's problem but it does describe an important aspect of Hashiguchi's solution.

We shall consider now the particular case of these problems when there is only one language in $\mathcal{F}$, or equivalently, there is only one variable X and the set to be expressed is X^*. Recall the definition of the finite power property, given in the Introduction, and note that the solution to either problem above (for one variable) can be expressed in terms of the finite power property for the only language in $\mathcal{F}$. This problem is already quite difficult and it will illustrate well the general case.

The problem of deciding whether or not a rational language has the finite power property was first formulated by J. A. Brzozowski in 1966 during the seventh SWAT (now FOCS) Conference. It was solved independently by Hashiguchi [12] and the author [40]. Our solution introduced the theory of multiplicities over the tropical semiring[5] (see [41]) which seems to be an important tool in minimizing the number of factors in expressions involving products of rational languages. We try to illustrate the idea briefly by an example.

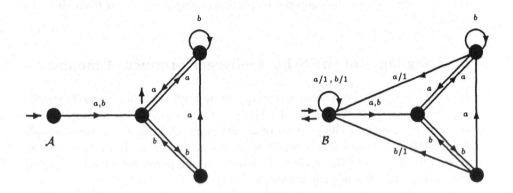

Fig. 1. A set X with the finite power property: $X^* = (1 \cup X)^4$.

Consider the language L recognized by the automaton $\mathcal{A}$ of Figure 1. Automaton $\mathcal{B}$ (without the multiplicities /1) is the automaton recognizing the language L^*, obtained by a standard construction; let i be its only initial and final state. Let us now assign a multiplicity 1 to each edge arriving at the final state i of $\mathcal{B}$ and multiplicity 0 to every other edge of $\mathcal{B}$ (zero multiplicities are not indicated in the figure). Let us postulate that the multiplicity of a path is the sum of multiplicities of its edges. The multiplicity of a word w is the least multiplicity of successful paths spelling w. These rules are easily remembered if one interprets the multiplicities as a "cost". Now, every $i - i$ path in $\mathcal{B}$, spelling $w \in L^*$, induces a factorization of w showing that $w \in L^n$, where n is the multiplicity of our path. It follows that the multiplicity of every word w in the behavior of $\mathcal{B}$ is

---

[5] This is the semiring consisting of the natural numbers extended with ∞ and equipped with the operations of minimums (as semiring addition) and addition (as semiring product).

the least exponent n, such that L^n contains w. Finally, the set L has the finite power property iff the words in L^* have bounded multiplicity. Or equivalently, iff the behavior of $\mathcal{B}$ is *limited*.

The last problem, deciding whether or not the behavior of an arbitrary finite automaton is limited is a basic ingredient in the solution of the star-height problem and many other related problems. It is a hard problem, first solved by Hashiguchi [13] and which since then has given rise to much research [21, 43, 42, 16, 57] which description is out of the scope of this paper.

We mention a recent result of D. Krob [20] which surprised everyone in the area. Krob has proved that the equivalence problem for finite automata with multiplicities in the tropical semiring is recursively undecidable. He did this by a very ingenious construction which solved Hilbert's tenth problem using only the very rudimentary arithmetic available in the tropical semiring and the equally rudimentary computing powers of finite automata. With such limited resources he was able to express the multiplication of natural numbers. Thus, Krob proved the undecidability of the equivalence problem using a reduction from Hilbert's tenth problem.

5 Languages of the Schützenberger product of monoids

In this section we prove a theorem incorporating work of Schützenberger, Straubing, Reutenauer and Pin [36, 46, 34, 31]. This result is one of the most important tools to work with products of rational languages. Our proof is a major simplification of earlier ones and is reminiscent of some of the early linguistic proofs related to the dot-depth problem. In a forthcoming paper we intend to explore the possible benefits of such a transparent proof.

Theorem 5 *Let A be a finite alphabet and let $M_0, M_1, \ldots, M_n$ be finite monoids. Then $\Diamond = \Diamond(M_0, M_1, \ldots, M_n)$ recognizes a language $L \subseteq A^*$ iff L can be expressed as a Boolean combination of languages of the form*

$$L_{i_0} a_1 L_{i_1} \cdots a_r L_{i_r}, \tag{1}$$

where $0 \leq r \leq n$, $0 \leq i_0 < i_1 < \cdots < i_r \leq n$, $a_i \in A$ (for $1 \leq i \leq r$), and $L_{i_j} \subseteq A^*$ is a language recognized by M_j (for $0 \leq j \leq r$).

Initially we give precise definitions of the terms of theorem 5. Let us consider monoids $M_0, M_1, \ldots, M_n$ and let $M = M_0 \times M_1 \times \cdots \times M_n$ be their direct product. The family K of subsets of M is a semiring under the operations of union and product of subsets of M. The *Schützenberger product* of the M_i's, denoted $\Diamond(M_0, M_1, \ldots, M_n)$, is the semigroup of $(n+1) \times (n+1)$ matrices $P = (P_{ij})$ over K whose elements satisfy the following properties:

1. $P_{ij} = \emptyset$, for every $0 \leq j < i \leq n$;
2. $P_{ij} \subseteq 1 \times \cdots \times 1 \times M_i \times \cdots \times M_j \times 1 \cdots \times 1$, for every $0 \leq i \leq j \leq n$;
3. P_{ii} is a unitary subset of K, for every $0 \leq i \leq n$.

For a monoid M and a language $L \subseteq A^*$ we say that M *recognizes* L if there exists a morphism $\mu \colon A^* \to M$ such that $L = f^{-1}fL$.

Lemma 6 *Every language of the form (1) is recognized by $\Diamond$.*

Proof. Initially we note that $\Diamond(M_{i_0}, \ldots, M_{i_r})$ is a submonoid of $\Diamond(M_0, \ldots, M_n)$; hence, there is no loss of generality if we assume that the language to be recognized is $L = L_0 a_1 L_1 \cdots a_n L_n$, where L_i is recognized by M_i. Assume that $\mu_i \colon A^* \to M_i$ are morphisms, for $0 \le i \le n$, such that μ_i recognizes the language L_i, i.e. $L_i = \mu^{-1}\mu L_i$. We define matrices $a\mu$, for $a \in A$, as follows:

$$
(a\mu)_{pq} = \begin{cases} (1, \ldots, 1, \mu_p a, 1, \ldots, 1) & \text{if } p = q; \\ (1, \ldots, 1) & \text{if } a = a_p \text{ and } q = p + 1; \\ \emptyset & \text{else.} \end{cases}
$$

Considering the unique extension of μ to a morphism, $\mu \colon A^* \to \Diamond$, we have, for every $w \in A^*$,

$$
(w\mu)_{pq} = \begin{cases} (1, \ldots, 1, \mu_p w, 1, \ldots, 1) & \text{if } p = q; \\ \{\, (1, \ldots, 1, \mu_p w_p, \ldots, \mu_q w_q, 1, \ldots, 1) \mid w \in A^* w_p \cdots a_q w_q A^* \,\} & \text{if } p \ne q. \end{cases}
$$

Thus, assuming that subset X_i of M_i is such that $L_i = \mu_i^{-1} X_i$, we have that $L = \mu^{-1} X$, where

$$
X = \{\, P \in \Diamond(M_0, \ldots, M_n) \mid P_{0n} \cap X_0 \times \cdots \times X_n \ne \emptyset \,\}.
$$

$\blacksquare$

To show the other implication in theorem 5 we consider a language $L \subseteq A^*$ recognized by $\Diamond$ and a morphism $\mu \colon A^* \to \Diamond$, such that $L = \mu^{-1}\mu L$. We shall study the morphism μ in detail. Initially, we define functions $\mu_{ij} \colon A^* \to K$ by putting $\mu_{ij} x = (\mu x)_{ij}$. Note that, for each $0 \le i \le n$, μ_{ii} is a morphism, which is easily identified with a morphism $A^* \to M_i$, but no similar property holds for the μ_{ij} in general. The next lemma says that μ_{ij} is essentially computed by the morphisms μ_{kk}. It contains the inspiration for our proof.

Lemma 7 *For every word $w \in A^*$, and for every $0 \le i, j \le n$,*

$$
\mu_{ij} w = \sum \mu_{i_0 i_0} w_{i_0} \mu_{i_0 i_1} a_1 \mu_{i_1 i_1} w_{i_1} \cdots \mu_{i_{k-1} i_k} a_k \mu_{i_k i_k} w_{i_k},
$$

where the sum extends over all $0 \le k \le n$, all $i = i_0 < i_1 < \cdots < i_k = j$, and all factorizations $w = w_{i_0} a_1 w_{i_1} \cdots a_k w_{i_k}$, with $a_i \in A$.

Proof. Let $w = b_1 b_2 \cdots b_r$ be the factorization of w in letters. The nature of matrix multiplication guarantees that

$$
\mu_{ij} w = \sum \mu_{i_0 i_1} b_1 \mu_{i_1 i_2} b_2 \cdots \mu_{i_{r-1} i_r} b_r,
$$

where the sum extends over all $i = i_0, i_1, \ldots, i_r = j$. Since $\mu_{pq} x = \emptyset$, whenever $p > q$, it is enough to consider sequences such that $i = i_0 \le i_1 \le \cdots \le i_r = j$.

Grouping now equal neighboring indices and remembering that each μ_{kk} is a morphism we arrive at the desired expression for $\mu_{ij}w$. ∎

This lemma suggests the following definition, crucial in the proof. An *object* is a sequence

$$o = (i_0, m_0, a_1, i_1, m_1, \ldots, a_k, i_k, m_k),$$

where $0 \le k \le n$, $0 \le i_0 < i_1 < \cdots < i_k \le n$, $a_i \in A$ and $m_j \in M_{i_j}$. Integer k is the *length* of the object o. There are finitely many objects and $\mathcal{O}$ will denote the set of all of them. Given μ we define the *value* of o as being

$$f(o) = m_0(\mu_{i_0 i_1} a_1) m_1 \cdots (\mu_{i_{k-1} i_k} a_k) m_k,$$

and do note that $f(o) \subseteq 1 \times \cdots \times 1 \times M_{i_0} \times \cdots \times M_{i_k} \times 1 \times \cdots \times 1$. For $u \in A^*$ we define its *contents* by

$$\text{cont}(u) = \{\, o \in \mathcal{O} \mid u = u_0 a_1 u_1 \cdots a_k u_k, \text{ with } \mu_{i_j i_j} u_j = m_j, \text{ for each } j \,\},$$

i.e. the contents of u consists of those objects for which u has a compatible factorization. Finally we define an equivalence relation, $\equiv \bmod \Diamond$, by

$$u \equiv v \bmod \Diamond \text{ iff } \text{cont}(u) = \text{cont}(v).$$

The reader will verify at once that $\equiv \bmod \Diamond$ is a congruence relation over A^* since $\text{cont}(ua)$, for $a \in A$, depends only on $\text{cont}(u)$ and a, but not on u itself. Besides, since there are only finitely many objects, we can conclude that $\equiv \bmod \Diamond$ is a congruence of finite index. We will denote by F_μ the quotient monoid $A^*/\equiv \bmod \Diamond$ and by π the natural projection $\pi : A^* \to F_\mu$.

Corollary 8 *The congruence $\pi^{-1}\pi$ is a refinement of the congruence $\mu^{-1}\mu$, i.e.,* $\pi^{-1}\pi \subseteq \mu^{-1}\mu$.

Proof. Observe initially that from Lemma 7 we can conclude that for every $u \in A^*$ and $0 \le i, j \le n$, $\mu_{ij}u$ depends only on $\text{cont}(u)$ and not on u itself. Assume that $u \equiv v \bmod \Diamond$. It follows that $\mu u = \mu v$. The proof is complete. ∎

Now we are ready to prove the second part of theorem 5.

Lemma 9 *Every language recognized by $\Diamond$ belongs to $\mathcal{F}$, where $\mathcal{F}$ is the family of Boolean combinations of languages of the form (1).*

Proof. Every language recognized by $\Diamond$ is a finite union of congruence classes $\mu^{-1}\mu$. Thus, it suffices to show that each such class is in $\mathcal{F}$.

Since $\pi^{-1}\pi$ is of finite index, in view of Cor. 8 each congruence class $\mu^{-1}\mu$ is a finite union of congruence classes of $\pi^{-1}\pi$. Hence, it suffices to show that each congruence class of $\pi^{-1}\pi$ is in $\mathcal{F}$. To do this, we associate a language $L(o)$ to every object o as follows:

$$L(o) = \{\, u \in A^* \mid o \in \text{cont}(u) \,\}.$$

442

Recalling the definition of an object and that each μ_{ii} is a morphism it is easy to see that

$$L(o) = (\mu_{i_0 i_0}^{-1} \mu_{i_0 i_0} m_0) a_1 (\mu_{i_1 i_1}^{-1} \mu_{i_1 i_1} m_1) \cdots a_k (\mu_{i_k i_k}^{-1} \mu_{i_k i_k} m_k).$$

Thus, $L(o)$ is of the form (1) and consequently belongs to $\mathcal{F}$.

We observe now that, for every $u \in A^*$,

$$\pi^{-1}\pi u = \bigcap_{o \in \text{cont}(u)} L(o) - \bigcup_{o \in \mathcal{O}-\text{cont}(u)} L(o).$$

It follows that each congruence class $\pi^{-1}\pi u$ is in $\mathcal{F}$ and this concludes the proof of the Lemma. ∎

Theorem 5 is established now by lemmas 6 and 9.

References

1. J. Almeida. On power varieties of semigroups. *J. Algebra*, 120:1–17, 1989.
2. J. Almeida. Implicit operations on finite $\mathcal{J}$-trivial semigroups and a conjecture of I. Simon. *J. Pure Appl. Algebra*, 69:205–218, 1990.
3. J. Almeida. *Semigrupos Finitos e Álgebra Universal*. IME-USP, São Paulo, 1992. in portuguese.
4. C. J. Ash. Pseudovarieties, generalized varieties and similarly described classes. *J. Algebra*, 92:104–115, 1985.
5. J. A. Brzozowski and R. Knast. The dot-depth hierarchy of star-free languages is infinite. *J. Comput. Syst. Sci.*, 16:37–55, 1978.
6. J. A. Brzozowski and I. Simon. Characterizations of locally testable events. *Discrete Math.*, 4:243–271, 1973.
7. J. R. Büchi. Weak second-order arithmetic and finite automata. *Z. Math. Logik Grundlagen Math.*, 6:66–92, 1960.
8. R. S. Cohen and J. A. Brzozowski. Dot-depth of star-free events. *J. Comput. Syst. Sci.*, 5:1–15, 1971.
9. S. Eilenberg. *Automata, Languages, and Machines, Volume A*. Academic Press, New York, 1974.
10. S. Eilenberg. *Automata, Languages, and Machines, Volume B*. Academic Press, New York, 1976.
11. C. C. Elgot. Decision problems of finite automata design and related arithmetics. *Trans. Amer. Math. Soc.*, 98:21–52, 1961.
12. K. Hashiguchi. A decision procedure for the order of regular events. *Theoretical Comput. Sci.*, 8:69–72, 1979.
13. K. Hashiguchi. Limitedness theorem on finite automata with distance functions. *J. Comput. Syst. Sci.*, 24:233–244, 1982.
14. K. Hashiguchi. Representation theorems on regular languages. *J. Comput. Syst. Sci.*, 27:101–115, 1983.
15. K. Hashiguchi. Algorithms for determining relative star height and star height. *Information and Computation*, 78:124–169, 1988.
16. K. Hashiguchi. Improved limitedness theorems on finite automata with distance functions. *Theoretical Comput. Sci.*, 72, 1990.

17. S. C. Kleene. Representations of events in nerve nets and finite automata. In Shannon, editor, *Automata Studies*, pages 3–41. pup, princeton, 1956.

18. R. Knast. A semigroup characterization of dot-depth one languages. *R.A.I.R.O. Informatique Théorique*, 17:321–330, 1983.

19. R. Knast. Some theorems on graph congruences. *R.A.I.R.O. Informatique Théorique*, 17:331–342, 1983.

20. D. Krob. The equality problem for rational series with multiplicities in the tropical semiring is undecidable. *Int. J. of Algebra and Computation*, 1993. in print.

21. H. Leung. On the topological structure of a finitely generated semigroup of matrices. *Semigroup Forum*, 37:273–287, 1988.

22. S. W. Margolis. On M-varieties generated by power monoids. *Semigroup Forum*, 22:339–353, 1981.

23. S. W. Margolis and J.-E. Pin. Minimal noncommutative varieties and power varieties. *Pacific J. Math.*, 111:125–135, 1984.

24. S. W. Margolis and J.-E. Pin. Power monoids and finite J-trivial monoids. *Semigroup Forum*, 29:99–108, 1984.

25. R. McNaughton. Symbolic logic for automata. Technical Report Tech. Note No. 60-244, Wright Air Development Division, Cincinnati, Ohio, 1960.

26. R. McNaughton. Algebraic decision procedures for local testability. *Math. Syst. Theor.*, 8:60–76, 1974.

27. R. McNaughton and S. Papert. *Counter-Free Automata*. The M.I.T. Press, Cambridge, Mass., 1971.

28. D. Perrin and J.-E. Pin. First-order logic and star-free sets. *J. Comput. Syst. Sci.*, 32:393–406, 1986.

29. J.-E. Pin. Hiérarchies de cocaténation. *R.A.I.R.O. Informatique Théorique*, 18:23–46, 1984.

30. J.-E. Pin. Semigroupe des parties et relations de Green. *Can. J. Math*, 36:327–343, 1984.

31. J.-E. Pin. *Variétés de Langages Formels*. Masson, Paris, 1984. English translation: Varieties of Formal Languages, Plenum, 1986.

32. J.-E. Pin and H. Straubing. Monoids of upper triangular matrices. In *Colloquia Mathematica Societatis Janos Bolyai, 39, Semigroups*, pages 259–272, Szeged, 1981.

33. J. Reiterman. The Birkhoff theorem for finite algebras. *Alg. Univ.*, 14:1–10, 1982.

34. C. Reutenauer. Sur les variétés de langages et de monoïdes. In *GI 79*, pages 260–265, Berlin, 1979. Springer-Verlag. Lecture Notes in Computer Science, 67.

35. J. Sakarovitch and I. Simon. Subwords. In M. Lothaire, editor, *Combinatorics on Words*, pages 105–144. Addison-Wesley, Reading, MA, 1983. Encyclopaedia of Mathematics, volume 17.

36. M. P. Schützenberger. On finite monoids having only trivial subgroups. *Information and Control*, 8:190–194, 1965.

37. M. P. Schützenberger. Sur certaines variétés de monoïdes finis. In E. R. Caianello, editor, *Automata Theory*, pages 314–319. Academic Press, 1966.

38. I. Simon. *Hierarchies of Events with Dot-Depth One*. PhD thesis, University of Waterloo, Waterloo, Ont., Canada, 1972. Department of Applied Analysis and Computer Science.

39. I. Simon. Piecewise testable events. In H. Brakhage, editor, *Automata Theory and Formal Languages, 2nd GI Conference*, pages 214–222, Berlin, 1975. Springer-Verlag. Lecture Notes in Computer Science, 33.

40. I. Simon. Limited subsets of a free monoid. In *Proc. 19th Annual Symposium on Foundations of Computer Science*, pages 143–150, Piscataway, N.J., 1978. Institute of Electrical and Electronics Engineers.

41. I. Simon. Recognizable sets with multiplicities in the tropical semiring. In M. P. Chytil, L. Janiga, and V. Koubek, editors, *Mathematical Foundations of Computer Science 1988*, pages 107–120, Berlin, 1988. Springer-Verlag. Lecture Notes in Computer Science, 324.

42. I. Simon. On semigroups of matrices over the tropical semiring. Technical Report RT-MAC-8907, Departamento de Ciência da Computação do IME-USP, São Paulo, 1989.

43. I. Simon. Factorization forests of finite height. *Theoretical Comput. Sci.*, 72:65–94, 1990.

44. J. Stern. Characterizations of some classes of regular events. *Theoretical Comput. Sci.*, 35:17–42, 1985.

45. H. Straubing. Recognizable sets and power sets of finite semigroups. *Semigroup Forum*, 18:331–340, 1979.

46. H. Straubing. A generalization of the Schützenberger product of finite monoids. *Theoretical Comput. Sci.*, 13:137–150, 1981.

47. H. Straubing. Finite semigroup varieties of the form $V * D$. *J. Pure Appl. Algebra*, 36:53–94, 1985.

48. H. Straubing. Semigroups and languages of dot-depth two. *Theoretical Comput. Sci.*, 58:361–378, 1988.

49. H. Straubing and D. Thérien. Partially ordered finite monoids and a theorem of I. Simon. *J. Algebra*, 119:393–399, 1988.

50. H. Straubing and P. Weil. On a conjecture concerning dot-depth two languages. *Theoretical Comput. Sci.*, 104:161–183, 1992.

51. W. Thomas. Classifying regular events in symbolic logic. *J. Comput. Syst. Sci.*, 25:360–376, 1982.

52. W. Thomas. An application of the Ehrenfeucht-Fraissé game in formal language theory. *Soc. Math. France, 2e série*, 16:11–21, 1984.

53. W. Thomas. A concatenation game and the dot-depth hierarchy. In *Computation Theory and Logic*, pages 415–426, Berlin, 1987. Springer-Verlag. Lecture Notes in Computer Science, 270.

54. W. Thomas. Automata on infinite objects. In J. van Leeuwen, editor, *Handbook of Theoretical Computer Science, Volume B, Formal Models and Semantics*, chapter 4, pages 133–191. Elsevier, elsevierp, 1990.

55. B. Tilson. Categories as algebra: an essential ingredient in the theory of monoids. *J. Pure Appl. Algebra*, 48:83–198, 1987.

56. B. A. Trakhtenbrot. Synthesis of logic networks whose operators are described by means of single-place predicate calculus. *Doklady Akad. Nauk. SSSR*, 118:646–649, 1958. in russian.

57. A. Weber. Exponential upper and lower bounds for the order of a regular language. Technical report, Fachbereich Informatik, Johann Wolfgang Goethe-Universitä, Frankfurt, 1992.

58. P. Weil. Inverse monoids of dot-depth two. *Theoretical Comput. Sci.*, 66:233–245, 1989.

On Regular Compatibility of Semi–Commutations

Edward Ochmański

Polska Akademia Nauk
Instytut Podstaw Informatyki,
Ordona 21, 01–237 Warszawa

Pierre–André Wacrenier

CNRS URA 369, LIFL, Bât.M3
Université de Lille 1
59655 Villeneuve d'Ascq

Abstract: A semi-commutation θ' is $\mathcal{REG}$-compatible with a semi-commutation θ iff the θ'-closure of any regular θ-closed language remains regular. The paper presents a decidable criterion, characterizing couples of $\mathcal{REG}$-compatible semi-commutations. The complexity of the problem is shown to be co-NP-complete.

Introduction

A semi-commutation (A,θ) is a finite alphabet A coupled with an irreflexive binary relation θ on A. This notion was introduced by Clerbout/Latteux [1] as a generalization of its symmetric version, called partial commutation. Numerous papers about various aspects of the semi-commutation theory were published since then. It was remarked already in [1] that any single semi-commutation rule represents a way of event occurences of an atomic petrinet (producer/consumer system). Several papers, starting from Hung/Knuth [5], proved semi-commutations form actually a powerful tool for study behaviour of concurrent systems, mostly petrinets.

Each semi-commutation (A,θ) induces the closure operation $f_\theta : 2^{A^*} \to 2^{A^*}$ (see Section 1). A language L is θ-closed iff $f_\theta(L)=L$, and $\mathcal{REG}_\theta$ denotes the family of θ-closed regular languages. Given two semi-commutations (A,θ) and (A,θ'), we say that θ' is $\mathcal{REG}$-compatible with θ iff $f_{\theta'}(L)$ is regular for any L in $\mathcal{REG}_\theta$.

The $\mathcal{REG}$-compatibility problem is the following: *Is it decidable, for any A,θ,θ', whether θ' is $\mathcal{REG}$-compatible with θ ?*. It is worth notice that the same problem narrowed to partial commutations (i.e. symmetric semi-commutation) is as trivial as possible. Namely, then θ' $\mathcal{REG}$-comp. θ iff $\theta' \subseteq \theta$, and there is nothing to prove (knowing that $\{a^n b^n \mid n \geq 0\}$ is not regular). On the contrary, the problem for semi-commutations stayed a long time unsolved. Where lies the crucial difficulty? In the fact $\mathcal{REG}_\theta$ for semi-commutations, unlike that for partial commutations, cannot be fully built with concurrent star, as the Roos' language (ab)*b(a+b)* (with aθb) shows (see [2]).

The paper presents the positive solution of the problem, giving a decidable criterion of $\mathcal{REG}$-compatibility. Complexity is established to be co-NP-complete. The course of events is the following:

In the preparatory part of the paper (Section 3) we define the notion of $Rank_\theta(L)$ and prove that $f_\theta(L)$ is regular for any regular L with finite $Rank_\theta(L)$ (Proposition 3.3). One must mention that the notion and the result generalize their partial commutation version of Hashiguchi [4]. The meaning of Propositon 3.3 goes far out of the paper. For example, the classical result of Clerbout/Latteux [1] (If L is regular, θ-closed and $\underline{\theta}$-strongly-connected, then $f_\theta(L^*)$ is regular) is provable quite easy (unlike the original proof) with Proposition 3.3.

Section 4 contains a discussion of the problem and the formulation of the main result (Theorem 4.6). A set of examples illustrates the discussion.

The "if" part is proved in Section 5. We show that if the criterion is fulfilled then $Rank_\theta(L)$ is finite for any L in $\mathcal{REG}_\theta$. Then, on account of Proposition 3.3, we have the "if" part proved.

For the converse (Section 6) we construct, whenever the criterion is not fulfilled, a Roos-like language R in $\mathcal{REG}_\theta$ such that its θ'-closure $f_{\theta'}(R)$ is not regular. It proves the "only if" part and completes the proof of Theorem 4.6.

Corollaries and complexity discussion of Section 7 conclude the paper. The $\mathcal{REG}$-compatibility problem is proved to be co-NP-complete.

1. Basic Notions

First, we recall some classical denotations. A^* means the free monoid generated by an alphabet A. Members of A are letters, members of A^* are words, ε is the empty word. Subsets of A^* are languages. Cardinality of A is denoted by $|A|$. For $w \in A^*$, alph(w) means the set of letters occuring in w, $|w|$ means the length of w, and $|w|_a$ means the number of occurrences of the letter a in the word w. For $B \subseteq A$, the projection $\Pi_B : A^* \to B^*$ is the morphism keeping letters of B and erasing those of A−B.

A *semi-commutation* is a pair (A, θ), where A is a finite alphabet and $\theta \subseteq A \times A$ is an irreflexive semi-commutation relation. The inverse of θ is the relation $\theta^{-1} = \{(b,a) \mid (a,b) \in \theta\}$, the complement of θ is the relation $\underline{\theta} = A \times A - \theta$. One can extend θ and $\underline{\theta}$ onto $A^* \times A^*$ as follows:

$u\theta v$ iff $alph(u) \times alph(v) \subseteq \theta$
$u\underline{\theta}v$ iff $alph(u) \times alph(v) \cap \underline{\theta}$ is nonempty.

Let (A,θ) be a semi-commutation. For $u,v \in A^*$, we write $u-_\theta\!\!->v$ iff there are $w,w' \in A^*$ and $(a,b) \in \theta$ such that $u=wabw'$ and $v=wbaw'$; the reflexive and transitive closure of $-_\theta\!\!->$ is denoted by $-_\theta\!\!->>$. The closure function $f_\theta : A^* \to 2^{A^*}$ and its extension $f_\theta : 2^{A^*} \to 2^{A^*}$ are the following: $f_\theta(w) = \{u \in A^* \mid w-_\theta\!\!->>u\}$ and $f_\theta(L) = \bigcup \{f_\theta(w) \mid w \in L\}$. A language $L \subseteq A^*$ is said to be θ-*closed* iff $f_\theta(L)=L$.

The fundamental notion of the semi-commutation theory is that of strong-connectivity:

Definition 1.1 (strong connectivity): A directed graph $G = \langle V; \to \rangle$ is strongly connected iff $(\forall x,y \in V)(\exists z_0,z_1,...,z_n \in V)$ such that $x=z_0 \to z_1 \to ... \to z_n=y$. The sequence $z_0,z_1,...,z_n$ is then called a path (in G) from x to y.

Let (A,θ) be a semi-commutation. A word $w \in A^*$ is $\underline{\theta}$-strongly-connected iff the graph $\langle alph(w) ; \underline{\theta} \cap alph(w) \times alph(w) \rangle$ is strongly connected; a word $w \in A^*$ is $\underline{\theta}$-connected iff it is $\underline{\theta} \cup \underline{\theta}^{-1}$-strongly-connected.

Let (A,θ') be an other semi-commutation; then θ' is strongly connected w.r.t. θ iff any $\underline{\theta}$-strongly-connected word $w \in A^*$ is $\underline{\theta}'$-strongly-connected.

2. Regular Languages

This paper is not a place for a review of numerous equivalent definitions of recognizability. The present definition is chosen because of its usefulness for our proving methods.

Definition 2.1: Given a language $L \subseteq A^*$ and a word $u \in A^*$, the *left quotient* of L by u is the language $L/u=\{v \in A^* \mid uv \in L\}$. A language $L \subseteq A^*$ is *recognizable* iff the family $\{L/u \mid u \in A^*\}$ of its left quotients by words of A^* is finite. It is *rational* iff one can build it from finite languages using the operations of union, product and star. Classes of recognizable and rational languages are denoted by $\mathcal{REC}$ and $\mathcal{RAT}$, respectively.

Kleene Theorem: If A is finite, then $\mathcal{REC}(A^*)=\mathcal{RAT}(A^*)$.

In the course of this paper we operate within finitely generated free monoids. In order to keep it in mind, members of $\mathcal{REC}=\mathcal{RAT}$ will be called regular languages and the class of regular languages will be denoted by $\mathcal{REG}$.

Let us introduce an useful notion of the k-syntactic relation:

Definition 2.2: Let k be an integer; let L be a language in A^*; let $X=(x_1,...,x_k)$ be a k-tuple in $A^* \times ... \times A^*$ (k times). The k-*syntactic* quotient of L by X is a subset of $A^* \times ... \times A^*$ (k+1 times) defined as follows:

$$(z_0,z_1,...,z_k) \in L//(x_1,...,x_k) \text{ iff } z_0 x_1 z_1 ... x_k z_k \in L.$$

The k-*syntactic relation* of L is an equivalence relation defined as follows:

$$(x_1,...,x_k) \equiv_{L,k} (y_1,...,y_k) \quad \text{iff} \quad L//(x_1,...,x_k) = L//(y_1,...,y_k).$$

The notion of the k-syntactic relation generalizes the well-known notion of syntactic relation (1-syntactic relation in our terms). Let us recall a well-known characterization of regular languages with the 1-syntactic relation, denoted by $\equiv_L$ in the sequel.

Fact 2.3: L is regular iff $\equiv_L$ has a finite index.

The following generalization easy follows from Fact 2.3:

Lemma 2.4: For any language $L \subseteq A^*$ and for any integer k:

L is regular iff $\equiv_{L,k}$ has a finite index.

Proof: If k=1 then we have Fact 2.3. One can easy show that if $(x_i) \equiv_L (y_i)$ for all i=1,...,k then $(x_1,...,x_k) \equiv_{L,k}(y_1,...,y_k)$. Thus the index of $\equiv_{L,k}$ does not exceed n^k, where n is the index of $\equiv_L$. For the converse observe that if $(x,\varepsilon,...,\varepsilon) \equiv_{L,k}(y,\varepsilon,...,\varepsilon)$ then $(x) \equiv_L (y)$. ◻

3. Regular Languages and Semi-Commutations

This section presents notions and results, forming a base for our main investigations. First, some combinatorial property of semi-commutative derivations:

Fact 3.1 ([6]): Let (A,θ) be a semi-commutation; let $w,u,v \in A^*$.

$w -_\theta ->> uv$ iff there is a factorization $w=v_0 u_1 v_1...u_n v_n$, such that

$u_1...u_n -_\theta ->> u$, $v_0 v_1...v_n -_\theta ->> v$, and $v_i \theta u_j$ for i<j.

The following notion generalizes the notion of "finite block testability", defined by Hashiguchi [4] for partial commutations.

Definition 3.2: Let (A,θ) be a semi-commutation; let L be a language in A^*; let $u,v \in A^*$ be words such that $uv \in f_\theta(L)$. We say $rank_{L,\theta}(u,v) \leq n$ (for an integer n) iff there is $w \in L$ such that $w=v_0 u_1 v_1...u_n v_n$, $u_1...u_n -_\theta ->> u$, $v_0 v_1...v_n -_\theta ->> v$, and $v_i \theta u_j$ for i<j. Thanks to Fact 3.1, $rank_{L,\theta}$ is a total function from $\{(u,v) | uv \in f_\theta(L)\}$ to the set N of integers, setting $rank_{L,\theta}(u,v) = \min\{n \in N | rank_{L,\theta}(u,v) \leq n\}$. We say $Rank_\theta(L)$ is finite iff there is an integer N such that $rank_{L,\theta}(u,v) \leq N$ whenever $uv \in f_\theta(L)$.

Now we can prove some sufficient condition.

Proposition 3.3: Let (A,θ) be a semi-commutation; let L be a regular subset of A^*.

If $Rank_\theta(L)$ is finite, then $f_\theta(L)$ is regular.

Proof: We shall prove that the number of different left quotients of $f_\theta(L)$ is finite. Let N be an integer bounding $\{rank_{L,\theta}(u,v) \mid uv \in f_\theta(L)\}$. Taking into account Fact 3.1 and Def.3.2 we get the following characterization of the set $f_\theta(L)/u$:

$v \in f_\theta(L)/u$ iff $uv \in f_\theta(L)$ iff there is $w \in L$ such that

(1) $w = v_0 u_1 v_1 ... u_N v_N$

(2) $u_1...u_N\!-\!_\theta\!->\!>u$ and $v_0 v_1...v_N\!-\!_\theta\!->\!>v$

(3) $v_i \theta u_j$ whenever $i<j$

Let us define the sets $W_\theta(x)$ for $x \in A^*$, and the sets $W_{\theta,N}(x_1,...,x_N)$ for $(x_1,...,x_N) \in A^* \times ... \times A^*$ (N times) as follows: $W_\theta(x) = \{w \in A^* \mid w\theta x\}$ and $W_{\theta,N}(x_1,...,x_N) = W_\theta(x_1...x_N) \times W_\theta(x_2,...,x_N) \times ... \times W_\theta(x_N) \times A^*$. Let us define the operation *COMB* from $2^{A^* \times ... \times A^*}$ to 2^{A^*} as follows: $COMB(X) = \{w \in A^* \mid w = x_1...x_N$ for some $(x_1,...,x_N) \in X\}$. Now we can reformulate the (1)-(2)-(3) characterization of left quotients of $f_\theta(L)$, using the introduced notions. Namely, for any $u \in A^*$, the left quotient $f_\theta(L)/u$ is equal to the set $\bigcup \{f_\theta[COMB(L//(u_1,...,u_N) \cap W_{\theta,N}(u_1,...,u_N))] \mid u_1...u_N\!-\!_\theta\!->\!>u\}$. Clearly, the family $\{W_\theta(x) \mid x \in A^*\}$ is finite, so the family $\{W_{\theta,N}(x_1,...,x_N) \mid x_i \in A^*$ for $1 \le i \le N\}$ is finite, too. Finiteness of the family $\{L//(x_1,...,x_N) \mid x_i \in A^*$ for $1 \le i \le N\}$ follows, by Lemma 2.4, from regularity of L. Therefore the family $\{f_\theta(L)/u \mid u \in A^*\}$ is finite, thus $f_\theta(L)$ is regular. $\quad\square$

> **Remark** that the converse of Prop.3.3 is not true, even for partial commutations: $A=\{a,b\}$, $\theta=\{(a,b),(b,a)\}$, $L=(ab)^*(a^*+b^*)$; then $f_\theta(L)=A^*$ is regular, although $Rank_\theta(L)$ is infinite (because $rank_{L,\theta}(a^n,b^n)=n$ for any integer n). This example answers negatively the first open problem of Hashiguchi [4].

The following fact, due to Clerbout/Latteux, will be used:

Fact 3.4 ([1]): If L and L′ are regular θ-closed languages, then $f_\theta(L \cup L')$ and $f_\theta(LL')$ are regular. Moreover, if all members of L are θ-strongly-connected, then $f_\theta(L^*)$ is regular.

4. Regular Compatibility

Let (A,θ) be a semi-commutation. The class of regular languages in A^* which are closed with respect to θ is denoted by $REG_\theta(A^*)$, or simply by REG_θ if there is no confusion about A. Precisely: $REG_\theta(A^*) = \{L \subseteq A^* \mid L \in REG$ and $f_\theta(L)=L\}$. Let us define the main notion of the paper:

Definition 4.1: Let (A,θ) and (A,θ') be two semi-commutations.

θ′ is *REG*-compatible with θ iff $f_{\theta'}(L) \in REG_{\theta'}$ for any $L \in REG_\theta$.

First observe that the partial commutation criterion $\underline{\theta} \subseteq \underline{\theta}'$ is useless in the semi-commutation case:

Example 4.2:

$\underline{\theta}': \quad a \qquad b$

$\underline{\theta}: \quad a \longrightarrow b$

$\underline{\theta}'': \quad a \longleftarrow b$

One can prove that both θ' and θ'' are $\mathcal{REG}$-compatible with θ (as $f_{\theta'}(L)=f_{\theta''}(L)=f_{\theta''}(L \cap a^*b^*)$ for any $L \in \mathcal{REG}_\theta$).

The aim of this paper is to characterize effectively the couples of $\mathcal{REG}$-compatible semi-commutations. In the rest of the paper θ and θ' are assumed to be two semi-commutation relations over a common, arbitrary but fixed, alphabet A.

Let us start with some necessary condition:

Lemma 4.3: If θ' is $\mathcal{REG}$-compatible with θ, then θ' is strongly connected w.r.t. θ.

Proof: Assume there is a word $w \in A^*$ that is $\underline{\theta}$-strongly-connected but not $\underline{\theta}'$-strongly-connected. Then, by Fact 3.4, $L=f_\theta(w^*)=f_\theta(f_\theta(w)^*)$ is regular. As w is not $\underline{\theta}'$-strongly-connected, there are $x,y \in \text{alph}(w)$ without a $\underline{\theta}'$-path from x to y in alph(w). Set $X=\{z \in \text{alph}(w) \mid \text{there is a } \underline{\theta}'\text{-path in alph(w) from x to z}\}$, $Y=\text{alph}(w)-X$. Set now $u=\Pi_X(w)$ and $v=\Pi_Y(w)$. Since u and v are non-empty words over disjoint alphabets, such that $w-_\theta \rightarrowtail vu$ and $uv-_\theta \rightarrowtail vu$, we have $f_{\theta'}(L) \cap v^*u^*=\{v^n u^n \mid n>0\}$. Thus $f_{\theta'}(L)$ is not regular. $\qquad \square$

Let us stop, for a moment, over the natural question about the converse of Lemma 4.3. Note that Example 4.2 does not disprove such a suspicion, and the following example neither.

Example 4.4:

$\underline{\theta}: \quad a \longrightarrow b \\ \qquad \nwarrow \; \nearrow \\ \qquad \quad c$

$\underline{\theta}': \quad a \qquad b \\ \qquad \nwarrow \\ \qquad \quad c$

We shall show soon that θ' is REG-compatible with θ.

Quite surprisingly, we meet a semi-commutation included in θ' that is strongly connected w.r.t. to θ, but not $\mathcal{REG}$-compatible with θ:

Example 4.5:

$\underline{\theta}: \quad a \longrightarrow b \\ \qquad \nwarrow \; \nearrow \\ \qquad \quad c$

$\underline{\theta}'': \quad a \qquad b \\ \qquad \nwarrow \; \nearrow \\ \qquad \quad c$

And this time θ'' is not $\mathcal{REG}$-compatible with θ. It will be also shown soon, using our main theorem.

Let us pose now the main theorem:

THEOREM 4.6: θ' is $\mathcal{REG}$-compatible with θ

if and only if

$(\forall u,v \in A^*)$ $u\theta'v$ implies $u\theta v$, whenever uv is strongly connected in $\underline{\theta} \cup \underline{\theta}'^{-1}$ and alph(u)∩alph(v)=∅.

Proof: See Sections 5 and 6. The "if" part follows from Prop.3.3 + Prop.5.1.

The "only if" - from Lemma 4.3 + Prop.6.4. ❑

The proof is quite precisely presented in Sections 5 and 6. The most involved technical parts (Claims 5.3, 6.2 and 6.3) are left to the full version of the paper.

> **Remark** that Theorem 4.6 gives a decidable criterion of $\mathcal{REG}$-compatibility. Actually, it suffices to check the words u,v∈A* with single letter's occurrences only. See Section 7 for the complexity discussion.

Examples 4.4 and 4.5 (continued): The graphs of $\underline{\theta} \cup \underline{\theta}'^{-1}$ and $\underline{\theta} \cup \underline{\theta}''^{-1}$ are:

In order to verify θ' $\mathcal{REG}$-comp. θ we have to check u=a and v=c only (ac is $\underline{\theta} \cup \underline{\theta}'^{-1}$-strongly connected and aθ'c). Since aθc, we deduce θ' is $\mathcal{REG}$-compatible with θ. On the contrary, when θ'' operates, the couple u=a and v=bc proves θ'' is not $\mathcal{REG}$-compatible with θ (since abc is $\underline{\theta} \cup \underline{\theta}''^{-1}$-strongly-connected, a$\theta''$bc and a$\underline{\theta}$bc).

The next two sections are devoted to the proof of Theorem 4.6.

5. The *"if part"* or Finite Ranks

As it was observed in the former sections, finiteness of $Rank_{\theta'}(L)$ for any L in $\mathcal{REG}_\theta$ is sufficient for $\mathcal{REG}$-compatibility of θ' with θ. Actually, the following proposition holds.

Proposition 5.1: Let θ and θ' be two semi-commutations on A, such that $(\forall u,v \in A^*)$ $u\theta'v$ implies $u\theta v$, whenever uv is $\underline{\theta} \cup \underline{\theta}'^{-1}$-strongly-connected and alph(u)∩alph(v)=∅.

Then $Rank_{\theta'}(L)$ is finite for any θ-closed language L⊆A*.

Proof: Let $uv \in f_{\theta'}(L)$. It follows from Fact 3.1 that then there is $w \in L$ such that:
(1) $w = v_0 u_1 v_1 ... u_n v_n$ (2) $u_1...u_n -_{\theta'} \rightarrow\!\!> u$ and $v_0 v_1...v_n -_{\theta'} \rightarrow\!\!> v$ (3) $v_i \theta' u_j$ if $i < j$.
Now we show that, although the independence $v_i \theta' u_j$ does not hold for all (i,j), it holds for "most" of the couples. Precisely:

> **Claim 5.2:**   If $u_{j_1} v_{i_1} u_{j_2} v_{i_2} ... u_{j_p} v_{i_p}$ (with $j_1, i_1, ..., j_p, i_p \in \{1,..,n\}$)
> be a subword of w (it means $j_1 \leq i_1 < j_2 \leq i_2 < ... < j_p \leq i_p$) such that
> ($\forall k \leq p$) $v_{i_k} \underline{\theta'} u_{j_k}$, then $p \leq |A|$.
>
> **Proof:** Let $k < l \leq p$ and $x_k \underline{\theta'} y_k$ for some $x_k \in \mathrm{alph}(v_{i_k})$, $y_k \in \mathrm{alph}(u_{j_k})$, and
> $x_l \underline{\theta'} y_l$ for some $x_l \in \mathrm{alph}(v_{i_l})$, $y_l \in \mathrm{alph}(u_{j_l})$. Then $x_k \neq x_l$, since $x_k \underline{\theta'} y_l$ and
> $x_l \underline{\theta'} y_l$. Hence p is bounded by the size of A.   □

It remains to check if "lengths" of "totally commutative" segments of w are limited. Actually, one can prove

> **Claim 5.3:**   Let θ and θ' satisfy the hypothesis of Proposition 5.1.
> Let $L \subseteq A^*$ be θ-closed, let $uv \in f_{\theta'}(L)$ and let $w \in L$ satisfy (1)-(2)-(3).
> Let $u_k v_k ... u_l$, for some $1 \leq k < l \leq n$, be a segment of $w = v_0 u_1 v_1 ... u_n v_n$ such
> that $v_i \theta' u_j$ for all $i, j \in [k, l-1]$.
> $$\text{If } rank_{L,\theta'}(u,v) = n \text{ then } l - k + 1 \leq |A|.$$
> **Proof:** Omitted in this version.   □

Now we are able to conclude the proof of Proposition 5.1. Clearly, $uv \in f_{\theta'}(L)$ iff ($\exists w \in L$) satisfying (1)-(2)-(3) and (4): $n = rank_{L,\theta'}(u,v)$. Take a subword $u_{j_1} v_{i_1} u_{j_2} v_{i_2} ... u_{j_p} v_{i_p}$ of $w = v_0 u_1 v_1 ... u_n v_n$ such that ($\forall k \leq p$) $v_{i_k} \underline{\theta'} u_{j_k}$, with a maximal "length" p. Since Claim 5.2, we have $p \leq |A|$. Next, for each $u_{j_k} v_{i_k}$, find $u_{j_{k'}} v_{i_{k'}}$ such that $j_k \leq j_{k'} \leq i_{k'} \leq i_k$, $v_{i_{k'}} \underline{\theta'} u_{j_{k'}}$ and [if $j_k \leq j_{k''} \leq i_{k''} \leq i_k$ and $v_{i_{k''}} \underline{\theta'} u_{j_{k''}}$ then $j_{k''} = j_{k'}$ and $i_{k''} = i_{k'}$]). This way, we have found a subword $u_{j_{1'}} v_{i_{1'}} u_{j_{2'}} v_{i_{2'}} ... u_{j_{p'}} v_{i_{p'}}$ such that any segment of our main factorization $v_0 u_1 v_1 ... u_n v_n$ lying between neighbouring pieces (i.e. between $u_{j_{k'}}$ and $v_{i_{k'}}$ or between $v_{i_{k'}}$ and $u_{j_{k+1'}}$) of our last subword satisfies the hypothesis of Claim 5.3. Thus "lengths" of these segments are bounded by $|A|$. The number of such segments is equal to $2p+1$, so $n \leq (2p+1)|A| + p$. Since $p \leq |A|$ (by Claim 5.2), we get $n \leq 2|A|^2 + 2|A|$.   □

6.   The *"only if part"* or Spoiling Regularity

Since Lemma 4.3, it remains to check the case θ' str.con. θ. We shall show how to construct, whenever the criterion of Theorem 4.6 is not fulfilled, a language R in $\mathcal{REG}_\theta$ such that $f_{\theta'}(R)$ is not in $\mathcal{REG}_{\theta'}$. The following example will illustrate the proof step by step.

Example 6.0:

θ:

θ':

$\theta \cup \theta'^{-1}$:

Clearly, θ' is strongly connected w.r.t. θ. Choosing $u=ab$ and $v=cd$, we have uv strongly connected in $\theta \cup \theta'^{-1}$, and $u\theta'v$ but $u\theta v$. So, it is just a case we are interested in.

Let us start with a graphic characterization:

Lemma 6.1 (Graphic Characterization): Let θ' str.con. θ. If there exist words $u, v \in A^*$, such that: (i) $alph(u) \cap alph(v) = \varnothing$ (ii) uv is $\theta \cup \theta'^{-1}$-str-con. (iii) $u\theta'v$ and $u\theta v$ then there exists a subalphabet $\{x_0, x_1, ..., x_n\}$ (with $n \geq 3$) of $alph(uv)$ such that:

1. $\{(x_0, x_1), ..., (x_{i-1}, x_i)\} \subseteq \theta'^{-1}$
2. $\{(x_{i+1}, x_{i+2}), ..., (x_{n-1}, x_n)\} \subseteq \theta \cup \theta'^{-1}$
3. $(x_0, x_n) \in \theta \cap \theta' \cap \theta^{-1}$
4. $(x_i, x_{i+1}) \in \theta \cap \theta' \cap \theta^{-1}$
5. $\{x_0, ..., x_i\} \times \{x_{i+1}, ..., x_n\} \subseteq \theta'$

$$\theta \cap \theta' \cap \theta^{-1} \qquad \overset{\theta'^{-1}}{\begin{array}{c} x_0 \to x_1 \to \cdots \to x_{i-1} \to x_i \\ \downarrow \qquad \qquad \qquad \qquad \downarrow \\ x_n \leftarrow x_{n-1} \leftarrow \cdots \leftarrow x_{i+2} \leftarrow x_{i+2} \\ \theta \cup \theta'^{-1} \end{array}} \qquad \theta \cap \theta' \cap \theta^{-1}$$

Proof: Obviously, $(x_i, x_{i+1}) \in \theta \cap \theta'$ for some x_i in u and x_{i+1} in v. As θ' str.con. θ, we have $(x_i, x_{i+1}) \in \theta \cap \theta' \cap \theta^{-1}$. Set $D = D(x_i) = \{y \in alph(uv) \mid$ there is a path from x_i to y in $\langle alph(uv); \theta' \rangle \}$ and $I = I(x_i) = alph(uv) - D$. Set $u' = \Pi_D(uv)$ and $v' = \Pi_I(uv)$. Clearly, $u'\theta'v'$, $u'\theta v'$, and $u'v'$ is $\theta \cup \theta'^{-1}$-strongly-connected. Therefore, there exists a shortest path in $\langle alph(v'); \theta \cup \theta'^{-1} \rangle$ from x_{i+1} to a letter x_n in v', such that there is an $\theta \cup \theta'^{-1}$-arc from x_n to a letter x_0 in u'. As $u'\theta'v'$, we have $(x_n, x_0) \in \theta \cap \theta'^{-1}$. Since x_0 is in D, there is a path from x_0 to x_i in θ'^{-1}. And $\{x_0, ..., x_i\} \times \{x_{i+1}, ..., x_n\} \subseteq \theta'$, since $\{x_0, ..., x_i\} \subseteq alph(u')$, $\{x_{i+1}, ..., x_n\} \subseteq alph(v')$ and $u'\theta'v'$. $\square$

Example 6.0 (step 1): The graph of Lemma 6.1, for $u=ab$ and $v=cd$, is the following:

$$\theta \cap \theta' \cap \theta^{-1} \qquad \overset{\theta'^{-1}}{\begin{array}{c} a \longrightarrow b \\ \downarrow \qquad \qquad \downarrow \\ d \longleftarrow c \\ \theta \cup \theta'^{-1} \end{array}} \qquad \theta \cap \theta' \cap \theta^{-1}$$

In order to simplify the construction we use an auxiliary semi-commutation ϑ, defined as follows: $\vartheta = A{\times}A - \{(x_k,x_{k+1}) \in \theta'^{-1}\} - \{(x_n,x_0),(x_i,x_{i+1})\} - \{(x,x) \mid x \in A\}$. Note that ϑ is the greatest semi-commutation including θ and keeping the properties (1-5). Obviously, $\mathcal{REG}_\vartheta \subseteq \mathcal{REG}_\theta$.

Example 6.0 (step 2): In our example ϑ is just equal to θ.

Now we are starting to construct a ϑ-closed regular language R, such that $f_{\theta'}(R)$ is not regular. Given a semi-commutation ϑ and a $\underline{\vartheta}$-connected word w, the auxiliary language $L_{\vartheta,w}$ is defined as follows:

$L_{\vartheta,w} =$ *if* w is $\underline{\vartheta}$-strongly-connected *then* $f_\vartheta(w^*)$

$$else \ f_{\vartheta \cap \vartheta^{-1}}[w^* f_\vartheta(D_{\vartheta,w}[alph(w)]^*)];$$

where $D_{\vartheta,w} = \{m \in A^* \mid (\exists m') \ w -_{\vartheta \cap \vartheta^{-1}} {>>} m' -_{\vartheta \cap \underline{\vartheta}^{-1}} {>} m$

$$or \ ww -_{\vartheta \cap \vartheta^{-1}} {>>} m' -_{\vartheta \cap \underline{\vartheta}^{-1}} {>} m\}.$$

Now we are able to define the language R:

Let A be the alphabet $\{x_0,...,x_n\}$. Let ϑ be a semi-commutation on A such that $(x_n,x_0) \in \underline{\vartheta}$ and $\underline{\vartheta} \subseteq \{(x_k,x_{k+1}) \mid k<n\} \cup \{(x_n,x_0)\} \cup \{(x,x) \mid x \in A\}$. Let $m_0 m_1 ... m_r$ be the factorization of $x_0 x_1 ... x_n$ such that $\{m_0 m_r\} \cup \{m_j \mid 0<j<r\}$ is the set of connected components of $\langle\{x_0,...,x_n\};\underline{\vartheta}\rangle$. We set $R = L_{\vartheta,m_1} \sqcup\!\sqcup L_{\vartheta,m_2} \sqcup\!\sqcup ... \sqcup\!\sqcup L_{\vartheta,m_{r-1}} \sqcup\!\sqcup L_{\vartheta,m_0 m_r}$.

Example 6.0 (step 3): For our word abcd we have the factorization m_0=a, m_1=bc, m_2=d. Next, we have D_{bc}={bbcc} and D_{ad}={da,daad,adda}. Hence,

$$L_{bc} = f_{\theta \cap \theta^{-1}}[(bc)^* f_\theta(bbcc(b+c)^*)] = (bc)^* bbb^* cb^* c(b+c)^* \text{ and}$$
$$L_{ad} = f_{\theta \cap \theta^{-1}}[(ad)^* f_\theta((da+daad+adda)(a+d)^*)] = (ad)^* dd^* a(a+d)^*.$$

This way, the language $R = L_{bc} \sqcup\!\sqcup L_{ad}$ has been built.

Claim 6.2: The language R is in $\mathcal{REG}_\vartheta$.

Proof: Regularity of L_w for $w \in \{m_1,...,m_{r-1},m_0 m_r\}$ is easily provable with Fact 3.4, several times called. Thus R is regular, as a shuffle product of regular languages. It remains to show that R is ϑ-closed; this part is left to the full version. $\square$

Example 6.0 (step 4): Regularity of R is obvious. Remark that ϑ-closeness of L_w for all $w \in \{m_1,...,m_{r-1},m_0 m_r\}$ suffices for ϑ-closeness of R. The ϑ-closeness of L_{bc} and L_{ad} directly follows from their rational expressions.

Now, assuming $x_0,...,x_n$ fulfil, together with ϑ and θ', the graphic characterization (1-5) of Lemma 6.1, one can prove:

Claim 6.3: The language $f_{\theta'}(R)$ is not regular.

Proof *(sketched)*: We use a regular language I such that $f_{\theta'}(R) \cap I$ is not regular. Set $u = x_0...x_i$ and $v = x_{i+i}...x_n$. We have to consider two cases: $i \neq 0$ and $i = 0$. If $i \neq 0$ then we set

$I=v^*u^*(x_1)^2...(x_n)^2(x_0)^2$. If i=0 we set $I=v^*u^*(x_k)^2...(x_n)^2(x_0)^2(x_1)^2...(x_{k-1})^2$, where x_k is the first letter of m_r.

The first case i≠0: one can prove that $f_{\theta'}(R)\cap I=\{v^pu^q(x_1)^2...(x_n)^2(x_0)^2\,|\,q{\le}p{+}1\}$.

The second case i=0: one can prove that if $x_k...x_nx_0$-θ'->>$x_0x_k...x_n$

then $f_{\theta'}(R)\cap I=\{v^pu^q(x_k)^2...(x_n)^2(x_0)^2(x_1)^2...(x_{k-1})^2\,|\,p{\ge}q{-}1\}\,|\,q{\le}p{+}1\}$

else $f_{\theta'}(R)\cap I=\{v^pu^q(x_k)^2...(x_n)^2(x_0)^2(x_1)^2...(x_{k-1})^2\,|\,p{=}q$ or $p{=}q{\pm}1\}$.

Hence $f_{\theta'}(R)$ is not regular. ◻

Example 6.0 (step 5): We have x_0=a, x_1=b, x_2=c, x_3=d, u=ab, v=cd, i=1 and $I=(cd)^*(ab)^*bbccddaa$. If q≤p then, shuffling $(bc)^qbbc^{p-q}cc$ of L_{bc} and $(ad)^qd^{p-q}ddaa$ of L_{ad}, we get $(abcd)^qbb(cd)^{p-q}ccddaa$ in R. Consequently, $(cd)^p(ab)^qbbccddaa$ belongs to $f_{\theta'}(R)$. If q=p+1 then, shuffling $(bc)^pbbbbcc$ of L_{bc} and $(ad)^p(ad)daa$ of L_{ad}, we get $(abcd)^p(ab)bbccddaa$ in R, and next $(cd)^p(ab)^{p+1}bbccddaa$ in $f_{\theta'}(R)$. This way $f_{\theta'}(R)\cap I$ is completed. Actually, if q>p+1 then a should be placed, during shuffling, into the bordered places in $(bc)^r\Box b\Box b...$; but then a letter d, staying between two bordered a's, blocks all right hand staying c's. We have $f_{\theta'}(R)\cap I=\{(cd)^p(ab)^qbbccddaa\,|\,q{\le}p{+}1\}$ proved. Hence $f_{\theta'}(R)$ is not regular.

Finally, recalling $\mathcal{REG}_\vartheta{\subseteq}\mathcal{REG}_\theta$, we conclude this section with

Proposition 6.4: If θ' is strongly connected w.r.t. θ and there exist words u,v∈A*, such that: (i) alph(u)∩alph(v)=∅ (ii) uv is $\underline{\theta}\cup\underline{\theta'^{-1}}$-strongly-connected (iii) uθ'v and u$\underline{\theta}$v, then there is a language R in $\mathcal{REG}_\theta$ such that $f_{\theta'}(R)$ is not regular.

7. Corollaries and Complexity

Due to the graphic characterization, checking whether two semi-commutations are not $\mathcal{REG}$-compatible is clearly in NP. We will prove the co-NP-completeness of the $\mathcal{REG}$-compatibility problem, showing it is co-NP-complete for the case θ⊆θ'.

First recall the notions of composition and confluence:

Composition: Let θ and θ' be two semi-commutations. Then $f_\theta{\circ}f_{\theta'}$ means the composition of f_θ and $f_{\theta'}$.

Confluency: A semi-commutation θ is said to be *confluent* iff (∀w,x,y∈A*)

if x <<-θ- w -θ->> y then (∃z∈A*) x -θ->> z <<-θ- y

Remark that if θ'⊆θ⁻¹ then θ' is always $\mathcal{REG}$-compatible with θ. Moreover, whenever θ⊆θ' we have:

Corollary 7.1: Let θ and θ' be two semi-commutations such that θ⊆θ'.

θ' is $\mathcal{REG}$-compatible with θ iff $f_{\theta'}=f_{\theta'{\cdot}\theta^{-1}}{\circ}f_\theta$.

Let us recall a characterization of confluence:

Fact 7.2 ([7]): Let θ be a semi-commutation. θ is confluent iff $f_{\theta^{-1}} \circ f_\theta = f_{\theta \cup \theta^{-1}}$

Hence, by 7.1 + 7.2, we get:

Corollary 7.3: $\theta \cup \theta^{-1}$ is $\mathcal{REG}$-compatible with θ iff θ is confluent.

Recall the related complexity result:

Fact 7.4 ([3]): The problem of confluence of semi-commutations is co-NP-complete.

And now 7.3 + 7.4 give:

Proposition 7.5: The $\mathcal{REG}$-compatibility problem is co-NP-complete.

Acknowledgements: The authors are extremely indebted to M.Clerbout, D.GonzaleZ, M.Latteux and Y.Roos for their meaningful collaboration over the presented problem.

Sponsors: This work has been partially sponsored by the EBRA Working Group 3166 ASMICS, by the PRC "Mathématiques et Informatique", and by the KBN Research Project 2 2047 32 03.

References

1. M.Clerbout/M.Latteux, *On a generalization of partial commutation;* 4th Hungarian Computer Science Conference's proceedings, pp.15-24 (1985); Extended version: *Semi-commutations;* Information & Computation 73, pp.59-74 (1987)

2. M.Clerbout/M.Latteux/Y.Roos/W.Zielonka, *Semi-commutations and rational expressions;* 19th ICALP proceedings, LNCS 623, pp.113-125 (1992)

3. V.Diekert/E.Ochmański/K.Reinhardt, *On confluent semi-commutations - decidability and complexity results;* 18th ICALP proceedings, LNCS 510, pp.229-241 (1991) Extended version to appear in Information & Computation.

4. K.Hashiguchi, *Recognizable closures and submonoids of free partially commutative monoids;* Theoretical Computer Science 86, pp.233-241 (1991)

5. D.V.Hung/E.Knuth, *Semi-commutations and Petri Nets;* Theoretical Computer Science 64, pp.67-82 (1989)

6. E.Ochmański, *Modelling concurrency with semi-commutations;* 17th MFCS proceedings, LNCS 629, pp.412-420 (1992)

7. Y.Roos/P.A.Wacrenier, *Composition of two semi-commutations;* 16th MFCS proceedings, LNCS 520, pp.406-414 (1991)

Algebraic Aspects of B-regular Series

Ph. Dumas

Algorithms Project,
INRIA Rocquencourt BP 105,
78153 Le Chesnay Cedex, France

Abstract. This paper concerns power series of an arithmetic nature
that arise in the analysis of divide-and-conquer algorithms. Two key
notions are studied: that of B-regular sequence and that of Mahlerian
sequence with their associated power series. Firstly we emphasize the
link between rational series over the alphabet $\{x_0, x_1, \ldots, x_{B-1}\}$ and
B-regular series. Secondly we extend the theorem of Christol, Kamae,
Mendès France and Rauzy about automatic sequences and algebraic
series to B-regular sequences and Mahlerian series. We develop here a
constructive theory of B-regular and Mahlerian series. The examples
show the ubiquitous character of B-regular series in the study of arithmetic functions related to number representation systems and divide-
and-conquer algorithms.

The interest of 2-regular sequences comes from their presence in many problems which touch upon the binary representation of integers or divide-and-
conquer algorithms, like sum-of-digits function, number of odd binomial coefficients, Josephus problem, mergesort, Euclidean matching or comparison networks. This explains why we study B-regular sequences that formalize the sequences which are solutions of certain difference equations of the divide-and-
conquer type. In other words we want to show that B-regular series (i.e. generating functions of B-regular sequences) are as important in computer science as
rational functions are common in mathematics.

Many properties of B-regular sequences like closure properties or growth
properties have been established by Allouche and Shallit. In particular they
showed that there is a link between B-regular sequences and rational series in
the sense of formal language theory. The transition from one to another uses
the B-ary representation of integers. There is already a long tradition about
recognizable sets and automatic sequences.

The link provides us with the well known machinery of rational series and
the first part of the paper is devoted to the illustration of its use. For example
we introduce the Hankel matrix of a regular series. This is the practical way to
find the rank of a regular series, to exhibit minimal recurrence relations or to
build up linear representations.

In the second part we compare B-regular series and Mahlerian series. Our
goal is to extend the theorem of Christol, Kamae, Mendès France and Rauzy
[6], which asserts that q-automatic series with coefficients in the finite field $\mathbb{F}_q$
are exactly algebraic series. To that purpose we introduce a more general notion
of Mahlerian series. We prove in particular that B-regular series are Mahlerian
series.

The reciprocal is more intricate but most useful. Indeed the theorem of Christol *et alii* is not adequate for theoretical computer science where the sequences have elements that are integer rather than elements of a finite fields. We give a partial answer to this problem, that permits to cover numerous cases of application.

In all the examples we have aimed at making the computations effective.

It is worth noting that we concentrate here on one facet of B-regular sequences, their algebraic closure properties. A complementary point of vue is the study of asymptotic behaviour of these sequences. One will find numerous examples in [9, 10].

1 Rational Series and B-regular Series

The properties of B-regular series come mainly from the properties of rational series in non commutative indeterminates and we build up a catalog where each notion about B-regular series is a translation of the corresponding notion about rational series. In view of the richness of the subject we limit ourselves to the essentials.

Let us begin with an example which gives the flavour of 2-regular series.

Example 1. Let us assume that we want to go from 0 to an integer n by leaps whose lengths are power of 2 and directions are forward or backward. The shortest path has a length w_n which may be defined by the conditions $w_0 = 0$, $w_n = 1$ if $n = 2^k$ and $w_n = 1 + \min(w_{n-2^k}, w_{2^{k+1}-n})$ if $2^k < n < 2^{k+1}$. For example we find $w_{14} = 2$ because $14 = 16 - 2$.

Another way to obtain this sequence (w_n) is to consider the two square matrices

$$A_0 = \begin{pmatrix} 1 & 0 & 0 & -1 \\ 0 & 0 & 0 & 1 \\ 0 & 1 & 1 & 1 \\ 0 & 0 & 0 & 0 \end{pmatrix}, \quad A_1 = \begin{pmatrix} 0 & 0 & -1 & 0 \\ 1 & 0 & 1 & 0 \\ 0 & 0 & 1 & 0 \\ 0 & 1 & 0 & 1 \end{pmatrix}$$

and the row and column matrices

$$\lambda = (\, 0 \quad 1 \quad 1 \quad 2 \,), \quad \gamma = (\, 1 \quad 0 \quad 0 \quad 0 \,)^T.$$

If the binary expansion of the integer n is $\epsilon_\ell \cdots \epsilon_1 \epsilon_0$, we have $w_n = \lambda A_{\epsilon_\ell} \cdots A_{\epsilon_1} A_{\epsilon_0} \gamma$. As an illustration

$$w_{14} = \lambda A_1 A_1 A_1 A_0 \gamma = 2.$$

This computation is akin to the definition of recognizable series and indeed B-regular series are merely a translation, as we shall see.

Let the alphabet $\mathcal{X}_B$ be formed of the digits $0, 1, \ldots, B-1$ used to write the integers in B-ary notation. To avoid confusion between figures and scalars, which lie in a ring $\mathbb{A}$, we represent figures by the indeterminates $x_0, x_1, \ldots, x_{B-1}$. We obtain B-regular series by translation of rational series [2].

Definition 1. A formal power series $f(z) \in \mathbb{A}[[z]]$ is a B-regular series if there exists a rational series $S \in \mathbb{A}^{\mathrm{rat}} \langle\!\langle \mathcal{X}_B \rangle\!\rangle$ in non-commutating indeterminates, whose support is included in the language $\mathcal{N}$ of integers B-ary expansions,

$$S = \sum_{u \in \mathcal{N}} (S, u)\, u \ ,$$

459

such that

$$f(z) = \sum_{n \geq 0} (S, \tilde{n}) \, z^n \ ,$$

where $\tilde{n}$ is the B-ary expansion of n.

Linear Representations. In the study of recognizable series, the linear representations come from the use of the division operators that trim a word of its leftmost letter. Classically the divisions are on the left but we favour the right operations, which correspond to the least significant digits. If the alphabet is $\mathcal{X}$ and w is a word, the right division w^{-1} acts on the series S according to the formula

$$Sw^{-1} = \sum_{u \in \mathcal{X}^*} (S, uw) \, u \ .$$

The division operators give us the section operators S_r, $0 \leq r <$ B, acting on $f(z) = \sum_n f_n z^n$ by the formula

$$S_r f(z) = \sum_{n \geq 0} f_{\mathrm{B}n+r} \, z^n \ .$$

Theorem 2 (Stability theorem). *A formal series is B-regular if and only if there exists an $\mathbb{A}$-module of finite type which is left stable by the section operators and contains the series.*

We obtain a linear representation of a B-regular series by expressing the section operators with respect to a generating family of that module. Moreover the linear representation permits us to exhibit a rational expression of the series S associated with the B-regular series: if $\Xi = \sum_{0 \leq r < \mathrm{B}} x_r A_r$ and $\Xi_+ = \sum_{0 < r < \mathrm{B}} x_r A_r$, we have $S = \lambda(I + \Xi_+ \Xi^*)\gamma$. This formula is only a translation of the fact that $\mathcal{N} = \varepsilon + \mathcal{X}_+ \mathcal{X}^*$, where ε is the empty word, $\mathcal{X} = \mathcal{X}_{\mathrm{B}}$ and $\mathcal{X}_+ = \{x_1, \ldots, x_{\mathrm{B}-1}\}$.

Example 2. The complexity of mergesort in the worst case satisfies the divide-and-conquer recurrence

$$T_n = T_{\lfloor n/2 \rfloor} + T_{\lceil n/2 \rceil} + n - 1 \ ,$$

with the initial conditions $T_0 = T_1 = 0$. The generating series $T(z)$ is 2-regular because the $\mathbb{Z}$-module generated by $T(z)$, $T(z)/z$, $2z/(1-z)^2$, $z(1+z)/(1-z)^2$ and $(1+z)/(1-z)^2$ is left stable by the two section operators S_0 and S_1. With respect to this basis, the matrices of S_0 and S_1 are

$$A_0 = \begin{pmatrix} 2 & 1 & 0 & 0 & 0 \\ 0 & 1 & 0 & 0 & 0 \\ 0 & 1 & 2 & 1 & 1 \\ 1 & 0 & 0 & 1 & 0 \\ 0 & 0 & 0 & 0 & 1 \end{pmatrix} \ , \quad A_1 = \begin{pmatrix} 1 & 0 & 0 & 0 & 0 \\ 1 & 2 & 0 & 0 & 0 \\ 1 & 0 & 0 & 1 & -1 \\ 0 & 0 & 0 & 0 & 0 \\ 0 & 1 & 2 & 1 & 3 \end{pmatrix} \ .$$

We take

$$\lambda = (\, 0 \ 0 \ 0 \ 0 \ 1 \,), \quad \gamma = (\, 1 \ 0 \ 0 \ 0 \ 0 \,)^T,$$

because the components of λ are the values at 0 of the series of the basis and γ gives the coordinates of $T(z)$.

Building a linear representation from the section operators gives the relation $\lambda A_0 = \lambda$ because the constant term of a series $g(z)$ is the constant term of $S_0 g(z)$ too. We call such a representation a standard linear representation. We have seen that every B-regular series $f(z)$ hides a rational series $S = \lambda(I + \Xi_+ \Xi^*)\gamma$, but for a standard representation it is simpler to introduce the rational series $R = \lambda \Xi^* \gamma$. Both series coincide on language $\mathcal{N} = \varepsilon + \mathcal{X}_+ \mathcal{X}^*$, but the first one extends $f(z)$ by 0 whereas the second one uses the rule $(R, x_0 w) = (R, w)$. Clearly each one determines the other and they have the same rank. By definition this is the rank of the series $f(z)$.

Recurrences. The B-regular series satisfy linear recurrences and the best way to find them is to use their Hankel matrices [5]. For the sake of simplicity, we assume the ring is a field $\mathbb{K}$.

The Hankel matrix of a series $f(z)$ is an infinite matrix whose rows are indexed by the integers and columns are indexed by the words in $\mathcal{X}_B^*$. The columns of the matrix are simply the sequences (f_n), (f_{Bn}), (f_{Bn+1}), $\ldots$, (f_{Bn+B-1}), $(f_{B^2 n})$, $\ldots$, if we arrange the words according to their length and lexicographic order.

Definition 3. The Hankel matrix of $f(z) \in \mathbb{K}[[z]]$ is an infinite matrix of type $\mathbb{N} \times \mathcal{X}^*$. The coefficient $H_{n,w}$ of that matrix is $f_{B^k n + r}$ if w has length k and r is the value of w for radix B.

Clearly a series is B-regular if and only if its Hankel matrix has finite rank. Moreover searching for relations between the columns of the matrix gives us recurrence relations.

Example 3. The van der Corput's sequence associates to an integer n with binary expansion $\epsilon_\ell \ldots \epsilon_0$ the rational number $v_n = \epsilon_0/2 + \epsilon_1/4 + \cdots + \epsilon_\ell/2^{\ell+1}$. It is 2-regular with rank 2 for it satisfies the recurrence

$$v_{2n} = v_n/2, \quad v_{2n+1} = 1/2 + v_n/2 \quad (n \geq 0) .$$

Its Hankel matrix begins with

$$\begin{pmatrix} 0 & 0 & 1/2 & 0 & 1/2 & 1/4 & 3/4 \\ 1/2 & 1/4 & 3/4 & 1/8 & 5/8 & 3/8 & 7/8 \\ 1/4 & 1/8 & 5/8 & 1/16 & 9/16 & 5/16 & 13/16 \\ 3/4 & 3/8 & 7/8 & 3/16 & 11/16 & 7/16 & 15/16 \\ 1/8 & 1/16 & 9/16 & 1/32 & 17/32 & 9/32 & 25/32 \\ 5/8 & 5/16 & 13/16 & 5/32 & 21/32 & 13/32 & 29/32 \\ 3/8 & 3/16 & 11/16 & 3/32 & 19/32 & 11/32 & 27/32 \\ 7/8 & 7/16 & 15/16 & 7/32 & 23/32 & 15/32 & 31/32 \end{pmatrix} .$$

The two columns with indices ε and x_1 (the first and the third) are independents. Expressing the columns with indices x_0, $x_0 x_1$ and $x_1 x_1$ according to these, we obtain the relations

$$\begin{cases} v_{2n} &= v_n/2 , \\ v_{4n+1} &= -v_n/4 + v_{2n+1} , \\ v_{4n+3} &= -v_n/2 + 3 v_{2n+1}/2 , \end{cases}$$

which are easy to verify in this case. What we want to emphasize is the shape of these relations and a picture will be clearer than a long comment (see Figure 1).

461

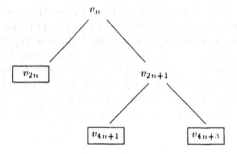

Fig. 1. The leaves of the tree give the shape of the recurrence relations.

This example epitomises the existence of a basis composed with sections $S_w f(z)$, such that the w are the addresses of the internal nodes of a B-ary tree. Furthermore to the leaves of the tree there correspond the recurrence relations; all the recurrences which express linear dependence between the sections are deduced from these [12].

Condensation. If $f(z)$ is B-regular and S is the associated rational series with support in $\mathcal{N} = \varepsilon + \mathcal{X}_+\mathcal{X}^*$, the commutative image [13, p. 147] is a rational series. We call it the condensate of $f(z)$ because it is simply

$$K f(t) = f_0 + \sum_{l \geq 1} \left(\sum_{B^{l-1} \leq n < B^l} f_n \right) t^l .$$

The condensation is useful for regular series just as density is for a regular language.

Example 4. The Taylor series of the logarithm is not B-regular for all B. The condensate of the series

$$\frac{1}{z} \ln \frac{1}{1-z} = \sum_{n \geq 0} \frac{z^n}{n+1}$$

is

$$F(t) = 1 + \sum_{l \geq 1} (H_{B^l} - H_{B^{l-1}}) t^l ,$$

with H_n the n-th harmonic number. Using the equality

$$H_{B^l} - H_{B^{l-1}} \underset{l \to +\infty}{=} \ln B + o(1)$$

and the transcendence of $\ln B$, we see that $F(t)$ is not rational, hence the conclusion.

Closure. The closure properties of rational series show immediately that the set of B-regular series is a module left stable by Hadamard product. Besides, the Cauchy product of two B-regular series is B-regular (assuming that the ring is Noetherian) and a rational function is B-regular if and only if its poles are roots of unity (here we suppose the ring is a field). These properties have been etablished directly by Allouche and Shallit [2], using computation on sequences.

For the sake of simplicity we assume that we use a field in the next theorem.

Theorem 4 (Closure theorem). *A rational function is B-regular if and only if its poles are roots of unity. The set of B-regular series is closed under*
— *linear combination,*
— *Hadamard product (term by term product),*
— *Cauchy product (function product),*
— *derivation.*

Example 5. Greene and Knuth [11, pp. 25–28] consider the sequence $f(n)$ defined by

$$f(n) = 1 + \min_i \left\{ \frac{i-1}{n} f(i-1) + \frac{n-i}{n} f(n-i) \right\},$$

which is relative to the search of an integer between 1 and n. The sequence $g(n) = nf(n)$ has second order difference given by

$$\Delta^2 g(n) = \begin{cases} 2 & \text{if } n \text{ is a power of 2} \\ 1 & \text{if } n \text{ is even but not a power of 2} \\ -1 & \text{if } n \text{ odd.} \end{cases}$$

Hence the generating series $g(z)$ is given by

$$g(z) = \frac{1}{(1-z)^2} \left(\frac{1}{1+z} + \sum_{k \geq 0} z^{2^k} \right)$$

and $g(z)$ is 2-regular as sum and product of 2-regular series.

Clearly the subject is not exhausted (we did not speak of Fatou lemma, of properties of coefficients, of decidability questions, *etc*).

2 Mahlerian Series and B-regular Series

As we want to extend the theorem of Christol *et alii* about automatic sequences, we recall at first the subject. Next we establish a general criterion and finally we apply the criterion to four cases:

1. a common case which is very useful because almost all divide-and-conquer recurrences are concerned,
2. the finite field case where we get back the theorem of Christol *et alii*,
3. the modular case, which provides examples where the ring is not an integral domain,
4. the algebraically closed field case, which completes the first case because it permits us to treat more complicated examples.

Let us recall the definition of a B-automatic sequence with values in a set $\mathcal{A}$. First a B-machine is a finite set of states, $\mathcal{S}$, with a distinguished initial state, i, and equipped with transitions $s \mapsto \epsilon.s$ ($0 \leq \epsilon < B$) from $\mathcal{S}$ into itself. Next we adjoin to this B-machine an application π from $\mathcal{S}$ into $\mathcal{A}$ and so we have a B-automaton. Finally for each integer n, we write its B-ary expansion $\epsilon_\ell \cdots \epsilon_0$ and we compute the state $s = \epsilon_\ell. \cdots .\epsilon_1.\epsilon_0.i$ by going through the automaton from the state i according to the digits of n. The value of the sequence for n is $\pi(s)$.

Clearly the B-automatic sequences with values in a ring are B-regular sequences. The matrices of the transitions, the initial state and the output application provide a linear representation. Conversely a B-regular sequence which takes only a finite number of values is B-automatic.

The theorem under consideration is the next one and has given rise to an extended literature [1, 7].

Theorem 5 (Christol, Kamae, Mendès France, Rauzy). *The generating series of q-automatic sequences with values in the finite field $\mathbb{F}_q$ are exactly the series algebraic over the field $\mathbb{F}_q(z)$ of rational functions.*

This theorem is based on the equality $f(z^q) = f(z)^q$ for a formal series with coefficients in $\mathbb{F}_q$ and this is the reason why algebraic series are in question. In fact the equations which come naturally in light in this situation are Mahlerian equations.

Definition 6. A Mahlerian equation is a functional equation of the form

$$c_0(z) f(z) + c_1(z) f(z^B) + \cdots + c_N(z) f(z^{B^N}) = b(z) \; ,$$

where $c_0(z)$, ..., $c_N(z)$ are polynomials. A Mahlerian series is a power series which satisfies a non trivial homogeneous Mahlerian equation.

Our purpose is to extend the theorem to regular series and to separate the radix B and the characteristic m of the ring we use. We show first that every B-regular series is B-mahlerian, at least when the ring is a field. Next we give some criteria which focus on the coefficient $c_0(z)$ and ensure that a solution of the equation is B-regular.

Minimal Equation. Let us assume that the ring is a field $\mathbb{K}$. In this case one can develop an arithmetic for the ring of operators $\mathbb{K}[z, M]$, where M refer to the Mahler operator $f(z) \mapsto f(z^B)$. Precisely there is a Euclidean left division, which causes the left ideals to be principal and every Mahlerian series posesses a minimal homogeneous equation [8].

The proof given by Allouche [1] to etablish that a q-automatic series over $\mathbb{F}_q$ is algebraic remains adequate to show that a B-regular series is B-mahlerian. Moreover it often gives a minimal equation for the series if one uses carefully a linear representation of the series. The idea is just to express $f(z)$, $f(z^B)$, etc in the basis corresponding to the representation and it leads to an effective method of computation.

Example 6. The series $o(z) = \prod_{k \geq 0} \left(1 + 2\, z^{2^k}\right)$ gives the number of odd coefficients in a row of Pascal's triangle [2, ex. 14] [14, seq. 109] [15]. Consequently the complementary series $e(z) = \dfrac{1}{(1-z)^2} - o(z)$ gives the number of even coefficients in a row. This series is 2-regular with rank 3 and a representation is

$$A_0 = \begin{pmatrix} 0 & -2 & -4 \\ 1 & 3 & 4 \\ 0 & 0 & 1 \end{pmatrix}, \quad A_1 = \begin{pmatrix} 2 & 0 & 0 \\ 0 & 0 & -2 \\ 0 & 1 & 3 \end{pmatrix}, \quad \begin{aligned} \lambda &= (\, 0 \;\; 0 \;\; 1 \,) \;, \\ \gamma &= (\, 1 \;\; 0 \;\; 0 \,)^T. \end{aligned}$$

The algorithm gives the equation

$$z^2 e(z) - \left(3z^2 - z + 1\right)\left(z^2 + z + 1\right)e(z^2)$$

$$+ \left(3 + 4z^2 + 11z^4 + 2z^8 + 6z^6\right)e(z^4) - 2\left(2z^4 + 1\right)\left(1 + z^4\right)^2 e(z^8) = 0 .$$

In fact the minimal equation, which is the lcm of the minimal equations for $1/(1-z)^2$ and $o(z)$, is

$$z^2 e(z) - [(1 + z^2)^2 + z^2(1 + 2z)]e(z^2) + (1 + z^2)^2(1 + 2z^2)e(z^4) = 0 .$$

Another proof, most in the spirit of this paper, consists in introducing the B-rational operators

$$F = \sum_{k \geq 0} c_k(z) M^k \in \mathbb{K}[[z, M]] ,$$

which are the images of the rational series S with support in $\mathcal{N} = \varepsilon + \mathcal{X}_+\mathcal{X}^*$ by the anti-morphism which associates to the letter x_r the operator $z^r M$. They are the natural intermediate between the rational series and the B-regular series, since every B-regular series is the value of a rational operator at the series 1. Using the closure properties of rational series and the arithmetic of operators, it is not difficult to prove that every B-rational operator satisfies an equality $QF = P$ where Q and P are two members of $\mathbb{K}[z, M]$ with the constraint $Q \neq 0$ and $\omega_M(Q) = 0$ (Q is a polynomial with respect to z and M and $\omega_M(Q)$ is the valuation of Q according to M). Now if $f(z)$ is a B-regular series it is written $f(z) = F.1$ where F is a rational operator; taking for Q a denominator of F, we have $Qf(z) = P.1$ hence a Mahlerian equation where the second member is a polynomial; it is not difficult to render it homogeneous.

General Criterion. For the rest of the paper we study the converse of the preceding property and we give first a general criterion to ensure that the solutions of a Mahlerian equation are B-regular.

Let us consider a Mahlerian equation

$$c_0(z)f(z) + c_1(z)f(z^B) + \cdots + c_N(z)f(z^{B^N}) = b(z)$$

where $b(z)$ is a B-regular series. We assume that the ring $\mathbb{A}$ is Noetherian and the coefficient of lowest degree in $c_0(z)$ is inversible in $\mathbb{A}$: we have $c_0(z) = Cz^\gamma g(z)$ with C inversible, γ a non negative integer and $g(0) = 1$. These constraints are normally fulfilled but we need to add the main condition: the set of the sections

$$S_{r_K} \cdots S_{r_1}\left(\frac{1}{g(z^{B^{K-1}}) \cdots g(z^B)g(z)}\right) = S_{r_K}\frac{1}{g}\left(S_{r_{K-1}}\frac{1}{g}\left(\cdots S_{r_1}\left(\frac{1}{g}\right)\right)\right),$$

where $K \geq 0$, $0 \leq r_k < B$ for $k = 1, \cdots, K$, is contained in a module of finite type. With these hypotheses a solution $f(z)$ of the equation is B-regular.

As we impose a condition only on coefficient c_0 and nothing on $c_1, \ldots, c_N$, there is no hope to find a necessary and sufficient condition. Nevertheless the hypothesis about the set of sections which appears in the criterion is exactly the condition which ensures that the Mahlerian infinite product

$$f(z) = \prod_{k \geq 0} \frac{1}{g(z^{B^k})}$$

is B-regular.

Common Case. If $g(z) = 1$, the main condition vanishes and we have an easy criterion to recognize a B-regular series. The case contains almost all the divide-and-conquer recurrences and in view of its importance, we extend the result to study vector of series instead of series. This permits us to treat sequences which admits a definition by case according to the residue modulo a power of B, say B^{k+1}, which expresses $B^{k+1}n + r$ according to the $B^l n + s$ with $0 \le l \le k$. The next assertion uses a natural extension of B-regularity to vector of series.

Theorem 7 (Common case). *We consider a vector of series*

$$F(z) = (\ f_1(z) \ \ldots \ f_d(z)\ )^T$$

and we assume the following hypothesis:
— *the ring is Noetherian,*
— *the vector of series satisfies an equation*

$$z^\gamma F(z) + \sum_{k=1}^N C_k(z) F(z^{B^k}) = B(z)$$

where $\gamma \ge 0$, $C_1(z)$, ..., $C_N(z)$ are some square matrices of polynomials and $B(z)$ is a column matrix whose components are B-regular series.

With these conditions, the components of $F(z)$ are B-regular series.

Example 7. Supowit and Reingold [16] encountered the sequence (C_n) defined by the recurrence

$$\begin{cases} C_{4n} &= a(C_{2n+1} + C_{2n-1}) + b \\ C_{4n+1} &= a(C_{2n+1} + C_{2n}) \\ C_{4n+2} &= a(C_{2n+1} + C_{2n+1}) + b \\ C_{4n+3} &= a(C_{2n+2} + C_{2n+1}) \end{cases}$$

for $n \ge 1$ and the initial conditions $C_0 = C_1 = 0$, $C_2 = b$, $C_3 = ab$, with $a = 1/\sqrt{2}$ and $b = \sqrt{3}$. The number b is only a scale factor and with a division by b we may suppose $b = 1$.

We call $f(z)$ the generating series of (C_n) and we refer to the section $S_w f(z)$ as $f_w(z)$. The recurrence gives us the system

$$\begin{cases} f_{00}(z) &= a(1+z)f_1(z) + 1/(1-z) \\ f_{01}(z) &= af_1(z) + af_0(z) \\ f_{10}(z) &= 2af_1(z) + 1/(1-z) \\ f_{11}(z) &= af_0(z)/z + af_1(z)\ . \end{cases}$$

If we express $f_0(z)$ and $f_1(z)$ with respect to $f_{00}(z)$, $f_{01}(z)$, $f_{10}(z)$ and $f_{11}(z)$ as $f_e(z) = f_{0e}(z^2) + z f_{1e}(z^2)$, we obtain an equation

$$F(z) = a\,C_1(z)F(z^2) + B(z)$$

in which the unknown is the vector $F(z) = (\ f_{00}(z)\ \ f_{01}(z)\ \ f_{10}(z)\ \ f_{11}(z)\ )^T$ and the coefficients are given by

$$C_1(z) = \begin{pmatrix} 0 & 1+z & 0 & z(1+z) \\ 1 & 1 & z & z \\ 0 & 2 & 0 & 2z \\ 1/z & 1 & 1 & z \end{pmatrix}, \qquad B(z) = \begin{pmatrix} 1/(1-z) \\ 0 \\ 1/(1-z) \\ 0 \end{pmatrix}.$$

In accordance with our result, we may assert that $F(z)$ and hence $f(z)$ is 2-regular.

Finite Fields and Rings. Let $p(z) \in \mathbb{A}[z]$ be a polynomial such that $p(0) = 1$. We say that T is the period of $p(z)$ if the sequence of coefficients of the formal power series $1/p(z)$ is periodic with period T. The study of the period [4] of

$$g(z^{B^{K-1}}) \cdots g(z^B)g(z)$$

provide us with cases in which we can guarantee that the main condition is satisfied.

Theorem 8 (Finite field). *Let a formal series $f(z)$ have coefficients in the field $\mathbb{F}_q$ with characteristic p and satisfy a Mahlerian equation whose right-hand side is B-automatic*

$$c_0(z)\, f(z) + c_1(z)\, f(z^B) + \cdots + c_N(z)\, f(z^{B^N}) = b(z) \ .$$

We assume that $c_0(z) = C\, z^\gamma g(z)$ with $\gamma \geq 0$, $g(0) = 1$. If p divides B or if the period T of $g(z)$ and the radix B have a common prime divisor, other than the characteristic p, then $f(z)$ is B-automatic.

It is worth noting that $g(z)$ does not matter in the first condition about B. This case extends directly the theorem of Christol, Kamae, Mendès France and Rauzy.

Example 8. The polynomial $g(z) = 1 + z^2 + z^3$, which lies in $\mathbb{F}_2[z]$, is 7-periodic. Hence a formal series $f(z) \in \mathbb{F}_4[[z]]$ which satisfies a Mahlerian equation of the shape

$$z^{1993}(1 + z^2 + z^3)f(z) + c_1(z)f(z^{21}) + c_2(z)f(z^{441}) = 0$$

is 21-regular. (Here $p = 2$, $q = 4$, $T = 7$ and $B = 21$.)

Starting from these results for the fields $\mathbb{F}_p$, it is not difficult to attain the quotient rings $\mathbb{Z}/(p^a)$. In fact if $g(z)$ has period t modulo p^a, it has period pt modulo p^{a+1}. Next the chinese remainder theorem permits us to consider rings $\mathbb{Z}/(m)$.

Theorem 9 (Modular case). *Let $f(z) \in \mathbb{Z}/(m)[[z]]$ be a formal series which satisfies*

$$c_0(z)f(z) + c_1(z)f(z^B) + \cdots + c_N(z)f(z^{B^N}) = b(z)$$

with right-hand side $b(z)$ B-automatic, $c_0(z) = C\, z^\gamma g(z)$, C invertible, $\gamma \geq 0$ and $g(0) = 1$. We assume that for every prime divisor p of m, one of the next two conditions is satisfied: i) p divides B, or ii) there exists a prime number p' which is different from p and divides both the radix B and the period $T(g,p)$ of $g(z)$ reduced modulo p. Then $f(z)$ is B-automatic.

Example 9. Let us consider the integer sequence (u_n) defined by the initial conditions $u_0 = 0$, $u_1 = 1$ and the recurrence relation

$$u_n = u_{n-1} + u_{n-2} + u_{\lfloor n/2 \rfloor} \ .$$

Clearly u_n is greater than the Fibonacci number F_{n-1} and the generating series

$$u(z) = z + 2\,z^2 + 4\,z^3 + 8\,z^4 + 14\,z^5 + 26\,z^6 + 44\,z^7 + 78\,z^8 + \cdots$$

is not 2-regular because its coefficients grow too rapidly. Nevertheless it is 2-regular when we reduce it modulo every integer. It suffices to look at the primary numbers p^a. If $p = 2$ the result is immediatly obtained for p equals B. Otherwise it suffices to remark that the period of $1 - z - z^2$ modulo an odd prime is even, because the Mahlerian equation which is to be considered is

$$(1 - z - z^2)u(z) - (1 + z)u(z^2) = z \ .$$

Example 10. A B-ary partition is an integer partition in which the parts are power of B. As an illustration there are nine 3-partitions of 16, namely 1^{16}, $1^{13}3$, $1^{10}3^2$, 1^73^3, 1^43^4, 13^5, 1^79, $1^43\,9$, 13^29 (we use the classical notation: 13^29 refers to $1 + 3 + 3 + 9$). The generating function of the number of B-ary partition is [3, p. 161]

$$p(z) = \prod_{k=0}^{+\infty} \frac{1}{1 - z^{B^k}}$$

and it satisfies the Mahlerian equation

$$(1 - z)p(z) = p(z^B) \ .$$

Because the period of $g(z) = 1 - z$ is 1 modulo every integer, we cannot use the second condition of our theorem, but the first one shows that $p(z)$ is B-regular if we reduce it modulo m and every prime divisor of m divides B. As an example the number of binary partition reduced modulo 8 may be defined by the 2-automaton

$$A_0 = \begin{pmatrix} 0 & 0 & 0 & 0 & 0 & 0 & 0 \\ 1 & 0 & 0 & 0 & 0 & 0 & 0 \\ 0 & 1 & 0 & 0 & 0 & 1 & 0 \\ 0 & 0 & 0 & 1 & 0 & 0 & 0 \\ 0 & 0 & 0 & 0 & 1 & 0 & 0 \\ 0 & 0 & 1 & 0 & 0 & 0 & 0 \\ 0 & 0 & 0 & 0 & 0 & 0 & 1 \end{pmatrix}, \quad A_1 = \begin{pmatrix} 0 & 0 & 0 & 0 & 0 & 0 & 0 \\ 1 & 0 & 0 & 0 & 0 & 0 & 0 \\ 0 & 0 & 0 & 0 & 0 & 0 & 0 \\ 0 & 0 & 1 & 1 & 0 & 0 & 0 \\ 0 & 1 & 0 & 0 & 0 & 1 & 1 \\ 0 & 0 & 0 & 0 & 0 & 0 & 0 \\ 0 & 0 & 0 & 0 & 1 & 0 & 0 \end{pmatrix},$$

$$\lambda = (\,1 \ 1 \ 0 \ 4 \ 2 \ 0 \ 6\,), \quad \gamma = (\,1 \ 0 \ 0 \ 0 \ 0 \ 0 \ 0\,)^T\,.$$

Algebraically Closed Field. Finally we apply our criterion to algebraically closed fields. Here the trick to obtain the main condition is to impose that

$$S_{r_K} \cdots S_{r_1} \left(\frac{1}{g(z^{B^{K-1}}) \cdots g(z^B)g(z)} \right)$$

have poles in a finite set with bounded multiplicities. This guarantees that they lie in a vector space of finite dimension. We obtain the following theorem.

Theorem 10 (Algebraically closed field). *Let* $f(z)$ *be a formal series with coefficients in an algebraically closed field. We assume that* $f(z)$ *satisfies a Mahlerian equation*

$$c_0(z)f(z) + c_1(z)f(z^B) + \cdots + c_N(z)f(z^{B^N}) = b(z)$$

in which $b(z)$ *is B-regular,* $c_0(z) = C z^\gamma g(z)$ *with* $C \neq 0$, $\gamma \geq 0$ *and* $g(0) = 1$. *If all the roots of* $g(z)$ *are roots of unity with an order (in the sense of group theory) which is not prime relative to B, then* $f(z)$ *is B-regular.*

Example 11. Let us consider the integer sequence (u_n) defined by $u_0 = 0$, $u_1 = 1$ and the recurrence

$$u_n = u_{n-1} - u_{n-2} + u_{\lfloor n/3 \rfloor} \quad (n \geq 2) \ .$$

Its generating function $u(z)$ is the solution of

$$(1 - z + z^2)u(z) - u(z^3) = z \ .$$

The roots of $1 - z + z^2$ are the primitive 6-th roots of unity, hence $u(z)$ is 3-regular. Besides its rank is 3. Moreover it is 3-automatic according to the equality

$$u(z) = (1 + z) \sum_{k,l \geq 0} (-1)^l z^{3^k(3l+1)} \ .$$

Acknowledgement. This work was (partially) supported by the ESPRIT Basic Research Action Nr. 7141 (ALCOM II).

References

1. J.-P. Allouche. Automates finis en théorie des nombres. *Expositiones Mathematicae*, 5:239–266, 1987.
2. J.-P. Allouche and J. Shallit. The ring of k-regular sequences. *Theoretical Computer Science*, 98:163–197, 1992.
3. G. E. Andrews. *The Theory of Partitions*, volume 2 of *Encyclopedia of Mathematics and its Applications*. Addison–Wesley, 1976.
4. E. R. Berlekamp. *Algebraic Coding Theory*. Mc Graw-Hill, revised 1984 edition, 1968.
5. J. Berstel and Ch. Reutenauer. *Rational series and their languages*, volume 12 of *EATCS monographs on theoretical computer science*. Springer, 1988.
6. G. Christol, T. Kamae, M. Mendès France, and G. Rauzy. Suites algébriques, automates et substitutions. *Bulletin de la Société Mathématique de France*, 108:401–419, 1980.
7. M. Dekking, M. Mendès France, and A. Van der Poorten. Folds! *Mathematical Intelligencer*, 4:130–138, 173–181, 190–195, 1982.
8. Philippe Dumas. *Récurrences Mahlériennes, suites automatiques, et études asymptotiques*. Doctorat de mathématiques, Université de Bordeaux I, 1993.
9. Philippe Flajolet and Mordecai Golin. Exact asymptotics of divide–and–conquer recurrences. Proceedings of ICALP'93, Lund., July 1993. This volume.
10. Philippe Flajolet, Peter Grabner, Peter Kirschenhofer, Helmut Prodinger, and Robert Tichy. Mellin transforms and asymptotics: Digital sums, July 1991. 23 pages. INRIA Research Report. Accepted for publication in *Theoretical Computer Science*.
11. D. H. Greene and D. E. Knuth. *Mathematics for the analysis of algorithms*. Birkhauser, Boston, 1981.
12. Ch. Reutenauer. Séries rationnelles et algèbres syntactiques. Master's thesis, Université Pierre et Marie Curie (Paris VI), 1980.
13. A. Salomaa and M. Soittola. *Automata-Theoretic Aspects of Formal Power Series*. Springer, Berlin, 1978.
14. N. J. A. Sloane. *A Handbook of Integer Sequences*. Academic Press, 1973.
15. Kenneth B. Stolarsky. Power and exponential sums of digital sums related to binomial coefficients. *SIAM Journal on Applied Mathematics*, 32(4):717–730, 1977.
16. K. J. Supowit and E. M. Reingold. Divide and conquer heuristics for minimum weighted Euclidean matching. *SIAM Journal on Computing*, 12(1):118–143, February 1983.

Products of Finite State Machines with Full Coverage

David M. Cohen[1] and Michael L. Fredman[2] *

[1] Bellcore
[2] Rutgers and UCSD

Abstract. Given a collection of finite state machines, $\{M_i\}$, with the same input alphabet, let M be the product machine, $M = \prod M_j$. In general, not every state in M is reachable. A natural question is whether there are any inherent limits to the number of reachable states in a system that is the product of many small finite state machines. This note constructs a family of product machines M where the number of states is *doubly* exponential in the number of states in any individual machine M_i and *every* product state is reachable.

Products of finite state machines such as discussed in this note occur when analyzing large collections of independently designed telecommunications services. These examples raise the possibility that product finite state machines modeling systems of independently designed services may have different characteristics from finite state machines modeling communications protocols. Consequently, analyzing collections of telecommunications services may require new heuristic methods.

1 Introduction

Given a collection of finite state machines, $\{M_i\}$, with the same input alphabet, let M be the product machine, $M = \prod M_j$. In general, not every state in M is reachable. A natural question is whether there are any inherent limits to the number of reachable states in a system that is the product of many small finite state machines. This note constructs a family of product machines M where the number of states is *doubly* exponential in the number of states in any individual machine M_i and *every* product state is reachable.

Products of finite state machines such as discussed in this note arise when analyzing large collections of independently designed telecommunications services. Analyzing them is of growing importance as telecommunications networks become increasingly sophisticated [4] [2]. Communications protocols have long been modeled as finite state machines and many heuristics exist to analyze them. One might hope to apply the same sorts of heuristics when analyzing collections of telecommunications services. However, a communications protocol usually imposes system-wide invariants that limit the reachable states, e.g. the sequence number of the last message sent is within a small constant of the sequence number of the last message acknowledged. A protocol's reachable state space is thus

* Supported by NSF Grant CCR-9008072.

often much smaller than its potential (Holzmann, page 225, [6]). Several heuristics used to analyze communications protocols rely on the reachable state space either being small or enjoying certain structural properties [6] [1]. The product machine examples constructed in this note, however, have large reachable state spaces. Moreover, except for Monte Carlo simulation, the sorts of heuristics that have been used successfully to analyze communications protocols have not performed successfully on our examples [3]. Consequently, analyzing collections of telecommunications services may require new heuristic methods.

2 General model

Let M_j be a family of finite state machines with the input alphabet $\{1, 0\}$. Let ϕ_j be the transition function for M_j, $\phi_j : \{0, 1\} \times M_j \to M_j$. The product machine $M = \prod M_j$ is defined as follows:

1. the set of states is the Cartesian product of the M_j
2. the input alphabet is $\{1, 0\}$
3. the transition function is defined:

$$\phi(i, x_1, \ldots, x_n) \mapsto (\phi_1(i, x_1), \ldots, \phi_n(i, x_n))$$

If there are n machines in the family M_j and each M_j has N states, then M has N^n potential states. The number of possible machines of size N is exponential in N, so that the number of states in the product machine can be doubly exponential in N. Are there such examples where every state is reachable?

In the general situation, local conditions can prevent a product state from being reached. For example, suppose we have machines A and B such that the mappings $x \mapsto \phi_A(0, x)$ and $y \mapsto \phi_B(1, y)$ aren't permutations of A and B. Then there are states $a \in A$ and $b \in B$ such that

$$\forall x \in A, \quad \phi_A(0, x) \neq a$$
$$\forall y \in B, \quad \phi_B(1, y) \neq b$$

If the most recent input is 0 then A isn't in state a, and if the input is 1 then B isn't in state b. Thus, the product state $a \times b$ in $A \times B$ isn't reachable.

Using the Chinese Remainder Theorem it is easy to construct product machines where every state is reachable but the number of states in such a machine is a single exponential in N. This note uses the theory of permutation groups to construct examples of product machines where every state is reachable and the number of factors is exponential in N, so that the number of of states is doubly exponential in N.

3 Full Coverage

Let p be a fixed odd prime, such that $p \neq 3, 11$, or 23 and $p \neq (q^k - 1)/(q - 1)$ for any prime q. We will construct a family of finite state machines, M_i, such that

- each machine M_i has p states,
- the number of machines in the family is exponential in p,
- every state in the product machine $M = \prod M_i$ is reachable.

Since there are an exponential number of machines in the family, the product machine, M, has a doubly exponential number of states, each of which is reachable.

The construction uses permutation groups. If T is a set, let $Sym(T)$ be the group of permutations on T and let $Alt(T)$ be the alternating subgroup of $Sym(T)$, i.e. the group of all even permutations. For a positive integer n, we let $[n]$ denote $\{1, ..., n\}$ and we let $Sym(n)$ and $Alt(n)$ denote $Sym([n])$ and $Alt([n])$ respectively. If G is a group of permutations of a set T, then the degree of G is the cardinality of T. Recall that a group G acts doubly transitive on T if and only if the subgroup of G that fixes any element x, i.e. the subgroup $\{g \mid g(x) = x\}$, acts transitively on T.

Let $S = \{1, ..., p\}$ be a set with p elements. Given two permutations s and t on S, define a finite state machine $M(s, t)$ as follows. The set of states is S, the input alphabet is $\{0, 1\}$, and the transitions in the state x for the inputs 1 and 0 are given by:

$$1 : x \mapsto s(x)$$
$$0 : x \mapsto t(x)$$

Since the actions of 1 and 0 on the set S defines a permutation of S, the action of any input string of 1's and 0's defines a permutation. Let F be the free group generated by the strings of 1's and 0's. Then the map $1 \mapsto s$ and $0 \mapsto t$ gives a homomorphism from F to $Sym(S)$.

The construction has two parts. We first show that for any fixed odd prime p, $p \neq 3, 11$, or 23 and $p \neq (q^k - 1)/(q - 1)$, there is a family Γ consisting of an exponential number of machines, $M(s, t)$, such that for each machine in Γ the subgroup of $Sym(S)$ generated by the actions of 1 and 0 on S is the alternating group. Secondly, we show that within this family the actions of F on the different machines are suitably independent so that we will be able to conclude that all states of the product machine M are reachable.

Throughout this paper, we describe a permutation π over S as being a cycle provided π consists of a single (full length) cycle with p elements.

Remark. The permutations s and t that will be chosen below to define the machines $M(s, t)$ will be cycles. Thus, for each word w in the free group F there is a string w' of 0's and 1's (free of inverses) whose action is equivalent to that of w. We obtain w' from w by replacing each exponent -1 with $p - 1$. Thus, all states of the product machine M are reachable via words consisting of 0's and 1's.

3.1 The action of F on S

We first show that the image of F is the alternating group. We need to establish some facts about permutation groups of prime degree.

Definition. Let $S = \{0, ..., p-1\}$ be the finite field of p elements, Z/p. Let L be the group of permutations of S of the form

$$L = \{x \mapsto cx + d \mid c, d \in S,\ c \neq 0\}.$$

Lemma 1. *Let t be the cycle $t : x \mapsto x + 1$ and let f be any relabeling of S such that the image of t under f is in L. Then $f(x) = ax + b$ for some a, b.*

Proof. Let t' be the image of t under the relabeling f. Thus, $t'(f(x)) = f(t(x))$. By assumption, $t' \in L$, so that it is given by $t' : x \mapsto cx + d$ for some c and d. Since t is a cycle, t' is also a cycle. If $c \neq 1$, then t' has the fixed point, $-d/(c-1)$. Since a cycle has no fixed point, $c = 1$. So $t' : x \mapsto x + d$, and therefore

$$f(x + 1) = f(t(x)) = t'(f(x)) = f(x) + d$$

It follows that

$$f(x) = d\,x + f(0)$$

$\square$

Observation. The proof of lemma 1 establishes the fact that all cycles t' in L have the form $t' : x \mapsto x + d$, and the number of such t' is $p - 1$.

Lemma 2. *Let t be the cycle $x \mapsto x+1$ and let f be a relabeling of S that takes t into L. Let s be an arbitrary permutation whose image s' under f is in L. Then $s \in L$.*

Proof. Since f takes t into an element of L, by Lemma 1 f has the form $f(x) = ax + b$. If under the relabeling f, the permutation s becomes $s' : x \mapsto cx + d$, then

$$a\,s(x) + b = f(s(x)) = s'(f(x)) = c\,f(x) + d = c(a\,x + b) + d$$

So $s(x) = cx + ((c-1)b + d)/a$, and hence $s \in L$. $\square$

Lemma 3. *The permutation group generated by the cycle $t : x \mapsto x + 1$ and any permutation s, $s \notin L$, is doubly transitive.*

Proof. A classical theorem of Burnside ([8] page 53) states that a transitive group of permutations on a set S of prime cardinality is either doubly transitive, or there is a relabeling of S, $f : S \to Z/p$, such that the image of the group under the relabeling is contained in L. By Lemma 2, if there is a relabeling f which takes the subgroup generated by t and s into L, then s itself is in L. So if s is not in L, then the group generated by s and t is doubly transitive. $\square$

Corollary. *The group generated by $x \mapsto x + 1$ and an arbitrary permutation s, $s \notin L$, is non-solvable.*

Proof. By a theorem of Huppert (Passman [8], page 253 and [7]), if G is a solvable doubly transitive permutation group on a set S of prime order then there is a relabeling of S such that G is contained in L. Let G be the group generated by s and t. By Lemma 3, it is doubly transitive. By Lemma 2, since s does not belong to L there is no relabeling f taking G into L. By Huppert's theorem, this implies that G is non-solvable. □

Corollary. *The group generated by any two cycles s and t of prime degree which do not commute is non-solvable.*

Proof. There is a labeling of S under which t', the image of t, is the cycle $x \mapsto x + 1$. Let s' be the image of S under this relabeling. Since s' is a cycle, if it were in L, it would have the form $s' : x \mapsto x + d$. Since all of these permutations commute with t', $s' \notin L$. Thus the group generated by t' and s' is non-solvable as is the group generated by s and t. □

Let $PSL(k, q)$ be the group of all k by k matrices over $GF(q)$ of determinant 1 modulo the subgroup of scalar matrices of determinant 1, i.e the projective special linear group. A consequence of the classification theorem for finite groups ([5] page 56) says that:

Theorem. *If G is a non-solvable doubly transitive permutation group of degree n which contains an n cycle, then one of the following holds (up to isomorphism):*

- G is either $Alt(n)$ or $Sym(n)$
- $n = 11$ and $G = PSL(2, 11)$, or G is the Mathieu group M_{11},
- $n = 23$ and G is the Mathieu group M_{23},
- $n = (q^k - 1)/(q - 1)$ for some prime power q and G is a subgroup of $Aut(PSL(k, q))$ containing $PSL(k, q)$

We now have the following:

Proposition. *Let p be a fixed odd prime, $p \neq 3, 11,$ or 23 and $p \neq (q^k - 1)/(q - 1)$, and let G be the subgroup of $Sym(p)$ generated either by two non-commuting cycles s and t or by the cycle $x \mapsto x + 1$ and an even permutation not in L, then G is the alternating group $Alt(S)$.*

Proof. By the corollaries and the Theorem, the subgroup G is isomorphic to either $Sym(n)$ or $Alt(n)$. Because s and t are even permutations, we conclude that G is the alternating group. □

3.2 Simultaneous action of F

We now consider the simultaneous action of F on several finite state machines. We want to show that the action is transitive. This is done in the following series of lemmas.

Let S be the finite field Z/p and fix t to be the permutation $x \mapsto x + 1$. For any permutation s, let ρ_s be the homomorphism from F to $Sym(S)$ given by $1 \mapsto t$ and $0 \mapsto s$. If s and r are any two permutations and $s = t^n r t^{-n}$ for some n, then for any sequence α of 1's and 0's, $\rho_s(\alpha) = t^n \rho_r(\alpha) t^{-n}$. Thus, for the respective kernels K_r and K_s of ρ_r and ρ_s, we have $K_r = K_s$. Now assume that s and r are two permutations not in L and that $s \neq t^n r t^{-n}$ for any n. We will first show that ρ_s and ρ_r are independent, i.e. that $K_r \neq K_s$. We then show that if we have such a set of pairwise independent maps, then all states of the product machine are reachable.

Lemma 4. *Let s and r be two different permutations such that $s \neq t^n r t^{-n}$ for any n, and such that images in $Sym(S)$ of ρ_s and ρ_r are the alternating group $Alt(S)$. Assume, moreover, that $|S| > 3$ and $|S| \neq 6$. Let K_s be the kernel of ρ_s and K_r the kernel of ρ_r. Then $K_s \neq K_r$.*

Proof. F/K_r is isomorphic to the group generated by r and t under the homomorphism ρ_r defined by $1 \mapsto t$ and $0 \mapsto r$. Since s and t generate $Alt(S)$, we conclude that F/K_r and $Alt(S)$ are isomorphic. Similarly we have an isomorphism $F/K_s \rightarrow Alt(S)$. If $K_r = K_s$, it follows that $r \mapsto s$ and $t \mapsto t$ induces an automorphism ρ of $Alt(S)$

It is well known ([9] page 314) that all automorphisms of $Alt(j)$ are inner provided $j > 3$ and $j \neq 6$. Consequently, $\rho(x) = uxu^{-1}$, for some permutation $u \in Sym(S)$. Since $\rho(t) = t$, $ut = tu$. Hence, $u(x + 1) = u(t(x)) = t(u(x)) = u(x) + 1$. Thus, $u = t^n$ for some n. Since $s = \rho(r)$, $s = t^n r t^{-n}$ contradicting the hypothesis of the lemma. Thus $K_r \neq K_s$. □

Observation. The relation ω between permutations defined by

$$\{(r, s) \mid s = t^n r t^{-n} \text{ for some integer } n\}$$

is an equivalence relation. The identity permutation and the cycles belonging to L each constitute singleton equivalence classes. All other equivalence classes have p permutations. Moreover, cycle structure is preserved within these classes. There are $((p - 1)! - (p - 1))/p$ classes consisting of cycles not belonging to L.

Lemma 5. *If A, B, and C are normal subgroups of a group G, such that $AC = BC = G$, and G/C is non-commutative. Then $A \cap B \not\subset C$.*

Proof. Let a be an arbitrary element of A and b an arbitrary element of B. Since A and B are normal, we have that $aba^{-1} \in B$, and $ba^{-1}b^{-1} \in A$. So

$$aba^{-1}b^{-1} \in A \bigcap B,$$

and we conclude $ab \equiv ba \pmod{A \cap B}$. Now suppose that $A \cap B \subset C$. Then $aba^{-1}b^{-1} \in C$, so $ab \equiv ba \pmod{C}$ for any $a \in A$ and $b \in B$. Since $AC = BC = G$, for any elements g and h in G we can find an element $a \in A$ and an element $b \in B$ such that $g \equiv a \pmod{C}$ and $h \equiv b \pmod{C}$. Thus $gh \equiv ab \equiv ba \equiv hg \pmod{C}$. This implies that G/C is commutative, contrary to assumption. □

Lemma 6. *If A, B, and C are normal subgroups of G and $AC = BC = G$ and G/C is non-commutative and simple, then $(A \cap B)C = G$.*

Proof. If G/C is non-commutative, then by lemma 5, $A \cap B \not\subset C$. Thus, $G' = (A \cap B)C$ is a normal subgroup of G and is not contained in C. Therefore, $G'/C = (A \cap B)C/C$ is a non-trivial normal subgroup of G/C.

Since G/C is simple, we conclude that $G'/C = G/C$, and therefore, $(A \cap B)C = G$. $\square$

Lemma 7. *Let $K_1, ..., K_n$ be a set of distinct normal subgroups such that each G/K_i is simple and non-commutative. Given any m subgroups, $K_{i_1} ... K_{i_m}$, and any K_j, $j \neq i_1, ..., i_m$, then*

$$(K_{i_1} \bigcap ... \bigcap K_{i_m})K_j = G.$$

Proof. By induction. First we consider the base case $m = 1$. Let $B = K_{i_1}$ and $C = K_j$. By assumption, B and C are distinct normal subgroups and G/B and G/C are simple. It follows that BC/C is a non-trivial normal subgroup of G/C and therefore, $BC = G$.

Now assume that $m > 1$ and the lemma is true for $m - 1$. Given any m subgroups $K_{i_1}, ... , K_{i_m}$ and a subgroup K_j, $j \neq i_1, ..., i_m$, let

$$A = K_{i_1} \bigcap ... \bigcap K_{i_{m-1}}$$
$$B = K_{i_m}$$
$$C = K_j$$

By the induction assumption applied to $K_{i_1}, ..., K_{i_{m-1}}$, and K_j, we have that $AC = G$. Similarly, $BC = G$. By lemma 6, we have that $(A \cap B)C = G$. This completes the induction step and the proof of the lemma. $\square$

Now let Γ denote the following family of machines $M(s,t)$. For each machine in the family t is given by $x \mapsto x + 1$. Next, consider the equivalence classes of ω consisting of p cycles, and choose Y to be a set of distinct representatives from these equivalence classes. The ensemble of cycles s defining the various machines $M(s,t)$ in Γ is given by Y. There are $((p-1)! - (p-1))/p$ machines in Γ.

Theorem. *et S be the field Z/p where p satisfies the restrictions stated in the Proposition of the previous Section. Let Γ denote the family of machines $M(s,t)$ defined above in terms of cycles s,t over S. Let M denote the product of the machines in Γ. Then every state of M is reachable.*

Proof. We will show that for any fixed component i and any state x in the product machine M, we can change the i-th component state x_i to an arbitrary state y_i while leaving the other components fixed. This implies that one can move from any product state x to any other product state y by moving along each component independently.

476

In order to change a specified component, we proceed to invoke lemma 7. The Proposition of the previous Section shows that the group generated by the actions of 0 and 1 for each machine $M(s,t)$ is the alternating group, which is simple and non-commutative. Lemma 4 shows that for distinct machines $M(s,t)$ the kernels in F of the respective homomorphisms are distinct. Choosing $G = F$ in lemma 7, we conclude that these kernels satisfy the hypothesis of Lemma 7.

Since the action of F on each individual machine $M(s,t)$ is transitive, there is a g in F such that $g(x_i) = y_i$. Let K_l denote the kernel corresponding to the machine of the l-th component, and let

$$H = \bigcap_{l \neq i} K_l$$

By Lemma 7, $F = HK_i$ so there is a decomposition $g = hk$ where $h \in H$ and $k \in K_i$. We now argue that h accomplishes the desired motion within M. Since k is in K_i, $k(x_i) = x_i$. Thus, $y_i = g(x_i) = hk(x_i) = h(x_i)$. Since h is in the intersection of the other kernels, h leaves the other components fixed and has the correct action on the i-th component. As remarked immediately preceding Section 3.1, there exists in F a string consisting of 0's and 1's, free of inverses, having the same effect as h. □

3.3 Summary

This note constructed examples of product machines where the number of product states is doubly exponential in the number of states in an individual machine and every product state is reachable.

Systems where every product state is reachable seem to be the exception as local conditions can prevent this from happening. However, while these local conditions prevent full coverage, they don't preclude having a doubly exponential number of reachable states. (As a trivial observation, starting with our construction, we can always add a new individual machine to the product which is isomorphic to one of the other machines. Full coverage of the new product state space is then precluded, but the size of the reachable state space remains unchanged, and hence doubly exponential.) We pose as an open problem how large the reachable state space is for products of random machines of a given size.

As noted in the Introduction, Monte Carlo simulation is one means for exploring the state space defined by the product machines constructed in this paper. Setting aside the fact that the state space is large, this approach would be additionally burdened if certain states are intrinsically hard to reach during the process of a random walk. Since the limiting distribution of the state space is readily shown to be uniform, particular states can be especially hard to reach only if the corresponding Markov chain fails to be rapidly mixing. We therefore pose as an open question whether our constructions, viewed as Markov chains, are rapidly mixing.

References

1. R. E. Bryant, Ordered Binary Decision Diagrams, ACM Computing Surveys, **24** (1992), 293-318.
2. E.J. Cameron,N. Griffeth, Y-J Lin, M. E. Nilson, W. Schnure, H. Velthuijsen, Towards a Feature Interaction Benchmark, to appear in IEEE Communications Magazine.
3. D. M. Cohen, Some Experiments Analyzing Flat Configurations of Finite State Machines, non-proprietary Bellcore Technical Memo, April 30 1992, TM-ARH-021362.
4. F. Dworak, T. Bowen, C. W. Chow, G. E. Herman, N. Griffeth, and Y-J Lin, Feature Interaction Problem in Telecommunication, Proceedings of the Seventh Int'l Conference on Software Engineering for Telecommunications Switching Systems, Bournemouth, UK, July 1989, pp 59 - 62.
5. D. Gorenstein, Finite Simple Groups: An Introduction to their Classification, Plenum Press, 1982.
6. G. J. Holzmann, Design and Validation of Computer Protocols, Prentice-Hall, 1991.
7. B. Huppert, Zweifach transitive auflosbare Permutationsgruppen, Mathematische Zeitschrift, **68** (1957), 126 - 150.
8. D. S. Passman, Permutation Groups, Benjamin, 1969.
9. W. R. Scott, Group Theory, Prentice-Hall, 1964.

AN EFFECTIVE VERSION OF STALLINGS' THEOREM IN THE CASE OF CONTEXT-FREE GROUPS

Géraud Sénizergues

LaBri
Université de Bordeaux I
351, Cours de la Libération 33405 Talence, France ** ***

Abstract. We give an algorithm producing from every p.d.a. $\mathcal{M}$ recognizing the word-problem for an infinite group G, a decomposition of G as an amalgamated product (with finite amalgamated subgroups) or as an HNN-extension (with finite associated subgroups).This algorithm has an elementary time-complexity.This result allows us to show that the isomorphism-problem for finitely generated virtually-free groups is primitive recursive,thus improving the decidability result of [Krstic,1989].

keywords: context-free groups, pushdown automata, Cayley graph, Thue-systems, complexity, graph of groups.

1 INTRODUCTION

1.1 Presentation of the result

Stallings theorem is a combinatorial group-theoretic theorem stating that every finitely generated group having at least two ends can be decomposed either as a non-trivial amalgamated product (with finite amalgamated subgroups) or as an HNN-extension (with finite associated subgroups) ([14], [5],[7]).

A context-free group is a group G defined by a presentation $< X; R >$ over a finite set X of generators, such that the word-problem for G on X can be solved by some pushdown automaton $\mathcal{M}$ (equivalently : such that the set of words $\{w \in (X \cup \overline{X})^* \mid w \xrightarrow{*}_R \epsilon\}$ is a context-free language)[1]. This class of groups is exactly the class of virtually-free groups ([10]) and is a strict sub-class of the class of automatic groups ([8]). It is known that every infinite c.f. group G has at least two ends ([10]), so that Stallings theorem applies on G.

** mailing adress:LaBri and UER Math-info, Université Bordeaux1
351 Cours de la libération -33405- Talence Cedex.
email:ges@geocub.greco-prog.fr
fax: 56-84-66-69
*** This work has been supported by the ESPRIT Basic Research Working Group "COMPUGRAPH II" and by the PRC MathInfo

In this paper we show that, given an effective description of G (i.e. a push-down automaton $\mathcal{M}$ recognising the word-problem on a finite alphabet of generators X) we can perform in five-fold exponential time the following task:

- compute the number of ends N_e of G (which may be $0, 2$ or ∞)
- in the case where $N_e \in \{2, \infty\}$, effectively decompose G as an amalgamated product (case 1) or as an HNN-extension (case 2) ;
- in case 1 compute finite sets of generators X_i for G_i (where $i \in \{1, 2\}$), pushdown automata $\mathcal{M}_i$ recognising the word-problem for G_i on X_i and finite subgroups K_i of G_i such that $G = < G_1 * G_2; K_1 = K_2 >$
- in case 2 compute a finite set of generators X_1 of a subgroup G_1, a p.d.a. $\mathcal{M}_1$ recognising the word-problem of G_1 on X_1, finite subgroups K_1, K_2 of G_1 and an element $t \in G - G_1$ such that $G = < G_1, t; t^{-1} K_1 t = K_2 >$.

The overall strategy for doing these computations is to follow the proof of Stallings theorem given in ([5], p41-56) and to make it constructive by using the p.d.a. $\mathcal{M}$. We use two kinds of arguments :

- "geometrical" arguments about the Cayley-graph of G (which strongly lean on the κ-triangulation property stated in [10] ;
- "language-theoretic" arguments about almost-invariant subsets of G or about left-stabilisers of almost-invariant subsets of G (they lean on a theorem of [3] concerning the right-linear rewriting systems defined in [4]).

1.2 Motivations

This algorithm is the first step of a work which aims to give an effective way to solve the following problems:

(P1) given a context-free group G, build a graph of groups (with finite vertex groups) admitting G as fundamental group (see definition p. 12 of [7])
(P2) given a context-free grammar which generates a group-language L defining a group G, build an equivalent NTS grammar G' generating L
(P3) given two c.f. groups G_1, G_2 (given by c.f. grammars) decide whether they are isomorphic.

The second step is done in [13] where we give an upper bound on the size of any minimal graph of groups admitting a given c.f. group G as its fundamental group; this bound is exponential with respect to the triangulation constant of the Cayley-graph of G. The present work shows that a solution to P1 can be computed in primitive recursive time from a description of G by an outer action of a finite group on a finitely generated free group (see the proof of theorem 17). Together with the second step it will show that P1 can be solved in primitive recursive time from a description of G by a pushdown automaton recognising its word-problem on some set of generators. Let us recall that P2 is solved in [2] by a construction which starts from a graph of groups with finite vertex groups, admitting G as its fundamental group. Problem P3 is solved in [9] by an algorithm working in exponential time from any "Culler's realizations" of G_1, G_2 (which can easily be deduced from their associated graphs of groups, see [9] p.123).

1.3 Organisation of the paper :

- in part 2 we recall some definitions and present our terminology concerning semi-Thue systems, automata, groups and graphs ;
- in part 3 we give the geometrical results concerning finite cocycles of the Cayley-graph of G and some consequences;
- in part 4 we give the language-theoretic results concerning right-linear rewriting systems and their consequences about almost-invariant subsets ;
- in part 5 we describe the whole decomposition algorithm, analyse its complexity and state the main results.

2 TERMINOLOGY and RECALLS

2.1 Semi-Thue systems

Let X be an alphabet. X^* is the free monoïd generated by X. ϵ denotes the empty string. A *semi-Thue system* S on X is a subset $S \subset X^* \times X^*$. The *one-step derivation* $\longrightarrow_S$ is defined for all strings $f, g \in X^*$ by : $f \longrightarrow_S g$ iff there exists $\alpha, \beta \in X^*$ and $(u,v) \in S$ such that $f = \alpha u \beta$ and $g = \alpha v \beta$. The *derivation-relation* $\overset{*}{\longrightarrow}_S$ is then the reflexive and transitive closure of $\longrightarrow_S$. $\longleftrightarrow_S$ denotes the symmetric closure of $\longrightarrow_S$ and $\overset{*}{\longleftrightarrow}_S$ is the reflexive and transitive closure of $\longleftrightarrow_S$. $\overset{*}{\longleftrightarrow}_S$ is the *congruence generated* by S. For every $w \in X^*$, by $[w]_{\overset{*}{\longleftrightarrow}_S}$ we denote the set $\{f \in X^* \mid w \overset{*}{\longleftrightarrow}_S f\}$. Similarly, the *one-step right-linear derivation* $\longrightarrow_{r,S}$ is defined for all strings $f, g \in X^*$ by: $f \longrightarrow_{r,S} g$ iff there exists $\alpha \in X^*$ and $(u,v) \in S$ such that $f = \alpha u$ and $g = \alpha v$. The *right-linear derivation* $\overset{*}{\longrightarrow}_{r,S}$ is then the reflexive and transitive closure of $\longrightarrow_{r,S}$ (this type of relation was originally defined in [4]).

2.2 Automata

A *finite automaton* on the alphabet X is a 5-tuple $\mathcal{B} = < X, Q, \delta, q_0, Q_+ >$ where Q is the finite set of states, $q_0 \in Q$ is the initial state, $Q_+ \subset Q$ is the set of terminal states and δ, the transition function, is a mapping : $\delta : Q \times X \to P(Q)$.

By $q \overset{f}{\longrightarrow}_\mathcal{B} q'$ we denote the fact that there exists some calculus of $\mathcal{B}$, starting with state q, reading f and reaching state q'.

A *pushdown automaton* on the alphabet X is a 6-tuple $\mathcal{A} = < X, Y, Q, \delta, q_0, y_0 >$ where Y is the finite stack-alphabet, Q is the finite set of states, $q_0 \in Q$ is the initial state, y_0 is the initial stack-symbol and δ, the transition function, is a mapping $\delta : YQ \times (X \cup \{\epsilon\}) \to \mathcal{P}(Y^*Q)$. Let $q, q' \in Q, \omega, \omega' \in Y^*, y \in Y, f \in X^*$

and $a \in X \cup \{\epsilon\}$; we note $(\omega yq, af) \longmapsto_{\mathcal{A}} (\omega\omega'q', f)$ if $\omega'q' \in \delta(yq, a)$. $\longmapsto_{\mathcal{A}}^{*}$ is the reflexive and transitive closure of $\longmapsto_{\mathcal{A}}$.

For every $\omega q, \omega'q' \in Y^*Q$ and $f \in X^*$, we note $\omega q \xrightarrow{f}_{\mathcal{A}} \omega'q'$ iff $(\omega q, f) \longmapsto_{\mathcal{A}}^{*}$ $(\omega'q', \epsilon)$.

$\mathcal{A}$ is said *deterministic* iff, for every $yq \in YQ$:

1. either $\mathrm{Card}(\delta(yq, \epsilon)) = 1$ and for every $a \in X$, $\mathrm{Card}\,(\delta(yq, a)) = 0$
2. or $\mathrm{Card}(\delta(yq, \epsilon)) = 0$ and for every $a \in X$, $\mathrm{Card}\,(\delta(yq, a)) \le 1$.

$\mathcal{A}$ is said *real-time* iff, for every $yq \in YQ$, $\mathrm{Card}(\delta(yq, \epsilon)) = 0$. Given some finite set $F \subseteq Y^*Q$ of configurations, the *language recognized by $\mathcal{A}$ with final configurations F* is

$$L(\mathcal{A}, F) = \{w \in X^* \mid \exists c \in F, y_0 q_0 \xrightarrow{f}_{\mathcal{A}} c\}$$

2.3 Groups

Presentations Let S be a semi-Thue system on X. $X^*/ \xleftrightarrow{*}_{S}$, is the set $\{[w]_{\xleftrightarrow{*}_{S}} \mid w \in X^*\}$. $X^*/ \xleftrightarrow{*}_{S}$ is naturally equipped with the associative composition law : $[w_1]_{\xleftrightarrow{*}_{S}}.[w_2]_{\xleftrightarrow{*}_{S}} = [w_1 w_2]_{\xleftrightarrow{*}_{S}}$, and admits the neutral element $[\epsilon]_{\xleftrightarrow{*}_{S}}$. Given a group G we say the pair $< X; S >$ (where S is a semi-Thue system on the alphabet X) is a *presentation of G* iff $G \approx X^*/ \xleftrightarrow{*}_{S}$ (i.e. G is isomorphic to $X^*/ \xleftrightarrow{*}_{S}$). A group G is said *context-free* iff there exists some finite alphabet Y and some semi-Thue system $S \subset Y^* \times Y^*$ such that $G \approx Y^*/ \xleftrightarrow{*}_{S}$ and $[\epsilon]_{\xleftrightarrow{*}_{S}}$ is a context-free language ([1]). Given such a presentation it is easy to modify it such that it takes the form : $Y = X \cup \overline{X}$ where $\overline{X}$ is an alphabet in one-to-one correspondance with X and for every $x \in X, (x\overline{x}, \epsilon) \in S$ and $(\overline{x}x, \epsilon) \in S$ (where $\overline{x}$ is the letter associated to x in the above one-to-one correspondance).

We then say that $< X \cup \overline{X}; S >$ is a *symmetric presentation*. Let us suppose that $G \approx (X \cup \overline{X})^*/ \xleftrightarrow{*}_{S}$ and

$$[\epsilon]_{\xleftrightarrow{*}_{S}} = L(\mathcal{M}, F)$$

(where $\mathcal{M}$ is a p.d.a. and F a finite set of configurations).
One can check that G is fully determined by $\mathcal{M}$ and F because $f \xleftrightarrow{*}_{S} g$ iff $f\tilde{\overline{g}} \in L(\mathcal{M}, F)$ (where $\overline{g}$ is the copy of g on $\overline{X}$ and $\tilde{\overline{g}}$ is the mirror image of $\overline{g}$).

Free product with amalgamation Let G_1, G_2 be groups admitting respectively the presentation $< X_1; R_1 >, < X_2; R_2 >$.Let $K_1 \subset G_1, K_2 \subset G_2$ be subgroups and $\varphi : K_1 \to K_2$ an isomorphism. Then the free product of G_1, G_2 amalgamating the subgroups K_1, K_2 by φ is defined by the presentation

$$< X_1 \cup X_2; R_1 \cup R_2; k = \varphi(k), k \in K_1 >$$

it will be noted

$$< G_1 * G_2; k = \varphi(k), k \in K_1 >$$

HNN-extensions (HNN stands for **H**ighman-**N**eumann- **N**eumann)

Let G be a group and K_1, K_2 be subgroups of G with $\varphi : K_1 \to K_2$ an isomorphism. If G admits the presentation $< X; R >$ then the HNN-extension of G, relative to K_1, K_2 and φ is the group $G_1 =< X \cup \{t, \bar{t}\}; R_1 >$ where $t, \bar{t}$ are new letters and R_1 is the semi-Thue system :

$$R_1 = R \cup \{(t\bar{t}, \epsilon), (\bar{t}t, \epsilon)\} \cup \{(\bar{t}k_1 t, \varphi(k_1)) \mid k_1 \in K_1\}$$

(in fact, in the above system R_1, k_1 denotes any word in X^* representing the element $k_1 \in K_1$)). For short we use the notation

$$G_1 =< G, t; t^{-1} k_1 t = \varphi(k_1), k_1 \in K_1 >$$

Almost-invariant subsets We define the relations $\subset_a$ (*almost-inclusion*), $=_a$ (*almost-equality*) between subsets of G by :

$$E \subset_a E' \quad \text{means that} \quad E \cap (G - E') \text{ is finite}$$

$$E =_a E' \quad \text{means that} \quad E \subset_a E' \text{ and } E' \subset_a E$$

A subset $E \in \mathcal{P}(G)$ is *almost-invariant* iff

$$\forall g \in G, Eg =_a E$$

The powerset $\mathcal{P}(G)$, equipped with the symmetric difference $\triangle$ is a vector-space over $\mathbb{Z}/2\mathbb{Z}$ and admits the subspaces :

$$\text{INV}(G) = \{E \in \mathcal{P}(G) \mid E \text{ is almost-invariant }\}$$
$$\text{FIN}(G) = \{E \in \mathcal{P}(G) \mid E \text{ is finite }\}$$

The *number-of-ends* of G is the dimension of the quotient-space $\text{INV}(G)/\text{FIN}(G)$. Hence G "has at least 2 ends" iff there exists some almost invariant subset E which is infinite and has infinite complement $G - E$. The number-of-ends of an arbitrary finitely generated group can be $0, 1, 2$ or ∞ ([5]).In the case of a context-free group it can only take values $0, 2$ or ∞ (1 is impossible, as shown in [10]).

2.4 Cayley graphs

Given a finitely generated group G and a finite set X_G of generators of G, the Cayley-graph of G over X_G is the following oriented, labeled graph $\Gamma = (V_\Gamma, E_\Gamma)$:

let X be an alphabet in one-to-one correspondance with X_G, $\overline{X}$ a disjoint alphabet in one-to-one correspondance with X_G^{-1}, such that for every $x_G \in X_G$, if $x \in X$ denotes x_G, $\overline{x} \in \overline{X}$ denotes x_G^{-1} ;

- V_Γ, the set of vertices, is equal to G
- $E_\Gamma = \{(g,x,g') \mid g,g' \in G, x \in X, g.x_G = g'\} \cup \{(g,\overline{x},g') \mid g,g' \in G, x \in X, g.x_G^{-1} = g'\}$.

Given a subset $E \subset V_\Gamma$, we define the *frontier* ΔE of E by :

$$\Delta E = \{v \in E \mid \exists v' \in V_\Gamma - E, \exists x \in X \cup \overline{X}, (v', x, v) \in E_\Gamma\}$$

The *cofrontier* ∂E of E is defined by :

$$\partial E = \{(v', x, v) \in E_\Gamma \mid v' \in V_\Gamma - E, x \in X \cup \overline{X}, v \in E\}$$

A *cocycle* ∂ of G is any subset ∂ of E_Γ such that there exists some subset E of V_Γ fulfilling $\partial = \partial E$. When $\partial \subset E_\Gamma$, by ∂^{-1} we denote the set

$$\partial^{-1} = \{(v, \overline{x}, v') \mid (v', x, v) \in \partial\}$$

(here we extend the notation $\overline{x}$ to every $x \in X \cup \overline{X}$ by setting $\overline{\overline{x}} = x$).

By $d(v, v')$ we denote the *distance* between two vertices v, v' in G : it is the minimal length of a path from v to v' in G.

We call *diameter of a cocycle* ∂ the number

$$\text{diam}(\partial) = \max\{d(v_1, v_2) \mid \exists x_1, x_2 \in X \cup \overline{X}, \exists v_1', v_2' \in V_\Gamma, (v_1, x_1, v_1') \in \partial \cup \partial^{-1}$$
and $(v_2, x_2, v_2') \in \partial\iota$

The cocycle ∂E is said *elementary* iff E and $V_\Gamma - E$ are both connected (i.e. the subgraphs generated by the sets of vertices $E, V_\Gamma - E$ are both connected). Here we call *end* of Γ any subset $E \subset V_G$ such that

$$\text{Card}(\partial E) < \infty \quad \text{and} \quad \text{Card}(E) = \infty$$

One must notice that E is an end of Γ iff, E, considered as a subset of G, is an infinite almost-invariant subset.

By $B(v, R)$ we denote the ball $\{v' \in V_\Gamma \mid d(v, v') < R\}$. Here we call *spherical end* of Γ any subset $E \subset V_\Gamma$ which is an infinite connected component of $\Gamma - B(1, R)$ for some radius R. It is simply called "end" in [10] but it is convenient here to consider a slightly more general notion of end ; (the reader should be aware that the notion of end defined in [5] is a third different notion which is not used here).

3 GEOMETRICAL PROPERTIES

Let us fix (from now and up to the end of this paper) some context-free group G given by an alphabet X, a p.d.a. $\mathcal{M} = < X \cup \overline{X}, P, Y, \delta, y_0, q_0 >$ a finite set $F \subset Y^*P$ such that G admits some presentation $< X \cup \overline{X}; R >$ and $[\epsilon]_{\underset{s}{\longleftrightarrow}} = L(\mathcal{M}, F)$. As noticed in 2.3, G is fully determined by $\mathcal{M}$ and F.

It is known that we can compute an integer $\kappa > 0$ such that the Cayley-graph Γ of G on the set of generators $\{[x]_{\underset{s}{\longleftrightarrow}} \mid x \in X\}$ is κ-triangulable ([10], theorem I p. 302)

Lemma 1. *Given an integer $R > 0$, we can compute the finite graph* $B(1, R)$.

Proof. Let us denote by T_R the tree whose vertices set V_R and edges set E_R are

$$V_R = \{w \in (X \cup \overline{X})^* \mid \ |w| < R\}$$

$E_R = \{(w, x, wx) \mid w \in V_R, x \in X \ \text{and} \ wx \in V_R\} \cup \{(wx, \bar{x}, w) \mid w \in V_R, x \in X$ and $wx \in V_R\}$

$B(1, R)$ is the quotient of the graph T_R by the bisimulation $\sim$: $w \sim w'$ iff $w\widetilde{w'} \in L(\mathcal{M}, \mathcal{F})$. As $\sim$ is computable, $B(1, R)$ is computable too.

Lemma 2. *Let $\partial \subset V_\Gamma \times (X \cup \overline{X}) \times V_\Gamma$ be a finite set of edges of Γ, whose initial and terminal vertices are all lying in* $B(1, R)$. *Let A, A' be two vertices belonging to some edges of ∂ . There exists some path from A to A', which does not use any edge of $\partial \cup \partial^{-1}$, iff there exists some path from A to A', lying in* $B(1, R + 2\kappa)$, *which does not use any edge of $\partial \cup \partial^{-1}$.*

The proof is technical and is omitted here.

Lemma 3. *Let $\partial \subset V_\Gamma \times (X \cup \overline{X}) \times V_\Gamma$ be a finite set of edges.*

1. *We can decide whether ∂ is a cocycle*
2. *We can decide whether ∂ is an elementary cocycle.*

Proof. Let $R = \text{diam}(\partial) + 1$. As properties (1), (2) are invariant by left-translation, we can suppose that all the vertices of ∂ lie in B(1,R). ∂ is a cocycle iff, for every $(C, x, A), (C', x', A') \in \partial$, there is no path from A to A', which does not use any edge of $\partial \cup \partial^{-1}$. By lemma 2 this property reduces to the same property in the graph $B(1, R + 2\kappa)$ which can be computed by lemma 1. A cocycle ∂ is elementary iff, for every (C, x, A), (C', x', A') which are both in ∂ or both in ∂^{-1} , there exists some path from A to A' which does not use any edge in $\partial \cup \partial^{-1}$. This can be tested by the same argument as above.

Lemma 4 ([11]). *If ∂ is a spherical cocycle, then $diam(\partial) \leq 3\kappa + 2$.*
(by "spherical"cocycle we mean the cofrontier of some spherical end).

485

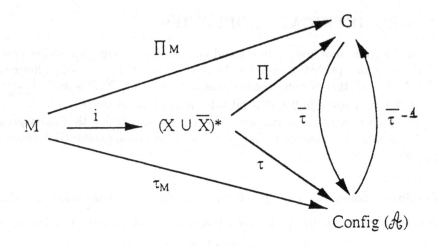

Diagram 1

This lemma is proved in [11], p 65.

In [11] the authors associate to every context-free graph some special deterministic p.d.a. $\mathcal{A}$ called *the canonical d.p.d.a* of Γ. The complete definition of $\mathcal{A}$ is technical, let us mention that if $\mathcal{A} = <X \cup \overline{X}, Z, Q, \delta_A, q_0, y_0 >$,then

(1) $L(\mathcal{A}, \{y_0 q_0\}) = L(\mathcal{M}, F) = [e]_{\xrightarrow{\ *\ }_R}$
   (i.e. $\mathcal{A}$ recognises the word-problem of G)

(2) the mapping $\overline{\tau} : G \to$ Config $(\mathcal{A})$, $[w]_{\xrightarrow{\ *\ }_R} \mapsto \alpha q \in Z^*Q \mid y_0 q_0 \xrightarrow{\ w\ }_\mathcal{A} \alpha q$
   is well-defined and bijective (Config $(\mathcal{A})$ is the set of accessible configurations of $\mathcal{A}$).

(3) $\forall g \in G, d(1_G, g) = \mid \overline{\tau}(g) \mid -1$
   (i.e. the distance from the neutral element to g is equal to the stack-height of the configuration representing g minus 1).

Theorem 5. *We can compute from the p.d.a. $\mathcal{M}$ defining the group G the canonical d.p.d.a. $\mathcal{A}$ of the Cayley-graph Γ of G.*

Sketch of proof. The stack-alphabet Z corresponds to the classes of spherical ends (under end-isomorphism), Q correspond to the maximum number of frontier points on any spherical end and δ_A encodes the edges of the spherical cocycles (see [11]). Hence $\mathcal{A}$ depends upon the spherical cocycles only and these cocycles can be computed by lemma 1 ,3 and 4.

Lemma 6. *Let ∂ be a finite elementary cocycle of Γ.*
Then $\mathrm{diam}(\partial) \leq \frac{1}{2}(3\kappa + 2)(\mathrm{Card}(\partial) - 1)$.

The proof is technical and is omitted here.

4 LANGUAGE-THEORETIC PROPERTIES

The main mathematical object which leads to a decomposition of G is an almost-invariant set $E \subset G$, which is infinite, has infinite complement and such that every $g \in G$ is in one of the four sets :

$$E_{+,+} = \{g \in G \mid gE \subset E\}$$
$$E_{+,-} = \{g \in G \mid gE \subset G - E\}$$
$$E_{-,+} = \{g \in G \mid g(G - E) \subset E\}$$
$$E_{-,-} = \{g \in G \mid g(G - E) \subset G - E\}$$

In order to compute such sets we define two ways for describing the elements of G by words (4.1), we then prove some properties of right-linear rewriting systems (4.2) and derive some consequences about the languages representing the sets $E_{\epsilon,\epsilon'}(\epsilon, \epsilon' \in \{+, -\})$ or other analogous sets (4.3).

4.1 Words representing the elements of G

There are two kinds of words representing an element $g \in G$:

1. the words $w \in (X \cup \overline{X})^*$ of minimal length such that $g = [w]_{\overset{*}{\longleftrightarrow}_R}$
2. the configuration $wq \in Z^*Q$ of the canonical automaton $\mathcal{A}$ which corresponds to the vertex g of Γ (noted $\overline{\tau}(g)$).

(We identify here the group G with the quotient-monoïd $(X \cup \overline{X})^* / \overset{*}{\longleftrightarrow}_R$). Let us define some more notations and vocabulary.
A word $w \in (X \cup \overline{X})^*$ is said minimal iff, for every $w' \in (X \cup \overline{X})^*$, $w \overset{*}{\longleftrightarrow}_R w' \Rightarrow |w| \leq |w'|$. We denote by M the set of all minimal words.
$\Pi : (X \cup \overline{X})^* \to (X \cup \overline{X})^* / \overset{*}{\longleftrightarrow}_R = G$ is the canonical projection.
$\tau : (X \cup \overline{X})^* \to \text{Config}(\mathcal{A})$ is the mapping "computed" by $\mathcal{A}$ in the following sense :

$$\forall w \in (X \cup \overline{X})^*, y_0 q_0 \overset{w}{\longrightarrow}_{\mathcal{A}} \tau(w)$$

($\tau(w)$ is uniquely defined by the above condition because $\mathcal{A}$ is deterministic, real-time and complete).
Π_M (resp. τ_M) is the mapping Π (resp. τ) restricted to M. i is the embedding of M into $(X \cup \overline{X})^*$. $\overline{\tau}$ is the unique map such that $\tau = \overline{\tau} \circ \Pi$ (this fact was recalled in section 3). $\overline{\tau}$ is a bijection.
The situation is summarised in the commutative diagram 1.

Lemma 7. *τ_M is a rational transduction.*

Sketch of proof. It suffices to notice that a computation of $\mathcal{A}$ on a minimal word w must be increasing (i.e. each transition used must strictly increase the stack-height).

Let us notice that $M = \text{domain}(\tau_M)$, hence M is rational.

4.2 Right-linear rewriting systems

Let $S \subset X^* \times X^*$ be a semi-Thue system.

Theorem 8 ([3]). *If S is finite, then $\xrightarrow{*}_{r,S}$ is a rational transduction.*

This theorem is proved in [3] even in the more general case where S is a recognisable subset of $X^* \times X^*$.

Let $K \subset X^*$. We define the language $H(S, K)$ (the "heart" of S relative to K) as :

$$H(S, K) = \{f \in X^* \mid \forall n \geq 0, \exists m \geq n, \exists k \in K, f \xrightarrow{m}_{r,S} k\}$$

Theorem 9. *If S is finite and K is rational, then $H(S, K)$ is rational.*

The proof is technical and is omitted here.

It is a refinement of theorem 5 of [3] which asserts that $H(S, X^*)$ is rational.

Let us consider some real-time p.d.a. $\mathcal{A} = < Y, Z, Q, \delta_A, q_0, y_0 >$ (for example, $\mathcal{A}$ could be the canonical automaton of Γ).

Let $R \subset Y^*, K \subset Z^*Q$ be two rational languages.

Lemma 10. *The two following languages are rational*

1. $\text{Config}(R, K) = \{\omega q \in Z^*Q \mid \exists f \in R, \omega q \xrightarrow{f}_{\mathcal{A}} K\}$
2. $\text{Config}_\infty(R, K) = \{\omega q \in Z^*Q \mid \text{there exist infinitely many words } f \in R \text{ such that } \omega q \xrightarrow{f}_{\mathcal{A}} K\}$

(the notation $\omega q \xrightarrow{f}_{\mathcal{A}} K$ means : $\exists k \in K, \omega q \xrightarrow{f}_{\mathcal{A}} k$))

Proof. Let $\mathcal{B} = < Y, Q', \delta, q_0', Q'_+ >$ be a f.a. recognising R. Let $\widehat{Z} = Z \cup \{[q, q'] \mid q \in Q, q' \in Q'\}$ be a new alphabet. We consider the semi-Thue sytem S constitued by all the rules

$$\omega_1[q_1, q_1')] \to \omega_2[q_2, q_2')]$$

such that

$$\omega_1, \omega_2 \in Z^*, q_1, q_2 \in Q, q_1', q_2' \in Q',$$
$$\exists y \in Y, \quad \omega_1 q_1 \xrightarrow{y}_{\mathcal{A}} \omega_2 q_2 \quad \text{is a transition of } \mathcal{A}$$
$$\text{and} \quad q_1' \xrightarrow{y}_{\mathcal{B}} q_2' \quad \text{is a transition of } \mathcal{B}$$

We then have :

$$\omega q \in Config(R, K) \iff \omega[q, q_0] \xrightarrow{*}_{r,S} K' \tag{1}$$
$$\omega q \in Config_\infty(R, K) \iff \omega[q, q_0] \in H(S, K') \tag{2}$$

where

$$K' = \{\omega'[q', q"] \mid \omega'q' \in K, q" \in Q'_+\} \tag{3}$$

By (1) and theorem 9, Config (R, K) is rational. By (2) and theorem 9, $Config_\infty(R, K)$ is rational.

4.3 Almost-invariant subsets as formal languages

The notion of rational language makes sense in any monoïd $(A, ., 1)$: the set of rational languages is the smallest subset of $\mathcal{P}(A)$ containing the finite subsets of A and closed by the operations:.(product of 2 subsets), $\cup$ (finite union) and $*$ (operation star). In the case of the monoïd G, rational subsets of G are related to rational languages of words by the following

Theorem 11. *Let $E \subset G$. The following properties are equivalent*

(1) E is a rational subset of G
(2) $\overline{\tau}(E)$ is a rational subset of $(Z \cup Q)^*$
(3) $\Pi_M^{-1}(E)$ is a rational subset of $(X \cup \overline{X})^*$

Sketch of proof. **(1)** $\Longrightarrow$ **(2)**: there exists some rational subset R of $(X \cup \overline{X})^*$ such that $E = \Pi(R)$.Hence $\overline{\tau}(E) = \tau(R)$. But τ preserves rationality.
(2) $\Longrightarrow$ **(3)**: $\Pi_M^{-1}(E) = \tau_M^{-1}(\overline{\tau}(E))$ and τ_M is a rational transduction (lemma 7).
(3) $\Longrightarrow$ **(1)**: $E = \Pi(\Pi_M^{-1}(E))$ and every homomorphic image of a rational set is rational

Lemma 12. *The set $Rat(G)$ of all rational subsets of G is closed under the operations $\cap$ (intersection of two subsets) and C (complement).*

Proof. As $Rat(G)$ is closed under $\cup$, it is sufficient to prove that it is closed under complement. Let $R \in Rat(G)$. $\Pi_M^{-1}(G - R) = M - \Pi_M^{-1}(R)$ and $Rat((X \cup \overline{X})^*)$ is closed under complement. As $M, \Pi_M^{-1}(R)$ are rational, $\Pi_M^{-1}(G - R)$ is rational too, hence $G - R$ is rational.

The idea of lemma 12 is borrowed to [12] where it is proved undermore general hypothesis.

Lemma 13. *Let $E \subset G$ be an almost-invariant subset. Then*

(1) E is rational
(2) given ∂E, we can compute a finite automaton recognising $\overline{\tau}(E)$.

Sketch of proof.

(1)
case 1: E is a spherical end. Then its frontier ΔE is such that $\overline{\tau}(\Delta E) = \{\omega q_i \mid 1 \le i \le p\}$ where $\omega \in Z^*$ is a fixed word and $p =\mathrm{Card}(\Delta E)$. Then $\overline{\tau}(E) = \omega Z^* Q \cap \mathrm{Config}\ (\mathcal{A})$, hence $\overline{\tau}(E)$ is rational.
case 2: E is a general almost-invariant subset. Let $R = \max\{d(1_G, c) \mid c \in \Delta E\}$. E is the finite union of a (finite) subset of $B(1, R)$ and some spherical ends associated to $B(1, R)$. Hence, by case 1, E is rational.
(2) The computation of the number R is straightforward. Let E_R be the unique subset of $B(1_G, R+1)$ such that $\partial E = \partial_B E_R$ (where B denotes $B(1, R+1)$ and $\partial_B E_R$ the cofrontier of E_R in the subgraph B). E is the union of E_R and the spherical ends whose frontier lies in E_R.

Lemma 14. *Let E, E' be two rational languages of G. Then the following languages are rational :*

(1) $L(E, E') = \{g \in G \mid gE \cap E' \neq \emptyset\}$

(2) $L_\infty(E, E') = \{g \in G \mid gE \cap E' \text{ is infinite}\}$

Proof.
$$L(E, E') = \Pi(\tau_M{}^{-1}(\text{Config}(R, K)))$$
$$L_\infty(E, E') = \Pi(\tau_M{}^{-1}(\text{Config}_\infty(R, K)))$$
where $R = \Pi_M^{-1}(E), K = \overline{\tau}(E')$.
Hence by lemma 10 and theorem 11, these languages are rational.

Lemma 15. *Let E be an almost-invariant subset of G (given by the cocycle ∂E). Then all the following sets are rational and finite automata recognising their inverse image by Π_M can be computed :*

(1) $E_{+,+}, E_{+,-}, E_{-,+}, E_{-,-}$
(2) $K = \{g \in G \mid gE =_a E\}$
(3) $H = \{g \in G \mid gE =_a E \text{ or } gE =_a G - E\}$
(4) $N = \{g \in K \mid \text{Card}(gE \cap (G - E)) = \text{Card}(g(G - E) \cap E)\}$
(5) $E' = \{g \in G \mid gE \subset_a E \text{ or } g(G - E) \subset_a E\}$
(6) $G_1 = \{g \in G \mid (E' - K)g = E' - K\}$
(7) $G_2 = \{g \in G \mid (E' - (H - K))g = E' - (H - K)\}$
(8) $P = \{g \in G \mid (E' - (H - K))g = E' - K\}$

Sketch of proof. We first remark that given rational subsets E_1, E_2 of G,
$$\alpha(E_1, E_2) = \{g \in G \mid gE_1 \subset E_2\}, \beta(E_1, E_2) = \{g \in G \mid gE_1 \subset_a E_2\}$$
are both rational languages by lemma 12, 14 and the following formula :
$$\alpha(E_1, E_2) = G - L(E_1, G - E_2); \beta(E_1, E_2) = G - L_\infty(E_1, G - E_2)$$
Hence points (1), (2), (3), (5) are proved.
By same means we can prove that $G_1^{-1}, G_2^{-1}, P^{-1}$ are rational. As the mapping $g \mapsto g^{-1}$ preserves rationality, points (6), (7), (8) are proved.
It remains to prove (4): if $\text{Card}(K) < \infty$ then $K = N$, hence N is rational ; if $\text{Card}(K) = \infty$, then N is a finite subgroup of K which is included in $B(1, \text{diam}(\partial) + 3)$.

5 EFFECTIVE DECOMPOSITION of G

We describe first the sequence of operations to be performed (we follow the proof given in p. 41-56 of [5](5.1), we explain then how every operation can be carried effectively (5.2), we evaluate the complexity of the algorithm (5.3) and then state the main result (5.4).

5.1 Sequence of operations

begin
(1) If $Card(G) < \infty$ **then begin** Num-ends $:=0$; Stop **end** ;
(2) Find an almost-invariant set E such that

$$\text{Card}(E) = \infty \text{ and } \text{Card}(G-E) = \infty \text{ and } G = E_{+,+} \cup E_{+,-} \cup E_{-,+} \cup E_{-,-}$$

(3) $K := \{g \in G \mid gE =_a E\}$
(4) If $\text{Card}(K) = \infty$ **then** Num-ends $:= 2$ **else** Num-ends $:= \infty$
(5) If Num-ends $= 2$ **then begin**

    (6) $N := \{g \in K \mid \text{Card}(gE \cap (G - E)) = \text{Card}(g(G - E) - E)\}$;
    $\{Card(N) < \infty; N \lhd K \lhd G; K/N \approx \mathbb{Z} \text{and} [G : K] \le 2\}$
    (7) if $K = G$ **then** "$G =< N, t; t^{-1}ut = \varphi(u), u \in N >$"
    (8) if $K \ne G$ **then begin** $\{G/K \approx \mathbb{Z}/2\mathbb{Z}\}$

        (9) let $a \in G - K, t \in K - N$ such that tN generates K/N
        (10) let k, l be integers such that
        $a^2 \equiv t^k \pmod{N}$ and $tat^{-1} \equiv at^l \pmod{N}$
        $\{l = -2 \text{ or } l = 0\}$
        (11) if l $=-2$ **then** "$G =< G_3 * G_4; N = N >$"
        $\{G_3 =< N, a >; G_4 =< N, ta >; [G3 : N] = [G4 : N] = 2\}$
        (12) if ($l = 0$ and $k = 2p$) **then**
        "$G =< G_5, t; ta't^{-1} = a'', tut^{-1} = \varphi(u), u \in N >$"
        $\{G_5 =< N, a' >, a' = at^{-p}\}$
        (13) if ($l = 0$ and $k = 2p + 1$) **then**
        "$G =< N, t'; t'ut'^{-1} = \varphi(u), u \in N >$"
        $\{t' = at^{-p}\}$
        end $\{8\}$

    end {of the case where Num-ends $= 2$ (line 5)}

(14) if Num-ends $= \infty$ **then begin**

    (15) $E' := \{g \in G \mid gE \subset_a E \text{ or } g(G - E) \subset_a E\}$
    (16) $H := \{g \in G \mid gE =_a E \text{ or } gE =_a G - E\}$
    $G_1 := \{g \in G \mid (E' - K)g = E' - K\}$
    $G_2 := \{g \in G \mid (E' - (H - K))g = E' - (H - K)\}$
    $P := \{g \in G \mid (E' - (H - K))g = E' - K\}$

    (17) if $P = \emptyset$ **then** "$G =< G_1 * G_2; K = K >$" ;
    (18) if ($P \ne \emptyset$ and $H \ne K$) **then** "$G =< G_1 * H; K = K >$" ;
    (19) if ($P \ne \emptyset$ and $H = K$) **then**
    "$G =< G_1, t; t^{-1}kt = \varphi(k), k \in K >$"; {where $t \in P$}
    end $\{14\}$

    end

5.2 Effectiveness of the operations

(1) M is a rational language (lemma). For every $g \in G, \Pi_M^{-1}(g)$ is finite. Hence $Card(G) < \infty$ iff $Card(M) < \infty$. This last property can be tested.

(2) There exists some almost-invariant subset E, infinite and having an infinite complement, such that ∂E has minimal cardinality (among all a.invariant subsets which are infinite and co-infinite), and such that

$$G = \bigcup_{(\epsilon,\epsilon') \in \{+,-\}} E_{\epsilon,\epsilon'} \quad ([5], \text{lemma } 3.2 \text{ p } 44).$$

There exists also some spherical end E_1 which is infinite and co-infinite. By minimality of E :

$$Card(\partial E) \leq Card(\partial E_1) \leq 2.Card(Q).Card(X)$$

∂E must contain some elementary cocycle ∂E_2 such that E_2 is infinite and co-infinite, and so, by minimality of $\partial E, \partial E$ is elementary.

Let us set $D = (3\kappa + 2). Card(Q). Card(X)$.

By lemma 6, diam $(\partial E) \leq D$, hence some translate of E lies in $B(1, D + 1)$. We can compute the ball $B(1, D + 1)$ (lemma 1), enumerate all the elementary cocycles of that ball (lemma 3) and test each of them for the property :

$$G = \bigcup_{(\epsilon,\epsilon') \in \{+,-\}} E_{\epsilon,\epsilon'}$$

(this can be done by lemma 15, point 1).

The sets given in **(3)**, **(6)**, **(15)**, **(16)** can be computed (i.e. finite automata recognising their inverse image by Π_M can be computed) by lemma 15.

The tests instructions **(4)**, **(7)**, **(8)**, **(17)**, **(18)**, **(19)** amount to test the equivalence of some finite automata.

(9) amounts to choose some words w_a, w_t such that

(9.1) $\quad w_a \in \Pi_M^{-1}(G) - \Pi_M^{-1}(K)$
(9.2) $\Pi(w_t)N$ is a generator of K/N

(9.1) is straightforward: it suffices to find some letter $a \in X$ such that $\Pi(a) \notin K$.

In order to find some w_t fulfilling **(9.2)** we compute a finite $Y \subset (X \cup \overline{X})^*$ such that $\Pi(Y)$ generates K :

$$Y = \{ax\overline{a} \mid \Pi(x) \in K\} \cup \{ax \mid \Pi(x) \notin K\}$$

($\Pi(Y)$ is the set of Schreier generators associated to the transversal $\{\Pi(\epsilon), \Pi(a)\}$)
The map $\varphi : K \to \mathbb{Z}$ defined by

$$\forall g \in K, \varphi(g) = Card(gE \cap (G - E)) - Card(g(G - E) \cap E)$$

is an homomorphism ([5], p31) such that $\mathrm{Ker}\varphi = N$.

Let $n = \mathrm{pgcd}\{\varphi(\Pi(y)) \mid y \in Y\}$. n can be computed. Every word w_t in $\Pi_M^{-1}(\varphi^{-1}(n))$ fulfills **(9.2)**.

(10) amounts to pick some words $(w_t)^k, (w_t)\ell$ respectively in the rational sets of words

- $(w_t)^* \cap \tau_M^{-1}(\Pi_M^{-1}(w_a^2 \Pi(N)))$
- $(w_t)^* \cap \tau_M^{-1}(\Pi_M^{-1}(w_t w_a \tilde{w}_t \tilde{w}_a) \Pi_M^{-1}(N)))$

It remains to compute finite sets of generators for the two factor-subgroups of decompositions **(17)**,**(18)** and for the base-subgroup of decomposition **(19)**.
Let us treate decomposition **(17)**:
given decompositions of each "old" generator $\Pi(x)(x \in X)$ over the subgroups G_1, G_2 :

$$(D_x) : \Pi(x) = g_{x,1} g_{x,2} ... g_{x,l(x)} \quad (\text{where } g_{x,j} \in G_1, G_2)$$

we can choose the following sets of "new" generators for G_i (where $i \in \{1, 2\}$:

$$Y_i = \{g_{x,j} \mid x \in X, 1 \le j \le l(x) \text{ and } g_{x,j} \in G_i\}$$

For every $x \in X$, we can build a decomposition of type (D_x) by determining some word in

$$(\Pi_M^{-1}(G_1) \cup \Pi_M^{-1}(G_2))^* \cap (\mathrm{L}(\mathcal{M}, F)\overline{x}^{-1})$$

Let X_i be a new alphabet and $\alpha_i : X_i \to Y_i$ a bijection. α_i entends to an homomorphism $\varphi_i : (X_i \cup \overline{X_i})^* \to (X \cup \overline{X})^*$ by setting :

$$\forall a \in X_i, \varphi_i(a) = \alpha_i(a), \varphi_i(\overline{a}) = \overline{\alpha_i(a)}$$

$\varphi_i^{-1}(\mathrm{L}(\mathcal{A}, y_0 q_0))$ is exactly the word-problem for G_i on the generating set Y_i. From $\mathcal{A}, \varphi_)$ we can compute a d.p.d.a. $\mathcal{A}_i$ and a finite set of configurations F_i such that $L_i = \mathrm{L}(\mathcal{A}_i, F_i)$. The cases of decompositions **(18)**,**(19)** can be treated similarly.

5.3 Complexity

In the following we denote by $T(h, n)$ a tower of h exponentials i.e.

$$T(0, n) = n \quad \text{and} \quad T(h + 1, n) = n^{T(h,n)}$$

complexity of the operations $\tau_M, \Pi_M^{-1}, \alpha, \beta$:

(τ_M, Π_M^{-1} are defined in section 4.1 and α, β are defined in the proof of lemma 15; we use below some g.s.m. $\mathcal{A}_M$ which computes τ_M)

$\Pi_M^{-1} : \quad \overline{\tau}(E) \to \Pi_M^{-1}(E)$
  time $\mathrm{O}(\|\mathcal{A}_M\| . \|\overline{\tau}(E)\|)$

produces a d.f.a from a d.f.a

τ_M : $\quad \Pi_M^{-1}(E) \to \overline{\tau}(E)$

$\quad$ **time** $O(\|\mathcal{A}_M\|.\|\overline{\tau}(E)\|)$

$\quad$ produces a n.f.a from a n.f.a

α : $\quad (\Pi_M^{-1}(E_1), \overline{\tau}(E_2)) \to \overline{\tau}(\alpha(E_1, E_2))$

$\quad$ **time** $2^{O(\|\Pi_M^{-1}(E_1)\|^6 . \|\overline{\tau}(E_2)\|^3 . \|\mathcal{A}\|^3)}$

$\quad$ produces a deterministic f.a from two n.f.a's

β : $\quad \Pi_M^{-1}(E_1), \overline{\tau}(E_2) \to \overline{\tau}(\beta(E_1, E_2))$

$\quad$ **time** $2^{O(\|\Pi_M^{-1}(E_1)\|^6 . (\|\overline{\tau}(E_2)\| + \|\mathcal{A}\|)^3 . \|\mathcal{A}\|^3)}$

$\quad$ produces a d.f.a from a n.f.a recognizing $\Pi_M^{-1}(E_1)$ and a d.f.a recognizing $\overline{\tau}(E_2)$

complexity of the algorithm :

$\quad$ let $n = \|(\mathcal{M}, F)\|$ where

$$\|(\mathcal{M}, F)\| = \sum_{wq' \in \delta(yq,a)} |wq'| + |yqa| + \sum_{f \in F} |f|$$

triangulation constant: $\kappa \leq n^n$

canonical d.p.d.a $\mathcal{A}$: $\|\mathcal{A}\| = O(T(3, n))$

we deduce from $\mathcal{A}$ a d.f.a $\mathcal{AC}$ recognizing $\text{Config}(\mathcal{A})$, a g.s.m. $\mathcal{A}_M$ computing τ_M (see the proof of lemma 7), and a d.f.a $\mathcal{D}_M$ recognizing M, with the following sizes $\|\mathcal{AC}\| = O(T(3, n))$, $\|\mathcal{A}_M\| = O(T(3, n))$, $\|\mathcal{D}_M\| = O(T(3, n))$.

instruction (1): time(1) $= O(T(3, n))$.

instruction (2): time(2) $= T(4, O(n))$.

instruction (3): time(3) $= T(4, O(n))$.

instruction (4): time(4) $= T(4, O(n))$.

instruction (6-9): time(6-9) $= T(3, O(n))$.

instruction (10): time(10) $= T(2, O(n))$.

instruction (15): time(15) $= T(4, O(n))$.

instruction (16): time(16) $= T(5, O(n))$.

instruction (17-19): time(17-19) $= T(5, O(n))$.

computation of generators for the factor-subgroups (or the base subgroup) done in time $T(5, O(n))$.

5.4 The main results

The above (rough) analysis proves the following

Theorem 16.

(1) *The algorithm defined in IV-1 produces from every p.d.a M (with set of final configurations F) of size n, recognizing a language of the form $[\epsilon]_{\equiv}$, where $X^* / \equiv = G$ is a group,*

- the number of ends of G, $N_e(G)$
- when $N_e(G) \in \{2, \infty\}$, it produces a decomposition of G either as a nontrivial amalgamated product (with finite amalgamated subgroups) or as an HNN-extension (with finite associated subgroups).

(2) the time complexity of this algorithm is $T(5, 0(n))$.

It is proved in [9] that the isomorphism problem is decidable for f.g. virtually-free groups. Using theorem 16 we can sharpen this theorem as

Theorem 17. *The isomorphism problem for finitely generated virtually free groups is primitive recursive.*

Sketch of proof. Let G, G' be finitely generated virtually free groups given by outer actions of finite groups A, A' respectively on finitely generated free groups F, F'.

From these actions we deduce for G, G' presentations of the form described in [10] p. 299, which in turn allow to build d.p.d.a's $\mathcal{M}$, $\mathcal{M}'$ recognizing the word problem for G (resp. G'). The sizes of $\mathcal{M}$, $\mathcal{M}'$ are equal to those of the outer actions.

The accessibility-length of G (resp. G') is $\leq$ rank(F) + Card(A) (resp. rank (F') + Card(A')).

A graph of groups $\mathcal{G}$ with only finite vertex-groups and with G as fundamental group can be obtained by iterating algorithm 5.1 at most (rank(F) + Card(A)) times. As the size of each p.d.a. obtained for a factor (or the base) at each step of decomposition is $T(5, O(n))$ where n is the size of the previous p.d.a, the whole computation will take a time which is $O(T(5.(\text{rank}(F) + \text{Card}(A)) + 1, n))$.

Some realization of G (resp. G') of the type described in the "Culler's realization theorem" can be computed in polynomial time from $\mathcal{G}$ (resp. $\mathcal{G}'$) by the method given in [9] p. 123. The final isomorphism test described in [9] p.137 can be done in time exponential with respect to the size of the realizations, hence neglectable with respect to the above tower of exponentials.

Remark. 1-We could give another proof of lemma 15 leaning on the fact that all the languages described in (1)...(9) can be defined by means of a logical formula with one free set-variable, in the language of monadic second order logic ; by an adaptation of Rabin's theory for S2S on the infinite tree to the case of an infinite context-free graph (see [11], [6]), we could conclude that the unique model of such a formula "corresponds" to a rational tree and is hence rational. The drawback of such a proof is that the complexity analysis of the corresponding algorithm would be more difficult and the complexity itself would be presumably higher.

2-We believe it would be possible to modify the algorithm of section 5.1 in such a way that its time-complexity becomes $T(3, O(n))$. The main modifications would consist in replacing some applications of lemma 14, by the construction of some "ad-hoc" d.f.a. based on geometric considerations. These modifications would result in an increasing complexity of our paper and a decreasing complexity of the algorithm. We plan to carry out these modifications in a further version of this work.

Aknowledgments

I thank P.Schupp for advising me to read the proof of [5] and D.Holt for making me aware of [9].

References

1. A.V. Anisimov. Group languages. *Kibernetica 4*, pages 18–24, 1971.
2. J.M. Autebert, L. Boasson, and G. Sénizergues. Groups and nts languages. *JCSS vol.35, no2*, pages 243–267, 1987.
3. L. Boasson and M. Nivat. Centers of context-free languages. *LITP technical report no84-44*, 1984.
4. J.R. Buchi. Regular canonical systems. *the collected works of J.R. Buchi*, 1990.
5. D.E. Cohen. *Groups of cohomological dimension one.* Lectures Notes in math.,Springer vol.245, 1972.
6. B. Courcelle. The monadic second-order logic of graphs ii: infinite graphs of bounded width. *Math. Systems Theory 21*, pages 187–221, 1990.
7. W. Dicks and M.J. Dunwoody. *Groups acting on graphs.* Cambridge University Press, 1990.
8. D.B.A. Epstein, J.W. Cannon, D.F. Holt, S.V.F. Levy, M.S. Paterson, and W.P. Thurston. *Word processing in groups.* Jones and Bartlett, 1992.
9. S. Krstic. Actions of finite groups on graphs and related automorphisms of free groups. *Journal of algebra 124*, pages 119–138, 1989.
10. D.E. Muller and P.E. Schupp. Groups, the theory of ends and context-free languages. *JCSS vol 26, no 3*, pages 295–310, 1983.
11. D.E. Muller and P.E. Schupp. The theory of ends, pushdown automata and second-order logic. *TCS 37*, pages 51–75, 1985.
12. J. Sakarovitch. Description des monodes de type fini. *Elektronische Informationsverarbeitung und Kybernetic 17*, pages 417–434, 1981.
13. G. Sénizergues. On the finite subgroups of a context-free group. *in preparation*, 199?
14. Stallings. On torsion-free groups with infinitely many ends. *Ann. of Math. 88*, pages 312–334, 1968.

On the Power of Periodic Iteration of Morphisms

Arto Lepistö

Department of Mathematics, University of Turku
SF-20500 Turku, Finland

Abstract. - In this paper we show that there exist infinite words generated by a periodic application of a finite number of morphisms such that they cannot be generated by iterating only one morphism and then applying a coding.

1 Introduction

One of the most frequently used way to generate infite words is to use D0L systems (cf. [Sa] and [Be]). In this method an infinite word is obtained from a given finite word w by applying iteratively a morphism h to the word w. Usually there is also an additional requirement "w is a prefix of $h(w)$", but this requirement is not essential. A natural generalization of this method, formalized in [CK], is to apply a finite number of morphisms in a periodic fashion. Let us say that words obtained in this way are obtained by D0L systems with periodic control. One well-known example of a word, which is easily obtained by a D0L system with periodic control, is the Kolakovski's infinite word [K]. We know that it cannot be generated by using a D0L system ([CKL]), while the question whether it can be generated by a CD0L system, i.e. by applying a coding to an infinite word obtained by a D0L system, is open.

Although we are not able to solve the above open problem we can settle a related one from [CK]. Namely, that there exist infinite words generated by D0L systems with periodic control which cannot be generated by CD0L systems. Our considerations below are based on subword complexity.

2 Preliminary considerations

Let Σ be a finite alphabet, h be a morphism from free semigroup Σ^+ into itself and w be a word in Σ^+ satisfying the condition "w is a proper prefix of $h(w)$". Then the word $h^i(w)$ is a prefix of the word $h^{i+1}(w)$ for all $i \in \mathbb{N}$ and therefore we can say that there exists an infinite word as a "limit". In other words, the word

$$\gamma = \lim_{n \to \infty} h^n(w) \in \Sigma^\omega$$

is well defined and such words are called *D0L words*, and the triples (Σ, h, w) generating such words are called *D0L systems*. Furthermore a *CD0L word* is a word obtained from a D0L word by a *coding*, i.e. by a morphism which maps alphabet Σ into itself.

Let H be a set of p morphisms from Σ^+ into itself, say $H = \{h_1, \ldots, h_p\}$. Then a triple (Σ, H, w) is referred to as a *D0L system with periodic control*, and it defines infinite words as follows. For a word $a_1 \ldots a_n$, with $a_i \in \Sigma$, let

$$H(a_1 \ldots a_n) = \alpha_1 \ldots \alpha_n,$$

where

$$\alpha_i = h_{i'}(a_i) \quad \text{if} \quad i' \equiv i \pmod{p}.$$

Now, if w is a proper prefix of $H(w)$, then the limit

$$\lim_{i \to \infty} H^i(w)$$

exists, and such words are called *D0L words with periodic control*. In our later considerations we assume that Σ is a binary alphabet, say $\{\alpha, \beta\}$, and p is an arbitrary natural number. Let us define p morphisms $h_1, \ldots, h_p$

$$h_1 : \begin{cases} \alpha \to \alpha\beta \\ \beta \to \alpha\alpha, \end{cases}$$

$$h_i : \begin{cases} \alpha \to \beta \\ \beta \to \alpha \end{cases} \quad \text{for } i \in \{2, \ldots, p\},$$

and consider the following D0L system with periodic control

$$(\{\alpha, \beta\}, \{h_1, \ldots, h_p\}, \alpha).$$

We set

$$F_p = \lim_{i \to \infty} H^i(w).$$

Then, for example the infinite word F_3 starts as

$$F_3 = \alpha\beta\alpha\beta\alpha\alpha\beta\beta\alpha\alpha\alpha\beta\alpha\beta\beta\alpha\alpha\beta\alpha\alpha\alpha\beta\beta\alpha\alpha\beta\beta\beta\alpha\alpha\alpha\beta\alpha\beta\alpha\alpha \ldots.$$

From now on we denote the complement of a letter a in Σ by $\bar{a}$, so the complements $\bar{\alpha}, \bar{\beta}$ will be β, α, respectively. The complement of a word is obtained by taking the complement of every letter. By $F^p_{(k,l)}$ we denote the subword of the word F_p, which starts from position k and has length l. By $l = \omega$ in previous notation we mean the suffix, which begins from kth letter, of the word F^p. For a mapping $f' : \Sigma^p \to \Sigma^*$ we say that the mapping

$$f : \Sigma^\omega \to \Sigma^\omega, \quad f(a_1 \ldots a_p a_{p+1} \ldots a_{2p} \ldots) = f'(a_1 \ldots a_p)f'(a_{p+1} \ldots a_{2p}) \ldots,$$

where $a_i \in \Sigma$ for all i, is a *morphic extension* of f' to the set Σ^ω. Now we obtain another method to generate F_p. Consider the morphic extension f of the following mapping f':

$$f' : \Sigma^p \to \Sigma^*, \quad a_1 \ldots a_p \to \alpha\bar{a}_1 \ldots \bar{a}_p, \quad \text{for all } a_i \in \Sigma.$$

Since f' equals to the mapping H restricted to Σ^p it follows that F_p is a fixed point of f.

Next we analyse the structure of F_p. By the definition of H we have

$$H(F^p_{(pk+1,p)}) = F^p_{((p+1)k+1,p+1)}.$$

On the other hand,

$$F_p = F^p_{(1,p)}F^p_{(p+1,p)}F^p_{(2p+1,p)} \cdots ,$$

so that every $(p+1)$th letter in the word F_p is α starting from the position one. By removing all these letters α from the word F_p we obtain another word, say G_p. Moreover, since $f(F_p) = F_p$ it follows from the structure of f that G_p is the complement of the word F_p. So obviously the word G_p is a fixed point of the morphic extension g of the following mapping g':

$$g' : \Sigma^p \to \Sigma^* , \quad a_1 \ldots a_p \to \beta \bar{a}_1 \ldots \bar{a}_p , \quad \text{for all } a_i \in \Sigma.$$

Because G_p is the complement of the word F_p we know from above that every $(p+1)$th letter in the word G_p is β. Similarly as before we conclude that removing those letters β from the word G_p results the word F_p. So the word F_p is obtained from itself by removing first letters α from every $(p+1)$th position, starting from the first one, and then letters β from every $(p + 1)$th position of the remaining word, starting again from the first one.

Now, insteed of removing letters as above let us change them to a new letter $\not{0}$, referred to as the *blank letter*. The iterative application of the above process yiedls a sequence $F_p, F^1_p, F^2_p, F^3_p, \ldots$ of words such that

$$F^n_p \sim \begin{cases} F_p , \text{ for all } n \in \{2,4,6,8,\ldots\} \\ G_p , \text{ for all } n \in \{1,3,5,7,\ldots\}, \end{cases}$$

where the relation $\sim$ is defined as follows. For infinite words F and G, the relation $F \sim G$ holds iff

$$\pi_{\not{0}}(F) = \pi_{\not{0}}(G),$$

where $\pi_{\not{0}}$ is the projection from the alphabet $\{\alpha, \beta, \not{0}\}$ into $\{\alpha, \beta\}$, i.e. is identity on $\{\alpha, \beta\}$ and erases $\not{0}$. In every step of the above construction we switch every $(p + 1)$th non-blank letter to the letter $\not{0}$. Equivalently, we can think of filling infinite blank word K instead of blanking letters from the word F_p. This yields a sequence $K_1, K_2, K_3, \ldots$ of words such that they have longer and longer common prefix with the word F_p. Consequently the following algorithm generates F_p as the limit:

Algorithm 1:

(1) Let r be the letter $\alpha \in \Sigma$ and K be the infinite word $\not{0}^\omega$.

(2) Replace every $(p + 1)$th occurrence of $\not{0}$ in the word H by the letter r, starting from the first blank letter $\not{0}$. Let H' be the word obtained.

(3) Change r to its complement, and set $H := H'$ and go to (2).

Clearly, after the ith application of the rule (2) we obtain K_i defined above.

Our goal is to count subwords in F_p. From this point of view algorithm 1 is not very suitable: It does not define directly a subword of certain length strating from a fixed position. To obtain this we define another very related allgorithm as follows:

Algorithm 2:

(1) Let r be the letter α, N be a positive integer and let

$$(\Gamma_n)_{n=0}^N$$

be a sequence of integers such that

$$\Gamma_n \in \{1, 2, \ldots, p+1\} \text{ for } n \in \{0, 1, \ldots, N\}.$$

Finally, set $i = 0$ and $I_0 = \emptyset^\omega$.

(2) Construct the word I_{i+1} from the word I_i by replacing every $(p+1)$th letter $\emptyset$ in the word I_i with the letter r in such a way that the Γ_ith occurrence of $\emptyset$ is the first to be replaced.

(3) Replace the letter r by its complement, increase i by one, as far as $i < N$ and return to (2).

In each iteration of algorithm 1 every $(p+1)$th occurrence of the blank letter $\emptyset$ is replaced by a specific letter from Σ. Algorithm 2 does exactly the same but starting from the Γ_ith position containing $\emptyset$. Now, let $F_{(k,\omega)}^p$ be a suffix of the word F_p, and consider how algorithm 1 defines it. Clearly, it does it by fixing in each iteration every $(p+1)$th blank, but starting from one of the first $(p+1)$ blanks positions and not from the first one. Consequently, an infinite number sequence consisting of numbers from set $\{1, \ldots, p+1\}$ defines $F_{(k,\omega)}^p$, in other words an infinite iteration of algorithm 2 for a suitable sequence produces $F_{(k,\omega)}^p$. Converse is not true: there are, of course, number sequences which does not correspond to any suffix of of the word F_p. But we show in lemma 1, that every finite iteration of algorithm can be extended to an infinite one corresponding a prefix of the word F_p.

3 Results

In this section we prove some results on subword complexity of the word F_p and we show that the word F_p cannot be generated by a D0L or CD0L system.

We denote $F \simeq G$ for infinite words F and G in $\{\alpha, \beta, \emptyset\}^\omega$ if these words have the same letters in those positions, where they both have non-blank letters. For finite words with the same length we define this relation in the same way. In the following lemma the words I_n are defined as in algorithm 2.

Lemma 1. *Let N and p be two natural number and $(\Gamma_n)_{n=0}^N$ be a finite sequence of numbers, where $\Gamma_n \in \{1, 2, \ldots, p+1\}$ for $n \in \{0, 1, \ldots, N\}$. Then there exists a suffix $F_{(k,\omega)}^p$ of the word F_p such that*

$$F^p_{(k,\omega)} \simeq I_N,$$

for some k.

Proof. Suppose that the sequence $I_1, I_2, \ldots, I_N$ is given by algorithm 2 using the number sequence $(\Gamma_n)^N_{n=1}$. The proof is induction on the number of iterations in algorithm 2.

In the first step we can choose $k = p - \Gamma_0 + 2$ and then clearly

$$F^p_{(k,\omega)} \simeq I_1.$$

Equivalently, this means that there is a suffix of the word F_p, starting from position $k \in \{1, 2, \ldots p + 1\}$, such that

$$F^p_{(n(p+1)+k,p+1)} \simeq I^1_{(n(p+1)+1,p+1)},$$

and

$$I^1_{(n(p+1)+1,p+1)} = I^1_{(1,p+1)},$$

holds for all $n \geq 0$.

Now we assume that for a fixed $m \geq 1$ it is possible to choose a suffix $F^p_{(k,\omega)}$ of the word F_p such that

$$F^p_{(n(p+1)^m+k,(p+1)^m)} \simeq I^m_{(n(p+1)^m+1,(p+1)^m)},$$

for all $n \geq 0$, and that for the word I_m

$$I^m_{(n(p+1)^m+1,(p+1)^m)} = I^m_{(1,(p+1)^m)},$$

holds for all $n \geq 0$.

There are p^m positions containing letter $\emptyset$ in the subword $I^m_{(1,(p+1)^m)}$ as one can easily verify by induction. And for every $n \geq 0$ there exists the smallest number $k'_{m,n} \leq (p + 1)$ of occurrences of the letter $\emptyset$ in the beginning of the word $I^{m+1}_{(n(p+1)^m+1,(p+1)^m)}$ such that

$$k'_{m,n} = \left| \{r \in \mathbb{N} \mid 1 \leq r \leq s , \; I^m_{(r,1)} = \emptyset \} \right|,$$

for some integer $s \in \mathbb{N}$ satisfying equations

$$I^m_{(s,1)} = \emptyset$$

and

$$I^{m+1}_{(n(p+1)^m+s,1)} \neq \emptyset.$$

Now, because we replace every $(p+1)$th occurrence of the letter $\emptyset$ from the word I_m and

$$\gcd(p^m, p + 1) = 1,$$

we know from elementary number theory that the sequence

$$(k'_{m,n})_{n=0}^{\infty}$$

is $(p+1)$-periodic containing all numbers from set $\{1, 2, \ldots, p+1\}$. Note that in case $m = 1$ number $(p+1)$ must be replaced by number 0. That is because in the subword $I^1_{(n(p+1)+1,(p+1))}$ there is only p occurrences of the letter $\not{0}$.

Because

$$\{k'_{m,0}, \ldots, k'_{m,p}\} = \{1, \ldots, p+1\}$$

(with $(p+1)$ replaced by 0 when $m = 1$) we can choose number k'' from the set $\{k'_{m,0}(p+1)^m, k'_{m,1}(p+1)^m, \ldots, k'_{m,p}(p+1)^m\}$ such that

$$\Gamma_m = \frac{k''}{(p+1)^m}.$$

By the $(p+1)$-periodicity of the sequence

$$(k'_{m,n})_{n=0}^{\infty}$$

it follows for the chosen k'' that the suffix $F^p_{(k'',\omega)}$ of the word F_p satisfies conditions

$$F^p_{(n(p+1)^{m+1}+k'',(p+1)^{m+1})} \simeq I^{m+1}_{(n(p+1)^{m+1}+1,(p+1)^{m+1})},$$

for $n \geq 0$. Moreover, by the very same reason we also conclude that the condition

$$I^{m+1}_{(n(p+1)^{m+1}+1,(p+1)^{m+1})} = I^{m+1}_{(1,(p+1)^{m+1})},$$

holds for $n \geq 0$. Consequently, we can set $k = k''$ to complete the induction step, as well as the whole proof of the lemma. □

As we have already mentioned each suffix F of F_p can be associated (by algorithm 1) with an infinite sequence of numbers from $\{1, \ldots, p+1\}$. Above lemma showed that any such finite number sequence can be extended to an infinite one corresponding to a suffix of the word F_p. Our next lemma shows that if two suffices of F_p, say F and G, have long common prefices then the number sequences associated with F and G possess also a long common initial part. In order to formulate this lemma let Λ_F denote the number sequence associated with a suffix F of the word F_p, i.e. if the ith component in Λ_F is Γ_i, then in the ith iteration of algorithm 2 the filling is started from the Γ_i:th blank position.

Lemma 2. *Let n, u and v be natural numbers such that $n \geq (p+1)^2$ and*

$$A = F^p_{(u,n)} = F^p_{(v,n)} = B.$$

Moreover, let F and G be two arbitrary infinite suffices of F_p having words A, B as prefices, respectively, and set

$$q_{p,n} = \max\{m \in \mathbb{N} \mid \sigma_m \geq (p+1)^2, \ \sigma_{k+1} = \left\lfloor \frac{p}{p+1}\sigma_k \right\rfloor, \ \sigma_1 = n, \ k \in \mathbb{N}\}.$$

Then the first $q_{p,n}$ terms in the sequences Λ_F, Λ_G are identical.

Proof. Proof is induction on number k of iterations in algorithm 1.

In case $k = 1$ we first define sets

$$K = \{m \in \mathbb{N} \mid I^1_{(u+m,1)} = \alpha\},$$

$$L = \{m \in \mathbb{N} \mid I^1_{(v+m,1)} = \alpha\}$$

and

$$K' = \{m \in \mathbb{N} \mid I^2_{(u+m,1)} = \beta\}.$$

Then both $r, s \in K$ and $r, s \in L$ imply $r \equiv s \pmod{(p+1)}$. On the other hand, let

$$r \not\equiv s \pmod{(p+1)},$$

for some $r \in K$ and $s \in L$. We claim that there exists $t \in \mathbb{N}$ such that

$$t \in K' \cap L.$$

This is because there are at least consecutive subwords

$$A_{(1,p+1)}, \ldots, A_{(p(p+1)+1,p+1)} \text{ and } B_{(1,p+1)}, \ldots, B_{(p(p+1)+1,p+1)}$$

of length $p + 1$ in the words A and B, respectively. (Note that $n \geq (p+1)^2$.) With the notations of the proof of lemma 1, the set $\{k'_{1,0}, k'_{1,1}, k'_{1,2}, \ldots, k'_{1,p}\}$ contains all numbers from the set $\{0, 1, 2, \ldots, p\}$ (cf. proof of lemma 1). But this contradicts with the definitions of sets K' and L. Therefore

$$r \equiv s \pmod{(p+1)}, \text{ for all } r \in K \text{ and } s \in L$$

and hence $K = L$ by algorithm 1. So the first terms in sequences Λ_F and Λ_G are the same.

In the induction step we have $1 < k \leq q_{p,n}$. By induction hypothesis assume that the first $k - 1$ terms in sequences Λ_F and Λ_G are identical. Because the words A and B are identical the words obtained by removing those letters, which occur in words $I^{k-1}_{(u+m,n)}$ and $I^{k-1}_{(v+m,n)}$ from the words A and B, respectively, are also identical. These words, say A' and B', are, by our earlier considerations in section 2, also subwords of the words F_p or G_p, and hence prefices of some suffices of F_p or G_p, say F' and G'. Moreover, the length of these words are at least $\sigma_k \geq (p+1)^2$ by the definition of the number $q_{p,n}$. Now as in case $k = 1$ we can determine that for these shortened words the first terms in the corresponding sequences $\Lambda_{F'}, \Lambda_{G'}$ are the same, so the first k terms in sequences Λ_F, Λ_G are identical by our induction hypothesis. This completes the proof. □

Let $\Pi(n, w)$ denote the number of different subwords of length n occurring in an infinite word w. Our goal is to estimate $\Pi(n, F_p)$.

Lemma 2 states that we can "almost" use the first $q_{p,n}$ terms from the sequence Λ_A to characterize the word A. Here "almost" means that there are at most $(p+1)^2 - 1$ positions in the word $I_{q_{p,n}}$ containing letter $\emptyset$, i.e. positions in which letters are not fixed.

From the definition of the number $q_{p,n}$ we obtain

$$n\left(\frac{p}{p+1}\right)^{q_{p,n}} \geq (p+1)^2.$$

This yields

$$q_{p,n} \leq \log_{\left(\frac{p+1}{p}\right)}\left(\frac{n}{(p+1)^2}\right).$$

On the other hand there is at most $2^{(p+1)^2-1}$ possible ways to choose letters in those at most $(p+1)^2 - 1$ positions, which are not fixed in the word $I_{q_{p,n}}$. Thus we obtain the following upper bound for $\Pi(n, F_p)$:

$$\Pi(n, F_p) \leq 2^{(p+1)^2-1}(p+1)^{q_{p,n}} \leq 2^{(p+1)^2-1}(p+1)^{\frac{\ln(n)-2\ln(p+1)}{\ln(p+1)-\ln(p)}},$$

for all $n \geq 1$. By lemmas 1 and 2 we obtain a lower bound for $\Pi(n, F_p)$:

$$\Pi(n, F_p) \geq (p+1)^{q_{p,n}},$$

for all $n \geq 1$. On the other hand, for those integers $r \geq 1$ satisfying the condition

$$n\left(\frac{p}{p+1}\right)^{r-1} - \sum_{i=0}^{r-1}\left(\frac{p}{p+1}\right)^i \geq (p+1)^2, \qquad (1)$$

we have

$$r \in \left\{ m \in \mathbb{N} \mid \sigma_m \geq (p+1)^2,\ \sigma_{k+1} = \left\lfloor \frac{p}{p+1}\sigma_k \right\rfloor,\ \sigma_1 = n,\ k \in \mathbb{N} \right\}. \qquad (2)$$

Now condition (1) can be rewritten as

$$r \leq \log_{\left(\frac{p+1}{p}\right)}\left(\frac{n}{p(p+2)+p\left(1-\left(\frac{(p+1)}{p}\right)^r\right)}\right).$$

so that equation (2) holds also for integers $r \geq 1$ satisfying the condition

$$r \leq \log_{\left(\frac{p+1}{p}\right)}\left(\frac{n}{p(p+2)}\right).$$

Thus we obtain for numbers $q_{p,n}$ a lower bound

$$q_{p,n} > \log_{\left(\frac{p+1}{p}\right)}\left(\frac{n}{p(p+2)}\right) - 1$$

$$= \log_{\left(\frac{p+1}{p}\right)}\left(\frac{n}{(p+1)(p+2)}\right).$$

So we can write

$$\Pi(n, F_p) > (p+1)^{\frac{\ln(n)-\ln((p+1)(p+2))}{\ln(p+1)-\ln(p)}}, \quad \text{for all } n \geq 1.$$

Thus
$$\gamma n^t < \Pi(n, F_p) \le \delta n^t,$$

where
$$t = \left(\frac{\ln(p+1)}{\ln(p+1) - \ln(p)} \right),$$

$$\gamma = ((p+1)(p+2))^{-t}$$

and
$$\delta = 2^{(p+1)^2 - 1}(p+1)^{-2t}.$$

Suppose now that $t \le 2$ for some $p \in \{2, 3, \ldots\}$. By the definition of t we derive
$$t = \left(\frac{\ln(p+1)}{\ln(p+1) - \ln(p)} \right) = \left(\frac{\ln(p)}{\ln(p+1) - \ln(p)} \right) + 1 \le 2.$$

From this we obtain $\ln(p+1) - \ln(p) \ge \ln(p) > 0$, which implies $\ln(p+1) \ge 2\ln(p)$. This yields $p + 1 \ge p^2$, and therefore $1 \ge p(p-1) \ge 2$. From this contradiction we conclude that $t > 2$ for all $p \in \{2, 3, \ldots\}$.

Now we are ready for our main result.

Theorem 1. *Infinite word F_p generated by a D0L system with periodic control cannot be obtained by any CD0L system.*

Proof. Let G be an infinite word obtained by a D0L system. Then due Ehrenfeucht, Lee and Rozenberg [ELR] we know that
$$\Pi(n, G) = O(n^2).$$

Because a CD0L word is only a coding of a D0L word this result holds also for CD0L words. However, we have shown above that
$$\gamma n^t < \Pi(n, F_p) \le \delta n^t,$$

where γ and δ are two positive constants and $t > 2$, proving the theorem. □

We get also another result concerning correspondence between the number p of morphisms and the subword complexity of F_p.

Theorem 2. *For any given real number r there is a infinite word generated by D0L system with periodic control such that its subword complexity is $\Omega(n^r)$.*

Proof. By the definition of t we obtain
$$\left(\frac{t}{p \ln(p+1)} \right) = (\ln((1 + p^{-1})^p))^{-1} \to 1 \text{ as } p \to \infty.$$

Therefore $t \to \infty$ and theorem follows. □

The following table show how the subword complexity of the word F_p grows when the number p of morphisms increases.

p	t	p	t
2	2.70951129	20	62.4003319
3	4.81884168	30	104.727227
4	7.21256744	40	150.392027
5	9.82746912	50	198.550706
6	12.6234289	100	463.815786
7	15.5726792	200	1063.31043
8	18.6548476	300	1714.98504
9	21.8543453	400	2400.58031
10	25.1588579	500	3111.41032
11	28.5584108	1000	6912.20874
12	32.0447600	2000	15206.6051
13	35.6109775	3000	24024.1050
14	39.2511595	4000	33181.3448
15	42.9602147	5000	42591.2250
16	46.7337075	10000	92109.0275
17	50.5677391	100000	1151293.55
18	54.4588553	1000000	13815511.6
19	58.4039748	10000000	161180958

Table 1. Correspondence between t and p.

4 Concluding remarks

Here we point out how our construction can be generalized. Let Σ be a finite alphabet of cardinality $q > 1$, $a \in \Sigma$ be a letter and let f be a mapping from the alphabet Σ into itself such that sequence $a, f(a), f^2(a), \ldots$ is ultimately periodic with period longer than one. We define morphisms $h_1, \ldots, h_p$ in the following way:

$$h_1 : \Sigma \to \Sigma^2 , \quad x \to af(x) , \text{ for all } x \in \Sigma,$$

$$h_i : \Sigma \to \Sigma , \quad x \to f(x) , \text{ for all } x \in \Sigma \text{ and } i \in \{2,3,\ldots,p\}.$$

Let G be the infinite word generated by this D0L system with periodic control, starting at a.

Our earlier considerations can be modified to this generalization. Results will be very similar to those we have already proved. For example, one can show, that

$$\gamma n^t < \Pi(n, G) \leq \delta n^t, \text{ where}$$

$$t = \left(\frac{\ln(p+1)}{\ln(p+1) - \ln(p)} \right),$$

$$\gamma = ((p+1)(p+2))^{-t}$$

and

$$\delta = q^{(p+1)^2 - 1}(p+1)^{-2t}.$$

We conclude with the following open problem:

Problem. Can we obtain an infinite word with exponential subword complexity by a D0L system with periodic control?

Acknowlegment

I am deeply grateful to J. Karhumäki for useful comments and for introducing the problem.

References

[Be] J. Berstel: Some resent results on squarefree words. Lecture Notes in Computer Science 166, 14-25. Berlin: Springer Verlag 1984.

[CK] K. Culik II and J. Karhumäki: Iterative devices generating infinite words. Lecture Notes in Computer Science 577, 531-544. Berlin: Springer Verlag 1992.

[CKL] K. Culik II, J. Karhumäki and A. Lepistö: Alternating iteration of morphisms and the Kolakovski sequence. In: G. Rozenberg, A. Salomaa (eds.): Lindermayer Systems, 93-106. Berlin: Springer Verlag 1992.

[ELR] A. Ehrenfeucht, K. Lee and G. Rozenberg: Subword complexities of various classes of deterministic developmental languages without interactions. Theoretical Computer Science 1, 59-75. 1975.

[K] W. Kolakovski: Self generating runs, Problem 5304. Amer. Math. Monthly 71. 1965.

[Sa] A. Salomaa: Jewels of formal language theory. Rockville, Maryland: Computer Science Press 1981.

If a D0L Language is k-Power Free then it is Circular

Filippo Mignosi

Dip. Mat. ed Appl., Università di Palermo
via Archirafi 34, 90123 Palermo, Italia

Patrice Séébold

L.I.T.P., Institut Blaise Pascal
2 place Jussieu, 75252 Paris Cedex 05, France

Abstract. We prove that if a D0L language is k-power free then it is circular. By using this result we are able to give an algorithm which decides whether, fixed an integer $k \geq 1$, a D0L language is k-power free; we are also able to give a new simpler proof of a result, previously obtained by Ehrenfeucht and Rozenberg, that states that it is decidable whether a D0L language is k-power free for some integer $k \geq 1$.

1 Introduction

The notion of k-power free words and of k-power free morphisms has been the subject of several works since Thue's paper in 1906 (see for instance references [1]-[3], [4]-[7], [9]-[14], [16]-[23], [25]-[27], [29], [31], [34]-[36]). The study of k-power free words (and the "symmetric" notion of repetition of subwords) is very important in the theory of formal languages, as stressed by Ehrenfeucht and Rozenberg in [12]: "The investigation of the combinatorial structure of languages forms an important part of formal language theory. One of the most basic combinatorial structures of languages is the repetition of subwords (in words of a language)."

An important family of languages, which has been extensively investigated, (see for instance [33], [34]) is that of D0L languages.

In [11] and [12], Ehrenfeucht and Rozenberg proved, in a beautiful but rather technical way, that it is decidable whether a D0L language is k-power free for some integer k. Their proof can give an upper bound on the number k but does not settle the following problem: fixed an integer $k \geq 1$, is it decidable whether a D0L language is k-power free?

Partial results to this problem were given in [1], [16], [17]. In [1] Berstel proved that it is decidable whether a D0L language over a three-letter alphabet is 2-power free (square free); in [16], [17] Karhumäki showed that it is decidable whether a D0L language over a two-letter alphabet is 3-power free (cube free). In this paper we settle positively the previous problem.

Our main result states that if a D0L language is k-power free then it is *circular*, this notion comes from the theory of dynamical systems (see [15], [24], [27], [28]) and it is close to the notion of circular code. It is possible to prove that, if the set $X(h) =$

{h(a) | a ∈ A} is a circular code then the language L(G) is circular (see [4]). One first formalization of the notion of circularity was given in [24] where a theorem analogous to our main result was incorrectly stated; since then it was an open question whether the basic ideas contained in [24] were correct. In [27] Mosse uses a definition which is just lightly weaker than our definition of circularity.

Roughly speaking, if the language L(G) is circular then the morphism h of the D0L System is "almost injective" when it is restricted to the set of subwords of the language L(G). We will give examples of D0L Systems G and G' having same morphism h but different axioms, such that L(G) is circular and L(G') is not,

As a consequence of our main result, we are able to give a new simpler proof of the result of Ehrenfeucht and Rozenberg in [11] and [12], and we give an algorithm which decides whether, fixed an integer k, a D0L language is k-power free.

2 Some Definitions

Let A be a finite set, called alphabet. We denote by A* the *free monoid* on A. The elements of A* are called *words* and the elements of A are called *letters* . Subsets of A* are called *languages*. We denote by 1 the empty word which is the identity of A*; we also denote by |v| the length of a word v.

A word u is a *subword* (or a *factor*) of a word w if there exist v, v' ∈ A* such that

$$w = vuv';$$

if v = 1 (v' = 1) then u is a *left (right) subword* of w. If L is a language, S(L) is the set of all the subwords of L.

If a word w is of the form

$$w = v....v = v^k$$

with v ≠ 1, v primitive, we say that w is a *k-power* of v; the number k ≥ 1 is called the *exponent* of the power and v is the *base* of the power. If a word w is of the form

$$w = v....vu = v^k u$$

with v ≠ 1, k ≥ 1 and u left subword of v, we say that w is a *fractional power* of v with *exponent* e = $\frac{|w|}{|v|}$ and v is the *base* of the power. Obviously a k-power is a fractional power with the same exponent and base.

A language is *repetitive* if for all positive integer k it contains a k-power.

A language L is *strongly repetitive* if there exists a subword v of a word of L such that for all positive integer k v^k is also a subword of a word of L.

A language L is *k-power free* if each word of L contains no subword which is a fractional power with exponent greater than or equal to k; If L is k-power free the *optimum* value α is given by

$$\alpha = \inf \{k \text{ real} \mid L \text{ is k-power free}\}.$$

Notice that the optimum value α can be reached by some exponent (as in the set of subwords of the binary Thue-Morse word, which contains no fractional power with exponent strictly greater than 2); in this case the language is not α-power free.

We call *morphisms* the homomorphisms from A* to B*.

To any endomorphism h defined on A* (A={a_1,...,a_n}) it is possible to associate a n×n matrix where the entry $m_{i,j}$ gives the number of occurrences of the letter a_i in h(a_j).

A *DOL System* is a triple

$$G = (A, h, w)$$

where A is an alphabet, h is an endomorphism (or morphism) defined on A^*, and w (referred to as the *axiom*) is a nonempty word. If for all $a \in A$ $h(a) \neq 1$ then G is *propagating* (PD0L; see [32])

The language of G is defined by

$$L(G) = \{ h^i(w) \mid i \geq 0 \}.$$

The set $X(h) = \{h(a) \mid a \in A\}$ is a code (see [4]) if and only if the morphism h is injective; if the morphism is injective then the D0L must be propagating .

Our next notion (definition 2) is the fundamental technical notion of this paper; it is a generalization of finite circular codes.

Definition 1: Let $G = (A, h, w)$ be a D0L system; a word v admits a *interpretation* by G if $v = s(0)x(1)x(2)...x(n)s(n+1)$ where $x(i) = h(a(i))$, $s(0)$, $s(n+1)$ are respectively a right and a left factor of $h(a(0))$, $h(a(n+1))$, $a(i) \in A$, and $a(0)a(1)a(2)...a(n)a(n+1)$ belongs to $S(L(G))$ (i.e. it is a subword of a word in $L(G)$). The word $a(0)a(1)a(2)...a(n)a(n+1)$ is called the ancestor of the interpretation.

Definition 2: A D0L language $L(G)$ is *circular* with *synchronization delay* D, if the following property holds: for all word v, if v admits two distinct interpretations, say $v = s(0)x(1)x(2)...x(n)s(n+1) = s'(0)x'(1)x'(2)...x'(t)s'(t+1)$ where $x(i) = h(a(i))$ and $x'(i) = h(a'(i))$, then whenever $|s(0)x(1)x(2)...x(i-1)| > D$ and $|x(i+1)...x(n)s(n+1)| > D$, there exists a number j such that $s(0)x(1)x(2)...x(i) = s'(0)x'(1)x'(2)...x'(j)$ with $a(i) = a'(j)$. That is, the two interpretations are synchronized at distance D from the borders.

A graphical view point is showed in Fig. 1.

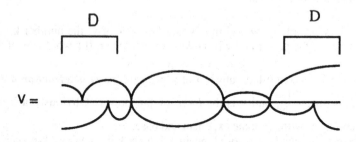

Fig. 1.

If a word v admits two distinct interpretations that, for all D, are not synchronized at distance D from the borders, we say that the two interpretations *never synchronize*.

Remark 1: We want to emphatize in Definition 1 the request that $a(0)a(1)...a(n)a(n+1)$ belongs to $S(L(G))$. Without this request, circularity would be equivalent to the fact that $\{h(a) \mid a \in A\}$ is a circular code and circularity would be a property of the morphism h and not of the language $L(G)$.

Remark 2: It is not difficult to see that if the property described in Definition 2 holds for all words u with $|u| \leq 2D+2m+1$, where $m = \max \{|h(a)| : a \in A\}$, then it holds for all words v (the idea is to "span" any word v with its subwords of length

2D+2m+1). This shows that it is decidable whether a D0L language is circular with a fixed synchronization delay D.

Examples: Let $G = \{\{a,b,c\}, h, c\}$ and $G' = \{\{a,b,c\}, h, a\}$, where $h(a) = ab$, $h(b) = a$, $h(c) = cc$. For all natural $i \geq 1$, the word c^{2i} is a subword of $L(G)$ and admits two interpretations that never synchronize: the first is $c^{2i} = c^2 c^2 ... c^2$ and the second is $c^{2i} = cc^2 ... c^2 c$. Since this holds for all natural $i \geq 1$, $L(G)$ is not circular.

The language $L(G')$ is circular with synchronization delay 1. In $L(G')$ there appear only the two letters a and b. Let v be a word that admit two interpretation and let $y(i)$ be the i-th letter of v, which is not the first letter of v nor the last; if $y(i) = b$ then it must be in the images of the letter a and both two interpretation must synchronize on $y(i)$. If $y(i) = a$ then, if the letter $y(i+1)$ is b then it must be in the images of the letter a and both two interpretation must synchronize on $y(i)$; if the letter $y(i+1)$ is a then $y(i)$ must be the images of the letter b and both two interpretation must synchronize on $y(i)$.

Sometimes if $L(G)$ is repetitive, strongly repetitive, k-power free or circular, we will say that G is repetitive, strongly repetitive, k-power free or circular respectively.

3 Main Results

The following definitions and Lemma 1 are contained in [12].

Definition 3: Let $G = (A, h, w)$ be a D0L system; a letter b has *rank zero* (in G) if $L(G_b)$ is finite, where $G_b = (A, h, b)$.

Definition 4: A D0L system $G = (A, h, w)$ is *pushy* if for all integer n there exists a subword v of $L(G)$ of length n which is composed by letters that have rank zero; otherwise G is *not pushy*. If a D0L system G is not pushy then $q(G)$ denotes max{ |v| | v is composed by letters that have rank zero }.

Lemma 1. (1) *It is decidable whether or not an arbitrary D0L system is pushy.*
(2) *If G is pushy then G is strongly repetitive.*
(3) *If G is not pushy then $q(G)$ is effectively computable.*

The following lemma says that if G is not pushy and if a letter b has not rank zero, then G_b is exponentially growing.

Lemma 2. *Let $G = (A, h, w)$ be a not pushy PD0L system. Let b a letter which has not rank zero.*

For all natural n, if $s = \lfloor \dfrac{n}{\#A(q(G)+2)} \rfloor + 1$ then $|h^n(b)| \geq 2^s$.

Proof. Since b has not rank zero then $|h^{\#A}(b)| \geq 2$. Since one at least of the letters composing $h^{\#A}(b)$ has not rank zero, $|h^{\#A(q(G)+2)}(b)| \geq q(G)+2$. Thus two at least of the letters composing $h^{\#A(q(G)+2)}(b)$ have not rank zero. The lemma is now straightforward.

Theorem 1. *Let $G = (A, h, w)$ be a propagating DOL system. If a word v of length n admits two distinct interpretations that never synchronize then there exists a subword of v which is a fractional power with exponent $e(n)$, where e is a function such that $e(m)$ tends to infinite as m tends to infinite.*

Proof. (Sketch) let $v = s(0)x(1)x(2)...x(L)s(L+1) = s'(0)x'(1)x'(2)...x'(t)s'(t+1)$ be the two distinct interpretations that never synchronize, where $x(i) = h(a(i))$ and $x'(i) = h(a'(i))$, $s(0)$, $s(L+1)$ are respectively a right and a left factor of $h(a(0))$, $h(a(L+1))$, $a(i) \in A$, and $s'(0)$, $s'(t+1)$ are respectively a right and a left factor of $h(a'(0))$, $h(a'(t+1))$, $a'(i) \in A$. Let us take $D = \lfloor \frac{n-2m-1}{2} \rfloor$ where $m = \max\{|h(a)| : a \in A\}$; there exists i such that $|s(0)x(1)x(2)...x(i-1)| > D$ and $|x(i+1)...x(L)s(L+1)| > D$ and for all j either $s(0)x(1)x(2)...x(i) \neq s'(0)x'(1)x'(2)...x'(j)$ or $a(i) \neq a'(j)$. Let us call (for reasons that will be clearer soon) i_1 the number i and $a(i_1,1)$ the letter $a(i)$; if j is the smallest integer such that $|s'(0)x'(1)x'(2)...x'(j)| > |s(0)x(1)x(2)...x(i)|$, let us call j_1 the number j and $a'(j_1,1)$ the letter $a'(j)$. By construction there exists at least one overlap between the words $h(a(i_1,1))$ and $h(a'(j_1,1))$. Let us call the overlap obtained by this construction the *natural overlap* between $h(a(i_1,1))$ and $h(a'(j_1,1))$.

If n is "big enough" then the length of the two ancestors $a(0)a(1)a(2)...a(L)a(L+1)$, $a'(0)a'(1)a'(2)...a'(t)a'(t+1)$ is greater than the length of the axiom w, and, consequently, each of them admits at least one interpretation. Let $s(0,2)x(1,2)x(2,2)...x(L_2,2)s(L_2+1,2)$ and $s'(0,2)x'(1,2)x'(2,2)...x'(t_2,2)s'(t_2+1,2)$ be the two interpretation, where $x(i,2) = h(a(i,2))$ and $x'(i,2) = h(a'(i,2))$; $s(0,2)$, $s(L_2+1,2)$ are respectively a right and a left factor of $h(a(0,2))$, $h(a(L_2+1,2))$, $a(i,2) \in A$ and $s'(0,2)$, $s'(t_2+1,2)$ are respectively a right and a left factor of $h(a'(0,2))$, $h(a'(t_2+1,2))$, $a'(i,2) \in A$. Let i_2 be such that $|s(0,2)x(1,2)x(2,2)...x(i_2-1,2)| \leq i_1 < |s(0,2)x(1,2)x(2,2)...x(i_2,2)|$ (this implies that $a(i_1,1)$ is "contained" in $h(a(i_2,2))$), and let j_2 be such that $|s'(0,2)x'(1,2)x'(2,2)...x'(j_2-1,2)| \leq j_1 < |s'(0,2)x'(1,2)x'(2,2)...x'(j_2,2|$. By construction there exists at least one overlap between the words $h^2(a(i_2,2))$ and $h^2(a(j_2,2))$ which contains as subword the natural overlap between $h(a(i_1,1))$ and $h(a'(j_1,1))$. Let us call the overlap obtained by this construction the *natural overlap* between $h^2(a(i_2,2))$ and $h^2(a'(j_2,2))$.

If n is "big enough" then we can iterate the above argument and construct a sequence of pairs of letters ($a(i_q,q)$, $a'(i_q,q)$), $1 \leq q \leq M$ for some M that tends to infinite as n and D tend to infinite; these pairs of letters have one beautiful property that naturally leads to the idea that is at the base of this proof. Before claiming this property we state some more notations.

Since now some indices are redundant, let us call ($a(i_q,q)$, $a'(i_q,q)$) simply (a_q, a'_q)

Let us suppose that $h^p(a_q)$ and $h^p(a'_q)$ with $p < q$, overlaps and let $u(q,p)$ be the word that is the common subword of $h^p(a_q)$ and of $h^p(a'_q)$. Let us call $u(q,q)$ the natural overlap between $h^q(a_q)$ and $h^q(a'_q)$. We remark that $u(q,p)$ is not in general uniquely determined while $u(q,q)$ is uniquely determined; in what follow we consider that, once made a choice, $u(q,p)$ is fixed.

When two word overlap there are always 4 cases: (1) $h^p(a_q) = v(q,p)u(q,p)$ and $h^p(a'_q) = u(q,p)z(q,p)$.   (2) $h^p(a'_q) = v(q,p)u(q,p)$ and $h^p(a_q) = u(q,p)z(q,p)$.

(3) $h^P(a_q) = v(q,p)u(q,p)z(q,p)$ and $h^P(a'_q) = u(q,p)$.   (4) $h^P(a'_q) = v(q,p)u(q,p)z(q,p)$ and $h^P(a_q) = u(q,p)$. We remark that in the case of the natural overlap $u(q,q)$ it follows by construction that $v(q,q)$ is also uniquely determined; this last remark is redundant in the cases (1) and (2) because $v(q,p)$ is determined by $u(q,p)$ but in the cases (3) and (4) it is not. In what follow we consider that, once made a choice, $v(q,p)$ is fixed.

Claim. Let $q>p>0$. $h^{q-p}(u(q,p)) \neq u(q,q)$ or $h^{q-p}(v(q,p)) \neq v(q,q)$.

Proof of the claim. Let us suppose by contradiction that $h^{q-p}(u(q,p)) = u(q,q)$ and $h^{q-p}(v(q,p)) = v(q,q)$; then also $h^{q-p}(z(q,p)) = z(q,q)$. Then it is not difficult to see that the overlap between $h^P(a_q)$ and $h^P(a'_q)$ is in the case (i) if and only if the natural overlap between $h^q(a_q)$ and $h^q(a'_q)$ is in the case (i). Let we set $h^{q-p-1}(u(q,p)) = b_0 b_1 b_2 ... b_d b_{d+1}$, $b_i \in A$; $h^{q-p-1}(u(q,p))$ is the ancestor of the interpretation of $u(q,q)$ = $h(b_0)h(b_1)h(b_2)...h(b_d)h(b_{d+1})$.

If we think to $u(q,q)$ as subword of $h^q(a_q)$ and to $u(q,p)$ as subword of $h^P(a_q)$, since $h^{q-p}(v(q,p)) = v(q,q)$, the above interpretation is a part of the first of the two distinct interpretation of v.

If we think to $u(q,q)$ as subword of $h^q(a'_q)$ and to $u(q,p)$ as subword of $h^P(a'_q)$, since $h^{q-p}(v(q,p)) = v(q,q)$, the above interpretation is a part of the second of the two distinct interpretation of v.

Therefore the two interpretation of v synchronize over $u(q,q)$. By the construction of $u(q,q)$ the two interpretation do not synchronize over $u(q,q)$, a contradiction and the claim is proved.

Since h is non erasing, by applying h^{N-q} in the statement of the Claim, we have the following consequence. Let $N>q>p>0$; $h^{N-p}(u(q,p)) \neq h^{N-q}(u(q,q))$ or $h^{N-p}(v(q,p))$ $\neq h^{N-q}(v(q,q))$.

The idea of the proof of Theorem 1 is now the following: if the number M of the pairs of letters (a_q, a'_q) is "large" then, by the pigeon holes principle there are "lot" of them (at least M/#A) that are equal, that is $(a_p, a'_p) = (a_q, a'_q) = ... = (a_N, a'_N)$, where $p < q < .... < N$.

Hence, the words $h^N(a_N)$ and $h^N(a'_N)$ overlaps, by the above consequence of the Claim, at least in M/#A distinct ways.

When two words u, v, overlaps in a "lot" of distinct ways then we expect that at least one of them contains, as subword, a fractional power with a large exponent; this consequence is not true in general and the cases where this consequence is not true are called "pathological". Two example of pathological cases are the following:

(1) the length of v is quite smaller than the length of u and u is equal to

$$u_1 v u_2 v u_3 v....u_{p-1} v u_p,$$ where the u_i are words.

(2) $v = u_p u_1....u_4 u_1 u_2 u_1 u_3 u_1 u_2 u_1$ and $u = u_1 u_2 u_1 u_3 u_1 u_2 u_1 u_4....u_1 u_p$ where the common words between v and u are: u_1, $u_1 u_2 u_1$, $u_1 u_2 u_1 u_3 u_1 u_2 u_1$, ..., $u_1....u_4 u_1 u_2 u_1 u_3 u_1 u_2 u_1$.

The proof of Theorem 1 now is technical and consist on proving that some pathological cases do not exist in a PD0L language and, if a pathological case is present, then it exists a fractional power with a large exponent.

Corollary. *If a DOL language is k-power free for some $k \geq 1$ then it is circular.*

Remark 3: It is possible, from the proof, to give an evaluation of the function $e(n)$ in the statement of Theorem 1 and, consequently, if a DOL language is k-power free then it is possible to give an evaluation in the above corollary of the synchronization delay D of the circularity as function of k.

For all DOL system $G = (A, h, w)$ it is possible to construct an elementary version $G' = (A', h', w')$ of G, where h' is injective and G' propagating (see for instance [30]). Since for all integer k, $L(G)$ is k power free (repetitive, strongly repetitive) if and only if $L(G')$ is k power free (repetitive, strongly repetitive), from now on the DOL systems will be always propagating, and we will continue writing "DOL" instead of "PDOL". Moreover we will suppose that $L(G)$ is infinite.

Proposition 1. *Let $G = (A, h, w)$ be a not pushy DOL system. There exists an effectively computable integer $\underline{n}$ such that if $v^{\underline{n}}$ is a subword of a word in $L(G)$, then for all positive integer k, v^k is a subword of a word in $L(G)$.*

Proof. We can suppose that v is a primitive word (see [21]). Since G is not pushy then, by lemma 1.3 it is possible to compute $q(G)$. Let us define $m = \max \{lh(a) : a \in A\}$ and set $\underline{n} = \max(1+q(G), 2|w|(2m)^{\#A})$; notice that $m \geq 2$ because $L(G)$ is infinite.

Since $\underline{n} > q(G)$ then $v^{\underline{n}}$ contains a letter which has not rank zero, that implies that v contains a letter which has not rank zero.

Since $\underline{n} > |w|$ then $v^{\underline{n}}$ admits a interpretation by G (see definition 1); let v_1 be the ancestor of this interpretation. If v_1 admits a interpretation let us call v_2 the ancestor of this interpretation. Let us iterate the above construction until either v_s does not admit a interpretation or $|v_{s+1}| < 2$. Let $v_s = a(0)a(1)a(2)...a(t)a(t+1)$; by construction $h^s(a(1)), ... , h^s(a(t))$ are subwords of $v^{\underline{n}}$, while $h^s(a(0)) = xy_0$ (respectively $h^s(a(t+1)) = y_{t+1}z$) where y_0 (respectively y_{t+1}) is a left subword (right subword) of $v^{\underline{n}}$. We claim that either $h^s(a(i))$ for some i , $1 \leq i \leq t$, or y_0 or y_{t+1} has length greater than or equal to $\dfrac{\underline{n}|v|}{2m|w|}$; if not then $|v^{\underline{n}}| = \underline{n}|v| < \dfrac{|v_s|\underline{n}|v|}{2m|w|}$, i.e. $|v_s| > 2m|w|$. Since $|v_s| > |w|$, v_s admits a interpretation and, since $|v_s| > 2m$, the ancestor v_{s+1} of v_s has length ≥ 2; a contradiction and the claim is proved. Let a_s be the letter obtained by the previous claim (if y_0 or y_{t+1} has length greater than or equal to $\dfrac{\underline{n}|v|}{2m|w|}$, then $a_s = a(0)$ or $a_s = a(t+1)$ respectively). By the definition of m it follows that there exists a letter a_{s-1}, between the letters composing $h(a_s)$, such that $h^{s-1}(a_{s-1})$ has length at least $\dfrac{\underline{n}|v|}{(2m)^2|w|}$ and is also a subword of $v^{\underline{n}}$. If $a_s = a(0)$ ($a_s = a(t+1)$) then there is also the possibility that $h^{s-1}(a_{s-1})$ contains a right subword (left subword) of length at least $\dfrac{\underline{n}|v|}{(2m)^2|w|}$ that is left subword (right subword) of $v^{\underline{n}}$; we stop considering these special cases because they can be treated in an analogous way as the general case. In analogous way we define a_{s-2}, a_{s-3}, ..., $a_{s-\#A}$ with the property that $h^{s-i}(a(s-i))$ is a subword of $v^{\underline{n}}$ with length at least $\dfrac{\underline{n}|v|}{(2m)^{i+1}|w|}$. By the pigeon holes principle there exist i, j , $0 \le i < j \le \#A$, such that $a_{s-i} = a_{s-j}$. From the choose of $\underline{n}$ we have that length of $h^{s-j}(a_{s-j}) \ge 2|v|$; since $h^{s-j}(a_{s-j})$ is a subword of $v^{\underline{n}}$ then $h^{s-j}(a_{s-j}) = v'v'u$ where v' is a conjugate to v (see [21]) and u is a word. But $h^{j-i}(h^{s-j}(a_{s-j})) = h^{s-i}(a_{s-i})$ is also a subword of $v^{\underline{n}}$, and, consequently $h^{j-i}(v'v')$ is a subword of $v^{\underline{n}}$; more precisely $h^{j-i}(v'v') = v^{\circ p}u$ where v° is another conjugate of v, u is a left factor of v° and $p \ge 2$ (since the morphism is non erasing). If $|h^{j-i}(v')| = |v^{\circ}| = |v'|$ then the morphism h^{j-i} generates a permutation of the letters composing v, and this implies that all the letters composing v have rank zero, that is impossible by the choice of $\underline{n}$ as noticed at the beginning of this proof. Therefore $|h^{j-i}(v')| > |v^{\circ}|$.

Now $h^{j-i}(v'v') = h^{j-i}(v')h^{j-i}(v')$ is a fractional power of base $h^{j-i}(v')$ and exponent 2; it is also a fractional power of base v°. From the theorem of Fine and Wilf (see [21]) it is also a fractional power of base x, where $|x| = gcm(|h^{j-i}(v')|, |v^{\circ}|)$. Since v is primitive then v° is primitive and, consequently, $v^{\circ} = x$. Hence $h^{j-i}(v') = v^{\circ q}$ for some integer $q \ge 2$; the proposition is now straightforward.

Theorem 2 (Ehrenfeucht and Rozenberg [12]). *If a D0L system G is repetitive then it is strongly repetitive.*
Proof. If G is pushy then it is strongly repetitive (Lemma 1.2). Suppose that G is not pushy and let $\underline{n}$ as in the above proposition; since G is repetitive, there exists a word v such that $v^{\underline{n}}$ is a subword of a word in L(G). Then, by the above proposition, for all positive integer k, v^k is a subword of a word in L(G), i.e. G is strongly repetitive.

Lemma 3. *Let G = (A, h, w) be a not pushy D0L system. If it is repetitive then it is not circular* (i.e. under the assumption that G is propagating and not pushy, the notion of circularity coincides with the notion of k-power free for some $k \ge 1$).
Proof. We give just the idea of the proof. Let us take for instance the D0L System G = {{c}, h, c}, where h(c) = cc; obviously $h^i(c) = c^{2i}$. The word c^{2i} admits two interpretations that never synchronize: the first is $c^{2i} = c^2c^2...c^2$ and the second is $c^{2i} = cc^2...c^2c$. Since this holds for all natural $i \ge 1$. the D0L System is not circular.
  Let us now consider the general case with G repetitive.
  Since G is strongly repetitive, let v be a primitive word such that for all k, v^k is a subword of a word in L(G). By the proof of Proposition 1 there exist integers j, p, $1 \le j \le \#A$, $p \ge 2$ such that $h^j(v) = v'^p$ where v' is a conjugate of v.
  Let us now make a generalization of definition 1 and 2 by replacing everywhere h with h^j , interpretation with j-interpretation, synchronize with j-synchronize and circular with j-circular. It is possible to prove that if a D0L language is circular (1-circular) with synchronization delay D then it is j-circular with synchronization delay m^jD, where m is defined as in Proposition 1.

Analogously as the previous example it is possible to prove that the word $(v'^P)^i$ admits two interpretations that never j-synchronize. Hence G is not j-circular and, consequently, it is not circular.

Theorem 3 (Ehrenfeucht and Rozenberg [12]). *It is decidable whether or not a D0L system G = (A, h, w) is k-power free for some integer k.*
Proof. From Lemma 1.1 we decide whether G is pushy or not; if the answer is yes then it is not k-power free (Lemma 1.2).

G is now not pushy. Let us take n such that $e(n) \geq \underline{n}$, where $e(n)$ is the function in Theorem 1 and $\underline{n}$ is as in Proposition 1. Let us check whether in all the subwords of length n+2m+1 (m=max {lh(a)l : a ∈ A}) of words in L(G) there are or not fractional powers of exponent $\underline{n}$. If such a fractional power is founded then by Proposition 1 the D0L system G is repetitive; if not then by Theorem 1 and by Remark 2 the D0L system G is circular with synchronization delay $D \leq \frac{n}{2}$. From Lemma 3 it is k-power free for some integer $k \geq 1$, q.e.d..

Remark 4: From the above proof it follows also that if a D0L system is k power free for some integer k then it is $\underline{n}$ power free, where $\underline{n}$ is described in Proposition 1.

Theorem 4. *It is decidable whether, fixed an integer k, a D0L system G = (A, h, w) is k-power free.*
Proof.(Sketch) First of all we decide, by using Theorem 2, whether G is n power free for some number k; if G is n power free then it is $\underline{n}$ power free, where $\underline{n}$ is described in Proposition 1. From Theorem 1 we get that it is circular with synchronization delay D calculable as function of $\underline{n}$.

The idea of the proof is to utilize the circularity to reduce the length of the basis of a fractional power without reducing "too much" the exponent. As second step, starting by fractional powers with bounded length, we evaluate the maximal exponent that they can "generate" by iterating h.

Let, for instance u be a fractional power with base v, exponent (for instance) greater than 2 and lvl >>D, lvl >>lwl. Let us open over u two "windows" of length 2D + 2m+1 (where m = max {lh(a)l : a ∈ A}; one at the beginning of u and the other at the beginning of the second occurrence of the base v in u (here we have supposed that u is "oriented" from left to right). The two windows "see" the same word x. Since lul >>lwl then u admits a interpretation; this interpretation induces two distinct interpretation on the word x. It follows, from the circularity of G, that the two distinct interpretation of x must synchronize in the middle of the two windows. Moving by step of one letter on the left the two windows, we can iterate the above argument and prove that the ancestor of the interpretation of u contains a fractional power of exponent "almost" greater as the exponent of u. More precisely the ancestor of the interpretation of u contains a fractional power u' with base v' such that lh(v')l is a conjugate of v and lul - lh(u')l ≤ 2D.

If lv'l is still >>D then we can repeat the above construction. Lemma 2 guaranties that, by iterating this argument, the length of the fractional power decreases exponentially. Starting from a fractional power u, we call reduced version of u any fractional power that we obtain with the above construction. There exists an integer N (calculable) such that for all fractional power u with $|u| \geq N$, there exists a reduced version of u that has length smaller than N.

Now we want to describe the second step of the proof but we need some more definitions. Let x be a subword of $z = a_0 a_1 a_2 \ldots a_n a_{n+1} = uxw, a_i \in A$; we say that x *contains the position j* if $|u| \leq j$ and $|ux| > j$. Let z be a subword of L(G) and let x be a fractional power subword of z with base v; we say that x is *maximal in z in the position j* if 1) it contains the position j, and 2)*either* $z = x$ *or* $z = uax$ (xau), $a \in A$, and ax (xa) is not a fractional power with same base *or* z =uaxbw, a and b $\in$ A, and ax, xb are not fractional powers with same base.

It is easy to see that h(x) has at least the same exponent of x. Let us define recursively x_n in the following way: if $h^{n-1}(z) = ux_{n-1}w$ with u and w words, x_n is the fractional power with base $h(v_{n-1})$ (where v_{n-1} is the base of x_{n-1}), subword of $h^n(z)$, which contains as subword $h(x_{n-1})$ and which is maximal in $h^n(z)$ in the position $|u|$. Informally we consider x_{n-1} as immersed in $h^{n-1}(z)$, then we apply the morphism h and finally we extend this new fractional power as much as possible. It is, in some sense, an inverse procedure of the previous step of proof. If we write $x_n = p_n h(x_{n-1})s_n$ then, from the previous step of proof, $p_n \leq D$ and $s_n \leq D$. It is also possible to prove that the sequence of pairs of words (p_n, s_n) is definitively periodic. At this point an analysis of the growth matrix of the D0L system (it is necessary to compute the Jordan normal form) allow us to evaluate the algebraic number α = sup { e | e is exponent of x_n} and to say whether this number is an exponent of an x_n or not. Comparing the number k of the statement of theorem to this number α for all sequences x_n, where $|x_0| \leq N$ complete the decision algorithm.

4 Conclusions and Further Remarks

At this moment our techniques cannot be extended to the k-freeness problem of morphism, because we deeply use the fact that if a word v has length greater than the length of the axiom, then it admits at least one interpretation. Probably our techniques can be extended to D0L Systems with finitely many axioms.

We believe that our Theorem 1 could be an useful tool for giving new proofs of some known results and we hope that it will help to settle other decidability problems concerning D0L systems. In [8] C. Choffrut proved a decidability result in the binary case of a long standing question about D0L locally catenative systems (see [32]); he says that his technique probably cannot be extended too much, and that "the most that can be expected is that it extends to morphisms with finite decifrability delay, but this is not too clear either". It is possible to prove that if a D0L system G is repetitive and locally catenative then lim L(G) is composed by periodic words; hence, by the results contained in [14], if G is repetitive then it is decidable whether it is locally catenative. We hope that the corollary to Theorem 1 will be a tool for solving the general case.

References

1. J. Berstel, "Sur les mots sans carré définis par un morphisme", in Springer Lectures Notes in Computer Science Vol 71 (1979), 16-25.
2. J. Berstel, "Some recent results on square-free words" (STACS 84) Tech. Rept. L.I.T.P. 84-6.
3. J. Berstel, "Motifs et répétitions", in Actes du Congres "Journées Montoises", 1990, 9-15.
4. J. Berstel and D. Perrin, "Theory of Codes", 1985 Academic Press.
5. F. J. Brandenburg, "Uniformly growing kth power free homomorphisms", T.C.S. 23 (1983), 69-82.
6. A. Carpi,"On the size of a square-free morphism on a three letter alphabet", Inf. Proc. Lett. 16 (1983), 231-235.
7. A. Cerny,"On a class of infinite words with bounded repetitions", RAIRO Inf. Th. 19 (1985), 337-349.
8. C. Choffrut, "Iterated Substitutions and Locally Catenative Systems: a Decidability Result in the Binary Case", in Proc. ICALP 90,Lecture Notes in Comp. Science, Springer (1990), 490-500.
9. M. Crochemore, "Sharp Characterizations of square free morphisms" T. C. S. 18 (1982) 221-226.
10. A. Ehrenfeucht and G. Rozenberg, "On the subword complexity of square-free DOL languages" T.C.S. 16 (1981), 25-32.
11. A. Ehrenfeucht and G. Rozenberg, "Repetitions in homomorphisms and Languages" in 9th ICALP Symposium, Lecture Notes in Comp. Science, Springer (1982), 192-196.
12. A. Ehrenfeucht and G. Rozenberg, "Repetitions of Subwords in DOL Languages", Information and Control 59 (1983), 13-35.
13. M. Harrison, "Introduction to Formal Language Theory" Addison-Wesley, Readings, Mass., 1978.
14. Harju and M. Linna,"On the periodicity of morphisms on free monoids", RAIRO Inf. Th. vol. 20 (1986), n°1, 47-54.
15. B. Host,"Valeurs propres des systèmes dynamiques définis par des substitutions de longueur variable" Erg. Th. and Dyn. Sys. 6 (1986), 529-540.
16. J. Karhumàki, "On cube free w-words generated by binary morphisms", in Proc. FCT'81, Lecture Notes in Comp. Science 117, Springer (1981), 182-189.
17. J. Karhumàki, "On cube free w-words generated by binary morphisms", Discr. Appl. Math. 5 (1983), 279-297.
18. V. Keranen, "On the k-freeness of morphisms on free monoids", STACS 87, Lecture Notes in Comp. Science 247, 180-187.
19. R. Kfoury,"A linear time algorithm to decide whether a binary word contains an overlap", RAIRO Inf. Th. 22 (1988), 135-145.
20. M. Leconte,"kth power free codes" in "Automata on infinite words", M. Nivat and D. Perrin editors, Lecture Notes in Comp. Science 192, Springer-Verlag, 1984,172-187.
21. M. Leconte,"A Characterization of power-free morphisms", T.C.S. 38(1) (1985), 117-122.
22. A. Lentin and M. P. Schutzenberger, "A combinatorial problem in the theory of free monoids", in Proc. University of North Carolina, (1967), Boss ed., North Carolina Press, Chapell Hill, 128-144.

23. Lothaire, "Combinatorics on words", Addison Wesley, Reading Mass. 1982.
24. J. C. Martin,"Minimal flows arising from substitutions of non constant length" Math. Sys. Th. 7 (1973), 73-82.
25. F. Mignosi, "Infinite word with linear subword complexity", T.C.S. 65 (1989), 221-242.
26. F. Mignosi, G. Pirillo, "Repetitions in the Fibonacci infinite word", RAIRO Inf. Th. vol. 26, n° 3 (1992), 199-204.
27. B. Mossé, "Puissance de mots et reconnaissabilité des points fixes d'une substitution" T.C.S. (1992)
28. M. Queffeleq,"Substitution dynamical systems - Spectral analysis" Lecture Notes in Math. 1294 (1987), Springer-Verlag.
29. A. Restivo and S. Salemi, "Overlap free words on two symbols", in "Automata on infinite words", M. Nivat and D. Perrin editors, Lecture Notes in Comp.Science 192, Springer-Verlag, 1984,198-206.
30. P. Séébold, "Sequences generated by infinitely iterated morphisms", Discr. Appl. Math. 11 (1985), 255-264.
31. P. Séébold, " An effective solution to the DOL-periodicity problem in the binary case", EATCS bull. 36 (1988), 137-151.
32. G. Rozenberg and A. Salomaa, "The mathematical theory of L Systems", Academic Press, 1980.
33. G. Rozenberg and A. Salomaa editors, "The book of L", Springer-Verlag, 1986.
34. A. Salomaa, "Jewels of Formal Language Theory", Computer Science Press, Washington, D. C., 1981.
35. Thue A., "Über unendliche Zeichenreihen", Norske Vid. Selsk. Skr. I. Mat.-Nat. Kl., Christiana 1906, Nr. 7, 1-22.
36. Thue A., "Über die gegenseitige Lege gleicher Teile gewisser Zeichenrein", Norske Vid. Selsk. Skr. I. Mat.-Nat. Kl., Christiana 1912, Nr. 1, 1-67.

Deciding True Concurrency Equivalences on Finite Safe Nets (Preliminary Report)

Lalita Jategaonkar * and Albert Meyer**

MIT Laboratory for Computer Science
Cambridge, MA 02139

Abstract. We show that the pomset-trace equivalence problem for finite safe Petri Nets is decidable, and is in fact complete for EXPSPACE. We also show that history-preserving bisimulation between such nets is complete for DEXPTIME, settling a question left open by Vogler. Our decision procedures are based on establishing correspondences between bounded-size partial orders of transition firings, from which the upper bounds follow immediately. Lower bounds follow by reduction of corresponding interleaving (language) equivalence problems with known complexity. Our methods also yield tight complexity bounds for several other true concurrency equivalences. The results are independent of the presence of hidden transitions.

1   Introduction

The computational complexity of the equivalence problem for nondeterministic finite-state automata under a variety of standard process semantics has been tightly characterized. In particular, trace equivalence and failure equivalence [4] are PSPACE-complete [10], while bisimulation [12] is PTIME-complete [1, 10]. It has been shown recently that these equivalence problems are exponentially harder for automata presented as finite "Mazurkiewicz nets" of synchronized state-machines [14]: namely, trace equivalence and failure equivalence of these nets are EXPSPACE-complete [11, 13] and bisimulation of these nets is DEXPTIME-complete [15].

The known results for "true" concurrency equivalences are much more limited. Vogler [21] has shown the decidability of history-preserving bisimulation [2, 14, 17, 19, 21] for finite safe Petri nets; however, he left open its complexity. Decidability of such a basic true concurrency property as *pomset-trace* equivalence [17] appears not to have been known. (An ordinary trace is a linear sequence of visible actions; pomset-traces generalize these to multi-sets of actions partially ordered to reflect causality and concurrency.)

Throughout this paper, we use the term *nets* to refer to marked, **safe** Petri Nets [21] whose transitions have labels from a fixed set $Act \cup \{\tau\}$, where Act is a set of "visible actions" and $\tau \notin Act$ is the "hidden action." A transition is *visible* (hidden) iff its label is visible (hidden). The *runs* of a net are its finite firing sequences [21]. A net is *finite* iff it has a finite number of places and transitions; the *size* of a net is the total number of its places and transitions.

* Supported by the AT&T GRPW Fellowship and ONR grant No. N00014–83–K–0125.
** Supported by ONR grant No. N00014–83–K–0125.

520

Definition 1. A *pomset* is a labeled partial order. Formally, a pomset, p, consists of a set Events_p whose elements are called *events*, a set Labels_p whose elements are called *labels*, a function $\text{label}_p\colon \text{Events}_p \to \text{Labels}_p$, and a partial order relation $\leq_p$ on Events_p. A function f is an *isomorphism* between pomset p and pomset q iff it is a label-preserving order-isomorphism, namely,

- $f\colon \text{Events}_p \to \text{Events}_q$ is a bijection,
- $\text{label}_p = \text{label}_q \circ f$,
- $e \leq_p e'$ iff $f(e) \leq_q f(e')$ for all $e, e' \in \text{Events}_p$.

The *places* of a transition t of a net N are the places directly connected to it, i.e., the union of the preset and postset of t. Let t_1, t_2 be transitions of a net N. We say that t_1 and t_2 are *statically concurrent* in N iff the places of t_1 are disjoint from the places of t_2.

A *transition-sequence* is a sequence of transitions of a net N. For transition-sequence $r = t_1 t_2 \ldots$, we write $|r|$ for the length of r. The *transition-pomset* of r has as events the integers from 1 to n, where the label of event i is t_i and the partial ordering is the transitive closure of the following "proximate cause" relation: event i *proximately causes* event j iff $i < j$ and t_i and t_j are *not* statically concurrent in N, cf. Figure 1.

The *visible-pomset* of r is the transition-pomset of r, restricted to events labeled with visible transitions; moreover, in the visible-pomset, the label of event i is the *label* of t_i (rather than t_i itself), cf. Figure 1. The *pomset-traces* of N are the visible-pomsets of *runs* of N.

For transition-pomsets and visible-pomsets, it is traditional to say that event e *causes* event e' iff $e < e'$ in the partial order.

Definition 2. Let N and N' be nets. Then N *pomset-trace approximates* N', written $N \sqsubseteq_{pt} N'$, iff every pomset-trace of N is isomorphic to some pomset-trace of N'. N and N' are *pomset-trace equivalent* iff each is $\sqsubseteq_{pt}$ the other.

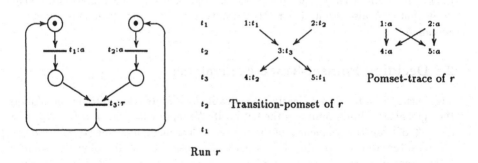

Fig. 1. An Example of a Transition-pomset and Pomset-trace

In contrast to trace equivalence, the decidability of pomset-trace equivalence for finite nets does not obviously reduce to equivalence of finite automata. The difficulty is that if a run of a net has a pomset-trace isomorphic to the pomset-trace of a run of another net, then whether a transition firable after one run yields the "same" pomset extension as a transition firable after the other run depends *a priori* on the entire pomset trace, which may be unboundedly large. Hence instead of searching for a suitable equivalence relation on the finite set of net markings, one has to consider equivalence relations on a potentially infinite set of pomset traces and final markings.

A similar difficulty appears in deciding whether finite nets are history-preserving bisimilar, which Vogler [21] overcomes by maintaining, instead of an entire pomset history, a partial order on the fixed set of places of the nets that reflects "most-recent" firings. We use a similar partial order, but instead of places, we find it technically smoother to keep track of the partial ordering between the most-recent firings of transitions. This idea leads to a decision procedure for pomset-trace equivalence, and a simple analysis of this procedure yields an EXPSPACE upper bound.[1] The same approach also gives a DEXPTIME decision procedure for history-preserving bisimulation.

Our lower bounds for these true concurrency equivalences follow easily from reductions from the corresponding interleaving equivalences, whose lower bounds in turn essentially follow from the results of [11, 13, 15]. We thus obtain a tight bound of EXPSPACE-completeness for pomset-trace equivalence. Likewise, we obtain DEXPTIME-completeness for history-preserving bisimulation, settling a question left open by Vogler [21].

Our methods also yield tight complexity bounds for several other true concurrency equivalences, summarized in Table 1. In particular, our EXPSPACE-completeness results for ST-traces and ST-failures solve problems left open by Vogler [23], who had earlier proved the decidability of these equivalences. Furthermore, our decidability results for pomset-bisimulation, pomset-ST-bisimulation, and maximality-preserving bisimulation settle questions alluded to by Vogler [20].

The paper is organized as follows. Section 2 describes our alternate characterization of pomset-trace equivalence, together with an EXPSPACE decision procedure. A similar analysis of history-preserving bisimulation is given in Section 3. Lower bounds for pomset-trace equivalence and history-preserving bisimulation are given in Section 4. A discussion of our other results and some open problems appears in Section 5.

2 Deciding Pomset-Trace Equivalence

The runs of a finite net are clearly recognizable by a finite state automaton, namely, the "global state" automaton of the net itself. We represent a pair $r = t_1 \ldots t_n$, $r'' = t_1'' \ldots t_n''$, of transition-sequences of the same length as an input string $(t_1, t_1'') \ldots (t_n, t_n'')$ for an automaton whose alphabet is pairs of transitions. So an "obvious" solution to the pomset-trace equivalence problem would be to define an effective procedure that, given any two finite nets as input, computes a finite-state automaton whose language consists of all the pairs of runs of the respective nets that have isomorphic pomset-traces. Such an automaton would easily yield a decision procedure for

---

[1] For expository purposes, we refer to bounds of the form $2^{O(n^k)}$ for fixed k as *exponential* in n. In the results presented here, k is at most 4.

Class	Equivalence	Complexity
Traces	Interleaving-traces	EXPSPACE-complete
	Step-traces [9, 16, 17]	
	ST-traces [17, 18]	
	Interval-pomset-traces [8, 22]	
	Pomset-traces [8, 17, 22]	
Failures/ divergences	Interleaving-failures [5]	EXPSPACE-complete
	Step-failures [9, 16, 17]	
	ST-failures [17, 18]	
	Interval-pomset-failures [8, 22]	
Bisimulation	Interleaving bisimulation [12]	DEXPTIME-complete
	Step-bisimulation [9, 17]	
	ST-bisimulation [17, 18]	
	History-preserving-bisimulation [2, 14, 17, 19, 21]	
	Maximality-preserving-bisimulation [6]	
	Pomset-bisimulation [3]	DEXPTIME-hard and in EXPSPACE
	Pomset-ST-bisimulation [19]	DEXPTIME-hard and in EXPSPACE

Table 1. Complexity results for finite safe Petri Nets

pomset-trace equivalence, since we could project the language it accepts onto the components of the pairs and check that the resulting languages include the set of runs of the respective nets.

However, such a finite-state automaton does not exist; the difficulty is that pairs of runs with isomorphic pomset-traces may generate the pomset-traces in different order, one getting unboundedly behind the other before catching up at the end.

We will show in this section that it suffices to consider pairs of runs that are "synchronous" in the sense that their behavior corresponds at each pair of transitions. We say that two runs r' and r'' are *equivalent up to concurrency* iff they have isomorphic transition-pomsets. We will show that:

- For all pairs of runs r and r' with isomorphic pomset-traces, there is a run r'' that is equivalent to r' up to concurrency, and r and r'' are "synchronous."
- The set of pairs of synchronous runs is recognizable by a finite automaton with size bounded by an exponential in the sizes of the nets.

Our decision procedure for pomset-trace equivalence is based on constructing such a finite-state automaton. To simplify the exposition, we consider first the case without hidden transitions.

2.1 Nets without Hidden Transitions

In this section, we assume that nets *do not contain hidden transitions*.

Definition 3. Let r and r' be transition-sequences of nets N and N', respectively. We say that r and r' are *synchronous* iff the identity function on $\{1, 2, \ldots, |r|\}$ is an isomorphism between the visible-pomset of r and the visible-pomset of r'.

In particular, if r and r' are synchronous, then they are of the same length.

A basic property of the causal partial order is that any linearization of a transition-pomset is a run. This easily implies:

Lemma 4. *Let r and r' be runs of nets N and N', respectively. If the pomset-traces of r and r' are isomorphic, then there is some run r'' of N' such that*

- *the transition-pomsets of r' and r'' are isomorphic, and*
- *r and r'' are synchronous.*

An important property of synchronous transition-sequences is that their equal-length prefixes are also synchronous.

Definition 5. Let p be a pomset and $e, e' \in \text{Events}_p$. Event e' is a *maximal cause* of event e in p providing $e' <_p e$ and there is no event $e'' \in \text{Events}_p$ such that $e' <_p e'' <_p e$.

Proposition 6. *Let r and r' be transition-sequences of length $n \geq 0$ and let t and t' be transitions of nets N and N', respectively. Then $r.t$ and $r'.t'$ are synchronous iff*

- *r and r' are synchronous,*
- *t and t' have the same label, and*
- *the maximal causes of event $n + 1$ are the same in the transition-pomsets of $r.t$ and $r'.t'$.*

Thus, in determining whether two pomset-traces "grow" synchronously, it suffices to keep track of the correspondence between maximal causes. We now observe that all maximal causes will necessarily be the most-recent firings of the corresponding transitions.

Definition 7. Let $r = t_1 \ldots t_n$ be a transition-sequence of a net N. Event i is a *most recent firing of transition t* in r iff $t_i = t$ and $t_j \neq t$ for $i < j \leq n$. Let $growth\text{-}sites(r)$ be the transition-pomset of r, restricted to the most-recent firings of the transitions in r, cf. Figure 2.

Proposition 8. *Let $r = t_1 \ldots t_n$ be a transition-sequence and t be a transition of a net N. Then the maximal causes of event $n + 1$ in the visible-pomset of $r.t$ are a subset of the events of $growth\text{-}sites(r)$.*

Proof. Suppose event i of the transition-pomset of $r.t$ is a maximal cause of event $n + 1$. Then by the definition of the causal partial ordering, event i must be a proximate cause of event $n + 1$, and hence transition t_i must not be statically concurrent with t. Therefore any later firing of t_i, that is, any event j with $i < j \leq n$ and $t_j = t_i$, would also be a proximate cause of t. But since event i proximately causes any such event j, this would contradict event i being a maximal cause of t. ∎

It now follows that whether two synchronous runs remain synchronous after firing another pair of transitions depends solely on the labels of these transitions, and on whether the causes of these transitions are the same in the growth-sites of the respective runs. It will be helpful to define a more general *growth-site correspondence* (*gsc*) between causes in growth-sites.

Definition 9. Let $r = t_1 \ldots t_n$ and $r' = t'_1 \ldots t'_m$ be transition-sequences of nets N and N', respectively. Then $gsc(r, r')$ is defined iff r and r' are synchronous. Furthermore, if r and r' are synchronous, then $gsc(r, r')$ is the partial identity function β: $growth\text{-}sites(r) \rightarrow growth\text{-}sites(r')$ such that $\beta(i) = j$ iff $i = j$ and $i \in carrier(growth\text{-}sites(r)) \cap carrier(growth\text{-}sites(r'))$, cf. Figure 2.

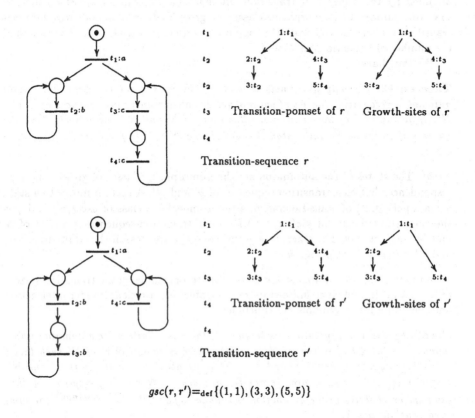

$$gsc(r, r') =_{\text{def}} \{(1, 1), (3, 3), (5, 5)\}$$

Fig. 2. An Example of Growth-Sites and Growth-Site Correspondence

We now state the key observation underlying our decision procedure: the growth-site correspondence of a pair of runs $r.t$ and $r'.t'$ is determined up to isomorphism by the isomorphism class of the growth-site correspondence between r and r'.

Definition 10. Let β and γ be partial functions whose domain and co-domain are pomsets. We say that β and γ are *isomorphic*, written $\beta \approx \gamma$, iff there is a pair of functions (I, J) such that

- I is an isomorphism between $dom(\beta)$ and $dom(\gamma)$,
- J is an isomorphism between $co\text{-}dom(\beta)$ and $co\text{-}dom(\gamma)$, and

525

$$- \gamma \circ I = J \circ \beta.$$

Lemma 11. *Let r_1, r_2 be transition-sequences and t a transition of net N; likewise for r_1', r_2', t' of net N'. If $\mathrm{gsc}(r_1, r_1') \approx \mathrm{gsc}(r_2, r_2')$, then $\mathrm{gsc}(r_1.t, r_1'.t') \approx \mathrm{gsc}(r_2.t, r_2'.t')$.*

We omit the proof.

The size of the growth-sites of any transition-sequence of a net is obviously bounded by the number of transitions in that net. We can thus easily conclude that the number of isomorphism classes of growth-site correspondences between transition-sequences of N and N' is bounded by an exponential in the maximum of the number of transitions in N and N'.

We thus have:

Theorem 12. *For any finite nets N and N', there is a deterministic finite-state automaton recognizing the set of pairs of synchronous transition-sequences of N and N'. If m and m' are the number of transitions in N and N', respectively, then the number of states in the automaton is bounded by $c^{\max\{m,m'\}^2}$ for some fixed constant $c > 1$.*

Proof. The states of the automaton are the isomorphism classes of growth-site correspondences between transition-sequences of N and N'. A state β moves to a state γ via a pair (t, t') of transitions iff β is the isomorphism class of $\mathrm{gsc}(r, r')$ and γ is the isomorphism class of $\mathrm{gsc}(r.t, r'.t')$ for some transition-sequences r and r' of N and N', respectively. The start state is the isomorphism class of the empty function, and all states are accepting. ∎

Since the runs of a finite net are finite-state recognizable by the transition system of the net itself, and since finite-state recognizable sets are closed under intersection and renaming input symbols, we conclude:

Corollary 13. *For any finite nets N and N', there is a finite-state automaton whose language is the set of runs r of N for which there is some run r' of N' such that r and r' are synchronous. If m and m' are the number of transitions in N and N', respectively, and n and n' are the number of places in N and N', respectively, then the number of states in the automaton is bounded by $d^{\max\{m,m'\}^2+\max\{n,n'\}}$ for some fixed constant $d > 1$.*

It is fairly straightforward to show that such an automaton can in fact be constructed in space proportional to the size of its transition table. The desired decidability result then follows as a corollary:

Theorem 14. *The pomset-trace equivalence problem for finite nets without hidden transitions can be decided in space exponential in the number of places and transitions in the nets.*

Proof. By Lemma 4 and Corollary 13, $N \sqsubseteq_{pt} N'$ iff the language of the finite-state automaton given in Corollary 13 is the set of all runs of N. It is easy to construct another finite-state automaton, of essentially the same size, recognizing the runs of N. So $N \sqsubseteq_{pt} N'$ iff these automata recognize the same language. But language equivalence is checkable in space proportional to the size of the automata [7]. ∎

2.2 Nets with Hidden Transitions

We briefly indicate how the results above extend to nets which *may contain hidden transitions*. We begin by modifying our definition of "synchronous" to take account of hidden transitions. This new definition will coincide with Definition 3 for nets without hidden transitions.

Definition 15. Let $r = t_1 \ldots t_n$ and and $r' = t'_1 \ldots t'_m$ be transition-sequences of nets N and N', respectively.

Let $\alpha_{r,r'}$ be the partial function on the integers such that $\alpha_{r,r'}(i) = j$ iff t_i is the kth transition of r with a visible label and t'_j is the kth transition of r' with a visible label, for some (necessarily unique) k.

Then r and r' are *synchronous* iff $\alpha_{r,r'}$ is an isomorphism between the visible-pomset of r and the visible-pomset of r'.

In particular, if r and r' are synchronous, then they have the same number of occurrences of visible transitions.

Lemma 4 continues to hold for this generalized notion of synchronous.

The notion of maximal cause must now be sharpened to be a maximal *visible* cause. Then Proposition 6 generalizes as follows:

Proposition 16. *Let r, r' be transition-sequences and let t, t' be visible transitions of nets N, N', respectively. Then $r.t$ and $r'.t'$ are synchronous iff*

- *r and r' are synchronous,*
- *t and t' have the same label, and*
- *$\alpha_{r,r'}$ restricted to the maximal visible causes of event $|r| + 1$ in the transition-pomset of $r.t$ is a bijection onto the maximal visible causes of event $|r'| + 1$ in the transition-pomset of $r'.t'$.*

Also, if t is a hidden transition, then $r.t$ and r' are synchronous iff r and r' are synchronous.

The notion of growth-sites extends to hidden transitions as follows:

Definition 17. Let r be a transition-sequence of a net N. Let *most-recent*(r) be the set of most recent firings in r of each transition. Let *max-visible-cause*(t, r) be the maximal visible causes of the most recent firing in r of transition t. Then *growth-sites*(r) is the restriction of the transition-pomset of r to

$$most\text{-}recent(r) \cup \bigcup \{ max\text{-}visible\text{-}causes(t, r) \mid t \text{ is a hidden transition} \}.$$

Proposition 8 now holds for the new definition of growth-sites by a similar proof.

Our definition of growth-site correspondences is also modified accordingly; this new definition will coincide with Definition 9 for nets without hidden transitions.

Definition 18. Let r and r' be transition-sequences of nets N and N', respectively. Then $gsc(r, r')$ is defined iff r and r' are synchronous. Furthermore, if r and r' are synchronous, then $gsc(r, r')$ is the 1-1 partial function β: *growth-sites*$(r) \to growth\text{-}sites(r')$ such that

$$graph(\beta) = graph(\alpha_{r,r'}) \cap (carrier(growth\text{-}sites(r)) \times carrier(growth\text{-}sites(r')))$$

Again, the growth-site correspondences are significant only up to isomorphism:

Lemma 19. *Let r_1, r_2 be transition-sequences of net N and let r'_1, r'_2 be transition-sequences of net N'. If $\mathrm{gsc}(r_1, r'_1) \approx \mathrm{gsc}(r_2, r'_2)$, then*

- $\mathrm{gsc}(r_1.t, r'_1.t') \approx \mathrm{gsc}(r_2.t, r'_2.t')$ *for any pair of* visible *transitions t and t' of N and N', respectively.*
- $\mathrm{gsc}(r_1.t, r'_1) \approx \mathrm{gsc}(r_2.t, r'_2)$ *for any* hidden *transition t of N.*
- $\mathrm{gsc}(r_1, r'_1.t') \approx \mathrm{gsc}(r_2, r'_2.t')$ *for any* hidden *transition t' of N'.*

We note that it follows directly from Definition 17 that the size of the growth-sites of any transition-sequence of a net is bounded by the square of the number of transitions in that net.

The earlier argument without hidden transitions now carries over:

Theorem 20. *The pomset-trace equivalence problem for finite nets that may contain hidden transitions can be decided in space exponential in the number of places and transitions in the nets.*

3 History-Preserving Bisimulation

We begin by defining history-preserving bisimulation on nets. Our definition induces the same equivalence as that of [2, 14, 17, 19, 21].

Definition 21. A set $\mathcal{R}$ of triples of the form (r, r', f) is a *history-preserving bisimulation* between nets N and N' iff

1. If $(r, r', f) \in \mathcal{R}$, then r and r' are runs of N and N', respectively, and f is an isomorphism between *pomset-trace(r)* and *pomset-trace(r')*.
2. $(\varepsilon, \varepsilon, \emptyset) \in \mathcal{R}$, where ε is the empty transition-sequence.
3. If $(r, r', f) \in \mathcal{R}$ and $r.t$ is a run of N, then then there is some, possibly empty, sequence of transitions $t'_1 \ldots t'_k$ and some function f' such that $((r.t), (r'.t'_1 \ldots t'_k), f') \in \mathcal{R}$ and f' restricted to *pomset-trace(r)* equals f.
4. If $(r, r', f) \in \mathcal{R}$ and $r'.t'$ is a run of N', then then there is some, possibly empty, sequence of transitions $t_1 \ldots t_k$ and some function f' such that $((r.t_1 \ldots t_k), (r'.t'), f') \in \mathcal{R}$ and f'^{-1} restricted to *pomset-trace(r')* equals f^{-1}.

Vogler [21] has given an alternate characterization of history-preserving bisimulation based on partially ordered sets of *places*, together with a decidability result. We give an alternate proof based on the approach presented in Section 2. We recall that the finite automaton described in Theorem 12, as well as its corresponding version that handles hidden transitions, is deterministic, and we let *update* refer to the state-transition function of the hidden-transition version of the automaton. We note that, in order to allow hidden transitions to move independently, the alphabet of this automaton consists of pairs (u, u'), where either u and u' are both *visible* transitions of the respective nets, or exactly one of u and u' is a *hidden* transition of the respective net and the other is a special symbol •. We refer to any sequence w of such pairs as a •-*pair-sequence*, and for $i = 1, 2$, we write $proj_i(w)$ to denote the projection of w onto its ith component alphabet, with all occurrences of $\bullet$ omitted. Furthermore, for any $\bullet$-pair-sequence w and any gsc β, we write $update(\beta, w)$ to mean the successive application of $update$ to each of the pairs in w. For any net N, we write $\text{init}(N)$ to denote the initial marking of N.

Definition 22. A set $\mathcal{V}$ of triples of the form (M, M', β) is an gsc-$bisimulation$ between nets N and N' iff

1. If $(M, M', \beta) \in \mathcal{V}$, then M and M' are markings of N and N', respectively, and β is an isomorphism class of growth-site correspondences between N and N'.
2. $(\text{init}(N), \text{init}(N'), \emptyset) \in \mathcal{V}$.
3. If $(M, M', \beta) \in \mathcal{R}$ and $M[t\rangle M_1$ for some transition t and some marking M_1, then there is some marking M_1' and some $\bullet$-pair-sequence w such that $proj_1(w) = t$, $M'[proj_2(w)\rangle M_1'$ and $(M_1, M_1', update(\beta, w)) \in \mathcal{V}$.
4. Vice-versa; if $(M, M', \beta) \in \mathcal{R}$ and $M'[t'\rangle M_1'$ for some transition t' and some marking M_1', then there is some marking M_1 and some $\bullet$-pair-sequence w such that $proj_2(w) = t'$, $M[proj_1(w)\rangle M_1$ and $(M_1, M_1', update(\beta, w)) \in \mathcal{V}$.

Lemma 23. *Nets are history-preserving bisimilar iff they are gsc-bisimilar.*

Page limitations force us to omit the proof.

As in Section 2.2, it is easy to see that for any finite net, the number of triples (M, M', β) is bounded by an exponential in the sizes of the nets. We use this fact in our decision procedure:

Theorem 24. *History-preserving bisimulation can be decided in* DEXPTIME *for finite nets that may contain hidden transitions.*

Proof. The algorithm to decide history-preserving bisimulation of nets N and N' is similar to the decision procedure for (interleaving) bisimulation by successive refinement. We start with a set $\mathcal{V}_0$ that contains all possible triples, and each step, we shrink this set. Specifically, we define inductively:

$$\mathcal{V}_0 = \{(M, M', \beta) \mid M, M' \text{ are markings of } N, N',$$
$$\text{and } \beta \text{ is a } gsc\text{-isomorphism class between } N \text{ and } N'\}$$

$$\mathcal{V}_{i+1} = \{(M, M', \beta) \in \mathcal{V}_i \mid \text{ for every transition } t \text{ and marking } M_1 \text{ with } M[t\rangle M_1,$$
$$\text{there is some marking } M_1'$$
$$\text{and some } \bullet \text{-pair-sequence } w$$
$$\text{such that } proj_1(w) = t, \; M'[proj_2(w)\rangle M_1'$$
$$\text{and } (M_1, M_1', update(\beta, w)) \in \mathcal{V}_i$$
$$\text{and vice-versa}\}$$

It is straightforward to show that N and N' are gsc-bisimilar iff

$$(\text{init}(N), \text{init}(N'), \emptyset) \in \mathcal{V}_k$$

for any k that exceeds the number of triples, and this number is easily bounded by an exponential in the sizes of N and N'. It is also easy to check that $\mathcal{V}_k$ can be computed in DEXPTIME in the size of N and N' (using a transitive closure technique as in [10] to calculate the existence of a $\bullet$-pair-sequence w). ∎

529

4 Lower Bounds

The lower bounds for trace equivalence and bisimulation essentially follow from previous results of Mayer&Stockmeyer on Mazurkiewicz nets and regular expressions with interleaving. In particular, Mayer&Stockmeyer [11] have shown the EXPSPACE-hardness of the language equivalence problem for regular expressions with interleaving. Our EXPSPACE lower bound for trace equivalence of finite safe Petri nets follows by a straightforward polynomial-time reduction.

Our proof of a DEXPTIME lower bound for bisimulation is a simple adaptation of Stockmeyer's result [15] for Mazurkiewicz nets: namely, we reduce the acceptance problem for polynomial-space Alternating Turing Machines to the bisimulation problem for finite safe Petri nets. In particular, we simulate the tape and finite-state control of polynomial-space Alternating Turing Machines by polynomial-time constructible safe Petri Nets. Our reduction to bisimulation is then essentially identical to that of Stockmeyer; we omit the proof here due to space limitations. Since Mazurkiewicz nets are somewhat more succinct than safe Petri Nets, our lower bound for bisimulation is a minor technical improvement of the results of Stockmeyer.

Theorem 25. *For finite nets, trace equivalence is polynomial-time reducible to pomset-trace equivalence.*

Proof. For any finite nets N_1, N_2 without hidden transitions, let N_i' be constructed by adding to N_i a single new, initially marked place which is placed in the preset and post-set of every transition of N_i. Clearly, N_i' is trace equivalent to N_i. Since no transitions in N_i' are statically concurrent, it is easy to see that N_1' and N_2' are trace equivalent iff they are pomset-trace equivalent; hence N_1 and N_2 are trace equivalent iff N_1' and N_2' are pomset-trace equivalent. This is a polynomial-time reduction from trace equivalence to pomset-trace equivalence. ∎

We then have as a simple corollary:

Corollary 26. *Pomset-trace equivalence of finite nets is EXPSPACE-hard.*

By a similar argument, we have:

Theorem 27. *For finite nets, bisimulation is polynomial-time reducible to history-preserving bisimulation.*

Corollary 28. *History-preserving bisimulation of finite nets is DEXPTIME-hard.*

We remark that all the results in this section hold as well for nets without hidden transitions.

5 Conclusions

Our methods also yield tight complexity bounds for several other true concurrency equivalences, summarized in Table 1. The proofs of the lower bounds are analogous to those for pomset-traces and history-preserving bisimulation, since it is easy to show that the true concurrency equivalences coincide with the corresponding interleaving equivalences on nets without hidden transitions and without concurrency. Some of the upper bounds can be obtained from fairly straightforward modifications of the growth-site correspondence isomorphism classes. Other upper bounds follow from reductions of true concurrency equivalences to interleaving equivalences, which are part of known full abstraction proofs [9, 8, 22, 23]. We remark that all these complexity results apply equally to process approximation as well as equivalence.

One open problem that we regard as especially significant is the complexity, and indeed decidability, of our earlier general pomset-failures semantics [8], which keeps track of concurrent divergences. We are currently working to extend our methods to handle this case.

Acknowledgments

We are grateful to Alex Rabinovich for some very helpful discussions, especially of lower bound proofs, and to Alain Mayer and Larry Stockmeyer for related discussions. We are also thankful to Rob van Glabbeek for helpful suggestions and information regarding previously known results.

References

1. C. Alvarez, B. J., J. Gabarro, and M. Santa. Parallel complexity in the design and analysis of concurrent systems. In *Proceedings of PARLE '91, Volume 505 of the Lecture Notes in Computer Science*, pages 288–303, 1991.
2. E. Best, R. Devillers, A. Kiehn, and L. Pomello. Concurrent bisimulations in Petri Nets. *Acta Inf.*, 28:231–264, 1991.
3. G. Boudol and I. Castellani. On the semantics of concurrency: Partial orders and transition systems. In *Proceedings of TAPSOFT '87, Volume 249 of the Lecture Notes in Computer Science*, pages 123–137, 1987.
4. S. D. Brookes, C. A. R. Hoare, and A. W. Roscoe. A theory of communicating sequential processes. *J. ACM*, 31(3):560–599, July 1984.
5. S. D. Brookes and A. W. Roscoe. An improved failures model for communicating processes. In *Seminar on Concurrency, Volume 197 of Lecture Notes in Computer Science*, pages 281–305, 1984.
6. R. Devillers. Maximality preserving bisimulation. *Theor. Comput. Sci.*, 102(1):165–184, Aug. 1992.
7. J. E. Hopcroft and J. D. Ullman. *Introduction to automata theory, languages, and computation.* Addison-Wesley, 1979.
8. L. Jategaonkar and A. R. Meyer. Testing equivalence for Petri nets with action refinement. In *Proceedings of CONCUR '92, Volume 630 of the Lecture Notes in Computer Science*, pages 17–31, 1992.
9. L. Jategaonkar and A. R. Meyer. Self-synchronization of concurrent processes. To appear in the Proceedings of *LICS*, 1993.
10. P. Kannelakis and S. Smolka. CCS expressions, finite state processes, and three problems of equivalence. *Inf. Comput.*, 86(1):43–68, 1990.
11. A. J. Mayer and L. J. Stockmeyer. The complexity of word problems – this time with interleaving. Technical report, IBM Research Division, Almaden Research Center, San Jose, CA, Sept. 1992.

12. R. Milner. *Communication and Concurrency.* Series in Computer Science. Prentice-Hall, Inc., 1989.

13. A. Rabinovich. Checking equivalences between concurrent systems of finite agents. In *Proceedings of ICALP '92, Volume 379 of the Lecture Series in Computer Science,* pages 696–707, 1992.

14. A. Rabinovich and B. Trakhtenbrot. Behavior structures and nets of processes. *Fundamenta Informaticae,* 11(4):357–404, 1988.

15. L. Stockmeyer, Jan. 1992. Unpublished notes.

16. D. Taubner and W. Vogler. Step failures semantics and a complete proof system. *Acta Inf.,* 27(2):125–156, Nov. 1989.

17. R. van Glabbeek and U. Goltz. Equivalence notions for concurrent systems and refinement of actions. In *Proceedings of MFCS '89, Volume 379 of the Lecture Series in Computer Science,* pages 237–248, 1989.

18. R. van Glabbeek and F. Vaandrager. Petri net models for algebraic theories of concurrency. In *Proceedings of PARLE '87, Volume 259 of the Lecture Notes in Computer Science,* pages 224–242, 1987.

19. W. Vogler. Bisimulation and action refinement. In *Proceedings of STACS '91, Volume 480 of the Lecture Notes in Computer Science,* pages 309–321, 1991.

20. W. Vogler. Bisimulation and action refinement. Technical report, Technische Universität München, 1991.

21. W. Vogler. Deciding history preserving bisimulation. In *Proceedings of ICALP '91, Volume 510 of the Lecture Notes in Computer Science,* pages 495–505, 1991.

22. W. Vogler. Failures semantics based on interval semiwords is a congruence for refinement. *Distributed Computing,* 4:139–162, 1991.

23. W. Vogler. Is partial order semantics necessary for action refinement? Technical report, Technische Universität München, 1991.

Timed Testing of Concurrent Systems

Walter Vogler*

Institut für Mathematik, Universität Augsburg
Universitätsstr. 8, D-8900 Augsburg

Abstract

We are concerned with timing considerations for concurrent systems where the time needed by the individual actions is not known beforehand; it has long been suspected that partial order semantics is useful here. We develop a suitable testing scenario to study this idea. With some view of timed behaviour, we can confirm that interval semiword semantics, a special partial order semantics, is indeed useful. With another view, our testing scenario leads to timed-refusal-trace semantics, where no relation to partial order semantics is obvious.

1 Introduction

A large number of action-oriented semantics for concurrent systems exist; they give varying information about the choices that are taken and about the independence of actions in a system run. To represent the latter information, a 'truely concurrent' semantics most often models a system run as a partial order.

An important argument in favour of a specific semantics is that it is observable in some sense; observability can be formalized by a testing scenario, see [DNH84]. Something we may observe about a system run is the time it takes. Folklore says that partial order semantics may be useful here; e.g. consider a system which can perform the partial order shown below.

$$a \longrightarrow b$$

$$c$$

If actions a and b take one unit of time each, while c takes two units, then we see from the partial order that the whole run takes two units. We would not be able to see this from the corresponding action sequences abc, acb and cab. Also, if we consider steps consisting of several simultaneous actions and, hence, the step sequences $\binom{a}{c}(b)$ and $(a)\binom{b}{c}$, we are not able to determine the duration of the run.

Of course, one could argue that in this situation we should replace c by the sequence $c'c''$, and then we would get the step sequence $\binom{a}{c'}\binom{b}{c''}$, which tells us what we want to know. This approach is not possible, if we do not know beforehand how long the actions will take; such a

*This work was partially supported by the ESPRIT Basic Research Working Group 6067 CALIBAN (CAusal calculI BAsed on Nets) and the Fakultät für Informatik, TU München.

phenomenon can easily occur in distributed systems, where actions involve synchronization or where other users might create varying loads. Our aim is to develop a suitable testing scenario for such a setting with unspecified timing. In this scenario, actions take varying times under varying circumstances, but nevertheless we are able to test different systems under the same circumstances. Having developed the testing scenario, we want to find out how the observable timed behaviour is related to partial order semantics.

We use safe timed Petri nets as system models where each transition is associated with a duration, which is a natural number, and we consider three versions of timing. Usually in Petri nets, a transition may occur if it is enabled, but it does not have to. Similarly, under *liberal* timing a transition may start if it is enabled, but it does not have to, and it may end at any time after its duration has passed. Most often, timed nets are combined with a different firing schedule; under *strict* timing – as we call it – a transition must start if it is enabled, and it ends exactly at the end of its duration. Finally, under *mixed* timing a transition may start if it is enabled, but once it has started, it must end exactly at the end of its duration; as an intuitive justification, one can think of conflict resolution mechanisms that need varying times but are not modelled explicitly in the Petri net. We call a net *untimed* if the duration is always 1. For untimed nets we can show that the variants of timed behaviour correspond quite directly to behaviour notions for nets without time.

A *test net* is a net which has a special action ω. A *timed test* consists of a test net O and a natural number d. In order to apply a test to a net N, we consider the parallel composition $N \parallel O$ where all actions except ω are synchronized. Now, N *may satisfy* the test, if $N \parallel O$ has a system run where ω is performed after at most d time units. N *must satisfy* the test, if $N \parallel O$ performs ω after at most d time units in each system run. We call nets *liberally, mixed* or *strictly test-equivalent*, if they may satisfy the same tests under liberal, mixed or strict timing. For the must-version, only strict timing is sensible; hence, we simply call nets *must-equivalent*, if they must satisfy the same tests under strict timing.

Our main results state that, for untimed nets, liberal and mixed test-equivalence coincide with interval-semiword equivalence, while strict test-equivalence and must-equivalence coincide with timed-refusal-trace equivalence; timed refusal traces are a refinement of refusal traces as defined by [Phi87].

Thus, under liberal and mixed timing, partial order semantics is indeed good for dealing with unspecified timing. What one should use here are interval semiwords, which define a partial order semantics that is not so much causality-based, but rather temporal in flavour. For strict test-equivalence and must-equivalence, it seems unlikely that some form of partial order semantics will be helpful.

The crucial points of our approach are:

- Synchronization is such that, if a takes τ_1 time units in N and τ_2 time units in O, then it takes $\max(\tau_1, \tau_2)$ time units in $N \parallel O$; hence, if N is untimed, then the timing is completely determined by O; this formalizes unspecified timing.

- The time bound d in a test (O, d), which has no counterpart in ordinary testing [DNH84], makes the test to a timed test. Without it, our results for liberal and mixed timing would fail.

Lack of space does not allow to give any proofs, not even all the definitions; they can be found in the full version. The final section contains a discussion of some closely related literature.

2 Basic Notions

We will deal with finite safe Petri nets whose transitions are labelled with actions from some infinite alphabet Σ'. We do not consider internal or silent actions here, but the alphabet contains two special actions ω and $wait$, which we will need for our testing scenario; we put $\Sigma = \Sigma' - \{\omega, wait\}$. Furthermore, we associate to each transition a duration or firing time; we assume that time is discrete, and therefore this duration is a positive natural number, see e.g. [Sta90].

Thus, a *discretely timed labelled Petri net* $N = (S, T, W, l, \tau, M_N)$ (or just a *net* for short) consists of finite disjoint sets S of *places* and T of *transitions*, the *weight function* $W : S \times T \cup T \times S \rightarrow \{0, 1\}$, the *labelling* $l : T \rightarrow \Sigma'$, the *firing time* $\tau : T \rightarrow I\!N$, and the *initial marking* $M_N : S \rightarrow I\!N_0$. We call a net *untimed* if all transitions have duration 1.

A *multiset* over a set X is a function $\mu : X \rightarrow I\!N_0$. We identify $x \in X$ with the multiset that is 1 for x and 0 everywhere else. For multisets, multiplication with scalars from $I\!N_0$ and addition is defined elementwise.

A *marking* is a multiset over S, a *step* is a multiset over T. A step μ is *enabled* under a marking M, denoted by $M[\mu\rangle$, if $\sum_{t \in \mu} \mu(t) \cdot W(s, t) \leq M(s)$ for all $s \in S$. The step is enabled under the *maximum* firing rule, if: whenever $M[\mu'\rangle$ and $\mu \leq \mu'$ (transition-wise), then $\mu = \mu'$.

If $M[\mu\rangle$ and $M'(s) = M(s) + \sum_{t \in \mu} \mu(t)(W(t, s) - W(s, t))$, then we denote this by $M[\mu\rangle M'$ and say that μ can *occur* or *fire* under M yielding the *follower marking* M'. Since transitions are special steps, this also defines $M[t\rangle$ and $M[t\rangle M'$ for $t \in T$.

This definition of enabling and occurrence can be extended to sequences as follows. A sequence w of steps is *enabled* under a marking M, denoted by $M[w\rangle$, and yields the follower marking M' when *occurring*, denoted by $M[w\rangle M'$, if $w = \lambda$ and $M = M'$ or $w = w'\mu$, $M[w'\rangle M''$ and $M''[\mu\rangle M'$ for some marking M''. If w is enabled under the initial marking, then it is called a *step sequence*, or – in case that $w \in T^*$ – a *firing sequence*. If all the steps occur under the maximum firing rule, then w is called a *maximum step sequence*.

We can extend the labelling of a net to steps by $l(\mu) = \sum_{t \in T} \mu(t) \cdot l(t)$; and then we can extend the labelling also to sequences of steps or transitions as usual. Next we lift the enabledness and firing definitions to the level of actions:

A sequence v of steps over Σ' is *image enabled* under a marking M, denoted by $M[v\rangle\rangle$, if there is some w with $M[w\rangle$ and $l(w) = v$. If $M = M_N$, then v is called an *image step sequence*; if additionally w is a maximum step sequence, then v is called an *image maximum step sequence*; if $w \in T^*$, then v is called an *image firing sequence*. We call two nets *(maximum-)step-sequence equivalent* if they have the same image (maximum) step sequences. We call two nets *language equivalent* if they have the same image firing sequences.

A marking M is *reachable* if there exists some $w \in T^*$ with $M_N[w\rangle M$. The net is *safe* if $M(s) \leq 1$ for all places s and reachable markings M. We assume that all nets considered in this paper are safe and without isolated transitions.

Due to lack of space, we cannot introduce partial order semantics and ST-semantics

[Gla90] here; we only mention the following. A partial order $(E, <)$ is an *interval order*, if for every $e \in E$ there is a closed real interval $I(e)$ such that $e < e'$ if and only if $x < y$ for all $x \in I(e)$, $y \in I(e')$. Interval semiword semantics [Vog92] is based on these interval orders, which may be seen as observations of system runs where each firing takes some time. Interval semiword equivalence coincides with ST-equivalence [Vog92]; the latter is needed in some proofs.

3   Timed Behaviour

To describe the timed behaviour, we have to distinguish the start t^+ of a transition t from its end t^-, which occurs some time later depending on τ, and similarly for the actions. If two a-actions start and then one ends, we want to know which one it is. For this purpose, we associate with a start and the corresponding end the same event e from some set Ev. This is very similar to ST-traces.

The state description in a timed behaviour contains a marking M, a set of currently firing transitions C and a function $\rho : C \to I\!N_0$, which gives the remaining firing times for the current transitions. Following e.g. [HR90] we model the passing of time explicitly: occurrence of the special action $\sigma \notin \Sigma'$ denotes the passing of one time unit, one 'tick of the clock'. This way, we can use sequences consisting of transition parts and of σ's; intuitively, transition parts between two consecutive σ's occur at the same time and the state reached immediately after the n-th σ is the state at time n.

As described in the introduction, we will consider three variants of timed behaviour. We use $[)_l$, $[)_s$ and $[)_m$ for a liberally, strictly or mixed timed firing.

Definition 3.1 Let Ev be some infinite set. For each transition t, t^+ is called the *start* of t, t^- the *end* of t; we assume that, for each set T of transitions, T^+ and T^- are disjoint copies of T. $T^\pm = \{t^+, t^- \mid t \in T\}$ is the set of *transition parts*. We also call the elements of $T^\pm \times Ev$ transition parts or transition starts and ends. Similar notions are defined for actions and sets of actions.

An *instantaneous description (ID)* of a net N is a triple (M, C, ρ) where M is a marking of N, $C \subseteq T \times Ev$ is the set of *current(ly firing) transitions* such that $proj_2$, the projection to the second component, is injective on C, and $\rho : C \to I\!N_0$ is the *residual firing time*. The initial ID is $ID_N = (M_N, \emptyset, \emptyset)$.

For ID's (M, C, ρ) and (M', C', ρ') we write $(M, C, \rho)[\varepsilon)_x$ and $(M, C, \rho)[\varepsilon)_x(M', C', \rho')$ where $x \in \{l, m, s\}$ if one of the following three cases applies:

i) $\varepsilon = (t^+, e)$, $t \in T$ with $M[t\rangle$, $e \in Ev \setminus proj_2(C)$.
   In this case $M' = M - W(., t)$, $C' = C \cup \{(t, e)\}$ and ρ' is defined by $\rho'(t, e) = \tau(t)$ and $\rho'|_C = \rho$. If $x = m$ or $x = s$, it is additionally required that $\forall (t, e) \in C : \rho(t, e) > 0$.

ii) $\varepsilon = (t^-, e)$, $(t, e) \in C$, $\rho(t, e) = 0$.
   In this case $M' = M + W(t, .)$, $C' = C - \{(t, e)\}$ and $\rho' = \rho|_{C'}$.

iii) $\varepsilon = \sigma$.
   In this case $M' = M$, $C' = C$ and $\rho' = \rho \dot{-} 1$ (where $0 \dot{-} 1 = 0$ and $(n+1) \dot{-} 1 = n$ for all

$n \in I\!N_0$). If $x = m$, it is additionally required that $\forall (t,e) \in C : \rho(t,e) > 0$. If $x = s$, it is additionally required that $\forall t \in T : \neg M[t\rangle$ and $\forall (t,e) \in C : \rho(t,e) > 0$.

If $ID_0[\varepsilon_1\rangle_x\, ID_1 \ldots [\varepsilon_n\rangle_x\, ID_n$ where $n \geq 0$ and $x \in \{l,m,s\}$, we write $ID_0[\varepsilon_1 \ldots \varepsilon_n\rangle_x\, ID_n$ or $ID_0[\varepsilon \ldots \varepsilon_n\rangle_x$, provided that $\varepsilon_1 \ldots \varepsilon_n$ is *well-formed*, i.e.:

a) if $\varepsilon_1 \ldots \varepsilon_n = w_1(t_1^-, e_1)w_2(t_2^+, e_2)w_3$, then $e_1 \neq e_2$;

b) if $\varepsilon_1 \ldots \varepsilon_n = w_1(t_1^+, e_1)w_2(t_2^-, e_2)w_3$, then w_2 contains σ.

If $ID_N[w\rangle_x\, ID$, then w is a *liberally-timed* ($x = l$) or a *mixed-timed* ($x = m$) or a *strictly-timed* ($x = s$) *firing sequence* of N; ID is *reachable* under liberal, mixed or strict timing. If $ID[\varepsilon\rangle_x\, ID'$, we write $ID[l_N(\varepsilon)\rangle\rangle_x\, ID'$, where $l_N(t^+, e) = (l_N(t)^+, e)$, $l_N(t^-, e) = (l_N(t)^-, e)$, and $l_N(\sigma) = \sigma$. We extend this notation to sequences as usual; if $\varepsilon_1 \ldots \varepsilon_n$ is a liberally-, mixed- or strictly-timed firing sequence, then $l_N(\varepsilon_1) \ldots l_N(\varepsilon_n)$ is a *liberally-, mixed- or strictly-timed action sequence* of N. The sets of these sequences are called the *liberal, mixed* or *strict language* of N and denoted by $LL(N)$, $ML(N)$ or $SL(N)$. Nets N_1, N_2 are *liberally-timed equivalent* if $LL(N_1) = LL(N_2)$, they are *mixed-timed equivalent* if $ML(N_1) = ML(N_2)$, and they are *strictly-timed equivalent* if $SL(N_1) = SL(N_2)$. □

In this definition, the generalization of $[\varepsilon\rangle_x$ to sequences $\varepsilon_1 \ldots \varepsilon_n$ is as usual except for the two additional clauses. The first of them, a), together with the condition $e \in Ev \setminus proj_2(C)$ of i) ensures that every event e is used at most once for a start of a transition. Thus it appears at most twice in $\varepsilon_1 \ldots \varepsilon_n$, namely in some (t^+, e) and in a pair with the next occurrence of t^-; this way, e can be used in the corresponding timed action sequence to connect the start of an action with its end.

The second clause, b), ensures that between two consecutive σ's we have just one (possibly empty) sequence of transition ends followed by just one (possibly empty) sequence of transition starts. Without b), consider a timed firing sequence $w_1(t_1^-, e_1)(t_2^+, e_2)w_2$; $w_1(t_2^+, e_2)(t_1^-, e_1)w_2$ would be well-formed, so it might be a timed firing sequence or it might not. In the latter case, we could conclude that t_1 provides the tokens needed by t_2; thus, we could draw conclusions about the causal ordering of the transition parts (t_1^-, e_1) and (t_2^+, e_2), which is counterintuitive since they happen at the same instant. With Clause b), $w_1(t_2^+, e_2)(t_1^-, e_1)w_2$ is not well-formed, hence not a timed firing sequence in any case.

The following theorem shows that the timed behaviour of untimed nets corresponds to behaviour notions that disregard the durations; this justifies to call a net untimed, if τ is 1 for all transitions. The proof of the first part is based on the close relationship between liberally timed behaviour and ST-traces.

Theorem 3.2 *For untimed nets, liberally timed equivalence coincides with interval semiword equivalence, mixed-timed equivalence coincides with step-sequence equivalence, and strictly timed equivalence coincides with maximum-step-sequence equivalence.*

4 Parallel Composition and Testing

In this section, we introduce parallel composition $\|_A$ with synchronization inspired from TCSP. If we combine nets N_1 and N_2 with $\|_A$, then – as usual – they run in parallel having to synchronize on actions from A. To construct the composed net, we have to combine each a-labelled transition t_1 of N_1 with each a-labelled transition t_2 from N_2 if $a \in A$. If such a combined transition occurs, N_1 needs $\tau_1(t_1)$ time units to perform a, while N_2 needs $\tau_2(t_2)$; we assume that in order to complete a they need $\max(\tau_1(t_1), \tau_2(t_2))$ altogether.

In the following definition of parallel composition, $*$ is used as a dummy element. (Naturally, we assume that $*$ is not a transition or a place of any net.)

Definition 4.1 Let N_1, N_2 be nets, $A \subseteq \Sigma'$. Then the *parallel composition* $N = N_1 \parallel_A N_2$ *with synchronization* over A is defined by

$$
\begin{aligned}
S &= S_1 \times \{*\} \cup \{*\} \times S_2 \\
T &= \{(t_1, t_2) \mid t_1 \in T_1, t_2 \in T_2, l_1(t_1) = l_2(t_2) \in A\} \\
&\quad \cup \{(t_1, *) \mid t_1 \in T_1, l_1(t_1) \notin A\} \\
&\quad \cup \{(*, t_2) \mid t_2 \in T_2, l_2(t_2) \notin A\} \\
W((s_1, s_2), (t_1, t_2)) &= \begin{cases} W_1(s_1, t_1) & \text{if } s_1 \in S_1,\ t_1 \in T_1 \\ W_2(s_2, t_2) & \text{if } s_2 \in S_2,\ t_2 \in T_2 \\ 0 & \text{otherwise} \end{cases} \\
W((t_1, t_2), (s_1, s_2)) &= \begin{cases} W_1(t_1, s_1) & \text{if } s_1 \in S_1,\ t_1 \in T_1 \\ W_2(t_2, s_2) & \text{if } s_2 \in S_2,\ t_2 \in T_2 \\ 0 & \text{otherwise} \end{cases} \\
M_N &= M_{N_1} \dot{\cup} M_{N_2}, \text{ i.e. } M_N((s_1, s_2)) = \begin{cases} M_{N_1}(s_1) & \text{if } s_1 \in S_1 \\ M_{N_2}(s_2) & \text{if } s_2 \in S_2 \end{cases} \\
l((t_1, t_2)) &= \begin{cases} l_1(t_1) & \text{if } t_1 \in T_1 \\ l_2(t_2) & \text{if } t_2 \in T_2 \end{cases} \\
\tau((t_1, t_2)) &= \max(\tau_1(t_1), \tau_2(t_2)), \text{ where } \tau_1(*) = 0.
\end{aligned}
$$

$\square$

Observe that the parallel composition of untimed nets is an untimed net again; for the class of untimed nets, Definition 4.1 coincides with the usual definition of $\parallel_A$ for nets without a firing-time function, which is studied e.g. in [Vog92].

In the present paper, the main purpose of parallel composition is to combine a net N with a test net. Designing suitable test nets O and looking at the behaviour of $N \parallel_\Sigma O$, we can get information on the behaviour of N. The net O may also be regarded as an observer of N; for the general approach of testing, see [DNH84]. A test net O is an ordinary net; in general, it has the special action ω denoting success. A net N can be tested, if it does not have the special actions ω and *wait*; N satisfies O if $N \parallel_\Sigma O$ eventually performs the action ω. It may happen that some system runs lead to ω, while others do not. In this case, N *may* satisfy O; N *must* satisfy O, if all system runs lead to ω. Nets are may-equivalent, if they may satisfy the same tests, they are must-equivalent if they must satisfy the same tests. May-equivalence usually coincides with language equivalence, while must-equivalence gives some form of failure equivalence; see [DNH84].

Under liberal timing, a test performed in the described way would be rather uninteresting. A successful system run could take arbitrarily long due to unnecessary waiting, and we would not have a *timed* test at all. As a consequence, we add to our tests a time at which success must be reached. In this paper, we will mainly consider may-equivalence based on these tests and on our three kinds of timing. Under liberal and mixed timing, a net is never forced to satisfy a test, since it may 'decide' to wait without doing anything; formally, we always have system runs consisting of arbitrarily many σ's. Hence, must-testing is only sensible in combination with strict timing.

Definition 4.2 A net N is *testable* if the special actions ω and *wait* do not occur as transition labels. (Recall that $\omega, wait \notin \Sigma$ and $\Sigma' = \Sigma \cup \{\omega, wait\}$.) A *liberal, mixed* or *strict test* (O, d) consists of a net O, a so-called *test net*, and some $d \in I\!N_0$. A testable net N *satisfies* a liberal (mixed, strict) test (O, d), if there is some $w \in LL(N \parallel_\Sigma O)$ (some $w \in ML(N \parallel_\Sigma O)$, some $w \in SL(N \parallel_\Sigma O)$) containing at most d σ's and some (ω^+, e).

Testable nets are *liberally* or *strictly test-equivalent* or *mixed-test-equivalent* if they satisfy the same liberal, strict or mixed tests.

A testable net N *must* satisfy a test (O, d) if every $w \in SL(N \parallel_\Sigma O)$ with more than d σ's contains some (ω^+, e). Testable nets are *must-equivalent* if they must satisfy the same tests. $\Box$

Observe that in the parallel composition $N \parallel_\Sigma O$ each transition of N is synchronized with some transition of O. (Transitions of N that do not 'find' an equally labelled synchronization 'partner' are automatically deleted.) If N is untimed, this has the effect that O not only observes all possible actions of N in some sense, it also specifies the time actions take; technically, we always have $\tau_{N\parallel_\Sigma O}((t_1, t_2)) = \tau_O(t_2)$. Thus, Definition 4.2 meets our intuitive aim to test untimed nets under varying circumstances where actions take varying times, and to test them in such a way that we can apply the same test with the same circumstances to different nets.

5 Liberal and Mixed Testing

Theorem 5.1 *Liberally timed equivalence is a congruence for parallel composition.*

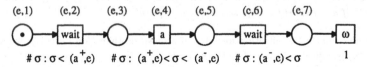

This theorem implies that liberally-timed equivalent nets are liberally test-equivalent. For the converse, one essentially constructs for each liberally-timed action sequence w a test net O as follows. For each occurrence of a, O has a part as shown above, where the ω-transition is the same for all parts. The time τ_1 for the first *wait* is the number of σ's before (a^+, e) in w, the time for the second *wait* is the number of σ's after (a^-, e) in w, and the time for the a-action is the number of remaining σ's. We apply the liberal test (O, d) where d is the total number of σ's in w. It is quite obvious that the only chance to reach ω in time is to start the first *wait* at once, to finish it after τ_1 σ's, then to start the a-action immediately and so on. Thus, if a net may satisfy the test, then it can perform w.

Theorem 5.2 *For testable nets, liberal test-equivalence coincides with liberally timed equivalence.*

From this and Theorem 3.2 we can draw the following conclusion: a timed test setting applied to untimed nets indeed justifies some form of partial order semantics, although this form is more temporal than causal.

Corollary 5.3 *For untimed testable nets, liberal test-equivalence coincides with interval semiword equivalence.*

It might seem that this result is not a good justification for partial order semantics, since liberal testing is based on liberally-timed firing sequences, which are in the case of untimed nets quite the same as interval semiwords. This might give the impression that we have justified interval semiwords by using interval semiwords, which does not look very surprising. But this view is not correct for several reasons.

First of all, interval semiwords correspond quite directly to liberally-timed firing sequences only for untimed nets; testing an untimed net N we have considered the liberally timed behaviour of nets $N \parallel_\Sigma O$, and these nets are in general not untimed. Thus, it is remarkable that liberal testing does not distinguish more untimed nets than interval semiwords. Indeed, adherents of causality-based partial order semantics should have expected that testing with variable timing constraints would justify some causality-based partial order semantics and not interval semiwords, which are somewhat temporal in flavour. Thus, it is maybe a little surprising that liberal test-equivalence is not finer than interval semiword equivalence.

To see non-triviality of Corollary 5.3, we can consider some variants of the testing scenario that are based on liberal timing but do not lead to interval semiword equivalence. In liberal testing without the time d, N passes the test O if $N \parallel_\Sigma O$ can perform (ω^+, e) eventually under liberal timing; it is easily seen that, in such a setting, liberal test-equivalence would coincide with language equivalence, although it would be based on liberally timed behaviour. Another variant would be to use only untimed test nets.

Proposition 5.4 *Untimed testable nets satisfy the same liberal tests (O, d) with untimed test nets O if and only if they are step-sequence equivalent.*

As an even better justification for interval semiwords than Corollary 5.3, we will close this section by considering mixed test-equivalence of untimed nets. Recall that the mixed-timed behaviour of untimed nets corresponds to ordinary step sequence semantics, which is generally not considered to be a 'true' partial order semantics.

Theorem 5.5 *Liberal and mixed test-equivalence coincide. Hence, for untimed testable nets, mixed test-equivalence and interval semiword equivalence coincide.*

6 Strict and Must-Testing

In order to determine the strictly timed behaviour of a composed net, we have to use liberal timing and, additionally, have to record the inability of the component nets to start or end actions. We do not have to record this inability just at the end as in failure semantics, but all along the system run; this is similar to refusal trace semantics [Phi87].

Definition 6.1 The *timed-refusal-trace semantics* $TRT(N)$ of a net N is the set of all timed refusal traces, which are the sequences constructed as follows. Let $w_1 \sigma w_2 \ldots w_n \sigma \in LL(N)$ such that no w_i contains σ, and let $ID_N[w_1\rangle\rangle_l \, ID_1[\sigma\rangle\rangle_l \, ID'_1[w_2\rangle\rangle_l \ldots [w_n\rangle\rangle_l \, ID_n[\sigma\rangle\rangle_l$. Then $w_1 X_1 \sigma \ldots X_{n-1} \sigma w_n X_n \sigma$ is a *timed refusal trace*, if for $i = 1, \ldots, n$

- $X_i \subseteq \Sigma' \cup (\Sigma'^- \times Ev)$
- for all $a \in X_i \cap \Sigma'$ we have $\neg M_i[a\rangle)$, where $ID_i = (M_i, C_i, \rho_i)$
- for all $(a^-, c) \in X_i \cap (\Sigma'^- \times Ev)$ we have j and k such that
    - $\neg ID_i[(a^-, c)\rangle\rangle_l$
    - (a^+, c) occurs in w_j and $j \leq i$
    - (a^-, c) occurs in w_k and $i < k$, or (a^-, c) does not occur and $k = n + 1$
    - for all $j \leq l < k$ we have $(a^-, c) \in X_l$

The sets X_i are called *refusal sets*. Nets N_1, N_2 are *timed-refusal-trace equivalent* if $TRT(N_1) = TRT(N_2)$. □

The refusal sets X_i contain some actions that cannot start under ID_i and some actions ends that cannot occur under ID_i. Note that the sets X_i contain just some of these actions or action ends; for example, one can choose all X_i to be empty.

The conditions regarding the action ends have the following intuitive meaning. If we have $(a^-, c) \in X_i$, then the timed refusal trace tells us that (a^+, e) occurred at some stage and, then, (a^-, e) could not occur until finally it occurred at the earliest possible moment (or it could not occur until the trace ended). This information is useful for constructing strictly-timed action sequences of composed nets. We also consider timed refusal traces where some (a^-, e) (possibly) does not occur at the earliest possible moment; such an (a^-, e) does not appear in any X_i. Such traces of N are needed when in a parallel composition $N \parallel_A N_1$ the end of (a, e) is determined by N_1.

Remark: The treatment of action ends is similar to the treatment of actions in [RR88], where hatted actions $\hat{a}$ are used to denote occurrence of a at the earliest possible moment. But note that in [RR88] all actions have the same duration; consequently, action ends are not treated explicitly and hatted actions denote action starts. Here, we treat action ends as hatted or unhatted, while action starts get a different, more detailed treatment. □

Theorem 6.2 *Timed-refusal-trace equivalence is a congruence with respect to parallel composition.*

The following theorem collects all implications between the equivalences we have defined.

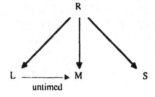

Theorem 6.3 *The thick arcs of the figure above indicate all implications that hold for nets in general between liberally-timed (L), mixed-timed (M), strictly-timed (S) and timed-refusal-trace (R) equivalence. The same holds for the class of untimed nets, except that here L implies M (thin arc).*

TRT-equivalence characterizes the remaining two test-equivalences.

Theorem 6.4 *For testable nets, timed-refusal-trace equivalence, strict test-equivalence and must-equivalence coincide.*

It can be shown that for strict tests (O, d) the time bound d is in fact superfluous. It has only been kept to have a uniform definition of timed tests.

Corollary 6.5 *Timed-refusal-trace equivalence is fully abstract with respect to parallel composition $\|_A$ and strictly timed equivalence.*

Theorem 6.4 is somewhat surprising if we compare it with classical results on test-equivalences. If we only consider untimed behaviour, may-testing reveals the language of a net, while must-testing corresponds to failure semantics. In failure semantics, one system run is described by an image firing sequence w together with a refusal set, which gives information on the final state reached by w. A refusal trace additionally contains refusal sets for the states passed during the system run. Timed refusal traces give even more information than refusal traces – but nevertheless they are revealed by a form of may-testing. That this form of may-testing is so powerful is obviously due to strict timing, which requires a very close synchronization between components of a parallel composition.

It is not clear at all how we could use some form of partial order semantics to represent TRT-semantics. For example, if $w \in LL(N)$ contains the subsequence $(a^+, e)\sigma(b^+, c')$, we might replace it by $(b^+, c')\sigma(a^+, c)$; this modification is in $LL(N)$ if and only if w is. The crucial point of using interval orders is that they abstract from the ordering of (a^+, c) and (b^+, e'), i.e. both sequences correspond to the same interval semiword. An analogous abstraction does not seem possible for traces in $TRT(N)$, if (a^+, e) is followed by a refusal set. I find it hard to imagine how this refusal information can be given without saying that a started before b – which is what we would want to abstract from.

7 Conclusion

Starting point for this paper was the idea that partial order semantics might be useful when each action has a duration which may vary from system run to system run. First of all, we have developed a testing scenario to study this idea. Two of our test-equivalences characterize a behaviour that can indeed be represented using partial orders, namely interval semiword behaviour. (Observe that this is not a causality-based partial order semantics.)

The other two test-equivalences allow one to observe timed refusal traces. Timed-refusal-trace semantics induces quite a strong equivalence; it distinguishes more nets than, for example, refusal trace semantics. Here, it does not seem as if partial orders can be of any use.

542

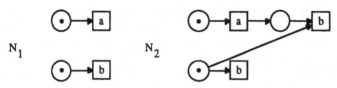

N_1 N_2

For unlabelled nets, a causality-based approach to the area of timing has been suggested in [Bes88]. Eike Best proposes to consider an ordinary process, to attach times to the transition occurrences in this process, and to take the length (w.r.t. the times) of a longest path in the process as the time taken by the process. If we translate this idea to a setting with labelled transitions and consider the nets shown above, we would conclude that they are not equivalent: in N_1 a system run always takes $\max(\tau(a), \tau(b))$ time units, while in N_2 it may also take $\tau(a) + \tau(b)$ time units.

But the two nets are interval-semiword equivalent. And indeed, I think they should be equivalent, since both nets are always ready to perform b if this is required by the environment. The dependent b of N_2 is only performed if the environment (or the net itself) decides to wait for the end of a; but then, the performance of N_1 will be just the same as the performance of N_2.

A lot of work has been done on timed concurrent systems. Most closely related to our approach seem to be the papers [RR88], [RR87], [HR90], [Hen91]. The first two papers study timed CSP where actions have a duration just as they have here. As a consequence, [RR88] and [RR87] distinguish the parallel performance of two actions from their arbitrary interleaving. The semantics in these papers are based on intuitive reasoning and not on testing scenarios. Nevertheless, the basic ideas behind the semantics of [RR87] are quite the same as those behind our timed-refusal-trace semantics, and it is already noted in [RR87] that they are somewhat similar to the ideas behind refusal trace semantics [Phi87]. Differences arise, since in [RR87] time is taken to be continuous, all actions have the same duration, and internal actions and divergence is considered.

The approaches in [HR90], [Hen91] are similar to our approach since both consider a testing scenario. In [HR90], a timed version of CCS and also the timed testing of untimed systems are considered. But actions do not have a duration and $a \mid b$, the parallel execution of a and b, is equated with $ab + ba$, the arbitrary interleaving of a and b. Furthermore, testing is only used as must-testing. Nevertheless, the semantics characterized by testing is based on some timed version of refusal traces. Testing in [HR90] does not involve a time bound, which is crucial for liberal testing as we have seen.

[Hen91] does not consider time, but actions with start and end. As an application of the ST-idea, may- and must-testing are studied where the test can explicitly require the start of an action or the end of some active action. May-testing in this scenario characterizes ST-equivalence, while must-testing characterizes some failure ST-equivalence. Considering the tests we have used in the proof of Theorem 5.2, there is a close relationship between our liberal testing and the may-testing of [Hen91]. But observe that our tests cannot explicitly require that some action starts or ends before some other action ends; this can only be required implicitly – using the crucial time bound.

An interesting extension of the approach presented here would be the inclusion of internal actions, especially when studying must-testing. Also, it might be fruitful to consider testing with restricted classes of test nets. In 5.4, we have already considered the class of untimed test nets. Related to the approach of [Bes88], another interesting class of nets would be the class of causal nets, which are used in the proof of 5.2.

References

[Bes88]   E. Best. Weighted basic Petri nets. In F.H. Vogt, editor, *Concurrency 88*, Lect. Notes Comp. Sci. 335, 257–276. Springer, 1988.

[DNH84]   R. De Nicola and M.C.B. Hennessy. Testing equivalence for processes. *Theoret. Comput. Sci.*, 34:83–133, 1984.

[Gla90]   R.J. v. Glabbeek. The refinement theorem for ST-bisimulation semantics. In M. Broy and C.B. Jones, editors, *Proc. IFIP Working Conference on Programming Concepts and Methods, Sea of Galilee, Israel*, 1990. To appear.

[Hen91]   M. Hennessy. Concurrent testing of processes. Technical Report 11/91, Dept. Comp. Sci. Univ. of Sussex, Brighton, 1991.

[HR90]   M. Hennessy and T. Regan. A temporal process algebra. Technical Report 2/90, Dept. Comp. Sci. Univ. of Sussex, Brighton, 1990.

[Phi87]   I. Phillips. Refusal testing. *Theoret. Comput. Sci.*, 50:241–284, 1987.

[RR87]   G.M. Reed and A.W. Roscoe. Metric spaces as models for real-time concurrency. In *Third Workshop on the Mathematical Foundations of Programming Language Semantics*, Lect. Notes Comp. Sci. 298, 331–343. Springer, 1987.

[RR88]   G.M. Reed and A.W. Roscoe. A timed model for communicating sequential processes. *Theoret. Comput. Sci.*, 58:249–261, 1988.

[Sta90]   P.H. Starke. Some properties of timed nets under the earliest firing rule. In G. Rozenberg, editor, *Advances in Petri Nets 1989*, Lect. Notes Comp. Sci. 424, 418–432. Springer, 1990.

[Vog92]   W. Vogler. *Modular Construction and Partial Order Semantics of Petri Nets*. Lect. Notes Comp. Sci. 625. Springer, 1992.

The Fork Calculus

Klaus Havelund
havelund@dmi.ens.fr
Ecole Normale Supérieure
Laboratoire d'Informatique
45 rue d'Ulm, 75005 Paris, France

*Kim G. Larsen**
kgl@iesd.auc.dk
Aalborg University
Institute for Electronic Systems
Department of Mathematics and Computer Science
Frederik Bajersvej 7, 9220 Aalborg, Denmark

Abstract

The Fork Calculus FC presents a theory of communicating systems in family with CCS, but it differs in the way that processes are put in parallel. In CCS there is a binary parallel operator $|$, and two processes p and q are put in parallel by $p|q$. In FC there is a unary **fork** operator, and a process p is activated to "run in parallel with the rest of the program" by $fork(p)$. An operational semantics is defined, and a congruence relation between processes is suggested. In addition, a sound and complete axiomatisation of the congruence is provided. FC has been developed during an investigation of the programming language CML [Rep91a], an extension of ML with concurrency primitives, amongst them a fork operator.

1 Introduction

The Fork Calculus FC is motivated by problems encountered while originally investigating semantic properties of the programming language CML (Concurrent ML) [Rep91a, Rep91b, BMT92]. In particular, we address the definition and axiomatisation of suitable equivalences between CML expressions. CML is an extension of ML with CCS-like concurrency primitives. The model behind CML is that of concurrently executing expressions that communicate by handshake message passing on typed channels. The concurrent aspects of CML, however, differs from CCS in a essential way: In CCS there is a binary parallel operator $|$, and two processes p and q are put in parallel by $p|q$. In CML the binary parallel operator has been replaced by a unary **fork** operator, and a process p is activated to "run in parallel with the rest of the program" by fork(p). The concurrency primitives of CML are provided as a set of "functions", from which the following may be derived[1]:

```
channel : unit -> 'a chan        transmit : 'a chan * 'a -> unit
fork    : (unit -> 'a) -> unit   accept   : 'a chan -> 'a
```

---

*The work of this author was supported by the Danish Natural Science Research Council project DART and partially by the ESPRIT Basic Research Action 7166, CONCUR2.

[1]There are minor differences in the choice of CML primitives, their types and names, in [Rep91a, Rep91b] and [BMT92]. In terms of the primitive features **sync**, **send** and **receive** of [BMT92], which we have chosen to follow, transmit and accept may be defined as: transmit(x) = (sync(send(x));()) and accept(x) = sync(receive(x)).

The function **channel** yields a fresh channel each time it is applied. The function **transmit** sends a value to a channel. The function **accept** reads a value from a channel. Finally, the function **fork** starts a separate evaluation of its argument function; that is: **fork(f)** starts the evaluation of **f()**. As an example, consider an implementation in CML of a function **calc:real->real** having the following specification: **calc(x)=cos(x)+sin(x)**. The implementation can be given as follows:

```
fun calc(x) =
    let val r1 = channel()
        val r2 = channel()
    in
    fork(fn () => transmit(r1,cos(x)));
    fork(fn () => transmit(r2,sin(x)));
    (accept(r1) + accept(r2))
    end;
```

The function evaluates the expressions **cos(x)** and **sin(x)** in parallel. First, two (local) channels **r1** and **r2** are allocated. Then, the two evaluations are forked; The two forked evaluations send their respective result back on the channels **r1** and **r2**.

Our ultimate goal is to define an appropriate equivalence between CML expressions. Obviously, we have a number of expectations to properties enjoyed by such an equivalence. As an example, consider that we reverse the order of the two fork expressions, thus forking the sinus calculation first. Then we would like the resulting function to be equivalent to the one above. The result in both cases is two parallel evaluations of the expressions **cos(x)** and **sin(x)** and we really do not care about how this result is obtained. In general, we will not want to observe the particular forking strategy — only the collected behaviour of the result. As an even more radical example, the implementation given above should satisfy the original specification **calc(x)=cos(x)+sin(x)**. Another natural and important requirement to our equivalence is that it is a *congruence* with respect to all CML constructs as this will allow compositional verification. In particular, equivalences between composite expressions should be inferable from equivalences of subexpressions.

Our work has been influenced by the work on Facile [PGM90], a language that integrates functional and concurrent programming in a way quite similar to CML — there is for example a fork operator. In [PGM90], Facile is given an operational semantics and a notion of equivalence is developed. The Facile equivalence is, however, not shown to be a congruence in the general case. This is caused by the fact that processes are values. We have concluded, that the issues of equivalence and compositionality in the presense of forking can best be studied in isolation from the other issues in CML, so we design a calculus, FC (Fork Calculus), that is close to CCS, but which provides a one-argument fork-operator instead of the two-argument parallel-operator found in CCS. Also, the unary prefix–operator of CCS is replaced by a dyadic operator for sequential composition. Although some of our techniques are related to those in [PGM90], this simplification gives us a congruence, and in addition we approach its complete axiomatisation.

The outline of the remainder of this paper is as follows: in section 2 we present the syntax and a structured operational semantics of our calculus FC. In section 3 we present the obvious (strong bisimulation) equivalence between processes based on the operational semantics of section 2. It, however, turns out that this equivalence is *not* a congruence with respect to the constructs of FC, a rather remarkable fact as strong bisimulation equivalence is preserved by almost all constructs introduced so far in process algebra (see e.g. [GV89]). In section 4, we provide an explicit characterization of the congruence induced by the strong bisimulation equivalence. In section 5, we offer a complete axiomatisation of this congruence.

2 Syntax and Semantics

The syntax of the calculus is as follows.

$$\mathcal{L} ::= nil \mid A \mid \mathcal{L}_1 + \mathcal{L}_2 \mid \mathcal{L}_1; \mathcal{L}_2 \mid fork(\mathcal{L}) \mid N$$
$$A ::= \tau \mid a? \mid a!$$

nil is the terminated process that can perform no actions. Amongst the actions A that a process can perform are τ, the internal action, input actions of the form $a?$, and output actions of the form $a!$, where a is a channel name. Two processes that run in parallel may synchronise on complementary actions, one being an input action and the other being an output action containing the same name. The choice between two processes is written as $\mathcal{L}_1 + \mathcal{L}_2$. Two processes can be sequentially composed by $\mathcal{L}_1; \mathcal{L}_2$. This has the traditional interpretation that $\mathcal{L}_1$ is evaluated first until it terminates (becomes *nil*) whereupon $\mathcal{L}_2$ continues. Note that FC here differs from CCS which instead of sequential composition has action prefixing. Sequential composition has greater precedence than choice.

The other main difference from CCS is the **fork** expression: a process is forked with **fork**$(\mathcal{L})$. It means that a separate evaluation of $\mathcal{L}$ is begun such that $\mathcal{L}$ is made to run in parallel with the rest of the program. The **fork** expression itself terminates immediately after starting the separate evaluation of $\mathcal{L}$. N is the call of a process, that has been named in a definition of the form $N \overset{def}{=} \mathcal{L}$. In the present theory we disallow recursion in order to obtain a complete axiomatisation, and we only introduce process naming to be able to write some more appealing (nonrecursive) examples. Except for the complete axiomatisation, it is very easy to extend the results of this paper to allow recursion.

So what are the consequences of this seemingly minor change compared to CCS: having sequential composition and forking instead of action prefixing and parallel composition? There are pragmatic as well as semantic consequences. As we shall see, the semantic consequences are quite drastic. Concerning the pragmatic consequences, let us study an example. Consider the following informal requirement specification:

A 'session' at a computer terminal consists of an 'initialisation' followed by a 'run'. The initialisation consists of a 'setup' phase followed by a 'dialog' phase. After the 'setup' phase, a report is sent to a paper printer which will 'print' the report.

This requirement specification can be directly presented in FC as follows (note that for convenience, we shall often leave out the '?' when writing input actions; actions are written with small letters by convention):

$$Session \overset{def}{=} Initialise; run$$
$$Initialise \overset{def}{=} setup; fork(print); dialog$$

The point to note is that we can locally in *Initialise* express the parallel activation of the printer (*print*) after the *setup* phase. This local activation of a process is not directly expressible in CCS, where we would write something like:

$$Session \overset{def}{=} setup.(print.nil \mid dialog.run.nil)$$

We see that it is not possible to give a name (*Initialise*) to the pair *setup* and *dialog*: one looses abstraction. So characteristic of the **fork** operator is that we can start a process locally where the need arises, and this gives a possibility of naming a sequential composition that performs parallel activation as a "side effect". Of course the above pragmatic difference between FC and CCS is just a matter of taste, and we shall in the following concentrate on the formal implications of having 'fork' and ';'.

First, we define an operational semantics for the language of the calculus. That is, the approach taken is that of structured operational semantics as introduced by Plotkin [Plo81] and later applied to CCS as described in [Mil89]. The difference between the semantics here and the two existing semantics of CML [Rep91b, BMT92] is (except for the different languages) that we let transitions be labelled with actions. Both in [Rep91b] and in [BMT92] transitions are basically not labelled. Labels are important from the point of view of defining an appropriate equivalence relation.

A labelled transition system is a triple $(St, Lab, \rightarrow)$, where St is the set of states (for example processes), Lab is the set of labels (actions performed by the processes) and $\rightarrow \subseteq St \times Lab \times St$ is the transition relation: $(st_1, l, st_2) \in \rightarrow$ may be interpreted as "the state st_1 is able to perform the action l and by doing so becomes the state st_2". Typically we use the notation $st_1 \xrightarrow{l} st_2$ for $(st_1, l, st_2) \in \rightarrow$. The transition relation thus defines the dynamic change of states as they perform actions.

The semantics of CCS is normally given in terms of a single labelled transition system where St is the set of CCS processes. In contrast to the CCS semantics, the FC semantics is divided into two layers, corresponding to two labelled transition systems. In the first layer we give semantics to processes seen in isolation (St is the set of processes). In the next layer, we give semantics to collections of processes running in parallel (St is the set of such process collections). When "running" a process, for example $fork(p); q$ we start out with a collection consisting of that process. After the forking, we have a collection containing two processes, p and q, running in parallel. We refer to a collection of processes as a program (thus St is the set of programs).

2.1 Processes

In this section we give semantics to processes seen in isolation. We shall do this by defining a labelled transition system $(\mathcal{L}, Lab, \hookrightarrow)$ where $\mathcal{L}$ is the set of processes introduced in section 2. Concerning the definition of the labels Lab, assume an infinite set of (channel) names $Chan$. Then Lab (the labels on process transitions) is gradually defined as follows:

$$
\begin{aligned}
Com &= \{a? \mid a \in Chan\} \cup \{a! \mid a \in Chan\} \\
Act &= Com \cup \{\tau\} \\
Lab &= Act \cup \{\phi(p) \mid p \in \mathcal{L}\}
\end{aligned}
$$

The set Com, ranged over by c, is the set of input-output communications that processes can perform. The set Act, ranged over by $\alpha, \beta, \gamma, \ldots$, includes in addition the τ action, and it is the set of actions that we will be able to observe in the end, when executing programs. The set Lab, ranged over by l, includes further labels of the form $\phi(p)$ ($p \in \mathcal{L}$) which arise from evaluation of processes of the form $fork(p)$. These labels will not be observable at the program layer, since at that level they will be converted into τ actions.

We now define the transition relation $\hookrightarrow \subseteq \mathcal{L} \times Lab \times \mathcal{L}$. Before defining this transition relation we define the predicate $Stop \subseteq \mathcal{L}$. We shall use the notation $Stop(p)$ instead of $p \in Stop$. Now $Stop$ is defined as the least subset of $\mathcal{L}$ satisfying the following:

$Stop(nil)$,
If $Stop(p_1)$ and $Stop(p_2)$ then $Stop(p_1 + p_2)$ and $Stop(p_1; p_2)$,
If $Stop(p)$ and $N \overset{def}{=} p$ then $Stop(N)$

The operational semantics of FC processes is then as follows.

Definition 2.1 (The transition relation $\hookrightarrow$) *Let $\hookrightarrow$ be the smallest subset of $\mathcal{L} \times Lab \times \mathcal{L}$ closed under the following rules:*

$$(Action) \quad \frac{}{\alpha \overset{\alpha}{\hookrightarrow} nil}$$

$$(Choice_1) \quad \frac{p_1 \overset{l}{\hookrightarrow} p_1'}{p_1 + p_2 \overset{l}{\hookrightarrow} p_1'} \qquad\qquad (Choice_2) \quad \frac{p_2 \overset{l}{\hookrightarrow} p_2'}{p_1 + p_2 \overset{l}{\hookrightarrow} p_2'}$$

$$(Sequence_1) \quad \frac{p_1 \overset{l}{\hookrightarrow} p_1'}{p_1 ; p_2 \overset{l}{\hookrightarrow} p_1' ; p_2} \qquad\qquad (Sequence_2) \quad \frac{p_2 \overset{l}{\hookrightarrow} p_2'}{p_1 ; p_2 \overset{l}{\hookrightarrow} p_2'} Stop(p_1)$$

$$(Fork) \quad \frac{}{fork(p) \overset{\phi(p)}{\hookrightarrow} nil} \qquad\qquad (Constant) \quad \frac{P \overset{l}{\hookrightarrow} P'}{A \overset{l}{\hookrightarrow} P'} A \overset{def}{=} P$$

The rules should be fairly simple to read. The *Action*-rule says that a process of the form α can perform the action α and become *nil*. The *Choice₁*-rule says that if p_1 can perform l and become p_1', then the sum $p_1 + p_2$ can also, and symmetrically by the *Choice₂*-rule. The sequencing rules explain how sequencing proceeds with the leftmost process until it has stopped (*Sequence₁*), whereupon the rightmost process continues (*Sequence₂*). The *Fork*-rule shows how the higher order labels $\phi(p)$ are created. When we come to the program semantics their use will be explained. Finally, the *Constant*-rule explains how the name of a process behaves as the defining body. Let us look at an example. The process $\alpha; fork(\beta); \gamma$ can evaluate as follows:

$$\alpha; fork(\beta); \gamma \overset{\alpha}{\hookrightarrow} nil; fork(\beta); \gamma \overset{\phi(\beta)}{\hookrightarrow} nil; \gamma \overset{\gamma}{\hookrightarrow} nil$$

Note that the forked process β just becomes part of the label, and that it is not further used. When executing programs, we will make sure that the forked process is put in parallel with the "rest of the program".

2.2 Programs

A program is a multiset[1] of processes. We let $\mathcal{L}_p$ denote the set of programs ($\mathcal{L}_p = MS(\mathcal{L})$). The semantics of programs is given in terms of the labelled transition system ($\mathcal{L}_p, Act, \longrightarrow$), where $\mathcal{L}_p$ is defined here and Act was defined in the previous section. Thus a program can perform the actions in the set Act; recall that these were of the form $a?$, $a!$ or τ. The fork actions $\phi(p)$ are thus not amongst program actions.

---

[1] A multiset can contain several copies of the same element, (in contrast to normal sets), corresponding to the fact that at a certain moment there may be several processes active with exactly the same structure. Formally, the multisets of A elements can be viewed as the elements in $MS(A) = A \rightarrow \mathbb{N}$. That is, a multiset of A elements is a total function from A to the natural numbers. Each A element is mapped to its number of occurrences. The union operator $\cup : (MS(A) \times MS(A)) \rightarrow MS(A)$ is defined by the equation $(S_1 \cup S_2)(a) = S_1(a) + S_2(a)$. A "finite" multiset S can be written $\{p_1, \ldots, p_n\}$ where the number of occurrences of a process q indicates the value $S(q)$. As an example, $\{p\}(p) = 1$ and $\{p\}(q) = 0$ whenever $p \neq q$.

We shall now define the transition relation: $\longrightarrow \subseteq \mathcal{L}_p \times Act \times \mathcal{L}_p$. We need the auxiliary function $rev : Com \rightarrow Com$, which for a given communication returns the complementary communication with which it can synchronise; i.e: $rev(a?) = a!$ and $rev(a!) = a?$. The operational semantics of FC programs is then as follows.

Definition 2.2 (The transition relation $\longrightarrow$) *Let $\longrightarrow$ be the smallest subset of $\mathcal{L}_p \times Act \times \mathcal{L}_p$ closed under the following rules:*

$$(Action^{\{\!\}}) \qquad \frac{p \overset{\alpha}{\hookrightarrow} p'}{\{\!p\!\} \overset{\alpha}{\longrightarrow} \{\!p'\!\}} \qquad\qquad (Fork^{\{\!\}}) \qquad \frac{p \overset{\phi(q)}{\hookrightarrow} p'}{\{\!p\!\} \overset{\tau}{\longrightarrow} \{\!p', q\!\}}$$

$$(Parallel_1^{\{\!\}}) \qquad \frac{P_1 \overset{\alpha}{\longrightarrow} P_1'}{P_1 \cup P_2 \overset{\alpha}{\longrightarrow} P_1' \cup P_2} \qquad (Parallel_2^{\{\!\}}) \qquad \frac{P_1 \overset{c}{\longrightarrow} P_1' , \; P_2 \overset{rev(c)}{\longrightarrow} P_2'}{P_1 \cup P_2 \overset{\tau}{\longrightarrow} P_1' \cup P_2'}$$

The $Action^{\{\!\}}$-rule just says that if a process can perform an action, then a program containing that process can perform the action. Note that α ranges over Act, which does not contain $\phi(p)$ actions. The $Fork^{\{\!\}}$-rule explains how a $\phi(\ldots)$ action results in a τ action at program level: the forking process and the forked process will after the transition be in parallel. Finally, the rule $Parallel_1^{\{\!\}}$ explains how a "subset" of a program may perform actions on its own. Note, that we need only one such rule as $\cup$ is clearly commutative. The $Parallel_2^{\{\!\}}$-rule shows how two distinct subsets of a program may communicate, resulting in a τ action.

3 Program and Process Equivalences

The purpose of this chapter is to define an equivalence relation $\sim \subseteq \mathcal{L} \times \mathcal{L}$ between FC processes. For this purpose we shall, however, first define an equivalence relation $\smile \subseteq \mathcal{L}_p \times \mathcal{L}_p$ between FC programs.

3.1 Program Equivalence

Our notion of equivalence is based on the concept of bisimulation [Mil89], which again is based on the idea that we only want to distinguish between two programs, if the distinction can be observed by an "observer" examining the actions that the two programs can perform. Note that in the following we shall regard the τ action just as observable as the other actions ($a?$ and $a!$) in Act. We shall for example distinguish $\{\!\alpha; \tau; \beta\!\}$ and $\{\!\alpha; \beta\!\}$. This will yield a rather strict congruence (fewer programs are congruent). We have chosen to make τ observable in our first attempt, since it is the classical choice: first a strong notion of equivalence is defined (where τ is observable), and then one abstracts from τ. The formal definition of $\smile$ proceeds in the standard way [Mil89] as follows. First, we define the notion of a bisimulation.

Definition 3.1 (Bisimulation) *A binary relation $S \subseteq \mathcal{L}_p \times \mathcal{L}_p$ is a bisimulation iff $(P, Q) \in S$ implies, for all $\alpha \in Act$,*

1. Whenever $P \overset{\alpha}{\longrightarrow} P'$ for some P' then $Q \overset{\alpha}{\longrightarrow} Q'$ for some Q' and $(P', Q') \in S$

2. Whenever $Q \overset{\alpha}{\longrightarrow} Q'$ for some Q' then $P \overset{\alpha}{\longrightarrow} P'$ for some P' and $(P', Q') \in S$

We write $P \smile Q$ where $(P, Q) \in S$ for some bisimulation S.

As usual it may be shown that $\smile$ is itself the largest bisimulation. Moreover, $\smile$ is easily shown to be a congruence with respect to $\cup$.

3.2 Process Equivalence

In the previous section we introduced an equivalence on programs, and we showed it to be a congruence with respect to the basic operator on programs: $\cup$. What we are really interested in is, however, not programs, but rather processes. Processes are the terms of our language, and programs are "just" semantic objects used for giving semantics to processes. So our definite goal is to define an equivalence on processes. This equivalence must additionally be a congruence with respect to the operators on processes (+ ; *fork*). In this section we shall come up with a process equivalence $\sim$, which seems rather natural and correct, but which, however, turns out not to be satisfactory due to lack of the congruence property. In the section to follow we will define an equivalence $\equiv$ that is also a congruence, in fact the congruence induced by $\sim$; but the present exercise can hopefully motivate the final solution.

We shall define an equivalence relation $\sim \subseteq \mathcal{L} \times \mathcal{L}$ between FC processes. Two processes p and q are said to be equivalent if $(p, q) \in \sim$, which is written more conveniently as $p \sim q$. The idea is to say that two processes are equivalent, if they are equivalent when regarded as programs. Put differently: to see whether two processes are equivalent, "run" them (as programs) and see whether they behave the same way. Formally, we thus define $\sim$ as follows:

Definition 3.2 (Process equivalence) *The relation $\sim \subseteq \mathcal{L} \times \mathcal{L}$ is defined as:*

$$p \sim q \Leftrightarrow \{\!\!\{p\}\!\!\} \smile \{\!\!\{q\}\!\!\}$$

As we shall see, the *fork* operator causes $\sim$ not to be a congruence. This is rather unusual since (strong) bisimilarity is normally preserved by operators. Consider two processes that are related by $\sim$:

$$\tau; \alpha \quad \sim \quad fork(\alpha)$$

To see this, consider the behaviours of the programs $\{\!\!\{\tau; \alpha\}\!\!\}$ and $\{\!\!\{fork(\alpha)\}\!\!\}$:

$$\{\!\!\{\tau; \alpha\}\!\!\} \quad \xrightarrow{\tau} \quad \{\!\!\{nil; \alpha\}\!\!\} \quad \xrightarrow{\alpha} \quad \{\!\!\{nil\}\!\!\}$$

$$\{\!\!\{fork(\alpha)\}\!\!\} \quad \xrightarrow{\tau} \quad \{\!\!\{nil, \alpha\}\!\!\} \quad \xrightarrow{\alpha} \quad \{\!\!\{nil, nil\}\!\!\}$$

Clearly these behaviours are bisimilar (as they are identical). Now, suppose that we put the two processes into the same context $\_; \beta$. Will it then hold that $\tau; \alpha; \beta \sim fork(\alpha); \beta$? Unfortunately no!. This can be seen from the behaviours of the programs $\{\!\!\{\tau; \alpha; \beta\}\!\!\}$ and $\{\!\!\{fork(\alpha); \beta\}\!\!\}$, as illustrated by the transition trees for the two programs in figure 1.

Thus, $\sim$ is not a congruence, and we have to repair this. In the following, we introduce a process relation that *is* a congruence. It is even the largest congruence induced by (contained in) $\sim$.

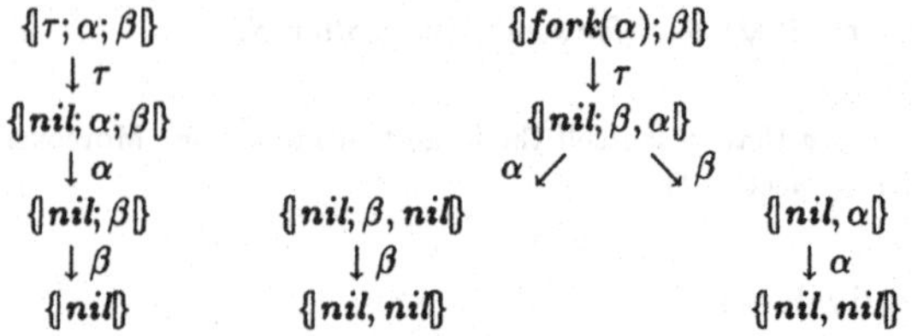

$$\begin{array}{cc}
\{\!|\tau; \alpha; \beta|\!\} & \{\!|fork(\alpha); \beta|\!\} \\
\downarrow \tau & \downarrow \tau \\
\{\!|nil; \alpha; \beta|\!\} & \{\!|nil; \beta, \alpha|\!\} \\
\downarrow \alpha & \alpha \swarrow \quad \searrow \beta
\end{array}$$

$$\begin{array}{ccc}
\{\!|nil; \beta|\!\} & \{\!|nil; \beta, nil|\!\} & \{\!|nil, \alpha|\!\} \\
\downarrow \beta & \downarrow \beta & \downarrow \alpha \\
\{\!|nil|\!\} & \{\!|nil, nil|\!\} & \{\!|nil, nil|\!\}
\end{array}$$

Figure 1: Different Transition Trees

4 Process Congruence

In this section we introduce a new process equivalence $\equiv$ being strictly finer than the previously given equivalence $\sim$. As one of the main results of this paper we prove that $\equiv$ is precisely the congruence induced by $\sim$; i.e. $\equiv$ is preserved by all operators of FC, and is the largest such equivalence included in $\sim$. The fact that $\sim$ is not a congruence is illustrated by the previous example demonstrating the difference between the two processes $\tau; \alpha$ and $fork(\alpha)$ when put into the context $\_; \beta$. The difference lies essentially in the ability of the action α to be in parallel with future computation, which is here represented by the action β.

It is this *ability to be in parallel with future computation* that we want to capture. Future computation is what computes after the *termination* of the observed process. When examining the two programs $\{\!|\tau; \alpha|\!\}$ and $\{\!|fork(\alpha)|\!\}$, we cannot detect this termination: both programs perform a τ action and then an α action, and that's it. The process $\tau; \alpha$, however, terminates after the second action (α), while the process $fork(\alpha)$ already terminates after the first action (τ), when the forking has been performed — the forked process α can then execute after this termination. We thus need to add some information that makes it possible to observe termination. This can be done by introducing a special event, π, that, when being performed, signals the successful termination of the observed process. For a given process p under observation, we shall examine $\{\!|p; \pi|\!\}$ rather than just $\{\!|p|\!\}$.

As an example, in order to observe the difference in terms of future computations between the processes $\tau; \alpha$ and $fork(\alpha)$, we "run" $\tau; \alpha; \pi$ and $fork(\alpha); \pi$ as programs. That is, we examine $\{\!|\tau; \alpha; \pi|\!\}$ and $\{\!|fork(\alpha); \pi|\!\}$. Both programs can perform the trace $\tau\alpha\pi$, but only the program $\{\!|fork(\alpha); \pi|\!\}$ can perform the trace $\tau\pi\alpha$, where the α action occurs after the π action. This may be illustrated by the transition trees for the two programs, which will be identical to the trees in figure 1 with π replacing β.

We are now able to give the following formal definition of the process congruence $\equiv$:

Definition 4.1 (Process congruence $\equiv$) *The relation* $\equiv \subseteq \mathcal{L} \times \mathcal{L}$ *is defined as* [2]:

$$p \equiv q \Leftrightarrow \{\!|p; \pi|\!\} \sim \{\!|q; \pi|\!\}$$

One of the main results of this paper is that $\equiv$ is the congruence (i.e. preserved by the operators of FC) induced by $\sim$. First of all, it is straightforward to show that $\equiv$ is an equivalence relation. That it is also a congruence is stated as the following theorem.

---

[2]This equivalence is similar to one of the equivalences defined in [PGM90]; however, no axiomatisation is provided in [PGM90].

Theorem 4.2 (Congruence Property) *Assume processes p_1, p_2 and q where $p_1 \equiv p_2$. Then:*

$$fork(p_1) \equiv fork(p_2) \qquad\qquad q; p_1 \equiv q; p_2$$
$$p_1 + q \equiv p_2 + q \qquad\qquad p_1; q \equiv p_2; q$$

That $\equiv$ is the congruence induced by $\sim$ is formulated as follows.

Theorem 4.3 (Induced Congruence Property) $\equiv$ *is the largest congruence contained in* $\sim$.

5 Strong Axiomatisation

In this section we present a sound and complete axiomatisation for the process congruence $\equiv$. The completeness of the axiomatisation is obtained in a classical manner through the use of normal forms — being process expressions with a very restricted use of the *fork*-operator. More precisely, the axiomatisation consists of a collection of basic equational axioms, and two expansion laws. The basic axioms achieve completeness for normal form processes, and the expansion laws (together with the basic axioms) enable arbitrary process expressions to be transformed into normal form, thus yielding completeness for the full calculus.

In more classical process calculi, expansion laws allow parallel composition to be replaced by non-determinism. In our calculus, the expansion laws will have an analogous purpose, namely that of replacing as much as possible forking with non-deterministic choice. However — as we shall see in the next section — our calculus seems to lack expressive power for suitable expansion laws to exist. To overcome this problem, we shall extend the calculus with an extra operator described below [3].

5.1 Searching for an Expansion Law

We need expansion laws, that describe how forking may be expanded (as much as possible) into non-determinism — similar to the expansion law of CCS that expands parallel composition into non-determinism. For example, consider the following instance of the CCS expansion law:

$$a.nil \,|\, b.nil \;=\; a.b.nil + b.a.nil$$

Let us try to search for a similar expansion law for the FC *fork* operator. We try to expand the corresponding FC-process $fork(a); b$. An initial guess can be the following:

$$fork(a); b \;=\; a; b + b; a$$

However, this equation is not sound (it does not hold when replacing $=$ with $\equiv$), and can therefore immediately be ignored. Intuitively, the reason is that the right hand side contains no information about a's capability to be in parallel with "the rest of the program". In the next seemingly correct equation we try to take this into account:

$$fork(a); b = a; b + b; fork(a) \qquad\qquad (1)$$

This equation is not sound either: the left hand side can perform a τ action as the first thing, while the right hand side can perform either an a action or a b action (note that since we want to

---

[3]This phenomenon is similar to the necessity of the leftmerge operator in PL in order to obtain a finite sound and complete equational axiomatisation as shown in [Mol90].

axiomatise strong process congruence $\equiv$, τ actions are observable). Trying to repair this problem we obtain:

$$fork(a); b \;=\; \tau; (a; b + b; fork(a)) \qquad (2)$$

This equation is not sound either: the left hand side can only perform one τ action, while the right hand side can perform two (the explicitly mentioned and the one caused by *fork*).

So it seems that we cannot in general expand forking! This leaves open the problem of how to establish equality between process expressions involving the *fork*-operator. The latter two attempts above suggest that we need a version of *fork* which is instantaneous without the initial internal transition caused by *fork*. Put alternatively, we lack the ability to express that something *has been* forked, with the initial τ action already having occurred previously. To gain this expressivity, we add a new instantaneous forking operator to our calculus. We call this operator *forked*, and we write *forked(p)* to mean 'fork p without a τ'. One can regard this operator alternatively by reading *forked(p)* as 'p has been forked', or shorter: 'forked p'. The latter reading suggests the following relationship between *fork* and *forked*:

$$fork(p) \;=\; \tau; forked(p)$$

Let us now try to write new versions of the equations (1) and (2), that contain the *forked* operator in appropriate positions. These equations can be shown sound on basis of the formal definition we give of the *forked* operator in the following section. The equations are:

$$forked(a); b \;=\; a; b + b; forked(a)$$
$$fork(a); b \;=\; \tau; (a; b + b; forked(a))$$

However, it remains to settle whether it is possible to find an operator *forked* satisfying the above equations. In the next section we give an affirmative answer by providing an operational semantics for this new operator.

5.2 Adding the 'Forked'-operator

The syntax is extended with the *forked* alternative:

$$\mathcal{L}^{\Phi} \;::=\; nil \,|\, \mathcal{A} \,|\, \mathcal{L}^{\Phi}{}_1 + \mathcal{L}^{\Phi}{}_2 \,|\, \mathcal{L}^{\Phi}{}_1; \mathcal{L}^{\Phi}{}_2 \,|\, fork(\mathcal{L}^{\Phi}) \,|\, forked(\mathcal{L}^{\Phi}) \,|\, N$$

The extended calculus is called FC$^{\Phi}$. The set *Lab* of actions that a process can perform is extended accordingly:

$$Lab \;=\; Act \cup \{\phi(p) \,|\, p \in \mathcal{L}^{\Phi}\} \cup \{\Phi(p) \,|\, p \in \mathcal{L}^{\Phi}\}$$

The new semantics of processes and programs is obtained by adding the following rules:

$$(\textit{Forked}) \quad \frac{}{\;forked(p) \overset{\Phi(p)}{\hookrightarrow} nil\;} \qquad\qquad (\textit{Forked} \text{\textbardbl}) \quad \frac{p \overset{\Phi(q)}{\hookrightarrow} p',\; \{p',q\} \overset{\alpha}{\longrightarrow} R}{\{p\} \overset{\alpha}{\longrightarrow} R}$$

The previous semantic definitions from section 2 — the sets *Com* and *Act* (however not *Lab*), and the operational semantic rules for the original operators — carry over unchanged to the extended calculus. Likewise do the definitions of the program equivalence $\smile$ and the process equivalences $\sim$ and $\equiv$ from sections 3 and 4. The proofs of the following properties also carry over: (1) $\smile$ is a congruence with respect to ∪, (2) ∼ is an equivalence (but not a congruence, as before), (3) ≡ is an equivalence.

The congruence property of ≡ does, however, not apply to the extended calculus. The reason for this can be illustrated by the following example. It is easily shown that $forked(nil) \equiv nil$. Now, consider the two processes $forked(nil) + \alpha$ and $nil + \alpha$. In order for ≡ to be a congruence, these two processes should be equivalent (show the same behaviour). They are, however, not equivalent since $forked(nil) + \alpha$ can "jump over" the α action while $nil + \alpha$ must perform the α action.

We choose to loosen the requirement that ≡ is a congruence. The congruence property holds for all the operators, except for the choice operator, which becomes conditioned. Let $Active(q)$, for any process $q \in \mathcal{L}^{\Phi}$, mean that q can perform an action. That is: $Active(q) \stackrel{def}{=} \exists \alpha \in Act, P \in \mathcal{L}_p^{\Phi} \cdot \{\!|q|\!\} \stackrel{\alpha}{\longrightarrow} P$. Then the loosened congruence property can be stated as follows: assume for two processes p_1, p_2 that $p_1 \equiv p_2$. Then for any process q:

$$p_1 + q \equiv p_2 + q \quad provided \ Active(q) \Rightarrow (Stop(p_1) \Leftrightarrow Stop(p_2))$$

The condition is motivated by our previous example, where q is α, and p_1 is $forked(nil)$ and p_2 is nil, thus the condition is not satisfied in this case. Note that $Stop(forked(nil))$ does not hold according the definition of $Stop$ which is unchanged for the extended calculus.

5.3 Basic Axioms and Inference Rules

The final axiom system $\mathcal{AS}$ consists of a set $\mathcal{AX}$ of equational axiom schemes, two expansion laws $\mathcal{E}_1$ and $\mathcal{E}_2$, using normal forms, and a set $\mathcal{I}$ of inference rules, that represents the fact that ≡ is an equivalence and (nearly) a congruence. In this section we shall present the basic equational axioms $\mathcal{AX}$.

Definition 5.1 (Basic axiom system $\mathcal{AX}$) The basic axiom system $\mathcal{AX}$ consists of the axioms[4]:

$$
\begin{array}{rclcrclcrcl}
fork(p) & = & \tau; forked(p) & \quad & p; nil & = & p & \quad & p + (q + r) & = & (p + q) + r \\
forked(\alpha; forked(p) + q) & = & forked(\alpha; p + q) & & nil; p & = & p & & p + q & = & q + p \\
forked(nil) & = & nil & & (p; q); r & = & p; (q; r) & & p + nil & = & p \\
& & & & (p + q); r & = & p; r + q; r & & p + p & = & p
\end{array}
$$

5.4 Normal Forms

Our way to completeness is classical in that it is based on *normal forms*. For processes in normal form, the basic axioms $\mathcal{AX}$ will be shown to be complete, and we shall in the next section present two expansion laws that will enable any process term to be transformed into a provable equivalent normal form process term.

Processes in normal form contain no applications of the *fork* operator, and applications of the *forked* operator occur last. One intuition behind this is that when observing a process we cannot observe the individual forkings; and as long as the original process has not terminated, we cannot observe which actions come from it and which actions come from the forked processes. We can, however, in contexts observe when the process terminates and what at that time has been

---

[4]The axiom $(p + q); r = p; r + q; r$ holds when $\neg Stop(p)$ and $\neg Stop(q)$.

forked. In principle a process is brought into normal form by first replacing applications $fork(p)$ by $\tau; forked(p)$, and then by moving the applications of $forked$ as much as possible "to the right". Note that we must deal with the $forked$ operator in normal forms, since we must keep track of what is potentially in parallel with future computation.

As an example, consider the process $fork(\alpha); \beta$. First, we can replace $fork(\alpha)$ with $\tau; forked(\alpha)$, thus obtaining $\tau; forked(\alpha); \beta$. Then we can consider the process $forked(\alpha); \beta$, and bring it into the form $\alpha; \beta + \beta; forked(\alpha)$. As result we obtain $\tau; (\alpha; \beta + \beta; forked(\alpha))$. We see that there is no application of the $fork$ operator, and that the application of the $forked$ operator occurs last. Let us now formally introduce normal forms:

Definition 5.2 (Normal form) *A process p is in normal form, if it is a term in N, where:*

$$N ::= \sum_i \alpha_i; N_i + \sum_j \beta_j; forked(B_j) \qquad \text{and} \qquad B ::= \sum_k \beta_k; B_k$$

A process p is in simple normal form, if it is a term in B.

Note that simple normal forms contain no applications of the $forked$ operator. That is, once we have reached the termination of a process (second alternative in the definition of N), what remains has all been forked, and to express this we only need one application of the $forked$ operator. That is, we do not care about any "further" forking.

5.5 Expansion Laws

The two expansion laws to be presented in this section will enable any process term to be transformed into normal form. To motivate the two expansion laws consider the case of a sequential composition of two process terms N and M already in normal form. Now assume N is of the following form:

$$N = \sum_i \alpha_i; N_i + \sum_j \beta_j; forked(B_j)$$

Then, using the laws for distributing ; over + and laws of associativity for ;, we obtain:

$$\vdash N; M = \sum_i \alpha_i; (N_i; M) + \sum_j \beta_j; (forked(B_j); M)$$

To enable this term to be transformed into a normal form we introduce the following expansion law:

Definition 5.3 (Expansion law $\mathcal{E}_1$)
Let: $A = \sum_i \alpha_i; A_i$, $N = \sum_j \beta_j; N_j$, $L = \sum_k \gamma_k; forked(C_k)$ *and* $M = N + L$ *where M is not nil. Then:*

$$forked(A); M = p + q + r + s + t \quad \text{where} \quad \begin{cases} p &= \sum_i \alpha_i; forked(A_i); M \\ q &= \sum_j \beta_j; forked(A); N_j \\ r &= \sum_k \gamma_k; forked(A); forked(C_k) \\ s &= \sum_{\alpha_i = rev(\beta_j)} \tau; forked(A_i); N_j \\ t &= \sum_{\alpha_i = rev(\gamma_k)} \tau; forked(A_i); forked(C_k) \end{cases}$$

To be able to inductively transform $forked(A); M$ into normal form, we see in definition 5.3 that we need to be able to handle terms of the form $forked(A); forked(B)$. This motivates the second expansion law below:

Definition 5.4 (Expansion law $\mathcal{E}_2$)

Let: $A = \sum_i \alpha_i; A_i$ and $B = \sum_j \beta_j; B_j$. Then:

$$forked(A); forked(B) = forked(p + q + r) \quad \text{where} \quad \left\{ \begin{array}{lcl} p & = & \sum_i \alpha_i; forked(A_i); forked(B) \\ q & = & \sum_j \beta_j; forked(A); forked(B_j) \\ r & = & \sum_{\alpha_i = rev(\beta_j)} \tau; forked(A_i); forked(B_j) \end{array} \right.$$

The basic axioms $\mathcal{AX}$, the two expansion laws $\mathcal{E}_1$ and $\mathcal{E}_2$ and the inference rules $\mathcal{I}$ constitute our proof system $\mathcal{AS}$, which we shall show to be (limited) complete. We write $\vdash p = q$ if the equivalence of p and q can be entailed within the proof system $\mathcal{AS}$.

5.6 Soundness and Limited Completeness

In this section we state, that the axiom system $\mathcal{AS}$ is sound and complete with respect to strong process congruence. That is, $\vdash p = q \Leftrightarrow p \equiv q$. The basic technique for showing completeness is classical; i.e. first to prove that each process term in the original *forked*-free calculus of section 2 is equivalent to a term in normal form, and then to prove completeness for normal forms. The fact that the completeness result only will apply to *forked*-free processes makes it "limited". First we state the soundness result.

Theorem 5.5 ($\mathcal{AS}$ is sound) *For all $p, q \in \mathcal{L}^\circledast$, whenever $\vdash p = q$ then $p \equiv q$.*

Note that the result holds for all p, q in FC$^\circledast$. The following proposition states that there exists a normal form for every process term in FC. Note that there does not exist a normal form for every process term in FC$^\circledast$; as an example, the process $forked(\alpha)$ has no normal form.

Proposition 5.6 (Normal forms for FC) *For all $p \in \mathcal{L}$, there exists a normal form N such that: $\vdash p = N$.*

The next step is to show completeness for normal forms.

Proposition 5.7 (Normal form completeness) *For all normal forms $M, N \in \mathcal{L}^\circledast$, whenever $M \equiv N$ then $\vdash M = N$.*

These two propositions can be used to prove the (limited) completeness result. The completeness result is limited in the sense that it only holds for process terms of FC (and not FC$^\circledast$).

Theorem 5.8 ($\mathcal{AS}$ is limited Complete) *For all $p, q \in \mathcal{L}$, whenever $p \equiv q$ then $\vdash p = q$.*

6 Conclusion and Future Work

In this paper we have identified and axiomatised a congruence $\equiv$ between FC–processes. Also, it has been demonstrated that $\equiv$ is the congruence induced by a natural strong bisimulation equivalence $\sim$.

In practice, however, both $\sim$ and $\equiv$ are too fine, as they are sensitive to internal computations. To obtain a more suitable equivalence, we may consider the *weak* bisimulation equivalence $\approx$ between processes, in which we abstract away from τ–transitions. Doing this, we will observe the same phenomena as we did for the strong equivalence: $\approx$ is not preserved by sequential composition. Applying the technique of this paper — i.e. defining $p \cong q$ iff $p; \pi \approx q; \pi$ — we obtain the coarsest equivalence contained in $\approx$ which is also preserved by ; (and *fork*). However, $\cong$ will not quite be a congruence as it will not be preserved by the choice–operator. This is a classical problem [Mil89], and we conjecture that the classical techniques for overcoming this problem will apply to $\cong$. Also, we conjecture that the congruence obtained in this manner will be completely axiomatized by the axiomatization $\mathcal{AS}$ presented in this paper augmented with the classical τ–laws [Mil89].

As immediate future work we intend to investigate the FC–calculus extended with primitives for dynamic channel creation and communication of channels. Further future work includes design of a (logical) specification language for specifying properties of FC programs. It should be shown that the designed specification language is *adequate* with respect to a suitable process–equivalence (for example the one defined here); i.e. two processes enjoy the same properties of the specification language precisely when they are behaviourally equivalent. One may consider a modification of the specification language which is defined in [HM85] for CCS, usually referred to as Hennessy-Milner logic.

A more long–term ambition is to extend our work to the full language of CML.

References

[BMT92] D. Berry, R. Milner, and D.N. Turner. A Semantics for ML Concurrency Primitives. In *Proceedings of the 19th ACM Symposium on Principles of Programming Languages*, 1992.

[GV89] J. F. Groote and F. W. Vaandrager. Structured Operational Semantics and Bisimulation as a Congruence. *LNCS*, 372, 1989.

[HM85] M. Hennessy and R. Milner. Algebraic Laws for Nondeterminism and Concurrency. *Journal of ACM*, 32(1), January 1985.

[Mil89] R. Milner. *Communication and Concurrency*. International Series in Computer Science. Prentice Hall, 1989.

[Mol90] F. Moller. The Importance of the Left Merge Operator in Process Algebra. *LNCS*, 443, 1990.

[PGM90] S. Prasad, A. Giacalone, and P. Mishra. Operational and Algebraic Semantics for Facile. In *Proceedings of ICALP90, LNCS 443*, 1990.

[Plo81] G. Plotkin. A Structural Approach to Operational Semantics. FN 19, DAIMI, Aarhus University, Denmark, 1981.

[Rep91a] J. H. Reppy. CML: A Higher-order Concurrent Language. In *ACM SIGPLAN'91 Conference on Programming Language Design and Implementation (SIGPLAN Notices 26(6))*, 1991.

[Rep91b] J.H. Reppy. An Operational Semantics of First–class Synchronous Operations. Technical Report TR 91-1232, Cornell University, Department of Computer Science, 1991.

Extended Transition Systems
for Parametric Bisimulation [1]

Paola Inverardi
I.E.I. - C.N.R.
Via S. Maria, 46
I-56100 Pisa
email: inverard@vm.cnuce.cnr.it

Corrado Priami
Università di Pisa
Dipartimento di Informatica
C.so Italia, 40
I-56100 Pisa
email: priami@di.unipi.it

Daniel Yankelevich
Università di Pisa
Dipartimento di Informatica
C.so Italia, 40
I-56100 Pisa
email: dany@newton.csc.ncsu.edu

1. Introduction

In the last years, a wide spectrum of semantic models for concurrency has been developed. Each model deals with different aspects of distributed concurrent systems. Moreover, there is no general accepted model. Indeed, different approaches may be used to specify different properties (or views) of the system. For example, final users of a system may just want to know how the system behaves in terms of its possible temporal sequences of actions, and thus the interleaving semantics [14] is suitable for them. On the other hand, designers usually need information about causal and spatial dependencies between events, and thus a truly concurrent semantics is more adequate for them.

A formalism able to describe many models in a single framework provides a general basis that permits to:

i. classify and compare the descriptive power of such models on firm grounds
ii. reuse general definitions and results
iii. describe different views of a system without changing almost nothing of the underlying theory.

These considerations leads to the development of parametric theories [5, 6, 8, 9, 15]. These approaches, starting from a very detailed description of systems given in the SOS style [17], provide abstraction mechanisms to recover many models presented in the literature. The parametric approach of [5, 6] roughly consists of the following four steps.

i. Define elementary transitions which describe the immediate evolution of the system;
ii. Construct computations of the system as paths in the transition system and give them a tree structure by ordering them by prefix;
iii. Introduce observations over computations to abstract from unwanted details, and decorate the trees above with observations, thus obtaining *observation trees*;
iv. Compare observation trees to determine which systems have an equivalent behaviour by means of a bisimulation relation.

Following this approach, many semantics can be captured just by slightly changing the observations of the third step (see [15, 20]).

An alternative approach [8] take proved transition systems [1] as privileged transition systems, where transitions are labelled with their proofs. Computations are defined as sequences of transitions, and are organized as trees, called *proved trees*. Their arcs are labelled with (encodings

[1] Work partially supported by Progetto Finalizzato Sistemi Informatici e Calcolo Parallelo

of) the proofs of the transitions and then are observed to recover many semantic models. Classical bisimulation [16] is defined over proved trees for comparing the behaviour of systems.

In [9] transition are considered to be terms of an algebra. The description of a system is driven to a tree-structured normal form in an axiomatic way. Also in this case, abstraction mechanisms allows to retrieve many models for the semantics of concurrent systems.

All approaches outlined above relies on tree structures to describe the behaviour of a system. Thus, they can finitely describe only systems having finite behaviour. This fact is a major drawback to perform bisimulation-based verifications. In fact, most of the approaches to automatic verification uses algorithms which rely on graph representation of the system [10, 13]. Moreover, almost any example of distributed systems has possibly infinite behaviours, and therefore it cannot be checked by using tree-like representations.

In this paper we propose a new kind of transition systems, called *Extended Transition Systems* (ETS), which extend previous approaches that deal with tree-structures to graphs. This model gives a parametric finite representation of a finite state system, by unifying many of the ideas of [5, 6] from one side and of [1, 8] from the other. Indeed, we start from the proved transition system and we label each node n with a regular expression describing all computations from the initial state to n. Hence, the number of the states in our representation does not increase with respect to the original transition system. We define abstraction mechanisms over ETS in order to get different views (observations) of a system. Also, a notion of parametric bisimulation is introduced. Moreover, we show that our parametric bisimulation coincides with the equivalences defined in [5, 6, 8]. We give some results to compute bisimulation for a class of observations, called *incremental*, and we briefly discus how this approach can be extended to other views. An immediate application of the results of this paper is the extension of parametric tools for verification of concurrent systems like [11] also for finite state systems. Indeed, if we apply our approach to a system with finite behaviour, we obtain the structures used by the tool of [11].

The paper is organized as follows. The following section recall the background of parametric theories. In Section 3 the extended transition systems are introduced and a notion of parametric bisimulation is defined over them. Also, we show that our equivalence coincides with the ones of [5, 6, 8]. Finally, Section 4 discusses how regular expressions can be observed.

2. Background

In this section we briefly recall the basic notions of the parametric theory based on *observation trees* [5, 6], on *proved transition systems* [1] and on *proved trees* [8]. We recall the basic definitions of those theories by considering systems specified in the well-known *Calculus of Communicating Systems* (CCS) [14].

Definition 2.1 (*CCS*)

Let Δ be a set of *names* (ranged over by $\alpha, \beta, \ldots$). Let $\bar{\ }$ be an involution on Δ, and call *complementary names* the elements of the set Δ^-. Then $\Lambda = \Delta \cup \Delta^-$ is the set of *labels* (ranged over by λ) and $A = \Lambda \cup \{\tau\}$ is the set of *actions* (ranged over by μ). The set T of closed CCS *terms* is expressed by the following BNF-grammar:

$$t ::= nil \mid x \mid \mu.t \mid (t \mid t) \mid (t + t) \mid t\backslash\alpha \mid t[\phi] \mid rec\ x.t$$

with the restriction that the term t in rec x.t is well-guarded, and where ϕ is a relabelling function preserving τ and $\bar{\ }$. ◊

In order to have a very concrete model for the description of distributed concurrent systems, the operational semantics of CCS is given in the SOS style [17] through the *proved transition system* (PTS) [1]. The transitions of PTS are labelled by encodings of their proofs. More precisely, we consider a variant of the Boudol' and Castellani's PTS, where the representation of synchronizations requires two rules for restriction as in [8]. Moreover, a rule for relabelling is introduced. First, we define the alphabet for the labelling of transitions, and then we report the proved transition system.

Definition 2.2 (*Proof Terms*)
Let $\vartheta \in \{\|_0, \|_1, +_0, +_1, \backslash_\alpha, \phi\}^*$.
The set of proof terms is $\Theta = \{\vartheta\mu \mid \mu \in A\} \cup \{\vartheta\langle\vartheta_0\lambda, \vartheta_1\lambda^-\rangle \mid \lambda \in \Lambda\}$, ranged over by θ. ◊

Definition 2.3 (*Proved Transition System, PTS [1]*)
The proved transition system PTS = $(T, \Theta, \_\theta\_\rightarrow)$, where T is the set of CCS terms, Θ is the set of proof terms and the transition relation $\_\theta\_\rightarrow \subseteq T \times \Theta \times T$ is defined by the following axiom and rules:

Act $\qquad\qquad \mu.t \_\mu\_\rightarrow t$

Sum $\qquad\qquad \dfrac{t \_\theta\_\rightarrow t'}{t + t'' \_+_0\theta\_\rightarrow t'} \qquad\qquad\qquad \dfrac{t \_\theta\_\rightarrow t'}{t'' + t \_+_1\theta\_\rightarrow t'}$

Rel $\qquad\qquad \dfrac{t \_\theta\_\rightarrow t'}{t[\phi] \_\phi\theta\_\rightarrow t'[\phi]}$

Res $\qquad\qquad \dfrac{t \_\vartheta\mu\_\rightarrow t'}{t\backslash\alpha \_\backslash_\alpha\vartheta\mu\_\rightarrow t'\backslash\alpha}, \mu \notin \{\alpha, \alpha^-\} \qquad \dfrac{t \_\vartheta\langle\theta_0, \theta_1\rangle\_\rightarrow t'}{t\backslash\alpha \_\backslash_\alpha\vartheta\langle\theta_0, \theta_1\rangle\_\rightarrow t'\backslash\alpha}$

Asyn $\qquad\qquad \dfrac{t \_\theta\_\rightarrow t'}{t \mid t'' \_\|_0\theta\_\rightarrow t' \mid t''} \qquad\qquad \dfrac{t \_\theta\_\rightarrow t'}{t'' \mid t \_\|_1\theta\_\rightarrow t'' \mid t'}$

Syn $\qquad\qquad \dfrac{t_0 \_\vartheta_0\lambda\_\rightarrow t'_0, t_1 \_\vartheta_1\lambda^-\_\rightarrow t'_1}{t_0 \mid t_1 \_\langle\vartheta_0\lambda, \vartheta_1\lambda^-\rangle\_\rightarrow t'_0 \mid t'_1}$

Rec $\qquad\qquad \dfrac{t[\text{rec } x.t/x] \_\theta\_\rightarrow t'}{\text{rec } x.t \_\theta\_\rightarrow t'}$ ◊

As it is already noted by Boudol and Castellani, it is immediate to recover the classical labelled transition system of CCS [14] from the above one. It is sufficient to delete the proof part of the labels of the transitions. We define the operational meaning of each CCS term t as the portion of the PTS that is generated by the term t, denoted by $[t]_{pts}$. Alternatively, the operational meaning of a CCS term t can be defined as the unfolding from t of the proved transition system as in [8]. The obtained tree is called *proved tree* and it is denoted by $[t]_{pt}$.

Example 2.1 (*Operational Construction of Proved Transition Systems*)
Consider the CCS term $t = \text{rec } x. \alpha.\beta.x \mid \text{rec } x. \gamma.x$. The PTS generated by the operational rules of Definition 2.3 is illustrated in Figure 2.1. ◊

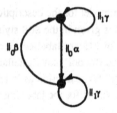

Fig. 2.1 - Proved transition system generated by the term rec x. $\alpha.\beta.x \mid$ rec x. $\gamma.x$

The definition of proved trees follows, assuming the standard syntax for trees as summations.

Definition 2.4 *(Proved Tree)*

The *proved tree* of a CCS term t is $[t]_{pt} = \Sigma_{i \in I} \theta_i \cdot [t_i]_{pt}$, where, $\forall i \in I$, $t -\theta_i \rightarrow t_i$ is a transition of the proved transition system. In the sequel, isomorphic trees will be identified. The set of proved trees generated by CCS terms will be denoted by PT. ◊

Given a tree, an arc is uniquely determined by its label and its depth. Indeed, proved trees cannot be simplified applying the axiom x+x = x, stating idempotence of summation, as tag $+_0$ is different from $+_1$. Therefore, in the formal summation $\Sigma_{i \in I} \theta_i \cdot [t_i]_{pt}$, $\forall i,j \in I$, $i \neq j$, we have $\theta_i \neq \theta_j$. Note also that the set I is always finite, i.e. the trees are finitely branching, because CCS terms are guarded.

Now, we define computations as sequences of transitions, i.e. paths in the PTS.

Definition 2.5 *(Computations)*

Let $[t]_{pts}$ be the proved transition system generated by t and let $t_0 -\theta \rightarrow t_1$ be a transition of $[t]_{pts}$. Then, t_0 is called the source of the transition and t_1 its target. The set C of computations of $[t]_{pts}$ is given by all sequences $t -\theta_0 \rightarrow t_1 -\theta_1 \rightarrow t_2 -\theta_2 \rightarrow t_3 -\theta_3 \rightarrow$ starting from t and such that the target of any transition coincides with the source of the next one. In the sequel, we use the notation $t = \xi \Rightarrow t_3$, where $\xi = \theta_0;\theta_1;\theta_2$ ranges over C. The empty computation is denoted by ϵ. Recall that the operator ";" is used for the sequential composition of transitions. Also, source and target are extended in the obvious way to computations. ◊

Alternatively to proved trees, a tree-like structure may be generated by ordering by prefix all computations outgoing from a starting state (corresponding to an agent) as the basic model of concurrent distributed systems. These structures are called observable trees [6]. Roughly speaking, an observable tree generated by an agent t is a tree, the nodes of which are the computations of t. The formal definition is the following.

Definition 2.6 *(Observable Trees)*

Let t be a CCS term and let $N = \{\xi \mid t = \xi \Rightarrow t_1$ with t_1 a reachable state of $[t]_{pts}\} \cup \{\epsilon\}$ be the set of all computations with source t and leading to any reachable state of $[t]_{pts}$. Let $\leq_{pre}$ be an ordering relation over N such that $\xi' \leq_{pre} \xi''$ iff $\xi'' = \xi\xi'$ with ξ possibly empty, $\xi, \xi', \xi'' \in N$. Then, the observable tree generated by t is $[t]_{OT} = \langle N, \leq_{pre} \rangle$.

Let n, n', n" $\in$ N. Then, a node n' is an *immediate successor* of a node n iff $n <_{pre} n'$ and there is no n" such that $n <_{pre} n" <_{pre} n'$. Also, n' is a *successor* of n iff $n \leq_{pre} n'$. Finally, n' is a *proper successor* of n iff n' is a successor of n and $n' \neq n$. ◊

Note that the relation $\leq_{pre}$ over computations corresponds to the prefix ordering over them. Observable and proved trees provide two variants of a parametric theory for concurrency: the former gives an *integral* view, while the latter provides for a differential approach.

Depending on the properties to investigate of a distributed concurrent system described through a CCS agent, many details contained in the nodes of the corresponding observable tree may be superfluous. Recall that from the proved transition system, many models for the semantics of concurrent system proposed in the literature can be retrieved by abstracting from unwanted details [8]. As an example, if we are simply interested in the temporal ordering of the events [14], it suffices to get as computations the sequences of action labels. Instead, if causality [3], locality [2], or both of them [12] are of interest also the concurrent structure of an agent, represented by parallel operators, must be recorded in the computations [4, 8, 15]. However, the computations that we use as nodes of observable trees contains many more information than the one mentioned above. Therefore, an abstraction step, called *observation*, is needed in order to get only the relevant information. Following the approaches of [5, 8, 15], the observation of an observable tree essentially consists in labelling its nodes with encodings of the relevant information that is contained in the corresponding computations. Roughly speaking, only the needed aspects of the experiment described by a node are made visible to the observer. More precisely, we have the following definition.

Definition 2.7 (*Observation Function*)
Let $\langle N, \leq_{pre} \rangle$ be an observable tree and let $\langle D, \leq \rangle$ be a partial ordering. Then, an observation function is a monotone function $O : \langle N, \leq_{pre} \rangle \rightarrow \langle D, \leq \rangle$ such that n $\leq_{pre}$ n', with n, n' $\in$ N, implies $O(n) \leq O(n')$. ◊

Now, we report the definition of observed tree, i.e., an observable tree with nodes labelled by the information that is extracted from computations.

Definition 2.8 (*Observed Trees*)
Let $\langle N, \leq_{pre} \rangle$ be an observable tree generated by a CCS term t and let O be an observation function. Then $\langle N, \leq_{pre}, O \rangle$ is the observed tree corresponding to $\langle N, \leq_{pre} \rangle$ according to O. ◊

The last step of the methodology sketched in the Introduction consists in comparing observed trees through bisimulations in order to determine which terms of the language have an equivalent behaviour according to a selected observation. Hence, we report the definition of bisimulation on observed trees.

Definition 2.9 (*Bisimulation on Observed Trees*)
Let $\langle N, \leq_{pre}, O \rangle$ and $\langle N', \leq_{pre}, O \rangle$ be two observed trees generated by the CCS terms t and t', respectively. Let R be a symmetric binary relation on $N \cup N'$. Assuming that n, $n_1, n_2 \in N$ and n', $n'_1, n'_2 \in N'$, the relation R is a *strong bisimulation* iff

$n_1 R n'_1$ implies that $O(n_1) = O(n'_1)$ and for every immediate successor n_2 of n_1 there exists an immediate successor n'_2 of n'_1 such that $n_2 R n'_2$ and for any n', $n'_1 \leq n' \leq n'_2$, it is $O(n') = O(n'_1)$ or $O(n') = O(n'_2)$.

Analogously, the relation R is a *weak bisimulation* iff

$n_1 R n'_1$ implies that $O(n_1) = O(n'_1)$ and for every immediate successor n_2 of n_1 there is a successor n'_2 of n'_1 such that $n_2 R n'_2$ and for any n', $n'_1 \leq n' \leq n'_2$, it is $O(n') = O(n'_1)$ or $O(n') = O(n'_2)$. ◊

The Example 2.2 shows all the steps of the described methodology, first reporting the operational construction of observable trees, and then illustrating how these trees are observed with the partial ordering observation of events.

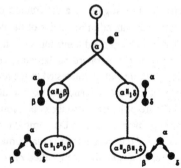

Figure 2.2 - Observable and Observed Tree generated by the CCS term t = α.(β.nil | δ.nil).

Example 2.2 (*Construction of Observable Trees and their Observation*)
Consider the CCS term t = α.(β.nil | δ.nil). According to the operational semantics, the observable tree originated by t is depicted in Figure 2.2, where the computations are the nodes of the tree. If we are interested, e.g., to causality, we label the nodes of the tree with the partial ordering of events generated by t. For instance, the computation $\alpha||_0\beta||_1\delta$ says that the action α causes both the event β and δ, but these two last actions are independent because one happens in the left part of a parallel composition and the other in the right part. Hence, the labelling of the corresponding node.   ◊

In the sequel, the reader is assumed familiar with regular expressions and with the usual notation for denoting them.

3. Extended Transition Systems

In this section we extend the theory of observable and observed trees [5] to graphs in order to cope with finite state processes. More precisely, we define node-labelled graphs called extended transition systems where any node n is a CCS term that is labelled with a regular expression which encodes all computations from the starting state to n. Therefore, since any state is a term of the language, and not a computation as in [5], it is possible to have finite parametric representations of regular processes. For the sake of readability, we first introduce an intermediate step which consists in restating the definition of bisimulation in order to consider the history of computations. This new definition is equivalent to Definition 2.9 for observed trees. Then, extended transition systems are defined and equipped with a notion of bisimulation. Finally, the bisimulation over extended transition systems is shown equivalent to the definition of the intermediate step. The following fact obviously derives from formal languages theory.

Fact 3.1 (*Computations and Regular Expressions*)
Let t be a CCS term. If $[t]_{pts}$ is finite state, then each computation ξ with source t in $[t]_{pts}$ is a regular language over the alphabet Θ which does not contain +.   ◊

The first step of the presentation is the definition of a bisimulation relation that keeps track of the history of computations. Before, we need some notation.

Notation 3.1 (*Sequences of moves*)
Let $[t]_{pts}$ be a proved transition system. Then, we use $t_0 \Rightarrow t_k$ if there is a computation $t_0 -\theta_0 \to t_1 -\theta_1 \to \dots t_{k-1} -\theta_{k-1} \to t_k$ in $[t]_{pts}$ with $\theta_i = \tau$ or $\theta_i = \vartheta \langle \vartheta_0 \lambda, \vartheta_1 \lambda \rangle$, $0 \le i \le k-1$. Also, $t_0 =\theta=> t_k$ denotes $t_0 \Rightarrow t_i -\theta_i \to t_{i+1} \Rightarrow t_k$, with $\theta_i = \vartheta \mu$. ◊

The following definition is an intermediate step towards the introduction of extended transition systems. It defines parametric bisimulation on proved transition systems by associating to each analyzed node all possible computations leading to it. This definition is clearly not effective even when dealing with finite state systems since to a node can be associated infinitely many computations.

Definition 3.1 (*Parametric Bisimulation on PTS*)
Let $[t]_{pts}$ and $[t']_{pts}$ be two proved transition systems, and let O be an observation function. Given two nodes t_1 and t'_1 of $[t]_{pts}$ and $[t']_{pts}$, respectively, let $t =\xi=> t_1$ and $t' =\xi'=> t'_1$. Then, a symmetric binary relation R on the union of the pairs ‹node, computation› of the two transition systems is a *strong parametric bisimulation* iff whenever $(t_1, t'_1, \xi, \xi') \in R$

- $t_1 -\theta \to t_2$ implies that there are t'_2 and θ' such that $t'_1 -\theta' \to t'_2$, $O(\xi;\theta) = O(\xi';\theta')$ and $(t_2, t'_2, \xi;\theta, \xi';\theta') \in R$;
- $t'_1 -\theta' \to t'_2$ implies that there are t_2 and θ such that $t_1 -\theta \to t_2$, $O(\xi;\theta) = O(\xi';\theta')$ and $(t_2, t'_2, \xi;\theta, \xi';\theta') \in R$.

Similarly, the relation R is a *weak parametric bisimulation* iff whenever $(t_1, t'_1, \xi, \xi') \in R$

- $t_1 -\theta \to t_2$ implies that there are t'_2 and θ' such that $t'_1 =\theta'=> t'_2$, $O(\xi;\theta) = O(\xi';\theta')$ and $(t_2, t'_2, \xi;\theta, \xi';\theta') \in R$;
- $t'_1 -\theta' \to t'_2$ implies that there are t_2 and θ such that $t_1 =\theta=> t_2$, $O(\xi;\theta) = O(\xi';\theta')$ and $(t_2, t'_2, \xi;\theta, \xi';\theta') \in R$.

Finally, $[t]_{pts}$ and $[t']_{pts}$ are strong or weak bisimilar iff $(t_1, t'_1, \varepsilon, \varepsilon) \in R$. We take the congruences induced by the largest above relations, and denote them by $\sim_p$ and $\approx_p$, respectively. ◊

In order to show the soundness of the above definition we have the following theorem which relates bisimulation defined on observation trees (OT), proved trees (PT) and proved transition systems (PTS).

Theorem 3.1 (*Soundness of Parametric Bisimulation on PTS*)
Given two CCS terms t and t', then $[t]_{OT} \approx [t']_{OT}$ iff $[t]_{pt} \approx_p [t']_{pt}$ iff $[t]_{pts} \approx_p [t']_{pts}$.
Proof:
$[t]_{pt} \approx_p [t']_{pt}$ iff $[t]_{pts} \approx_p [t']_{pts}$ follows noticing that the definition of parametric bisimulation on proved trees (see [8]) compares proved transitions, while the one on proved transition systems compares proved computations. The implications $[t]_{OT} \approx [t']_{OT}$ iff $[t]_{pt} \approx_p [t']_{pt}$ follows from the isomorphism between proved trees and observation trees [8]. ◊

We now introduce a new kind of transition systems that are labelled on nodes by ordered summations of regular expressions instead of being labelled on arcs by proofs of transitions. However, the fact of labelling transitions or nodes does not change very much the equivalences or the theory. Note that it is possible to identify any node t' of a transition system $[t]_{pts}$ with the set C $(t') = \{\xi_i \mid t =\xi_i=> t'$ and ξ_i is a computation in $[t]_{pts}\}$ of all computations that have as target the considered node. In order to define bisimulations on ETS we represent the set $C(t')$ as an ordered summation of regular expressions $\mathcal{R} = \Sigma_i r_i$, where each r_i does not contain +. Indeed, in the comparison step of the bisimulation it is necessary to correctly augment the two computations that are currently compared. Hence, we implicitly assume an ordering (from left to right) on the arcs outgoing from nodes of ETSs. By convention, any node is uniquely identified by a string of integers. For instance, the string 1.2.1 denotes the first node of the second son of the root. This avoids possible shuffles of computations that could result in the equivalence of agents which are not. We are now able to define the extended transition systems.

Definition 3.2 (*Extended Transition System*)
Let t be a CCS term and $[t]_{pts}$ its corresponding PTS. The extended transition system (ETS) originated by t and denoted by $[t]_{ets}$ is obtained by labelling any node t' of $[t]_{pts}$ with $\mathcal{R} = \Sigma_i r_i$, i.e., the ordered summation of regular expressions over the alphabet of proof terms representing the computations from t to t'. The regular expressions in $\mathcal{R}$ are denoted as r[k], where k = $h_i.j$, h_i is the ordered position of the ith immediate predecessor t_i of t' with respect to the initial node and j is the position of t' among all the nodes generated from t_i. ◊

Note that given a finite state proved transition system, the corresponding extended transition system can be constructed by using an algorithm which generates a regular expression from an automata. We use as automata the proved transition system originated by a CCS term and as language the proofs of transitions. The regular expression that we associate to a node t' is the one obtained by choosing it as acceptance state of the automata. This approach is very similar to ideas of *path expressions* [18], where regular expressions are used to describe all paths between two nodes of a directed graph. An algorithm to construct path expressions is presented in [19].

The next step introduces the notion of bisimulation over the ETS. Note that differently from Definition 3.1, the following definition provides an effective checking algorithm when dealing with finite state systems. In fact, in this case the number of nodes to be examined is finite as well as the size of their labels.

Definition 3.3 (*Parametric Bisimulation on Extended Transition Systems*)
Let $[t]_{ets}$ and $[t']_{ets}$ be two ETS, and let O be an observation function. Given two nodes t_1 and t'_1 of $[t]_{ets}$ and $[t']_{ets}$, let $\Sigma_i r_i$ and $\Sigma_j r'_j$ be their corresponding labels. Then, a relation R_e on the nodes of the transition systems is a *strong parametric bisimulation* iff whenever $(t_1, t'_1, r_1[h], r'_1[k]) \in R_e$

- $t_1 -\theta \rightarrow t_2$ implies that there exist t'_2 labelled by $\mathcal{R}_2$ such that $t'_1 -\theta' \rightarrow t'_2$, $O(r_2[s]) = O(r'_2[q])$ and $(t_2, t'_2, r_2[s], r'_2[q]) \in R_e$, where $r_2[s]$ and $r'_2[q]$ are such that $s = h.x$ and $q = k.y$, with x, y the positions of t_2 and t'_2 among all the nodes generated from their immediate predecessors, respectively;

- $t'_1 -\theta' \rightarrow t'_2$ implies that there exist t_2 labelled by $\mathcal{R}_2$ such that $t_1 -\theta \rightarrow t_2$, $O(r_2[s]) = O(r'_2[q])$ and $(t_2, t'_2, r_2[s], r'_2[q]) \in R_e$, where $r_2[s]$ and $r'_2[q]$ are such that $s = h.x$ and $q = k.y$, with x, y the positions of t_2 and t'_2 among all the nodes generated from their immediate predecessors, respectively;

Analogously, the relation R_e on the nodes of the transition systems is a *weak parametric bisimulation* iff whenever $(t_1, t'_1, r[h], r'[k]) \in R_e$

- $t_1 -\theta \rightarrow t_2$ implies that there exist t'_2 labelled by $\mathcal{R}'_2$ such that $t'_1 = \theta' => t'_2$, $O(r_2[s]) = O(r'_2[q])$ and $(t_2, t'_2, r_2[s], r'_2[q]) \in R_e$, where $r_2[s]$ and $r'_2[q]$ are such that $s = h.x$ and $q =$

k.y, with x, y the positions of t_2 and t'_2 among all the nodes generated from their immediate predecessors, respectively;

- $t'_1-\theta'\rightarrow t'_2$ implies that there exist t_2 labelled by $\mathcal{R}_2$ such that $t_1=\theta\Rightarrow t_2$, $O(r_2[s]) = O(r'_2[q])$ and $(t_2, t'_2, r_2[s], r'_2[q]) \in R_e$, where $r_2[s]$ and $r'_2[q]$ are are such that $s = h.x$ and $q = k.y$, with x, y the positions of t_2 and t'_2 among all the nodes generated from their immediate predecessors, respectively.

Finally, $[t]_{ets}$ and $[t']_{ets}$ are bisimilar iff for all r[i] in the label of t there exists r'[k] in the label of t' such that $(t, t', r[i], r'[k]) \in R_e$, and *viceversa*. As usual, we take the congruences induced by the largest above relations, and denote them again by $\sim_p$ and $\approx_p$. ◊

Note that the above definition of parametric bisimulation deals with the observation of a regular expression. This topic is the argument of the next section. The soundness of Definition 3.3 is guaranteed by the following theorem.

Theorem 3.2 (*Soundness of Parametric Bisimulation on ETS*)
Given two CCS terms t and t', $[t]_{ets} \approx_p [t']_{ets}$ iff $[t]_{pts} \approx_p [t']_{pts}$.
Outline of the proof:
Given a node t_i of $[t]_{ets}$, the regular expression $\mathcal{R}_i$ associated to t_i is a finite representation of all computations from t to t_i. Hence, a step of comparison in ETS corresponds to many (possibly infinite) steps of comparison in PTS. Moreover, the assumption that the labels of the nodes in the ETSs are ordered summations assures that different computations are not shuffled during the bisimulation process. Hence, a comparison step in ETS corresponds to all and only the steps in PTS. The proof carries on as follow: if $[t]_{ets} \approx_p [t']_{ets}$ there exists a bisimulation R such that $[t]_{ets}$ R $[t']_{ets}$. Starting from R a bisimulation R' can then be defined such that $[t]_{pts}$ R' $[t']_{pts}$. The same applies by first assuming $[t]_{pts} \approx_p [t']_{pts}$. ◊

4. Observations and Regular Languages

In this section we discuss the problem of dealing with the equivalence of labels in ETSs. Indeed, since the labels to be compared in the ETS are regular expressions that in general describe an infinite set of computations, we want to determine if the (possibly infinite) set of observations of two labels are the same or not. More precisely, if O is the obvious extension of an observation function to sets, we want to know if $O(\mathcal{R}) = O(\mathcal{R}')$, where $\mathcal{R}$ and $\mathcal{R}'$ are the regular expressions labelling two nodes of an ETS. As a first result, we report the following fact.

Fact 4.1 (*Languages and Observations*)
Let $\mathcal{R}$ and $\mathcal{R}'$ be two regular expressions, and let $L(\mathcal{R})$ and $L(\mathcal{R}')$ be the languages denoted by $\mathcal{R}$ and $\mathcal{R}'$, respectively. Then, $L(\mathcal{R}) = L(\mathcal{R}')$ implies $O(\mathcal{R}) = O(\mathcal{R}')$. ◊

Clearly, the above fact gives a sufficient condition for checking equivalences by using well-known techniques from formal languages theory. There are cases when the languages of two regular expressions are not equal, but their observations in a particular model coincide. In order to deal with these cases we distinguish observations in *incremental* and *non-incremental*, according to [6].

Definition 4.1 (*Incremental Observations*)
Let $\xi_1, \xi'_1, \xi_2, \xi'_2$ be computations and let O be an observation function. Then, O is called in-

cremental if $O(\xi_1) = O(\xi'_1)$ and $O(\xi_2) = O(\xi'_2)$ imply $O(\xi_1 \cdot \xi'_1) = O(\xi_2 \cdot \xi'_2)$, where $\cdot$ denote concatenation of computations. ◊

For any incremental observation O it is very easy to translate the structure of regular expression of computations into observations. More precisely, we have the following lemma.

Lemma 4.1 (*Languages and Incremental Observations*)
Let O be an incremental observation function and let $O(\mathcal{R}) = \mathcal{R}_1$ and $O(\mathcal{R}) = \mathcal{R}_1$. Then, $O(\mathcal{R}) = O(\mathcal{R})$ if and only if $L(\mathcal{R}_1) = L(\mathcal{R}_1)$.
Proof:
Since O preserves the constructors of regular expressions +, ., and * (see Definition 4.1), it is possible to concatenate observations and to compute finite iterations of them from a basic value. Hence, the observation of a regular expression is itself a regular expression on a different alphabet. Finally, two regular expressions are equivalent if their languages are equal. ◊

Example 4.1 (*Observing Extended Transition Systems*)
Consider the CCS term $t = rec\ x.\ \alpha.\beta.x \mid rec\ x.\ \gamma.x$, whose PTS is illustrated in Figure 2.1. The corresponding ETS is reported in Figure 4.1(a). Also, consider the CCS term $t' = rec\ x.\ (\gamma.x + \alpha.(rec\ y.\ (\gamma.y + \beta.x)))$. The ETS of t' is shown in Figure 4.1(b). Clearly, $[t]$ and $[t']$ are not bisimilar in any observation that distinguishes the parallel composition from interleaving and nondeterminism. Hence, let O be the classical interleaving observation function, that is incremental. We have $O\ (((\|_1\gamma)^*.(\|_0\alpha.(\|_1\gamma)^*.\|_0\beta)^*)^*) = O\ (((+_0\gamma)^*.(+_1\alpha.(+_0\gamma)^*.+_1\beta)^*)^*) = (\gamma^*.(\alpha.\gamma^*.\beta)^*)^*$ and also $O\ ((\|_1\gamma)^*.\|_0\alpha.(\|_1\gamma)^*.(\|_0\beta.(\|_1\gamma)^*.\|_0\alpha.(\|_1\gamma)^*)^*) = \gamma^*.\alpha.\gamma^*.(\beta.\gamma^*.\alpha.\gamma^*)^* = O\ ((+_0\gamma)^*.+_1\alpha.(+_0\gamma)^*.(+_1\beta.(+_0\gamma)^*.+_1\alpha.(+_0\gamma)^*)^*)$. Thus, by application of Lemma 4.1 the bisimulation that proves the equivalence of t and t' is the following
$\{\ (p,\ q,\ ((\|_1\gamma)^*.(\|_0\alpha.(\|_1\gamma)^*.\|_0\beta)^*)^*,\ ((+_0\gamma)^*.(+_1\alpha.(+_0\gamma)^*.+_1\beta)^*)^*),$
$(p',\ q',\ ((\|_1\gamma)^*.\|_0\alpha.(\|_1\gamma)^*.(\|_0\beta.(\|_1\gamma)^*.\|_0\alpha.(\|_1\gamma)^*)^*,$
$((+_0\gamma)^*.+_1\alpha.(+_0\gamma)^*.(+_1\beta.(+_0\gamma)^*.+_1\alpha.(+_0\gamma)^*)^*)\ \}.$
Note that in this example instead of using ordered summations of regular expressions to label the nodes of the ETS, we use a single expression because the two transition systems to be checked have the same structure, hence it is correct to use the well-known law for regular expressions $(e_1 + e_2)^* = (e_1^*e_2^*)^*$ ◊

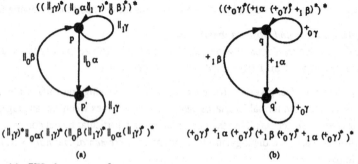

Figure 4.1 - ETS of $t = rec\ x.\ \alpha.\beta.x \mid rec\ x.\ \gamma.x$ (a) and of $t' = rec\ x.\ (\gamma.x + \alpha.(rec\ y.\ (\gamma.y + \beta.x)))$ (b).

For non-incremental observations, the situation is more complex. Indeed, these observations do not preserve the structure of computations and therefore Lemma 4.1 does not apply. In order to cope with this problem, we decompose any non-incremental observation into an incremental one and an abstraction function f. Thus, we use Lemma 4.1 for the incremental component of the observation and then we apply f during the comparison steps. The existence of the decomposition is ensured by the following fact.

Fact 4.2 (*Decomposition of non-incremental Observations*)
Let O be a non-incremental observation function. There exists an incremental observation function O' and an abstraction function f such that $O = f \cdot O'$, where $\cdot$ denotes function composition. ◊

In the following example we show how it is possible to obtain a non-incremental observation like partial orders from a more concrete and incremental one like spatial histories [9] (also called concurrent histories in [7]).

Example 4.2 (*Decomposition of non-incremental observations*)
Consider the CCS term $t = (\alpha.nil \mid \gamma.(\gamma.nil + \beta.nil))[\phi] + \delta.nil$ where ϕ is such that $\phi(\gamma) = \alpha$. A possible computation of t is $\xi = +_0\phi\|_0\alpha \; \phi\|_1\gamma \; \phi\|_1+_1\beta$. If ξ is observed as a spatial history, we get the representation of Figure 4.2(a). The right partial order observation of ξ is represented in Figure 4.2(b). The two structures are almost the same, it is easy to define an abstraction function f that simply discards the initial and final nodes of the spatial history to get the corresponding partial order. ◊

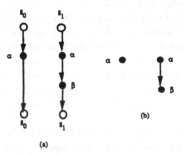

Figure 4.2 - Spatial History and Partial Order of the computation $\xi = +_0\phi\|_0\alpha \; \phi\|_1\gamma \; \phi\|_1+_1\beta$.

Finally, note that if we consider a term with finite behaviour, the language associated to each node of the extended transition system is described by a summation of regular expressions that represents finite languages. In other words, any node is labelled by the tree of computations (represented as formal summation) leading to it and therefore it can be observed with incremental and also non incremental observations as done in [8, 15]. As an example consider the proved transition system originated by the CCS term $t = \alpha.\beta.\delta.nil + \gamma.\delta.nil$ and depicted in Figure 4.3. The regular expression attached to the final state of $[t]_{pts}$ is $\mathcal{R} = +_0\alpha\beta\delta + +_1\gamma\delta$.

Figure 4.3 - Proved Transition System originated by the term $\alpha.\beta.\delta.nil + \gamma.\delta.nil$

5. Conclusions

In this work we have defined a parametric model for describing the semantics of finite states systems. It relies on the parametric theories of observation trees [5, 6] and proved trees [8]. A notion of parametric bisimulation is introduced over extended transition systems and it is shown that this equivalence coincide with the ones already presented in literature. The results presented in this paper are fundamental for a practical use of a parametric theory in automatic verification of systems.

Following the definitions given above, it is immediate to derive an algorithm for parametric bisimulation when incremental observations are considered. The extension to other observations is under development following the approach of decomposing any non-incremental observation into an incremental one and an abstraction function. The basic idea is use standard techniques from fix-point theory to prove properties on regular languages that may permit to make this decomposition effective.

References

[1] Boudol, G., Castellani, I., *A non-interleaving semantics for CCS based on proved transitions*, Fundamenta Informaticae, XI (4), 1988, 433 - 452.

[2] Boudol, G., Castellani, I., Hennessy, M., Kiehn, A., *A Theory of Processes with Localities*, in Proc. CONCUR'92, LNCS , Springer-Verlag, 1992.

[3] Darondeau, Ph., Degano, P., *Causal Trees*, in Proc. ICALP '89, LNCS 372, 1989, 234 - 248.

[4] Degano, P., De Nicola, R., Montanari, U., *On the Operational Semantics of Distributed Concurrent Systems*, in Proc. IFIP'88 (David, Boute, and Shriver Eds), North-Holland, 1990, 3 - 32.

[5] Degano, P., De Nicola, R., Montanari, U., *Universal Axioms for Bisimulations*, Tech. Rep. TR 9/92, Dipartimento di Informatica, Università di Pisa, to appear in Theoretical Computer Science.

[6] Degano, P., De Nicola, R., Montanari, U., *Observation Trees*, in Proc. NAPAW'92.

[7] Degano, P., Montanari, U., *Concurrent Histories: A Basis for Observing Distributed Systems*, J.C.S.S., 34, 1987, 422 - 461.

[8] Degano, P., Priami, C., *Proved Trees*, in Proc. ICALP'92, LNCS 623, Springer, 1992, 629 - 640.

[9] Ferrari, G., Gorrieri, R., Montanari, U., *An Extended Expansion Theorem*, in Proc. TAPSOFT'91, LNCS 494, Springer-Verlag, 1991, 29 - 48.

[10] Inverardi, P., Priami, C., *Evaluation of Tools for the Analysis of Communicating Systems*, EATCS Bullettin, n. 45, 1991.

[11] Inverardi, P., Priami, C., Yankelevich, D. *Verifying concurrent systems in SML*, in Proc. of ACM SIGPLAN Workshop on ML and its Applications, San Francisco, June 1992.

[12] Kiehn, A., *Local and Global Causes*, Report Technische Universität Munchen 342/23/91 A, 1991.

[13] Korver, H., *The Current States of Bisimulation Tools*, Tech. Rep. P9101, CWI, 1991.

[14] Milner, R., *Communication and Concurrency*. Prentice Hall International, London 1989.

[15] Montanari, U., Yankelevich, D., *A Parametric Approach to Localities*, in Proc. ICALP'92, LNCS 623, Springer-Verlag, 1992, 617 - 628.

[16] Park, D., *Concurrency and Automata on Infinite Sequences*, in Proc. GI, LNCS 104, Springer-Verlag, 1981, 167 - 183.

[17] Plotkin, G., *A Structural Approach to Operational Semantics*. Tech.Rep. DAIMI FN-19, Aarhus Univ, 1981.

[18] Tarjan, R., *A Unified Approach to Path Problems*, J. ACM 28, 3, 1981, 577 - 593.

[19] Tarjan, R., *Fast Algorithms for Solving Path Problems*, J. ACM 28, 3, 1981, 594 - 614.

[20] Yankelevich, D., *Parametric Views of Process Description Languages*, PhD Thesis Università di Pisa, TD 23/93, 1993.

Temporal Logic and Categories of Petri Nets

Carolyn Brown* and Doug Gurr[†]

Chalmers University of Technology, Göteborg, Sweden

Abstract. We present a novel method for proving temporal properties of the behaviour a Petri net. Unlike existing methods, which involve an exhaustive examination of the transition system representing all behaviours of the net, our approach uses morphisms dependent only on the static structure of the net. These morphisms correspond to refinements. We restrict the analysis of dynamic behaviours to particularly simple nets (test nets), and establish temporal properties of a complex net by considering morphisms between it and various test nets. This approach is computationally efficient, and the construction of test nets is facilitated by the graphical representation of nets. The use of category theory permits a natural modular approach to proving properties of nets.

Our main result is the syntactic characterisation of two expressive classes of formulae: those whose satisfaction is preserved by morphisms and those whose satisfaction is reflected.

1 Introduction

Proving properties of the operational behaviour of Petri nets is computationally expensive, as most existing techniques [1] involve an exhaustive examination of the labelled transition system representing all possible markings and behaviours of the net. In this paper we describe a novel technique for proving properties of the behaviour of a Petri net by considering only the static structure of the net. Our approach exploits the simplicity of the graphical presentation of a net: it is sufficiently powerful to prove a wide range of properties but has complexity which is linear in the size of the net.

Our technique builds on our existing results concerning categories of Petri nets. In [2, 3, 4, 5] we studied a category **Net** whose objects are unmarked Petri nets. We proved in [5] that whenever there is a morphism from N to N' in **Net** then subject to a natural condition on the initial markings of the nets, N' can simulate any evolution of N. This result gives rise to a methodology for proving properties of the dynamic behaviour of a net by exhibiting morphisms in **Net**: such morphisms depend only on the static structure of the nets. The method involves constructing a number of simple "test" nets whose behavioural properties can either be inferred by inspection or proved using existing model-checking techniques. These test nets should be small enough that their properties can be established quickly and easily. We then establish properties of a more complex net by exhibiting morphisms between it and the test nets, and using the fact that the image net must be able to simulate the behaviour of the source net.

Some examples of this technique were given in [3], including proofs of liveness properties and of mutual exclusion properties. We now prove that our technique can establish properties which cover the full spectrum of Manna and Pnueli's hierarchy of temporal properties [9]. The main advantage of a technique based on the static structure of the net is that the complexity of model-checking is linear in the size of the net. An additional advantage is that the graphical presentation of a simple

---

* E-mail: cbrown@cs.chalmers.se   [†]Currently employed by the UK Department of Transport

test net is a great aid to envisaging properties of its behaviour. The advantage of using category theory is that it gives rise to a compositional, modular proof system: this permits a structured approach to proving properties of large nets.

In [16], Winskel considered a category of nets which is essentially a subcategory of MNet$^+$. He suggested that, informally, morphisms in his category of nets appeared to preserve liveness properties and to reflect safety properties. This judgement was based on the usual description of a safety property as expressing the fact that "something bad never happens" and a liveness property expressing the fact that "something desirable is guaranteed to happen." Our results show that the situation is more complex than this: we give a syntactic characterisations of formulae which are preserved, reflected or respected in a different sense by morphisms. Human insight is needed both in choosing morphisms and in designing suitable, efficient test nets, while checking that we have a morphism and that a test net satisfies a formula can be readily and efficiently automated.

In Section 2 we recall the elementary definitions of Petri net theory and give examples of the proof technique. In Section 4 we define a temporal logic $\mathcal{T}$ for describing net behaviours and define a notion of satisfaction of a $\mathcal{T}$ formula by a marked net. In Section 3 we generalise the relevant results from [4, 5] and in Section 5 we give a syntactic characterisation of properties which are preserved or reflected by morphisms in our category. This fundamental result shows when we can deduce properties of a complex net from the existence of morphisms between it and test nets satisfying those properties. The check that a pair of functions $\langle f, F \rangle$ is a morphism from N to N' is linear in the size of the nets N and N', and so our technique is relatively efficient.

2 Definitions concerning Petri Nets

We recall some elementary definitions of Petri net theory: details may be found in [14].

DEFINITION 1. *A Petri net, denoted N, is a 4-tuple $\langle E, B, pre, post \rangle$ where E and B are sets, and pre and post are functions from $E \times B$ to $\mathbb{N}$.*

We shall call elements of E *events* and elements of B *conditions*. We shall call *pre* and *post* the pre- and post-condition relations of N respectively. With each of the multirelations *pre* and *post* we associate a function of the same name from E to $B^{\oplus}$ (the free abelian monoid on B, with unit the empty multiset $\emptyset$) defined by

$$pre(e) = \sum_{b \in B} pre(e, b)b \quad \text{and} \quad post(e) = \sum_{b \in B} post(e, b)b.$$

We call $pre(e)$ the pre-condition set and $post(e)$ the post-condition set of e. A *loop* arises if the pre- and post-condition sets of an event intersect non-trivially. A *1-loop* is a loop such that for every $b \in pre(e) \cap post(e)$ we have $pre(e, b) = post(e, b) = 1$. All loops which are not 1-loops are *multi-loops*. We shall only consider the class of nets without multi-loops, which we call **Petri**.

The state of a net is described by a finite multiset over B (that is, a multiset which is zero on all but finitely many $b \in B$), called a *marking*, which indicates which conditions hold, and in what multiplicities. A *marked net* is a pair $\langle M, N \rangle$, where N is a net and M is a marking of N.

The occurrence of an event, called a firing, transforms the state of the net by consuming its pre-condition set and producing its post-condition set. We say $\langle M, N \rangle$ enables $\Sigma n_i e_i$ if the marking M contains the multiset $\Sigma n_i pre(e_i)$. The multiset $\Sigma n_i e_i$ of events, called a *step*, can then fire concurrently. We denote this firing $M \xrightarrow{\Sigma n_i e_i} M - \Sigma n_i pre(e_i) + \Sigma n_i post(e_i)$. A *step sequence* σ is a sequence of steps $M \xrightarrow{s_0} M_1 \xrightarrow{s_1} \ldots$. We consider all step sequences to be infinite, extending finite computations by considering a trivial identity step to be repeated indefinitely.

3 Categories of Nets: extending existing results

In the past [2, 3, 4, 5] we have considered primarily unmarked nets, structural properties of nets and modular specification using categorical constructions on nets. We derived results about a net's behaviour for all initial markings or for those markings meeting a given condition. It is clear that the behavioural properties of a net depend crucially on its initial marking: for example, in the net

$$N = \quad \begin{array}{c} \end{array} \quad {}^2$$

with marking $2b_0$, some event is always enabled and throughout every computation, e_0 is always eventually enabled. However, the net $\langle b_0, N \rangle$ possesses neither of these properties. In this paper we therefore work with explicit markings, modifying our earlier definitions and results accordingly. (In the notation of Section 4, if $\theta(\alpha_i) = e_i$ for $i = 0, 1$ then $\langle 2b_0, N \rangle \models_\theta \square \exists x. E(x)$ and $\langle 2b_0, N \rangle \models_\theta \square \Diamond E(\alpha_0)$ but $\langle b_0, N \rangle \models_\theta \neg(\square \exists x. E(x) \vee \square \Diamond E(\alpha_0))$.)

It is our intention to prove properties of a net N by exhibiting morphisms between N and various test nets T_i. This approach is most efficient if our test nets are small. We can use smaller test nets if, rather than insisting that a morphism from N to N' map events of N to events of N' (as in our earlier work), we allow an event of N to be mapped to a finite step sequence of N' (as will be done in proving absence of starvation in Section 3.2). With this aim, we now generalize the results of [3, 5]: such a generalization is somewhat in the spirit of [10].

3.1 A Category of Nets for proving Temporal Properties

Intuitively, a computation is either an event (possibly idle) or the parallel or sequential composition of two computations. The parallel composition of computations c and d, written $c + d$, occurs when they can fire simultaneously, consuming $pre(c) + pre(d)$ and producing $post(c) + post(d)$. The sequential composition of c and d, written $c ; d$, occurs when c can fire to reach a marking in which d is enabled. We extend the pre and post-condition relations of a net from events to step sequences in the evident way, putting

$$pre(c_0 ; c_1) = pre(c_0) + pre(c_1) - post(c_0), \qquad post(c_0 ; c_1) = post(c_1) + post(c_0) - pre(c_1),$$
$$pre(c_0 + c_1) = pre(c_0) + pre(c_1) \qquad \text{and} \qquad post(c_0 + c_1) = post(c_0) + post(c_1).$$

Suppose we have a function $F: B' \rightarrow B$ which maps the conditions in a refining net N' to the conditions in the original net N which they implement. Let M be a marking of N and M' a marking of N'. Whenever M' contains enough resources to implement all the resources marked in M, we expect the simulating net $\langle M', N' \rangle$ to be able to simulate any computation of $\langle M, N \rangle$. This relationship between markings is formalized in the following definition.

DEFINITION 2. *Let F be a function from a set B' to a set B. The relation $F^+ \subseteq B^\oplus \times B'^\oplus$ is given by*

$$\langle M, M' \rangle \in F^+ \quad \text{if and only if} \quad MF \leq M',$$

that is, if and only if for each $b' \in B'$ we have $M(Fb') \leq M'(b')$.

We now define a category of marked nets in which morphisms from $\langle M, N \rangle$ to $\langle M', N' \rangle$ map events of a N to step sequences (or computations) of N'.

DEFINITION 3. *The category* **MNet**$^+$ *is defined by the following data:*

- *objects are marked nets* $\langle M, N \rangle$ *where* N *is an element of* **Petri,**
- *a morphism from* $\langle M, E, B, pre, post \rangle$ *to* $\langle M', E', B', pre', post' \rangle$ *is a pair of functions* $\langle f, F \rangle$ *with* $f \colon E \to E'^+$ *and* $F \colon B' \to B$ *such that* $\langle M, M' \rangle \in F^+$ *and in* **Set** *we have*

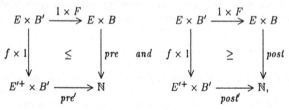

that is, for each $e \in E$ *and each* $b' \in B'$

$$pre\langle e, Fb' \rangle \geq pre'\langle fe, b' \rangle \quad and \quad post\langle e, Fb' \rangle \leq post'\langle fe, b' \rangle,$$

- *and composition is function composition in each component.*

Morphisms in **MNet**$^+$ are defined on the purely static structure of nets, but capture precisely a notion of simulation between the dynamic behaviours of nets, as the following results show.

Proposition 4. *Let* $\langle f, F \rangle$ *be a morphism from* $\langle M_0, N \rangle$ *to* $\langle M'_0, N' \rangle$ *in* **MNet**$^+$. *Then for all* $e \in E$, *if* $M_0 \xrightarrow{e} M_1$ *in* N *then* $M'_0 \xrightarrow{fe} M'_1$ *in* N' *and* $\langle M_1, M'_1 \rangle \in F^+$.

Corollary 5. *Let* $\langle f, F \rangle$ *be a morphism from* $\langle M_0, N \rangle$ *to* $\langle M'_0, N' \rangle$ *in* **MNet**$^+$. *For* $i \in \{0, \ldots, n\}$ *let* $s_i = \sum_1^{k_i} n_j c_j$ *be a multiset of events of* N. *Extend* f *to multisets of events by putting* $f(t+s) = f(t) + f(s)$. *If* $\langle M_0, N \rangle$ *enables the step sequence* $M_0 \xrightarrow{s_0} M_1 \xrightarrow{s_1} \cdots M_n$ *then* $\langle M'_0, N' \rangle$ *enables the step sequence* $M'_0 \xrightarrow{fs_0} M'_1 \xrightarrow{fs_1} \cdots M'_n$.

Proposition 4 shows that if a pair of markings $\langle M, M' \rangle$ is in F^+, then the net $\langle M', N' \rangle$ can simulate any one–step evolution of $\langle M, N \rangle$, in the sense that whenever $\langle M, N \rangle$ enables an event e, $\langle M', N' \rangle$ enables the step sequence fe. Evidently for any marking M of N we can construct a marking M' of N' such that $\langle M, M' \rangle \in F^+$, and thus Corollary 5 shows that N' can simulate any evolution of N. We say that N' *simulates* N.

DEFINITION 6. *Let* $\langle M, N \rangle$ *and* $\langle M', N' \rangle$ *be nets and let* $f \colon E \to E'^+$ *and* $F \colon B' \to B$ *be functions. Then* $\langle M', N' \rangle$ *simulates* $\langle M, N \rangle$ *(and* $\langle f, F \rangle$ *is a simulation), if and only if* $\langle M, M' \rangle \in F^+$ *and for all pairs of markings* $\langle M_0, M'_0 \rangle \in F^+$,

$$if \ M_0 \xrightarrow{e} M_1 \ then \ M'_0 \xrightarrow{fe} M'_1 \ and \ \langle M_1, M'_1 \rangle \in F^+$$

By Corollary 5, every morphism in **MNet**$^+$ is a simulation. The converse also holds:

Proposition 7. *Let* N *and* N' *be elements of* **Petri** *and let* $\langle f, F \rangle$ *be a simulation from* $\langle M, N \rangle$ *to* $\langle M', N' \rangle$ *which preserves 1-loops, that is,*

$$if \ pre(e, Fb') = post(e, Fb') = 1 \ then \ pre'(fe, b') = post'(fe, b') = 1.$$

Then $\langle f, F \rangle \colon \langle M, N \rangle \longrightarrow \langle M', N' \rangle$ *in* **MNet**$^+$.

The results of this section are important because they show that, not only do the morphisms of **MNet**$^+$ have a meaningful computational interpretation, but further, all simulations between nets without multi-loops are morphisms in **MNet**$^+$.

3.2 An Example: proving a safety and a liveness property

We illustrate a proof of a safety property and a liveness property, using an example taken from [12]. Olderog presents the nets N_1 and N_2 below, and wishes to examine the relationship between them. As he says, "Intuitively, N_2 is obtained from N_1 by *abstracting* from the actions NCr_i, Req_i and Out_i, $i = 1, 2$, in N_1, i.e. by transforming them into internal actions τ and then forgetting about the τ's". We shall give a morphism which effects such an abstraction. For simplicity, in the net N_1 we have only named those conditions which will be in the image of our morphisms or in the initial marking of N_1.

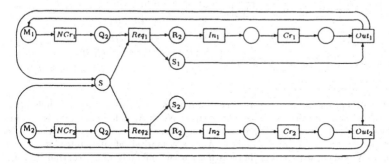

The net N_1: mutual exclusion

Given marking C, the net N_2 below forces a choice between the evolutions Beg_1 ; End_1 and Beg_2 ; End_2:

The net N_2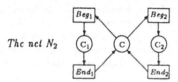

It is readily proved that every behaviour of the net $\langle C, N_2 \rangle$ is a sequence of form Beg_a ; End_a ; Beg_b ; End_b ; Beg_c ; End_c ; ... where a, b and c range over $\{1, 2\}$. We shall add to the net N_2 a trivial event $*$, which has empty pre- and post-condition set. The resultant net $\langle C, N_2 + \bot \rangle$ is the coproduct in $\mathbf{MNet}^+$ of N_2 with the marked net $\bot = \langle \emptyset, \{*\}, \{*\}, 0, 0 \rangle$ (where 0 denotes the empty multirelation). There is a morphism $\langle f, F \rangle$ in $\mathbf{MNet}^+$ from $\langle M_1 + M_2 + S, N_1 \rangle$ to $\langle C, N_2 + \bot \rangle$ given by:

$$f(Req_i) = Beg_i \qquad f(Out_i) = End_i \qquad f(c) = * \text{ for all other events } c$$
$$F(C) = S \qquad F(C_i) = S_i$$

By Corollary 5, the existence of this morphism shows that the net $\langle C, N_2 + \bot \rangle$ can simulate any behaviour of the net $\langle M_1 + M_2 + S, N_1 \rangle$. Since the behaviour of the image net is so restricted (indeed, $\langle C, N_2 + \bot \rangle$ is minimal in the sense of Definition 17), this proves an important feature of the marked net $\langle M_1 + M_2 + S, N_1 \rangle$, that it can never reach a state in which Req_2 can occur if Req_1 has occurred and Out_1 has not. This, together with the analogous property for Req_2, ensures that $\langle M_1 + M_2 + S, N_1 \rangle$ preserves mutual exclusion of the behaviours In_1 ; Cr_1 ; Out_1 and In_2 ; Cr_2 ; Out_2. This example is particularly simple. Note, however, for any net $\langle M, N \rangle$ intended as a mutual exclusion algorithm, the existence of a morphism from $\langle M, N \rangle$ to $\langle C, N_2 + \bot \rangle$ can be used to demonstrate that $\langle M, N \rangle$ preserves mutual exclusion.

The net $\langle C, N_2 \rangle$ describes the behaviour of the shared resource, abstracting away from the competing processes. A different abstraction is given in the net $\langle m_1 + m_2 + s, N_3 \rangle$ below, which describes only the possible states of the processes (critical, requesting entry to the critical region, or neither of these) and how these interact. There is a morphism $\langle g, G \rangle$ in $\mathbf{MNet}^+$ from $\langle m_1 + m_2 + s, N_3 \rangle$ to $\langle M_1 + M_2 + S, N_1 \rangle$ given by:

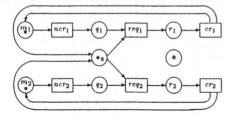

$$g(ncr_i) = Ncr_i \quad g(req_i) = Req_i$$
$$g(cr_i) = In_i \; ; \; Cr_i \; ; \; In_i$$
$$G(M_i) = m_i \quad G(Q_i) = q_i$$
$$G(R_i) = G(S_i) = r_i \quad G(S) = s$$
$$G(b) = * \text{ for all other conditions } b \text{ of } N_1$$

We shall assume strong fairness in the sense that if any event of N_3 is enabled infinitely often, it occurs infinitely often. Note that no behaviour of either N_1 or N_3 is finite, and N_1 is minimal for $\langle g, G \rangle$: under these conditions, $\langle g, G \rangle$ preserves strong fairness. Clearly, if q_1 is marked in N_3 but req_1 never occurs, then q_1 is always marked. Also, s is marked infinitely often. Hence req_1 is enabled infinitely often and by strong fairness must occur infinitely often, contradicting the assumption that req_1 never occurs. We deduce that N_3 satisfies a liveness property which might be called "absence of starvation", stating that if a process requests entry to its critical region, it eventually enters it. This property is preserved by $\langle g, G \rangle$ and thus N_1 also satisfies absence of starvation. This small example illustrates two ways in which morphisms reduce the complexity of model-checking: conditions can be identified and computations can be collapsed to single events (r_1 corresponds to both S_1 and R_1 while cr_1 corresponds to $In_1 \; ; \; Cr_1 \; ; \; Out_1$).

In Section 5.1 we make the results of this section precise by expressing mutual exclusion and absence of starvation as temporal logic formulae and showing that the existence of the morphisms $\langle f, F \rangle$ and $\langle g, G \rangle$ can be used to prove that N_1 satisfies both properties, without explicitly considering the set of possible behaviours of N_1.

4   A Temporal Logic for Enablement

The main purpose of modal and temporal logics is the specification of complex concurrent systems. A specification is the conjunction of formulae each describing a property required of a system: our technique facilitates the proof that a net satisfies each conjunct in its specification. Classifying properties helps to prevent underspecification: we know, for example, that a full specification must describe both safety and liveness properties. The categorical approach offers a basis for successive refinements (since we can compose morphisms) and for a compositional proof system exploiting structure in our category of processes.

The examples of Section 3.2 gave simple test nets possessing properties of mutual exclusion and absence of starvation, and used morphisms to demonstrate that a more complex net also had these properties. A key point is that we proved properties of the complex net without reference to its dynamic behaviour. We now prove that this technique applies to a large class of properties, which we characterise syntactically in Section 5. In this section we develop a simple modal language $\mathcal{M}$

and temporal language $\mathcal{T}$ for discussing net behaviours. We give interpretations of $\mathcal{M}$ and $\mathcal{T}$ in any marked net, define a notion of satisfaction and demonstrate the expressiveness of our logics. This section formalises the arguments of Section 3.2, and indicates the expressive power of the formulae for which our technique can be applied.

Modal logics use modalities to express the effects of events firing. For each step s, the operator $[s]$ means "after every s-step", while its dual $\neg[s]\neg$, abbreviated $\langle s \rangle$, means "after some s-step". We assume disjoint collections of variables (ranged over by $x, x_0, \ldots$) and constants (ranged over by $\alpha, \alpha_0, \alpha_1, \ldots$). A *term* of $\mathcal{M}$ is either a variable, a constant, a multiset of constants or a sequence of two terms. $\mathcal{M}$ is the modal language given by:

$$\phi ::= \mathrm{tt} \;\Big|\; \neg\phi \;\Big|\; \phi \wedge \phi \;\Big|\; \langle t \rangle \phi \;\Big|\; \forall x.\phi \qquad \text{for } t \text{ a closed term and } x \text{ a variable.}$$

We define formulae ff, $\phi \vee \psi$, $\phi \rightarrow \psi$, $\exists x.\phi$, $[t]\phi$ and $\phi \leftrightarrow \psi$ (logical equivalence) in the usual, classical way. The quantifiers $\forall$ and $\exists$ bind variables, and a formula is closed if it has no free variables. Closed terms are ranged over by t. We write $\phi[e/x]$ to stand for ϕ with e substituted for all free occurrences of x, subject to the usual renaming of bound variables. We define an interpretation of an $\mathcal{M}$ formula ϕ in a marked net inductively in terms of an interpretation of the constants α_i which occur in ϕ as computations of the net. An *interpretation* of $\mathcal{M}$ in a marked net $\langle M, N \rangle$ is a partial function θ from the constants α_i of $\mathcal{M}$ to the computations E^+ of N. $dom(\theta)$ denotes the set of constants on which θ is defined. We extend θ homomorphically to closed terms.

DEFINITION 8. *The satisfaction relation $\models_\theta$ between marked nets and closed formulae of $\mathcal{M}$ relative to an interpretation θ of $\mathcal{M}$ in $\langle M, N \rangle$ is defined as follows:*

1. $\langle M, N \rangle \models_\theta \mathrm{tt}$
2. $\langle M, N \rangle \models_\theta \neg\phi$ *iff it is not the case that $\langle M, N \rangle \models_\theta \phi$*
3. $\langle M, N \rangle \models_\theta \phi \wedge \psi$ *iff $\langle M, N \rangle \models_\theta \phi$ and $\langle M, N \rangle \models_\theta \psi$*
4. $\langle M, N \rangle \models_\theta \forall x.\phi$ *iff for all $\alpha \in dom(\theta)$ we have $\langle M, N \rangle \models_\theta \phi[\alpha/x]$*
5. $\langle M, N \rangle \models_\theta [t]\phi$ *iff whenever $M \xrightarrow{\theta t} M'$ we have $\langle M', N \rangle \models_\theta \phi$.*

The satisfaction relation is then determined for the derived operators. For example, we have:

$\langle M, N \rangle \models_\theta \phi \vee \psi$ iff $\langle M, N \rangle \models_\theta \phi$ or $\langle M, N \rangle \models_\theta \psi$

$\langle M, N \rangle \models_\theta \phi \rightarrow \psi$ iff   if $\langle M, N \rangle \models_\theta \phi$ then $\langle M, N \rangle \models_\theta \psi$

$\langle M, N \rangle \models_\theta \exists x.\phi$ iff   there exists $\alpha \in dom(\theta)$ such that $\langle M, N \rangle \models_\theta \phi[\alpha/x]$

$\langle M, N \rangle \models_\theta \langle t \rangle \phi$ iff   there exists M' such that $M \xrightarrow{\theta t} M'$ and $\langle M', N \rangle \models_\theta \phi$.

Rules 1 to 4 give satisfaction a standard meaning in the style of Tarski: in particular, they reflect the fact that our logic is classical. The interesting rule is 5, which expresses the interaction of the modal operators with evolution of the net. Thus $\langle M, N \rangle \models_\theta \langle \alpha \rangle \phi$ if M can evolve under $\theta(\alpha)$ to a marking in which ϕ is satisfied. Similarly, $\langle M, N \rangle \models_\theta \exists x.\langle x \rangle \phi$ if it is possible to satisfy ϕ after a computation interpreting some constant.

Let t be a closed term of $\mathcal{M}$. Define $E(t)$ to be the formula $\langle t \rangle \mathrm{tt}$. Then $\langle M, N \rangle \models_\theta E(t)$ exactly when the computation in $\langle M, N \rangle$ which interprets the term t is enabled. It follows from the definition of satisfaction that $\langle M, N \rangle \models_\theta \neg E(t)$ if and only if $\langle M, N \rangle \models_\theta \langle t \rangle \mathrm{ff}$, that is, precisely when the computation interpreting t is not enabled. Observe that if α is interpreted by the identity step id_{nb} then $\langle M, N \rangle \models_\theta E(\alpha)$ whenever the condition b is marked in $\langle M, N \rangle$ with at least n tokens. In general such properties as mutual exclusion or freedom from deadlock can be expressed in terms of the enabling of events. For example, the fact that two events e_0 and e_1 cannot occur concurrently is expressed by the formula $\neg E(\alpha_0 + \alpha_1)$, where α_i is interpreted in $\langle M, N \rangle$ by e_i.

We wish to specify and reason about both the overall behaviour of a net and individual enabled steps: we therefore turn our attention from steps to step sequences, and extend $\mathcal{M}$ to the temporal logic $\mathcal{T}$ by considering the modal formulae which hold on computation paths rather than at individual states. $\mathcal{T}$ is given by:

$$\phi ::= \mathbf{tt} \;\Big|\; \neg\phi \;\Big|\; \phi \wedge \phi \;\Big|\; \forall x.\phi \;\Big|\; [t]\phi \;\Big|\; \Box\phi \quad \text{for } t \text{ a closed term.}$$

DEFINITION 9. *The interpretation of a closed formula ϕ of $\mathcal{T}$ relative to an interpretation θ of $\mathcal{T}$ in a marked net $\langle M, N \rangle$ is a set of infinite sequences of terms $\sigma = t_0 ; t_1 ; \ldots$ given as follows:*

$\sigma \in [\![\mathbf{tt}]\!]_\theta$ *for any σ*

$\sigma \in [\![\neg\phi]\!]_\theta$ *iff it is not the case that $\sigma \in [\![\phi]\!]_\theta$*

$\sigma \in [\![\phi \wedge \psi]\!]_\theta$ *iff $\sigma \in [\![\phi]\!]_\theta \cap [\![\psi]\!]_\theta$*

$\sigma \in [\![\forall x.\phi]\!]_\theta$ *iff for all $\alpha \in dom(\theta)$ we have $\sigma[\alpha/x] \in [\![\phi]\!]_\theta$*

$\sigma \in [\![[t]\phi]\!]_\theta$ *iff whenever there exists k such that $t = \theta(t_0 ; t_1 \ldots ; t_k)$ then $t_{k+1} ; t_{k+2} ; \ldots \in [\![\phi]\!]_\theta$*

$\sigma \in [\![\Box\phi]\!]_\theta$ *iff for each i we have $t_i ; t_{i+1} ; \ldots \in [\![\phi]\!]_\theta$.*

The satisfaction relation $\models$ between marked nets and closed formulae of $\mathcal{T}$ relative to θ is given by $\langle M, N \rangle \models_\theta \phi$ iff every computation of $\langle M, N \rangle$ is the image under θ of some $\sigma \in [\![\phi]\!]_\theta$.

This interpretation gives the usual meaning to the derived operators. Thus $\langle M, N \rangle \models_\theta \Diamond\phi$ precisely when every computation of $\langle M, N \rangle$ eventually satisfies ϕ, while $\langle M, N \rangle \models_\theta \langle t \rangle \phi$ precisely when $\langle M, N \rangle$ can evolve under $\theta(t)$ to $\langle M', N \rangle$ and $\langle M', N \rangle \models_\theta \phi$. We could define $\models_\theta$ relative to certain fairness or liveness assumptions, considering, for example, only those step sequences which are *weakly* or *strongly fair* [8]. In his temporal logic for occurrence nets [15], Reisig restricts attention to behaviours in which no condition ever contains more than one token.

The language $\mathcal{T}$ expresses many interesting properties of nets, both positive (what can be enabled) and negative (what cannot be enabled). For example, mutual exclusion of events interpreting α_0 and α_1 is expressed by satisfaction of the formula $\Box \neg E(\alpha_0 + \alpha_1)$ while freedom from deadlock is expressed by satisfaction of the formula $\Box \exists x.E(x)$.

In practice, the graphical representation of nets facilitates the creative process of constructing test nets. It appears difficult to find an algorithm which constructs a test net corresponding to a given formula (especially in the case of negation). Each test net can be used to establish a property for many different complex nets, which justifies considerable effort in constructing test nets. An efficient (smaller) test net offers savings each time it is used.

This paper's main aim is to demonstrate by means of modal and temporal logic the wide range of properties which our technique can be used to prove. A related goal, which we do not explore here, is to develop a sound and complete proof system for our net model. In addition to the usual proof rules for modal logic [7] and temporal logic [8], the net model satisfies proof rules corresponding to properties of nets, including the evident rules reflecting the following facts

- $\langle M + pre(\theta(t)), N \rangle \models_\theta E(t)$ for any marking M of N,
- if $\langle M, N \rangle \models_\theta E(t_0 ; t_1)$ then $\langle M, N \rangle \models_\theta E(t_0)$ and $\langle M, N \rangle \models_\theta \Diamond E(t_1)$ and
- if $\langle M, N \rangle \models_\theta E(t_0 + t_1)$ then $\langle M, N \rangle \models_\theta E(t_0) \wedge E(t_1)$.

Further rules reflect the interaction between satisfaction and structure in the category $\mathbf{MNet}^+$.

5 The Interaction of the Logics with the Categorical Framework

In this section, we show more precisely how the satisfaction of modal and temporal logic formulae interacts with morphisms and structure in MNet. This is necessary for compositional and modular reasoning about the properties satisfied by net behaviours.

Let $\mathcal{L}$ be the sublanguage of the modal language $\mathcal{M}$ without negation or quantification, given by:

$$\phi ::= \text{tt} \mid \text{ff} \mid \langle t \rangle \phi \mid [t]\phi \mid \phi \wedge \phi \mid \phi \vee \phi \quad \text{for } t \text{ a closed term.}$$

The language $\mathcal{L}$ is of particular interest because, if t is restricted to constant terms, $\mathcal{L}$ characterises strong bisimulation of processes in CCS in the sense that two finitely branching processes are strongly bisimilar if and only if they satisfy the same formulae of $\mathcal{L}$.

DEFINITION 10. *Satisfaction of a formula ϕ of T is preserved by morphisms in* MNet$^+$ *if whenever* $\langle f, F \rangle : \langle M_0, N \rangle \longrightarrow \langle M_0', N' \rangle$ *in* MNet$^+$ *then for any interpretation θ of T in N_0,*

$$\text{if } \langle M_0, N \rangle \models_\theta \phi \text{ then } \langle M_0', N' \rangle \models_{f\theta} \phi.$$

Satisfaction of ϕ is reflected by morphisms in MNet$^+$ *if*

$$\text{if } \langle M_0', N' \rangle \models_{f\theta} \phi \text{ then } \langle M_0, N \rangle \models_\theta \phi.$$

For brevity, we shall write "ϕ is preserved (reflected)" instead of "satisfaction of ϕ is preserved (reflected) by morphisms in MNet$^+$".

Proposition 11. If ϕ is a formula of $\mathcal{L}$ containing no instance of $\langle t \rangle$ then ϕ is reflected.

Proof: We use induction on the structure of ϕ. The interesting case is when $\langle M_0', N' \rangle \models_{f\theta} [t]\phi$. Whenever $M_0 \xrightarrow{\theta(t)} M_1$ in N, we know that $M_0' \xrightarrow{f(\theta(t))} M_1'$ in N', and so $\langle M_1', N' \rangle \models_{f\theta} \phi$, by assumption. Now $\langle f, F \rangle : \langle M_1, N \rangle \to \langle M_1', N' \rangle$ in MNet$^+$, and so, by inductive hypothesis, $\langle M_1, N \rangle \models_\theta \phi$. Hence, by definition, $\langle M_0, N \rangle \models_\theta [t]\phi$. □

Proposition 12. If ϕ is a formula of $\mathcal{L}$ containing no instance of $[t]$ then ϕ is preserved. □

Note that $[t]\phi$ is not preserved: for the net N of Section 3, we have $\langle id, id \rangle : \langle \emptyset, N \rangle \to \langle 2b_0, N \rangle$ in MNet$^+$. If $\theta(\alpha) = e_0$ then $\langle \emptyset, N \rangle \models_\theta [\alpha]E(\alpha)$ (since e_0 is not enabled), but $\langle 2b_0, N \rangle \not\models_\theta [\alpha]E(\alpha)$.

The above results state that certain safety properties expressible as formulae of $\mathcal{L}$ are preserved by morphisms in MNet$^+$, while certain liveness properties are reflected. It is important to note that we code up the change of interpretation by replacing θ by $f\theta$. Since the formula ϕ does not change, a single test net satisfying ϕ witnesses the fact that both $\langle M, N \rangle$ and $\langle M', N' \rangle$ satisfy the property described by ϕ. We now generalise these results to our temporal language T.

DEFINITION 13. *A state formula of T is a formula of T which contains no instance of $\Diamond$ or $\Box$ (that is, it involves no temporal operator). A positive state formula is a formula of T which can be proved equivalent in classical logic to a state formula containing no negations.*

Proposition 14. Let θ be an interpretation of T in a net $\langle M, N \rangle$ and let $\langle f, F \rangle$ be a morphism from $\langle M, N \rangle$ to $\langle M', N' \rangle$ in MNet$^+$. Let ϕ be any positive state formula of T. Whenever $\langle M', N' \rangle \models_{f\theta} \Box \neg \phi$ then $\langle M, N \rangle \models_\theta \Box \neg \phi$.

579

Proof: By a simple structural induction on ϕ. We give the case where ϕ is $E(t)$.

Suppose $\langle M', N'\rangle \models_{f\theta} \Box\neg E(t)$. By definition of satisfaction, the computation $f(\theta(t)$ is never enabled in any evolution of $\langle M', N'\rangle$. By Proposition 4, whenever $\theta(t)$ is enabled in $\langle M, N\rangle$ then $f(\theta(t))$ is enabled in $\langle M', N'\rangle$. Since $f(\theta(t))$ is never enabled in $\langle M', N'\rangle$, it must be the case that $\theta(t)$ is never enabled in $\langle M, N\rangle$, and so $\langle M, N\rangle \models_\theta \Box\neg E(t)$. $\quad\Box$

Thus safety properties of the form "an event e is never enabled" are reflected.

Proposition 15. Satisfaction of the following formulae is reflected by morphisms in MNet$^+$:

$\Box\neg E(\alpha)$ $\theta(\alpha)$ is never enabled
$\forall x.\neg E(x)$ no $\theta(\alpha)$ is enabled (relative deadlock) $\Box$

Proposition 16. Satisfaction of the following formulae is preserved by morphisms in MNet$^+$:

$E(t)$ $\theta(t)$ is enabled
$\exists x.E(x)$ some $\theta(\alpha)$ is enabled
$\Box\Diamond\exists x.E(x)$ infinitely often, some $\theta(\alpha)$ is enabled $\Box$

These three formulae express various liveness properties, which are relative in the sense that they concern only the computations which interpret some constant α in the domain of θ. In reaching the marking enables $\theta(\alpha)$, the net may execute steps which do not interpret any constant.

Definition 17. *Let $\langle f, F\rangle: N \to N'$ be a morphism in* MNet$^+$. *We say that the image net N' is minimal if every computation of N' is the prefix of the image of a computation of N.*

Thus minimality of a net depends on a particular morphism $\langle f, F\rangle: N \to N'$. Note that if f restricts to a surjection of E onto E', then N' is minimal. If N' is a test net for a formula ϕ which is reflected, then minimality is a natural condition ensuring that N' is efficient in the sense of having no redundant behaviour.

Proposition 18. Let ϕ be any of $E(\alpha)$, $\exists x.E(x)$, $\Box\Diamond\exists x.E(x)$ and $\Diamond\Box E(\alpha)$. Satisfaction of ϕ is reflected by morphisms with minimal image.

Proof: We use minimality to show that if a computation of the image net does not satisfy ϕ, then the corresponding computations of the domain net also fail to satisfy ϕ. $\quad\Box$

For brevity, we write "ϕ is minimally preserved (reflected)" rather than "satisfaction of ϕ is preserved (reflected) by morphisms in MNet$^+$ with minimal image".

Proposition 19. The following formulae are minimally preserved and minimally reflected:

$\Diamond E(\alpha)$ $\theta(\alpha)$ will eventually be enabled
$\Box\forall x.E(x)$ all computations interpreting constants are continuously enabled
$\Box\Diamond\exists x.E(x)$ infinitely often some computation interpreting a constant is enabled. $\Box$

If we extend T with arbitrary disjunctions then we obtain the following proposition:

Proposition 20. Let $\langle f, F\rangle: \langle M, N\rangle \to \langle M', N'\rangle$ with $\langle M', N'\rangle$ minimal. Each of the following formulae is minimally preserved:

$\Box E(t)$ $\theta(t)$ is continuously enabled,
$\Box\Diamond E(t)$ $\theta(t)$ is enabled infinitely often
$\Diamond E(t)$ $\theta(t)$ is eventually enabled.

Furthermore, if $\langle M', N' \rangle \models_{f\theta} \Box E(t)$ then $\langle M, N \rangle \models_\theta \Box \bigvee_I E(t_i)$, where I indexes $\{t_i \mid f\theta(t_i) = f\theta(t)\}$,

if $\langle M', N' \rangle \models_{f\theta} \Box \Diamond E(t)$ then $\langle M, N \rangle \models_\theta \Box \Diamond \bigvee E(t_i)$, and

if $\langle M', N' \rangle \models_{f\theta} \Diamond E(t)$ then $\langle M, N \rangle \models_\theta \Diamond \bigvee E(t_i)$.

Proof: Suppose for example that $\langle M', N' \rangle \models_{f\theta} \Box E(t)$. We show that $\langle M, N \rangle \models_\theta \Box \bigvee_I E(t_i)$. In every computation of $\langle M', N' \rangle$ the computation $\theta(t)$ is continuously enabled. By minimality, in every computation of $\langle M, N \rangle$, there is always a computation enabled whose image under f equals $f(\theta t)$. Let I index the set $\{t_i \mid f\theta(t_i) = f\theta(t)\}$. Then $\langle M, N \rangle \models_\theta \Box \bigvee_I E(t_i)$. $\Box$

Note that, if in the proof of Proposition 20 $f\theta(t') = f\theta(t)$ implies that $t' = t$, then $\langle M, N \rangle \models_\theta \Box E(t)$.

Proposition 21. Let $\langle f, F \rangle : \langle M, N \rangle \to \langle M', N' \rangle$ with $\langle M', N' \rangle$ minimal. Each of the following formulae is minimally reflected:

$$\Box \Diamond \neg E(t) \qquad \theta(t) \text{ is disabled infinitely often}$$
$$\Diamond \neg E(t) \qquad \theta(t) \text{ will eventually be disabled.}$$

Furthermore, if $\langle M, N \rangle \models_\theta \Box \Diamond \neg E(t)$ then $\langle M', N' \rangle \models_{f\theta} \Box \Diamond \bigvee \neg E(t_i)$ and

if $\langle M, N \rangle \models_\theta \Diamond \neg E(t)$ then $\langle M', N' \rangle \models_{f\theta} \Diamond \bigvee \neg E(t_i)$. $\Box$

It is readily shown that if the formulae ϕ and ψ are preserved (reflected) by morphisms in **MNet**$^+$ then the formulae $\phi \wedge \psi$, $\phi \vee \psi$, $\phi \to \neg \psi$, $\langle t \rangle \phi$ and $\Diamond \phi$ are preserved (respectively reflected) while the formulae $\neg \phi$, $[t] \neg \phi$ and $\Box \phi$ are reflected (respectively preserved).[2] These observations, combined with the preceding propositions and the proof rules for temporal and modal logic, determine a relatively large and expressive class of formulae which are either preserved or reflected by morphisms in **MNet**$^+$. These formulae occur at all levels of Manna and Pnueli's hierarchy [8, 9]. Thus if ϕ and ψ are state formulae,

$\Box \phi$ describes a safety property. Many such formulae, including mutual exclusion $\Box \neg E(t_0 + t_1))$, are reflected: some (for example $\Box E(t)$) are preserved.

$\Diamond \phi$ describes a termination property, guaranteeing a one-time goal. An example is $\Diamond E(\alpha)$, which is both minimally preserved and minimally reflected.

$\Box \Diamond \phi$ describes a recurrence property or response property. An example is $\Box(E(t_0) \to \Diamond E(t_1))$, which is minimally preserved and minimally reflected.

$\Diamond \Box \phi$ describes a persistence property. As an example, $\Diamond \Box E(t)$ is minimally reflected.

$\Diamond \Box \phi \vee \Box \Diamond \psi$ describes a progress property. An example is $\Box(\Box \Diamond E(t_0) \to \Box \Diamond E(t_1))$ (strong fairness) which is minimally preserved and reflected.

5.1 Proving Properties of Nets

We now outline the formal proofs that the net $\langle M_1 + M_2 + S, N_1 \rangle$ of section 3.2 preserves mutual exclusion and satisfies absence of starvation. For mutual exclusion, putting $\theta(\alpha) = Out_1 + Out_2$ and $\theta(\beta) = Cr_1 + Cr_2$ we have $\langle C, N_2 \rangle \models_{f\theta} \Box \neg E(\alpha)$. By Proposition 14, $\langle S + M_1 + M_2, N_1 \rangle \models_\theta \Box \neg E(\alpha)$. Since $N_1 \models_\theta [\beta] E(\alpha)$, we deduce that $\langle S + M_1 + M_2, N_1 \rangle$ can never enable Cr_1 and Cr_2

---

[2] Using this fact we can deduce some of the above propositions from others.

581

simultaneously. Thus entry to the critical regions Cr_1 and Cr_2 is mutually exclusive. For absence of starvation, we shall assume an invertible interpretation θ in $\langle m_1 + m_2 + s, N_3 \rangle$ with inverse η. Plainly $\langle m_1 + m_2 + s, N_3 \rangle \models_\theta \Box \Diamond E(\eta\, id_s)$ and $\langle m_1 + m_2 + s, N_3 \rangle \models_\theta (E(\eta\, id_{q_i}) \wedge \neg \Diamond E(\eta\, cr_i)) \to \Box E(\eta\, id_{q_i})$ for $i \in \{1,2\}$. The assumption of strong fairness implies that $\langle m_1 + m_2 + s, N_3 \rangle \models_\theta \Box \Diamond E(\eta\, req_i) \to \Box \Diamond E(\eta\, cr_i)$. We deduce that $\langle m_1 + m_2 + s, N_3 \rangle \models_\theta E(\eta\, req_i) \to \Diamond E(\eta\, ncr_i)$ by applying the proof rules of temporal logic. Thus N_3 satisfies absence of starvation. Satisfaction of $E(\alpha)$ is preserved and satisfaction of $\Diamond E(\alpha)$ is reflected, by minimality. Hence satisfaction of $E(\eta\, req_i) \to \Diamond E(\eta\, ncr_i)$ is preserved and N_1 satisfies absence of starvation.

6 Future Work

This paper sketches an approach and presents some preliminary results concerning the applicability of that approach. It remains to establish a sound and complete proof system for our logic and to consider a logical characterisation of the simulation preorder. An important aspect of future research is the use of structure in our category to modularise proofs. $MNet^+$ has coproducts (representing choice) and products of a kind (representing parallel composition of processes). There is certainly a relationship between the formulae satisfied by a compound net and the formulae satisfied by its components, which we would like to make precise (compare [16]). Future work will consider the use of relations rather than functions, thus approaching still more closely the simulations of process algebra [11, 13].

References

1. H. R. Andersen and G. Winskel, *Compositional Checking of Satisfaction*, in K. G. Larsen and A. Skou, editors, Proc. 3rd Workshop on Computer Aided Verification, 1991, Aalborg, LNCS 575.
2. C. T. Brown, *Linear Logic and Petri Nets: Categories, Algebra and Proof*, PhD thesis, University of Edinburgh, Technical Report ECS-LFCS-91-128, 1990.
3. C. T. Brown and D. J. Gurr, *Refinement and Simulation of Nets – a categorical characterisation*, in K. Jensen, editor, Proc. 13th Int. Conf. on Applications and Theory of Petri Nets, LNCS 616, 1992.
4. C. T. Brown and D. J. Gurr, *Timing Petri Nets Categorically*, in W. Kuich, editor, Proc. ICALP, LNCS 623, 1992.
5. C. T. Brown, D. J. Gurr and V. C. V. de Paiva, *A Linear Specification Language for Petri Nets*, Tech. Report DAIMI PB – 363, Århus University, 1991, to appear in Math. Structures in Comp. Science.
6. J.W. de Bakker, W.-P. de Roever, and G. Rozenberg, editors, *Proc. Workshop on Linear Time, Branching Time and Partial Order in Logics and Models for Concurrency*, LNCS 354, 1988.
7. D. Kozen, *Results on the Propositional μ-calculus*, Theoretical Computer Science, 27:333–354, 1983.
8. Z. Manna and A. Pnueli, *The Anchored Version of the Temporal Framework*, in [6], pages 201–284.
9. Z. Manna and A. Pnueli, *A Hierarchy of Temporal Properties*, in Proc. ACM Symposium on Principles of Distributed Computing, Quebec, 1990.
10. J. Meseguer and U. Montanari, *Petri nets are Monoids: A new algebraic foundation for net theory*, in Proc LICS, 1988.
11. R. Milner, *Communication and Concurrency*, Prentice Hall, 1989.
12. E. R. Olderog, *Nets, Terms and Formulas*, CUP, 1991.
13. D. M. R. Park, *Concurrency and Automata on Infinite Sequences*, LNCS 104, Springer–Verlag, 1980.
14. W. Reisig, *Petri Nets: an Introduction*, EATCS Monographs on Theoretical Computer Science, Springer–Verlag, 1985.
15. W. Reisig, *Towards a Temporal Logic for Causality and Choice in Distributed Systems*, in [6]:603–627.
16. G. Winskel, *A Category of Labelled Petri Nets and Compositional Proof System*, in Proc LICS, 1988.

Decidability of a partial order based temporal logic

Kamal Lodaya[1], R. Ramanujam[1], P.S. Thiagarajan[2]

[1] The Institute of Mathematical Sciences, Madras 600 113, INDIA
[2] School of Mathematics, SPIC Science Foundation, 92 G.N. Chetty Road, T. Nagar, Madras 600 017, INDIA

1 Introduction

In the past decade, a variety of temporal logics have been proposed to reason about distributed programs and systems [Eme, Sti]. As opposed to the approach taken by Hoare logic [Apt] and dynamic logic [Har], where programs are explicitly used in the syntax of formulas, temporal logics have been interpreted over behaviours of programs rather than programs themselves. Typically, a transition system is used to model the state space of a program. A *run* (computation) of the program is a sequence of states permitted by the transition system. Formulas of the logic are interpreted over the states visited by a run. Depending on whether quantification is allowed over runs, one has branching or linear time temporal logics. In the case of concurrent systems, the states of the transition system represent *global* states of the distributed program, and a run denotes the *interleaved* execution of actions.

An alternative approach – which we have followed – is to have a single ("unfolded") structure represent the behaviour of a distributed program. In such a structure, causality, choice and concurrency can be explicitly defined and separated from each other. Furthermore, viewing a global state as only a potential state of affairs, one attaches logical assertions to *local* states of the computations generated by the program.

Axiomatizing models of distributed systems in this way is in the spirit of classical modal logic [HC], where one speaks of a logic *characterizing* a class of structures. The main motivation here is to identify operators which would directly express notions such as communication and concurrency. In the logic considered here, the focus of attention is communication between agents.

Consider a system of n (≥ 1) sequential agents which communicate with each other asynchronously via point-to-point unbounded buffers. Such systems often appear in the literature on distributed algorithms [CM]. One way of representing the "unfolded" behaviour of such a system is through n trees which are interconnected in some coherent fashion. This would be a generalization of the "timing diagrams" of Lamport [Lam]. (A timing diagram represents n interconnected linear orders.) The individual trees are meant to denote the local sequential behaviour of the agents. The interconnections capture the communication pattern established during the course of the runs permitted by the system.

Such behavioural objects can be formalized as *Communicating Sequential Agents* (CSAs) [LRT]. They can also be viewed as structured versions of prime event structures [NPW]. In [LRT] we proposed a temporal logic with future and indexed past modalities for CSAs. The semantics of the logic was chosen so that the modalities represent the notion of an agent gaining information about another through the *reception* of messages but not by *sending* them. We showed completeness results for this logic over CSAs and many subclasses of CSAs. In [LR], these results were further improved upon.

Decidability of the CSA-logics has turned out to be an interesting problem. Traditionally, decidability of tense logics has been proved via translation to $S2S$, the monadic second order theory of two successors (see [Bur] for an example). This gives a nonelementary decision procedure [Rab]. Encoding our logics into $S2S$ over trees seems difficult and generalizing $S2S$ to interpret over partial orders is a hard problem. On the other hand, the standard filtration techniques [HC] can be easily seen to violate the condition that each agent be tree-like.

In this paper, we consider the logic defined in [LR] and prove elementary decidability of that logic. This leads us to decidability results for the logics over subclasses of CSAs studied in [LRT]. Our results show that partial order based temporal logics, even with explicit reference to agents, need not be unmanageably expressive.

Our proof relies upon new techniques for performing filtrations over partial orders. Recording the right amount of information about the past at a local state turns out to be quite nontrivial.

It is perhaps worth noting that there are very few decidability results for logics based on the partial order semantics of concurrency. One such result is due to Pinter and Wolper [PW]. Their logic is interpreted over runs of the system. Our approach is different in the use of agents as well as in the interpretation over the entire structure rather than over runs. A similar remark applies to the logic of Penczek [Pen], which, although interpreted over event structures, has operators suited to describing (partially ordered) runs.

2 Definitions and Results

In this section, we present a model of distributed systems called n-ACSAs, a temporal logic for local reasoning in n-ACSAs and state the results of our paper. For the sake of brevity, we merely introduce the logic and models here; see [LR, LRT] for a detailed treatment.

Definition 2.1 *An* n-ACSA *(n Asynchronously Communicating Sequential Agents) is a triple $S = (E, \leq, \eta)$, where*

1. *E is a set of event occurrences.*

2. *$\leq$ is a partial order on E called the causality relation.*

584

3. $\eta : E \rightarrow \{1, \ldots, n\}$ *is a naming function.*

4. $\forall e \in E : \forall i : 1 \leq i \leq n \cdot \{e' \mid e' \leq e, \eta(e') = i\}$ *is totally ordered by* $\leq$.

The following points can be noted about n-ACSAs:

1. *Causality* - We interpret $e_1 \leq e_2$ to mean that it is necessary for e_1 to occur before e_2 does. For instance, sending a message has to precede receiving it.
2. *Conflict* - Consider two incomparable event occurrences e_1 and e_2. We say they are in conflict, either if $\eta(e_1) = \eta(e_2)$, or if there exist e'_1 and e'_2 such that $\eta(e'_1) = \eta(e'_2), e'_1 \leq e_1, e'_2 \leq e_2$ and e'_1 and e'_2 are incomparable. Thus conflicting event occurrences never occur in the same computation. Now, we can see that condition (4) in Definition 2.1 ensures that no event occurrence causally depends on conflicting event occurrences. This forces agents to be tree-like - we refer to this property as backward linearity within agents.
3. *Concurrency* - Consider incomparable event occurrences e_1 and e_2 which are not in conflict. Necessarily, they are in distinct agents. We interpret this to mean concurrent occurrence of e_1 and e_2 and the same computation can include both.

A unique agent is associated with each event occurrence by the naming function η. Thus the sending of a message and its receipt are to be separated into distinct events performed by different agents. It is in this sense that our model supports asynchronous communication.

Let $e \in E$ and $\eta(e) = i$. $\downarrow e \overset{\text{def}}{=} \{e' \mid e' \leq e\}$ is the local state of agent i when e has "just" occurred. We say that an n-ACSA is *finitary* if for every e in E, $\downarrow e$ is finite. The motivation for defining finitary n-ACSAs is that any computation of a real system can be traced back to some starting point, so the past of any event occurring during the computation must be finite.

Figure 1 is an example of a 2-ACSA consisting of a *producer* agent (marked 1) and a *consumer* agent (marked 2), communicating via an unbounded buffer. The producer can produce zero or more items and then quit. The consumer can consume items produced by the producer as long as the items are available in the buffer. The "quit" events in agent 1 are labelled q.

n-ACSAs arise naturally as behavioural representations of distributed systems. Consider a structure $D = (TS_1, TS_2, \ldots, TS_n)$ where, for $i \in \{1, \ldots, n\}$, the TS_i are transition systems representing agent i. The alphabet of TS_i will allow internal actions of agent i, send to j and receive from j actions, for $j \neq i$. Two action sequences are termed equivalent if their projections onto the alphabets of each individual agent are identical. The equivalence classes are called *traces*. The set of traces under a standard prefix ordering will give rise to an n-ACSA. The proof of this result follows that in [MT].

We now define a logic that is to be interpreted over n-ACSAs.

Let $Prop = \{p_0, p_1, \ldots\}$ be a countable set of atomic propositions. The formulas of the language $\mathcal{L}_n$ are defined inductively as follows:

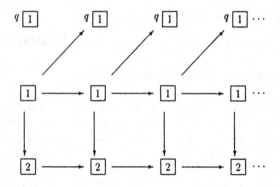

Fig. 1. A 2-ACSA

- Every member of *Prop* is a formula.
- If α and β are formulas, then so are $\neg\alpha, \alpha \lor \beta, \Diamond\alpha$ and $\Diamond_i\alpha$, $i \in \{1, \ldots, n\}$.

A *model* is a pair $M = (S, V)$ where S, the *frame*, is an n-ACSA and V, the *valuation*, is a function from E to 2^{Prop}.

The notion of a formula α being true in a local state e of a model M, denoted $M, e \models \alpha$, is defined inductively as follows:

  (i) $M, e \models \alpha$ iff $\alpha \in V(e)$, for $\alpha \in Prop$.
  (ii) $M, e \models \neg\alpha$ iff $M, e \not\models \alpha$.
  (iii) $M, e \models \alpha \lor \beta$ iff $M, e \models \alpha$ or $M, e \models \beta$.
  (iv) $M, e \models \Diamond_i\alpha$ iff $\exists e' \leq e : \eta(e') = i$ and $M, e' \models \alpha$.
  (v) $M, e \models \Diamond\alpha$ iff $\exists e' : e \leq e'$, $\eta(e) = \eta(e')$ and $M, e' \models \alpha$.

Note that $\Diamond_i$ behaves like a normal past modality – it covers all events that lie in the i-past of e. However $\Diamond\alpha$ is different: in agent j, it asserts that there is a possible future for agent j satisfying α. The asymmetry between past and future arises from the fact that in distributed systems, the past of other agents can be completely obtained by messages, while the possibilities for the future are only locally known.

Define $\boxminus_i\alpha \stackrel{\text{def}}{=} \neg\Diamond_i\neg\alpha$ and $\Box\alpha \stackrel{\text{def}}{=} \neg\Diamond\neg\alpha$.

Examples of reasoning with this logic can be found in [LMRT, LR, LRT].

As usual, a formula α is *satisfiable* if there is a model $M = (S, V)$, $S = (E, \leq, \eta)$ and $\exists e \in E$ such that $M, e \models \alpha$. It is *finitary satisfiable* if it is satisfiable in a model $M = (S, V)$ where S is finitary. A formula α is *valid* if $\neg\alpha$ is not satisfiable. It is *finitary valid* if $\neg\alpha$ is not finitary satisfiable.

Here are some formulas. $(F1) - (F4)$ are valid, whereas $(F5)$ is not. However, $(F5)$ is finitary valid.

$(F1)\ \Box_i\alpha \supset \Box_j\Box_i\alpha$

$(F2)\ \Box_i\Box(\alpha \supset \Diamond_i\alpha)$

$(F3)\ \Box_i(\Diamond\alpha \equiv \Box_i\Diamond\alpha)$

$(F4)\ \Diamond_i\alpha \wedge \Diamond_i\beta \supset \Diamond_i(\alpha \wedge \Diamond_i\beta) \vee \Diamond_i(\beta \wedge \Diamond_i\alpha)$

$(F5)\ \Diamond_i\alpha \supset \Diamond_i(\alpha \wedge \Box_i(\neg\alpha \supset \Box_i\neg\alpha) \wedge \Box_j\Box_i\neg\alpha),\ \ j \neq i$

The following theorem constitutes the main contribution of the paper:

Theorem 2.2 *1. Satisfiability of formulas in $\mathcal{L}_n$ is decidable in nondeterministic double exponential time.*

2. Finitary satisfiability of formulas in $\mathcal{L}_n$ is decidable in nondeterministic double exponential time.

We can also consider systems with unboundedly many agents. Let $\mathbf{N}$ denote the set $\{0, 1, \ldots\}$. We can define an *ACSA* (Asynchronously Communicating Sequential Agents) to be a tuple $S = (E, \leq, \eta)$, where E and $\leq$ are as before, but $\eta : E \to \mathbf{N}$ is a naming function such that the range of η is finite. Thus, the system allows a finite but unbounded number of agents. The logic, however, needs to allow for countably many past-indexed modalities. Define $\mathcal{L}$ to be the language whose formulas are built up as before, except that we include $\Diamond_i\alpha$ as a formula, whenever α is a formula and $i \in \mathbf{N}$. The notions of satisfiability and finitary satisfiability for formulas in $\mathcal{L}$ over ACSAs and finitary ACSAs, respectively, can be suitably defined. We have the following result also:

Theorem 2.3 *1. Satisfiability of formulas in $\mathcal{L}$ over ACSAs is decidable in nondeterministic double exponential time.*

2. Finitary satisfiability of formulas in $\mathcal{L}$ (over finitary ACSAs) is decidable in nondeterministic double exponential time.

We can also extend our frames to allow synchronous communication.

Definition 2.4 $S = (E, \leq, \eta)$ *is a CSA (Communicating Sequential Agents) when*

1. $(E, \leq)$ *is a partially ordered set of event occurrences.*

2. $\eta : E \to \wp_{fin}(\mathbf{N})$ *is a naming function assigning to each e in E a non-empty finite subset of $\mathbf{N}$.*

3. $\forall e \in E : \forall j \in \mathbf{N} : \{e' \mid e' \leq e, j \in \eta(e')\}$ *is totally ordered by $\leq$.*

We interpret $j \in \eta(e)$ as the agent j participating in the event e. Thus $\eta(e) = \{1, 2\}$ can stand for a synchronization "handshake" between agents 1 and 2. Note that only finitely many agents can synchronize at a time. *Finitary* CSAs can be defined by restricting each event to have a finite past.

Our logical language also needs to be changed slightly. We refer to [LRT] for details. Our result goes through for the richer frames as well:

Satisfiability as well as finitary satisfiability over CSAs of the logic defined in [LRT] is decidable in nondeterministic double exponential time.

3 Proof Ideas

In this section, we give a sketch of the proof of Theorem 2.2(1). The other theorems can be proved similarly. The full paper will contain detailed proofs of all the theorems mentioned in Section 2.

It can be easily checked that the logic $\mathcal{L}_n$ lacks the *finite model property*: consider the formula $\Box(\alpha \supset \Diamond\neg\alpha) \wedge \Box(\neg\alpha \supset \Diamond\alpha)$. We define a notion of *quasi-models* and show that the logic does possess the *finite quasi-model property*. Thus a formula is satisfiable if and only if it is finitely quasi-satisfiable. In fact, given a formula α of length m, we show that α is satisfiable iff it is satisfiable in a quasi-model of size $2^{2^{cm}}$ for some constant $c > 0$ determined by the logical language. This gives us the required decision procedure.

While models are based on partial orders, the quasi-models use pre-orders.

Definition 3.1 *A* quasi-frame *is a tuple* $F = (W, \sqsubseteq, \eta)$, *where* $(W, \sqsubseteq)$ *is a pre-order and* $\eta : W \to \{1, \ldots n\}$ *is a naming function such that*

$$\forall w \in W : \forall j \in \{1, \ldots, n\} : \{w' \sqsubseteq w \mid \eta(w') = j\} \text{ is totally ordered by } \sqsubseteq.$$

A *quasi-model* is a pair $Q = (F, V)$, where $F = (W, \sqsubseteq, \eta)$ is a quasi-frame and $V : W \to 2^{Prop}$ is the valuation. The notion $Q, w \models^q \alpha$ can be defined as for models. Quasi-satisfiability and quasi-validity are suitably defined. It can be checked that the formulas $(F1) - (F4)$ of the previous section are also quasi-valid.

The notion of *subformula closure* of a formula turns out to be crucial for proving decidability.

Definition 3.2 *Let* α *be a formula.*

1. $CL'(\alpha)$ *is the least set of formulas containing* α *and satisfying the conditions*

   (a) $\neg\beta \in CL'(\alpha)$ *implies* $\beta \in CL'(\alpha)$.

   (b) $\beta \vee \gamma \in CL'(\alpha)$ *implies* $\{\beta, \gamma\} \subseteq CL'(\alpha)$.

   (c) $\Diamond_i\beta \in CL'(\alpha)$ *implies* $\beta \in CL'(\alpha)$.

(d) $\Diamond \beta \in CL'(\alpha)$ *implies* $\{\beta\} \cup \{\boxminus_j \Diamond \beta \mid j \in \{1, \ldots, n\}\} \subseteq CL'(\alpha)$.

2. $CL(\alpha) \stackrel{\text{def}}{=} CL'(\alpha) \cup \{\neg \beta \mid \beta \in CL'(\alpha)\}$.

For any α, $CL(\alpha)$ is finite and linear in the size of α.

The proof of decidability consists of two parts: unfolding and folding. The former shows that every quasi-satisfiable formula is also satisfiable. The latter shows that every model for a formula can be "folded down" into a finite quasi-model for it.

Lemma 3.3 (Unfolding) *If α is quasi-satisfiable in a finite quasi-model, then it is satisfiable.*

The proof of the unfolding lemma closely follows classical lines: for example, the one in [HC] to obtain irreflexive structures. We make countably many copies of every element in the quasi-model and connect up suitably so that antisymmetry is ensured. In fact, if $Q = ((W, \sqsubseteq, \eta), V)$ is the given quasi-model, we define a model $M = ((E, \leq, \eta'), V')$ where $E \stackrel{\text{def}}{=} W \times \mathbf{Z}$. (Here $\mathbf{Z}$ denotes the set of integers.)

Proving the second part is hard, and hence we give the proof strategy below.

Lemma 3.4 (Folding) *If α is a satisfiable formula, then α is quasi-satisfiable in a quasi-model of size $2^{2^{cm}}$, where $m = |\alpha|$ and $c > 0$ is a constant.*

Proof. Fix a satisfiable formula α_0. Let $M = (S, V)$ be the given model such that $S = (E, \leq, \eta)$ and for some $e_0 \in E$, we have $M, e_0 \models \alpha_0$. Throughout the rest of this section, we refer implicitly to $S = (E, \leq, \eta)$ and let CL denote $CL(\alpha_0)$.

Definition 3.5 *Define $\mu : E \to 2^{CL}$ by $\mu(e) \stackrel{\text{def}}{=} \{\Diamond_i \gamma \in CL \mid M, e \models \Diamond_i \gamma\}$.*

It is obvious from the definition that whenever we have $e_1 \leq e_2$ in M, we also have $\mu(e_1) \subseteq \mu(e_2)$. Further, when $\Diamond_i \alpha \in \mu(e)$, there exists e' such that $e' \leq e$, $\eta(e') = i$ and $M, e' \models \alpha$. In fact, this assertion can be made stronger. Among all e' which satisfy these conditions, we can look for the "virtually earliest" one. This notion is defined below.

Definition 3.6 *Suppose $\Diamond_i \alpha \in \mu(e)$. We say e' is a witness for $(e, \Diamond_i \alpha)$ iff the following conditions hold:*

1. $e' \leq e$, $\eta(e') = i$ and $M, e' \models \alpha$.

2. for every $e'' \leq e$, if $\eta(e'') = i$ and $M, e'' \models \alpha$, then $\mu(e') \subseteq \mu(e'')$.

We say e' is a witness for e if it is a witness for $(e, \Diamond_i \alpha)$ for some $\Diamond_i \alpha \in \mu(e)$.

Proposition 3.7 *If $\Diamond_i\alpha \in \mu(e)$, then there exists a witness e' for $(e, \Diamond_i\alpha)$. Moreover,*

1. *If e_1 and e_2 are both witnesses for $(e, \Diamond_i\alpha)$, then $\mu(e_1) = \mu(e_2)$.*

2. *If e is a witness for $(c_1, \Diamond_i\alpha)$ and $c_1 \leq c_2$, then e is a witness for $(e_2, \Diamond_i\alpha)$ as well.*

The idea of using witnesses allows us to "prune" the given model M. The pruning procedure retains the set E in the given model, but orders fewer event occurrences from distinct agents:

Proposition 3.8 *$(E, \ll, \eta)$ is a frame, where $e_1 \ll e_2$ iff*

- *$e_1 \leq e_2$, and*
- *$\eta(e_1) = \eta(e_2)$ or there is a witness e_3 for e_2 such that $e_1 \leq e_3 \leq e_2$ and $\eta(e_1) = \eta(e_3)$.*

Observe that for e_1, e_2 such that $\eta(e_1) = \eta(e_2)$, we have $e_1 \ll e_2$ iff $e_1 \leq e_2$.

The following proposition assures us that we might as well forget about the given model and work with the "pruned" structure $(E, \ll, \eta)$.

Proposition 3.9 *Let $e \in E$.*

1. *If $M, e \models \Diamond_i\alpha$ then $\exists e' \ll e$: $\eta(c') = i$ and $M, c' \models \alpha$.*

2. *If $M, e \models \Diamond\alpha$, then $\exists c'$: $\eta(c') = \eta(e)$, $c \ll e'$ and $M, e' \models \alpha$.*

We now proceed to define the equivalence relation on E which will give us the required filtration.

Definition 3.10 *1. $\Pi : E \to 2^{(\{1,\ldots,n\} \times 2^{CL})}$ is given by:*

$$\Pi(e) \overset{\text{def}}{=} \{(\eta(c'), \mu(e')) \mid e' \ll e\}.$$

2. $\sim \subseteq E \times E$ is given by: $e_1 \sim e_2$ iff $(\eta(e_1) = \eta(e_2)$ and $\Pi(e_1) = \Pi(e_2))$.

Proposition 3.11 *Suppose $e_1 \sim c_2$. Then the following hold:*

1. *$\mu(e_1) = \mu(e_2)$.*

2. *If e_3 is a witness for $(e_1, \Diamond_i\alpha)$, then there exists a witness e_4 for $(e_2, \Diamond_i\alpha)$ such that $\mu(e_3) = \mu(e_4)$.*

The following lemma asserts that $\sim$ behaves like a "past bisimulation" with respect to $\ll$.

Lemma 3.12 *Suppose $e_1 \sim e_2$ and $e_3 \ll e_1$. Then there exists $e_4 \ll e_2$ such that $e_3 \sim e_4$.*

To get an idea of how this lemma is proved, assume the hypothesis. By definition of $\sim$, we can find $e_4 \ll e_3$ such that $\mu(e_3) = \mu(e_4)$ and $\eta(e_3) = \eta(e_4)$. This is far from proving Π equality for e_3 and e_4. Now suppose $e \ll e_3$. We can find $e' \ll e_2$ of the same μ and η as e. If we can manage to transport e' to the past of e_4, we are done, as that would prove $\Pi(e_3) \subseteq \Pi(e_4)$. If $\eta(e') = \eta(e_4)$, we can use backward linearity to get the result. Otherwise, $\eta(e)$ and $\eta(e_3)$ are also different: so find e'' between e and e_3 which is a witness for some formula $\diamondsuit_i \alpha$, use Proposition 3.7(2) and Proposition 3.11 to find a witness in the past of e_2, observe that $\diamondsuit_i \alpha \in \mu(e_4)$ and thus use Proposition 3.7 to transport $\mu(e'')$ to $\Pi(e_4)$. The rest of the proof proceeds as in the previous case.

With these preliminaries, we are now ready to define the desired filtration of the given model. So far we have considered only modal equivalence; that is, two equated events (in the given model) satisfy the same modal formulas in CL. To take care of the propositions, we now introduce a refinement of the equivalence relation we have been using so far:

Definition 3.13 $\approx \subseteq E \times E$ *is defined by:*

$$e_1 \approx e_2 \text{ iff } e_1 \sim e_2 \text{ and } V(e_1) \cap CL = V(e_2) \cap CL.$$

Below, we use $[e]$ to denote the equivalence class of e under $\approx$, where $e \in E$.

Proposition 3.14 $Q \overset{\text{def}}{=} (F, V')$ *is a quasi-model, where $F = (W, \sqsubseteq, \eta')$ and V' are defined as follows:*

1. $W \overset{\text{def}}{=} \{[e] \mid e \in E\}$.

2. $[e_1] \sqsubseteq [e_2]$ *iff $\exists e, e' : e \sim e_1, e' \sim e_2$ and $e \ll e'$.*

3. $\eta'([e]) \overset{\text{def}}{=} \eta(e)$.

4. $V'([e]) \overset{\text{def}}{=} V(e) \cap CL$.

Note that in the definition of $\sqsubseteq$ we have used $\sim$ and not $\approx$. To show that F is indeed a quasi-frame, we make heavy use of Lemma 3.12. The lemma also enables us to prove:

Lemma 3.15 $\forall \gamma \in CL : \forall e \in E : M, e \models \gamma$ *iff $Q, [e] \models^q \gamma$.*

Since $M, e_0 \models \alpha_0$, we get $Q, [e_0] \models^q \alpha_0$ and thus α_0 is quasi-satisfiable. Further, the quasi-model we constructed has size bounded by 2^{2^m}, where $m = |CL|$. This completes the proof of Lemma 3.4. □

When proving Theorem 2.2(2) for the finitary case, our unfolding cannot use the construction of Lemma 3.3 since the model produced is not finitary. We have to discover a condition on quasi-models which allows unfolding in the future direction, yet preserves the satisfaction of past formulas. Formulating such a condition, folding models so that they produce quasi-models satisfying this condition and discovering an unfolding construction make the proof quite nontrivial. The details will be provided in the full paper.

Admittedly, our decision procedures have a very high complexity. It is far from clear that this is the best that can be done. For instance, using automata-theoretic techniques as in [VW] might give a better decision procedure.

Acknowledgement: We thank Madhavan Mukund for lengthy discussions on the decidability of this and other logics.

References

[Apt] K.R. Apt: Ten years of Hoare logic: a survey – Part I, *ACM Trans. Prog. Lang. Syst.* **3**,4 (1981) 431-483.

[Bur] J.P. Burgess: Decidability for branching time, *Studia Logica* **XXXIX** (1980) 203-218.

[CM] K.M. Chandy, J. Misra: *Parallel program design: a foundation* (Addison-Wesley, 1988).

[Eme] E.A. Emerson: Temporal and modal logic, in J. van Leeuwen (ed.): *Handbook of theoretical computer science* B (Elsevier, 1990) 995-1072.

[HC] G.E. Hughes, M.J. Creswell: *A companion to modal logic* (Methuen, 1982).

[Har] D. Harel: Dynamic logic, in D. Gabbay, F. Guenthner (eds.): *Handbook of philosophical logic* II (Reidel, 1984) 497-604.

[Lam] L. Lamport: Time, clocks and the ordering of events in a distributed system, *Commun. ACM* **21**,7 (Jul 1978) 558-565.

[LMRT] K. Lodaya, M. Mukund, R. Ramanujam, P.S. Thiagarajan: Models and logics for true concurrency, *Sādhanā* **17**, Part 1 (Indian Academy of Sciences, Mar 1992) 131-165.

[LR] K. Lodaya, R. Ramanujam: Tense logics for local reasoning in distributed systems, *Proc. 11th FST & TCS, LNCS* **560** (1991) 71-88.

[LRT] K. Lodaya, R. Ramanujam, P.S. Thiagarajan: Temporal logics for communicating sequential agents: I, *Int. J. Found. Comput. Sci.* **3**,2 (1992) 117-159.

[MT] M. Mukund, P.S. Thiagarajan: A Petri net model of asynchronously communicating sequential processes, in R. Narasimhan (ed.): *A perspective in theoretical computer science – commemorative volume for Gift Siromoney* (World Scientific, 1989) 165-198.

[NPW] M. Nielsen, G. Plotkin, G. Winskel: Petri nets, event structures and domains I, *Theoret. Comput. Sci.* **13** (1980) 86-108.

[Pen] W. Penczek: A temporal logic for event structures, *Fund. Inform.* **XI** (1988) 297-326.

[PW] S. Pinter, P. Wolper: A temporal logic for reasoning about partially ordered computations, *Proc. 3rd ACM PODC* (1984) 28-37.

[Rab] M.O. Rabin: Decidability of second order theories and automata on infinite trees, *Trans. Amer. Math. Soc.* **141** (1969) 1-35.

[Sti] C. Stirling: Temporal logics for CCS, *Proc. REX 88, LNCS* **354** (1989) 660-672.

[VW] M. Vardi, P. Wolper: Automata theoretic techniques for modal logics of programs, *J. Comput. Syst. Sci.* **32**,2 (1986) 183-221.

Local Model Checking for Context-Free Processes

Hardi Hungar[1] and Bernhard Steffen[2]

[1] Computer Science Dept., University Oldenburg, D-2900 Oldenburg, Germany
[2] Lehrstuhl für Informatik II, RWTH Aachen, D-5100 Aachen, Germany

Abstract.
We present a local model checking algorithm that decides for a given context-free process whether it satisfies a property written in the alternation-free modal mu-calculus. Heart of this algorithm is a purely syntactical sound and complete formal system, which in contrast to the known tableau techniques, uses intermediate higher-order assertions. These assertions provide a finite representation of all the infinite state sets which may arise during the proof in terms of the finite representation of the context-free argument process. This is the key to the effectiveness of our local model checking procedure.

1 Introduction

Model-checking provides a powerful tool for the automatic verification of behavioral systems. The corresponding standard algorithms fall into two classes: the iterative algorithms (cf. [10, 5, 8, 9]) and the tableaux-based algorithms (cf., e.g. [3, 2, 6, 13, 15, 16]). Whereas the former class usually yields higher efficiency in the worst case, the latter allows *local* model checking (cf. [15]), which avoids the investigation of for the verification irrelevant parts of the process being verified. Local model checking has been exploited by Bradfield and Stirling [3, 2] in order to construct a sound and complete tableau system for the full mu-calculus [12], which can deal with *infinite* transition systems. However, in this tableau system, a purely syntactical characterization of the validity of a formula cannot always be achieved. Thus their proof method is not effective in general.

In this paper we develop a local model checking algorithm that decides the alternation-free modal mu-calculus for *context-free* processes, i.e. for processes that are given in terms of a context-free grammar, or equivalently, as mutually recursive systems of finite state-labeled transition systems. We adopt the second viewpoint in this paper, which directly leads to our notion of *procedural* transition systems. These process representations are standard finite-state labeled transition systems that are extended by introducing *recursive procedures* or, alternatively, *recursive action refinements*. The resulting processes may of course be infinite.

For this class of processes, an *iterative* model checking algorithm has already been developed in [4]. The central idea behind that algorithm is to raise the standard iterative model-checking techniques to *higher order*: in contrast to the usual approaches, in which the set of formulae that are satisfied by a certain state are iteratively computed, this algorithm iteratively computes a *property transformer* for each state class of the finite process representation. These property transformers can then simply be applied to solve the model-checking problem.

Here, we also exploit the idea of higher-order reasoning. Heart of our model checking algorithm is a purely syntactic sound and complete formal system, which in contrast to the known tableau techniques (cf. e.g. [3, 2, 6, 13, 15]), uses intermediate higher-order assertions. These assertions allow to compositionally deal with the sequential composition operator which implicitly arises in procedural transition systems: parts of the transition system, which belong to a particular procedure incarnation (expansion of a certain call transition), are sequentially composed with the part of the transition system representing the process behavior after the return from the called procedure. This is the key to the effectiveness of our local model checking procedure, because it allows the finite representation of all the infinite state sets which may arise during the proof in terms of the finite representation of the context-free argument process.

2 Processes and Formulae

In this section we introduce *process graphs* as the basic the structure for modelling behavior, and more specifically, *context-free process systems* as finite representations of infinite process graphs, as well as the (alternation-free) modal mu calculus as a logic for specification.

2.1 Context-Free Process Systems

Definition 1 [11]. A *process graph* is a quadruple $G = \langle S, Act, \rightarrow, s_0 \rangle$, where:

- S is a set of *states*;
- Act is a set of *actions*;
- $\rightarrow \subseteq S \times Act \times S$ is the *transition relation*; and
- $s_0 \in S$ is a distinguished element, the "start state".

Intuitively, a process graph encodes the operational behavior of a process. The set S represents the set of states the process may enter, Act the set of actions the process may perform and $\rightarrow$ the state transitions that may result upon execution of the actions. Unrooted process graphs, i.e. process graphs without a specified start state, are also called *labeled transition systems*.

In the remainder of the paper we use $s \xrightarrow{a} s'$ in lieu of $\langle s, a, s' \rangle \in \rightarrow$, and we call s' an *a-derivative* of s. Finally a process graph is said to be *finite-state*, when S and Act are finite.

As in [4], we represent *context-free processes*, which may have infinitely many states, by means of *context-free process systems*. A context-free process system is essentially a set of named finite process graphs whose set of actions contain the names of the system's process graphs. Transition labeled with such a name are meant to represent the denoted process graph. Thus the names of the process graphs correspond to the non-terminals and the atomic actions to the terminals of a context-free grammar. An alternative way to interpret those transitions is to think of them as *procedure calls*, where each named process graph stands for a procedure declaration.

Definition 2. A *procedural process graph* (PPG) is defined as a quintuple $P = \langle \Sigma_P, Trans, \rightarrow_P, \sigma_P^s, \sigma_P^e \rangle$, where:

595

- Σ_P is a set of *state classes*;[3]
- $Trans =_{df} Act \cup \mathcal{N}$ is a set of *transformations*,
  where Act is a set of *actions* and $\mathcal{N}$ is a set of *names*;
- $\to_P = \to_P^{Act} \cup \to_P^{\mathcal{N}}$ is the *transition relation*,
  where $\to_P^{Act} \subseteq \Sigma_P \times Act \times \Sigma_P$ and $\to_P^{\mathcal{N}} \subseteq \Sigma_P \times \mathcal{N} \times \Sigma_P$; and
- $\sigma_P^s \in \Sigma_P$ is a class of *"start states"* and $\sigma_P^e \in \Sigma_P$ is a class of *"end states"*.

Additionally a PPG P must satisfy the following three constraints:

1. The class of "start states" σ_P^s must be *initial* in P, i.e. there must not exist any $\alpha \in Trans$ and $\sigma' \in \Sigma_P$ with $\langle \sigma', \alpha, \sigma_P^s \rangle \in \to_P$;
2. The class of "end states" σ_P^e must be *terminating* in P, i.e. there must not exist any $\alpha \in Trans$ and $\sigma' \in \Sigma_P$ with $\langle \sigma_P^e, \alpha, \sigma' \rangle \in \to_P$; and
3. P must be *guarded*, i.e. all initial transitions of P must be labeled with atomic actions.

Conditions 1 and 2 guarantee that thinking of named process graphs as procedures is consistent: procedures can only be entered through the start state and left through the end state. Condition 3 avoids infinite branching.

P is called *simple*, if it does not contain any calls, or equivalently, if it is a process graph with a distinguished end state. The set of all simple PPGs is denoted by $\mathcal{G}$. Moreover a PPG P is said to be *finite* if Σ_P and $Trans$ are finite.

The definition of *context-free process systems* is now straightforward.

Definition 3. A *context-free process system* (CFPS) is defined as a quadruple $\mathcal{P} = \langle \mathcal{N}, Act, \Delta, P_0 \rangle$, where

- $\mathcal{N} = \{N_0, \ldots, N_{n-1}\}$ is a set of *names*;
- Act is a set of *actions*;
- $\Delta =_{df} \{ N_i = P_i \mid 0 \le i < n \}$ is a finite set of *PPG definitions* where the P_i are finite PPGs with names in $\mathcal{N}$ and
- P_0 is the *"main"* PPG.

The system of Figure 1 is an example of a CFPS which can not be replaced by a finite process graph. Its language is the set $\{ a^n b^n \mid n \ge 1 \}$.

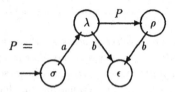

Fig. 1. A context-free process system for $a^n b^n$.

As before for process graphs, we use $\sigma \xrightarrow{\alpha} \sigma'$ instead of $\langle \sigma, \alpha, \sigma' \rangle \in \to$. – A CFPS $\mathcal{P}$ serves as a finite representation of the *complete expansion* of P_0, which is defined as follows.

[3] As will be explained, members of Σ_P represent classes or sets of states in the usual sense.

Definition 4. Let P be a PPG of a CFPS $\mathcal{P}$. The *complete expansion* of P wrt. $\mathcal{P}$ is the simple PPG which results from successively replacing in P each transition $\sigma \xrightarrow{P_i} \sigma'$ by a copy of the corresponding PPG P_i, while identifying σ with $\sigma_{P_i}^s$ and σ' with $\sigma_{P_i}^e$. We denote the complete expansion of P wrt. $\mathcal{P}$ by $Exp_{\mathcal{P}}(P)$.

Figure 2 illustrates the stepwise expansion for the system presented in Figure 1.

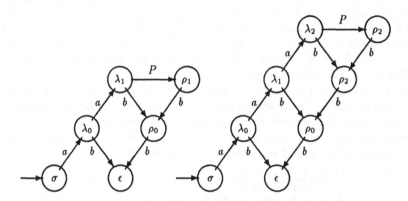

Fig. 2. First two steps of the expansion of P.

Given a state $s \in \mathcal{S}$ of a complete expansion $Exp_{\mathcal{P}}(P)$, we say that s belongs to the state class $\sigma \in \Sigma_{P_i}$ if it arose as a copy of σ during the expansion. Thus a state class stands for a possibly infinite set of states of the corresponding complete expansion.

In order to assign a unique state class to each state of the complete extension, we need to eliminate the ambiguity which results from the the identification in Definition 4 of the start and end node of a new procedure incarnation with already existing nodes. This can simply be done by defining start and end state classes as to be empty except for the main procedure, where they contain exactly one element: the global start resp. end state. In the following, given a state s of the expansion, we will denote its state class by $[s]$, and the (return) state of the expansion, which completes the procedure incarnation to which s belongs, by $end(s)$. Note that $end(s)$ does not belong to the same procedure incarnation as s, but to the surrounding one.

Finally, we introduce some notations which concern PPGs. If $P = \langle \Sigma_P, Trans, \rightarrow_P, \sigma_P^s, \sigma_P^e \rangle$ is a PPG and σ is a state class of P, then we denote with $P^{(\sigma)}$ the PPG $\langle \Sigma_P, Trans, \rightarrow_P, \sigma, \sigma_P^e \rangle$, which is essentially the PPG P, where the initial state class changed from σ_P^s to σ.[4] If P_1 and P_2 are two PPGs, then we define their sequential composition $P_1; P_2$ as the PPG

$$\langle \Sigma_{P_1} \cup \Sigma_{P_2} \setminus \{ \sigma_{P_2}^s \}, Trans_{P_1} \cup Trans_{P_2}, \rightarrow_{P_1} \cup \rightarrow_{P_2'}, \sigma_{P_1}^s, \sigma_{P_2}^e \rangle$$

where $\rightarrow_{P_2'}$ denotes the transition relation which results from substituting in $\rightarrow_{P_2}$ all occurrences of $\sigma_{P_2}^s$ by $\sigma_{P_1}^e$.

---

[4] This change may not result in a 'proper' PPG, as σ is in general not initial in $P^{(\sigma)}$. However, this does not matter, because there are no calls to $P^{(\sigma)}$.

2.2 Mu Calculus

The following negation–free syntax defines a sublanguage of the mu-calculus, which in spite of being as expressive as the full mu-calculus allows a simpler technical development.

$$\Phi ::= f\!\!f \mid t\!\!t \mid X \mid \Phi \wedge \Phi \mid \Phi \vee \Phi \mid [a]\Phi \mid \langle a\rangle\Phi \mid \nu X.\Phi \mid \mu X.\Phi$$

In the above, $a \in Act$, and $X \in Var$, where Var is a set of variables. The fixpoint operators νX and μX bind the occurrences of X in the formula behind the dot in the usual sense. Properties will be specified by *closed* formulae, i.e. formulae that do not contain any free variable. A formula is *alternation free* if no ν-subformula has a free variable which, in the context of the whole formula, is bound by a μ, and vice versa. The set of closed alternation-free formulae is denoted by $\mathcal{M}$.

There are no atoms in this calculus other than $t\!\!t$ and $f\!\!f$, in order to simplify the presentation. It is, however, straightforward to add further constants, as long as the corresponding valuations respect the partioning into state classes.

Formulae are interpreted with respect to a fixed (possibly infinite) labeled transition system $\langle S, Act, \rightarrow\rangle$, and an environment $e : Var \rightarrow 2^S$.

$$[\![X]\!]e = e(X)$$
$$[\![\Phi_1 \vee \Phi_2]\!]e = [\![\Phi_1]\!]e \cup [\![\Phi_2]\!]e$$
$$[\![\Phi_1 \wedge \Phi_2]\!]e = [\![\Phi_1]\!]e \cap [\![\Phi_2]\!]e$$
$$[\![[a]\Phi]\!]e = \{\, s \mid \forall s'.\ s \xrightarrow{a} s' \Rightarrow s' \in [\![\Phi]\!]e \,\}$$
$$[\![\langle a\rangle\Phi]\!]e = \{\, s \mid \exists s'.\ s \xrightarrow{a} s' \wedge s' \in [\![\Phi]\!]e \,\}$$
$$[\![\nu X.\Phi]\!]e = \bigcup\{S' \subseteq S \mid S' \subseteq [\![\Phi]\!]e[X \mapsto S']\}$$
$$[\![\mu X.\Phi]\!]e = \bigcap\{S' \subseteq S \mid S' \supseteq [\![\Phi]\!]e[X \mapsto S']\}$$

Intuitively, the semantic function maps a formula (with free variables) to the set of states for which the formula is "true". Accordingly, a state s satisfies X if s is an element of the set bound to X in e. A process graph satisfies a formula if its start state satisfies the formula, and a formula is valid in a context-free process system if it is valid in its complete expansion.

One way to examine the meaning of a formula is by inspecting its immediate subformulae, while repeatedly *unfolding* fixpoints. This procedure is formalized in the rules for the construction of a tableau. The set of formulae generated from some formula Φ is called the *closure* of Φ.

Definition 5. The *closure* $CL(\Phi)$ of a (closed) formula Φ is inductively defined as follows.

$$CL(\Phi_1 \vee \Phi_2) = \{\Phi_1 \vee \Phi_2\} \cup CL(\Phi_1) \cup CL(\Phi_2)$$
$$CL(\Phi_1 \wedge \Phi_2) = \{\Phi_1 \wedge \Phi_2\} \cup CL(\Phi_1) \cap CL(\Phi_2)$$
$$CL(\langle a\rangle\Phi) = \{\langle a\rangle\Phi\} \cup CL(\Phi)$$
$$CL([a]\Phi) = \{[a]\Phi\} \cup CL(\Phi)$$
$$CL(\nu X.\Phi) = \{\nu X.\Phi\} \cup CL(\Phi[\nu X.\Phi/X])$$
$$CL(\mu X.\Phi) = \{\mu X.\Phi\} \cup CL(\Phi[\mu X.\Phi/X])$$

Note that, although a fixpoint may be unfolded infinitely often, the closure of a formula (which is different from the set of subformulae, due to the unfoldings of fixpoints) is always finite.

2.3 Higher-Order Semantics

The validity of a formula is defined with respect to single states. To define the validity of a formula for a state class does not make much sense: the truth value might not be the same for different representatives (copies) of the same state class. But if two states s and s' belong to the same state class and the corresponding end states $end(s)$ and $end('s)$ satisfy the same set of formulae, then so do s and s'. This is the key observation motivating the *higher-order semantics* from [4]: It is consistent with the usual semantics to view a (named) PPG as a *property transformer*, i.e. as a system which yields the set of formulae which are valid at the start state, relative to the assumption that the set of states, to which the transformer is applied, are valid at the end state. This can be formalized as follows [4].

Definition 6. Let $P = \langle S, Act, \to_P, \sigma_P^s, \sigma_P^e \rangle$ be a simple PPG. Then we interpret P as the function $[\![P]\!] : 2^{\mathcal{M}} \longrightarrow 2^{\mathcal{M}}$ which is defined as follows.

$$[\![P]\!](M) = \{ \Phi' \in \mathcal{M} \mid \forall P' \in \mathcal{G}, \ P' \cap P = \emptyset. \ \sigma_P^e \models_{P;P'} M \implies \sigma_P^s \models_{P;P'} \Phi' \}$$

That the higher order semantics is consistent with the usual semantics of simple PPGs in terms of its valid formulae, is a consequence of the following theorem.

Theorem 7 (Consistency of Higher-Order Semantics).
Let P be a simple PPG and Φ be a closed formula. Then we have:

$$\sigma_P^s \models \Phi \qquad \Longleftrightarrow \qquad \Phi \in [\![P]\!](\mathcal{F}_{deadlock}),$$

where $\mathcal{F}_{deadlock}$ is the set of all propositions that are "true" at a "deadlocked state", i.e.:

$$\mathcal{F}_{deadlock} =_{df} \{ \Phi \mid s \models \Phi \ \ in \ \mathcal{T} = \langle \{ s \}, Act, \emptyset \rangle \}.$$

A very important fact about the higher-order semantics is the following.

Fact 8. *Let $M, M' \subseteq \mathcal{M}$ be consistent and $M \cap CL(\Phi) = M' \cap CL(\Phi)$.*
Then
$$\Phi \in [\![P]\!]M \qquad iff \qquad \Phi \in [\![P]\!]M'.$$

Thus finite parts of the higher-order semantics only depend on finite parts of the arguments. This is essential for the completeness of the tableau system (and for the effectiveness of the model checking procedure of [4]).

The extension of the higher order semantics for simple PPGs to CFPSs is now straightforward. We simply associate with each state class σ of some P_i the property transformer which is induced by the complete expansion of $P_i^{(\sigma)}$.

Definition 9. Let $\mathcal{P} = \langle \mathcal{N}, Act, \Delta, P_0 \rangle$ be a CFPS and $\sigma \in \Sigma_{P_i}$ be a state class of P_i. Then we define: $[\![\sigma]\!]^{\mathcal{P}} =_{df} [\![Exp_{\mathcal{P}}(P_i^{(\sigma)})]\!].$

Higher-order semantics will not be used formally within this paper. It merely serves as a mean to motivate the form of the assertions and the rules of the tableau system: intermediate assertions in a derivation are pairs of formulae that can be thought of to be of higher order.

Definition 10. A *higher-order assertion* is a pair $\langle \Phi, \Psi \rangle$ of (alternation-free) formulae. A *higher-order sequent* is a pair consisting of a state class and a higher-order assertion, and it is written in the form $\sigma \vdash \langle \Phi, \Psi \rangle$. Given a CFPS and a state class σ, the sequent $\sigma \vdash \langle \Phi, \Psi \rangle$ is *valid*, iff $s \in [\![\Phi]\!]$ for any copy s of σ provided that $end(s) \in [\![\Psi]\!]$. If σ is an end state class, the sequent is valid if $[\![\Phi]\!] \supseteq [\![\Psi]\!]$, i.e. if $\Psi \Rightarrow \Phi$.[5]

3 The Tableau System

One way to characterize the difference between regular and context free process is the generalization from action prefixing to the usual sequential composition, which is equivalent to the generalization from left recursion to general (parameterless) recursion in this setting. In fact, the main problem of the construction of a tableaux system for context-free processes, which directly works on a CFPS representation, is to compositionally deal with the sequential composition, which implicitly arises when dealing with CFPS: parts of the transition system, which belong to a particular procedure incarnation (expansion of a certain call transition), are sequentially composed with the part of the transition system representing the process behaviour after the return from the called procedure. The solution to this problem are the modality rules, which like the composition rule of the Hoare Calculus, require the right guess of the intermediate formula. The rest of the rules are an adaptation of the usual tableau rules (cf. eg. [13, 15, 6, 3, 2]), which organizes the verification of the intermediate formulae. Formally our tableau is given below:

Start Rule

$$P_0 \vdash \Phi$$
$$\overline{\qquad\qquad\qquad\qquad\qquad\qquad}$$
$$\sigma_{P_0}^s \vdash \langle \Phi, \Theta \rangle \quad \sigma_{P_0}^e \vdash \Theta$$

Global End Rules

$$\sigma_{P_0}^e \vdash \Phi \wedge \Psi$$
$$\overline{\qquad\qquad\qquad\qquad\qquad}$$
$$\sigma_{P_0}^e \vdash \Phi \quad \sigma_{P_0}^e \vdash \Psi$$

$$\frac{\sigma_{P_0}^e \vdash \Phi \vee \Psi}{\sigma_{P_0}^e \vdash \Phi} \qquad \frac{\sigma_{P_0}^e \vdash \Phi \vee \Psi}{\sigma_{P_0}^e \vdash \Psi}$$

$$\frac{\sigma_{P_0}^e \vdash \nu X.\Phi}{\sigma_{P_0}^e \vdash \Phi[tt/X]} \qquad \frac{\sigma_{P_0}^e \vdash \mu X.\Phi}{\sigma_{P_0}^e \vdash \Phi[ff/X]}$$

[5] Note that the start state classes of procedure definitions are empty!

Conjunction and Disjunction Rules

$$\frac{\sigma \vdash \langle \Phi \wedge \Psi, \Theta \rangle}{\sigma \vdash \langle \Phi, \Theta \rangle \quad \sigma \vdash \langle \Psi, \Theta \rangle}$$

$$\frac{\sigma \vdash \langle \Phi \vee \Psi, \Theta \rangle}{\sigma \vdash \langle \Phi, \Theta \rangle} \qquad \frac{\sigma \vdash \langle \Phi \vee \Psi, \Theta \rangle}{\sigma \vdash \langle \Psi, \Theta \rangle}$$

Modality Rules

$$\frac{\sigma \vdash \langle [a]\Phi, \Theta \rangle}{\sigma' \vdash \langle \Phi, \Theta \rangle \ \dots \ \sigma_P^s \vdash \langle [a]\Phi, \Psi \rangle \quad \sigma'' \vdash \langle \Psi, \Theta \rangle}$$

$$(\text{all } \sigma' \text{ where } \sigma \xrightarrow{a} \sigma' \text{ and all } P, \sigma'' \text{ where } \sigma \xrightarrow{P} \sigma'')$$

$$\frac{\sigma \vdash \langle \langle a \rangle \Phi, \Theta \rangle}{\sigma' \vdash \langle \Phi, \Theta \rangle} \ (\sigma \xrightarrow{a} \sigma') \qquad \frac{\sigma \vdash \langle \langle a \rangle \Phi, \Theta \rangle}{\sigma_P^s \vdash \langle \langle a \rangle \Phi, \Psi \rangle \quad \sigma'' \vdash \langle \Psi, \Theta \rangle} \ (\sigma \xrightarrow{P} \sigma'')$$

Fixpoint Rules

$$\frac{\sigma \vdash \langle \nu X.\Phi, \Theta \rangle}{\sigma \vdash \langle \Phi[\nu X.\Phi/X], \Theta \rangle} \qquad \frac{\sigma \vdash \langle \mu X.\Phi, \Theta \rangle}{\sigma \vdash \langle \Phi[\mu X.\Phi/X], \Theta \rangle}$$

Local End Rules

$$\frac{\sigma_P^e \vdash \langle \Phi, \Psi \wedge \Theta \rangle}{\sigma_P^e \vdash \langle \Phi, \Psi \rangle} \qquad \frac{\sigma_P^e \vdash \langle \Phi, \Psi \wedge \Theta \rangle}{\sigma_P^e \vdash \langle \Phi, \Theta \rangle}$$

Intuitively, $\sigma \vdash \langle \Phi, \Theta \rangle$ means that σ satisfies Φ, whenever the end node of its corresponding procedure incarnation satisfies Θ. In particular, $\sigma_{P_0}^s \vdash \langle \Phi, \Theta \rangle$ means that the start node of the CFPS satisfies Φ, i.e. $P_0 \vdash \Phi$, whenever $\sigma_{P_0}^e$ satifies Θ, i.e. whenever $\sigma_{P_0}^e \vdash \Theta$. This explains the Start Rule. Whereas the following five (unconditional) End Rules provide the mean to verify $\sigma_{P_0}^e \vdash \Theta$, all the other rules are required for the verification of $\sigma_{P_0}^s \vdash \langle \Phi, \Theta \rangle$. Here, the Conjunction and Disjunction Rules are obvious and the Local End Rules correspond to the usual Thin Rules. The remaining Modality Rules are the heart of the calculus. On their standard action transition part they are the straightforward adaptations of the rules for the usual tableau systems, and for call transitions they reflect the implicit sequential composition mentioned above: they split the proof into two parts, the part within the called procedure and the part after the return.

Definition 11 (Successful Tableaux). A finite tableau built according to this rules is *successful* if every of its leaves is successful. A leaf n is *successful* if either

- $n = \sigma_{P_0}^e \vdash tt$
- $n = \sigma \vdash \langle tt, \Theta \rangle$

- $n = \sigma_{P_0}^e \vdash [a]\Phi$
- $n = \sigma \vdash \langle[a]\Phi, \Theta\rangle$, where σ is no end node and there is no σ' s.t. $\sigma \xrightarrow{a} \sigma'$
- $n = \sigma_P^e \vdash \langle\Theta, \Theta\rangle$, or
- $n = \sigma \vdash \langle\Phi(\nu X.\Psi), \Theta\rangle$, where $\Phi(\nu X.\Psi) \in CL(\nu X.\Psi)$ and there is a node on the path from the root of the tableau to n labelled with the same sequent.

A formula Φ is *derivable* for a CFPS $\mathcal{P}$ if there is a successful tableau for $P_0 \vdash \Phi$.

Whereas the correctness of the first five conditions is rather obvious, the last condition is a generalization of the usual condition for ν-success. Note that for $\Phi(\nu X.\Psi)$ to reappear in the derivation, a maximal fixpoint subformula must have been unfolded. An example for a successful tableau is given in Figure 3, where M abbreviates $\mu Y.[b]Y$ and N stands for $\nu X.([a,b]X \wedge M)$. It establishes that no infinite b-sequences are possible in the CFPS of Figure 1.

In the remainder of the paper we are going to show that the construction of successful tableaux is an effective, sound and complete verification method for context–free processes. The only other system dealing with infinite models is Bradfield's system of [2], which we will call the B-system. This system is more general than ours, because it applies to the full mu-calculus, which requires the introduction of propositional constants, and to arbitrary transitions systems, which leads to an intricate, semantics-based notion of successful tableau. Our restriction to context–free processes and alternation–free formulae avoids propositional constants and the intricate definition of μ-success on the price of a slightly more complicated definition of ν-success.

Instead of giving a formal proof for the soundness of our tableau system here, we will informally present the relevant arguments. First note that all rules are backwards sound, i.e. if the sequents below the line are valid, then so is the sequent above the line.[6] Thus, if a sequent at the top of a tableau is false, then one of the leaves must also be false. Moreover, except for the ν-success leaves, all successful leaves are obviously true. In order to justify our generous condition for ν-success, we will only argue here that a similarly generous condition can be added to the B-system without changing the set of derivable assertions. This can be done by providing a simple transformation of a "generous" tableau into a tableau of the B-system: Whenever a formula recurs on a path of the "generous" tableau, then one of its topmost fixpoint subformulae must have been unfolded. Thus, starting at the recurring leaves, we can simply redo part of the derivation until we reach the point where the unfolded fixpoint subformula recurs. The new leaves of the resulting tableau are now guaranteed to satisfy the usual condition of ν-success. The iterative application of this transformation yields a tableau of the B-system. – A formal soundness proof will be given in the full version of the paper.

Theorem 12 (Soundness). *Every derivable sequent is valid.*

---

[6] There is a subtlety here: strictly speaking, for the modality rules this is not true, because σ_P^e is the empty set if $P \neq P_0$. But since the assertion starts with a modal operator, it can consistently be viewed as an assertion about the following state classes. Reformulating the rules accordingly would also be a way to cope with this anomaly.

$$P \vdash N$$

$$\cfrac{}{\epsilon \vdash N \wedge M} \qquad \cfrac{\sigma \vdash \langle N, N \wedge M \rangle}{}$$

$$T_\epsilon \qquad \sigma \vdash \langle [a,b]N \wedge M, N \wedge M \rangle$$

$$\sigma \vdash \langle [a,b]N, N \wedge M \rangle \qquad \sigma \vdash \langle M, N \wedge M \rangle$$

$$\bullet\, \lambda \vdash \langle N, N \wedge M \rangle \qquad \sigma \vdash \langle [b]M, N \wedge M \rangle$$

$$\lambda \vdash \langle [a,b]N \wedge M, N \wedge M \rangle$$

$$\lambda \vdash \langle [a,b]N, N \wedge M \rangle \qquad\qquad \lambda \vdash \langle M, N \wedge M \rangle$$

$$\sigma \vdash \langle [a,b]N, N \wedge M \rangle \qquad \rho \vdash \langle N \wedge M, N \wedge M \rangle \qquad \epsilon \vdash \langle N, N \wedge M \rangle \qquad T_\lambda$$

$$\lambda \vdash \langle N, N \wedge M \rangle \hookrightarrow \bullet \qquad\qquad T_\rho \qquad\qquad \epsilon \vdash \langle N, N \rangle$$

$$T_\epsilon = \cfrac{}{\epsilon \vdash N \wedge M}$$

$$\cfrac{\epsilon \vdash N}{\epsilon \vdash [a,b]tt \wedge M} \qquad \cfrac{\epsilon \vdash M}{\epsilon \vdash [b]\!f\!f}$$

$$\epsilon \vdash [a,b]tt \qquad \epsilon \vdash M$$

$$\epsilon \vdash [b]\!f\!f$$

$$T_\rho = \cfrac{}{\rho \vdash \langle N \wedge M, N \wedge M \rangle}$$

$$\rho \vdash \langle N, N \wedge M \rangle \qquad\qquad \rho \vdash \langle M, N \wedge M \rangle$$

$$\rho \vdash \langle [a,b]N \wedge M, N \wedge M \rangle \qquad \rho \vdash \langle [b]M, N \wedge M \rangle$$

$$\rho \vdash \langle [a,b]N, N \wedge M \rangle \qquad \rho \vdash \langle M, N \wedge M \rangle \qquad \epsilon \vdash \langle M, N \wedge M \rangle$$

$$\epsilon \vdash \langle N, N \wedge M \rangle \qquad \rho \vdash \langle [b]M, N \wedge M \rangle \qquad \epsilon \vdash \langle M, M \rangle$$

$$\epsilon \vdash \langle N, N \rangle \qquad \epsilon \vdash \langle M, N \wedge M \rangle$$

$$\epsilon \vdash \langle M, M \rangle$$

$$T_\lambda = \cfrac{}{\lambda \vdash \langle M, N \wedge M \rangle}$$

$$\lambda \vdash \langle [b]M, N \wedge M \rangle$$

$$\epsilon \vdash \langle M, N \wedge M \rangle \qquad \sigma \vdash \langle [b]M, tt \rangle \qquad \rho \vdash \langle tt, N \wedge M \rangle$$

$$\epsilon \vdash \langle M, M \rangle$$

Fig. 3. Eample tableau for the CFPS of Figure 1.

Due to the presence of fixpoint formulae proving our tableau system complete is highly complicated. We will therefore start by motivating and explaining two special features of our system, the necessity of the generous ν-success and the (apparent) absence of the μ-success.

The generous condition for ν-success is required, because in our tableaux, the sequent with a ν-formula Φ is not guaranteed to recur on every path, whereas a sequent with some element of its closure (where Φ is a subformula) must recur. The reason for this is that Φ itself might only appear within a procedure, infinitely often at the side of the derivation path. Since any assertion about an end state class is a leaf in the tableau, there would be no path connecting two such occurences. But in such a situation, the first component of the assertion about the start state class, which will recur, would be some $\Psi \in CL(\Phi)$ containing Φ as a subformula, as required by the recurrence condition. An example for this situation is given in Figure 4. The sequent marked with $\bullet$ recurs, and there is no way to get around this sequent recurring by means of the recurrence of a ν-formula.

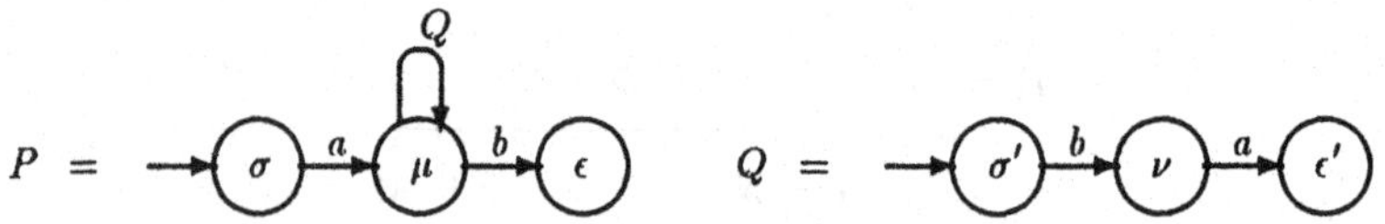

$$P = \quad \xrightarrow{} (\sigma) \xrightarrow{a} (\mu) \overset{Q}{\circlearrowleft} \xrightarrow{b} (\epsilon) \qquad\qquad Q = \quad \xrightarrow{} (\sigma') \xrightarrow{b} (\nu) \xrightarrow{a} (\epsilon')$$

$$\cfrac{\cfrac{\cfrac{P \vdash \nu X.\,[a][b]X}{\sigma \vdash \langle \nu X.\,[a][b]X,\ \nu X.\,[a][b]X \rangle}}{\cfrac{\sigma \vdash \langle [a][b]\nu X.\,[a][b]X,\ \nu X.\,[a][b]X \rangle}{\bullet\ \mu \vdash \langle [b]\nu X.\,[a][b]X,\ \nu X.\,[a][b]X \rangle}} \qquad \cfrac{\epsilon \vdash \nu X.\,[a][b]X}{\epsilon \vdash [a][b]tt}}{}$$

$$\epsilon \vdash \langle \nu X.\,[a][b]X,\ \nu X.\,[a][b]X \rangle \qquad\qquad T \qquad\qquad \bullet\ \mu \vdash \langle [b]\nu X.\,[a][b]X,\ \nu X.\,[a][b]X \rangle$$

$$\cdots$$

where T is the following (successful) tableau:

$$T = \cfrac{\cfrac{\cfrac{\sigma' \vdash \langle [b]\nu X.\,[a][b]X,\ [b]\nu X.\,[a][b]X \rangle}{\nu \vdash \langle \nu X.\,[a][b]X,\ [b]\nu X.\,[a][b]X \rangle}}{\nu \vdash \langle [a][b]\nu X.\,[a][b]X \rangle,\ [b]\nu X.\,[a][b]X}}{\epsilon' \vdash \langle [b]\nu X.\,[a][b]X,\ [b]\nu X.\,[a][b]X \rangle}$$

Fig. 4. An example for the necessity of a more general recurrence rule for ν-formulae

Our system does not require an explicit μ-success, although we deal with an infinite state space. Suppose we try to prove the validity of a μ-formula for a state class and within the tableau, the same sequent appears again. In the B-system, this may mean success, depending on whether the following order is well-founded: $s \sqsubseteq s'$ iff s being in the first sequent is the reason for s' being in the second. (Intuitively, the formula is valid because for the minimal elements w.r.t. this ordering, a successful tableau must contain another argument why they satisfy the formula). In a similar situation with our system, the order is never well-founded, because the two states belong to the same state class: Either s and s' are in the same copy of the named process graph, then $s = s'$ (introducing a cycle), or s' is in a later copy, but then the copying can be repeated infinitely often. The order would only be well-founded, if s' were in an earlier copy. But then, there is no path in our tableau: The path would have to go through some node with an assertion about $[end(s)]$, and such nodes are leaves in our tableaux. Therefore, a sequent with a μ-formula does not recur explicitly in a successful tableau. The safe recurrence of μ-formulae is hidden.

The tableaux constructed in the completeness proof are built around sequents $\sigma \vdash \langle \Psi, \Theta \rangle$ of a very specific form: Θ is the conjunction of $\{\Theta_1, \ldots, \Theta_k\} =_{df} \{\Gamma \in CL(\Psi) \mid end(s) \models \Gamma\}$ for some s out of σ, .i.e the conjunction of *all* subformulae valid at the corresponding end state. This 'completeness' is essential for the success of the tableau construction procedure.

Let us illustrate this by means of an example. If σ is a state class of which the corresponding end state class is an a-derivative, the sequent $\sigma \vdash \langle \langle a \rangle \Phi \vee \langle a \rangle \Psi, \Phi \vee \Psi \rangle$ is valid but not derivable. However, this sequent violates the specific form, as any state which satisfies $\Phi \vee \Psi$ satisfies one of the disjuncts. In our setting, Φ or Ψ must be a conjunct of the second component, which guarantees the successful application of the Disjunction Rule. Fact 8 provides the argument for the general case.

Theorem 13 (Completeness). *For every CFPS $\mathcal{P}$ and every $\Phi \in \mathcal{M}$ with $P_0 \vdash \Phi$ there is a successful tableau.*

The number of state classes and the closure of a formula Φ are finite. Thus only a finite number of sequents and a finite number of intermediate formulae need to be considered during the construction of a tableau, which yields:

Theorem 14 (Effectiveness). *The tableau system provides an effective model checking procedure for context-free processes and alternation-free formulae.*

4 Conclusions and Future Work

We have presented a local model checking algorithm that decides the alternation-free modal mu-calculus for *context-free* processes. Heart of this algorithm is a purely syntactic sound and complete formal system, which in contrast to the known tableau techniques, uses intermediate higher-order assertions. These assertions provide a finite representation of all the infinite state sets which may arise during the proof in terms of the finite representation of the context-free argument process. This finiteness is the key to the effectiveness of our local model checking procedure.

Currently we are looking at two elaborations of our proof method. First, a modification to improve the worst-case time complexity along the lines of [1, 14]: by keeping track of intermediate results it should be straightforward to almost arrive at the worst case time complexity of the iterative algorithm of [4]. Second, an extension to deal with the full modal mu-calculus. One problem with this is to find the right condition for ν-success. Just introducing propositional constants (as in [15]) will not suffice: remember that a different success condition is already needed for the alternation-free mu-calculus. – Our algorithm is going to be implemented as part of the Concurrency Workbench [7].

Acknowledgements: We thank Olaf Burkart and Colin Stirling for discussions and comments on previous versions of this paper.

References

1. Andersen, H., *Model checking on boolean graphs.* ESOP '92, LNCS 582 (1992), 1-19.
2. Bradfield, J.C., *Verifying temporal properties of systems.* Birkhäuser, Boston (1992).
3. Bradfield, J.C., and Stirling, C. P., *Verifying temporal properties of processes.* Proc. CONCUR '90, LNCS 458 (1990), 115-125.
4. Burkart, O., and Steffen, B., *Model checking for context-free processes.* CONCUR '92, LNCS 630 (1992), 123-137.
5. Clarke, E.M., Emerson, E.A., and Sistla, A.P., *Automatic verification of finite state concurrent systems using temporal logic specifications.* ACM TOPLAS 8 (1986), 244-263.
6. Cleaveland, R., *Tableau-based model checking in the propositional mu-calculus.* Acta Inf. 27 (1990), 725-747.
7. Cleaveland, R., Parrow, J., and Steffen, B., *The concurrency workbench.* Workshop Automatic Verification Methods for Finite-State Systems, LNCS 407 (1989), 24-37.
8. Cleaveland, R., and Steffen, B., *Computing behavioral relations, logically.* ICALP '91, LNCS 510 (1991).
9. Cleaveland, R., and Steffen, B., *A linear-time model-checking algorithm for the alternation-free modal mu-calculus.* CAV 91, LNCS 575 (1992), 48-58.
10. Emerson, E.A., and Lei, C.-L., *Efficient model checking in fragments of the propositional mu-calculus.* 1st LiCS (1986), 267-278.
11. Huynh, D.T., and Tian, L., *Deciding bisimilarity of normed context-free processes is in* Σ_2^p. Tech. Rep. UTDCS-1-92, Univ. Texas Dallas (1992).
12. Kozen, D., *Results on the propositional μ-calculus.* TCS 27 (1983), 333-354.
13. Larsen, K. G., *Proof systems for satisfiability in Hennessy-Milner logic with recursion.* TCS 72 (1990), 265-288.
14. Larsen, K.G., *Efficient local correctness checking.* CAV '92.
15. Stirling, C. P., and Walker, D. J., *Local model checking in the modal mu-calculus.* TAPSOFT '89, LNCS 351 (1989), 369-383.
16. Winskel, G., *A note on model checking the modal mu-calculus.* ICALP '89, LNCS 372 (1989), 761-772.

Computing on Structures

Serge Abiteboul[1] and Victor Vianu[2]

[1] INRIA, BP 105, 78153 Le Chesnay CEDEX, France
email: abitebou@inria.inria.fr
[2] CSE C-0114, UC San Diego, La Jolla, CA 92093, USA
email: vianu@cs.ucsd.edu

1 Introduction

One of the exciting recent developments in complexity theory is the discovery of
a very intimate connection between computational complexity and logic. This intimate connection was first discovered by Fagin, who showed that the complexity
class NP coincides with the class of properties expressible in existential 2nd-order
logic [Fag74] (cf. [JS74]). Another demonstration of this connection was given by
Immerman and Vardi, who discovered tight relationships between the complexity
class P and inflationary fixpoint logic [Imm86, Var82] and between the class PSPACE
and noninflationary fixpoint logic [Var82]. This initiated, during the 1980s, a new
branch of complexity theory, which focuses on the *descriptive complexity* of problems,
i.e. the complexity of describing problems in some logical formalism [Imm87b].

The tight connection between descriptive and computational complexity, typically referred to as the connection between "logic and complexity", was then pro-
claimed by Immerman [Imm87a], and studied by many researchers[3].

Although the relationship between descriptive and computational complexity is
intimate, it is not without its problems, and the partners do have some irreconcilable
differences. While computational devices work on *encodings* of problems, logic is
applied directly to the underlying mathematical structures. As a result, machines
are able to enumerate objects that are logically unordered. For example, while we
typically think of the set of nodes in a graph as unordered, it does become ordered
when it is encoded on the tape of a Turing machine. This "impedance mismatch"
does not pose any difficulty in the identification of NP with existential 2nd-order
logic (in [Fag74]), since the logic can simply assert the existence of the desired order.
The mismatch with logic becomes apparent, however, at complexity classes below
NP. For example, the relationship between the class P and inflationary fixpoint logic
is more complicated as a result of the mismatch. Although inflationary fixpoint logic
can describe P-complete problems, there are some very easy problems in P that are
not expressible in inflationary fixpoint logic (e.g., checking whether the cardinality
of the structure is even [CH82]). It is only when we assume built-in order that we
get that P coincides with the class of properties expressible in inflationary fixpoint
logic [Imm86, Var82]. Similarly, it is only when we assume a built-in order that we
get that PSPACE coincides with the class of properties expressible in noninflationary
fixpoint logic [Var82].

---

[3] The focus here is on the connection between finite-model theory and complexity. The
connection between logic and complexity has also a proof-theoretic aspect; see [Bus86,
GSS90, Lei91] and [Imm89] for a survey.

We shall present in this paper various devices operating directly on structures (without encoding). The motivation and benefits for doing this are manyfold. On a fundamental level, encodings of structures seem to be a technical device rather than an intrinsic feature. This point has already been made by several mathematicians such as Tarski [Tar86] or Harvey Friedman [Fri71] (see Section 5). It has only come up more recently in the context of databases, where devices computing on structures model more acurately database computation carried out against an abstract interface hiding the internal representation of data. Thus, the primary benefit of studying devices and languages computing on structures is that they clarify issues which are somewhat obscured in classical devices such as Turing machines. For example, they yield new notions of complexity, quite different from classical computational complexity. These new notions reflect more acurately the actual complexity of computation, which, like database computation, cannot take advantage of encodings of structures.

A related reason for studying devices operating on structures is that this seems a natural way to eliminate the "impedance mismatch" between logic, operating on structures, and devices operating on encodings of structures. Indeed, the investigation of devices computing on structures yields an order-free correspondence between some *classical* questions in computational and descriptive complexity. This order-free correspondence is obtained via the new devices, which act as a mediator between logic and classical devices. A typical result of this type is that *fixpoint* is strictly included in *while* iff P is strictly included in PSPACE [AV91]. Similarly, we present logical analogs of all inclusions between the complexity classes from P to EXPTIME, in terms of various fixpoint logics. Such results are consequences of a powerful normal form for several languages and devices, which provides a bridge between computation without order and computation with order. The removal of the order assumption is technically significant because questions about logical expressiveness over ordered structures are typically much harder than their unordered counterparts; see for example [dR84].

We focus in this paper on the *relational machine* of [AV91, AV91c, AVV92a, AVV92b], and the *generic machine* of [AV91]. Section 5 discusses briefly various ancestors and cousins of these devices from [CH80, Cha81, CH82, Fri71, Lei89a].

2 FO, fixpoint, and while

We review informally three languages which play a central role in our discussion: *FO*, *fixpoint*, and *while*. To begin, we recall some terminology and notation of relational databases [Ull88, Kan91]. This is interchangeable with the closely analogous terminology of logic and finite model theory.

A *database schema* S is a finite set of predicates of fixed arity (denoted $P, Q, R, ...$). A *relational database* over S is a finite structure over the predicates in S. A query φ is a mapping from finite structures over an *input* schema to finite structures of the same domain (i.e., the same set of elements as the input) over an *output* schema. The mapping must be computable and *generic*: for each automorphism ν of an input $\mathbf{I}$, $\varphi(\nu(\mathbf{I})) = \nu(\varphi(\mathbf{I}))$. A query language or computing device is called *complete* if it expresses exactly all queries. Complexity classes of queries are defined based on

608

Turing complexity in the classical fashion. For example, the P class consists of all queries φ such that there is a TM which, given on the tape a standard encoding $enc(I)$ of an input I, produces a standard encoding of $\varphi(I)$, in time polynomial in $|enc(I)|$.

Most database query languages are based on extensions of first-order logic without function symbols (FO). Many of these extensions converge around two central classes of queries: the *fixpoint* queries and the *while* queries. We briefly present the languages FO, *fixpoint*, and *while*.

The FO formulas over predicate symbols $\{R_1, ..., R_n\}$ are built from atomic formulas $R_i(x_1, ..., x_m)$ (R_i of arity m) and equality $x = y$ using the standard connectives $\vee, \wedge, \neg$ and quantifiers $\exists, \forall$. The semantics is also standard. Codd introduced a many-sorted algebraïzation of FO called relational algebra that we denote here $\mathcal{A}$ (see [Ull88]) which involves π (projection), $\times$ (cross product), $\cup$ (set union), $-$ (set difference), and $\sigma_{i=j}$ (select from a relation the tuples where the i-th and j-th co-ordinates are equal). It is also important to note that FO is in (uniform) AC_0 [Imm87a], so FO queries can be evaluated in constant parallel time with polynomial resources.

The *fixpoint queries* (*fixpoint*, also FP) [CH82] are constructed using the first-order constructors as in FO together with a fixpoint operator (μ). The fixpoint operator binds a predicate symbol R that is free and that appears only positively (i.e., under an even number of negations) in the formula. The semantics is given by the least fixpoint of the formula.

The *while* language [Cha81, CH82] also provides an inductive definition of relations up to a fixpoint. $\mathcal{A}$ is extended with (i) sorted relational variables $(X, Y, ...)$, (ii) assignment of FO queries to variables, and (iii) a *while* construct allowing to iterate a program while some first-order condition (e.g., $X = \emptyset$) holds[4].

We will see that the same expressive power as FP can be achieved using an *inflationary fixpoint logic* (IFP) [GS86], where the iteration of the formula is cumulative, so converges even if the formula is not monotonic in the bound predicate. Also, *while* is equivalent to *noninflationary fixpoint logic* (NFP) [AV89]. The operator NFP iterates an arbitrary FO formula up to a fixpoint, which may or may not exist. Therefore, it is only partially defined.

We are concerned with the expressive power and complexity of languages like *fixpoint* and *while*. These turn out to depend in an essential way on assumptions on the database, such as the presence or absence of a total order on the domain. A database is said to be *ordered* if one particular binary relation *succ* provides a successor relation on the elements of the domain. With such an order, *fixpoint* expresses exactly P [Imm86, Var82] and *while* expresses precisely PSPACE [Var82]. On the other hand, both languages collapse to FO on sets, i.e. the set of queries they express on inputs consisting of unordered sets coincides with the FO queries on such inputs. This shows, in particular, that *while* cannot compute many "simple" queries such as the *even* query on a set.

A normal form for *while* provides a bridge between computation without order and computation with order. It says, intuitively, that each *while* computation over

---

[4] One could define a *cumulative while* using cumulative assignment. The language thereby obtained has exactly the expressive power of *fixpoint*.

an unordered domain can be reduced to a *while* computation over an *ordered* domain via a *fixpoint* query. More precisely, a *while* program in the normal form consists of two phases. The first is a *fixpoint* query which performs an analysis of the input. It computes an equivalence relation on tuples which is a congruence with respect to the rest of the computation, in that equivalent tuples are treated identically throughout the computation. Thus, each equivalence class is treated as an indivisible "block" of tuples, which is never split later in the computation. The *fixpoint* query outputs these equivalence classes in some order, so that each class can then be thought of abstractly as an integer. The second phase consists of a *while* query which can be viewed as computing on an *ordered* database obtained by replacing each equivalence class produced in the analysis phase by its corresponding integer. The result that *fixpoint* = *while* iff P = PSPACE is a direct consequence of this normal form. We will come back to this and similar results in Section 3.3.

The *while* queries, and indeed most query languages, are characterized by the fact that they manipulate the input using some finite set of FO queries. The first device (computing on structures) that we consider, called "relational machine", models precisely this type of computation.

3 Relational Machines

The *relational machine (RM)* [AV91, AV91c, AVV92a] extends the *while* queries in the following way. The *while* queries can be viewed as the result of coupling a finite set of FO queries with a finite-state control. In relational machines, the finite-state control of *while* is extended to a computationally complete device. It consists of a Turing Machine (TM) augmented with a finite set of fixed-arity relations forming a *relational store*. We describe it next.

3.1 Description and normal form

The machine works as follows. The input is given in designated relations of the store, and the result is computed in designated output relations. The tape of the machine is a work tape and is initially empty. In addition to changing its internal state, moving the head on the tape and writing on the tape, the machine can check whether the store satisfies some FO condition, and assign to a relation the result of an FO query on the store. An RM has *arity* k if all relations in the store have arity at most k and the maximum number of variables in its FO queries is at most k.

Thus, the relational machine provides arbitrary computation interacting with the database by FO queries posed against an abstract interface (the relational store). This models accurately database application programs, which often use a FO relational language (say, SQL) embedded in a full programming language (say, C). The TM part of our machine models the use of C, whereas the FO queries on the relational store correspond to the SQL queries.

Since a relational machine has a TM component, it can perform arbitrarily complex computations on the tape. Thus the relational machines are complete for ordered inputs. However, it is not complete in general. Indeed, it cannot compute *even*, and in fact collapses to FO on sets. This wide variation in expressive power generalizes the situation for the *while* language and has similar causes. Like *while*, the relational machine interacts with the databases via a finite set of *FO* queries, which limits its ability to distinguish among tuples in the input. Essentially, relational machine can perform *any* computation on equivalence classes of tuples it can distinguish. As for *while*, the information about these equivalence classes can be computed by a *fixpoint* query.

This yields a generalization of the normal form for *while* to relational machine, which essentially says that any relational machine computation can be reduced to a relational machine computation over an ordered input via a *fixpoint* query. More precisely, for each relational machine M, there exists an equivalent machine which works in four phases. The first phase is equivalent to a *fixpoint* query which performs the analysis of the input exactly like for *while*. In the second phase, the result of the analysis is coded on the tape using the integers representing the equivalence classes. (This is done in P.) Next, the computation is carried out exclusively on the tape. The content of a relation is represented at all times by a sequence of integers representing the equivalence classes it contains. Lastly, if the simulation halts, the representation of the result (a sequence of integers) is decoded from the tape into the output relations. This last phase is done in P and is not needed if the machine is an acceptor.

3.2 Robustness

A particularly appealing feature of relational machines is their robustness. First, RM is equivalent to an extension of the while language with integer arithmetic. Let $while_N$ [Cha81, CH82] be the *while* language augmented with (i) integer variables $i, j, ...$, initialized to zero; (ii) *increment*(i) and *decrement*(i) statements; and (iii) tests of the form $i = 0$ in termination conditions of loops. From the equivalence between TM's and counter machines, it is is immediate that RM is equivalent to $while_N$.

It is also possible to extend relational machines with more flexible interfaces to the relational store without changing the expressive power. One such extension allows dynamic generation of queries. That is, one can add a "query tape" to the machine. The machine can generate dynamically (encodings of) *FO* queries (using a bounded number of variables) on the query tape. The machine can request at any time the application of the query on the tape against the relational store, and use it either as a test in the control or to assign the result to a relation in the store. An orthogonal extension allows addressable relations, i.e. the relational store has a variable, unbounded number of relations of bounded arity. Neither extension affects expressive power.

Finally, there is a natural correspondence between RM and infinitary logic. Infinitary logic with finitely many variables (denoted $L^\omega_{\infty\omega}$) (see [Ba77]) is first-order logic (*FO*) extended by allowing disjunctions and conjunctions of infinite sets of formulas. Although it generally has non-effective syntax, and can define non-computable queries, $L^\omega_{\infty\omega}$ subsumes most query languages and thus provides an elegant unifying formalism [ACY91, KV90b]. It is easy to see that RM is also subsumed by $L^\omega_{\infty\omega}$. Moreover, RM corresponds *precisely* to the natural effective fragment of $L^\omega_{\infty\omega}$, which we describe next.

We define a semantic notion of recursively enumerable (r.e.) formula. The notion of r.e. requires the set of models of the sentence to be r.e. More precisely, a set S of finite structures over some schema σ is *recursively enumerable* (r.e.) if there exists a recursive enumeration $\mathbf{I}_1, ..., \mathbf{I}_i, ...$ of structures over σ such that $\mathbf{I}$ is in S iff some structure isomorphic to $\mathbf{I}$ belongs to the enumeration.

The main result on the connection between RM and $L^\omega_{\infty\omega}$-formulas whose sets of models are r.e. is the following (note that this also yields a syntactic normal form for such formulas). Let S be a set of finite structures over some fixed schema. The following are equivalent:

(i) S is accepted by some relational machine;

(ii) $S = models(\varphi)$ for some $\varphi \in L^\omega_{\infty\omega}$ and S is r.e.;

(iii) For some k, $S = models(\bigvee A)$, for some recursive set A of FO sentences using k variables[5].

The connection between relational machines and $L^\omega_{\infty\omega}$ is developed in [AVV92b]. It is also important to note that it yields a characterization of the discerning power of relational machines in terms of certain infinite 2-player pebble games, which we outline next.

The *k-pebble game* between the Spoiler and the Duplicator on the l-tuples ($l \leq k$) $\mathbf{u}$ and $\mathbf{v}$ of a structure $\mathbf{I}$ has the following rules. Each of the players has k pebbles, say $p_1, ..., p_k$ and $q_1, ..., q_k$, respectively. The game starts with the Spoiler choosing one of the tuples $\mathbf{u}$ or $\mathbf{v}$, placing $p_1, ..., p_l$ on the elements of the chosen tuple (i.e., on $u_1, ..., u_l$ or $v_1, ..., v_l$), and placing the pebbles $p_{l+1}, ..., p_k$ on some elements of $\mathbf{I}$. The Duplicator responds by placing the pebbles $q_1, ..., q_l$ on the elements of the other tuple, and placing the pebbles $q_{l+1}, ..., q_k$ on some elements of $\mathbf{I}$. In each following round of the game, the Spoiler moves some pebble p_i (or q_i) to another element of $\mathbf{I}$, and the Duplicator responds by moving the corresponding pebble q_i (or p_i).

Let a_i (resp., b_i), $1 \leq i \leq k$, be the elements of $\mathbf{I}$ under the pebbles p_i (resp., q_i), $1 \leq i \leq k$, at the end of a round of the game. If the mapping h with $h(a_i) = b_i$, $1 \leq i \leq k$, is not an isomorphism between the substructures of $\mathbf{I}$ with universes $\{a_1, ..., a_k\}$ and $\{b_1, ..., b_k\}$ respectively, then the Spoiler wins the game. The Duplicator wins the game if he can continue playing "forever", i.e. if the Spoiler can never win the game.

If the Duplicator wins the k-pebble game on the tuple $\mathbf{u}$ and $\mathbf{v}$ of a structure $\mathbf{I}$, then we say that $\mathbf{u}$ and $\mathbf{v}$ are k-equivalent, denoted $\mathbf{u} \equiv_k \mathbf{v}$, over $\mathbf{I}$. The relation $\equiv_k$ characterizes the discerning power of k-ary relational machines: The tuples $\mathbf{u}$ and $\mathbf{v}$ are k-equivalent over a structure $\mathbf{I}$ if and only if no k-ary relational machine M can discern between $\mathbf{u}$ and $\mathbf{v}$ over $\mathbf{I}$.

The results on the robustness of RM allow to identify the factors that have essential impact on its expressive power. Thus, it is clear that the limit on the arity of the relations in the store, and on the number of variables in FO formulas used to manipulate it, are determining factors. In contrast, expressive power is insensitive to

---

[5] We note that the normal form provided by (iii) can be viewed as the effective counterpart of a similar result shown for the full $L^k_{\infty\omega}$ in [KV92]. It is also shown in [KV92] that every formula of $L^k_{\infty\omega}$ is equivalent to a countable disjunction of FO^l-formulas, for some $l \geq k$. Furthermore, it follows from [DLW91] that this holds also for $l = k$.

variations such as whether the number of relations in the store is fixed or variable, and whether the set of FO queries used is fixed or generated dynamically.

3.3 Relational Complexity

As seen above, relational machines subsume a wide variety of query languages. We would like to use RM to gain better understanding of the complexity of queries expressed in such languages. This can be done by studying complexity classes for RM, defined by the amount of resources (space, time) required in RM computations on given inputs. However, the definition poses an interesting problem. Recall that for classical devices, like TM, the measure of the input is its size. For relational machines, the size of the input (as for TM) is not an appropriate measure for relational machines. This is because, unlike Turing machines, relational machines have limited access to their input, and in particular cannot generally compute its size.

The discerning power of k-ary RM was captured by the equivalence relation $\equiv_k$. Indeed, recall that $\mathbf{u} \equiv_k \mathbf{v}$ iff $\mathbf{u}$ and $\mathbf{v}$ are not distinguished by any RM of arity k; and computations of k-ary relational machines are determined by the k-equivalence classes. Intuitively, relational machines are complete on the equivalence classes of tuples they can distinguish. This is best understood by looking at the extremes. As shown in [AV91], relational machines are complete on ordered inputs (where all distinct tuples can be distinguished from each other), but they collapse to first-order logic on unordered sets (where the number of k-equivalence classes is bounded by a constant independent on the size of the input). Thus, it seems natural to measure the input size with respect to $\equiv_k$.

Let the k-size of a structure I, denoted $size_k(\mathrm{I})$, be the number of $\equiv_k$-classes of k-tuples over I. As in [AV91, AV91c], we propose to measure the time or space complexity of k-ary relational machines as a function of the k-size of their input. This measure, however, can reasonably serve as a basis for measuring complexity only if it can be calculated by relational machines. The techniques of [AV91, AV91c] can now be used to show that relational machines *can* measure[6] k-size.

From now on we measure the complexity of k-ary relational machines in terms of the k-size of their input. For instance, we can define the relational complexity class P_r (relational polynomial time), $\mathrm{NPSPACE}_r$, etc. We already know the effective enumerability of these classes. (Note that, in contrast, it is not clear how to get effective enumerability if we define relational complexity in terms of the actual size of the input.)

Let C denote a Turing complexity classes and C_r denotes the analog relational complexity class. All complexity classes considered here include P. It is easily seen that, for C at least P, $C_r \subset C$. Note that, a priori, known relationships between deterministic, nondeterministic, and alternating complexity classes, such as PSPACE $=$ NPSPACE $=$ APTIME, need not hold for relational complexity classes, since these relationships are typically the result of simulations that use order. However, the normal form for RM allows to prove the following: For each complexity classes C, C' containing P, $C = C'$ iff $C_r = C'_r$.

---

[6] An alternate proof of the result, which makes an explicit connection with the pebble games, was recently given in [DLW91].

3.4 Relational complexity and fixpoint logics

A measure of the naturalness of relational complexity is that, as will be shown in this section, there is a seemless match between relational complexity and various fixpoint logics. We begin by defining several such logics.

We already considered inflationary fixpoint logic IFP. A more powerful logic results if one iterates general 1st-order operators, until a fixpoint is reached (which may never happen). In this case we may have non-terminating computations, unlike inflationary fixpoint logic, where the iteration was guaranteed to converge. Noninflationary fixpoint logic (NFP) coincides with the query language *while* and thus captures the complexity class PSPACE.

IFP and NFP are obtained by iterating inflationary and noninflationary 1st-order operators, respectively. In both cases, the iteration is sequential and deterministic. Certain problems, however, seem to defy description by such iterations (e.g., nonuniversality of finite automata over a binary alphabet). One can consider a *nondeterministic iteration* of 1st-order operators. *Nondeterministic fixpoint logics* are obtained by augmenting 1st-order logic with the nondeterministic (inflationary and noninflationary) fixpoint formation rules, under the restriction that negation cannot be applied to nondeterministic fixpoints[7].

Another type of fixpoint logic is obtained by allowing alternation in the control of the iteration. This yields alternating fixpoint logics. Let Φ and Ψ be 1st-order operators. This pair of operators generates *convergent trees* of stages that are obtained by successively applying, till convergence is reached, either one of Φ and Ψ or both of Φ and Ψ. (See [AVV92a] for more motivation on the fixpoint logics.)

The discussion so far shows that fixpoint logics can be parameterized along two dimensions: the power of their iteration construct, deterministic vs. nondeterministic vs. alternating, and the power of their 1st-order operators, inflationary vs. noninflationary. This gives rise to six fixpoint logics. We use the notation $FP(\alpha, \beta)$ to refer to a fixpoint logic with iteration of type α and operators of type β. Thus, the logics IFP and NFP will be denoted $FP(D, i)$ and $FP(D, n)$, respectively, and $FP(A, n)$ denotes alternating noninflationary fixpoint logic.

The link between relational complexity and the fixpoint logics is provided by:

$$FP(D, i) = \text{P}_r; \qquad FP(D, n) = FP(N, n) = FP(A, i) = \text{PSPACE}_r;$$
$$FP(N, i) = \text{NP}_r; \qquad FP(A, n) = \text{EXPTIME}_r.$$

An immediate consequence is that $FP(A, i)$, $FP(D, n)$ $FP(N, n)$ all have the same expressive power[8].

---

[7] The nondeterminism described above resides in the *control*, i.e. the choice of the formula to be applied at each stage. This should be contrasted with the *data nondeterminism* of [AV91a], which allows to nondeterministically choose an arbitrary tuple from a relation. Data nondeterminism is strictly stronger than control nondeterminism. For instance, with data nondeterminism, one can (nondeterministically) order the domain elements and use the constructed order to compute the parity of the set of domain elements.

[8] These results also demonstrate how complexity theory can yield *unconditional* results about expressive power of logics. An example where complexity theory yields *conditional* results about expressive power of logics appeared in [Fag74]. Fagin showed that existential and universal second-order logics coincide iff Hamiltonicity is expressible in universal second-order logic.

3.5 Relational complexity as mediator

A consequence of Fagin's results is that NP=co-NP if and only if existential and universal 2nd-order logic have the same expressive power. This equivalence of questions in computational and descriptive complexity is one of the major features of the connection between the two branches of complexity theory. It holds the promise that techniques from one domain could be brought to bear on questions in the other domain.

Unfortunately, the order issue complicates matters. The results by Immerman and Vardi show that P=PSPACE if and only if inflationary and noninflationary fixpoint logics have the same expressive power over *ordered* structures. Because of this restriction, the above equivalence provides a translation of the P vs. PSPACE question to a descriptive complexity question, but does not provide a translation of the inflationary vs. noninflationary question to a computational complexity question. Thus, it is desirable to obtain an order-free correspondence between questions in computational and descriptive complexity. (See also [IL90] for a discussion of the order issue from another perspective.)

We can now provide a partial solution to the order issue, by using relational machines as a mediator between classical complexity and fixpoint logics. On one hand, we showed that questions about containments among standard complexity classes can be translated to questions about containments among relational complexity classes. On the other hand, the expressive power of fixpoint logic can be *precisely* characterized in terms of relational complexity classes. This tight three-way relationship among fixpoint logics, relational complexity and standard complexity yields in a uniform way logical analogs to all containments among the complexity classes P, NP, PSPACE, and EXPTIME. For example[9], P = PSPACE iff $FP(D, i) = FP(D, n)$, P = NP iff $FP(D, i) = FP(N, i)$, NP = PSPACE iff $FP(N, i) = FP(N, n)$, and PSPACE = EXPTIME iff $FP(A, i) = FP(A, n)$. This also enables us to translate known relationships among complexity classes, such as the equality of PSPACE, NPSPACE, and APSPACE, into results about the expressive power of fixpoint logics. This fulfills the promise of applying results from one domain to another domain and shows that some of the most tantalizing questions in complexity theory – P vs. PSPACE, NP vs. PSPACE, and PSPACE vs. EXPTIME – boil down to *one fundamental issue*: the relative power of inflationary vs. noninflationary 1st-order operators.

4 The Generic Machine

In previous sections, we focused on the relational machine, a very powerful device which is nonetheless not complete. In this section, we consider a complete extension of the relational machine, called *generic machine*. This yields yet a new kind of complexity, *generic complexity*.

The *generic machine* (GM) of [AV91] differs from the relational machine in the interaction between the tape and the relational store. GM allows loading the content of relations on the tape, and storing tuples back into relations. To load a relation in

---

[9] The first equivalence was shown in [AV91] by a direct proof using the normal form for *while*.

a deterministic way, tuples cannot be put on the tape in some arbitrary sequence. A natural solution is to introduce parallelism. A load operation therefore involves spawning a new copy of the machine for each tuple loaded. All copies then compute synchronously in parallel. There is a mechanism for merging parallel machines. The output is only obtained after all machines are merged into a single one, which ensures genericity of the global computation. It was shown in [AV91] that GM can express all queries.

There are many alternative ways of defining complete devices operating directly on structures. Recall that *while* cannot go beyond PSPACE because (i) it uses, throughout the computation, only domain elements from the input, and (ii) it uses relations of fixed arity. The addition of integers as in *while$_N$* is one way to break the space barrier. The parallelism of GM is another. Yet another is to relax (i) or (ii). Relaxing (i) is done by allowing the creation of new domain elements, not present in the input. Relaxing (ii) yields an extension of *while* with *untyped algebra*, i.e. an algebra of relations with variable arities. We next describe two complete languages obtained by relaxing (i) and (ii).

The first is an extension of *while* allowing the creation of new domain elements throughout the computation called *while$_{new}$*. The language *while* is modified as follows: (i) there is a new instruction $R := new(S)$, where R and S are relational variables and $arity(R) = arity(S) + 1$; and (ii) the looping construct is of the form *while R do s*, where R is a relational variable. The semantics of (i) is the following. Relation R is obtained by extending each tuple of S by one distinct new domain, not occurring in the input, the current state, or in the program. The semantics of *while R do s* is that statement s is executed while R is nonempty.

Note that the *new* construct is, strictly speaking, nondeterministic. Indeed, the new domain elements are arbitrary, so several possible outcomes are possible depending on their choice. However, the different outcomes differ *only* in this choice. Therefore, we must consider only *well-behaved while$_{new}$* programs whose answer never contains domain elements introduced by the new statements. It is possible to give a syntactic restriction on *while$_{new}$* programs which guarantees good-behavior, can be checked, and yields a class of programs equivalent to all well-behaved *while$_{new}$* programs.

One can show that the language of well-behaved *while$_{new}$* programs is complete[10]. This is proved using new domain elements to denote enumerations of domain elements.

A second extension of *while* (historically, the first language shown to be complete [CH80]) that we call *while$_{uty}$* is obtained by relaxing the fixed-arity requirement present in the languages encountered so far. This is done by using an *untyped* version of relational algebra instead of the familiar typed version.

Based on GM, we can define complexity classes proper to generic computation, focusing on generic analogs of PTIME (GEN-PTIME) and PSPACE (GEN-PSPACE). These

---

[10] One may also consider queries containing new domain elements in the answer. Such queries arise naturally in the context of object-oriented databases where new object identifiers appear in query results. It is interesting to note that *while$_{new}$* is not complete with respect to this extended notion of query which leads to introduce other constructs [AK89].

classes are robust. Indeed, the natural polynomial time and space restrictions of $while_{uty}$ and $while_{new}$ coincide respectively with GEN-PTIME and GEN-PSPACE. Similar results are obtained for other computation models in [AK89, DV91].

The classes GEN-PTIME and GEN-PSPACE are studied in [AV91]. In particular, it is shown that, in agreement with several known nonexpressibility results, *even* is a hard query relative to the notion of generic complexity provided by GM. Indeed, *even* is in GEN-EXPSPACE but not in GEN-PSPACE. Such results point to a trade-off between complexity and computing with an abstract interface.

5 Other work on computing on structures

A number of mathematicians have been interested in computation carried out directly on structures. Several recursion theorists and logicians have adressed the issue, motivated by the question of how tied recursion theory is to the particular structure of integers, or to representations by ordered strings. Typical in that respect is the work of Harvey Friedman on *formal algorithmic procedures (fap)* [Fri71]. The different motivation generally renders this and similar models incomparable to models directly motivated by database queries, such as relational machines. Nonetheless, we briefly describe next some of his and other work that is related, at least in spirit, to our discussion.

Let σ be a first-order signature (language) with predicate and function symbols. Equality is assumed present and always interpreted as equality. A *formal algorithmic procedure (fap)* over σ is a program using finitely many variables $x_1, \ldots, x_k$ (representing domain elements), the predicate and function symbols of σ, and consisting of a finite concatenation of labeled instructions of the form:

- if $R(x_{i_1}, \ldots, x_{i_r})$ then i else j,
  where R is a predicate symbol of σ of arity r, x_{i_j} are variables, and i, j are instruction labels;
- $x_{i_0} = f(x_{i_1}, \ldots, x_{i_r})$,
  where f is a function symbol of σ of arity r and x_{i_j} are variables; and,
- stop.

Suppose a structure over σ is given, as well as an initialization for the first n ($n < k$) variables. The semantics of the instructions is the obvious one. Note that, at each point in the computation, each variable either holds a value or is undefined if no value has been assigned to it. Thus, a fap can be viewed as an acceptor of n-tuples over the domain of σ: $\langle a_1, \ldots a_n \rangle$ is accepted iff the program stops and x_k is defined; otherwise (x_k is underfined or the computation does not stop) $\langle a_1, \ldots, a_n \rangle$ is rejected. In particular, each fap p over σ defines a partial mapping from structures I over σ to n-ary relations over the same domain as σ (denoted also by p), as follows:

if p does not terminate on some n-tuple of elements in I, $p(I)$ is undefined, otherwise $p(I) = \{\langle a_1, \ldots, a_n \rangle \mid p \text{ accepts } \langle a_1, \ldots, a_n \rangle\}$

Clearly, such a mapping is a query (by the definition of Chandra and Harel). It is easily verified that any query defined by a fap is in LOGSPACE. Furthermore, Hartmanis [Har72] and later Gurevich [Gur88], showed that the set of queries computed by fap on ordered structures is *exactly* LOGSPACE. Leivant [Lei89a] reviews these results in the context of a syntactic variant of the fap called *sequential on-site acceptor*. This also provides insight into the connection with FO; since FO is less than LOGSPACE even on ordered structures, fap compute non-FO queries. On the other hand, there are simple FO queries that fap obviously cannot compute, such as the projection of a relation.

There are several ways to add power to fap. One way, considered by Friedman, is to add counting capability to fap in the style of $while_N$. This is done by allowing integer variables, increment and decrement instructions, and an *if k=0 then i else j* instruction. This yields the *fap with counting (fapc)*. This is strictly more powerful than fap, and complete on ordered structures. The fapc is weaker than $while_N$ since, like the fap, it cannot compute the projection of a relation.

Another way to augment the power of the fap is proposed by Leivant in [Lei89a]. This consists in allowing (second order) typed relational variables $X, Y, \ldots$ in addition to domain variables, and instructions of the form:

- $cX(x_{i_1}, \ldots, x_{i_r})$, where $c \in \{+, -\}$, r is the arity of X, and x_{i_j} are domain variables;
- if $X(x_{i_1}, \ldots, x_{i_r})$ then i else j.

The first instruction provides tuple insertion and deletion into variable relations, and the second extends the *if* instruction to such variables. Let us call such programs *second order fap (SO fap)*. Clearly, SO fap can be evaluated in PSPACE. On ordered structures, they express precisely PSPACE [Lei89a]. Without order, they are strictly included in *while*.

As an analog of Turing machine to arbitrary structures, Friedman proposes *generalized Turing algorithms (gTa)* [Fri71]. In addition to usual tape symbols called *auxialliary*, a gTa can place on the tape elements from the structure. The machine can tell if it scans an auxiliary symbol or a data element, but can only read auxiliary symbols. The manipulation of data elements on the tape remains generic. More precisely, a gTa starts with an n-tuple of domain elements in adjacent squares on the tape, the head on the leftmost square, and the other squares blank. Besides usual moves, it can switch the content of adjacent squares, test membership of an r-tuple of consecutive square values into a relation and replace a value by the result of applying a function in the structure to a tuple of consecutive values. Acceptance is defined in the natural way. Clearly, a gTa defines a query from structures to relations consisting of the n-tuples accepted by the machine. Friedman shows that fapc are strictly weaker than gTa. Interestingly, fap augmented with *stacks* of data elements are equivalent to gTa.

Friedman's intention for gTa is to compute all "reasonable" functions on structures. Clearly, this does not fit the database domain, since gTa cannot compute many queries (like the projection of a relation) which are considered essential. The emphasis in Friedman's and other similar investigations is on lifting classical theorems of recursion theory to models of computation such as gTa. Leivant uses his version of fap, on-site acceptors, to obtain descriptive complexity characterizations of complexity classes, but his results assume ordered structures, so the focus is again different from our study of relational machines. Yet another related line of investigation concerns *program schemata* [LP89, LPP70], which are essentially the same

618

as fap. The emphasis here is on program verification. See the survey [She85] for an excellent overview of Friedman's work on fap, and related work.

The notion of computation or algorithm which use only properties of given structures, has been of interest to other logicians and computer scientists from various points of view. Gurevich points out the naturaleness of such algorithms [Gur88]. Tarski discusses in [Tar86] *logical notions*, i.e. notions which are invariant under isomorphisms of the domain of discourse. Thus a generic query is a logical notion; and, a computational device becomes a logical notion when its definition depends only on the information present in the structure it operates on. Turing machines are not logical notions with respect to the an arbitrary structure, but are so relative to its encoding on the tape; relational machines, generic machines, fap and gTa are logical notions with respect to the structure.

References

[ACY91] Afrati, F., S.S. Cosmadakis, M. Yannakakis, On Datalog vs. polynomial time, *Proc. 10th ACM Symp. on Principles of Database Systems*, 1991.

[AK89] S. Abiteboul and P.C. Kanellakis. Object identity as a query language primitive. In *Proc. ACM SIGMOD Symp. on the Management of Data*, pages 159–173, 1989. to appear in *J. ACM*.

[AV89] S. Abiteboul and V. Vianu. Fixpoint extensions of first-order logic and Datalog-like languages. In *Proc. 4th IEEE Symp. on Logic in Computer Science*, pages 71–79, 1989.

[AV90] S. Abiteboul and V. Vianu. Procedural languages for database queries and updates. *Journal of Computer and System Sciences*, 41:181–229, 1990.

[AV91] S. Abiteboul and V. Vianu. Generic computation and its complexity. In *Proc. ACM SIGACT Symp. on the Theory of Computing*, pages 209–219, 1991.

[AV91a] S. Abiteboul and V. Vianu. Datalog extensions for database queries and updates. *Journal of Computer and System Sciences*, 43:62–124, 1991.

[AV91c] S. Abiteboul and V. Vianu. Computing with first-order logic. To appear in *Journal of Computer and System Sciences*.

[AVV92a] S. Abiteboul, Moshe Y. Vardi, and V. Vianu. Fixpoint logics, relational machines, and computational complexity. In *Proc. Conf. on Structure in Complexity Theory*, Boston, 1992.

[AVV92b] S. Abiteboul, Moshe Y. Vardi, and V. Vianu. Computing with infinitary logic. To appear in *Int'l. Conf. on Database Theory*, Berlin, 1992.

[Ba75] Barwise, J., *Admissible Sets and Structures*, Springer-Verlag, 1975.

[Ba77] Barwise, J., On Moschovakis closure ordinals, *J. Symbolic Logic*, 42 (1977), pp. 292–296.

[BF85] Barwise, J., S. Feferman (eds.), *Model-Theoretic Logics*, Springer-Verlag, 1985.

[Bus86] S. R. Buss. *Bounded Arithmetics*. Bibliopolis, 1986.

[CH80] A.K. Chandra and D. Harel. Computable queries for relational data bases. *Journal of Computer and System Sciences*, 21(2):156–178, 1980.

[CH82] A.K. Chandra and D. Harel. Structure and complexity of relational queries. *Journal of Computer and System Sciences*, 25(1):99–128, 1982.

[Cha81] A.K. Chandra. Programming primitives for database languages. In *Proc. ACM Symp. on Principles of Programming Languages*, pages 50–62, 1981.

[CKS81] A. Chandra, D. Kozen, and L. Stockmeyer. Alternation. *Journal of the ACM*, 28:114–133, 1981.

[Com88] K. J. Compton. An algebra and a logic for NC^1. In *Proc. 3rd IEEE Symp. on Logic in Computer Science*, pages 12–21, 1988.

[DLW91] A. Dawar, S. Lindell, and S. Weinstein. Infinitary logic and inductive definability over finite structures. Research report, Univ. of Pennsylvania, 1991.

[DV91] K. Denninghoff and V. Vianu, The Power of Methods with Parallel Semantics, In Proc. Intern. Conf. on Very Large Data Bases, pages 221-232, 1991.

[Fag74] R. Fagin. Generalized first-order spectra and polynomial-time recognizable sets. In R. M. Karp, editor, Complexity of Computation, SIAM-AMS Proceedings, Vol. 7, pages 43-73, 1974.

[Fag75] R. Fagin. Monadic generalized spectra. Zeitschrift für Mathematische Logik und Grundlagen der Mathematik, 21:89-96, 1975.

[F90] Fagin R., Finite-Model Theory—a Personal Perspective, Proc. 3rd Int'l. Conf. on Database Theory, Springer-Verlag, Lecture Notes in Computer Science 470, 1990, pp. 3-24, to appear in Theoretical Computer Science.

[Fed81] T. Feder. Stable networks and product graphs. PhD thesis, Stanford University, 1981.

[Fri71] H. Friedman. Algorithmic procedures, generalized turing algorithms, and elementary recursion theory. In R.O.Gangy and C.M.E.Yates, editors, Logic Colloquium '69, pages 361-389. North Holland, 1971.

[Goe89] A. Goerdt. Characterizing complexity classes by higher-type primitive-recursive definitions. In Proc. 4th IEEE Symp. on Logic in Computer Science, pages 364-374, 1989.

[Gra84] E. Grandjean. The spectra of first-order sentences and computational complexity. SIAM Journal on Computing, 13:356-373, 1984.

[Gra85] E. Grandjean. Universal quantifiers and time complexity of random access machines. Mathematical System Theory, 13:171-187, 1985.

[Gur83] Y. Gurevich. Algebras of feasible functions. In Proc. 24th IEEE Symp. on Foundations of Computer Science, pages 210-214, 1983.

[Gur84] Y. Gurevich. Toward logic tailored for computational complexity. In M. M. Richter et al., editor, Computation and Proof Theory, Lecture Notes in Mathematics 1104, pages 175-216. Springer-Verlag, 1984.

[Gur88] Y. Gurevich. Logic and the challenge of computer science. In E. Börger, editor, Current trends in theoretical computer science, pages 1-57. Computer Science Press, 1988.

[GS86] Y. Gurevich and S. Shelah. Fixed-point extensions of first-order logic. Annals of Pure and Applied Logic, 32:265-280, 1986.

[GSS90] J-Y. Girard, A. Scedrov, and P. SCott. Bounded linear logic: a modular approach to polynomial time computability. In S. R. Buss and P. Scott, editors, Feasible Mathematics, pages 195-207. Birkhauser, 1990.

[Har72] J. Hartmanis. On nondeterminacy in simple computing devices. Acta Informatica, 1:336-344, 1972.

[IL90] N. Immerman and E. S. Lander. Describing graphs: a first-order approach to graph canonization. In A. Selman, editor, Complexity Theory Retrospective, pages 59-81. Springer-Verlag, 1990.

[Imm82] N. Immerman. Upper and lower bounds for first-order expresibility. Journal of Computer and System Sciences, 25:76-98, 1982.

[Imm86] N. Immerman. Relational queries computable in polynomial time. Information and Control, 68:86-104, 1986.

[Imm87a] N. Immerman. Expressibility as a complexity measure: results and directions. In Second Structure in Complexity Conference, pages 194-202, 1987.

[Imm87b] N. Immerman. Languages that capture complexity classes. SIAM Journal of Computing, 16:760-778, 1987.

[Imm89] N. Immerman. Descriptive and computational complexity. In J. Hartmanis, editor, Computational Complexity Theory, Proc. Symp. Applied Math., Vol. 38, pages 75-91. American Mathematical Society, 1989.

[JS74]   N. G. Jones and A.L. Selman. Turing machines and the spectra of first-order formulas. *Journal of Symbolic Logic*, 39:139–150, 1974.

[Kan91]   P. C. Kanellakis. Elements of relational database theory. In J. Van Leeuwen, editor, *Handbook of Theoretical Computer Science*, pages 1074–1156. North Holland, 1991.

[KV90a]   Ph. G. Kolaitis and M. Y. Vardi. 0-1 laws for infinitary logics. In *Proc. 5th IEEE Symp. on Logic in Computer Science*, pages 156–167, 1990.

[KV90b]   Ph. G. Kolaitis and M. Y. Vardi. On the expressive power of Datalog: tools and a case study. In *Proc. 9th ACM Symp. on Principles of Database Systems*, pages 61–71, 1990. Full version appeared in IBM Research Report RJ8010, March 1991.

[KV92]   Kolaitis, P., M.Y. Vardi, Fixpoint vs. infinitary logic in finite-model theory, to appear in *Proc. 7th IEEE Symp. on Logic in Computer Science*, 1992.

[Lei89a] D. Leivant. Descriptive characterization of computational complexity. *Journal of Computer and System Sciences*, 39:51–83, 1989.

[Lei89b] D. Leivant. Monotonic use of space and computational complexity over abstract structures. Unpublished manuscript, 1989.

[Lei90]   D. Leivant. Inductive definitions over finite structures. *Information and Computation*, 89:95–108, 1990.

[Lei91]   D. Leivant. A foundational delineation of computational feasibility. In *Proc. 6th IEEE Symp. on Logic in Computer Science*, pages 2–11, 1991.

[Lin91]   S. Lindell. An analysis of fixed point queries on binary trees. *Theoretical Computer Science*, 85:75–95, 1991.

[LP89]   D. Luckham and D. Park. The undecidability of the equivalence problem for program schemata. Technical Report UCSC-CRL-89-40, UCSC, December 1989. to appear in *ACM Transactions on Database Systems*.

[LPP70]   D. Luckham, D. Park, and M. Paterson. Formalized computer programs. *Journal of Computer and System Sciences*, 4:220–249, 1970.

[Mos74]   Y. N. Moschovakis. *Elementary Induction on Abstract Structures*. North Holland, 1974.

[dR84]   M. de Rougemont. Uniform definability on finite structures with successor. In *Proc. 16th ACM Symp. on Theory of Computing*, pages 409–417, 1984.

[Saz80b] V. Yu. Sazonov. Polynomial computability and recursivity in finite domains. *Elektronische Informationverarbeitung und Kybernetik*, 16:319–323, 1980.

[She85]   J. C. Shepherdson. Algorithmic procedures, generalized turing algorithms, and elementary recursion theory. In L.A.Harrington et al., editor, *Harvey Friedman's research on the foundations of mathematics*, pages 285–308. North Holland, 1985.

[Sto77]   L. J. Stockmeyer. The polynomial-time hierarchy. *Theoretical Computer Science*, 3:1–22, 1977.

[Tar86]   A. Tarski. What are logical notions? *History and Philosophy of Logic*, 7:143–154, 1986. (Ed. J.Corcoran).

[TU88]   J. Tiuryn and P. Urzyczyn. Some relationships between logic of programs and complexity theory. *Theoretical Computer Science*, 60:83–108, 1988.

[Ull88]   J.D. Ullman. *Principles of Database and Knowledge Base Systems: Volume I and II*. Computer Science Press, 1988.

[Var82]   M.Y. Vardi. The complexity of relational query languages. In *Proc. ACM SIGACT Symp. on the Theory of Computing*, pages 137–146, 1982.

A partial solution for D-unification based on a reduction to AC1-unification

Evelyne Contejean

Max-Planck-Institut für Informatik
Im Stadtwald
D-6600 Saarbrücken, Germany
contejea@mpi-sb.mpg.de

Abstract. We show that deciding unification modulo both-sided distributivity of a symbol $*$ over a symbol $+$ can be reduced to AC1-unification for all unification problems which do not involve the $+$ operator. Moreover, we can describe "almost all" solutions in a finite way, although there are in general infinitely many minimal solutions for such problems. As a consequence, $*$-problems appear as a good candidate for a notion of solved-form for D-unification.

1 Introduction

Equations are ubiquitous in mathematics as well as in computer science. Unification is solving equations in some particular domains, namely free term algebras or term algebras modulo an equational theory. Unification was first introduced by Herbrand [3], and rediscovered by Robinson as a basic mechanism for resolution in first order logic [10]. Unification is also the basic mechanism for computing critical pairs [7], and the main inference rule of the completion procedure.

On the other hand, the very old and famous 10th Hilbert problem of solving Diophantine equations has been proved undecidable by Matijasevic [9]. The challenge now is to find the maximal subsets of Peano arithmetic for which unification is decidable. Such a candidate is actually provided by the two axioms of left and right distributivity of a symbol $*$ over a symbol $+$. Arnborg and Tidén have shown that one-sided (left *or* right) distributivity has a decidable unification problem, whereas adding a unit element for $*$ and associativity of $+$ makes unification undecidable [12]. Szabo has proved the same result when associativity of $+$ is added to both-sided distributivity [11].

In this paper, we give a partial solution for unification modulo both-sided distributivity. More precisely, we show that if a problem does not contain any $+$ function symbol, solvability modulo D and solvability in the free algebra are equivalent.

Describing all solutions of a problem P , however, is more difficult. In a first step, we show that all solutions (modulo D) are instances of the linearized form λ of the most general unifier of P in the free algebra. Not all of them, however, are solutions. The appropriate instances are topped by an AC1 solution of the problem $P\lambda$ in the theory where $*$ is AC1.

The paper is organized as follows: the second section contains the needed formal apparatus. Section 3 is devoted to $*$-problems. It introduces "indexed distributivity" as a main tool used throughout the paper. Section 4 studies the algebra of structures which are the terms used in order to represent the tops of solutions modulo distributivity. This algebra has a unique decomposition property similar to the unique decomposition property of natural numbers into prime numbers. Hence, the algebra of structures can be seen as a free commutative monoid. The description of almost all solutions of a *-problem follows as a corollary.

2 Definitions

We assume that the reader is familiar with the notions of *term algebra, position in a term, substitution, equational theory, equational proof, rewrite proof* surveyed in [2]. We recall briefly the most important ones. Given a *signature* $\mathcal{F}$, that is, a set of function symbols with their arity, and a set $\mathcal{X}$ of variables, the term algebra $\mathcal{T}(\mathcal{F}, \mathcal{X})$ is the free $\mathcal{F}$-algebra over $\mathcal{X}$. An equational axiom is an unordered pair of terms $< l, r >$ of $\mathcal{T}(\mathcal{F}, \mathcal{X})$, also denoted by $l = r$. An equational theory presented by a set of equational axioms E is the reflexive transitive closure of $\longleftrightarrow_E$, the smallest relation containing E which is compatible with the term structure of $\mathcal{T}(\mathcal{F}, \mathcal{X})$. As in [2], we use postfixed notations for substitution applications.

In the following, we may not always distinguish a set of equational axioms with its associated equational theory.

Definition 2.1 *D is the equational theory presented by*
$$x * (y + z) = (x * y) + (x * z) \qquad (D_l)$$
$$(x + y) * z = (x * z) + (y * z) \qquad (D_r)$$

The axioms of D are usually oriented from left to right in this paper:

Definition 2.2 (Developed normal form) *Let t be a term in $\mathcal{T}(\{+, *\}, \mathcal{X})$. Its (possibly many) irreducible forms with respect to the following set of rules:*
$$x * (y + z) \rightarrow (x * y) + (x * z)$$
$$(x + y) * z \rightarrow (x * z) + (y * z)$$
are called developed normal forms.

Definition 2.3 *$AC1$ is the equational theory presented by*
$$x * (y * z) = (x * y) * z \qquad (A)$$
$$x * y \quad = y * x \qquad (C)$$
$$x * 1 \quad = x \qquad (1)$$

Definition 2.4 (E-Unification Problem) *Let $\mathcal{T}(\mathcal{F}, \mathcal{X})$ be a term algebra, and E an equational theory over $\mathcal{T}(\mathcal{F}, \mathcal{X})$. A E-unification problem is a first order formula, where the logical connectives are $\exists$, $\wedge$ and $\vee$, and the atoms are either T, or F, or some equation $s =_E^? t$ between two terms of $\mathcal{T}(\mathcal{F}, \mathcal{X})$. The solutions σ of such a problem are the substitutions of $\mathcal{T}(\mathcal{F}, \mathcal{X})$ that satisfy the formula when $=_E^?$ is interpreted as $=_E$.*

In this paper, we deal with unification problems modulo $AC1$, D, or in the free algebra.

Definition 2.5 (∗-Problems) *A ∗-equation in $T(\{+, ∗\}, \mathcal{X})/D$ is an equation $s =^?_D t$, where s and t are terms of $T(\{∗\}, \mathcal{X})$. A ∗-problem is a unification problem in the algebra $T(\{+, ∗\}, \mathcal{X})/D$ in which all equations are ∗-equations.*

Definition 2.6 (Variable Identification) *A variable identification of $T(\mathcal{F}, \mathcal{X})$ is a substitution, the codomain of which is contained in the set of variables $\mathcal{X}$.*

Definition 2.7 (Well-balanced ∗-Problems) *A well-balanced ∗-equation in $T(\{+, ∗\}, \mathcal{X})/D$ is an equation $t\sigma =^?_D t\tau$, where t is a term of $T(\{∗\}, \mathcal{X})$ and σ and τ are two variables identifications. A well-balanced ∗-problem is a unification problem in the algebra $T(\{+, ∗\}, \mathcal{X})/D$ in which all equations are well-balanced ∗-equations.*

One should notice that terms occurring in ∗-problems do not contain any $+$ function symbol. Moreover, in the well-balanced case, both terms of an equation are the same except for their leaves.

3 General ∗-Problems

This section is devoted to the proof of our first main result: if P is a unification ∗-problem then P is solvable modulo D if and only if it is solvable in the free algebra. Moreover all its solutions modulo D are instances of the linearized form of its most general unifier in the free algebra.

The proof of this theorem needs some technical tools, some of which are based on rewriting techniques. To record some information about the application of distributive steps, we will mark "distinct" ∗ function symbols by distinct indexes. Two occurrences of ∗ in a term will be considered identical if and only if they come from the duplication of a same ∗ symbol when using distributivity.

3.1 Indexation

Definition 3.1 (Marked term) *Let $\mathcal{X}$ be a set of variables, and $\mathcal{I}$ be a set whose members are called hereafter "indexes". A marked term with respect to $\mathcal{I}$ is either*
- a variable x in $\mathcal{X}$, or
- $s + t$ where s and t are marked terms with respect to $\mathcal{I}$, or
- $s ∗_i t$ where s and t are marked terms with respect to $\mathcal{I}$ and i is an index of $\mathcal{I}$.

Indexed distributivity, called DI in the following, is a version of distributivity which cops with marked terms. DI is presented by the indexed axioms:

$$x_I ∗_i (y_J + z_K) = (x_I ∗_i y_J) + (x_I ∗_i z_K) \qquad (DI_l)$$
$$(x_I + y_J) ∗_i z_K = (x_I ∗_i z_K) + (y_J ∗_i z_K) \qquad (DI_r)$$

where i is any index and the variables x_I, y_J and z_K can be instanciated by marked terms.

Indexed distributivity has been introduced in order to study distributivity. Hence we would like that D and DI have the "same" equivalence classes. More precisely, we mean that if t_I is a marked term, and t is the term obtained by erasing its indexes, then the class of t modulo D is exactly the class of t_I modulo DI after erasing all indexes. Unfortunately this is not always true. For example, the class modulo DI of $(x ∗_1 y) + (x ∗_2 z)$ is equal to $\{(x ∗_1 y) + (x ∗_2 z)\}$, whereas the class modulo D of $(x ∗ y) + (x ∗ z)$ is equal to $\{(x ∗ y) + (x ∗ z), x ∗ (y + z)\}$.

Definition 3.2 (Compatible indexation) *Let t_I be a marked term and t be the unmarked term derived from t_I. t_I has a* compatible indexation *if any sequence of rewrite steps modulo D starting from t can be obtained by erasing all indexes in some sequence of rewrite steps modulo DI starting from t_I.*

Example 3.3 $(x *_1 y) + (x *_2 z)$ *has not a compatible indexation.* $(x *_1 y) + (x *_1 z)$ *has a compatible indexation.*

Any term in $T(\{+, *\}, \mathcal{X})$ can be marked in such a way that the obtained term has a compatible indexation. The obvious but useless solution is to mark all $*$ function symbols with the same index.

Definition 3.4 (Finer indexation) *Let t_I and t_J be two marked terms such that the terms obtained by erasing their indexes are equal to the same term t. t_I has a* finer indexation *than t_J if t_J is equal to t_I after applying an index identification.*

Lemma 3.5 *Let t be a term in $T(\{+, *\}, \mathcal{X})$. t can be marked in such a way that the obtained term t_I has a unique minimal (finest) compatible indexation, up to renaming.*

Sketch of the proof : t has finitely many $*$ function symbols. Hence, up to renaming, t can be marked by finitely many distinct indexations. Among these indexations, there are some compatible ones, hence t has a finite non empty set of compatible indexations. This set owns at least a minimal indexation with respect to the above ordering. Two minimal indexations of t can be superimposed, yielding a finer compatible indexation. Hence the three indexations are equal up to an index renaming. $\Box$

Minimal compatible indexations are very useful in order to decide when a term can be factored out, that is, when an axiom of distributivity can be applied from right to left. Indeed when two $*$ function symbols are marked with the same index, such a factorization is possible, and we will show that there is no need to look at the subterms below them. This is important for unification since the terms that have to be unified are known, but the substitution that has to be applied in order to make them equal is *a priori* unknown.

Lemma 3.6 *Let t_I be a marked term with a compatible (respectively minimal compatible) indexation and s_J be a marked term equal modulo DI to the term t_I. Then s_J has a compatible (respectively minimal compatible) indexation.*

Lemma 3.7 *Let t_I be a marked term with a compatible indexation. Then all subterms of t_I have a compatible indexation.*

Our purpose, in this section, is to concentrate on $*$ function symbols. We define a new notion of position which takes only $*$ function symbols into account. Thanks to this notion, we can prove lemma 3.9 which is the key to proposition 3.12.

Definition 3.8 ($*$-position) *Let t_I be a marked term, and p a position of t_I. The $*$-position $\mathcal{D}_*(t_I, p)$ associated with p in t_I is equal to*
- Λ *if p is equal to Λ*
- $\mathcal{D}_*(t_I, q)$ *if p is equal to $q \cdot n$, where n is either 1 or 2, and $t_I(q) = +$,*
- $\mathcal{D}_*(t_I, q) \cdot (n, *_i)$ *if p is equal to $q \cdot n$, where n is either 1 or 2, and $t_I(q) = *_i$.*

Lemma 3.9 *Let t_I be a marked term with a minimal compatible indexation. For every index i occurring in t_I, the set $\mathcal{P}_*(t_I, i) = \{\mathcal{D}_*(t_I, p) \mid t_I(p) = *_i\}$ is a singleton set.*

Definition 3.10 *Let t_I be a marked term with a minimal compatible indexation, and i be an index occurring in t_I. The $*$-position of i in t_I is equal to $\mathcal{P}_*(t_I, i)$. The pseudo-position of i in t_I is the pair $(\mathcal{P}_*(t_I, i), n)$, where n is the number of distinct indexes occurring on the left hand side of the minimal position of i (that is, at a smaller position with respect to the lexicographic ordering) and which have the same $*$-position than i.*

It should be noticed that two distinct indexes have distinct pseudo-positions.

Lemma 3.11 *Let t_I and s_J be two DI-equal marked terms with a minimal compatible indexation, and let i be an index which occurs in t_I (hence in s_J). Then the pseudo-positions of i in t_I and in s_J are the same.*

Proposition 3.12 *Let t_I be a marked term with a minimal compatible indexation. Then all subterms of t_I have a minimal compatible indexation.*

Proof : This proof is quite technical. Actually, we show by induction on the pair (n_*, n_+), where n_* (respectively n_+) is equal to the number of $*$ (respectively $+$) function symbols in a developed normal form of t_I, that $t_I|_1$ and $t_I|_2$ have minimal compatible indexations. The key point is to prove minimality since lemma 3.7 ensures compatibility. $\square$

We can now state the

Proposition 3.13 *Let t_I be a marked term with a minimal compatible indexation. If t_I contains a subterm $t_I|_p$ of the form $(a_I *_i b_I) + (c_I *_i d_I)$, then this subterm can be factored out, that is*

$$
\begin{aligned}
(a_I *_i b_I) + (c_I *_i d_I) &=_{DI} \alpha_J *_i (\beta_J + \gamma_J) \\
a_I *_i b_I &=_{DI} \quad \alpha_J *_i \beta_J \\
c_I *_i d_I &=_{DI} \quad \alpha_J *_i \gamma_J \\
&\quad\; or \\
(a_I *_i b_I) + (c_I *_i d_I) &=_{DI} (\alpha_J + \beta_J) *_i \gamma_J \\
a_I *_i b_I &=_{DI} \quad \alpha_J *_i \gamma_J \\
c_I *_i d_I &=_{DI} \quad \beta_J *_i \gamma_J
\end{aligned}
$$

Proof: According to proposition 3.12, $t_I|_p$ has a minimal compatible indexation. If this term cannot be factored out, all sequences of rewrite steps modulo DI starting from $t_I|_p$ do not contain any step at position Λ. This is in contradiction with the minimality of the indexation, since the marked term $(a_I *_{i_1} b_I) + (c_I *_{i_2} d_I)$, where i_1 and i_2 are two distinct copies of i, has a finer compatible indexation. $\square$

3.2 Solutions of *-problems

It is very easy to decide whether a given unification *-problem P has a solution modulo D: one simply has to check the existence of a solution modulo the free theory which is decidable [3, 2]. Moreover if P is satisfiable, its most general unifier in the free theory, "combined" with appropriate $AC1$ unifiers can be used to represent "almost all" solutions.

Proposition 3.14 *Let P be a *-problem. P has a solution modulo D if and only if it has a solution modulo the empty equational theory.*

Proof : It is obvious that a substitution which is a solution for P modulo the free theory is also a solution for P modulo D. Hence we only have to show that if there exists a substitution τ which is a solution modulo D for P, there exists a substitution σ which is a solution for P modulo the free theory. We may assume without restriction that τ is in developed normal form. Let $s =^?_D t$ be an equation in P. The two terms $s\tau$ and $t\tau$ are equal modulo D, and so are their developed normal forms. Their left-most maximal *-subterms are equal since the recursively defined S_l

$$
\begin{array}{rcll}
S_l(x) & = & x & \text{if } x \in \mathcal{X} \\
S_l(t_1 + t_2) & = & S_l(t_1) & \\
S_l(t_1 * t_2) & = & S_l(t_1) * S_l(t_2) &
\end{array}
$$

provides obviously the left-most maximal *-subterm for a term which is in developed normal form, and gives the same result for all D-equal terms. Moreover $S_l(s\tau)$ (respectively $S_l(t\tau)$) is equal to $s\{x \mapsto S_l(x\tau) \mid x \in \mathcal{D}om(\tau)\}$ (respectively $t\{x \mapsto S_l(x\tau) \mid x \in \mathcal{D}om(\tau)\}$) since s (respectively t) does not contain any $+$ function symbols. Hence the following equality holds:
$$ s\{x \mapsto S_l(x\tau) \mid x \in \mathcal{D}om(\tau)\} = t\{x \mapsto S_l(x\tau) \mid x \in \mathcal{D}om(\tau)\} $$
The substitution $\{x \mapsto S_l(x\tau) \mid x \in \mathcal{D}om(\tau)\}$ is a solution for P in the free theory. □

We now proceed with the reduction of *-problems to well-balanced *-problems.

Definition 3.15 (Linear substitution) *A substitution σ is* linear *if any variable x in its codomain occurs exactly once in the multiset $\{y\sigma \mid y \in \mathcal{D}om(\sigma)\}$.*

Lemma 3.16 *Any substitution σ can be decomposed into a linear substitution λ and a variable identification ι: $\sigma = \lambda\iota$*

When P has no solution, there is no well-balanced instance of P. The following proposition shows that solving P boils down to solving its most general well-balanced instance.

Proposition 3.17 *Let P be a solvable *-problem, $\sigma_0 = \lambda_0\iota_0$ its most general unifier, where λ_0 is a linear substitution and ι_0 a variable identification. Let σ be a solution of P modulo D. Then $\sigma =_D \lambda_0\rho$ for some ρ.*

Sketch of the proof : The proof is by induction on n_*, the number of $*$ function symbols of λ_0. Let σ be a solution of P, let $s =_D^? t$ be an equation of P which is not well-balanced and p be a position such that $t(p)$ is a $*$ function symbol and $s(p)$ is a variable x. $s\sigma$ can be marked with a minimal compatible indexation, yielding a minimal compatible indexation over $t\sigma$ (lemmas 3.5 and 3.6). Let us denote by i the index occurring at position p in the marked version of $t\sigma$. i does not occur anywhere else in the marked version of $t\sigma$ since all $*$-positions of $*$ function symbols are not equal to the $*$-position of i in $t\sigma$. Thanks to properties of pseudo-positions, it is then possible to show that the marked version of $(s\sigma)|_p$ is the only subterm in $s\sigma$ which contains $*_i$. Moreover $*_i$ occurs along all paths from the root to the leaves in $(s\sigma)|_p$ and it is the first encountered indexed $*$ symbol. Thanks to the factorization proposition, we then know that $(s\sigma)|_p$ is D-equal to a term $u_1 * u_2$. The problem $P\{x \mapsto x_1 * x_2\}$, where x_1 and x_2 are some fresh variables, has a solution that has less $*$ function symbols than λ_0 and the induction hypothesis applies. Since there is a one-to-one mapping from the solutions of P to the solutions of P', we can conclude that σ is D-equal to an instance of λ_0. □

4 Well-balanced $*$-Problems

Well-balanced $*$-problems always admit solutions. The most trivial one is a substitution which maps all variables on a single variable. In this case, two terms occurring in the same equation become syntactically equal. Hence, the question is not the solvability of such problems, but a full description of their solutions. In [6], Kirchner and Klay have proved that distributivity is not syntactic [5, 6], by giving an infinite set of uncomparable solutions for the very simple equation $x * y =_D^? u * v$. We introduce a representation of the solutions which enables us to represent such an infinite set by a single scheme. Actually, we cannot represent all solutions, but only the "upper part" of each solution, that is the part without any $*$ function symbol. Such an upper part is also a solution for a well-balanced $*$-problem. The schemata we use in order to represent the solutions of a well-balanced $*$-problem can also help for the general case, see [1]. This section is devoted to the study of these schemata, and emphasizes the strong and astonishing relationship between both-sided distributivity and the theory of associativity and commutativity with a unit element.

First, we formally define the "upper part" of a term, which belongs to a particular term algebra called the algebra of structures. This notion is quite natural for a certain class of terms, but in the general case, we need some lemmas in order to prove the uniqueness of this upper part.

4.1 Upper part of a term

Definition 4.1 (Algebra of structures) $\mathcal{T}(\{+, \square\})$ *is the* algebra of structures.

Definition 4.2 (Upper part of a term in normal form) *Let t be a term in $\mathcal{T}(\{+, *\}, \mathcal{X})$ in developed normal form. The* upper part *of t is the unique maximal term (with respect to the size) u of the algebra of structures, such that there* *exist a term s and a substitution σ satisfying*

$$t \equiv s\sigma \qquad u \equiv s\{x \mapsto \Box \mid x \in \mathcal{V}ar(s)\}$$

The upper part of t is denoted by $\hat{t}$.

Remark : $\{x \mapsto \Box \mid x \in \mathcal{V}ar(s)\}$ is not exactly a substitution since it does not define an endomorphism. This "pseudo-substitution" defines an homomorphism from $\mathcal{T}(\{+, *\}, \mathcal{X})$ to $\mathcal{T}(\{+, \Box\})$.

The formal definition is quite complicated, but the computation of an upper part is rather simple: since t is in developed normal form, all $+$ function symbols are above the $*$ symbols. Hence, the upper part of a term in developed normal form can be obtained by replacing all $*$-headed terms and variables by the $\Box$ symbol.

Example 4.3 *Consider the term* $(x + (x * z)) + (x * y)$. *Its upper part is equal to* $(\Box + \Box) + \Box$.

When orienting the two axioms of distributivity as in definition 2.2, a critical pair appears between the obtained rules. Hence a term can have several developed normal forms. If we extend our notion of upper part to terms which are not in developed normal form, we cannot ensure the uniqueness property. This problem is solved by considering classes of structures modulo an equivalence relation $\sim_D$ derived from the equational theory D.

Definition 4.4 (D-equivalence) *Two structures s and t are D-equivalent if*
$$s\{\Box \mapsto x * y\} =_D t\{\Box \mapsto x * y\}$$
This is denoted by $s \sim_D t$.

An important remark is that if t_1 and t_2 are in developed normal form, there is a normal from of $t_1 * t_2$ the upper part of which is equal to $\hat{t_1}\{\Box \mapsto \hat{t_2}\}$. This normal form is obtained by applying D_r as far as possible and then D_l.

Hence we introduce the following:

Definition 4.5 (Composition of structures) *Let t_1 and t_2 be two structures. The composition of t_1 and t_2 is the structure denoted $t_1@t_2$ obtained by replacing all leaves of t_1 by t_2: $t_1@t_2 = t_1\{\Box \mapsto t_2\}$*

Lemma 4.6 $\mathcal{T}(\{+, \Box\})$ *and* $\mathcal{T}(\{+, \Box\})/\sim_D$ *are semi-groups with respect to composition.*

This lemma shows a relationship between D and $A1$, but it is actually a relationship between D and $AC1$.

Lemma 4.7 *The composition of structures is commutative in* $\mathcal{T}(\{+, \Box\})/\sim_D$.

Proof : Let s and t two structures, we will show that $s@t$ and $t@s$ are D-equivalent. By applying D_r as far as possible to all subterms $t\{\Box \mapsto x * y\}$ occurring in $s@t\{\Box \mapsto x * y\}$, one gets $s\{\Box \mapsto (t\{\Box \mapsto x\}) * y\}$. Then apply D_l to the whole term as far as possible, in order to obtain $(s\{\Box \mapsto x\}) * (t\{\Box \mapsto y\})$. A developed normal form of this term can now be computed by applying first D_r as far as possible and then D_l as far as possible. This normal form is equal to $t@s\{\Box \mapsto x * y\}$. $\Box$

Corollary 4.8 $T(\{+,\square\})/\sim_D$ *is a commutative semi-group with respect to @.*

Remark : Sometimes, we will use the notation $\underset{i\in I}{@}\,s_i$ instead of $s_{i_1}@\ldots@s_{i_n}$ if $I = \{i_1,\ldots,i_n\}$. The composition has these key properties: it is assocative, has a unit element equal to $\square$, and is compatible with D-equivalence.

4.2 Decomposition of structures

The quotient algebra $T(\{+,\square\})/\sim_D$ has a unique decomposition property, similar to the decomposition property of natural numbers. This does not imply, however, that it is a factorial ring.

Definition 4.9 (Decomposition of structures) *Let s be a structure in $T(\{+,\square\})$. $s_1@s_2$ is a decomposition of s if s and $s_1@s_2$ are D-equivalent. If s_1 (or s_2) is equal to the empty structure $\square$, the decomposition is trivial. A non empty structure is prime if all its decompositions are trivial. A decomposition is maximal if it is reduced to $\square$ or if all its members are prime structures.*

The following property means that $T(\{+,\square\})/\sim_D$ is actually the free commutative semi-group generated by the set of "letters" identified as the equivalence classes of the prime structures.

Proposition 4.10 *Let r be a structure. r has exactly one maximal decomposition up to permutation.*

Sketch of the proof : Let $s_1@\ldots@s_k$ and $t_1@\ldots@t_l$ be two maximal decompositions of r. These two structures are D-equivalent, hence there is a sequence of rewrite steps modulo D between the two terms $s \equiv (s_1@\ldots@s_k)\{\square \mapsto x*y\}$ and $t \equiv (t_1@\ldots@t_l)\{\square \mapsto x*y\}$. We can always choose a sequence such as the one below:

$$s \overset{(\neq\Lambda)^*}{\underset{D}{\longleftrightarrow}} w \overset{\Lambda}{\underset{D}{\longleftarrow}} (u\{\square\mapsto x\}) * (v\{\square\mapsto y\}) \overset{*}{\underset{D}{\longleftrightarrow}} (u'\{\square\mapsto x\}) * (v'\{\square\mapsto y\}) \overset{\Lambda}{\underset{D}{\longrightarrow}} w' \overset{(\neq\Lambda)^*}{\underset{D}{\longleftrightarrow}} t$$

The proof of the proposition is by induction on the pair made of the number of $+$ function symbols occurring in r and the number of rewrite steps at position Λ in the middle part of the sequence

$$(u\{\square\mapsto x\}) * (v\{\square\mapsto y\}) \overset{*}{\underset{D}{\longleftrightarrow}} (u'\{\square\mapsto x\}) * (v'\{\square\mapsto y\}) \qquad \square$$

4.3 Top of a term

Proposition 4.11 *Let s and t be two D-equal terms in $T(\{+,*\},\mathcal{X})$, and s' and t' some developed normal forms of s and t. Then the upper parts of s' and t' are D-equivalent.*

Sketch of the proof : The proof is by induction on the triple $(n_+(s'), n_*(s'), n_\Lambda(s',t'))$, where $n_+(s')$ (respectively $n_*(s')$) is the number of $+$ (respectively $*$) function symbols in s' and $n_\Lambda(s',t')$ is the number of rewrite Λ-steps modulo D in a sequence between s' and t'. $\square$

The intuitive meaning of this result is that every proof modulo distributivity between two terms in developed normal form can be performed by using only the top-most *-symbols. As a consequence, two distinct developed normal forms of a term t have the same upper part modulo $\sim_D$.

Definition 4.12 (Top of a term) *Let t a term of $T(\{+,*\}, \mathcal{X})$, and t' one of its developed normal forms. The top of t is the class of the upper part of t' modulo D-equivalence, denoted by $\hat{t}$.*

In the following, for short, we will identify the top which is a set of structures with one (not anyone) of its members.

4.4 Solutions of well-balanced *-problems

All previous definitions of upper part and top extend naturally to substitutions.

Lemma 4.13 *Let P be a well-balanced *-problem without equations between variables and σ b a solution of P. Then the top of σ (replacing $\square$ by any variable in $\mathcal{X}$) is a solution of P.*

Proof : Let $t\iota =_D^? t\iota'$ be an equation of P, where t is a linear term and ι and ι' are two variable identifications. Since σ is a solution of P, $t\iota\sigma =_D t\iota'\sigma$ holds. Hence, according to proposition 4.11, $t\iota\sigma$ and $t\iota'\sigma$ have the same top:

$$\underset{x\in Var(t)}{@} \widehat{x\iota\sigma} \sim_D \widehat{t\iota\sigma} \sim_D \widehat{t\iota'\sigma} \sim_D \underset{x\in Var(t)}{@} \widehat{x\iota'\sigma}$$

P does not contain any equation between two variables, hence t is an instance of $x * y$. By definition of D-equivalence,

$$(\underset{x\in Var(t)}{@} \widehat{x\iota\sigma})\{\square \mapsto t\}\{x \mapsto \square \mid x \in Var(t)\} \underset{D}{=} (\underset{x\in Var(t)}{@} \widehat{x\iota'\sigma})\{\square \mapsto t\}\{x \mapsto \square \mid x \in Var(t)\}$$

This equality can be rephrased as $t\iota\hat{\sigma} =_D t\iota'\hat{\sigma}$. $\square$

Corollary 4.14 *Let P be a well-balanced *-problem, σ a solution of P and $\hat{\sigma}$ the top of σ. Then $\hat{\sigma}\{\square \mapsto x * y\}$ is a solution of P.*

Thanks to the property of uniqueness for the maximal decomposition of a structure, we can describe all tops of the solutions of a well-balanced *-problem as instances of the most general unifier of an $AC1$ problem. $AC1$ is unitary, and the most general unifier of a problem can be easily computed by solving systems of linear Diophantine equations [4].

Proposition 4.15 *Let P be a well-balanced *-problem, σ a solution of P and ρ_{AC1} the most general solution of P modulo the equational theory $AC1$ of $*$. Then there exists a semi-group homomorphism h from $T(\{*\}, \mathcal{X})/AC1(*)$ to $T(\{+,\square\})/ \sim_D$ such that*

$$\hat{\sigma} \equiv \rho_{AC1}h$$

Conversely, let h' be any semi-group homomorphism from $T(\{*\}, \mathcal{X})/AC1(*)$ to $T(\{+,\square\})/ \sim_D$. Then $\rho_{AC1}h'\{\square \mapsto x * y\}$ is a solution of P.

Proof : First, we prove that $\hat{\sigma} \equiv \rho_{AC1}h$. Consider an equation of P, $t\iota =_D^? t\iota'$, where t is a linear term. σ is a solution of P, hence $t\iota\sigma =_D t\iota'\sigma$ holds. These two terms have the same top. On the other hand, we have two decompositions of this top, $@_{x \in Var(t)}(x\iota\hat{\sigma})$ and $@_{x \in Var(t)}(x\iota'\hat{\sigma})$. We can derive two maximal decompositions by decomposing the $x\iota\hat{\sigma}$ and $x\iota'\hat{\sigma}$ as far as possible. There are finitely many distinct (up to D-equivalence) prime structures occurring in the decompositions: $s_1, s_2, \ldots, s_n$. Let us associate a variable x_i with s_i for $1 \le i \le n$. For each variable y of P we can build an arbitrary term u_y in $T(\{*\}, \mathcal{X})$ whose multiset of variables is equal to the multiset of variables attached to the prime structures occurring in the maximal decomposition of $y\hat{\sigma}$. According to proposition 4.10, the maximal decompositions derived from $@_{x \in Var(t)}(x\iota\hat{\sigma})$ and $@_{x \in Var(t)}(x\iota'\hat{\sigma})$ are equivalent up to permutation, that is, the multisets of their prime structures are the same. Hence the multisets of variables of $t\iota\{x\iota \mapsto u_{x\iota} \mid x \in Var(t)\}$ and $t\iota'\{x\iota' \mapsto u_{x\iota'} \mid x \in Var(t)\}$ are the same and these two terms are equal modulo the equational theory $AC1$.

Consider the substitution τ defined in $T(\{*\}, \mathcal{X})$ by $\tau \equiv \{y \mapsto u_y \mid y \in Var(P)\}$. $t\iota\tau =_{AC1} t\iota'\tau$ holds for all equations $t\iota =_D^? t\iota'$ of P. Hence τ is a solution of P modulo $AC1$. Since $AC1$ is unitary when there is no constant, τ is an instance of the most general solution of P, $\tau \equiv \rho_{AC1}\tau'$. Let g be the semi-group homomorphism from $T(\{*, 1\}, \mathcal{X})/AC1$ to $T(\{+, \square\})/ \sim_D$ such that $x_i g = s_i$ for all i, $1 \le i \le n$, and $yg = \square$ if $y \notin \{x_1, \ldots, x_n\}$. $\hat{\sigma}$ is equal to $\underbrace{(\rho_{AC1}\tau')}_{\tau} g \equiv \rho_{AC1} \underbrace{(\tau'g)}_{h}$.

Now, we prove that $\rho_{AC1}h'\{\square \mapsto x * y\}$ is a solution of P for all semi-group homomorphisms h' from $T(\{*, 1\}, \mathcal{X})/AC1$ to $T(\{+, \square\})/ \sim_D$. Let $t\iota =_D^? t\iota'$ be an equation of P. ρ_{AC1} is the minimal solution of P modulo the equational theory $AC1$, hence the two terms $t\iota\rho_{AC1}$ and $t\iota'\rho_{AC1}$ are equal modulo $AC1$. Since h' is a semi-group homomorphism, $(t\iota\rho_{AC1})h'$ and $(t\iota'\rho_{AC1})h'$ are D-equivalent and by definition $(t\iota\rho_{AC1})h'\{\square \mapsto x * y\} =_D (t\iota'\rho_{AC1})h'\{\square \mapsto x * y\}$. Here, it should be noticed that h' maps the whole terms $t\iota\rho_{AC1}$ and $t\iota'\rho_{AC1}$ to structures, and that all $*$ function symbols of t and ρ_{AC1} become $@$. By $(\rho_{AC1}h'\{\square \mapsto x * y\})$, we mean a substitution in $T(\{+, *\}, \mathcal{X})$, such that only the $*$ function symbols of ρ_{AC1} are replaced by $@$, hence the following equalities hold:

$$t\iota(\rho_{AC1}h'\{\square \mapsto x * y\}) =_D (t\iota\rho_{AC1})h'\{\square \mapsto (t\{u \mapsto x * y \mid u \in Var(t)\})\}$$
$$t\iota'(\rho_{AC1}h'\{\square \mapsto x * y\}) =_D (t\iota'\rho_{AC1})h'\{\square \mapsto (t\{u \mapsto x * y \mid u \in Var(t)\})\}$$

since t contains only $*$ function symbols, $(t\{u \mapsto x * y \mid u \in Var(t)\})$ is an instance of $x * y$, hence $t\iota(\rho_{AC1}h'\{\square \mapsto x * y\}) =_D t\iota'(\rho_{AC1}h'\{\square \mapsto x * y\})$. □

There are infinitely many semi-group homomorphisms from $T(\{*\}, \mathcal{X})/AC1(*)$ to $T(\{+, \square\})/ \sim_D$, but ρ_{AC1} is unique and can be used to schematize all tops of solutions of P.

By putting together proposition 4.15 and proposition 3.17, we get a description of the solutions of any $*$-problem P.

Corollary 4.16 *Let P be a solvable $*$-problem, λ_0 the linearization of its most general unifier in the free theory, and ρ_{AC1} the most general unifier of $P\lambda_0$ modulo $AC1$. Let σ be a solution of P modulo D. There exist a substitution ρ of $T(\{+, *\}, \mathcal{X})$ and a semi-group homomorphism h from $T(\{*\}, \mathcal{X})/AC1(*)$ to $T(\{+, \square\})/ \sim_D$ such that $\sigma =_D \lambda_0\rho$ and $\hat{\rho} = \rho_{AC1}h$.*

Conversely, let h' be a semi-group homomorphism from $T(\{*\}, \mathcal{X})/AC1(*)$ to $T(\{+, \square\})/\sim_D$. Then the substitution $\lambda_0(\rho_{AC1} h'\{\square \mapsto x * y\})$ is a solution of P.

5 Conclusion

We have introduced new tools (indexed distributivity and the algebra of structures) which enable us to check very easily the solvability modulo D of a *-problem and to represent its infinite set of solutions with a single scheme. The most surprising result is that D-unification of *-problems boils down to $AC1$-unification. The question of course, is whether this can be generalized to arbitrary problems. We believe it can, and based on the previous tools, we have solved the general problem under the technical assumption that there exists no cycle of some special form called "cycles of non-null weight" [1]. We therefore conjecture that unification modulo distributivity is decidable, but the algorithm appears to be at least as complex as Makanin's algorithm [8]. Moreover, it is interesting to notice that both of them use the solutions of Diophantine equations, for solving positions equations in Makanin's algorithm, and for computing $AC1$-solutions in our algorithm.

References

1. Evelyne Contejean. Éléments pour la décidabilité de l'unification modulo la distributivité. Thèse de Doctorat, Université de Paris-Sud, France, Avril 1992.
2. Nachum Dershowitz and Jean-Pierre Jouannaud. Rewrite systems. In J. van Leeuwen, editor, *Handbook of Theoretical Computer Science*, volume B, pages 243–309. North-Holland, 1990.
3. J. Herbrand. Recherches sur la théorie de la démonstration. Thèse d'Etat, Univ. Paris, 1930. Also in: Ecrits logiques de Jacques Herbrand, PUF, Paris, 1968.
4. Alexander Herold and Jorg H. Siekmann. Unification in abelian semi-groups. *Journal of Automated Reasoning*, 3(3):247–283, 1987.
5. Claude Kirchner. Méthodes et outils de conception systématique d'algorithmes d'unification dans les théories equationnelles. Thèse d'Etat, Univ. Nancy, France, 1985.
6. Claude Kirchner and Francis Klay. Syntactic theories and unification. In *Proc. 5th IEEE Symp. Logic in Computer Science, Philadelphia*, June 1990.
7. Donald E. Knuth and Peter B. Bendix. Simple word problems in universal algebras. In J. Leech, editor, *Computational Problems in Abstract Algebra*, pages 263–297. Pergamon Press, 1970.
8. G.S. Makanin. The problem of solvability of equations in a free semigroup. *Akad. Nauk. SSSR*, 233(2), 1977.
9. J. V. Matijasevic. Enumerable sets are diophantine. *Soviet Mathematics (Dokladi)*, 11(2):354–357, 1970.
10. J. A. Robinson. A machine-oriented logic based on the resolution principle. *Journal of the ACM*, 12(1):23–41, 1965.
11. P. Szabo. Unifikationstheorie erster ordnung. Technical Report Thesis, Fakultat fur Informatik, University Karlsruhe, Karlsruhe, West Germany, 1982.
12. Erik Tiden and Stefan Arnborg. Unification problems with one-sided distributivity. *Journal of Symbolic Computation*, (3):183–202, 1987.

Efficient Analysis of Concurrent Constraint Logic Programs

Michael Codish[1]   Moreno Falaschi[2] *
Kim Marriott[3]   William Winsborough[4] **

[1] Department of Computer Science, K.U. Leuven, Belgium.
[2] Dipartimento di Elettronica e Informatica, Via Gradenigo 6/A, Padova, Italy.
[3] Department of Computer Science, Monash University, Australia.
[4] Department of Computer Science, Penn State University, PA, USA.

Abstract. The standard operational semantics of concurrent constraint logic languages is not confluent in the sense that different schedulings of processes may result in different program behaviors. While implementations are free to choose specific scheduling policies, analyses should be correct for all implementations. Moreover, in the presence of parallelism it is usually not possible to determine how processes will actually be scheduled. Efficient program analysis is therefore difficult as all process schedulings must be considered. To overcome this problem we introduce a confluent semantics which closely approximates the standard (non-confluent) semantics. This semantics provides a basis for efficient and accurate program analysis for these languages. To illustrate the usefulness of this approach we sketch analyses based on abstract interpretations of the confluent semantics which determine if a program is suspension and local suspension free.

1 Introduction

Confluence, that is independence of scheduling of reductions, is an important and desirable semantic property of declarative languages. In particular, it allows a program to be understood using any convenient scheduling as other schedulings lead to "isomorphic" results. For example, confluence holds in the lambda calculus because of the Church-Rosser property, and it holds in logic programming because of the Switching Lemma [8]. In the context of concurrency, confluence is an even more desirable property [9] as concurrent programs are notoriously difficult to reason about and to analyze and, without confluence, all possible scheduling rules, and hence interleavings, must be considered. In concurrent languages we are also interested in non-terminating computations. In this case we will understand confluence as independence of scheduling for all "fair" reduction sequences in the sense that the possible outcomes of the computations are the same. However, because of the interaction between non-determinism and synchronization, confluence does not hold for many concurrent languages. In particular it does not hold for concurrent constraint logic languages, the class of languages we are interested in analyzing. In

---
* Partially supported by ESPRIT Basic Research Action 6707 ('Parforce')
** Supported in part by NSF CCR-9210975

these languages implementations are free to choose a particular process scheduling policy. However, as shown in Example 1 (Section 2), the standard operational semantics is not confluent with respect to different schedulings. Efficiency is therefore problematic in analyses which are directly based on the standard semantics as they must consider all possible process schedulings so as to ensure correctness for any implementation.

For this reason we introduce a confluent semantics which approximates the standard (non-confluent) semantics of the concurrent constraint logic languages and use this as a basis for accurate and efficient program analysis. Correctness of the analysis holds because the confluent semantics approximates the standard semantics in the sense that (1) any successful reduction sequence in the usual semantics is also a valid reduction sequence in the confluent semantics, and (2) suspension in the usual semantics implies suspension in the confluent semantics. Accuracy holds because the standard semantics is "nearly" confluent — in fact, for deterministic programs and programs without synchronization the two semantics coincide — and so the approximation is very close. Finally, because of confluence, an analysis based on this semantics need only be proven correct for a single scheduling rule. This provides for accuracy as the analysis can choose a scheduling which gives the most precise answer and also provides for efficiency as there is no need to examine the potentially exponential or even infinite number of different but "isomorphic" reduction sequences corresponding to other schedulings.

To illustrate the usefulness of the confluent semantics as a basis for abstract interpretation, we sketch analyses for detecting "suspension" and "local suspension". Local suspension occurs when a process in a system can never be reduced as it requires input from other processes in its environment to continue[5]. Suspension is an acute form of local suspension in which the computation halts as no process in the system can be scheduled.

The main contribution of this paper is a semantic basis for efficient and accurate analysis of concurrent constraint logic programming languages. Our specific technical contributions are twofold. First to show that our semantics is confluent and that it approximates the standard semantics. Our second contribution is the definition and analysis for local suspension which has not been previously studied in the context of concurrent logic languages. To our knowledge the idea of basing the analyses of a concurrent language on an approximating confluent semantics is new.

Concurrent constraint logic languages and the ask/tell paradigm were introduced by Saraswat [12]. Also see Shapiro [13]. Independence of scheduling in the confluent semantics for finite computations in a sense generalizes the standard result for logic programming, i.e. Theorem 9.2 in [8], Theorem 4 in [15] for moded equational programs, and Theorem 3.7 in [11] for determinate concurrent constraint programs. Independence of scheduling in the confluent semantics for fair infinite computations generalizes Theorem 6.5 [7] for logic programming. Our definition of suspension is the one generally assumed in the context of concurrent (constraint) logic languages [12, 13]. The definition of local suspension and its corresponding analysis are novel. Local suspension is similar to the notion of deadlock of an agent in CSP [6]. Codognet et al. [4] and Codish et al. [3] have also investigated the analysis of concurrent logic

---

[5] In the case of non-terminating computations we require that scheduling is fair.

languages, and in particular analyses for the detection of possible suspension. Both of these papers give restrictions on the analyses which ensure independence of scheduling for finite computations, allowing efficient implementation. The present work is an improvement for two reasons. Firstly, previous work does not consider confluence of non-terminating computations and so cannot be simply modified to give analyses for local suspension. Secondly, our approach simplifies proofs of correctness as such "efficient" analyses can be seen as direct abstractions of the confluent semantics. The suspension and local suspension analyses we give have some similarities to analyses of CSP, for example see [1, 2], and to the work of Peng and Purushothaman [10] as our analyses essentially construct a graph of possible states of the processes and arcs which link possible reductions between those states. However there are significant differences reflecting the different underlying models of concurrency. In particular we must handle asynchronous communication and dynamic creation and deletion of processes and communication channels.

The rest of this paper is organized as follows. In the next section we give several motivating examples which illustrate the main ideas. In Section 3 we make precise the usual operational semantics of concurrent constraint logic programs. In Section 4 we give the confluent semantics. Finally in Section 5 we define suspension and local suspension and sketch analyses for their detection based on the confluent semantics. Section 6 concludes.

2 Motivating Examples

The operational semantics of concurrent constraint logic programs is formalized in the next section. However, the intuitive idea is that processes are identified with atoms which communicate and synchronize through a common store of constraints. Computation starts with an initial environment or "state" containing a set of processes and the current constraint store. Computation proceeds by repeatedly using clauses in the program to *reduce* processes in the state. Reduction using the clause $C = H : - Ask : Tell \mid B$ can occur if H matches the process, and the current constraint implies Ask and is consistent with $Tell$. Reduction occurs by replacing the process by the body of the clause, B, and adding $Tell$ to the current store. Thus processes communicate by "telling" a constraint to the store, and synchronize by "asking" the store if a particular constraint is implied by it. Reduction continues until there are no processes left, in which case the current constraint is an *answer* of the original state, or until no process can be reduced. A process in a state is *stuck* if (1) it cannot be reduced by any clause, and (2) at least one of the clauses defining the process has constraints which are consistent with the current store. The initial state *suspends*, or *leads to suspension* if some sequence of reductions leads to a state in which all processes are stuck.

The operational semantics for a program and initial state is given as a *transition system* which is a graph with states as nodes and arcs indicating reductions, where the initial state is the "source". We adopt the convention of underlining the scheduled atom in a state and labeling the arc with the clause it is reduced with. Different transition systems result from different process schedulings. In the following examples we take (conjunctions of) syntactic equations over the Herbrand universe as constraints.

Example 1. Consider the following program P and state $s = \langle p(x), q(y); x = y \rangle$.

```
1)  p(x) :- x=a : true | s(z).        4)  q(y) :- true : y=a | true.
2)  p(x) :- x=a : true | true.        5)  q(y) :- true : y=b | true.
3)  p(x) :- true : x=b | true.        6)  s(z) :- z=a : true | true.
```

Using a left-to-right scheduling rule the program behaves deterministically as $p(x)$ can only reduce with clause (3). Thus under this scheduling rule the state s does not suspend and computation terminates with answer $x = b \wedge y = b$. The behavior, however, is radically different if a right-to-left scheduling rule is applied. In this case the program is no longer deterministic. It has three possible reduction sequences, one which leads to suspension (as the atom $s(z)$ is stuck) and others which give answers $x = a \wedge y = a$ and $x = b \wedge y = b$ respectively.

This demonstrates that analyses based directly on a standard operational semantics must consider all possible schedulings. In order to achieve independence of scheduling, we must guarantee that whenever a process is enabled it can make the same choices regardless of when it is scheduled. There are two issues to consider: (1) an enabled process which is scheduled later in the standard semantics may reduce with more clauses, and (2) an enabled process in the standard semantics may later become disenabled (and not fail) (see Example 2). The basic idea of the confluent semantics is to separate synchronization from non-determinism by interpreting synchronization at the procedure level instead of at the clause level. Namely, if every instance of an atom is either inconsistent with all clauses or can reduce with some clause in the standard semantics, then it can reduce with all consistent clauses in the confluent semantics. By considering all instances, we are sure that enabled processes do not suspend later (and hence can be scheduled); by reducing all consistent clauses, we are sure that we consider all potential choices at the time of scheduling.

The intuition behind basing analyses on a confluent semantics is that any reduction sequence in the standard semantics has an "isomorphic" reduction in the confluent semantics in which the reduction order is possibly changed and suspensions occur possibly sooner. Thus an analysis based on the confluent semantics inherits the ability to detect suspension by considering only the transition system for a single scheduling rule as a program is suspension free for all schedulings in the standard semantics if it is suspension free for any one scheduling rule in the confluent semantics.

Example 2. Consider the following program P and state
$s = \langle p(x_1, y_1), q(x_2, y_2); x_1 = x_2 \wedge y_1 = y_2 \rangle$.

```
1)  p(x,y) :- true : x=a | true.    3)  q(x,y) :- true : x=b | true.
2)  p(x,y) :- y=b : true | true.    4)  q(x,y) :- true : x=a | true.
```

With a left-to-right scheduling rule the standard computation is successful and gives $x_1 = a$. With a right-to-left scheduling the (standard) computation suspends after reducing $q(x_2, y_2)$ with the third clause. This illustrates that independence of scheduling for $p(x_1, y_1)$ does not hold in the standard semantics. In the confluent semantics both left-to-right and right-to-left schedulings will reduce $q(x_2, y_2)$ because it is not the case that all instances of $p(x_1, y_1)$ which do not fail can reduce with some of the clauses.

The previous examples suggest that the confluent semantics is a good basis for suspension analyses. In practice, however, we would like a more refined analysis which detects also "local suspension", that is when some process can never be reduced. For example the initial state $\langle clock, q(x); true\rangle$ with the program:

```
1)    clock :- true : true | clock.
2)    q(x) :- x = a : true | true.
```

does not suspend as *clock* can always be scheduled, but does have local suspension because the process $q(x)$ can never be reduced.

Local suspension analyses can also be based on the confluent semantics. The following example illustrates the intuition behind basing such analyses on the confluent semantics. The program exemplifies a common technique called *incomplete messages* for specifying two-way communication between a pair of processes.

Example 3. Consider the following program P with state $s = \langle p(x_1), c(x_2); x_1 = x_2\rangle$.

```
(1) p(x) :- true : x = [msg(y)| x1] | read(y), p(x1).
(2) p(x) :- true : x = [ ] | true.
(3) c(x) :- x = [msg(y)| x1] : true | write(y), c(x1).
(4) c(x) :- x = [ ] : true | true.
(5) read(y) :- y = a : true | true.
(6) write(y) :- true : y = a | true.
```

For any reasonable scheduling no process will be stuck forever. However an "unfair" scheduling which only schedules $p(x_1)$, will produce *read* processes that will remain forever stuck because they require $c(x_2)$ to be scheduled. For this reason when considering local suspension we restrict our attention to fair schedulings in which any process which is not stuck is eventually reduced. Now independence of process scheduling holds for all fair infinite reduction sequences in the confluent semantics. Thus, to show that a program and state are free of local suspension we need only construct a transition system based on the confluent semantics, which is local-suspension free and which has fair scheduling. In this case a suitable (and finite) transition system is obtained by consecutively scheduling p, c,read and write.

Example 3 also demonstrates the efficiency obtained by considering only one scheduling policy, as there are an infinite number of different process schedulings. The actual analyses for suspension and local suspension which we develop are simple abstractions from the confluent semantics in which the constraints are replaced by constraint descriptions and similar states are merged into the same state. The analyses work by constructing a confluent transition system over these "abstract states" with the desired property.

3 The Standard Operational Semantics

This section presents an operational semantics for concurrent constraint logic programs which formalizes the one described in the previous section. The definitions are parametric with respect to the underlying constraint system. Moreover, almost the same definitions apply when defining the confluent semantics and the suspension analyses.

We let Con_C be a fixed set of (concrete) constraints that is closed under conjunction and existential quantification. Elements of Con_C are regarded modulo logical equivalence. Typical examples of Con_C are constructed from syntactic equations over the Herbrand universe, or linear arithmetic equalities and inequalities. We let $fail$ denote the unsatisfiable constraint and $true$ the always satisfiable constraint. We write $\theta \leq \theta'$ if θ logically implies θ'. Thus Con_C is a lattice ordered by $\leq$ with bottom element $fail$ and top element $true$. For a finite set V of variables and $\theta \in Con_C$ we use $\exists_V \theta$ as shorthand for the constraint $\exists v_1 \exists v_2 ... \exists v_n \theta$ where $\{v_1, ..., v_n\} = V$. We use $\bar{\exists}_s \theta$ as shorthand for $\exists_{vars(\theta) \setminus vars(s)} \theta$ where $vars(s)$ denote the set of variables occurring in syntactic object s. Intuitively, $\bar{\exists}_s \theta$ restricts the constraint θ to the variables in syntactic object s.

We adopt a slightly non-standard notion of goals. The standard notion of a "goal" or "environment" is captured by a state that consists of a $goal$ and the current constraint store. Here, a $goal$ is a (possibly empty) set of atoms that do not share variables. The empty goal is denoted by $true$ and the set of goals is denoted by $Goal$. Consequently, inter-process communications are always specified in a constraint, and as a result it is sufficient to base analyses on descriptions of constraints.

Let Con be a lattice. The $set\ of\ states$ constructed from Con is defined by $State = Goal \times Con$. Associated with $State$ are the projections $goal : State \to Goal$ and $con : State \to Con$ defined by $goal\langle g, \theta \rangle = g$ and $con\langle g, \theta \rangle = \theta$. The $concrete$ states constructed from Con_C are denoted $State_C$. We will also be interested in states constructed from abstract constraints which are descriptions of concrete constraints.

A $program$ is a finite set of guarded clauses. A $guarded\ clause$ (or $clause$) is a formula of the form $A : -Ask : Tell \mid B$ where A is an atom, called the $head$, Ask and $Tell$ are unquantified concrete constraints and B, called the $body$, is a goal. The set of programs is denoted $Prog$.

A $(variable)\ renaming$ is a bijection on the set of variables. The set of renamings is denoted by Ren. Renamings are naturally extended to mappings from terms to terms, etc. Often we will be interested in terms, atoms, clauses or constraints modulo variable renaming. We write $p \sim q$ and say that p is a $renaming$ of q if there is a renaming ρ such that $\rho(p) = q$. For program P and a syntactic object s, $C \ll_s P$ denotes that C is a renaming of a clause in P such that $vars(C) \cap vars(s) = \emptyset$.

The operational semantics is given in terms of reductions between states. This is modeled using a try function and a $resolve$ function. The try function indicates if an atom (in a state) can be reduced with a given clause while the $resolve$ function specifies the effect of the reduction on the constraint store. We let $Atom$ denote the set of atoms, and $Clause$ the set of clauses.

Definition 1. The $concrete\ resolve\ function$, $resolve_C : Atom \times Con_C \times Clause \to Con_C$, is defined by $resolve_C(A, \theta, C) = (A = H \wedge Ask \wedge Tell \wedge \theta)$ and the $concrete\ try\ function$, $try_C : Atom \times Con_C \times Clause \to \{fail, success, delay\}$, by

$$try_C(A, \theta, C) = \begin{cases} fail & \text{if } resolve_C(A, \theta, C) = fail \\ success & \text{if } resolve_C(A, \theta, C) \neq fail \text{ and } \theta \leq \bar{\exists}_A(A = H \wedge Ask) \\ delay & \text{otherwise} \end{cases}$$

where $C = H : - Ask : Tell \mid B$.

A constraint has an associated "stuck" relationship that holds for an atom if under the constraint the atom cannot be successfully reduced with any clause, but does delay for some clause.

Definition 2. Let $P \in Prog$ and $\theta \in Con_C$. Atom A is *stuck* in θ (for P), written $stuck_C^P(A, \theta)$, iff: (1) $\exists C \ll_V P$. $try_C(A, \theta, C) = delay$; and (2) $\forall C \ll_V P$. $try_C(A, \theta, C) \neq success$, where $V = vars(\langle A; \theta \rangle)$.

Typically, implementations of the operational semantics use a particular process scheduling policy, such as selection of the leftmost non-stuck process. We model a scheduling policy as an arbitrary choice of atoms from the state's goal that satisfies a suitable scheduling relation.

Definition 3. Let $P \in Prog$. A (concrete) *scheduling relation*, $sched^P \subseteq State_C \times Goal$, is defined in terms of a corresponding relation $stuck^P \subseteq Atom \times Con_C$ by: $sched^P(s, B)$ iff: (1) $B \subseteq goal(s)$; (2) $A \in B \Rightarrow \neg stuck^P(A, con(s))$; and (3) $\exists A \in goal(s) . \neg stuck^P(A, con(s)) \Rightarrow B \neq \emptyset$.

In the following we will be interested in two concrete scheduling relations. The *standard* scheduling relation denoted $sched_C^P$ which is defined in terms of the relation $stuck_C^P$ defined in Definition 2; and the *confluent* scheduling relation defined in the next section. Reduction is defined in terms of a set of selected atoms.

Definition 4. Let $P \in Prog$ and $s, s' \in State_C$. The state s' is a *concrete resolvent* of s with atom A and defining clause $C = H : - Ask : Tell \mid B$ iff $A \in goal(s)$ and $s' = \langle (goal(s) \setminus \{A\}) \cup B; resolve_C(A, con(s), C) \rangle$. In this case A is said to be the *selected atom* and C the *corresponding clause*.

The standard reduction relation for P, $reduce_C^P \subseteq State_C \times State_C \times Atom$, is defined by $reduce_C^P(s, s', A)$ iff s' is a concrete resolvent of s with A and $C \ll_s P$ such that $try_C(A, con(s), C) = success$.

In the following the superscript will be omitted from $stuck_C^P$, $sched_C^P$ and $reduce_C^P$ when clear from the context. The operational semantics is defined as a *transition system*, which is a graph that has states as nodes. The initial state is a "source node" and edges correspond to *reductions* between the states. Thus reduction sequences correspond to paths in the graph starting from the source. Different transition systems for the same initial state and program result from different scheduling rules.

Definition 5. Let $P \in Prog$, *State* be a set of states, $s \in State$ and let *reduce* $\subseteq State \times State \times Atom$ and *sched* $\subseteq State \times Goal$ be a reduction relation and a scheduling relation respectively. A *transition system* $\mathcal{G}$ for P and s is a graph with each node n labeled by a state, denoted by $state(n)$, and a set of selected atoms, denoted by $sel(n)$ such that: (a) every node in $\mathcal{G}$ is reachable from a distinguished node called the source, which is labeled with state s; (b) for all nodes n, $sched(state(n), sel(n))$; and (c) there is an edge from n to n' iff $\exists A \in sel(n).reduce(state(n), state(n'), A)$.

Note that *reduce* determines which clauses can be used while *sched* determines which goals are scheduled. The standard operational semantics is given by the *standard transition systems* which are transition systems constructed from concrete states and the standard scheduling and reduction relations.

The execution sequences of a program are modeled by its *derivations*. We will be interested in successful, suspending, and failed derivations as well as the answers from successful derivations.

Definition 6. Let $\mathcal{G}$ be a transition system on states *State* for $s_1 \in$ *State* and $P \in$ *Prog*. A *derivation* in $\mathcal{G}$ is a (possibly infinite) maximal sequence of states $s_1 \rightarrow s_2 \rightarrow \cdots$ such that there is a path in $\mathcal{G}$ with s_i the state label of the ith node in the path. When we also wish to indicate the selected atom and clause at each stage, we write the derivation as $s_1 \xrightarrow{A_1; C_1} s_2 \xrightarrow{A_2; C_2} \cdots$. We let $deriv(\mathcal{G})$ denote the *set of derivations* in $\mathcal{G}$.

Definition 7. Let $\mathcal{G}$ be a standard transition system on *State*$_C$ for $s \in$ *State*$_C$ and $P \in$ *Prog*. A (finite) derivation which ends in a state s' is: *successful* if $goal(s') = true$; *suspended* if $goal(s') \neq true$ and $\forall A \in goal(s')$. $stuck_C(A, con(s')))$; and is otherwise *failed*. An *answer* of $\mathcal{G}$ is a constraint $\bar{\exists}_s con(s')$ where s' is the last state of a successful derivation in $\mathcal{G}$.

As we are concerned with confluence we must make precise what it means for two different transition systems to be "isomorphic" up to process scheduling and formalize a notion of fairness.

Definition 8. Let $\mathcal{G}$ and $\mathcal{G}'$ be transition systems for s and P. Let $\mathcal{D}$ and $\mathcal{D}'$ be derivations of $\mathcal{G}$ and $\mathcal{G}'$, respectively, with $\mathcal{D} = s_1 \xrightarrow{A_1; C_1} s_2 \xrightarrow{A_2; C_2} \cdots \xrightarrow{A_i; C_i} s_{i+1} \cdots$ where the s_i are indexed by I, a possibly infinite initial subsequence of the positive integers. We say that $\mathcal{D}$ is *isomorphic* to $\mathcal{D}'$ iff there exist a renaming $\mathcal{D}''$ of $\mathcal{D}'$ and a bijection $f : I \longrightarrow I$ such that $\mathcal{D}'' = s_1 \xrightarrow{A_{f(1)}; C_{f(1)}} s_2' \xrightarrow{A_{f(2)}; C_{f(2)}} \cdots \xrightarrow{A_{f(j)}; C_{f(j)}} s_{j+1}' \cdots$. We say that $\mathcal{G}$ and $\mathcal{G}'$ are *isomorphic* if their derivations are isomorphic.

Definition 9. An infinite derivation $s_1 \xrightarrow{A_1; C_1} s_2 \xrightarrow{A_2; C_2} \cdots$ is *fair* if for every $i \in \mathbb{N}$, $A \in goal(s_i) \wedge \neg stuck(A, con(s_i)) \Rightarrow (\exists j \geq i . A = A_j)$. A transition system is *fair* iff all of its infinite derivations are fair.

The following definitions formalize the notions of suspension and local suspension.

Definition 10. A state $s \in$ *State*$_C$ *suspends* for program P iff $goal(s) \neq true$ and for all $A \in goal(s)$, $stuck_C(A, con(s))$. Let $\mathcal{G}$ be a transition system on *State*$_C$ for P and s. A derivation of $\mathcal{G}$ *suspends* iff it is finite and ends in a suspended state. A transition system *suspends* iff it has a derivation that suspends. A state s *leads to suspension* for P iff there is a standard transition system for P and s that suspends.

Definition 11. Let $\mathcal{G}$ be a transition system on *State*$_C$ for program P and $s \in$ *State*$_C$. A derivation $s_1 \rightarrow s_2 \rightarrow \cdots$ of $\mathcal{G}$ *locally suspends* iff it is not failed and $\exists i . \exists A \in goal(s_i) . \forall j . (j \geq i \Rightarrow stuck_C(A, con(s_j)))$. A transition system *locally suspends* iff it has a derivation that locally suspends. A concrete state s *leads to local suspension* for program P iff there is a fair standard transition system for P and s that locally-suspends.

4   A Confluent Semantics

In this section we present a confluent semantics which approximates the standard operational semantics. The basic idea is to separate synchronization from non-determinism by interpreting synchronization at the procedure level. This is achieved by: (1) scheduling an atom only if it can be scheduled in the standard semantics and cannot become stuck under further instantiation, and (2) synchronizing a clause not by its own synchronization condition but rather by a combined condition consisting of a disjunction of the conditions from the clauses of the given procedure. Hence, if an atom can reduce with any clause, then it can reduce with all clauses which are consistent with the current constraint.

Definition 12. Let $P \in Prog$. The *confluent reduction relation*, $reduce_{C\mathcal{F}} \subseteq State_C \times State_C \times Atom$, is defined by $reduce_{C\mathcal{F}}(s, s', A)$ iff s' is a concrete resolvent of s with A and $C \ll_s P$ such that $try_C(A, con(s), C) \neq fail$. The *confluent scheduling relation*, $sched_{C\mathcal{F}}^P$ is the concrete scheduling relation determined by

$$stuck_{C\mathcal{F}}^P(A, \theta) = \exists \theta' \leq \theta.\ stuck_C^P(A, \theta').$$

A *confluent transition system* is a transition system constructed from $State_C$ with the scheduling relation $sched_{C\mathcal{F}}^P$ and the confluent reduction relation $reduce_{C\mathcal{F}}$.

The following theorem justifies our use of "confluent". It states that independence of scheduling holds for finite derivations and for infinite derivations in the case that the transition systems are fair.

Theorem 13. *Let $\mathcal{G}, \mathcal{G}'$ be confluent transition systems for s and P and let $\mathcal{D}$ be a non-failing derivation of $\mathcal{G}$. Then, (1) $\mathcal{D}$ is finite iff there is a finite non-failing derivation of $\mathcal{G}'$ isomorphic to $\mathcal{D}$; and (2) if $\mathcal{G}$ and $\mathcal{G}'$ are fair then $\mathcal{D}$ is infinite iff there is an infinite derivation of $\mathcal{G}'$ isomorphic to $\mathcal{D}$.*

This means that if $\mathcal{G}$ and $\mathcal{G}'$ are confluent transition systems for a given program and initial state, then they will have the same answers, and each will suspend if and only if the other does. This is the main technical contribution of the paper. It is easy to construct an example showing that if the fairness requirement is dropped, then the theorem no longer holds. The following proposition states that the confluent semantics approximates the standard semantics.

Proposition 14. *If $\mathcal{G}$ is a (fair) standard transition system for s and P which (locally) suspends, then any (fair) confluent transition system $\mathcal{G}'$ for s and P (locally) suspends.*

As a consequence of Theorem 13 and Proposition 14, suspension analyses can be based on a single scheduling rule and the resultant transition system. Furthermore, local suspension analyses can be based on any one fair transition system.

For many programs, P, the confluent and standard semantics are equivalent in the sense that for all $s \in State_C$, $\mathcal{G}$ is a standard transition system for s and P if and only if it is a confluent transition system for s and P. These are programs that are not affected by lifting the interpretation of synchronization from the clause level to the procedure level. In particular, P-Prolog [14] and P-Prolog$_x$ [13] programs are specifically defined in this way.

Definition 15. A program P is *confluent* iff for all atoms A, constraints θ and clauses $C \ll_{(A;\theta)} P$ and $C' \ll_{(A;\theta)} P$,

$$try_C(A, \theta, C) = success \Rightarrow try_C(A, \theta, C') \neq delay.$$

In particular, programs for which the asks are mutually exclusive are confluent because they are deterministic in the strong sense that, if an atom succeeds with some clause, it will fail with all other clauses.

Proposition 16. *The confluent and standard transition semantics are equivalent for confluent programs.*

Consequently, independence of the scheduling rule holds for confluent programs using the *standard semantics*.

5   Suspension and Local Suspension Analyses

Analyses for these properties are couched as abstract interpretations [5] of the confluent semantics in which constraints are replaced by constraint descriptions. Correctness is argued by providing an approximation relation, $\propto$, which relates the descriptions to the objects they describe. Correctness of the analyses is based on the following theorem.

Theorem 17. *A state $s \in State_C$ does not lead to suspension for P if there exists a confluent transition system for s and P that does not suspend. Furthermore, s does not lead to local suspension for P if there exists a fair confluent transition system for s and P that does not locally suspend.*

In a suspension (or local suspension) analysis, one is interested in knowing which atoms in a state are "possibly" stuck. This requires keeping information about how variables in a state will be affected if other variables in that state become more instantiated after a reduction. In [3] we have given several such domains.

We induce a state description from Con_A essentially by leaving the goal component as it is, and abstracting the constraint component of the state. We note that such an analysis may not terminate for programs in which the number of atoms (that is processes) increases through the computation. In [3] we have shown how to provide for such cases by collapsing processes that are renamings of one another into the same abstract process. If this is done, termination is guaranteed for all programs.

Definition 18. Let $Goal^* \subseteq Goal$ be some (fixed) maximal set such that no two goals in $Goal^*$ are variable renamings. Let Con_A be a constraint description. Define the *induced (abstract) states*, $State_A$, to be $Goal^* \times Con_A$. Let $t \in State_A$, $s \in State$ and $\rho \in Ren$. Define $t \propto_\rho s$ iff: (1) $goal(t) = \rho(goal(s))$; and (2) $con(t) \propto \rho(\bar{\exists}_{goal(s)} con(s))$. We say that t approximates s, written $t \propto s$, iff $\exists \rho \in Ren.t \propto_\rho s$.

Reduction of abstract states is essentially the same as for concrete (confluent) reduction. To ensure correctness of the analysis we require that abstract reduction relation $reduce_A$ approximates the confluent reduction relation $reduce_{CF}$, namely that $reduce_A \subseteq State_A \times State_A \times Atom$ satisfies the following for all $A \in Atom$, $s, s' \in State_C$ and $t \in State_A$,

$$t \propto_\rho s \; \& \; reduce_{C\mathcal{F}}(s, s', A) \Rightarrow \exists t' \in State_A.reduce_A(t, t', \rho(A)) \; \& \; t' \propto s'.$$

This ensures that, if there is a reduction in the confluent semantics, there will be a corresponding reduction in the approximating abstract semantics. We must also define what it means for an atom to be stuck in an abstract constraint. As we are interested in detecting possible suspension and local-suspension we should err on the side of being stuck. Thus an atom is stuck in the abstract constraint whenever the atom is stuck in some concrete constraint described by the abstract constraint. That is, atom A is stuck in the abstract constraint θ, written $stuck_A(A, \theta)$ iff $\exists E \in Con_C . \theta \propto E \; \& \; stuck_{C\mathcal{F}}(A, E)$. The definitions for scheduling relation, suspended state, derivation, etc., are as for the concrete states except that abstract stuckness replaces concrete stuckness. An abstract transition system is a transition system with states $State_A$, a scheduling relation $sched_A$ defined in terms of $stuck_A$, and an abstract reduction relation $reduce_A$. We analyze a state s and program P for possible suspension by constructing a single abstract transition system for s and P. If this system contains no suspended derivations, then s and P definitely do not lead to suspension (for any scheduling rule) with respect to the standard transition system, otherwise they may. In general, the domain of abstract constraints must be chosen carefully so that abstract transition graphs are guaranteed to be finite and checking for suspended derivations is possible. Similarly we analyze s and P for possible local suspension by constructing a single fair abstract transition system for s and P. If this system contains no locally suspended states, then s and P definitely do not locally suspend (for any fair scheduling rule), otherwise they may. Correctness of these analyses is a consequence of the following theorem.

Theorem 19. *Let $\mathcal{G}$ be an abstract transition system for a state s and program P. If $\mathcal{G}$ is fair and does not lead to (local) suspension then any standard transition system for s and P does not lead to (local) suspension.*

6 Conclusion

We have introduced a confluent semantics for concurrent constraint logic languages which provides a basis for their efficient and accurate analysis. We have shown the usefulness of this approach by using it to develop analyses for suspension and local suspension. We stress that the approach is of general applicability. It can be used to develop analyses for various program properties which are independent of scheduling in the confluent semantics. In particular it can be used to develop analyses for other reactive properties such as deadlock and local deadlock which are extreme forms of suspension and local suspension in which adding further processes to the initial system cannot remove the eventual suspension. Moreover, it can be applied to non-reactive properties such as detecting determinism or analysing success and fail patterns. Another application is to optimize implementations by applying a scheduling rule for which a program is shown not to locally suspend. In this case speed-ups may be obtained as there is no need to test for synchronization.

Acknowledgment

We acknowledge the suggestions of the (anonymous) referees of a previous version of this paper.

References

1. S.D. Brookes and A.W. Roscoe. Deadlock Analysis in Networks of Communicating Processes. *Distributed Computing*, 4:209–230, 1991.
2. K.M. Chandy and J. Misra. Deadlock Absence Proofs for Networks of Communicating Processes. *Information Proc. Letters*, 9(4):185, 1979.
3. M. Codish, M. Falaschi, and K. Marriott. Suspension Analyses for Concurrent Logic Programs. *ACM Transactions on Programming Languages and Systems*, 1993. To appear.
4. C. Codognet, P. Codognet, and M. Corsini. Abstract Interpretation for Concurrent Logic Languages. In S. Debray and M. Hermenegildo, editors, *Proc. North American Conf. on Logic Programming'90*, pages 215–232. The MIT Press, Cambridge, Mass., 1990.
5. P. Cousot and R. Cousot. Abstract Interpretation: A Unified Lattice Model for Static Analysis of Programs by Construction or Approximation of Fixpoints. In *Proc. Fourth ACM Symp. Principles of Programming Languages*, pages 238–252, 1977.
6. C.A.R. Hoare. *Communicating Sequential Processes*. Prentice-Hall, 1985.
7. J.-L. Lassez and M. J. Maher. Closures and Fairness in the Semantics of Programming Logic. *Theoretical Computer Science*, 29:167–184, 1984.
8. J. W. Lloyd. *Foundations of Logic Programming*. Springer-Verlag, Berlin, 1987. Second edition.
9. R. Milner. *Communication and Concurrency*. Prentice-Hall Int. (UK), 1989.
10. W. Peng and S. Purushothaman. Data flow analysis of communicating finite state machines. *ACM Transactions on Programming Languages and Systems*, 13(2):399–442, 1991.
11. V. Saraswat, M. Rinard, and P. Panangaden. Semantic Foundation of Concurrent Constraint Programming. In *Proc. Eighteenth Annual ACM Symp. on Principles of Programming Languages*, 1991.
12. V. A. Saraswat. *Concurrent Constraint Programming Languages*. PhD thesis, Carnegie-Mellon University, January 1989. Also in *ACM Distinguished Dissertation Series*.
13. E. Y. Shapiro. The family of concurrent logic programming languages. *ACM Computing Surveys*, 21(3):412–510, 1989.
14. R. Yang and H. Aiso. P-Prolog: a parallel language based on exclusive relation. In E. Y. Shapiro, editor, *Proc. Third Int'l Conf. on Logic Programming*, volume 225 of *LNCS*, pages 255–269. Springer-Verlag, Berlin, 1986.
15. K. Yelick and J. Zachary. Moded type systems for logic programming. In *Proc. Sixteenth Annual ACM Symp. on Principles of Programming Languages*, pages 116–124. ACM, 1989.

A confluent reduction for the extensional typed λ−calculus with pairs, sums, recursion and terminal object

Roberto Di Cosmo*   Delia Kesner §

Abstract

We add extensional equalities for the functional and product types to the typed λ-calculus with not only products and terminal object, but also sums and bounded recursion (a version of recursion that does not allow recursive calls of infinite length). We provide a confluent and strongly normalizing (thus decidable) rewriting system for the calculus, that stays confluent when allowing unbounded recursion. For that, we turn the extensional equalities into *expansion* rules, and not into contractions as is done traditionally. We first prove the calculus to be weakly confluent, which is a more complex and interesting task than for the usual λ-calculus. Then we provide an effective mechanism to simulate expansions without expansion rules, so that the strong normalization of the calculus can be derived from that of the underlying, traditional, non extensional system. These results give us the confluence of the full calculus, but we also show how to deduce confluence without the weak confluence property, using only our technique of simulating expansions.

1 Introduction

Over the past years there has been a growing interest in the properties of λ-calculus extended with various different type constructors, in particular pairs and sums, used to represent common data types. For these type constructors it is customary to provide a set of equalities that are then turned into computation rules: this is the case, for example, of the elimination rules for pairs:

$$(\pi_1) \quad \pi_1(\langle M, N \rangle) \quad = \quad M \qquad (\pi_2) \quad \pi_2(\langle M, N \rangle) \quad = \quad N$$

They tell us how to operationally *compute* with objects of these types: if we have a pair $\langle M, N \rangle$, then we can decompose it to access its first or second component.

There is anyway something else that one likes to do with λ-calculus, besides using λ-terms as programs to be computed: one would like to *reason* about programs, to prove that they enjoy certain properties. Here is where extensional equalities come into play. In the case of functions, for example, since the only operational way to *use* a function is to apply it to an argument, we do not really want to consider a term M of function type different from the term $\lambda x.Mx$ where x does not occur free in M: both terms, when applied to an argument N, give the same result MN. Similarly for pairs, the only operational way to *use* a pair is by projecting out the first or the second component, so we do not want to consider a term M of product type different from the term $\langle \pi_1(M), \pi_2(M) \rangle$: the result of accessing any of these two terms via a first or second projection is the same term $\pi_1(M)$ or $\pi_2(M)$.

These facts can be incorporated in the calculus in the form of equalities, that one can read in at least two different ways:

*DMI-LIENS (CNRS URA 1347) Ecole Normale Supérieure - 45, Rue d'Ulm - 75230 Paris France
e-mail:dicosmo@dmi.ens.fr

§INRIA Rocquencourt - Domaine de Voluceau, BP 105 - 78153 Le Chesnay Cedex, France and CNRS and LRI - Bât 490, Université de Paris-Sud - 91405 Orsay Cedex, France - e-mail:kesner@lri.lri.fr

- *an operational way:* these equalities just state possible *optimizations* of a program. Since a term $\langle \pi_1(M), \pi_2(M) \rangle$ is more complex then M, but behaves the same way, it is convenient to replace all its occurrences by M, as this transformation will yield an equivalent, but more efficient and smaller program. Similarly, we will replace every occurrence of $\lambda x.Mx$ by M.

- *a theoretical way:* these equalities state a relation between a program and its type. They just tell us that whenever a term M has a functional type, then it must really be a function, built by λ-abstraction, so we ought to replace it by $\lambda x.Mx$ if it is not already a function. Similarly, a term M of product type has to be really a pair, built via the pair constructor, or otherwise it must be replaced by $\langle \pi_1(M), \pi_2(M) \rangle$.

As we will briefly see in the Survey, a lot of research activity has focused on the operational reading of these equalities in the tradition of λ-calculus, while only a little on the theoretical one. In this paper we will show how this last reading of the equalities provides a confluent and strongly normalizing reduction system for the simply typed λ-calculus with pairs, sums, unit type (or terminal object) and a bounded recursion operator. We also show that the same reduction system stays confluent when allowing unbounded recursion, while of course loosing the strong normalization property.

2 Survey

Due to the deep connections between λ-calculus, proof theory and category theory, works on extensional equalities have appeared with different motivations in all these fields.

By far, the best known extensional equality is the η axiom that we informally introduced above, written in the λ-calculus formalism as

$$(\eta) \qquad \lambda x.Mx = M \qquad \text{provided } x \text{ is not free in } M$$

This axiom, also known as *extensionality*, has traditionally been turned into a reduction, carrying the same name, by orienting the equality from left to right, interpreting operationally equality as a *contraction*. Such an interpretation is well behaved as it preserves confluence [CF58].

In the early 70's, the attention was focusing on products and the extensional rule for pairs, called *surjective pairing*, which is the analog for product types of the usual η extensional rule.

$$(SP) \qquad \langle \pi_1(M), \pi_2(M) \rangle = M$$

With the previous experience of the η rule, it is easy to understand how, at that time, most of the people thought that the right way to turn such an equality into a rewrite rule was also from left to right, as a contraction. But in 1980, J.W. Klop discovered [Klo80] that, if added to the usual confluent rewrite rules for pure λ-calculus, this interpretation of SP breaks confluence[1].

Anyway, this first negative result was shortly after mitigated in [Pot81] for the simply typed λ-calculus with η and SP contractions, by providing a first proof of confluence and strong normalization, later on simplified in different ways (see [Tro86] or [GLT90], for example). From then on, the contraction rule for SP was not considered harmful in a typed framework, until the seminal work by Lambek and Scott [LS86]. There, the decision problem of the equational theory of Cartesian Closed Categories (ccc's) is solved using a particular typed λ-calculus equipped with not only η and SP equalities, but also with a special type $\mathbf{T}$ representing the *terminal object* of the ccc's[2]. This

---

[1] See [Bar84], p. 403-409 for a short history and references.
[2] This is the *Unit* type in languages like ML.

distinguished atomic type comes with a further extensional axiom asserting that there is exactly one term $*$ of type $\mathbf{T}$:

$$(Top) \qquad M : \mathbf{T} = *$$

Now, the type $\mathbf{T}$ has the bad property of destroying confluence, if the extensional equalities η and SP are turned into contraction rules: the following are the critical pairs that arise immediately, as first pointed out by Obtulowicz, (see [LS86]):

$$
\begin{array}{lllll}
\langle *, \pi_2(x) \rangle & {}_{Top}\!\!\Leftarrow & \langle \pi_1(x), \pi_2(x) \rangle & \Rightarrow_{SP} & x \\
\langle \pi_1(x), * \rangle & {}_{Top}\!\!\Leftarrow & \langle \pi_1(x), \pi_2(x) \rangle & \Rightarrow_{SP} & x \\
(\lambda x : \mathbf{T}.M*) : \mathbf{T} \to A & {}_{Top}\!\!\Leftarrow & (\lambda x : \mathbf{T}.Mx) : \mathbf{T} \to A & \Rightarrow_{\eta} & M \\
(\lambda x : A.*) : A \to \mathbf{T} & {}_{Top}\!\!\Leftarrow & (\lambda x : A.Mx) : A \to \mathbf{T} & \Rightarrow_{\eta} & M
\end{array}
$$

It is indeed possible, but not easy, to extend the contractive reduction system in order to recover confluence. A first step towards such a confluent system was taken by Poigné and Voss, who were not inspired by category theory, but by the implementation of algebraic data types [PV87]. In their paper, they study a calculus that includes $\lambda^1\beta\eta\pi*$, and notice that to solve the previous critical pairs one needs to add an infinite number of reduction rules (that can be anyway finitely described). Then confluence of such an extended system can be proved by showing weak confluence and strong normalization. Unfortunately, the critical pair for $(\lambda x : A.Mx) : \mathbf{T} \to A$ is missing there, and the strong normalization proof is incomplete.

More recently, Curien and the first author got interested in a polymorphic extension of $\lambda^1\beta\eta\pi*$, that arose in the study of the theory of object oriented programming and of isomorphisms of types [CDC91]. They give a complete (infinite) set of reduction rules for the calculus, which is proved confluent using just weak confluence, weak normalization and some additional properties.

Meanwhile, in the field of proof theory, Prawitz was suggesting [Pra71] to turn these extensional equalities into *expansion* rules, rather than contractions. Building on such ideas, but motivated by the study of coherence problems in category theory, Mints gives a first faulty proof that in the typed framework *expansion rules*, if handled with care, are weakly normalizing and preserve confluence of the typed calculus [Min79][3].

This idea of using expansion rules seems to have passed unnoticed for a long time, even if the so called η-long normal forms were well known and used in the study of higher order unification problems [Hue76]: only in these last years there has been a renewed interest in expansion rules. In recent work [Jay92], still motivated by category theoretic investigation, Jay explores a simply typed λ-calculus with just $\mathbf{T}$ and a natural number type $\mathbf{N}$ as base types, equipped with an induction combinator for terms of type $\mathbf{N}$. He introduced expansion rules for η and SP that are exactly the same as the ones originally used by Mints, and in [JG92] this calculus is proved confluent and strongly normalizing. Category theory is also the motivation of Cubric [Cub92], who repaired the bug in the original proof by Mints showing confluence and weak normalization (but not strong normalization). Another recent related work is [Aka93], where an interesting divide-and-conquer approach is proposed to prove confluence and strong normalization of Mints' calculus.

2.1 Our work

The present paper is inspired by all the previous works, but especially by [Jay92] and [PV87]. We use expansion rules to provide a confluent rewriting system for the typed λ-calculus with not only products and terminal object, but also sums and recursion. This result is derived from the confluence of a restricted system where recursion is bounded (recursive calls of infinite length are not allowed), which is proved to be weakly confluent and strongly normalizing.

---

[3]The same idea is present in [Min77].

We show that strong normalization of the full system can be reduced to that of the system without expansion rules, for which the traditional techniques can be used. For that purpose, we show that any one step reduction in the calculus with expansions can be *simulated* by a non-empty reduction sequence in the calculus without expansions. It turns out that this result is powerful enough to prove directly also the confluence property, as shown in section 6.

Since the reduction with expansion rules is not a congruence, several fundamental properties that hold for the well known typed λ-calculi have to be reformulated in the expansionary framework in a different way as we will shortly see in Section 4. For this reason we believe that the system with expansion rules deserves to be studied much more carefully, so we will undertake the task of proving directly weak confluence: this will lead us to uncover many of the essential features of this reduction.

We introduce now the calculus and its reduction system in section 3, then we investigate the key properties of the new reduction system: weak confluence (section 4) and strong normalization (section 5). In section 6 we derive the confluence property in two different ways and finally in the conclusion we discuss some further applications of our proof techniques. Due to space limitations, we cannot provide the full proofs, and we refer the interested reader to [DCK93] for full details.

3 The Calculus

It is now time to introduce the calculus we will deal with in this paper. There are two versions, one with bounded recursion, and the other with unbounded recursion, that differ just in the term formation rule and in the equality rule for recursive terms. We will now introduce the calculus with bounded recursion and then describe how the unbounded version can be obtained from it.

3.1 Types and Terms

The set of types of our calculus contains a distinguished type constant $\mathbf{T}^4$, a denumerable set of atomic or base types, and is closed w.r.t. formation of function, product and sum, i.e. if A and B are types, then also $A \to B$, $A \times B$ and $A + B$ are types.

For each type A, we fix a denumerable set of variables of that type. We will use $x, y, z, \ldots$ to range over variables, and for a term M we write $M : A$ to mean that M is a term of type A.

The term formation rules of the calculus can then be presented as follows.

$\Gamma \vdash * : \mathbf{T}$

$x_1 : T_1, \ldots, x_n : T_n \vdash x_i : T_i \ (1 \leq i \leq n),$ where the x_i's are pairwise distinct

If $\Gamma \vdash M : A \to B$ and $\Gamma \vdash N : A$ then $\Gamma \vdash (MN) : B$

If $\Gamma, x : A \vdash M : B$ then $\Gamma \vdash \lambda x . A.M : A \to B$

If $\Gamma \vdash M : A$ and $\Gamma \vdash N : B$ then $\Gamma \vdash \langle M, N \rangle : A \times B$

If $\Gamma \vdash M : B_1 \times B_2$ then $\Gamma \vdash \pi_i(M) : B_i \ (i = 1, 2)$

If $\Gamma \vdash M : B_i$ then $\Gamma \vdash in^i_{B_1 + B_2}(M) : B_1 + B_2 \ (i = 1, 2)$

If $\Gamma \vdash P : A_1 + A_2$ and $\Gamma \vdash M_i : A_i \to D \ (i = 1, 2)$ then $\Gamma \vdash Case(P, M_1, M_2) : D$

If $\Gamma, x : A \vdash M : A$ then $\Gamma \vdash (rec \ x : A.M)^i : A \ (i \geq 0)$

Notation 3.1 (Free variables, substitutions) *The set of free variables of a term M will be noted $FV(M)$. We write $[N_1, \ldots, N_n/x_1, \ldots, x_n]$ (often abbreviated $[\overline{N}/\overline{x}]$) for the typed substitution mapping each variable $x_i : A_i$ to a term $N_i : A_i$. We write $M[\overline{N}/\overline{x}]$ for the term M where each variable x_i free in M is replaced by N_i.*

---

[4]This stands for the terminal object in ccc's or for the *Unit* type in languages like ML.

3.2 Equality

Besides the usual identification of terms up to α conversion (i.e. renaming of bound variables), our calculus is equipped with the following equalities between terms.

$$
\begin{array}{llll}
(\beta) & (\lambda x:A.M)N = M[N/x] & (Top) & M = * \text{ if } M:\mathbf{T} \\
(\pi_1) & \pi_1(\langle M_1, M_2\rangle) = M_1 & & \\
(\pi_2) & \pi_2(\langle M_1, M_2\rangle) = M_2 & (\eta) & \lambda x:A.Mx = M \text{ if } \left\{ \begin{array}{l} x \notin FV(M) \\ M:A \to B \end{array} \right. \\
(\rho) & Case(in_C^1(R), M_1, M_2) = M_1 R & (\delta) & \langle \pi_1(M), \pi_2(M)\rangle = M \text{ if } M:A \times B \\
& Case(in_C^2(R), M_1, M_2) = M_2 R & (rec) & (rec\ y:C.M)^{i+1} = M[(rec\ y:C.M)^i/y] \\
\end{array}
$$

The index i that is attached to each rec term is a *bound* on the depth of the recursive calls that can originate from it. With such a bound, it is possible to insure the strong normalization of the associated reduction system.

The unbounded system is obtained from the bounded one by simply erasing all the bound indexes from the formation and equality rules (and the associated reduction rules). As we will show later, the bounded system can simulate any finite reduction of the unbounded system, and this fact will make it easy to extend the confluence result for the bounded system to the unbounded one. For simplicity, we will explicitly note the bound index only when necessary, dropping it whenever the properties we discuss hold in both systems.

3.3 The confluent rewriting system

The non extensional equality rules and the rule for $\mathbf{T}$ can be turned into a confluent rewriting system by orienting them from left to right, as follows

$$
\begin{array}{llll}
(\beta) & (\lambda x:A.M)N & \overset{\beta}{\longrightarrow} & M[N/x] \\
(\pi_i) & \pi_i(\langle M_1, M_2\rangle) & \overset{\pi_i}{\longrightarrow} & M_i, \text{ for } i = 1, 2 \\
(\rho) & Case(in_C^i(R), M_1, M_2) & \overset{\rho}{\longrightarrow} & M_i R, \text{ for } i = 1, 2 \\
(rec) & (rec\ y:C.M)^{i+1} & \overset{rec}{\longrightarrow} & M[(rec\ y:C.M)^i/y], \text{ for } i \geq 0 \\
(Top) & M & \overset{Top}{\longrightarrow} & * \text{ if } M:\mathbf{T} \text{ and } M \neq * \\
\end{array}
$$

But when we want to turn the extensional equalities for functions and pairs into expansions, as explained very clearly by Jay, we must be careful to avoid the following reduction loops:

$$
\begin{array}{lclcl}
\lambda x.M & \rightsquigarrow & \lambda y.(\lambda x.M)y & \rightsquigarrow & \lambda y.M[y/x] = \lambda x.M \\
\langle M, N\rangle & \rightsquigarrow & \langle \pi_1(\langle M, N\rangle), \pi_2(\langle M, N\rangle)\rangle & \rightsquigarrow & \langle M, N\rangle \\
MN & \rightsquigarrow & (\lambda x.Mx)N & \rightsquigarrow & MN \\
\pi_i(P) & \rightsquigarrow & \pi_i(\langle \pi_1(P), \pi_2(P)\rangle) & \rightsquigarrow & \pi_i(P) \\
\end{array}
$$

To break the first two loops we must disallow expansions of terms that are already λ-abstractions or pairs:

$$
(\eta)\quad M \overset{\eta}{\longrightarrow} \lambda x:A.Mx \text{ if } \left\{ \begin{array}{l} x \notin FV(M) \\ M:A \to B \text{ and } M \text{ is not a } \lambda\text{-abstraction} \end{array} \right.
$$
$$
(\delta)\quad M \overset{\delta}{\longrightarrow} \langle \pi_1(M), \pi_2(M)\rangle \text{ if } \left\{ M:A \times B \text{ and } M \text{ is not a pair} \right.
$$

But this is not enough: to break the last two loops we must also forbid the η expansion of a term in a context where this term is applied to an argument, and SP expansion of a term when such a term is the argument of a projection. This means that we cannot define the one-step reduction relation $\Longrightarrow$ on terms as the least congruence on terms containing the above reductions $\longrightarrow$, as is done usually. Instead, one defines formally $M \Longrightarrow M'$ starting from $\longrightarrow$ by induction on the structure of the term. The definition is the same as a congruence closure but for the two last cases.

Definition 3.2 (One-step reduction)

- If $M \longrightarrow M'$, then $M \Longrightarrow M'$
- If $M \Longrightarrow M'$, then $(rec\ x : A.M)^i \Longrightarrow (rec\ x : A.M')^i$

  $Case(M, N, O) \Longrightarrow Case(M', N, O)$ $\quad in_C^1(M) \Longrightarrow in_C^1(M')$ $\quad \langle M, N \rangle \Longrightarrow \langle M', N \rangle$

  $Case(N, M, O) \Longrightarrow Case(N, M', O)$ $\quad in_C^2(M) \Longrightarrow in_C^2(M')$ $\quad \langle N, M \rangle \Longrightarrow \langle N, M' \rangle$

  $Case(N, O, M) \Longrightarrow Case(N, O, M')$ $\quad \lambda\,x : A.M \Longrightarrow \lambda\,x : A.M'$ $\quad NM \Longrightarrow NM'$

- If $M \Longrightarrow M'$ but $M \overset{\neg\eta}{\longrightarrow} M'$, then $MN \Longrightarrow M'N$
- If $M \Longrightarrow M'$ but $M \overset{\neg\delta}{\longrightarrow} M'$, then $\pi_i(M) \Longrightarrow \pi_i(M')$ for $i = 1, 2$

where $\overset{\neg\eta}{\longrightarrow}$ stands for a $\longrightarrow$ step that is not an η step, and similarly for δ.

Notation 3.3 *The transitive and the reflexive transitive closure of* $\Longrightarrow$ *are noted* $\Longrightarrow^+$ *and* $\Longrightarrow^*$ *respectively. Similarly we define* $\overset{\infty}{\Longrightarrow}$ *,* $\overset{\infty}{\Longrightarrow}{}^+$ *and* $\overset{\infty}{\Longrightarrow}{}^*$ *for the unbounded system.*

It is also useful to define a notion of *influential positions* of a term: informally, a position in a term is *influential* if it prevents an expansion rule from being applied at the root of the subterm found at that position. For example, M occurs at an influential position in the term MN, as η expansion is forbidden on M, no matters if it is a λ-abstraction or not. Obviously, a position in a term can be influential for η or for δ, but not for both. This notion can be properly formalized, by induction on the structure of the terms, as shown in the full paper.

This calculus also enjoys the subject reduction property, so reductions preserve types.

Proposition 3.4 (Subject Reduction) *If* $\Gamma \vdash R : C$ *and* $R \Longrightarrow^* R'$, *then* $\Gamma \vdash R' : C$

4 Weak Confluence

In this section we set off to prove that the reduction system proposed above is actually weakly confluent, i.e. that whenever $M' \Longleftarrow M \Longrightarrow M''$ we can find a term M''' s.t. $M' \Longrightarrow^* M''' {}^* \Longleftarrow M''$. The proof is fairly more complex here than in the case of λ-calculus where extensional equalities are interpreted as contractions, and this is due to the fact that the reduction relation $\Longrightarrow$ introduced above *is not a congruence on terms*.

4.1 Some difficulties

In particular, in the simply typed λ-calculus if $M \Longrightarrow^* M'$ then $\pi_i(M) \Longrightarrow^* \pi_i(M')$, and if also $N \Longrightarrow^* N'$, then $MN \Longrightarrow^* M'N'$, but this is no longer true now: indeed, we have $x : A \to B \Longrightarrow \lambda z : A.xz$, but xN does not reduce to $(\lambda z : A.xz)N$.

These properties still hold for those reduction sequences $M \Longrightarrow^* M'$ that do not involve expansions at the root:

Remark 4.1 *Let* $M \equiv M_0 \Longrightarrow M_1 \ldots M_{n-1} \Longrightarrow M_n \equiv M'$ *be a reduction sequence where none of the M_i's is expanded at the root. Then* $\pi_i(M) \Longrightarrow^* \pi_i(M')$, *for $i = 1, 2$, and, if* $N \Longrightarrow^* N'$, *then* $MN \Longrightarrow^* M'N'$.

4.2 Solving Critical Pairs

In this calculus, it is no longer true that reduction is stable by substitution, as in the traditional λ-calculus: if $P \Longrightarrow P'$, $N \Longrightarrow N'$, it is not true in general that $P[N/x] \Longrightarrow^* P'[N'/x]$.

Indeed, $x : A \to B \Longrightarrow \lambda z : A.xz$, but $x[\lambda y : A.w/x] = \lambda y : A.w$ cannot reduce in our system to $\lambda z : A.(\lambda y : A.w)z = \lambda z : A.xz[\lambda y : A.w/x]$, and $(yM)[x/y] = xM$ cannot reduce to $(\lambda z : A.xz)M = (yM)[\lambda z : A.xz/y]$.

We can prove some weaker properties: if $P \Longrightarrow P'$, then $P[N/x]$ and $P'[N/x]$ have a common reduct (Lemma 4.2), and similarly $P[N/x]$ and $P[N'/x]$ when $N \Longrightarrow N'$ (Lemma 4.3). This suffices for our purpose of proving weak confluence of the reduction system.

Lemma 4.2 (Substitution Lemma (i))
If $P \Longrightarrow P'$, then $P[N/x] \Longrightarrow^* P'[N/x]$ or $P'[N/x] \Longrightarrow^* P[N/x]$. Moreover, if no expansion take place at the root position of P, then there are no expansions at root positions in the reduction sequences $P[N/x] \Longrightarrow^* P'[N/x]$ and $P'[N/x] \Longrightarrow^* P[N/x]$.

Lemma 4.3 (Substitution Lemma (ii))
If $N \overset{R}{\Longrightarrow} N'$, then $M[N/x] \Longrightarrow^* M'' \,{}^*\!\!\Longleftarrow M[N'/x]$ for some term M''. These reduction sequences contain expansions at the root only if $M \equiv x$ and R is an expansion applied at the root of N.

Example 4.4 *Take $M = \langle xy, x \rangle$, $N = w$ and $N' = \lambda z : A.wz$. Then*

$$M[N/x] = \langle wy, w \rangle \Longrightarrow \langle wy, \lambda z : A.wz \rangle \Longleftarrow \langle (\lambda z : A.wz)y, \lambda z : A.wz \rangle = M[N'/x]$$

Lemma 4.2 and 4.3 suffice to prove that all critical pairs arising from a term M by a β-reduction and another reduction rule can be solved. The other critical pairs are treated in full details in [DCK93]. We can then state the following:

Proposition 4.5 (Critical Pairs are solvable)
If $M \to M'$ and $M \Longrightarrow M''$, then $\exists R$ such that $M' \Longrightarrow^* R$ and $M'' \Longrightarrow^* R$.

4.3 From Solved Critical Pairs to Full Weak Confluence

It is to be noted that the solvability of critical pairs we just proved as Proposition 4.5 does not allow us to deduce the weak confluence of the calculus via the famous Knuth-Bendix Critical Pairs Lemma. That Lemma holds only for algebraic rewrite systems, and not for the λ-calculus, that has the higher order rewrite rule β. We need to prove local confluence explicitly, and to do so the following remark is useful.

Remark 4.6 (Expansion rules) *In case the two reductions $M' \longleftarrow M \Longrightarrow M''$ do not involve η (resp. δ) rules applied at the root positions of M, it is possible to close the diagram without using η (resp. δ) rules at the root, except in the three cases shown below: external π's and internal η, external β and internal δ. Notice that M is not a λ-abstraction in the first diagram, N is not a λ-abstraction in the second and $M[N/x]$ is not a pair in the third one.*

$$\pi_1(\langle M, N \rangle) \overset{\eta}{\Longrightarrow} \pi_1(\langle \lambda x.Mx, N \rangle) \qquad \pi_2(\langle M, N \rangle) \overset{\eta}{\Longrightarrow} \pi_2(\langle M, \lambda x.Nx \rangle)$$

$$
\begin{array}{ccc}
\pi \Big\downarrow & & \Big\Vert \pi \\
M \overset{\eta}{\Longrightarrow} \lambda x.Mx & &
\end{array}
\qquad
\begin{array}{ccc}
\pi \Big\downarrow & & \Big\Vert \pi \\
N \overset{\eta}{\Longrightarrow} \lambda x.Nx & &
\end{array}
$$

$$(\lambda x : A.M)N \overset{\delta}{\Longrightarrow} (\lambda x : A.\langle \pi_1(M), \pi_2(M) \rangle)N$$

$$
\begin{array}{ccc}
\beta \Big\downarrow & & \Big\Vert \beta \\
M[N/x] \overset{\delta}{\Longrightarrow} \langle \pi_1(M[N/x]), \pi_2(M[N/x]) \rangle & &
\end{array}
$$

With this additional knowledge, we can prove that $\Longrightarrow$ is actually weakly confluent.

Theorem 4.7 (Weak Confluence) *If $M' \Longleftarrow M \Longrightarrow M''$ then there exist a term M''' such that $M' \Longrightarrow^* M''' {}^* \!\!\Longleftarrow M''$ (i.e. the reduction relation $\Longrightarrow$ is weakly confluent). Furthermore, if the reductions in $M' \Longleftarrow M \Longrightarrow M''$ do not contain η (resp. δ) rules applied at the root of M, it is possible also to close the diagram without applying η (resp. δ) rules at the root, except in the cases shown in the previous Remark 4.6.*

5 Strong Normalization

We provide in this section the proof of strong normalization for our calculus. The key idea is to reduce strong normalization of the system with expansion rules to that of the system without expansion rules and for this, we show how the calculus without expansions can be used to simulate the calculus with expansions. We will use a fundamental property relating strong normalization of two systems:

Proposition 5.1 *Let $\mathcal{R}_1$ and $\mathcal{R}_2$ be two reduction systems and $\mathcal{T}$ a translation from terms in $\mathcal{R}_1$ to terms in $\mathcal{R}_2$. If for every reduction $M_1 \xrightarrow{\mathcal{R}_1} M_2$ there is a non empty reduction sequence $P_1 \xrightarrow{\mathcal{R}_2}{}^+ P_2$ such that $\mathcal{T}(M_i) = P_i$, for $i = 1, 2$, then the strong normalization of $\mathcal{R}_2$ implies that of $\mathcal{R}_1$.*

Proof. Suppose $\mathcal{R}_2$ is strongly normalizing and $\mathcal{R}_1$ is not. Then there is an infinite reduction sequence $M_1 \xrightarrow{\mathcal{R}_1} M_2 \xrightarrow{\mathcal{R}_1} \ldots$ and from this reduction we can construct an infinite reduction sequence $\mathcal{T}(M_1) \xrightarrow{\mathcal{R}_2}{}^+ \mathcal{T}(M_2) \xrightarrow{\mathcal{R}_2}{}^+ \ldots$ which leads to a contradiction. $\square$

The goal is now to find a translation of terms mapping our calculus into itself such that for every possible reduction in the original system from a term M to another term N, there is a reduction sequence from the translation of M to the translation of N, that is *non empty* and *does not* contain any expansion. Then the previous proposition allows us to derive the strong normalization property for the full system from that of the system without expansion rules, which can be proved using standard techniques.

5.1 Simulating Expansions without Expansions

The first naïve idea that comes to the mind is to choose a translation such that expansion rules are completely impossible on a translated term. This essentially amounts to associate to a term M its η-δ normal form, so that translating a term corresponds then to executing all the possible expansions.

Unfortunately, this simple solution is not a good one: if M reduces to N via an expansion, then the translation of M and that of N are the same term, so to such a reduction step in the full system corresponds an *empty* reduction sequence in the translation, and this does not allow us to apply proposition 5.1.

This leads us to consider a more sophisticated translation that maps a term M to a term M° where expansions are not fully executed as above, but just *marked* in such a way that they can be executed during the simulation process, if necessary, by a rule that is not an expansion.

Let us see how to do this on a simple example: take a variable z of type $A_1 \times A_2$, where the A_i's are atomic types different from $\mathbf{T}$. By performing a δ expansion we obtain its normal form w.r.t. expansion rules: $\langle \pi_1(z), \pi_2(z) \rangle$. Instead of executing this reduction, we just mark it in the translation by applying to z an appropriate *expansor* term $\lambda x : A_1 \times A_2.\langle \pi_1(x), \pi_2(x) \rangle$. As for

$\langle \pi_1(z), \pi_2(z) \rangle$, it is in normal form w.r.t. expansions, so the translation does not modify it in any way. Now, we have the reduction sequence

$$z^\circ \equiv (\lambda x : A_1 \times A_2.\langle \pi_1(x), \pi_2(x) \rangle)z \rightarrow_\beta \langle \pi_1(z), \pi_2(z) \rangle$$

where the translation of z reduces to the translation of $\langle \pi_1(z), \pi_2(z) \rangle$, and the δ expansion from z to $\langle \pi_1(z), \pi_2(z) \rangle$ is simulated in the translation by a β-rule. Clearly, in a generic term M there are many positions where an expansion can be performed, so the translation will have to take into account the *structure* of M and insert the appropriate expansors at all these positions.

Anyway, expansors must be carefully defined to correctly represent not only the expansion step arising from a redex already present in M, but also all the expansion sequences that such step can create: if in the previous example the type A_1 is taken to be an arrow type and the type A_2 a product type, then the term $\pi_1(z)$ can be further η-expanded and the term $\pi_2(z)$ can be expanded by a δ-rule, and the expansor $\lambda x : A_1 \times A_2.\langle \pi_1(x), \pi_2(x) \rangle$ cannot simulate these further possible reductions. This can only be done by storing in the expansor terms all the information on possible future expansions, that is fully contained in the *type* of the term we are marking.

Definition 5.2 (Translation) *To every type C we associate a term, called the expansor of type C and denoted Δ_C, defined by induction as follows:*

$$\Delta_{A \to B} = \lambda x : A \to B.\lambda z : A.\Delta_B(x(\Delta_A z))$$
$$\Delta_{A \times B} = \lambda x : A \times B.\langle \Delta_A(\pi_1(x)), \Delta_B(\pi_2(x)) \rangle$$
$$\Delta_A \qquad \text{is empty, in any other case}$$

We then define a translation M° for a term $M : A$ as follows:

$$M^\circ = \begin{cases} M^{\circ\circ} & \text{if } M \text{ is an abstraction or a pair} \\ \Delta_A^k M^{\circ\circ} & \text{for any } k > 0 \quad \text{otherwise} \end{cases}$$

where $\Delta_A^k M$ denotes the term $\underbrace{(\Delta_A \ldots (\Delta_A M) \ldots)}_{k \ \text{times}}$ and $M^{\circ\circ}$ is defined by induction as:

$$
\begin{array}{llll}
x^{\circ\circ} & = x & (\lambda x : B.M)^{\circ\circ} & = \lambda x : B.M^\circ \\
*^{\circ\circ} & = * & (rec\ y : A.M)^{i\circ\circ} & = (rec\ y : A.M^\circ)^i \\
\langle M, N \rangle^{\circ\circ} & = \langle M^\circ, N^\circ \rangle & Case(R, M, N)^{\circ\circ} & = Case(R^\circ, M^\circ, N^\circ) \\
(MN)^{\circ\circ} & = (M^{\circ\circ} N^\circ) & \pi_i(M)^{\circ\circ} & = \pi_i(M^{\circ\circ}) \\
in_C^i(M)^{\circ\circ} & = in_C^i(M^\circ) &
\end{array}
$$

This corresponds exactly to the marking procedure described before, but for a little detail: in the translation we allow *any* number of markers to be used (the integer k can be any positive number), and not just one as seemed to suffice for the examples above.

The need for this additional twist in the definition is best understood with an example. Consider two atomic types A and B and the term $(\lambda x : A \times B.x)z$: if k is fixed to be one (*i.e.* we allow only one expansor as marker) then its translation $((\lambda x : A \times B.x)z)^\circ$ is $\Delta_{A \times B}((\lambda x : A \times B.\Delta_{A \times B}x)\Delta_{A \times B}z)$. Now $(\lambda x : A \times B.x)z \xrightarrow{\beta} z$, so we have to verify that $((\lambda x : A \times B.x)z)^\circ$ reduces to z° in at least one step. We have:

$$\Delta_{A \times B}((\lambda x : A \times B.\Delta_{A \times B}x)\Delta_{A \times B}z) \Longrightarrow \Delta_{A \times B}\Delta_{A \times B}\Delta_{A \times B}z$$

However, even if both $\Delta_{A \times B}^3 z$ and $\Delta_{A \times B}z$ reduce to the same term $\langle \pi_1(z), \pi_2(z) \rangle$, it is not true that $\Delta_{A \times B}^3 z \Longrightarrow^* \Delta_{A \times B}z$. Anyway, if we admit $\Delta_{A \times B}^3 z$ as a possible translation of z we will have the desired property relating reductions and translations. Hence, to be precise, our method associates to each term not just one translation, but a whole family of possible translations, all with the same structure, but with different numbers of expansors used as markers.

What is important for our proof is that when we are given a reduction $M_1 \Longrightarrow M_2 \ldots \Longrightarrow M_n$ in the full calculus, then no matter which possible translation M_1° we choose for M_1, the reductions used in the simulation process all go through possible translations M_i° of the M_i.

Translations preserve types and leave unchanged terms where expansions are not possible.

Lemma 5.3 (Type Preservation) *If* $\Gamma \vdash M : A$, *then* $\Gamma \vdash M^\circ : A$ *and* $\Gamma \vdash M^{\circ\circ} : A$.

Lemma 5.4 *If* M *is in normal form or in* η-δ *normal form, then* $M^\circ = M$.

The next step is to prove that we can apply proposition 5.1 to our system, *i.e*, for every one step reduction from M to N in the full system, there is a non empty reduction sequence in the system without expansions from any translation of M to a translation of N.

The following property is essential to show that every time we perform a β-reduction on a term M in the original system, any translation of M reduces to a translation of the term we have obtained via $\rightarrow_\beta$ from M. Take for example the reduction $(\lambda x : A.M)N \rightarrow_\beta M[N/x]$. We know that $((\lambda x : A.M)N)^\circ = \Delta_A^k((\lambda x : A.M^\circ)N^\circ)$ and we want to show that there is a *non empty* reduction sequence leading to $M[N/x]^\circ$. Since $\Delta_A^k((\lambda x : A.M^\circ)N^\circ) \rightarrow_\beta \Delta_A^k M^\circ[N^\circ/x]$, we have now to check that the term $(M[N/x])^\circ$ can be reached. We state the property as follows:

Lemma 5.5 *If* $\Gamma \vdash M : A$, *then* $\forall k \geq 0$, $\Delta_A^k M^\circ[\overline{N^\circ}/\overline{x}] \Longrightarrow^* (M[\overline{N}/\overline{x}])^\circ$ *and no expansions are performed in the reduction sequences.*

Using 5.5 we can show now:

Theorem 5.6 (Simulation) *If* $\Gamma \vdash M : A$ *and* $M \Longrightarrow N$, *then* $M^\circ \Longrightarrow^+ N^\circ$ *and there are no expansions in the reduction sequences.*

5.2 Strong Normalization of the Full Calculus

Having shown that our translation satisfies the hypothesis of Proposition 5.1, all we are now left to prove is that the bounded reduction system without expansion rules is strongly normalizing. This can be established by one of the standard techniques of reducibility, and does not present essential difficulties once the right definitions of *stable term* or *reducible terms* are given. In the full paper we provide two proofs, one adapting the proof provided by Poigné and Voss in [PV87], and the other adapting Girard's proof from [GLT90]. These standard techniques apply straightforwardly, but the interested reader will nevertheless find in the full paper all the details.

It is then finally possible to state the following

Theorem 5.7 (Strong normalization)
The reduction $\Longrightarrow$ *for the bounded system with expansions is strongly normalizing.*

Proof. By proposition 5.1, theorem 5.6 and the strong normalization of the bounded calculus without expansions . $\square$

6 Confluence of the Full Calculus

We can immediately deduce the confluence property for the bounded system from the weak confluence and strong normalization properties, however, we can also provide an extremely simple and neat proof that does not need the weak confluence property for the expansionary system.

Theorem 6.1 (Confluence) *The relation* $\Longrightarrow$ *is Church-Rosser.*

Proof. Let M be a term s.t. $P_1 \,{}^*\!\!\Longleftarrow M \Longrightarrow^* P_2$. Since $\Longrightarrow$ is strongly normalizing, we can reduce the terms P_i to their normal forms $\overline{P_i}$. Then we have $\overline{P_1} \,{}^*\!\!\Longleftarrow M \Longrightarrow^* \overline{P_2}$, and by theorem 5.6 $\overline{P_1}^\circ \,{}^+\!\!\Longleftarrow M^\circ \Longrightarrow^+ \overline{P_2}^\circ$ without expansions in the reduction sequences. As the system without expansions is confluent (we showed that it is strongly normalizing, and weak confluence without expansions can be shown as easily as for the simply typed lambda calculus), we can close the internal diagram with $\overline{P_1}^\circ \Longrightarrow^* R \,{}^*\!\!\Longleftarrow \overline{P_2}^\circ$. Now, $\overline{P_i}^\circ =_{lemma\ 5.4} \overline{P_i}$ and therefore we can complete the proof using the reductions $P_1 \Longrightarrow^* \overline{P_1} \Longrightarrow^* R \,{}^*\!\!\Longleftarrow \overline{P_2} \,{}^*\!\!\Longleftarrow P_2$ (notice that $\overline{P_1} = R = \overline{P_2}$). $\square$

In order to show confluence of the full calculus we relate in the first place the bounded reduction $\Longrightarrow$ and the unbounded one $\overset{\infty}{\Longrightarrow}$, and then we use the confluence of $\Longrightarrow$ to show the confluence of $\overset{\infty}{\Longrightarrow}$. This very same technique, that originates from early work of Lévy [Lév76], was used in [PV87]. The connection between the reductions $\Longrightarrow$ and $\overset{\infty}{\Longrightarrow}$ comes from the following:

Remark 6.2 *If $M \Longrightarrow^* N$, then $|M| \overset{\infty}{\Longrightarrow} |N|$, where $|M|$ is obtained from M by removing all the indices from the rec terms.*

Lemma 6.3 *For any reduction sequence $M_0 \overset{\infty}{\Longrightarrow} M_1 \overset{\infty}{\Longrightarrow} \ldots \overset{\infty}{\Longrightarrow} M_n$, there exists an indexed computation $N_0 \Longrightarrow N_1 \Longrightarrow \ldots \Longrightarrow N_n$ such that $|N_i| = M_i$, for $i = 0 \ldots n$.*

Confluence of the full calculus results now from the confluence of the bounded calculus.

Theorem 6.4 $\overset{\infty}{\Longrightarrow}$ *is Church Rosser.*

7 Conclusion and Future Work

We have provided a confluent rewriting system for an extensional typed λ-calculus with product, sum, terminal object and recursion, which is also strongly normalizing in case the recursion operator is bounded. There are mainly two relevant technical contributions in this paper: the weak confluence proof and the simulation theorem.

On one hand, let us remark once again that the weak confluence property for a context-sensitive reduction system is not as straightforward as for the reduction systems that are congruencies. The proof is no longer just a matter of a boring but trivial case analysis, so we had to explore and analyze here the fine structure of the reduction system, showing clearly how substitution and reduction interact in the presence of context-sensitive rules.

The simulation theorem, on the other hand, turns out to be the real key tool for this expansionary system: it allows to reduce *both* confluence *and* strong normalization properties to those for the underlying calculus without expansions, that can be proved using the standard techniques. In a sense, this is all that you really need to prove.

It is also important to remark that our techniques can be applied to many other calculi with expansionary rules. For example, we can accommodate in our calculus the limited form of extensionality for the sum type[5] which is commonly used in proof theory(see [Gir72], for example),

---

[5]The extensional equality for sums is very problematic in its full form, see [Dou90] for a detailed discussion.

namely $Case(P, \lambda x.inl(x), \lambda x.inr(x)) = P$. We refer the interested reader to [DCK93] for more details. Finally, these techniques are also well-behaved in polymorphic calculi, like Girard's Systems F and F_ω, which will be the argument of forthcoming work.

References

[Aka93] Y. Akama. On mints' reductions for ccc-calculus. *TLCA*. LNCS 664, Springer Verlag, 1993.

[Bar84] H. Barendregt. *The Lambda Calculus; Its syntax and Semantics*. North Holland, 1984.

[CDC91] P.L. Curien and R. Di Cosmo. A confluent reduction system for the λ-calculus with surjective pairing and terminal object. *ICALP 91*, LNCS 510, pages 291–302.

[CF58] H.B. Curry and R. Feys. *Combinatory Logic*, volume 1. North Holland, 1958.

[Cub92] D. Cubric. On free ccc. Distributed on the types mailing list, 1992.

[DCK93] R. Di Cosmo and D. Kesner. Simulating expansions without expansions. Technical report, INRIA, 1993.

[Dou90] D. Dougherty. Some reduction properties of a lambda calculus with coproducts and recursive types. Technical report, Wesleyan University, 1990. E-mail: ddougherty@eagle.wesleyan.edu.

[Gir72] J.Y. Girard. *Interprétation fonctionnelle et élimination des coupures dans l'arithmétique d'ordre supérieure*. Thèse de doctorat d'état, Université de Paris VII, 1972.

[GLT90] J.Y. Girard, Y. Lafont, and P. Taylor. *Proofs and Types*. Cambridge University Press, 1990.

[Hue76] G. Huet. Résolution d'équations dans les langages d'ordre $1, 2, \ldots, \omega$. Thèse de doctorat d'état, Université de Paris VII, 1976.

[Jay92] C. Barry Jay. Long $\beta\eta$ normal forms and confluence (revised). Technical Report ECS-LFCS-91-183, LFCS, 1992. University of Edimburgh.

[JG92] C. Barry Jay and N. Ghani. The virtues of eta-expansion. Technical Report ECS-LFCS-92-243, LFCS, 1992. University of Edimburgh.

[Klo80] J.W. Klop. Combinatory reduction systems. *Mathematical Center Tracts*, 27, 1980.

[Lév76] J.J. Lévy. An algebraic interpretation of the $\lambda\beta\kappa$-calculus and a labelled λ-calculus. *TCS*, 2:97–114, 1976.

[LS86] J. Lambek and P.J. Scott. *An introduction to higher order categorical logic*. CUP, 1986.

[Min77] G. Mints. Closed categories and the theory of proofs. *Zapiski Nauchnykh Seminarov Leningradskogo Otdeleniya Matematicheskogo Instituta im. V.A. Steklova AN SSSR*, 68:83–114, 1977.

[Min79] G. Mints. Teorija categorii i teoria dokazatelstv.I. *Aktualnye problemy logiki i metodologii nauky*, pages 252–278, 1979.

[Pot81] G. Pottinger. The Church Rosser Theorem for the Typed lambda-calculus with Surjective Pairing. *Notre Dame Journal of Formal Logic*, 22(3):264–268, 1981.

[Pra71] D. Prawitz. Ideas and results in proof theory. *Proc. 2nd Scand. Logic Symp.*, pages 235–307, 1971.

[PV87] A. Poigné and J. Voss. On the implementation of abstract data types by programming language constructs. *JCSS*, 34(2-3):340–376, April/June 1987.

[Tro86] A.S. Troelstra. Strong normalization for typed terms with surjective pairing. *Notre Dame Journal of Formal Logic*, 27(4), 1986.

Modularity of Termination and Confluence in Combinations of Rewrite Systems with λ_ω

Franco Barbanera[1]* and Maribel Fernández[2]

[1] Dipartimento di Informatica, Corso Svizzera 185, 10149 Torino, Italy.
E-mail: barba@di.unito.it
[2] LRI Bât. 490, CNRS/Université de Paris-Sud, 91405 Orsay Cedex, France.
E-mail: maribel@lri.fr

Abstract. We prove that termination and confluence are modular properties in combinations of the typed λ-calculus of order ω with (first or higher order) term rewrite systems, provided that the first order rewrite system is conservative (non-duplicating) and the higher order rewrite system satisfies some suitable conditions (the general schema) and does not introduce critical pairs.

1 Introduction

In the last years, many research efforts have been devoted to the study of the interactions between two closely related models of computation: the one based on β-reduction on λ-terms and the one formalized by means of rewrite rules on algebraic terms. Many interesting results (see [8], [9], [17], [3], [2], [14]) have been obtained concerning the *modularity* of *strong normalization* (or *termination*) and *confluence* of the combined relation. A property is called modular if the combination of two systems having this property inherits it.

Confluence and strong normalization are very useful properties in practice; strong normalization ensures that all reduction sequences are finite, whereas confluence establishes a kind of consistency of computations because it ensures that when two different terms u and v can be obtained by reducing some term t, there exists a common reduct of u and v. In [8] and [17] it is shown that the system obtained by combining a terminating first order many-sorted term rewrite system with the second order typed λ-calculus is again terminating with respect to β-reduction and the algebraic reductions induced by the rewrite rules, i.e. strong normalization is a modular property in this case. The same result is proven for confluence in [9]. In [14] both results are extended to combinations of first and higher order rewriting systems with second order λ-calculus, provided that suitable conditions are satisfied. Such conditions are that the higher order rules satisfy the so-called *general schema* (a generalization of primitive recursive definitions) and that the first order rules are *conservative* (also called *non-duplicating*), that is, the number of occurrences of each variable in the right

---

* *To Bianca and Massimo*

hand side is less than or equal to the number of occurrences of the variable in the left hand side.[3]

This last result is also valid when type assignment systems for λ-calculus are considered instead of explicitly typed calculi: in [4] it is shown that termination and confluence are modular properties of combinations of the intersection type assignment system (an extremely powerful system defined in [6]) with first and higher order algebraic rewrite systems, provided that the first order reductions are conservative and the higher order rules satisfy the general schema of Jouannaud and Okada. We rely on the results of [4] to obtain the main results of this paper.

Indeed the restriction to conservative reductions is also required to get modularity of termination in combinations of algebraic rewrite systems alone. In [20], Y. Toyama proved that confluence is modular for disjoint unions of term rewrite systems and conjectured that termination was also modular, but later H. Barendregt and J.W. Klop gave a counterexample to modularity of termination using a non-conservative rewrite system (see [19]). Modularity of termination for disjoint sums of conservative systems was proven in [18]. In practice, this restriction is not significant: most implementations of rewrite systems use sharing, and shared-reductions are always conservative since all the occurrences of a variable in a right hand side are shared.

A (practical) motivation for the investigation of combinations of λ-calculi with rewrite systems is that they provide an alternative for the design of new programming languages: the *algebraic functional languages* [14]. These languages allow algebraic definitions of data types and operators (as in equational languages like OBJ) and definition of higher order functions (as in functional languages like ML), in a unified framework. By the Curry-Howard isomorphism, some of these languages can also be seen as logical systems. From this point of view, it is better to consider more powerful type disciplines for λ-calculus than the ones considered up to now, such as the typed λ-calculus of order ω (Girard's system F_ω [12]) or the Calculus of Constructions of Coquand and Huet [10]. As pointed out in [8], it would be useful to know whether the modularity results above hold also in these cases: confluence and termination ensure the consistency of the logical system.

We will show in this paper that this is true for the combination of the λ-calculus of order ω (λ_ω in the following) with first and higher order rewrite systems, provided that the first order systems are conservative and the higher order systems satisfy the general schema of Jouannaud and Okada.

We will prove first the modularity of the strong normalization property. For this we give a proof based on a translation from λ_ω-terms to terms of the system described in [4], for which strong normalization is known. This mapping preserves all reduction sequences, and hence the strong normalization property of the former system is a direct consequence of the strong normalization property of the latter. Our proof of strong normalization generalizes to the problem discussed

---

[3] Although not explicitly required in [14], the restriction to non-duplicating first order rules is necessary for the modularity of termination.

in this paper the proof in [2].

After proving the modularity of the strong normalization property, we will show that local confluence (or weak confluence) is also modular in combinations of λ_ω with first and higher order rewriting systems, provided that the higher order rules do not introduce critical pairs. To prove this we use an argument similar to the one used in [4] to prove the confluence of the combination of rewriting systems and type assignment systems. Since in strongly normalizing systems local confluence and confluence are equivalent, we get also a proof of confluence for the system λ_ω extended with first and higher order rewriting.

The modularity of strong normalization in combinations of λ_ω with first and higher order rewrite systems (a result interesting in itself) is also a first step towards proving the modularity of strong normalization in combinations of the Calculus of Constructions (λ_C in the following) with first and higher order rewrite systems: λ_ω is a subset of λ_C where types depending on terms are not allowed. An example of type depending on a term (taken from [5]) is $A^n \rightarrow B$ with n a natural number, defined by $A^0 \rightarrow B = B$; $A^{n+1} \rightarrow B = A \rightarrow (A^n \rightarrow B)$.

However, the generalization of this result to combinations of λ_C with rewrite systems is not straightforward. One of the difficulties concerns the Conversion Rule, which states that if a term t in λ_C has type T and T is convertible to T' then t has also type T'. Of course, in the extension of λ_C with algebraic features the convertibility of types involves, besides β-conversion, the rewrite relation induced by the rewrite system, since types may depend on terms. Then one has to show that this relation has the same useful properties that β-conversion has. This problem will be the subject of future work.

2 Adding algebraic features to the typed λ-calculus of order ω

In the following we assume familiarity with typed λ-calculi and the way to present them used below (for more details see [5] and [7]). Let us define now $\lambda_{\omega RH}$, the algebraic extension of the system λ_ω (called F_ω in [12]).

We consider a denumerable set S of *sorts* and define by induction the set $\mathcal{T}_S$ of *arrow types based on* S:

- If $s \in S$ then $s \in \mathcal{T}_S$
- If $\sigma_1, \ldots, \sigma_n, \sigma \in \mathcal{T}_S$ then $\sigma_1 \ldots \sigma_n \rightarrow \sigma \in \mathcal{T}_S$.

An *extended signature* $\mathcal{F}$ contains *first* and *higher order function symbols*: $\mathcal{F} = \bigcup_{\tau \in \mathcal{T}_S} \mathcal{F}_\tau$ where $\mathcal{F}_\tau$ denotes a set of function symbols of type τ. We will assume that $\mathcal{F}_\tau \cap \mathcal{F}_{\tau'} = \emptyset$ if $\tau \neq \tau'$. Let $s_1 \ldots s_n, s \in S$, and $\tau = s_1 \ldots s_n \rightarrow s$, then $\mathcal{F}_\tau$ is a set of first order function symbols. We denote by Σ the set of all first order function symbols and by f, g its elements. We use F, G to denote higher order function symbols. When it is clear from the context, we use f to denote a generic (first or higher order) element of $\mathcal{F}$.

System $\lambda_{\omega RH}$ is based on a set T of *pseudo-expressions* built out of variables (term and type variables), function symbols and sort symbols using application, abstraction and universal quantification. Pseudo-expressions are defined by the following abstract syntax:

$$T ::= x \mid * \mid \square \mid f \mid s \mid TT \mid \lambda x{:}T.T \mid \Pi x{:}T.T$$

where x ranges over the category of variables (divided into two groups: Var^* and $Var^\square$), $*$ and $\square$ are special constants (denoting respectively the set of types and the set of kinds of the system), s ranges over the set S of sorts and f ranges over the set $\mathcal{F}$ of function symbols. A *declaration* for a variable x is an expression of the form $x : A$, where $A \in T$. If $A \in S$ we say that x is a first order variable.

In the following we shall denote simultaneous substitutions by $\{x_1 \mapsto N_1, \dots, x_n \mapsto N_n\}$. Postfix notation will be used for their application, e.g. $M\{x_1 \mapsto N_1, \dots, x_n \mapsto N_n\}$ denotes the simultaneous substitution of N_i for x_i ($1 \leq i \leq n$) in M. When applying a substitution we must take care of bound variables, as usual. We shall use the symbol ϕ to denote a generic substitution.

On pseudo-expressions, the notions of β-reduction and β-conversion are defined by the contraction rule: $(\lambda u{:}A.B)C \rightarrow_\beta B\{u \mapsto C\}$

In the following Γ will denote a *context*, that is, a finite sequence of declarations. The empty sequence will be denoted by $\langle\rangle$ and if $\Gamma = \langle x_1 : A_1, \dots, x_n : A_n\rangle$ then $\Gamma, x : B = \langle x_1 : A_1, \dots, x_n : A_n, x : B\rangle$.

A *well-formed term* for λ_{wRH} *of type B in Γ* is a pseudo-expression A such that it is possible to derive $\Gamma \vdash A : B$ using a subset of the *term formation rules* listed below.

Axioms

$$\langle\rangle \vdash * : \square$$

$$\langle\rangle \vdash s : * \qquad \text{for each } s \in S$$

$$\langle\rangle \vdash f : \sigma_1 \to \dots \to \sigma_n \to \sigma \qquad \begin{array}{l}\text{for each } f \in \mathcal{F}_{\sigma_1 \dots \sigma_n \to \sigma} \\ (\sigma_1 \to \dots \to \sigma_n \to \sigma \text{ is short for} \\ \Pi x_1{:}\sigma_1.\Pi x_2{:}\sigma_2 \dots \Pi x_n{:}\sigma_n.\sigma).\end{array}$$

General Rules

Start rule
$$\frac{\Gamma \vdash A : p}{\Gamma, u{:}A \vdash u : A} \qquad \text{if } p \in \{*, \square\}, u \in Var^p \text{ and } u \notin \Gamma$$

Weakening rule
$$\frac{\Gamma \vdash A : B \quad \Gamma \vdash C : p}{\Gamma, u{:}C \vdash A : B} \qquad \text{if } p \in \{*, \square\}, u \in Var^p \text{ and } u \notin \Gamma$$

Application rule
$$\frac{\Gamma \vdash F : \Pi u{:}A.B \quad \Gamma \vdash C : A}{\Gamma \vdash FC : B\{u \mapsto C\}}$$

Conversion rule
$$\frac{\Gamma \vdash A : B \quad \Gamma \vdash B' : p \quad B =_\beta B'}{\Gamma \vdash A : B'} \qquad \text{if } p \in \{*, \square\}.$$

Specific rules

The specific rules are all introduction rules and are parametrized by $*$ and $\square$; more precisely, they are (p_1, p_2) rules, with $p_1, p_2 \in \{*, \square\}$.

$$\Pi\text{-intro} \qquad \frac{\Gamma \vdash A : p_1 \qquad \Gamma, u : A \vdash B : p_2}{\Gamma \vdash \Pi u : A.B : p_2}$$

$$\lambda\text{-intro} \qquad \frac{\Gamma \vdash A : p_1 \qquad \Gamma, u : A \vdash b : B \qquad \Gamma, u : A \vdash B : p_2}{\Gamma \vdash \lambda u : A.b : \Pi u : A.B}$$

The term formation rules of λ_{wRH} are all the axioms and general rules and a particular subset of the set of specific rules, namely $(*, *), (\Box, *), (\Box, \Box)$. The specific term-formation rules have the following informal meaning: $(*, *)$ allows of forming terms depending on terms, $(*, \Box)$ allows of forming types depending on terms, $(\Box, *)$ allows of forming terms depending on types, $(\Box, \Box)$ allows of forming types depending on types. The set of terms of λ_{wRH} is denoted in the following by Λ_{wRH}.

2.1 Algebraic terms and rewrite rules

The set of *higher order algebraic terms of type* σ in λ_{wRH} is inductively defined by:

1. If $f \in \mathcal{F}_{\sigma_1 \ldots \sigma_n \to \sigma}$ (either first or higher order) and $M_1, \ldots, M_n$ $(n \geq 0)$ are algebraic terms of type $\sigma_1, \ldots, \sigma_n$ in Γ then $f M_1 \ldots M_n$ is an algebraic term of type σ in Γ.

2. If $x : \sigma_1 \ldots \sigma_n \to \sigma \in \Gamma$, with $\sigma_1 \ldots \sigma_n \to \sigma \in T_S$, and $M_1, \ldots, M_n$ $(n \geq 0)$ are algebraic terms of type $\sigma_1, \ldots, \sigma_n$ in Γ then $x M_1 \ldots M_n$ is an algebraic term of type σ in Γ.

It is easy to see that if M is algebraic, and $\Gamma \vdash M : \sigma$, then the β-normal form of σ belongs to T_S. First order algebraic terms are algebraic terms in which only first order function symbols and first order variables occur.

We define now two sets of rewrite rules on algebraic terms:

1. a set R of *first order rewrite rules* whose elements are denoted by $r : t \to t'$ where t, t' are first order algebraic terms of the same sort in some context Γ, i.e. the rewriting rules of R are assumed sound with respect to types. Besides, in $r : t \to t'$, t cannot be a variable and the set of variables in t' must be a subset of the variables in t. R is *conservative* (also called *non-duplicating*) if for all $r : t \to t' \in R$ and for all variables x in t, the number of occurrences of x in t' is less than or equal to the number of occurrences of x in t.

2. a set HOR of *higher order rewrite rules* satisfying the *general schema* ([14]):

$$F \vec{l}[\vec{X}, \vec{x}] \vec{Y} \vec{y} \to v[(F \vec{r_1}[\vec{X}, \vec{x}] \vec{Y} \vec{y}), \ldots, (F \vec{r_m}[\vec{X}, \vec{x}] \vec{Y} \vec{y}), \vec{X}, \vec{x}, \vec{Y}, \vec{y}]$$

where $\vec{X}, \vec{Y}$ are sequences of higher order variables; $\vec{x}, \vec{y}$ are sequences of first order variables; F is a higher order function symbol that can not appear in $\vec{l}, v, \vec{r_1}, \ldots, \vec{r_m}$; both sides of the rule have the same type in some context Γ, the left hand side is an algebraic term and the right hand side v is a term in λ_{wRH}; $\vec{l}, \vec{r_1}, \ldots, \vec{r_m}$ are all terms of sort-type; $\vec{X} \subseteq \vec{Y}$ and $\forall i \in [1..m]$, $\vec{l} \rhd_{mul} \vec{r_i}$ (where $\lhd$ denotes strict subterm ordering and $\rhd_{mul}$ denotes the multiset extension of $\rhd$). The notation $t[t_1, \ldots, t_n]$ means that $t_1, \ldots, t_n$ are subterms of t.

The higher-order rules can be considered as definitions of new functionals of the language. There is a restriction that we have to impose on the set HOR: mutually recursive definitions are forbidden. This restriction, however, together with the one that the higher order variables in $\vec{l}$ must be included in $\vec{Y}$, could easily be removed (the first by introducing product types and packing mutually recursive definitions in a same product and the second by reasoning on a transformed version of F). The restriction that terms in $\vec{r_i}$ are subterms of terms in $\vec{l}$, however, is essential in the proof of strong normalization of the combined language (see also [14] and [4]).

Although restricted, the general schema is interesting from a practical point of view: it allows for the introduction of functionals by primitive recursion on a first order data structure, as in the definition of the functional map in the following example (taken from [14]):

$append\ nil\ l = l$
$append\ (cons\ x\ l)\ l' = cons\ x\ (append\ l\ l')$
$append\ (append\ l\ l')\ l'' = append\ l\ (append\ l'\ l'')$
$map\ X\ nil = nil$
$map\ X\ (cons\ x\ l) = cons\ (X\ x)\ (map\ X\ l)$

Here, the first order function $append$ is defined algebraically (the third rule establishes the associativity of append on lists, and makes the definition non-primitive recursive), while the higher order function map is defined recursively on the structure of lists. See [14] for more examples and applications of the general schema.

Each rule in R and HOR induces a rewrite relation in $\lambda_{\omega RH}$: Let $M, M' \in \lambda_{\omega RH}$, $r : t \to t' \in R$ (resp. $r : t \to t' \in HOR$). Then $M \to^r M'$ if there exists a subterm P of M such that $P \equiv t\{x_1 \mapsto N_1, \ldots, x_n \mapsto N_n\}$ (where obviously $N_1, \ldots, N_n \in \lambda_{\omega RH}$) and M' is obtained from M by replacing the term $t'\{x_1 \mapsto N_1, \ldots, x_n \mapsto N_n\}$ for P. Notice that since $N_1, \ldots, N_n \in \lambda_{\omega RH}$ these can contain λ-terms. We write $M \to_R M'$ (resp. $M \to_{HOR} M'$) if $M \to^r M'$ for some $r : t \to t' \in R$ (resp. $r : t \to t' \in HOR$). By $\to_R^*$, $\to_{HOR}^*$ we denote the reflexive and transitive closure of $\to_R$, $\to_{HOR}$ respectively.

In the following $\to_{mix}$ denotes the reduction relation on terms of $\lambda_{\omega RH}$ obtained by the union of $\to_\beta$, $\to_R$ and $\to_{HOR}$. $\to_{mix}^*$ denotes its transitive and reflexive closure, as usual.

2.2 Basic properties of $\lambda_{\omega RH}$

We will use the notation $\Gamma \vdash M : A$ to denote the fact that indeed we can derive $\Gamma \vdash M : A$ in the system $\lambda_{\omega RH}$. We let $\Gamma \vdash A : B : C$ stand for $\Gamma \vdash A : B$ and $\Gamma \vdash B : C$. $A \to B$ is short for $\Pi u : A.B$ when u is not a free variable in B. Finally, we denote by $Context(\lambda_{\omega RH})$ the set of all sequences of declarations for $\lambda_{\omega RH}$.

If $\Gamma \vdash A : B : *$, then A is called an *object* and B is called a *type*. The set of all objects in $\lambda_{\omega RH}$ is denoted in the following by $Object(\lambda_{\omega RH})$, and the set of all types by $Type(\lambda_{\omega RH})$. If $\Gamma \vdash A : B : \square$ then A is called a *constructor* and B is called a *kind*. The set of all the constructors in $\lambda_{\omega RH}$ is denoted in the following by $Constructor(\lambda_{\omega RH})$, and the set of all the kinds by $Kind(\lambda_{\omega RH})$. Notice that $*$ is a particular kind and that types are particular constructors. It can be shown that a term is either an object, a constructor or a kind.

Let $\Gamma \in Context(\lambda_{\omega RH})$, and $\Pi z\colon B_1.B_2$, $\lambda z\colon B_1.B_2$, $B_1, B_2 \in \Lambda_{\omega RH}$. In the following we use the terminology:

1. $\Pi z\colon B_1.B_2$ is *formed by* (p_1, p_2) in Γ if there are specific rules $(p_1, p_2) \in \lambda_{\omega RH}$ such that $\Gamma \vdash B_1 \colon p_1$ and $\Gamma, x\colon B_1 \vdash B_2 \colon p_2$.

2. $\lambda z\colon B_1.B_2$ is *formed by* (p_1, p_2) in Γ if there are specific rules $(p_1, p_2) \in \lambda_{\omega RH}$ such that $\Gamma \vdash \lambda z\colon B_1.B_2 : \Pi z\colon C_1.C_2$ and $\Pi z\colon C_1.C_2$ is formed by (p_1, p_2) in Γ.

3. $B_1 B_2$ is *formed by* (p_1, p_2) in Γ if there are specific rules $(p_1, p_2) \in \lambda_{\omega RH}$ such that $\Gamma \vdash B_1 : \Pi z\colon C_1.C_2$ and $\Pi z\colon C_1.C_2$ is formed by (p_1, p_2) in Γ.

The following lemmas were proved in [11] for General Type Systems and hold also for the system in which we are interested (i.e. $\lambda_{\omega RH}$).

Lemma 1 Unicity of formation. *Let $\Gamma \in Context(\lambda_{\omega RH})$, $B \in \Lambda_{\omega RH}$. If B is formed by (p_1, p_2) in Γ and B is formed by (p_1', p_2') in Γ' then $p_1 \equiv p_1'$ and $p_2 \equiv p_2'$.*

The Unicity of Formation Lemma allows us to use the terminology "formed by" without mentioning the context Γ.

Lemma 2. *Let $\Gamma \in Context(\lambda_{\omega RH})$, $t \in \Lambda_{\omega RH}$, and K be the set inductively defined by:*

$- * \in K$
$- k_1, k_2 \in K \Rightarrow k_1 \to k_2 \in K.$

then $t \in Kind(\lambda_{\omega RH})$ implies $t \in K$ and $\langle\rangle \vdash t : \square$.

Lemma 3. *Let $A, t \in \Lambda_{\omega RH}$. If $A \in Constructor(\lambda_{\omega RH})$ and t is a subexpression of A then $t \in Kind(\lambda_{\omega RH})$ or $t \in Constructor(\lambda_{\omega RH})$.*

The relation $\to_{mix}$ enjoys the following important property:

Theorem 4 Generalized Subject Reduction for $\lambda_{\omega RH}$. *Let B, B', C in $\Lambda_{\omega RH}$ and $\Gamma \in Context(\lambda_{\omega RH})$. Then $\Gamma \vdash B : C$ and $B \to_{mix}^* B'$ implies $\Gamma \vdash B' : C$.*

3 Strong Normalization and Confluence of $\to_{mix}$ in $\lambda_{\omega RH}$

The strong normalization of the combination of typed λ-calculus of order ω with terminating first order rewrite systems was proved in [2]. In this section we will extend that result, showing that λ_ω, enriched with first and higher order rewriting, is strongly normalizing whenever the first order rewrite system is terminating and conservative, and the higher order rewrite system satisfies the general schema. Moreover, we will prove that if the first order rewrite system is also confluent and the higher order rules do not introduce critical pairs then $\lambda_{\omega RH}$ is also confluent.

3.1 Strong Normalization of $\rightarrow_{mix}$

The following lemma was proved in [12] for λ_ω (i.e. without algebraic features), but it holds also for $\lambda_{\omega RH}$ because the function symbols in $\mathcal{F}$ can be seen as free variables in β-reductions.

Lemma 5 [12]. *If $M \in \Lambda_{\omega RH}$ then M is β-strongly normalizable.*

In order to show that each term of $\lambda_{\omega RH}$ is $\rightarrow_{mix}$-strongly normalizable we use the type assignment system $\wedge TRH$ of [4]. This system, but for its algebraic component, is the system devised in [6] without the universal type and the $\leq$ relation on types. It is a very powerful system indeed, since it can type precisely the set of strongly normalizable λ-terms (for a detailed proof see [1]).

Let us recall briefly the system $\wedge TRH$. A type assignment system is defined by specifying a set of terms, a set of types and a set of type inference rules. For $\wedge TRH$ we have

1. The set $T_{\wedge RH}$ of types is inductively defined by:
   (a) $\alpha_1, \alpha_2, \ldots \in T_{\wedge RH}$ (*type variables*, a denumerable set which we shall denote by V_T)
   (b) S (the set of sorts) is included in $T_{\wedge RH}$
   (c) $\sigma, \tau \in T_{\wedge RH} \Rightarrow \sigma \rightarrow \tau \in T_{\wedge RH}$ (*arrow types*).
   (d) $\sigma, \tau \in T_{\wedge RH} \Rightarrow \sigma \wedge \tau \in T_{\wedge RH}$ (*intersection types*). Intersection is associative, commutative and idempotent.
2. The terms we consider are pure λ-terms built out of a denumerable set of variables and a set of constants. The set of constants has exactly the function symbols of $\mathcal{F}$ as elements.
3. A basis is a set of statements of the form $x : \sigma$, where x is a variable and $\sigma \in T_{\wedge RH}$. If x does not occur in the basis B, then $B, x : \sigma$ denotes the basis $B \cup \{x : \sigma\}$. The type inference rules are the following :

$$(Ax) \quad B, x : \sigma \vdash x : \sigma \qquad (Ax) \quad B \vdash f : \sigma, \text{ if } f \in \mathcal{F}_\sigma$$

$$(\rightarrow I) \quad \frac{B, x : \sigma \vdash M : \tau}{B \vdash \lambda x.M : \sigma \rightarrow \tau} \qquad (\rightarrow E) \quad \frac{B \vdash M : \sigma \rightarrow \tau \quad B \vdash N : \sigma}{B \vdash (MN) : \tau}$$

$$(\wedge I) \quad \frac{B \vdash M : \sigma \quad B \vdash M : \tau}{B \vdash M : \sigma \wedge \tau} \qquad (\wedge E) \quad \frac{B \vdash M : \sigma \wedge \tau}{B \vdash M : \sigma}$$

We will express that it is possible to derive $B \vdash M : \sigma$ in system $\wedge TRH$ by simply stating $B \vdash M : \sigma$. A term will be called *typeable* in $T_{\wedge RH}$ if there exists a basis B and a type σ such that $B \vdash M : \sigma$.

Briefly, the idea of the strong normalization proof is the following: We define a "type erasing" function on terms of $\lambda_{\omega RH}$ that gives pure λ-terms as result and then we prove that erased terms are typeable in $\wedge TRH$ (this is done in three steps: first we reduce the complexity of the λ_ω structure of a term M by reducing it in β-normal form, then we prove that the erasures of terms in normal form are typeable in $\wedge TRH$, finally we exploit the preservation of intersection types by

β-expansion to prove that the erasure of M too is typeable in $\wedge TRH$). After that we show that an infinite $\rightarrow_{mix}$-reduction sequence on a term of $\lambda_{\omega RH}$ induces an infinite reduction sequence on the corresponding erased term. Since we know that $\wedge TRH$ is strongly normalizing, we deduce that $\lambda_{\omega RH}$ is strongly normalizing.

The erasing function $|\ |: Object(\lambda_{\omega RH}) \rightarrow \Lambda$ is inductively defined by

1. $|x| = x$ if $x \in Var^*$.
2. $|f| = f$ if $f \in \mathcal{F}$.
3. $|\lambda x{:}A.q| = \lambda x.|q|$ if $\lambda x{:}A.q$ is formed by $(*, *)$.
4. $|\lambda x{:}A.q| = |q|$ if $\lambda x{:}A.q$ is formed by $(\square, *)$.
5. $|pq| = |p||q|$ if pq is formed by $(*, *)$
6. $|pQ| = |p|$ if pQ is formed by $(\square, *)$.

We shall prove that $|M| \in \Lambda_{\wedge RH}$ (the set of typeable terms in $\wedge TRH$) whenever $M \in Object(\lambda_{\omega RH})$ (Theorem 9 below). To do this we use some lemmas. In the following a type A will be called *arrow-ground* if its β-normal form $A\downarrow_\beta$ belongs to $\mathcal{T}_S$.

Lemma 6. *Let* $M \in Object(\lambda_{\omega RH})$ *such that* $\Gamma \vdash M : A$ *and* $|M|$ *is in* β-*normal form. Then there exist* B *and* σ *such that* $B \vdash |M| : \sigma$. *Moreover,*

1. *if* A *is an arrow-ground type then* $\sigma \equiv A\downarrow_\beta$
2. *if* $x : \delta \in \Gamma$ *with* δ *an arrow-ground type, then* $x : \delta\downarrow_\beta \in B$.

Lemma 7. *Let* $M \in Object(\lambda_{\omega RH})$, $|M| \equiv Q\{x \mapsto P\}$, *where* P *is a term such that*

1. *if* x *is not a free variable in* Q *then* P *is in* β-*normal form and*
2. $\exists P' \in Object(\lambda_{\omega RH})$ *s.t.* $|P'| \equiv P$.

Then $\exists B, \sigma$ *s.t.* $B \vdash Q\{x \mapsto P\} : \sigma \Rightarrow \exists B'$ *s.t.* $B' \vdash (\lambda x.Q)P : \sigma$

We can now prove that the erasure of a term $M \in Object(\lambda_{\omega RH})$ is β-strongly normalizable, by showing that a β-reduction on $|M|$ induces a β-reduction on M. The β-strong normalization of $|M|$ is crucial to prove that indeed $|M| \in \Lambda_{\wedge RH}$ and, from this, that M is $\rightarrow_{mix}$-strongly normalizable.

Lemma 8. *Let* $M \in Object(\lambda_{\omega RH})$. *If* $|M| \rightarrow_\beta N$ *then there exists* $M' \in Object(\lambda_{\omega RH})$ *such that* $N \equiv |M'|$ *and* $M \rightarrow_\beta M'$.

Theorem 9. *If* $M \in Object(\lambda_{\omega RH})$, *then there exist* B, σ *s. t.* $B \vdash |M| : \sigma$.

Proof. $|M|$ is $\rightarrow_\beta$-strongly normalizable by Lemma 5 and Lemma 8. Then all the reduction strategies allow us to obtain the β-normal form of $|M|$, in particular the rightmost-innermost reduction strategy, according to which a contraction $(\lambda x.Q)P \rightarrow_\beta Q\{x \mapsto P\}$ is performed only if P is in β-normal form. Hence we can find B and σ by applying Lemma 6 to the β-normal form of $|M|$ and iterating Lemma 7 backward along the chain of reduction steps which leads from $|M|$ to its β-normal form. $\square$

So, we have proved that if $M \in Object(\lambda_{\omega RH})$ then $|M| \in \Lambda_{\wedge RH}$. In fact we can also prove that for algebraic terms we can obtain the same type:

Lemma 10. *If* $\Gamma \vdash M : \tau$ *is an algebraic term in* $\lambda_\omega RH$ *, then* $|M| \in \Lambda_{\wedge RH}$, *and* $|M|$ *is typeable with* $\tau \downarrow_\beta$ *from a basis* B *such that: if* $x : \tau' \in \Gamma$, *then* $x : \tau' \downarrow_\beta \in B$.

Each rule $r : A \rightarrow B \in R \cup HOR$ in $\lambda_\omega RH$ induces a reduction relation $\rightarrow^r_{\wedge RH}$ on $\Lambda_{\wedge RH}$: $|A|\phi \rightarrow^r_{\wedge TRH} |B|\phi$ for any substitution ϕ in $\wedge TRH$ such that if Γ is the context for A and B and $x : \sigma' \in \Gamma$ then $x\phi$ is typeable with type $\sigma' \downarrow_\beta$. Lemma 10 ensures that this is a good definition.

We define $\rightarrow_{R_{(\wedge TRH)}} = \bigcup\limits_{r \in R} \rightarrow^r_{\wedge TRH}$, $\rightarrow_{HOR_{(\wedge TRH)}} = \bigcup\limits_{r \in HOR} \rightarrow^r_{\wedge TRH}$ and $\rightarrow_{mix_{(\wedge TRH)}} = \rightarrow_\beta \cup \rightarrow_{R_{(\wedge TRH)}} \cup \rightarrow_{HOR_{(\wedge TRH)}}$ Since it will always be clear from the context, we shall denote in the same way a reduction on terms of $\lambda_\omega RH$ and the corresponding one on terms in $\Lambda_{\wedge RH}$, i.e. we shall omit the subscript $(\wedge TRH)$. The following theorem is fundamental for the proof that $\lambda_\omega RH$ terms are $\rightarrow_{mix}$-strongly normalizing.

Theorem 11 [4]. $\rightarrow_{mix}$ *is strongly normalizing on terms of* $\Lambda_{\wedge RH}$ *if* R *is conservative and* HOR *satisfies the general schema.*

Conservativity of R is essential here. A counterexample to this theorem in the case of non-conservativity is shown in [4].

We can now prove the main theorem of this section. A β-reduction on a $\lambda_\omega RH$ term such that the β-redex is formed by (p_1, p_2), will be called, in the following, a $\beta(p_1, p_2)$-reduction.

Theorem 12. *Assume that* R *is conservative and that* HOR *satisfies the general schema. If* $M \in \Lambda_\omega RH$ *then* M *is* $\rightarrow_{mix}$*-strongly normalizable.*

Proof. By Lemma 2, we only need to consider the cases $M \in Constructor(\lambda_\omega RH)$ and $M \in Object(\lambda_\omega RH)$. If $M \in Constructor(\lambda_\omega RH)$, then, since $\lambda_\omega RH$ objects can not occur in constructors (Lemma 3), each reduction in M is actually a β-reduction. Hence, strong normalization of M follows from Lemma 5. If $M \in Object(\lambda_\omega RH)$, then we assign to M the pair $\mathcal{I}(M) = \langle |M|, M \rangle$. By Theorem 9, $|M| \in \Lambda_{\wedge RH}$ and then by Theorem 11 $|M|$ is $\rightarrow_{mix}$-strongly normalizing. By Lemma 5, M is $\rightarrow_\beta$-strongly normalizable. Then the ordering $\geq \equiv (\rightarrow_{mix}, \rightarrow_{\beta(\square,\square)} \cup \rightarrow_{\beta(*,\square)})_{lex}$ is well founded on these pairs. Moreover, $M \rightarrow_{mix} M'$ implies $\mathcal{I}(M) > \mathcal{I}(M')$, so there is no infinite reduction sequence. □

The *second order* λ-*calculus* is included in λ_ω. Then, as a by-product of Theorem 12 we also obtain the $\rightarrow_{mix}$-strong normalization of the second order λ-calculus enriched with first and higher order rewriting. This property was already proved in [14] using the classical method of candidates of reducibility.

3.2 Confluence of $\rightarrow_{mix}$

We first recall the definition of confluence: a reduction relation $\rightarrow$ is called *confluent* if for all t such that $t \rightarrow^* v_1$ and $t \rightarrow^* v_2$ for some v_1, v_2, there exists v_3 such that $v_1 \rightarrow^* v_3$ and $v_2 \rightarrow^* v_3$. Local confluence is a closely related (weaker) property: $\to$ is called *locally confluent* if for all t such that $t \to v_1$ and $t \to v_2$ for some v_1, v_2, there exists v_3 such that $v_1 \to^* v_3$ and $v_2 \to^* v_3$. For strongly normalizing relations, local confluence is equivalent to confluence (Newman's Lemma [15]). So we shall prove in the rest of this subsection that $\to_{mix}$ is locally confluent on $\lambda_{\omega RH}$. The following lemmas show that the confluence of $\to_R$ for algebraic terms transfers to $\lambda_{\omega RH}$-terms, and that for the class of higher order rewrite systems which we consider, the absence of critical pairs implies confluence (note that this is not true for arbitrary higher order rewrite systems, as shown in [16]). Due to lack of space we can not include the proofs of these lemmas here.

Lemma 13. *If R is confluent and strongly normalizing on the set of algebraic terms of $\lambda_{\omega RH}$ then $\to_R$ is locally confluent on $\Lambda_{\omega RH}$.*

Lemma 14. *Let HOR be a higher order rewrite system satisfying the general schema. If there is no critical pair, then $\to_{HOR}$ is confluent on $\lambda_{\omega RH}$.*

Now let us prove that $\to_{mix}$ is locally confluent.

Theorem 15 Local Confluence of $\to_{mix}$ in $\lambda_{\omega RH}$. *If R is confluent over the set of algebraic terms, and there are no critical pairs between rules in R and HOR and between rules in HOR, then $\to_{mix}$ is locally confluent on $\lambda_{\omega RH}$.*

Proof. It suffices to show the commutativity of β-, $\to_R$- and $\to_{HOR}$-reductions on overlapping redexes. But since $\to_\beta$ is confluent, $\to_{HOR}$ is confluent (by Lemma 14) and $\to_R$ is confluent (by Lemma 13), it is sufficient to prove that, for all t such that $t \to_{mix} v_1$ at position p using one of the reduction relations, and $t \to_{mix} v_2$ at position $p.q$ using a different reduction relation, there exists a v_3 such that $v_1 \to^*_{mix} v_3$ and $v_2 \to^*_{mix} v_3$.

Let t' be the term obtained from t by replacing the subterm at position $p.q$ by a new variable x. Since there are no critical pairs, t' is still reducible at position p: $t' \to_{mix} v'$. If x appears in v' at positions $m_1, \ldots, m_n$ then $t|_{p.q}$ appears in v_1 at the same positions. Let t'' be the term obtained after reducing v_1 at positions $m_1, \ldots, m_n$. Then $v_2 \to_{mix} t''$ at position p. $\square$

For example, the class of higher order rewriting systems defining higher order functions by primitive recursion (structured recursion) on first order data structures, verify the required hypothesis and then $\to_{mix}$ is confluent in this case.

4 Conclusions and further work

The results proved here allow for the use of the well known principle of Divide et Impera to prove consistency of logical systems based on combinations of λ_ω with algebraic rewrite systems (both first and higher order), provided that the first order reductions are conservative, and that higher order rules satisfy the general schema. Unfortunately, the extension of these results to more powerful systems such as the Calculus of Constructions is not straightforward. This is no doubt a topic worth of further investigation.

References

1. S. van Bakel. Complete restrictions of the intersection type discipline. *Theoretical Computer Science*, 102:135-163, 1992.
2. F. Barbanera. Adding algebraic rewriting to the calculus of constructions: Strong normalization preserved. In *Proc. of the 2nd Int. Workshop on Conditional and Typed Rewriting*, LNCS 514, 1990.
3. F. Barbanera. Combining term rewriting and type assignment systems. *International Journal of Foundations of Computer Science*, 1:165–184, 1990.
4. Franco Barbanera and Maribel Fernández. Combining first and higher order rewrite systems with type assignment systems. In *Proceedings of the International Conference on Typed Lambda Calculi and Applications, Utrecht, Holland*, LNCS 664, 1993.
5. H. Barendregt. Introduction to generalised type systems. *Journal of Functional Programming*, 1991.
6. H. Barendregt, M. Coppo, and M. Dezani-Ciancaglini. A filter λ-model and the completeness of type assignment. *Journal of Symbolic Logic*, 48(4):931–940, 1983.
7. S. Berardi. *Type dependence and constructive mathematics*. PhD thesis, Mathematical Institute, Torino, Italy, 1990.
8. Val Breazu-Tannen and Jean Gallier. Polymorphic rewriting conserves algebraic strong normalization. *Theoretical Computer Science*, 1990. to appear.
9. Val Breazu-Tannen and Jean Gallier. Polymorphic rewriting conserves algebraic confluence. *Information and Computation*, 1992. to appear.
10. Thierry Coquand and Gérard Huet. The calculus of constructions. *Information and Computation*, 76:95–120, February 1988.
11. H. Geuvers and M.J. Nederhof. Modular proof of the strong normalization for the calculus of constructions. *Journal of Functional Programming*, vol.1 (2), 1991.
12. J.-Y. Girard. *Interprétation fonctionelle et élimination des coupures dans l'arithmétique d'ordre supérieur*. Thèse d'Etat, Univ. Paris VII, France, 1972.
13. J.-Y. Girard, Y. Lafont, and P. Taylor. *Proofs and Types*. Cambridge Tracts in Theoretical Computer Science. Cambridge University Press, 1989.
14. Jean-Pierre Jouannaud and Mitsuhiro Okada. Executable higher-order algebraic specification languages. In *Proc. 6th IEEE Symp. Logic in Computer Science, Amsterdam*, pages 350–361, 1991.
15. M. H. A. Newman. On theories with a combinatorial definition of 'equivalence'. *Ann. Math.*, 43(2):223–243, 1942.
16. T. Nipkow. Higher order critical pairs. In *Proc. IEEE Symp. on Logic in Comp. Science, Amsterdam*, 1991.
17. Mitsuhiro Okada. Strong normalizability for the combined system of the types lambda calculus and an arbitrary convergent term rewrite system. In *Proc. ISSAC 89, Portland, Oregon*, 1989.
18. Michaël Rusinowitch. On termination of the direct sum of term rewriting systems. *Information Processing Letters*, 26:65–70, 1987.
19. Y. Toyama. Counterexamples to termination for the direct sum of term rewriting systems. *Information Processing Letters*, 25:141–143, April 1987.
20. Y. Toyama. On the Church-Rosser property for the direct sum of term rewriting systems. *Journal of the ACM*, 34(1):128–143, April 1987.

From Domains to Automata with Concurrency

Felipe BRACHO [1] and Manfred DROSTE [2]

Abstract

We investigate an operational model of concurrent systems, called automata with concurrency relations. These are labelled transition systems $\mathcal{A}$ in which the event set is endowed with a collection of binary concurrency relations which indicate when two events, in a particular state of the automaton, commute. This model generalizes asynchronous transition systems, and as in trace theory we obtain, through a permutation equivalence for computation sequences of $\mathcal{A}$, an induced domain $(D(\mathcal{A}), \leq)$. Here, we construct a categorical equivalence between a large category of ('cancellative') automata with concurrency relations and the associated domains. We show that each cancellative automaton can be reduced to a minimal cancellative automaton generating, up to isomorphism, the same domain. Furthermore, when fixing the event set, this minimal automaton is unique.

1 Introduction

In the study of programming languages like CCS [Mi] and CSP [Ho], labelled transition systems have been frequently used to give an operational semantics of concurrent processes. A labelled transition system may be defined to be a quadruple $(S, E, T, *)$ where S is a set of states, E is a set of events, $T \subseteq S \times E \times S$ is the transition relation, and $* \in S$ is the start state. Recently, several authors have considered labelled transition systems with an additional binary relation $\|$ on E incorporating direct information about concurrency. Then two transitions $t = (s, e, r), t' = (s, e', r')$ are defined to 'commute' whenever $e \parallel e'$. Such asynchronous transition systems, which generalize Mazurkiewicz traces [Ma], were investigated by Bednarczyk [Be] and Shields [Sh]. Similar structures have been used to provide a semantics for CCS [BC] and to model properties of computations in term rewriting systems, in the lambda calculus [BD, BL, HL, Le] and in dataflow networks [St2, St3]. For further background, we refer the reader to [WN].

In the previous model, a single binary relation on E was used to represent the concurrency information for all pairs of transitions. Here, we investigate a more general model in which the concurrency information for two transitions depends not only on the two arriving events, but also on the present state of the transition system. Hence, we consider transition systems (automata) $\mathcal{A} = (S, E, T, *)$ together with a collection of binary concurrency relations $\|_s$ ($s \in S$) on E which reflect when two events commute in a particular state $s \in S$. Such *automata with concurrency relations* were introduced in [D1, D2], where their domains of computation sequences were investigated, also, independently and in a slightly

---
[1] IIMAS, Universidad Nacional Autónoma de México, A.P. 20-726, 01000 México D.F.
[2] Mathematik und Informatik, Universität GHS Essen, 4300 Essen, Germany

different form, in [KP], where applications are given. They arise naturally, for instance, when considering the dynamic behaviour of place/transition nets with capacities in Petri net theory, see [DS].

Similarly as for asynchronous transition systems and as in trace theory, the concurrency relations of the automaton $\mathcal{A}$ induce a natural definition of permutation equivalence for (finite or infinite) computation sequences of $\mathcal{A}$; intuitively, two computation sequences are equivalent, if they represent 'interleaved views' of a single computation (for the origins of this notion of equivalence, see [BL, HL, Le]). Moreover, the set $D(\mathcal{A})$ of equivalence classes of computation sequences carries a non-trivial partial order which is naturally induced by the prefix-ordering of computation sequences. In [D1,D2], an order-theoretic characterization was given of all the partial orders $(D(\mathcal{A}), \leq)$ where $\mathcal{A}$ is an automaton with concurrency relations. These *weak concurrency domains* turned out to be closely related with event domains and dI-domains which arose in studies of denotational semantics of programming languages (cf. [Cu, Wi]).

In this paper, we investigate categories of automata with concurrency relations and of weak concurrency domains. Let us say that an automaton with concurrency relations $\mathcal{A}$ *generates* a domain $(D, \leq)$, if $(D, \leq)$ is order-isomorphic to the domain $(D(\mathcal{A}), \leq)$. In general, a given domain $(D, \leq)$ may be generated by many (non-isomorphic) automata $\mathcal{A}$. This indicates that we should endow the domains $(D(\mathcal{A}), \leq)$ with more structure. In fact, as we will show, $\mathcal{A}$ induces on the compact elements and on the prime intervals of its domain $(D(\mathcal{A}), \leq)$ two labelling functions in a natural way. These take values in the state set S and the event set E of $\mathcal{A}$, respectively. This leads to a functor $\mathbf{D}$ from the category *Aut* of all automata with concurrency relations into the category *LDom* of all labelled weak concurrency domains. We show that this functor induces, in fact, an equivalence between the large subcategory of *Aut* comprising all *cancellative* automata and the category of all *nicely labelled* weak concurrency domains. (For precise definitions, see section 2.) As a consequence we obtain a characterization of when a given weak concurrency domain $(D, \leq)$ can be generated by a finite cancellative automaton $\mathcal{A}$.

An important tool for these results is the notion of a *reduction* of $\mathcal{A}$ to $\mathcal{A}'$; this is defined to be an epimorphism from $\mathcal{A}$ to $\mathcal{A}'$ reflecting the enabling and concurrency of events at states. We show that such a reduction of $\mathcal{A}$ to $\mathcal{A}'$ does not change (up to isomorphism) the induced domain $D(\mathcal{A})$ of computation sequences.

Next we consider, for a given weak concurrency domain $(D, \leq)$, the class of all cancellative automata $\mathcal{A}$ generating $(D, \leq)$. This class contains, with respect to reductions, a greatest automaton $\mathcal{A}_{max}$; i.e., $\mathcal{A}_{max}$ can be reduced to any other cancellative automaton generating $(D, \leq)$, and $\mathcal{A}_{max}$ is unique up to isomorphism.

Similarly as in classical formal language theory, each cancellative automaton $\mathcal{A}$ generating $(D, \leq)$ can be reduced to a 'minimal' such automaton $\mathcal{A}_{min}$; here 'minimal' means that any further reduction of $\mathcal{A}_{min}$ is an isomorphism. However, here in general $\mathcal{A}_{min}$ is not unique up to isomorphism. Somewhat surprisingly, however, if we consider only automata with (in a certain sense) a fixed event set, then this class of automata contains, with respect to state-reductions, also a uniquely determined minimal automaton.

For further results and proofs we refer the reader to the full paper [BDr].

Acknowledgement. Most of this work was done while the second named author was a visitor at the Universidad Nacional Autónoma de México in spring and summer 1992. He would like to thank his colleagues for their hospitality and a wonderful time.

2   Automata and labelled domains

In this section, we will introduce automata with concurrency relations and their induced domains of concurrent computation sequences. Also we will show how these domains can be endowed, in a natural way, with two labelling functions, for events and states, respectively.

Definition 2. 1 An *automaton with concurrency relations* is a quintuple $\mathcal{A} = (S, E, T, *, \|)$ where

1. S and E are countable sets; $* \in S$ is a distinguished element;

2. T is a subset of $S \times E \times S$ such that whenever $(s, e, s'), (s, e, s'') \in T$, then $s' = s''$; we require that for each $e \in E$ there are $s, s' \in S$ with $(s, e, s') \in T$.

3. $\| = (\|_s)_{s \in S}$ is a family of irreflexive, symmetric binary relations on E; it is required that whenever $e_1 \|_s e_2$ $(e_1, e_2 \in E)$, there exist transitions $(s, e_1, s_1), (s, e_2, s_2), (s_2, e_1, r)$ and (s_1, e_2, r) in T.

The elements of S are called *states*, the elements of E *events* and the elements of T *transitions*. Intuitively, a transition $t = (s, e, s')$ represents a potential computation step in which event e happens in state s of $\mathcal{A}$ and $\mathcal{A}$ changes from state s to s'. We write $ev(t) = e$, the event of t. The element $*$ is the *start state*. The *concurrency relations* $\|_s$ describe the concurrency information for pairs of events at state s. In general, the events that concur at a state s do not have to bear upon those that concur in another state. Thus the concurrency relations $\|_s$ $(s \in S)$ are viewed as being independent of each other. Later on we will impose additional restrictions on $\mathcal{A}$. A *finite computation sequence* in $\mathcal{A}$ is either empty (denoted by ε), or a finite sequence $u = t_1...t_n$ of transitions $t_i \in T$ of the form $t_i = (s_{i-1}, e_i, s_i)$ for $i = 1, ..., n$; it can be depicted as:

$$s_0 \xrightarrow{e_1} s_1 \xrightarrow{e_2} ... \xrightarrow{e_n} s_n.$$

We call s_0 the *domain* of u, denoted $dom(u)$, and s_n the *codomain*, denoted $cod(u)$. An infinite sequence $(t_i)_{i \in \mathbb{N}}$ of transitions $t_i = (s_{i-1}, e_i, s_i)$ $(i \in \mathbb{N})$ is called an *infinite computation sequence* of $\mathcal{A}$; its domain is s_0. A computation sequence is called *initial* if its domain is $*$, the start state. We let

$CS(\mathcal{A})(CS^0(\mathcal{A}), CS_*(\mathcal{A}), CS^0_*(\mathcal{A}))$ denote the sets, respectively, of all (all finite, all initial, all finite initial) computation sequences of $\mathcal{A}$. The *composition* uv of a finite computation sequence u and an arbitrary computation sequence v with $dom(v) = cod(u)$ is defined in the natural way by concatenating u and v. Formally, we put $u\varepsilon = \varepsilon u = u$. We call u a *prefix* of w, if u is finite and $w = uv$ for some computation sequence v.

Now we want the concurrency relations of $\mathcal{A}$ to induce an equivalence relation on $CS(\mathcal{A})$ so that equivalent computation sequences are not differentiated by the order in which the concurrent events appear. For this we proceed as follows: we call two finite computation sequences $t = t_1...t_n$ and $u = u_1...u_n$ *strongly equivalent* if we obtain t from u by replacing for some $1 \leq i < n$, an occurrence $u_i u_{i+1}$ of the form $(q, a, p)(p, b, r)$ by $t_i t_{i+1}$ of the form $(q, b, s)(s, a, r)$ with $a \parallel_q b$ in $\mathcal{A}$. We then let $\sim$ be the reflexive and transitive closure of strong equivalence on $CS^0(\mathcal{A})$.

It easily follows from the above that $\sim$ is an equivalence relation and that any two equivalent sequences have the same length, domain and codomain. Also for any $a \in E$, the number of occurrences of a is the same in any two equivalent sequences.

The prefix relation together with $\sim$ induces a preorder on $CS^0(\mathcal{A})$ by letting $u \leq v$ iff $v \sim uw$ for some $w \in CS^0(\mathcal{A})$. This gives rise to a preorder in $CS(\mathcal{A})$ where for $u, v \in CS(\mathcal{A})$ we put $u \leq v$ if for every prefix u' of u there exists a prefix v' of v such that $u' \leq v'$. Then put $u \sim v$ iff $u \leq v$ and $v \leq u$, and let $[u]$ denote the equivalence class with respect to $\sim$. We order these classes by $[u] \leq [v]$ iff $u \leq v$. Then let $D(\mathcal{A}) = \{[u] : u \in CS_*(\mathcal{A})\}$ and call $(D(\mathcal{A}), \leq)$ the *domain of concurrent computation sequences associated with* $\mathcal{A}$. Given a partial order $(D, \leq)$, we say that $\mathcal{A}$ *generates* $(D, \leq)$ if $(D, \leq)$ is isomorphic to $(D(\mathcal{A}), \leq)$. It is proved in Droste [D2] that this is indeed a domain where the compact or finite elements are given by $D^0(\mathcal{A}) = \{[u] : u \in CS^0_*(\mathcal{A})\}$. We will later show that this construction induces a functor between the categories of automata and certain kinds of domains and functions. Let us now turn to the domains that are induced by the automata we have defined.

We introduce some notation. Let $(D, \leq)$ be a domain, i.e. an ω-algebraic complete partial order (cpo). We denote the set of *compact (= isolated, finite)* elements of $(D, \leq)$ by D^0. We say that $(D, \leq)$ is *finitary*, if for all $x \in D^0$, the set $\{d \in D^0 : d \leq x\}$ is finite. For $x, y \in D$ with $x < y$ we write $x \prec y$ if there is no $z \in D$ with $x < z < y$. We denote by $[x, y]$ such a pair, and we call it a *prime interval* of D. Let Int_D denote the collection of all prime intervals of D. Also, for prime intervals $[x, y], [x', y']$ of D we put $[x, y] \prec [x', y']$ if $x' \neq y$, $x \prec x'$ and $y \prec y'$. We let $\succ\!\!\prec$ denote the smallest equivalence relation on Int_D containing $\prec$.

Let $\mathcal{A} = (S, E, T, *, \parallel)$ be an automaton with concurrency relations. It is immediate from the definition of $(D(\mathcal{A}), \leq)$ that for $x, y \in D^0(\mathcal{A})$ we have that $x \prec y$ iff $x = [u]$ and $y = [ut]$ for some $u \in CS^0_*(\mathcal{A})$ and $t \in T$. Since the number of occurrences of any fixed event e in two equivalent finite computation sequences is the same and all $u \in x$ have the same codomain, it follows that

t is uniquely determined by x and y. We will write $x \stackrel{e}{\prec} y$ when for some $u \in CS^0_*(A)$, $t \in T$ we have $x = [u]$, $y = [ut]$, and $ev(t) = e$. Since, conversely, t is uniquely determined by $dom(t)$ and $ev(t)$, we also obtain that $x \stackrel{e}{\prec} y$ and $x \stackrel{e}{\prec} y'$ imply $y = y'$.

Suppose now that $[x, y] \prec [x', y']$ in $(D(A), \leq)$. Let $x = [u]$, $y = [ut_1]$ and $x' = [ut_2]$ with $t_1, t_2 \in T$. Since $y \prec y'$ and $x' \prec y'$, we have $y' = [ut_1t'_1] = [ut_2t'_2]$ with $t'_1, t'_2 \in T$. Let $e_i = ev(t_i)$, $e'_i = ev(t'_i)$ $(i = 1, 2)$. Since the number of occurrences of e_1 (respectively e_2) in $ut_1t'_1$ is the same as in $ut_2t'_2$ and $e_1 \neq e_2$ by $y \neq x'$, we obtain that $e'_1 = e_2$ and $e'_2 = e_1$. Hence $x \stackrel{e}{\prec} y$ and $[x, y] \prec [x', y']$ imply $x' \stackrel{e}{\prec} y'$. We summarize these observations in the following lemma.

Lemma 2. 2 Let $A = (S, E, T, *, \|)$ be an automaton with concurrency relations. Let $x, y, z, x', y' \in D^0(A)$ with $x \prec y, x \prec z$ and $x' \prec y'$, and let $e, e' \in E$.

(a) If $x \stackrel{e}{\prec} y$ and $x \stackrel{e'}{\prec} z$, then $y = z$ iff $e = e'$.

(b) $[x, y] \prec [x', y']$ and $x \stackrel{e}{\prec} y$ imply $x' \stackrel{e}{\prec} y'$.

Let $(D, \leq)$ again be a finitary domain, and let $x, y \in D^0$ with $x < y$. A sequence $(x_i)_{i=0}^n$ in D^0 of the form $x = x_0 \prec x_1 \prec \ldots \prec x_n = y$ will be called a *covering chain* from x to y. Such a covering chain will be said to be *strongly equivalent* to any other covering chain from x to y of the form $x = x_0 \prec \ldots \prec x_i \prec z \prec x_{i+2} \prec \ldots \prec x_n = y$ with $z \neq x_{i+1}$, for some $0 \leq i \leq n - 2$. We define *equivalence* on the set of all covering chains in D as the reflexive and transitive closure of strong equivalence.

Definition 2. 3 ([D2]). A finitary domain $(D, \leq)$ is called a *weak concurrency domain* if it satisfies the following two conditions for any $x, y, z \in D^0$:

(R) If $x \prec y, x \prec z$ and $[x, y] \prec [x, z]$, then $y = z$;

(E) Any two covering chains from $\perp$ to x are equivalent.

Let A be an automaton with concurrency relations. Lemma 2.2 shows that $(D(A), \leq)$ satisfies axiom (R). Besides, any finite initial computation sequence $t_1 \ldots t_n$ with $ev(t_i) = e_i$ gives rise to a covering chain $\perp = x_0 \stackrel{e_1}{\prec} x_1 \stackrel{e_2}{\prec} \ldots \stackrel{e_n}{\prec} x_n$ in $D(A)$ from $\perp$ to x_n, where $x_i = [t_1 \ldots t_i](i = 1, \ldots, n)$. It is easy to see that this correspondence preserves strong equivalence, thus also equivalence; hence $(D(A), \leq)$ satisfies axiom (E). So, $(D(A), \leq)$ is a weak concurrency domain. Conversely, each weak concurrency domain $(D, \leq)$ is generated by some automaton A with concurrency relations [D2]. Here, in general A is not determined uniquely by $(D, \leq)$. However, as will be seen, the class of all automata A generating a fixed weak concurrency domain $(D, \leq)$ can be well structured. Any domain $(D(A), \leq)$ carries a natural labelling of its prime intervals $[x, y]$, as indicated by Lemma 2.2. This motivates the following definition.

Definition 2. 4 Let $(D, \leq)$ be a finitary domain and E a set. A mapping $l_E : Int_D \to E$ will be called an *event-labelling function* if it is onto and satisfies the following two conditions for any $x, y, x', y', z \in D^0$:

1. $[x, y] \asymp [x', y']$ implies $l_E([x, y]) = l_E([x', y'])$.

2. $x \prec y, x \prec z$ and $l_E([x, y]) = l_E([x, z])$ imply $y = z$.

Then $(D, \leq, l_E)$ will be called an *event-labelled domain*. In this case, for $x, y \in D^0$, we will write $x \overset{e}{\prec} y$ to denote that $x \prec y$ and $l_E([x, y]) = e$.

Note that any event-labelled domain satisfies axiom (R). Conversely any finitary domain $(D, \leq)$ satisfying axiom (R) carries an event-labelling function l mapping each prime interval $[x, y]$ onto its equivalence class with respect to $\asymp$. If $\mathcal{A}$ is an automaton with concurrency relations, we can also define a function $l_E : Int_{D(\mathcal{A})} \to E$ by putting $l_E([x, y]) = e$ if $x = [u], y = [ut]$ for some $ut \in CS^0_*(\mathcal{A})$ with $t \in T$ and $ev(t) = e$. By Lemma 2.2, l_E is an event-labelling function on $(D(\mathcal{A}), \leq)$. We call l_E the *induced* event-labelling function. Next we note that the correspondence $[u] \mapsto cod(u)$ $(u \in CS^0_*(\mathcal{A}))$ defines a function from $D^0(\mathcal{A})$ into S, which we also denote, simply, by cod. Similarly as before for events, its properties motivate the following definition.

Definition 2. 5 Let $(D, \leq, l_E)$ be an event-labelled domain and S a set. A mapping $l_S : D^0 \to S$ will be called a *state-labelling function* if it is onto and satisfies the following condition:

1. Whenever $x, y, x' \in D^0$ with $x \overset{e}{\prec} y$ and $l_S(x) = l_S(x')$, then there is $y' \in D^0$ with $x' \overset{e}{\prec} y'$ and $l_S(y') = l_S(y)$.

Then $(D, \leq, l_E, l_S)$ will be called a *labelled domain*. Moreover, it will be said to be *nicely labelled* (and l_S is a *nice* state-labelling function) if:

2. Whenever $x, y_i, z, x', y'_i, z'_i \in D^0$ with $x \overset{e_i}{\prec} y_i \overset{e_{3-i}}{\prec} z$ and $x' \overset{e_i}{\prec} y'_i \overset{e_{3-i}}{\prec} z'_i$ for $i = 1, 2, y_1 \neq y_2$ and $l_S(x) = l_S(x')$, then $z'_1 = z'_2$.

In pictures:

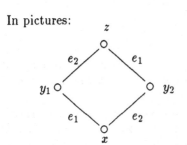
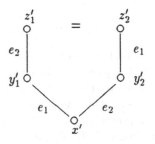

Clearly, for any event-labelled domain $(D, \leq, l_E)$, the identity mapping id_{D^0} on D^0 is a nice state-labelling of $(D, \leq, l_E)$.

Now let $\mathcal{A}$ be an automaton with concurrency relations, and let l_E be the induced event-labelling of $(D(\mathcal{A}), \leq)$. Then $cod : D^0(\mathcal{A}) \to S$, as defined before, is a state-labelling of $(D(\mathcal{A}), \leq, l_E)$. For, if $x, y, x' \in D^0(\mathcal{A})$ with $x \overset{e}{\prec} y$ and $cod(x) = cod(x')$, then for some $u, u' \in CS^0_*(\mathcal{A})$ and $t \in T$, we have $x = [u]$, $y = [ut]$, $ev(t) = e$, $x' = [u']$ and $cod(u) = cod(u')$; so $y' = [u't] \in D^0(\mathcal{A})$, $x' \overset{e}{\prec} y'$ and $cod(y') = cod(y)$. We put $\mathbf{D}(\mathcal{A}) = (D(\mathcal{A}), \leq, l_E, cod)$, and we call $\mathbf{D}(\mathcal{A})$ the *induced labelled domain* of $\mathcal{A}$. In general, $\mathbf{D}(\mathcal{A})$ is not nicely labelled. To have this we need additional assumptions on $\mathcal{A}$.

Definition 2. 6 Let $\mathcal{A}$ be an automaton with concurrency relations in which each state is reachable.

(a) $\mathcal{A}$ is *cancellative*, if whenever there exist x, y_1, y_2, z in $D^0(\mathcal{A})$ with $x \overset{e_i}{\prec} y_i \overset{e_{3-i}}{\prec} z$ for $i = 1, 2$, then $e_1 \parallel_{cod(x)} e_2$.

(b) ([D1]) $\mathcal{A}$ is *concurrent*, if whenever (q, a, p), (q, b, r), $(q, c, s) \in T$ are such that $a \parallel_q b, a \parallel_q c$ and $b \parallel_p c$, then also $b \parallel_q c$, $a \parallel_r c$ and $a \parallel_s b$.

Note that $\mathcal{A}$ is cancellative iff for any finite initial computation sequences ut_1t_2, $ut'_1t'_2$ with $t_i, t'_i \in T$ ($i = 1, 2$), $ut_1t_2 \sim ut'_1t'_2$ implies $t_1t_2 \sim t'_1t'_2$, which explains the name. It is easy to see that if $\mathcal{A}$ is cancellative, then $\mathbf{D}(\mathcal{A})$ is nicely labelled. The requirement for concurrent automata can be illustrated by the following diagram:

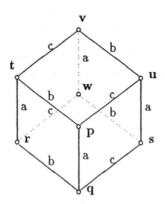

The black lines indicate the transitions which exist by the assumption that $a \parallel_q b, a \parallel_q c, b \parallel_p c$. The dotted lines indicate the transitions which are forced to exist by the requirements: $b \parallel_q c$, $a \parallel_r c$ and $a \parallel_s b$.

Concurrent automata were studied in detail in Droste [D2]. They correspond in a precise sense to automata with residual operations which were investigated by Stark [St1], Panangaden and Stark [PS] and Bachmann and Dung [BD]. They occur naturally in λ-calculus, networks of communicating processes and reductions in non-deterministic term rewriting, see [Le,St1,BD,HL].

Proposition 2. 7 Let $\mathcal{A}$ be a concurrent automaton. Then $\mathcal{A}$ is cancellative.

Proof. By [D2, (3.3)], $\mathcal{A}$ can be transformed into an 'automaton with residual operation'. By Stark [St4], these automata are cancellative.

It will be shown below that any weak concurrency domain can be generated by a cancellative automaton. Hence, with respect to the class of generated domains, the assumption that the underlying automata are cancellative is no essential restriction. However, concurrent automata generate more specific domains, as shown in [D1,2]. A domain $(D, \leq)$ is a *Scott-domain*, if each non-empty subset of D which has an upper bound in D has a supremum in D. A finitary Scott-domain $(D, \leq)$ is called a *concurrency domain*, if it satisfies condition (R) (see Definition 2.3) and (C) for any $x, y, z \in D^0$:

(C) Whenever $x \prec y$, $x \prec z$, $y \neq z$ and $\{y, z\}$ has an upper bound in D, then $y \prec y \sqcup z$ and $z \prec y \sqcup z$.

Any such domain also satisfies condition (E) of Definition 2.3, and as shown in [D2], concurrent automata generate precisely the concurrency domains.

3 Categories of automata and labelled domains

We will introduce morphisms between automata and between labelled domains and then construct a functorial equivalence between the categories of cancellative automata and of nicely labelled domains. First let us define morphisms between automata.

Definition 3. 1 Let $\mathcal{A} = (S, E, T, *, \|)$ and $\mathcal{A}' = (S', E', T', *', \|')$ be two automata with concurrency relations, and let $f : S \to S'$, $g : E \to E'$ be functions. The pair (f, g) is called a *morphism* from $\mathcal{A}$ to $\mathcal{A}'$, if the following conditions are satisfied:

1. Whenever $(s, e, r) \in T$, then $(f(s), g(e), f(r)) \in T'$;

2. whenever $e \|_s e'$ and $g(e) \neq g(e')$, then $g(e) \|'_{f(s)} g(e')$;

3. $f(*) = *'$.

Note that this is just the kind of morphism we would obtain from model theory or universal algebra if we view S and E as unary and T and $\|$ as ternary relations on $S \cup E$; thus a morphism preserves states, events, transitions, the start state and maps concurrent or equal events of $\mathcal{A}$ to concurrent or equal events of $\mathcal{A}'$. A slightly restricted version of these morphisms (obtained by deleting the assumption that $g(e) \neq g(e')$ in condition (3)) and the interplay between the induced category of automata with concurrency relations and a category of Petri nets were studied, e.g., in Droste and Shortt [DS]. Clearly morphisms compose and (id_S, id_E) is the identity morphism. We let *Aut* denote the category of all automata with concurrency relations, and morphisms as above as arrows, and we let $CAut$ denote its full subcategory comprising all cancellative automata. Next we define the morphisms between labelled domains.

Definition 3. 2 Let $\mathcal{D} = (D, \leq, l_E, l_S)$, $\mathcal{D}' = (D', \leq, l_{E'}, l_{S'})$ be two labelled domains. A triple (φ, f, g) of functions $\varphi : D \to D', f : S \to S', g : E \to E'$ will be called a *morphism* from $\mathcal{D}$ to $\mathcal{D}'$, if it satisfies the following conditions:

1. $\varphi : (D, \leq) \to (D', \leq)$ is continuous, $\varphi(D^0) \subseteq D'^0$ and $\varphi(\perp) = \perp'$;

2. whenever $x, y \in D^0$ with $x \overset{e}{\prec} y$, then $\varphi(x) \overset{g(e)}{\prec} \varphi(y)$, i.e. $l_{E'}([\varphi(x), \varphi(y)]) = g \circ l_E([x, y])$.

3. $l_{S'} \circ \varphi |_{D^0} = f \circ l_S$.

If here φ is an order-isomorphism, we call (φ, f, g) an *order-morphism*. If, moreover, f and g are bijective, we call (φ, f, g) an *isomorphism*.

We let $NLDom$ denote the category of all nicely labelled weak concurrency domains, with morphisms (φ, f, g) as arrows.

Now let $\mathcal{A}, \mathcal{A}'$ be two automata with concurrency relations, let $\mathbf{D}(\mathcal{A}) = (D(\mathcal{A}), \leq, l_E, l_S)$, $\mathbf{D}(\mathcal{A}') = (D(\mathcal{A}'), \leq, l_{E'}, l_{S'})$ be the induced labelled domains, and let $(f, g) : \mathcal{A} \to \mathcal{A}'$ be a morphism. We define a mapping $\varphi : D(\mathcal{A}) \to D(\mathcal{A}')$ as follows. If $x = [u] \in D(\mathcal{A})$ where $u = (s_0 \overset{e_1}{\longrightarrow} s_1 \overset{e_2}{\longrightarrow} ...)$ is a finite or infinite initial computation sequence of $\mathcal{A}$, let $u' = (f(s_0) \overset{g(e_1)}{\longrightarrow} f(s_1) \overset{g(e_2)}{\longrightarrow} ...)$, and put $\varphi(x) = [u']$. Since (f, g) is a morphism, it follows easily that φ is well-defined (irrespective of the particular choice of u). We call (φ, f, g) the *induced morphism* from $\mathbf{D}(\mathcal{A})$ to $\mathbf{D}(\mathcal{A}')$, and we put $\mathbf{D}(f, g) := (\varphi, f, g)$.

Now we can state our first main result:

Theorem 3. 3 The correspondence $\mathbf{D} : CAut \to NLDom$ induces an equivalence of categories. It cuts down to an equivalence between the full subcategories of all concurrent automata and nicely labelled concurrency domains, respectively.

From this, the following consequences are straightforward:

Corollary 3. 4 For each nicely labelled weak concurrency domain $\mathcal{D}$ there exists, up to isomorphism, a unique cancellative automaton $\mathcal{A}$ which generates $\mathcal{D}$.

Corollary 3. 5 Let $(D, \leq)$ be a domain. The following are equivalent:

1. $(D, \leq)$ can be generated by a finite cancellative automaton.

2. $(D, \leq)$ is a weak concurrency domain, and there exist event- and state-labelling functions l_E, l_S for $(D, \leq)$ with E and S finite such that $\mathcal{D} = (D, \leq, l_E, l_S)$ is nicely labelled.

Next we introduce particular kinds of morphisms between automata which will be very useful in what follows. If $\mathcal{A}$ is an automaton, we say that an event $e \in E$ is *enabled* at a state $s \in S$, if there is a transition (s, e, r) in T.

Definition 3. 6 Let $\mathcal{A} = (S, E, T, *, \|), \mathcal{A}' = (S', E', T', *', \|')$ be two automata with concurrency relations. A morphism $(f, g) : \mathcal{A} \to \mathcal{A}'$ is called a *reduction* of $\mathcal{A}$ to $\mathcal{A}'$, if the following conditions are satisfied:

1. $f : S \to S'$ is onto;

2. whenever $s \in S$ and $e' \in E'$ is enabled in $f(s)$, then there exists $e \in E$ which is enabled in s with $g(e) = e'$;

3. whenever $s \in S$ and $e'_1, e'_2 \in E'$ with $e'_1 \|'_{f(s)} e'_2$, then there are $e_1, e_2 \in E$ with $e_1 \|_s e_2$ and $g(e_i) = e'_i$ $(i = 1, 2)$;

4. g is *locally injective*, i.e. whenever $e_1, e_2 \in E$ are enabled in $s \in S$ and $e_1 \neq e_2$, then $g(e_1) \neq g(e_2)$.

Condition (2) says that g maps $En_E(s) = \{e \in E : e \text{ is enabled in } s\}$ onto $En_{E'}(f(s))$ for each $s \in S$, in particular T onto T'. We note that if $f : S \to S'$ is onto, then condition (2) implies that $g : E \to E'$ is onto. For, if $e' \in E'$, choose a transition $(s', e', r') \in T'$ and $s \in S$ with $f(s) = s'$, then $e' = g(e)$ for some $e \in E$. Condition (3) says that g maps $\|_s$ onto $\|'_{f(s)}$ $(s \in S)$, which combined with the assumption of local injectivity of g tells us that for any $e_1, e_2 \in E$ enabled in s we have that $e_1 \|_s e_2$ iff $g(e_1) \|'_{f(s)} g(e_2)$. Observe that g may be locally injective without being injective. Now we will show that if there is a reduction from $\mathcal{A}$ to $\mathcal{A}'$, then $\mathcal{A}$ and $\mathcal{A}'$ generate the same domain. More precisely:

Theorem 3. 7 Let $\mathcal{A}, \mathcal{A}'$ be two automata with concurrency relations, and let $(f, g) : \mathcal{A} \to \mathcal{A}'$ be a reduction. Then the induced morphism $(\varphi, f, g) : D(\mathcal{A}) \to D(\mathcal{A}')$ is an order-morphism.

Proof. By Theorem 3.3, it suffices to show that φ is an order-isomorphism. Let $x, y \in D^0(\mathcal{A})$. Also by 3.3, $x \leq y$ implies $\varphi(x) \leq \varphi(y)$. So assume now that $\varphi(x) \leq \varphi(y)$. We claim that $x \leq y$. We may assume that $x = [u]$, $y = [v]$ where $u, v \in CS^0_*(\mathcal{A})$ have the form:

$$u = (s_0 \xrightarrow{e_1} s_1 \xrightarrow{e_2} s_2 \to \dots \xrightarrow{e_n} s_n) \text{ and } v = (r_0 \xrightarrow{e^*_1} r_1 \xrightarrow{e^*_2} r_2 \to \dots \xrightarrow{e^*_m} r_m)$$

with $s_0 = r_0 = *$ and $m, n \in \omega$. Then $\varphi(x) = [u']$, $\varphi(y) = [v']$ with

$$u' = (f(s_0) \xrightarrow{g(e_1)} f(s_1) \xrightarrow{g(e_2)} f(s_2) \to \dots \xrightarrow{g(e_n)} f(s_n)),$$

$$\text{and } v' = (f(r_0) \xrightarrow{g(e^*_1)} f(r_1) \xrightarrow{g(e^*_2)} f(r_2) \to \dots \xrightarrow{g(e^*_m)} f(r_m)).$$

We proceed in two steps. First assume $\varphi(x) = \varphi(y)$; we show that $x = y$. For this, we may suppose that the computation sequences u', v' are strongly equivalent (and different) in $CS(\mathcal{A}')$. In particular, $n = m$. Then for some $j \leq n - 2$ we have:

1. $f(s_i) = f(r_i)$ and $g(e_i) = g(e_i^*)$ for each $i \leq j$ and each $i > j+2$,

2. $f(s_j) \xrightarrow{g(e_{j+1})} f(s_{j+1}) \xrightarrow{g(e_{j+2})} f(s_{j+2}) \approx f(r_j) \xrightarrow{g(e_{j+1}^*)} f(r_{j+1}) \xrightarrow{g(e_{j+2}^*)} f(r_{j+2})$, and thus:

3. $g(e_{j+1}) = g(e_{j+2}^*) \neq g(e_{j+2}) = g(e_{j+1}^*)$ and $g(e_{j+1}) \|'_{f(s_j)} g(e_{j+1}^*)$.

Since (f, g) is a reduction, we obtain first $e_i = e_i^*$ and $s_i = r_i$ for each $1 \leq i \leq j$. Then we have: e_{j+1} and e_{j+1}^* are enabled in $s_j = r_j$, hence $e_{j+1} \|_{s_j} e_{j+1}^*$ because of (3), as noted before. This implies that e_{j+1}^* is enabled in s_{j+1}, and thus $e_{j+1}^* = e_{j+2}$ by local injectivity of g. Similarly $e_{j+1} = e_{j+2}^*$. So $e_{j+1} \|_{s_j} e_{j+2}$. Thus $s_{j+2} = r_{j+2}$, and again $e_i = e_i^*$, $s_i = r_i$ also for each $j+2 \leq i \leq m$. This proves that u is strongly equivalent to v, giving $x = [u] = [v] = y$ as we needed to show.

Now we deal with the general case that $\varphi(x) \leq \varphi(y)$. There exists $w' \in CS^*(\mathcal{A}')$ with $u'w' \sim v'$. Let w' have the form $w' = (s_n' \xrightarrow{e_{n+1}'} s_{n+1}' \to \ldots \xrightarrow{e_{n+k}'} s_{n+k}')$ with $s_n' = f(s_n)$; then $s_{n+k}' = f(r_m)$. Since (f, g) is a reduction, inductively we obtain a computation sequence $w = (s_n \xrightarrow{e_{n+1}} s_{n+1} \to \ldots \xrightarrow{e_{n+k}} s_{n+k})$ with $g(e_{n+i}) = e_{n+i}'$ and $f(s_{n+i}) = s_{n+i}'$ for each $1 \leq i \leq k$. Clearly $x = [u] \leq [uw]$ and $\varphi([uw]) = [u'w'] = [v'] = \varphi([v])$. Then $[uw] = [v] = y$ as shown above, hence $x \leq y$.

Similarly to the above, where we constructed the computation sequence w for w', we obtain that φ maps $D^0(\mathcal{A})$ onto $D^0(\mathcal{A}')$. Hence φ is an order-isomorphism from $(D^0(\mathcal{A}), \leq)$ onto $(D^0(\mathcal{A}'), \leq)$ thus also from $(D(\mathcal{A}), \leq)$ onto $(D(\mathcal{A}'), \leq)$.

Finally, using Theorems 3.3 and 3.7 it is possible to derive the following result (see [BDr]):

Theorem 3. 8 Let $(D, \leq)$ be a weak concurrency domain.

(a) There exists a cancellative automaton $\mathcal{A}_{max}$ generating $(D, \leq)$ such that for every other cancellative automaton $\mathcal{A}$ that generates $(D, \leq)$ we have:

  1. There exists a reduction from $\mathcal{A}_{max}$ to $\mathcal{A}$.

  2. Any reduction from $\mathcal{A}$ to $\mathcal{A}_{max}$ is an isomorphism.

(b) For any cancellative automaton $\mathcal{A}$ generating $(D, \leq)$ we can find a cancellative automaton $\mathcal{A}_{min}$ also generating $(D, \leq)$ such that:

  1. There exists a reduction from $\mathcal{A}$ to $\mathcal{A}_{min}$.

  2. Any reduction from $\mathcal{A}_{min}$ to an automaton with concurrency relations is an isomorphism.

As noted in the introduction here $\mathcal{A}_{min}$ in general is not unique up to isomorphism.

REFERENCES

AR I.J. Aalbersberg, G. Rozenberg: Theory of traces, Theoret. Comp. Science **60** (1988), 1-82.

BD P. Bachmann, Phan Minh Dung: Nondeterministic computations – structure and axioms, *Elektron. Inf.verarb. Kybern. EIK* **22** (1986), 243-261.

Be M. Bednarczyk: Categories of asynchronous systems, Ph.D. Thesis, University of Sussex, 1987.

BL G. Berry, J.-J. Levy: Minimal and optimal computations of recursive programs, *J. ACM* **26** (1979), 148-175.

BC G. Boudol, I. Castellani: A non-interleaving semantics for CCS based on proved transitions, *Fundam. Inform.* **11** (1988), 433-452.

BDr F. Bracho, M.Droste: Domains and automata with concurrency, internal report, Universidad Nacional Autónoma de México and Universität Essen, Nov. 1992.

Cu P. L. Curien: Categorical Combinators, Sequential Algorithms and Functional Programming, Research Notes in Computer Science, Pitman, London, 1986.

D1 M. Droste: Concurrency, automata and domains, in: 17th ICALP, *Lecture Notes in Computer Science* **443**, Springer, 1990, 195-208.

D2 M. Droste: Concurrent automata and domains, *Intern.J. of Foundations of Comp. Science*, in press.

DS M. Droste, R.M. Shortt: Petri nets and automata with concurrency relations – an adjunction, in: 'Semantics of Programming Languages and Model Theory' (M. Droste, Y. Gurevich eds.), Gordon and Breach Science Publ., Reading 1993, in press.

Ho C.A.R. Hoare: Communicating sequential processes, *Comm. ACM* **21** (1978), 666-676.

HL G. Huet, J.-J. Levy: Call-by-need computations in non-ambiguous linear term rewriting systems, IRIA-LABORIA Report 359 (1979).

KP S. Katz, D. Peled: Defining conditional independence using collapses, in: 'Semantics for Concurrency' (M.Z Kwiatkowska, M.W. Shields, R.M. Thomas, eds.), Proc. of the Int. BCS-FACS Workshop at Leicester, 1990, Springer, 262-280.

Le J.-J. Levy: Optimal reductions in the lambda calculus, in: 'To H. B. Curry: Essays on Combinatory Logic, Lambda Calculus and Formalism' (J.P. Seldin, J.R. Hindley, eds.), Academic Press, New York, 1980, 159-191.

Ma A. Mazurkiewicz: Concurrent program schemes and their interpretations, DAIMI Report PB-78, Aarhus University, Aarhus, 1977.

Mi R. Milner: A Calculus of Communicating Systems, *Lecture Notes in Computer Science* **92**, Springer, 1980.

PS P. Panangaden, E.W. Stark: Computations, residuals and the power of indeterminacy, in: 15th ICALP, *Lecture Notes in Computer Science* **317**, Springer 1988, 439-454.

Sh M.W. Shields: Concurrent machines, *Comp. J.* **28** (1985), 449-465.

St1 E.W. Stark: Concurrent transition systems, *Theoret. Comp. Science* **64** (1989), 221-269.

St2 E.W. Stark: Compositional relational semantics for indeterminate dataflow networks, in: Proc., Category Theory and Computer Science, *Lecture Notes in Computer Science*, **389**, Springer, 1989, 52-74.

St3 E.W. Stark: Dataflow networks are fibrations, in: 'Category Theory and Computer Science', Proc. Paris, *Lecture Notes in Computer Science*, **530**, Springer, 1991, 261-281.

St4 E.W. Stark: Connections between a concrete and an abstract model of concurrent systems, in: 5th Conference on the Mathematical Foundations of Programming Semanties, *Lecture Notes in Computer Science*, **442** Springer, 1989, pp. 53-79.

Wi G. Winskel: Event structures, in: Petri Nets: Applications and Relationships to Other Models of Concurrency, *Lecture Notes in Computer Science* **255**, Springer, 1987, pp. 325-392.

WN G. Winskel, M. Nielsen: 'Models for Concurrency', draft copy of Oct. 1991, in: Handbook of Logic in Computer Science (S. Abramsky, D.M. Gabbay, T.S.E. Maibaum, eds.), to appear.

What is a Universal Higher-Order Programming Language?

Ramarao Kanneganti and Robert Cartwright *

Department of Computer Science
Rice University
Houston, TX 77251-1892

Abstract. Classic recursion theory asserts that all conventional programming languages are equally expressive because they can define all partial recursive functions over the natural numbers. This statement is misleading because programming languages support and enforce a more abstract view of data than bitstrings. In particular, most real programming languages support some form of *higher-order* data such as potentially infinite streams (input and output), lazy trees, and functions. In this paper, we develop a theory of higher-order computability suitable for comparing the expressiveness of sequential, deterministic programming languages. The theory is based on the construction of a new universal domain T and corresponding universal language KL. The domain T is universal for "sequential" domains; KL can define all the computable elements of T, including the elements corresponding to computable sequential functions. In addition, T preserves maximality of finite elements in embeddings, so the termination behavior of programs is preserved by embeddings in T.

1 Background and Motivation

Classic recursion theory [18, 7, 13] asserts that all conventional programming languages are equally expressive because they can define all partial recursive functions over the natural numbers. This statement, however, is misleading because real programming languages support and enforce a more abstract view of data than bitstrings. In particular, most real programming languages support some form of *higher-order* data such as potentially infinite streams (input and output), lazy trees, and functions. In contrast to conventional data objects like numbers, characters, arrays, and lists, *higher-order* data objects do not have finite canonical representations. As a result, computations involving higher-order objects cannot be modeled as ordinary computations over the natural numbers. The integrity of higher-order data abstractions critically depends on the fact that programs obey constraints on how higher-order representations are manipulated. Since classic recursion theory ignores these constraints, it does not address the expressiveness of languages that manipulate higher-order data.

---
* This research was partially supported by the National Science Foundation under the grant CCR-9122518.

To assess the expressiveness of real languages, we need to develop a theory of computability that includes higher-order data. To be comprehensive, this theory must accommodate all of the data objects that occur in conventional languages, including ordinary finite data objects and higher-order data objects such as lazy trees and functions. In this paper, we develop a theory of higher-order computability suitable for sequential, deterministic programming languages. The theory is based on the construction of a new universal domain T suitable for embedding all "sequential" domains. Roughly speaking, a Scott-domain (see Section 4) is sequential if its elements can be represented as lazy trees. The sequential domains correspond to "filiform concrete data structures" studied by Berry and Curien [2], which are a restriction of "concrete domains" originally introduced by Kahn and Plotkin [12].

We show that the new universal domain T has two important properties:

1. Every "sequential" domain D can be embedded by a retraction as a subdomain D' of T such that the maximality of finite elements is preserved.
2. There is a simple metalanguage called KL that is *universal* for T: every computable element of T and every computable "sequential" operation on T can be expressed in KL. Since T is universal for "sequential" domains, KL is a universal "sequential" higher-order programming language.

The preservation of finite maximal elements by the embedding retraction is critically important from the perspective of computability theory. Finite maximal elements are the denotations of terminating computations. If the embedding of a domain D into T fails to preserve the finite maximality of elements, then the termination behavior of computations over D cannot be simulated by programs written in KL.

2 Previous Work

The issue of higher-order computation has previously been studied in two contexts: (*i*) the extension of classic recursion theory to computable functionals [14, 10] and (*ii*) *domain theory* [17, 15], the mathematical framework underlying denotational semantics. In the classic theory of computable functionals, functions are represented intensionally as bitstrings. Since programs can inspect the representations of higher order data objects, this model of higher order computation does not capture the linguistic restrictions imposed by real programming languages.

Scott and Plotkin developed domain theory to address this issue. In domain theory, denotational definitions for programming languages are written in a metalanguage *LAMBDA* corresponding to a universal domain U (either $P\omega$ [17] or T^ω [15]). In essence, a denotational definition of a programming language is a functional program written in *LAMBDA* that maps source program phrases into their meanings, which are data objects in the universal domain. The language *LAMBDA* appears to be a promising candidate for a universal, higher-order programming language for higher-order computation. Unfortunately, the model of computation underlying *LAMBDA* is too abstract to simulate the behavior of real programs faithfully. In particular, *LAMBDA* eliminates the distinction between terminating and non-terminating computations: the evaluation of an expression M in *LAMBDA* simply enumerates all finite approximations to the data object d denoted by M. This enumeration process cannot terminate because no approximation in U is maximal.

Cartwright and Demers [4] recently developed a new formulation of domain theory that addresses the issue of program termination. They constructed a new universal domain ∇ and metalanguage *Cons* that distinguish terminating and non-terminating computations; ∇ includes finite approximations that are maximal. Any Scott-domain (see Section 5.2) that is *effectively* presented can be effectively embedded inside ∇ such that the finiteness and maximality of elements are preserved. The evaluation of an expression M in *Cons* terminates iff M denotes a finite maximal element of ∇.

However, their theory has two liabilities. First, the syntax of the universal language *Cons* is not recursive; a programmer must prove that a program written in *Cons* is well-formed. Second, the continuous function space construction does not preserve maximality information. Given effective presentations of the domains A and B, it is not possible in general to construct an effective presentation for the domain $A \rightarrow_c B$ (the continuous functions from A to B).

3 Our Intuition: Continuous Functions Are Too General

We can trace the liabilities of ∇ directly to the properties of the continuous function space construction. The domain constructor $\rightarrow_c$ is contravariant in its first argument. If a domain A has infinite *ascending* chains of elements, then the domain $A \rightarrow_c B$ (where B is non-trivial) has infinite *descending* chains of elements. As a result, a universal domain U that accommodates the continuous functions as a subspace and preserves the finiteness of embedded elements must contain infinite descending chains. The presence of these chains makes it difficult to devise a metalanguage.

We can avoid the pathologies caused by infinite descending chains by using a more restrictive formulation of functions than the *continuous* functions. There is a subspace of the continuous functions called the observably sequential functions that encompasses all of the functions definable in practical *deterministic* programming languages [6]. The observably sequential functions exclude continuous functions that cannot be evaluated without multiple threads of control. In practice, *non-sequential* functions are unimportant in deterministic computation. We are not aware of any practical deterministic language that can define non-sequential functions like por, the "parallel-or" function.[2] Even pedagogic functional languages like Miranda and Haskell do not support this class of functions because it would encourage insidiously inefficient programming.

The rest of the paper is organized as follows. In Section 4, we introduce the class of domains, called *OS*-domains, suitable for sequential computation. In

---

[2] por(x, true) = true; por(true, y)= true; and por(false, false) = false.

Section 5, we present a domain T that is universal for OS-domains. We show how to embed any OS-domain in T while preserving the maximality of finite elements. We also present a language KL for defining operations on the domain T. In Section 6, we prove that KL is universal by showing that every computable element of the domain T is expressible in KL.

4 OS-Domains

In this section, we define the class of OS-domains; the acronym OS stands for "observably sequential". These domains have the structure required to support observably sequential computation.

A *Scott-domain* $(D, \sqsubseteq)$ is the ideal completion of a *Scott-basis* $(E, \leq)$, which is a partial order closed under least upper bounds for finite bounded subsets. The *finite elements* of the domain are the principal ideals generated by the elements of the Scott-basis E. As is customary in the literature, we will identify all Scott-domains that are order-isomorphic—eliminating the distinction between a Scott-basis and the corresponding finite elements.

OS-domains are Scott-domains with special structure: they can be generated from a subset of finite elements called the *prime basis*. The topological constraints governing OS-domains are formulated as constraints on the prime basis. These notions are formally defined as follows.

Definition 4.1. (*Partial Order*) A *partial order* S is a pair $\langle S, \sqsubseteq \rangle$ consisting of a set S of objects, called the *universe*, and a binary relation $\sqsubseteq$ over S such that $\sqsubseteq$ is *reflexive*, *antisymmetric*, and *transitive*. If $a \sqsubseteq b$, we say that a *approximates* b. An element a *precedes* b, written as $a \prec b$, if $a \sqsubseteq b$ and there are no elements between a and b in the partial order. A subset $R \subseteq S$ is *downward closed* iff all the elements in S approximating a member of R belong to R. ∎

Given the preceding definition, we can concisely define the notion of a prime-basis as follows.

Definition 4.2. (*Prime Basis*) A triple $(P, \leq, C)$ is a *prime basis* iff

[PO] $(P, \leq)$ is a countable partial order.
[UP] Each element of the partial order $(P, \leq)$ has at most one predecessor.
[F] each element of P is approximated by only a finite number of elements in P.
[C] $C = \{Q_1, Q_2, \ldots\}$ is a partitioning of P into non-empty *conflict* sets (or C-sets) $Q_1, Q_2, \ldots$ such that $p, q \in Q_i$ implies that p and q have the same set of predecessors.

A prime basis $(P, \leq, C)$ is *error-rich* iff each C-set $Q \in C$ has two designated elements error_1^Q, error_2^Q that are maximal in $(P, \leq)$. In addition, every C-set must contain at least one non-error element. ∎

An OS-domain is the "prime-closure" of an error-rich prime basis.

Definition 4.3. (*Prime-Domain, OS-domain*) A *prime-domain* is a partial order $(D, \sqsubseteq)$ generated from a prime basis $(P, \leq, C)$ where

1. the elements of D are *downward-closed* subsets of P that do not contain conflicting primes (distinct primes from the same C-set).
2. the relation $\sqsubseteq$ is the subset ordering $\subseteq$ on D.

The domain generated by the prime basis $(P, \leq, C)$ is denoted $\mathbf{D}(P, \leq, C)$. If the prime basis $(P, \leq, C)$ is error-rich, then the prime-domain $\mathbf{D}(P, \leq, C)$ is an *OS*-domain. ∎

Most domains encountered in the literature are prime-domains. The most notable exceptions are the domains generated by continuous function construction. Consider the following simple examples.

1. The flat domain $\mathbf{B}_\perp$ of truth values $\{\mathsf{tt}, \mathsf{ff}\}$ is a prime-domain.
2. The flat domain $\mathbf{N}_\perp$ of natural numbers is a prime-domain; every number is a prime element.
3. The continuous function space $\mathbf{B}_\perp \to_c \mathbf{B}_\perp$ is not a prime-domain; the prime functions (the "one-step" functions) cannot be partitioned into C-sets.

5 A Universal Sequential Domain

To perform arbitrary sequential computations, we need to construct a universal domain U in which any sequential domain can be embedded. We can reduce sequential computation over an arbitrary domain D to sequential computation over U by embedding D in U.

Our universal domain T is a domain of lazy binary trees over the natural numbers and error elements. We define the prime basis for the domain T as follows.

1. The set of primes P is given by the inductive definition:

$$P = \mathsf{error}_1 \mid \mathsf{error}_2 \mid n \in \mathsf{N} \mid \langle \perp, \perp \rangle \mid \langle \perp, \perp \rangle \mid \langle \perp, p \rangle \mid \langle p, \perp \rangle \qquad p \in P$$

2. The ordering relation $\leq$ on P is defined by the rules:

$$x \leq x \qquad \text{for} \quad x \in \mathsf{N} \cup \{\mathsf{error}_1, \mathsf{error}_2\}$$
$$\langle a, b \rangle \leq \langle c, d \rangle \quad \text{iff} \quad [(a = \perp) \text{ or } (a \leq c)] \text{ and } [(b = \perp) \vee (b \leq d)]$$

3. The *conflict* sets (C-sets) are defined by the equivalence closure of the relation C' over P:

$$(0, \mathsf{error}_i), \ (0, \langle \perp, \perp \rangle) \in C''$$
$$(0, n) \in C' \qquad \text{for} \quad n \in \mathsf{N}$$
$$(\langle a, \perp \rangle, \langle b, \perp \rangle), \ (\langle \perp, a \rangle, \langle \perp, b \rangle) \in C' \qquad \text{for} \quad (a, b) \in C'$$

The prime basis P generates the domain T of lazy binary trees over natural numbers and errors. Every tree corresponds to a distinct set of prime approximations. Each prime approximating the tree t identifies the value of a node in t. If two trees are inconsistent, there is a node where the trees have different values other than $\perp$.

Each C-set in the domain T identifies a *position* in the tree; the elements of the C-set specify different values for the node identified by the C-set. Hence two trees are inconsistent iff they are approximated by two different prime elements from the same C-set. We refer to C-sets by capital letters such as Q, R and S. A position Q in a tree is *open* iff the tree has $\perp$ at that position. We say that a tree A is *strictly below* a tree B at position Q iff the tree A has a $\perp$ and B has a node value other than $\perp$ at position Q. Similarly, we say that a tree a *precedes* Q, written $a \prec Q$, iff a is is open at the position Q and in all the positions less than Q, a is defined, *i.e.*, it has non-$\perp$ values at those positions.

The universal sequential domain has the property that any sequential domain D can be embedded in T. Moreover, there is a sequential function ρ_D over T such that $\rho_D(\mathsf{T}) = D'$ where D' is isomorphic to D. To formulate the class of embeddings we must define the OS-functions.

5.1 OS-Function Space Construction

The observably sequential functions from T into T are a subset of continuous functions, $\mathsf{T} \rightarrow_c \mathsf{T}$. These functions propagate any error element that they encounter during the evaluation of the input. More precisely, if a function encounters an error element error_i in its input while it is computing the node value for a position Q, it must output the value error_i at position Q of the output element. We formally define this class of functions in the following definitions.

Definition 5.1. (*Sequentiality Index*) For a continuous function $f : \mathsf{T} \rightarrow \mathsf{T}$, an open position R in a is the *sequentiality index* for the input a and an open position Q in $f(a)$, iff for any $x \supset a$ such that $f(x)$ is strictly above $f(a)$ at position Q, x is strictly above a at R. ∎

If R is the sequentiality index at an input a and an output position Q, then the function f explores the input at position R to generate an output at the position Q. If the function f propagates errors, then it must generate the value error_i at position Q if it encounters the value error_i at R. A function f with such a behavior has a *sequential* strategy to evaluate its arguments. Moreover, the behavior of f over error elements determines that evaluation strategy. Since this information is a part of the graph of f, f is called *observably* sequential function, or OS-function for short.

Definition 5.2. (*Observably Sequential Function*) A continuous function $f : \mathsf{T} \rightarrow \mathsf{T}$ is *observably sequential* if it is

sequential: for every pair (a, Q) where Q is an open position in $f(a)$ has a sequentiality index if for some $x \supset a$, the position Q in $f(x)$ is defined; and it is

error-sensitive: if R is the sequentiality index of f for the input a and the output position Q, $\text{error}_1^Q \in (f(a \cup \text{error}_1^R))$ and $\text{error}_2^Q \in f(a \cup \text{error}_2^R)$. ∎

Every OS-function has a unique evaluation strategy manifest in its graph.[3] If an OS-function f has two sequentiality indices R, R' for input a and open position Q in $f(a)$, it is easy to show that f is not continuous.[4] Since the sequentiality indices for an OS-function f are unique, it makes sense to introduce a function seq_f, where $seq_f(a, Q)$ is the sequentiality index of f for input a and output position Q.

The function space $\mathbf{T} \to_{os} \mathbf{T}$ is an OS-domain. Its prime basis $(P_\to, \leq_\to, C_\to)$ can be described as follows:

$P_\to$: The members of P can be divided into two disjoint subsets:

1. **Output Primes:** An OS-function f in $\mathbf{T} \to_{os} \mathbf{T}$ is an output prime iff there exists a finite element a and a prime element p in $\mathbf{T}$ such that f is a minimal function satisfying the constraint $f(a) = p$ and for all $a' \subset a$, $f(a') \subset f(a)$. The function f has a C-set *label* $\langle a, Q, F' \rangle$ where Q is the position of p and $F' = \{g \in \mathbf{T} \to_{os} \mathbf{T} \mid g \subset f\}$.

2. **Schedule Primes:** an OS-function f in $\mathbf{T} \to_{os} \mathbf{T}$ is a *schedule prime* iff there exists a finite element a and C-sets R, Q in $\mathbf{T}$ where $a \prec R$ such that f is a minimal function with the property $f(a \sqcup \text{error}_i^R) = \text{error}_i^Q$ and $f(a) \subset \text{error}_1^Q$. The function f has the C-set *label* $\langle a, Q, F' \rangle$ where $F' = \{g \in \mathbf{T} \to_{os} \mathbf{T} \mid g \subset f\}$.

$\leq_\to$ The prime functions are ordered under usual pointwise ordering, *i.e.*, $f \leq g$ iff $\forall x \in \mathbf{T} : f(x) \leq g(x)$.

$C_\to$ The partitioning of $P_\to$ determined by the equivalence relation $\sim$ on $P_\to$ where

$$p \sim q \Leftrightarrow \text{the C-set } label \text{ of } p = \text{the C-set } label \text{ of } p.$$

It is easy to verify that $(P_\to, \leq_\to, C_\to)$ forms a prime basis. The two designated error elements of a C-set with label $\langle a, Q, F' \rangle$ are $F' \cup \{(a, \text{error}_1^Q)\}$ and $F' \cup \{(a, \text{error}_2^Q)\}$. We also need to verify that $\mathbf{D}(P_\to, \leq_\to, C_\to)$ is isomorphic to the domain $\mathbf{T} \to_{os} \mathbf{T}$. The proof breaks down into two parts. First, we can prove that any function in the domain $\mathbf{D}(P_\to, \leq_\to, C_\to)$ is an OS-function. Second, we can prove that any finite function in $\mathbf{T} \to_{os} \mathbf{T}$ is the least upper bound of its prime approximations in $P_\to$. Together, these two facts imply that $(P_\to, \leq_\to, C_\to)$ generates the OS-function domain $\mathbf{T} \to_{os} \mathbf{T}$.

---

[3] Sequential algorithms [1] do not have this property; hence they are not order-extensional. OS-functions can be thought of as order-extensional interpretations of sequential algorithms.

[4] Otherwise, on the input extending a with error_1 at R and error_2 at R' the function has to generate the least upper bound of two inconsistent elements, error_1 and error_2, at position Q.

5.2 Embeddings that Preserve Maximality

The universal domain T is universal for the class of OS-domains. That is, any OS-domain can be embedded in T by an OS-function such that the maximality of the finite elements is preserved. In addition, any prime-domain can be embedded in T by enriching it with sufficient number of error elements. Since $T \rightarrow_{os} T$ is an OS-domain, it can be embedded in T by an OS-function. This embedding allows functions to be represented as trees.

To capture the behavior of computations in a domain D after it has been embedded in T, the embedding must preserve the maximality of finite elements in D; otherwise the termination behavior of computations will be different in D and its image in T. A computation over a domain terminates if the result of the computation is a finite maximal element. The corresponding computation over T does not terminate if the finite maximal elements in D are mapped to non-maximal elements in T.

Any OS-domain D can be effectively embedded in T, preserving the maximality of finite elements. To do so, the domain D must be presented *effectively*. The presentations of domains used in classical domain theory [17, 15] do not include maximality information; hence they are not suitable for maximality preserving embeddings. Therefore, we need to introduce a new definition of effective presentation.

In our formulation of domain theory, an effective presentation $\mathcal{P}$ of the domain $\mathbf{D}(P, \leq, C)$ is a tuple $\langle \mathbf{E}, \mathbf{c}, \mathbf{pr}, \mathbf{arity}, \mathbf{size} \rangle$ such that:

1. $\mathbf{E} : P \rightarrow \mathbf{N}$ is an injective function that enumerates the prime elements of the domain excluding errors in topologically sorted order. That is, if an element a approximates b, a is enumerated before b. The error elements are not enumerated because their presence is implied by the fact that $\mathbf{D}(P, \leq, C)$ is an OS-domain.
2. $\mathbf{c} : range(\mathbf{E}) \rightarrow \mathbf{N}$ is a function that maps the index of the prime element to its C-set code. That is, $\forall i, j > 0 : \mathbf{c}(i) = \mathbf{c}(j)$ iff $p_i, p_j \in Q$ for $Q \in C$. The range of the function $\mathbf{c}$ is the set of C-set numbers.
3. $\mathbf{pr}$ is a recursive function over $\mathbf{N}$ defined by $\mathbf{pr}(i) = j$ iff $p_i \prec p_j$.
4. $\mathbf{arity}$ is a recursive function that maps the index of a prime element to the number in $\mathbf{N} \cup \{\omega\}$ of C-sets above that element;[5] and
5. $\mathbf{size}$ is a recursive function that maps the index of a C-set to its cardinality in $\mathbf{N} \cup \{\omega\}$.

All flat domains such as numbers, booleans, and non-lazy lists obviously have effective presentations. Moreover the domain constructions like cartesian products, disjoint unions, lifting, OS-function construction preserve the effective presentation. As a result, all the domains we encounter in deterministic sequential computation can effectively be embedded in T while preserving the maximality of finite elements.

In particular, the OS-function construction preserves maximality information. If two domains D and E have effective presentations, the corresponding

---

[5] A prime element may have ω C-sets above it.

OS-function space $D \to_{os} E$ has an effective presentation. The functions **arity** and **size** for the function space can be computed from the functions **arity** and **size** of the domains D and E. The details of the effective presentation of OS-functions is given in appendix I.

A domain D is embedded in T by a function f_d mapping its prime elements into T. For each prime p, $f_d(p)$ is computed by inserting a subtree into the tree corresponding to predecessor of p. Since all the prime elements are enumerated in topologically sorted order, the embedding can be defined inductively. The details of the embedding are given in appendix II. An arbitrary element of the domain D can be embedded by embedding all its prime approximations.

5.3 A Universal Language for Sequential Computation

To embed an arbitrary domain D, we must define an idempotent function f_D over T such that its range $f_D(\mathsf{T})$ isomorphic to D. Thus, sequential computation over D can be performed in the universal domain. Therefore, to perform sequential computation over arbitrary sequential domains, we must design a language that can express all computable OS-functions over T. In this section, we describe such a *universal* language KL (Kleene's Language) for the domain T.

The language KL includes a binary operator $Apply : \mathsf{T} \times \mathsf{T} \to_{os} \mathsf{T}$ and a set of constants: $\{0, \text{error}_i, 1^+, 1^-, \text{pair?}, \text{left}, \text{right}, \text{cons}, \text{if0}\}$. These primitives construct trees, select subtrees, and perform arithmetic operations on natural numbers. All the constants except 0 and error_i are the elements of $\mathsf{T} \to_{os} \mathsf{T}$ (embedded in T); they are interpreted as functions by $Apply$. In figure 1, we present the constants in $\mathsf{T} \to_{os} \mathsf{T}$ as uncurried functions instead of the explicit tree representations for clarity.

Nullary Operations:
$$0 = \ulcorner 0 \urcorner \qquad \text{error}_i = \text{error}_i$$

Unary Operations:
$$1^+ = \{n \to n+1\} \cup \{\text{error}_i \to \text{error}_i\}$$
$$1^- = \{0 \to 0\} \cup \{n+1 \to n\} \cup \{\text{error}_i \to \text{error}_i\}$$
$$\text{pair?} = \{\langle \bot, \bot \rangle \to 0\} \cup \{n \to 1\} \cup \{\text{error}_i \to \text{error}_i\}$$
$$\text{left} = \{\langle x, \bot \rangle \to x\} \cup \{\text{error}_i \to \text{error}_i\}$$
$$\text{right} = \{\langle \bot, y \rangle \to y\} \cup \{\text{error}_i \to \text{error}_i\}$$

Binary Operations:
$$\text{cons} = \{x \times y \to \langle x, y \rangle\}$$

Ternary Operations:
$$\text{if0} = \{0 \times x \times \bot \to x\} \cup \{1 \times \bot \times y \to y\}$$
$$\cup \{\text{error}_i \times \bot \times \bot \to \text{error}_i\}$$

Fig. 1. Primitive Operators of KL

In the tradition of Kleene [13], programs in KL are sets of recursive definitions over the primitive operations using *Apply*. Thus, a function is defined by composition and application of other functions and recursion. The denotation of a function defined by a recursive definition is the least fixed point of corresponding functional[3].

All the primitive operations and *Apply* over T are observably sequential. Since composition, application, and least fixed points preserve observable sequentiality, KL can express only the *OS*-functions.

$$1^+(n) \longrightarrow n+1 \qquad\qquad 1^+(\text{error}_i) \longrightarrow \text{error}_i$$
$$1^-(0) \longrightarrow 0 \qquad\qquad 1^-(n+1) \longrightarrow n$$
$$1^-(\text{error}_i) \longrightarrow \text{error}_i \qquad\qquad \text{pair?}(\langle a,b \rangle) \longrightarrow 0$$
$$\text{pair?}(n) \longrightarrow 1 \qquad\qquad \text{pair?}(\text{error}_i) \longrightarrow \text{error}_i$$
$$\text{left}(\langle a,b \rangle) \longrightarrow a \qquad\qquad \text{left}(\text{error}_i) \longrightarrow \text{error}_i$$
$$\text{right}(\langle a,b \rangle) \longrightarrow b \qquad\qquad \text{right}(\text{error}_i) \longrightarrow \text{error}_i$$
$$\text{cons}(a)(b) \longrightarrow \langle a,b \rangle \qquad\qquad \text{if0}(0)(a)(b) \longrightarrow a$$
$$\text{if0}(n+1)(a)(b) \longrightarrow b \qquad\qquad \text{if0}(\text{error}_i)(a)(b) \longrightarrow \text{error}_i$$

Fig. 2. Rewrite Rules for KL

Figure 2 defines the operational semantics of KL, where $f(x)$ abbreviates $Apply(f,x)$. The operational semantics defined by these rewrite rules exactly match the mathematical semantics. In other words, the evaluation of an expression M yields the potentially infinite canonical form for the tree d denoted by M. The evaluation of M terminates iff d is finite and maximal.

Compatibility with λ-Notation: It is easy to define an alternate syntax for KL based on λ-notation. In that notation, λ-abstractions are abbreviations for terms constructed by the combinators S and K, and the primitive operations $\{1^+, 1^-, \text{left}, \text{right}, \text{cons}, \text{pair?}, \text{if0}\}$. The combinators S and K are definable by recursive equations in KL, but the definitions are a bit tedious. A similar definition of S and K using recursion equations appears in [5]. Since the set of *OS*-domains and *OS*-functions form a cartesian closed category [8], we know that S and K must be *OS*-functions, because they are definable in the categorical combinators [9]. However, in our proofs we find it more natural to write programs as recursion equations.

6   Computability and Universality

KL can be used to perform arbitrary sequential computations over an *OS*-domain if it can express all computable *OS*-functions. The proof for the expressiveness of KL has two parts: First we must show that any partial recursive function over the natural numbers can be defined in KL. Second, we must show that any element or OS-function that is computable on the domain T can be defined in KL.

We show that the language KL is partially recursive by encoding an arbitrary partial recursive function in the language. It is well known [16] that any partial recursive function can be expressed by the operations: $0, 1^+, 1^-$, selection, composition, primitive recursion, and minimization. All these operations can be expressed in KL over the natural numbers.

A programming language $\mathcal{L}$ is universal for a domain D iff the language can express all the computable elements and the functions of the domain. If we encode the prime elements of D as natural numbers, an element in D is computable if the prime approximations are recursively enumerable. An OS-function is computable if its graph, $i.e.$, the set $\{(\mathbf{b}, f(\mathbf{b}))\}$ where $\mathbf{b}$ are finite elements, is recursively enumerable. Since the OS-functions can be embedded in T and interpreted by $Apply$, it is sufficient to show that KL can define all the computable elements of T to prove the universality of KL.

We can encode the prime elements of the Universal Domain T as natural numbers as follows. Each prime element can be uniquely represented by the number $\langle p, e \rangle$ where $\langle .,. \rangle$ is a recursive bijective function and p and e are the numerical representations of $path$ and $node$ respectively.

If the prime approximations to a computable element d are r.e., then there is a partial recursive function f_d such that $f_d(m) = n$ iff $\langle m, n \rangle$ is the index of a prime approximation to d. Since every partial recursive function can be written in KL f_d also can be defined as $\mathbf{f}$ in KL. From $\mathbf{f}$, it is easy to construct d recursively.

Full abstraction of KL: Since every finite element of the domain is computable, every finite element can be defined in KL. From that fact we can prove that the domain T is a full abstract model for KL as follows. If KL is not fully abstract, then there are two terms M and N that are operationally equivalent but denotationally different. Since their denotations are different, there must be a prime element (a tree node) in one of the denotations, but not the other. Therefore, we can write a simple program P using left and right operations that extracts the differentiating node. Hence P distinguishes M and N contradicting the assumption that they are operationally equivalent. Thus, we conclude that in KL denotational equivalence implies operational equivalence.

7 Conclusions and Directions for Further Research

Our investigation of OS-domains provides strong support for the claim that KL is a universal programming language for sequential computation. Any OS-domain D can be embedded in the domain T by a sequential retraction that preserves the maximality of finite elements. Moreover, any computable function f over D is definable in KL over the embedded image of D. Since the maximality of finite elements is preserved by the embedding, the image of f in KL behaves exactly like f—including termination behavior.

We are currently investigating whether practical languages such as the functional subset of Scheme constitute universal sequential programming languages. We are also studying the problem of designing a comprehensive data definition language for sequential computation based on T. Research on data specification [11] has focused on defining first-order data domains, yet higher-order data plays an important role in models of programming languages. We are designing a new dialect of Scheme that includes a comprehensive data definition facility capable of specifying arbitrary higher-order (observably sequential) data as well as conventional first-order data.

References

1. G. Berry and P-L. Curien. Sequential algorithms on concrete data structures. *Theor. Comput. Sci.*, 20:265–321, 1982.

2. G. Berry and P.-L. Curien. Theory and practice of sequential algorithms: the kernel of the applicative language cds. In J. Reynolds and M. Nivat, editors, *Algebraic Methods in Semantics*, pages 35–88. Cambridge University Press, London, 1985.

3. R. Cartwright. Recursive programs as definitions in first order logic. *SIAM Journal of Computing*, 13:374–408, 1984.

4. R. Cartwright and A. Demers. The topology of program termination. In *Proc. Symposium on Logic in Computer Science*, pages 296–308, 1988.

5. R. Cartwright and J. Donahue. The semantics of lazy (and industrious) evaluation. In *Proc. 1982 ACM Symposium on Lisp and Functional Programming*, pages 253–264, 1982.

6. Robert Cartwright and Matthias Felleisen. Observable sequentiality and full abstraction. In *Conference Record of the Nineteenth Annual ACM Symposium on Principles of Programming Languages*, pages 328–342, January 1992.

7. Alonzo Church. An unsolvable problem of elementary number theory. *Americal Journal of Mathematics*, 58:345–363, 1936.

8. P.-L. Curien. Observable algorithms on concrete data structures. In *Proc 7th Symposium on Logic in Computer Science*, 1992.

9. P.L. Curien. *Categorical Combinators, Sequential Algorithms and Functional Programming*. Research Notes in Theoretical Computer Science. John Wiley & Sons, Inc., New York, 1986.

10. Martin Davis. Computable functionals of arbitrary finite type. In A. Heyting, editor, *Constructivity in Mathematics*. North Holland Publishing Company, Amsterdam, 1959.

11. E. Wagner J. Goguen, J.Thatcher. An initial algebra approach to the specification, correctness, and implementation of abstract data types. Technical Report 6487, IBM Research Report, 1976.

12. G. Kahn and G. Plotkin. Structures de donneés concreètes. Technical Report 336, INRIA LABORIA, 1978. Now available in English.

13. Stephen C. Kleene. General recursive functions of natural numbers. *Mathematische Annalen*, 112:727–742, 1936.

14. G. Kreisel, D. Lacombe, and J. R. Scoenfield. Partial recursive functionals and effective operations. In A. Heyting, editor, *Constructivity in Mathematics*. North Holland Publishing Company, Amsterdam, 1959.

15. G.D. Plotkin. T^{ω} as a universal domain. *J. Comput. Sci.*, 17:209–236, 1978.

16. Hartley Rogers. *Theory of Recursive Functions and Effective Computability.* McGraw-Hill, New York, 1967. McGraw-Hill series in higher mathematics.

17. D.S. Scott. Data types as lattices. *SIAM J. Computing*, 5:522–587, 1976.

18. Alan M. Turing. Computability and λ-definability. *The Jounal of Symbolic Logic*, 2:153–163, 1937.

Appendix I: Effective Presentation of Function Spaces

In this appendix, we show how to construct an effective presentation $\mathcal{P}$ of the function space $D_1 \rightarrow_{os} D_2$ given the effective presentations $\mathcal{P}_1$ and $\mathcal{P}_2$ for D_1 and D_2. Since the *finite* elements of D_i are the least upper bounds of sets of primes, we can assign unique codes in $\mathbf{N}$ to the *finite* elements of D_i using standard methods for encoding sequences. Let the indices I, J range over the indices of finite elements and i, j, k range over the indices of prime elements. We refer to the finite element with index I as a_I and the prime element with index i as p_i. We superscript elements with their domains whenever it is necessary to avoid confusion.

The index of each prime function is defined inductively as follows. Let the index of the $\bot \rightarrow_{os} \bot$ be 0. Let f be a prime function immediately above f'. Let the index of f' be l. Then,

$$\mathbf{E}(f) = \begin{cases} \langle\langle 0, I, k\rangle, l\rangle & \text{if } f \text{ is an output prime determined by } f', a_I, \text{ and } p_k \\ \langle\langle 1, \langle I, m\rangle, n\rangle, l\rangle & \text{if } f \text{ is a schedule prime with } seq_f(a_I, C_m) = C_n \end{cases}$$

where $\langle \cdot, \cdot \rangle$ is the standard bijective pairing function on $\mathbf{N}$. It is clear from the above encoding that the enumeration is topologically sorted.

pr is the function that selects the second component of a tuple $\langle i, j \rangle$ since p_j is the immediate predecessor of the prime element $p_{\langle i, j\rangle}$.

The function **c** is defined by the equations:

$$\mathbf{c}(\langle\langle 0, I, k\rangle, l\rangle) = \langle\langle I, \mathbf{c}_2(k)\rangle, l\rangle$$
$$\mathbf{c}(\langle\langle 1, \langle I, m\rangle, n\rangle, l\rangle) = \langle\langle I, m\rangle, l\rangle$$

From the above encoding, it is easy to show that elements in the same C-set are mapped to same number.

The function **arity** is defined by the equations:

$$\mathbf{arity}(\langle\langle 0, I, k\rangle, l\rangle) = \mathbf{arity}_2(k)$$
$$\mathbf{arity}(\langle\langle 1, \langle I, m\rangle, n\rangle, l\rangle) = \mathbf{size}_1(n)$$

The number of C-sets above an output prime f depends on the number of C-sets above the final output p_k of f. The function f may generate incremental outputs in all the directions above p_k; therefore $\mathbf{arity}(f) = \mathbf{arity}_2(k)$. If f is a schedule prime with $si_f(a_I, C_m) = C_n$, f may generate a C-set for each element in the input C-set C_n; therefore $\mathbf{arity}(f) = \mathbf{size}_1(n)$.

The function **size** is defined as follows. Let the index of the C-set Q be $\langle\langle I, m\rangle, l\rangle$. Let S_I be the set of indices primes on the "fringe" of a_I, i.e., if $i \in S_I$ then $p_i \in a_I$ and there is no $p_j \in a_I$ such that $\mathbf{pr}(j) = i$. Then,

$$\mathbf{size}(\langle\langle I, m\rangle, l\rangle) = \mathbf{size}_2(m) + \sum_{i \in S_I} \mathbf{arity}_1(i)$$

where the addition operator $+$ has been extended to the domain $\mathbb{N} \cup \{\omega\}$. We can easily verify that the function **size** gives the cardinality of the C-set in $D_1 \to_{os} D_2$. It is clear that the number of output primes in the C-set Q is exactly the number of primes in the output C-set C_m. The C-set Q has a schedule prime for each direction above a_I. Thus, the preceding definition of **size** computes the number of elements in the C-set.

Appendix II: Embedding in the Universal Domain

In this appendix, we show how to embed an effectively presented domain D within T. We define the embedding function f mapping each prime element p_i into T by induction on i. At each stage in the construction of f, we prove the following hypotheses.

1. f maps the prime element p_i to a tree formed by substituting a subtree s_i for a $\perp$ leaf in the tree corresponding to its predecessor. The subtree s_i has same number of $\perp$'s as the number of C-sets above p_i.
2. If $p, q \in C_i$ (the same set in the partitioning), then the trees $f(p)$ and $f(q)$ are inconsistent.
3. If $p \leq q$, then $f(p) \sqsubseteq f(q)$.
4. If a finite element a represented by the set A of prime elements is maximal, the tree $\bigsqcup\{f(p) \mid p \in A\}$ is maximal.

Base Case: f maps p_0, which must be $\perp$, to $\langle n, \perp^n\rangle$ where n is the number of C-sets above $\perp$.

Induction Step: Assume that we have embedded all the primes in the enumeration from p_0 through p_{i-1}. We define $f(p_i)$ as follows:

Let k be the cardinality of the set of the already enumerated elements that are in conflict with p_i. Let s_i, the subtree for p_i be $\langle\langle\langle\mathbf{size}(\mathbf{c}(p_i)), k\rangle, \mathbf{arity}(p_i)\rangle, \perp^l\rangle$, where l is the number of C-sets above p_i. Note that l can be ω. Let q be the element immediately below p_i. By induction, q has been embedded in T as a tree $f(q)$. The element q was embedded in T by adding a subtree s_q to the image of q's predecessor. (In the special case where $q = \perp$, let s_q be $f(\perp)$.) In the subtree s_q, insert s_i (the subtree corresponding to p_i) at position $g(p_i)$, where the function $g(p_i)$ is defined as follows. If a prime p' belonging to the same C-set as p_i has been enumerated, then $g(p_i) = g(p')$. Otherwise, $g(p_i)$ is the number of distinct C-sets above q that are already enumerated. By the induction hypothesis, the position $g(p_i)$ has $\perp$ in the subtree s_q.

It is easy to show that by the preceding construction satisfies the the hypotheses.

Author Index

Lecture Notes in Computer Science

For information about Vols. 1–615
please contact your bookseller or Springer-Verlag

Vol. 655: M. Bidoit, C. Choppy (Eds.), Recent Trends in Data Type Specification. X, 344 pages. 1993.

Vol. 656: M. Rusinowitch, J. L. Rémy (Eds.), Conditional Term Rewriting Systems. Proceedings, 1992. XI, 501 pages. 1993.

Vol. 657: E. W. Mayr (Ed.), Graph-Theoretic Concepts in Computer Science. Proceedings, 1992. VIII, 350 pages. 1993.

Vol. 658: R. A. Rueppel (Ed.), Advances in Cryptology – EUROCRYPT '92. Proceedings, 1992. X, 493 pages. 1993.

Vol. 659: G. Brewka, K. P. Jantke, P. H. Schmitt (Eds.), Nonmonotonic and Inductive Logic. Proceedings, 1991. VIII, 332 pages. 1993. (Subseries LNAI).

Vol. 660: E. Lamma, P. Mello (Eds.), Extensions of Logic Programming. Proceedings, 1992. VIII, 417 pages. 1993. (Subseries LNAI).

Vol. 661: S. J. Hanson, W. Remmele, R. L. Rivest (Eds.), Machine Learning: From Theory to Applications. VIII, 271 pages. 1993.

Vol. 662: M. Nitzberg, D. Mumford, T. Shiota, Filtering, Segmentation and Depth. VIII, 143 pages. 1993.

Vol. 663: G..v. Bochmann, D. K. Probst (Eds.), Computer Aided Verification. Proceedings, 1992. IX, 422 pages. 1993.

Vol. 664: M. Bezem, J. F. Groote (Eds.), Typed Lambda Calculi and Applications. Proceedings, 1993. VIII, 433 pages. 1993.

Vol. 665: P. Enjalbert, A. Finkel, K. W. Wagner (Eds.), STACS 93. Proceedings, 1993. XIV, 724 pages. 1993.

Vol. 666: J. W. de Bakker, W.-P. de Roever, G. Rozenberg (Eds.), Semantics: Foundations and Applications. Proceedings, 1992. VIII, 659 pages. 1993.

Vol. 667: P. B. Brazdil (Ed.), Machine Learning: ECML – 93. Proceedings, 1993. XII, 471 pages. 1993. (Subseries LNAI).

Vol. 668: M.-C. Gaudel, J.-P. Jouannaud (Eds.), TAPSOFT '93: Theory and Practice of Software Development. Proceedings, 1993. XII, 762 pages. 1993.

Vol. 669: R. S. Bird, C. C. Morgan, J. C. P. Woodcock (Eds.), Mathematics of Program Construction. Proceedings, 1992. VIII, 378 pages. 1993.

Vol. 670: J. C. P. Woodcock, P. G. Larsen (Eds.), FME '93: Industrial-Strength Formal Methods. Proceedings, 1993. XI, 689 pages. 1993.

Vol. 671: H. J. Ohlbach (Ed.), GWAI-92: Advances in Artificial Intelligence. Proceedings, 1992. XI, 397 pages. 1993. (Subseries LNAI).

Vol. 672: A. Barak, S. Guday, R. G. Wheeler, The MOSIX Distributed Operating System. X, 221 pages. 1993.

Vol. 673: G. Cohen, T. Mora, O. Moreno (Eds.), Applied Algebra, Algebraic Algorithms and Error-Correcting Codes. Proceedings, 1993. X, 355 pages 1993.

Vol. 674: G. Rozenberg (Ed.), Advances in Petri Nets 1993. VII, 457 pages. 1993.

Vol. 675: A. Mulkers, Live Data Structures in Logic Programs. VIII, 220 pages. 1993.

Vol. 676: Th. H. Reiss, Recognizing Planar Objects Using Invariant Image Features. X, 180 pages. 1993.

Vol. 677: H. Abdulrab, J.-P. Pécuchet (Eds.), Word Equations and Related Topics. Proceedings, 1991. VII, 214 pages. 1993.

Vol. 678: F. Meyer auf der Heide, B. Monien, A. L. Rosenberg (Eds.), Parallel Architectures and Their Efficient Use. Proceedings, 1992. XII, 227 pages. 1993.

Vol. 679: C. Fermüller, A. Leitsch, T. Tammet, N. Zamov, Resolution Methods for the Decision Problem. VIII, 205 pages. 1993. (Subseries LNAI).

Vol. 682: B. Bouchon-Meunier, L. Valverde, R. R. Yager (Eds.), IPMU '92 – Advanced Methods in Artificial Intelligence. Proceedings, 1992. IX, 367 pages. 1993.

Vol. 683: G.J. Milne, L. Pierre (Eds.), Correct Hardware Design and Verification Methods. Proceedings, 1993. VIII, 270 Pages. 1993.

Vol. 684: A. Apostolico, M. Crochemore, Z. Galil, U. Manber (Eds.), Combinatorial Pattern Matching. Proceedings, 1993. VIII, 265 pages. 1993.

Vol. 685: C. Rolland, F. Bodart, C. Cauvet (Eds.), Advanced Information Systems Engineering. Proceedings, 1993. XI, 650 pages. 1993.

Vol. 686: J. Mira, J. Cabestany, A. Prieto (Eds.), New Trends in Neural Computation. Procedings, 1993. XVII, 746 pages. 1993.

Vol. 687: H. H. Barrett, A. F. Gmitro (Eds.), Information Processing in Medical Imaging. Proceedings, 1993. XVI, 567 pages. 1993.

Vol. 688: M. Gauthier (Ed.), Ada - Europe '93. Proceedings, 1993. VIII, 353 pages. 1993.

Vol. 689: J. Komorowski, Z. W. Ras (Eds.), Methodologies for Intelligent Systems. Proceedings, 1993. XI, 653 pages. 1993. (Subseries LNAI).

Vol. 690: C. Kirchner (Ed.), Rewriting Techniques and Applications. Proceedings, 1993. XI, 488 pages. 1993.

Vol. 691: M. Ajmone Marsan (Ed.), Application and Theory of Petri Nets 1993. Proceedings, 1993. IX, 591 pages. 1993.

Vol. 692: D. Abel, B.C. Ooi (Eds.), Advances in Spatial Databases. Proceedings, 1993. XIII, 529 pages. 1993.

Vol. 693: P. E. Lauer (Ed.), Functional Programming, Concurrency, Simulation and Automated Reasoning. Proceedings, 1991/1992. XI, 398 pages. 1993.

Vol. 694: A. Bode, M. Reeve, G. Wolf (Eds.), PARLE '93. Parallel Architectures and Languages Europe. Proceedings, 1993. XVII, 770 pages. 1993.

Vol. 695: E. P. Klement, W. Slany (Eds.), Fuzzy Logic in Artificial Intelligence. Proceedings, 1993. VIII, 192 pages. 1993. (Subseries LNAI).

Vol. 696: M. Worboys, A. F. Grundy (Eds.), Advances in Databases. Proceedings, 1993. X, 276 pages. 1993.

Vol. 697: C. Courcoubetis (Ed.), Computer Aided Verification. Proceedings, 1993. IX, 504 pages. 1993.

Vol. 700: A. Lingas, R. Karlsson, S. Carlsson (Eds.), Automata, Languages and Programming. Proceedings, 1993. XII, 697 pages. 1993.